W9-CTH-646

Nineteenth-Century Literature Criticism

Guide to Gale Literary Criticism Series

For criticism on	Consult these Gale series
Authors now living or who died after December 31, 1959	*CONTEMPORARY LITERARY CRITICISM (CLC)*
Authors who died between 1900 and 1959	*TWENTIETH-CENTURY LITERARY CRITICISM (TCLC)*
Authors who died between 1800 and 1899	*NINETEENTH-CENTURY LITERATURE CRITICISM (NCLC)*
Authors who died between 1400 and 1799	*LITERATURE CRITICISM FROM 1400 TO 1800 (LC)* *SHAKESPEAREAN CRITICISM (SC)*
Authors who died before 1400	*CLASSICAL AND MEDIEVAL LITERATURE CRITICISM (CMLC)*
Authors of books for children and young adults	*CHILDREN'S LITERATURE REVIEW (CLR)*
Dramatists	*DRAMA CRITICISM (DC)*
Poets	*POETRY CRITICISM (PC)*
Short story writers	*SHORT STORY CRITICISM (SSC)*
Black writers of the past two hundred years	*BLACK LITERATURE CRITICISM (BLC)*
Hispanic writers of the late nineteenth and twentieth centuries	*HISPANIC LITERATURE CRITICISM (HLC)*
Native North American writers and orators of the eighteenth, nineteenth, and twentieth centuries	*NATIVE NORTH AMERICAN LITERATURE (NNAL)*
Major authors from the Renaissance to the present	*WORLD LITERATURE CRITICISM, 1500 TO THE PRESENT (WLC)*

ISSN 0732-1864

Volume 82

Nineteenth-Century Literature Criticism

Excerpts from Criticism of the
Works of Novelists, Poets, Playwrights,
Short Story Writers, Philosophers, and Other
Creative Writers Who Died between 1800
and 1899, from the First Published Critical
Appraisals to Current Evaluations

Suzanne Dewsbury
Editor

GALE GROUP

Detroit
New York
San Francisco
London
Boston
Woodbridge, CT

STAFF

Suzanne Dewsbury, *Editor*
Gianna Barberi, *Associate Editor*
Tom Schoenberg, *Assistant Editor*
Lynn Spampinato, *Managing Editor*

Maria L. Franklin, *Permissions Manager*
Kimberly F. Smilay, *Permissions Specialist*
Kelly A. Quin, *Permissions Associate*
Erin Bealmear, Sandra K. Gore, *Permissions Assistants*

Victoria B. Cariappa, *Research Manager*
Corrine Boland, Tamara C. Nott, Tracie A. Richardson, *Research Associates*
Timothy Lehnerer, Patricia Love, *Research Assistants*

Dorothy Maki, *Manufacturing Manager*
Stacy Melson, *Buyer*

Michael Logusz, *Graphic Artist*
Randy Bassett, *Image Database Supervisor*
Robert Duncan, *Imaging Specialist*
Pamela A. Reed, *Imaging Coordinator*

This book is printed on acid-free paper that meets the minimum requirements of American National Standard for Information Sciences—Permanence Paper for Printed Library Materials, ANSI Z39.48-1984.

Library of Congress Catalog Card Number 84-643008
ISBN 0-7876-3258-9
ISSN 0732-1864
Printed in the United States of America

10 9 8 7 6 5 4 3 2 1

Contents

Preface vii

Acknowledgments xi

Preface

Since its inception in 1981, *Nineteenth-Century Literature Criticism* has been a valuable resource for students and librarians seeking critical commentary on writers of this transitional period in world history. Designated an "Outstanding Reference Source" by the American Library Association with the publication of its first volume, *NCLC* has since been purchased by over 6,000 school, public, and university libraries. The series has covered more than 300 authors representing 29 nationalities and over 17,000 titles. No other reference source has surveyed the critical reaction to nineteenth-century authors and literature as thoroughly as *NCLC*.

Scope of the Series

NCLC is designed to introduce students and advanced readers to the authors of the nineteenth century, and to the most significant interpretations of these authors' works. The great poets, novelists, short story writers, playwrights, and philosophers of this period are frequently studied in high school and college literature courses. By organizing and reprinting commentary written on these authors, *NCLC* helps students develop valuable insight into literary history, promotes a better understanding of the texts, and sparks ideas for papers and assignments. Each entry in *NCLC* presents a comprehensive survey of an author's career or an individual work of literature and provides the user with a multiplicity of interpretations and assessments. Such variety allows students to pursue their own interests; furthermore, it fosters an awareness that literature is dynamic and responsive to many different opinions.

Every fourth volume of *NCLC* is devoted to literary topics that cannot be covered under the author approach used in the rest of the series. Such topics include literary movements, prominent themes in nineteenth-century literature, literary reaction to political and historical events, significant eras in literary history, prominent literary anniversaries, and the literatures of cultures that are often overlooked by English-speaking readers.

NCLC continues the survey of criticism of world literature begun by Gale's *Contemporary Literary Criticism (CLC)* and *Twentieth-Century Literary Criticism (TCLC)*, both of which excerpt and reprint commentary on authors of the twentieth century. For additional information about *TCLC, CLC,* and Gale's other criticism series, users should consult the Guide to Gale Literary Criticism Series preceding the title page in this volume.

Coverage

Each volume of *NCLC* is carefully compiled to present:

- criticism of authors, or literary topics, representing a variety of genres and nationalities
- both major and lesser-known writers and literary works of the period
- 4-8 authors or 4-6 topics per volume
- individual entries that survey critical response to an author's work or a topic in literary history, including early criticism to reflect initial reactions, later criticism to represent any rise or decline in reputation, and current retrospective analyses.

Organization

An author entry consists of the following elements: author heading, biographical and critical introduction, list of principal works, excerpts of criticism (each preceded by a bibliographic citation and an annotation), and a bibliography of further reading.

- The **Author Heading** consists of the name under which the author most commonly wrote, followed by birth and death dates. If an author wrote consistently under a pseudonym, the pseudonym will be listed in the author heading and the real name given in parentheses on the first line of the biographical and critical introduction. Also located at the beginning of the introduction to the author entry are any name variations under which an author wrote, including transliterated forms for an author whose language uses a nonroman alphabet.

- The **Biographical and Critical Introduction** outlines the author's life and career, as well as the critical issues surrounding his or her work. References are provided to past volumes of *NCLC* in which further information about the author may be found.

- Most *NCLC* entries include a **Portrait** of the author. Many entries also contain reproductions of materials pertinent to an author's career, including manuscript pages, title pages, dust jackets, letters, and drawings, as well as photographs of important people, places, and events in an author's life.

- The list of **Principal Works** is chronological by date of first publication and identifies the genre of each work. In the case of foreign authors with both foreign-language publications and English translations, the English-language version is given in brackets. Unless otherwise indicated, dramas are dated by first performance, not first publication.

- **Criticism** in each author entry is arranged chronologically to provide a perspective on changes in critical evaluation over the years. All titles of works by the author featured in the entry are printed in boldface type to enable the user to easily locate discussion of particular works. Also for purposes of easier identification, the critic's name and the publication date of the essay are given at the beginning of each piece of criticism. Unsigned criticism is preceded by the title of the journal in which it appeared. Publication information (such as publisher names and book prices) and some parenthetical numerical references (such as page and line references to specific editions of works) have been deleted at the editors' discretion to provide smoother reading of the text. Footnotes that appear with previously published pieces of criticism are reprinted at the end of each essay or excerpt. In the case of excerpted criticism, only those footnotes that pertain to the excerpted text are included.

- A complete **Bibliographic Citation** provides original publication information for each piece of criticism.

- Critical excerpts are prefaced by **Annotations** providing the reader with a summary of the critical intent of the piece. Also included, when appropriate, is information about the critic's reputation, individual approach to literary criticism, and particular expertise in an author's works, as well as information about the relative importance of the critical excerpt. In some cases, the annotations cross-reference excerpts by critics who discuss each other's commentary.

- An annotated list of **Further Reading** appearing at the end of each entry suggests secondary sources on the author. In some cases it includes essays for which the editors could not obtain reprint rights.

Cumulative Indexes

- Each volume of *NCLC* contains a cumulative **Author Index** listing all authors who have appeared in Gale's Literary Criticism Series, along with cross-references to such biographical series as *Contemporary Authors* and *Dictionary of Literary Biography*. Useful for locating authors within the various series, this index is particularly valuable for those authors who are identified with a certain period but who, because of their death dates, are placed in another, or for those authors whose careers span two periods. For example, Fyodor Dostoevsky is found in *NCLC*, yet Leo Tolstoy, another major nineteenth-century Russian novelist, is found in *TCLC* because he died after 1899.

- Each *NCLC* volume includes a cumulative **Nationality Index** which lists all authors who have appeared in *NCLC*, arranged alphabetically under their respective nationalities.

- Each new volume in Gale's Literary Criticism Series includes a cumulative **Topic Index**, which lists all literary topics treated in *NCLC, TCLC, LC 1400-1800*, and the *CLC* Yearbook.

- Each new volume of *NCLC*, with the exception of the Topics volumes, contains a **Title Index** listing the titles of all literary works discussed in the volume. In response to numerous suggestions from librarians, Gale has also produced a **Special Paperbound Edition** of the *NCLC* title index. This annual cumulation lists all titles discussed in the series since its inception. Additional copies of the index are available on request. Librarians and patrons have welcomed this separate index: it saves shelf space, is easy to use, and is recyclable upon receipt of the following year's cumulation. Titles discussed in the Topics volume entries are not included in the *NCLC* cumulative index.

Citing *Nineteenth-Century Literature Criticism*

When writing papers, students who quote directly from any volume in Gale's Literary Criticism Series may use the following general forms to footnote reprinted criticism. The first example pertains to material drawn from periodicals, the second to material reprinted from books:

[1]Kim McQuaid, "William Apes, Pequot: An Indian Reformer in the Jackson Era," *The New England Quarterly*, 50 (December 1977), 605-25; excerpted and reprinted in *Nineteenth-Century Literature Criticism*, Vol. 73, ed. Janet Witalec (Farmington Hills, Mich.: The Gale Group, 1999), pp. 3-4.

[2]Richard Harter Fogle, *The Imagery of Keats and Shelley: A Comparative Study* (Archon Books, 1949); excerpted and reprinted in *Nineteenth-Century Literary Criticism*, Vol. 73, ed. Janet Witalec (Farmington Hills, Mich.: The Gale Group, 1999), pp. 157-69.

Suggestions Are Welcome

In response to suggestions, several features have been added to *NCLC* since the series began, including annotations to excerpted criticism, a cumulative index to authors in all Gale literary criticism series, entries devoted to criticism on a single work by a major author, more illustrations, and a title index listing all literary works discussed in the series.

Readers who wish to suggest authors, single works, or topics to appear in future volumes, or who have other suggestions, are cordially invited to write: The Editors, *Nineteenth-Century Literature Criticism*, The Gale Group, 27500 Drake Rd., Farmington Hills, MI 48331-3535; call toll-free at 1-800-347-GALE.

Acknowledgments

The editors wish to thank the copyright holders of the excerpted criticism included in this volume and the permissions managers of many book and magazine publishing companies for assisting us in securing reproduction rights. We are also grateful to the staffs of the Detroit Public Library, the Library of Congress, the University of Detroit Mercy Library, Wayne State University Purdy/Kresge Library Complex, and the University of Michigan Libraries for making their resources available to us. Following is a list of the copyright holders who have granted us permission to reproduce material in this volume of *NCLC*. Every effort has been made to trace copyright, but if omissions have been made, please let us know.

COPYRIGHTED EXCERPTS IN *NCLC*, VOLUME 82, WERE REPRODUCED FROM THE FOLLOWING PERIODICALS:

American Literary Realism: 1870-1910, v. 22, Spring, 1990. © 1990 by McFarland & Company, Inc., Publishers. Reproduced by permission.—*boundary 2,* v. XIX, Fall, 1992. Copyright © Duke University Press, 1992. Reproduced by permission.—*The Charles Lamb Bulletin,* April, 1990; July, 1991. Both reproduced by permission.—*Forum for Modern Language Studies,* v. XII, July, 1976. For "Mundane Magic: Some Observations on Chamisso's Peter Schlemihl" by Martin Swales. Reproduced by permission of the publisher and the author.—*The German Quarterly,* v. XLVII, November, 1974; v. LV, January, 1982. Copyright © 1974, 1982 by the American Association of Teachers of German. Both reproduced by permission.—*Journal of the History of Ideas,* v. 56, July, 1995. Copyright 1995 by Journal of the History of Ideas, Inc. Reproduced by permission.—*Legacy: A Journal of Nineteenth-Century American Women Writers,* v. 3, Fall, 1986; v. 6, Fall, 1989. Copyright 1986, 1989 by The Pennsylvania State University. Both reproduced by permission of The Pennsylvania State University Press.—*Literature and Psychology,* v. XVII, 1967. Copyright © 1968 by Leonard F. Manheim and Morton Kaplan. Reproduced by permission.—*MELUS: Society for the Study of the Multi-Ethnic Literature of the United States,* 1991. Copyright, *MELUS: The Society for the Study of Multi-Ethnic Literature of the United States*, 1991. Reproduced by permission.—*Monatshefte,* v. LXIX, Spring, 1977. Copyright © 1977 by the Board of Regents of the University of Wisconsin System. Reproduced by permission of The University of Wisconsin Press.—*The New Criterion,* v. 10, November, 1991. For "Hazlitt's Passions" by Joseph Epstein. Copyright © 1991 by The Foundation for Cultural Review. Reproduced by permission of the author.—*South Atlantic Review,* v. 57, May, 1992. Copyright © 1992 by the South Atlantic Modern Language Association. Reproduced by permission.—*Southern Studies,* v. XXV, Fall, 1986 for "Constance Woolson's Southern Sketches" by Sharon L. Dean. Reproduced by permission of the author.—*Studies in English Literature, 1500-1900,* v. 35, 1995. © William Marsh Rice University 1995. Reproduced by permission of The Johns Hopkins University Press.—*Studies in Romanticism,* v. 14, Winter, 1975; v. 29, Summer, 1990; v. 36, Fall, 1997. Copyright 1975, 1990, 1997 by the Trustees of Boston University. All reproduced by permission.—*Tennessee Studies in Literature,* v. XII, 1967. Copyright © 1967 by The University of Tennessee Press. Reproduced by permission of The University of Tennessee Press.

COPYRIGHTED EXCERPTS IN *NCLC*, VOLUME 82, WERE REPRODUCED FROM THE FOLLOWING BOOKS:

Bloom, Harold. From an introduction to *William Hazlitt.* Edited by Harold Bloom. Chelsea House Publishers, 1986. © 1986 by Chelsea House Publishers, a division of Chelsea House Educational Communications, Inc. Introduction © 1986 by Harold Bloom. All rights reserved. Reproduced by permission.—Butler, Marilyn. From "Satire and the Images of Self in the Romantic Period: The Long Tradition of Hazlitt's Liber Amoris" in *English Satire and the Satiric Tradition.* Edited by Claude Rawson. Basil Blackwell, 1984. First appeared in *Yearbook of English Studies.* © Modern Humanities Research Association 1984. All rights reserved. Reproduced by permission of Modern Humanities Research Association and the author.— Caccavari, Peter. For "Exile, Depatriation and Constance Fenimore Woolson's Traveling Regionalism" in *Women, America, and Movement: Narratives of Relocation.* Edited by Susan L. Roberson. University of Missouri Press, 1998. Copyright © 1998 by The Curators of the University of Missouri. All rights reserved. Reproduced by permission.—Chadwick, C. From *Rimbaud.* The Athlone Press, 1979. © C. Chadwick 1979. Reproduced by permission.—Enright, Nancy. From "William Hazlitt and His 'Familiar Style'" in *Essays on the Essay: Redefining the Genre.* Edited by Alexander J. Butrym. The University of Georgia Press, 1989. © 1989 by the Univer-

PHOTOGRAPHS APPEARING IN *NCLC*, VOLUME 82, WERE RECEIVED FROM THE FOLLOWING SOURCES:

Adelbert von Chamisso

1781-1838

(Born Louis Charles Adelaide. Also known as Adalbert.) French-born German poet, novelist, travel-writer, linguist, and botanist.

INTRODUCTION

Chamisso was a noted German lyric poet who is generally remembered for his classic novel *Peter Schlemihls wundersame Geschichte* (1814; *The Wonderful History of Peter Schlemihl*). Taking its title from the Yiddish word schlemihl—which denotes an unlucky or simple person—*Peter Schlemihl* is ostensibly a *Märchen,* or fairy tale; although scholars consider it a work of serious fiction. The story follows Schlemihl as he enters into a deal with the devil, exchanging his shadow for a purse of endless wealth. The work is generally seen as a social satire with elements of fantasy, allegory, and confessional autobiography. In addition to *Peter Schlemihl,* Chamisso also composed a number of popular poems, including those of his song-cycle *Frauenliebe und Leben,* and a travel journal, *Reise um die Welt mit der Romanzoffischen Entdeckungs-Expedition,* that is numbered among the finest of the nineteenth century.

Biographical Information

Chamisso was born in Château de Boncourt, France, in 1781. As a youth, he fled with his family to Prussia in order to avoid the social turmoil of the French Revolution. Chamisso adopted German as his new tongue, and subsequently wrote all of his mature works in this language. He joined the Prussian army in 1798 and served for the next eight years. While still in the military, he helped create the Nordsternbund, a group of Romantic poets in Berlin, and between 1804 and 1806 co-edited the society's journal *Musenalmanach,* in which were published several of his earliest poems. Over the next several years, Chamisso returned to France and later participated in the literary salons of Madame de Staël at Geneva and Coppet. He returned to Berlin in 1812 and focused on the study of botany, which he had begun at Coppet. Taking advantage of a period of leisure in 1813, he began to write his novel *Peter Schlemihl* and published it the following year. In 1815 Chamisso embarked on a scientific voyage around the world aboard a Russian ship under the direction of Captain Otto von Kotzebue. Engaged as a botanist on the vessel, Chamisso recorded his experiences in diary form and later published these journals as *Reise um die Welt.*

After returning to Europe, Chamisso accepted a post as curator at the Berlin Botanical Gardens, serving there until his death in 1838.

Major Works

Chamisso's most read and studied work, *Peter Schlemihl,* presents the story of a man who naively makes a contract with the devil. An exile newly arrived in Germany, Schlemihl encounters a confidence man clad all in gray. This man, the devil in disguise, impresses Schlemihl with a magical purse, from which he draws a seemingly limitless number of valuable objects. He ensnares Schlemihl by offering the purse in exchange for the man's shadow, something he points out is clearly of no value. Schlemihl agrees to the trade. Initially delighted with his easily attained wealth, Schlemihl finds himself ostracized from society because of his eerie lack of a shade. He sinks into a deep despair that lasts for a year and a day, until the devil reappears and offers to return the shadow if Schlemihl will sign away his soul. Able to evade the devil's trickery and keep his soul, Schlemihl nevertheless remains alienated from society at the novel's end. His fortunate acquisition of some magical boots in the final segment of the story, however, offers him a measure of contentment. Using the boots, Schlemihl finds he can traverse a distance of seven leagues in a single step, allowing him to exist outside of society while satisfying his wanderlust and interest in botanical study. Among Chamisso's other works, his *terza rima* poem "Salas y Gomez," inspired by the cliffs of the Pacific island of that name, plays upon the motif of Robinson Crusoe, as its narrator imagines a lone shipwreck survivor on the desolate rock. "Die alte Waschfrau" ("The Old Washerwoman") is generally considered Chamisso's most popular poem, and features the humble laundress figure that would become a stock character in German literature of the nineteenth century. In the travelogue *Reise um die Welt,* Chamisso recounts his journey by sea across the globe through a series of anecdotes, many of them humorous. In particular, he notes the idyllic splendor of the South Pacific islands, and praises the unspoiled lives and fascinating art of the Pacific islanders. His remaining works include a study of Hawaiian grammar entitled *Über die Hawaiische Sprache* and several essays on botany.

Critical Reception

Chamisso claimed that he wrote *Peter Schlemihl* in order to amuse the children of his friend Eduard Hitzig, and in part out of boredom. Thomas Mann and others since have observed that the romantic novel, though appealing to children, was intended for more sophisticated audiences as well. This assessment has been supported by a number of scholars who have endeavored to unravel the ambiguities of the novel. While stressing its symbolic nature, most commentators have avoided allegorical explanations of the work. Many have focused on the motif of Schlemihl's lost shadow, which has inspired various interpretations, including readings that it is a metaphor for Schlemihl's status as an exile alienated from society. Critics have also commented on the protagonist's pretensions to wealth and social esteem in the work. Psychoanalytic assessments have been forwarded, and the story has been read as a kind of cautionary tale related to material greed and to the pitfalls of business dealings in general. Other studies have perceived Schlemihl as a disinterested scholar who values solitary contemplation over social contact. Overall, modern commentators, while disagreeing on specific interpretations, have lauded the depth of Chamisso's social insight and the complexity of his narrative technique and characterization in *Peter Schlemihl.* Likewise, many critics of Chamisso's collected writings have acknowledged his significant contributions to nineteenth-century German lyric poetry and travel-writing.

PRINCIPAL WORKS

Peter Schlemihls wundersame Geschichte [*The Wonderful History of Peter Schlemihl*] (novel) 1814
Das Schloß Boncourt (poetry) 1927
Frauenliebe und Leben (poetry) 1830
Gesammelte Werke. 6 vols. (novel, travel writing, and poetry) 1836
Reise um die Welt mit der Romanzoffischen Entdeckungs-Expedition (travel writing) 1836
Über die Hawaiische Sprache (linguistics) 1837

CRITICISM

Thomas Mann (essay date 1911)

SOURCE: "Chamisso," in *Essays of Three Decades,* trans. by H. T. Lowe-Porter, Alfred A. Knopf, 1948, pp. 241-58.

[*In the following essay, originally published in 1911, Mann surveys Chamisso's life and writings, concentrating on his novel* Peter Schlemihl, *which he calls "one of the most charming youthful works in German literature."*]

Among our schoolbooks was one that stood out from all the rest. On the outside it looked dry and forbidding, like any textbook. But within it gave of its contents with lovely human charm. Actually, strange as it may seem, it was an amusing book, full from cover to cover of delightful things which got our interest straightway, with no dry bits in between. We read it without being told, for sheer enjoyment; we read on ahead of the class, and felt none of the usual pangs when the lesson hour came and the books lay open on the desks. It was almost like a game and the exercises they set us out of it were easy and amusing. We answered every question like a flash, in eager, excited voices. And if there was one of us who took no interest, let him be as redoubtable as he might in any other field, we put him down for a dull fellow.

This book must have been added to the school curriculum by some exceptionally kindly hand. It was called, quite simply, *The German Reader.* It was given us solely to the end that we should look at the language, our mother tongue—or rather that we should listen to it—as it smiled to see itself in verse. *The German Reader* contained a gay and varied collection of good stories, both rhymed and unrhymed, in prose and verse. If I were to come across it again, I wager that I could turn straightway to my old favourites.

There was the comic ballad about the fellow who was so upset because his pigtail hung down behind—he wanted it before. There was the humorous-serious anecdote about the Szekler Assembly—and it is my belief that its easy, unimpeachable structure of triplets with the single line so happily rounding out everything at the end gave me my earliest instance of masterly performance in that kind. There was the fine ode to an old washerwoman; what an enchantment that was, how it made my heart beat every time I came to the closing strophe:

Und ich, an meinem Abend, wollte . . .

I too at evening of my day. . . .

There was the tale of an evil deed, long hidden and unknown; I always fancied that the "flickering sunbeams" played on these pages to bring the crime to the light of day. We read the long-drawn-out tale of Abdullah and the eighty camels. The dervish appeared to him (the more unearthly in our eyes because we did not know exactly what a dervish was), and Abdullah became very wealthy and then a blind beggar all in one day, because of his own greed. Then there was the fearsome and fantastic story of the "right barber." The child giantess spread out her little cloth and scooped peasant and plough into it with her hands. The brave wives of Winsperg carried their husbands pick-a-back out of the gate. And lastly in a succession of rhymed chapters was unfolded the magic dream-poem of Cousin Anselmo and his ingratitude.

At the end of all these pieces was signed their author's name, a foreign-sounding one: Chamisso. The same name was on a richly bound volume I found in the glass bookcase in the smoking-room at home. This second book contained things such as our good little textbook could not boast; some of them frightful, like the story of the sunken castle, for a long time my greatest favourite, particularly on account of the "brazen minion" who was so brazen as to walk in her shoes over fine white bread. She seemed just that much more bedevilled because in fact I had no clear idea what a minion was. These earliest impressions are no doubt amazingly distorted by my childishly undeveloped powers of imagination. Did I not promptly, whenever my stomach was upset, dream the frightful dream of the men in the Zoptenberg? It was I myself and not the godly Johannes Beer from Schweidnitz who saw the three gaunt sinners sitting in the black-hung hall at the round table by the dim lamp. It was I who saw the curtain gape, behind it the horrid heap of ribs and skulls, the remnant of their crimes. I understood just enough Latin to give me goose-flesh when the three miscreants stammered their gloomy *"Hic nulla, nulla pax!"* Looking at the verses to-

day I am struck afresh by the capital performance. How crisp and lively is the indirect discourse that is fitted into the verse! With what deftness and economy are chosen and applied those tools of the language calculated to arouse the most fear and horror! The cold and shuddering breath of the unwholesome place, the staring, shaking anguish of the accursèd ones, their stammering, teeth-chattering, pointing, starting, mowing, mouthing—how capital all that was! . . . And when evening came, we sat quietly at our ease and listened to our mother at the piano, singing the serene and lovely song-cycle of *Frauenliebe und Leben.*

This poet, whose name was so early familiar to us, this German author who was set before us lads as our first and best model, was a stranger, a foreigner. French songs were his lullabies. The air, the water, the nourishment of France shaped his body, the rhythm of the French tongue was the medium of all his thoughts and feelings till he was half-grown. Only then, at fourteen, did he come over to us. He never managed to converse with fluency in German. He reckoned in French. Tradition says that up to the last when he composed he first recited aloud in French and only after that poured his inspirations into a metrical mould—but after all, the result was masterly German.

It is amazing, it is even unheard-of. True, there have been cases of gifted men who were so drawn to the genius of a stranger folk that they changed their nationality, immersed themselves utterly in the ideas and problems of the people with whom they felt this affinity, and learned to use their pens ad equately, even elegantly, in a tongue their fathers did not speak. But what is correctness, what even elegance, compared to the deep intimacy the artist must have! The knowledge of the ultimate mysteries and refinements, the uttermost control of his craft in tone and movement, in the reflex workings of words on one another, of their sensuous appeal, their dynamic, their special stylistic, ironic, pathetic value; that mastery—to put in a word what, after all, is unanalysable—of the delicate and powerful mechanism of language, which produces the literary artist and is indispensable to poet and writer. He who is born and called one day to enrich the literature of his land will quite early find himself peculiarly concerned with his mother tongue. The Word: there it is, it belongs to everybody, yet it seems to belong to him more in particular, in a more inward and gratifying sense than to anyone else. It is his earliest wonder, his first delight, his childish pride, the field of his private and unpraised efforts, the source of his strange and undefined superiority. At fourteen years, if the individual sustain this unusual relation to the Word, there may already have been some private beginnings. And then, at this age, to be set amongst strangers speaking strange thoughts in a strange tongue! Even though some latent, unexplained sympathy were already present; even though there was some unconscious adjustment to the German tempo and German laws of thought; still, and even so, how much conscious labour, how much wooing for the favour of our tongue was needed to make a German poet out of a French child!

And he hesitates long. Long considers it presumptuous to regard himself seriously as belonging to the German Parnassus. He is forty-one years old when he writes to a French friend: "When we were boys I wanted to be a poet; you too made German verses, though probably such flights have ceased ere now. With me not quite. I still sing, when song comes to my mind; I even collect these fugitive blossoms into a herbarium for myself and my loved ones for future times. But they remain in the family circle, as they should." Five years later, to Varnhagen's sister: "That I was and am no poet is abundantly clear; but the taste for it is still there." And only in the following year (1828) when he was attracting increasing notice from the public: "I almost think I am a German poet." One hears in his voice the pride, the still questioning joy with which he feels the garland on his head, his awe at the dignity which the nation bestowed by popular applause. A German poet: in those days that was something to be in the world. The word on the lips of a people of poets and thinkers was at the height of its significance. The romantic movement had put its seal on the European conception of poetry. Poetry—that was romanticism. But the romantic—that was German. In the letter I quoted, the easy equation of "to be a poet" with "to make German verses" is worth remark. Never was an epithet more intimately fused with its noun than in the phrase *"der deutsche Dichter."* To be a German, that almost meant to be a poet. To be a poet, that almost meant to be German. This may help us to understand the astonishing fact that the poetic talent of a foreigner could so happily strike root into the soil of the German language.

The fine poem **Boncourt Castle** is a metrical treatment of Chamisso's biography. It moved a warm-hearted monarch to tears. It describes the old feudal seat in Champagne, whose castle court sheltered the poet's childhood. Today the plough turns the soil on which it stood. Sadly but without rancour, the poet invokes a blessing on the dear earth now summoned to bring forth fruit; on the ploughman who tills it; and at the end the exiled grandson of the lords of Chamisso at Boncourt, with that melancholy resignation which suits so well the romantic poets, girds himself to travel the far spaces of the earth, a wandering singer, lute in hand.

The boy was born in 1781 and christened with the names Louis Charles Adelaide. The family were driven out in 1790 by the political tempest of the Revolution. They wandered for years in great privation through the Low Countries, Holland, Germany, and at last into Prussia. Here in Berlin, in 1796, they succeeded in getting for young Adelaide or Adalbert the position of page to the Queen Consort of Friedrich Wilhelm II. Two years later he begins his military career as ensign in a Berlin regiment of foot. In 1801 he is made lieutenant. When the First Consul permitted the lad's parents to return to France, Adalbert remained where he was. His literary production seems to have begun by then. He writes French verse, then German verse. Friendships grow up with like-minded youths, Varnhagen and Hitzig; and the fruit of these alliances is an *Almanac of the Muses,* which came out from 1804 to 1806, and, unripe as its contents were, won for young Chamisso the fatherly kindness of Fichte. Private studies in Greek, Latin, and incidentally in the living languages of Europe went on at the same time. Then years of war interrupted the service of the muse. Chamisso took part in the Weser campaign, was imprisoned in Hamelin, quit the service, and went back to Berlin. Meanwhile he had been orphaned. And now in Berlin, without hope for the future, he spent lonely, unfruitful years. A summons to the land of his fathers, to Napoléonville, as professor at the *lycée* released him from an intolerable situation. He hastened to France, whither in the days of his Berlin exile his heart may have fondly turned—or perhaps only thought it ought to turn. Nothing came of the professorship. The young *homme de letters* was drawn into the orbit of Madame de Staël, that "magnificent, amazing woman," whom he admired not least as a power not subservient to the Emperor. He followed the proscribed heroine to Geneva and Coppet. And from there he writes to Fouqué, scion of the Normans: "Here I live, love, pursue my quiet German course; nowhere have I been more blockheadedly German than in Paris." Then, in 1812, he returned of his own free will to Berlin and continued at the university the scientific studies that he had embarked on in Paris. The events of the years 1813 to 1815, in which he could not take an active part, tear him asunder time after time, as he says in a *curriculum vitæ* composed by himself. "What my nearest friends shrieked at me when I left, I now say to myself: the times held no sword for me; yet it is maddening to be an idle spectator at such a popular movement of happy warriors." Shamefacedly, self-conflicted, he withdrew into solitude. It was a repetition, even harder to bear, of the restless period after his resignation from the army. Whither should he turn? He might be no German, yet felt a stranger to his French homeland. A newspaper came into his hands with a notice about a forthcoming Russian voyage of discovery "to the North Pole," under Otto von Kotzebue. He pricked up his ears, friends came forward to help, even the Privy Councillor August von Kotzebue, in Königsberg, was appealed to, and an earlier wish-dream of Chamisso's came unexpectedly true. In June 1815 he was appointed scientist on the forthcoming voyage of discovery to the South Seas and round the world. Hamburg, Copenhagen, Plymouth, Tenerife, Brazil, Chile, Kamchatka, California, the Sandwich Islands, Manila, the Cape of Good Hope, London, St. Petersburg—it was three years of luxurious gratification of his romantic wanderlust and love of the exotic; beyond doubt the richest, most rewarding years of his life, which filled the storehouse of his mind with an inexhaustible treasure of pictures and material and endowed him with food for contemplation for his whole productive life. The immediate literary fruit of these years was the attractive book *Travels round the World,* in its scientific aspect a volume of "Comments and Opinions on a Voyage of Discovery under Kotzebue." Actually, the most important result of the experience was of a personal and human kind. In those wild and distant scenes through which he passed, Chamisso's feeling for home, which had vacillated so long, became once for all fixed—and fixed upon Germany. Wanderlust and love of home are certainly not mutually exclusive. They may be friendly allies, and precisely in romantic souls may kindle and enhance the one the other. Chamisso's gentle heart, with its craving for companionship, had suffered from the conflict of double nationality and the indecision of not knowing in which soil he wanted to strike root. His travels taught him that when he turned his thoughts and feelings "homeward" it was to Germany they went. He found that all his hopes and humours, his love of language, science, and friendship bound him to her. By the dispensation of fate he had now in fact and in truth become at heart a German. Today we believe less in heart and more in blood and race; perhaps we even exaggerate this belief into a superstition. Thus we may have our doubts and in fact, under the pressure of a general devotion to the binding force of blood, may find that the case of Chamisso would be subjectively hardly possible. But in his time it was, and that must do us; the inward experience, like all powerful personal convictions, could and did preserve and demonstrate itself objectively through his German work. He landed in Swinemünde in October 1818, and greeted his German home in verse, begging her, in exchange "for so much love," for just one thing, that on her soil he might find a stone whereon one day to pillow his head and fall asleep. The verses belong to the loveliest, most moving, and most moved that he ever wrote. Thirteen years later, a fifty-year-old man, in like fervent syllables, he sang his thanks to "his dear German home" for all the friendliness she had shown to the *"gebeugten Gast."* That was not little; for it seems that along with the inner peace happiness and well-being accrued from without. Friedrich Wilhelm of Prussia, long an admirer of his art, took Chamisso under his protection, and made him assistant at the Botanical Gardens and Director of the Royal Herbaria, with pay sufficient. The homeless one founded a home, he married, there would be a little house, "and the modest little space is large enough to hold a new-awakened, gay and ample life." Peace and the esteem of his fellows spur him on, his reputation increases, in dignity and discipline his talent unfolds to mastery. Heine, his greater contemporary, admiringly says "with every year he grows younger and fuller of bloom." The next generation, to whom he had ever been a kindly counsellor and inspiration, held him in honour. Since 1832 he had, with Schwab and Gaudy, been publishing the German *Almanac of the Muses,* and in 1835 he was invited to become a member of the Academy of Science. But premonitions of death now began to be voiced in his verse. **"Dream and Waking,"** written in 1837, is the retrospect, sad and glad, of one who feels himself at his journey's end. His lungs were attacked, and in the summer of 1838, at the height of his fame, he fell asleep. Fifty years later, Berlin, which might well regard him as her son, erected a monument to him in Monbijou Place.

He was a tall, mild man with long, straight hair and noble, almost beautiful features. Capable of friendship with children and savages, he loved to remember the Radak Islanders whose guest he had once been and whose beauty and nearness to nature he praises in the style of Rousseau. The Ulea-Indian Kadú, who served him in the South Seas, he considered "one of the finest characters" he had met in his life and one of the human beings he "loved the most." His scientific works, for instance the *Conspectus of Useful and Harmful Plants That Grow Wild or Cultivated in Northern Germany,* to mention one of them, are considered "valuable." But it is as poet that his name survives.

Chamisso's collected poems, which he first brought himself to publish in 1831, are only in small part in lyric. The immediately lyrical is infrequent, and not always happy; the hymnic, dithyrambic, ecstatic is wholly lacking. The somewhat unexciting epic, the well-wrought objective work, make up by far the larger part of his product; preambles and preludes such as:

Ich bin schon alt, es mahnt der Zeiten Lauf
Mich oft an längst geschehene Geschichten,
Und die erzähl' ich, horcht auch niemand auf.
So weiss ich aus der Chronik und Gedichten,
Wie bei der Pest es in Ferrara war,
Und will davon nur einen Zug berichten—

Now I am old, the passage of the years
Minds me of things that in past time
befell,
And I relate them, though nobody hears;
From chronicle and verse I know full
well
How in Ferrara in the plague it was,
And of them all one only I will tell.

That sort of thing indicates his attitude as a poet; even the flowery and lyrical, like *Frauenliebe und Leben* and *Lebens-Lieder und Bilder* come within the epic-dramatic compositions, unities of strophe and antistrophe, monologue and rejoinder. What strikes one is the abrupt, almost pathological contradiction between the ethereal delicacy of Chamisso's production in this kind and his indisputable fondness for strong, even horrible subjects. Public opinion did not criticize him from the first angle, of course; but it probably did from the second, and his partisans have cited in his behalf the friendship that bound him to the criminalist Hitzig. It was Hitzig, they said, who provided the poet in search of material with such exotic, not to say horrid subjects. The apology is as untenable as the reproach—which has also been levelled against Heinrich von Kleist. One might with more justice suppose that a friendship with the editor of criminalist periodicals was itself the consequence of Chamisso's requirement of objective material from the field of the abnormal and horrible. For the over-delicate and the brutal are complementary cravings of the romantic temperament. It is precisely this contrast that places Chamisso's works with all their Latin clarity and definition in the category of the romantic in literature.

Poems showing such a tendency to horrible subject-matter are, for instance, **"Don Juanito Marques Verdugo de los Leganes,"** a story also used by Balzac, about a young Spanish grandee who on heroic grounds brings himself to execute the French blood-judgment on his own family; **"Retribution,"** the excruciating anecdote of the executioner who in his sleep marks with his branding-iron the frightful betrayer of his daughter; the famous *terza rima* composition **"Salas y Gomez,"** which, first appearing in the Wendish *Musenalmanac* of 1829, made a real sensation in the world of belles-lettres and permanently established the literary standing of the author. Today we do not quite follow the admiration which greeted this terrifying Robinsonade. Is not its poetic value rather problematic? What made the poet illuminate with his art the lamentable tale of the young business man cast away on an island, peopled only by water-birds, who gets to be a hundred years old and scratches his misery on three slate tablets? On his voyage round the world Chamisso had seen the bare cliffs of Salas y Gomez and, shuddering, said to himself that a man cast away there could probably sustain life all too long on birds' eggs. That might be ground enough to make him fill more than three hundred lines of verse with those shudderings; but not quite ground enough for us to find the thing particularly interesting. What we do admire without reservation is the form of the poem, the wrought bronze of the language. Certainly, Platen wrote the most perfect German sonnets; but with equal certainty Chamisso deserves the title of most masterly wielder of the *terza rima*.

However, Chamisso was no formalist, and as a conscientious artist scarcely at all dealt in the explicitly artificial. The ghazal, for instance, used with dazzling effect by Rückert and Platen, does not appear in his work. Other classic forms—the sonnet, the Sapphic ode, the Nibelung strophe—are not prominent either. And most lovable of all, as is lyric poetry in general, are two or three apparently artless things, quite simple in form, light and brief as dreams are, but quivering with feeling and extraordinarily forthright in their simplicity, like all confessions:

> *Was Soll Ich Sagen?*
>
> *Mein Aug' ist trüb, mein Mund ist stumm,*
> *Du heissest mich reden, es sei darum.*
>
> *Dein Aug' ist klar, dein Mund ist rot,*
> *Und was du nur wünschest, das ist ein Gebot.*
>
> *Mein Haar ist grau, mein Herz ist wund,*
> *Du bist so jung, und bist so gesund.*
>
> *Du heissest mich reden, und machst mir's so schwer,*
> *Ich seh' dich an, und zittre so sehr.*

"The Old Washerwoman" is probably Chamisso's most popular poem; **"Salas y Gomez"** won him the applause of connoisseurs. But European name, yes, a world reputation he achieved in a narrative prose work. Today, almost a hundred years after it was written, this title book will, I am convinced, have the same immediate and profound appeal.

The Marvellous Tale of Peter Schlemihl was, to begin with its literary history, written in the year 1813. At that time the poet, in a state of desperation, both personally and politically speaking, was botanizing on the estate of his friends the Itzenplitz family. He himself said he undertook the work to distract his mind and amuse the children of a friend (Eduard Hitzig). There are a few scraps of information about some small incidents that helped to shape the fable. Chamisso says in a letter: "I had lost on a journey my hat, portmanteau, gloves, handkerchief, my whole movable property. Fouqué asked me whether I had not also lost my shadow, and we began imagining such a mishap. Another time, turning the pages of La Fontaine, I read about a very obliging man in a company who turned all sorts of things out of his pockets as they were asked for. If one were to encourage the fellow, I thought, he might even take out a coach and four as well. With that the Schlemihl was born. And when once in the country I had leisure and was bored, I began to write." Wilhelm Rauschenbusch, the publisher of the two-volume Grote edition of Chamisso, a personal acquaintance of the author, adds that an essential factor in the development of the fable was a walk Chamisso once took with Fouqué at Nennhausen, the Fouqué estate. "The sun threw long shadows, so that little Fouqué, to judge from his, looked almost as tall as tall Chamisso. 'Look, Fouqué,' says Chamisso, 'what if I just rolled up your shadow and you had to walk along beside me without one!' Fouqué found the idea frightful, and Chamisso teasingly went on to exploit the subject." Need of distraction, then, playing uncle to some children, a travelling mishap, a chance remark about a book, a jest among friends, idleness and boredom—these are certainly modest motives and occasions for the origin of a composition which may justly be called immortal. Certainly that is the way stories arise. But the story that here arose received in the hands of a poet qualities calculated to charm the world. French and English, Dutch and Spanish translated it, America pirated it from England, and in Germany it was reprinted with the drawings of Cruickshank, the illustrator of Dickens. Hoffmann, when it was read aloud to him, is said to have hung on the reader's lips, beside himself with pleasure and suspense. One can readily believe it.

Is it in order to set down a few recollections, a few advance pointers about the charm of the tale? First: Peter Schlemihl has been called a fairy-tale; or even, because of the poet's idle assertion that he wrote it for the children of a friend, it has been called a fairy-tale for the young. That it is not. However indefinite its terrain, it is too much the novel; with all its whimsical vein, it is too modern, feverish, too much in earnest to come within the rubric of the fairy-tale. For the same reasons, in my opinion and experience, it is not particularly suitable for children. The story begins in a quite realistic, commonplace vein, and the real artistry of the writer lies in his knowing how to keep up the realistic bourgeois atmosphere to the end, all the while relating in the greatest detail the most fabulous and impossible circumstances. This in such a way that Schlemihl's adventures impress the reader as "strange" in the sense of a destiny seldom or never before visited upon an erring human being by the will of God; but never actually "strange" in the sense of an unnatural or irresponsible or "fairy" story. The autobiographical, confessional form, as contrasted with that of the typical fairy-tale, contributes to emphasize its truthfulness and reality. So, if I were challenged to classify Peter Schlemihl, I think I should call it a fantastic novelette or long story.

The theme derived from La Fontaine is happily employed on the very first page with the altogether discreet introduction of the grey man, that "silent, lean, tall, and gaunt elderly person" who at Lord John's garden party in all modesty and helpfulness produces, to the horror of the narrator, not only a dispatch-case and telescope, but a Turkish rug, a sizable marquee, and three bridled riding-horses out of his "tight-fitting" coat-tail pocket. It is the Devil; and he is capitally drawn, especially in the scene between him and Schlemihl on the lawn. No cloven hoof, no demonry,

no diabolic glitter. An over-courteous, embarrassed man, who blushes (a pricelessly convincing touch) when he introduces the crucial conversation about the shadow. Schlemihl, hovering between horror and respect, treats him with aghast politeness. What this extraordinary amateur offers him in exchange for his shadow are good old familiar things: the genuine magic root, the mandrake; magic pennies; thieves' thalers; the napkin of Roland's squire; a gallows-mannikin; Fortunatus's wishing-cap, "newly refurbished." The story here refers to familiar and taken-for-granted paraphernalia of saga and fairy-tale, and this sustains its atmosphere of the legitimate and reliable. The befooled Schlemihl chooses the lucky purse; and then follows that priceless moment when the grey man kneels down and with admirable deftness loosens Schlemihl's shadow from the grass, lifts it from head to foot, rolls it up, folds it, and puts it in his pocket.

But now, of course, everybody—man, woman, and street Arab—straightway perceives that Schlemihl has no shadow and overwhelms him with scorn, pity, or horror. On this point I am not quite so sure as I was in the matter of the lucky purse. If a man meets me when the sun is shining and he casts no shadow, would I notice its absence? And if I did, would I not simply conclude that there was some peculiar optical factor unknown to me that made him seem to lack one? Well, no matter. Precisely the impossibility of checking up on and deciding this question is the real point of the book; granting the premise, everything follows with shattering consistency.

For what comes next is the portrayal of an apparently advantaged and enviable but actually romantically miserable existence, dwelling solitary in its own mind with a sinister secret—and certainly no poet has ever before succeeded in bringing home to the reader the emotions of such a man or depicting them with such convincing simplicity, realism, and sympathy.

The deciding factor is that the author managed from the start to convince us of the value and importance of a good healthy shadow for the respectability of a human being. So that we find such expressions as "sinister secret" and the like at worst only a bit exaggerated; we are prepared to see a man without a shadow as the most afflicted and repulsive human being under the sun. We see the wealthy Schlemihl leave his house by night and moonlight, wrapped in a voluminous cloak, with his hat drawn over his brows, driven by the tormenting desire to test the general opinion and read his doom out of the mouths of passers-by. We see him cringe beneath the pity of the women, the mockery of the young, the scorn of grown men, especially the portly ones, "who themselves cast a good broad shadow." We see him staggering heartbroken home when a sweet innocent child chances to cast her eye upon him from close at hand and at sight of his shadowless state veils her lovely face and passes on with averted gaze. His sense of guilt at this incident is boundless. And the narrative rises again to one of its most extraordinary heights in the episode with the painter, whom Schlemihl approaches in a roundabout way and asks whether he could paint a man an artificial shadow. The artist makes the chilling reply that whoever has no shadow should not walk in the sun, that is the safest and most reasonable way—and quits him with a "piercing" look.

The story goes on to tell with great fidelity to detail how Schlemihl tries to adjust himself more or less to his affliction. To his valet, a sturdy fellow with a kind face, he has in a weak moment confided his shameful infirmity; and the good soul, although horrified, conquers his feelings and, defying all the world, remains loyal and helps Schlemihl all he can. He supports his master, walks everywhere in front of or with him, and, being taller and broader, he covers him at critical moments with his own imposing shadow. Thus Schlemihl is able to go among people and play his part in society. "I had indeed," says he, "to pretend to many oddities of conduct. But all such eccentricities become the man of means." Defeats and humiliations are not lacking and presently comes that touching episode which is an immortal theme of romantic poetry: the love of the marked man, hunted, infamous, accursed, for a pure and unsuspecting maiden, to whom he turns like any simple, bourgeois human being.

I mean the unhappy idyll with the forester's daughter; there we have all the typical elements of the theme: the simple, foolish, match-making mother; the decent, distrustful father who "does not look so high"; the wooer's pangs of conscience, the intuitions of the girl, her tender attempt to penetrate her lover's secret, and her woman's cry: "If you are wretched, bind me to your wretchedness, that I may help you bear it." The old tale is told with such freshness, such convincing gravity, such veracity and detail, one loses sight of the fact that the premises are fantastic, since the poet himself seems wholly to have forgotten it. Nowhere is the story so little a fairy-story as here, nowhere so entirely a romance, reality, serious life. Those lines of verse seem to preside over this prose, lines fearful, fervid, strangely bold in their simplicity, like all confessions:

> *Du heissest mich reden und machst mir's so*
> *schwer,*
> *Ich seh' dich an und zittre so sehr.*

One would like to tell the whole story over again, put one's finger on every paragraph; but here is the rest of it. Nothing happier than the last chapter, where the Evil One, "as though used to such treatment," silently bows his head and stoops his shoulders and lets himself be thrashed by the faithful Bendel. Nothing more amusing than the point of the jest: "Now the whole affair of course became clear to me: the man must

have had the invisible bird's nest which makes invisible him who has it but not his shadow, and then he threw it away!" Yes, yes! And no finer conclusion imaginable than the one invented by the poet. It is a good and soothing end, though at the same time an austere one, remote from the childlike optimism of the fairy-tale, where everything ends in wedding bells and "if they are not dead they live there still."

Schlemihl, shut out by early sin from human society, never returns to it and never regains his shadow. He remains solitary, he goes on doing penance. But he finds in nature a substitute for bourgeois happiness. By a fortunate chance, he is drawn to contemplate her and spends his life in the service of natural science. The author accompanies with a wealth of accurate geographical detail the account of his hero's travels in the seven-league boots—here again employing the method of supporting fantasy with realistic detail. An illustration of his carefulness as well as of his unobtrusive way of making plausible the fantastic is the brilliant little inspiration of the "brake-shoe." Innocently, with all the simplicity in the world, the idea of the brake-shoe is transferred to the slippers which Schlemihl draws on over his boots when he wants to take ordinary and not seven-league strides. Thus the writer succeeds in giving the whole impossibility a character of bourgeois realism which in the legend it never possessed. Now, a grotesque figure, magnificently satisfied with his lot, Schlemihl covers the backbone of this earth, striding and studying. He establishes the geography of unexplored regions, he botanizes and zoologizes in the grand manner, and he will take care to have his manuscripts submitted before his death to the University of Berlin. "I have faithfully striven," he says, "with all that I had of silent, stern, unintermitted effort, to depict what came before my inward eye; and my self-satisfaction has depended on making what I described coincide with the original." Here the fantastic improvisation of the poet's imagination merges into a confession. And is it only here that the confession occurs?

Chamisso has made it easy for his contemporaries and posterity to see that his Schlemihl is himself. Repeatedly and with evident pleasure he has used external detail to play upon the identity between the poet and his fictional hero. Why must Schlemihl's faithful servant be called Bendel? The name recurs in a humorous poem telling how Chamisso as a young lieutenant went to sleep over his Homer and failed to report for duty:

> *Stiefletten, Bendel, schnell! ich seh*
> *erschrocken,*
> *Dass sich bereits der Obrist eingefunden.*

> Quick, Bendel, quick! My boots! I see appalled
> The colonel's come, already he's advancing.

So he actually had a servant of that name. There is a letter to Hitzig wherein he fancifully relates how the shadowless world-wanderer personally brought him the manuscript of his memoirs. The description of this man, even down to the tight-fitting black coat, is Chamisso's own—why? His explicit denial fits almost better: "The shadow," he asserts in the introductory poem **"To My Old Friend Peter Schlemihl"**:

> *Den Schatten hab' ich, der mir angeboren,*
> *Ich habe meinen Schatten nie verloren.*

>   The shadow I was born with, good or
> ill,
>   I never lost it, and I have it still.

He goes on to lament:

> *Mich traf, obgleich unschuldig wie das Kind,*
> *Der Hohn, den sie für deine Blösse hatten.—*
> *Ob wir einander denn so ähnlich sind?!*
> *Sie schrien mir nach: Schlemihl, wo ist dein*
> *Schatten?*

>   Guiltless as any babe I had to bear
>   Their scorn when they your follies
> would deride:
>   Whether or not we like each other are,
>   "Schlemihl, where is your shadow?"
> still they cried.

This seems to be literally true, for Hitzig relates to Fouqué that some Berlin lad had mocked Chamisso on the street and called after him: "Just wait, Peter Schlemihl!" But we need not assume that the popularity of his double grieved the poet. Poets who give themselves away want at bottom to be recognized; for with them it is not so much a matter of the fame of their work as the fame of their life and suffering. But then, what was the experience, what was the suffering this poet had in common with his hero? Wherein lies his inner solidarity with poor Peter Schlemihl? How far is the little book a confession? And what does it mean to have no shadow? People have racked their brains over the mystery ever since the book appeared, they have devoted theses to it and answered it all too clearly and precisely by saying that the man without a shadow is the man without a country. But that would be to narrow down too much the "deeper meaning" of a motif which in the first instance was only a grotesque fancy. Schlemihl is no allegory; Chamisso was not the man to whom an intellectual idea was ever the primary thing in his production. "Only life," he said, "can recapture life." But precisely because that is true, he would not have been able without some basis of experience to fill out a comic idea into something so full of life and novelistic veracity. Need of distraction, avuncular benevolence, could never by themselves have enabled him to write the tale if he had not known

himself to be in a particular situation that gave him power to animate it with verisimilitude out of his own personal lot.

But again, what was this peculiar and personal lot? Chamisso wrote a charming foreword to the French edition of *Peter Schlemihl*. Towards the end of it he says that his tale has fallen into the hands of thinking people who, accustomed to reading in order to be edified, are troubled because they want to know what the shadow was. And then, with a straight face, he proceeds to quote in French from an old tome the definition of the shadow:

> *De l'ombre.*

> *Un corps opaque ne peut jamais être éclairé qu'en partie par un corps lumineux, et l'espace privé de lumière qui est situé du côté de la partie non éclairée, est ce qu'on appelle ombre. Ainsi l'ombre, proprement dite, représente un solide dont la forme dépend à la fois de celle du corps lumineux, de celle du corps opaque, et de la position de celui-ci à l'égard du corps lumineux. L'ombre considéré sur un plan situé derrière le corps opaque qui la produit n'est autre chose que la section de ce plan dans le solide qui représente l'ombre.*

> (Hauy, *Traité élémentaire de physique. T. 11. 1002 et 1006.*)

> *"C'est donc de ce solide,"* Chamisso comments, *"dont il est question dans la merveilleuse histoire de Pierre Schlémihl. La science de la finance nous instruit assez de l'importance de l'argent, celle de l'ombre est moins généralement reconnue. Mon imprudent ami a convoité l'argent dont il connaissait le prix et n'a pas songé au solide. La leçon qu'il a chèrement payé, il veut qu'elle nous profite et son expérience nous crie: songez au solide."*

"Songez au solide!" Here, then, is the ironic moral of the book, whose author knew only too precisely what it means to lack solidity, human regularity, bourgeois stability. "Thus," he writes in the autobiographical sketch we have from him, "in the years when the boy is growing to manhood I stood alone. I made verses. . . . Doubtful of myself, without station or occupation, bowed down and crushed, I spent in Berlin a gloomy time." He knew the torments of youth, the problems of the young man who, without any normal future to look forward to, cannot test his powers. Wounded in his ego, he sees mockery and scorn wherever he turns, especially from the stout and solid, "who themselves cast a good broad shadow." He had perhaps even stranger insights into the fluctuating unreality and precariousness of his existence. By birth a Frenchman, he had made Germany his home and could say to himself that if chance had so willed, he might just as well have made it anywhere else. Somewhere in his writings he expressly declares that he had discovered in himself the gift of feeling at home everywhere. His extraordinary talent for languages was no doubt part of this feeling—we know that he possessed not only German but all sorts of other tongues as well, even Hawaiian. What was he, who was he anyhow? Nothing, everything? A creature, not a person, uncircumscribable, everywhere and nowhere at home? There may have been days when he felt that out of sheer vagueness and unreality he himself cast no shadow.

The shadow has become, in *Peter Schlemihl,* a symbol of all bourgeois solidity and human belongingness. It is spoken of as money is spoken of, as something which one has to respect if one wants to live among men; which one can only get rid of if one is minded to live exclusively for himself and his better self. The ironic summons: *"Songez au solide!"* applies to the bourgeois, as we would say today, to the philistines, to use the word of the romantics. But irony almost always implies making a superiority out of a lack. The whole little book is nothing but a profoundly experienced description of the sufferings of the marked and solitary man. It tells us that young Chamisso knew with painful vividness how to esteem the value of a healthy shadow.

Well, he got one! The pretty verses by his friend Hitzig, sent to Fouqué, the third member of the group, to announce the news of Chamisso's betrothal, explain that Schlemihl need no longer go without a shadow, that in fact he has three: first, the shadow of the Prussian eagle, which graciously hovers over him with its wings; second, the shadows of the trees in the Botanical Gardens, whose well-paid head he is; and finally, most beautiful of all, the shadow which has vowed not to leave him more—"Antonie—do we need more words?" And Chamisso himself sent a picture of his bride to Fouqué with the lines:

> *Den Schlemihl genannt sie ·hatten,*
> *Reich in seiner Schatten Zier,*
> *Gönnet jetzt von seinem Schatten*
> *Strafend einen Schatten dir.*
> He whom once they knew as Schlemihl,
> Brave in shadow clothed anew,
> Here a shadow of his shadow
> *En revanche* now gives to you.

It is the old story. Werther shot himself, but Goethe remained alive. Schlemihl, shadowless, strides booted over hill and dale, a natural scientist, "living to himself alone." But Chamisso, after producing a book from his sufferings, hastened to outgrow his problem-child phase. He settles down, becomes the father of a family and an academician, master of his craft. Only the eternally bohemian finds that stupid. One cannot be interesting

forever. Either you die of your interestingness, or you become a master.—But *Peter Schlemihl* is one of the most charming youthful works in German literature.

Hermann J. Weigand (essay date 1965)

SOURCE: "Peter Schlemihl" in *Surveys and Soundings in European Literature,* Princeton University Press, 1966, pp 208-22.

[*In the following essay, originally published in 1965, Weigand offers a thematic analysis of* Peter Schlemihl, *interpreting the work as a tongue-in-cheek satire on "salesmanship and business ethics."*]

Peter Schlemihl, an immortal classic that charmed the reading public of Europe and America on its first appearance a century and a half ago, is the story of a man who got involved with the devil by selling him his shadow. That so great a poet as Hugo von Hofmannsthal nevertheless chose to omit it from his collection, *Deutsche Erzähler,* is due, I believe, not to any deficiencies on Chamisso's part, but rather to Hofmannsthal's own deep involvement with the motif of the shadow and its symbolism along totally divergent lines as developed in his *Die Frau ohne Schatten,* the text of Richard Strauss's opera, and later elaborated in a story bearing the same title. *Peter Schlemihl* should have been written by an American, because it is an illustration of the peculiarly American techniques of salesmanship as taught in the best manuals of the craft. *Peter Schlemihl* is a parable on the central Christian theme summed up in the words of Jesus: "For what shall it profit a man, if he shall gain the whole world, and lose his own soul" (Mark 8:36). *Peter Schlemihl* is a serious, realistic story built on fantastic premises; it is a two-act drama full of acute emotional tension and shot through with iridescent flashes of wit, humor, satire, and paradox. *Peter Schlemihl* is the psychological case study of an insecure individual beset by anxieties and phobias that shape up to a full-fledged psychoneurosis. He is cured in the end without benefit of the psychoanalyst's couch; he continues to bear the scars of his harrowing experience, but he has achieved an adjustment to conditions that guarantees him a life of satisfying concentrated activity and relative happiness. Making its appeal on so many counts, the story of Peter Schlemihl offers high entertainment to readers of the most various interests.

Peter's story takes the form of a personal confession addressed to his most intimate friend, Adelbert von Chamisso, the author. It is released to the public through the indiscretion of two of Chamisso's literary friends. The exchange of letters that heads the story in lieu of a preface must not be skipped by the discerning reader: they are an integral part of the intricate web of relationships that constitute the many-faceted charm of the story.

Peter Schlemihl is, on the face of it, a variant of the theme that received its most famous treatment in Goethe's *Faust,* the first part of which had appeared when Chamisso wrote his story. Among other, later treatments of the theme, Jeremias Gotthelf's *Die schwarze Spinne* (1842) deserves special mention. In all three cases the basic situation is the same: an individual or, as in Gotthelf's story, a community, gets involved with the devil, and in all three instances the devil is ultimately foiled in line with the tradition of folklore that shows the devil, for all his wiles, to be no match for the powers of good. But Chamisso's originality in the handling of the theme shows up at a glance. In Goethe's *Faust,* an individual of superman aspirations, contemptuous of the limits set to human existence, despairing of penetrating the ultimate mystery of being by ordinary means, enters open-eyed into a conditional pact and wager with the devil, with his soul as the stake. Faust's devil is a cavalier who hides his essentially evil design under an entertaining and often attractive mask of impish roguery. In Gotthelf's story of *The Black Spider* the community of peasants, tortured by impossible exactions of their overlords, is pressured into agreeing to the devil's terms, and he can afford to dispense with any attempt to conceal his identity. In *Peter Schlemihl,* on the other hand, the devil sets about ensnaring the soul of a simple, God-fearing man who would shrink in horror if overtly approached by the Evil One. He must accordingly go about the business of ensnaring Peter with the utmost circumspection. To this end, having first dazzled the unsuspecting Peter by a series of magical tricks, he approaches Peter as the deferential salesman bent first of all on putting his prospect at his ease. Though unable withal to overcome Peter's instinctive aversion to his sinuous, slimy, indefinable personality, he tempts him with the equivalent of an offer of something for nothing—a very large something indeed, an inexhaustible purse. The nothing he wants in exchange is the shadow that he sees Peter casting "with a certain disdainful nonchalance."

What is this shadow, what does it stand for? Readers asked this question of Chamisso when the story appeared, and interpreters have labored ever since to equate it with something positive and substantial. The conjecture most often voiced is that Chamisso equated the loss of Peter's shadow with his own loss of his homeland. Chamisso's family were refugees who fled from France in the wake of the Revolution. But Chamisso never endorsed this interpretation. Any attempt to see the shadow in terms of being rooted in a specific milieu must fail. It does not fit Peter's case. Peter's swap is an act of impulsive choice, and the gradual chain of involvement which Peter experiences could be deduced only from such a premise. The value

of the shadow is given as a mere nothing according to all standards of human usefulness. A closer parallel might be found in Goethe's *Werther*. Finding himself inadvertently an uninvited guest at a social gathering of aristocrats, Werther suffers a most humiliating rebuff. He is taken aside by a well-wisher and informed that his presence is embarrassing to some of the highborn ladies—all this because, though attached to the Count's retinue and enjoying his personal benevolence, he has no "von" to his name, no magical three-letter word that serves as a card of admission to such company. But even such identification of the shadow with a specific social status is no equivalent for Peter's complete ostracism from all human society.

To read Peter's story in terms of an allegory is to take a false lead. We must take the shadow "for what it is worth." It is worth nothing in practical terms, but its absence makes Peter a marked man. In this way the missing shadow can serve as a symbol for anything that can produce such an effect on a man. The shadow in question, however, is not just an ordinary shadow. Since the devil has a hand in the business, it assumes magical properties. It can be manipulated, rolled up and unfolded for display like a substantial physical object. A second characteristic of equal importance is the fact that when Peter shows himself in the open, its absence is noticed by everybody at once. Such attention to an attribute of totally negligible value runs counter to all observable habits of human behavior.

These, then, are the fantastic premises on which Peter's story is built. By a free—if ill-considered—choice he has swapped his shadow for a very valuable consideration. By this choice he has lost his freedom of movement, his spontaneity. He can no longer be his natural self in the open. So far as he ventures to live among men, his whole personality will be geared to furtiveness and deception.

This basic situation, derived from fantastic premises, is the starting point for a development that unfolds with close adherence to realism and psychological plausibility. These same words would aptly describe Kafka's techniques in some of his most notable successes. *Peter Schlemihl* is in this respect a forerunner of *The Metamorphosis.*

Peter's story unfolds as a two-act drama. It is a contest of wills, a tug of war. The devil is the aggressor and Peter is on the defensive. For a long time Peter is unaware of the aggressor's long-range design. The supersalesman plots his course with wily calculation and infinite patience. A whole year elapses before he shows his hand. The tug of war runs its course in two distinct campaigns. The aggressor's initial strategy is, after exhaustive preparations, to close in on his unsuspecting victim with a double-pronged frontal attack calculated to achieve a total breakthrough. The plan, apparently foolproof, engineered with consummate ingenuity and executed without a flaw, nevertheless fails. A chance event, a circumstance beyond the range of foresight and calculation, at the last moment turns victory into rout. With Mephisto our salesman could vent his chagrin in the exclamation "Ein grosser Aufwand schmählich ist vertan!" [A lavish effort has been disgracefully wasted!] But his tenacity is not yet ready to give up the game as lost. In a second round he follows a strategy keyed to the new situation. He lays siege to the fortress, confident that a campaign of attrition will force its ultimate surrender. If this paln also fails, only an imperceptive reader will attribute the outcome to bungling. Such an imputation should bring a blush to the master salesman's cheek.

But in order to follow the moves deployed we must take a good look at Peter and follow it up by a second closer look.

While omitting any specific data on Peter's background, his story acquaints us very quickly with his circumstances and his personality. In the course of the first few pages we gather that Peter is a young man of good moral character, breeding, and education. He is very poor, but his dress and manner attempt to put on a brave show of respectability.[1] Bearing a letter of recommendation to Thomas John, a millionaire, he is enormously impressed by the display of wealth and aware of the gulf in social status it interposes between himself and those who enjoy it. For characterizing Peter's disposition, the language of modern psychology offers the handiest terms. Peter has an acute sense of inferiority. We may call it a complex because it shows up as insecurity in his social behavior. He impulsively toadies to his prospective patron by echoing his dictum that anyone not worth a million must be accounted a rogue. In stealing away from the garden party where he is out of place, Peter is apprehensive of being taken to task for walking across the grass. He overreacts to the uncanny stranger's compliments. In the course of this interview he fluctuates between a desire to shrink and hide from the eerie magician and an impulsive burst of condescension toward a man who apparently has lost his wits. He ends up with an equally impulsive lunge at the proffered bait. Without question, Peter suffers from ego-deficiency. Having no defined social status of his own, he overcompensates in his responses. We see this so well later, when Peter's image of himself is determined by the evil glances shot at him. Inner-directed by his moral education, he nevertheless succumbs to the pressure of the social environment to the point of lapsing into a state of hopelessly other-directed bewilderment. Eventually, the pressure of tacit social disapproval and the anguish over the outcome of his passion combine to make Peter fall prey to a full-fledged guilt psychoneurosis.

This is what the salesman had counted on and waited for in order to apply the squeeze and close the pincers of his attack. But this is anticipating.

Now for that second closer look at Peter of which we spoke above. We have been seeing him as the artless simpleton entrapped by the wiles of a master salesman into a disastrous bargain. That is the surface version of Peter's story. But Peter's strange autobiography is a personal confession, addressed to his friend Adelbert von Chamisso, the author, and this friend is none other than Peter's double. As shown by the letters that introduce the story in lieu of a preface, Chamisso is playing a game—a game that abounds in wit, humor, hilarious fun, satire, irony, parody, and paradox. Chamisso, at the time of the writing, is a man of settled pursuits, a student of plant and animal science, chiefly concerned with the collecting and classifying of plants, but through Peter's mouth, at the close of the story, he also confesses to the more ambitious hope of contributing to the establishment of a "natural system"—not genetically, it is to be presumed, forty years before Darwin, but by ranging all the phenomena under observation in graduated series of typological relationships. In the story of *Peter Schlemihl* Chamisso delights in portraying his personality at a more youthful, immature stage of its development a decade earlier. He portrays his alter ego as involved in the turmoil of unattainable wishes and plunged into the vortex of a consuming passion that threatens his sanity and his integrity. Chamisso introduces Peter as his unmistakable double in looks and features, idiosyncrasy of costume, habits and disposition, including the gaucherie and lack of alertness that made him the butt of his friends' good-natured teasing.

The mask is fully transparent even to the present-day reader, who may never have heard of Hitzig, the biographer of Hoffmann, and is likely to associate Fouqué's name only with his immortal story of the mermaid Undine. One of its delightful devices is that Peter makes his confession with a straight face, with deep emotion and—tongue-in-cheek. The twinkle of his eye can be caught in any phase of his recital—in the puns and word plays, the literary allusions, the profound reflections, the dripping sentimentality of style in the recital of the love story, and in his half-hearted attempts to explain and excuse his unchivalrous conduct. A startling instance revealing Peter's double personality is his matter-of-fact account of that extraordinary dream of seeing Chamisso seated in his study among his plant specimens and skeletons, flanked by the tomes of the great authorities Haller, Linné, and Humboldt, but—dead. The heart of this Chamisso is stilled. It has forsworn the dance of devastating passion that will be the high point of Peter's confession. The mask is lifted to the limit at an early point of the story when Peter, appearing shadowless in public for the first time, finds himself "reviewed" and pelted with horse apples by the whole gang of "literary" juveniles. The wag in Peter is at his best in his sundry explanations of how he lost his shadow—the shadow that froze to the ground in the mythical cold of the Russian winter; the shadow sent out for repair because of damage suffered from the step of a heavy-footed lout; the shadow that faded out (and has not yet come back) along with the loss of hair and nails in the wake of a disease. This is in the best tradition of the great Baron Münchhausen. Contrast these admittedly ludicrous inventions of a desperate demented man with Peter's straight-faced account of the objects that successively came out of the stranger's pocket—telescope, rug, tent, plus three saddled riding horses. He concludes with guileless candor: "My dear Chamisso, you would not believe these things had I not seen them myself."

A fantastic story built on this premise, the identity of the narrator with the recipient of his confession, their thin disguise penetrated at every moment by the flashing of impish lights—such a story, almost needless to say, calls for a double act of participation by the reader. The tense emotional drama will hold him in its grip. At the same time the witty double-play will afford no end of intellectual amusement. Like a light melody embroidering its graceful loops around a somber theme, the two attitudes will not interfere with or neutralize each other. They will rather afford that complex entertainment felt by the Romantic generation of German writers to be the essence of great literature.

With these preliminaries disposed of, we can turn our attention to the plot, the unfolding of the master salesman's grand strategy.

Knowing that Peter will repent of his bargain upon realizing that it brands him as a marked man, the cunning salesman disappears, leaving word that he will return for another business talk in "a year and a day." The phrase "über Jahr und Tag," originally a well-defined term of legal parlance, is a very vague measure of time in ordinary usage. That Peter takes the phrase literally and misses by one the count of the days elapsed is part of the same hypnotic spell to which he had succumbed in watching the stranger's sleight-of-hand manipulation of his inexhaustible pocket. This explanation is, of course, left to the reader's conjecture because Peter reports his error without suspecting that he has been tricked. We put it down as part of the devil's practice to deceive by telling the truth. What the devil counts on in his game is the force of habit. Within a year Peter will find it impossible to be without his wealth. At the same time the constant threat of exposure, the ever-present need to be on his guard, will undermine his personality, weak to begin with, and soften him up for the deal to be proposed. Peter's career as a man of wealth, it is true, got off to an auspicious start. But it could be foreseen that his short-lived flirtation with Fanny, during which

he displayed a pose of self-confidence and ready wit quite alien to his bashful and impulsive nature, would end in disaster and precipitous flight. Thus, in his new place of residence, Peter finds himself in a tragi-comical predicament, passively forced to assume the role of the highborn man of mystery, Graf Peter, wrapped in an aura of gloom, a fraud against his will. That he now falls in love in earnest with a simple innocent girl and pins all his hopes on finding her a sympathetic partner of his loneliness might also have been predicted. That it did occur, enormously enhanced the tempter's prospects of success. If the force of habit is great, the motive force of a passionate love is without limit.

The devil plays his cards well. He engineered Rascal's betrayal of his master and the forester's three-day ultimatum to coincide with the time of his expected return. He lets the climactic day pass without showing himself, while Peter wears himself out with anxious waiting. The next day, when anxiety, anguish, despair, and desolation have driven Peter to roaming aimlessly on a deserted heath, the devil finds that the time is ripe at last for the frontal attack. Accosting Peter familiarly, he offers to extricate him from his predicament by the return of his shadow in exchange for the signature involving his soul. Peter demurs, not unexpectedly perhaps, but this is only the opening phase of a complicated battle of movement. Now the tempter comes forward with his offer to lead him unseen under the screen of his *Tarnkappe* to the forester's lodge and let him gaze his fill on the face of his beloved Mina. Again Peter declines, because he senses the trap, and he remains adamant in his refusal to commit his soul. But the tempter still has a whole bag of tricks up his sleeve. He produces Peter's shadow and carefully adjusting it to his own person, struts up and down with the shadow following him. This maneuver, while exposing Peter to sadistic torture, is dictated by a more practical design: Bendel approaches, having tracked his master like a faithful dog, but the tempter's business is with Peter alone, and Bendel must be removed from the scene. He accomplishes this with ingenious cunning. Ignoring Bendel's threats and impervious to the hail of blows from Bendel's stout blackthorn, he arches his shoulders and stalks away with measured step, continuing in this way until both he and Bendel have disappeared from Peter's sight.

Alone again, Peter spends the day and the night on the heath in aimless despair. The next day, the day that will irrevocably decide Mina's fate, sees the tempter execute his supreme maneuver. Of a sudden, startled by a sound, Peter sees an apparently masterless human shadow walking by. Instantly he makes a dash to capture it in the quixotic hope that it will cling to his person. But the shadow takes flight, and Peter exhausts his last energies in hot pursuit. As it makes for a wooded area, where it would be lost to sight, Peter redoubles his efforts. He gains on the shadow. It suddenly wheels about, and Peter collides with a solid body. The full force of the impact throws Peter to the ground, his arms locked around a man under him and visible. The denouement of this encounter represents the capital *tour de force* of Chamisso's wit. With lightning speed our guileless *Ingénu* hero has grasped a desperately intricate chain of reasoning. "Now the situation resolved itself for me in the most natural way in the world." Obviously the stranger, carrying the invisible bird's nest that makes its bearer invisible but not his shadow (a requisite of folklore featured in the title of one of Grimmelshausen's novels), had dropped it under the force of the impact, thereby becoming visible. The nest must betray its location by a diminutive shadow. A glance at the ground, a quick grab, and Peter held in his hand the priceless nest that made him totally invisible since he had no shadow to begin with. The tempter had calculated only too well. Without wasting a thought on the identity of the stranger whose property he had unlawfully appropriated, Peter felt himself irresistibly drawn to the scene of his passion, now that he could do so without having to endure the odious company of the tempter. But events prove that he had walked into a trap. There is the stranger seated at his side, gloating over his misery, both of them screened by a magic net. And this time Peter would have infallibly succumbed to the combined pressure of love, heart-rending pity, a sense of honor and nervous exhaustion, had not "an event intervened in place of a deed," when the blood-stained pen was thrust into his hand to sign: Peter fell into a deep swoon from which he awoke only after Mina had been lost to him forever. In his confession Peter speaks of this event in sober and apologetic terms. To us it is clear nonetheless that he has been saved by the intervention of divine grace. The devil's frontal attack, launched with incredible cunning and patience to win the soul of a man who is weak but essentially good, has failed. With this, the curtain rings down on act one of the drama.

Act two of the drama can be passed in quick review. We can be certain to begin with that it can bring nothing to match the climactic tension of the first act. And as we watch the continuation of the contest, we are not likely to place our bets on the devil as the winner. That the devil does not give up after having suffered so stunning a defeat does credit to his tenacity. He still has a powerful hold on Peter by virtue of the inexhaustible purse. But after the loss of Mina he can no longer hope to further his ends by an appeal to Peter's noblest impulses. That he must alter his tactics to conform to a basically changed situation is evident. Having failed in his great frontal strategic thrust, he resorts to a strategy of attrition. Habituation, the motive on which he based his calculation from the outset, may yet bring his victim to terms, he reasons. He offers Peter the use of his shadow on a loan basis coupled with his own personal services, hoping thereby gradually to wear down that instinctive aversion to his slimy

person which kept Peter from signing. The temptation to enjoy both the purse and the shadow exercises an enormous lure. Once more, in the course of their journeyings, our moral friend succumbs to the weakness of the flesh. He tries to abscond with the loaned shadow, but the ruse fails. He is put to shame by the observation of the complaisant servant that, while not making any profession of such high moral standards as Peter, he on his own part has simply followed the rules of decent behavior without resorting to violence or trickery.

There comes the moment of the second climax. Having had to listen to his companion's glib philosophical sales talk day after day, Peter is ready at last to face a showdown. Did the salesman have a signature from Mr. Thomas John, he asks. Oh, in the case of so good a friend that formality was altogether superfluous, he replies. What has become of him? Peter continues. By God, I want to know. At this, the devil reluctantly reaches into his pocket and draws forth the livid corpse of Thomas John whose lips utter the words: "Justo judicio dei judicatus sum; justo judicio dei condemnatus sum."

This denouement comes as a complete surprise. How is it possible that the devil, having played a superbly astute and infinitely tenacious game, should suddenly throw down his hand and call it quits? Is it possible that he writes off the pursuit of this particular soul as a bad investment, an investment of time and energy out of proportion to any possible yield? Or is he just a stupid devil after all who finds his tenacity outmatched by Peter's resistance? But does not this conclusion nullify the carefully built-up image of the devil as an aggressor who never lets go? Is it possible on the other hand, that the author, having run out of ideas, spoils the end of the story by a lame conclusion? Time and again I have known students to read this critical episode without raising an eyebrow. Does the foreign language operate as a barrier? I am persuaded that some of them, at least, read their comics with more discernment. However, even an interpreter like Benno von Wiese (*Die deutsche Novelle,* Düsseldorf, 1956) glosses over the scene without remarking on the tempter's incredible psychological inconsistency.

They have all missed the point, and yet the point is incredibly simple. Every child who has read the *Arabian Nights* knows that if you find yourself being carried aloft through space by a djinn and if in this plight you utter the words, "There is no power and no protection except in Allah the Sublime," the story will continue: "At these words a fiery dart fell from heaven and burned the djinn to ashes." It is an axiom of the game that if the devil is commanded something in the name of God, the infernal one must comply. Peter in his emotional outburst had inadvertently used the name of God. With that, the devil's game was up. This denouement was subtly prepared for at an earlier point of the story. When the devil first proffered the swap of Peter's shadow for his signature, Peter had replied: "If our bargain can be rescinded, well and good, in God's name." At this the tempter's brow had darkened.

Once more, divine grace, operating through the mechanics of a fortuitous outburst, has come to the aid of a good man. But in order to clinch the victory, Peter now has to rise to the great act of renunciation. There is no flinching from the decision. Casting the ill-gotten purse into the abyss, Peter now solemnly adjures the tempter in the name of the living God, to betake himself hence and show his face no more.

This is the end of the dramatic contest. The devil's frontal attack failed at the moment he thought victory in his grasp; his campaign of attrition has likewise come to naught. Both times divine intervention had mercy on the good man's frailty and saved his soul. But one cannot do business with the devil and expect to get off scot-free. Peter's shadow is lost to him forever. As the German phrase goes: "Er hat Haare gelassen." [He suffered the consequences.]

The story proper ends here. The appended sequel, centered on the divine gift of the Seven League Boots, an *Ersatz* (compensation) for the forfeited contact with human society, is a story of pure adventure. It is not lacking in exciting and hazardous incidents, but it is without a trace of the anguishing dramatic tension of the first story. It has the same fanciful touch, it is told with the same delightful attention to realistic detail in a miraculous setting, the same superb *Anschaulichkeit,* but it requires no analysis. The sequel is not a comedown in any sense, and the unity of personality is felicitously sustained. Here, incidentally, we have a rare instance, where a knowledge of the author's biography contributes to the inherent charm of the story. Peter's acquisition of the Seven League Boots projects a wish fulfillment on the part of his double. It turned out to be a prophetic anticipation of what was to happen. A few years after the writing of **Peter Schlemihl,** Chamisso participated in a great voyage of exploration as the expedition's official botanist. It took him to the polar regions, the South Seas, and the Andes. And like Peter, who wept at finding himself barred from exploring the reaches of the continent beyond the Indonesian archipelago, Chamisso too was denied setting foot on Australian soil. Like Peter, he had to learn that every human undertaking is doomed to fall short of fulfillment.

At the risk of appearing old-fashioned, we cannot take leave of our story without scrutinizing its moral. Peter himself, in his tongue-in-cheek manner, concludes with a moral tailored to his own state of social isolation. **Peter Schlemihl** is, among other things, a great satire on salesmanship and on business ethics generally. The warning "caveat emptor," let the buyer be on his guard, is sounded by implication all through the story. There are broad satirical references to the technique of getting rich quick by the practice of declaring bankruptcy. The whole story can be read as a negative illustration of the idealistic code of ethics formulated by Germany's greatest philosopher. Immanuel Kant found a variety of ways to word the ethical imperative. It is the second phrasing of the principle that most aptly applies to the circumstances of our story. In this phrasing the maxim reads as follows: "Always act in such a way as to treat your fellowman as an end in himself, never as a means only." No ethical precept has ever been devised that bears so directly on business ethics. It is the ABC of the businessman that he is performing a service, that he is enriching the lives of his customers by supplying existing wants and creating new ones. The compelling motive behind all this fine talk is invariably to make money. Even the businessman who serves genuine needs is bound to think of his transactions primarily in terms of profit. He is bound to think of his prospective customers primarily as means. If he also thinks of them as ends in themselves, that is a luxury that he can generously afford only on the basis of a sound balance sheet. We may generalize: The peaceful coexistence of the world of business enterprise and the realm of absolute ethics poses an antinomy that defies solution. Social life is a phenomenon with a built-in paradox.

The Kantian maxim, however, applies to the buyer as well as to the seller. It is no less unethical on the part of the purchaser to strike a profitable bargain by taking advantage of the seller's ignorance of the value of his offerings. Peter, surely, could not have swapped his shadow for the inexhaustible purse without feeling that he was taking unfair advantage of the eager salesman. Without question, it was this thought that implanted the germ of a sense of guilt in Peter's conscience that later blossomed into a full-fledged psychoneurosis of criminal involvement. (By contrast, an example of a rigorous—if quixotic—sense of rectitude comes to mind from Adalbert Stifter's famous novel *Der Nachsommer.* Here the white-haired Baron von Risach, the incarnation of mellow humane wisdom, tells his young protégé how he acquired the noble antique marble statue that graces the landing of the staircase in his "Rosenhaus." Seeing the statue in an Italian village, unvalued and exposed to the weather, he bought it from its owner under the impression that it was a plaster copy. But in the process of having it set up in his Austrian estate, its weight led to the discovery that it was a marble original, and the removal of the encrusted layers of paint and dirt confirmed the Baron's realization that he had inadvertently acquired a rare treasure. He forthwith proceeded to ascertain its true value and to recompense the unsuspecting owner with an adequate sum. Without this, he could not have enjoyed its possession with a clear conscience. This incident goes to show how, among the landed gentry of Europe, a stigma continued to attach to the mercantile profession long after the industrial revolution had set on its course.)

Perhaps the most ingenious feature of our whimsical story is the two systems of value presented. They may be ranged in a single mathematical series as (1) the shadow, (2) gold, (3) the immortal soul. In this series, the shadow appears as the equivalent of zero value, the inexhaustible purse is a finite value, and the immortal soul, which we can render as personal integrity, is of infinite value. In discussing this graded series of values, the devil deftly turns the three on the central axis to an angle of 180 degrees. The purse, the finite value, is left unchanged in its central position while the other two values are reversed. The shadow takes on the value of infinity, while the immortal soul, personal integrity, takes its place at the zero end of the scale. We remember how the glib salesman refers to the soul as this unknown quantity, this "X." A neater reversal of the values of the world and those of the spirit cannot be imagined. Consider the squeeze that the devil applies to Peter in trying to make him rescue Mina from Rascal's clutches. He appeals to Peter's warmest, noblest human impulses in order to induce him to agree to the absolute renunciation of his personal integrity in order to achieve a limited good. The motif of the sacrifice of self is posed here in its most paradoxical form. Peter's logic, of course, is too untrained to penetrate the maze of this dilemma. Speaking tongue-in-cheek as the simple man of feeling, he leaves the logic to us.

Chamisso returned to the problem of values in a delightful preface written for a new French edition of **Peter Schlemihl** in 1837. Having been pressed by curious readers, he tells us, to explain the meaning of the shadow, he gravely proceeds to quote section and paragraph from a French treatise on mathematical physics, to give a scientific definition of a shadow. Reducing the learned verbiage of the long quotation to simplest terms, we learn that a shadow, properly speaking, is a three dimensional object of solid geometry. The shape and size of this solid are determined, first, by the shape and size of the source of illumination and those of the opaque body that blocks the transmission of light and, secondly, by the distance that separates them. What we ordinarily refer to as a shadow is in reality only any one of an infinite number of possible cross sections of that solid, the real shadow. Therefore, Chamisso concludes his explanation, "Songez au solide," go for what is solid!

We would end here if a recent interpreter had not taken issue with Thomas Mann's delightful essay on Chamisso and doubted the ironic ring of this admonition. So we may be pardoned for spelling it out. Already in Imperial Rome the standard gold coin of the realm was known as the "solidus," the solid. Throughout the western world the term "solid" is still used to differentiate a well-founded business establishment from a fly-by-night venture. The rating of a business as solid comprises its evaluation in terms of plant, cash, other material assets and "good will"—the foundations of credit, the equivalent of the inexhaustible purse. Thus our tongue-in-cheek author has come full circle to fix the reader's eye upon the hypnotic dazzle of gold.

Notes

[1] "His newly turned coat." Thrifty Germans of the old school still make it a practice to have the tailor turn their worn woollens inside out. There may be nothing but the reversed position of buttons and buttonholes to indicate that the garment has been rebuilt.

Paul Neumarkt (essay date 1967)

SOURCE: "Chamisso's *Peter Schlemihl*," in *Literature and Psychology*, Vol. XVII, Nos. 2 and 3, 1967, pp. 120-27.

[*In the following essay, Neumarkt interprets* Peter Schlemihl *as an introverted personality type with repressed extrovert tendencies.*]

Chamisso's novel **Peter Schlemihl** has remained a literary delight ever since Chamisso conceived the idea that a man's shadow was not necessarily an epiphenomenon tied up with the existence of the human personality but rather a possession to be taken care of, tended, cherished; a possession, above all, capable of being lost. An individual may "lose his shadow" in many parts of the world, probably quite frequently. The chances are that the individual whose shadow has gone astray is not even aware of the extraordinary circumstance he finds himself in. Neither are his coevals in a world in which time and space have become commodities, subject to the exigencies of demand and supply. The busy engineer who is engaged in translating his blueprints into remote-controlled vehicles penetrating space to its outer reaches, and the business magnate who is ready to support such phantastic endeavours by supplying astronomical sums of money, are all too much occupied to ponder on so trivial a matter as the shadow cast by a vestigial entity known as the human body. That a man should, however, be aware of the fact that his shadow may perchance have slipped from what he has thought to be his legitimate possession, is indeed remarkable. That this selfsame individual should, moreover, make an effort to retrieve the lost treasure is no doubt indicative that the said person has turned from the logical to the psychological. People of marked individuality have always found it difficult to get along in a world dominated by collective values. The individual who has "turned psychological" is for all practical purposes a displaced person. He lives in a world which is strange to him, and in which he feels himself a stranger.

Shrugged off by his matter-of-fact contemporaries, he pursues his rather eccentric, if not quixotic, endeavors to recapture a vanished shadow. At best he is left alone to roam the universe, mocked at and ridiculed. If he is bold enough, in addition, to boast of his doubtful undertakings, he runs the risk of being labeled a lunatic. In this case he may soon find himself put away in a structure with heavy iron bars adorning his windows, and a gigantic chart attached to his bedstead, indicating his particular afflication.

This then is the story of Peter Schlemihl which stunned the reading public when it first appeared in 1813. In the course of a few years it was translated into French, Italian, and English. The question most frequently asked was, What was the poet's intention when he created the figure of Peter Schlemihl. The poet himself has given us a clue as to how he wanted the shadow to be understood. In his foreword accompanying the French translation Chamisso indicates that it is the hero's shadow rather than his material aspect, leading the hero astray, that should occupy the minds of the readers. Thus he states:

> Un corps opaque ne peut jamais etre éclairé qu'en partie par un corps lumineux, et l'espace privé de lumière qui est situé du coté de la partie non éclairé, est ce qu'on appelle 'ombre.' Ainsi, 'l'ombre' proprement dite, représente un solide dont la forme dépend à la fois de celle du corps lumineux, de celle du corps opaque, et de la position de celui-ci à l'égard du corps lumineux. . . . C'est donc de ce solide dont il est question dans la merveilleuse historie de Pierre Schlémihl. La science de la finance nous instruit assez de l'importance de l'argent, celle de l'ombre est moins généralement reconnue. Mon imprudent ami a convoité l'argent dont il connaissait le prix et n'a pas songé au solide. La leçon qu'il a chèrement payée, il veut qu'elle nous profite et son expérience nous crie: songez au solide.[1]

The foregoing quotation puts us, without delay, into the situation which constitutes the core as well as the purpose of this paper. Psychological insight has always been a much cherished quality in any type of conative activity. As a science, in the present-day meaning of that term, psychology had, in Chamisso's own time, scarcely achieved any role of significance. The fact that the poet speaks about *"l'ombre . . . un solide"* leads us, however, to the assumption that what he had in mind was more than the intangible entity which is perceptible whenever an object obstructs the passage of light. To sound this 'solide,' to delineate it as to shape, colour, and depth is more specifically the very purpose of the present analysis.

The life history of Peter Schlemihl constitutes an attempt at depicting the development of the hero's psyche from undifferentiated origins within the personal and collective unconscious. It is an analytical

problem that arrogates to itself the full scope of psychological implication. Jung maintains that the "integration of the shadow, i. e., the personal unconscious, in its process of gaining consciousness, constitutes the first step in the analytical process."[2] In other words, the integration of the shadow causes a neurosis which is essential in the process of analysis because the unconscious part of the personal psyche is thereby rendered conscious. "The shadow originates from the repression of thought, impulses and feelings not acceptable to the persona [i. e., mask]. It also contains the unexpressed attitudes and functions of the persona. That is, in an extravert, the shadow contains introverted tendencies; in an introvert it contains extraverted tendencies."[3]

Peter Schlemihl is the introverted type, as can easily be deduced from the beginning of the story. He withdraws, is shy, reticent, and finds it difficult to engage people in conversation. He is, nevertheless, drawn to mix among people, to acquire wealth and status. Consciously he rejects the symbols associated with extraversion. He flees from Mr. John's party, which frightens him with all its splendour and extravagance, but he is magically drawn to the selfsame elements that reside within his personal unconscious, i. e., his shadow. Thus the integration of the shadow in his conscious plans is tantamount to lifting the contents of the personal unconscious of the shadow sphere and exposing them to the full impact of conscious understanding. "If we think of the conscious as the source of light and of the persona as being erected to allow us to see into the outer world and protect ourselves from it, we can visualize the persona as casting a shadow. If we face the light, as we do except when we are asleep . . . we do not see our shadow, and prefer to be unaware of it."[4] Since the personal unconscious and the shadow are synonymous terms, it follows that the repressed thoughts, impulses, and feelings which make up the personal unconscious, are held in abeyance. By the same token the conscious ego must be on guard lest the repressed contents, dwelling so near the surface, break through the protective wall created by the persona (mask). If the ego, however, is weakened, the defenses are overrun by the negative forces of the shadow, gain the upper hand, and assume leadership. We can then say that the individual is no longer in possession of his shadow, simply because there is no longer a mask (persona) to cast a shadow. When the "Man in Grey" challenges Peter in a direct confrontation, the latter succumbs. The sinister forces lurking deeply within his shadow have already overrun the persona and have established themselves firmly in Peter's conscious ego. One of the first actions after this fateful event is Peter's acquisition of new, stylish garments, fashionable living quarters, and other paraphernalia associated with the extraverted disposition. The shy, reticent introvert has been overcome by the formerly repressed, but now dominant, functions associated with extraversion and collective values.

With the upward movement of repressed contents residing in the personal unconscious, the persona is of necessity affected. Psychologically speaking the individual identifies himself with these erstwhile repressed elements so that "the subject is himself convinced that his manner of behaviour to his inner processes is . . . his unique and actual character. In such a case the unconsciousness of the persona results in its projection upon an object more especially of the same sex, thus providing a foundation for many cases of more or less admitted homosexuality, and of father-transferences in men or mother-transferences in women."[5] The crumbling of the defence mechanism is tantamount to the identification of the individual with his shadow, i. e., personal unconscious. Thus we can adequately explain this process as the cessation of the existence of the shadow. At the same time, however, as the place of the persona has been occupied by the shadow, the former is projected upon an outside object. The projection of the persona is therefore not that of the originally unconscious contents but rather of contents that have been rendered unconscious *a posteriori*. This explains why Chamisso calls Peter's object of projection the "Man in Grey." It is Peter that is originally in possession of his shadow. It is he that wears the 'black' coat. When he loses his shadow it becomes the possession of the "Man in Grey". This is an indication that the shadow, having been exchanged for a purse of gold, is no longer representative of the dark, personal unconscious sphere of the hero, but rather of the much lighter shade of the mask, i. e., persona. By means of projection the persona has been rendered unconscious, i. e., dark, but not dark enough to constitute a genuine shadow. The admixture of the sparkle of gold, in terms of Jung the 'Logos principle', has transformed the impenetrable blackness of the shadow and given it a greyish nuance. It is this vicarious expression of shadow that the "Man in Grey" represents. Since the persona is originally associated with and centered around the conscious ego, its projection refers, as pointed out above, to the same sex. This enables us to explain Peter's association with the "Man in Grey" as a projection in the above sense of father-transference. Our assumption is further supported by the fact that Peter indulges in numerous love affairs but never reaches the point where love is fully consummated. He moves ahead to the brink of passionate involvement but always manages to withdraw short of the climactic experience of love. His basic fear of heterosexual relationship would be in support of Jung's suggestion that regressive homosexual tendencies might possibly be involved. If we take into consideration that the shadow "contains inferior, childish, or primitive qualities which, ... because they are closely connected with the problem of the persona, can often play a disastrous role,"[6] it is possible to explain Jung's indication of homosexuality as a fixation of unresolved childhood complexes which prevent the hero from reaching the full experience of the objective in his love affairs. "Such cases are always people with defective external adaption and comparative unrelatedness because the identification with the soul begets an attitude with a predominant orientation towards the inner processes, whereby the object is deprived of its determining influence."[7] Whenever the object is deprived of its influence, libidinal charges flow away from the object in the direction of the subject. Thus it becomes clear that Peter Schlemihl represents primarily the introvert type, while his repressed extravert tendencies constitute part of his unconscious psyche. This fact is of great importance since it constitutes the basic premise which is later upset by the loss of the shadow and finally readjusted in a process of growing awareness which establishes the basic premise in a modified sort of way.

Peter's association with the "Man in Grey" in terms of father-transference is of significance in Schlemihl's first dream, which depicts the poet withdrawn in his laboratory. Turning to the poet Peter relates: "I saw you sitting . . . at your desk between a skeleton and a bundle of dried plants . . . I looked at you for a long time . . . you did not move, you did not breathe either, you were dead."[8] The hero actually addresses the poet in the dream. This is an unusual, if not to say, strange means of technical subterfuge by which the poet as narrator actually makes himself part of the *dramatis personae* he has created. This points to Chamisso's involvement and identification with the personality of Peter Schlemihl. The poet himself considered his own introvert disposition the dominating feature of his conscious psyche, i. e., his true nature. This is corroborated by Max Koch, the editor of his *Collected Works,* who stresses that the poet could at times be seen withdrawing into a corner, in the midst of gay company, without uttering a word for hours on end.[9] His lifelong interest in botany reveals simultaneously a vigorous, scientific propensity occupying an inferior position in the poet's psyche, which, at times, caused him doubt whether he was really entitled to call himself a full-fledged poet. Even at so late a date as the successful publication of his **Peter Schlemihl** he felt prompted to remark to one of his friends that he had not considered himself a poet in the past and did not think he was one in the present.[10] The conflict between the writer and the scientist in him was finally decided in favour of the former. This is brought out in Chamisso's fragmentary drama **Faust.** It is within this framework that his preoccupation with language and writing rather than his involvement with science gains the upper hand. "You can only think through the medium of language, only observe nature through your senses . . . only see your own shadow, but to really comprehend is impossible for us,"[11] the poet declares. Thus the dream in which he depicts himself as dead constitutes an unconscious wish fulfillment, the Goethean "Stirb und Werde" (die and become), by means of which he will emerge in full realization of his creative potential as a recognized poet and writer. The dream makes final his conscious decision to keep his involvement with science in abeyance so that it does not interfere with his creative activity. The poet's lingering doubt of his own ability as a writer is an expression of his dire need for approval and recognition of his poetic work on the part of his literary coevals.

After having embarked upon his new venture in life, the transference is removed from the father image referring to the poet and projected upon the "Man in Grey". It is not surprising that the dream contents reflect the sterile laboratory atmosphere in which the skeleton and the dried plants dominate, as both are reduced to symbolic existence divorced from the living source of nature. The figure of the dead poet reflects the changed situation of the hero himself as Peter's basically introvert disposition has been superseded by extravert libidinal contents, hitherto relegated to the sphere of repression. The poet striving for recognition has emerged from the solitude of his basically introvert disposition to take his due place among his contemporaries. With growing success in the literary field he gains enough security to exclaim with modest confidence that he has finally reason to accept himself as one of Germany's poets.[12] In terms of psychology this means that the "undifferentiated function and the underdeveloped attitude . . . our 'dark side', the inborn collective predisposition,"[13] has broken through the protective wall of the conscious ego, represented by the persona. Being "the real counterpart of our conscious ego . . . this dark mass of experience that is seldom or never admitted to our conscious lives"[14] declares its right to exist by sweeping away considerations and relationships which existed prior to its coming into its own.

Chamisso is well aware that the unresolved conflict in Peter Schlemihl's psyche must ultimately be resolved. The dialectical character of the introvert-extravert polarity harbours the persona-shadow constellation which is the plausible adjunct of man's moral existence. Thus the second dream is introduced as a sort of anticipatory motif foreshadowing a possible solution of Peter's endless afflictions. The second dream thus depicts a rather pleasant scene:

> "Mina, a wreath of flowers in her hair, glided past me and smiled at me in a friendly manner. The honest Bendel was also covered with flowers and sped by with friendly greetings. I saw others as well, and, I believe, you too Chamisso, in the distant crowd. A bright light shone, but it did not cast a shadow, and, what is even stranger, it did not look bad,—flowers and songs, love and friends among palmgroves."[15]

The second dream depicts the undifferentiated state wherein man has either not yet developed a shadow, or has already overcome the moral foundation of our world in which the shadow is an exigency not to be dispensed with. Both possibilities, the yearning to return to the state of childhood bliss, and the projection into the future, when man will ultimately return to the scene of infantile carefreeness are, in fact, expressions of regressive nostalgia. They depict the Paradisaical atmosphere where man's soul is no longer two-dimensional. The basically introvert disposition longs to resolve the psychic discord by coming to terms with the inferior extravert tendency prevalent in the hero's unconscious psyche. The withdrawal from life is characteristic of the introvert type. Note how Peter's essentially introvert disposition comes to the fore as soon as the conflict is hypothetically resolved in the world of dream: Mina and Bendel, in festive garb, glide by him, smiling and greeting in a friendly manner. The poet's own position is somewhat changed on this carefree, blissful occasion. He appears very much alive, but rather remote from the center of collective activity. There is, however, no joyous embrace as could be expected in so happy a reunion. Note further his subsequent statement: "I could not hold the moving . . . lovely figures."[16]

With the emergence of his introvert disposition in primary function within his psyche, his unconscious desire to mix with people is now thwarted. Peter expresses the wish to hold on to his friends, but finds himself unable to do so. Within the sphere of Paradise, however, this dilemma is reconciled in so far as his extravert propensity assumes its rightful place in the hero's psyche, leaving the primary position to be occupied by the native introvert tendencies. If the first dream was explained as the upsurge of undifferentiated contents from the personal as well as the collective unconscious with emphasis on the emergence of extravert characteristics, the second dream constitutes a reversal of this process as the dream made it clear to the poet that his close friends were slipping from his grip. They were within eyeshot, to be sure, but not within physical reach. The realization of this dilemma is, however, not traumatic. In fact, the environment depicted is rather pleasant, as it dwells on the motif of Paradisaical bliss and equanimity where the struggling dialectical forces are reconciled. The essentially introvert contents are about to find and establish a *modus operandi* with the inferior extravert function, hitherto inflated beyond proportion. In fact, the ensuing activities of the hero point in that direction when he tells the poet about the seven-league boots that enable him to lead his life independent of human society. The symbol of the seven-league boots is thus additional indication that the therapeutic process is about to find speedy solution. By getting away from his erstwhile extravert involvements he will not only do justice to his indigenous introvert nature, but will *ipso facto* help the latter to regain its rightful place in the psyche. At the same time he is now aware of the fact that this cannot be accomplished at the expense of the inferior extravert elements but rather with their co-operation. If the latter are consciously recognized instead of ignored, the sphere of consciousness has been successfully complemented and the hitherto inflated extravert contents relegated to their indigenous psychic background. Thus Peter Schlemihl's monumental work *Historia stirpium-planetarum utriusque orbis,* and *Flora universalis terrae* are to be regarded as contributions of the hero's truly introvert frame of mind. His last earthly companion is not a human being, but characteristically enough a poodle to which he is very much attached.

With his decision to bequeath his scientific work to the Berlin University the initially divergent trends are ultimately and realistically resolved. Peter is concerned with the public that is to be the final recipient of his earthly endeavours, but this public is now reached in an indirect way, via the lecture hall and library of an institute of higher learning. This is a true indication that the extravert tendency is in genuine operational relationship to the primary introvert disposition of the hero. With the realization that the attainment of absolute Paradisaical equanimity is practically impossible in our 'valley of sorrow' Chamisso's work draws to a close on a note of resigned, if not subdued, satisfaction.

In conclusion it should be noted that as soon as the hero is able to shed light on the particular problems plaguing him, the "Man in Grey" disappears. This is, in fact, an indication that the persona or introvert disposition of the hero is no longer harrassed by upsurging extravert, repressed contents from the personal unconscious, i. e., shadow. The previously displaced persona, representing Peter's introvert disposition and projected upon the "Man in Grey", has now returned to its rightful owner. The "Man in Grey" vanishes from our sight as Peter understands his psychic dilemma and evaluates it in objective terms.

When we first set out to discover the nature of Peter Schlemihl's shadow in analytical terms it was clear that Chamisso's emphasis of the term *'solide'* was ample indication of the direction such undertaking would have to follow. The poet lived long before the emergence of psychology as a science in its own right. He was, however, intuitively aware of the fact that the shadow was a concrete entity of manifold symbolical connotations. The term *'solide'* is, for our purposes, first and foremost a denotative quantum. It represents an entity having depth, colour, and shape. To observe this entity throughout the personality transformation of the hero it was incumbent upon us to recognize the extent of the hero's projections and regressions in order to reach an understanding of his actions and their motivational causes. By means of

the foregoing analysis the shadow has been lifted out of its cryptic, symbolical context and, for the first time, brought within the intellectual grasp of the present day reader. it is in this light that Chamisso's work *Peter Schlemihl* takes on added significance in the age of depth psychology.

Notes

[1] *Chamissos Gesammelte Werk,* "Peter Schlemihl", ed. by Max Koch, (Stuttgart, Cotta'sche Buchhandlung), vol. II p. 282. (All subsequent quotations from this source henceforth referred to as *Peter Schlemihl.*) The translation from the German original is my own.

[2] C. G. Jung, *Welt der Psyche,* (Zürich, Rascher Verlag, 1954), p. 101. The translation from the German original is my own.

[3] Robert A. Clark, *Six Talks on Jung's Psychology,* (Pittsburgh, Pennsylvania, The Boxwood Press, 1953), p. 34.

[4] *Ibid.,* pp. 33-34.

[5] C. G. Jung, *Psychological Types,* transl. by H. Godwin Baynes, (New York, Pantheon Books, 1962), p. 598.

[6] Jolande Jacobl, *The Psychology of C. G. Jung,* transl, by Ralph Manheim, (London, Routledge and Kegan Paul, 1962), p. 109.

[7] C. G. Jung, *Psychological Types,* p. 598.

[8] *Peter Schlemihl,* p. 290.

[9] *Chamissos Gesammelte Werke,* "Biographische Einleitung," p. 17, passim.

[10] *Ibid.,* p. 49. passim.

[11] *Chamissos Gesammelte Werke,* "Faust," p. 350.

[12] *Chamissos Gesammelte Werke,* "Biographische Einleitung," p. 49, passim.

[13] Jolande Jacobi, op., cit., p. 107.

[14] *Ibid.,* p. 109.

[15] *Peter Schlemihl,* p. 325.

[16] *Loc. cit.*

Niklaus R. Schweizer (essay date 1973)

SOURCE: *A Poet Among Explorers: Chamisso in the South Seas,* Herbert Lang. 1973, pp. 13-18, 27-46.

[*In the following excerpt, Schweizer recounts Chamisso's experiences, recorded in poetry and prose, concerning his voyage to the South Seas.*]

When the Russian brig *Rurik,* Captain Otto von Kotzebue, sailed out of the harbor of Copenhagen on August 17, 1815, heading for the Bearing Strait and the hopeful discovery of the fabled Northeast Passage, a civilian of unusual qualities could be seen aboard. Adelbert von Chamisso, author of the intriguing **Peter Schlemihl,** had joined the expedition, financed by Count Romanzoff of Reval (Tallinn) in the capacity of an honorary scientist, a *Titulargelehrter.* His duties consisted of the observation and recording of whatever interesting natural phenomena the expedition was to encounter, and since his own discipline was that of a botanist, he concentrated on the discovery and description of new and little known plants. A Hawaiian tree fern bearing his name, *cibotium chamissoi,* and a doctor honoris causa, awarded by the University of Berlin upon his return in 1819, testify to his expertise as a botanist.

His overriding interests on this voyage, however, were not bestowed upon botany. Chamisso somewhat deprecatingly referred to his botanical activities as the collecting of so much hay.[1] Not exotic plants prompted him to volunteer for the hardship and the isolation a voyage around the world was bound to entail in those days, but rather the lure of remote cultures which promised to arise beyond the vast horizon of the Pacific. For Chamisso, like many of his contemporaries, was an ardent admirer of Jean Jacques Rousseau and Johann Gottfried Herder, and he shared with them the desire to go back to unspoiled nature and the love for the simple poetry of unsophisticated man, the *Volkslied.* Unlike his fellow romantics, who dreamt of the remotest islands, but were fortunate if they ever managed to cross the Alps, Chamisso was heading for the incredible expanses of the Great Ocean. Thus we deal with the unique spectacle presented by a romantic poet who actually reached the goal of his most daring reveries.

The magic of the South Seas was to capture Chamisso for the rest of his life. Far from suffering a disappointment when setting foot upon the islands of the Pacific, his experiences there served to bring his great gifts to full fruition. A heightened awareness of cultures very different from Europe's civilization, a host of exotic impressions and images, and a deep love for Polynesia and Micronesia were the real treasures which he brought back to Germany.

Curiously enough, he had already presaged his circumnavigation in his short novel **Peter Schlemihl,** published in 1814, at a time when he could not have foreseen his voyage aboard the *Rurik.* Schlemihl, having sold his shadow to the devil and having acquired magic boots, *Siebenmeilenstiefel,* roamed the world from east to west and west to east, but ironically was barred from New Holland and the islands of the South Seas, the very islands the *Rurik* was bound to visit extensively during the winter months of 1816 and 1817. Chamisso thus had singled out the *Zoophyteninseln,* as he called the coral islands of the Pacific,[2] as objects of special interest which in the true romantic tradition were to remain shrouded in eternal mystery.

As the *Rurik* was gaining the open sea on that fateful morning of August 17, 1815, the obstacles which had prevented Schlemihl from visiting the Pacific Islands and had forced him to stare wistfully in their direction from vantage points at Cape Horn and Lamboc ceased to exist for Chamisso himself. A sturdy brig proved to be a more dependable means of conveyance than a pair of magic boots. The brave little ship enabled Chamisso to write the very first grammar of the Hawaiian language; a number of interesting treatises on the Hawaiian Islands and the atolls of Ratak, in the Marshall Islands; **"Salas y Gomez,"** one of his best poems; a poem entitled **"Gerichtstag auf Huahine"**; and the inspired translation of a Tongan song. **"Salas y Gomez"** belongs to works reflecting the Robinson Crusoe motif; the other two poems, along with his comments on life in Hawaii and Ratak should be counted among the first writings extolling the romance of the South Seas, contributing doubtlessly to a kind of *Südseeromantik* to which Germany seems to have a better claim than any other European nation.

Chamisso had been born in France in the year 1781 as the son of an old aristocratic family. When the French Revolution broke out, his father, Louis Marie Comte de Chamisso, was forced to hasten into exile with his family, and for a number of years the Chamissos lived in Germany. Later they were allowed to return to France, but Adelbert chose to remain in Germany, a country for which he was feeling increasing affection and loyalty and which he adopted as his own.

Chamisso was not the first German intellectual to sail around the world. The incomparable Johann Georg Forster, destined to die a mysterious death in Paris during the chaotic days of the French Revolution, and his father, Johann Reinhold Forster, had accompanied Captain James Cook on his second voyage of 1772-1775; and the Swiss Johann Wäber, a burgher of Berne who had anglicized his name to John Webber, had served as Cook's official draftsman and painter on his third and last expedition. Wäber, who was present at the discovery of the Sandwich Islands, made a number of priceless drawings of old Hawaii and returned with a considerable collection of Hawaiian artifacts including a precious royal feather cloak, which he donated to the Historical Museum at Berne.[3] Chamisso, however, surpassed his predecessors by virtue of his keen understanding of the civilizations in the South Seas and his determination to open the region to the imagination of his German readers.

That a French nobleman, turned German, should circumnavigate the world aboard a Russian ship in the early nineteenth-century, demonstrates that then as now the world has always been open to those who have the moral fiber to avail themselves of an auspicious constellation. Having suffered an identity crisis during the Napoleonic wars which pitted his old and new homelands against each other, a crisis artistically expressed in **Peter Schlemihl,** Chamisso was desperately searching for an expedient to end his drifting. On the occasion of a visit to his friend Julius Eduard Hitzig in Berlin he discovered a poorly written newspaper article announcing a prospective Russian expedition to the "North Pole."[4] Otto von Kotzebue was listed as the commander of the expedition. He was no other than the son of the dramatist August von Kotzebue, who resided in Königsberg, possessed considerable influence with the Russian government, and was personally known to Hitzig. A letter was dispatched to the elder von Kotzebue, and a few weeks later Adam Johann von Krusenstern, who had led an earlier Russian expedition around the world and was August's brother-in-law, answered affirmatively on behalf of the Russian admiralty.

After the usual stormy voyage around Cape Horn the *Rurik* reached the Pacific in the beginning of February, 1816. A short visit to Chile followed and then the actual exploration began. The ship sailed past the uninhabited island of Salas y Gomez, a lonely rock which later inspired Chamisso to write the famous poem with the same title, visited Easter Island, discovered Romanzoff Island named in honor of the ship's patron, sighted the Rurik chain, and sailed to Petropavlovsk in Kamtschatka by way of Krusenstern Island and the northern group of the Ratak chain. Thus, the charms of the Pacific Islands could not yet be enjoyed for long, since the ship had first to carry out the initial exploration along the coast of Russian America, modern Alaska, before she could call at the Sandwich Islands. Kotzebue's instructions for the summer of 1816 called for the discovery of a suitable anchorage which would serve as a base camp for the exploration by land and by sea of the Northeast Passage presumed to connect the Pacific with the Atlantic.

Everything went well that year. The *Rurik* passed the Bering Strait proper and discovered an ideal anchorage in a huge bay which was appropriately named Kotzebue Sound. An island which provided protection against the waves rolling in from the Chukchi Sea, a part of the Arctic Ocean, was destined to bear our poet's name. The dubbing of Chamisso Island moved him sufficiently to manifest his feelings in a number of grandiloquent distichs, characterized by a good deal of self-irony:

*Bei Benennung der Chamisso-Insel im
Kotzebue-Sund*

Endlich verherrlichet sieht nach den übrigen
  allen auch sich selbst,
    Der schon lange der Schar sich anzureihen
    gestrebt.
Mitten in deiner Welt, der geschmälerten,
  fürstlich begabten,
    Reicher Vespucius, laß üben mich
    rühmlichen Raub;
Bleibet dir doch der Ehre genug: [oliqou te
  philou te][5]
  Gönne den dürftigen Raum mir, dem
  geringeren Mann!
Lächle, du großer Maglan, aus dem wokigen
  Throne hernieder,
    Nicht mißgönnend den Platz fern mir am
    anderen Pol!
Von der schwankenden Höh', der schwindelnd
  erklimmeten, huldreich
    Neige zu mir den Blick, palmengetragener
    Kunth!
Aber du stoße mit Macht in deine Trompeten,
  Fallopius,
    Laß sie dröhnend der Welt künden ein neues
    Gestirn.[6]

Two famous navigators, Amerigo Vespucci and Ferdinand de Magellan, as well as the botanist Karl Sigismund Kunth, professor at the University of Berlin and a friend of Chamisso, and the Italian Gabriel Fallopia, are supplicated to grant our poet his insignificant island, notwithstanding the minute loss censequently incurred by their own grandeur. A Magellan smiling down from his throne in the clouds, a Kunth gazing at Chamisso from the top of a palm, and finally the ludicrous image of a Fallopia trumpeting on his fallopian tubes the discovery of a new celestial body into the world, a slightly indelicate pun on the German term *Muttertrompete,* demonstrate sufficiently how lightly Chamisso took the honor of his addition to topography.

The *Rurik's* mission in northern waters planned for the summer of 1816 had been carried out and the ship was to sail to the Sandwich Islands and the atolls in the western Pacific to spend the winter in the tropical zone. Kotzebue chose a route which led him first to San Francisco, at that time an insignificant fort in a neglected peripheral province of Spain's colonial empire. The Russian ship, flying the Tsar's imperial flag normally reserved for men-of-war, arrived in time to mediate in the dispute between Don Paolo Vicente de Sola, governor of California, and the commander of the Russian colony at Port Bodega, Kuskoff, who in his capacity as administrator in the services of the Russian America Company had established a fort on ground claimed by Spain and had lost no time to arm it with a dozen cannons manned by twenty Russians and some fifty Eskimos from Kodiak. Fort Ross, situated half a day's journey from San Francisco, specialized not only in supplying Russian ships and remote possessions with victuals, but also carried on a highly profitable commerce in contraband against the interests of Spain. Chamisso had the honor of serving as interpreter in the delicate deliberation between Kotzebue, the Spanish governor, and Kuskoff, an effort which like many similar endeavors led to a politely worded protocol destined to disappear in the Chanceries of Russia and Spain without further consequence.[7]

After this political interlude in California the *Rurik* weighed its anchor and set course for the Sandwich Islands. Fortune had it that a passenger had come aboard in San Francisco who turned out to be the personal physician of King Kamehameha I of Hawaii. John Elliot de Castro, a rather quixotic adventurer of English and Portuguese descent, proved to be a fairly tolerable teacher of the Hawaiian language to Chamisso, who within a few days demonstrated his remarkable ability to acquire a working knowledge of a language totally unrelated to the Indo-European family. This strange tutor, who had once been imprisoned in Buenos Aires for smuggling tobacco and who had dreamt of accumulating a fortune by fishing pearls in the Pearl River on the island of Oahu, thus contributed, indirectly at least, to the writing of the first Hawaiian grammar.

In the introduction to the grammar of 1837 Chamisso deplored that the hitherto published books written in Hawaiian did not attempt to preserve the ancient Polynesian traditions. The authors, missionaries newly arrived from New England, were solely interested in imposing their own cultural values on a civilization vastly different from theirs, and were not inclined to allow reminiscences of the old way of life to endanger their efforts.

The ancient customs, the laws, the former social organization, the religious practices, even the histories and legends were totally ignored and consigned to the stream of oblivion at the very time when they could have offered a clue to scholars by shedding light on the mysterious origins of the Polynesian race and consequently the origin of man in general. Chamisso, who according to Captain von Kotzebue had been the first European visitor to participate in a *tabu* ceremony of considerable duration in a *heiau,* was justly indignant about the state of affairs. "Indeed," he exclaimed, "should one not call out to these pious missionaries: the thirst after knowledge which distinguishes man from the animal is divine, too, and it is not a sin, when a man desires to cast his glance back on his own history, in which God reveals himself in progress. But it is too late! Before the new has been given an opportunity to

emerge, the old already disappeared!"[23] Thus, the possibility for a synthesis of the old and the new was lost.

Ideas such as these reveal the essentially romantic attitude of Chamisso, who was peculiarly attracted by peoples living in a more "primitive" and therefore more "natural" state, and who fused the ideas of Rousseau and Herder into a concept running counter to the desire of the emissaries of western civilization, bent as they were on changing the lifestyle of alien cultures according to their own models. Influenced by Herder's historicism, the belief that no culture is inherently superior or inferior to another, that each civilization is justified by virtue of the influences and forces which have shaped it, he took exception to the missionaries' attitude, who in the tradition of the Enlightenment proclaimed that their own values were the best and should be extended to others.

Chamisso's admiration for the Pacific Islanders in particular is illustrated in his account of a visit to Romanzoff Island, (Tikéi), discovered by the *Rurik* in the Tuamotu Islands in the beginning of the Pacific voyage. Chamisso was commanded by von Kotzebue to explore the island with two sailors. After having reached the shore with great difficulty he found no natives on the island, but a number of uninhabited huts suggested frequent Polynesian visitors. Investigating one of these simple huts Chamisso experienced a feeling of reverence comparable only to the attitude of veneration with which he would have visited Goethe's country house, indeed his very study:

> Wir durchwandelten nun fröhlich den Wald und durchforschten die Insel. Wir lasen alle Spuren der Menschen auf, folgten ihren gebahnten Wegen, sahen uns in den verlassenen Hütten um, die ihnen zum Obdach gedient. Ich möchte das Gefühl vergleichen mit dem, das wir in der Wohnung eines uns persöhnlich unbekannten, teuren Menschen haben würden; so hätte ich Goethe's Landhaus betreten, mich in seinem Arbeitszimmer um-gesehen.[24]

Chamisso clearly saw himself from the beginning in the role of an advocate for the islanders of the South Seas. In particular he protested against the usage of the term "savages" to denote the inhabitants of the Pacific Islands. With the linguist's precision he declared that the term, when properly used, applies only to roving hunters, men who know neither agriculture nor the pastoral forms of life, men who have no settlements and whose only possessions consist of the arms used on the chase. True to Herder's philosophy he pointed out that the standards of cultural achievement applied in Europe, such as the invention of a monetary system or the art of writing, are irrelevant to these remote tribes "living under this blissful sky for the moment and for pleasure, without a yesterday and without a tomorrow:"

Ich ergreife diese Gelegenheit, auch hier gegen die Benennung "Wilde" in ihrer Anwendung auf die Südsee-Insulaner feierlichen Protest einzulegen. Ich verbinde gern, so viel ich kann, bestimmte Begriffe mit den Wörtern, die ich gebrauche. Ein Wilder ist für mich der Mensch, der ohne festen Wohnsitz, Feldbau und gezähmte Thiere, keinen andern Besitz kennt als seine Waffen, mit denen er sich von der Jagd ernährt. Wo den Südsee-Insulanern Verderbtheit der Sitten Schuld gegeben werden kann, scheint mir solche nicht von der Wildheit, sondern vielmehr von der Uebergesittung zu zeugen. Die verschiedenen Erfindungen, die Münze, die Schrift u.s.w., welche die verschiedenen Stufen der Gesittung abzumessen geeignet sind, auf denen Völker unseres Continents sich befinden, hören unter so veränderten Bedingungen auf, einen Maßstab abzugeben für diese insularisch abgesonderten Menschenfamilien, die unter diesem sonnigen Himmel ohne gestern und morgen dem Momente leben und dem Genusse. (100-101)

Hitzig summed up Chamisso's love for the unadulterated and his profound distate for the excessively civilized way of life in a eulogy entitled "Einzelne Züge zur Charakteristik Chamisso's:"

Aus der eben erörterten Eigenthümlichkeit Chamisso's [seiner ausgesprochenen Liebe für das Natürliche] ging auch seine Vorliebe für Naturvölker hervor, unter welchen er sich auf seiner Reise frei von alle dem gefühlt, was ihm in unserm civilisierten Zustande unerträglich schien. Es war ihm voller Ernst, als er einst gegen Hitzig den Wunsch aussprach, an heißen Sommertagen in eignem Garten nackt, mit der Pfeife im Munde, spazieren zu können, ohne dadurch Anstoß zu erregen, und er wäre auch wohl der Mann gewesen dies auszuführen, hätte er auf dem Lande statt in einer volkreichen Stadt gewohnt. In unsrer Kleidung überhaupt, in der Einrichtung unsrer Wohnungen, in allen unseren geselligen Formen, erblickte er nur lästige Fesseln, und sehnte sich in früheren Jahren, wo die Reiseeindrücke noch frisch waren, oft zurück nach seinem Lieblingseilande Radack [Ratak], wo er mit seinen geliebten Insulanern gelebt hatte wie ein Eingeborner.[25]

On the atolls of Ratak, visited by the *Rurik* twice, each time after Hawaii, Chamisso had befriended an islander by the name of Kadu, who had originated from the Carolines, and with whom Chamisso explored the world of the low-lying coral islands, the reefs, and the customs of their inhabitants whom Chamisso praised as "uncorrupted." He took his new friend along on the attempt of the *Rurik* to discover the Northeast Passage in the summer of 1817, which ended in ultimate failure due to von Kotzebue's ill health. Chamisso experienced with Kadu a deep relationship with a true child of nature. The islander became Chamisso's own "noble savage," although Chamisso himself would have taken exception to this very term, and a friendship of a special kind developed, since the two met on an equal footing, and not as in the case of the proverbial association of Robinson Crusoe and his goodman Friday on the basis of master and servant.

Chamisso showed his love for innocent nature in a humorous anecdote related in *Reise um die Welt.* During his first stay in Hawaii he was faced on one of his many botanical excursions with the necessity of crossing a river flowing into the harbor of Honolulu. He undressed in order to swim or wade through the stream, but the water reached only to his knees. Suddenly he heard a hearty peal of laughter emanating from an approaching outrigger canoe. A lady of high birth was delighted to happen upon the poet in his embarrassing situation and she behaved as a European young blood would if he were to surprise an innocent young lady bathing. But laughing in Hawaii was the most natural of all spontaneous reactions, and king as well as commoner, according to Chamisso, had the right to laugh at each other without incurring censure.

The Hawaiians certainly used this right at the expense of Chamisso on various occasions, and the poet, by paying them back in kind, gained their admiration and affection. An amusing encounter which he experienced with a swarm of children and which turned him unwittingly into a sort of Hawaiian Pied Piper may illustrate this point and demonstrate his deep understanding for the mentality of the Polynesians:

Arocha! [aloha] ist der Friedensgruß, den jeder jedem bietet und der mit gleichem Gegengruß erwidert wird. Auf jedes *'Arocha!'* das einem zugerufen wird, antwortet man *'Arocha!'* und ziehet seines Weges, ohne sich umzusehen. Als ich einst botanisieren ging und von Hana-ruru [Honolulu] meinen Weg nach den Taropflanzungen genommen hatte, fiel es mir auf, daß, wo schon die Häuser zu Ende waren, das Grüßen noch kein Ende nahm; und war doch auf dem freien Felde links und rechts Niemand zu sehen. *'Arocha!'* ward mir in allen Tönen unabläßig nachgerufen, und ich erwiderte treuherzig jeden Gruß. Ich sah mich unvermerkt um und ward gewahr, daß ich einen Troß Kinder hinter mir her nachzöge, die es belustigte, den *Kanaka haore* [kanaka haole 'Ausländer'] sein *Arocha!* wiederholen zu lassen. Wartet nur! meinte ich; und ich zog mit großer Geduld begrüßt und gegengrüßend den Schwarm mir nach bis in die Engpäße der Tarofelder, über Gräben, Gehege, Wasserleitungen und Erdwälle. Da kehrte ich mich unversehens um und lief mit erhobenen Armen und entsetzlichem Geheul auf sie zu; sie, im ersten Schrecken, ergriffen die Flucht und stürzten über einander und die Wasserbehälter. Ich lachte sie aus, sie lachten, und wir schieden als Freunde: *Arocha!*[26]

As can be easily seen in this passage, Chamisso was gifted with a warm humor and a lively imagination, and he loved to take his friends by surprise. In the summer of 1823 he played a little trick on a lady of rank and one of the female members of the romantic circle of Berlin, Henriette Herz von Fürst, who was spending the warm season on an estate near the capital. One day Henriette's servant came rushing into her drawing room, a look of consternation on his face and a calling card in his hand. The card read, "Ein Wilder von den Sandwichsinseln" and the servant confessed that the man in question looked savage, indeed. The stranger entered, with flowing long hair, unshaved, wrapped in a green, woollen cloak of the type worn by Kalmucks, with his specimen box slung across one shoulder, and a chest slung across the other. The chest contained a barometer, and Chamisso, for the mysterious savage dressed not unlike Schlemihl turned out to be no other, was on his way to measure various barometrical pressures at Greifswald. His identity established, he was invited to stay overnight, and his adventures in Hawaii must needs have been discussed at length that evening.

In contrast to the somewhat rigid attitude the missionaries displayed toward the native culture, an attitude attacked by Chamisso on several occasions, the Hawaiians had apparently little difficulty to assimilate concepts and thoughts which were totally alien to them. They were greatly aided in this process by their language, which, as Chamisso observed with astonishment in the introduction to his grammar, embraced with wonderful ease the abstract terms used in the fields of western philosophy, architecture, the sciences, the trades, finances, printing, the northern climate, in short all the concerns and institutions associated with the "polite world." Such a flexibility of the Hawaiian language impressed Chamisso greatly.[27] He decided to compile a dictionary of Hawaiian, he called it a "vocabulary," but had to abandon the project when a Herr Deppe returned from Honolulu in late 1837 or early 1838 with a number of new books, among which Chamisso discovered *A Vocabulary of Words in the Hawaiian Language* by Lorrin Andrews, printed in 1836 by the press of Lahainaluna, the first school in the Islands, and indeed the first college preparatory school west of the Rocky Mountains. He had already compiled many words under the letter 'a,' by far the most common sound in the Hawaiian language and prominent in all Polynesian languages,[28] but had to acknowledge that a person residing in Hawaii enjoyed a natural advantage over him. Deppe reported, however, that the missionaries had still not managed to write a grammar. The first article of a grammatical nature to be published in Hawaii, entitled "Peculiarities of the Hawaiian Language," appeared in the *Hawaiian Spectator* in 1838.[29] The author, the indefatigable Lorrin Andrews, also wrote a grammar of some length in 1854, *Grammar of the Hawaiian Language*,[30] followed by William Dewitt Alexander's *A Short Synopsis of the Most Essential Points in Hawaiian Grammar*.[31] The astonishing fact remains that the first Hawaiian grammar was published in the German language.

The dances of the Hawaiians appeared to Chamisso to be as natural and endearing as their language was musical and charming. In *Reise um die Welt* he depicted the performance of two ritual dances organized by the governor of Honolulu, Kalaimoku, on December 4 and 6, 1816. What Chamisso saw was the ancient *hula;* he called it the *hurrahurra.* He was not so much impressed by the dancing girls, many of whom he nevertheless conceded to be extraordinarily beautiful, as by three men who performed the most artful and elegant motions. The beauty of the dancing and the enthusiastic reaction of the audience, who showered gifts upon the performers, moved him to contrast the *hula* with what he considered the sadly debased form of the contemporary ballet. He poses the searching question why the "unnatural antics" of European ballet dancers are considered art, while those who are really endowed with an aesthetic sense are commonly termed "savages." Suggesting pointedly that it may be well to ponder the proper application of the word "barbarian," he adds that it is certainly to be regretted that no eminent painter reached the Islands to capture on canvas the exquisite beauties of the *hula:* "For time is running out. On Tahiti, on Hawaii, the missionaries are hiding the beautiful bodies of the Polynesians under their unshapely dresses, all manifestations of joyful art come to a close, and the *tabu* of the Sabbath casts its pall over the children of pleasure."[32]

The official draftsman of the von Kotzebue expedition, the Russian painter and lithographer Lodovik (Louis) Choris, famous for his portrait of Kamehameha in the red vest,[33] made two sketches of the *hula,* which he incorporated into his work *Voyage pittoresque autour du monde,*[34] but Chamisso felt compelled to warn against consulting his productions. He argued that Choris was not the man to do justice to the *hula,* and that it could be only wished that the genius of art were to forgive him for having trespassed into a sacred sphere. Today we are inclined to be more favorably disposed toward the sketches in question, which are among the few representations extant of the prechristian *hula.*

In *Bemerkungen und Ansichten,* the collection of essays written upon Chamisso's return from the voyage in 1819, he proves still more enthusiastic in his praise of the *hula.* The *hula* is seen by him as an original form of art combining poetry, music, and dancing into an expression of *joie de vivre* designed to enrich existence with beauty. He discovers a certain similarity between the Polynesian dances and the lyrics of the Pindaric ode, inasmuch as the words eulogize the glory of a chief or prince. The chanting is rather monotonous, but reaches a higher harmony due to the accompanying beating of the drums and due to its function to give the motions of the dance direction. The dancing is the central element of the *hula,* and in dancing the human figure is permitted to unfold in the most magnificent manner, showing itself in an easily flowing succession of natural and beautiful postures. The whole body participates; dancing is not restricted to the feet, which simply sustain the dancer, but envelopes the arms and the muscles of the dancer and enlivens his face. Chamisso pays a high tribute to the *hula* by comparing it to the chorus of ancient Greek tragedy, before the dialogue intervened:

> Der Gesang hebt langsam und leise an und wird allmälich und gleichmäßig beschleunigt und verstärkt, indem die Tänzer vorschreiten und sich ihr Spiel belebt.—Alle führen dieselben Bewegungen aus. Es ist, als stünde derselbe Tänzer mehreremal wiederholt vor uns. Wir werden bei diesen Festspielen O-Waihi's [Hawaiis] an den Chor der Griechen, an die Tragödie, bevor der Dialog hervorgetreten war, erinnert, und wenden wir den Blick auf uns zurück, so erkennen wir, auf welchen Abweg wir lächerlicherweise geraten sind, den Tanz in die Bewegung der Füsse zu bannen. Diese Festspiele berauschen mit Freude die O-Waihier. Ihre gewöhnlichen Lieder werden in demselben Sinn, stehend oder sitzend, getanzt; sie sind von sehr verschiedenem Charakter, aber stets mit anmutigen Bewegungen des Körpers und der Arme begleitet. Welche Schule eröffnet sich hier dem Künstler, welcher Genuß bietet sich hier dem Kunstfreunde dar![35]

Chamisso, in the spirit of Rousseau, contrasts this idyllic scene with the sombre spectacle of a European ballet, staged in the dimly lit labyrinth of the civilized theater. The happy inhabitants of the Pacific Islands, accustomed to perform their undulating dances in unconfined nature and under the canopy of coconut trees, could hardly be induced to enter one of these pits—Chamisso uses the intriguing term *Mördergrube*—and would presumably be even less inclined to accept the explanation that a joyous event was taking place. That the Europeans were at that very moment so insensitive as to construct a modern theater in Athens to perform their "artless ballets," Chamisso considered the ultimate disregard for nature.

It is not surprising though regrettable that the pragmatic American and European settlers of the Sandwich Islands appeared to disagree with Chamisso. They displayed little interest in Polynesian art, but were rather fascinated with Europe's artists and particularly with some of her lesser authors. On Oahu, as well as on Guam, in Manila, and even in the Aleutian Islands[36] the fame of August von Kotzebue greeted the *Rurik* and resulted in special favors extended to the son of the dramatist and to his crew. Chamisso received his share of the glory which evidently had been spread around the globe by American merchantmen. He attributed this remarkable feat of America's men of commerce and her sailors to their mobility on one hand and to their ignorance of the beauties of romantic poetry, to which they had not yet been exposed, on the other.

In Honolulu mediocre European drama was thus adjudged to be more valuable than the splendors of Polynesian art. The ancient *hula* was threatened with almost complete extinction,[37] while the Kotzebues thrived.

At one occasion at least Chamisso saw to it that some islanders were exposed to better taste. Having been treated by the natives of Ratak to some of their songs, he was asked to reciprocate with a performance of his own. We are amused to learn that he chose "Generalbeichte" (1802), a shorter poem by Goethe, which begins with the line: "Lasset heut im edeln Kreis . . ." Chamisso's selection was appropriate enough. Goethe's anacreontic exhortation not to fall prey to the Philistines, not to live a shallow existence, but to drink deep of wine and love,[38] found its confirmation in the remarkable vitality of the Ratakians, who in complete freedom from the fetters of narrow notions lived a simple, yet fulfilled existence. Chamisso recited the poem with such emphasis and fervor that the islanders began to imitate him and in due time reached a degree of authenticity in rendering the German verse.

On a more serious note it should be observed that Chamisso became sufficiently interested in the Pacific Islanders, and particularly the Hawaiians, that he requested von Kotzebue's permission to remain in the Sandwich Islands until the projected return of the *Rurik* in the fall of 1817. If the permission had been granted, Chamisso would have spent nearly a year in Hawaii, but the unwillingness of his captain to explore the Northeast Passage without his naturalist aboard deprived the world of what would certainly have turned out to be a fascinating study of ancient Hawaii. That the *Rurik* ultimately failed in her quest to find a shorter route from the Pacific to Europe does little to console us for this cultural loss. Chamisso would have been the first, and it seems the only scholar of some weight to live for an extended period in Hawaii at a time when Kamehameha I still ruled the Islands, when the *tabu* system was still in full force, and when the missionaries had not yet arrived.

Much later, in 1836, Chamisso renewed his endeavor to spend a year or two in Hawaii. On the first of September of that year he applied to Alexander von Humboldt to bring his desire to the attention of the king of Prussia. Referring to an obstreperous cough, acquired in 1833 and indicative of a diseased lung which caused his death in 1838, Chamisso pointed to the desirability of a sea-voyage and a change in climate. Hawaii was blessed with warm and healthy weather and would appear to be an ideal place to regain his health. With his knowledge of the Hawaiian language he would be in an advantageous position to enrich the sciences with valuable discoveries and to shed light upon the culture and the traditions of the

Polynesian race, uncovering perhaps the hypothetical archaic language from which the modern Polynesian languages had sprung. He told Humboldt that it was high time for such a venture, if the last vestiges of a disappearing culture were to be recorded for posterity. A Prussian ship was bound for the Sandwich Islands that fall, and Chamisso felt that it would be better to die in the active pursuit of knowledge than to linger on in a state of passivity. In the midst of his audience with Humboldt, Chamisso was unfortunately seized by one of his terrible fits of coughing which usually lasted for half an hour. Humboldt saw all too clearly that death was waiting in the wings, and the plan came to naught.

Even in 1836 Chamisso would have been the first visiting scholar to deal systematically with Hawaiian history and traditions. He would have had a Hawaiian counterpart, however, in the person of David Malo, who at that time happened upon the scene. Malo was one of the first graduates of Lahainaluna school. Originally fiercely proud of the culture of his forefathers, he became a convert to Christianity at Lahainaluna and developed a tendency to reject Polynesian civilization. He was, nevertheless, prevailed upon to write a history of Hawaii, *Moolelo Hawaii* (ca. 1840), a somewhat contradictory and poorly-organized work reflecting the format of the *Old Testament*. For all its faults the book is nevertheless quite a classic, and if we were to exercise a certain degree of imagination, we could speculate about the results of a cooperation between Malo and Chamisso. Reality forbade such a cooperation, and Malo, at least as much hampered as he was helped by his newly acquired faith, did not receive much assistance in writing the story of his people, while Chamisso, separated from his islands by half the globe, tried his best to write his grammar in Germany, using whatever books he could collect.

It would stand to reason that Chamisso, fascinated as he was with the Pacific Islands, would have written a considerable number of poems on Hawaii, or on Ratak, a group of atolls which he considered an earthly garden of Eden. However, when we search his works for South Seas poetry, we find essentially only three poem[s], **"Salas y Gomez"** (1829), **"Idylle"** (1830), and **"Ein Gerichtstag auf Huahine"** (1832). These poems are nevertheless quite important. They all belong to the category of exotic literature, which under the influence of Daniel Defoe's *Robinson Crusoe* (1719) and Rousseau's back-to-nature movement had grown to a stature of its own, and to which Chamisso contributed also a translation of Malayan[39] songs, entitled **In malayischer Form** (1821).

The sighting of Salas y Gomez, an uninhabited rock near Easter Island, from the deck of the *Rurik* in 1816, caused Chamisso in 1829 to write the famous poem. An earlier expedition had reportedly discovered the wreck of a ship on the rugged coast of the island. This disaster suggested to Chamisso the story of Robinson Crusoe, and in the tradition of Defoe he created a moving poem on the fate of a lone survivor.

In contrast to many *Robinsonaden* the hero of Chamisso's poem is not a Rousseauite, who fatigued with Europe's civilization finds solace in a South Seas paradise. He is rather a lively Spanish merchant, struggling desperately against the hostile environment and experiencing a life-in-death situation reminiscent of Samuel Taylor Coleridge's *Ancient Mariner* (1798). Having sustained a miserable existence for more than fifty years on a diet of bird eggs, he finally finds consolation in a state of humble resignation. The poem ends on a note of reconciliation with God and a trust in the mercy of the Supreme Being:

> Laß weltverlassen sterben mich allein
> Und nur auf deine Gnade noch vertrauen!
> Von deinem Himmel wird auf mein Gebein
> Das Sternbild deines Kreuzes niederschauen.[90]

The poem reaches a climax, when a rescue party discover the hero seconds before his demise. His story is feared to remain an eternal enigma, but three slabs are found on which the stranded merchant recorded his tortuous experiences for posterity, and his message constitutes the essence of the work.

The hero's reconciliation with God notwithstanding, a deep gloom pervades **"Salas y Gomez,"** contrasting strangely with the serene world of the Pacific and Chamisso's idyllic descriptions of the South Sea Islands. We are confronted here with a mysterious and dark side of Chamisso's mind, which is evident in a number of his poems. In **"Traum und Erwachen"** (1838) he sets his Ratakian friend Kadu a literary monument by having him appear as a shocking phantom in a frightening nightmare. This rather unorthodox approach to a celebration of affection finds a parallel in the same poem when his mother removes her veil, reveals a bare skull, and proceeds to pull the poet into her grave.[41] Of an equally gothic nature are **"Die Giftmischerin"** and **"Das Kruzifix,"** poems with a decidedly morbid turn which caused some severe criticism when they first appeared. It is apparent that Chamisso never quite overcame some of the doubts and fears expressed in **Schlemihl.** In fact he took delight in nourishing his interest in the sensational and the macabre by visiting his neighbor and friend Eduard Hitzig, who would produce for his persual the latest reports on lurid incidents published in various journals in the field of criminology.

"Idylle," a translation of a Tongan poem, and the Malayan songs, a collection of three poems on love and death characterized by an elegant simplicity, lead us again into a harmonious world and belong to the first Pacific *Volkslieder,* or folksongs, ever to have appeared in Europe. The poetry of the "noble savage" was thus directly introduced to his Continental admirers, and Chamisso's translation lent added support to the idealized image of "natural man."

Performing translations was one of the main concerns of the age. August Wilhelm Schlegel in his lectures in Berlin had expounded the necessity of translating all the valuable works created throughout the world into the German language. Since he and his romantic contemporaries equated Germany with the very essence of humanism, it followed that the German language should reflect all the beauties of literary feelings and thoughts ever conceived anywhere. Schlegel devoted a good portion of his talents to the famous translation of Shakespeare's works which was completed by Ludwig Tieck. Goethe's concept of *Weltliteratur,* developed during his last years in his correspondence with Thomas Carlyle, proclaimed a similar aim and did much to strengthen the appeal of foreign works. Translating was rightfully considered a most challenging activity, an art in its own rights, and Chamisso, who had listened personally to Schlegel, was attracted by the difficulties and promises this kind of literary endeavor entailed. He translated some French poems, dealt with a number of Lithuanian songs and a small portion of the *Edda,* and rendered several early works by Hans Christian Andersen into German.

The translation of the Tongan poem is of special interest. Having appeared originally in William Mariner's careful study of Tongan culture, the song attracted the attention of Wilhelm von Humboldt, who in *Über die Kawisprache auf der Insel Jawa* translated it into German. Humboldt's translation is the work of an accomplished linguist who with great exactitude accounts for every word and consequently loses the inherent poetic qualities.[42]

Chamisso, on the other hand, shows his poetic talents and his romantic leanings in his rendition of the poem. Instead of clinging closely to the original his version leads in a crescendo to the praise of the joys of life in which the Tongans indulge by dint of contrast cast upon them by the constant threat of renewed warfare. The flowers, the brown maidens, their enticing pleas to the men to join them on their intended visit to the outer beach carry all the elements of the South Seas romance so cherished by Germans to this very day. "Idylle" in Chamisso's translation is a *carpe diem* poem in the best tradition and celebrates the noble and profound feelings Chamisso had discovered the Polynesians to be capable of.

As if his translation needed an apology to ensure that even the most sceptical reader would not consider the South Sea Islanders savages anymore, Chamisso added an introduction to set matters right:

In fremder Zunge schallt ein Lied herüber,
Aus jenem meerumspühlten Sitz der Freude,
Dem heil'gen Tonga.—'Wilde' hörtest Du
Die Sänger schelten, aber mir erschienen
Die so sie schalten, selber nur Barbaren.
Laß in der Sprachen Dir gefälligen
Verwirrung auch erklingen diesen Sang.
Befleißen will ich mich, die Worte Dir
Zu deuten, weigert auch sich unbeholfen
Der Ernst der Muttersprache sich zu fügen,
Dem kindergleichen Laute der Natur.

Introduction and translation appeared first in the *Chaos,* a privately circulated journal edited by Ottilie von Goethe, Goethe's daughter-in-law, in Weimar in the years 1829-1832. Chamisso affixed the date of November 6, 1830.[43] The idea of the childlike quality of the Tongan language, upon which Chamisso touches in the two last lines of the introduction, and which he contrasts with the serious nature of German, is reminiscent of his comments concerning the Hawaiian language, and demonstrates the characteristic linguistic bias of the followers of Rousseau. In their desire to turn the clock back to a simpler and more innocent existence, they erroneously expected the languages spoken by the so-called "children of nature" to be far less developed than the highly civilized and consequently "corrupted" languages of Europe.

"Ein Gerichtstag auf Huahine" contains as its central motif one of Chamisso's favorite topics, the gradual decline of the Polynesian peoples in the face of the all-encompassing onslaught of European civilization. The poem celebrates the advent of a set of written laws which in May of 1822 reached Huahine, an outer island near Tahiti.

Unfortunately, the law, inspired by the missionaries, brings gloom to both Tarute, the plaintiff, whose breadfruitfree has been felled by the Queen's carpenter, and to the Queen of Tahiti, who appears in the role of the accused. The commoner Tarute, although he is found to be in the right according to the new law, would prefer to live in the days of old, when men existed for war and joy only. The Queen, on the other hand, is deeply humiliated and forced to abrogate a good deal of her former royal power and dignity. The poem is reminiscent of Chamisso's observation in **Reise um die Welt** that the gloom of the Sabbath very nearly destroyed the *joie de vivre* of the Polynesians. The key passage of this poem in terza rima deserves to be quoted. Tarute contrasts life under the old god Oro with existence under the supervision of the missionaries. The old days may have been cruel and rather gory, but a vigorous life-force did manifest itself which now has yielded to desiccated penance:

'Uns ist das Licht der heitern Lust
  verglommen,—

Ihr saget ja, daß ihr an Christum glaubt!—
Und soll die Zeit des Blutes
  wiederkommen?'

'Nehm' auch mein Leben, wer mein Gut mir
  raubt;
  Und mög' ich liegen auf Oros Altar,
  Wie blutig einst schon meines Vaters
  Haupt!'

'Als seine Tempel standen, ja, da war
  Die volle freud'ge Kraft noch unbezwungen,
  Die wogend Krieg und süße Lust gebar.'

'Ward in der Männerschlacht der Speer
  geschwungen,
  Galt doch das Leben nur dem Dienst der
  Lust,
  Und nur das Lied der Freude ward
  gesungen.'

'Nun schlägt der Sünder an die hohle Brust;
  Gesang und Waffenschall sind gleich
  verhallt;
  Der stille Sabbat jammert den Verlust.'

'Ich selber bin nun worden schwach und alt,
  Und wieder zweifelnd frag' ich das Gericht:
  Gilt euer Recht? gilt wieder die Gewalt?'[44]

The question may be raised why Chamisso chose to translate a Tongan poem and immortalize the islands of Huahine and Salas y Gomez, but neglected to sing about Hawaii or Ratak, islands which he had actually visited and cherished deeply. Salas y Gomez he had only seen from afar, while Huahine and Tonga had remained hidden behind the blue horizons of the vast Pacific. Elisabeth Ehrlich in an article entitled "Das französische Element in der Lyrik Chamissos"[45] maintains that Chamisso demonstrates a certain lack of appreciation for nature which is essentially French, since French as well as Latin lyrical poetry is characterized by a dearth of the pictorial. There may be some truth in this thought, but she must have been unaware of his lyrical translation of **"Idylle"** and the Malayan songs, as well as his **"Gerichtstag auf Huahine,"** when she asserts that his circumnavigation of the globe gave rise to scientific observations and objective descriptions of events and customs encountered, but did not result in a single essentially lyrical poem: "Seine Weltreise zeitigt wissenschaftlich-exakte Arbeiten und die sachliche Beschreibung der *Reise um die Welt,* die— außer dem tagebuchartigen Festhalten der Ereignisse und sachlichen Naturbeschreibungen— die Schilderung menschlicher Sitten und Gebräuche enthält, aber kein einziges wirkliches lyrisches Gedicht."(56)

As far as the purely human element was concerned, which Chamisso according to Elisabeth Ehrlich did

cultivate, the South Sea Islands would have had a great deal to offer. Why did he fail to write a poem about Kamehameha the Great, *ka Napoliōna o ka Pākīpika,* "the Napoleon of the Pacific," as he was proudly called by the Hawaiians, a monarch for whom he had found moving words in prose? Did not Ka'ahumanu, the old king's gigantic consort, present him with a fitting object for his attention, or could he not have praised the unspoiled and innocent existence of the Ratakians? Mysterious forces shape a poem in a sensitive mind, and it would be an idle endeavor to probe Chamisso's psyche for an answer. Presumably his linguistic and botanical efforts in Hawaii prevented him from mounting winged Pegasus, but whatever the reasons may have been, this omission is regrettable. Alfred Lord Tennyson, who had never left Europe, felt impelled to celebrate Kapiolani's courageous defiance of Pele, the goddess of volcanoes. He did this in 1892, almost seventy years after the fearless Kapiolani, a high chiefess, had descended into the steaming crater of Kilauea on the Island of Hawaii to prove to her people the power of the Christian God and the weakness of Polynesian deities.[46] Kapiolani's determination soon became a standard theme on Europe's pulpits, but Chamisso remained silent. We can only surmise that he would have contributed a number of poems on Hawaii, if he had been able to stay a year or two in the Islands.

Nevertheless, our romantic traveler, having executed what most of his contemporaries dared only to dream about, namely a voyage to the most distant isles, continued to be fascinated by them all his life, notwithstanding some of his less enchanting adventures in those regions and the boredom of a life spent chiefly aboard a ship ruled with military discipline in the isolation of the world's greatest ocean. Particularly Hawaii claimed his continuous interest, which manifested itself not only in his studies of its language and culture, but also in details of a more intimate nature, such as his signing of a letter to his friend Louis de la Foye, dated August 18, 1830, with *arocha,* (aloha) or his frequent use of the word *tabu.* Chamisso, indeed, was whimsical enough to place his study, which was graced by a portrait of the Tahitian Queen Pomare II, and all his books in his house in Schöneberg under the severe restrictions imposed by this magic ban.

His Polynesian habits apparently affected also his family, for his oldest son would greet his father in the Hawaiian way with a ringing *arocha.* On his deathbed Chamisso was heard to speak a good deal of Hawaiian in his delirium before he finally lapsed into his native French shortly before passing away on the morning of August 21, 1838.

In his last years his Hawaiian studies had been his main moral support which he mustered against his increasingly troublesome lung condition. His final letter to Louis de la Foye ends with the exhortation: "Lebe Du wohl und erzürne Dich gegen irgend eine Arbeit, wie ich gegen das Hawaiische, das ich doch untergekriegt habe."[47]

His friends took his fascination for the South Seas in stride. Hitzig once wrote Friedrich de La Motte-Fouqué, who in 1814 had published *Peter Schlemihl* without Chamisso's permission, that he had received enough punishment for such an illoyal act by virtue of the haunting knowledge that Chamisso must have addressed his grief even to his friend, the late Tameiameia on O-Wahu.[48] The same light note can be seen in a collection of poems presented to Chamisso on his fifty-first birthday in 1832 by some poetic contemporaries.[49] Chamisso was hailed as the king of the tranquil islands of the South Seas. Thereupon a journalist, who had befriended the poet, wrote a humorous article praising "His Majesty" for several achievements and holding him up to his fellow monarchs in Europe as an example worthy to be followed. This jest in turn had the consequence that several others took up the thread in Germany, and that a St. Petersburger paper referred in great earnest, and as Chamisso put it "bona fide," to his realm in the Pacific.[50]

Goethe possibly had Chamisso in mind when he commented to Eckermann in one of his darker moods that the Europeans found themselves in a rather unattractive situation characterized by general artificiality and a lack of the comforts of love and truthfulness. "Indeed," he added, "one should often wish to have been born on one of the South Sea Islands as a so-called savage to enjoy life for once without the tinge of falsehood, to enjoy it in complete purity:"

> Es geht uns alten Europäern übrigens mehr oder weniger allen herzlich schlecht; unsere Zustände sind viel zu künstlich und kompliziert, unsere Nahrung und Lebensweise ist ohne die rechte Natur und unser geselliger Verkehr ohne eigentliche Liebe und Wohlwollen.—Jedermann ist fein und höflich, aber niemand hat den Mut, gemütlich und wahr zu sein, so daß ein redlicher Mensch mit natürlicher Neigung und Gesinnung einen recht bösen Stand hat. Man sollte oft wünschen, auf einer der Südseeinseln als sogenannter Wilder geboren zu sein, um nur einmal das menschliche Dasein, ohne falschen Beigeschmack, durchaus rein zu genießen.[51]

Today Chamisso is remembered in Europe chiefly for *Peter Schlemihl* and some of his poems, such as **"Das Schloß Boncourt"** (1827) and occasionally **"Salas y Gomez,"** while in Hawaii he is recalled for his work on the Hawaiian language and his interest in Polynesia in general. On the Continent his experiences in the Pacific have not yet met with the interest they deserve, although Hugo von Hofmannsthal saw fit to include a passage entitled "Auf Radack" in *Deutsches Lesebuch; Eine Auswahl deutscher Prosastücke aus dem Jahrhundert 1750-1850,*[52] an anthology dealing with examples of good prose written in that period. The time has arrived that both elements in Chamisso be recognized

as two complementing aspects of the same man, so that we may obtain a greater appreciation of his astonishing versatility. The recently published new edition of Chamisso's travelogue *Reise um die Welt*[53] may contribute to such a fuller understanding of the poet and his life.

Notes

[1] 'Das tat ich sonst, das tu' ich annoch heute,
   Ich pflücke Blumen, und ich sammle Heu;
   Botanisieren nennen das die Leute,
   Und anders es zu nennen, trag' ich Scheu;
   So schweift das Menschenkind nach trockner Beute
   Das Leben und die Welt hindurch, die Reu'
   Ereilet ihn, und, wie er rückwärts schaut,
   Der Abend sinkt, das Haar ist schon ergraut.'

In "Aus der Beringsstraße," *Chamissos Werke,* ed. Hermann Tardel (Leipzig und Wien: Meyers Klassiker Ausgaben, 1907), I, 15-16, hereafter cited as *Werke.*

[2] Cf. *Werke,* II, 343.

[3] Cf. Karl H. Henking, "Ein Königsornat von Hawaii im Bernischen Historischen Museum," *Jahrbuch des Bernischen Historischen Museums,* XXXIV, (1954) 231-244; "Die Südsee- und Alaskasammlung Johann Wäber: Beschreibender Katalog," *JBHM,* XXXV und XXXVI, 325-389.

[4] "Da kam mir zufällig einmal bei Julius Eduard Hitzig ein Zeitungsartikel zu Gesicht, worin von einer nächst bevorstehenden Entdeckungsexpedition der Russen nach dem Nordpol verworrene Nachricht gegeben ward. 'Ich wollte, ich wäre mit diesen Russen am Nordpol!' rief ich unmuthing aus und stampfte wohl dabei mit dem Fuß. Hitzig nahm mir das Blatt aus der Hand, überlas den Artikel und fragte mich: 'Ist es dein Ernst?'—'Ja!'—'So schaffe mir sogleich Zeugnisse deiner Studien und Befähigung zur Stelle. Wir wollen sehen, was sich thun läßt.'"

Reise um die Welt mit der Romanzoffischen Entdeckungs-Expedition (1836) in: *Werke,* III, 23.

[5] Footnoted by Chamisso as "zwar wenig, aber gern," *Ilias* I, p. 167.

[6] *Werke,* II, 65.

[7] The fort, built in 1812, remained in Russian possession until 1841, when it was sold to General August Sutter.

. . . . .

[22] For an excellent discussion of Chamisso's grammar see: Samuel H. Elbert and Mary Kawena Pukui,

"Previous Studies of Hawaiian Grammar," the first chapter in their *Hawaiian Grammar* (University of Hawaii Press, in press).

[23] "Sollte man diesen frommen Missionaren nicht zurufen: Er ist auch von Gott, der Durst nach Erkenntnis, der den Menschen von dem Vieh unterscheidet, und es ist nicht Sünde, wenn er auf seine eigene Geschichte zurückzuschauen begehrt, worin sich Gott im Fortschritt offenbaret? Aber zu spät! Bevor sich das Neue gestaltet hat, ist das Alte bereits verschollen." *Werke,* II, 364.

[24] *Werke,* III, 102.

[25] *Adelbert von Chamisso's Werke,* ed. Julius Eduard Hitzig (Berlin, 1856), VI, 265.

[26] *Werke,* III, 173-174.

[27] Samuel H. Elbert suggested at a meeting of the American Association of Teachers of German, Hawaii Chapter, on December 2, 1969, that Hawaiian would be rather useful as an international language, because of its facility of absorbing novel scientific and technical concepts.

[28] According to a recent study conducted by Samuel H. Elbert with a computer the letter 'a' appears with a frequency of almost 25%. It occurs far more often than the other four vowels or the seven consonants of Hawaiian.

[29] (Honolulu, 1838), I, 392-420.

[30] (Honolulu: Mission Press, 1854).

[31] (Rutland, Vermont: Charles E. Tuttle Company, 1968), first published in 1864.

[32] "Es wird nun schon spät. Auf O-Tahiti, auf O-Waihi verhüllen Missionshemden die schönen Leiber, alles Kunstspiel verstummt, und der Tabu des Sabbats senkt sich still und traurig über die Kinder der Freude." *Werke,* III, 178.

[33] Cf. Jean Charlot, *Choris and Kamehameha* (Honolulu: Bishop Museum Press, 1958).

[34] (Paris, 1822).

[35] *Werke,* III, 502.

[36] "Sämtliche Bibliotheken auf den Aleutischen Inseln, soweit ich solche erkundet habe, bestaden in einem vereinzelten Bande von der russischen Übersetzung von Kotzebue." *Werke,* III, 43.

[37] In recent years a heartening renaissance of Hawaiian dancing and music has been taking place. The ultimate credit for having saved the *hula* should be accorded to the last Hawaiian King, David Kalakaua, who reigned from 1873-1891.

[38] Cf. *Gedenkausgabe der Werke, Briefe und Gespräche,* ed. Ernst Beutler (Zürich, 1949), II, pt. 1, 89-90.

[39] Chamisso uses the term "Malayan" as defined by William Marsden in *A Grammar of the Malayan Language* (London, 1812).

[40] *Werke,* I, 399.

[41] Cf. *Werke,* I, 424-427.

[42] Cf. ed. J. K. E. Buschmann (Berlin, 1839), III, 457.

[43] No. 52, 205-207.

[44] *Werke,* I, 319-320.

[45] *Germanische Studien,* no. 118 (Berlin, 1932).

[46] Cf. "Kapiolani," *The Poems of Tennyson,* ed. Christopher Ricks (London, 1969), pp. 1450-1452; "Kapiolani, Chiefess of Hawaii," *The Friend* (Honolulu, 1893), L1, 33.

[47] *Werke,* (1856), VI, 256.

[48] "Hielte ich Dich nicht für Dein eigenmächtiges Verfahren (denn mir hast Du 1814 ja kein Wort von der Herausgabe des Manuskripts gesagt) hinlänglich dadurch bestraft, daß unser Chamisso bei seiner Weltumsegelei, in den Jahren 1815 bis 1818, sich gewiß in Chili und Kamtschatka, und wohl gar bei seinem Freunde, dem seligen Tameiameia auf O-Wahu, darüber beklagt haben wird, so forderte ich noch jetzt öffentlich Rechenschaft darüber von Dir." Letter, dated "Berlin, im Januar 1827," *Werke* (1856), IV, 248.

[49] *An Ad. v. Chamisso zu seinem 51ten Geburtstag, Berlin 1832. Mit Gedichten von W. Wackernagel, K. Simrock und Fr. Kugler.*

[50] Cf. letter addressed by Chamisso to de La Foye, Berlin, June 2, 1832. *Werke* (1856), VI, 238.

[51] "Gespräche mit Goethe," ed. Johann Peter Eckermann, *Gedenkausgabe* (Zürich, 1949), XXIV, 685-686.

[52] (München, 1923).

[53] Ed. Walther Migge (Stuttgart: Deutsche Verlags-Anstalt, 1970).

Ralph Flores (essay date 1974)

SOURCE: "The Lost Shadow of Peter Schlemihl," in *The German Quarterly,* Vol. XLVII, No. 4, November, 1974, pp. 567-84.

[In the following essay, Flores examines the magical and realistic elements of Peter Schlemihl, *viewing the novel as a complex study of its protagonist's alienation from society.]*

Critics have recognized Chamisso's **Peter Schlemihls Wundersame Geschichte** to be an odd work—one for which the categories of literary history and criticism may seem to be adequate, yet one which seems to elude those categories in a somewhat disturbing way. Most critics have noted that the work, like other Romantic tales, is mixed in its modality: it combines the paraphernalia of magic (mandragora, a bird's nest, seven-league boots) with a "realistic" and quasi-autobiographical depiction of the exigencies of bourgeois life. Such is the point of departure, for example of Oskar Walzel's commentary.[1] Again, Stuart Atkins notes Grillparzer's remark that the story is "schlecht gemacht," suggesting that it lacks unity; then, in tracing affinities and influences, he views the work as a *Märchen* lacking the succinctness or naiveté of a "true" *Volksmärchen,* being tearfully sentimental but also a humorous satire on sentimentalism.[2] H. A. Korff, in his *Geist der Goethezeit,* designates the work as one of the first "modern" *Märchen,* since unlike the *Märchen* of Brentano and Fouqué, with their knights and fantasy, this work depicts the bourgeois realm of the present; it is "eine Satire auf die bürgerliche Welt der Wirklichkeit und in diesem Sinne ein echt romantisches Produkt."[3]

Valid as these observations may be, they do not touch upon the uneasiness suggested (if not resolved) by the positions of other commentators. Benno von Wiese, for example, questions Korff's observations, and, by implication, all attempts to put the work into a literary-historical niche without having sufficiently pondered the work's strangeness. Peter Schlemihl's wanderings, he notes, are anything but Romantic: the story is devoid of Romantic yearnings for the *Blaue Blume* or for the higher realms of dream and art. Indeed, in **Peter Schlemihl,** the usual Romantic "quest" has reversed its direction: "Das Märchenmotif des verkauften Schattens wird zum dichterischen Gleichnis für [den] verlorenen Bezug zur alltäglichen bürgerlichen Welt."[4] Similarly, Thomas Mann, in his remarks on the story, draws attention to its realistic, bourgeois elements—pointing out, for example, that the devil, presented without demonic trappings (cleft feet, hellish wit, odor), appears as a polite and deferential gentleman. Mann, like most critics, is aware that Peter Schlemihl's shadowlessness is not allegorical in any simple, specifiable sense; he discounts the notion that a man without a shadow must be a man without a country. But Mann goes on merely to cite Chamisso's perversely unilluminating remarks prefacing the French edition, about the physics of shadow-making: "La science de la finance nous instruit assez l'importance de l'argent, celle de l'ombre est moins généralement reconnue."[5] Ulrich Baumgartner is more speculative,

and notices the tragic aspects of Schlemihl's plight: "Er unterscheidet nicht zwischen Ich und der Welt, zwischen seinen geringen Möglichkeiten und den umfassenden der Welt der Gesellschaft, sondern er bringt seinen Wunsch nach einer gewissen Stellung und Bedeutung, die er zu verstehen mag, in Gegensatz zu einer dunkeln, unverständlichen Welt, die er scheut und vor der er Angst hat."[6] Since Baumgartner is primarily concerned to place the work in its historical and social context, he does not examine the paradoxical phenomenon of what he calls a "tragedy" involving the loss of a mere shadow. What requires elucidation, in other words, is how shadowlessness can become dynamically entwined with ordinary social phenomena—some of them ominous and disturbing, if not tragic. This in turn, will engage us in the question of how the work's "magical" and "realistic" constituents are interrelated. The task is not an easy one.

It has been begun, however, by Hermann J. Weigand, who attempts to systematize—indeed schematize—the major elements of the story. The story, according to him, presents two systems of value:

> They may be ranged in a single mathematical series as (1) the shadow, (2) gold, (3) the immortal soul. In this series, the shadow appears as the equivalent of zero value, the inexhaustible purse is a finite value, and the immortal soul, which we can render as personal integrity, is of infinite value. In discussing this graded series of values, the devil deftly turns the three on the central axis to an angle of 180 degrees.[7]

Granted that these are the important values in the work, to set these values in a mathematical sequence is only deceptively instructive; we are still left in puzzlement about the qualitative interconnections between them, and here Professor Weigand offers scant help. On his reading, Peter is simply a foolish consumer who makes a very unwise investment, and the story is a "great satire on salesmanship and business ethics" whose moral "sounded by implication all through the story [is] *caveat emptor.*"[8] Such a reading is unsettling precisely because of its initial plausibility: there seems, indeed, to be an inversion of values in the story, involving a misestimation of the relative worth of money, shadow, and soul. But to assume that the story is a satire on business ethics, and that Peter Schlemihl's error is no more serious than a mistaken purchase, is merely to accept the very values by which Peter is socially ostracized. In this story, surely, society and its values are hardly displayed in a favorable light, and Peter's position in relation to society (and the demonic man in gray) is more ambiguous than any mathematical representation is likely to suggest.

The issues posed by the story are more complex than they appear; critics have been only partially successful in attempting to allay bewilderment by adducing formulae or by viewing the work in the perspective of standard literary-historical categories. A different approach seems called for at this point, one which would examine the story's psychological and social dynamics and draw upon the musings of other writers on money, shadows, and the soul. We would do well to examine the meaning of shadowlessness (or of shadows) from as many different viewpoints as possible, with particular interest in writers who are somewhat removed from strictly "literary" concerns. In gaining what Kenneth Burke might call "perspectives by incongruity," we should be able to see the work from fruitfully odd angles. I thus propose to look backward to one literary antecedent, Dante, and forward to a number of writers—Locke, Nietzsche and Marx—who although they might be loosely placed in the tradition of Romanticism, are valuable in providing ways for exploring the qualities and issues of Chamisso's tale.

A useful starting point, in considering the tale, is the concept of priority. The story of Peter Schlemihl involves an absence or misvaluation of priorities. What happens, for example, prior (in time) to Peter's disembarkation is not specified; we can only infer that, wherever he came from or however he was educated, Peter had never learned the priority (in value) of his shadow over other values. When he arrives on land, his mind is rather naive with regard to social norms; the tale depicts his painful education into "necessary" priorities. But whether his education is (or even could be) complete or satisfying is dubious: in the story, an absence or misestimation of priorities seems inevitable, not only on the part of Peter, but (to a possibly greater or lesser extent) of virtually everyone else as well. In recognition of the arbitrariness as well as importance of priorities, the reader is forced to step back from the story's immediate events to attend to the interplay of priorities as a psycho-social phenomenon. Since priorities and their rationales are largely tacit, this attending to the interplay of priorities is also a process of hypothetical supplementation.

The burden of supplementation falls most immediately and exigently upon Peter Schlemihl, who in his ignorance and desperation is concerned with social acceptability; but the burden of supplementation also falls upon the reader. The story is a challenging one, after all, because (as with Kafka's stories) the act of attentive reading is at the same time a continual and deceptive attempt to interpret ambiguous elements and attitudes, an attempt culminating in the uneasy awareness that any interpretation can, like a shadow, be arbitrarily overvalued. The reader of Peter Schlemihl is disconcerted by critical "conclusions" about the work because the work, even with its delightful folktale qualities, is also puzzling and ominous; it offers an experience of impenetrability which confident affirmations necessarily ignore and even offend against.

I

Peter Schlemihl is an "outsider" (the story opens with his arrival from somewhere by ship) who desires to be a member of the wealthy class. When he first appears, Schlemihl seems to have some potentially profit-making scheme in mind. But the scheme, if there is one, is never specified or carried out, since it apparently becomes unnecessary: in exchange for his shadow, a nameless man in gray offers Schlemihl a magical bag which produces endless pieces of gold. At the time he makes the deal, Schlemihl does not imagine the loss of his shadow to be a serious matter; but it soon becomes apparent from the outraged and astonished exclamations of passersby, his shadowlessness constitutes a grave breach of social decorum. As readers, we can well understand the kinds of emotions expressed by the passersby, but not immediately the cause of these emotions. We are confronted with a lack of "fit" between the outrage expressed and the shadowlessness which seems to engender that outrage. We have several avenues of possible recourse: we can question the emotions being expressed, assuming that something is wrong with the passersby, who would seem more justified to be astonished or indifferent than to be offended; or we can assume that in Chamisso's fiction, a human shadow (or its lack) must "mean" something. We cannot, however, be quite sure what the shadow "means," either to the local offended citizenry or in any possible larger "literary" or "historical" sense. (To an extent which will become more and more apparent, we, like Schlemihl, are outsiders.) We are gradually forced to examine the entire configuration of givens (the gray man, shadowlessness, the responses of passersby, the narrational details) with a sense that more is occurring than we understand. We become engaged in the familiar process by which children learn—joyfully, painfully, intuitively—the mores and manners of their families and societies.

Schlemihl, however, has no peers, and his social elders do not treat him as a child. He is placed in the position of having seriously but unwittingly misbehaved, and he is compelled, on account of uncontrollable circumstances, to continue to misbehave. In his conspicuous impropriety, Schlemihl finds himself in a society which is privy to an assumption (appearing as superior insight) which is so well understood as to remain tacit. As readers, we vacillate between a respect for the annoyance and indignation of the passersby and a disdain for their foolishness in being upset over nothing more than a missing shadow. At the same time, however, we know that it is precisely the seeming foolishness, the arbitrariness, of social norms which give those norms their awesome authority: the norms need no sanction or justification; they are simply to be obeyed and respected. On one level, we are in sympathy with Schlemihl's desperate attempts to disguise his shadowlessness (by using the power of his money, by going out only at night, by standing behind Bendel's shadow). At another level, however, we find ourselves looking for clues as to why shadows are cherished and what they could possibly mean.

Meaning, we discover, emerges negatively: a shadow is a necessary but not sufficient condition for respectability and human intercourse. Literally and positivistically, this seems foolish. Unless he were a magician or a prankster, a man without a shadow would present a phenomenon to be studied (and presumably explained) by the laws and theories of optical physics. He would not be subjected to outrage and rejection. Yet consider the matter again: a man without a shadow would be a rather bizarre creature. He would seem to have a body, and yet at the same time would not seem to be ensconced, like ordinary mortals, in "this muddy vesture of decay." Shadows, as an indication of body, are an indication of mortality and the flesh. Having a shadow involves belonging to the society of mortal things. Schlemihl assumes a part in the human world but seems exempt from the human condition. Indeed, Schlemihl is exempt from a major aspect of that condition: by means of his money sack he is freed from the curse of labor. Here the connection between money and shadow begins to emerge: however meaningful they may be in themselves, money and shadow must also be considered—in this story—in conjunction. As propaedeutic to such a conjunction, let us reflect upon the terms separately.

II

Perhaps the most painful concrete consequence of Schlemihl's shadowlessness is the disruption of his engagement to Mina.[9] One expression, in particular, of this disruption is worth remarking. When her father becomes suspicious and accuses Schlemihl of being without a shadow, Mina exclaims in dismay that she herself had had such a presentiment ("'O meine Ahnung, meine Ahnung! . . . ja, ich weiß es längst, er hat keinen Schatten!'" [V. 41].[10] This is admirably unclear: is Schlemihl's defect peculiar to him alone or do shadowless men constitute an undesirable social class? Paradoxically, both alternatives apply: Mina and others behave toward Schlemihl as though he belonged to a class of undesirables—those without shadows—but Schlemihl's plight is devastating because (apart from the devotion of Bendel), his torments are his alone; he is totally isolated; he encounters no fellows in his sufferings. The peculiarity of his plight notwithstanding, Schlemihl's shadowlessness evokes a disapprobation which is not relative to any particular society: he is offensive no matter where he wanders. How is this to be accounted for?

In questing for an answer, we might do well to entertain the possibility, so strongly suggested in the story, that shadowlessness is at least in some respects an unfortunate state of mind, since metaphorically our shadows perpetuate concourse between our deeper selves and our social performances. By selling his shadow, Peter "gives away" a major part of himself, and thereby condemns himself to a continual psychic imbalance;

for the bulk of his story, we observe Schlemihl in incessant doubt and self-turmoil. At the moments of his major decisions (when exchanging his shadow or when about to sign away in blood his soul) Schlemihl is overcome by swoons, as though unconscious forces flooded into his conscious mind and led to the conditions which follow.[11] When Peter exchanges his shadow for the magical money bag (the first unfortunate event from which all others follow), he is not in full possession of "himself." He becomes entranced by his own repetitive and automatic seizing upon coins, expressed in incantatory rhythms ("Ich griff hinein und zog zehn Goldstücke daraus, und wieder zehn, und wieder zehn, und wieder zehn; ich halt ihm schnell die Hand hin: 'Topp! der Handel gilt, für den Beutel haben Sie meinen Schatten!'" [I. 17]). But passive though he may be in the early parts of the story, Peter Schlemihl is more than a mere victim to unconscious forces; he takes a resolute stand in finally banishing the gray man once and for all. Should there have been any doubt, however, these observations give backing to the possibility that we would do well to view shadowlessness as a human phenomenon rather than a problem in physics.

For a more refined specification of the phenomenon, we must look to our literary tradition, which provides a rich harvest of examples: images of shadows as more or as less than human figures (as stalking ghosts, for example, or as underworld shades who are not quite alive or dead).[12] At one particular point in the tradition we meet a figure without a shadow. In the third canto of *Purgatorio,* Dante the pilgrim is astonished to discover that his master Virgil is shadowless. The pilgrim, aware of the red sun rising behind him, is startled to find the figure of only his own shadow and is afraid of having been abandoned. In his terror, he turns aside, provoking Virgil's chastisement and explanation:

> And my Comfort turned full to me then to
>   say:
>   "Why are you still uncertain? Why do you
>   doubt
>   that I am here and guide you on your
>   way?
>
> Vespers have rung already on the tomb
>   of the body in which I used to cast a
>   shadow.
>   It was taken to Naples from Brindisium.
>
> If now I cast no shadow, should that fact
>   amaze you more than the heavens which
>   pass the light
>   undimmed from one to another?
>
> [E 'l mio conforto: "Perchè pur diffidi?"
>   A dir mi comiciò tutto rivolto;
>   "Non credi tu me teco, e ch' io ti guidi?

Vespero è già colà, dov'è sepolto
   Lo corpo, dentro al quale io facea ombra:
   Napoli l' ha, e da Brandizio è tolto.

Ora, se innanzi a me nulla s' adombra,
   Non ti maraviglia più che de' cieli,
   Che l' uno a l' altro raggio non
ingombra."][13]

The main point here is immediately apparent: the mortal body, by nature, casts a shadow; so it is no wonder that the figures seen by Dante, which are no longer alive, should no longer be with shadow. More intriguing, however (and quite relevant to *Peter Schlemihl*), are two seemingly unrelated observations: that Dante the pilgrim, in his need to see a shadow, lacks faith in the person and presence of his guide, and that Virgil's body itself cannot cast a shadow, because of being ensepulchered within a tomb and moreover (as if to clinch the point) it is now evening in Naples. Virgil speaks of "lo corpo dentro al quale io facea ombra," as though somehow the process of life itself involves the making of shadows. Obviously his meaning is not merely that any physical, solid body, when illuminated, gives off a shadow, but rather that a living, earthly body, in the human world (the world which contains Naples and Brindisi) gives off a shadow.

The opposition between two realms, one in which shadows are made, the other, beyond life, in which they are not, suggests different, less explicit oppositions. The shadow externalized itself in the visible, earthly world; but a converse activity may be required to see "into" (empathize with) another member of that world. Dante the pilgrim, in seeking for a shadow, seeks for the kind of "proof" and "assurance" which shadows, in a living person, might provide, not seeing that a need for assurance may preclude faith in that person. A shadow is a "figure" of something else; the external figure cast by a shadow is usually a distorted image of the person who casts the shadow. In the highest realms of *Paradiso,* minds are perfectly luminescent and shadowless to one another; but in lower realms, and on earth, the weaker lights of human minds are inconstant and penumbral. They illuminate one another fitfully; they "make" shadows as well as light; indeed, darkness and light are the conditions of one another. The "I" ("io") makes shadows which can be seen by others, and thus contributes to the play of light and shadows which is so familiar and assumed a part of the ordinary mortal world. Dante, the living pilgrim, brings his shadowed vision with him and must trust in the compassionate presence and guiding insight of his once mortal guide.

III

What we learn about shadows from Dante's Virgil has a bearing on *Peter Schlemihl.* Schlemihl, in responding to social beliefs about the importance of visible shadows, comes to share that society's attitude against shadowlessness. The social judgments against Schlemihl are made, for the most part, by strangers rather than by friends or by intimates, and thus are based on external appearances. (Persons are seen in their outward figures as having and playing roles.) Even when characters sympathetic to Schlemihl are involved, such as Bendel and Mina, the social bias against shadowlessness is unavoidable: the bias, whose rationale is never questioned, is a fact which they have to accept. It is important to the story that although Schlemihl's lack of a shadow transgresses social norms, those norms are never explicitly stated or justified: the seriousness of his transgression is not immediately revealed; Schlemihl apprehends what the norms might be through the varying reactions of a succession of individuals. The early reactions to Schlemihl's shadowlessness are of a wide range: (1) concern, (2) a reminder of carelessness or forgetfulness, (3) indignation, as though Schlemihl had been improperly dressed, and (4) mockery from young schoolboys, who throw pieces of mud at him (II. 18, 19). Schlemihl's response to the last of these reactions is to throw money at the boys—his first gesture of self-protection, one which is soon to become habitual with him. They throw mud; he throws money. He counterattacks with something more "substantial" than their mud and "shows" them that he is better than he seems, all the while seeming to be bribing them. Here, as elsewhere, Peter Schlemihl gives the impression of a man who wants desperately to be a member of society, who is deeply impressionable and sensitive to manners, yet who—for these very reasons, perhaps—seems ignorant of "prior" matters; matters which, more basically, give the social order its sustenance and value. To a deeper extent than might be apparent, Schlemihl is implicated in his own increasing alienation.

At the outset, Schlemihl arrives on shore, pushes his way through the scurrying people ("das wimmelnde Volk"), as though superior to them. The opening narrative has concision, purposiveness, and directness: Schlemihl has "modest plans" and makes his way to the home of a rich man, Herr John. But the world of the rich which so dazzles Peter Schlemihl is not quite real: appetites are satisfied with delicacies and wishes are immediately granted. Here is a *Gesellschaft* ("society" as well as "company": a word without any ready English equivalent), the members of which speak lightly of important matters and importantly of light matters—an inversion of what is *leicht* and what is *wichtig.* Any possible reservations about what Peter sees, however, are superseded by his admiration. What repeatedly amazes Peter Schlemihl, even more than the magical feats of the gray man, is the lack of amazement of the *Gesellschaft* at such feats. Peter sees before him a *Gesellschaft* in which magical feats seem to have become an expected convenience—the normal and routine way in which desires are realized. In his amazement at the lack of amazement, Schlemihl fails to discern what he sees: in this *Gesellschaft* there is scant concern for others; the people here gossip maliciously about absent friends and fail to offer thanks to anyone. Neither the feats nor the person of the gray man are noticed: the *Gesellschaft* is narcissistically self-enclosed, and seems to have developed a habitual blindness to anyone outside its present circle.

Peter Schlemihl fails to recognize a dichotomy which might alert the reader: on one side, an extreme scraping and fawning on the part of the gray man, on the other an extreme indifference and unceremoniousness on the part of the *Gesellschaft*. Peter seems, in this situation, to have no self of his own and thus wants very much to be defined, to be told how to respond ("[ich] rieb mir die Augen, nicht wissend was ich dazu denken sollte . . ." [I. 14]). In his astonishment, Peter fails to suspect that the entire setting might be a performance: he is captivated by a well-performed magical show. Peter's astonishment, in short, helps to weaken his natural resistance: he has just seen that immediate and repeated fulfillment of wishes is not only possible, but (among a certain class) a routine and socially acceptable convenience. The distinguishing feature of the members of this *Gesellschaft* is their wealth. It is natural, in Peter's eyes, that wealth and magic should be connected; thus he is prepared to accept, without thought or hesitation, the gray man's offer of a magical money sack. Peter's experiences at the *Gesellschaft* at Herr John's occur before he makes a deal with the gray man, which in turn is prior to all the misfortunes which follow. In both cases, it seems clear, the priority is more than temporal: from an ordering of values in these episodes, other orderings inescapably follow.

Thus just as the show at Herr John's is theatrical and illusory, money too, it turns out, is theatrical and illusory. Gold provides Schlemihl with a temporary and only apparent respite from feelings of alienation, for gold is only a mediator and an abstraction, intensifying rather than relieving Schlemihl's need for direct and personal human contact. After Schlemihl engages in an orgy of gold-throwing, surrounding himself with piles of gold and revelling in the gold's sound and glitter (II. 20), he finds himself burdened with his earlier foolishness. The gold seems somehow indecent; it cannot be left lying around on the floor. Yet it will not fit back into the pouch (whose "magic" is apparently irreversible). Schlemihl's laborless production of gold has been counterbalanced by an odd phenomenon: gold, which usually is the reward for labor, has now become the curse of labor—since Schlemihl does not want to attract attention to himself, he must secretly and laboriously haul his gold away, out of the public eye.

Schlemihl's gold has made him more alone than ever: "Ich lag, . . . fern von jedem menschlichen Zuspruch,

bei meinem Golde darbend, . . . um dessentwillen ich mich von allem Leben abgeschnitten sah" (III. 24). Schlemihl here comes to see that he is isolated from human contact not only because of his shadowlessness, but because of his money as well. In repeatedly giving money to those who find him offensive, Schlemihl is compelled to commit against others the misdeed which had been committed against him by the gray man. The effect is to weaken still further Schlemihl's genuine relationships with other people, and to produce an illusory and compensatory sense of identity. As Karl Marx has argued, money deludes us into believing that we are someone else and can thus attain rectification for all our defects.[14] Money undermines and subverts natural human capacities and associations: communal relationships are replaced by exploitation and dependency.[15] In this light, there is something odd about Schlemihl's deal (*Handel*) with the gray man; most deals involve an exchange of money or its equivalent, but this one involves an endless source of money. It is no irony that Schlemihl must have recognized, even in his swoon, that this was a deal to end all deals. But whatever feelings of exploitation may have flitted through his mind, Schlemihl is the exploited more than the exploiter. The gray man can afford all too easily to treat the money sack as a toy, suggesting his complicity in a strange and perhaps ominously powerful social order which can dispense so blithely with gold.

Granted its alienating powers, money is nonetheless a means not only of separation, but of union.[16] It brings men together in order for them to benefit from one another's various and specialized talents. Money is a fluid form of property (the "blood" of the commonwealth, Hobbes calls it), and is of stable value under socially "healthy" conditions. Without getting into the murkier regions of economics, we can venture the generally accepted assumption that property rights have some connection with labor. On John Locke's formulation, "every man has a property in his own person. . . . The labour of his body and the work of his hands are properly his."[17] Schlemihl's shadow might seem to be a property in his own person, to do with what he might. But without having labored, Schlemihl exchanges it for what is given value through labor: the gold he gains is not properly his, since he has not mixed his labor with it.

Schlemihl's plight involves other and deeper elements, as well. The binding power of a commonwealth is partially based upon fear and loyalty among its citizens: a whole tradition of thinkers have speculated upon the origins of society in a "social contract." Whatever the reality of the "social contract" (as a principle if not as an empirical locus in time), this "prior" contract supports and justifies lesser contracts and the framework of law. An example of a lesser contract is Schlemihl's enforced agreement with Mina's father to obtain a shadow within three days' time or else forfeit the girl. Schlemihl cannot fulfill this lesser contractual relationship, it can be argued, because he has broken the larger and prior contract in trading his shadow for an endless source of unearned wealth, freeing himself hypothetically (if not in intention) from all fear and loyalty to anyone else. Here the psychological and social strands of the story can be connected: Schlemihl is "guilty" for having committed himself blindly (and irrevocably) to an anti-social compact. This compact might in some sense be "pre-social" and is deeply connected, as well, to "later" social orderings and Schlemihl's lack of a place in those orderings. One possible genesis for the feeling of guilt is suggested, in general terms, by Nietzsche: " . . . jener moralische Hauptbegriff 'Schuld' [hat] sein Herkunft aus dem sehr materiellen Begriff 'Schulden' genommen."[18] This seems applicable: Peter Schlemihl is "indebted" to the gray man in a manner which prevents the incurring of other kinds of indebtedness. Schlemihl's *Schuld* is both an indebtedness (to the gray man) and a feeling of guilt (towards his fellow men); he cannot deal fairly with the latter and his prior *Schuld* is demonstrated by his later states and incapacities. On these grounds, Schlemihl lacks a social-economic "person" with the pertinent rights of such a person. In other words, on account of his deal with the gray man, Schlemihl is *schuldig* in a way which he can never make good in public. It seems that he knows, deep within, that the gray man was not merely a man among men, and that to admit to having had dealings with the gray man would be to jeopardize whatever small and temporary social status he might perchance have attained. His feeling of *Schuld*, which seems (and to some extent is) social in origin, can nonetheless never be exposed to social scrutiny. Schlemihl's prior transaction with the gray man precludes rather than facilitates ordinary day-to-day social transactions: no sequent canon of justice or fair play could arise from such a transaction. The so-called *"Gesellschaft"* at Herr John's, which set the atmosphere for Schlemihl's deal, was permeated with unreal and narcissistic fantasies given magical fulfillment.

IV

Schlemihl was predisposed by temperament and situation to have dealings with the man in gray, who might even be designated as a double for Schlemihl. Schlemihl is led into an identification with the gray man (whom he instinctively finds repugnant): both seem to be outsiders, both maintain a deferential and respectful distance from the *Gesellschaft* they observe, both are hardly noticed or welcomed, both of them sneak away. When the gray man approaches and Peter returns his overly courteous bow, it becomes clear that the gray man gives expression to (externalizes) Peter's own deepest wishes and returns them to Peter himself. Peter's feeling is naturally ambivalent: he is personally repulsed by the gray man and thinks the offer "insane," yet is secretly delighted to be treated with such politeness; despite his feelings of aversion, he "fits" his voice to the humility of the gray man (I. 17). Schlemihl at first assumes that the gray man is insane, yet he all too sincerely adapts himself to that insanity (I. 17). The gray man's display of sentiments similar to Schlemihl's is an astute seductive ploy—similar feelings and mutually advantageous possessions connected with those feelings lead reasonably to an exchange. Schlemihl's similarity to the gray man continues even after he has exchanged the shadow. Schlemihl with his endless wealth has an influential power at his command. Yet like the gray man's, Peter's power is poisoned at the source: the gray man was personally repulsive, and Peter is repulsive for his shadowlessness.

If Peter's double is the gray man, Peter's double is also, however, "Chamisso" (the implied *persona* to whom he writes).[19] Peter's character is refracted in two directions—on one side, toward the gray man, and on the other side, toward "Chamisso." As the story progresses, Schlemihl's partial identification with the gray man (his bad double) gradually gives way to his identification with "Chamisso" (his good double). Three refracted images of Peter Schlemihl (gray man, Peter Schlemihl, "Chamisso") are roughly parallelled by the three kinds of "society" through which Schlemihl passes: the group at Herr John's, the social order which ostracizes Schlemihl and the larger world of nature through which Schlemihl wanders in his seven-league boots.

In the world of Herr John and in the world which cherishes shadows, Schlemihl is forced (and is willing) to play roles. Whenever Peter gains a temporary place in society, his position is delineated theatrically. Schlemihl repeatedly finds himself to be an actor; he meets his beloved Mina during a flamboyantly theatrical procession and is mistaken for the King of Prussia, who himself was travelling under the name of a count (IV. 34); Peter accepts the gratuitous title of Count and then tries to live up to it (to play it). Again, his sincere and deeply emotional relationship with Mina is seen, in retrospect, to have been inextricably entwined with a badly-played stage part (" . . . die gemeine Posse beschließt eine Verhöhnung" [IV. 29]). The emptiness of Schlemihl's social position inevitably mirrors the emptiness of the *Gesellschaft* he earlier admired. Schlemihl can easily forgive Raskal's thefts, since the distinction between taking and being given has become blurred. Raskal's embezzlements can hardly harm a man of endless wealth, who might just as easily have given what was stolen. By the same reasoning, however, Schlemihl's attitude is merely a role: his forgiveness seems false and his charity empty.

As a role-player, Schlemihl continually lies, in order to countenance his shadowlessness. Each of Schlemihl's "stories" is designed to "explain" his shadowlessness, and thus, to a certain extent, each of these stories is in competition with the larger story which Schlemihl addresses to his friend Chamisso. There are several competing stories: to the painter, Schlemihl recounts (in the third person) that while travelling in Russia, his shadow froze to the ground and could not be torn loose; to the forester, Schlemihl says that his shadow was stepped on by a rough man and is being repaired; finally, to a peasant he meets, Schlemihl claims that he suffered a serious illness in which his shadow was irretrievably lost (III. 25; V. 42; IX. 66). Each time he recollects having made up a story, Schlemihl admits that he lied and each time that he lies, the lie is ineffective in winning for him the pity or forgiveness he craves. What is to prevent us from assuming, however, that Schlemihl might have produced his biggest lie of all for us, and that we, his readers, are his most gullible victims? The story, after all, is very much a "story," with its magical paraphernalia and its set of "bad" and "good" characters.

An answer is implied in the final sections of the work. There, Schlemihl no longer needs to assume theatrical postures. In gaining his seven-league boots, Schlemihl gains a point "outside" the human world, from which to measure and classify the natural world, of which the human world is only a part. Schlemihl becomes almost god-like in his ability to change places and seasons. From this point of view, human society and the gray man fade into a single perspective: the gray man attacks the human world by making use of methods and values of that world. The gray man is a perpetual actor, with allegiance to no law, and yet makes claim to (has pretensions of) "legal" ownership of Schlemihl's shadow, which will not "stick" to Schlemihl without the gray man's consent (when Schlemihl tries to make off with the shadow, it returns to its "gesetzmäßigen Eigentümer" [VIII. 60]).

Schlemihl, through "Chamisso," validates the truth of his tale. The tale is only partially a matter of magical or story-telling capacities; it is also a matter of social pressures within and against which the truth of his tale emerges. The false stories, on Schlemihl's part, were attempts to avoid revealing his creditor and to minimize or undo his *Schuld*. With his friend "Chamisso," Schlemihl presumably establishes a small but solid society in which truth is possible. As Schlemihl becomes more and more alienated from society, the number of addresses to his author increases: Schlemihl, it seems, can be cured of his habitual mendacity only when he has broken all concrete ties with humanity except his tie with (or as) the author. "Chamisso" is the sole confessor of Schlemihl and the sole possessor of Schlemihl's "full" story. The story, we discover, has a built-in system of narrative integrity: the isolation of Schlemihl at the end is necessary to deprive him of any motivation for lying—he becomes a "disinterested" servant of truth. The larger narrative encompasses and

replaces the smaller, false narratives which it contains; it tells the "real" story of Schlemihl. It is, however, a discomfiting testimony, giving bitter perspective upon the price of truthfulness: Peter's "better" self reveals itself only outside of ordinary human context and community.

V

Its system of narrative self-validation notwithstanding, ***Peter Schlemihls wundersame Geschichte*** is questionable. For reasons not necessarily having to do with the veracity or perceptiveness of the narrator, the story has not yielded to critical generalizations, nor have readers been dispelled of their puzzlement. To a certain extent, this is fortunate: the "wundersame Geschichte" produces an appropriate sense of pleasurable amazement. Yet another element—ominous but familiar—confounds our responses. This element has to do with our sense of the potency of social sanctions and the frightening vulnerability and plurality of possible justifications for such sanctions. "Romantic" elements mollify the story's terror, but only for readers innocent enough to be content with saccharine gratifications. For such readers, the story ends well: Schlemihl has learned from his experiences, the "devil" is exorcised, Schlemihl has become "good" and "useful," he has discovered his "true" self, he has made himself at home all over the world, and the story itself—which is, after all, only a story—even has a moral: *caveat emptor*. Many readers, however, will not be so easily mollified: the magic is too entangled with the illusions by which terrifying social sanctions are nourished and exacted. Magic is a tool to the nameless man in gray, and it results less in delight than in agony and dehumanization.

We are now in a position to understand the reader's uneasiness and the inadequacy of critical commentary. The story offers a series of incompatible but equally exigent alternatives, without suggesting any possible resolution between them. The story attacks as well as defends its protagonist, whose ostracism is both deserved and thrust upon him. Money, which plays an important role in changing Schlemihl, could be viewed as a cause of separation (as Marx contended) and as a necessary binding of the commonwealth (as Hobbes and Locke contended). The ambiguity is not resolved by considering the valuation of money in conjunction with other potential values—such as the shadow, the soul, or human society—because with each of these, the same ambiguity obtains. The shadow, for example, seems to represent an important part of the person, and Schlemihl, in underestimating its value, underestimates the entire realm of mortal affairs; on the other hand, however, the shadow seems to be given social value only out of entrenched but foolish and narrow-minded prejudice. The soul itself, although intimately connected with the other values, seems to be the only element which might nonetheless be purified.

In his final dealing with the gray man, Schlemihl is neither passive nor swooning (as in his earlier dealings); his language is resolute and commanding. He asks for Herr John: "'bei Gott, ich will es wissen!'" (VIII. 64). The invocation of God's name reminds us that the divine order (according to which the corpse of John claims to have been justly judged) is supra-social, thus providing the story with a counterbalance to the arbitrariness of merely social norms. Another counterbalance is apparent in Schlemihl's newly-found selfhood. Here, for the first time, Schlemihl's attitude is not merely reactive to social expectations; he himself dismisses the gray man. Schlemihl wants to know, and his desire for a knowledge independent of social pressures is a major impetus for his studies of nature. Schlemihl's repeated crises gradually give way to a "higher" self which takes pure knowledge as its object and which is not constricted by social prejudices. But there can be no doubt that this outcome is unsatisfactory. Schlemihl is condemned to know only the surfaces of the external world, and on account of physical limitations, is hindered even there (X. 70). His abstract investigations, a result of his exclusion from the concrete human world, are for the betterment of "humanity" in the abstract. Earlier in the story, Schlemihl experiences alienation in immediate social contexts; here, alienation is a matter of scientific knowledge. The gradual progression from one kind of alienation to another is embodied in many techniques of aesthetic distancing, particularly in techniques of magic. The shadow-tale and the seven-league-boots tale at first seem unrelated: from an external viewpoint, the author has simply linked together two discrete folktales. But in both tales, magical powers are the origin and instruments for realistically portrayed feelings of alienation. In the shadow tale, as we have seen, the rationale for Schlemihl's ostracism is suggested with indirectness, this very indirectness being a part of the experience of exclusion. In the seven-league-boots tale, however (which begins after Schlemihl has abandoned society and dismissed the gray man), indirectness is no longer necessary: feelings of homelessness and distance are at once magnified and concretized in a kaleidoscopic shifting of geographical locations.

Both kinds of magic serve to strip Schlemihl of all but his soul in its purely cognitive capacities. Peter seems to have gained a "self," but can there really be a self at all without a human world (in Dante's sense)? The chilling end of Peter Schlemihl is to be most alive when dead to the human world. Unlike Dante the pilgrim, who learns from Virgil to cherish and understand the bases for a civilized order, Peter Schlemihl, without a guide, learns little, if anything, to justify society as he experiences it. Like Dante, Peter leaves the living human world, but unlike Dante, Peter knows no prospect of return.

Notes

[1] Introduction to *Chamissos Werke,* in *Deutsche National-Literatur,* 148 (Stuttgart, n.d.), esp. pp. xliv-lxi.

[2] "*Peter Schlemihl* in Relation to the Popular Novel of the Romantic Period," *Germanic Review* 21 (1946), 191-208.

[3] *Geist der Goethezeit,* 4 (Leipzig, 1953), p. 348.

[4] *Die Deutsche Novelle,* 1 (Düsseldorf, 1964), p. 106.

[5] "Chamisso," in Thomas Mann's *Gesammelte Werke,* 9 (Oldenberg, 1960), pp. 46-55.

[6] *Adalbert von Chamissos Peter Schlemihl,* Wege zur Dichtung 42. (Leipzig, 1944), p. 40.

[7] *Surveys and Soundings in European Literature,* ed. A. Leslie Willson (Princeton, 1966), p. 221.

[8] *Ibid.,* p. 219.

[9] Elsewhere, too, Schlemihl's shadowlessness terrifies a woman with whom he is involved, disrupts the relationship, and forces him to realize that a major change in his life is required (III. 28). Shadowlessness is connected with Schlemihl's sexual identity and thus deeply with his psychological dynamics.

[10] References to *Pteer Schlemihls wundersame Geschichte* are to the Reclam edition (Stuttgart, 1965), which is based on Max Koch's edition.

[11] Carl G. Jung has used the term "shadow" to indicate a negative but essential part of the psyche. On his line of thinking, any person whose shadow-side is undeveloped or repressed must fall into a state of psychic paralysis (*Two Essays on Analytical Psychology, trans.* R. F. C. Hull [New York, 1953]), p. 313, note 5. The appeal of *Peter Schlemihl* is partly to the unconscious; the story is puzzling partly because Schlemihl is quite unaware of the workings of the unconscious and considers his problems to be "outer" problems of social adjustment rather than problems of the integrity of the self in its social relations.

[12] One underworld source, from Lucian, has been noted by Grillparzer. See Atkins, 191, n. 1.

[13] *Purgatorio,* trans. John Ciardi (New York, 1957); *La Divina Commedia,* ed. C. H. Grandgent (Boston, 1933), canto 3, lines 22-30.

[14] "Geld," in *Ökonomische-philosophische Manuskripte* (1844), *Werks,* Ergänzungsband 1 [Berlin, 1968], p. 564; "Das, was ich *bin* und *vermag,* ist . . . keineswegs durch meine Individualität bestimmt. Ich *bin* häßlich, aber ich kann mir die *schönste* Frau kaufen" [Marx's italics].

[15] "Bedürfnis, Produktion und Arbeitsteilung," in *Werke,* p. 547: "Jeder Mensch spekuliert darauf, dem andern ein *neues* Bedürfnis zu schaffen, um ihm einem neuen Opfer zu zwingen, um ihn in eine neue Abhängigkeit zu versetzen . . . Jeder sucht eine *fremde* Wesenskraft über den andern zu schaffen, um darin die Befriedigung seines eigenen eigennützigen Bedürfnisses zu finden" [Marx's italics].

[16] *Ibid.,* p. 565: "Wenn das *Geld* das Band ist, das mich an das *menschliche* Leben, das mir die Gesellschaft, das mich mit der Natur und den Menschen verbindet, ist das Geld nicht das Band aller *Bande?* Kann es nicht alle Bande lösen und binden? Ist es darum nicht auch das allgemeine *Scheidungsmittel?* Es ist die wahre *Scheidemünze,* wie das wahre Bindungsmittel, die *chemische* Kraft der Gesellschaft?" [Marx's italics].

[17] *The Second Treatise of Civil Government,* chap. V, sect. 27 in *Two Treatises of Government,* ed. Thomas I. Cook (New York, 1947).

[18] *Zur Genealogie der Moral,* in *Werke,* ed. Karl Schlechta (München, n.d.), sect. 8, p. 811.

[19] Chamisso writes in his letter to Hitzig (27 September 1813) that Peter Schlemihl is a part of himself and (in the prefatory poem) indicates more specific resemblances.

Martin Swales (essay date 1976)

SOURCE: "Mundane Magic: Some Observations on Chamisso's *Peter Schlemihl,*" in *Forum for Modern Language Studies,* Vol. XII, No. 3, July, 1976, pp 250-62.

[*In the following essay, Swales investigates the ambiguous shadow motif of* Peter Schlemihl "*as the paradigm for that uncertain moral and social situation which the novel so brilliantly explores.*"]

By any standards, **Peter Schlemihl** is a most engaging story.[1] On several occasions, Chamisso asserted that the work was originally written to amuse children, and its combination of verbal and situational humour leaves one in little doubt that it fulfils this purpose admirably. One wonders, however, whether careful textual study would not reveal the story to be much more than a beguiling fantasy. Certainly a number of critics have felt that **Peter Shlemihl** must be taken as a completely

serious work of art, and scholarly interpreters have argued that the shadow embodies a deeper meaning which transforms the harmless children's entertainment into an allegory of great moral and social import. It has, for example, been suggested that the shadow is a symbol representing outward honour, the fatherland, national identity, the social persona, the world of appearances, the integrity of the personality, solidarity with the human community, participation in bourgeois society. While the story certainly does invite this kind of reading, yet one feels that a degree of violence has to be done to the work in order to transform it into an explicit allegory. Furthermore, the shadow poses certain interpretative problems. My objections to the overtly symbolic readings are that they tend to overlook the crucial interpretative ambiguity of the shadow itself. The shadow, as it functions in the story, is both a nothing and a something, both worthless and infinitely precious. No reading that ignores this dialectic can do justice to the story. Moreover, the shadow acquires meaning not in and of itself, but entirely within the context of people's attitudes to it. Its meaning resides in what it tells us about the people who react to it, who interpret it, who notice it. In itself, it is—and remains—simply a shadow. For this reason it is not, strictly speaking, a symbol. It does not reliably embody anything—apart from its own insubstantial existence. But this is not to say that it is devoid of overall interpretative significance within the story. If the kind of distinction I have in mind sounds like hair-splitting, one can perhaps clarify the point by means of a comparison. Hugo von Hofmannsthal's *Die Frau ohne Schatten* is also concerned with shadowlessness. But Hofmannsthal's story operates with a consistently sustained allegorical intensity (and clarity) that Chamisso never achieves. In Hofmannsthal's work the attainment of a shadow is, interpretatively, a known quantity throughout: it represents the acceptance of—and entry into—full humanity. There is no trace of the kind of ambiguity that pervades Chamisso's story. Furthermore, the high seriousness of allegorical intention in *Die Frau ohne Schatten* is apparent in the style, in the narrative tone, in the depiction of events. There is none of the humour, none of the down-to-earth, almost mundane treatment of the magical such as we get in **Peter Schlemihl.** Indeed, actual social reality has little place in Hofmannsthal's story (although it would seem to be very much part of its theme), precisely because Hofmannsthal will not allow himself to document a specific social world in the way that Chamisso does. In *Die Frau ohne Schatten* everything is handled allegorically: the characters move through an overtly denotative landscape. And the magical elements are symptomatic of the story's whole detachment from concrete realities. But in **Peter Schlemihl** the supernatural is obliged to exist in and work through the everyday social world. This is the source of much of the humour in **Peter Schlemihl**—and of its deepest import. The dialectic of the real and the magical, of concrete and abstract, informs the whole of Chamisso's story, and prevents it from operating at the level of unrelieved allegorical abstraction.

An analysis of the opening pages of *Peter Schlemihl* will, I hope, suggest some of the specific qualities of this remarkable story and the narrative control with which they are handled.

The story begins with a preface which consists of three letters, one from Chamisso to his publisher Hitzig, one from Hitzig to Fouqué, and one from Fouqué to Hitzig. The letters tell us how the story of Peter Schlemihl—told in his own words—came to be published. It transpires that both Chamisso and Hitzig knew Schlemihl: Chamisso on one occasion even took him along to one of his publisher's literary teas. Peter, having written down his life story, leaves it one night for his friend Chamisso. The latter is obviously touched by what he reads, although he cannot help feeling that much more could have been made of it if the tale had been entrusted to a professional writer—such as Jean Paul. But, as it stands, it has the authority of personal confession. Fouqué apparently shares Chamisso's admiration for the story—and has it published. Obviously, this introduction serves one overriding purpose: it asserts that the story we are about to read is true, that the man who wrote it actually lived: he was a friend of well-known German authors and publishers. And therefore the magical events which he describes did, in fact, occur in the recognizable world of North German society in the early years of the nineteenth century. Indeed, it is made clear that when Schlemihl delivered the manuscript to Chamisso's house, he was wearing his seven league boots at the time, which accounts for his rather strange attire—"und bei dem feuchten, regnichten Wetter Pantoffeln über seine Stiefel" (410)[2]. It follows, then, that magic can exist in the world of early nineteenth-century literary Berlin, a world whose objective existence we can verify from standard histories of literature. It is important to note that this opening serves to underpin not only the authenticity of the tale we are about to read but also its interpretative relevance to an unmistakably real social world. Moreover, although the introductory section is only very brief, consisting as it does of three letters, it continues as an implicit presence throughout Schlemihl's narration. Time and time again he refers to 'mein lieber Chamisso', thus reminding us of the real world that will see fit to publish his manuscript. Hence, the whole urgency of the moral teaching which he seeks to express is both derived from and relevant to the society which exists as an objective historical entity.

We then begin with Peter's narration. He describes his arrival in Germany after a long and wearisome sea voyage. His first contact with the bustling, lively society around him occurs when he tries to find accommodation for the night: "Ich begehrte ein Zimmer, der Hausknecht mass mich mit einem Blick und führte mich unters Dach" (413). This encounter sets the seal on what is to follow. Peter has arrived in an acquisitive, money-conscious society from which his relative poverty excludes him. He immediately sets off for Thomas John's residence, armed with his letter of introduction. He has no difficulty in recognizing the wealthy owner of the mansion: "Ich erkannte gleich den Mann am Glanze seiner wohlbeleibten Selbstzufriedenheit" (413). The formulation here is noteworthy: it derives wit and satirical energy from the surprising yoking of abstract and concrete, and this is a register that will be sustained throughout Peter's narration. The satire is continued in the very next sentence: "Er empfing mich sehr gut, wie ein Reicher einen armen Teufel" (413). We find ourselves in a world which is dominated by money, by worldly concerns. Furthermore, it is significant that in this story, which is so full of magical events, including even several appearances by the Devil himself, the first reference to the Devil is completely without metaphysical resonance. Schlemihl is an "armer Teufel". The Devil exists as a component in the colloquial speech of wealthy, leisured society—and as a metaphor expressing the attitudes inherent in that society. Peter manages to give Thomas John the letter of introduction, and the latter receives it with manifest casualness and lofty self-assurance. The patronizing quality in his behaviour is suggested by a witty formulation, a formulation which once again unites abstract and concrete, metaphorical and physical: "Er brach das Siegel auf und das Gespräch nicht ab" (413 f.).

The company moves towards the garden amidst social chatter: "es ward getändelt und gescherzt, man sprach zuweilen von leichtsinnigen Dingen wichtig, von wichtigen öfters leichtsinnig" (414). Here the behaviour of the society receives explicit moral evaluation: the important becomes trivial and the trivial important. But the full implications of this are something to which Peter is largely blind: he is infatuated with the glittering world around him, and is dominated by a burning desire to participate in it (as we see from his full-blooded assent to Thomas John's remark: "Wer nicht Herr ist wenigstens einer Million, der ist, man verzeihe mir das Wort, ein Schuft!" [414]—which involves a simple equation of worldly success and moral value). Peter, then, is in an ambivalent situation: he is dazzled by a world of which he is not yet part. He has the detachment which enables him to feel—and to see—the strangeness of the way of life which this society embodies, and yet it is a detachment which is not allowed to ripen into a fully critical attitude because he desperately wants to become part of the world which he observes.

At this stage in the story, the man in grey makes his first appearance. One of the ladies scratches her hand on a thorn, and requests sticking plaster. A somewhat

HEATH'S GERMAN SERIES.

Peter Schlemihls

Wundersame Geschichte.

WITH AN INTRODUCTION AND NOTES,

BY

SYLVESTER PRIMER, Ph.D.,

Professor of Modern Languages, College of Charleston, S. C.

BOSTON, U. S. A.

D. C. HEATH & CO., PUBLISHERS

1894

insignificant man whom Peter has hitherto not noticed produces the desired article—"und reichte der Dame mit devoter Verbeugung das Verlangte. Sie empfing es ohne Aufemerksamkeit für den Geber und ohne Dank" (414). This incident is the first of many: the man in grey shows a quite remarkable ability to minister to the needs of the company. He produces a Dollond tele-scope (the mention of the make underscores the point that the grey man is the inexhaustible purveyor of the practical articles and manufactured goods by which this society sets such store). The telescope is used by the company—but it is not returned to its owner. He then provides "mit bescheidener, ja demütiger Gebärde" (415), a Turkish carpet which is accepted as a matter of course: "Bediente nahmen ihn in Empfang, als müsse es so sein" (415). Only Schlemihl is astonished at the grey man's inexhaustible supply of goods, and yet he is uncertain what to make of his own surprise "besonders da niemand etwas Merkwürdiges darin fand" (415). His attempts to find out more about the grey man fail: nobody seems to know him, nor even to want to know him. His remarkable powers are taken for granted. Fanny now turns to ask if he has a tent with him, and the man, "als widerführe ihm eine unverdiente Ehre" (416), produces even this. This is the first time that anyone has spoken to the man—and, characteristically, it is a request for further goods. The grey man obliges—"und keiner fand noch etwas Ausserordentliches darin" (416). Peter becomes more and more troubled: "Mir war schon lange unheimlich, ja graulich zumute" (416). But there is more to come, and the grey man produces three horses from his pocket. And the hapless Peter can only reassure the friend for whom he is writing the story (Chamisso) that all these things really happened: "Wenn ich dir nicht beteuerte, es selbst mit eigenen Augen angesehen zu haben, würdest du es gewiss nicht glauben" (416). Schlemihl feels so unsettled that he decides to leave the party, but he is foiled by the grey man.

Before one analyzes the conversation that ensues, it is appropriate to summarize the interpretative implications of the behaviour of the grey man up to this point. First, one should notice that the magic is introduced gradu-ally into the story: only when the grey man produces the carpet from his pocket does the reader begin to suspect that he is some supernatural figure. Quite apart from the fact that the opening feats involve deeds which are well within the realm of physical possibility, we do not suspect anything unusual about the grey man be-cause he is so much anchored in a carefully docu-mented social role—that of the servant. And that social role is not changed in the slightest even when the tasks he performs become more and more prodi-gious. He continues to behave as the perfect servant, ready to fulfil any and every whim of his wealthy masters. And it is because the framework of his behaviour is one of social normality that none of the guests at Thomas John's garden party thinks twice about the physical impossibility of his last two actions. This is a society which is used to having every con-ceivable wish granted immediately. It is a society that is completely dependent on the ready supply of goods and services, that is used to the fact that physical dif-ficulty and practical obstacles can always be overcome, providing one has enough money. Everything—the physically possible and the physically impossible—exists on the same level, the level of instantaneous availability. And the man in grey (the Devil) knows that the society is vulnerable in terms of its complete dependence on an army of servants who will carry out every command and fulfil every wish. Hence, by as-suming the role of perfect social servant, he gains power over the members of that society. He himself does not draw attention to the prodigies he performs—this would be inappropriate in terms of his chosen social function. He behaves with the silent, devoted deference that the society expects, and for this reason he stifles any pos-sible awareness on the part of the social world that there is something unusual or sinister about him. Only Peter, who is not yet a member of that society, notices how unusual the behaviour of the man in grey is. But his infatuation with the wealthy society around him prevents him from drawing the necessary conclusions from this perception: he does not see that if the grey man's behaviour is sinister, then the kind of social ethos which it serves and helps to reinforce is also sinister. There is one particularly revealing moment in the scene when Peter comments: "ich fürchtete mich fast noch mehr vor den Herren Bedienten als vor den bedienten Herren" (415). The verbal wit, the neatly turned pun is, as I have already suggested, typical of much of the narration. And it involves not simply gra-tuitous linguistic exuberance, but an important percep-tion of the particular social situation before him. The servants are, in fact, as much "masters" as the masters whom they serve. And this is to develop into one of the major themes of the story.

Because the grey man has noticed Schlemihl's over-whelming desire to join the acquistive society from which he is at present excluded, he approaches Peter and suggests a bargain to him. And in proposing the bargain, he adopts precisely the register which he has already employed with such effectiveness: "Er nahm sogleich den Hut vor mir ab und verneigte sich so tief, als noch niemand vor mir getan hatte" (416). Peter is terrified and responds in the same vein: "Ich nahm den Hut auch ab, verneigte mich wieder und stand da in der Sonne mit blossem Haupt wie angewurzelt" (416). Whereupon the man in grey intensifies the expressions of his subservience: "Er selber schien sehr verlegen zu sein; er hob den Blick nicht auf, verbeugte sich zu verschiedenen Malen, trat näher und redete mich an mit leiser, unsicherer Stimme, ungefähr im Tone eines Bettelnden" (416 f.). This section reads like a kind of comic ballet. Both participants seem to be terri-fied: each seeks to outdo the other in expressions of subservience. For all the comedy of the scene, however, there is something important at stake here. Paradoxically, reverence, awe, subservience, service can mean power. And what ensues is a contest in which the winner is the one who can end as the 'servant' of the other. The battle is continued at a verbal level. The man in grey begins:

> "Möge der Herr meine Zudringlichkeit entschuldigen, wenn ich es wage, ihn so unbekannterweise aufzusuchen, ich habe eine Bitte an ihn. Vergönnen Sie gnädigst—"—"Aber um Gottes willen, mein Herr!" brach ich in meiner Angst aus, "was kann ich für einen Mann tun, der"—wir stutzten beide und wurden, wie mir deucht, rot. (417)

Both Devil and his prospective victim blush. Both play the role of servant—"Möge der Herr meine Zudringlichkeit entschuldigen", "was kann ich für einen Mann tun". And the result is, at this stage, a draw. The Devil renews the attack and makes his opening move:

> Während der kurzen Zeit, wo ich das Glück genoss, mich in Ihrer Nähe zu befinden, hab ich, mein Herr, einigemal—erlauben Sie, dass ich es Ihnen sage—wirklich mit unaussprechlicher Bewunderung den schönen, schönen Schatten betrachten können, den Sie in der Sonne, und gleichsam mit einer gewissen edlen Verachtung, ohne selbst darauf zu merken, von sich werfen, den herrlichen Schatten da zu Ihren Füssen. Verzeihen Sie mir die freilich kühne Zumutung. Sollten Sie sich wohl nicht abgeneigt finden, mir diesen Schatten zu überlassen? (417)

The language here is significant. First, one notes the obsequiousness (the reference to the "pleasure of being near you"), the self-deprecating reticence in "erlauben Sie, dass ich es Ihnen sage". Then comes the most insidious suggestion of all. The grey man compliments Schlemihl on the superlative excellence of his shadow, an excellence which he has attained without even making the slightest effort ("ohne selbst darauf zu merken"). The Devil imputes to Schlemihl a kind of aristocratic insouciance ("edle Verachtung"), and suggests his own inferiority by putting himself in the position of being the man who notices and admires an achievement which Schlemihl does not even recognize as existing—let alone perceive as excellent.

Of course, Schlemihl is not unaware of the strangeness of what his companion is proposing to him. But he concludes that the man in grey is not just odd—he must be mad. And this crucial step forces him into a role of superiority:

> Er muss verrückt sein, dacht ich, und mit verändertem Tone, der zu der Demut des seinigen besser passte, erwiderte ich also: "Ei, ei, guter Freund, habt Ihr

> denn nicht an Eurem eigenen Schatten genug? das heiss ich mir einen Handel von einer ganz absonderlichen Sorte." (417)

The arrogant tone, the inherent loftiness is the sign that Schlemihl has lost the battle. The sheer charm of being superior, of having someone of the grey man's extraordinary capabilities at his disposal proves too much. The Devil makes his proposal that in exchange for the shadow he will offer Schlemihl some of the many treasures which he has in his pocket. The mention of the pocket recalls to Schlemihl what he has seen only minutes before, and he regrets his patronizing tone: "ich wusste nicht, wie ich ihn hatte guter Freund nennen können" (417). And instinctively he tries to get out of the present dangerous situation in which he has landed himself by returning to the subservient role: "Ich nahm wider das Wort und suchte es, wo möglich mit unendlicher Höflichkeit wieder gutzumachen" (417). And when he speaks, he refers to himself as the "most humble servant" of the man in grey. But he makes one crucial mistake: instead of repudiating the bargain that has been proposed, he asserts its impracticability. As we have already seen, physical difficulties are no problem for the man in grey: "Ich erbitte mir nur Dero Erlaubnis, hier auf der Stelle diesen edlen Schatten aufheben zu dürfen und zu mir zu stecken; wie ich das mache, sei meine Sorge" (417). The objection on practical grounds allows the Devil to interrupt with the simple assertion (so much part of his role) that such difficulties can safely be left to him. With the subservience of the good salesman he lists the various articles which he has to offer, culminating in the offer of a "free trial": "Belieben gnädigst der Herr diesen Säckel zu besichtigen und zu erproben" (418). Schlemihl pulls gold coins out of the bag and without any further hesitation accepts the bargain. The Devil shakes his hand, and "mit einer bewunderungswürdigen Geschicklichkeit" (418) he lifts the shadow from the grass, rolls it up, folds it, and puts it in his pocket. The ending of the first encounter between Schlemihl and the man in grey is as unspectacular, as ordinary, as bound to the practicalities of concrete existence and social aspirations as has been the whole of their conversation. The Devil remains true to his role as impeccable—and indispensable—social servant: the magic gift he offers Schlemihl has a practical purpose within the real world—it will allow him access to moneyed society. And money, in this world, has almost magical powers: it dissolves practical difficulties and obstacles. It gives life an almost fairy-tale ease and weightlessness by making reality conform to every whim. Thereby, however, it removes a whole dimension from everyday living, that human dimension which initially allowed Schlemihl to notice and be critical of the behaviour of Thomas John's guests, which allowed him to be troubled by the man in grey.[3]

The opening chapter of the story is a superlative achievement in that it skilfully combines all the various strands of meaning, all the stylistic features which are to inform the whole work. Obviously, the chapter is most memorable for its casual, almost underhand introduction of the supernatural into the everyday, of the magical into the real. The fact that the extraordinary works through the ordinary is the deepest source of the story's meaning. It is also the source of much of the humour in the work, a humour which is not secondary or irrelevant, but which is an important artistic expression of the theme. Obviously one notices immediately the comedy of incident which results from the intermingling of the magical and the mundane. There is the catalogue of the man in grey's increasingly stupendous achievements, the prosaic way in which he takes possession of the shadow once the bargain is made, there is the battle for the "Vogelnest", and the delightfully practical touch that Schlemihl has to wear slippers over his magic boots "denn ich hatte erfahern, wie unbequem es sei, seinen Schritt nicht anders verkürzen zu können, um nahe Gegenstände gemächlich zu untersuchen, als indem man die Stiefel auszieht" (457). More significant, however, is the linguistic comedy which results from a comparable intermingling of the abstract and the concrete, of the grandiose and the everyday. The tension between these two registers means that the story never loses contact with the simple facts of social experience. One remembers the curiously puncturing quality of the following description of Schlemihl's despair: "O, was hätt ich nicht da für einen Schatten gegeben! Ich musste meine Scham, meine Angst, meine Verzweiflung tief in den Grund meines Wagens verbergen" (427). What we expect here is the phrase "tief in den Grund meines Herzens". What we read is the relentless reminder of the sheer unrelieved *practicality* of the problem: Schlemihl has to hide his grief where no one will notice his shadowlessness.[4] More important are those moments where the strangeness of Schlemihl's situation makes the language he uses comment on itself. When our hero encounters a shadow running along without an owner, he concludes that the man in question must be wearing the magic bird's nest. He introduces his explanation with the following words: "Nun ward mir auch das ganze Ereignis sehr natürlich erklärbar" (441). Obviously, the explanation given is—on our terms—anything but "natural", but, in the context of Schlemihl's existence, it is perfectly "natural". The language here reminds us that what is "natural" is largely a question of interpretative context—amd not of factual possibility or impossibility. A similar effect is achieved when the Devil refers to himself as "ein armer Teufel" (437), or when he justifies his behaviour with the time-honoured phrase "der Teufel ist nicht so schwarz, als man ihn malt" (449). Both the tone—and the sentiments expressed—are in keeping with the undaemonic grey man: he is, after all, only an impeccable social servant, a man who has power in so far as the prevailing social ethos allows him to be powerful. Indeed, at one point, he sounds like a

thoroughly reliable pawnbroker: "Apropos, erlauben Sie mir noch, Ihnen zu zeigen, dass ich die Sachen, die ich kaufe, keineswegs verschimmeln lasse, sondern in Ehren halte, und dass Sie bei mir gut aufgehoben sind" (438). In such moments of linguistic subtlety Chamisso sustains that interplay of the magical and the mundane which is central to the story's meaning.

The function of the shadow is consistent with the dialectic that informs both the events and the language of the story. Interpretatively, the shadow is linked with a whole series of supernatural occurrences and is at the same time embedded in the moral and social attitudes of real people. In this sense, it conveys a whole complex of meanings—without in itself being the reliable symbol "for" any one thing. Indeed, the shadow fulfils an ambiguous function within the context of people's attitudes to Peter's plight. At one level, all the characters with whom he comes into contact sense that there is something wrong about his lack of a shadow. And, in part at least, their judgment stands as an indictment of the main character, as a reliable indication of his betrayal of his own humanity. On the other hand, much of their instinctive revulsion reflects not simply on Peter but on themselves: they seem spiteful and small-minded, as in the self-righteous, uncaring reaction of the boys: "Ordentliche Leute pflegten ihren Schatten mit sich zu nehmen, wenn sie in der Sonne gingen" (419). The shadow may be important, but it is not all-important. Precisely this dialectic is embodied in the attitude of Bendel, who is both critical and compassionate. His first comment is: "Weh mir, dass ich geboren ward, einem schattenlosen Herrn zu dienen!" (424). But he then modifies this to "Was die Welt auch meine, ich kann und werde um Schattens willen meinen gütigen Herrn nicht verlassen" (424), whereby he distances himself from the uncharitable and prejudiced views of wordly wisdom.

The essential point about the shadow is that while Peter's ability to dispose of it is, by definition, a "magical" event, the implications of this action (both before and after the event) are moral and social—rather than metaphysical. Of course, the metaphysical dimension does enter the story when the man in grey offers Peter the traditional Devil's pact (involving the soul of his victim). But interpretatively, this confrontation represents an essentially metaphorical underpinning of the moral vision which is the substance of the story.

What Chamisso offers us is much more than a straightforward social satire, much more than a simple assertion that "money is the root of all evil". Rather, he conveys the confusion, the psychological and moral uprootedness that the inherent paradoxes of this specific kind of society implant in the individual. Early in the story, when Peter has for the first time experienced the unpleasant consequences that his shadowlessness brings, he reflects: "dass, um so viel das Geld auf Erden

Verdienst und Tugend überwiegt, um so viel der Schatten höher als selbst das Gold geschätzt werde" (419). Schlemihl is here talking not of his own personal attitudes—but of the consensus of worldly opinion. And the crucial term is "schätzen". Society's "Schätzung" is ambivalent. On the one hand, people rate money far above moral virtue (in that they are prepared to sell even human values and relationships—Minna's parents will make sure that their daughter is married off to the highest bidder). On the other hand, money can only be worshipped with impunity in certain socially acceptable contexts (marriage is one, profitable evasion of creditors is another—one thinks, for example, of the "Handelsmann, der Bankerott gemacht hatte, un sich zu bereichern, der allgemeine Achtung genoss und einen breiten, obgleich etwas blassen Schatten von sich warf" [430]). Schlemihl's moral guilt is one that is shared by most of the people with whom he comes into contact. What distinguishes him is the radical consequences of his attitude, consequences that are extreme to the point of involving magic. The actual sale of the shadow puts Schlemihl beyond the pale. And yet, in moral terms, the damage done to other people by his thoughtless action is much less than that done by the many "acceptable" bargains. And here we come to one crucial aspect of the shadow in this story: when the Devil first proposes his transaction to Schlemihl, he says: "für diesen unschätzbaren Schatten halt ich den höchsten Preis zu gering" (417). Once again, we meet the verb "schätzen". And it is in this whole question of evaluation within both social and moral value-scales that the central meaning of the shadow—and of Chamisso's story-resides.

In the word "unschätzbar" two value-scales—and their largely contradictory relationship to one another—are suggested. Within the context of the practical, monetary value-scale of the acquisitive society portrayed in this story, the shadow is quite simply worthless. But in terms of a different, less easily definable value-scale, the shadow is priceless, it is invaluable precisely because it is of a different order from those things which can be assessed in terms of quantifiable exchange-value, of price. The social universe to which Peter so eagerly desires access is almost exclusively dominated by the first scale. And even when it notices Peter's shadowlessness and repudiates him for it, it does so at the debased—and reified—level of Minna's father: "ich gebe Ihnen drei Tage Frist, binnen welcher Sie sich nach einem Schatten umtun mögen" (436). One notes the use of the indefinite article here: any shadow will do, it does not have to be Peter's. The people impute a false value to the shadow when they conceive of its as a thing, as something one owns, as part of one's socially necessary equipment (like money, clothes, possessions). Hermann Weigand makes the interesting point that the shadow, once handled by the Devil, assumes magical properties in that "it can be manipulated, rolled up and unfolded for display, like a substantial physical object."[5] Everything

the Devil touches becomes reduced to the level of a barterable object. And when Peter refuses the final exchange which the man in grey offers him, he vindicates the scale of values to which he has hitherto been blind, the value of the "unschätzbar". At this point he distances himself from the norms of the society around him. For the obsession with material possessions, with goods and services, affects the quality of life of the members of this society. Everything is, as it were, for sale: everything is potentially available. The only distinctions are those of quantity (of how many currency units article A costs as against article B). There is no awareness of ultimately qualitative distinctions, of the fact that article A may be of a different order from article B. And this involves a drastic reduction of man's possible evaluative responses to the world in which he lives. In a strange way—for all the materialism of the society—reality is converted into something weightless and abstract.[6] Ready exchangeability removes distinctions, above all removes the human capacity to perceive and act upon distinctions. Hence, the entry of magic into this social world constitutes a radical expression of the kind of human ethos which prevails; in no sense does it suggest a transcendence of the materialist ethos.

When Peter sells his shadow for money, he disposes of one part of the simple clutter which surrounds human existence on this planet. He sells part of the *donnée* of the human universe, a part which cannot be evaluated in terms of practical use or monetary significance. And thereby he starts on the path towards selling his soul. But Peter is able to call a halt to this process: he instinctively recoils from the final exchange possibility, although the Devil's arguments are splendidly persuasive and consistent. The Devil offers him, in essence, a repeat of the first bargain: the opportunity to exchange something of no demonstrable value for something that is of immediate practical use. The only change vis-à-vis the first bargain is that the shadow has now become the "solid" piece of goods—the soul is the useless appendage:

> Und, wenn ich fragen darf, was ist denn das für ein Ding, Ihre Seele? Haben Sie es je gesehen, und was denken Sie damit anzufangen, wenn Sie einst tot sind? Seien Sie doch froh, einen Liebhaber zu finden, der Ihnen bei Lebenszeit noch den Nachlass dieses X, dieser galvanischen Kraft order polarisierenden Wirksamkeit, und was alles das närrische Ding sein soil, mit etwas Wirklichem bezahlen will, nämlich mit Ihrem leibhaftigen Schatten, durch den Sie zu der Hand Ihrer Geliebten und zu der Erfüllung aller Ihrer Wünsche gelangen können. (437)

The language here subtly stresses the pragmatic value-scale. If the soul is not a thing of demonstrable usefulness (and only *things* are of demonstrable usefulness), then it can simply be disposed of.

The Devil argues that, whereas the soul is not a "Ding", the shadow is in every sense "leibhaftig". Furthermore, the Devil reasserts his role of the eager servant-cum-buyer: Schlemihl should be glad to find someone who is prepared to offer substantial payment for such insignificant trifles as the soul. (The appeal has been used before in the first bargain when the Devil comments on the casualness with which Schlemihl performs the task of casting a good shadow). But this is one attempt at salesmanship where the Devil fails—although his defeat is due more to deeply ingrained, instinctive responses in Schlemihl than to any precise understanding of the issues involved.

It is, in my view, important to insist on the predominantly social reading of the story which I have given above, because it helps to account not simply for the sequence of events in the work but also for its narrative mode. It also highlights the importance of certain carefully articulated themes. I have, for example, already insisted on the frequency with which the Devil plays the role of impeccable servant. The relationship of master and servant is a vital concern in the story. The wealthy society to which Schlemihl gains access is dependent upon being served by both people and goods. And in this process the "masters" become the slaves of the "servants". It is important to note that when Schlemihl is betrayed, it is by the one figure who has real power over him—the servant Raskal. Hence, Schlemihl needs the offices of his good servant Bendel at every turn in order to keep unpleasant consequences at bay. This is, at one level, the simple result of practical difficulties that stem from his shadowlessness. At another level, however, much more is involved. The story of Schlemihl's life is a radical enactment of implications inherent in the social experience of his time: and his utter dependence on being protected by his servant is symptomatic of the encapsulated existence led by the wealthy figures who gather at Thomas John's garden party. Whole dimensions of human experience (and of human responses) have to be kept at bay, and the welter of servant figures expresses the sheer timorousness, the existential fragility of the world which their masters inhabit.

Ultimately, Schlemihl is able to repudiate and break out of this world. The ending of the story is conciliatory in that Schlemihl, while remaining an outcast, is enabled by the lucky acquisition of some seven league boots to find a purpose in life. This purpose seems, at first sight, a rather peculiar one. Obviously, the hero's ability to travel, to explore the natural world, is a source of comfort to him: but one must note the specific nature of the exploration which is involved. Schlemihl is not concerned to observe spectacular natural phenomena: rather, his relationship to nature is as prosaic as the slippers which he has to wear over his magic boots. He becomes a scientist, a cataloguer of natural phenomena, who lists not the great wonders of the world, but simply the ordinary stuff of which this planet is made up. Literary-historical explanations of the ending (which refer us to the "Biedermeier" ethos, to the basically conservative mood which succeeds the excesses of Romanticism) are not, in themselves, sufficient to account for the ending to this story. Purely within the context of the work, however, the ending in my view makes perfect sense. If Schlemihl's sin in selling his shadow consists in the inability to cherish the simple, and, in itself, unremarkable and unimportant clutter of life on earth, then surely his career as a botanist is the sustained enactment of the lesson he has learnt. The Schlemihl of the closing pages of the story is someone who devotes his life to the careful, reverent cataloguing of the facts of this world. These facts are not in themselves significant: but they acquire significance in terms of the kind of response which they can elicit from man. As with the shadow, the human attitude is all-important, and is the source of meaning. And a reverent cherishing of such things implies the awareness of a value-scale which operates completely without reference to notions of monetary quantifiability—or of practical usefulness. Schlemihl's botanizing activities are the assertion of the value of the "unschätzbar", of the worth of the invaluable.

In Chamisso's story, the whole complex of themes is brought into interpretative focus by means of the shadow. That shadow is a nothing and a something, an insubstantial factor within human existence, but one that can have value nonetheless, it is a possession— but of an utterly intangible kind, an absence and a presence. Within the money-conscious society of this story the concrete facts of man's life are rendered insubstantial by their interchangeability, whereas money, that very agent of interchangeability, that abstraction from actual goods and objects, becomes the one and only hard fact. In this blurred and topsy-turvy world the shadow—and the interpretative problem it poses for us the readers—functions as the paradigm for that uncertain moral and social situation which the story so brilliantly explores.

Notes

[1] Apart from the studies acknowledged in specific footnotes, I should like also to record my gratitude to the following analyses: U. Baumgartner, *Adalbert von Chamissos "Peter Schlemihl"* (Wege zur Dichting, 42), Fraunfeld/Leipzig, 1944; Thomas Mann, *Chamisso* in T.M., *Das essayistische Werk* (ed. Bürgin) I, Frankfurt am Main, 1968; and Franz Schulz, "Die erzählerische Funktion des Motivs vom verlorenen Schatten in Chamissos *Peter Schlemithl*", GQ 45 (1972) 429 ff.

[2] References throughout are to *Chamissos Werke* (ed. Heinrich Kurz), I, Hildburghausen (Verlag des Bibliographischen Instituts), 1870.

[3] See Ernst Loeb's perceptive article "Symbol und Wirklichkeit des Schattens in Chamissos *Peter Schlemihl*", *GRM* N.F. 15 (1965), 398 ff. Loeb suggests that Schlemihl sells his shadow for a life of ease, that he attempts to buy "light" without "dark", whereas living involves both light and dark, both hard and easy.

[4] See Atkins's argument that *Peter Schlemihl* is a satire on the lacrymose effusions of contemporary novel-writing. (*GR,* 21 [1946], 191 ff.).

[5] Hermann J. Weigand, *Surveys and Soundings in European Literature* (ed. A. Leslie Willson), Princeton, 1966, p. 210.

[6] Compare Benno von Wiese's telling point: "Trotz seiner sozialen Funktion oder vielleicht gerade auf Grund dieser sozialen Funktion behält das Geld etwas Chimäres, Flüssiges und Wandelbares und daher durchaus Unzuverlässiges." (*Die deutsche Novelle von Goethe bis Kafka,* I, Düsseldorf, 1956, p. 111). See also Ralph Flores, "The lost Shadow of Peter Schlemihl", *GQ* 47 (1974), 576-7.

Irving Massey (essay date 1976)

SOURCE: "Singles and Doubles: *Peter Schlemil,*" in *The Gaping Pig: Literature and Metamorphosis,* University of California Press, 1976, pp. 138-55.

[*In the following essay, Massey begins by comparing* Peter Schlemihl *and* Frankenstein, *and continues by discussing the ways in which polarities and oppositional schemes operate in Chamisso's novel.*]

Peter Schlemihl is a book that shows nemerous situational similarities to *Frankenstein*. Both books are tragedies of science; both involve doubles (in fact, Peter Schlemihl himself has at least two doubles—his shadow and the devil); both raise the question of what happens, or what should happen, when the intellectual force is detached from its embodiment. But the answers the two books produce are quite different, even though the materials they manipulate are similar, even to such details as the ice fields that furnish the setting for the crucial scenes. Both books create an individual who is unnatural, who is outside the webwork of human relationships and has no means of reentering it. The crucial difference is that in *Frankenstein* (as in *Jekyll and Hyde*) the scientist is set aside, and the center of attention shifts at the end of the book to the monster, who represents the scientist's bodily existence; whereas in *Peter Schlemihl* the materially minded Peter loses his physical substantiality and finally himself becomes an archscientist, a kind of monster of pure science.

The Story

In its bare outline, *Peter Schlemihl* seems a slight story about a man who sells his shadow to the devil (but refuses to trade in his soul to recover the shadow). It is a humorous variant of the Faust legend which Chamisso had already attempted a decade earlier. The action is amusing and can be understood as merely didactic or comical in intent, though the darker strokes that fall across the clear outlines of the tale cannot be overlooked either. Like Huckleberry Finn or Robinson Crusoe[1] Peter Schlemihl finds that he cannot escape from the shadow of socialization (devil, Jim, or Friday) as easily as he thinks.

Peter is a young man of no consequence, someone who might appropriately be described as a "poor devil." He arrives, as it were, from nowhere, disembarking from a ship and going directly to the home of a wealthy burgher who, he hopes, will advance his fortunes. There he meets a man who, though physically nondescript, just a sort of shadow, extracts from the pocket of his coat a band-aid, binoculars, a huge carpet, a tent to cover it, and three riding horses in full harness. All this is by way of preliminary display to persuade Peter to enter into a compact: namely, the exchange of his shadow for Fortunatus's inexhaustible money purse. The transaction has no sooner been made than Peter begins to realize the inconveniences that will follow; still, his first reaction is to shut himself up in his room and wallow in his gold until he falls asleep.

Science as Excuse for Isolation

Thus far, the story moves in a straight line, developing its plot with perfect economy. But when Peter drops off to sleep, a new element is suddenly introduced, which seems to have nothing to do with the action. For no apparent reason, at this juncture Peter begins to dream of his friend Chamisso (actually the author of the book), to whom these memoirs of Peter's are addressed. He envisions Chamisso (who was a naturalist as well as a writer) sitting in his study. On one side of him stands a skeleton, on the other a bundle of dried plants; before him, on the desk, lie his scientific books. In his dream, Peter studies Chamisso and his room attentively through a glass door, almost as if he were examining a botanical specimen. And indeed, Chamisso might as well have been a specimen, for, in the dream, "du rührtest dich aber nicht, du holtest auch nicht Atem, du warst tot" ("but you didn't move, nor did you breathe; you were dead").

It is not clear whether Chamisso is actually dead, or whether he is just frozen by the dream; but in either case, there is an uncanny feeling of a sudden arrest that has befallen this briskly moving story; Chamisso at his desk is somewhat like the man in "Bartleby" who is struck dead by summer lightning, but remains standing at his window. The paralysis that halts the action is in startling contrast to the rapidity and freedom with which events and feelings have been following each other so far. Abruptly, one is not sure whether the matrix of the story is action or stasis, whether one is dealing with the absolute, fixed world of the naturalist's study or with the world of desire that goes its blind but lively way outside the glass doors. One thing is very clear; in his perception of Chamisso's fate, Peter is being granted a premonition of his own. Chamisso does not realize that he himself, author of the story and naturalist though he may be, is dead; and Peter does not yet know that he will come to share Chamisso's condition. Author and character will be united in a common destiny of death-in-life. Both will be reduced to nothing by the terms in which they deal, money, words, or taxonomic structures. It is not their destiny to overcome the threat and the fear of transitive, competitive experience, either through love or by an act of the imagination that would join the hostilities of language in the centaur of metaphor. All such challenges will be avoided by recourse to a system of classification that reduces content to zero and allows classification to become everything, that in fact pretends to avoid the responsibilities of expression altogether. The death-into-science of Peter is the pretext under which he may keep his emotions alive—but at the cost of making himself invisible, of ceasing to express, communicate, and give content to his being through action.

Later in the story, Peter will have another dream, this time of a paradise in which none of his friends has a shadow, yet where all is well. Later, too, he will lie, "invisible" to his friends in the disguise of his long beard, watching them again through the glass door of his incognito while they pursue their lives undisturbed by his disruptive presence.

From the time of his first dream, Peter Schlemihl is committed to the fixity of the metamorphic state, which will eventually be symbolized by the world of ice that he first encounters after he has resigned himself to solitude, friend no longer of either man or devil.[2] Accident and action alike, Peter eventually realizes, lead him to the same end.[3] For him the temptations of gold and sex are masks for a more serious danger. There is never any possibility that Peter will sell his soul to the devil: he is far too anxious to keep it for himself. The excessive desire for worldly advantage is merely a pretext to create a predicament which will force him to withdraw from the world entirely, to become a priest of science, who will look on human love only from afar (cf. Lucius).

The remaining events of the story follow the pattern that has been outlined. Tied to the devil, his new shadow, Peter is unable to attend to the normal necessities of life, as Frankenstein had been, once he was

saddled with his double, the monster. His struggles, now ludicrous, now pathetic, to avoid the inevitable outcome, only lead him more rapidly toward the necessary dénouement. He tries to get an artist to paint him a new shadow. He declares that his shadow has been damaged and is out for repairs; that he has suffered a serious illness and his hair, nails, and shadow have fallen out. But all in vain. He loses the girl to whom he is engaged when her parents learn that he has no shadow. The novelette quickly assumes the elegiac or posthumous tone that alone befits the circumstances. As Peter tries to repeat his story with the living emotion with which it should be fraught, he laments (though, in truth, the reader feels no such lack), "Now I beat in vain against a rock that no longer yields any living spring, and the God has abandoned me."[4] When he is finally driven from his sobbing bride by her indignant father, "I staggered away, and I felt as if the world had closed behind me."[5]

The Shadow and Polarity

The devil, of course, offers to set everything to rights (that is, return Peter's shadow) with one small stipulation: that Peter surrender his soul. And, after all, why should Peter protest so much, express such outrage over such a trifle? What is a soul, anyway? It isn't even as real as a shadow. All it is is a kind of "X," a *polarisierende Wirksamkeit* (polarizing force). To be sure, readers of Hegel and of Lévi-Strauss, students of logic, might hesitate before surrendering their "X," and especially their concept of polarity, but why Peter Schlemihl? Perhaps there is something in him which warns him that his entire destiny is bound up with the undefined quantity from which all definitions and all mathematical series take their start,[6] as well as with the problem of polarity. Having surrendered one of his dimensions, his physical reality (for what body does not cast some shadow? And in the end his seven-league boots only make him doubly transparent), Peter can no longer hope to function as a force that distinguishes between the real and the unreal; but he can still operate within the domain of pure consciousness as a kind of scanning mechanism that polarizes, organizes, and classifies its own counters, that can aspire only to the completion of a symbolic system without ever touching down in the unconsciousness that is reality. His capacity for classification, which is indeed a polarizing function, is preserved intact, but it can never renew its content through contact with the randomness and variety of experience, either through a recognition of the infinity of all subject matter, or through an awareness of the subjective status of the observer within his own system.

Peter Schlemihl may be a slender staff on which to lean the whole weight of the problem of polarity, but it is very explicitly brought up in the book itself. Chamisso was himself, of course, a scientist and classifier of genera, and, besides, similar issues have arisen too often in the context of this study (for instance, in *The Golden Ass*) to be ignored. The whole question of metamorphosis depends in part on the distinction and confusion of genera. I should like to offer a comment on the nature of polarity in relation to dialectics, which may throw at least an oblique light on Peter Schlemihl's predicament, left as he is in the end with nothing but the fixities of an oppositional scheme in which to operate.

Oppositional Schemes

Buber says, "The life of human beings is not passed in the sphere of transitive verbs alone" (*I and Thou*, I:iii). Sartre adds (*Being and Nothingness*, "Introduction," vi), "Being is . . . neither passivity nor activity. Both of these concepts are *human* and designate human conduct or the instruments of human conduct."[7] Extrapolating from the relationships which obtain between human beings, in which there is always someone acting and someone being acted upon, we project the threat-defense syndrome upon our relationship with our natural surroundings, using a language derived from the conflicts between human beings to describe a world which has no such relation to us. The colors in the sunset do not want to hurt us. But in our language, and in our way of thinking about the world as well, we are always Xerxes lashing the Hellespont, or Pharnuces sitting in judgment upon a treacherous horse (Herodotus, *Histories*, book VII). The work of someone like Dorothy Wordsworth consists of the effort to melt the hostile knot of self, which is perception in the I—it relationship. When the heart melts, it can itself become the vision, and a reciprocity has been established that goes beyond the transitive view of nature. "We lay upon the sloping Turf. Earth and sky were so lovely that they melted our very hearts. The sky to the north was of a chastened yet rich yellow fading into pale blue and streaked and scattered over with steady islands of purple melting away into shades of pink. It made my heart almost feel like a vision to me" (*Grasmere Journal*, June 20, 1802).

This is not a reciprocity that creates a double transitive (for that would be at least as bad as the single transitive of hostile perception). It is a reciprocity in which the stand-off between man and nature, which is based upon the psychological model of action and reaction, is left behind, and the locus of perception is no longer established within one thing looking at another. The heart may as well be the vision as the landscape, once the perceiver has abandoned his privileged position. One is, finally, on the same footing as what one is looking at, and the "objectivity" or "subjectivity" of one's appraisal is cancelled away, the present winning for itself in this respect what is usually the exclusive prerogative of memory.[8]

By a process similar to the one which projects our antagonisms as people (or not even our antagonisms: the ordinary condition in which one human consciousness perceives and reacts to the messages and the pressures of another human consciousness) onto the natural world and our relation to it, we project our own hostile oppositional patterns onto the world in the very foundations of our logic. If it be true, as Heraclitus,[9] Aristotle, Hegel, or Frege would have it, that our thinking is based on comparisons, on something-nothing, zero-one, or other models in which something is set up *against* something else (with all the attendant implications of negation as the motor that drives on thought, in either a sceptical or a Hegelian system) then we are indeed projecting our oppositions on the whole of reality.[10] I am not thinking here in Durkheimian terms, and deriving logical models such as polarity from the two sides of a village or from other social patterns.[11] What seems to be happening is rather that we cannot understand that reality may choose to exist in its discrete forms, as individual phenomena that have no relation to each other, and we assume that it must exist as an infinite number of oppositions and interactions, in the same way as people relate to each other. Things exist individually (not even in the relations of a syllogistic or a causal syntax) but we force a relationship on them (a conflicting or "oppositional" relationship) by hypostatizing the adjectives that we attach to them and turning those modifiers into realities rather than conditions, whether modifiers such as "left-right", "even-odd," or "hot-cold." But a thing in itself is never even or odd, left or right, more hot than cold; these aspects exist only in the minds that contemplate things, and set them against each other, get them to fight. If this is the nature of our logic (perhaps even of our language) it is small wonder that a theory of negation is always so important an element in it. (I am here arguing against the position taken by Heidegger in the *Introduction to Metaphysics*,[12] and lean towards the Fichtean opinion that perception of identities precedes perception of difference.)

Metaphor as Mitosis

It may have been in an attempt to deal with this problem that Coleridge elaborated his theory of imagination. His notion of the imagination is a way of converting or overcoming the competitive force of the binary (or the force of the negative within the binary) by an "organic fusing." On the other hand, once one has assumed that the negative nature of our standard logic gives us the true nature of reality, and has come to see even metaphor itself as evidence of the comparative process, there may be no way back to a reunification.[13] Perhaps one should begin by assuming that metaphor is a way of seeing things as being different from themselves rather than as being similar to other things. Maybe the perception of beauty separates a thing into itself and its analogue (or at least something which has hitherto been thought of as its analogue), rather than analogy producing the perception of beauty. In fact, I am inclined to think that the experience of beauty involves the unconscious awareness of a contradiction in perception. The metaphor seeks that which is, in some sense, most unlike itself. (Homer Brown suggests to me the example "The stationary blasts of waterfalls," from *The Prelude* vi:626; or it could be a square stone house by the St. Lawrence gulf, like a French pastry set down a little too firmly, having been carried for a bit in its cardboard box, with one or two corners tilted up slightly—light pastry, malleable cream corners, coconut-sprinkled—all as unlike stone as it is possible for them to be.) Coleridge would say that imagination "reveals itself in the balance or reconciliation of opposite or discordant qualities."[14] I am saying that imagination does not reconcile; it demands opposition, but as a way of defining and giving body to the thing itself. It is like Lévi-Strauss's totemic crow, except that instead of picking on a point of resemblance it pivots on a point of difference. Like rhyme, it uses sameness merely as a way of justifying difference (for rhyme too is simply a way of forcing one into unexpected associations).[15] Lévi-Strauss tells us that eaglehawk and crow are both carnivores; but one is a hunter, the other (carrion-eater) a thief: "the natural species are classed in pairs of opposites, and this is possible only on condition that the species chosen have in common at least one characteristic which permits them to be compared."[16] And Lévi-Strauss adds, in true Coleridgean phrase, that totemism shows "how to make opposition, instead of being an obstacle to integration, serve rather to produce it" (p. 89).[17] In my view, the accessory elements (points of resemblance), at least in metaphor (I pretend to no competence in ethnology) are just supports for the point of difference; perhaps they are pretexts for it, or even ways of masking the fact that the essential thing is the point of difference.

It may appear that my own explanation of metaphor leads right back toward the categories of difference and opposition that I have just repudiated. But to emphasize difference is not necessarily to fall again into the Hegelian-Heideggerian trap of dialectic, the trap of linguistic violence. Metaphor uses opposites to detach itself from violence, to allow the new truth to step forth like Venus from her conch, naked and untrammelled by the nets of association.

To word my point anew: I have begun by saying that the basic experience (as in Dorothy Wordsworth) is one of identity *not* contrast; yet I go on to argue that aesthetic perception is one of opposites or contradiction. But these are not opposites being compared and fused; it is the self-division of the image, too full, that makes it into two, itself and its opposite. Unity, when subjected to the mode of desire, issues in duality. But the duality does not consist in pushing things which one initially perceives as being in conflict with each other together until they (hopefully) merge; it is a duality that remains duality, in which the tension that

binds the relationship is at the origin, rather than at the outcome.[18] A perception originates in unity and bifurcates; it then remains split, like a tuning fork, the parts vibrating but not competing with each other; in the Coleridge-Lévi-Strauss model, a wishbone effect is created, where one is irresistibly driven to pull the halves apart, returning them to the separateness which was their natural state.

In any case; the incongruity in experience, the articulated metaphor, once perceived, in turn creates the characteristic space that makes the object distinct. (After all, Coleridge's theory of metaphor, for all its organicism, emphasizes difference not similarity). Words themselves create a space between themselves and experience: a time-space, because they take time to speak or read, and a life-space, because they postpone action. Metaphor is even more space-forming because it is not instrumental; it does not point in the direction of consuming its object; it is an "Aufhebung" of the impulse to consume. The thing is held in suspense, it does not pass directly into use; that is why it calls for a verbal resolution. One cannot picture an animal as seeing something metaphorically, because to see it that way you have to hold it in suspense in your mind or perception, and to do so is already a linguistic act. A metaphoric perception is already half communication. (If it were not articulated it would be a superstition [and even animals do seem to be susceptible to phobias and superstitions]; one might actually *believe* the low waves running along a tropic shore to be black pigs, instead of seeing them metaphorically that way). A seeing that cannot be completed in any action demands to spill over into words or find some kind of relief. The intensity of perception forces one to divide the thing perceived and so ease one of the excess of its presence. It is a bit like mitosis—the thing swells until it breaks in two. It is not dissatisfaction with the thing itself that leads one on to metaphor, it is excess of satisfaction.

The Story Continued

I suggest, then, that in order to combat the principle of comparison and opposition within the theory of metaphor, we stand Coleridge's idea on its head, so that the mind would act to separate things rather than to bring them together. A philosophy of individualizing difference may be more cheerful than a philosophy involving one in endless comparisons and polarities.[19] At least, that is what one could conclude from a reading of **Peter Schlemihl.** If we continue to follow Peter through the vicissitudes of his story, we will soon be led back to the danger that seems to dog his every step: the threat of his being reduced to a mere problem in polarity, or, even worse, to a mere designator of polarities and contrasts. (With Poe in "How to Write a *Blackwood* Article," Peter might plead, "Put in something about the Supernal Oneness. Don't say a syllable about the Infernal Twoness.") After he loses his beloved, Mina, to his scoundrelly servant, Rascal, he wanders off in a daze through desert areas that prefigure the polar (and polarizing) wastes where he will eventually realize his vocation and his destiny. He pursues a bodiless shadow (cast by the devil) and, seizing the nest of invisibility which the devil has been carrying, finds himself suddenly without either shadow or visible body. Peter keeps slipping up and down the scale of absence and presence, from the time when he has first compromised his substantiality by selling his shadow, until we come to fear that he will disappear altogether one day. And in fact, to get rid of the clinging devil, he finally does have to get rid of himself (that which casts a shadow; p. 455). As I have mentioned, he has a dream of all his friends, as shadowless as himself, inhabiting a paradisal world, where no one needs a shadow; but, as he has learned, people without shadows might as well be dead, and the shadowless Chamisso of this dream is not altogether different from the dead or petrified Chamisso in the scientist's cabinet of Peter's previous vision.

It is not long after Peter abandons the devil that his earthly, all-too-human shoes wear out, and he must replace them with the abstract seven-league-boots of science. A few steps, and "about me the stillness of death reigned, the ice on which I stood stretched beyond the limits of vision. . . . "[20] The boots have brought him to a deathlike silence, another frozen world like that of Chamisso in his study. But no sooner does Peter realize what has befallen him than he drops to his knees, shedding tears of joy and gratitude! He has been shown his vocation, and he is content with it. "Excluded from human company by early transgression, I was directed towards Nature, which I had always loved, as a substitute; the earth was given to me as my garden, study as the guide and impulse of my life, science as my goal."[21]

The rest of his life Peter will devote to the classification of species. Only once does he come in contact with people again. After an accident that results from his attempt to avoid a polar bear, Peter falls ill and is tended by his former servant, Bendel, and his former beloved, Mina, in a hospital they have established in his name, the Schlemihlium. Disguised by his long beard, Peter is nothing but "number 12" to them; to all intents and purposes invisible, he can overhear their conversation from a position not unlike that of Chamisso in his study, alive, yet not quite alive. He is a sort of Specimen, an object of scientific care whose inner nature is remote from all inquiry. When he leaves the Schlemihlium, Peter leaves a note for his friends, assuring them that he is indeed better off than he had been: "Your old friend is also better off than he was before, and if he is doing penance, it is the penance of reconciliation."[22] The last word on human relationships, especially when they have gone beyond the merely human, must be reconciliation.

But in Peter Schlemihl, the reconciliation with others has to be incidental to Peter's destiny, which takes him definitively away from people. Speaking simply, one could say that science is an attempt to make a success of solitude. This story demonstrates a withdrawal from synthesis, and the discovery of a solution to the problem of the relationship between "something" and "nothing" on the side of zero, of the nonconcrete, the state of "absence" represented by scientific noninvolvement. It argues that a settlement of the conflict between the real and unreal, or rather the substantial and the abstract in human life, does not require an interpenetration, confluence, or reconciliation of the two. Peter Schlemihl returns to what may at first look like common sense after his adventure with Faustian overreaching, but it is the substitution of withdrawal for excess, of science for greed. Peter, as we have seen, remains without shadow and without contact with other human beings. He becomes a classifier of plants—and that activity is what is supposed to close the space between him and reality. If he can succeed in making his system completely adequate to its subject, so that his grid will touch every species of living thing on earth, he will have closed the gap (or so he seems to think) between the abstract and the real, achieved something comparable to contact with other people, to marrying Mina. But of course this cannot be, for Peter has reduced himself to a cipher—to that "X" that the devil had called the soul. He has stripped off both the inner shadow (the devil) and the outer one that betokens his body, and has left himself, without darkness and without substance, as an assigner of meaning, as the line between the word as idea and the word as thing signified; as a space in which the verbal order and an absolute preexistent order (the world) are one and are possible as one. He has settled the conflict between abstraction and reality by deleting both physical reality, with its infinite alternatives and confusions, and subjective reality. By eliminating himself, by getting rid of his opacity, he has made science absolute, done away with all lingering uncomfortable questions about the motivation of his work or the hypotheses underlying his method. The all is within his grasp; if not the all desired by sinful Faustian man, at least the all of the scientist who believes that he can make his ideas, some idea, commensurate with the world. Foucault has described this ambition of classical taxonomy[23] and its disappearance in the new milieu of Cuvier's thought (p. 280). Foucault actually sees classical taxonomy as a linguistic perhaps more than a scientific or even descriptive activity. In order to know species, we must classify them; in order to classify them, we must produce names for all of them; nature becomes knowable only to the extent that we can supply names for its inhabitants. At some horizon, perhaps, as Peter Schlemihl seems to hope, all the names for all the things will have been provided and we will be able to celebrate the marriage of nature with language (if not of Peter with Mina). As a replacement for his right to dream (his "night-side," of which the devil has robbed him),[24] Peter can still have the dream of an universal order, the shadow of a supernal harmony.

Peter is easily seen as a member of the "je est un autre" series, one of the large metamorphic brotherhood for whom the self becomes the archstranger. Even something as close to one as one's shadow can become detached; the most intimate and impalpable evidence of one's very existence is removable and objectifiable. First the shadow is shown to be provisionally detachable; then the self itself (as in the case of the scientist) is permanently detached. Nor does virtue show one the road back to the recovery of the self. In the end, as in the case of Gogol's "Overcoat," we realize that the moral issue which had seemed to be the theme of the story at the beginning was a red herring.[25] Peter's situation does not really change between the beginning and the end of the story (as Lucius's in *The Golden Ass* does not change); his original poverty merely equals his later lack of shadow, and he is an outsider at the beginning as he is an outcast at the end. A refusal to do business with the devil would not have earned him the entrée to life; in fact, life, a "normal" life, is the real immorality, the really immoral alternative, in both Chamisso's and Gogol's stories. To remain below the level of meaning and of participation is their only salvation; for Akaki, in his copying of copies of nothing, until there is an implosion of language into magic figure; the same for the student Anselmus in Hoffmann's "Golden Pot"; for Peter, it lies in an outward movement, the extension of the abracadabra of classification to embrace the world in a universal linguistic act that is meant to be something like love.

Yet these tales have been written, and their authors cannot share their characters' innocence of the act of writing and of having meddled with meaning; a kind of dialogue of guilt and innocence seems to be established in these stories, between author and character, or between creature and creator, finally among author, character, and reader. The author spares his reader the self-damage of the act of writing, yet more than occasionally (as in "The Sandman," for instance) tries in turn to avoid part of the injury by passing it on to a character in his story. He attempts to force the character to do the writing or to act out the unwanted story-book situation for him; sometimes he even has the character project the injury to a third remove (as in "St. Julien," where the protagonist would force the animals to assume responsibility for his own self-destructive impulses). The real purpose of the epistolary novel or the "MS. found in a bottle" may be to free the author from the guilt of writing by having another seem to write for him. Writing is stealing meaning from God; language beyond or behind meaning, absolute language unspoiled by human interference,[26] in fact seems to be the definition of God . . . in general. The writer (I think here of Stevenson) being

in any case past Akaki's wordless stage, is willing to assume the guilt of writing in view of a promise or hope of reconciliation, as his act of communication is at least not for his private purpose and so flows back, bringing others with him, into the absolute language of God. . . .

Comparisons with Frankenstein

To return to a simple comparison of *Peter Schlemihl* with *Frankenstein:* if, in the first book, a solution is sought on the side of nonsubstance, so that Peter, reduced to a mere cipher, "X," or *"polarisierende Wirksamkeit,"* can continue to exist without the man of flesh and blood from which this volatile essence has been boiled off, then *Frankenstein* suggests the opposite resolution: the scientist is eliminated, the human being remains. In *Peter Schlemihl* the human can be rescued from the devil and enabled to survive only under the protection of the neutral scientific attitude; in *Frankenstein* the human principle frees itself from the negative but then, without it, must burn up in the ice. It burns, but surrounded by the ice of negation; and it is destroyed. One cannot live without zero, nor can object be without its perceiver, empty though he may be.

This digest, of course, pretends to summarize what finally remains a pair of impenetrably mysterious states. We have said enough about the peculiar condition of the monster at the end of *Frankenstein;* Peter's destiny seems simpler, but may finally be even less commensurate with our summary. The monster can at least take things into his own hands, and invite the final metamorphsis which all of us must undergo. But Peter, poor wandering Jew that he has become, has no further potential for change. He cannot put an end to things so that they may, at least in the reader's mind, offer the opportunity of a fresh beginning. He can move neither forward nor back. Being the same from both sides (swift beyond visibility, and shadowless), he has had his metamorphic potential closed off. The devil has it in his keeping. In his own way, he rejoins the society of the single, those who, like the hardly seen Mr. Hyde, have nothing left to change to; for whom all change has come to an end. Peter may continue to subdivide the world, but no possibility of division within himself, of recapturing the schizoid state, remains.

Reconciliation

Yet there is some way in which Peter, misanthrope though he may be, invites not only Hyde but even Frankenstein's monster back into his society. I have said that *Peter Schlemihl* shows that the human can be preserved only under the protective cloak of the neutral scientific attitude. The purpose of the book, then, is not to destroy the human but to preserve it, at whatever cost. The empty, virtually nonexistent Peter, passing like his own transparent shadow through the "Schlemihlium," which has been named for the space of his former life, hardly strikes us as a monster of the laboratory. His whole science is an attempt to convey, by the only means at his command, a love for the world as a whole which he has been forbidden to express towards individuals by any direct means. The later Peter is tender and invisible, like Frankenstein's monster himself. He appears only once; to turn in the notebook in which he has relieved us as well as Chamisso of the burden of the truth of his story, through the telling of it.

Notes

1 Homer Brown, "The Displaced Self in the Novels of Daniel Defoe," *ELH* 38 (December, 1971):573.

2 There is a similar preoccupation with ice in "Adelberts Fabel."

3 Adelbert von Chamisso, *Gesammelte Werke* (Gutersloh, 1964), p. 265.

4 P. 242: "da schlag' ich vergebens an einen Felsen, der keinen lebendigen Quell mehr gewährt, und der Gott ist von mir gewichen."

5 P. 254: "Ich schwankte hinweg, und mir war's, als schlösse sich hinter mir die Welt zu."

6 *The Language of the Self,* (Baltimore, 1968), pp. 42, 261. Cf. Leclaire, *Psychanalyser* (Paris, 1968), pp. 63, 155. The shadow is, of course, the ideal illustration of the "nothing signifying something" in Lacanian psychology. See also Hans Jonas, *On the Gnostic Religion,* 2nd. ed., rev. (Boston, 1963), pp. 123-124, on Mana as the unidentifiable absent presence, or "X" dimension of the soul. I am obliged to Paul Piehler for this reference.

7 Sartre, *Being and Nothingness* (New York, 1969), p. 27. (*L'Être et le néant* [Paris, 1943], p. 32: "L'être . . . n'est ni passivité ni activité. L'une et l'autre de ces notions sont humaines et désignent des conduites humaines ou les instruments des conduites humaines.") The sentence from Buber reads, "Das Leben des Menschenwesens besteht nicht im Umkreis der zielenden Zeitwörter allein." Cf. Roland Barthes, *Le Plaisir du Texte* (Paris, 1973), pp. 48-52. Even Vico (*The New Science,* section 405), complains of man's ignorance, which induces him to describe nature in terms of his own experiences. Interestingly, this discussion of language leads Vico on to the topic of metamorphosis (sections 410-411).

8 Cf. Coleridge, *Anima Poetae* (Boston and New York, 1895), p. 209. The contemplation of Nature rescues one from unhappiness; "till the lulled grief lose itself in fixed gaze on the purple heath-blossom, till the present beauty becomes a vision of memory." Cf. *Notebooks* I, entry 921, on suppressing the oppositional elements in perception.

9 See Eberhard Jüngel, *Zum Ursprung der Analogie bei Parmenides und Heraklit* (Berlin, 1964), p. 37-39. For Hegel's view of identity, difference, and contradiction, see the *Wissenschaft der Logik,* Book II, sec. i, ch. 2. (Homer Brown has drawn my attention to n. 3 in particular.)

10 Cf. Nietzsche, *Genealogie der Moral,* I, xiii. In his efforts to get away from a zero-one logic, Nietzsche, too, accuses language of creating a model that we follow blindly in our thinking; but his objection is to the separation of subject from verb, rather than to transitive structures as such.

11 *Les Formes élémentaires de la vie religieuse* (Paris, 1960), p. 17.

12 Heidegger, *An Introduction to Metaphysics* (New Haven and London, 1964), p. 138, as well as pp. 157, 168, etc. (*Einführung in die Metaphysik* [Tübingen, 1953], pp. 106, 120, 128-129, etc.)

13 I find it significant that, despite his organic theory of metaphor, in "Theory of Life" Coleridge speaks of polarity as "the highest law, or most general form, under which this tendency acts." ("This tendency" being the individuation characteristic of life.) See *Selected Poetry and Prose of Coleridge,* ed. Donald A. Stauffer (New York, 1951), p. 578.

14 *Biographia Literaria* (Oxford, 1907), II:12.

15 Cf. Michael Riffaterre, "Criteria for Style Analysis," *Word* 15 (1959):154-174, esp. p. 158, as quoted in Stanley Fish, *Self-Consuming Artifacts,* (Berkeley, 1972), p. 419: stylistic devices "Prevent the reader from inferring or predicting any important feature. . . . For unpredictability will compel attention. . . . "

16 *Totemism* (Boston, 1968) iv, III:87-88.

17 Claude Lévi-Strauss, *Le Totémisme aujourd'hui* (Paris, 1962), p. 126: " . . . les espèces naturelles sont classées en couples d'oppositions, et cela n'est possible qu'à la condition de choisir des espèces qui offrent au moins un caractère commun, permettant de les comparer." P. 128: "Le totémisme se ramène ainsi à une façon particulière de formuler un problème général: faire en sorte que l'opposition, au lieu d'être un obstacle à l'intégration, serve plutôt à la produire." On metaphor as the affirmation of difference, see below, ch. 10, "Metamorphosis and Metaphor."

18 To paraphrase Fichte: "In vain shall we look for a link of connection between tenor and vehicle, if they

are not first and simply apprehended as a unity." "Tenor and vehicle" are, of course, "subject and object" in Fichte. See Robert Adamson, *Fichte* (Philadelphia and Edinburgh, 1892), p. 128.

In his Buffalo lectures on Nietzsche (November, 1973), Bernard Pautrat presented the concept of contradiction in a manner consistent with its treatment in the present chapter. As Pautrat understands it, contradiction for Nietzsche occurs within a single thing, with its elements occupying the *same* space, rather than between two separate entities.

Meaning itself is described in similar terms by the pre-Saussurean school of linguists in the nineteenth century. I quote from Adolf Tobler (1835-1910), "Versuch eines Systems der Etymologie," *Zeitschrift für Völkerpsychologie und Sprachwissenschaft,* I (1860):360: words with antithetical meanings do not arise separately; "vielmehr entspringen beide [Bedeutungen] aus einer, in sich polaren Grundbedeutung . . ." ("both [meanings], rather, spring from a single basic meaning which is in itself polarized"). See the author's "Some Antecedents of Saussure," *Linguistische Berichte* 30 (April, 1974): 66-68.

On literature as nonviolent contradiction, see also Roland Barthes, *Le Plaisir du texte* (Paris, 1973), pp. 9-10, 41, 51; cf. Albert Rothenberg, "Cognitive Processes in Creation" (forthcoming) and Monroe C. Beardsley, *Aesthetics* (New York, 1958), pp. 161-162.

[19] The reading of Heraclitus developed by Jean Bollack and Heinz Wismann in *Héraclite ou la séparation* (Paris, 1972), provides strong support for this position, as well as for several of the other arguments I have advanced in this chapter. For instance: "Les deux contraires ne forment pas une somme, et moins encore l'ensemble des opposés, une somme de contraires. Chacun se constitue dans un rapport singulier, d'où l'expression distributive de la totalité fractionée. . . . *L'art,* c'est encore de se séparer . . ." (pp. 30-31; cf. paragraph in text following n. 18, above. "The two contraries do not form a sum, and even less does the totality of the opposed elements form a sum of contraries. Each one establishes itself in a singular relation, which is why the fractioned whole is expressed in a distributive manner. . . . *The art,* once more, is to be separate . . ."). The editors demartialize the Heraclitean dialectic (pp. 42, 43, 46): things exist individually, rather than in a state of conflict, even when they stand in a relation of contradiction to each other (cf. "Metaphor as Mitosis," above).

[20] P. 278: "um mich herrschte die Stille des Todes, unabsehbar dehnte sich das Eis, worauf ich stand. . . . "

[21] P. 279: "Durch frühe Schuld von der menschlichen Gesellschaft ausgeschlossen, ward ich zum Ersatz an die Natur, die ich stets geliebt, gewiesen, die Erde mir zu einem reichen Garten gegeben, das Studium zur Richtung und Kraft meines Lebens, zu seinem Ziel die Wissenschaft."

[22] P. 286: "Auch Eurem alten Freunde ergeht es nun besser als damals, und büsset er, so ist es Busse der Versöhnung."

[23] *Les Mots et les choses* (Paris, 1966), pp. 172-175. Foucault's reasoning follows from Nietzsche's. For a discussion of Nietzsche's conception of science which is directly applicable to *Peter Schlemihl,* see Sarah Kofman, "Nietzsche et la métaphore," *Poétique* 5 (1971):77-98, esp. pp. 83-85.

[24] I am indebted to Le Roy Perkins's unpublished paper on "Dominoes and *Peter Schlemihl*" for the following suggestions:

"The devil tries to buy our shadow-doubles, our darker selves, the unconscious followers of our bodies, in short, our dreams. Peter loses his dreams."

"The devil appears in grey (both black and white), and hence is a mediator or middleman between waking and sleeping, a dealer in shadows, the man who buys our dreams."

"Having no shadow, no repository for his darkness, Peter is forced into the burden of consciousness, made to go about 'Carrying my sinister secret in my heart. . . . '"

"The major characters, like dominoes, have their halves, their shadow-doubles. Bendel (Rascal), Mina (Fanny), Peter (the devil, who is *also* a scientist)."

[25] But then, every literary statement probably subverts itself. Perhaps paradox is the essence of thought. (See below, ch. 9, n. 39; and ch. 1, n. 6.)

I would risk a definition of the uncanny as that literary genre in which the author attempts to escape duality, by co-opting the energy of the counter-story that runs beneath the surface of every story. (Instead of remaining an unconscious force, it is taken into the author's own hands.)

It will be apparent from my interpretation of Hoffmann's "The Sandman" as a conflict between the author and his character that I do not regard it (in spite of Freud's analysis) as belonging to the genre of the uncanny. See ch. 6, n. 1, for further references concerning this question.

[26] See E. Bernhardt-Kabisch, "Wordsworth's Ghostly Language," unpublished, ch. 5, n. 8 above.

Colin Butler (essay date 1977)

SOURCE: "Hobson's Choice: A Note on *Peter Schlemihl*," in *Monatshefte: Für Deutschen Unterricht, Deutsche Sprache und Literatur,* Vol. LXIX, No. 1, Spring, 1977, pp 5-16.

[*In the following essay, Butler summarizes some critical assessments of* Peter Schlemihl, *observing that despite its ambiguities the work is finally a fairy tale in which the protagonist finds contentment apart from society.*]

> Als ich mich ins Fremdenbuch einschrieb und im Monat Juli blätterte, fand ich auch den vielteuern Namen Adelbert von Chamisso, den Biographen des unsterblichen Schlemihl. Der Wirt erzählte mir: dieser Herr sei in einem unbeschreibbar schlechten Wetter angekommen, und in einem eben so schlechten Wetter wieder abgereist.
>
> —Heinrich Heine, *Die Harzreise*

Although many commentators have pronounced on *Peter Schlemihl* with confidence, any comparison of their several utterances soon reveals the peculiar intractability of a work which, like James' *The Turn of the Screw,* provides enough information of one kind or another for interpretations to be ventured but not quite enough to make them definitive. Thus, for example, following Chamisso's not altogether helpful "explanation" of the shadow in the preface to a much later French translation that "C'est donc de ce solide dont il est question . . . Mon imprudent ami a convoité l'argent dont il connaissait le prix et n'a pas songé au solide,"[1] Thomas Mann, clearly with his mind on his own problems, asserts that "Der Schatten ist im *Peter Schlemihl* zum Symbol aller bürgerlichen Solidität und menschlichen Zugehörigkeit geworden";[2] Josef Nadler, ever alert to the "gemeinvölkische Frage," tribalizes and particularizes this line of thought: "Der Schatten, den der Mensch wirft, wird durch das erzeugt, was ihn von außen her beleuchtet: Volkstum, Bekenntnis, Familie, Rang, Stand, Beziehungen, Ruf und Name";[3] Benno von Wiese, in pursuit of "das soziale Ich," repeats Thomas Mann's point and concludes that "im Schatten geht es um das Zwischenmenschliche, das Verbindende, um die Kontaktstellen, um das Umgreifende im sozialen Dasein";[4] and H. A. Korff, arguing for "die Macht der Imponderabilien, die den Menschen erst zum vollgewichtigen Gesellschaftswesen machen," sees in *Peter Schlemihl* "eine Satire auf die bürgerliche Welt" (in contrast to von Wiese: "die im Symbol des Schattens gefaßte Existenz als bürgerlich-soziales Ich und die Geltung der gesellschaftlichen Ordnungen wird voll anerkannt"), and, like Nadler, feels obliged to particularize: "Volle Wirklichkeit im bürgerlichen Sinne aber hat . . . um die Satire fortzuführen, nur wer 'aktenkundig' ist, einen Geburtsschein, beglaubigte Eltern, Heimatberechtigung und tausend andere Dinge

hat."[5] However, Korff is wise enough to add that none of these is actually mentioned ("Diese Imponderabilien, deren konkrete Form der Dichter klugerweise im Dunkeln läßt . . ."), and this is surely significant, for the "soziale Umwelt" (von Wiese) is so tenuously realized in the story that the question arises whether such phrases as "die Geltung der gesellschaftlichen Ordnungen (von Wiese) and "bürgerliche Wirklichkeit" (Korff), let alone lists of particulars of doubtful accreditation, are really *à propos*. Hermann Pongs, for instance, suggests that "Chamissos eigne Lebenstragik," in a much more diffuse and apparently Angst-ridden sense, is the focal point: "*Peter Schlemihls wundersame Geschichte* hat ihre geniale Pointe in dem fehlenden Schatten, der, an sich ein Nichts, dennoch von unersetzlichem Wert ist, wenn man ihn nicht hat. Die phantastischsten Abenteuer bekommen von dieser Pointe her ihren tiefen, nie ganz auszudeutenden Sinn. Chamissos eigne Lebenstragik ist hier mit eingegangen und gibt dem märchenhaften Gebilde die sich immer wieder bewährende Wirklichkeit";[6] Georg Lukács links Chamisso with Hoffmann and concludes that in *Peter Schlemihl* "dient die Realistik zur Steigerung der Unheimlichkeit, der Phantastik";[7] Ernst Loeb is persuaded that the sale of the shadow signifies existential inauthenticity: "Eben nun dies ist der Schatten,—Verschattung und Dunkelseite des Lebens, ohne die allerdings auch das Licht seine Wesensbestimmung und Bedeutung verlöre . . . Uns scheint hier . . . Peters Vergehen offenkundig geworden,-ein Vergehen, das eben darin besteht, daß er das Licht ohne Schatten und damit das Leben zu einem Preis kaufen will, zu dem es nicht feil ist";[8] and Stuart Atkins, while not offering an interpretation of the story as a whole, further complicates the task for others by his well-argued contention that much of the heavy stuff in *Peter Schlemihl* is a deliberate parody of the sentimental excesses of contemporary writers.[9]

When we look at the formal descriptions the work has accumulated, we find a similar collective uncertainty. Thomas Mann opts for a "Fabel," Nadler a "Märchen," as does Korff; Pongs prefers an "allegorische Stimmungsnovelle," Loeb a "Märchennovelle," which, however, should be seen more as symbolical than allegorical;[10] Werner Feudel ("Was jedoch unter der Hand des Dichters entstand . . . [war] zu sehr dem Bereich der modernen Wirklichkeit verhaftet, um der Gattung des Märchens eingeordnet werden zu können") concurs in Mann's second shot, a "phantastische Novelle";[11] von Wiese speaks of "diese in ein Märchen verkleidete Novelle" and comes to prefer "Märchennovelle" to "Novellenmärchen"; and Chamisso himself progressed from "Abenteuer" through "Schicksale" to "wundersame Geschichte."[12] This is more than a terminological quibble, for the choice of *genre* (or mixture of *genres*) implies not only the areas of human experience the author is interested in (morals, imagination, society, Angst, parody or whatever) but also the degree to which he is able to comprehend them and consequently to treat them appropriately. Benno von Wiese comes to see an explanation of the mixed mode of **Peter Schlemihl** in the time in which it was written: "Solche Vorwegnahme [des neuen bürgerlichen Bewußtseins des Realismus] mußte im Jahre 1813 noch mit einer Erzählform bezahlt werden, die nicht eindeutig sein konnte, sondern sich schwebend zwischen Märchen und Novelle, zwischen Allegorie und Symbol bewegte." "Schwebend" may well be no more than a rhetorical flourish, for von Wiese's essay is nothing if not clear in its distinctions and seems to depart from the proposition that this clarity is justified by the text. Yet "schwebend" is perhaps after all the right word, not in the service of a "Weltdeutung als vage durchzuspürender Sinn" as Pongs would have it, but (what von Wiese seems not to have had in mind) as indicative of a failure on Chamisso's part to come to grips with his own material in a way which goes beyond the implied literary-historical determinism of von Wiese's remark. The claims of the imagination, consolidated during the previous decade and a half as one of the finest of human capabilities, clearly lie beyond both Chamisso's competence and allegiance; yet a residual hankering after the fantastic seems to prevent a realistic form from emerging entire. Does this bespeak confusion, or is a mixed mode exactly right? Ulrich Baumgartner claims "daß die Konzeption der Geschichte in eine Zeit fiel, als für den Dichter die Problematik (das Verhältnis Ich—Welt) in ihrem vollen Unfang noch bestand, während die Fassung, wie sie uns vorliegt, das Werk einer Zeit ist, in der sich der Dichter von diesem Druck der Unlösbarkeit befreit hatte."[13] This allows him to argue, correctly I think, that everything in the story is subordinated to the "Endsituation," which, again correctly, he regards as a consolation. But by confining himself rigorously to "die seelische Entwicklung des Dichters," Baumgartner falls securely into a trap of his own making: an absence of critical perspective. Since, however, Baumgartner is by no means alone in this, it would seem useful to attempt to supply the difference.

Peter Schlemihl is introduced to the reader and to the level of society with which he aspires to make contact as an obscure and impoverished young man arriving from a place or places unknown to solicit the assistance of Thomas John in gaining, it would appear, financial and social advancement. Why this new beginning has become necessary is not made clear, for we are told only that Schlemihl had previously sacrificed wealth to his conscience, though why the two should be mutually exclusive is divulged neither by means of direct explanation nor by a description of previously obtaining circumstances such as to allow appropriate inferences to be made. Nor is it clear whether John or some other person is to function as employer or benefactor, though since John and his associates are dubiously funded and happy to be so ("Er [John] selbst

hatte sein Wohlgefallen daran, und ihn kümmerte es nicht, daß er nicht wisse, woher er sie habe"),[14] one might expect, if "die Geltung der gesellschaftlichen Ordnung" is to be a real consideration, that a more representative account of both earned and unearned income would be provided, if not here, then elsewhere. That such an account is absent—by the time Schlemihl gets around to trying to earn a living, the magical loss of his shadow disqualifies him, and a career as a miner is rendered unnecessary by angelic intervention—suggests that the nature and consequences of social living, whether as the object of validation or of satire, are a priori not Chamisso's primary concern. This in turn both informs and vitiates such moralizing utterances as "Es mußte schon die Ahnung in mir aufsteigen, daß, um so viel das Gold auf Erden Verdienst und Tugend überwiegt, um so viel der Schatten höher als selbst das Gold geschätzt werde."[15] The first part makes a proposition, the general as distinct from the particular truth of which is, by the very particularity of Chamisso's examples, impossible to judge, while the second obscures the moral dimension of the acquisition of wealth implied (with significant imprecision) in the first part by removing the issue to the personal psychology of the misfit. For if society esteems wealth more than moral integrity, then Schlemihl should have no more problems in finding acceptance than John; and if Chamisso had wanted to explore the issues of moral choice and adaptation entailed by living as a social being, he would not have removed Schlemihl from the outset. Thus the loss of the shadow, society being represented, albeit on the scantiest evidence, as being undiscriminating, indicates a radical and private sense of not-belonging (hence the attraction of the Schlemihl figure),[16] to which society's structure, be it expressed either in moral terms ("Gold" / "Verdienst und Tugend") or in specific institutional terms à la Nadler and Korff, is largely irrelevant. That Chamisso sees fit to confine himself to a very diffuse and excluding "out there" suggests that the biography of Peter Schlemihl is to have a logic of its own. It remains to be seen why the Märchen is chosen as its dominant mode of expression.

Whatever may have gone awry in Schlemihl's earlier life, it is clear that what prompts him to sell his shadow is a strongly-felt need for social assimilation, to which he regards the acquisition of wealth as indispensable. Such demeaning phrases as "meine kleine Habseligkeit" and "der Hausknecht maß mich mit einem Blick und führte mich unters Dach"[17] draw the attention not to a sense of dignity invulnerable to assault—there is no Resolution and Independence here—but to a sense of insecurity activated by conspicuous indigence. Indeed, during John's display of unlimited affluence and its concomitant of social prestige, Schlemihl falls over himself to concur in his own denigration: "Wer nicht Herr ist wenigstens einer Million,' warf er hinein, 'der ist, man verzeih' mir das Wort, ein Schuft!'—'O, wie wahr!' rief ich aus mit vollem, überströmendem Gefühl.";[18] and it is his humiliating consignment to the obscure periphery of John's gathering which brings about his association with the Man in Grey ("man bekümmerte sich nicht mehr um den grauen Mann als um mich selber").[19] Thus it is not surprising that, despite an instinctive but unclear Angst, Schlemihl should agree to barter his shadow not for an instrument of clear criminality like Wechselpfennige, nor for an everlasting supply of good eating, but for a guaranteed supply of money like John's. Yet why the *shadow* rather than something less visible? We know that the hypothesized loss of a shadow was the original inspiration of the story,[20] but such knowledge solves nothing. What needs to be explained is why the means by which Schlemihl seeks to secure social acceptance is precisely that which will ensure his permanent exclusion. The gravity and the irreversibility of the sale point psychologically to the *parti pris* of the outsider: the feeling of not belonging promotes a desire for acceptance, but that acceptance is felt in advance by the author and will be discovered by the protagonist to be in any case unobtainable. As Cruickshank well communicates in his illustrations for Bowring's English translation of 1823, there is a sense of the weird and unsettling to the idea of a lost shadow that has more to do with personality than with moral dereliction.[21] Following the ostensible causality of the story, von Wiese contends that "die Schattenlosigkeit hat die Isolierung zur Folge." But it seems more accurate to maintain the reverse.

Perhaps this should be pursued a little further. To succumb to the blandishments of wealth and position, particularly if not motivated by congenital cupidity but by a sense of exclusion compounded by inexperience ("und in mir war noch keine Besinnung"), is of itself not such a terrible thing as Chamisso makes out: it all depends on its consequences. In *Middlemarch,* for example, Fred Vincy is in a very similar position to Schlemihl when the former speculates on old Featherstone's will (the realist equivalent of the "Fortunati Säckelchen") to shore up his lofty materialism. Yet even though he does some damage, he is allowed to retrieve the situation by signing up with Caleb Garth (not the Devil!) and to reorganize his life in accordance with a revised set of values. In *Adam Bede,* however, Arthur Donnithorne goes too far, and a new and commensurately unsatisfactory situation ensues. By making Schlemihl's mistake irrevocable from the outset—there is never any suggestion that the shadow will be restored except on terms which are known to be unacceptable—Chamisso ensures that Schlemihl will remain an outsider irrespective of what may happen subsequently. The false absolute of the Märchen—irrevocability in excess of the occasion—abrogates the realist notions of choice and consequences by foreclosing *ab initio* all other options than exclusion; which was the given condition to begin with.

The loss of the shadow, then, both symbolizes and confirms in practice Schlemihl's not-belonging, but as long as he does not realize this, he will involve himself in a series of incidents which mark the pre-ordained futility of his situation. One of the first people to challenge him is the "Schildwacht," representative and sentinel of social order; and the children of the place are quick to point out that "Ordentliche Leute pflegten ihren Schatten mit sich zu nehmen, wenn sie in die Sonne gingen!"[22] What social satire there is in this story emerges here: "ordentliche Leute" are apparently meant to be seen as morally undiscriminating provided appearances are right, and the frustration of Schlemihl's situation is intensified by the sardonic reflection that he has to bear not only "den Hohn der Jugend" but also "die hochmütige Verachtung der Männer, besonders solcher dicken, wohlbeleibten, die selbst einen breiten Schatten warfen."[23] However, that he is rejected by the pure and impure alike also strengthens the contention that the loss of the shadow means that Schlemihl is not intended to gain acceptance on any terms, moral or otherwise, and that this is then less a reflection on society than on himself. Feeling "von allem Leben abgeschnitten" (the generalization is significant), he tries to fake integration by seeking to acquire a painted shadow and is prepared to tell lies about the loss of the original, sensitive though he is to the untenability of his situation; and eventually he contrives "eine Rolle in der Welt zu spielen" by means of a false identity (Graf Peter) and an equally false *modus vivendi* (in society but out of the light). Clearly a better state of affairs would be for him to be out of society and in the light, and this is what the end of the story amounts to. To that extent, the intervenient episode with Mina is supererogatory, for Schlemihl's fate is sealed before he ever meets her. It does, however, raise in acute fashion the degree to which Chamisso was able to handle the consequences of the situation he has created and for that reason needs looking at in some detail.

That Mina is intended to be the antithesis of the worldly Fanny is obvious enough. Schlemihl's half-hearted, or better, no-hearted, attempt to enter upon an *affaire* with the latter is represented as a competition of vanities, in accordance with the principle well established by now that a mistaken sense of values conduces to mistaken endeavors ("Ich war nur eitel darauf, sie über mich eitel zu machen, und konnte mir, selbst mit dem besten Willen, nicht den Rausch aus dem Kopf ins Herz zwingen"),[24] whereas the relationship with Mina, clearly of considerable moral potential, is signalled by the apostrophe "O mein guter Chamisso, ich will hoffen, du habest noch nicht vergessen, was Liebe sei!"[25] (one notes the anticipatory past tense, which serves, as we shall see, less to record past events than to write them off: though Chamisso uses the more elegant terms of "Schicksal" and "weise Fügung.") Like Esther Lyon, Emma Bovary, Nettchen of "Kleider machen Leute" (of whom more in a moment) and many another post-Romantic impressionable young lady, Mina is given to thinking in terms of a literary image of "the hero" which is out of true with prosaic reality: "Sie war indes weit entfernt, meine Worte richtig zu deuten; sie ahnte nun in mir irgend einen Fürsten, den ein schwerer Bann getroffen, irgend ein hohes, geächtetes Haupt, und ihre Einbildungskraft malte sich geschäftig unter heroischen Bildern den Geliebten herrlich aus."[26] At this level her immaturity, indicated by her high-flown imagination, and Schlemihl's, indicated by his imposture, complement each other. But since one is also intended to descry a fundament of good in both on which a lasting relationship might well be built, provided that it has the opportunity to come into being, one is compelled to consider whether the ostensible impediments to their eventual union are wholly persuasive.

Technically, the difficulty is the absence of Schlemihl's shadow, which one is tempted to understand as his manifest lack of social legitimacy, for as far as Mina's father is concerned, "erscheinen Sie binnen drei Tagen vor mir mit einem wohlangepaßten Schatten, so sollen Sie mir willkommen sein," an assurance which is echoed by the Man in Grey when, in trying to induce Schlemihl to sell his soul, he remarks "Sie sollen in dem Förstergarten willkommen sein, und alles ist nur ein Scherz gewesen."[27] Accordingly, it could be argued that an eminently suitable relationship is simply the victim of a social sanction (appearances), the dubiety of which is confirmed by Mina's subsequent betrothal to Raskal; and that Schlemihl is *pari passu* being punished for generally attempting to exploit a morally indefensible position (his false identity), and particularly for involving Mina. Certainly, this is Schlemihl's own retrospective assessment of the situation: "Wer leichtsinnig nur den Fuß aus der geraden Straße setzt, der wird unversehens in andere Pfade abgeführt, die abwärts und immer abwärts ihn ziehen; er sieht dann umsonst die Leitsterne am Himmel schimmern, ihm bleibt keine Wahl, er muß unaufhaltsam den Abhang hinab und sich selbst der Nemesis opfern";[28] and it is true that had not Schlemihl entered into his initial agreement with the Man in Grey, he would not have been handicapped in this manner, he would not have met Mina, and the present predicament would not then have ensued. But this only serves to bring us back to the false absolute of the loss of the shadow.

In "Kleider machen Leute," Keller was later to treat an exactly similar theme: two immature people, the one attracted to glamorous figures, both living and literary, the other falsely representing himself as such, in a social environment which is equally ready to be swayed by appearances. In that story Nettchen's accession to self-possession in the moment of crisis ("Keine Romane mehr!") leads to a recognition of Strapinski's sustaining qualities and, for all the irony of the ending, to a new beginning being made possible. But that is precisely what Chamisso is not prepared to envisage,

neither at this point in his story, when it might be argued that Mina does not have Nettchen's freedom of action and Schlemihl is unable to rise to the consequences of his situation (he faints), *nor at the end,* when both are older and wiser and yet a new beginning is eschewed. Had Schlemihl been seeking to profit from his spurious ennoblement in a nefarious manner—there is, after all, a distant echo of Faust and Gretchen in all this—that would have been understandable, although a resumption of relations on a new and better footing (one thinks in this respect of "Die Marquise von O") would not even then have been entirely out of the question. But there is no doubt that Schlemihl's affection for Mina and his desire to establish a proper relationship with her are beyond reproach. For all that he indulges in some doubtful magicking on the side, a maneuver on Chamisso's part which secures the narrative within the constraints of the Märchen; his refusal to barter away his soul for the wherewithal to achieve hymeneal bliss bears adequate testimony to the unimpaired presence of his "besseres Selbst," and it is an odd contrivance on Chamisso's part that it should be precisely that which separates him from Mina—unless, of course, Chamisso was intent upon introducing a love story that was in any case incapable of fulfilment. Ernst Loeb, who maintains that "der Versuchung, die Erzählung durch das zusätzliche Motiv des Liebesopfers zu komplizieren, weicht der Dichter aus" (without saying why), argues that the issue here is that of preserving Schlemihl's essential integrity: "Wird er, dem mit einer *äu\g?\eren* Lüge zu leben so bitter schwer wurde, diese nun gegen eine *innere* eintauschen, die seinen menschlichen Wert zerstört?"[29] The important thing, apparently, is to keep Schlemihl's "besseres Selbst" intact (hence the fainting) like caviar in a bottle for the great moral decision which is to come later ("Indem er den Beutel von sich schleudert und in Einsamkeit und Armut geht, nimmt er sein Schicksal bewußt in eigene Hände und führt die große Wende herbei").[30] This, however, begs the question of why later and not now, which is after all an authorial decision, and to rest one's case on the exigencies of a contrived situation, even if one secularizes the soul by calling it "der Wert des Lebens," is to fall prey to a curious kind of literal-mindedness; for "der Wert des Lebens" is not of itself an absolute, no more than is "Lebensmeisterung," which Loeb in the same essay sees as Schlemihl's eventual achievement: both have to be, or should be, defined by their context. The context ensures that both exclude Mina or any other comparable relationship, which brings us back to the question of why, and to answer it on Chamisso's terms is merely to recommence the circle.

It has already been implied that it is necessary to Chamisso's intentions that the Märchen element of his story be taken *au pied de la lettre.* After Schlemihl sells his shadow he has to function as a shadowless man who is seen as such: no change of heart will redeem, it, not even his taking "sein Schicksal bewußt in eigene Hände," for the absent shadow is an integral part of that fate. Similarly here. We have to accept that the *only* way Schlemihl can secure Mina is literally by selling his soul, for otherwise (as Keller saw, and appropriately expressed in a realist mode, in which real choices may be made) the possibility of marriage *and* integrity would be entailed; whereas for Schlemihl the issue is unconditional: marriage *or* integrity, union *or* solitude; and, clearly, solitude it then has to be, albeit of a torch-bearing kind. Now, given that it is unthinkable that Schlemihl should sell his soul (it is an indication of Chamisso's inadequacy here that it is impossible to imagine what kind of relationship would have obtained had he done so), no decision is then necessary, or thinkable for that matter; and so "Notwendigkeit . . . eine weise Fügung" is invoked (in itself difficult to square with the eventual possibility of free moral choice—"authorial direction" makes more sense), Schlemihl faints ("ein Ereignis an der Stelle einer Tat"),[31] and his moment of decision is postponed until its terms are more manageable. As the ending reveals, the same "weise Fügung" will take care of Mina and Bendel, thus saving Schlemihl the trouble.

In virtue of the dictates of Chamisso's preferred mode—having neither the flexibility of Realism nor the painful responsibility of tragedy—the issue of self-sacrifice has been trivialized in favor of the issue of self-preservation. This self, "sein wahres Selbst" according to Korff, who speaks more truly than he knows, might best be described as non-extensible, either into society or into a significant human relationship. Fully acknowledged and appropriately cast, this could give rise to a work of particular poignancy expressive of the disjunction between genuine human needs and the possibility of their fulfilment, and is in fact the origin of what pathos there is in *Peter Schlemihl.* Yet the full force of this situation is vitiated by Chamisso's refusal to bring Schlemihl's non-extensible self and life "unter den Menschen" into a sufficiently pregnant juxtaposition, as is the related dilemma of "Gold" and "das Gewissen"; and again the reality of the situation is subverted by Chamisso's reliance on the Märchen.

In the aftermath of his first frenzied indulgence of his tainted money, Schlemihl has a dream. He sees Chamisso sitting in an enclosed space ("dein kleines Zimmer") at his desk, surrounded by items of particular personal significance: botanical specimens, a medical student's skeleton, a volume of Goethe, a copy of his friend Fouqué's *Der Zauberring,* and botanical studies by Haller, Alexander von Humboldt, and Linnaeus. The principal elements of this dream are enclosure, solitude, repleteness, and an easy death. That all of these are unavailable to Schlemihl at the moment of dreaming should not be allowed to conceal the fact that this is the glimpse of an ideal which will eventually be substantially realized once the appropriate

rectifications have been made. Following his rejection of the Man in Grey, which allows him to keep both his soul *and* some of his money (a curate's egg of a situation if ever there was one), he again has a dream, which is worth quoting in full:

> Anmutige Bilder verwoben sich mir im luftigen Tanze zu einem gefälligen Traum. Mina, einen Blumenkranz in den Haaren, schwebte an mir vorüber und lächelte mich freundlich an. Auch der ehrliche Bendel war mit Blumen bekränzt und eilte mit freundlichem Gruße vorüber. Viele sah ich noch, und wie mich dünkt, auch dich, Chamisso, im fernen Gewühl; ein helles Licht schien, es hatte aber keiner einen Schatten, und was seltsamer ist, es sah nicht übel aus—Blumen und Lieder, Liebe und Freude, unter Palmenhainen.[32]

Schlemihl is unable to interpret this dream, but it seems straightforward enough. It takes place in a world which is removed from the hardships of common reality, and the relationships in it are transformed accordingly; it generates a cosy emotional fog; a shadow is no longer important; economic reality is excluded; and all is forgiven. The way is set for life on a new footing.

The means to this are, significantly, the magic seven-league boots, purchased from a convenient angel with money provided by the Man in Grey. Since, however, according to the plot the original transaction also cost Schlemihl his social legitimacy, which in turn cost him Mina, it follows *post hoc, ergo propter hoc* that Mina's real worth was a pair of boots (albeit *this* pair of boots in *this* situation), a conclusion which Chamisso implicitly endorses:

> denn klar stand plötzlich meine Zukunft vor meiner Seele. Durch frühe Schuld von der menschlichen Gesellschaft ausgeschlossen, ward ich zum Ersatz an die Natur, die ich stets geliebt, gewiesen, die Erde mir zu einem reichen Garten gegeben, das Studium zur Richtung und Kraft meines Lebens, zu ihrem Ziel die Wissenschaft.[33]

The mode of the Märchen has its advantages as well as disadvantages. To feel that the earth is a rich garden and a present at that is altogether more comforting than to feel that it is a complex of difficulties, and it is then easy to understand the attractions of the bachelor life of the private scholar for the man who has been shown to be incapable of anything else. Schlemihl's choice of habitation is apposite: a tomb-like Theban cave, where a dog provides companionship, and nicotine smoothes over the rough patches. It may not be perfect ("O mein Adelbert, was ist es doch um die Bemühungen der Menschen!"),[34] but it is the best available in the circumstances.

Thomas Mann sees this voluntary limitation on the powers of magic symbolized by Schlemihl's "Hemmschuhe" as a sign of Chamisso's underlying sense of reality ("Indem hier der geläufige Begriff der Hemmschuhe ohne weiteres und mit der unschuldigsten Miene auf die Pantoffeln übertragen wird . . . erhält das ganze Wunder einen Charakter bürgerlicher Wirklichkeit, den es im Märchen niemals desaß."),[35] and it is true that insofar as Schlemihl's suffering disposition is accommodated rather than replaced, Chamisso avoids an obvious temptation. But in doing so, he succumbs to another: that of allowing the Märchen to solve all his other problems. The Schlemihlium remains financed by magic means, thus absolving Schlemihl of the need actually to do anything for Mina and Bendel. This in turn consolidates the allededly irretrievable consequences of his "frühe Schuld," which allows him to love and suffer at a distance to the disadvantage of nobody else; for they are consequences of no consequence save for himself, Mina and Bendel having meanwhile found "das stille, innerliche Glück":

> " . . . seit ich meinen langen Traum ausgeträumt habe und in mir selber erwacht bin, geht es mir wohl; seitdem wünsche ich nicht mehr und fürchte nicht mchr dcn Tod. Seitdem denke ich heiter an Vergangenheit und Zukunft. Ist es nicht auch mit stillem innerlichen Glück, daß Sie jetzt auf so gottselige Weise Ihrem Herrn und Freunde dienen?"— "Sei Gott gedankt, ja, edle Frau. Es ist uns doch wundersam ergangen; wir haben viel Wohl und bitteres Weh unbedachtsam aus dem vollen Becher geschlürft. Nun ist er leer; nun möchte einer meinen, das sei alles nur dic Probe gcwcscn, und, mit kluger Einsicht gerüstet, den wirklichen Anfang erwarten. Ein anderer ist nun der wirkliche Anfang, und man wünscht das erste Gaukelspiel nicht zurück und ist dennoch im ganzen froh, es, wie es war, gelebt zu haben."[36]

So it was, after all, a fairy tale, a provisional rehersal for a life which is simultaneously incipient and already set for its close. Responsibility is admitted, yet Schlemihl's "besseres Selbst" is directed to other things, damage is done, but a "weise Fügung" picks up the pieces. There is little point in talking of "das soziale Ich" where its entailments are so rigorously ignored; and there is as little point in trumpeting "Lebensmeisterung" when, to the very end, "unter den Menschen" and one's "besseres Selbst" are kept categorically apart.[37]

Notes

[1] Quoted in Adalbert von Chamisso, *Peter Schlemihls wundersame Geschichte,* ed. James Boyd (Oxford, 1956), p. xxvii and dated November 1837.

[2] Thomas Mann, "Chamisso" (1911), *Gesammelte Werke,* IX, 2., durchgesehene Auflage, (Frankfurt, 1974), p. 56. For a discussion of Mann's obvious identification with Chamisso and Schlemihl see Arthur Burkhard, "Thomas Mann's Appraisal of the Poet," *Publications of the Modern Language Association of America,* XLVI (1931), 913.

[3] Josef Nadler, *Die Berliner Romantik 1800-1814* (Berlin, 1921), p. 122. Nadler continues: "In *Peter Schlemihl* aber schrieb er, vom Tragischen ins Tragikomische gewendet, die Geschichte jener ungezählten Fremden, die ihren Schatten verloren, als sie Deutsche wurden" (pp. 124-125).

[4] Benno von Wiese, *Die deutsche Novelle* (Düsseldorf, 1963), p. 110.

[5] H.A. Korff, *Geist der Goethezeit,* IV (Leipzig, 1953), p. 349.

[6] Hermann Pongs, *Das Bild in der Dichtung,* II, 2. Auflage (Marburg, 1963), p. 177.

[7] Georg Lukács, *Deutsche Realisten des 19. Jahrhunderts* (Bern, 1951), p. 59.

[8] Ernst Loeb, "Symbol und Wirlichkeit des Schattens in Chamisso's *Peter Schlemihl,*" *Germanisch-Romanische Monatsschrift,* Neue Folge, XV (1965), 402-403.

[9] Stuart Atkins, "*Peter Schlemihl* in Relation to the Popular Novel of the Romantic Period," *The Germanic Review,* XXI (1946), 19-208.

[10] In *Die deutsche Literatur in Text und Darstellung: Romantik II,* ed. Hans-Jürgen Schmitt (Stuttgart, 1974), p. 125; and "Symbol und Wirklichkeit des Schattens," p. 398.

[11] Werner Feudel, *Adalbert von Chamisso: Leben und Werk* (Leipzig, 1971), pp. 71-72.

[12] Boyd, p. xxiii.

[13] Ulrich Baumgartner, *Adalbert von Chamissos Peter Schlemihl* (Frauenfeld/Leipzig), 1944, p. 51.

[14] Boyd, p. 13.

[15] Boyd, p. 9.

[16] Chamisso to his French translator in 1821: "Schlemihl oder besser Schlemiel ist ein hebräischer Name und bedeutet Gottlieb, Theophil oder *aimé de Dieu.* Dies ist in der gewöhnlichen Sprache der Juden die Benennung von ungeschickten oder unglücklichen Leuten, denen nichts in der Welt gelingt . . . Der Name ist beizubehalten." Quoted in Max Zeldner, "A Note on 'Schlemiel'", *The German Quarterly,* XXVI (1953), 116-117.

[17] Boyd, p. 1.

[18] Boyd, p. 2.

[19] Boyd, p. 3.

[20] Chamisso to K.B. von Trinius, 1829: "Ich hatte auf einer Reise Hut, Mantelsack, Handschuhe, Schnupftuch und mein ganzes bewegliches Gut verloren; Fouqué frug: ob ich nicht meinen Schatten verloren habe? und wir malten uns das Unglück aus." Quoted in Boyd, p. xxiv, who also records the variant wherein Chamisso, who was walking in the sun next to his shorter friend Fouqué, is said to have horrified the latter by exclaiming, "Sieh, Fouqué, wenn ich dir nun deinen Schatten aufrollte und du ohne Schatten neben mir wandern müßtest!"

[21] Bowring robustly insists, however, that "the story is a moral one. I leave its development to my readers. It would be little flattering to them to suspect they required my assistance, in order to discover the obvious lessons it conveys." *Peter Schlemihl,* tr. Sir John Bowring, 3rd edition (London, 1861), p. 5.

[22] Boyd, p. 9.

[23] Boyd, p. 12.

[24] Boyd, p. 18.

[25] Boyd, p. 25.

[26] Boyd, p. 28.

[27] Boyd, pp. 33 and 34.

[28] Boyd, p. 45.

[29] "Symbol und Wirklichkeit des Schattens," p. 406.

[30] Ibid., p. 407. Cf. Ralph Flores, "The Lost Shadow of Peter Schlemihl," *The German Quarterly,* XLVII (1974), 572: "When Peter exchanges his shadow for the magical money bag . . . he is not in full possession of 'himself' . . . But passive though he may be in the early parts of the story, Peter Schlemihl . . . takes a resolute stand in finally banishing the gray man once and for all." But not the swag!

[31] Boyd, p. 46.

[32] Boyd, pp. 56-57.

[33] Boyd, p. 60.

[34] Boyd, p. 63.

[35] "Chamisso," p. 52.

[36] Boyd, p. 67.

[37] Cf. the concluding stanza of "An meinen alten Freund Peter Schlemihl" (1834):

Wir geben uns die Hand darauf, Schlemihl,
Wir schreiten zu und lassen es beim alten:
Wir kümmern uns um alle Welt nicht viel,
Es desto fester mit uns selbst zu halten.
Wir gleiten so schon näher unserm Ziel,
Ob jene lachten, ob die andern schalten;
Nach allen Stürmen wollen wir im Hafen
Doch ungestört gesunden Schlafes schlafen.

Quoted in Boyd, p. xli (my italics).

Marko Pavlyshyn (essay date 1982)

SOURCE: "Gold, Guilt and Scholarship: Adelbert von Chamisso's *Peter Schlemihl,* in *The German Quarterly,* Vol. LV, No. 1, January, 1982, pp. 49-63. '

[*In the following essay, Pavlyshyn considers the ending of* Peter Schlemihl *and the implications of Schlemihl's role as a scientist who refuses to participate in society.*]

Adelbert von Chamisso's ***Peter Schlemihls wundersame Geschichte*** (written in 1813, published 1814) is one of the more frequently interpreted German prose texts of the early nineteenth century. Dörte Brockhagen's Forschungsbericht lists twenty-one studies of the work for the period 1945-76 alone.[1] Since then, at least three new titles have appeared, all of considerable importance.[2] Yet critical interest has centered upon a limited number of issues—the genre under which the tale is best classified ("Märchen" or "Novelle"?), the applicability to it of the descriptive categories "romantic" and "realistic," and the interpretation of the symbolic significance of the shadow motif—to the relative neglect of other, equally significant questions. One such critical gap, to which the present paper addresses itself, is the examination of the scholarly idyll at the end of the tale in relation to the themes of knowledge and guilt.

Several opinions have been advanced concerning Schlemihl's final situation. Benno von Wiese suggests that it reflects Chamisso's approval of self-denial and self-limitation in disinterested scholarly contemplation as the only satisfactory solution for one estranged from the unedifying world of society and money.[3] But although von Wiese rightly states that the tale admits of no possible world but that of civil society,[4] he omits to discuss the nature of the relationship developed in the tale between this social world and the researcher Schlemihl. Martin Swales partly fills this lacuna by interpreting both Schlemihl's final condition and his original misdemeanor in economic terms. The sale for money of his own shadow makes him guilty of alienating and degrading to the status of an exchange commodity something that is at once personal and non-material.[5] While this aspect of Swales' argument is persuasive, his account of Schlemihl's botanical activity—the painstaking collection and documentation of the details of nature—as a penance for his previous materialism does not do justice to the complexity and ambiguity of the ending. In a more recent discussion of the work, Colin Butler demonstrates with finesse that such an ambiguity exists, but evaluates it as a weakness. He expresses disapproval of the so-called "happy end": as an illusory reconciliation made possible by the narrative convention of the "Märchen" form, it is evidence of the tale's moral indifference. Responsibility and guilt, elements of the central character's consciousness which should be the link between his private self and the social world, are merely dismissed; reality is "subverted" by Chamisso's "reliance on the 'Märchen.'"[6] Butler does not concede that the non-resolution of obvious problems may in this case be a deliberate structural device with a complex, interpretable and socially significant meaning. It seems that the realistic aesthetic of the large-scale nineteenth-century novel, from which Butler draws many of his examples for comparisons with *Schlemihl,* has led him to demand verisimilitude of psychological causation as a prerequisite of responsible social argumentation in literature.

There is little point in taking issue with this position other than by offering an alternative interpretation, according to which Chamisso is more sensitive to his social environment than Butler admits.

I

The portion of Chamisso's story which deals with Peter Schlemihl's existence as a scientist, though small, nevertheless contains surprisingly complete accounts, both of Schlemihl's scientific practice, and of his personal ideology. The two stand in profound contradiction.

Though embellished by the fairy-tale motif of the magical seven-league boots, Schlemihl's botanical, zoological and meteorological studies correspond closely to authentic research undertaken on contemporary voyages of discovery. They coverage almost exactly, for instance, with what were to be Chamisso's own duties as official scientist on the expedition of the Russian ship *Rurik* (1815-1818).[7] On the basis of Schlemihl's own description, his activity would seem to be motivated by the notion that knowledge worth having consists of a fullness of unadorned facts intelligently interpreted after thorough collation and comparison:

> Ich streifte auf der Erde umher, bald ihre Höhen, bald die Temperaturen ihrer Quellen und der Luft messend, bald Tiere beobachtend, bald Gewächse untersuchend; ich elite von dem Äquator nach dem Pole, von der einen Welt nach der andern, Erfahrungen mit Erfahrungen vergleichend.[8]

Yet Chamisso does not permit Schlemihl to espouse the positivist ideal of science which would be logically appropriate to his practice. Instead, he contrives for Schlemihl the following confession concerning his vocation:

> Ich fiel in stummer Andacht auf meine Knie and vergoß Tränen des Dankes—denn klar stand meine Zukunft *vor meiner Seele*. Durch frühe Schuld von der menschlichen Gesellschaft abgeschlossen, ward ich zum Ersatz an die Natur, die ich stets geliebt, gewiesen, die Erde mir zu einem reichen Garten gegeben, das Studium zur Richtung und Kraft meines Lebens, zu ihrem Ziel die Wissenschaft. Es war nicht ein Entschluß, den ich fate. Ich habe nur seitdem, was *da* hell und vollendet im Urbild vor mein inneres Auge trat, getreu in stillem, strengem, unausgesetztem Fleiß darzustellen gesucht, und meine Selbstzufriedenheit hat von dem Zusammenfallen des Dargestellten mit dem Urbild abgehangen. (pp. 60-61; my emphasis.)

The grammatical ambiguity of the word "da" in this passage makes it possible that Schlemihl is saying onc of two equally curious things: either the vision of that single inspired moment provides him with an all-embracing "Urbild" (perhaps an instantaneous perception of all the knowledge which he later unravels in detail in the course of his scientific labors), or a series of such direct perceptions guides him in the process of observation. In either case, a special organ of supra-sensual cognition is at work. The terms in which the passage is couched carry associations remote from scientific rationality. "Seele" is part of the Christian vocabulary adopted by the literature of sentimentality; "Urbild" suggests Platonic and idealist contexts; "inneres Auge" belongs to the theory of the Romantic imagination. The terminology underscores the fact that, whichever meaning applies, Schlemihl deliberately distances himself from rigorous positivism and insists on the spiritual dimension of his scientific knowledge, preserving in it an element of revelation. The product of his scholarly labors, the "Darstellung," presumably as it is manifest in his written records, bears the imprint of something more than the empirical world.

When Schlemihl's methodological theorizings are confronted with the reader's evidence of his scientific practice, however, it becomes evident that the role of the subjective force which he claims accompanies his pursuit of knowledge is limiting, rather than productive. In a confessional passage he writes, "ich habe . . . vieles auf sich beruhen lassen, vieles zu wissen und zu begreifen Verzicht geleistet, und bin, . . . meinem geraden Sinn vertrauend, der Stimme in mir, so viel es in meiner Macht gewesen, auf dem eigenen Wege gefolgt" (p. 53). Yet the actual results of Schlemihl's pursuit of the Inner Voice are not profound insights, but some Latin publications and a quantitative expansion of geographical, meteorological and botanical information.

These would seem to be the fruits, not of a life in-spired by a vision, but a career guided by scholarly skepticism and caution, and dedicated to painstaking research so rigidly positivist that it almost neglects interpretation in favor of factual precision: "Ich habe die Tatsachen *mit möglicher Genauigkeit* in klarer Ordnung aufgestellt *in mehreren Werken,* meine Folgerungen und Ansichten *flüchtig* in einigen Abhandlungen niedergelegt" (my emphasis; p. 66). What, within the poetic logic of the work, is the reason for the inconsistency between Schlemihl's expressed self-consciousness as a scien-tist and the principles implicit in his work?[9] The answer becomes transparent through the special func-tion which accrues in Schlemihl's discourse to the term "Seele." In Schlemihl's account of his revelation quoted above, the phrase "vor meiner Seele," usually a con-versational cliché approximating the English "before the mind's eye," is recharged with meaning: Schlemihl speaks of the soul as the cognitive organ through which he has perceived, "im Urbild," his future vocation. The reader is reminded that Schlemihl's soul is a partici-pant in the plot: had it been in the devil's hands at the time, no vision would have occurred. Schlemihl's sci-entific venture, in fact, is dependent upon his posses-sion of a soul. (Lest this appear an overinterpretation of a stylistic accident, it should be noted that Chamisso is fond of the meaningful revitalization of clichés[10] and that an identical usage of "Seele" occurs at another important point in the narrative, discussed below.)[11] And yet, for all the significance which Schlemihl as narrator *retrospectively* ascribes to the soul, he had at first displayed little interest in it. His initial rejection of the gray man's proposal to exchange his soul for his shadow is not the result of principles: "Er [the gray man] war mir von Herzensgrunde verhaßt, und ich glaube, daß mich dieser persönliche Widerwille mehr als Grundsätze oder Vorurteile abhielt, meinen Schatten, so notwendig er mir auch war, mit der begehrten Unterschrift zu erkaufen" (p. 43).

Schlemihl is indifferent to any Christian connotations of the loss of the soul until after he has lost his chances of social happiness with Mina. Only then does the ap-pearance from the gray man's pocket of the damned soul of the rich merchant Thomas John move Schlemihl to throw away the purse of Fortunatus, thus ensuring that the devil shall never tempt him with the return of the shadow again. This is an act of salvage, ensuring that at least the soul, an abstraction by which Schlemihl had previously put little stock, will remain with him when shadow, social prominence, marriage and money have been lost. If Schlemihl carries over his soul into his new life and stylizes it as the cognitive starting-point and ideological cornerstone of his scientific enterprise, he does so out of psychological need. Only by making a virtue of necessity can he give the severe limitations imposed upon his life a positive interpretation. The contradiction between Schlemihl's science and his ide-ology remains real: the preserved spiritual dimension of his scientific endeavors is a mere play on words, a case of intellectual self-delusion for the sake of a bear-able self-image.

II

Chamisso's *Schlemihl* is so structured as to challenge its early-nineteenth-century reader to make a judg-ment of the situation at the end of the tale, which the hero-narrator paints as an idyll of limited content-ment and meaningful activity. Chamisso provides com-plex evidence for such a judgment—evidence, as this paper will now suggest, whose interpretation draws the reader to reflections on aspects of his social environment.

In a narrow sense, Schlemihl's enterprises as a scien-tist are morally indifferent, insofar as they are carried out in isolation and thus have no effects, good or bad, on the human sphere. However, Schlemihl's activities in pursuit of knowledge *can* be judged by their asso-ciation with phenomena which, in the given argu-mentative framework, have an unambiguous moral significance.

In *Peter Schlemihl* it stands the natural sciences in good stead to be seen as the alternative to the acqui-sition of knowledge by speculation, which is assigned a distinctly negative value. This point is made in a passage which has escaped critical attention hitherto,[12] but which merits attentive consideration. After fleeing on horseback in the depths of night from the town where he had wooed Mina and had survived the threat to his soul, Schlemihl is joined on his path by a pedes-trian, who, after a number of social niceties, begins a monologue. Schlemihl reports:

> Er entfaltete seine Ansichten von dem Leben und der Welt und kam sehr bald auf die Metaphysik, an die die Forderung erging, das Wort aufzusuchen, das aller Rätsel Lösung sei. Er setzte die Aufgabe mit vieler Klarheit auseinander und schritt fürder zu deren Beantwortung.
>
> . . . Nun schien mir dieser Redekünstler mit großem Talent ein fest gefügtes Gebäude aufzuführen, das in sich selbst begründet sich emportrug, und wie durch eine innere Notwendigkeit bestand. Nur vermißte ich ganz in ihm, was ich eben darin hätte suchen wollen, und so ward es mir zu einem bloßen Kunstwerk, dessen zierliche Geschlossenheit und Vollendung dem Auge allein zur Ergetzung diente; aber ich hörte dem wohlberedten Manne gerne zu, der meine Aufmerksamkeit von meinen Leiden auf sich selbst abgelenkt, und ich hätte mich ihm willig ergeben, *wenn er meine Seele wie meinen Verstand in Anspruch genommen hätte.* (My emphasis; p. 53.)

The pedestrian, whose identity as the gray man is ini-tially concealed both from Schlemihl and from the reader, sets himself the task of discovering the word which is the answer to all riddles. On the "Märchen" level this undertaking is of a kind with the other folktale motifs in the narrative, and in particular it provides the intellectual equivalent of Fortunatus' magic purse. The latter is the source of infinite wealth, the former promises absolute knowledge. In the tradition of the fairy-tale, the riddle is a constraint on the freedom of the hero; correctly answered, it guarantees his liberty to proceed towards his happy end.[13] The motif found a place in Romantic literature—it plays a role in Klingsohr's "Märchen" in Novalis' *Heinrich von Ofterdingen,* to mention only the best-known example[14]—and the pursuit of the magic word or the mysterious language is a favored symbol of the quest and yearning for infinite human freedom in the perfection of knowledge. The pedestrian's self-imposed task, then, reflects an intellectual ambition familiar to the period.

The proposed solution to the conundrum bears the qualities of a speculatively deduced philosophical system: inner cohesion, completeness, and mutual interdependence of all its parts. It constitutes an argument for the proposition that the totality of knowledge resides in a system of rational speculation. The philosophical fashion reflected here is, of course, that of all-embracing philosophical systems which had been initiated by Leibniz and intensified by the concentration of philosophical interest since Kant and Fichte on the self and its cognitive activity as the ordering principle of the world.

Schlemihl's reaction is ambivalent, although it ends in his rejection of the pedestrian's mental experiment. Although he admires the system's aesthetic qualities, admitting freely the great rhetorical mastery of the speaker, he does not find the speech persuasive, as he would have, had it affected his *soul* as it did his mind. A revitalized cliché again alerts the reader to the fact that had Schlemihl sold his soul to the devil, the rejection would not have taken place. Only after it has been made clear that the pedestrian's philosophical propositions are seductive, but not convincing to one still in the possession of a soul, comes the light of dawn which identifies the pedestrian as the gray man and therefore German Idealism as a thing of the devil.

There is, of course, a venerable literary and demonological tradition in which the devil is a sophistical debater and a master of abstract logic. The reason why it should be invoked here in order to demonize speculative rationalism is not clarified within the text, but easily enough understood in terms of a personal antipathy on the author's part. Chamisso had rejected Kantian and Fichtean thought, as well as the speculative and systematic approach to natural phenomena fostered by Schelling, at the time of his turn to the natural sciences.[15] In *Peter Schlemihl* this judgment stands unsubstantiated on the argumentative

level of the text—which does not diminish its role in the poetic logic of the work. The scene is a deliberately constructed scenario in which Schlemihl distances himself from such philosophizing, and affords the reader an opportunity to judge this move positively, preparing him to give the unassuming empirical method of contributing to knowledge a high evaluation when he encounters it on the final pages.

On the other hand, from a different perspective, the natural sciences appear in a negative light. They are placed severely in question by their association, through the intermediary motif of gold, with the devil. The advocate of the intellectual bugbear of philosophical Idealism is also the author of the more palpable evil in the story: gold, or, more precisely, the exchange for gold of an inalienable thing—a shadow. Swales has argued that the initial guilt of Peter Schlemihl stems from his acquiescence in converting into a commodity a naturally given companion of human life:[16] he fails to resist the corrupt materialism which accompanies wealth and dehumanizes all values. The most complete satire on this form of reification occurs in the gray man's attempt to persuade Schlemihl to relinquish his soul:

> Und, wenn ich fragen darf, was ist denn das für ein Ding, Ihre Seele? Haben sie es je gesehen, und was denken Sie damit anzufangen, wenn Sie einst tot sind? Seien Sie doch froh, einen Liebhaber zu finden, der Ihnen bei Lebenszeit noch den Nachlaß dieses X, dieser galvanischen Kraft oder polarisierenden Wirksamkeit, und was alles das närrische Ding sein soll, mit etwas Wirklichem bezahlen will, nämlich mit Ihrem leibhaftigen Schatten, durch den Sie zu der Hand Ihrer Geliebten und der Erfüllung aller Ihrer Wünsche gelangen können. (pp. 42f.)

According to this remarkable diatribe, nothing—not even a soul—can have any value unless it be an object. Of course, a soul fails to meet the definition of an object espoused by the materialist and the utilitarian: it cannot be seen, nor can it be put to use. From the gray man's viewpoint, it can at best be considered a luxury article, a hobby item, of interest only to a limited clientele of collectors such as himself. In trying to persuade Schlemihl to part with his (intrinsically) "invaluable" soul, the devil argues that the soul is "valueless" (in the market place). He can therefore claim to be magnanimous in offering to accept it in return for something with a socially proven market value: Schlemihl's "corporeal shadow." To borrow for a moment from a familiar terminology, we encounter here a formulation of the distorted relationship between exchange value and use value in capitalist society. The humorous paradox in the phrase "leibhaftiger Schatten" highlights the capacity of the commercial process arbitrarily to create value, even if this involves turning common sense upside down and imparting to the immaterial the illusion of substance.

The immaterial things whose degeneration into exchangeable commodities is paralleled by the sale of the shadow, the tale suggests, are the indistinct, but nonetheless real elements of human relationships: respect, admiration, even love. Schlemihl discovers that his new gold can transform all of these into purchasable articles. The transformation does not initially require an act of his volition; at the outset it costs him no more than a passive lie. With time, the business of maintaining an untruth becomes more circumstantial. Initially, the populace of the town to which Schlemihl flees from Thomas John's circle is its own dupe for assuming him to be an incognito king; but he thereafter nurtures the illusion, adding deliberate deceit to his initial involuntary guilt. Where Schlemihl tries to preserve his human emotions from corruption, the evil generated by his gold brings him to grief: his love for Mina founders when the scandalous origin of his wealth becomes public knowledge. A relationship which he strenuously strove to retain at a human, rather than a financial level ultimately falls prey to the commercial principle which Schlemihl in that instance had tried to circumvent: Mina is purchased from her parents by his former servant Rascal, a less scrupulous but more consistent exploiter of wealth than Schlemihl. The wealth which makes possible this abomination has its origin in the same purse that Schlemihl had received for his shadow. The consequences of that unhappy act of exchange, therefore, include suffering for the initial "beneficiary" and for those who innocently come within his ambit.

The very act of the enjoyment of the gold is painted as sordid, shameful and guilty; it is performed in secret in a frenzy of self-humiliation:

> Was denkst du, Chamisso, daß ich nun anfing!—O mein lieber Chamisso, selbst vor dir es zu gestehen, macht mich erröten. Ich zog den unglücklichen Säckel aus meiner Brust hervor, und mit einer Art Wut, die, wie eine flackernde Feuersbrunst, sich in mir durch sich selbst mehrte, zog ich Gold daraus, und Gold, und Gold, und immer mehr Gold, und streute es auf den Estrich, und schritt darüber hin, und ließ es klirren, und warf, mein armes Herz an dem Glanze, an dem Klange weidend, immer des Metalles mehr zu dem Metalle, bis ich ermüdet selbst auf das reiche Lager sank und schwelgend darin wühlte, mich darüber wälzte. So verging der Tag, der Abend, ich schloß meine Tür nicht auf, die Nacht fand mich liegend auf dem Golde, und darauf übermannte mich der Schlaf. (p. 24)

The celebration of the newly acquired gold is described as a physical, indeed, an orgiastic excess, as an eruption of uncontrollable and irrational forces; it is followed by bad conscience, exhaustion, revulsion and remorse. Material greed, this passage would suggest, is a component of the subconscious, usually repressed; its explosions are followed by the regrets of the discriminating, rational judgment. If, as this excerpt apparently demonstrates, avarice is a repressed, but in fact natural element of Schlemihl's psychic composition, then it would seem that the guilt associated with it may well be real and palpable, but it is not the product of his own responsible acts. There exists, in other words, an a priori connection between gold and guilt independent of volition—a conclusion confirmed by the circumstances under which Schlemihl assumes what he comes to regard as his "frühe Schuld" (p. 60). Unlike the sale of a soul, the sale of a shadow is not immediately recognizable to him (nor to the reader) as a culpable act. Only the association in folklore of the shadow with the soul makes the event somewhat uncanny. Add the fact that Schlemihl enters the agreement in a kind of avaricious trance rather than in the full possession of his faculties—this is reiterated no fewer than three times[17]—and it is difficult at any single point to discover a willfully guilty act.

On the basis of these observations, one can readily enough discover in the gold motif implications for features of the modern economy that were discernible by the early nineteenth century.[18] Schlemihl's eagerness to possess the magic purse without understanding the consequences brings to mind the individual's desire to benefit from the capitalist economy without understanding its workings; Schlemihl's failure to escape the devil except by throwing away the purse suggests the individual's difficulty in opting out of the prevailing economic system. The miraculous flow of gold from Fortunatus' purse is reminiscent of the speculative generation of wealth, for which opportunities multiplied during the eighteenth century; it is a metaphor for the growing abstraction of the connection between wealth and its sources.[19] It is not, however, the intention here to refine and elaborate these analogies. Their purpose is to draw attention to the fact that a historical localization of the function of the gold motif (and its critical ramifications) is both possible and plausible, before we address ourselves to the closer examination of Schlemihl's scholarship.

It is a consequence of the yoking together of gold and guilt that any connection which might be established between gold and Schlemihl's science must throw a shadow (so to speak) over the latter. Chamisso goes out of his way to ensure that such a relationship is established. Schlemihl discovers some time after his acquisition of the seven-league boots that his former servant Bendel has used the remaining hoards of his otherwise unsanctified ("sonst nicht gesegnetes," p. 64) gold to establish a foundation which finances the building and upkeep of a hospital. Institutional charity is supported by money whose origins are far from respectable. Furthermore, Schlemihl uses the remnants of the devil's gold which he finds in his pockets as the financial basis of his scientific enterprise. When the seven-league boots are purchased with the tainted gold,

Chamisso even refers to a cash transaction ("bare Bezahlung," p. 59) in order to remind the reader of this fact. As for the books, the sextant, and the other instruments which Schlemihl requires—he purchases them, as he says without discomfiture, "mit dem Rest meines Zaubergoldes" (p. 62).

What is to be made of the fact that in *Peter Schlemihl* activities which the narrative structure invites the reader from one viewpoint to approve, are directly dependent on agencies which, in a context developed elsewhere, are to be condemned? Why is science to be seen as a by-product of the evil of wealth? When considered in connection with the historical development of scientific disciplines in Chamisso's day, the paradox seems less strange. Chamisso, who found his way to the natural sciences only after rejecting philosophy and poetry as his chief occupations, was accustomed to reflect on his own relationship to science, as numerous places in his correspondence confirm.[20] It is not surprising that *Peter Schlemihl* appears to give evidence of a well-developed (and skeptical) attitude to the social role of scientific activity.

From the middle of the eighteenth century onward, structural changes in the funding of scientific research began to occur throughout Europe. For reasons which included the growing complexity of scientific disciplines, the need for more expensive personnel and equipment, and the increasing urgency of research to commerce, industry and the military establishments, the sciences found new patrons. In England, where much scientific enterprise served the progress of the Industrial Revolution, these patrons were largely private. Institutions to promote and reward scientific and technological ingenuity, such as the Society for the Encouragement of Arts, Manufactures and Commerce and the Royal Institution of Great Britain were established by public subscription or by wealthy entrepreneurs.[21] Industrialists engaged scientists and engineers for research with the goal of enhancing efficiency and productivity.[22] On the continent, where neither the Industrial Revolution nor the private patronage of science had yet taken hold, the sciences were nevertheless blessed with a significant increase in funding from "enlightened" governments motivated, as a contemporary chronicler of German universities puts it, by the "Genius des Jahrhunderts"[23] and by a competitive spirit between rival courts. The ability to subsidize universities, astronomical observatories, herbariums, botanical gardens, libraries and academic salaries was, especially in Germany, a measure of the glory of the absolute monarch and, like ostentatious patronage of the arts, an important aspect of his self-representation.

Although the actual conditions for the pursuit of knowledge improved, the decline of the self-financing amateur scientist in favor of the scientist as the employee, whether of an industrial concern or of a state-funded university, inevitably put severely into question the concept of a disinterested and free science. In England scientists found themselves for the first time pursuing objectives defined, not by their own disciplines, but by industry. In Germany, newly organized universities provided scholars with salaries which permitted them to live without personal hardship; on the other hand, the universities were stripped of their traditional privileges, often including the right of self-censorship and the right to appoint professors.[24]

Nowhere did the dependence of the scientist on the public or private patron become more acute than in those branches of knowledge whose furtherance required extensive data. The progress of geography, zoology, meterology, anthropology, astronomy, and botany (Chamisso's special interest) demanded the collection of empirical data from all parts of the globe by means of exploratory expeditions employing ships and hundreds of men, and lasting several years. Such ventures were obviously beyond the reach of individual scholars or even unassisted scholarly groups, and depended on governments or outstandingly rich private patrons. Scientific activity was therefore necessarily combined with the pursuit of economic and political interests. These interests, however, were entirely beyond the control of the scholar himself; still less under his control were the sources of the money which subsidized his research. Against the background of this state of affairs the morally ambiguous connection between the motifs of gold and scholarship in *Peter Schlemihl* becomes more than an accident of narrative necessity.

Two historical examples may serve to illustrate the kind of practical dilemma of science which finds an echo in *Schlemihl*. The three voyages of Captain James Cook between 1768 and 1780 were explicitly dedicated to scientific goals: the observation of the transit of Venus from a station in the South Seas; the verification of the existence or otherwise of a southern continent in the Pacific; and the discovery of a northern passage from the Bering Strait to Hudson Bay. The scientific character of at least the first two voyages was visible in the role played by the Royal Society in initating and organizing them. But the voyages also bear witness to the integration of scientific objectives with those of an empire-building commercial state. The British Parliament voted £25,000 from the public purse to finance the second voyage,[25] not because the first had successfully performed its astronomical objective—it had not. The financial support carried the character of an investment. The failure of the third voyage to find a passage from the northern Pacific to the Atlantic was more than compensated by the discovery of the Sandwich Islands (Hawaii), whose convenience as a half-way harbor between China and North America was immediately exploited by trade. From the perspective of the scientist in whose name this activity was carried out, the gains to knowledge stand in uncertain balance with the negative effects of the voyages. Georg Forster's record of Cook's second voyage repeatedly deals with the question whether the discovery of new peoples in the South Seas is sufficient justification for the social disruption, disease and exploitation which contact with Europeans is bound to bring.[26]

If this example illuminates the moral ambiguity of the consequences following upon the collaboration of science and money, the early history of Chamisso's own journey is a particularly strident case of science benefiting from what in terms of our discussion hitherto may be called "tainted gold." The expedition was funded privately by the Russian aristocrat Nikolai Petrovich, Count Rumjantsev (1754-1826), a patron of the sciences on a large scale.[27] (Chamisso's report on the journey slightly deforms his name, in keeping with contemporary German practice, to "Romantsoff.") Apart from the expedition of the *Rurik,* he was concerned with numerous similar voyages, financed scholarly publications and editions of historical sources, provided support to Russian scholars and established a major library and museum. These ventures were funded from the profits of Rumjantsev's enormous landholdings in the Ukraine. The estates had been acquired by Rumjantsev's father, partly through purchase, but largely as gifts for his services to the crown as field marshall and as governor-general of the Ukrainian territories. In the latter position, Rumjantsev sen. distinguished himself particularly by supervising in 1783 the introduction of serfdom. The voyage of the *Rurik,* whose scientific undertakings were to benefit mankind in general, was financed through wealth generated by the labor of Rumjantsev's newly enserfed peasants.

As a result of its dependence on money, scientific research which is entirely laudable, or at least value-free when viewed in terms of its internal justifications and objectives, becomes enmeshed in social causes and consequences of a morally uncertain character, which the scientist is often incapable of seeing, much less controlling. Such a situation is reflected in the interconnection of gold and scholarship in *Peter Schlemihl.*

III

The evidence has now been marshalled for the evaluative judgment of Peter Schlemihl which the tale demands of its reader. Such a judgment can be no simple one. We know that Schlemihl's guilt rests on no consciously culpable act. He has sold his shadow under mitigating circumstances, ignorant of the true state of affairs, deceived by a cunning adversary and urged by subconscious inclination. But his involuntary guilt in this context is balanced by involuntary innocence in another. When he freely makes the Faustian choice to sell his soul rather than lose Mina to Rascal, circumstance intervenes: he loses consciousness. In the former case he cannot be held responsible for his action; in

the second he is prevented from implementing his will. Clearly, he is not in control of his own destiny, and not to be judged as one would judge a Faust. Schlemihl must be seen to inhabit a moral half-way house. On the one hand he is tainted with the guilt of materialism, into which he has been imperceptibly drawn. In this respect he re-enacts the non-deliberate process by which the individual finds himself entangled in the contingencies of the socio-economic system within which he has no choice but to live. On the other hand, when all is said and done, he discovers that he has not accepted the final consequences of the materialist's demonic world. Even so, he continues to be a victim of false consciousness: he remains innocently unaware of the paradox involved in renouncing the devil, yet keeping part of the gold. It is the privilege of Schlemihl as scholar and scientist to benefit (admittedly to a limited extent) from the sinister processes which create wealth, and yet to have the moral satisfaction of renouncing a pact with the devil.

In *Peter Schlemihl,* then, the reader is invited to see the hero as led along a compromise course between the extremes of absolute guilt and absolute uprightness. Here moral compromise is a workable modus vivendi, not involving extreme hardship, but at the same time offering only moderate satisfaction; here provision is made for a human being to develop a favorable self-image which, though remote from the truth, gives life an illusory dimension of meaning. Within a model of reality in which the individual is denied knowledge and responsibility, the reader's judgment of Schlemihl cannot be a stern one. The affect appropriate to such a reality is humor (and not the pathos of tragic choice, for whose absence Butler would criticize Chamisso).[28]

To underscore the perceived triviality of human fate, Chamisso's humor banalizes whatever elements in it display even the potential of sublimity. Thus the devil is no Mephistopheles; he appears instead as a salesman. Schlemihl himself, deprived of the grandeur of personal decision, retains no more stature at the end of the tale than a comic figure. The secondary literature has tended, unjustifiably, to evaluate Schlemihl's final fate in emphatically positive terms. Feudel speaks of his "heroische Entsagung"[29] and Flores considers his enhanced mobility "godlike,"[30] but in fact Schlemihl as a scientist undergoes continual trivialization. Gero von Wilpert has demonstrated that Chamisso systematically exploits the possibilities of the shadow motif for its comic potential.[31] The same could be shown for the motif of the seven-league boots, which determines the character of Schlemihl's life as a scientist. When Chamisso combines the wit involved in the imaginative exploitation of the motif with slapstick effects, Schlemihl plays the clown: he scours the continents from one side of the globe to the other (there is a long itinerary of his ports of call) within a single afternoon;

after a fall into the Arctic Ocean he oscillates fever-ishly between the torrid and frigid zones, between night and day, in order to find an appropriate temperature for drying off. It is difficult to accommodate such comically grotesque elements in a seriously affirmative interpretation of Schlemihl's scholarship. Furthermore, Chamisso makes Schlemihl the object of an ironic jest between author and reader by having him remain un-aware of the comical contradictions in his new lifestyle. Following the tradition of Christian hermits, Schlemihl settles in a cave in the desert of Thebais. Into this region, with its history of devout self-abnegation, he introduces vestiges of middle-class comfort: his cave is "eine der verborgensten, die zugleich geräumig, bequem und den Schakalen unzugänglich war" (p. 61). He equips himself with the other attributes of a bachelor's domestic comfort—a tobacco pipe and a dog. By revealing himself as a paradoxically *convenient* hermit, he opens himself to derision as that whipping boy of Romantic literature, a Philistine.

The relativization of Schlemihl's scientific phase, how-ever, does not always take comic forms. The most se-rious shortcoming of his existence as a scientist is its isolation from life situations, which receives anticipa-tory formulation early in the plot. After his orgy of gold production, Schlemihl has a dream. It takes the form of a static scene, reminiscent in its arrangement of a baroque emblem and therefore inviting allegori-cal interpretation. At the center is Schlemihl's friend Chamisso in his study. He is surrounded by the at-tributes of his profession as biologist and writer—a skeleton, pressed botanical specimens, works of lit-erature on the sofa, scientific books open on the desk. The strangest and most significant element, which is revealed last and provides the exegetic key, is the fact that Chamisso is dead. It becomes clear that all the elements of the dream—zoology, botany, literature—deal with life only at second remove. The picture of death, therefore, anticipates Schlemihl's life, which will have to do with dead plants, dead animals, and the dead impressions of life in books. As if this were not enough, the skeleton, symbol not only of death but of vanitas, suggests that even the value of Schlemihl's activities will be placed radically in doubt. (It need scarcely be added that the presence of Chamisso as the center-piece of this dream—it is, when interpreted, a nightmare—is a self-inflicted irony that reflects Chamisso's doubts, amply documented in his corre-spondence,[32] about his own work as a natural scientist.)

In fact, the trivialization of Schlemihl's scientific achievements occurs in the final paragraphs of the tale, where it can exert maximum influence on the reader's parting impression of the book. Not unexpect-edly, the situation is humorously conceived: Schlemihl cannot reach New Holland, evidently because his seven-league boots cannot cross the Timor Sea even by a process of island-hopping. (Seven German miles

are about 52.5 km; even with today's geographical knowledge, the feat would be impossible.) Schlemihl's scientific insights remain incomplete:

> Das merkwürdige, zum Verständnis der Erde und ihres sonnengewirkten Kleides, der Pflanzen- und Tierwelt, so wesentlich notwendige Neuholland und die Südsee mit ihren Zoophyten-Inseln waren mir untersagt, und so war, im Ursprunge schon, alles was ich sammeln und erbauen wollte, bloßes Fragment zu bleiben verdammt (pp. 61f.).

In this differentiated, subtle, perceptive and, indeed, prophetic portrait of the modern scientist and the busi-ness of modern scientific scholarship, the last words equate fragmentation with damnation. It is true that systematic philosophy is derided in *Peter Schlemihl* as rhetorical deception; but the empirical method pro-vides no emotional compensation for the totality of world view which it disenfranchised; the undimin-ished yearning for that unity is echoed in the final "verdammt." Fragmentation, too, is the social experi-ence of Schlemihl as the modern individual who dis-covers that the alternative to an unreserved affirmation of the demonism of the economic leviathan is isola-tion, non-participation and social irrelevance.

Notes

[1] Dörte Brockhagen, "Adelbert von Chamisso" in *Literatur in der sozialen Bewegung,* ed. Alberto Martino, Günter Häntzschel and Georg Jäger (Tübingen: Niemeyer, 1977), pp. 373-423.

[2] They are, in chronological order, Martin Swales, "Mundane Magic: Some Observations on Chamisso's *Peter Schlemihl,*" *Forum for Modern Language Stud-ies,* 12 (1976), pp. 250-62; Colin A. Butler, "Hobson's Choice: a Note on *Peter Schlemihl,*" *Monatshefte,* 69 (1977), pp. 5-16; and Gero von Wilpert, "A. von Chamisso *Peter Schlemihls wundersame Geschichte*" in his *Der verlorene Schatten. Varianten eines literarischen Motivs* (Stuttgart: Kröner, 1978), pp. 20-50. Butler's provocative article, though rarely in agreement with the present author's views, provided numerous stimuli to this paper. Winfried Freund, *Adelbert von Chamisso. Peter Schlemihl. Geld und Geist. Ein* bürgerlicher *Bewußtseinsspiegel* (Paderborn: Schöningh, 1980) could not be consulted before the completion of the manu-script. The book does not, however, touch upon the issues to be discussed here.

[3] Benno von Wiese, "Adelbert von Chamisso, *Peter Schlemihls wundersame Geschichte*" in his *Die deutsche Novelle von Goethe bis Kafka. Interpretationen,* in 2 vols. (Düsseldorf: Bagel, 1956), I, 97-116, here pp. 102-04.

[4] *Ibid.,* p. 106.

[5] Swales, p. 261f.

[6] Butler, p. 13.

[7] See Chamisso's register of his activities in his letter to Hitzig from the voyage, in Adelbert von Chamisso, *Werke,* in 6 vols., 2nd ed. (Leipzig: Weidmann'sche Buchhandlung, 1842), VI, 48. This edition is subsequently referred to in the Notes as *Werke.*

[8] Adelbert von Chamisso, *Sämtliche Werke,* in 2 vols., ed. Jost Perfahl and Volker Hoffmann (München: Winkler, 1975), I, 63. All page numbers in the text refer to the first volume of this edition.

[9] Some critics have noticed no conflict between Schlemihl's theory and practice. Von Wiese, for instance, asserts that for Schlemihl the world is not the object of "Gefühl," but of "forschender Verstand" (p. 114), whereas in fact it is the object of both of these.

[10] Cf. Stuart Atkins, "*Peter Schlemihl* in Relation to the Popular Novel of the Romantic Period," *GR,* 21 (1946), pp. 191-208, here p. 203; von Wilpert, p. 49.

[11] See p. 54 below.

[12] To my knowledge, the only critic who mentions this passage even obliquely is von Wiese (p. 106).

[13] Mathilde Hain, *Rätsel* (Stuttgart: Metzler, 1966), Sammlung Metzler 53, p. 36.

[14] Novalis, *Schriften* (Darmstadt: Wissenschaftliche Buchgesellschaft, 1960-1976), I, 301.

[15] "Mir ist das müßige Construiren a priori und Deduciren und Wissenschaft aufstellen von jedem Quark und Haarspalten, zum Ekel geworden." *Werke,* V, 376; see also *Werke,* V, 398.

[16] Swales, pp. 261-62.

[17] ". . . er hatte mit dem einen Wort [Fortunati Glücksäckel] meinen ganzen Sinn gefangen"; "in mir war noch keine Besinnung"; "Ich kam endlich zu Sinnen" (p. 23).

[18] Cf. Werner Feudel, *Adelbert von Chamisso. Leben und Werk* (Leipzig: Reclam, 1971), p. 73.

[19] P. Rohrmann, "The Central Role of Money in the Chapbook *Fortunatus.*" *Neophilologus,* 59 (1975), pp. 262-72 describes the motif in its sixteenth-century formulation as a reflex to conditions prevailing in early capitalism.

[20] E.g., *Werke,* V, 351, 376, 378, 391; VI, 39-40, 52, 57.

[21] A. Wolf, *A History of Science, Technology and Philosophy in the 18th Century,* in 2 vols., 2nd ed. (London: Allen and Unwin, 1962), II, 42; Jürgen Kuczynski, *Wissenschaft und Wirtschaft bis zur industriellen Revolution* (Berlin [East]: Akademie-Verlag, 1970), p. 122.

[22] Kuczynski, pp. 130f.

[23] Christoph Meiners, *Geschichte der Entstehung und Entwicklung der hohen Schulen unseres Erdteils,* in 4 vols. (Göttingen: Johann Friedrich Römer, 1802-1805, Rep. Aalen: Scientia, 1973), II, 42.

[24] *Ibid.,* IV, 204-05 and 214-17.

[25] George Forster, *Werke,* vol. I (*A Voyage Round the World*) (Berlin [East]: Akademie-Verlag, 1968), p. 17.

[26] *Ibid.,* pp. 133, 182.

[27] "Nikolai Petrovich Rumjantsev" and "Petr Aleksandrovich Rumjantsev Zadunajskij" in *Entsyklopedicheskij Slovar,* in 82 vols. (Leipzig: F. A. Brockhaus; St. Petersburg: I. A. Efron, 1890-1904).

[28] Butler, p. 13.

[29] Feudel, p. 78.

[30] Ralph Flores, "The Lost Shadow of Peter Schlemihl," *GQ,* 49 (1974), pp. 567-84, here p. 580.

[31] Von Wilpert, pp. 42-49.

[32] *Werke,* VI, 52, 53.

FURTHER READING

Biography

Ampère, M. J. J. Review of *Adalbert von Chamisso's Werke. The Foreign Quarterly Review* XXXVI, No. LXXII (1845): 412-37.
    Recounts Chamisso's life and examines selections from his best-known poems.

Bisson, L. A. "The First French Edition of *Peter Schlemihl.*" In *German Studies Presented to Professor H. G. Fiedler, M. V. O.,* pp. 26-32. Oxford: Clarendon Press, 1938.
    Anecdotal account of Chamisso's relationship to his French publisher and a potential translator.

Criticism

Atkins, Stuart. "*Peter Schlemihl* in Relation to the Popular Novel of the Romantic Period." *The Germanic Review* XXI, No. 3 (October 1946): 191-208.

Examines sentimental elements in *Peter Schlemihl* that some critics have considered flaws in the work, to which Atkins responds by observing the satirical function of these episodes.

Koepke, Wulf. "Introduction." In *Peter Schlemihl,* by Adelbert von Chamisso, pp. v-xxix. Columbia, S. C.: Camden House, 1993.

Summarizes Chamisso's life, assesses the relationship of *Peter Schlemihl* to German Romanticism, and surveys modern interpretations of the novel.

Reeve, W. C. "*Die alte Waschfrau:* A Nineteenth-Century Literary Motif." *Seminar: A Journal of Germanic Studies* XX, No. 2 (May 1984): 95-115.

Explores representations of Chamisso's humble, wise, and self-effacing washerwoman in subsequent German literature.

Riedel, Walter. "The Lost Shadow: Henry Kreisel's and Carl Weiselberger's Use of Adelbert von Chamisso's Literary Motif." *Canadian Review of Comparative Literature* XIV, No. 2 (June 1987): 211-22.

Discusses the adaptation of Chamisso's theme of a lost shadow to the contexts of exile.

Zeldner, Max. "A Note on 'Schlemiel.'" *The German Quarterly* XXVI, No. 2 (April 1953): 115-17.

Probes the origins of the term *schlemiel* (or *schlemihl*) as an unlucky, clumsy, or simple person.

William Hazlitt

1778-1830

English essayist, critic, and biographer. For additional information on Hazlitt's life and career, see *NCLC*, Volume 29.

INTRODUCTION

William Hazlitt was one of the leading prose writers of the Romantic period. Influenced by the concise social commentary in Joseph Addison's eighteenth-century magazine, the *Spectator*, and by the personal tone of the essays of Michel de Montaigne, Hazlitt was one of the most celebrated practitioners of the "familiar" essay. Characterized by conversational diction and personal opinion on topics ranging from English poets to washerwomen, the style of Hazlitt's critical and autobiographical writings has greatly influenced methods of modern writing on aesthetics. His literary criticism, particularly on the Lake poets, has also provided readers with a lens through which to view the work of his Romantic contemporaries.

Biographical Information

Hazlitt was born in Wem, Shropshire, and educated by his father, a Unitarian minister whose radical political convictions influenced the reformist principles that Hazlitt maintained throughout his life. In 1793 Hazlitt entered Hackney Theological College, a Unitarian seminary, where he studied philosophy and rhetoric and began writing the treatise on personal identity titled *An Essay on the Principles of Human Action* (1805). During this time Hazlitt began to question his Christian faith and, considering himself unsuited to the ministry, withdrew from the College and returned to Wem.

In 1798 Hazlitt was introduced to Samuel Taylor Coleridge whose eloquence and intellect inspired him to develop his own talents for artistic expression. Shortly afterward he followed the example of his older brother, John, and began to pursue a career as a painter. Hazlitt lived in Paris and studied the masterpieces exhibited in the Louvre, particularly portraits painted by such Italian masters as Raphael and Leonardo, whose technique he adopted. Commissioned by Coleridge and William Wordsworth to paint their portraits, Hazlitt spent the summer of 1803 at their homes in the Lake District. His political views and quarrelsome nature, however, offended the poets. Moreover, his moral conduct was suspect,

and his friendship with them ended when he was forced to leave the Lake District in fear of reprisals for his assault on a woman. As a painter, Hazlitt achieved little success. He moved to London in 1804 and began to direct his energies toward writing.

In London Hazlitt became a close friend of Charles and Mary Lamb, at whose weekly social gatherings he became acquainted with literary society. Through the Lambs he also met Sarah Stoddart, whom he married in 1808. During this time Hazlitt wrote philosophical works that were criticized for their dense prose style. In 1811 Hazlitt began working as a journalist; he held the positions of parliamentary correspondent for the *Morning Chronicle,* drama critic and political essayist for Leigh Hunt's *Examiner,* and columnist for the *Edinburgh Review.* The liberal political views expressed in Hazlitt's writing incurred resentment from the editors of and contributors to Tory journals such as *Blackwood's Magazine* and the *Quarterly Review,* who attacked Hazlitt's works and his character. In 1818 Hazlitt published a collection of his lectures on English literature and in 1822 John Scott of the *London Magazine* invited him to contribute essays to a feature entitled "Table-Talk." The reflective pieces he wrote were well received and are now among Hazlitt's most acclaimed works. During this period of success, however, Hazlitt's marriage was failing and he became involved in an unfortunate affair with the daughter of an innkeeper. He chronicled his obsession with this young woman in *Liber Amoris; or, the New Pygmalion* (1823). After a divorce from his wife, Hazlitt entered into a second unsuccessful marriage with a rich widow. He continued to write until his death in 1830, producing numerous essays, a series of sketches on the leading men of letters of the early nineteenth century entitled *The Spirit of the Age* (1825), and a biography of Napoleon Bonaparte (1826-30).

Major Works

Hazlitt's most important works are often divided into two categories: literary criticism and familiar essays. Of his literary criticism Hazlitt wrote, "I say what I think: I think what I feel. I cannot help receiving certain impressions from things; and I have sufficient courage to declare (somewhat abruptly) what they are." Representative of his critical style is *Characters of Shakespeare's Plays* (1817), which contains subjective, often panegyrical commentary on such individual characters as Macbeth, Othello, and Hamlet. This work introduces Hazlitt's concept of "gusto," a term he used to refer to qualities of passion and energy that he considered necessary to great art. In accord with his impressionistic approach to literature, Hazlitt's concept of gusto also suggests that a passionate and energetic response is the principal criterion for gauging whether or not a work achieves greatness. Hazlitt felt that Shakespeare's sonnets lacked gusto and judged them as passionless and unengaging despite the "desperate cant of modern criticism." Hazlitt was no less opinionated on the works of his contemporaries. In the final section of *Lectures on the English Poets* (1812) he criticized Coleridge and Wordsworth, whose emphasis on nature and the common aspects of life acknowledged, in his view, "no excellence but that which supports its own pretensions." In addition to literature, Hazlitt also focused on drama and art in his critical essays, many of which are collected in *A View of the English Stage* (1818) and *Sketches of the Principal Picture-Galleries in England* (1824).

The many and varied familiar essays that Hazlitt wrote for magazine publication and collected in the volumes of *The Round Table, Table-Talk,* and *The Plain Speaker* are usually considered his finest works. Critics differentiate between the essays of *The Round Table* and those in *Table-Talk* and *The Plain Speaker:* the former contain observations on "Literature, Men, and Manners" in a style that tends to imitate the essays of Addison and Montaigne, while the latter focus on Hazlitt's personal experiences in a more original, conversational style. Often beginning with an aphorism, Hazlitt's familiar essays are characterized by informal diction and an emotional tone. This informal style, in Hazlitt's words, "promises a greater variety and richness, and perhaps a greater sincerity, than could be attained by a more precise and scholastic method." Hazlitt described his essays as "experimental" rather than "dogmatical," in that he preferred to use the model of common conversation to discuss ordinary human experiences rather than to write in what he believed was the abstract and artificial style of conventional nonfiction prose. Among other things, Hazlitt's essays express discomfort with his reputation as irascible ("On Good Nature"), attack those who question his abilities as a writer ("The Indian Juggler"), extol the benefits of common sense, which, he felt, comprises "true knowledge" ("On the Ignorance of the Learned"), and otherwise defend his character.

Critical Reception

Hazlitt's critics had a wide range of reactions to the style and content of his familiar writing. Hazlitt's political opinions caused bitter antagonism with Coleridge and Wordsworth, as well as a great majority of his countrymen. Modern critics Harold Bloom and Lionel Trilling, however, consider Hazlitt to be "the pre-eminent master in English" in the genre of the familiar essay. In addition, many modern critics note Hazlitt's unique ability to write on a wide range of literary subjects with a depth of taste John Keats considered one of "three things superior in the modern world."

While modern literary historians generally agree on Hazlitt's acumen as a critic and essayist, lively debate has continued since Hazlitt's death on the merit of *Liber Amoris,* which—for good or ill—has become Hazlitt's most puzzling legacy. An account of Hazlitt's infatuation with Sarah Walker, *Liber Amoris* has been considered alternatively a pathetic attempt at catharsis, a precursor of Freudian psychoanalytic method, a personal confession, an analysis of the idea of infatuation, a critique of Romanticism, and, according to Gerald Lahey, "a parable of the entire Romantic period trying to come to terms with its flawed visionary conception of reality." Recently the critical treatment of *Liber Amoris* has become something of a gauge for determining the relevance of Hazlitt's familiar style for contemporary readers: if this, the most personal of Hazlitt's writings, has merit beyond its autobiographical curiosity, the familiar essay may remain an effective genre in the modern period and Hazlitt's position as a forebearer of modern literary practices will be secured.

PRINCIPAL WORKS

An Essay on the Principles of Human Action (essay) 1805

A Reply to the "Essay on Population," by the Rev. T. R. Malthus (essay) 1807

Characters of Shakespeare's Plays (criticism) 1817

The Round Table: A Collection of Essays on Literature, Men, and Manners. 2 vols. [with Leigh Hunt] (essays) 1817

Lectures on the English Poets (criticism) 1818

A View of the English Stage (criticism) 1818

Lectures on the English Comic Writers (criticism) 1819

Letter to William Gifford, Esq. (letter) 1819

Political Essays, with Sketches of Public Characters (essays) 1819

Lectures Chiefly on the Dramatic Literature of the Age of Elizabeth (criticism) 1820

Table-Talk. 2 vols. (essays) 1821-22

Characteristics: In the Manner of Rochefoucauld's Maxims (aphorisms) 1823

Liber Amoris; or, the New Pygmalion (dialogues and letters) 1823

Sketches on the Principal Picture-Galleries in England (essays) 1824

The Spirit of the Age (essays) 1825

Notes of a Journey through France and Italy (travel essays) 1826

The Plain Speaker: Opinions on Books, Men, and Things. 2 vols. (essays) 1826

The Life of Napoleon Bonaparte. 4 vols. (biography) 1826-30

Conversations of James Northcote, Esq., R. A. (dialogues) 1830

Literary Remains of the Late William Hazlitt. 2 vols. (essays) 1836

Sketches and Essays (essays) 1839; also published as *Men and Manners,* 1852

Winterslow: Essays and Characters Written There (essays) 1850

The Complete Works of William Hazlitt. 21 vols. (essays, criticism, letters, dialogues, and biography) 1930-34

The Letters of William Hazlitt (letters) 1978

CRITICISM

Robert Ready (essay date 1975)

SOURCE: "The Logic of Passion: Hazlitt's *Liber Amoris,*" in *Studies in Romanticism,* Vol. 14, No. 1, Winter, 1975, pp. 41-57.

[*In the following essay, Ready evaluates* Liber Amoris *as a literary exploration into the nature of the sympathetic imagination.*]

No matter what their attitudes toward his involvement with Sarah Walker, most readers of Hazlitt's *Liber Amoris; or, The New Pygmalion* (1823) have been more concerned with the book as biography than they have with the book as literature.[1] Assuming that Hazlitt's only sustained narrative, and one of his longest works, can be viewed critically as well as biographically, I hope to demonstrate the integral position of *Liber Amoris* in Hazlitt's recurrent theme of the sympathetic imagination and to sketch the chief structural and imagistic characteristics of the text.

I

In **"On the Spirit of Obligations"** (1823), Hazlitt responded to the hostile reception *Liber Amoris* received. "What I would say to any friend who may be disposed to foretel a general outcry against any work of mine, would be to request him to judge and speak of it for himself, as he thinks it deserves" (XII, 79).[2] If we accede to this request, by examining *Liber Amoris* within the context of Hazlitt's other writings, we may find it illuminating to determine what connection the work has to the theme many commentators find at the center of the Hazlitt canon. From the time he wrote *An Essay on the Principles of Human Action* (1805), "the natural disinterestedness of the human mind," or the sympathetic imagination, was the fundamental proposition of Hazlitt's thinking and writing. This statement needs multiple qualification beyond the scope of this essay, but essentially, his belief that egoism can and must be transcended by the conjunction of feeling and imagination germinates the convictions and the dramatic tensions of Hazlitt's morality, politics, criticism and familiar essays. "Hazlitt's principle of the sympathetic imagination," writes Ralph Wardle, " . . . is, in fact, the keystone of most of his thinking, political and aesthetic as well as philosophical. For he recognized his own sympathetic imagination as the noblest of his faculties: thanks to it he could *feel with* other human beings, real or fictional. . . . "[3]

Liber Amoris is about sympathy in a negative way, a retelling of the Pygmalion legend as a dramatization of an unsympathetic imagination, a lover's attempt to force an earthly girl into the mold of a goddess. The book is Hazlitt's major demonstration of passion blocking the sympathetic perception of an existence separate from one's own.

H. . . . I would gladly die for you.

S. That would give me no pleasure. But indeed you greatly overrate my power.

H. Then that is because you are merciful, and would spare frail mortals who might die with gazing.

S. I have no power to kill.

H. . . . if such is thy sweetness where thou dost not love, what must thy love have been? I cannot think how any man, having the heart of one, could go and leave it.

S. No one did, that I know of.

H. . . . By Heaven, you are an angel! You look like one at this instant! Do I not adore you—and have I merited this return?

S. I have repeatedly answered that question. You sit and fancy things out of your own head, and then lay them to my charge.

(IX, 101, 102, 103, 108)

The modern term "pedestalism" accurately describes H's vision of S. Each time his insistence that she be what he says she is to him crowds her and each time her curt responses guard the little room he leaves her.[4] Often enough she tells him to come down, or at least to let her come down from on high. When he says, "Thou art to me more than thy whole sex," she replies straight enough, "I require no such sacrifices" (IX, 101). *Liber Amoris,* then, is a record of what Hazlitt knows to be a most basic human failing—the inability to allow a person to be other than what we want her (or him) to be.

Benjamin Robert Haydon wrote to Mary Russell Mitford that Hazlitt meant "with certain arrangements" to publish his conversations with Sarah Walker and his letters to P. G. Patmore "as a tale of character."[5] Given H's bitter "a more complete experiment on character was never made" (IX, 160), the tale may seem to be the woman's, yet the sheer preponderance of H's dialogue and first-person narration shows the focus to be on the man. Intellectually, Hazlitt had long rued the sight of a man trapping himself in his own fixed ideas. In an aside to **"Mr. Kean's Iago"** (1814), he wrote of those "whose romantic generosity and delicacy ought not to be sacrificed to the baseness of their nature, but who treading securely the flowery path, marked out for them by poets and moralists, the licensed artificers of fraud and lies, are dashed to pieces down the precipice, and perish without help" (XX, 401). How ideals of love can become obsessive is explained in an essay of the following year. **"Mind and Motive"** (1815) argues against self-interest as the dominant principle of action by citing instances of self-destructive behavior. John Kinnaird has demonstrated in what way Hazlitt's theory of the natural benevolence of the mind was finally matched by his realization that the mind can just as naturally sympathize with "power," that is, with an act not conducive to its own or another's good.[6] In **"Mind and Motive"** Hazlitt writes, "The two most predominant principles in the mind, besides sensibility and self-interest, are imagination and self-will, or (in general) the love of strong excitement, both in thought and action." He continues: "The attention which the mind gives to its ideas is not always owing to the gratification derived from them, but to the strength and truth of the impressions themselves, *i.e.,* to their involuntary power over the mind. This observation will account for a very general principle in the mind, which cannot, we conceive, be satisfactorily explained in any other way, we mean *the power of fascination.*" As an instance of the involuntary power of imagination, Hazlitt cites "the necessity which lovers have for confidants, auricular confession," and he concludes: "There are a thousand passions and fancies that thwart our purposes and disturb our repose . . . they assimilate all objects to the gloom of our own thoughts, and make the will a party against itself. This is one chief source of most of the passions that prey like vultures on the heart, and embitter human life" (XX, 44-47). We see that long before he met Sarah Walker, Hazlitt planted a warning before the "flowery path" and gave evidence that imagination can veer into destructive passion.

Even at the time of Hazlitt's intense misery over Sarah Walker, he occasionally shows a double perspective on what was happening to him. **"On the Conduct of Life,"** written in February, 1822, in Scotland, shows him in a black mood, but more importantly it shows him observing the irrational self-laceration of his obsession. He advises his son, to whom this essay is addressed, to choose a woman carefully in order to avoid ridicule and a lack of understanding and sympathy: "We trifle with, make sport of, and despise those who are attached to us, and follow those that fly from us. 'We hunt the wind, we worship a statue, cry aloud to the desert'" (XVII, 98-99). The quotation, varied from Ambrosio's eulogy for the shepherd Chrysostom in *Don Quixote,* functions ironically if we remember Marcela's plea that she is not responsible for the self-destructive passion of Chrysostom.[7] In a stylized passage that he later suppressed from **"On the Conduct of Life,"** Hazlitt warns his son not to "let your blood stagnate in some deep metaphysical question, or refine too much in your ideas of the sex, forgetting yourself in a dream of exalted perfection" (XVII, 396).

The literary significance, however, of the "book of love" Hazlitt formed out of his dream of Sarah Walker emerges in part from its kinship with some of the literary subjects of the time. P. P. Howe states that *Liber Amoris* is Hazlitt's *"Werther* or *Nouvelle Héloise"* (IX, 263). The influence of these recognizable antecedents on Hazlitt ought not shift attention away from the distinct nature of *Liber Amoris* as a work concerning imaginative projection in love. This theme places *Liber Amoris* in a tradition of writing that emerges distinctly in Hazlitt's own period and becomes particularly central to twentieth-century works. Thus in England, *Liber Amoris* suggests the Romantic preoccupation with a certain figure of woman which produced Blake's "Tirzah," Coleridge's "Lewti" and "Christabel," and Keats's "Lamia" and "La Belle Dame." In France Benjamin Constant published *Adolphe* in 1816, a work that also makes structural use of the device of an "editor" publishing the manuscript of a love affair of a man now dead. It has also been noted that Stendhal and Hazlitt had some correspondence prior to this period, that Stendhal's *De l'amour* appeared in 1822 and that Stendhal's theory of crystallization, by which one projects attributes onto one's beloved, finds perfect embodiment in *Liber Amoris.* It is doubtful, though, that Hazlitt knew *De l'amour* at this time, and he did not really come to know Stendhal until the two met in 1824.[8] A review of *De l'amour* did appear in the *New Monthly Magazine* at the end of 1822 (the same magazine in which Hazlitt's **"On Great and Little Things"** appeared in 1822, an essay which is a notable example of crystallization in its long reference to Sarah Walker). Hazlitt could have read this skeptical review that summarized Stendhal's theory of crystallization and the progressive stages of love. The review ended by exhorting "M. Beyle" to flesh out his theory in a novel.[9]

Like *De l'amour, Liber Amoris* should be read as one of the earliest studies of the projective psychology of love. I use the word "study" advisedly, because obviously Hazlitt did not discover the literary material inherent in the projective psychology of love. That material is as old as the Pygmalion legend itself, and one could trace Pygmalion motifs through all of love literature. But as a "tale of character," an extensive treatment of the particular trouble the lover's imagination gets him into, *Liber Amoris* previews a twentieth-century interest in the phenomenon.

To read Thomas Hardy's *The Well-Beloved: A Sketch of a Temperament* (1897) is to find the closest literary analogue to Hazlitt's book; both delineate temperaments that try to duplicate their experience in art with intractable human material.[10] Three other writers should be mentioned: Proust, whose narrator projects his youthful love fantasies onto Gilberte and whose character Swann forges an unlikely idol from Odette; Yeats, who frequently employs themes similar to Hazlitt's Pygmalion theme in such poems as "The Hero, the Girl and the Fool," "The Statues," "The Mask," "Towards Break of Day," "The Grey Rock," "A Memory of Youth," "On Woman," "Broken Dreams," "The Tower" (Part II), "Among School Children," and "The Living Beauty"; and Sartre, whose overview of the futility of the love enterprise

is that love is perpetual conflict, ultimately an impossibility, since the ideal of both lovers is the appropriation of the beloved's "freedom" or "subjectivity" (*Being and Nothingness,* "Concrete Relations with Others," Section I). Finally, we are not very far away from Jung's concept of the anima when we find Hazlitt writing in **"On Great and Little Things"** (1822), "The image of some fair creature is engraven on my inmost soul . . ." (VIII, 236), and in **"On the Knowledge of Character"** (1821): "The idol we fall down and worship is an image familiar to our minds. It has been present to our waking thoughts, it has haunted us in our dreams, like some fairy vision" (VIII, 311).[11]

I doubt that *Liber Amoris* was read by any of these other writers; nor is my point to read these writers back into Hazlitt. Yet to go on reading *Liber Amoris* as if it served only Hazlitt's personal ends of confession or catharsis is to tear it out of its proper literary perspective and to treat it as a freak. The frequency with which modern writers have turned to the subject of love's projective psychology shows that *Liber Amoris* anticipates later works as much as it looks to Rousseau and Goethe. It is one of the first extended treatments in a line of modern writing on men who try to make women fit their illusions. In this modern line, Hazlitt's special perspective is that love's projective imagination is an unsympathetic imagination. He does not subtitle his book "The New Pygmalion" without irony. Hazlitt and his character H are the "new" Pygmalions in that Pygmalion's statue was given breath and life, whereas the new Pygmalions have to learn so painfully that their beloveds already have a life and breath of their own.

II

W. E. Henley remarked that *Liber Amoris* "is unique in English."[12] The anonymous *Examiner* critic of a hundred years previous had written: "*Liber Amoris* is a novelty in the English language." "Q." bore down precisely when he summarized the book as the tale of a "highly gifted individual, who having suited himself with a train of very tasteful and elegant associations in relation to female beauty, perfection, and sentiment, is led by a few casual coincidences to infer a perfect adaptation, where nothing of the kind existed."[13] *Liber Amoris* moves on a train of association, and much of the book's great uniqueness, its novelty, results from this movement. We may characterize the structure of Hazlitt's book from his understanding of the associative logic of passion.

Writing of Shakespeare, Hazlitt says that "the greatest strength of genius is shewn in describing the strongest passions." Shakespeare's descriptions of the strongest passions, as in *Cymbeline,* work by "the force of natural association, a particular train of thought suggesting different inflections of the same predominant feeling, melting into, and strengthening one another, like chords in music." ***Liber Amoris,*** the product of Hazlitt's strongest passion, works in this manner. It is the manner of what Hazlitt calls, in his essay on *King Lear,* "the logic of passion": "We see the ebb and flow of the feeling, its pauses and feverish starts, its impatience of opposition, its accumulating force when it has time to recollect itself, the manner in which it avails itself of every passing word or gesture, its haste to repel insinuation, the alternate contraction and dilatation of the soul" (IV, 271, 184, 259).

For Hazlitt, Shakespeare is the very model of the sympathetic imagination. Shakespeare's plays embody the logic of passion because Shakespeare has sympathized with the ebb and flow, the fits and starts of passion. The passion in ***Liber Amoris*** is the passion of an unsympathetic imagination, the obsession of a lover who refuses to accept a woman as she is. It takes sympathy to follow the logic of this obsession and to recreate that logic in a literary structure. Hazlitt the artist sympathizes with the associative logic of H's unsympathetic passion. The result is the particular structure of ***Liber Amoris.***

Hazlitt presents the logic of H's passion in three parts, each of which offers a different perspective on character and action. The work does not have a linear structure. Its progression is a series of movements backward and forward. One result of this kind of progression is a number of shifts in the base line of time, that is, in the time of the narrator in each of the book's three sections.[14]

In the fourth conversation of Part I, we learn that S has been rejected by a previous lover. The fifth scene doubles back in time to depict the first time S told of this rejection. This scene not only precedes the fourth chronologically, but also the second scene. For in the fifth scene, S says that "he is one to whom I feel the sincerest affection, and ever shall, though he is far distant" (IX, 104). In the second scene H imagines himself in Italy: "Ah! dearest creature, I shall be 'far distant from you,' as you once said of another, but you will not think of me as of him, 'with the sincerest affection'" (IX, 101). This shift in time points out that the associative logic of passion remembers conversations according to their importance in the development of the relationship rather than their order in time. Short and honed-down, the scenes of Part I enrich one another, but they are without sequence, except for the last two.

The time when the beginning letters of Part II are written overlaps with the time when the final conversations of Part I are written. In the first letter of Part II, H tells C. P., "I have begun a book of our conversations" and he describes the quarrel that made up the penultimate conversation of Part I (IX, 116-117). Since we are then to think of H's letters in Part II as beginning a good deal before most of the conversations took shape, the result is that the process of writing ***Liber Amoris*** becomes part of the dramatic action. The base line in time of Part II overtakes Part I when Letter III of Part I reports that the conversations have been finished.

Time displacement avoids straight linear narration in favor of a fragmented or angular presentation of a shattering experience. Since no one perspective sees multiple angles of the exprience, Hazlitt forces our perception of character and action to fragment. We must supply our own continuity. (Thus, Letter VI of Part II is written on a steamboat going back to Scotland; that H has returned to London and thrown a violent scene goes quite unexplained until Part III.) The continuity Hazlitt constructs is psychological rather than narrative; it is the continuity of the logic of passion in H's associating mind as he remembers and writes.

This associating mind, to return to the incisive remark of the *Examiner* reviewer, is that of "a highly gifted individual," who has "suited himself with a train of very tasteful and elegant associations in relation to female beauty, perfection, and sentiment." Hazlitt has significantly altered his own personality in creating H. Not only, for example, has he edited out the obscenities in his original letters to Patmore, but he has also given a good deal more coherence to some of the disconnected ravings we find in the original letters.[15] The cooler, more even H who results from this revision is indeed a tasteful, elegant and highly gifted individual. Hazlitt's character is a man who often perceives life through the mediation of art. He continually thinks in terms of previous literature, of writers, and of images both plastic and literary.

The first conversation, a microcosm of the whole, demonstrates the complex mediation by which H transforms S. "The Picture" immediately allies with the Pygmalion motif. H shows S a miniature by Raphael.

> H. Don't you think it like yourself?
>
> S. No: it's much handsomer than I can pretend to be.
>
> H. That's because you don't see yourself with the same eyes that others do.

She changes the subject, asking what the picture is. He replies: "Some say it is a Madona [*sic*]; others call it a Magdalen, and say you may distinguish the tear upon the cheek, though no tear is there. But it seems to me more like Raphael's St. Cecilia, 'with looks commercing with the skies,' than anything else" (99-100).[16]

His reply is packed. By being associated with the patron saint of music, S now belongs to its harmony, and the other dialogues sometimes speak of her in terms of music. H's own St. Cecilia also has "'looks commercing with the skies,'" that is, her harmony bridges to higher harmony, perhaps the music of the spheres. The quotation is line 39 of Milton's *Il Penseroso,* where the poet addresses Melancholy, the "pensive Nun, devout and pure" (l. 31). S's reticence may suggest melancholy; but following immediately after the Cecilia reference, the quotation, by evoking *Il Penseroso* re-enforces the high seriousness of H's vision of S. Furthermore, H seems to refer to the whole passage from Milton:

> Com, but keep thy wonted state,
> With eev'n step and musing gate,
> And looks commercing with the skies,
> Thy rapt soul sitting in thine eyes:
> There held in holy passion still,
> Forget thy self to Marble, till
> With a sad Leaden downward cast,
> Thou fix them on the earth as fast.
>
> (ll. 37-44)

Liber Amoris makes a good deal of S's graceful manner of walking and the singular expression of her eyes. It persistently uses "marble" to describe her, sometimes adoringly, sometimes bitterly. And of course, something akin to "holy passion" is attributed to her several times. Also, as this conversation ends, H speaks of "your mouth full of suppressed sensibility, your downcast eyes, the soft blush upon that cheek" (99-100). The features he sees could well be those of the "pensive Nun, devout and pure," and S's "downcast eyes" recall specifically line 43 of the poem (with perhaps another echo, Spenser's "Epithalamion," l. 234, "her eyes still fastened on the ground").

In addition to this Miltonic mode; other literary references abound in *Liber Amoris.* H is Aeneas: "But even in another world, I suppose you would turn from me" (103; see *The Aeneid,* Book VI, 469-473). He sarcastically refers her to the Carthaginian wars: "Her's is the Fabian method of making love and conquests" (118). As he returns to Scotland on "a sort of spectre-ship, moving on through an infernal lake, without wind or tide, by some necromantic power," like the Mariner he feels "the eternity of punishment in this life" (121); and, like the Coleridge of "Dejection: An Ode," he has "conversed too long with abstracted truth" (124). One has, in fact, only to glance at Howe's notes to see the fabric H weaves out of literary and mythological references throughout *Liber Amoris.* "Those lines in Tibullus seem to have been written on purpose for her. . . . Or what do you think of those in a modern play, which might actually have been composed with an eye to this little trifler—" (143). When he asks S's sister to convey three books to S "in lieu of three volumes of my own writings" and the young girl replies, "'AND THOSE ARE THE ONES THAT SHE PRIZES THE MOST!'" [*sic*], H swells into "If there were ever words spoken that could revive the dead . . ." (148-149). This almost hyper-literary sensibility, so imbued with quotations that give substance to his unreciprocated love, and so betokened by the physical presence of books themselves, has only to be equipped with several passages relating his communion with or disjunction from the picturesque and sublime in nature (125, 126, 128-131, 138, 140-141), to create the complete man of feeling who projects the world from his own center and whose fallacies are truly pathetic.

Literary references, the overlay of nature topoi familiar from the literature of the time, books, and the reader's unbroken awareness of the process of this epistolary work are further reinforced by a complex system of image and symbol. The overall illusion-reality theme is elaborated in imagery of two main types: what I will term a lamia group (such as serpent, poison, witch, enchantress) and a Pygmalion group (such as statue, picture, marble, stone). There are also brief but important instances of flower and weed images. Hazlitt's complex uses of imagery flow naturally from the sub-title, "The New Pygmalion." The associative logic of H's passion continually works changes on a set body of images. I will first sketch the movement of the imagery in Parts I and II in order to devote space to imagery in the climactic Part III.

The fourth conversation, "The Flageolet," first develops the Pygmalion motif: "Cruel girl! you . . . resemble some graceful marble statue. . . . I could worship you at this moment." He reverses the motif in an important pre-figuring of a crisis point in Part III: "You see you can mould me as you like" (103). The sixth conversation, "The Quarrel," concludes by introducing the imagery which Hazlitt later inverts to close *Liber Amoris:* "Thou wert to me a little tender flower, blooming in the wilderness of my life; and though thou should'st turn out a weed, I'll not fling thee from me, while I can help it." He then entreats her, "Kiss me, thou little sorceress!" (109). As the conversations began about a picture, they end focusing on a statue, when H asks if he resembles her old lover:

> S. No, Sir. . . . But there was a likeness.
>
> H. To whom?
>
> S. To that little image! (*looking intently on a small bronze figure of Buonaparte on the mantelpiece*).

The Pygmalion theme is now complete; they both have their images. H's final gloss ironically counterpoints the theme: "[. . . And then I added 'How odd it was that the God of my idolatry should turn out to be like her Idol, and said it was no wonder that the same face which awed the world should conquer the sweetest creature in it!' . . .]" (111-112). Part I ends with two letters followed by a note "Written in a blank leaf of Endymion" (presumably Keats's); he wishes for the picture "to kiss and talk to" and begs pardon for the quarrel: "I hope the *little image* made it up between us &c" (113-114). That the note is written in a blank leaf of *Endymion* allies H with the prototype of a man who falls in love with an ideal woman. And the note may also have further connection with Keats's *Lamia* volume (1820): "—But by her dove's eyes and serpent-shape, I think she does not hate me; by her smooth forehead and her crested hair, I own I love her; by her soft looks and queen-like grace (which men might fall down and worship) I swear to live and die for her!" (114).

In Letter I of Part II, H tells C. P., "I have begun a book of our conversations (I mean mine and the statue's . . .)." H recounts the quarrel swiftly, prefaced by "She cajoled me out of my little Buonaparte as cleverly as possible," and concluding with "So I must come back for it." H encloses the first of the two letters to S that ended Part I; he remarks that the letter "might move a stone" (116-117). Letter II encloses her frigid reply and begins to dress his fears and imaginings. He is of two minds about her: "I suspect her grievously of being an arrant jilt, to say no more—yet I love her dearly." His role as cynical lover is contained in the phrase "before you set about your exposition of the new Apocalypse of the new Calypso," certainly a facile remark but in line with the enchantress-witch complex. H goes on to relate additional conversations, but he now remembers her remarks as nonsequiturs or as coy and ambiguous: "After all, what is there in her but a pretty figure, and that you can't get a word out of her" (117-118).

Despair in the third letter intensifies the "arrant jilt" suspicion through the lamia imagery: "If I knew she was a mere abandoned creature, I should try to forget her; but till I do know this, nothing can tear me from her, I have drank in poison from her lips too long— alas! mine do not poison again" (119). Reassured in Letter IV that S is chaste, H raises the Pygmalion strain: "my heart's idol . . . the dear saint . . . the sweet apparition" (119-20). This relative altitude continues in Letter V as H launches into her praise: "I could devour the little witch. If she had plague-spot on her, I could touch the infection: if she was in a burning fever, I could kiss her, and drink death as I have drank life from her lips. . . . It is not what she says or what she does—it is herself that I love" (121). The morbid imagery recurs from "The Quarrel," where H exclaimed, "wert thou a wretched wanderer in the street, covered with rags, disease, and infamy, I'd clasp thee to my bosom, and live and die with thee, my love" (109). In Letter VI, the Buonaparte

statue symbolizes S's old lover: she "only played with my credulity till she could find some one to supply the place of her unalterable attachment to *the little image.*" His own Pygmalion sickness worsens as he writes, "I cannot forget *her;* and I can find no other like what *she seemed,*" and as he closes by asking P to see if any reconciliation is possible or if she is "quite marble" (122). Disaffected from nature in Letter VIII—"The sky is marble to my thoughts"—an inanimate figure haunts him: "I wake with her by my side, not as my sweet bedfellow, but as the corpse of my love. . . . " An apostrophe following Letter VIII recasts the theme of the inanimate: "'Stony-hearted' Edinburgh! What are thou to me? . . . City of palaces, or of tombs—a quarry, rather than the habitation of men! . . . Thy cold grey walls reflect back the leaden melancholy of the soul!" (125-126). Thus divorce from both nature and city is expressed in terms of inanimate substance. The logic of passion, through its preoccupation with the hard, unresponsive beloved, links all other things in a chain of similar images.

In Letter IX, H distances himself sufficiently to ponder the illusion-reality split: "fancying a little artful vixen to be an angel and a saint"; "my life (that might have been so happy, had she been what I thought her)"; "For this picture, this ecstatic vision, what have I of late instead as the image of the reality?" The lamia returns: "I see the young witch seated in another's lap, twining her serpent arms round him, her eye glancing and her cheeks on fire. . . . " Even so, he plans still to offer marriage and begs that his letter be seen as "the picture of a half-disordered mind" (127-129). A descriptive passage in Letter X then recasts familiar images: " . . . the river winded its dull, slimy way like a snake along the marshy grounds: and the dim misty tops of Ben Leddi, and the lovely Highlands (woven fantastically of thin air) mocked my embraces and tempted my longing eyes like her, the sole queen and mistress of my thoughts!" Once more, by relating images he has employed for S with images in nature, H expresses the associative psychology of passion. Nature fuses the morbid and the inanimate into a climactic death fantasy: "As I trod the green mountain turf, oh! how I wished to be laid beneath it—in one grave with her—that I might sleep with her in that cold bed, my hand in hers, and my heart for ever still—while worms should taste her sweet body, that I had never tasted!" (130-131).

Letter XI oscillates, as did Letter IX, between hard-hitting analysis of S and dejection at her loss. S is the "well practiced illusion," while H writes of himself, "abased and brutalised as I have been by that Circean cup of kisses, of enchantments, of which I have drunk!" (132). The last mythological reference was to Calypso in Letter II. Choice of witch figures intensifies with H's changing mind about S. The flip reference to Calypso gives way to Circe, whose enchantment was vicious and lethal. Short and business-like, Letter XII directs P to tell M, S's brother-in-law, that H will propose marriage. This letter is followed by pieces entitled "Unaltered Love" and "Perfect Love." The former shows that H is, in a major respect, exactly where he started: " . . . I will make a Goddess of her, and build a temple to her in my heart, and worship her on indestructible altars, and raise statues to her" (133). "From C. P., Esq." then relates the outcome of P's visit to M, to the effect that H ought to come back and propose. Letter XIII is jubilant: "She is an angel from Heaven, and you cannot pretend I ever said a word to the contrary!" He has seen a painting (*Hope Finding Fortune in the Sea*) whose female figure mirrored S— "If it is not the very image of her, I am no judge." With the picture motif returns the statue motif: " . . . I have had her face constantly before me, looking so like some faultless marble statue, as cold, as fixed and graceful as ever statue did" (137-138).

Part III is a self-contained narrative of events between H's sudden visit to London through the final break with S: he returns to London, throws a violent scene following the most distancing reception from S, returns to Scotland until his divorce is finalized, comes back only to see S in the street one day with another man. Part III concludes with H's analysis of her character.

He begins, "My dear K—, It is all over, and I know my fate" (140). Physical motion is also fated in Part III, as a kind of enchantment or magnetism seems to control H, forcing him to play out the drama almost unwittingly. When S is "frank and cordial" to him for the first time—"This of course acted as a spell on me." He goes out with his son, but "I found that I still contrive'd to bend my steps towards her, and I went back to take tea" (143). There follows a maddening interview with S; he snaps, and screams out his anguish. Again he tries to get away and again he is riveted back: " . . . I was no sooner in the street, than the desolation and the darkness became greater, more intolerable; and the eddying violence of my passion drove me back to the source, from whence it sprung" (146). These two motions out and back anticipate the book's climax, where motion is choreographed, the figures encountering one another as if in a passing dream:

> I passed a house in King Street where I had once lived, and had not proceeded many paces, ruminating on chance and change and old times, when I saw her coming towards me. I felt a strange pang at the sight, but I thought her alone. Some people before me moved on, and I saw another person with her. *The murder was out. . . .* We passed at the crossing of the street without speaking. . . . I turned and looked—they also turned and looked—and as if

by mutual consent, we both retrod our steps and passed again, in the same way. I went home. I was stifled.

(157)

After so long in his obsessive maze, the way out comes simply, and the effect is masterful. The two previous movements have solidified its power.

Hazlitt maintains an increasingly symbolic use of the Buonaparte statue before the King Street climax. When H first returns from Scotland, he finds the statue back on his mantelpiece, which he considers "a sort of recognition of old times." He spins the fact that she has kept it into new hope, and the evening when he breaks loose in rage begins as he tries to get S to sit and talk with him. When she refuses, he says, "'Well, then, for the sake of *the little image!*' The appeal seemed to have lost its efficacy; the charm was broken; she remained immoveable" (144). After she leaves, he rails hysterically, and grabbing the statue, smashes it to pieces. The next day he picks up the pieces and sends them contritely to S. He tries to bring the next conversation around to sentimental matters, but she puts him off: "'I was sadly afraid the *little image* was dethroned from her heart, as I had dashed it to the ground the other night.'—'She was neither desperate nor violent'" (152). Upon his return from Scotland, he asks her to get the statue repaired. Within a few days her mother tells him that S is out doing just that: "My heart, my poor fond heart, almost melted within me at this news." The next morning she returns with the statue whole again. They shake hands in reconciliation, "and she went waving out of the room" (155-156). This is the day before King Street, after which we hear no more of the statue, except for one contemptuous reference to the *"little image"* so suddenly displaced from her breast by the new suitor.

Hazlitt continues to orchestrate the other image clusters through Part III. As they first speak of the Buonaparte again: "Her words are few and simple; but you can have no idea of the exquisite, unstudied, irresistible graces with which she accompanies them, unless you can suppose a Greek statue to smile, move, and speak" (143). Poison and death: "I had drank in the poison of her sweetness too long ever to be cured of it; and though I might find it to be poison in the end, it was still in my veins. My only ambition was to be permitted to live with her, and to die in her arms" (147). His fantasy of picking her off the street returns: "I felt that my soul was wedded to hers; and were she a mere lost creature, I would try to snatch her from perdition" (148).

Through Part III, H continues thinking of S in the Pygmalion terms. When he asks her to get the Buonaparte fixed, he marvels at her face, the "finest expression that ever was seen . . . but without speaking a word, without altering a feature. It was like a petrifaction of a human face in the softest moment of passion" (155). Before King Street she is his "earthly Goddess"; afterwards he sees only a "pale cold form" and a "lifeless image" (156, 159). Life has finally left Pygmalion's substance.

The most climactic use of imagery in Part III merges the lamia and Pygmalion groups shortly before the King Street denouement:

> It was a fable. She started up in her own likeness, a serpent in place of a woman. She had fascinated, she had stung me, and had returned to her proper shape, gliding from me after inflicting the mortal wound, and instilling deadly poison into every pore; but her form lost none of its original brightness by the change of character, but was all glittering, beauteous, voluptuous grace. Seed of the serpent or of the woman, she was divine! I felt that she was a witch, and had bewitched me. Fate had enclosed me round about. *I* was transformed too, no longer human (any more than she, to whom I had knit myself) my feelings were marble; my blood was of molten lead; my thoughts on fire. I was taken out of myself, wrapt into another sphere, far from the light of day, of hope, of love. I had no natural affection left; she had slain me, but no other thing had power over me. (153)

We saw the reverse Pygmalion theme briefly in Part I, "The Flageolet." Here in Part III, the metamorphosis of the artist is complete. Hazlitt also ends his book by reversing the flower-weed imagery of "The Quarrel": "Her image seems fast 'going into the wastes of time,' like a weed that the wave bears farther and farther from me. Alas! thou poor hapless weed, when I entirely lose sight of thee, and for ever, no flower will ever bloom on earth to glad my heart again!" (162).

At the end H sees the whole affair as a "frightful illusion" (159). And though, as the final long indictment of S shows, he does not blame himself, he does discern that she resented his vision: "She in fact knows what she is, and recoils from the good opinion or sympathy of others, which she feels to be founded on a deception; so that my overweening opinion of her must have appeared like irony, or direct insult" (162). As difficult as it is for him to believe other than that "she still *is* what she so long *seemed,*" he will not relinquish the original vision for having been tricked and deluded by it. Tortured, he is far from broken, and confesses nothing. The anima, if you will, remains: "I know all this; but what do I gain by it, unless I could find some one with her shape and air, to supply the place of the lovely apparition?" (160).

We may infer that as long as H longs for apparitions he will fail to see real existences. Hazlitt's "tale of character" tells how what is protects itself against what one would have. Wrenched out of his own worst years to be a negative example in his pervasive concern with the practical and aesthetic value of sympathy, *Liber Amoris* articulated the logic of passion and dramatized that no person can successfully appropriate the being of another. Hazlitt spoke from experience in **"On Personal Identity"** (1828) when he wrote that despite a man's high intentions, a woman resents being insistently thought of as something she is not. "We are not," the essay concludes, "to be cozened out of our existence for nothing" (XVII, 273).

Notes

[1] Two recent full-length studies of Hazlitt illustrate this continued neglect of *Liber Amoris*. In well over a hundred pages on the Walker episode in Ralph Wardle's *Hazlitt* (Lincoln: U. of Nebraska Press, 1971), most of the discussion the book receives as a literary work is four pages summarizing the history of its critical reception. Roy Park, *Hazlitt and the Spirit of the Age* (Oxford: Clarendon Press, 1971), does not mention *Liber Amoris*. Herschel Baker, *William Hazlitt* (Cambridge, Mass: Harvard U. Press, 1962), excoriates the "shabby liaison" (p. 410), but he does not evaluate the work beyond positing its function as Hazlitt's "necessary cathartic" (p. 427). In the twentieth century the book has been most extensively defended (but again, not particularly analyzed) by: P. P. Howe, "Hazlitt and 'Liber Amoris'," *The Fortnightly Review,* 99 (1916), 300-310; Catherine Macdonald Maclean, *Born Under Saturn* (New York: Macmillan, 1944); Charles Morgan, *Liber Amoris and Dramatic Criticism* (London: Peter Nevill, 1948); Stanley Jones, "Hazlitt and John Bull: A Neglected Letter," *RES* [*Review of English Studies: A Quarterly Journal of English Literature and the English Language*], 17 (1966), 163-170. Ronald Blythe includes the work in his *William Hazlitt: Selected Writings* (Baltimore: Penguin, 1970).

[2] References to Hazlitt's writings are to *Complete Works of William Hazlitt,* ed. P. P. Howe, 21 vols (London: J. M. Dent and Sons, 1930-34).

[3] Wardle, p. 85, his italics. Park's recent work also reiterates the crucial nature of the concept: "The *Essay,* therefore, established the imagination as the moral faculty, and its central importance in this respect never altered in any of his subsequent ethical writings" (p. 47).

[4] Biographical accounts persist in caricaturing nineteen-year-old Sarah Walker on the basis of the comments Hazlitt ascribes to S. Christopher Salvesen, *Selected Writings of William Hazlitt* (New York: Signet, 1972), p. 14, calls Sarah Walker "intellectually inert"; S, at least, seems quite capable of warding off H's

etherialized, rhetorical view of her. As for the frequent implication that Sarah Walker was a sexual tease, moral disapproval has to contend with another of S's direct statements of her own personality: "I am no prude, Sir" (IX, 108).

[5] *Diary of Benjamin Robert Haydon,* ed. Willard B. Pope, 5 vols, (Cambridge, Mass.: Harvard U. Press, 1960-63), II, 382.

[6] John Kinnaird, "William Hazlitt's Philosophy of the Mind," Diss. Columbia University, 1959, esp. pp. 298-316; see also Kinnaird, "Hazlitt as Poet," *SiR* [*Studies in Romanticism*], 12 (1973), 434n.

[7] Cervantes, *The Adventures of Don Quixote,* Part I, chapters XII-XIV. The quotation occurs in several other essays of the Walker period (VIII, 97, 236; XX, 227) and will also be found in "Mind and Motive" (XX, 50).

[8] See Charles Morgan's introduction to his edition of *Liber Amoris,* pp. 7-28. Robert Vigneron discusses the relationship between Hazlitt and Stendhal and their mutual borrowings in "Stendhal et Hazlitt," *MP* [*Modern Philology: A Journal Devoted to Research in Medieval and Modern Literature*], 35 (1938), 375-414.

[9] "On Love," *New Monthly Magazine,* 5 (1822), 423-431.

[10] The similarity between Hardy's novel and *Liber Amoris* is most apparent in Pierston's relations with the second Avice. She is his washerwoman, and for a time serves him as a domestic in his London lodgings, where he treats her with respect and offers a plan to educate and marry her. At one point he likens her to a Rubens figure, just as H sees S as a Raphael figure.

[11] "Every man carries within him the eternal image of woman, not the image of this or that particular woman, but a definite feminine image. . . . Since this image is unconscious, it is always unconsciously projected upon the person of the beloved, and is one of the chief reasons for passionate attraction or aversion. . . . [This projection often] turns out to be an illusion with destructive consequences . . ." (C. G. Jung, "Marriage as a Psychological Relationship," trans. R. F. Hull, *The Collected Works of C. G. Jung,* ed. Herbert Read et. al., 18 vols. [London: Routledge & Kegan Paul, 1953-], XVII, 198-199). It is worth noting, too, that *Liber Amoris* dramatizes the duality of "overvaluation" and "debasement" that Freud saw in the way men sometimes choose love-objects (see particularly "On the Universal Tendency to Debasement in the Sphere of Love," *The Complete Psychological Works of Sigmund Freud,* trans. and ed. James Strachey, 24 vols. [London: The Hogarth Press and the Institute of Psycho-Analysis, 1953-], XI, 179-190).

[12] W. E. Henley, *Essays* (London: Macmillan, 1921), p. 113.

[13] *The Examiner,* 22 (1823), pp. 315, 313.

[14] Wardle notes that Hazlitt "might even have been anticipating some of the experiments in chronology made by later novelists" (p. 363n).

[15] The changes Hazlitt made in his original material warrant a separate discussion. But one has only to compare LetterV of Part II with its counterpart, the second in the original letters in the edition of *Liber Amoris* "privately printed" by Richard Le Gallienne and W. Carew Hazlitt in 1894, to see that Hazlitt's originally chaotic train of thought became more shaped and pointed in the book. Nothing occurs in *Liber Amoris* to match the harried notations of the acidic little journal Hazlitt kept in March, 1823 (*The Journals of Sarah and William Hazlitt 1822-1823,* ed. Willard Hallam Bonner, The University of Buffalo Studies, XXIV, No. 23, 1959). The overall editing process is most visible in Part II: material from original letters (Le Gallienne) 1, 3, 2, 8, 6, 9, and 11 respectively becomes material for letters 3, 4, 5, 7, 8, 11, and 13 in *Liber Amoris.* Wardle fills in various deletions Le Gallienne and W. Carew Hazlitt made from the original letters (now in the Lockwood Memorial Library of the State University of New York at Buffalo).

[16] Remaining page references, unless otherwise indicated, are to Vol II of *Complete Works.*

Marilyn Butler (essay date 1984)

SOURCE: "Satire and the Images of Self in the Romantic Period: The Long Tradition of Hazlitt's *Liber Amoris,*" in *English Satire and the Satiric Tradition,* edited by Claude Rawson, Basil Blackwell, 1984, pp. 209-25.

[*In this essay, Butler examines the satirical elements that appear in some Romantic writings, as well as the extent to which* Liber Amoris *can be considered a satiric commentary on contemporary doctrines of the imagination.*]

Satire is a mode with which we do not as a rule associate the Romantic period. Among the trees of the literary forest a few scrubs can still be picked out: minor satirical verse like Mathias's *Pursuits of Literature,* Gifford's *Baviad* and *Maeviad,* the contributions of Canning and Frere to *The Anti-Jacobin,* and the Smith brothers' *Rejected Addresses.* These sold well at the time but have not worn well since, for future generations have become convinced that the Spirit of the Age was very different. Symptomatically, the two substantial writers whose bent was unequivocally satirical, Byron and Peacock, are generally represented in the twentieth century as, one way or another, marginal (though some unease is often expressed, very reasonably, at the demotion of Byron that this entails). As satirists, Byron and Peacock attract similar criticisms. They are irresponsible jesters, without clear satirical aims in view, even to themselves, and anachronisms, lacking a proper understanding of the age they were born into.

But an age's self-image may not be as distinct as posterity's view of it. The so-called Romantics did not know at the time that they were supposed to do without satire. Obvious if sometimes superficial changes in fashion had come about with the passing of time and with the marked growth of the educated reading public. Pope's closed couplet had been under attack since the late eighteenth century, and in the early nineteenth century sophisticated writers could no longer appeal with confidence to a social norm and a moral consensus. But it is easy to exaggerate the break with the recent literary past, or with that portion of it we now designate Augustanism. Swift remained a much-admired writer. Byron's well-known tribute to Pope may have been controversial; Scott's even better-advertised tribute to Dryden was less so. Though the writers of the period are often linked with Shakespeare, partly because it is the era of the brilliant Shakespeare criticism of Coleridge and Hazlitt, in their poetry they are more inclined to draw on Milton, who was probably the most admired classic English writer precisely on account of his intellectuality and his public role. If Peacock is to be dismissed as an eccentric, it may not count for much that in a list of favourite great writers he named Rabelais, Burton, Swift, Fielding, and Sterne. It *is* significant, and typical (but not stereotypical), that Lamb and Hazlitt both defended Restoration comedy against those who wanted comedy without 'disagreeables'.

Admittedly it became fashionable to announce, as Shelley and Keats did in very similar terms, 'didactic poetry is my abhorrence'. Satire is not merely didactic, but has to be specifically and pellucidly so, or it cannot be effective. Shelley's poetry remains essentially didactic, and even Keats's seems far more so than he allows; all that these two poets can really be claiming is that their means are generally allusive, fanciful, pictorial, and narrative rather than directly argumentative. Yet even if it is relatively rare for either Shelley or Keats to write formal satires, their sense of the scope and social function of poetry remains in large part traditional. The old questions asked by Jonson in 'To Penshurst', by Dryden in *Absalom and Achitophel*, and by Pope in *The Dunciad*—how to judge a good way of life or a good man or a good poet—are also asked by Byron in *Childe Harold* III

and IV, by Shelley in *Prometheus Unbound* and *The Triumph of Life*, and by Keats in *The Fall of Hyperion*.

Nineteenth-century readers gradually came to expect good creative writing to be self-referential, and did not cavil if writers took themselves and their problems very seriously. Readers also became less inclined to want, and less inclined to notice, satire, intellectual analysis, debate, and controversy. But in what we now call the Romantic period, writing directly about the self was still problematical. On the one hand, the reader seems to demand, and the writer to strive for, a new fullness of self-expression: the qualities prized include sincerity, emotional intensity, and particularity in rendering place, especially the haunts of childhood. On the other hand, as this paper will demonstrate, any work which appears to have self-expression or self-validation as its goal is liable to set up an ethical backlash, a complaint that the individual is not autonomous, that society has claims, and that artists are as much bound by moral law as anyone else. This hostile response is not confined to the reviews, where it would be predictable, since many were written for sections of the public suspicious of the arts and of the increasingly self-important claims of artists. The critique of Romantic autobiography, which is also a critique of a growing aestheticism, seems interesting precisely because it occurs within the major poetry and prose of the first three decades of the century. It is the proposition of this paper that some well-known Romantic self-portraits are satirical portraits, and even the rest frequently a source of satire in others.

For modern critics, Wordsworth's *Prelude* has a central position in English Romanticism. Its innovation is to adapt epic, a genre concerned with society, to the topic of a single private life: an epic about the growth of a poet's mind is, properly, a contradiction in terms. Where Milton's *Paradise Lost* was ornamented with similes which spanned the story of mankind in time and space, in fact and fiction, Wordsworth derives his illusion of depth from 'spots of time' which throw out their unexpected lines of sight into the poet's own private experience. Classic antecedents for *The Prelude* are identifiable, not only by Milton but by autobiographers like St Augustine and Rousseau. Citing them normally operates to stress that Wordsworth's treatment is revolutionary not only in his 'naturalness' but in his self-absorption, raised to the level of a new metaphysical system.

As it happened, Wordsworth's contemporaries outside the circle of his friends did not know *The Prelude*, but they did know 'Tintern Abbey' (1798), that intense exploration of private memory and of the poet's relationship with his sister, and *The Excursion* (1814), in which the poet seems to present himself in the guise of two personae, the Wanderer and the Solitary. The preface and first book of *The Excursion* (1814), firmly declaring its subject to be the inner life, functioned for younger contemporaries as *The Prelude* does for us. The verse preface speaks of 'ill sights' among 'the tribes | And fellowships of men . . . the fierce confederate storm | Of sorrow, barricadoed evermore | Within the walls of cities' (ll. 73, 78), and in these circumstances it declares that it is better to muse in solitude:

> Of the individual Mind that keeps her own
> Inviolate retirement, subject there
> To conscience only, and the law supreme
> Of that Intelligence which governs all—
> I sing—'fit audience let me find though few'.
>
> (l. 19)

The quotation from Milton, with his public and universal subject, must have struck alert readers as paradoxical. It was on this kind of evidence that Keats, following Hazlitt's lead, thought of Wordsworth as the Egotistical Sublime.

And yet, other poems by Wordsworth, also well known at the time, themselves ridiculed the notion of the self-satisfied and self-absorbed poet. An unmistakably detached and even satirical attitude to the poet's persona emerges in 'Anecdote for Fathers' and 'We Are Seven', both of which appeared in *Lyrical Ballads* in 1798, and above all in 'Resolution and Independence', first published in 1807, which humblingly contrasts the conceited, absorbed literary man with the leech-gatherer, representative of humanity at one with nature. The curious fact is, then, that Wordsworth himself was a pioneer critic of that notion of the solipsistic poet with which readers of his own day and ours have identified him. And not uninstructed readers alone: Wordsworth's supposedly uncritical image of himself became an important negative inspiration to Shelley and Keats.

Shelley's poem *Alastor* (1816), written the year after *The Excursion* appeared, features a Narrator who tells the story of another idealistic young poet. The latter figure, whom we can distinguish from the Narrator by calling him the Visionary, tries to live by the light of Nature and by an altruism fostered narcissistically within his own mind and imagination; he cuts himself off from sympathy with his own species, and dies. Victorian readers were evidently quick to take the Visionary for Shelley himself, and Mary Shelley in her editorial note on the poem in 1839 contributes to that identification by writing of the bleak autobiographical circumstances in which the poem emerged. But the immediate model for the visionary Poet in *Alastor* is, surely, the Wanderer as a young man, described approvingly by Wordsworth in *The Excursion,* Book 1. The Wanderer's life has been devoted to virtue and to

religious idealism, and has apparently been entirely solitary, which means, among other things, celibate:

> There he kept
> In solitude and solitary thought
> His mind in a just equipoise of love.
> Serene it was, unclouded by the cares
> Of ordinary life; unvexed, unwarped
> By partial bondage.
>
> (l. 353)

In short, Wordsworth seems to redefine 'love' so that it needs no second party, just as he redefines religion so that it needs neither a church nor an independent deity:

> sometimes his religion seemed to me
> Self-taught, as of a dreamer in the woods;
> Who to the model of his own pure heart
> Shaped his belief.
>
> (l. 409)

Shelley's poem guys such a creed when the Visionary fails to notice an Arab maiden who offers him 'sweet human love'. The only sexual experience he proves capable of is a perverse and onanistic one, with a fantasy-woman projected in his dreams; and this figure is, significantly, equated with his own thoughts and his words when making poetry:

> Her voice was like the voice of his own soul
> Heard in the calm of thought . . .
> Knowledge and truth and virtue were her
>   theme,
> And lofty hopes of divine liberty,
> Thoughts the most dear to him, and poesy,
> Himself a poet.
>
> (ll. 153, 158)

In the Narrator's introduction to the Visionary's story, and in his summing up afterwards, there are specific quotations from Wordsworth, especially from the 'Intimations' Ode: 'natural piety' (*Alastor,* l. 3), 'obstinate questionings' (l. 26), and 'too deep for tears' (l. 713). It has thus become almost standard to identify the Narrator with Wordsworth; what should follow, and generally does not, is the equally Wordsworthian derivation of the other principal figure, the Visionary. By evoking the lifestyle of the Wanderer, but interpreting his solitariness as narcissistic and doom-laden, Shelley turns the idealization into a critique. The attack is brought home to Wordsworth personally, since Shelley reads the Wanderer as Wordsworth's complacent representation of his decision as a young man to forsake progressivism for a visionary, private, self-nurtured religion. On the contrary, Shelley believes that withdrawal led to Wordsworth's death as a poet, a point he reiterates in the sonnet, 'To Wordsworth', which appeared in the *Alastor* volume:

> In honoured poverty thy voice did weave
> Songs consecrate to truth and liberty—
> Deserting these, thou leavest me to grieve,
> Thus having been, that thou shouldst cease to
>   be.

In his 'Preface' to *Alastor,* Shelley hints hard that he means us to associate *both* poet-characters with the single figure of Wordsworth. The 'Preface' ends with Shelley quoting ironically those lines from *The Excursion,* Book 1, in which the Wanderer really does speak of human love, his own for his 'daughter' Margaret: 'the good die first | And they whose hearts are dry as summer dust | Burn to the socket' (l. 500).[1] The 'Preface', like the poem, has apparently been about two types of men: the failed imaginative youths, and the delinquents who keep aloof from sympathies with their kind. Wordsworth has been both, which is why his portrait in *Alastor* is a complex one.

Shelley's poem mars its own critical case by conveying a confusing element of sympathy with doomed idealists (even Wordsworth), so that it is perhaps not surprising that it has generally been taken for a classic instance of that poetic indulgence it sets out to satirize. The same fate has met another immature exercise in the same kind, Keats's *Endymion.* The models for Endymion's behaviour are, presumably, both the youthful Wanderer and the Visionary in *Alastor.* The clues that Keats is thinking of Shelley's Visionary are that he gives his own hero some of the same adventures, including sexual encounters with two girls, one belonging to the human world (Keats has an Indian maiden where Shelley had an Arab), the other a dream-figure, who in the Keats poem is the moon-goddess Cynthia. True, Keats does not set out with quite the same overtly critical and intellectual intentions as Shelley. He identifies more naïvely and heartily with his hero, who is allowed to choose the right option at each juncture. Endymion goes ahead and makes love to his Indian girl, as it happens a wise move which earns him his moon goddess after all. This does not alter the fact that Keats in *Endymion* makes the same general point as Shelley in *Alastor:* solitary idealists do no good to themselves or to anyone else, and love as an ideal, though universally professed by literary altruists, can be put into practice only in relationships with others.

What is surprising about Keats's poem is not that it accuses Wordsworth of narcissism and asexuality—these were the commonplaces of the day in critics hostile to Wordsworth—but that it goes out of its way to implicate Shelley too. Keats cannot, it is clear, read the Poet in *Alastor* as a critical portrait. He must think he is setting Shelley straight when he has Endymion make love to the Indian; though the failure of Shelley's

hero to make love to his Arab looks now like a distanced ironic way of making the very same point. Here is evidence of a pattern that is to be repeated many times, more frequently with reference to Byron's Childe Harold of Canto III than even to the Wanderer. Writers put forward an unromantic anti-type to correct what they see as a too-romantic prototype, each time overlooking an element suspicious of egotism in the first writer. This cannot be thought of as an example of unconscious Bloomian 'misreading' by the second author, since it occurs in conscious and virtually satirical locations. The cumulative effect of the practice is to lead us to underestimate the element of scepticism actually present in Romantic portraiture of poets.

Given the pattern, one begins to wonder where, if anywhere, a 'pure' Romantic autobiography is to be had. Byron wrote a number, if he is to be identified with the heroes of a number of his early and middle poems (the Giaour, the Corsair, Lara, Manfred), though for late twentieth-century readers the debunking tone of Byron's journals and letters also makes him an arch-critic of romanticizing. Otherwise, Wordsworth's Wanderer is surely too dramatized and fictionalized a figure to stand in for his creator. Coleridge gives a fillip to the writer's status with his demon-poet in 'Kubla Khan', and he supplies copious if abstruse further documentation in *The Lay Sermons* and the *Biographia Literaria;* but the very difficulty and eclecticism of that material is off-putting, and anyone attempting to track Coleridge as an autobiographer (let alone approach him as a biographer) has been inclined to lose heart.

According to some readings, another contender for a 'straight' Romantic autobiography might be Hazlitt's eccentric 'novel', the ***Liber Amoris*** of 1823, which, as the agonized record of a man in the grip of a sexual obsession, has been commonly regarded as an uncomfortably artless example of the Romantic compulsion towards self-expression. But is the hero of the ***Liber Amoris*** Hazlitt? Is he an emanation of Hazlitt's persona as a writer, being subjected to criticism and mockery? Is he a yet more detached figure, a composite of other characters in life and in books? The divergent possibilities make it a classic instance of the period's sceptical and divided approach to the self.

Hazlitt in February 1822 was forty-four, and in the grip of a mid-life crisis. His first marriage, to Sarah Stoddart in 1808, had broken down by mutual agreement, and Hazlitt now set off to Scotland to obtain a divorce. At Stamford on the way north he began writing first recollections and then a series of letters, some direct to the daughter of his London landlord, Sarah Walker, most to his friend P. G. Patmore, a few to another friend, J. S. Knowles. Hazlitt was attempting to memorialize, perhaps to exorcize, perhaps even yet to consummate, his passion for the nineteen-year-old

Sarah. He agonized to Patmore over the details of her past behaviour to him, the conversations they had had, the wording of her brief inarticulate replies. Was she a goddess? was she a slut? was she just a coarse, dull teenager? To conform with Scottish divorce law, Hazlitt had to put in three months' residence in Scotland, and he spent the spring, from February to May 1822, at an inn at Renton, Berwickshire, thirty miles from Edinburgh, composing his increasingly steamy series of letters and, in the act of writing, further intensifying his emotions.

The correspondence as Hazlitt actually penned it has long been known. Indeed one letter from Hazlitt to Patmore was published by a journal hostile to Hazlitt, the Tory *John Bull,* in July 1823, only two months after the publication of an edited 'formal' version of the same letter in the **Liber Amoris.** But the real-life series appeared in its entirety only in 1978, in the Sikes, Bonner, and Lahey edition of the **Letters of William Hazlitt.** The publishers of that edition, faced with the unenviable task of advertising the coldest and most impassive of Romantic letter-writers, understandably dwell on the merits of the torrid letters of 1822:

> In an age of self-revealing, 'confessional' autobiography, such as that of Rousseau and De Quincey, there is no comparable example of such savagely honest, of such appealing yet unsparingly ruthless self-exposure as appears in Hazlitt's letters which recount the intense struggle of the Romantic temperament with its own violently shifting moods. These letters . . . alone constitute a primary document for the study of the Romantic imagination.[2]

To dwell upon the honesty of the self-exposure is, however, a dubious move. Hazlitt had made a journalistic living variously in the second decade of the century, often with political articles for such liberal papers as the Hunt brothers' *Examiner* and *Yellow Dwarf,* but his métier was probably theatre criticism, and the line in his writing between theatre and life had long since become indistinct. The 'unsparingly honest' letters to Patmore are written in a highly conscious literary manner, full of dramatic cross-references which Hazlitt sometimes cut before publication. Excised phrases of this sort include 'is it not to write whore, hardened, impudent, heartless whore after her name?'; 'musing over my only subject (Othello's occupation, alas! is gone)'; 'thinking her human and that "below was not all the fiend's"' (pp. 263, 269). From the start he depicts a series of scenes in which he plays, by turns, the parts of Young Werther, Hamlet, Othello, Iago, and Lovelace. The last two roles are significant: Hazlitt's self-image includes the notion of the ingenious contriver who is himself like a stage-manager, or like the author's surrogate within his fiction. It is, then, the most self-conscious, the most continuously literary of love

affairs, though some of the sense of contrivance arises because Sarah has scarcely any words of her own, and seems to be waiting, like an actress, for her part to be written. Hazlitt, stage-managing as well as writing and performing, takes all the initiatives and dictates the course of the scenes. He tries Sarah physically by pulling her on to his knee and fondling her; he tests her morally by trusting her with his most prized possession, a little bronze statue of Napoleon. In late May, when he had served his Scottish time but not completed the divorce proceedings, he paid a flying visit to his London lodgings, where he found Sarah chillier than he had hoped for. In his rage he smashed the statue, and thus by a fine symbolic act pronounced the end of the affair.

As if the letters did not reveal an incurable self-dramatizer, they were clearly begun with at least half an eye to publication; by mid-March 1822 Hazlitt was certainly thinking not of a private record but of a book.[3] Henceforth, as he went on wooing Sarah by letter, he did so in the declared knowledge (declared to Patmore but not to Sarah) that he was making copy. The painful feelings were no doubt genuine; the fact that they were stage-managed does not imply that they were under control. Hazlitt at the time was under that compulsion pioneered by the Ancient Mariner, of telling all his friends about his sorrows and, when his friends were not at home, of telling their servants instead.[4] He extended the practice from London to Edinburgh, where he took the professional risk of laying bare his soul to the rather proper and very eminent Francis Jeffrey, editor of the *Edinburgh Review* and one of the leading journalistic patrons of the day.

From its inception as letters to its appearance as a novel, the book is always an inextricable blend of the lover's compulsive self-dramatization and the writer's professional calculation. *The Liber Amoris or the New Pygmalion* was published anonymously early in May 1823. Each of its three sections is based fairly closely on an original document or group of documents, two of which survive. Part I, seven fragments of dialogue between H— and S—, derives from a manuscript notebook (now in the Lockwood Memorial Library of the State University of New York at Buffalo); this must be the notebook Hazlitt told Patmore he had begun at Stamford in February 1822. Part II is based on the letters Hazlitt sent Patmore from Renton, with various cuts, rearrangements, and rewriting: the originals survive in various libraries. Part III is made up of the more polished retrospective letters Hazlitt apparently wrote later in the summer to his new friend, the Scottish dramatist J. S. Knowles, telling of the closing stages of the affair. But two further passages of 'real' material, not used in the novel for, presumably, decency's sake, show Hazlitt at his most Lovelacean, his most knowingly literary. One is in a letter of 18 June, in which he describes an overheard kitchen conversation between his 'goddess', her mother, and her brother in such bawdy terms that to his fevered imagination the lodging-house has now taken on the appearance of a brothel. The other is an extraordinary sequence entered in a separate notebook between 4 and 16 March 1823, and thus potentially a fourth episode for the book. The entries record the last and most flamboyantly literary of Hazlitt's contrivances, his procuring of a friend, F—, to test Sarah's virtue by attempting to seduce her. The notebook, which is given as an appendix in the Lahey edition of the **Letters,** consists of Hazlitt's summary of F—'s dealings with Sarah, including a last episode in which they scampered together up the lodging-house stairs, 'he all the way tickling her legs behind' (p. 388). This last document demonstrates not merely that the 'private' material can be more gripping than what was printed in the edition of 1823; it also shows that, if a clear line ever existed in Hazlitt's mind between living his story and making a book of it, this had now broken down. Why was F— procured? To tell Hazlitt something about Sarah that, nine months after their parting, he still emotionally had to know? It was, surely, to discover something about her that readers of the drama needed to know; though in the end Sarah, least manipulable of heroines, proved as incommunicable to F— as she had been to H—.

Ever since the appearance of the **Liber Amoris** in 1823, no clear distinctions between the character H—and the author Hazlitt, the 'novel' and the 'real' manuscripts, have ever proved possible to maintain. When the Tory *John Bull* maliciously printed the unexpurgated letter, it claimed that it did so in the public interest, part of the 'truth' having been improperly withheld. Reviewers and columnists immediately identified Hazlitt, no difficult matter when half London was in his confidence, and their descriptions of the **Liber Amoris** show that they thought they were dealing with the truth and nothing but the truth, even if it was not quite the whole truth. Later in the century the *Dictionary of National Biography* treated the book without demur as an autobiography. Hazlitt, *DNB* supposes, must have been half mad when he wrote it, but 'sane enough to get £100 for rivalling Rousseau's *Confessions*'.

But in fact the crucial question, 'What kind of an autobiography is it?', cannot be settled either by way of the textual evidence (since no text is more private or honest than another) or by biographical speculation. The anecdotes of contemporary literary men tend to support *DNB*'s hypothesis that Hazlitt was deranged, and this is a view which fits well enough a reading of the **Liber Amoris** as 'the intense struggle of the Romantic temperament with its own violently shifting moods'. But writers themselves and their families and friends often give very poor evidence about why a book was written, because its significant context need not be the private firsthand experience they have witnessed so much as the books of other writers, the taste of the public, and the state of the market. Viewed with these considerations in mind, the **Liber Amoris** becomes less unaccountable and considerably less insane.

In early 1822 Hazlitt was in difficulties not only with both his Sarahs, but with his journalistic employers and a number of his creditors; he was to be arrested for debt on 12 February 1823. The political polemic which had been one staple of his writing for the past seven years had become unfashionable, in the quieter and less controversial times that came with the end of the post-war economic crisis and the temporary slackening of reform agitation. Editors wanted something lighter, more personal, and perhaps profitably titillating— such as both Lamb and De Quincey had in their different styles been achieving during 1821 in John Scott's new *London Magazine,* with the first *Essays of Elia* and the serialized *Confessions of an English Opium Eater.* Of these two new journalistic successes, De Quincey's brilliant impressionistic autobiography must have irked Hazlitt more. While Lamb was a friend of Hazlitt's, De Quincey was an ally and political adherent of the Tory Lake poets. A clear hint that Hazlitt was enviously aware of De Quincey as a journalistic rival came later in 1823, when Hazlitt sent a letter to the *London Magazine* claiming that a recent article by De Quincey against Malthus had used an argument in which Hazlitt had anticipated him.[5]

Above all, the *Confessions* made a target because the book could be read as a classic instance of one of those self-flattering idealizing Portraits of the Artist which stimulated emulation and annoyance in the period. De Quincey adapts the exalted conception of the artist and of his imagination that he has found in the work of Wordsworth and Coleridge, cleverly naturalizing the rather grand concepts by telling a story set in the London streets. Instead of glimpsing a tantalizing Muse, as the younger Romantics and their poetic contemporaries had become over-fond of doing, he found and then lost again the haunting young prostitute, Ann, in Oxford Street. The Oriental visions of Beckford, Southey, and Coleridge in 'Kubla Khan' become the no less fantastic and lavishly written, but more psychologically explicable, consequences for De Quincey's dream-life of his ten-year addiction to laudanum. But De Quincey has not lost sight of the theoretical potential of the dream-vision, which in the idealist view of art beginning to emanate from Germany, and being popularized by Coleridge, can stand symbolically for another world created and peopled by the artist's imagination. The *Confessions* works as an *apologia pro vita sua,* because it isolates the artist again from the common world in which he is placed, elevating him to a special magical category on account of his gift of imagination.

De Quincey himself, in the opening passage of his *Confessions,* complains of *his* most obvious model, the *Confessions* of Rousseau, because it is too self-indulgent. That charge was often levelled against Rousseau's sexually-permissive narrative, from an England in the grip of a moralistic religious revival. But when De Quincey is the accuser the effect conveyed, more strongly than ever, is of the pot calling the kettle black. De Quincey's own *Confessions,* with their exculpatory approach to addiction, their narcissistic descriptions of dreams, their unrelenting egotism, advertise their author at least as provocatively as Rousseau's book does. So flamboyantly is this the case, indeed, that it comes as no surprise to discern in Hazlitt's Romantic autobiography of the following year what is in effect a counter-example to De Quincey's.

Countering De Quincey meant feeling for the point at which his approach was specially vulnerable. The generalized ground for complaint against Wordsworth, the leading writer of the Lake school, was, as we have seen, his solipsism; a typical counter-move proposed human love, or rather the consummation of the sexual act with one girl, who is explicitly not a mere figment of the fictional poet's fantasy-life and so functions as a challenge to his egotism. Though De Quincey has the London street-girl in his autobiography, and though he insists that his attitude to her is affectionate and benevolent, he has actually drawn a strangely muted and one-sided relationship. It is not, of course, sexual: that, perhaps, makes a rhetorical point against Rousseau, whose early sexual exploits become the burden of the narrative in his *Confessions.* But if De Quincey describes a mere friendship, bestowing material and physical comfort, the sceptical reader cannot help noticing that it is the waif Ann who gives and the adolescent De Quincey who takes. The key relationship in De Quincey's book thus maintains the asexuality and unsociability which had become a matter of complaint in the work of Wordsworth, De Quincey's main literary mentor. Hazlitt ripostes by taking as the subject of his 'memoirs' a common London girl with whom he longs to have sexual intercourse, but whose very nature is hidden by his over-intellectualizing.

Where De Quincey admits to an autobiography (and even, by choosing the title *Confessions,* evokes the most notoriously self-indulgent of autobiographies), Hazlitt claims, however notionally, to be writing a novel. The formal manœuvre cannot have been adopted in order to hide the author's identity, or he would have changed initials and place-names and other details that made identification certain. Fictionalizing the story is a device for objectifying it, above all for setting up a distance and some measure of control between the author and H—, now formally a character and not Hazlitt himself. Hazlitt was sufficiently conscious of the technical distinction to make a point of it to the painter B. R. Haydon, who passed on to Mary Russell Mitford that the conversations with Sarah and the letters to Patmore were to be published as 'a tale of

character'.[6] It is a critical not an apologetic portrait that Hazlitt thinks he is after, and other intellectual novels within his milieu supply a precedent for this. William Godwin's *Fleetwood* (1805) and *Mandeville* (1817) each make a critical study of an introverted intellectual, through two heroes so neurotically self-absorbed that they are incapable of successfully loving a woman. Godwin's novels fell under the usual curse of books on this topic, of being misread as examples of precisely that complacent misanthropy they were intended to dispel. *Mandeville* becomes one of the satiric targets of Peacock's *Nightmare Abbey,* which borrows its gloomy setting and its misanthropic hero, and lampoons Godwin's novel ('Devilman') as though it is itself uncritical. But *Fleetwood, or the New Man of Feeling* comes nearer to supplying Hazlitt with a useful model, one which its full title, with its revisionist implications, already points to: there is a significant tradition of intellectual novel-writing, as we shall see, which uses the debunking sub-title, 'or the . . . ', followed by a pretentious term for an artist. Fleetwood is a Wordsworthian man who has lived solitarily among the Welsh mountains; in middle age, too late, he tries to find happiness in marriage and is instead consumed by egotism and jealousy. The precedents are thus available for a novel which is apparently autobiographical but in spirit critical, itself introverted in pursuit of a critique of introversion. The precedents are also available to have it misread, but of this Hazlitt may have been unaware.

There is documentary corroboration that in the very month in which Hazlitt began to compile the ***Liber Amoris,*** he was sketching an outline Portrait of the Artist, one which incorporated the very criticism which De Quincey's book might have been expected to provoke. The sketch in question appears in yet another letter of an essentially open, public type, Hazlitt's Chesterfieldian **'Letter to his Son'** which was meant from the beginning for inclusion in ***Table Talk.***[7] In advising his son what kind of man to be, Hazlitt bitterly advocates that he should not become a writer, since writers do not prosper in that sphere (the sexual) with which Hazlitt equates, apparently both ironically and seriously, success and happiness in life. The passage was so nakedly autobiographical that much of it was cut when the 'Letter' was first published in 1825, and only appeared in full when Hazlitt's son himself edited his father's ***Posthumous Remains*** in 1836. Hazlitt has just plainly referred to his ill success with Sarah Walker: 'There is no forcing liking . . . Women care nothing about poets, or philosophers, or politicians. They go by a man's looks and manner.' But in some profound sense, he goes on to argue, authors bring this rejection on themselves:

> Authors feel nothing spontaneously. . . . Instead of yielding to the first natural and lively impulses of

things, in which they would find sympathy, they screw themselves up to some farfetched view of the subject in order to be unintelligible. Realities are not good enough for them . . . They are intellectual dram-drinkers; and without their necessary stimulus, are torpid, dead, insensible to every thing. . . . Their minds are a sort of Herculaneum, full of old petrified images;—are set in stereotype, and little fitted to the ordinary occasions of life.

What chance, then, can they have with women?. . . . Do not, in thinking to study yourself into the good graces of the fair, study yourself out of them, millions of miles. Do not place thought as a barrier between you and love; do not abstract yourself into the regions of truth, far from the smile of earthly beauty. . . . Should you let your blood stagnate in some deep metaphysical question, or refine too much in your ideas of the sex, forgetting yourself in a dream of exalted perfection, you will want an eye to cheer you, a hand to guide you, a bosom to lean on, and will stagger into your grave, old before your time, unloved and unlovely . . .

A spider, my dear, the meanest creature that lives or crawls, had its mate or fellow; but a scholar has not mate or fellow. For myself, I had courted thought, I had felt pain; and Love turned away his face from me. I have gazed along the silent air for that smile which had lured me to my doom . . . And as my frail bark sails down the stream of time, the God of Love stands on the shore, and as I stretch out my hands to him in vain, claps his wings, and mocks me as I pass.[8]

The significance of this extraordinary passage is that it both reflects Hazlitt's obsession with Sarah Walker and objectifies it, so that it becomes the basis for a satirical view of the modern artist as an impotent and marginal figure. There is a possible allusion to De Quincey in the phrase, 'they are intellectual dram-drinkers'. There is a much clearer anticipation of the entire plot and theme of the *Liber Amoris,* with an emphasis that points up the full implications of the subtitle of that work: *the New Pygmalion.* Aesthete, narcissist, Pygmalion fell in love with the statue he had made, an icon of his own creation. Inserting the word 'new' has the effect of updating the portrait, and of debunking it further. Really, Hazlitt seems to sigh, no matter how up-to-the-minute the cult of the artist, there is nothing new under the sun.[9]

The power and fascination of the *Liber Amoris,* most underrated of Romantic autobiographies, derives precisely from the interplay between what is personal to Hazlitt, genuinely obsessive, and what has a generalized reference to the lives of all artists. H— has two icons, which correspond to Hazlitt's in real life: Sarah herself, sometimes goddess and sometimes whore; and the little bronze statue, or bust, of Napoleon. The pres-

ence of these two successive passions in Hazlitt's life is a matter of record, and was already publicly on record by 1823. Hazlitt had even told the public that he saw a continuity between his old veneration for Napoleon, itself an extension of his youthful revolutionary idealism, and the passionate love he now felt for Sarah Walker. In an essay entitled **'On Great and Little Things'**, written in January 1821 and printed in the *New Monthly Magazine* (n.s. 4, 1822), he first alludes unmistakably to his unhappy love affair ('to see beauty is not to be beautiful, to pine in love is not to be loved again') and then, in an upsurge of hope, imagines both love and the political hopes of earlier days restored to him: 'The sun of Austerlitz has not set. It still shines here— in my heart; and he, the son of glory, is not dead, nor ever shall, to me'. (Hazlitt admittedly appended the footnote to the paragraph: 'I beg the reader to consider this passage merely as a specimen of the mock-heroic style, and as having nothing to do with any real facts or feelings'.) Within the *Liber Amoris,* Sarah too makes the statue stand for her unrequited sexual desires, since Bonaparte's face reminds her of a man with whom she has been in love. In the stage-direction with which Hazlitt completes the final dialogue of Part I, 'The Reconciliation', H— and Sarah appear precariously at one in their contemplation of the statue:

> I got up and gave her the image, and told her it was her's by every right that was sacred . . . I pressed it eagerly, and she took it. She immediately came and sat down, and put her arm round my neck, and kissed me, and I said, 'Is it not plain we are the best friends in the world, since we are always so glad to make it up?' And then I added, 'How odd it was that the God of my idolatry should turn out to be like her Idol, and that it was no wonder that the same face which awed the world should conquer the sweetest creature in it!' How I loved her at that moment! (p. 82)

So long as the bust survives, it can be used, even if ominously, to symbolize their different sexual fantasies. When H— smashes it on his last visit to Southampton Buildings in May 1822, the crash involves not just the icon he has made of Sarah, and thus the current love affair, but the old, thwarted, superseded passions of both, and thus, by implication, the human comedy implicit in the making and breaking of icons.

But if here the *Liber Amoris* generalizes, elsewhere it particularizes. No autobiographical document of the period, and certainly not the novels with which the *Liber Amoris* was compared by an admiring reviewer, Rousseau's *Julie* and Goethe's *Werther,* in fact delved so minutely into the psychopathology of frustrated sexual love.[10] Sarah's behaviour is almost as intriguing to the reader as it was to Hazlitt, for she copes erratically with his long campaign of sexual harassment, sometimes by avoiding her persecutor, most often by a discouraging reserve, but sometimes with passive acquiescence. Hazlitt grows almost delirious with joy when he fancies himself encouraged, as he does when Sarah's young sister says that Sarah prizes his books; he is then plunged into deeper torment as it becomes plain in the course of the next week that Sarah is keeping out of sight (p. 155). He fully recognizes the humiliating spectacle he must make to others, a man of rich inner resources the slave to a girl without conversation, in whom most of his friends do not even see good looks. In the unpublished parts of the letters, still more than in the *Liber Amoris,* he moans over the pleasure, even in memory, of fondling her body, even through clothes, and he moans too at his own abject dependence on her.[11] When *John Bull* alludes to the hero of the muted published version as a 'disappointed dotard' and an 'impotent sensualist', it has the text(s), read unironically, on its side.

Powerful and extraordinary though it is on its own, Hazlitt's Portrait of the Artist seems incomplete until we have contemplated it superimposed upon other portraits. Along with his fellow writers, Hazlitt was caught up in a collective enterprise in which the notion of the stereotypical intellectual was explored, corrected, given Identikit features, one contribution fitting over and losing itself in the last. Hazlitt's sorrowing and ridiculous Pygmalion gains from his dialogic relationship with De Quincey's tormented but vindicated Dreamer. Together, moreover, these two books advance the stereotype and show up hòw thin, sentimental, and bombastic it was before. De Quincey with his sluttish Muse in Oxford Street, Hazlitt with his in Southampton Buildings, Holborn, are both modern literary men, aeons away from the idealizations of the poets or from the canvasses of historical painters. For its full revisionist impact, the work of De Quincey and Hazlitt should be seen in the context of the craze, at its height across Europe in the first two decades of the nineteenth century, for a mythologized pantheon of artist-heroes: Homer, Tiresias, Dante, Tasso, and Milton recur, victimized but also resplendent, in the poetry of Byron and Shelley, Goethe and Foscolo, and in the paintings of late neo-Classical artists, particularly in France.[12] The figures of Ann and Sarah need comparing, too, with the poets' impressive idealized meetings with their Muses, who for Foscolo are the Graces, for Keats Greek divinities and Queens of the Underworld.

Yet, even though De Quincey and Hazlitt are like one another and unlike the poets in their realistic treatment of detail and setting, they cannot be compared with one another as iconoclasts: it is only Hazlitt who pits literary realism against literary idealism. The *Examiner*'s reviewer hailed the *Liber Amoris* as a very philosophical book, in the tradition of Bishop Berkeley and Sir William Drummond, the sceptical thinker admired by Shelley: these comparisons are not clearly explained, but it is possible to see why a sympathetic fellow-liberal made them.[13]

Since that time the *Liber Amoris* has not received much recognition, and certainly not the *Examiner*'s kind of intellectual recognition. Today copies of it are hard to find, and readers even of Hazlitt have often never heard of it. Nevertheless the book represents a crucial breakthrough in Hazlitt's career. He was not only working Sarah, the real girl, out of his system; by interpreting their story symbolically he was defining his position in relation to some extreme contemporary versions of the doctrine of the Imagination, which, in Hazlitt's rendering, kills. The book is of key importance for him because it marks the final transition from his activities in the second decade of the century, when he was a critic and a political journalist, to his final phase as an autobiographical essayist. Oddly, Hazlitt exclaimed with relief to his publisher Colburn as, on 3 March 1822, he finished the second volume of his *Table Talk:* 'I have done with essay writing for ever' (*Letters,* p. 238). What he was really achieving was an extension and enrichment of his life as an essayist, since henceforth these fragments could be seen against a larger project, a critical, intellectual, and generalized portrait of himself. The essayist who wrote **'On Going a Walk'**, **'Indian Jugglers'**, **'On Being a Good Hater'** remained an autobiographer, as he remained the author of dramatic monologues and the manipulator of real-life experience. The persona and the voice is developed in the *Liber Amoris;* so is the train of critical thinking that contextualizes the portrait, without which Hazlitt's career as a whole would lack an intellectual dimension.

But then the same point might be made about Romantic autobiography, and about most English Romantic writing as we habitually represent it: without its critical element, its corrections, critiques, parodies, and satires, it lacks an intellectual dimension apparent (if uncertainly) to writers and readers of the age. With the passing of time, critics seem to have become less rather than more aware of the satirical and intellectualist strain in Romantic writing. The problem is that all modern professional persons of letters are Romantics, one way or another, and the premises on which most of our procedures rest are biased in favour of aestheticism. Biographers, psychobiographers, editors, textual critics, deconstructionists, critics of the poem or the poet in isolation, take, as a matter of course, the specialized, narrowly restricted view that in the early nineteenth century was still encountering intelligent criticism. The sympathetic portrait of the solitary artist, lifted by his calling above the ordinary obligations of life, initially aroused resistance because it demanded to be read on its own terms, which put aesthetics above ethics. The satirical counter-portrait is hard to read (and was already hard when it first appeared) because it refuses 'Romantic' self-sufficiency. The meaning of a work remains incomplete until it is read alongside another work: *Alastor* alongside *The Excursion,* Book I; the **Liber Amoris** alongside *The Confessions of an English Opium Eater.*

For some tastes, the case for aestheticism was proved philosophically by Kant, Schelling, Hegel, and their adherents (there is a philosopher's equivalent of the Whig Idea of Progress). If this is the case, the gestures of the English younger Romantic generation were a futile rearguard action, soon overtaken by history, or by revelation. From a more sceptical point of view, the sudden prestige of aestheticism around 1800 is itself a historical phenomenon, no more above criticism than any other movement of ideas, and certainly not immune from the observation that the intellectuals and artists who fostered it had an interest. From that angle of vision, it is pleasant to see Romantic aestheticism meeting, at the outset, some pockets of resistance.

Notes

[1] Shelley's version of line 501 in the 'Preface' to *Alastor* reads: 'And those whose hearts are dry as summer's dust'.

[2] *The Letters of William Hazlitt,* edited by Herschel Moreland Sikes, assisted by Willard Hallard Bonner and Gerald Lahey (New York 1978; London 1979); publisher's advertisement on dustjacket. References to Hazlitt's letters are to this edition. Though floridly written, this description is not otherwise untypical. Compare the extended, 'romantic' accounts in Catherine M. Maclean, *Born Under Saturn: A Biography of Hazlitt* (London, 1943), pp. 415-99; Cyril Connolly, 'Hazlitt's *Liber Amoris*', *London Magazine,* November 1954; Ralph M. Wardle, *Hazlitt* (Lincoln, Nebraska, 1971), pp. 300-65.

[3] *Letters,* p. 246. A postscript to the letter reads: 'I have begun a book of our conversations (I mean mine and the statue's), which I call *Liber Amoris*'. The text of this letter becomes Letter I of Part II of the published *Liber Amoris.*

[4] The amusing account of Hazlitt's communicativeness by B. W. Proctor (the writer Barry Cornwall) is quoted in Richard Le Gallienne's privately printed edition of the *Liber Amoris* (London, 1894), p. xiv. References are to this edition.

[5] *London Magazine,* November 1823. De Quincey writes on the subject in October and (replying to Hazlitt) December 1823. See *Letters,* pp. 329-32.

[6] *Diary of Benjamin Robert Haydon,* edited by Willard B. Pope, 5 vols (Cambridge, Massachusetts, 1960-63), II, 382, cited by Robert Ready, 'The Logic of Passion: Hazlitt's *Liber Amoris*', *Studies in Romanticism,* 14

(1975), 41-57. This article is one of the few discussions to take seriously the claims of the *Liber Amoris* as a work of art: Ready sees it as a carefully fashioned, if eccentric, novel.

[7] 'I had a letter from my little boy the other day, and I have been writing him a long essay in my book on his conduct in life' (Hazlitt to Sarah Walker (9 March 1822), *Letters,* pp. 243-44).

[8] *Letters,* pp. 223-25. Though the 'Letter' was included in *Table Talk* (1825), the entire passage quoted here was omitted.

[9] One precedent for Hazlitt's full title, Godwin's *Fleetwood, or the New Man of Feeling,* has already been noted. But Godwin's daughter, Mary Shelley, also wrote an admonitory fable about the intellectual life: *Frankenstein, or the Modern Prometheus* (1818). The themes of Hazlitt's and Mary Shelley's books have much in common. Frankenstein, too, is a creative figure, purportedly a scientist but allegorically, surely, an artist, who sets out with exaggerated notions of the benefits that he, like the fire-bearer Prometheus, is bringing to mankind. What he actually succeeds in bringing is a murderous Monster, an intensely lonely creature who is the mirror-image of Frankenstein's own egotism. For *Frankenstein*'s link with *Alastor* and with the critique of Wordsworth's *Excursion,* see my *Peacock Displayed* (London, 1979), p. 72.

[10] *Examiner,* No. 798 (11 May 1823): quoted in *Liber Amoris,* p. xxiii. It is interesting that even this sympathetic reviewer remarked on the resemblance neither to Godwin's novels (for which see text) nor to Benjamin Constant's *Adolphe, and the Red Notebook* (1816), which anticipates the *Liber Amoris* in that it purports to be the edited manuscript of a lover now dead.

[11] Hazlitt to P. G. Patmore (31 May 1822), *Letters,* p. 263.

[12] See Jon Whitely, 'Homer Abandoned: A French Neoclassical Theme', in *The Artist and the Writer in France,* edited by F. Haskell, A. Levi, and R. Shackleton (Oxford, 1974) pp. 40-51. Whitely estimates that no fewer than sixteen French painters before 1830 used mythical themes from Homer's life, further amplified in modern times to suggest that the blind artist was peculiarly neglected and unfortunate.

[13] *Examiner,* No. 798 (11 May 1823); quoted in *Liber Amoris,* p. xxiii.

Harold Bloom (essay date 1986)

SOURCE: Introduction to *William Hazlitt,* edited by Harold Bloom, Chelsea House Publishers, 1986, pp. 1-13.

[*In the following introduction to a collection of critical essays on Hazlitt, Bloom contends that Hazlitt's "poetics of power" chronicles the difficult relationship between imagination and experience, oneself and others.*]

I

David Bromwich, Hazlitt's best critic, shrewdly says of Hazlitt's key word *gusto* that it "accords nicely with the belief that taste adds to our nature instead of correcting it." I take it that Hazlitt's *gusto* is an aesthetic displacement of the Dissenting Protestant version of grace, which corrects our nature without abolishing it. The son of a radical Dissenting Minister, Hazlitt himself was always a Jacobin with a faith in Napoleon as the true heir of the Revolution. Unswerving in his politics, Hazlitt also remained an unreconstructed early Wordsworthian, unlike Wordsworth himself, a difference that Hazlitt bitterly kept in mind, as here in his observations on Wordsworth's *The Excursion:*

> In the application of these memorable lines, we should, perhaps, differ a little from Mr. Wordsworth; nor can we indulge with him in the fond conclusion afterwards hinted at, that one day *our* triumph, the triumph of humanity and liberty, may be complete. For this purpose, we think several things necessary which are impossible. It is a consummation which cannot happen till the nature of things is changed, till the many become as united as the *one,* till romantic generosity shall be as common as gross selfishness, till reason shall have acquired the obstinate blindness of prejudice, till the love of power and of change shall no longer goad man on to restless action, till passion and will, hope and fear, love and hatred, and the objects proper to excite them, that is, alternate good and evil, shall no longer sway the bosoms and businesses of men. All things move, not in progress, but in a ceaseless round; our strength lies in our weakness; our virtues are built on our vices; our faculties are as limited as our being; nor can we lift man above his nature more than above the earth he treads. But though we cannot weave over again the airy, unsubstantial dream, which reason and experience have dispelled,
>
> What though the radiance, which was once so
>   bright,
> Be now for ever taken from our sight,
> Though nothing can bring back the hour
> Of glory in the grass, of splendour in the
>   flower:
>
> yet we will never cease, nor be prevented from returning on the wings of imagination to that bright dream of our youth; that glad dawn of the day-star of liberty; that spring-time of the world, in which the hopes and expectations of the human race seemed opening in the same gay career with our own; when France called her children to partake her equal blessings beneath her laughing skies; when the stranger was met in all her villages with dance and festive songs, in celebration of a new and golden era; and when, to the retired and contemplative student, the prospects of human happiness and glory were seen ascending like the steps of Jacob's ladder, in bright and never-ending succession. The dawn of that day was suddenly overcast; that season of hope is past; it is fled with the other dreams of our youth, which we cannot recall, but has left behind it traces, which are not to be effaced by Birthday and Thanksgiving odes, or the chaunting of *Te Deums* in all the churches of Christendom. To those hopes eternal regrets are due; to those who maliciously and wilfully blasted them, in the fear that they might be accomplished, we feel no less what we owe—hatred and scorn as lasting!

In effect, the aesthetic loss of Wordsworth's visionary gleam is associated here with the spiritual loss of revolutionary hope. All loss, for the critic Hazlitt, is ultimately a loss of gusto, since *gusto* is Hazlitt's version of Blake's "exuberance," as in: "Exuberance is Beauty." One sees this clearly when he transfers the term *gusto* from painters to writers:

> The infinite quantity of dramatic invention in Shakespeare takes from his gusto. The power he delights to shew is not intense, but discursive. He never insists on any thing as much as he might, except a quibble. Milton has great gusto. He repeats his blow twice; grapples with and exhausts his subject. His imagination has a double relish of its objects, an inveterate attachment to the things he describes, and to the words describing them.
>
> ————Or where Chineses drive
> With sails and wind their *cany* waggons *light.*
>
> Wild above rule or art, *enormous* bliss.
>
> There is a gusto in Pope's compliments, in Dryden's satires, and Prior's tales; and among prose-writers, Boccaccio and Rabelais had the most of it. We will only mention one other work which appears to us to be full of gusto, and that is the *Beggar's Opera.* If it is not, we are altogether mistaken in our notions on this delicate subject.

Shakespeare's gusto is in his exuberance of invention, Milton's in his exhaustive tenacity at battering the object, as it were. An aesthetic category comprehensive enough to include also Pope, Dryden, and Prior, on the one side, and Boccaccio, Rabelais, and John Gay, on the other, is perhaps too broad to be of use to practical criticism. Hazlitt's own gusto or critical exuberance proved capable of overcoming this difficulty, and he gave us a poetics of power still unsurpassed in its potential:

> The language of poetry naturally falls in with the language of power. The imagination is an exaggerating

and exclusive faculty: it takes from one thing to add to another: it accumulates circumstances together to give the greatest possible effect to a favourite object. The understanding is a dividing and measuring faculty, it judges of things not according to their immediate impression on the mind, but according to their relations to one another. The one is a monopolising faculty, which seeks the greatest quantity of present excitement by inequality and disproportion; the other is a distributive faculty, which seeks the greatest quantity of ultimate good, by justice and proportion. The one is an aristocratical, the other a republican faculty. The principle of poetry is a very anti-levelling principle. It aims at effect, it exists by contrast. It admits of no medium. It is everything by excess. It rises above the ordinary standard of sufferings and crimes. It presents a dazzling appearance. It shows its head turretted, crowned, and crested. Its front is gilt and bloodstained. Before it "it carries noise, and behind it leaves tears." It has its altars and its victims, sacrifices, human sacrifices. Kings, priests, nobles, are its train-bearers, tyrants and slaves its executioners.— "Carnage is its daughter."—Poetry is right-royal. It puts the individual for the species, the one above the infinite-many, might before right. A lion hunting a flock of sheep or a herd of wild asses is a more poetical object than they; and we even take part with the lordly beast, because our vanity or some other feeling makes us disposed to place ourselves in the situation of the strongest party. So we feel some concern for the poor citizens of Rome when they meet together to compare their wants and grievances, till Coriolanus comes in and with blows and big words drives this set of "poor rats," this rascal scum, to their homes and beggary before him. There is nothing heroical in a multitude of miserable rogues not wishing to be starved, or complaining that they are like to be so; but when a single man comes forward to brave their cries and to make them submit to the last indignities, from mere pride and self-will, our admiration of his prowess is immediately converted into contempt for their pusillanimity. The insolence of power is stronger than the plea of necessity. The tame submission to usurped authority or even the natural resistance to it has nothing to excite or flatter the imagination: it is the assumption of a right to insult or oppress others that carries an imposing air of superiority with it. We had rather be the oppressor than the oppressed. The love of power in ourselves and the admiration of it in others are both natural to man: the one makes him a tyrant, the other a slave.

This is from Hazlitt's discussion of *Coriolanus* in his **Characters of Shakespeare's Plays.** The quality of excess is central to Hazlitt's insight here, which tells us that meaning gets started (rather than being merely repeated) by excess, by overflow, and by a sense of potential, a sense of something evermore about to be. The dialectic of this poetics of power depends upon an interplay of Shakespearean and Wordsworthian influences upon Hazlitt. From Shakespeare, Hazlitt takes an awareness that character may be fate, yet only personality bestows some measure of freedom. From Wordsworth, Hazlitt received a new consciousness of how a writer could begin again despite the strength and persistence of cultural traditions. The freedom of personality, in Falstaff, *is* freedom because ego ceases to be persecuted by superego. The originality of writing, in Wordsworth, is the disappearance of subject matter, and its replacement by subjectivity. Taken together, the ego of free wit and the triumph of a fresh subjectivity make up the manner and matter of Hazlitt's characteristic achievement, an essay at once familiar and critical, firmly literary yet also discursive and speculative.

In his loving meditation, **"On the Periodical Essayists,"** Hazlitt lists his precursors: Montaigne, Steele (rather than Addison), Johnson (despite Hazlitt's dislike of his style), Goldsmith. Had Edmund Burke been a familiar essayist rather than an orator, Burke certainly would be Hazlitt's nearest ancestor. Instead, Hazlitt makes a second to Johnson in a great procession of critical essayists that goes on to Carlyle, Emerson, Ruskin, Pater, and Wilde. (I omit Coleridge because of his obsession with method, and Arnold because of his authentic incompetence.) The procession ceases in our century because the mode now seems inadequate, not so much to the apparent complexities of modernist literature (after all, many of those now resolve themselves into more complications), but to the waning of the self, with all the perplexities attendant upon that waning. A curious irony of modern literature made Freud, the analyst of such waning, also the only twentieth-century essayist worthy to be the coda of the long tradition that went from Montaigne on through Johnson, Hazlitt, and Emerson until it culminated in Freud's older contemporaries, Ruskin, Nietzsche, and Pater.

II

Hazlitt's poetics of power seems to me more Freudian than any of the psychopoetics—orthodox or Lacanian—that currently drift uselessly in Freud's wake. Like Freud, Hazlitt knows that the poets— Shakespeare, Milton, Wordsworth—were there before him, which is a very different realization than any that penetrate the blindnesses of what now passes for "Freudian literary criticism." The poets are still there before Freud, better guides to the interpretation of Freud than he could ever be to the reading of consciousnesses even more comprehensive and coherent than his own. Hazlitt, in his best theoretical essay, **"On Poetry in General,"** begins with the fine realization: "Poetry then is an imitation of Nature, but the imagination and the passions are a part of man's nature." Passion, or pathos, or sublimity, or power (the four are rightly one, according to Hazlitt) remove poetry from the domain of all conventional considerations of psychology and morality:

> We are as fond of indulging our violent passions as of reading a description of those of others. We are as prone to make a torment of our fears, as to luxuriate in our hopes of good. If it be asked, Why do we do so? the best answer will be, Because we cannot help it. The sense of power is as strong a principle in the mind as the love of pleasure. Objects of terror and pity exercise the same despotic control over it as those of love or beauty. It is as natural to hate as to love, to despise as to admire, to express our hatred or contempt, as our love or admiration.
>
> Masterless passion sways us to the mood
> Of what it likes or loathes.
>
> Not that we like what we loathe; but we like to indulge our hatred and scorn of it; to dwell upon it, to exasperate our idea of it by every refinement of ingenuity and extravagance of illustration; to make it a bugbear to ourselves, to point it out to others in all the splendour of deformity, to embody it to the senses, to stigmatize it by name, to grapple with it in thought, in action, to sharpen our intellect, to arm our will against it, to know the worst we have to contend with, and to contend with it to the utmost. Poetry is only the highest eloquence of passion, the most vivid form of expression that can be given to our conception of anything, whether pleasurable or painful, mean or dignified, delightful or distressing. It is the perfect coincidence of the image and the words with the feeling we have, and of which we cannot get rid in any other way, that gives an instant "satisfaction to the thought." This is equally the origin of wit and fancy, of comedy and tragedy, of the sublime and pathetic. When Pope says of the Lord Mayor's show,—
>
> Now night descending, the proud scene is
>   o'er,
> But lives in Settle's numbers one day more!
>
> —when Collins makes Danger, "with limbs of giant mould,"
>
>   —Throw him on the steep
> Of some loose hanging rock asleep:
>
> when Lear calls out in extreme anguish,
>
> Ingratitude, thou marble-hearted fiend,
> How much more hideous shew'st in a child
> Than the sea-monster!
>
> —the passion of contempt in the one case, of terror in the other, and of indignation in the last, is precisely satisfied. We see the thing ourselves, and shew it to others as we feel it to exist, and as, in spite of ourselves, we are compelled to think of it.

> The imagination, by thus embodying and turning them to shape, gives an obvious relief to the indistinct and importunate cravings of the will.—We do not wish the thing to be so; but we wish it to appear such as it is. For knowledge is conscious power; and the mind is no longer, in this case, the dupe, though it may be the victim of vice or folly.

To speak of poetry as giving "an obvious relief to the indistinct and importunate cravings of the will" is to have more than anticipated Freud. Hazlitt's quotation from *The Merchant of Venice* is the center of one of Shylock's great speeches:

> Some men there are love not a gaping pig;
> Some that are mad if they behold a cat;
> And others, when the bagpipe sings i' th'
>   nose,
> Cannot contain their urine; for affection,
> Mistress of passion, sways it to the mood
> Of what it likes or loathes.

"Masterless passion" is as likely a reading as "Mistress of passion," the text being uncertain, and better suits Hazlitt's emphasis upon the cravings of the will. Hazlittian exuberance, *gusto,* teaches us to admire Shylock even as we admire Coriolanus. Few passages even in Hazlitt are as superbly memorable as when he shows us how the grandest poetry can be the most immoral, here in *Coriolanus:*

> This is but natural, it is but natural for a mother to have more regard for her son than for a whole city; but then the city should be left to take some care of itself. The care of the state cannot, we here see, be safely entrusted to maternal affection, or to the domestic charities of high life. The great have private feelings of their own, to which the interests of humanity and justice must courtesy. Their interests are so far from being the same as those of the community, that they are in direct and necessary opposition to them; their power is at the expense of *our* weakness; their riches of *our* poverty; their pride of *our* degradation; their splendour of *our* wretchedness; their tyranny of *our* servitude. If they had the superior knowledge ascribed to them (which they have not) it would only render tham so much more formidable; and from Gods would convert them into Devils. The whole dramatic moral of *Coriolanus* is that those who have little shall have less, and that those who have much shall take all that others have left. The people are poor; therefore they ought to be starved. They are slaves; therefore they ought to be beaten. They work hard; therefore they ought not to be treated like beasts of burden. They are ignorant; therefore they ought not to be allowed to feel that they want food, or clothing, or rest, that they are enslaved, oppressed, and miserable. This is the logic of the imagination and the passions; which seek to

aggrandize what excites admiration, and to heap contempt on misery, to raise power into tyranny, and to make tyranny absolute; to thrust down that which is low still lower, and to make wretches desperate; to exult magistrates into kings, kings into gods; to degrade subjects to the rank of slaves, and slaves to the condition of brutes. The history of mankind is a romance, a mask, a tragedy, constructed upon the principles of *poetical justice;* it is a noble or royal hunt, in which what is sport to the few is death to the many, and in which the spectators halloo and encourage the strong to set upon the weak, and cry havoc in the chase though they do not share in the spoil. We may depend upon it that what men delight to read in books, they will put in practice in reality.

Though Hazlitt is an intellectual of the permanent Left, of the French Revolution, he is too great a critic not to see that poetry worships power without regard to the morality of power. Indeed, his poetics of power compels us to see more than that, which is that Plato was right in fearing Homer's effect upon society. Poetical justice is antithetical to societal justice, and the noble or royal hunt of the imagination does not make us better citizens or better human beings, and very likely may make us worse.

III

Hazlitt, like Johnson before him, and the great progression of Carlyle, Emerson, Ruskin, Pater, and Wilde after him, teaches us several unfashionable truths as to the nature of authentically *literary* criticism. It must be experiential; it must be at least somewhat empirical or pragmatic; it must be informed by love for its subject; above all it must follow no method except the personality of the critic himself. Coleridge never ceased to quest for method, and lost the critical gift in consequence, while Matthew Arnold drowned what gift he had by assuring himself that they handled these matters better on the Continent. Hazlitt is a literary critic; our contemporary imitators of Continental philosophy may be human scientists or ideological rebels or what they will, but they are not literary critics. Hume's philosophy teaches the critic to fall back upon personality because every other possibility has been collapsed by skepticism. German thought persuaded Coleridge to posit an "organic" unity in imaginative works, but such organicism and its resultant unities can be seen now as banal fictions. Hazlitt, like Johnson, refuses to carry philosophical aesthetics into the pragmatic realms of criticism. I read Coleridge when and as I have to, but I read Hazlitt for pleasure and insight. Whether he writes on **"The Indian Jugglers"** or **"On Going a Journey"** or **"On a Sun-Dial,"** Hazlitt reminds us always that life and literature are, for him, the one interpenetrated reality.

I remember **"The Indian Jugglers"** partly for its vivid celebration of the jugglers' skill:

> Coming forward and seating himself on the ground in his white dress and tightened turban, the chief of the Indian Jugglers begins with tossing up two brass balls, which is what any of us could do, and concludes with keeping up four at the same time, which is what none of us could do to save our lives, nor if we were to take our whole lives to do it in. Is it then a trifling power we see at work, or is it not something next to miraculous? It is the utmost stretch of human ingenuity, which nothing but the bending the faculties of body and mind to it from the tenderest infancy with incessant, ever-anxious application up to manhood, can accomplish or make even a slight approach to. Man, thou art a wonderful animal, and thy ways past finding out! Thou canst do strange things, but thou turnest them to little account!— To conceive of this effort of extraordinary dexterity distracts the imagination and makes admiration breathless. Yet it costs nothing to the performer, any more than if it were a mere mechanical deception with which he had nothing to do but to watch and laugh at the astonishment of the spectators. A single error of a hair's-breadth, of the smallest conceivable portion of time, would be fatal: the precision of the movements must be like a mathematical truth, their rapidity is like lightning. To catch four balls in succession in less than a second of time, and deliver them back so as to return with seeming consciousness to the hand again, to make them revolve round him at certain intervals, like the planers in their spheres, to make them chase one another like sparkles of fire, or shoot up like flowers or meteors, to throw them behind his back and twine them round his neck like ribbons or like serpents, to do what appears an impossibility, and to do it with all the ease, the grace, the carelessness imaginable, to laugh at, to play with the glittering mockeries, to follow them with his eye as if he could fascinate them with its lambent fire, or as if he had only to see that they kept time with the music on the stage— there is something in all this which he who does not admire may be quite sure he never really admired anything in the whole course of his life. It is skill surmounting difficulty, and beauty triumphing over skill.

Remarkable as descriptive writing, this acquires hidden power when subsequently it is revealed as a literary paradigm, leading Hazlitt to the profound observation: "No act terminating in itself constitutes greatness." The act of writing *Paradise Lost* is precisely one that does not terminate in itself. Hazlitt's insight is that the canon is constituted by works that engender further works that do not terminate in themselves. **"On Going a Journey"** begins by advising that "the soul of a journey is liberty, perfect liberty, to think, feel, do just as one pleases." A few pages later the essay achieves perceptions into our involuntary perspectivism that both anticipate and correct Nietzsche:

There is hardly anything that shows the short-sightedness or capriciousness of the imagination more than travelling does. With change of place we change our ideas; nay, our opinions and feelings. We can by an effort indeed transport ourselves to old and long-forgotten scenes, and then the picture of the mind revives again, but we forget those that we have just left. It seems that we can think but of one place at a time. The canvas of the fancy has only a certain extent, and if we paint one set of objects upon it, they immediately efface every other. We cannot enlarge our conceptions; we only shift our point of view. The landscape bares its bosom to the enraptured eye; we take our fill of it; and seem as if we could form no other image of beauty or grandeur. We pass on, and think no more of it; the horizon that shuts it from our sight also blots it from our memory like a dream. In travelling through a wild barren country, I can form no idea of a woody and cultivated one. It appears to me that all the world must be barren, like what I see of it. In the country we forget the town, and in town we despise the country. "Beyond Hyde Park," says Sir Fopling Flutter, "all is a desert." All that part of the map that we do not see before us is a blank. The world in our conceit of it is not much bigger than a nutshell. It is not one prospect expanded into one another, county joined to county, kingdom to kingdom, lands to seas, making an image voluminous and vast; the mind can form no larger idea of space than the eye can take in at a single glance. The rest is a name written on a map, a calculation of arithmetic. For instance, what is the true signification of that immense mass of territory and population, known by the name of China to us? An inch of paste-board on a wooden globe, of no more account than a China orange! Things near us are seen of the size of life: things at a distance are diminished to the size of the understanding. We measure the universe by ourselves, and even comprehend the texture of our own being only piece-meal.

"On a Sun-Dial" is a nostalgic reverie explaining why Hazlitt has never bothered to own a watch or a clock. In the midst of this brief study of the nostalgias, we are suddenly given a memorable theory of romance, as applicable to Hawthorne as to Wordsworth:

Surely, if there is anything with which we should not mix up our vanity and self-consequence, it is with Time, the most independent of all things. All the sublime, all the superstition that hang upon this palpable mode of announcing its flight, are chiefly attracted to this circumstance. Time would lose its abstracted character, if we kept it like a curiosity or a jack-in-a-box: its prophetic warnings would have no effect, if it obviously spoke only at our prompting, like a paltry ventriloquism. The clock that tells the coming, dreaded hour— the castle bell, that "with its brazen throat and iron tongue, sounds one unto the drowsy ear of night"—the curfew, "swinging slow with sullen roar" o'er wizard stream or fountain, are like a voice from other worlds, big

with unknown events. The last sound, which is still kept up as an old custom in many parts of England, is a great favourite with me. I used to hear it when a boy. It tells a tale of other times. The days that are past, the generations that are gone, the tangled forest glades and hamlets brown of my native country, the woodsman's art, the Norman warrior armed for the battle or in his festive hall, the conqueror's iron rule and peasant's lamp extinguished, all start up at the clamorous peal, and fill my mind with fear and wonder. I confess, nothing at present interests me but what has been— the recollection of the impressions of my early life, or events long past, of which only the dim traces remain in a smouldering ruin or half-obsolete custom. That *things should be that are now no more,* creates in my mind the most unfeigned astonishment. I cannot solve the mystery of the past, nor exhaust my pleasure in it.

One sees, after reading this, why Wordsworth's "Ode: Intimations of Immortality" was Hazlitt's poem-of-poems, as it was Emerson's and Ruskin's. Hazlitt's regret is hardly for actual immortality, which he dismisses with splendid vigor in his **"On the Fear of Death."** It is rather what he adumbrates in his superb **"On the Feeling of Immortality in Youth"**:

Objects, on our first acquaintance with them, have that singleness and integrity of impression that it seems as if nothing could destroy or obliterate them, so firmly are they stamped and rivetted on the brain. We repose on them with a sort of voluptuous indolence, in full faith and boundless confidence. We are absorbed in the present moment, or return to the same point— idling away a great deal of time in youth, thinking we have enough and to spare. There is often a local feeling in the air, which is as fixed as if it were of marble; we loiter in dim cloisters, losing ourselves in thought and in their glimmering arches; a winding road before us seems as long as the journey of life, and as full of events. Time and experience dissipate this illusion; and by reducing them to detail, circumscribe the limits of our expectations. It is only as the pageant of life passes by and the masques turn their backs upon us, that we see through the deception, or believe that the train will have an end. In many cases, the slow progress and monotonous texture of our lives, before we mingle with the world and are embroiled in its affairs, has a tendency to aid the same feeling. We have a difficulty, when left to ourselves, and without the resource of books or some more lively pursuit, to "beguile the slow and creeping hours of time," and argue that if it moves on always at this tedious snail's-pace, it can never come to an end. We are willing to skip over certain portions of it that separate us from favourite objects, that irritate ourselves at the unnecessary delay. The young are prodigal of life from a superabundance of it; the old are tenacious on the same score, because they have little left, and cannot enjoy even what remains of it.

As a commentary upon our common experience, both when young and when old, this compels the chill of a self-recognition beyond illusion and delusion alike. But it is also a powerfully implicit commentary upon Wordsworth's Great Ode, and upon very nearly everything else in Wordsworth that truly matters. Hazlitt's strength, matched among critics in the language only by Johnson and by Ruskin, is that he never allows us to forget the dark and antithetical relationship between the power of the imagination and the power of human experience. Imaginative gain and experiential loss are identical in Hazlitt, who, unlike Wordsworth, understands that there is no knowledge that is not purchased by the loss of power, no power that is not purchased at the expense both of others and of the self.

Nancy Enright (essay date 1989)

SOURCE: "William Hazlitt and His 'Familiar Style'," in *Essays on the Essay: Redefining the Genre,* edited by Alexander J. Butrym, University of Georgia Press, 1989, pp. 116-25.

[*In the essay that follows, Enright discusses the careful balance between stiff overformality and amateurish lack of style that characterizes the ideal of Hazlitt's "Familiar Style."*]

> Coming forward and seating himself on the ground in his white dress and tightened turban, the chief of the Indian Jugglers begins with tossing up two brass balls, which is what any of us could do, and concludes with keeping up four at the same time, which is what none of us could do to save our lives, not if we were to take our whole lives to do it in. Is it then a trifling power we see at work, or is it not something next to miraculous?

—**"The Indian Jugglers"** (*Works,* VIII)

The wonder and admiration that William Hazlitt felt for the Indian jugglers and tightrope walkers grew perhaps out of his devotion to *balance* in the area of writing. For Hazlitt defines the essay according to the terms of what he calls "the Familiar Style." This style consists of a balancing act between various extremes and opposites.

In his essay **"On the Familiar Style"** (*Works,* VIII, 242), Hazlitt delineates the terms of his definition, responding to attacks against his "underformality." Criticized for vulgarity and lack of polish (**"On the Familiar Style"**) and called a "slangwhanger" (Chesire 101-102), Hazlitt defends himself by explaining the difference between a Familiar Style and mere lack of style. He insists that creating the balance between a proper structure and style on the one hand and a pleasing naturalness on the other requires hard work and much skill: "It is not easy to write a familiar style. . . . There

is nothing that requires more precision and, if I may so say, purity of expression, than the style I am speaking of" ("**Familiar Style,**" *Works,* VIII, 242).

Hazlitt clearly describes the two barriers the good essayist must not cross, overformality and underformality, in order to achieve this proper *balance,* a balance not maintained in his *Liber Amoris* or in his letters and journal. The Familiar Style "utterly rejects not only all unmeaning pomp, but all low, cant phrases, and loose, unconnected, slipshod allusions" ("**Familiar Style,**" *Works,* VIII, 242). The essayist must be direct and clear without being offensively blunt or overly emotional. Of course, what might have offended Hazlitt's nineteenth-century audience and what would alienate twentieth-century readers differ considerably, and realistically a writer can never achieve a perfectly accessible and fully audience-directed style. However, as an ideal toward which one aims, the balance between over- and underformality is an important goal for the essayist who wishes to avoid merely ventilating emotion or writing to a limited clique of readers. The Familiar Style is informed not by censureship or "policing" of expression but rather by a sensitivity to clarity and an awareness of audience.

This distinction is clearly seen when Hazlitt's discussion of a particular concept in an essay is compared with his treatment of it in another form of writing, such as one of the letters in his *Liber Amoris.* This work, decidedly not an essay, consists of a series of conversations, written in script form, between Hazlitt's thinly veiled persona, H, and a young lady named Sarah Walker; it also includes letters to her, less often from her, and, most often, to friends about her. In one such letter Hazlitt describes his passion in the following words: "The barbed arrow is in my heart—I can neither endure it, nor draw it out; for with it flows my life's blood" (Letter 7, *Liber Amoris* II, 138 *Works,* VIII, 124). Contrast the preceding example with the following discussion of passion in one of Hazlitt's essays: "Passion is the undue irritation of the will from indulgence or opposition; imagination is the anticipation of unknown good; affection is the attachment we form to any object from its being connected with the habitual impression of numberless sources and ramifications of pleasure. The heart is the most central of all things" ("**On Novelty and Familiarity,**" *Works,* XII, 310). Note the distancing of tone and the control evidenced in the essay, though both essay and letter describe passion. Or again, examine another example, the subject of which is disappointment in love, taken from Hazlitt's essay **"On Great and Little Things,"** in which the tone and voice are certainly personal. Hazlitt is obviously discussing something deeply important to him, but the frenzy and the clichés, evident in the letter, are gone, replaced by more objective, distanced tone and vocabulary: "To see beauty is not to be beautiful, to pine in love is not to be loved again—I always was inclined to raise and magnify the power of Love" (*Works* VIII, 236-37). Hazlitt's choice of words in the essays is prompted not by his emotional need to ventilate, as it is, at least to a greater degree, in the letter, but by a desire to communicate an idea to his audience in the clearest, most accessible way he can. One might argue that the comparison is weakened by the fact that in the letter Hazlitt is talking about a personal passion, whereas in the essays he is discussing passion in general, though in the second passage the context is an indirect reference to Sarah Walker. However, even when he is specifically describing his own negative emotions, his sense of failure and disappointment toward the end of his life, in his essay **"On the Pleasure of Hating,"** he avoids what might be called the vulgarity and the lack of control evidenced, not inappropriately so, in the letters, the journal, and even the *Liber*. In the essays, the balance is maintained: "Mistaken as I have been in my public and private hopes, calculating others from myself and calculating wrong; always disappointed where I placed most reliance; the dupe of friendship, and the fool of love; have I not reason to hate and to despise myself? Indeed I do; and chiefly for not having hated and despised the world enough" (*Works,* XII, 136). Compare the preceding paragraph to the following excerpt from a letter to P. G. Patmore in the *Liber* concerning Sarah Walker. Hazlitt's persona, H, laments, "To what a state am I reduced, and for what? For fancying a little artful vixen to be an angel and a saint, because she affected to look like one, to hide her rank thoughts and deadly purposes. Has she not murdered me under the mask of tenderest friendship?" (*Liber Amoris* II, Letter 9, *Works,* VIII, 127). Or again, compare the excerpt from the essay **"The Pleasure of Hating,"** quoted earlier, with the following expression of identical feelings of failure and general disillusionment in Letter 8 of the *Liber:* "I am pent up in burning and impotent desires which can find no vent or object. I am hated, repulsed, bemocked by all I love" (26, *Works,* VIII, 125). Both letter and essay express the same depth of despair, but the wildness, the sense of cathartic expurgation through the process of writing itself, is controlled in the essay, as it need not be in the letter. And Hazlitt's personal letters go beyond those in the *Liber,* which, as Robert Ready observes, are themselves edited to fit the overall theme and structure of that work and given "a good deal more coherence" than "some of the disconnected ravings we find in the original letters" (Ready 54). Note, for example, the following excerpt from this personal letter from Hazlitt to P. G. Patmore: "I would give a thousand worlds to believe her anything but what I suppose. *I love her, Heaven knows* [italics Hazlitt's]. W. H. You say I am to try her after she agrees to have me: No: but I hate her for this, that she refuses me, when she could go to—[several words obliterated] aye, and with a grave air,—I'm mad! so much for sentiment" (*Works,* IX, 273). These letters offer an even more striking contrast

with the essays. They remind me of the sort of writing composition that students do when told to "free-write" or to write in their journals. Ideas and perhaps deep feelings are flung out on paper, and only later do they achieve coherence and clarity in essay form. The sense of balance in the Familiar Style allows writers to express their deepest emotions but always with an awareness of their audience's sensibilities; when an essayist remains merely self-indulgent and ambiguous or disorganized, he or she has not gone far enough with revision or editing for clarity's sake.

Audience awareness also demands careful word choice, leading to writing that is precise, another attribute of the Familiar Style which also involves balance. Though the essayist need not be as technically precise, perhaps, as the scientist, philosopher, or theologian must be, he or she needs to choose words with greater care than does the conversationalist. Hazlitt says: "Out of eight or ten words equally common, equally intelligible, with nearly equal pretensions, it is a matter of some nicety and discrimination to pick out the very one, the preferableness of which is scarcely perceptible, but decisive" (**"On the Familiar Style,"** *Works,* VIII, 243). For example, notice the use of the word "dalliance" in the following excerpt from **"The Pleasure of Hating"**: "Pleasure asks a greater effort of the mind to support it than pain, and we turn, after a little *dalliance,* from what we love to what we hate" (emphasis mine). Hazlitt could have conveyed virtually the same sentence meaning with several other words—"while," "time," "flirtation"—but "dalliance" conveys just the right sense of short, fleeting time combined with a sense of something being loosely and playfully held. Again, note the use of the word "governed" in **"Conversations as Good as Real III"** (*Works,* XX, 295): "A man's understanding often had no more influence over his will than if they belonged to two different persons; nor frequently so much, since we sometimes consented to be *governed* by advice, though we could not control our passions if left to ourselves" (emphasis mine). In the context, the word "governed" denotes influence; however, "governed" also implies a sense of authority and of force not found in the word "influenced" and is thereby connected with the term "control" used in the next phrase. Hazlitt saw this ability to choose the precisely correct word as his strong point (Nabholtz 98); Hazlitt states, "I only used the word which seemed to me to signify the idea I wanted to convey, and I did not rest until I got it" (**"Letter to William Gifford,"** *Works,* IX, 30; quoted in Nabholtz).

This precise use of words helps to give the Familiar Style its quality of being like "heightened conversation." Again, the sense of balance is important. While Hazlitt asserts, "To expect an author to talk as he writes is ridiculous" (**"Characteristics,"** *Works,* IX, Letter

281, p. 208), he says that a good essay should give the effect of conversation in terms of voice and personal expressiveness while heightening this effect with the precise use of appropriate words. Says Hazlitt, "To write a genuine or truly English style, is to write as anyone would speak in common conversation, who had a thorough command and choice of words, or who could discourse with ease, force, and perspicuity, setting aside all pedantic and oratorical flourishes" (**"Familiar Style,"** *Works,* VII, 242). Nothing could sound more simple and "conversational" than the following statement from Hazlitt's essay **"On Novelty and Familiarity":** "I have spun out this Essay in a good measure from the dread I feel of entering upon new subjects" (*Works,* XII, 309). What could be more personal or appear more spontaneous than a writer's confession of a feeling of inadequacy about writing? However, a close reading will discover that the words "spun out" are indeed carefully chosen and implicitly metaphorical, suggesting a weaving of words and implying an analogy between spinner/craftsman and writer/craftsman. Or notice the key words in Hazlitt's description of the "newly ennobled" lady in **"On Vulgarity and Affectation":** "She rises into the air of gentility from the ground of a city life, and flutters about there with all the fantastic delight of a butterfly that has just changed its caterpillar state" (*Works,* VIII, 165). What words or phrases could better suggest the ephemeral quality of the state he is describing than "rises into air," "flutters," "fantastic delight," "butterfly"? The sentence is written in simple and clear English vocabulary, but the precisely chosen words "heighten" its effect.

Together with careful word choice, artful sentence structure also gives Hazlitt's Familiar Style the sense of being heightened conversation. Notice the parallelism in this highly personal and expressive yet carefully written excerpt from **"A Farewell to Essay Writing"** (*Works,* XVII, 314): "Beautiful Mask! I know thee! When I can judge of the heart from the face, of the thoughts from the lips, I may again trust myself!" Or note the similar use of parallelism in the following excerpt from **"On Paradox":** "With one party, whatever is, is right: with their antagonists, whatever is, is wrong" (*Works,* VIII, 147). The balance of the sentence structure unobtrusively gives the writing a poetic quality not usually found in ordinary speech while allowing it to retain its sense of naturalness and spontaneity.

Using the precise word in its proper context requires effort but not stultifying and excessive self-consciousness in a writer. Here again the balance of the Familiar Style avoids the extreme of overly rigorous precision of language. Like the Indian Juggler, the essayist must keep the equilibrium between naturalness of tone and carefully chosen vocabulary. While "the first word that occurs" is certainly not always the best, it may,

says Hazlitt, "be a very good one; and yet a better may present itself on reflection or from time to time" (**"Familiar Style,"** *Works,* VIII, 244). The good essayist is comfortable enough with subject and self to relax about vocabulary, allowing ultimately for better word choice. Hazlitt says a change in wording "should be suggested naturally . . . and spontaneously, from a fresh and lively conception of the subject" (**"Familiar Style,"** *Works,* VIII, 244). Unlike the philosophical or scientific writer, the essayist of the familiar style need not rigorously labor over the technically correct term. The subject, as always, is key; if the words elucidate the subject as clearly as possible, the essayist has done his or her job. Even the general organization of the essay must be determined by the subject and not rigorously imposed upon it. As John Nabholtz points out, Hazlitt's essays are not amorphous, as some people have said, but organized naturally around subject and purpose rather than made to fit a rhetorical pattern. Says Hazlitt: "A clear and comprehensive mind is, I conceive, shewn, not in the extensiveness of the plan which an author has chalked out for himself, but in the order and connection observed in the arrangement of the subject and the consistency of the several parts" (**"Reply to the Essay on Population,"** *Works,* I, 186-87; quoted in Nabholtz). Hazlitt makes this point very clearly in his description of the Familiar Style: "It is not pomp or pretension, but the adaptation of the expression to the idea that clenches a writer's meaning" (**"Familiar Style,"** *Works,* VIII, 244). Therefore, the proper choice of words and the correct organizational pattern flow from the desire to communicate as easily and effectively as possible with one's audience. If that desire becomes tainted with the urge to impress or mystify, meaning becomes lost in the words instead of being expressed through them.

Using what Hazlitt calls "common words" in their clearest application will result in universality, another important quality of the Familiar Style. The desire to communicate something to an audience leads the essayist to avoid pretension on the one hand and slang or ambiguity on the other; once again, we see that balance is key to Hazlitt's conception of the essay. Words are chosen for the clearest exposition of the subject and are used in their most widely recognized meaning. Says Hazlitt, "A truly natural or familiar style can never be quaint or vulgar for this reason, that it is of universal force and applicability, and that quaintness and vulgarity arise out of the immediate connection of certain words with coarse and disagreeable, or with confined ideas" (**"Familiar Style,"** *Works,* VIII, 242).

This distinction often arises in composition classes. If the teacher as well as the students can consistently remember the fulfillment of the goal of communication as the yardstick by which to measure all word choices, then much confusion may be avoided. Having taught composition on the college level for eight years, I know that many student writers need to see why it is important to choose words that their audience will clearly understand and to avoid words that will either alienate or confuse their readers. Thus the desire for clarity and universality, not for an overly pristine sense of formality, makes the use of slang words or colloquialisms generally inappropriate in a college essay though entirely appropriate in a letter, a journal, or ordinary speech. Words such as "hassle" (used as a noun) or "party" (used as a verb), for example, make perfect sense when used among student speakers, but in an essay intended for a general audience, these terms may be wrong. As Hazlitt puts it, a colloquialism "has a stamp exclusive and provincial" (**"On Vulgarity and Affectation,"** *Works,* VIII, 162). A quality that Hazlitt finds particularly annoying is *affected* vulgarity, for like any other affectation, it falsifies writing: "Nothing is vulgar that is natural, spontaneous, unavoidable. Grossness is not vulgarity, ignorance is not vulgarity, awkwardness is not vulgarity; but all these become vulgar when they are affected and shown off on the authority of others, or to fall in with *the fashion* or the company we keep" (**"On Vulgarity and Affectation,"** *Works,* VIII, 161). Colloquialisms often fit the above description, since they are frequently expressions in vogue, fleeting in popularity and changeable of meaning.

However, far from saying that informality is wrong in itself, Hazlitt himself uses slang, colloquialisms, and obscenity in his letters and journal but generally eschews such language in his essays, where his aim is the clarity and universality of the Familiar Style. Notice, for example, his use of the word "set" in the following excerpt from his journal notes during the period of his infatuation with Sarah Walker: "She then went out and gave one of her *set* [emphasis mine] looks at the door" (*Journals,* March 4, 1823). Hazlitt seems to have a special, personal meaning for the word "set"—appropriate for his journal but not for an essay, were he to use it in one without an explanation. In fact, he makes a point of saying that he avoids such a practice: "I never invented or gave a new and unauthorized meaning to any word but one single one (the term 'impersonal' applied to feelings) and that was in an abstruse metaphysical discussion to express a very difficult question" (**"Familiar Style,"** *Works,* VIII, 244). Notice the contrast that Hazlitt stresses between language of the Familiar Style, which should always advance the audience's ease of understanding, and that of another sort of writing, here metaphysics, wherein technical precision must impose itself over audience accessibility. Another example of Hazlitt's use of terminology inappropriate for the Familiar Style is his calling Sarah Walker "a bitch" and "an artful little vixen" and other such appellations in his letters or journal while avoiding such terminology in the essays.

Of course, no writer can ever achieve a style that is totally universal. Like all of the qualities of the Familiar Style, its universality is also an ideal toward which the essayist aims; the essayist can never be completely and equally accessible to *all* audiences. However, the concept of universality can do much to help students and teachers go beyond the mere arbitrariness of what is considered "acceptable" or "unacceptable" for a formal essay as opposed to what is appropriate in preliminary free writing or journal writing. If the clearest communication possible with one's audience is the goal in the essay, as Hazlitt suggests, the decision about which phrase works and which one does not becomes simplified. And student writers, understanding the *reason* why certain colloquialisms or slang words are considered inappropriate for a specific audience or type of assignment, can avoid the mistaken idea that all such informal language is bad *in itself* when used in the proper context.

This understanding can alleviate the confusion into which some student writers fall as they try to avoid informality, which they have been taught to do without understanding why, by using an excessively formal and inflated style. The result is writing in what Hazlitt calls "the florid style . . . the reverse of the familiar" (*Works,* VIII, 246). While the Familiar Style "is employed as an unvarnished medium to convey ideas," the Florid Style "is resorted to as a spangled veil to conceal the want of them" (**"Familiar Style,"** *Works,* VIII, 246). Unfortunately, the latter problem is more difficult to correct than the former. To such writers, the pageantry of words seems impressive, and often they cannot understand exactly what the writing teacher (or editor) finds objectionable. However, Hazlitt says such writers are guilty of another sort of "vulgarity" which is perhaps even worse than that which they are trying to avoid: "Gentility is only a more select and artificial vulgarity" (**"On Vulgarity and Affectation,"** *Works,* VIII, 157). The root problem in both cases is falsehood, "taking manners, actions, words, opinions on trust from others, without examining one's own feelings or weighing the merits of the case" (**"On Vulgarity and Affectation,"** *Works,* VIII, 157). As with all of the other attributes of the Familiar Style, the key here is once again to convey the subject in the most direct and honest way possible, maintaining the balance between a confusing overformality and a limiting colloquialism. An inflated style, like a "vulgar" one, as Hazlitt calls it, impedes honest communication.

Hazlitt notes a further solution for this problem of artificiality in his discussion of the naturalness of the Familiar Style. For Hazlitt, the source of all good writing is Truth: all that is real, expressed in words as it is experienced in the heart of the writer. For him, any other sort of writing is mere "pride and ignorance—pride in outside show . . . and ignorance of the true worth and hidden structure of both words and things" (**"Familiar Style,"** *Works,* VIII, 247). In his essay **"On Novelty and Familiar Things,"** Hazlitt states, "That the tongue or the pen or the pencil can describe the workings of nature with the highest truth and eloquence without being prompted by or holding communication with the heart . . . I utterly deny" (*Works,* XII, 298). One cannot *pretend* to a Familiar Style; one must be speaking from the heart. In Hazlitt's words, "What we impart to others we have within us" (**"Novelty and Familiar Things"**). The writing teacher and the student writer both experience the frustration of reading and producing, respectively, works that proceed from a desire for a grade, a desire to imitate "textbook style" writing, a desire to please; however, if students can be guided toward producing works that on one level or another proceed from the heart, they will have moved a long way toward becoming serious and interesting writers. Any essayist, guided by Hazlitt's principles of the Familiar Style, can move in the direction of writing that fits Harold Bloom's description of Hazlitt's literary essay: "It must be experiential; it must be at least somewhat empirical or pragmatic; it must be informed by love of its subject; above all it must follow no method except the personality of the critic himself" (Bloom 8).

Hazlitt's Familiar Style of essay writing can therefore be defined as *a means for the mind to express the feelings of the heart,* as it is stirred by nature, that is, anything and everything. Yet it must do so in a manner that retains the balance, the sense of audience awareness, that distinguishes self-expressiveness from mere self-indulgent expression. The Essay, with its adaptability and limitless range of potential subjects, is the perfect vehicle for such expression. Its possible subject matters are vast because the capacity of the human mind to interpret and experience its surroundings is vast. "What a Proteus is the human mind!" exclaims Hazlitt; "All that we know, think of, or can admire, in a manner becomes ourselves" (**"On Personal Identity,"** *Works,* XVII, 274). Hazlitt's own essays, particularly when they are contrasted with his other writings, exhibit the Familiar Style he advocates in their clarity, their universality, their naturalness, and, most important, their balance. Though Hazlitt humbly contrasts his ability as a writer with the dexterity of the Indian Juggler, his Familiar Style is a valiant attempt to reproduce as well as to define, through "the inefficiency and slow progress of intellectual compared to mechanical excellence" (**"Indian Jugglers,"** *Works,* VIII, 79), something of the balancing act he so admired.

Notes

Bloom, Harold. "Introduction." In *Modern Critical Views: William Hazlitt,* ed. and introd. Harold Bloom. New York: Chelsea House, 1986.

Chesire, Ardner R., Jr. "William Hazlitt: Slangwhanger." *Wordsworth Circle,* 7 (1976): 101-102.

Hazlitt, William. *The Complete Works in Twenty-One Volumes: Centenary Edition.* Ed. P. P. Howe. After the edition of A. R. Waller and Arnold Glover. New York: AMS Press, 1967.

———. *The Journals of Sarah and William Hazlitt, 1822-1831.* Ed. Willard Hallard Bonner. *University of Buffalo Studies,* vol. 24, no. 3, February 1959.

Nabholtz, John R. "Modes of Discourse in Hazlitt's Prose." *Wordsworth Circle,* 10 (1979): 97-106.

Ready, Robert. "The Logic of Passion: *Liber Amoris.*" In *Modern Critical Views: William Hazlitt,* ed. and introd. Harold Bloom. New York: Chelsea House, 1986.

James Mulvihill (essay date 1990)

SOURCE: "The Anatomy of Idolatry: Hazlitt's *Liber Amoris,*" in *The Charles Lamb Bulletin,* n.s. No. 70, April, 1990, pp. 195-203.

[*In the following essay, Mulvihill attempts to reevaluate* Liber Amoris, *which he contends is not an unseemly self-exposure, but an analysis of the feeling of infatuation itself.*]

It has been said that we know too much about the Romantics. Certainly, we know too much about the author of **Liber Amoris; or, The New Pygmalion** (1823), for, preoccupied with the autobiographical origins of this, William Hazlitt's only work of fiction, readers have largely misread the book itself. In this strange, obsessive little work Hazlitt recounts, in compulsive detail, his unrequited and disastrous infatuation with a lodging-house maid named Sally Walker. It is 'something between a work of art and a case history', according to Cyril Connolly, while Lord David Cecil has memorably said that 'No one ever edited his personality for publication less.'[1] Only recently have critics begun to regard **Liber Amoris** as something more than a literary monstrosity, interesting only as a document of unseemly self-exposure.[2] Rather than merely the thinly-disguised record of a middle-aged infatuation, **Liber Amoris** is an exhaustive and erudite analysis of the idea of infatuation which happens to find its starting-point in a middle-aged infatuation. The confessional aspect must be viewed in the context of this overarching analytical purpose, and equally as the literary form consciously chosen as best able to carry within itself the more transparent mode of 'anatomy' or investigation and analysis of private feelings and mental states in this work.

According to Frye, the 'anatomy' (or Menoppean satire) 'presents us with a vision of the world in terms of a single intellectual pattern.' Its satiric focus is not moral or social but intellectual, for the anatomist sees evil and folly 'as diseases of the intellect, as a kind of maddened pedantry which the *philosophus gloriosus* at once symbolizes and defines'— the latter being Frye's term for the pedant-hero of the anatomy. Bakhtin terms this figure the 'hero-ideologist', and states that the aim of what he calls the *menippea* is 'to test the idea and the man of the idea'.[3] The defining trait of *Liber Amoris,* similarly, is its obsessive intellection. In the final section of this work, the narrator H—concludes that a 'more complete experiment on character was never made' (160).[4] While a reference to 'character' may suggest the social and psychological emphases of the novel, the term 'experiment' describes Hazlitt's anatomistic approach to his subject, for in *Liber Amoris* 'character' is an idea, a hypothesis to be rigorously tested and debated. Much as Bakhtin's *menippea* concerns itself with 'moral-psychological experimentation' and creates '*extraordinary situations* in which to provoke and test a philosophical idea', so *Liber Amoris* is a sort of 'moral-psychological' crucible— Godwin's *Political Justice* is described in *The Spirit of the Age* as 'an *experimentum crucis* to show the weak sides and imperfections of human reason as the sole law of human action' (11. 23)— in which Hazlitt decompounds H—'s infatuation with S— and analyzes its elements, observing their actions and reactions in various situations. Hence the 'propositions' put forward by H— at one point as he ponders his love for S— (124), and his appeals to his correspondent C. P— as 'a philosopher' (118). (A reviewer in the *Examiner* in fact noted a philosophical bent in this work.[5]) Moreover, 'character' here is ancillary to a more dominant preoccupation of Hazlitt's, which is the idea of idolatry, a concept introduced in the very subtitle, *The New Pygmalion.*

Every other idea and motif is subsumed by this central preoccupation to form the 'single intellectual pattern' that is H—'s vision of the world in *Liber Amoris.* Each episode, each circumstance of H—'s courtship of S—, is, as Bakhtin observes of even the most fantastic Menippean interludes, 'subordinated to the purely ideological function of provoking and testing the truth.'[6] Like the Shakespeare of *Twelfth Night* he describes elsewhere, Hazlitt 'runs riot in a conceit and idolises a quibble' (4. 314), for the obsessive nature of anatomy perfectly suits this work's theme of idolatry and the disputatious bent of its author. Hazlitt, or rather his narrator, is *philosophus gloriosus* in love.

Within its largely dialogic-epistolary framework, *Liber Amoris* exhibits the medley style typical of the anatomy, containing verse, manuscript notations, *pensees,* and miniature familiar essays, and underlying this multiform structure is the anatomist's preoccupation with examining an idea from as many points of view and by means of as many methods as possible. H—'s analysis of his idolatrous bent must of necessity include all its possible vehicles, for idolatry is pre-eminently a formal impulse— a compulsion to objectify, and obsessive need to impose form upon desire. Hence the various manners in which H— attempts to approach the object of his desires: the dialogues of Part I in which he tries to coerce the indifferent S— into reflecting, or rather echoing, his ideas concerning her; the letters to S— in which, his attempts at dialogue having failed, H— modulates into supplicating monologue; the letters to C.P— and J.S.K— in which H— attempts to validate his obsession with S— by appealing to the sympathy and understanding of another, H—'s retreats into subjectivity, on the one hand, in pensees and miniature familiar essays, and, on the other hand, H—'s sober, objective references to his situation and prospects in journal-like fragments of italicized narrative ('*To this letter I have received no answer, not a line*' [114]). Thus it is possible for Hazlitt to exhibit H—'s monomaniacal obsession from the different perspectives of the genres through which H— variously attempts to objectify his desires in S—.

The anatomy's playful, multiform nature may also indicate a parodic impulse. Marilyn Butler has recently argued that *Liber Amoris* is in fact a satire and that works like it and Shelley's *Alastor* present a 'critique of Romantic autobiography'. Butler does not relate this thematic preoccupation to the actual form of *Liber Amoris,* but certainly the genres variously employed by Hazlitt in this work are, with the exception of the critical/dialectical form of the dialogue, conventional forms of self-revelation: letters, pensees, familiar essays, journal entries. Perhaps, though, Hazlitt's concern is less with confession than with obsession, the confessional mode serving chiefly as a vehicle for this satiric preoccupation. Significantly, many of the allusions and quotations in *Liber Amoris* point to such works of sentimental obsession as Shakespeare's *Romeo and Juliet, Othello, Hamlet, Troilus and Cressida* and the sonnets, Byron's *Sardanapalus,* Keats' *Endymion,* and Mackenzie's *Man of Feeling.* One of these allusions, for instance, takes the intriguing form of a jotted note 'WRITTEN IN A BLANK LEAF OF ENDYMION' (114). Reminiscent in its bibliographic playfulness of Sterne, this reference dovetails nicely into the intellectual pattern of *Liber Amoris,* for Keats' elusive feminine ideal issues from the same epipsychic impulse as S—, the protean Venus-Lamia figure of H—'s obsessive worship. While carrying no subversive overtones separately, in the prevailingly analytical context of *Liber Amoris* such intertextual elements suggest the satiric/parodic pattern of anatomy. The numerous quotations, often an irritating mannerism elsewhere in Hazlitt, are here perfectly suited to both subject and form. Collectively they constitute something like the chaotic, fragmentary record left by Carlyle's Teufelsdrockh of his infatuation with the obscure Blumine—'confused masses of Eulogy and Elegy, with their mad Petrarchan and Werterean ware lying madly scattered among all sorts of quite extraneous matter'[7]—and as in the case of *Sartor Resartus* the disorder and the extraneousness are only apparent. The formal conventions of romantic confession, courtly love, portraiture, tragedy, metaphysical drama, the novel of sensibility, and so on, in this seeming miscellany of recondite erotica, have been manipulated into the satiric self-portrait that is Hazlitt's anatomy of idolatry.

It is in keeping with its paradoxical nature that the anatomy should be so variegated in its form and references and yet so obsessively focused on some ruling idea. Thus, for instance, Herr Teufelsdrockh's clothes philosophy informs every one of the bewildering array of subjects raised in *Sartor Resartus* as Carlyle's Professor 'undertakes to make manifest, in its thousandfold bearings, this grand Proposition, that Man's earthly interests 'are all hooked and buttoned together, and held up, by Clothes.'[8] In *Liber Amoris,* as I have suggested, every other idea is subsumed by Hazlitt's ruling preoccupation with the concept of idolatry, its 'grand Proposition', in the words of the love-lorn H—, is that 'nothing touches me but what has a reference to her' (123)—namely, S—, his heart's idol' (119). 'I will make a Goddess of her', cries the infatuated H—, 'and build a temple to her in my heart, and worship her on indestructible altars, and raise statues to her' (133). But idolatry is not restricted only to affairs of the heart in *Liber Amoris.* '[w]e are more in love with a theory than a mistress', Hazlitt writes elsewhere (18. 306), and this statement holds true even with reference to H—'s mistress, for in the end it is not S—but the nature of H—'s obsession with her that is the central preoccupation of this work. Moreover, while 'love's projective psychology', as Robert Ready terms it,[9] is the immediate subject of *Liber Amoris,* the underlying principle of which this psychological phenomenon is an aspect—namely idolatry—this underlying principle in its many other manifestations, political and aesthetic as well as erotic, is finally the subject of Hazlitt's anatomizing intelligence. What is central to this Book of Love, then, is the theory behind H—'s love for his mistress.

The terms 'idol' and 'idolatry' recur throughout Hazlitt's writings in numerous contexts, aesthetic and political. Hazlitt, indeed, believed that he lived in an age of idolatry. In an essay **'On the Spirit of Monarchy'**, published the same year as *Liber Amoris,* he suggests that man's progress from the 'brute idols' of primitive superstition to the graven images restored in the name of Legitimacy after Waterloo has not been so great after all:

> It was thought a bold stride to divert the course of our imaginations, the overflowings of our enthusiasm, our love of the mighty and the marvellous, from the dead to the living *subject,* and there we stick. We have got living idols, instead of dead ones; and we fancy that they are real, and put faith in them accordingly. Oh, Reason! when will thy long minority expire? (19. 259)

Hazlitt himself, as John Kinnaird notes, is often 'an infatuated idolater of "greatness" ' in his writings,[10] and chief among the idols, living and dead, to whom he pays homage are Shakespeare and Napoleon, as well as lesser gods like Edmund Kean the actor. Though arising in part from what in an essay on **'Mind and Motive'** Hazlitt terms *the power of fascination'* (20.45), and thus something passive and susceptible, idolatry is also for Hazlitt a species of self-aggrandizement by which a subject willfully establishes its own preconceived ideal in an object. 'The idol we fall down and worship', states Hazlitt, 'is an image familiar to our minds' (8. 311), is in effect created in our own image, but not necessarily in our best image. In Hazlitt's estimate, the great folly of the age is the newly-revived cult of Legitimacy—wholly a product of idolatrous projection:

> The contrivers or re-modellers of this idol, beat all other idol-mongers, whether Jews, Gentiles or Christians, hollow. The principle of an idolatry is the same: it is the want of something to admire, without knowing what or why: it is the want of an effect without a cause; it is a voluntary tribute of admiration which does not compromise our vanity: it is setting something up over the rest of the world, to which we feel ourselves to be superior, for it is our own handywork; so that the more perverse the homage we pay to it, the more it pampers our self-will: the meaner the object, the more magnificent and pompous the attributes we bestow upon it; the greater the lie, the more enthusiastically it is believed and greedily swallowed. (7. 150)

Idolatry is at once a desire to worship otherness and a projection of self. Its deception, then, lies within both idol and idolater, for the one is not what it seems, while the other seems to adore what it cannot, and will not, know beyond itself. The 'stupid idol', according to Hazlitt in *The Spirit of the Age,* is 'set up on its pedestal of pride for men to fall down and worship with idiot fear and wonder at the thing themselves have made, and which, without that fear and wonder, would itself be nothing!' (11. 7).

Throughout the dialogues of *Liber Amoris* the debate between idol and idolater— 'this running fight of question and answer', as H— calls it (152)— turns on just such an epistemological impasse. When, in the opening dialogue of Part I, 'The Picture', H— warns S— that 'if you are never to be mine, I shall not long be myself' (99), he indicates the investment of ego involved in his hoped-for possession of S—. His insistence that she resembles the female subject of a certain picture he owns is thus nothing more than a pampering of his own self-will. The ensuing exchange amounts to an indirect, though remarkably dense, pathology of imaginative projection that is not without its ironic edge, as, like the worshippers of Legitimacy in Hazlitt's description above, H— attempts to re-model his reluctant idol:

> S. Do not, I beg, talk in that manner, but tell me what this is a picture of.
>
> H. I hardly know, but it is a very small and delicate copy (painted in oil on a gold ground) of some fine old Italian picture, Guido's or Raphael's, but I think Raphael's. Some say it is a Madonna; others call it a Magdalen, and say you may distinguish the tear upon the cheek, though no tear is there. But it seems to me more like Raphael's St. Cecilia, 'with looks commercing with the skies', than anything else.— See, Sarah, how beautiful it is! Ah! dear girl, these are the ideas I have cherished in my heart, and in my brain; and I never found any thing to realize them in earth till I met with thee, my love! While thou didst seem sensible of my kindness, I was but too happy: but now thou hast cruelly cast me off.
>
> S. You have no reason to say so: you are the same to me as ever.
>
> H. That is, nothing. You are to me everything, and I am nothing to you. Is it not too true?
>
> S. No.
>
> H. Then kiss me, my sweetest. Oh! could you see your face now— your mouth full of suppressed sensibility, your down-cast eyes, the soft blush upon that cheek, you would not say the picture is not like because it is too handsome, or because you want complexion. Thou art heavenly-fair, my love— like her from whom the picture was taken— the idol of the painter's heart, as thou art of mine! Shall I make a drawing of it, altering the dress a little, to shew you how like it is?
>
> S. As you please.— (99-100)

And here the debate ends, only to be picked up in the ensuing dialogue, and in the dialogue after that, and so forth.

Ostensibly, there are only two perspectives here: that of the taciturn and somewhat sullen S—, and that of H—, effusive and desperate. But whereas S— speaks in only the monotone of everyday speech, H—'s longer, more animated speeches exhibit a greater dynamic range; they are, in Bakhtin's phrase, 'internally dialogized'. H— is by turns courtly lover, connoisseur of art, man of letters, painter, and hopeless wretch, and underlying his many voices is the ground bass of idolatry, for in each mode he attempts to objectify his 'idea' of S—, cherished in both his 'heart' and 'brain'. She is variously a Madonna and a Magdalen— by Guido or Raphael— or perhaps she is Raphael's St. Cecilia, though the quotation accompanying this identification suggests that she is also Milton's melancholy goddess in 'Il Penseroso'. Thus she is virgin and whore, patron saint of music and muse of melancholy: she is, in short, anything H— can make of her in his various modes. He ends by offering to remake her once again by drawing a revised copy of the copy to which he originally compared her. *Liber Amoris* does indeed, as Butler nicely puts it, draw out 'the human comedy implicit in the making and breaking of icons'.[11]

For her part, S— maintains a stubborn insistence on the integrity of her literal identity and on her feelings toward H—. '[Y]ou are the same to me as ever', she tells him, and when he hysterically demands to know whether he is nothing to her, her answer is a simple 'No'. S—'s final 'As you please' to H—'s offer to draw her suggests the irresolution characteristic of the anatomy, a genre, according to Philip Stevick, 'strong on tensions but rather disinclined to resolve them'.[12] Hence the numerous dinner debates in Peacock that achieve gustatory but never intellectual resolution. Moreover, S—'s concluding words only give expression to the intellectual uncertainty that has underlain H—'s extravagant propositions throughout the dialogue. When S— asks him about the female subject of his picture, he answers, 'I hardly know', and the identifications that follow are speculative and even contradictory.

Variations on this theme run through *Liber Amoris* as Hazlitt examines idolatry in its many possible permutations. In the example above, H—'s habit of abstracting an image of his intellectual ideal in S— is implicitly paralleled with the process by which a painter's model is transformed into 'the idol of the painter's heart' (100). Not surprisingly, H— often refers to the sculptor's art in his idealizing of S—. 'Since I wrote to you about making a formal proposal', H— tells his correspondent C.P—, 'I have had her face constantly before me, looking so like some faultless marble statue, as cold, as fixed and graceful as statue ever did'. Here H— betrays his desire to appropriate and 'fix' S—'s very self much as the sculptor imprisons beauty and grace in his frozen, immobile medium, 'for I think', H— adds, 'she was made on purpose for me' (137-38). The statue motif also recalls the Pygmalion myth of the subtitle, for indeed the impulse to idolize is not restricted to the pictorial arts. The poet's ideal embodiments, too— whether Milton's Eve (126), the mistress of Shakespeare's sonnets (133), the elusive Cynthia of

Keats' *Endymion* (114)— these ideal feminine embodiments are the graven images that at once possess and are possessed by the poet. Even the book as physical artifact bears a totemic significance as witnessed by H—'s reverence for those books— authored by him, significantly— that he has made gifts of to S— (148-9). Most revered, of course, is the Book itself, this Book of Love that H— has consecrated in the name of his devotion to S—. Catherine MacDonald MacLean observes that while Hazlitt might have hoped to loosen the grip of his obsession by writing about it, he merely gave it more tangible form in a book which 'served him also at times as, a graven image'.[13]

It is in the dialogues concerning 'the little image', however, that the full scope of Hazlitt's intellectual preoccupation with idolatry becomes evident. In an episode entitled 'The Reconciliation', H— queries S— about a former lover and wonders if she was first drawn to him by his likeness to this lover. S— denies this but does claim a likeness between her old lover and a small bronze figure of Buonaparte on H—'s mantle. In a passage of italicized narrative H— describes how he was moved by this admission to give her the figure: *'And then I added "How odd it was that the God of my idolatry should turn out to be like her Idol, and said it was no wonder that the same face which awed the world should conquer the sweetest creature in it!" '* (112). The 'little image' clearly has a totemic significance, serving as an objectification of H—'s love for S—. Moreover, this tiny statue is such a potent symbol for H—'s worship of a woman because it carries the associations of an equally idolatrous political devotion. In *Political Essays* (1819) Hazlitt describes the spiritual malaise from which Napoleon saved disaffected liberals during the reactionary retrenchment of Legitimacy that set in following the French Revolution, claiming that 'He who saves me from this conclusion, who makes a mock of this doctrine, and sets at nought its power, is to me not less than the God of my idolatry . . . He who did this for me, and for the rest of the world, and who alone could do it, was Buonaparte' (7. 10). Hazlitt's justification of his idolatry— for it *is* justification, directed at those disillusioned by the barbarities of a warlike god— implicitly distinguishes, without wholly divorcing, the man from the ideal projection that issues as graven image. 'It is true, I admired the man', states Hazlitt in the preface to his *Life of Napoleon Buonaparte,* 'but what chiefly attached me to him, was his being, as he had been long ago designated, "the child and champion of the Revolution." Of this character he could not divest himself, even though he wished it. He was nothing, he could be nothing but what he owed to himself and to his triumphs over those who claimed mankind as their inheritance by a divine right' (13. ix). Thus Napoleon is the object in which the projective imagination of the idolater sets up its sacred idea, the living icon of revolutionary liberation opposed to the false god of Legitimacy. Divested of this 'character', he would be 'nothing' in the eyes of his jacobin idolater.

Napoleon had since fallen of course, so that the devotee of S— had already experienced what it was to have the god of his idolatry overthrown. From all contemporary accounts, Napoleon's defeat at Waterloo shattered Hazlitt and become the sole, obsessive topic of his conversation for some time afterwards, as his traumatic infatuation for Sally Walker would six years later. Indeed, though Hazlitt once described the abstract theorizing of the French Revolution as being much more seductive than a mistress (18. 306), it is clear that to the author of *Liber Amoris* attachments so apparently different in mind may be similar in degree, for informing both is the projective imaginative intensity of the idolater. Hazlitt, in the years following Napoleon's defeat, felt increasingly the solitary righteousness of one devoted to a fallen god. 'To have an object always in view dearer to one than one's self', he writes in 1821, 'to cling to a principle in contempt of danger, of interest, of the opinion of the world,— this is the true *ideal,* the high and heroic state of man' (20.99), and he speaks with the knowledge of one who has experienced the lonely rigours of being a Buonapartist in post-Waterloo England. In *Liber Amoris* H— assumes a similar role with respect to his quixotic devotion to S—, contemplating in Part II a life dedicated to the faithful worship of his 'Goddess' despite her hostility. 'And thus', he concludes, 'my love will have shown itself superior to her hate; and I shall triumph and then die. This is my idea of the only true and heroic love!' (134). The spurned lover and the alienated jacobin become martyrs to their own peculiar idols. *Liber Amoris* must be one of the very few instances where sexual failure serves to sublimate political zeal.

But a thin line divides consecration from desecration. In one of his letters to J.S.K.— in Part III, H— describes an emotional episode in which he is alternately ideolater, appealing to S—'s attachment to *'the little image',* and iconoclast, cursing her name and destroying the symbols of his love for her:

> I tore the locket which contained her hair (and which I used to wear continually in my bosom, as the precious token of her dear regard) from my neck, and trampled it in pieces. I then dashed the little Buonaparte on the ground, and stamped upon it, as one of her instruments of mockery. (145)

The idolater, in all his intellectual folly, is here decisively upset— 'discrowned', to use Bakhtin's term for the anatomy's overthrowing of the hero-ideologist[14]— humiliated and exposed as surely as the Peacockian crotcheteer inevitably finds himself the object of his creator's retributive slapstick. This episode plumbs the secret capacity of the idolater for blasphemy, the emotional relief of destroying what has been so carefully enshrined in the heart and cherished in spite of the most painful persecution—indeed, cherished all the more for the persecution and resented for this reason too. Hence the exquisite remorse that follows this act of release, the recriminations and the renewed devotions. S— has 'the little image' mended, though new pieces have had to be used in its repair, to which H— says ' "I didn't care how it was done, so that I had it restored to me safe, and by her" ' (156). But it will never be quite the same, just as H— can never quite trust S— completely, and the final rupture occurs soon after.

From a new historicist perspective, this episode could be viewed as yet another of the historical suppressions that characterize the Romantic ideology. An impulse toward idolatry and desecration alike is viewed elsewhere by Hazlitt as distinguishing the age. With respect to the violent fluctuations of Godwin's reputation, Hazlitt asks in *The Spirit of the Age:* 'Is the very God of our idolatry all of a sudden to become an abomination and an anathema?' (11.17).

It is to this tendency that Hazlitt credits the success of such contemporary luminaries as Reverend Edward Irving, who 'keeps the public in awe by insulting all their favourite idols' (11. 41), and Lord Byron, who 'hallows in order to desecrate, takes a pleasure in defacing the images of beauty his hands have wrought, and raises our hopes and our belief in goodness to Heaven only to dash them to the earth again, and break them in pieces the more effectually from the very height they have fallen' (11. 75). Surely the smashing of the 'little image' just two years before lies somewhere behind these passages. In *Liber Amoris* H—'s infatuation with S— develops along lines similar to the course of political sensibility during the post-Waterloo period, at least as seen from Hazlitt's morbidly disillusioned perspective. While it would be wrong to see in H—'s smashing of the 'little image' a rejection of the Napoleonic ideal— based, that is, on anything we know of the history of Hazlitt's beliefs—perhaps this act indicates a revulsion from the idolatrous intensity of his Buonapartism. According to Kinnaird, Hazlitt's fascination with Napoleon was 'compounded variously of combative idealism and vengeful contempt for idealism, of fear, envy, baffled pride, and the identification of the impotent with compensatory or oppressive strength'.[15] Thus Hazlitt might certainly have recognized in himself the very idolatrous impulse he saw imaged in the noxious hegemony of Legitimacy, that 'lie' so 'greedily swallowed' by its worshippers. Through H—'s destruction of Buonaparte's image, therefore, Hazlitt rejects not the man, or the libertarian idea he associates with the man, but the obsession that fuses man and idea into an object of idolatrous regard. S— has been fashioned by H— into

just such an object, only to be symbolically destroyed in the cruel dissection of her character that concludes *Liber Amoris*— and from the same willful compulsion to desecrate that has led to the destruction of the 'little image'. Moreover, the terms which the disaffected H— uses to describe this fallen idol of his heart—she is to him now only a 'phantom', a 'mockery', and a 'frightful illusion' (153, 159)— are similar to those in which Hazlitt elsewhere describes the 'phantom of the imagination' Legitimacy (7. 151). Hazlitt could never bring himself to describe his Buonapartism in such terms, but the deception in which idols and their idolaters are implicated is finally no different in nature than that involving the 'little image' and the middle-aged radical.

H—'s last words, then, that 'no flower will ever bloom on earth to glad my heart again' (162), carry both a personal and a public meaning. In an essay **'On the Pleasure of Hating'**, written the same year, Hazlitt bitterly reflects that 'mistaken as I have been in my public and private hopes, calculating others from myself, and calculating wrong, always disappointed where I placed most reliance, the dupe of friendship, and the fool of love, have I not reason to hate and to despise myself? Indeed I do, and chiefly for not having hated and despised the world enough' (12. 136). Hazlitt can only be referring here to his disappointments in love and politics, as in a later essay **'On the Fear of Death'** (1825) in which he dismisses his life, saying, 'My public and private hopes have been left a ruin, or remain only to mock me' (8. 325). It was a common enough strain among liberals and radicals at the time, this public/personal *topos* finds its critique in figures such as Wordsworth's Solitary in *The Excursion* and Peacock's Shelley-like Scythrop Glowry in *Nightmare Abbey* in reaction to much less critical presentations in works like Byron's *Childe Harold*. In the ironic self-portrait presented in *Liber Amoris,* Hazlitt, in the obsessive manner of the anatomist, examines this spirit of the age under the rubric of idolatry, tracing his peculiar intellectual bent through its various permutations in love, art, and politics. 'A more complete experiment on character was never made', claims H—, for indeed it is the testing 'of the idea and the man of the idea' with which Hazlitt is ultimately concerned in his anatomy of idolatry.

Notes

1 Cyril Connolly, 'Hazlitt's "Liber Amoris" ', *London Magazine* 1 (November, 1954), 58, *The Fine Art of Reading* (London, Constable, 1957), p. 247.

2 For example, in his recent *English Fiction of the Romantic Period* (London, Macmillan), Gary Kelly characterizes this work as a 'Romantic lyrical quasi-novel'. Similarly, Marilyn Butler speaks of this work's 'inception as letters to its appearance as a novel';

'Satire and the Images of Self in the Romantic Period: The Long Tradition of Hazlitt's *Liber Amoris,*' in *English Satire and the Satiric Tradition,* ed. Claude Rawson (Oxford: Basil Blackwell, 1984), p. 216. See also Robert Ready, 'The Logic of Passion: Hazlitt's *Liber Amoris', Studies in Romanticism,* 14 (Winter, 1975), 41-57. On the other hand, Gerald Lahey, in the introduction to his recent edition of *Liber Amoris* (New York: Gotham Library, 1980) still emphasizes the traditional autobiographical view of this work.

[3] Northrop Frye, *Anatomy of Criticism* (Princeton: Princeton University Press, 1971), pp. 310, 309, Mikhail Bakhtin, *Problems of Dostoevsky's Poetics,* trans. R. W. Rotsel (Munster: Ardis, 1973), pp. 91, 122.

[4] *The Complete Works of William Hazlitt,* ed. P. P. Howe (London: J. M. Dent and Sons, 1932), v. 9. Hereafter, all further references to *Liber Amoris* will be taken from this volume and edition. References to Hazlitt's other works will be identified by volume as well as page.

[5] Cited by Butler, 223.

[6] Bakhtin, pp. 95, 94.

[7] Butler, p. 210, Thomas Carlyle, *Sartor Resartus: The Life and Opinions of Herr Teufeldsrockh* (London: Curwen Press, 1931), pp. 175-6.

[8] Carlyle, p. 63.

[9] 'The Logic of Passion', 46.

[10] *Hazlitt: Critic of Power* (New York: Columbia University Press, 1978), p. 36.

[11] Bakhtin, p. 114, Butler, p. 222.

[12] Stevick, 164.

[13] Catherine MacDonald MacLean, *Born Under Saturn* (New York: Macmillan, 1944) p. 440.

[14] Bakhtin, p. 102.

[15] Kinnaird, p. 327.

James Mulvihill (essay date 1990)

SOURCE: "Hazlitt and 'First Principles'," in *Studies in Romanticism,* Vol. 29, No. 2, Summer, 1990, pp. 241-55.

[*In this essay, Mulvihill contends that Hazlitt's method of inferring character is not impressionistic, as has been claimed, but empiricist, using seemingly insignificant traits to discover the general principles of character.*]

As Recently As 1981, Marilyn Butler termed William Hazlitt's writings "impressionistic and personal."[1] Thus to at least one eminent student of romanticism a response to Hazlitt premised on his apparently "idiosyncratic critical posture" (Butler 173) remains adequate even after decades of scholarship arguing the contrary. Such a view reflects the persistence of what John Kinnaird has called "the myth of Hazlitt's 'critical impressionism.'"[2] In this view, Hazlitt's *forte* as a critic is "emotive self-dramatization, rather than sustained thought" (Butler 171)—Hazlitt being somehow incapable of "a defined, consistent philosophy of life" or even "a consistent point of view," according to an earlier commentator.[3]

"Thus," says Hazlitt, "people continually find fault with the colours of style as incompatible with the truth of the reasoning, but without any foundation whatever" (12: 46).[4] Does "emotive self-dramatization" necessarily preclude "sustained thought"? **"My First Acquaintance with Poets,"** to cite a familiar example, is infused with the poignant recollection of emotion and incident which forms the other pole to the testiness that the Lake poets could also provoke in Hazlitt. Nevertheless, underlying its personal portrait of Coleridge is a preoccupation with more abstract concerns, for "Coleridge in truth," says Hazlitt, "met me halfway on the ground of philosophy" (17: 115). Hazlitt's account of their famous walk along the Shrewsbury road combines the personal/circumstantial with the abstract/general:

> I observed that he continually crossed me on the way by shifting from one side of the foot-path to the other. This struck me as an odd movement; but I did not at that time connect it with any instability of purpose or involuntary change of principle, as I have done since. He seemed unable to keep on in a strait line. (17: 113)

Here Hazlitt perceives the general cause working out through a particular effect. While a man's manner of walking, even so eccentric a manner as this, may seem a rather slender—even impressionistic—basis for judging his principles, there is a certain inductive logic to Hazlitt's method. "When Sir Isaac Newton saw the apple fall," Hazlitt mentions elsewhere, "it was a very simple and common observation, but it suggested to his mind the law that holds the universe together" (12: 358). Similarly, an innocuous event on the Shrewsbury road, though at the time suggesting nothing more than a wayward gait, indicates, through hindsight and the observation of many other such occurrences, the underlying principle—a wayward intellect. Eighteen years later, Hazlitt would observe of the author of the *Lay Sermons* that "[h]e moves in an unaccountable diagonal between truth and falsehood, sense and nonsense, sophistry and commonplace. . . . All his notions are floating and unfixed" (7: 116-17). Moreover, this principle is capable of a wider application, as Hazlitt demonstrates in his essay **"On Consistency of Opinion"**: "There is no use in shifting from place to place, from side to side, or from subject to subject. You have always to begin again, and never finish any course of study or observation" (17: 33). Indeed, to Hazlitt in the years following Waterloo, the wayward, fluctuating principle he had observed in Coleridge two decades before must have seemed as universal as Newton's law.

If they were isolated occurrences, such passages might constitute no more than figures of speech—among a good many other figures of speech in Hazlitt. Yet they point to an important concern of Hazlitt the critic and essayist that is still obscured by the impressionistic myth. In his account of Coleridge on the Shrewsbury road Hazlitt displays what he calls "depth" in his essay **"On Depth and Superficiality"**:

> *Depth* consists then in tracing any number of particular effects to a general principle, or in distinguishing an unknown cause from the individual and varying circumstances with which it is implicated, and under which it lurks unsuspected. It is in fact resolving the concrete into the abstract. . . . the mind, instead of being led away by the last or first object or detached view of the subject that occurs, connects all these into a whole from the top to the bottom, and by its intimate sympathy with the most obscure and random impressions that tend to the same result, evolves a principle of abstract truth. (12: 355)

A meandering gait, an eccentric prose style, unreliable political views—these seemingly "obscure and random impressions" are only the beginning of a process in which "particular effects" are traced to a "general principle." Hazlitt, as I will show, is not in his methods an impressionist finally, but an empiricist for whom "random impressions" are the means to an end.

II

While Hazlitt was critical of the way empirical thinkers tended to reduce mind and thought into physical phenomena,[5] physical analogy is nevertheless an important element in his writings. Like Hogarth, who to him "embodied and made tangible the very thoughts and passing movements of the mind" (6: 133), Hazlitt instinctively thinks in the most palpable, concrete terms, not so much rejecting the materialist thesis as qualifying and refining it to reflect his own critical observations. Thus, in his essay **"On Liberty and Necessity,"** even while he refutes the billiard-ball analogy used by necessitarians to depict the mind as a passive agent, he counters in kind with a physical analogy of his own: "[S]uppose I push against a heavy body; if it be square it will not move: if it be cylindrical it will. What the difference of form is to the stone, the difference of disposition is to the mind" (2: 269). In **"Prospectus of**

a History of English Philosophy" he argues similarly that the mind "is free, as the body is free, when it is not subject to a power out of itself, though its operations still depend on certain powers and principles within itself" (2: 118). Moreover, it is only a lateral step from the analogy between mind and matter to that between the social and the natural worlds, for "[t]he material universe is infinitely divisible, and so is the texture of human affairs" (8: 240).

Hazlitt is influenced mainly by Thomas Hobbes in his use of physical analogy. Indeed, "the celebrated philosopher of Malmesbury," as he is called in *The Spirit of the Age* (11: 53), receives pride of place in Hazlitt's **"Lectures on English Philosophy,"** delivered in 1812, where his radical nominalism is described in terms that might be used of Hazlitt himself: "[A]ll his ideas seemed to lie like substances in his brain: what was not a solid, tangible, distinct, palpable object was to him nothing" (2: 126).[6] At the root of the model of man and society posited by Hobbes is Galileo's law of inertia—that motion, not rest, as philosophers since Aristotle had assumed, is the natural state of things in the physical universe. "'When a body is once in motion,'" states Hobbes in a passage cited by Hazlitt, "'it moveth (unless something else hinder it) eternally'" (2: 131). What Hobbes did was to apply Galileo's mechanics to the human sphere, describing man's sensations, desires, and motives as the results of internal motions termed by Hobbes "appetites" and "aversions," and man himself as a body in motion within the larger body politic.[7] Thus, in Hazlitt's rendering of Hobbes's leading proposition, "as nothing exists out of mind but matter and motion, so it is itself with all its operations nothing but matter and motion" (2: 144).

Hazlitt, it is true, can be critical of Hobbes's thoroughgoing materialism. Yet, he admires the "comprehension and precision" with which Hobbes accounts for "every movement of the mind" (2: 134) and indeed, as the latter phrase indicates, is strongly drawn by this psychological application of the laws of motion. In his essay **"On Liberty and Necessity,"** which is essentially Hobbesian in orientation, Hazlitt seems to admit wholeheartedly the materialist analogy:

> By the principle of moral or philosophical necessity is meant then that the mind is invariably governed by certain laws which determine all its operations; or in other words, that the regular succession of cause and effect is not confined to mere matter, while the impulses of the will are left quite unaccounted for, self-caused, perfectly contingent and fantastical. (2: 245)

Hazlitt and Hobbes both argue that these "impulses of the will" appear "contingent and fantastical" only because they operate in a more complex manner than the motions of mere matter and are therefore more difficult to predict (2: 246). Moreover, if the motions within an individual mind are complex and diverse, the motions of numerous individuals within society are manifoldly so. In the *Leviathan* Hobbes states that although "the voluntary actions, and inclinations of all men" tend similarly to the same end, the attainment of happiness, they differ as to means—"which ariseth partly from the diversity of passions, in divers men; and partly from the difference of the knowledge, or opinion each one has of the courses, which produce the effect desired" (Hobbes 161).

To Hazlitt, too, man and society are complex entities, "containing numberless modifications of reason and prejudice, of thought and passion" (4: 67), that act and re-act against each other like charged particles of matter. Hazlitt has thus derived from Hobbes a dynamic model of humanity in which each constituent element moves according to its own impulses or is impeded by other bodies of opposite tendency, according to consistent if complicated principles. Hence "the shocks of accident and fluctuations of opinion" (4:4) that Hazlitt observes in everything from manners and morals to literature and politics. "Spirit of contradiction!" he cries, almost as if to his own peculiar muse, "when wilt thou cease to rule over sublunary affairs, as the moon governs the tides? Not till the unexpected stroke of a comet throws up a new breed of men and animals from the bowels of the earth; nor then neither, since it is included in the very idea of all life, power, and motion. *For* and *against* are inseparable terms" (19: 303).

Hazlitt's Shakespeare criticism is a case in point, occupied as it is with analyzing "the distinct and complicated reaction of the character upon circumstances" (5: 211). Thus Shakespearean tragedy is essentially a study in attraction and repulsion:

> In Shakespeare there is a continual composition and decomposition of its elements, a fermentation of every particle in the whole mass, by its alternate affinity or antipathy to other principles which are brought in contact with it. Till the experiment is tried, we do not know the result, the turn which the character will take in its new circumstances. (5: 51)

In the Elizabethan age itself Shakespeare is a kind of imaginative nucleus and his contemporaries "a mighty phalanx of kindred spirits closing him round, moving in the same orbit, and impelled by the same causes in their whirling and eccentric career" (6: 181). In Hazlitt's own age, the apostate Lake Poets "oscillate, with a giddy and sickening motion, from one absurdity to another" (8: 151), their erratic motions reflected in microcosm in Coleridge, whose mind "is in a constant estate of flux and reflux. . . . He is no sooner borne to the utmost point of his ambition, than he is hurried away

from it again by the same fantastic impulse" (7: 117). As an essayist, Hazlitt is preoccupied with "reducing things to their principles" (11: 54), isolating the element that gives his subject, whether the Elizabethan drama or political apostates, its characteristic tendency or determination. "The actions, and events, and feelings of human life, the passions and pursuits of men," he believes, "could no more go on without the interference of the understanding than without an original principle of physical sensibility" (2: 220-21). Here, then, the role of the "understanding" in the determination and motivation of character is comparable to that of "an original principle of physical sensibility" in animating the body, though not identical. Hence the curious double signification of such terms in Hazlitt as "impulse," "bias," "tendency," "direction," "disposition," "impetus," "resistance," "direction," and "inclination"—terms that at once denote abstract ethical or intellectual relations and concrete, physical ones. Of course, language is filled with once figurative expressions that have settled into a neutral abstract existence, but in Hazlitt the original mind/matter duality inherent in such terms exerts a surprisingly durable rhetorical force.

In the **"Character of Lord Chatham,"** for example, political principle seems to resolve itself into a physical principle as Hazlitt isolates the springs of action in Chatham: "The feelings and the rights of Englishmen were enshrined in his heart; and with their united force braced every nerve, possessed every faculty, and communicated warmth and vital energy to every part of his being. The whole man moved under this impulse" (7: 297). The term "impulse" is suggestive less of conscious, intellectual motive here than of involuntary physical impetus—the necessary impetus under which Chatham acted. " '[N]othing taketh beginning from itself,' " according to Hobbes in a passage quoted by Hazlitt, " 'but from the action of some other immediate agent without itself' " (2: 247). No political temporizer, Chatham is nevertheless like Hobbes's physical agent, which must ultimately take its impetus from "some immediate agent without itself"—in this case, the "united force" of English libertarianism. "[D]ecided character," according to Hazlitt, is "a marked determination to an extreme point" (8: 318), and it is on the basis of the principle which lends it this "determination" or "impulse" that character is defined.

Moreover, the term "principle" is itself potentially dualistic, signifying physical law as well as philosophical or moral motive. Hazlitt's usage often alternates between these categories, as, on one hand, in a discussion of the human soul in his portrait of Jeremy Bentham in *The Spirit of the Age*—"The soul, by reason of its weakness, is an aggregating and an exclusive principle; it clings obstinately to some things, and violently rejects others" (11: 8-9)—and, on the other, in his reflections on the political reversals that have thrust William Godwin into near obscurity: "Could so many young men of talent, of education, and of principle have been hurried away by what had neither truth, nor nature, not one particle of honest feeling nor the least show of reason in it?" (11: 17). The latter excerpt here is in effect "mind" to the former's "matter." Hazlitt depicts soul or mind as an active moral agent that is nevertheless subject to external forces: an "aggregating and an exclusive principle," it alternately attracts and repels, because "it must do so" (11: 9). Thus too are those men of principle formerly attracted by the doctrines of *Political Justice* now repelled by them.

Is truth, then, so relative? The answer is a qualified yes. In his **"Character of Mr. Burke,"** Hazlitt asserts "that truth is *many*. There are as many truths as there are things and causes of action and contradictory principles at work in society." He does, to be sure, extend this relativism only so far, for "[i]n making up the account of good and evil, indeed, the final result must be one way or the other." Nevertheless, "the particulars on which that result depends are infinite and various" (7: 308). Thus, "instead of referring to any distinct or positive fact," important truths or principles "must point out the combined effects of an extensive chain of causes, operating gradually, remotely, and collectively, and therefore imperceptibly" (7: 304-5).

When Hazlitt writes of political apostates, then, that "[t]hey have changed sides to preserve the integrity of their principles and the consistency of their characters" (7: 132), his irony is only partial, for there are principles, and then there are first principles. "Depth," we recall, consists in "distinguishing an unknown cause from the individual and varying circumstances with which it is implicated." In his essay **"On Consistency of Opinion"** Hazlitt thus traces inconsistent principles to an anterior principle, finding apostates to be "made up of mere antipathies—a very repulsive sort of personages—at odds with themselves, and with every body else" (17: 24). Of the Lake poets he concludes similarly:

> They must be conspicuous, dogmatical, exclusive, intolerant, on whichever side they are: the mode may be different, the principle is the same. A man's nature does not change, though he may profess different sentiments. A Socinian may become a Calvinist, or a Whig a Tory: but a bigot is always a bigot; an egotist never becomes humble. (19: 277)

"General principles," indeed, "are not the less true or important because from their nature they elude immediate observation" (7: 305). Surely such a realization lies somewhere behind Hazlitt's account of that portentous walk with Coleridge.

III

Turning to the miscellaneous mass of Hazlitt's work—the literary criticism, the art criticism, the political writings, the familiar essays—we find as many principles at work as there are topics: hence the "spirit of contradiction" that bears sway over this intellectual universe where "*for* and *against* are inseparable terms." There is no progression without contraries, and the stubborn resistance of mind, like that of matter, must exist in constant friction with its opposing principle or sink into "the *vis inertiae* of custom and indolence" (17: 331). Sympathy and tolerance depend, paradoxically, on antipathy, for "[a]ll opinions, by constant collision and attrition, become, if not equally probable, equally familiar. Men's minds are slowly weaned from blind idolatrous bigotry and intolerant zeal, by the continually increasing number of points of controversy and the frequency of dispute" (20: 102). Moreover, even such humanistic qualities as sympathy and tolerance may themselves fall prey to the "*vis inertiae*" if not resisted by some contrary principle. As Hazlitt suggests in his essay **"On Novelty and Familiarity,"** a principle of atrophy is inherent in even an inquiring intellect: "The facility which habit gives in admitting new ideas, or in reflecting upon old ones, renders the exercise of intellectual activity a matter of comparative insignificance; and by taking away the resistance and the difficulty, takes away the liveliness of impulse that imparts a sense of pleasure or of pain to the soul" (12: 296). For mind and matter alike, attraction and repulsion, impulse and motion, action and reaction, resistance and coalescence, are innate and necessary principles: "When people have done quarrelling about one set of questions they start another. Motion is necessary to mind as much to matter; and for 'an ultimate end,' Hobbes denies that there is any such thing" (20: 334).

Hazlitt's analogies are drawn not from one but many sciences, applied and theoretical: physics, chemistry, mechanics, electricity and magnetism, geometry, optics, and astronomy among them. Moreover, they find applications in many subjects. "His penetrating eye," writes Hazlitt of a rival drama critic, "is infinitely delighted with the picturesque appearance of so many imperceptible deviations from a right line, and mathematical inclinations from the perpendicular" (20: 6). In a more speculative vein, Hazlitt finds that "[t]he mind resembles a prism, which untwists the various rays of truth, and displays them by different modes and in several parcels" (20: 298). Yet, too, "[t]here are indeed certain minds that seem formed as conductors to truth and beauty, as the hardest metals carry off the electric fluid, and round which all examples of excellence, whether in art or nature, play harmless and ineffectual" (16: 189-90). Just as "[t]ragedy is human nature tried in the crucible of affliction" (12:

346), so the grammatical analyses of the *Diversions of Purley* reduce language to its primary elements: "Mr. Tooke, in fact, treated words as the chemists do substances; he separated those which are compounded of others from those which are not decompoundable" (11: 55). Physical laws seem similarly to apply in the sphere of political reform, for according to Hazlitt "public opinion might be said to rest on an inclined plane, tending more and more from the heights of arbitrary power and individual pretension to the level of public good" (12: 374). Indeed, "[t]he lever, the screw, and the wedge, are the great instruments of the mechanical world: opinion, sympathy, praise and blame, reward and punishment, are the lever, the screw, and the wedge, of the moral world" (20: 63).

All these metaphors are premised on Hazlitt's notion of physical analogy, and each, whether drawn from chemistry or mechanics, operates in an essentially Newtonian universe where matter and motion are governed by certain basic principles. That Hazlitt himself ever read Newton is uncertain, although he need not have. "I believe firmly in the Newtonian system," he writes in his **"Aphorisms on Man,"** "though I have never read the *Principia*" (20: 330). Hobbes's application of Galileo seems to have provided Hazlitt with the initial impulse for this general tendency—and it is just that, a tendency, a pervasive tendency it is true, but not a thorough-going system in either the Newtonian or Hobbesian senses. Moreover, it is a tendency more immediately observable in Hazlitt as an aspect of usage than of cosmology. This is not to reduce Hazlitt's physical analogies to mere detached impressionistic figures of speech, however, for an underlying principle is always present beneath seemingly "random impressions." In the following passage, Hazlitt discusses Hogarth's art in terms at once abstract and concrete: "There is a perpetual collision of eccentricities—a tilt and tournament of absurdities—the prejudices and caprices of mankind are let loose, and set together by the ears, as in a bear-garden" (18: 98). Here the movement is from general principle to particular circumstances: first the preconditions of motion and resistance and then their particular occurrences in Hogarth as we advance from a "perpetual collision" of elements, in this case "eccentricities," through the more concrete and peculiar "tilt and tournament," to the pre-eminently circumstantial and Hogarthian image of the "bear-garden." Each half of the equation is equally necessary: the finely descriptive impression of Hogarth's art and the principle detected beneath it.

Nevertheless, even in its final equation the above figure still retains an abstract dimension, for this is no particular picture by Hogarth and neither are these particular people in a picture, but general human qualities, "prejudices and caprices" constituting the informing principles isolated by Hogarth's

satiric genius. Indeed, elsewhere Hazlitt goes even further and identifies the very principle of "art" in Hogarth:

> Hogarth's pictures are true history. Every feature, limb, figure, group, is instinct with life and motion. He does not take a subject and place it in a position, like a lay figure, in which it stirs neither limb nor joint. The scene moves before you. . . . The muscles pull different ways, or the same way, at the same time, on the surface of the picture, as they do in the human body. What you see is the reverse of *still life*. There is a continual and complete action and reaction of one variable part upon another, as there is in the Elgin Marbles. (18: 161)

"The principle of life and motion is, after all, the primary condition of all genius" (11: 135), and it is this vital impulse that characterizes "Gin Lane" as much as the "Ilissus."

This principle finds an application not only in Hazlitt's general estimate of art, but in more specific connections as well. In Hazlitt's analysis the characters of Shakespeare often seem more like physical agents operating in a universe of matter and motion than figures on the tragic stage. Thus even such an unnatural villain as Iago, "a man who will not suffer himself or any one else to be at rest" (18: 201), adheres to the principle of inertia (as opposed to the Aristotelian assumption of "natural place") a century before the *Principia* was published. Unlike her tormentor, Desdemona is more acted upon than acting, but the terms in which her passiveness is described also carry an implicit suggestion of Newtonian mechanics:

> Bating the commencement of her passion, which is a little fantastical and self-willed (though that may be accounted for in the same way from an inability to resist a rising inclination) her whole character consists in having no will of her own, no prompter but her obedience. Her romantic turn is only a consequence of the domestic and practical part of her disposition. (20: 87)

In this passage are combined the material necessity of an efficient causation with the moral imperatives of tragic character, as Hazlitt's usage—i.e., "resist," "inclination," "disposition"—equivocates between psychological motive and physical impulse. Such a tendency can also be traced in the novel criticism. In Godwin's *Cloudesley,* for example, "the spirit of the execution is lost in the inertness of the subject-matter" (16: 395), while the hero "remains a characterless, passive, inefficient agent to the last" (16: 394). Hazlitt detects the same weakness in the novels of Sir Walter Scott whose heroes "are worked out of very listless and inert materials. . . . Instead of acting, they are acted upon, and keep in the background and in a neutral position" (17: 252). Such as they are—for they are conventional heroes of romance—they "follow the general law of their being" (17: 252).

Like other talented Tories, Scott is problematic for Hazlitt. The insipidity of his leading characters notwithstanding, Scott the novelist is a man of genius, while Scott the poet lacks "power"—that imaginative impulse capable of animating "the inert, scattered, incoherent materials presented to it" (11: 59)—and Scott the Tory is down-right regressive, holding "that the moral world stands still, as the material one was supposed to do of old" (11: 58). Thus in one mind are combined the principle of motion and its absence: "The cells of his memory are vast, various, full even to bursting with life and motion; his speculative understanding is empty, flaccid, poor, and dead" (11: 58). Scott is largely an exception among Tories, however, and Burke another matter. William Gifford and his like present no such complications. The editor of the *Quarterly Review* "cannot bear the slightest jostling or irregularity of motion":

> Flashes of thought, flights of fancy, idiomatic
> expressions, he sets down among the signs of the
> times—the extraordinary occurrences of the age
> we live in. They are marks of a restless and
> revolutionary spirit: they disturb his composure
> of mind, and threaten (by implication) the safety
> of the state. His slow, snail-paced, bed-rid habits
> of reasoning, cannot keep up with the whirling,
> eccentric motion, the rapid, perhaps extravagant
> combinations of modern literature. He has long
> been stationary himself, and is determined that
> others shall remain so. (11: 116)

In Gifford's liberal rival Francis Jeffrey, by contrast, "there is a constitutional buoyancy and elasticity of mind . . . that cannot subside into repose, much less sink into dulness" (11: 132).

The reactionary bias detected in literary Tories like Scott and Gifford is no isolated anomaly in the age. Hazlitt detects its stultifying influence in all those who oppose "the progress of natural refinement" that he identifies with the *zeitgeist* (12: 128-29). "They will always stand in the way," Hazlitt complains of these forces of reaction, "and oppose the *vis intertiae* of custom and indolence (at least) to every project of amelioration and reform" (17: 331). Thus Lord Eldon, "true to the call of prejudice, of power, to the will of others and to his own interest," stands against all innovation, "fixed and immovable" (11: 146). Likewise characterized by this innate antipathy to progress, George Canning runs a "heedless career" (11: 154) in support of that bugbear of reform, Legitimacy, his ruling impulse: "It is the principle of his interference and of his forbearance. It makes him move forward, or retreat, or stand still" (11: 156). Indeed, if Hazlitt isolated a single principle behind this reactionary tem-

per, it is Legitimacy: "It smites with its petrific mace, it deadens with its torpedo touch, the Minister, the Parliament, the people, and makes this vast, free, enlightened, and enterprising country, a body without a soul, an inert mass" (11: 157).

Although an active principle is not of itself an infallible indicator of that vital impulse Hazlitt detects in genius, it is nevertheless a requisite. In *The Spirit of the Age* Hazlitt concludes of Bentham that "we should find a difficulty in adducing from his different works (however elaborate or closely reasoned) any new element of thought" (11: 8). The tacit metaphor of the chemical "element" suggests the dynamic, interactive aspect of Hazlitt's model of genius, for a "truth discovered" is "like a new substance in nature" (11: 7), acting and reacting with other elements in nature. Having "not struck out any great leading principle" (11: 7), Bentham is relegated to the realm of the "passive" according to a scheme outlined by Hazlitt in his essay, **"On Liberty and Neccessity."** There the term "active" is defined as "the positive determinate tendency or the additional impulse to the production of any effect," and "passive" as "an indifference in any agent to this or that motion, except as it is acted upon by, and transmits the efficacy of other causes" (2: 268). What Hazlitt goes on to develop here is essentially a theory of originality based on the laws of motion:

> Any thing is so far active as it modifies and re-acts upon the original impulse; it is passive in as far as it neither adds to, nor takes from that original impulse, but merely has a power of receiving and continuing it. This I take to be the practical and philosophical meaning of the terms. *This distinction, therefore, applies equally to matter and mind.* (2: 268-69; my italics)

Thus is Bentham's system a mere "inventory," "a very nicely dovetailed mosaic pavement of legal commonplaces" (11: 14), for his "*forte* is arrangement," and he has given no "new or decided impulse to the human mind" (11: 7).

This passive principle Hazlitt detects in many other connections besides Bentham's philosophy. Sir Joshua Reynolds is "an industrious compiler, or skilful translator, not an original inventor in art" (18: 53). Although he is granted his place in English painting, Reynolds is finally like Hazlitt's passive agent, neither adding to nor taking from the original impulse, for "[t]he art would remain, in all its essential elements, just where it is, if Sir Joshua Reynolds had never lived" (18: 53)—that is, not English art *per se* but art in general, for Hazlitt is now speaking of first principles, and here Reynolds has added no new essential element. Of French art as a whole Hazlitt concludes:

> A premature and superficial sensibility is the grave
> of French genius and of French taste. Beyond the

momentary impulse of a lively organisation, all the rest is mechanical and pedantic; they give you rules and theories for truth and nature, the Unities for poetry, and the dead body for the living soul of art. (12: 332)

A vital, original art draws on nature rather than pre-cept:

> There is no alliteration or antithesis in the style of the Elgin Marbles, no setness, squareness, affectation, or formality of appearance. . . . The sculptor does not proceed on architectural principles. His work has the freedom, the variety, and stamp of nature. The form of corresponding parts is indeed the same, but it is subject to inflection from different circumstances. (18: 148)

In Shakespeare, similarly, "nothing is made out by formal inference and analogy, by climax and antithesis: all comes, or seems to come, immediately from nature" (5: 50), in contrast to Shakespeare's editor, Dr. Johnson, whose criticism is governed "by rule and system, by climax, inference, and antithesis" (4: 175).

As in politics and philosophy, then, so in art and letters. Whether in the "inert mass" of reactionary imposture, Bentham's static classifications, or the retarding pedantry of neoclassical dicta, the principle is the same. But even vital, original impulses are subject to corruption, for the mind, "that unequal compound," is "alternately swayed by individual biasses and abstract pretensions" (20: 319). The author of *Political Justice,* William Godwin has clearly given a "first impulse" to mind, and his philosophy, though "true and sound" (11: 19) in its first conception, has been characterized subsequently by violent action and reaction. With his "overcharged" opinions, he once "carried with him all the most sanguine and fearless understandings of the time," whereas now these same opinions repel those whom they formerly attracted (11: 17). In their own erratic, extreme career, indeed, these opinions have been "warped and debased by the example, the vices, and follies of the world" (11: 18)—namely, by those in whom inconstancy of principle is the anterior principle. In the case of Thomas Malthus, the original impulse has from the start been misguided. "He has not left opinion where he found it," allows Hazlitt, but "given it a wrong bias" (11: 104). With the appearance of Godwin's utopian projections in *Political Justice,* "the hopes and the imaginations of speculative men could not but rush forward into this ideal world as into a *vacuum* of good" (11: 106), and one notable speculator, Malthus, claimed to have carried Godwin's principles to their extreme logical end and to have exposed their fallacy—"but a wrong bias was thus given, and the author's theory was thus rendered warped, disjointed, and sophistical from the very outset" (11: 105).

Hazlitt isolates this "principle of fluctuation and reaction" (11: 9) in many others, too, for in his analysis the mind is a highly unstable compound. But Coleridge is always the cautionary instance. His mind is *"tangential"* (11: 29), and the three-page account given in *The Spirit of the Age* of his intellectual career is dizzying in its momentum and irregularity.[8] In the end, Hazlitt concludes "[i]t was not to be supposed that Mr. Coleridge could keep on at the rate he set off; he could not realize all he knew or thought, and less could not fix his desultory ambition" (11: 34). The "mouldering" ruin that remains is of course the Sage of Highgate, a very different figure from the radical thinker "who some twenty years ago, threw a great stone into the standing pool of criticism . . . which gave a motion to the surface and a reverberation to the neighbouring echoes, which has not since subsided" (11: 28)—and yet demonstrating the same principle, as Coleridge's companion of a quarter century before on the Shrewsbury road well knew.

IV

Although Hazlitt believed that mental and physical phenomena were "two things entirely distinct" (20: 13), there is no denying the pervasiveness of physical analogy in his critical language. Certainly it does not assume the shape of a system as it does in empirical psychology; Hazlitt does not view himself as a Newton among critics. Neither, however, is it merely an idiosyncrasy of Hazlitt's impressionism. As much as Hobbes, Hazlitt refuses "to resolve the solid fabric of the universe into an essence of Della-Cruscan witticism and conceit" (12: 318), and his use of physical analogy indicates an assumption that the mental world is governed by discoverable efficient causes, that "[t]here must be a principle, a fund of activity somewhere, by and through which our sensibility operates" (20: 47). Neither idiosyncratic nor systematic, Hazlitt uses the methods of empiricism to achieve a criticism that combines sensitive observation with inductive inference. The result is dynamic rather than static, a crucible revealing "ideas in their first concoction" (8: 57).

Notes

[1] Marilyn Butler, *Romantics, Rebels, and Reactionaries* (Toronto: Oxford UP, 1981) 170.

[2] John Kinnaird, *William Hazlitt: Critic of Power* (New York: Columbia UP, 1978) 163.

[3] Lord David Cecil, "Hazlitt's Occasional Essays," *The Fine Art of Reading* (Indianapolis: Bobbs-Merrill, 1957) 247, 248.

[4] *The Complete Works of William Hazlitt,* edited by P. P. Howe (Toronto: J. M. Dent and Sons, 1932).

Hereafter, all further references in the text will be to this edition cited by volume and page.

5 "An exceedingly technical and scientific mode of reasoning," Hazlitt cautions in his essay "On Reason and Imagination," is "scarcely attainable in the mixed questions of human life" (12: 52). David Bromwich characterizes Hazlitt "as a thinker committed to the procedures of empirical philosophy but convinced that the tradition ought to be revised—arguing always from experience, and drawing his illustrations from ordinary life; but unwilling to resolve mental into physical phenomena, when he came to define experience itself": *Hazlitt: The Mind of a Critic* (New York: Oxford UP, 1983) 29.

6 In his "Farewell to Essay-Writing" Hazlitt says of himself: "I have brooded over an idea till it has become a kind of substance in my brain" (17: 317). The phrase is originally used of Wordsworth's Pedlar in *The Excursion* 1: 136-38.

7 See C. B. Macpherson's Introduction to Thomas Hobbes, *Leviathan,* ed. C. B. Macpherson (Harmondsworth: Penguin, 1982) 161. Further references in the text are to this edition.

8 Cf. Hazlitt's review of the *Lay Sermons:* "[T]he general character of Mr. Coleridge's intellect, is a restless and yet listless dissipation, that yields to every impulse, and is stopped by every obstacle; an indifference to the greatest trifles, or the most important truths: or rather, a preference of the vapid to the solid, of the possible to the actual, of the impossible to both; of theory to practice, of contradiction to reason, and of absurdity to common sense. Perhaps it is as well that he is so impracticable as he is: for whenever, by any accident, he comes to practice, he is dangerous in the extreme. Though his opinions are neutralized in the extreme levity of his understanding, we are sometimes tempted to suspect that they may be subjected to a more ignoble bias" (16: 102).

John L. Mahoney (essay date 1991)

SOURCE: "William Hazlitt: The Essay as Vehicle for the Romantic Critic," in *The Charles Lamb Bulletin,* n.s. No. 75, July, 1991, pp. 92-98.

[*In the following essay, Mahoney contends that Hazlitt's essay represents a move away from the formal treatise—and toward a more familiar style of writing about aesthetics that would become popular in the nineteenth century.*]

Genre is, of course, an old critical issue. As M. H. Abrams and others remind us, it is apparent in the ancient classical tendency to divide literature into epic-narrative, poetic-lyric, and dramatic, and it per-

sists with varying degrees of emphasis throughout the history of literary theory.[1] From the Renaissance to the neoclassic period, genres were strictly defined and were not to be mixed lightly lest their basic purity be defiled. There was also an order of rank with epic and tragedy regarded as major forms and lyric as minor. The more striking appearances of forms like the novel, biography, and the essay in the eighteenth-century and the further refinement of categories like poetry, fiction, and drama in the late eighteenth and early nineteenth-century create new effects, however, especially a certain weakening of confidence in the stability of genre theory.

Abrams places great emphasis on the emergence of certain kinds of poems—James Thompson's *The Seasons* with its combination of natural description and philosophy, the short lyric—as part of his thesis in *The Mirror and the Lamp* that a new concern with expression of the feelings of the writer further weakens a hierarchy of genres. One might question his somewhat sweeping generalization that from the Romantic period until the recent past, genres have been conceived as convenient but rather arbitrary ways to classify literature,[2] but he does capture nicely the thinning boundary lines between genres in the period.

Alastair Fowler's recent book, *Kinds of Literature: An Introduction to the Theory of Genres and Modes* enters a salutary warning that 'we have to allow for the fact that the complete range of genres is never equally, let alone fully available in any one period. Each age has a fairly small repertoire of genres that its readers and critics can respond to with enthusiasm. And the repertoire easily available to its writers is smaller still: the temporary canon is fixed for all but the greatest or strongest or most arcane writers.'[3] Each age makes its own adjustments. Epic gave way to the novel in the eighteenth-century; the realistic novel has been challenged by fabulations in our time only to see a surge of biography that seems to satisfy a demand for real people in real situations.

Enough for the backgrounds of genre questions. Our focus in this essay is the borderline of genres, that fascinating area where one form is actually moving toward another or, as I see it, where each of the two forms is being used in the service of the other. I am concerned with literary criticism and the essay, and I will consider William Hazlitt as a special example of the blending or merging of two nineteenth-century genres, and—even more important for me—as a precursor of the trend away from writing aesthetics and criticism in a formal treatise and toward the more personal, familiar essay that was to become so popular throughout the century.

A brief word about the use of the term 'essay'. Abrams is again helpful in his ability to capture tersely certain general characteristics associated with the essay in any age. He regards it as 'any brief composition in prose that undertakes to discuss a matter, express a point of view, or persuade us to accept a thesis on any subject whatever.'[4] We can build on this description, seeing the essay as formal or informal, aware of its audience, and using a general and non-technical approach to engage that audience. It had a long history before it was given its present name in Michel de Montaigne's *Essais* (1580) and a good deal of its validity in Francis Bacon's *Essays* (1597). Leslie Fiedler sees Montaigne as a clear prototype and the beginnings of the form in that larger cultural phenomenon which he calls 'the discovery of the self,' a phenomenon which he locates at a point between the flowering of the Renaissance and the outbreak of the French Revolution as the middle classes took their place somewhat closer to the aristocracy.[5]

In eighteenth-century England, with a widening reading audience and the rapid development of periodicals, Addison and Steele in the *Spectator* and *Tatler* and Samuel Johnson in the *Rambler, Idler,* and *Adventurer* set a standard for the form, but seemed so concerned with the didactic bent of the time that the personal often gave way to a somewhat public voice articulating ideas in a rather formal manner and structure. Yet their success became the impetus for that later outburst of essay writing by figures like De Quincey, Hunt, Lamb, Hazlitt, and many others. While some may find examples of what Fiedler regards as whimsy and cuteness in these early nineteenth-century essayists, there is in the essays—and the lectures—of Hazlitt a striking difference, on that seems apt in the context of our thesis.

Hazlitt is, of course, an informal essayist we remember from our earliest readings; think of **'On the Love of Life,' 'On Good-Nature,' 'On Familiar Style,' 'On Pedantry.'** He takes pains to locate himself in the tradition of the essay. Montaigne is his hero, if not his exact model, 'the first who had the courage to say as an author what he felt as a man' (VI,92,)[6] a writer frank, sincere, modest in his expectations of himself. Hazlitt prefers Addison's *Tatler,* its 'sterling wit and sense' (VI,97), to the *Spectator* with 'the greater gravity of its pretensions, its moral dissertations and critical reasonings' (VI,99). Johnson's *Rambler* 'is a collection of moral Essays, or scholastic theses, written on set subjects' (VI,100).

At the same time Hazlitt is a major literary theorist and practical critic, whether advancing ideas about the force of gusto or the power of the sympathetic imagination or advancing critiques of Shakespeare's plays or Wordsworth's poetry. Indeed, the great contributions of contemporary critics from W. J. Bate to Herschel Baker to W. P. Albrecht, to most recently John Kinnaird and David Bromwich have left little

doubt as to Hazlitt's importance. Yet he is seldom excessively formal in his mode of presentation or organization of argument, seldom casual in his approach to a text or performance. He is a man of strong opinions about the success or lack of success of a work of art or about how art engages the human personality. Actually he writes essays that tread the border between the personal dimension of Montaigne and the more formal dimension of Addison or Johnson. If, as David Bromwich puts it, 'criticism is as creative as poetry,' combining 'interpretative vividness and the expressive power of utterance,'[7] then Hazlitt has stretched the boundaries of essay and literary criticism to create a new kind of critical essay, the kind that would attract more writers and command a wider audience. In stretching these boundaries, he strengthens each genre, bringing each to the service of the other, with criticism the greater beneficiary.

Why the essay, we ask, in conjunction with Hazlitt? Well, we have already alluded to the explosion of periodical publishing in his time; the greater number of literate readers interested in good writing about the arts. Then there is the obvious matter of making a living, always a pressing matter for him. There seems to be no end to his activity—in 1813, critic for the *Champion,* then the *Edinburgh Review;* in 1817, drama critic for *The Times;* from January to March, 1818, lecturer on the English poets; in 1820, contributor of dramatic criticism and **'Table Talk'** to the *London Magazine;* in 1821, publisher of **Table Talk or Original Essays,** with a second volume in 1822. And more.

But these are too obvious answers to a complex question. Hazlitt simply seemed restless and dissatisfied with the form and spirit of criticism in his own and the previous age. He speaks of the 'dry and meagre mode of dissecting the skeletons of works, instead of transfusing their living principles, which prevailed in Dryden's Prefaces, and in the criticisms written on the model of the French school about a century ago.' To him a 'genuine criticism should, as I take it, reflect the colours, the light and shade, the soul and body of a work' (VIII,217). The critics he deplores never get to the soul of a work, never communicate what passion has been moved and how. He is similarly bothered by the obsession with current tastes and fashions, with the burden of the present (to vary a critical phrase in fashion today).

Snobbery is a great *bête noire*. Such critics 'discern no beauties but what are concealed from superficial eyes, and overlook all that are obvious to the vulgar part of mankind' (VIII,225). Total mastery of a subject, he contends, brings dangers, frustrating an audience, separating the critic from the larger society, no small tragedy for Hazlitt (VIII,282). With an almost prophetic sense, especially as we think of the current battles in our own literary academy today, he debunks two ex-

TABLE-TALK;

68/80

OR,

ORIGINAL ESSAYS.

BY WILLIAM HAZLITT.

LONDON:

JOHN WARREN, OLD BOND-STREET.

MDCCCXXI.

tremes, one critic who would 'torture the most obvious expression into a thousand meanings, and enter into a circuitous explanation of all that can be urged for or against its being in the best or worst style possible . . . not to do justice to his author . . . but to do himself homage' (VIII,214), and another critic committed to the principle that 'the more you startle the reader, the more he will be able to startle others with a succession of smart intellectual shocks' (VIII,216).

Well, enough for Hazlitt's dislikes although in these negatives we can see his values and especially his vision of the essay in the service of a new kind of criticism. The good essay 'plays the whole game of human life over before us' (VI,91). There should be in such an essay what he admired in Montaigne, originality and the strong presence of the self in advancing critical judgements. David Bromwich, is, of course, correct in saying that when Keats went to hear Hazlitt's lectures at the Surrey Institution, 'he went to hear not criticism, but Hazlitt.'[8] Hazlitt wants his readers to know how he feels, how he has been engaged, not whether the work fits some body of rules or meets with some general and popular approval. He strikes us as a guide leading us through his personal museum of artistic delights, sharing his pleasures, offering his reasons of the heart and head.

Nor is the intensity of his involvement without a logic, a logic of passion. He is content to isolate one or two excellences—the sympathy of Shakespeare, the epic power of Milton, the variety of Chaucer. He eschews abstract argument in favour of strategic metaphor and quotation that illuminate and enliven. True to his empirical-associationist background, he is always ready to make quick and pointed connections to bolster a point.

We might follow Hazlitt at work first in some general commentary and then in a full analysis of one of his critical essays. Take the famous essay **'On Gusto,'** for example. Aesthetics is a major concern, of course, but note the directness, the immediacy, the personal dimension of its opening. Gusto is 'power of passion defining any object.' Then follows at once the concrete example from painting, 'the colouring of Titian. Not only do his heads seem to think—his bodies seem to feel.' Then analogy bolsters his enthusiastic argument as he compares Titian with other painters. His flesh-colour is 'like flesh, and like nothing else. It is as different from that of other painters, as the skin is from a piece of white or red drapery thrown over it.' Further examples range widely in order to involve the reader. 'Rubens made his flesh-colour like Flowers; Albano's is like ivory; Titian's is like flesh, and like nothing else.' (IV,77). Then back to reinforcement of the argument: 'In a word, gusto in painting is where the impression made on one sense excites by affinity those of another' (IV,78).

Nor is gusto of one kind. Michaelangelo's forms 'everywhere obtrude the sense of power upon the eye. His limbs convey an idea of muscular strength, of moral grandeur, and even of intellectual dignity: they are firm, commanding, broad, and massy, capable of executing with ease the determined purpose of the will' (IV,78). Claude Lorrain's landscapes, however, lack gusto. 'They are perfect abstractions of the visible images of things; they speak the visible language of nature truly. They resemble a mirror or a microscope . . . He saw the atmosphere, but he did not feel it' (IV,79).

Shakespeare is his favourite example of gusto. He finds the same quality of delineation in his representation of passion as he does in his treatment of character. In a typically long Hazlitt sentence, he uses style to suggest his argument about this delineation, piling image upon image to dramatize his point. Shakespeare, he argues, gives us 'not some one habitual feeling.' 'It is passion modified by passion, by all the other feelings to which the individual is liable, and to which others are liable with him; subject to all the fluctuations of caprice and accident; calling into play all the resources of the understanding and all the energies of the will; irritated by obstacles or yielding to them; rising from small beginnings to its utmost height; now drunk with hope, not stung to madness, now sunk in despair, now blown to air with a breath, now raging like a torrent.' Iago, as Hazlitt sees him boasting about his seduction of Othello, 'enters at this moment, like the crested serpent, crowned with his wrongs and raging for revenge! The whole depends upon the turn of a thought. A world, a look, blows the spark of jealousy into a flame; and the explosion is immediate and terrible as a volcano.' The dialogues in *King Lear,* in *Macbeth,* nearly all those where there is this intensity, exemplify 'this dramatic fluctuation of passion' (V,51-52).

As suggested earlier, we will close with a fuller analysis of Hazlitt's less celebrated, but no less insightful essay **'On Milton's *Lycidas*'** from *The Examiner* of August 6, 1815 (No.15 of the Round Table series). It seems to capture well the Hazlitt essay in the service of criticism. The speaker is personal, companionable, eager to express and share his pleasure in the poem, to isolate a limited number of key features and build an argument utilizing strategic quotation and telling metaphor.

After citing the closing lines of the poem—' At last he rose, and twitch'd his mantle blue: / Tomorrow to fresh woods, and pastures new' as his epigraph, he proceeds immediately and enthusiastically to his argument. Of all Milton's shorter poems, '*Lycidas* is the greatest favourite with us,' Samuel Johnson's objections to its 'pedantry and lack of feeling' notwithstanding. At the same time he is reluctant to overestimate it as a monumental work, given the age of the author at the time of composition. Yet it is 'the final emanation of classical sentiment in a youthful scholar—"most musical, most melancholy." '

Hazlitt's special kind of critical argument accompanies his personal involvement. He is lyrical in noting how 'a certain tender gloom overspreads' the poem, and yet is quick to observe how there is 'a forgetfulness of his subject in the serious reflections that arise out of it.' Typically metaphor reinforces argument or indeed becomes a part of it as he confronts the text. 'The gusts of wind come and go like the sound of music borne on the wind.' There is, of course, the loss of a friend, yet, and here Hazlitt seems almost to anticipate the argument of John Crowe Ransom many years later,[9] the lament triggers 'with double force, the reality of those speculations which they had indulged together; we are transported to classic ground, and a mysterious strain steals responsive on the ear while we listen to the poet, "With eager thought warbling his Doric lay" ' (IV,31).

Again quotations from the test rather than abstract theorizing support the argument. Twenty-five celebrated lines—the mourning voice of the speaker, one Greek shepherd mourning the death of another—are cited 'for the truth and sweetness of the natural descriptions' and 'the characteristic elegance of the allusions.'

> Together both, ere the high lawns appear'd
> Under the opening eye-lids of the morn,
> We drove a-field
>
> . . . . .
>
> But O the heavy change, now thou art gone,
> Now thou art gone, and never must return!
>
> . . . . .
>
> As killing as the canker to the rose,
> Or taint-worm to the weaning herds that graze,
> Or frost to flowers that their gay wardrobe
>   wear,
> When first the white-thorn blows;
> Such, Lycidas, thy loss to shepherd's ear!

Another fifteen lines are quoted, those following the apostrophe to Fame, quoted enthusiastically as examples of 'perfect art.' The lines begin with 'Oh fountain Arethuse, and thou honoured flood, / Smooth-sliding Mincius, crown'd with vocal reeds, / that strain I heard was of a higher mood; / But now my oat proceeds.' Playing the companionable role of the essayist drawing his readers into a circle of admiration, he says, 'Nor do we wish for anything better.' Still unconcerned about elaborate explication of text but aware of the pitfalls of pure impressionism, he proceeds to praise the meter, the evocative sound of the proper names. He offers no apologies to some of the contemporary snob-

bish criticism about allusions to the classics. 'To ask the poet not to make use of such allusions as these,' he argues, 'is to ask the painter not to dip in the colours of the rainbow, if he could.' He dismissed the charge of 'pedantry and affectation'. Pedants consistently are blind to the beauties of both nature and art. Milton saw both and saw the fascinating interrelationships of the two, the ways in which one could enhance the other. 'He was a passionate admirer of nature; and, in a single couplet of his, describing the moon,—"Like one that hath been led astray / Through the heaven's wide pathless way,"—there is more intense observation, and intense feeling of nature (as if he had gazed himself blind in looking at her), than in twenty volumes of descriptive poetry' (IV,32-33).

How interesting and helpful Hazlitt is in pointing up both Milton's power of imaginative association as a poet and his own associative technique as essayist in the matter of Milton's combining the classical and Christian in those lines in which Hazlitt finds a 'wonderful correspondence in the rhythm . . . to the ideas which they convey!' The yoking of classical ('Camus, reverent sire') and Christian ('The pilot of the Galilean lake') seems inappropriate only to the mechanical understanding; it is thoroughly natural to the associative imagination. Such seeming opposites 'constantly co-exist' in the imagination. Hazlitt, making a serious critical point with the light touch of the essayist, argues that 'every classical scholar, however orthodox a Christian he may be, is an honest Heathen at heart' (IV,34).

Further he develops the growing romantic emphasis on the power of fiction, not technically, but in the manner of familiar essayist, drawing the reader into a comfortable and familiar metaphorical world. 'And, as we shape towers and men, and armed steeds, out of the broken clouds that glitter in the distant horizon, so, throned above the ruins of the ancient world, Jupiter still nods sublime on the top of blue Olympus . . . and still we hear—"The Muses in a ring / Age round about Jove's altar sing. . . . Have sight of Proteus coming from the sea, / And hear old Triton blow his wreathed horn" ' (IV,34). For Hazlitt, even if these imaginative creations really existed, they could not have moved the human psyche more deeply.

The **'Lycidas'** essay rounds to a close nicely with a return to his praise of the poem as the best of the shorter works and a rejoinder to Johnson's remark that Milton's genius was too capacious to show itself in smaller world, contending that *Paradise Lost* 'is not more distinguished by strength and sublimity than by tenderness and beauty. The last were as essential qualities of Milton's mind as the first' (IV,36).

In Hazlitt the Romantic phenomenon of genres evolving from genres is an interesting one. Whether discussing aesthetic issues or considering major figures like Shakespeare and Milton, or reviewing contemporary stage production, he brings to the writing of essays and the delivery of lectures the perceptiveness of the critic and to criticism the charm and accessibility of the essay.

Notes

[1] See *A Glossary of Literary Terms,* 4th ed. (New York: Holt, Rinehart and Winston, 1981), 70-71.

[2] *Literary Terms,* 71.

[3] (Cambridge, Mass.: Harvard University Press), 226-27.

[4] *Literary Terms,* 55.

[5] *The Art of the Essay,* 2nd ed. (New York: Thomas Crowell Company, 1969), 1.

[6] All quotations from Hazlitt are from *The Complete Works of William Hazlitt,* ed. P.P. Howe (London and Toronto: J. M. Dent and Sons, Ltd., 1930). Volume numbers are in Roman and page numbers in Arabic numerals.

[7] *Hazlitt: The Mind of a Critic* (New York: Oxford University Press, 1983), ix.

[8] *Hazlitt,* 14.

[9] See "A Poem Nearly Anonymous" [Lycidas] in *Milton Criticism: Selections from Four Centuries* (Rhinehart and Company, Inc., 1950) 225-238.

Joseph Epstein (essay date 1991)

SOURCE: "Hazlitt's Passions," in *The New Criterion,* Vol. 10, No. 3, November, 1991, pp. 33-44.

[In the following essay, Epstein places Hazlitt's writings within the context of his business and personal life.]

In *The Birth of the Modern,* his panoramic history of world society between 1815 and 1830, Paul Johnson refers to William Hazlitt as "a truly great writer, perhaps the first truly modern writer in England." Johnson, working an extremely crowded canvas, never gets around to saying just why he thinks Hazlitt is perhaps the first truly modern writer in England. Yet his is an assertion that gains immediate assent; it feels, somehow, right. Among Hazlitt's contemporaries, Coleridge was certainly more wide-ranging, Wordsworth in his particular line deeper, Lamb more winning. But Hazlitt, for a multiplicity of reasons, feels more like our contemporary, which is another way of saying that he seems more modern.

Hazlitt, Our Contemporary—it sounds, I fear, like one of those rather dreary lectures read in a patches-on-the-elbows brown tweed jacket from yellowing paper, in which one attempts to make the case for the relevance of a writer whose work is obviously deader than a Rudy Vallee lyric. I should like to go at things from a different angle, since Hazlitt's writings are for the most part clearly and vibrantly alive, and attempt to show that his modernity, which is very real, does not always honor either him or us.

Hazlitt was an extraordinary writer, yet he was also a writer who had more flaws than the normal man. This might not matter but for the fact that much of what he wrote itself insists on doing away with the distinction between the man and the writer in him. He could be deeply stupid on some subjects and quite close-minded on others. He was awkward, passionate, shy, brilliant, and often foolish, a man of absolute integrity who was probably a genius, the word we fall back upon to explain talent of a power for which we cannot otherwise account. As Hazlitt said apropos of Cobbett, so more pertinently may one say apropos of Hazlitt: "It is easy to describe second-rate talents, because they fall into a class and enlist under a standard: but first-rate powers defy classification or comparison, and can be defined only by themselves."

About William Hazlitt's own talent there cannot be much argument. Paul Johnson notes that Hazlitt "has strong claims to be considered the first British art critic of significance," and Kenneth Clark called him "the best English critic before Ruskin." Thomas McFarland, in his book *Romantic Cruxes* (1988), writes that "he may be the finest pure critic of literature that English culture has brought forth"; and by pure critic Professor McFarland means a critic who does not write out of a moral or cultural program—he cites Matthew Arnold and T. S. Eliot—but rather deals directly with works of literary art. Keats marveled at Hazlitt's unerring "depth of Taste" in all things having to do with art. "We are mighty fine fellows," Robert Louis Stevenson once remarked to William Henley, "but we cannot write like William Hazlitt." P. G. Patmore, describing his friend Hazlitt's mental quickness, wrote: "Hazlitt could perceive and describe 'at sight' the characteristics of anything without any previous study or knowledge whatever, but by a species of intellectual intuition." Hazlitt himself said that he "never worshiped the Echo," by which he meant that he came by his views and opinions absolutely on his own.

William Hazlitt was born in dissent—no minor biographical fact—and died in discouragement. His was a short, disorderly, tumultuous, sad, and finally immensely impressive life. He lived fifty-two years, wrote several books, made many enemies, and died both broke and, it is fair to say, broken-hearted. Perhaps no writer of his quality was attacked so viciously in his lifetime as he, though he must have valued his enemies, at any rate to the extent of never for a moment having wanted them on his side, and he certainly came near giving as good as he got. (Keats held that Hazlitt "is your only good damner, and if ever I am damn'd—damn me if I shouldn't like him to damn me.") Perpetually harried by financial worry, he wrote nearly all his works under pressure and on the run. He produced brilliant criticism under the constraints of journalism; in his familiar essays he produced literature almost by the way, and into the bargain much improved the form by opening it up to more serious subjects. He was tactless, abrasive, dogmatic, obsessive, in many ways quite hopeless, and yet one of the few authentic heroes of literature.

William Hazlitt was born in 1778, the third surviving child of a dissenting minister of the Unitarian church who was never to live in anything approaching comfort. Upon his father's death, Hazlitt referred to him as his anchor, but the Reverend William Hazlitt was an anchor that bobbed about a good bit, going from one inadequate living to another. He had favored the side of America during the Revolutionary War, and this cost him favor and hence tenure at various churches he served. In 1783, he sailed for New England with his family, and after four years and much disappointment and illness discovered that the New World was not the solution either. Hazlitt wrote that he remembered "once hearing a shrewd man say that he would never send a son of his to my father, lest the boy should be so schooled in truth as to be disqualified from getting his living in the world." Hazlitt's father knew, and soon so would his son, that the things he most honored the world cared for but little. "One image," his son wrote, "he had set up in his mind: it was Truth. One idol he had: it was Justice. One aspiration he had: it was Liberty." Hazlitt loved his father, and wrote that "when I think of the thing I am, I know that all I most care to remember in what I have been and done, has come to me through him."

Between the ages of nine and fifteen Hazlitt lived, quite happily, in the market town of Wem, in Shropshire, on the border of Wales, where his father had his modest clerical living. At fifteen, he was sent off to the New College at Hackney, a Unitarian academy, on a scholarship that stipulated he study for the ministry. But before that the great formative event of Hazlitt's youth, and indeed of his life, had taken place: the Revolution in France. He was eleven when it occurred, but it would be at the center of much that he thought and did in the forty-one years left to him. "It seems to me," he later wrote, "as if I had set out in life with the French Revolution, and as if all that had happened before that were but a dream." And all afterwards, perhaps, something of a nightmare. "The light of the Revolution, dabbled though it now was

with drops of crimson gore, still circled my head like a glory," he wrote. Hazlitt not only had his politics early fixed by the French Revolution, but early, too, learned the seriousness of politics. In 1791, the Birmingham home of the dissenting minister Joseph Priestly, a friend of Hazlitt's father, was robbed and burned by a mob goaded into action by Priestly's reply in opposition to Edmund Burke's *Reflections on the French Revolution*. In politics, people of that day, as we should say today, played hardball.

By fifteen, then, Hazlitt had a nearly fully formed politics of his own. When the French Revolution went bloody, he blamed it on England's war against France, which he thought whipped up French hatred at the mere thought that the old monarchy, with all its abuses, might be restored. He saw the great, the central, the indispensable problem of his time as that of the need to free mankind from the tyranny of monarchy, which was, in his view, everywhere an obstacle to progress, hope, decency, and truth. His politics having been formed over the problem of liberty—to him in his certitude it was neither a question nor an issue—his friends and enemies followed therefrom. On his deathbed, he worried about the Bourbons regaining the throne of France.

The adolescent Hazlitt must have been a bit of a prig, moral-political division, so passionate, so full of politics was he, like those children who have been reading *The Nation* or *The New Republic* since the age of eleven and have all the answers at fourteen. In his forties, Hazlitt wrote to his son that it was "my misfortune perhaps to be bred up among Dissenters, who look with too jaundiced an eye at others and set too high a value on their own peculiar pretensions." The youthful Hazlitt was a perfect little red-hot Jacobin. But—a crucial but—he was not that alone. He was a boy whose imagination was fired by Bible stories, whose heart was stirred by *Tom Jones*, whose life was permanently altered at seeing Sarah Siddons play Lady Macbeth, whose timbers were shivered by reading Schiller's tragedy *The Robbers*. Even as a boy he was used to reasoning things out on his own. He had considerable powers of reflection, and would go off by himself and think things through. An opinion once taken on he seldom deserted.

What Hazlitt did desert, not long after his entrance at New College, was the notion of following his father into the Unitarian ministry. For one thing, the world at large had great allure for him. For another, though Hazlitt would always remain respectful of the religion of his father, he was too set in his own difficult ways ever to hope to find and keep a living as a minister. He must early have sensed the oddity of his own personality. The man who would one day be known as one of the great practitioners of the essay was not, for example, able to write assigned essays in school; writing was already too important for him to expend it upon trivial classroom work.

Hazlitt had a temperament problem, which did not allow him to be other than he was, and an integrity problem, which did not allow him to change himself for anyone. Normally, these might be considered happy problems. But they turned out to be both the making of him and the cause behind much of his difficulty in life. Sensing his faith and his reason in conflict, Hazlitt decided that, if he was not to live with contradiction in his own soul, he would have to forgo a career in the ministry, even if this would cause his father sadness. "You have done everything in your power to make your son a wise and useful man," the head of the New College at Hackney wrote to Hazlitt's father upon William's announcing his not wishing to become a minister, which meant his withdrawal from the school, "and may we not hope that he will be a wise and useful man in some other sphere of life? What that other sphere will be I cannot point out. . . . "

Neither for a good while could Hazlitt. He left school at seventeen. Dissenters were not then allowed admission to Oxford or Cambridge. For a painfully long spell he worked away—with excruciating slowness—on an ambitious essay that set out to prove that men were not inherently selfish. "For many years of my life I did nothing but think," he later wrote. "I had nothing else to do but solve some knotty point, or dip into some abstruse author, or look into the sky, or wander by the pebbled sea-side. . . . " As so often with Hazlitt, who was wont to find the bad in the good and the good in the bad, he also later wrote, referring to these years: "I can write fast enough now. Am I better than I was then? Oh no! One truth discovered, one pang of regret at not being able to express it, is better than all the fluency and flippancy in the world."

He lived with his father or sometimes with his older brother John, a painter of miniatures. Owing to a family connection, he knew William Godwin, author of *Political Justice,* through whom he came to meet Coleridge, one of the decisive influences on his life. Working on his essay, which he titled "On the Disinterestedness of the Human Mind," he wrote to his father to report that he has "ventured to look at high things." He also let his father know that the work proceeded slowly, though he felt he wrote more easily than he once did. Around this time he discovered the prose of Edmund Burke, which he later allowed that he had tried half a dozen times, unsuccessfully, to describe, but which quite simply blew him away. Reading Rousseau, which he also did around this time, made for another Eureka moment in his life. Burke and Rousseau, two altogether contradictory figures, were further influences on Hazlitt.

The essay on the disinterestedness of the human mind, begun in 1796, was eventually published in 1805 under the title *An Essay on the Principles of Human Action.* In between times, Hazlitt set out on a new career, that of portrait painter, which, after his early failures at religion and philosophy, was to prove his third false start. The landscape painter Philipp Hackert once told Goethe, when the poet showed an interest in painting, that "you have talent, but you are incompetent." Something of the reverse was true of Hazlitt, who was competent but, by his own high reckoning, without talent. Stanley Jones, in his excellent biography of Hazlitt, a measured work of genuine scholarship that serves well both its subject and its readers, remarks of Hazlitt's painting that in it he "never threw off the paralysis of imitation nor moved forward to the frontiers of originality that he later successfully crossed in his writing."[1] Hazlitt had several commissions to do portraits, but his perfectionism joined to his strong sense of his own inadequacy—Titian, Rembrandt, and above all Raphael were among his models—stood in the way of his completing many of them.

Although Hazlitt failed as a painter, his interest in painting made him all the better as a writer. It not only made him an impressive art critic—he was among the first to recognize the genius in the early paintings of Turner and splendid at describing all that went on in a painting—but it gave something akin to a painterly quality to his prose generally. ("A genuine criticism," he would later write, "should, as I take it, reflect the colours, the light and shade, the soul and body of a work.") Something similar might be said about the ultimate utility of his failure at philosophy. He would describe his own prose as endowed with the thought of a metaphysician and the tact of a painter. Of course, if one succeeds, as Hazlitt later did with his essays, then in retrospect it seems as if even one's starkest failures have contributed to that success.

Not everyone would agree about the degree of Hazlitt's success as an essayist. As a useful corrective to the all but locked-in reputation of Hazlitt as great essayist, one can scarcely do better than to read Leslie Stephen on Hazlitt. In a brilliant criticism in *Hours in a Library,* Stephen says straightaway that he thinks Hazlitt not capable of "the highest kind of excellence." He thinks him a man "whose personal and public sentiments [were] so invariably blended in his mind that neither he nor anybody else could have analyzed their composition." He thinks Hazlitt a man wrapped within multiple masks of "cunning egotism," and that it does not in any way redound to his credit that all his life he held to the same views: "A man whose opinions at fifty are his opinions at fourteen has opinions of very little value," he writes. (Hazlitt had claimed that "a person who forgets all the sentiments and principles to which he was most attached at nineteen can have no sentiments ever after worth being attached to.") His politics, moreover, "were simply the expression, in a generalized form, of his intense feeling of personality." He was "no genuine democrat," for no party was good enough for him, and, writes Stephen, "he hates 'both mobs,' or in other words, the great mass of the human race." ("Mankind are a herd of knaves and fools," Hazlitt wrote. "It is necessary to join the crowd, or get out of their way, in order not to be trampled to death by them.") Everything that Leslie Stephen says is dead-on, devastatingly true, but, somehow, it isn't quite the whole truth.

Precocious and yet a slow starter, Hazlitt dabbled and dithered. He spent four months in Paris, copying the great masters in the Louvre. He wrote a grammar, did abridgments, edited and completed the memoirs of Thomas Holcroft, published an attack on Malthus's theory of population, continued to take on commissions for portraits, and functioned as something of an odd-jobs man in the arts. But he didn't really get underway until financial pressure had set in in earnest, and once it had it never left him. Henceforth, writes Catherine Macdonald Maclean, one of Hazlitt's earlier biographers, "never in all his life . . . even on his deathbed, was he to know respite from financial anxiety and literary labour."

It was his marriage, in 1808 (when he was thirty), and the subsequent birth of two sons—one of whom died in infancy—that forced Hazlitt to strap on the harness of more regular employment. As Leslie Stephen rightly put it, Hazlitt, in his thirties, with a wife and son, "at last discovered the great secret of the literary profession, that a clever man can write when he has to write or starve." Not his marriage but the need to support it by steady literary production was the making of William Hazlitt, who, given his dreaminess, his penchant for brooding at great length over subjects, his perfectionism, might have ended an obscure footnote in literary history: a sometimes sullen chap who used from time to time to show up at Charles and Mary Lamb's "Wednesdays" and occasionally explode into passionate utterance over politics.

As for Hazlitt's marriage—it was the first of two—it is part of his history with women, and a grievously sad history that is. William Hazlitt, to put it very gently, had a woman problem and an especial talent for looking to the wrong women to solve it. His friend P. G. Patmore said that he never knew Hazlitt when he wasn't in love; and part of the difficulty here is that he seems never to have been in love with the women he married. "A cynic," wrote Paul Elmer More, "might point a moral from the fact that the only events of Hazlitt's life which were utterly free from the intrusion of passion were his two ventures into matrimony." Hazlitt's taste in women, but not in wives, ran to country girls or chambermaids—"humble beauties," as he referred

to them—in any event, to women well below him in intellectual sophistication. Poor, foolish man, he wanted both to idealize women and to make them over; his *Liber Amoris,* which caused such a scandal in its day and seems so pathetic in ours, carries the subtitle of "The New Pygmalion." Much the largest portion of **"On the Conduct of Life; or Advice to a School-Boy,"** Hazlitt's essay in the form of a letter to his son, is about women, and all of it is cautionary, ending with his telling the boy that "Love turned away his face from me." He meant it did so his lifelong.

In his diary, Henry Crabb Robinson claimed that, "like other gross sensualists, [Hazlitt] had a horror of the society of ladies, especially of smart and handsome and modest young women." A gross sensualist seems off the mark. Any consideration of Hazlitt's tortured relations with women has to go back to what is known as the incident at Keswick. This incident—misadventure? contretemps?—took place in the Lake District in 1803, when Hazlitt was twenty-five and an itinerant portrait painter. Nobody knows precisely what happened, but the best guess is that Hazlitt made advances to a village girl who not only repulsed his advances but set the village toughs on him, so that Hazlitt was fortunate to escape with his life. "The minx made a fool of him," Stanley Jones economically puts it, "and the episode ended in ludicrous catastrophe and ignominious flight."

No further mention need have been made of it, except that Wordsworth, in response to Hazlitt's review of the *Excursion* in later years, loosed the story, with colorful details added, in the long-standing method of going after the character of the critic when you can't bear the criticism. With the Keswick story as ammunition, Wordsworth tried to ruin Hazlitt's friendship with Charles Lamb, Henry Crabb Robinson, and others. More devastatingly, however, it was later used by Hazlitt's quite unscrupulous enemies on *Blackwood's Magazine,* where, in painting him as a brute out of control, the story was used as political propaganda against him. (These same enemies claimed Hazlitt was a drunk and referred, famously in that day, to "pimpled Hazlitt," though Hazlitt was apparently not more than a regular drinker in a hard-drinking age and had a clear complexion.) Wordsworth must have first heard the story of the incident at Keswick from Coleridge, who later claimed that Hazlitt, on the run, came to him, and that he gave him "all the money I had in the world, and the very shoes off my feet to escape over the mountains." That detail about the shoes off his feet makes one wonder what Coleridge was smoking the day he retold it.

The relationship between Hazlitt and Coleridge is a story in itself, and one that scholars of romanticism are apparently not yet agreed upon. Thomas McFarland, for example, in *Romantic Cruxes,* thinks the relationship central: he flicks a wet noodle at David Bromwich, who, in his book *Hazlitt: The Mind of a Critic* (1983), seeks to minimize its importance. One thing is clear, and this is that Hazlitt returned again and again to the subject of Coleridge, and in his work would cross a crowded street to spit on his shoes. In his essay **"On Depth and Superficiality,"** for example, Hazlitt refers to Coleridge as "a great but useless thinker." In **"On the Prose Style of Poets,"** he claims Coleridge's prose "swelling and turgid—everlastingly aiming to be greater than his subject; filling his fancy with fumes and vapours in the pangs and throes of miraculous parturition, and bringing forth only *still-births*." But in his *Lectures on the English Poets,* Hazlitt says that Coleridge is "the only person I ever knew who answered to the idea of a man of genius," adding that "his thoughts did not seem to come with labour and effort; but as if borne on the gusts of genius, and as if the wings of his imagination lifted him from off his feet."

Hazlitt's most impressive portrait of Coleridge appears in his essay—one of his very best—**"My First Acquintance with Poets."** This essay was written in 1823, long after the two men, Hazlitt and Coleridge, had complicated their relationship to the point of alienation, and it is a tribute to the generosity in Hazlitt that he recalls with such large-hearted fidelity how impressed he initially was by Coleridge and how important he once was to him. Hazlitt was not yet twenty, Coleridge twenty-six upon their first meeting, and the occasion was a sermon Coleridge was to deliver at a Unitarian church in Shrewsbury, ten miles' distance from Wem. Hazlitt made the trek on muddy roads in January to hear him, for Coleridge was already a celebrated figure. Coleridge launched into his sermon "like an eagle dallying with the wind." Listening to him, Hazlitt heard "the music of the spheres. Poetry and Philosophy had met together." And in one of those passionate, slit-your-own-gut-open sentences, sometimes telling you rather more than you wish to know, Hazlitt, early in the essay, acknowledges his intellectual debt to Coleridge:

> My soul has indeed remained in its original bondage, dark, obscure, with longings infinite and unsatisfied; my heart, shut up in the prison-house of this rude clay, has never found, nor will it ever find, a heart to speak to; but that my understanding also did not remain dumb and brutish, or at length found a language to express itself, I owe to Coleridge.

In *The Spirit of the Age,* Hazlitt takes the machine gun to Coleridge, leaving an intellectual corpse riddled with holes. The theme of this essay is how Coleridge blew everything by talking away his gifts. "If Mr. Coleridge had not been the most impressive talker of his age, he would probably have been the finest writer; but he lays down his pen to make sure of an auditor,

and mortgages the admiration of posterity for the stare of an idler." Hazlitt notes the tangential quality of Coleridge's mind, its dilatoriness and digressiveness. As a prose writer, Coleridge's mind was the scene of a bloody battlefield in which prolixity often battled obscurity to a dead draw. Or, as Hazlitt puts it in a single shot that plunks three balls into the pocket: "If our author's poetry is inferior to his conversation, his prose is utterly abortive." Yet in his *Lectures on the English Poets,* published seven years earlier, Hazlitt notes of Coleridge that "he is the only person from whom I ever learnt anything." He then adds: "There is one thing he could learn from me in return, but *that* he has not."

Hazlitt does not say what that "one thing" is, but a reasonable guess would be that what Coleridge could have learned from him was political constancy. Everything that Hazlitt says about Coleridge is true enough, but behind it, even so, was the feeling of betrayal that he felt against Coleridge and the Lake Poets—Wordsworth and Southey chief among them. To put it in one unkind, very modern, hyphenated word that he himself does not use, Hazlitt thought that they were "sell-outs." Hazlitt was above party politics, was not a Whig and certainly not a Tory, but he did think himself a member of the party of liberty ("of all the loose Terms in the world," wrote Edmund Burke, "Liberty is the most indefinite"), and it was this party that the Lake Poets had, in Hazlitt's mind, deserted.

Hazlitt, as Professor Jones remarks, "took public events hard," and none harder than those connected with France and that nation's revolution. It won't do to press the analogy too hard, but in several respects Hazlitt was to the French Revolution what many modern intellectuals—they still walk the streets— have been to the Russian Revolution. Unlike these contemporary counterparts, Hazlitt did not attempt to cover up revolutionary bloodshed, though he did sometimes justify it. Where opinions on the French Revolution are divided, Hazlitt is never quite to be trusted. He allows for Wordsworth's originality and power, but you sense him pulling back from a larger appreciation of him because Wordsworth later concluded that there might just have been other dawns when it was perhaps even more blissful to be alive and more heavenly to be young than that of the dawn of the French Revolution. Hazlitt will allow that Southey's "prose-style can scarcely be too much praised," add that "he is steady in his attachments, and is a man, in many particulars admirable, and in all respectable," but cannot forbear closing: "his political inconsistency alone excepted." Over the subject of Napoleon, Hazlitt was able to get into a fight with Charles Lamb for Lamb's political indifference, which, given the latter's famous good nature, apparently wasn't an easy thing to do.

William Hazlitt was in that category of persons who, in order to like them, one has *really* to like them. I happen to be in the category of persons who *really* like Hazlitt, but one has to admit that he must have been a very great trial to his friends and a delight to his enemies in the large exposed target he gave them. Geoffrey Keynes, his bibliographer, has remarked that no one who reads Hazlitt remains neutral about him. Virginia Woolf wrote that "no man could read him and maintain a simple and uncompounded idea of him." In **"On Depth and Superficiality,"** Hazlitt wrote of himself:

> I am not, in the ordinary acceptation of the term, a *good-natured man;* that is, many things annoy me besides what interferes with my own ease and interest. I hate a lie; a piece of injustice wounds me to the quick, though nothing but the report of it reach me. Therefore I have made many enemies and few friends; for the public know nothing of well-wishers, and keep a wary eye on those that would reform them.

That is fair enough, even if a bit self-glorifying, but Hazlitt, being Hazlitt, cannot of course let it go at that, and so must close the passage by zinging Coleridge, who "used to complain of my irascibility in this respect, and not without reason. Would that he had possessed a little of my tenaciousness and jealousy of temper; and then, with his eloquence to paint the wrong, and acuteness to detect it, his country and the cause 'of liberty might not have fallen without a struggle." His loyal friend Lamb said of Hazlitt: "I wish he would not quarrel with the world at the rate he does; but the reconciliation must be effected by himself, and I despair of living to see that day." Nor would he.

But in order to admire Hazlitt you don't even have to like him. His talent, which was doubtless inseparable from his crotchets, his intellectual aggression, his thorny nature, simply commands admiration. "The virtue of his work," wrote Paul Elmer More, "lies not in his analytic criticism, which can be studied apart from his own language, but in the fusion of passion and insight." That is precisely wherein Hazlitt's power lay. In most writing, passion brings opacity and obscurity in its wake; the angrier one becomes the cloudier and more muddled one's thought. With Hazlitt passion in argument seemed to result in even greater penetration. He was easily the greatest polemicist of his own highly polemical age, and perhaps one of the greatest polemicists in all of intellectual history.

Professor Jones makes the useful point that Hazlitt's polemical exchanges were more than mere argument against enemies, and they would be of no interest if they were. ("Nothing," as Cyril Connolly once rightly put it, "ages like hate.") Instead they were a mode of thought that in his hands turned argument into literature. Professor Jones writes:

> All such exchanges are evidence of [Hazlitt's] disinclination to pontificate, of his dislike of the egotistical; his views are commonly defined dramatically, on specific occasions, by opposition to those of others. Ultimately grounded in principle, they are immediately polemical; they manifest his leaning towards the marriage of the general and the particular, of the abstract and the concrete, of the universal and the individual. He saw the clash of argument as a means of escaping from self-communion into the dramatic and so of acceding to universality, a means of liberation from the sterility of the immured self.

The Hazlitt of the fiery polemics, of the impassioned art criticism, of the jaunty writing about the theater, the literary critic, the familiar essayist, and the writer who finally belonged to literature had first to serve his apprenticeship in daily journalism. This he began in 1812, at the age of thirty-four, covering the House of Commons for the *Morning Chronicle,* for which he received his first steady income, four guineas a week. His own obvious talent soon freed him from the gallery of the House of Commons and the tedium of reporting the empty utterances of politicians, and he was set to writing drama criticism, which he did surpassingly well. Presently he was writing on other subjects— art, literature, politics—and his writing began to appear in other papers, including Leigh Hunt's *Examiner* and *The Times.* Fearless, confident, knowing his own views and not much concerned with the views of others, except to topple them, he was among the first critics to recognize and support the genius of Turner in painting, Edmund Kean in acting, Keats in poetry.

Hazlitt's earlier prose was that of a toy philosopher, stiff, slow, awkward, the writing of a student imitating quite well but nonetheless still imitating a metaphysician. But now he realized that, if he were to make his way as a journalist, he would have to write as a man writing to men; he sought to achieve what, in his essay **"On the Prose Style of Poets,"** he called the "genuine master-spirit of the prose-writer," which was "the tone of lively sensible conversation." He later told the painter James Northcote that, when he began to write for the newspapers, he "had not till then been in the habit of writing at all, or had been a long time about it; but I perceived that with the necessity, the fluency came. Something I did, *took;* and I was called upon to do a number of things all at once. I was in the middle of the stream, and must sink or swim." He swam, as we now know, not merely well but like an Olympian.

Hazlitt's essays have immense flow. He once compared Edmund Burke's prose to a diamond. "It has always appeared to me that the most perfect prose-style, the most powerful, the most dazzling, the most daring, that which went the nearest to the verge of poetry, and yet never fell over, was Burke's." If Burke's prose was comparable to a diamond, Hazlitt's own prose most closely resembles a cascade, a waterfall, a body of beautiful white water, a rapids. One has to attend closely to all that he says, as one does to every stretch of white water, for crags, tree limbs, and odd debris float past. Surprises are contained in the codas of sentences, as for example in the following from the paragraphs on the poet Tim Moore in *The Spirit of the Age:* "Or modern poetry in its retrograde progress comes at last to be constructed on the principle of the modern opera, where an attempt is made to gratify every sense at every instant, and where the understanding alone is insulted and the heart mocked." Formulations come fast and furious: "the want of passion is but another name for the want of sympathy and imagination"; "mere good-nature (or what passes in the world for such) is often no better than indolent selfishness"; "the principle of life and motion is, after all, the primary condition of genius"; and "there is nothing so tormenting as the affectation of ease and freedom from affectation." As for invective, he could serve it up, vast quantities of it, at typhoon' intensity. Of William Gifford, he wrote:

> Mr. Gifford was originally bred to some handicraft. He afterwards contrived to learn Latin, and was for some time an usher in a school, till he became a tutor in a nobleman's family. The low-bred, self-taught man, the pedant, and the dependent on the great, contribute to form the Editor of the *Quarterly Review.* He is admirably qualified for this situation, which he has held for some years, by a happy combination of defects, natural and acquired; and in the event of his death it will be difficult to provide him a suitable successor.

"I think what I feel," Hazlitt noted in the preface to his *View of the English Stage;* "I say what I think." Many people say what they think they feel, but to say it just so is the trick. "To write a genuine familiar or truly English style," Hazlitt wrote in **"On Familiar Style,"** "is to write as any one would speak in common conversation, who had a thorough command and choice of words, or who could discourse with ease, force, and perspicuity, setting aside all pedantic and oratorical flourishes." This Hazlitt could do, consummately.

Still, he was better at the sentence than at the paragraph, and better at the paragraph than at the complete composition. Much in Hazlitt is unshapely; many of his essays—even his superior ones—end up in the air, which is to say arbitrarily, unsatisfactorily, badly. In explanation, if not extenuation, of this, it is well to remember that Hazlitt turned out his prose at a fierce rate. At one point he went off to his country cottage at Winterslow where in a month's time he wrote nine full essays. One is inclined to wonder what he might have

done had he worked more slowly. But then one is brought up by the recollection of Karl Kraus's withering aphorism about a journalist being someone who, given time, writes worse.

It was a point of pride with Hazlitt, as it ought to be with any writer capable of honestly saying as much, that "I never wrote a line that licked the dust." At the same time, he did not mind kicking a goodly amount of dust over his friends. Hazlitt was eager to write for the *Edinburgh Review,* for example; that magazine paid him well, and its editor, Francis Jeffrey, on more than one occasion proved his friend by bailing him out of financial difficulty and on others did a good bit in his service by cleaning up his prose for publication. But Hazlitt did not see this as in any way debarring him from writing the following in *The Spirit of the Age:*

> The faults of the *Edinburgh Review* arise out of the very consciousness of critical and logical power. In political questions it relies too little on the broad basis of liberty and humanity, enters too much into mere dry formalities, deals too often in *moot-points,* and descends too readily to a sort of special-pleading in defence of *home* truths and natural feelings. In matters of taste and criticism, its tone is sometimes apt to be supercilious and *cavalier* from its habitual faculty of analysing defects and beauties according to given principles, from its quickness in deciding, from its facility in illustrating its views. In this latter department it has been guilty of some capital oversights.

Which Hazlitt doesn't in the least mind going on to point out and elaborate upon.

For a powerfully intelligent man Hazlitt had a powerfully high quotient of naïveté. He did not so much overrate the truth as he overrated its powers of persuasion. It is so that the truth will set you free, but you ought to know that, enunciated tactlessly enough, it is likely to leave you no shortage of enemies to have to deal with in your freedom. "All the former part of my life I was treated as a cipher," Hazlitt wrote when he began to be well known, "and since I have got into notice, I have been set upon as a wild beast." He was accused of dishonesty, of writing ungrammatically, of being brutish with women. It was his politics, with his take-no-hostages polemical style, that set the wolves on his trail. Professor Jones puts the case well: "The reputation he gained by his criticism was constantly jeopardized by the enmity stirred up by his political writings, and it was owing to these that he was pursued with abuse for the rest of his life, and abandoned to disparagement and neglect after his death."

That Hazlitt was so harassed by enemies makes all the stranger his decision to publish, in 1823, *Liber Amoris,* his account of his dreary love affair with Sarah Walker, one of the daughters of the tailor in whose home he,

Hazlitt, took lodgings in London after he and his wife had separated (though not yet divorced). Hazlitt's love affair with Sarah Walker was his mid-life *Human Bondage,* played without a clubfoot but, in reading Hazlitt's own pathetic account of it, with something one is inclined to view as close to a clubhead. Sarah Walker was nineteen, Hazlitt forty-two, when, in 1820, they first met. She brought him his morning tea, and allowed him to caress her before she set out on her other morning rounds. "I cannot describe the weakness of mind to which she has reduced me," he wrote, in a letter that appears in the thinly fictionalized account provided in *Liber Amoris.* But he was wrong; the book does describe, all too clearly, how stupefied he became.

Many are the views of Hazlitt's sad unconsummated love for Sarah Walker. The best face put upon it is perhaps that drawn by Professor Gerald Lahey, the editor of a scholarly edition of *Liber Amoris,*[2] who sees in it "a parable of the entire Romantic period trying to come to terms with its flawed visionary conception of reality." Yet one wonders if this isn't what the English used to call over-egging the pudding. What Hazlitt seems to have done is vastly overrate a not very attractive young woman from the workaday lower-middle class. The painter Benjamin Haydon nicely caught Hazlitt's situation: "the girl really excited in him a pure, devoted and intense love. His imagination clothed her with that virtue which her affected modesty induced him to believe in, and he is really in love with an ideal perfection, which has no existence but in his own mind." Hazlitt told the young woman he would divorce his wife for her; and in fact he did, striking the modern literary note in being perhaps the first famous writer to be under the gun for alimony and child support.

Hazlitt seems to have told everybody he saw about his infatuation with and ill-treatment at the hands of this young woman, including his eleven-year-old son. In fact, she didn't especially treat him ill, unless one is ready to call ill-treatment her refusal to go along with his fantasies about her. She was quite correct, when he asked her to come live with him, to tell him "that it would be no use if I did [for] you would always be hankering after what could never be." She was rightly put off with his talking so much about her not only to friends but to her own family. At one point he went so far as to assign another man the task of attempting to seduce Sarah in order to test her moral standards. (She passed.) In short, Hazlitt made a pest, a jerk, a royal fool of himself.

One thing to make a fool of yourself, another to publish an account of your foolishness, which Hazlitt did in *Liber Amoris.* Why did he do it? Some contend that he needed to do so to burn Sarah Walker out of his system; some that it took great courage for him to do

so; some that, having done so, proved Hazlitt no gentleman, which, when it came to women, it is probably fair to say that he wasn't, having, in this realm, only three settings on his emotional dial: worshipful, vengeful, and indifferent. My own guess is that he probably did so because he was the pure type of the writer, as we have come to know it in our day, who cannot let anything like a serious experience go unwritten about.

Liber Amoris, despite occasional touching passages, does not have any real standing as literature. What is of interest about it is that for its time it marks a new candor in confession—and a very modern candor in its unpleasantness, its lack of interest in redemption, and, one must add, its self-deception. Hazlitt knows that he has made a fool of himself, but blames this alternately on the guile of Sarah Walker, on the overwhelming power of love, on everyone and everything but himself. *Liber Amoris* feels very much a predecessor of the Norman Mailer, Robert Lowell, Sylvia Plath school of sloppy confession without remorse that has had a strong run in recent decades.

Was Hazlitt, in *Liber Amoris,* attempting to emulate Montaigne, whose "inexpressible frankness and sincerity, as well as power" he much admired, Montaigne in whom there "is no attempt at imposition or concealment, no juggling tricks or solemn mouthing, no laboured attempts at proving himself always in the right, and every body else in the wrong"? If so, he made a rum job of it. This most gifted of English essayists, persistent student of human nature though he wished to be, seems to have had little talent for introspection. He was nearly always in battle, always agitated, always angry, a paranoid who made his own real enemies. He was too much the moralizer and too little the moralist. Montaigne looked to himself to understand the world. Hazlitt looked at the world in puzzlement over why it did not understand him. Not quite the same thing.

Yet the pathetic affair with Sarah Walker seems to have increased Hazlitt's strength as a writer. When he published *Characteristics, In the Manner of Rochefoucauld's Maxims* in 1823, the year after his affair with Sarah Walker, he noted that the only point on which he dared to claim comparison with the French master was that neither of them had a theory to maintain. But, in fact, after the events recounted in *Liber Amoris* Hazlitt's essays took on a greater richness owing to an implicit theory. This had to do with his renewed appreciation of the mixed qualities of motives in life, of the element of irrationality often in even the most mundane of human affairs. In his essay **"The Main-Chance,"** he set out to show how small a part reason plays in life next to parts played by passion and sheer human oddity. In **"My First Acquaintance with Poets,"** he remarks upon the exhaustion of enjoyment and hope as one grows older: "As we taste the pleasures of life, their spirit evaporates, the sense palls; and nothing is left but the phantoms, the lifeless shadows of what *has been!*" Hazlitt suffered but not for nothing.

Although he claimed that Sarah Walker was "my life" and that "it is gone from me, and I am grown spectral," he still had expenses to meet, his writing was much in demand by newspapers and magazines, his political passions were undimmed, he had his son's future to think about, he wished to see the Louvre again and Italy for the first time. He even remarried, unsuccessfully, and in the last years of his life set out on a mammoth biography of Napoleon, his hero of heroes, a work of justification which he had hoped would be his own greatest literary monument. (When Napoleon went down at Waterloo, Hazlitt took the defeat personally. "He seemed prostrated in mind and body," Benjamin Haydon wrote, "he walked about unwashed, unshaved, hardly sober by day and always intoxicated by night, literally, without exaggeration, for weeks; until at length, wakening as it were from a stupor, he at once left off all stimulating liquors, and never touched them after.") He wrote the brilliant pieces that make up *The Spirit of the Age* in 1825, but melancholy suffuses his later familiar essays. "I turn back from the world that has deceived me," he wrote in **"A Farewell to Essay-Writing,"** "to nature that has lent it a false beauty, and that keeps up the illusions of the past." In this same essay he remarks upon our indifference to that which is worthy in life, caught up as we are in "the present vexation, the future disappointment."

Hazlitt had a sufficiency of his own present vexations and future disappointments: the many attacks on him (William Gifford's *Quarterly* claimed his essays oozed a trail of "slime and filth"); the sadness of his relations with women; the endless broken friendships; the dismantling of the French Revolution and the defeat of Napoleon—nothing, it must have seemed to him, worked out. All that was left to him was pride in his integrity and the surprising number of his books (when young he "had no suspicion that I should ever become a voluminous writer"). He once said that he took pleasure in life only from paintings, books, and nature. Notably absent from this list is people. Referring to the writer in general but to himself more pertinently, he wrote that "the coldness and jealousy of his friends not unfrequently keep pace with the rancour of his enemies."

Not long before he died—of stomach cancer, in September of 1830—this almost instinctively disputatious man asked only three things of life before he departed it: that he die with someone he loved beside him, that he have some evidence of hope for mankind of the sort that the French Revolution gave him when young, and that he leave "some sterling work" behind him. Only

the latter, as we now know, came about. Still this often disagreeable man, whose truculent personality rendered him lonely most of his days, can never be removed from the small but courageous company of those writers who knew not how to lie or to fudge, but could only convey the complicated truths they found in their own troubled hearts.

Notes

[1] *Hazlitt: A Life,* by Stanley Jones; Oxford University Press, 424 pages, $84; $22 paper.

[2] *Liber Amoris, or, The Modern Pygmalion,* edited, with an introduction and notes, by Gerald Lahey (New York University Press, 1980).

Edward W. Bratton (essay date 1991)

SOURCE: "William Hazlitt's Curious Concept of Taste," in *South Atlantic Review,* Vol. 57, No. 2, May, 1992, pp. 1-9.

[*In the essay that follows, originally published in 1991, Bratton explores some examples of Hazlitt's judgments of taste in an effort to determine the paradoxes of his overarching theory and its relevance to the twentieth century.*]

John Keats praised William Hazlitt's "depth of taste" as one of "three things superior in the modern world" (*Letters* 1: 204-05)—even when that taste was negatively employed. "Hazlitt," Keats wrote, "is your only good damner, and if ever I am damn'd (damn me if) I shoul'nt like him to damn me" (*Letters* 1: 252). Not everyone responds to Hazlitt so generously. Virtually all the world agree on his contrariness and his bad habit of letting his personal experience obtrude on the "real" subjects of his essays and criticism. In order accurately to reflect Hazlitt's methods here, therefore, I shall in an appropriately contrary way begin with my personal experience of Hazlitt's literary taste in operation, then—perhaps—work my way back to his concept of that aesthetic capability.

My first acquaintance with William Hazlitt was through his essay **"The Fight,"** and was in several ways both appropriate and paradoxical. My wife and I had both abandoned good jobs and better prospects to become undergraduates together again, this time at a university, where, with (quite literally) a fifty-cent dog named Bo and on a G. I. Bill check of $110 a month, I was to major in English for, of all things, the fun of it, and with no prospects. A certain tension soon developed between the demands of the mind and those of the belly. In terms of diet, the fun was quickly translated into broken chicken wings, six pounds for a dollar in a block of ice, plain wrapper, from a Swanson's frozen-dinner plant nearby, along with damaged canned goods, at a nickle a can, from a local shipping facility. The labels were always removed, but the codes imprinted on the lids of the cans were a foreign language I learned well by trial and error, though for no college credit. The repetition of one code in particular imprinted it on my mind forever—MDLB: More Damn Lima Beans. Bo and I had them even for breakfast, and a long endless line of identical, mealy, sickly-green lima beans has pursued me even in my dreams.

In that personal context I first read and relished the "supreme boxing classic of literature," paradoxically written by one who had never before that time even seen a prize fight and published only over strong editorial objections—curiously enough, because an essay on **"The Fancy,"** or boxing, was considered in bad taste (Wilcox 5). Further abuse of our stomachs to cater to my mind produced in a few months the grand sum of $65, which could still unaccountably bring, cradled in a shredded *London Times,* a set of the gilt-edged-and-titled twenty-one-volume limited Centenary Edition of *The Complete Works of William Hazlitt,* edited by P. P. Howe. Never was hunger so well fed. I soon learned that Hazlitt seemed almost always passionately living or writing a paradox and/or a political, critical, or intellectual fight.[1] When knocked down by an exasperated John Lamb, then asked to shake hands and forgive, Hazlitt responded, "Well, I don't mind if I do. I am a metaphysician and nothing but an idea hurts me" (Howe, *Life* 192). There is both tension and tolerance in that reported scene, as there typically is in a good paradox or oxymoron, which is but a paradox collapsed. As critic, Hazlitt had an original gift for shaping the seeming contradiction which engages the reader's mind to prove its kernel of truth. Thus he indicates that successful comedies have rendered comedy unsuccessful (4: 10); that Byron's poetry is "a tissue of superb commonplaces; even his paradoxes are *commonplace*" (11: 76); that Sir Walter Scott is "a *prophesier* of things past" (11: 57); that Shelley has a philosophical "maggot in his brain" and "where he has attempted little, he has done most" (8: 148; 16: 266); that the "strength [of Wordsworth's "homely muse"] . . . arises from the excess of his weakness," making him "the greatest poet of the . . . day, only because he is the greatest egotist" (8: 44-45; 11: 86). And we have Lamb's description of Hazlitt's mixture of contraries in criticizing Coleridge: it "is like saluting a man: 'Sir, you are the greatest man I ever saw,' and then pulling him by the nose" (Robinson 1: 202).

I have termed Hazlitt's concept of taste curious partly because it is so frequently paradoxical in theory no less than in operation and expression, involving in several ways both the tension of contraries and their housing (if not resolution) in figurative and critical tolerance. "Magnanimity" and "moderation" (Foot 64;

Bate 282) may well be the most courageous nouns ever used to label Hazlitt's taste and thought, but they may also be the most nearly accurate.[2] His concept of taste is also curious simply because it is odd, out of critical antiquity, and does not rise so far above the literary text and author to the current level of theoretical ether. Taste, Hazlitt insists, is more a matter of fact and feeling than of theory, a sympathetic and strenuous grasp of the moral and intellectual and sensitive aspects of art, enabling the critic, not to compete with, but to "reflect the colours, the light, the shade, the soul and body of a work" and to return us to it with greater understanding and relish (20: 386; 5: 6; 8: 217). Hazlitt's concept may have some useful currency of suggestion and reminder still, grounded as it is in the immediate experience of literature, the fun of it as one might say. And in developing that concept, Hazlitt wrestled with some persistent questions of literary interpretation and evaluation (two inseparables). His answers are hardly definitive, but then neither are those of anyone else, which is why the questions persist.

In that connection, I want to return—figuratively only—to those lima beans. I have used them to flavor my account of Hazlitt's taste less hesitantly than I might have because I find an American beer similarly employed in the most recent, extensive, and knowledgeable discussion of the same topic elsewhere. At least that discussion defines Hazlitt's critical term "gusto" as a special "word for taste" and analyzes the slogan "real gusto in a great, light beer" as showing "as tactful an understanding as one could wish" of Hazlitt's concept (Bromwich 228-29). I wonder who wrote the slogan. I'm still one up on that discussion, of course, with my dog Bo as companion in taste, for whom, incidentally, there is very specific precedent in Hazlitt's own comments on taste (but you'll have to read my footnote).[3] Lima beans. I find in them an experiential emblem of distasteful, mealy sameness—almost a sick parody of sustenance—so perfectly countered by Hazlitt in his essays and criticism. Hazlitt opposed any notion that the arts are mechanically "progressive" (4: 160-64), but just as clearly thought that they—and our critical means of tracking them—necessarily undergo change according to the age and culture. I hardly need remind you how a language is translated from the living to the dead. So literature and criticism which do nothing more than repeat the past. Thus Hazlitt tells us from a remarkably current perspective that "criticism is an art that undergoes a great variety of changes, and aims at different objects at different times" (8: 214). Little wonder that he was the first English critic to give anything like adequate and serious attention to the comparatively new literary form of the novel (Patterson), the first to publish an incisive and capacious critique of Wordsworth's revolutionary poetry through 1814 (19: 9-25), and the only critic of his age publicly to apply discriminating taste to the various ages and types of English literature from Chaucer through his own contemporaries.

In practice, Hazlitt clearly kept to his theoretical cloth and could do so handily even today, which has brought both critical challenge and expansion to the literary heritage we have taught as our own and to which we owe incalculable debts. Perhaps we might say that yesterday's conception of that heritage as a single shaft of light has passed through the prism of our souls and has become a rainbow of perspectives. And in the dance of those colors, how current seems Hazlitt's remark that "we may be sure . . . when we see nothing but grossness and verbiage in a writer that is the God of [an age's] or a nation's idolatry, it is we and not they who want true taste and feeling." In matters of critical taste, there can be no fixed, hereditary line, he observes, no "aristocracy of letters," and no "true superiority but what arises . . . [from] the presupposed ground of equality . . . [and] the free communication and comparing of ideas" (8: 205-08). Amidst the extremes of "political correctness," how timely seems this antique concept of Hazlitt's, how balanced to have come from such a biased and rabid partisan, an admitted lover of quarrels (8: 79) and author of a psychologically astute essay on **"The Pleasure of Hating."** "A toleration," he insists, "not an uniformity of opinion, is as much as can be expected" in matters of taste (8: 222).

Hazlitt defined taste as "nothing but sensibility to the different degrees and kinds of excellence in . . . works of art" (17: 57; 20: 263). It is perhaps curious, but consistent with his "Catholic spirit of criticism" (20: 270), for so Romantic a critic to dismiss the silly question of whether Pope was a poet by observing that "if he was not a great poet . . . he was a great writer of some sort" (20: 89). Hazlitt found his "singular" model "of good [and Catholic] taste" in the old friend and critical mentor of his youth, the dissenting minister and sometime poet Joseph Fawcett, "who had Paine's Rights of Man and Burke's Reflections on the French Revolution bound up in one volume, and . . . said, that, both together, they made a very good book" (17: 65). A persistent supporter of the French Revolution, Hazlitt carried Fawcett's paradox one step further when, as he says, "in a fit of extravagant candour," he wrote a generous assessment of Edmund Burke in 1807, ten years later produced a "craftily qualified" essay on Burke, and then—with honest, admirable bravado—published both in his 1819 volume of **Political Essays** (7: 226, 301). Hazlitt's brilliance once pushed even Wordsworth to exclaim, "The Dog writes strong" (9: 6), which was the way of "the Dog" when he balanced accounts, those of others or his own.

Even more curious than Hazlitt on Burke, and more pertinent to the present occasion, is another instance of Hazlitt's apparent political incorrectness related to his concept of taste. In the book extolling the beer slogan, it seems somehow appropriate that one can playfully flip three pages and also find "the common reader's taste" presented as a kind of centerpiece of Hazlitt's critical position. The passage contrasts Hazlitt's stance with "Coleridge's [critical] defection to the university-man's view" in the following terms: "*Coleridge is the first important critic in English to divest the common reader of authority and entrust the survival of great works to a specially trained clerisy.* Hazlitt, on the other hand, inherits the Johnsonian feeling about the common reader's taste and judgments, as the only measure of 'duration' in literature" (Bromwich 232). There is, of course, some truth in all that. But I want to play at Hazlitt a bit and write also the truth of the other side. It is well to recall how much like what we would define as a university-man Hazlitt was: that Coleridge found his young friend to have "the most metaphysical head he ever met with" (9: 3); that Hazlitt published books on philosophy, social science, and Shakespeare; edited collections of oratory, poetry, and drama; and produced encyclopedia entries and an English grammar on advanced principles; that he was the foremost English critic of theater and, arguably, of painting of his age; and that he delivered (sometimes repeated) several series of lectures on philosophy, on poetry, on comic writers, and on the Age of Elizabeth—incidentally, with the likes of John Keats as student. One is reminded of the disjunction between DeQuincey's remark that Hazlitt "has read nothing" and his act of plagiarizing from him.

Political bias is endlessly charged against Hazlitt's criticism, which might suggest that this strident political democrat and author of the ringing sentences of **"Who Is the People?"** would naturally place "the Common reader's taste" at the center of his critical thought. But the paradoxical nature of Hazlitt's undemocratic view of taste is pervasive in his works. He was no common leveler of literature, but consistently praised originality of artistic genius and varieties of excellence, which he thought typically "not intelligible to the common reader" (20: 387). He could lament, and attack, the narrow audience appeal of such a literary egotist as Wordsworth, yet consistently judge him the greatest poet of the age; and Walter Scott he considered only an "excellent mimic" of a great poet, despite his large following of common readers (5: 154-55). He believed that genius, "to please generally . . . must exaggerate . . . [the] shewy, . . . [and] insipid, that which strikes the greatest number of persons with the least effort of thought" (18: 107), and that "the principle of universal suffrage, however applicable to matters of government, . . . is by no means applicable to matters of taste, which can only be decided upon by the most refined understandings . . ." (18: 46), a trait possessed by "persons of strong natural sensibility for any art, and who have paid the closest attention to it"—that is, "those who have studied the subject . . ." (20:

386). And so on and on.[4] Hazlitt's words are more suggestive of the SAMLA community than a community of common readers. And despite contrary views, I see little confusion here or elsewhere in Hazlitt between critical and political judgments, perhaps another timely quality of his literary taste.

Anyone who has taught a genuinely successful seminar in literature can appreciate Hazlitt's aphorism that "truth is not one, but many; and an observation may be true in itself that contradicts another equally true, according to the point of view from which we contemplate the subject" (9: 228). That might be termed a multiple paradox, but not a limitless one; truth is *many,* not *any.* And it is a paradox clearly operative with Hazlitt's critical taste, in his evaluations/interpretations of literature. Just a few years ago, Paul Armstrong concluded a fine essay in a similar vein:

> The question,of what we "ought" to believe [about literature and literary works] can only be decided by discussion and argument within the community. While such exchanges do not lead to agreement about a single, indubitable truth, they do introduce testing and evaluation. . . . Literary criticism is a pluralistic universe, but there are limits to its pluralism. (349)

Hazlitt would be comfortable in such a critical neighborhood, a community of accountability characterized by the tension of differing convictions and the necessary tolerance for their discussion and evaluation. Despite his general reputation as a kind of loose cannon of critical impressionism, Hazlitt declared: "The reputation ultimately . . . affixed to works of genius, is stamped upon them by authority, ["accumulating" over time,] by the imperfect and yet more than casual agreement among" "well--informed minds" (18: 48; 20: 386-87). Consequently, "There is not an absolute standard, [but] at least a comparative scale, of taste . . . ," one pertaining to that "not which does, but which would please universally, supposing . . . all to have paid an equal attention to any . . . [art] and to have equal relish for it" (20: 386-87). Thus does Hazlitt answer with a paradox the ancient (and current) paradox of literary judgment/evaluation—that it is at once individual and not arguable, yet universal and arguable.

If Hazlitt's curious concept of taste be antique, then, it is also of real and present value. When Cleanth Brooks was presented SAADE's John Hurt Fisher Award at SAMLA a year ago today, he remarked that he was at Yale, where "the house is on fire," adding with apparent disapproval: "The author is nothing. We've abolished the author"—and one suspects by implication, the text. Professor Brooks lamented our current emphasis on means, then asked and answered: "What has happened to the ends of life [in our literary concerns]? Oh, Ann Landers and the advertisers will take care of that." Hazlitt's "depth of taste" can occasionally, brilliantly remind us that it was not always so, perhaps need not be. The old, bold agreements about what literature and its relation to life ought to be (to the extent they existed) have faded as naturally as leaves. But there will be, Hazlitt insists, always other autumns, other winters, for other leaves.

Almost exactly two hundred years ago, another house was set fire, the meeting-house of Joseph Priestly; and a thirteen-year-old William Hazlitt was quick to the defense of another kind of genius in his first publication, a letter to the *Shrewsbury Chronicle* admonishing those who were like wrens, as he put it, "pecking at an eagle."[5] The terms of Hazlitt's defense of Priestly in this letter are remarkably suggestive of his mature defense of literary genius—as Houck points out, he considered its preservation and the assurance of its safe passage to the future, along with the nurturing of promising genius like that of a John Keats, the chief obligations of the critic. Hazlitt long ago emphasized that "all genius is, in a great measure, national and local, arising out of time and circumstance," yet is also endowed with an inner nature distinctly individual and enduring beyond time and circumstance in its greatness, as with a Cervantes, a Moliere, a Shakespeare (20: 390-91; 8: 77-89). And Hazlitt was excruciatingly conscious of how slippery and limiting language can be, but also how liberating, that it is a complex system to which genius on every front denies closure, is forever expanding, imbuing with new potential to reflect and to convey two other immense complexities, human perception and human response—and, again, to do so beyond the challenging and informing crossroads of history and language. And James Dickey provided us a superb dissertation on and demonstration of precisely that last evening (see *SAR* 57.1 [1992]: 1-14). After applying his critical taste in commentary that would earn his station "near the top of those who have written greatly on the greatest of all writers" (Baker 310), Hazlitt could provide yet another remarkably honest display of his own Shakespearian capability in vigorously writing the truth of various sides of an issue—even against himself. He understood and said, "Taste limps after genius . . ." (6: 187). "If we wish to know the force of human genius, we should read Shakespeare. If we wish to see the insignificance of human learning, we may study his commentators" (8: 77).

In reading Hazlitt, J. B. Priestly writes, "You risk both indigestion and satiety but eat joyously and are well nourished" by his "variety, frankness, intensity, richness" (5). Certainly with Hazlitt's curious concept of taste and his downright Shakespearian critical displays of it, one is fed anything but a line of mealy, sickly-green sameness, signifying nothing. . . .

Notes

* This was the 1991 South Atlantic Modern Language Association Presidential Address, delivered on 15 November 1991 at the Hyatt Regency Hotel in Atlanta, Georgia.

[1] Hazlitt specifically rebutted the charge of being paradoxical merely to start "the most specious novelty" or to contradict received or "vulgar opinion" (8: 146-56).

[2] Hazlitt's less well-known definition of truth is pertinent: "Truth is not one thing, but has many aspects and many shades of difference; it is neither all black nor all white; sees something wrong on its own side, something right in others; makes concessions to an adversary, allowances for human frailty, and is nearer akin to charity than the dealers in controversy or the declaimers against it are apt to imagine" (20: 306-07).

[3] In "Outlines on Taste" Hazlitt writes: "A merely ignorant spectator, walking through a gallery of pictures, no more distinguishes the finest than your dog would, if he was to accompany you" (20: 388).

[4] For example: 4: 83, 163, 367; 5: 144; 7: 84; 8: 19; 9: 42; 12: 133-34, 320; 17: 207-08; 18: 182-83; 20: 38, 152, 156, 242, 278, 301-02.

[5] *Letters* 59. I reverse young Hazlitt's preference between two comparisons he uses.

Works Cited

Armstrong, Paul B. "The Conflict of Interpretations and the Limits of Pluralism." *PMLA* 98 (1983): 341-52.

Baker, Herschel. *William Hazlitt.* Cambridge, MA: Harvard UP, 1962.

Bate, Walter Jackson. *Criticism: The Major Texts.* New York: Harcourt, 1952.

Bromwich, David. *Hazlitt: The Mind of a Critic.* New York: Oxford UP, 1983.

Foot, Michael. "Hazlitt's Revenge on the Lakers." *The Wordsworth Circle* 14 (1983): 61-68.

Hazlitt, William. *The Complete Works of William Hazlitt.* Ed. P.P. Howe. 21 vols. London: J. M. Dent, 1930-34.

———. *The Letters of William Hazlitt.* Ed. Herschel Moreland Sikes, Willard Hallam Bonner, and Gerald Lahey. New York: New York UP, 1978.

Houck, James A. "Hazlitt on the Obligations of the Critic." *The Wordsworth Circle* 4 (1973): 250-58.

Howe, P. P. *The Life of William Hazlitt.* New ed. London: Hamish Hamilton, 1947.

Keats, John. *The Letters of John Keats.* Ed. Hyder E. Rollins. 2 vols. Cambridge, MA: Harvard UP, 1958.

Patterson, Charles I. "William Hazlitt as a Critic of Prose Fiction." *PMLA* 68 (1953): 1001-16.

Priestly, J. B. *William Hazlitt.* London: Longmans, 1960.

Robinson, Henry Crabb. *Henry Crabb Robinson on Books and Their Writers.* Ed. Edith J. Morly. 3 vols. London: J. M. Dent, 1938.

Wilcox, Stewart C. *Hazlitt in the Workshop: The Manuscript of "The Fight" Transcribed, with Collation, Notes, and Commentary.* Baltimore: Johns Hopkins UP, 1943.

Raymond Martin and John Barresi (essay date 1995)

SOURCE: "Hazlitt on the Future of the Self," in *Journal of the History of Ideas,* Vol. 56, No. 3, July, 1995, pp. 463-81.

[*In the following essay, Martin and Barresi examine Hazlitt's theories of personal identity, focusing particularly on how they relate to modern philosophies.*]

> There are moments in the life of a solitary thinker which are to him what the evening of some great victory is to the conqueror and hero . . . milder triumphs long remembered with truer and deeper delight. And though the shouts of multitudes do not hail his success . . . [yet] as time passes . . . [such moments] still awaken the consciousness of a spirit patient, indefatigable in the search of truth and a hope of surviving in the thoughts and minds of other men.[1]

William Hazlitt's moment occurred in 1794, when he was sixteen years old. In that moment Hazlitt thought he realized three things: that we are *naturally* connected to ourselves in the past and present but only imaginatively connected to ourselves in the future, that with respect to the future we are *naturally* no more self-interested than other-interested, and that for each of us our future selves should have the same moral and prudential status as that of anyone else's future self.

Whether these realizations are genuine is, of course, debatable. Some today would say that they are. What is not debatable is that when in his *Essay on the Principles of Human Action* Hazlitt explained and defended these realizations, he sketched theoretical possibilities and drew explosive morals from them that would not occur to other personal identity theorists until our own times.[2] For instance, he was the first to see in what are now called fission examples a basis for questioning whether the preservation of identity is what matters primarily in an individual's "self-interested" concern to survive. He was also the first to suggest a genuinely modern developmental account of the origin of our self-concepts. It is not too much to say that had Hazlitt's views received the attention they deserved, the philosophical discussion of personal identity may well have leaped ahead one hundred and fifty years and the psychological discussion have been significantly advanced.

Hazlitt's views did not receive the attention they deserved; far from it. Keats's idea of the "negative capability" of the imagination was based on a careful study of Hazlitt's *Essay.* Coleridge once mentioned the *Essay* in print but only briefly.[3] In the seventh edition of the *Encyclopedia Britannica* Mackintosh remarked in a footnote to his discussion of Butler that "the very able work" done by Hazlitt in the *Essay* "contains original views" on the nature and origin of "the private appetites."[4] But few others, and no mainstream philosophers, seem even to have noticed. Discouraged, Hazlitt turned from metaphysics to painting, politics, and aesthetic criticism.

In the twentieth century, especially during the last few decades, Hazlitt's star has risen. His writings have been reprinted, additional correspondence has been published, and there have been several books written about him. However, it is as critic and stylist and not also as personal identity theorist that Hazlitt's reputation has grown. Most commentators on his thought have been reluctant even to discuss the *Essay* in detail. Howe, an early and influential biographer, called it "a book by a metaphysician for metaphysicians" and added that "the few words we may say of it here" concern only "its relation to Hazlitt's other works and to his character."[5] More recently, Jones begins his account of Hazlitt's life and thought with Hazlitt's marriage, in 1808, three years after the publication of the *Essay!*[6] Among those who have considered the *Essay* in detail, Kinnaird, who had as his professed aim to write "a biography of [Hazlitt's] mind," does not mention Hazlitt's discussion of fission examples.[7] Nor does Bromwich, in his otherwise excellent study, except briefly and in a footnote.[8] More importantly, no mainstream personal identity theorist, so far as we know, has ever even mentioned, much less discussed, any aspect of Hazlitt's views.

In sum, Hazlitt as personal identity theorist, like Vico before him, is a fascinating example of what is sometimes dismissed as a romantic fiction: the original and penetrating thinker whose insights and perspec-tives are so far ahead of his own times that they drop through the cracks of history. The purpose of the present paper is to retrieve Hazlitt's account of personal identity and to explain the importance of his insights, particularly in terms of the ways in which he anticipated subsequent developments in philosophy and psychology.

Hazlitt's Insights

Hazlitt wrote that he was led to his central realizations by wondering "whether it could properly be said to be an act of virtue in anyone to sacrifice his own final happiness to that of any other person or number of persons, if it were possible for the one ever to be made the price of the other?" The question arose for him as he was reading, in d'Holbach's *System of Nature,* a speech put into the mouth of a supposed atheist at the Last Judgment. Suppose, Hazlitt wondered, I could save twenty other persons by voluntarily consenting to suffer for them. "Why," he asked, "should I not do a generous thing, and never trouble myself about what might be the consequence to myself the Lord knows when?" (133-34).

Hazlitt answered his question on behalf of common sense:

> [H]owever insensible I may be to my own interest at any future period, yet when the time comes I shall feel differently about it. I shall then judge of it from the actual impression of the object, that is, truly and certainly; and as I shall still be conscious of my past feelings, and shall bitterly regret my own folly and insensibility, I ought, as a rational agent, to be determined now by what I shall then wish I had done, when I shall feel the consequences of my actions most deeply and sensibly. It is this continued consciousness of my own feelings which gives me an immediate interest in whatever relates to my future welfare, and makes me at all times accountable to myself for my own conduct. (134-35)

But Hazlitt was dissatisfied with this answer.

> I cannot . . . have a principle of active self-interest arising out of the immediate connection between my present and future self, for no such connection exists or is possible. I am what I am in spite of the future. My feelings, actions, and interests must be determined by causes already existing and acting, and are absolutely independent of the future. (139)

Where there is no "intercommunity of feelings," he claimed, "there can be no identity of interests" (139).

Hazlitt conceded that in relation to the past and present, people are naturally self-interested. We remember only our own past experiences and are directly "conscious" only of our own present experiences.

[Any] absolute distinction which the mind feels in comparing itself with others [is] confined to two faculties, viz., sensation, or rather consciousness, and memory. The operation of both these faculties is of a perfectly exclusive and individual nature; and so far as their operation extends (but no farther) is man a personal, or if you will, a selfish being. (110-11)

The reasons for this, Hazlitt insisted, are physiological. Memories depend on physical traces of prior sensations, and these traces are not communicated between individuals. Present sensations depend on the stimulation of one's nerves, and "there is no communication between my nerves, and another's brain, by means of which he can be affected with my sensations as I am myself" (111).

In the case of the future, however, Hazlitt stressed that people are neither "mechanically" nor "exclusively" connected to themselves. They cannot be, he thought, since no one's future yet exists. Instead, people are connected both to their own futures and to the futures of others by means of their faculties of anticipation. These, he claimed, unlike the faculties of memory and sensation, are a function of *imagination* and thus do not respect the difference between self and other:

[Imagination] must carry me out of myself into the feeling of others by one and the same process by which I am thrown forward as it were into my future being and interested in it. I could not love myself, if I were not capable of loving others. Self-love, used in this sense, is in its fundamental principle the same with disinterested benevolence. (3)

In other words, Hazlitt maintained that to feel future-oriented concern for someone, one first must project oneself imaginatively into the feelings of that person; and imagination, functioning naturally, that is, independently of its having acquired a bias through learning, projects as easily into the feelings of others as into one's own future feelings.

Today it may seem that Hazlitt exaggerated the extent to which memory is independent of imagination and underestimated our mechanical connections to our future selves. Perhaps so. Still, he was right in insisting on there being a crucial difference in our relations at any given time to our past and future selves: we are already affected by our past selves and in a way that substantially diminishes our having to rely on imagination; and even though our present selves will mechanically connect to our future selves we are not yet affected by those connections and hence have to rely more importantly on imagination to connect psychologically to our future selves.

According to Hazlitt, people are naturally concerned about whether *someone* is pleased or suffers as a conse-

quence of their actions (33). This is because "there is something in the very idea of good, or evil, which naturally excites desire or aversion." But, he claimed, before the acquisition of self-concepts people are indifferent about whether those who may be pleased or suffer are themselves or others: "a child first distinctly wills or pursues his own good . . . not because it is his but because it is good" (34). As a consequence, "what is personal or selfish in our affections" is due to "time and habit"; the rest is due to "the principle of a disinterested love of good as such, or for it's own sake, without any regard to personal distinctions" (34). Hazlitt thought that these insights provided a basis for founding morality not on self-interest, which he regarded as an "artificial" value, but on the "natural" concern people have to seek happiness and avoid unhappiness, regardless of whose happiness it is. He concluded that "we are not obliged at last to establish generosity and virtue 'lean pensioners' on self-interest" (48-49).

Hazlitt proposed such ideas in an era when English moral theory was still dominated by the need to come to terms with psychological and ethical egoism. In the view of several philosophers, including Hazlitt, Butler had already refuted Hobbes, but the idea that humans are naturally selfish had been revived and popularized by Helvetius and d'Holbach and the new economists, following Mandeville's lead, were increasingly giving scientific sanction to the idea that the pursuit of private interest promotes the public good, thereby encouraging a tendency to base public morality on a view of humans as fundamentally self-interested. The mature Adam Smith, for instance, conceded that "it is not from the benevolence of the butcher, the brewer, or the baker, that we expect our dinner, but from their regard to their own interest," which, he thought, is constrained by "the invisible hand" of competition to promote the common good.[9]

Among others whose views Hazlitt took seriously, Locke, Tucker, and Paley had held that humans are originally selfish but can subsequently develop benevolent motives.[10] Hazlitt, of course, did not accept that humans are originally selfish. Hume, Hartley, and Priestley were, like Hazlitt, sympathetic to the view that humans are neither originally selfish nor benevolent; however, they believed that humans become either selfish or benevolent by empirical "associations" of pleasure and pain. Hazlitt rejected associationism, partly on the grounds that one could not always explain through associations how people respond so quickly and competently to things they see for the first time (143-69). Butler, on the other hand, anticipated Hazlitt in thinking that humans are naturally disinterested, but he was committed to a traditional, substantial account of personal identity and rejected as patently absurd the idea that each of us does not have an absolute interest in our future selves.[11]

Others before Hazlitt had considered the possibility that a person's so-called future self is metaphysically an "other." In the early eighteenth-century debate between Clarke, Boyle Lecturer and "chief lieutenant of Newton," and Collins, a friend of Locke's and at the onset of the debate a relative unknown, Clarke argued that on Locke's theory personal identity would be destroyed since consciousness is not indivisible but "a Number of Particular Acts" which "perish the Moment they begin," in effect, a "Multitude of distinct and separate Consciousnesses."[12] This debate went through two editions by 1712 and was reprinted in 1731 and again in 1738. Hazlitt may well have been aware of it.

Nor was Hazlitt even the first to wonder about fission examples. Surprisingly, Locke was: " . . . it must be allowed, that if the same consciousness . . . can be transferred from one thinking substance to another, it will be possible that two thinking substances may make but one person. For the same consciousness being preserved, whether in the same or different substances, the personal identity is preserved."[13] Reid had even commented on fission examples, albeit briefly: "This doctrine [Locke's view of personal identity] hath some strange consequences, which the author was aware of, Such as, that, if the same consciousness can be transferred from one intelligent being to another, which he thinks we cannot shew to be impossible, than two or twenty intelligent beings may be the same person."[14]

Yet Hazlitt's innovations . . . even apart from his revolutionary discussion of fission . . . are still genuine. He can be distinguished from all of his predecessors, including those who, like him, may have rejected the idea that humans are naturally selfish, first, by the degree to which he emphasized (and the uses to which he put) the thesis that people are mechanically related to their own presents and pasts but only imaginatively related to their futures: second, by his insistence that the natural use of imagination does not respect the distinction between self and other; and third, by his account of the growth of selfish motives in humans by appeal to their acquisition of self-concepts. Because of the first two of these elements in his view Hazlitt was led to ask a question which did not arise as starkly or in the same form for any of his predecessors and to which the third element was his answer: if people connect to the future through imagination, which does not respect the difference between self and other, why is the force of habit almost invariably on the side of selfish feelings?

Hazlitt answered that when very young children behave selfishly it is not because they like themselves better but because they know their own wants and pleasures better (34-35). In older children and adults, he thought, it is because they have come under the control of their self-concepts, which is something that happens in three stages. First, young children acquire an idea of themselves as beings who are capable of experiencing pleasure and pain. Second, and almost "mechanically" (since physiology insures that children remember only their own pasts), children include their own pasts in their notions of themselves. Finally, imaginatively, they include their own futures.

Hazlitt thought that to progress through all three of these stages the child must form a self-concept and that this requires that it first discriminate its own mental activities from those of others. This involves "perceiving that you are and what you are from the immediate reflection of the mind on its own operations, sensations or ideas" (105).

> It is by comparing the knowledge that I have of my own impressions, ideas, feelings, powers, etc. with my knowledge of the same or similar impressions, ideas, etc. in others, and with the still more imperfect conception that I form of what passes in their minds when this is supposed to be essentially different from what passes in my own, that I acquire the general notion of self. If I had no idea of what passes in the minds of others, or if my ideas of their feelings and perceptions were perfect representations, i.e., mere conscious repetitions of them, all proper personal distinction would be lost either in pure self-love, or in perfect universal sympathy. (108)

Hazlitt here is addressing the delicate issue of how the child's formation of self-concepts is related to its development of empathy and sympathy. So far as we know, no one had considered this issue before. As we shall see, developmental psychologists are preoccupied with it now.

Why, though, since our "mechanical" connections to ourselves are entirely restricted to present sensations and past memories, do young children imaginatively include only their own futures and not the futures of others in their ideas of self? Hazlitt's answer was that it is the "greater liveliness and force with which I can enter into my future feelings, that in a manner identifies them with my present being." This notion of identity being once formed, he adds, "the mind makes use of it to strengthen its habitual propensity, by giving to personal motives a reality and absolute truth which they can never have" (140). This happens, he thought, because "we have an indistinct idea of extended consciousness and a community of feelings as essential to the same thinking being"; as a consequence, we assume that whatever "interests [us] at one time must interest [us] or be capable of interesting [us] at other times" (10-11).

Hazlitt rejected as "wild and absurd" the idea that we have an "absolute, metaphysical identity" with ourselves in the future. He claimed that a bias in favor of ourselves in the future could never "have gained the assent of thinking men" but for "the force" with which a future-oriented idea of self "habitually clings to the mind of every man, binding it as with a spell, deadening its discriminating powers, and spreading the confused associations which belong only to past and present impressions over the whole of our imaginary existence" (6). We have been misled, Hazlitt thought, by language: by "a mere play of words" (6, 27).

In Hazlitt's view both children and adults fail to look beyond the common idioms of personal identity and as a consequence routinely mistake linguistic fictions for metaphysical realities. To say that someone has a "general interest" in whatever concerns his or her own future welfare "is no more," he insisted, "than affirming that [he or she] shall have an interest in that welfare, or that [he or she is] nominally and in certain other respects the same being who will hereafter have a real interest in it" (10-11). No amount of mere telling "me that I have the same interest in my future sensations as if they were present, because I am the same individual" can bridge the gulf between the "real" mechanical connections I have to myself in the past and present and the merely verbal and imaginary connections I have to myself in the future (28-29).

Since people have no mechanical connections to themselves in the future, it follows, Hazlitt thought, that so far as a person's "real" interests are concerned, one's self in the future is essentially an other. So, for instance, if you've injured yourself (in the past), you may suffer as a consequence (in the present).

> [But] the injury that I may do to my future interest will not certainly by any kind of reaction return to punish me for my neglect of my own happiness. In this sense, I am always free from the consequences of my actions. The interests of the being who acts, and of the being who suffers are never one. (31)

In sum, so far as your real self-interest is concerned, it makes no difference "whether [you] pursue [your] own welfare or entirely neglect it" (31). Your suffering in the future is only nominally your suffering.

The Philosophy of Personal Identity

From Plato until the late seventeenth century almost all Western personal identity theorists relied on the notion of a person's soul, or on some sort of non-material substance, to explain personal persistence.[15] Spinoza was the first European thinker to break with this tradition, but he had only an implied theory of personal identity. Locke was the first influential personal identity theorist to develop a relational, rather than a substance, account.[16] Remarkably, though, Locke accepted

on faith that people have immaterial souls. His point was that even if they do, personal identity cannot be understood by appeal to them. Instead, he thought, it must be understood by appeal to something that is at least indirectly observable: a person's psychological and/or physical relations to earlier and later stages of him or herself.

Since Locke, all influential personal identity theorists have given a relational account. Until recently their battles with each other have been mainly over which relations . . . psychological or physical . . . are primary. In Locke's view psychological relations, particularly memory relations, are primary. He used his prince and cobbler example to show that because someone could remember having had experiences that he or she had while in another body people could switch bodies, a consideration thought by many to refute physical-continuity theories of *identity*. Eventually, however, physical-continuity theorists, who have tended also to give pride of place to memory, turned the tables on Lockenas by giving a physical-continuity account of *memory*. Martin and Deutscher, for instance, argued in an influential paper that only genuine (as opposed to mere-seeming) memories could sustain personal identity and only memories brought about by their normal physical causes could be genuine.[17]

In the late 1960s a second revolution in personal identity theory was precipitated by the attempt to understand the implications of fission examples. In David Wiggins's initial illustrations a person divides amoeba-like into two or more physically and psychologically equivalent descendant persons.[18] Since each such descendant bears the same relation to his or her common pre-fission ancestor, each has an equal claim to be regarded as the same person as that ancestor. Yet if both fission-descendants were the same person as the pre-fission ancestor, then by the transitivity of the identity relation . . . the rule that if A is identical to B, and B to C, then A is identical to C . . . each fission-descendant would also be the same person as the other. Since it would be bizarre to regard two (or more) such fission-descendants as the same person as each other (think, for instance, of the legal and moral complications) many theorists concluded that none of the fission-descendants is the same person as the pre-fission ancestor.

In the opinion of many philosophers, what this means is, first, that although in the situations depicted in such examples the relation between any one fission-descendant and his or her pre-fission ancestor *intrinsically* may have all that is required to preserve identity, still identity is lost (that is, the pre-fission person does not persist); and yet, second, that the pre-fission person nevertheless may obtain what matters primarily in his or her "self-interested" concern to survive.

The latter can happen since from the prefission person's selfish point of view, transforming into fission-descendants might in the circumstances be a better selfish choice than ordinary survival.[19]

Such science-fiction fission scenarios had a basis in real life situations. In the late 1930s psychosurgeons began performing an operation in which they severed the corpus callosums of severe epileptics in an effort to reduce the severity of their seizures. This procedure had the bizarre side-effect, not discovered until the 1960s, of creating two independent centers of consciousness within the same human skull. These centers lacked introspective access to each other and could be made to acquire information about the world and to express it behaviorally independently of each other. Most dramatically they sometimes differed volitionally, expressing their differences using alternate sides of the same human bodies they jointly shared. For instance, one patient was reported to have hugged his wife with one arm while he pushed her away with the other; another tried with his right hand (controlled by his left, verbal hemisphere) to hold a newspaper in front of himself, thereby blocking his view of the television, while he tried with his left hand to knock the paper out of the way.[20]

Typical of the sort of hypothetical fission examples that philosophers have considered is one in which you are asked to imagine that you have a health problem that will result soon in your sudden and painless death unless you receive one of two available treatments.[21] The first treatment is to have your brain removed and placed into the empty cranium of a body that is otherwise qualitatively identical to your own. The second is to have your brain removed, divided into functionally identical halves (each of which, imagine, is capable of sustaining your full psychology), and then to have each of these halves put into the empty cranium of a body of its own, again one that is brainless but otherwise qualitatively identical to your own.

In the first treatment there is a ten-percent chance the transplantation will take. If it takes, the survivor who wakes up in the recovery room will be physically and psychologically like you just prior to the operation except that the survivor will know that he or she has had the operation and he or she will be healthy. In the second there is a ninety-five-percent chance both transplantations will take. If they both take, the survivors who wake up in the recovery room will be physically and psychologically like you just prior to the operation except that each of them will know that he or she has had the operation and each will be healthy. If the transplantation in the first treatment does not take, the would-be survivor will die painlessly on the operating table. If either transplantation in the second treatment does not take, then the other will not either,

and both would-be survivors will die painlessly on the operating table. Everything else about the treatments . . . suppose . . . is the same and as attractive to you as possible: for instance, both are painless, free of charge, and result, if successful, in survivors who recover quickly.

Many philosophers, as we have seen, believe that identity would be retained in the first (non-fission) treatment but lost in the second (fission). But if you would persist through the first treatment but not the second, then only by sacrificing your identity can you greatly increase the chances of *someone's* surviving who is qualitatively just like you. Would it be worth it . . . that is, would it be worth it for egoistic (or self-regarding) reasons? Most who consider this example feel strongly that it would be, hence (apparently) that being continued by fission-descendants can matter as much, or almost as much, as personally persisting. As a consequence philosophers have been forced to face the possibility that one might survive *as someone else* whose existence one values as much as one's own and, hence, they have also been forced to divide two questions they had previously treated as one: the traditional question, "What are the necessary and sufficient conditions under which personal identity is preserved (over time)?" and the new one, "What are the conditions under which one secures (over time) what matters primarily in survival?"

Depending on which theorist is asking this new question, it may mean, "What are the conditions under which one secures what *actually does* (or, *would,* on reflection) matter primarily in survival?" or it may mean, "What are the conditions under which one secures what *rationally ought* to matter primarily in survival?" Among contemporary theorists, Shoemaker, Nozick, and Lewis have tended to focus on the former, psychological version of the new question, while Parfit and, more recently, Sosa and Unger have tended to focus on the latter, normative version.[22] Neither version had been raised earlier, except by Hazlitt, who slid back and forth in his own discussion between concern with how one actually does feel about one's future self and with how "one ought as a rational agent" to feel. Until the 1960s all other personal identity theorists simply assumed that one's persisting as the same person one now is must be both what does and what should matter primarily in survival, an assumption that, if true, would guarantee that both the traditional question and the new one have the same answer. No personal identity theorist *assumes* this any more.

In assessing Hazlitt's philosophical accomplishments and potential impact it is important to remember that the seemingly new ideas that were mainly responsible for ushering in this most recent 1960s-phase of philosophical theorizing about personal identity do not require for their appreciation that one looks at the issues through the lens of any late twentieth-century philosophical theory, such as the semantics of modal logic. To be sure, some philosophers have appealed to such theories to grapple with the puzzles which fission examples have provoked. But the examples could easily have provoked the same puzzles if they had occurred to anyone a hundred or even two hundred years earlier. We now know that they did occur to someone and that they did provoke many of the same puzzles. They occurred to Hazlitt.

Over a hundred and fifty years before fission examples entered the philosophical mainstream Hazlitt asked essentially the same questions that provoked the recent revolution in personal identity theory. How would the subsequent debate over personal identity have been different if mainstream theorists such as Mill and Sidgwick had grappled with Hazlitt's questions and examples? We can only speculate. So far as we know, none of them ever read Hazlitt's **Essay**. But virtually everything that produced the theoretical revolution in the 1960s was already present in Hazlitt's work. So, the ingredients were in place for Hazlitt to have had a profound affect.

It was not just in his asking the new question and in inventing a fission example to support his answer to it that Hazlitt anticipated subsequent developments. As we have seen, he also stressed that when someone remembers in any actual circumstance, there is a "mechanical" and "natural" relation between his or her memory episode, which is in the present, and the original experience of the events remembered, which is in the past. This observation by itself came close to anticipating Martin and Deutscher's influential point, made in 1966, about the implications for personal identity theory of a physical-continuity account of memory. But unlike Martin and Deutscher, Hazlitt did not use his observation about the physical basis of memory against Locke. Instead, he took seriously the possibility that in certain hypothetical circumstances, involving, say, divine intervention, "consciousness' might be continued (and hence, perhaps, memories might be preserved) by an unusual, non-physical, causal mechanism. This consideration led him directly to fission examples, which gave him a much more powerful objection to Locke.

Hazlitt's consideration of fission examples occurred in the context of his critique of the Lockean idea that one's identity extends as far as one's consciousness extends. What, Hazlitt asked, would a theorist committed to this idea say "if that consciousness should be transferred to some other being?" How would such a person know that he or she had not been "imposed upon by a false claim of identity?" (135-36). He answered, on behalf of the Lockeans, that the idea of one's consciousness extending to someone else "is ridiculous": a person has "no other self than that which arises from this very consciousness." But, he countered, after our deaths:

> this self may be multiplied in as many different beings as the Deity may think proper to endue with the same consciousness; which if it can be so renewed at will in any one instance, may clearly be so in a hundred others. Am I to regard all these as equally myself? Am I equally interested in the fate of all? Or if I must fix upon some one of them in particular as my representative and other self, how am I to be determined in my choice? Here, then, I saw an end put to my speculations about absolute self-interest and personal identity. (136)

What these extraordinary observations mean is, first, that Hazlitt saw that, hypothetically, psychological continuity might not continue in a single stream but instead might divide. Second, in asking the *two* questions . . ."Am I to regard all of these as equally myself? Am I equally interested in the fate of all?" . . . he correctly separated the question of whether *identity* tracks psychological continuity from that of whether *self-concern* tracks it. Finally, in direct anticipation of what would not occur to other philosophers until the 1960s, Hazlitt concluded that because of the possibility of fission neither identity nor self-concern necessarily tracks psychological continuity. Thus, he used his theological speculations in the same spirit and to the same effect, as philosophers in our own times have used hypothetical examples drawn from science-fiction scenarios.

Hazlitt also used fission examples to call into question whether in cases in which there is no fission a person's present self-interest extends to his or her self in the future. He began by asking:

> How then can this pretended unity of consciousness which is only reflected from the past, which makes me so little acquainted with the future that I cannot even tell for a moment how long it will be continued, whether it will be entirely interrupted by or renewed in me after death, and which might be multiplied in I don't know how many different beings and prolonged by complicated sufferings without my being any the wiser for it, how I say can a principle of this sort identify my present with my future interests, and make me as much a participator in what does not at all affect me as if it were actually impressed on my senses? (138)

His answer was that it cannot.

> It is plain, as this conscious being may be decompounded, entirely destroyed, renewed again, or multiplied in a great number of beings, and as, whichever of these takes place, it cannot produce the least alteration in my present being . . . that what I am does not depend on what I am to be, and that there is no communication between my future interests and the motives by which my present conduct must be governed. (138-39)

Hazlitt concluded:

> I cannot, therefore, have a principle of active self-interest arising out of the immediate connection between my present and future self, for no such connection exists, or is possible . . . My personal interest in any thing must refer either to the interest excited by the actual impression of the object which cannot be felt before it exists, and can last no longer than while the impression lasts, or it may refer to the particular manner in which I am mechanically affected by the idea of my own impressions in the absence of the object. I can therefore have no proper personal interest in my future impressions, . . . The only reason for my preferring my future interest to that of others, must arise from my anticipating it with greater warmth of present imagination. (139-40)

Such ideas were not be taken seriously again until the 1960s.

The Psychology of Empathy, Sympathy, and Identification

The theoretical consideration of empathy, in something close to the way contemporary psychologists understand it, began with Spinoza but has its most significant roots in Vico and Herder, who highlighted it in their attempts to characterize historical understanding.[23] Empathy was given its classic psychological formulation by Lipps.[24] The theoretical consideration of sympathy began in earnest with the British moralists, especially with Hutchenson, and was discussed in England throughout the eighteenth century. It was later considered by Schopenhauer in his investigation of "compassion."[25] Sympathy received its classic formulation in Scheler's famous study.[26]

In its current theoretical sense empathy occurs when one person understands a situation from another's perspective. Ordinarily this understanding has both a cognitive and an affective component. For instance, if another person is in an embarrassing situation, then to be empathic with his or her embarrassment we must understand from the embarrassed person's point of view why the situation is embarrassing as well as represent to ourselves somehow his or her embarrassed feelings. But to be empathic we do not have to feel embarrassed ourselves or feel any urge to help the other.

Sympathy requires more . . . not only that we be empathic with the other but also that we adopt for ourselves at least some of the other's relevant objectives through a process of identification with the other. So, for instance, if embarrassment causes someone to want to remove him or herself from an embarrassing situation, then, all else being equal, the sympathetic person will also want that the embarrassed person be removed from the situation and will be disposed to help him or her accomplish that objective.

Some contemporary theorists have supposed that both empathy and sympathy involve an appreciation of the psychological orientation of another through imaginative simulation. An empathic or sympathetic person simulates another person's point of view by imagining having that point of view, that is, either by imagining being him or herself in the other person's situation or by imagining being the other person in the other person's situation.[27] In both cases the empathic or sympathetic person uses his or her own mind, "off-line," to imagine the other's point of view.[28] In the case of sympathy such off-line empathic simulation comes partially on-line in the form of identification with the other, which includes a disposition to help the other.

Currently, there are two major theoretical alternatives to simulation accounts of empathy. According to one, empathic social understanding depends not on simulation but on appeal to a "theory of mind." According to the other, it depends on one's adopting a certain sort of "intentional stance" toward the other by which one attempts to rationalize the other's activities.[29]

For present purposes the important point is that on any of these theoretical perspectives (simulation, theory inference, or stance adoption), for people (or animals) to appreciate the mental states or activities of another they have somehow to be able to translate a *third*-person *perception* of the other into something like a *first*-person *representation* of the other's point of view. This skill apparently requires a self-concept of some sort that can be applied to others as well as to oneself, that is, it requires a way of representing the other that is also applicable to oneself and that deserves to be called a self-concept when it is applied to oneself. Barresi and Moore have theorized that the acquisition of such a self-concept requires the prior development of an interpersonal representation of mental activities, which is formed initially to facilitate a person's conceptualization of behavioral activities that he or she engages in jointly with others. That is, in their view it is by reflecting on coordinated first- and third-person aspects of an overt activity that an agent later becomes able to interpret *third*-person information about another's behavior in the same way as *first*-person information about him or herself.[30]

Only humans and perhaps great apes seem to have this skill. Lower organisms, even as high as monkeys, while they may have a sophisticated repertoire of behaviors that are provoked by a third-person perception of another's activities, are unable to interpret activities of self and other from a homologous point of view. Thus, any self-concepts that lower animals may have do not provide a third-person perspective of their own activities or a first-person perspective of the activities of others. That is why lower animals cannot recognize themselves in mirrors even though they can recognize others in mirrors and also why they cannot imitate novel activities of others.

This difference between humans (and perhaps great apes) on the one hand and lower animals on the other, shows up in the relation between emotional contagion, which is widespread in both humans and animals, and empathy or sympathy. In emotional contagion . . . so-called "animal sympathy" . . . one acquires an emotion simply by observing it in another. For instance, very young infants may respond to the crying of other infants by crying themselves. Such contagion is not real empathy or sympathy, in our use of the terms, since it requires neither an understanding of the emotion as belonging to the other nor concern for the other.

Even though in emotional contagion the others whose emotional (and, sometimes, cognitive) attitudes are adopted tend to be conspecifics with whom the individual has bonded, theorists believe that lower animals always, and higher animals often, adopt these attitudes without understanding why they adopt them. If this is right, then emotional contagion is no more than a sharing of emotional orientation cued to the other's activity. That is, the sort of primitive social understanding that is available to lower animals, even though it involves distinguishing significant others from other organisms and objects, does not involve an empathic appreciation of the other's point of view or a sympathetic response to that point of view. For instance, although a maternal monkey may respond helpfully to the cries of its infant, in this view it does not interpret these cries as an expression of the infant's distress. Rather the cries simply arouse distress in the mother about the infant's situation. Support for this view comes in part from the observation that in situations where the infant monkey may be in danger but does not express its fear the mother may not act to help the infant. Thus, animal altruism based purely on emotional contagion may be just a response to the activity of others based on third-person knowledge of relations between expressive characteristics and likely causes or consequents. By contrast truly empathic organisms can appreciate the needs of others as such whether or not the others themselves are aware of their own needs. This is because empathic organisms can interpret the meaning of situations from another's point of view even in the absence of expressive activity by the other.

In humans, unlike lower animals, emotional contagion is typically a stage on the way to affective empathy and sympathy. As Hoffman in particular has shown, there is in a human child, from about ten to eighteen months of age, a gradual development of its ability to understand the source of its contagiously acquired emotions.[31] For instance, an infant of ten months typically responds to the distress (crying) of another by becoming distressed itself, but then it consoles only itself while ignoring the other. Later, apparently realizing that it shares a common emotion with the other, it intermittently consoles the other as well as itself. Eventually, the infant may no longer cry itself but, now recognizing that it is the other who is sad, may simply try to console the other. Subsequently, the normal child's sympathetic responses show an increasing sensitivity to the particular needs of the other, not merely by consoling the other but by responding more specifically to the other's mental states and motivations based on a better appreciation of the other's point of view.

In sum, when lower animals either provide aid to those under their care or take advantage of others in situations where identity of interests does not occur, it is due not to concern or lack of concern for the other but to their pursuing ends toward which they are moved by the situation, without regard to whether these ends are in their own or another's interests. That is, lower animals and, as Hazlitt suggested, very young humans are simply unaware of the distinction between their own interests and those of others since they are not even aware of interests as such. However, at the critical developmental transition of a year and a half the human child is perfectly balanced between egoism and altruism. It is able to recognize that its spontaneous "animal" sympathy to another's distress is not a response to its own situation, which it can now recognize as different from another's, yet it still feels an impulse to relieve the distress it experiences by helping the other. Such spontaneous altruism sometimes issues in actions apparently against the child's own long-term self-interest, such as when the child gives its favorite doll to the other. It is only with repeated experience that the child can begin to recognize the potential for conflict between its current sympathetic response to others and its own current or long-term interests, and it is only through acquiring a habit of thinking about and identifying with its own current or future interests that the child learns to inhibit spontaneous sympathy in favor of self-interest.

Contemporary studies, then, suggest that initially children are neither self-interested nor other-interested, neither altruists nor egoists, but only later become so. Such studies thus support Hazlitt's claim that children are "naturally disinterested," at least in relation to the future. They also suggest that he was substantially correct in emphasizing the importance of acquiring self-concepts in the development of self-interest as a motivating force. In addition, by assigning an important role in empathy to representing others' points of view and in sympathy to determining appropriate responses to others' needs, such studies support Hazlitt's insistence on the importance of imagination in the development of moral sensibility. Finally, such studies tend to confirm Hazlitt's view that learning to be self-interested depends on the development of forms of identification that connect the child to itself in the future and separate it from others.

Notes

We are grateful to Stiv Fleishman, Ingmar Persson, and two referees of this journal for helpful comments on earlier versions of this paper. We especially thank Ronald Tetreault for drawing our attention to Hazlitt's *Essay.*

[1] William Hazlitt, *Essay on the Principles of Human Action and some Remarks on the Systems of Hartley and Helvetius* (London, 1805; reprinted, with an introduction, by John R. Nabholtz, Gainesville, Fla., 1969), 133 (page numbers noted parenthetically refer to 1969 reprint).

[2] *Ibid.*

[3] On Hazlitt's influence on Keats, see W. J. Bate, "The Sympathetic Imagination in Eighteenth-Century Criticism," *English Literary History,* 12 (1945) and his *John Keats* (Oxford, 1966), 239f; D. Bromwich, *Hazlitt* (Oxford, 1983), 374. Coleridge's comment on Hazlitt's *Essay* is in his *Lay Sermons* (London, 1817; Cambridge, 1972), 187.

[4] Sir James Mackintosh, "Dissertation on the Progress of Ethical Philosophy, Chiefly during the Seventeenth and Eighteenth Centuries," *Miscellaneous Works of the Right Honourable Sir James Mackintosh* (Philadelphia, 1847), 94-198.

[5] P. P. Howe, *The Life of William Hazlitt* (London, 1947), 76.

[6] Stanley Jones, *Hazlitt: A Life* (Oxford, 1989). Prima facie, Hazlitt's views in the *Essay* had a profound effect on his philosophy of art, a major preoccupation of which is the artist's ability to transcend his or her own limited identity and enter into sympathetic union with an object of contemplation. John L. Mahoney, *The Logic of Passion* (Salzburg, 1978), 108, says that "It is this sense of projection, of widening . . . our sympathies . . . , and of representing this new range of sympathy with concreteness and vitality, that one sees the essence of Hazlitt's theory." James Engell, *The Creative Imagination* (Cambridge, Mass., 1981), 199, says that Hazlitt's *Essay* provides "the psychological basis for his criticism."

[7] J. Kinnaird, *William Hazlitt* (New York, 1978), 24-30, 58.

[8] Bromwich, *op. cit.,* 418, n. 32. Nor have philosophers done better. For instance, James Noxon, "Hazlitt as moral philosopher," *Ethics,* 73 (1963), 279-83, gives a sympathetic account of Hazlitt's ethical views and briefly sketches Hazlitt's theory of personal identity but fails to appreciate its importance, and J. B. Schneewind, *Sidgwick's Ethics and Victorian Moral Philosophy* (Oxford, 1977), 148, mentions only that "Hazlitt in his early days wrote philosophical essays in one of which he put forward some original and interesting objections to egoism."

[9] Adam Smith, *Wealth of Nations,* ed. Edward Cannon (New York, 1937), 14.

[10] Howe, *op. cit.,* 77; Kinnaird, *op. cit.,* 24-25.

[11] Joseph Butler, *The Analogy of Religion, Natural and Revealed* (London, 1852), II, 6-8; see also, Leonard M. Trawick III, "Sources of Hazlitt's 'Metaphysical Discovery,'" *Philological Quarterly,* 42 (1963), 280.

[12] As soon as Locke's views on personal identity were published they provoked a storm of protest. In addition to Clarke and Collins the disputants included Stillingfleet, Shaftesbury, Berkeley, Mandeville, Prior, Watts, and such lesser-knowns as Henry Lee, Richard Burthogge, Thomas Burnet, Catherine Trotter, Winch Holdsworth, Henry Felton, John Sergeant, and Peter Browne, as well as anonymous pamphleteers and writers in *The British Apollo* and *The Spectator.* For a few details see Christopher Fox, *Locke and the Scriblerians* (Berkeley, 1988), ch. 3.

[13] John Locke, *An Essay Concerning Human Understanding,* ed. A. C. Fraser (Oxford, 1894), bk. 2, ch. 27, sec. 13.

[14] Thomas Reid, *Essay on the Intellectual Powers of Man,* 1785, *The Works of Thomas Reid,* ed. William Hamilton (Edinburgh, 1863). Also G. W. Leibniz, *New Essay Concerning Human Understanding,* tr. A. G. Langley (New York, 1891), 255-56.

[15] There were exceptions, such as the medieval Aristotelian, Gersonides, but none that had an important impact on the subsequent personal identity debate. See Rabbi Levi ben Gershom, *The Logic of Gersonides: A Translation of Sefer ha-Heqqesh ha-Yashar,* ed. Charles H. Manekin (Dordrecht, 1992).

[16] Spinoza, *Ethica ordine geometrico demonstrata* (c. 1679), in *Spinoza Opera,* ed. C Gebhardt (4 vols.; Heidelberg, 1924); Locke, *op. cit.*

[17] C. B. Martin, and Max Deutscher, "Remembering," *The Philosophical Review,* 75 (1966), 161-97.

[18] David Wiggins, *Identity and Spatio-Temporal Continuity* (Oxford, 1967), 50.

[19] David Lewis (*Philosophical Papers* [New York, 1983], I, 55-77), has questioned whether fission does undermine identity. Raymond Martin has argued ("Identity, Transformation, and What Matters in Survival," D. Kolak and R. Martin [eds.], *Self & Identity* [New York, 1991], 289-301) that non-fission examples can be used to show the relative unimportance of identity. We here stick to the fission case, asking the reader to focus on what is crucial about it . . . not fission but the apparently egoistically motivated trading of continued identity for other benefits.

[20] For more details see the essays by R. Sperry, R. Puccetti, T. Nagel, and D. Parfit, in Kolak and Martin, *ibid.*

[21] See Sydney Shoemaker, "Personal Identity: A Materialist Account," S. Shoemaker and R. Swinburne (eds.), *Personal Identity* (Oxford, 1984), 119.

[22] Sydney Shoemaker, "Persons and Their Pasts," *American Philosophical Quarterly,* 7 (1970), 269-85, and *ibid.;* Robert Nozick, *Philosophical Explanations* (Cambridge, Mass., 1981), ch. 1; David Lewis, *op. cit.;* Derek Parfit, "Personal Identity," *The Philosophical Review,* 80 (1971), 3-27 and *Reasons and Persons* (Oxford, 1984), part III; Ernest Sosa, "Surviving Matters," *Nous,* 24 (1990), 305-30; Peter Unger, *Identity, Consciousness, and Value* (New York, 1991).

[23] Spinoza, *op. cit.,* Pr. 27; G. B. Vico, *The New Science,* tr. T. G. Bergin and M. H. Frisch (Ithaca, 1986); L. Wispe, "The distinction between sympathy and empathy: To call forth a concept a word is needed," *Journal of Personality and Social Psychology,* 50 (1986), 314-21, and *The Psychology of Sympathy* (New York, 1991).

[24] T. Lipps, "Einfuhlung, inner Nachahmung, and Organempfindaungen," *Archiv fur die gesamte psychologie,* 2 (1903), 185-204.

[25] A. Schopenhauer, *On the Basis of Morality,* tr. E. F. J. Payne (New York, 1965).

[26] M. Scheler, *The Nature of Sympathy,* tr. P. Heath (London, 1954); cf. P. Mercer, *Sympathy and Ethics: A Study of the Relationship between Sympathy and Morality with special reference to Hume's Treatise* (Oxford, 1972).

[27] G. G. Gallup, "Self-awareness and the emergence of mind in primates," *American Journal of Primatology,* 2 (1982), 237-48; Alvin Goldman, "Empathy, Mind, and Morals," *Proceedings and Addresses of the American Philosophical Association,* 66 (1992), 17-41; "Ethics and Cognitive Science," *Ethics,* 103 (1993), 337-60; and "The Psychology of Folk Psychology," *Behavioral and Brain Sciences,* 16 (1993), 15-28; P. L. Harris, *Children and Emotion* (Oxford, 1989); and "From Simulation to Folk Psychology: The Case for Development," *Mind & Language,* 7 (1992), 120-44; N. Hum-phrey, *Consciousness Regained* (Oxford, 1984); R. Gordon, "Folk Psychology as Simulation," *Mind & Language,* 1 (1986), 158-71.

[28] S. P. Stich and S. Nichols, "Folk Psychology: Simulation or Tacit Theory?" *Mind & Language,* 7 (1992), 35-71.

[29] For references and discussion of these alternative views, see Goldman, *op. cit.,* 1992.

[30] John Barresi and C. Moore, "Sharing a Perspective Precedes the Understanding of that Perspective," *Behavioral and Brain Sciences,* 16 (1993), 513-14; "Knowledge of the psychological states of self and others is not only theory-laden but also data-driven," *Behavioral and Brain Sciences,* 16 (1993), 61-62; and "Intentional Relations and Social Understanding," *Behavioral and Brain Sciences,* in press.

[31] M. L. Hoffman, "Empathy, its development and prosocial implications," C. B. Keasey (ed.), *Nebraska Symposium on Motivation, Social Cognitive Development* (Lincoln, 1977), XXV.

Jonathan Gross (essay date 1995)

SOURCE: "Hazlitt's Worshiping Practice in *Liber Amoris,*" in *Studies in English Literature, 1500-1900,* Vol. 35, No. 4, Autumn, 1995, pp. 707-21.

[*In the following essay, Gross argues that* Liber Amoris *"reveals the growth of [Hazlitt's] fetishistic imagination," which both fueled his creative sensibilities and helped refine his theory of religious practice.*]

> [A]nd I will make a Goddess of her, and build a temple to her in my heart, and worship her on indestructible altars, and raise statues to her: and my homage shall be unblemished as her unrivalled symmetry of form.
>
> *Liber Amoris* (9:133)

William Hazlitt's infatuation with a lodging-house girl has caused almost as much pain to his recent literary commentators as it did to him.[1] Various writers on Hazlitt have expressed their outrage at an event in his life which seems to have no place in his literary career.[2] Henry Crabb Robinson called *Liber Amoris* "disgusting," Richard Le Gallienne termed it "silly," and Frank Swinnerton spoke of it as "that tragic piece of futility."[3] *The Literary Gazette* and *New European Magazine* were disturbed by the honesty of the portrait, while *Blackwood's* dismissed it as "a *veritable* transcript of the feelings and doings of an individual living LIBERAL."[4] More recently, Herschel Baker, in a chapter of his biography on Hazlitt entitled "A Mind Diseased," reluctantly discusses the episode which "has always given pain to Hazlitt's admirers and satisfaction to the prurient."[5] Stanley Jones rescues the work from the charge of embarrassing naiveté by claiming, with the authority of R. H. Horne and Marilyn Butler, that the work is ironic: "[i]t is the dialogue of the lover and his coy mistress, couched on his side in language that dramatizes the familiar romantic dichotomy between the emotional and the intellectual."[6] Anxious to restore artistry to Hazlitt's confessional work, Jones reminds the reader that Hazlitt is "not so much recording his own unhappy story as elaborating a study of a man in love."[7]

I am interested in recovering a more personal Hazlitt, a man whose infatuation with Sarah Walker was closely connected with both his early ambition to become a painter and his admiration for the career of Napoleon Bonaparte. Critics have overlooked the personal key to *Liber Amoris* in favor of a more literary and perhaps decorous reading.[8] Yet Hazlitt wrote a number of essays for *Table-Talk* which, as Robert Ready has observed, "present the writer instead of the writing" and give us insight into the method employed in his next work, *Liber Amoris.* Drawing briefly on the logic of his metaphors in *Table-Talk,*[9] I argue that *Liber Amoris* reveals the growth of his fetishistic imagination; to read at the fault lines of Hazlitt's book of love is to discover a critical intelligence both sustained and swayed by this powerful capacity for worship.

I

E. Tangye Lean argues that Napoleonists like Lord Byron, Charles James Fox, William Godwin, William Hazlitt, Lord and Lady Holland, and Leigh Hunt were engaged in a revolt against their fathers which was suppressed, thus condemning them to lifelong fidelity as the children of outcast leaders. Though rather broadly applied, Lean's argument seems particularly compelling in the case of William Hazlitt. Hazlitt remained loyal to his father, a Unitarian minister, long after he had made his break with the Unitarian faith in 1795.[10] Hazlitt's father, who intervened on behalf of American prisoners transported to Kinsale, Ireland, was a figure of extraordinary, if embattled, prestige to Hazlitt. Hazlitt could no more have betrayed his father than he could have "stabbed the Good Samaritan in the back," Lean argues.[11] Yet a betrayal was necessary. Hazlitt's father saw no value in the art, philosophy, or literature that was to become the centerpiece of his son's adult life. Though he wrote numerous essays attacking Nonconformists for their indifference to art, Hazlitt never criticized his father for his religious convictions. The result of this need to rebel against his father coupled

with the practical inability to do so created what Lean calls the English Napoleonist, who perpetually sees evil at home, and good in foreign governments. "[W]hereas the normal outcome in adult life is to see the representative of the good father at the head of the country and the bad figure in the world outside," Lean states, "there was an acquired reversal in the Napoleonist which made him see the goodness outside and the evil at home."[12]

Lean, perhaps too jingoistically, reduces the oppositional politics of the Napoleonists to a pathology. At the same time, however, it is clear that *Liber Amoris* is a pathological work, one that reveals a strain in Hazlitt's identity. Hazlitt himself asserts that the hero of his tale may be supposed to have died of "a sickly frame and morbid state of mind" (9:97). In this thinly veiled biography, which Freud might have called a pathography,[13] Hazlitt reveals his susceptibility to scopophilia and fetishism. The worshiping practice evident in his previous writings is exposed in *Liber Amoris* by the pressure of five intersecting events: the fall of Napoleon, the failure of his artistic ambitions, the death of his father, his unrequited love for Sarah Walker, and his separation from his wife, Sarah Stoddart.

An essay that appeared in the second volume of *Table-Talk,* "On Dreams," gives us some authority for reading *Liber Amoris* in this way.[14] Written two years after his father's death in 1820, this essay shows Hazlitt in an act of religious worship:

> I dreamt I was there [in the Louvre] a few weeks ago, and that the old scene returned—that I looked for my favourite pictures, and found them gone or erased. The dream of my youth came upon me; a glory and a vision utterable, that comes no more but in darkness and in sleep: my heart rose up, and I fell on my knees, and lifted up my voice and wept, and I awoke. I also dreamt a little while ago, that I was reading the *New Heloise* to an old friend, and came to the concluding passage in Julia's farewell letter, which had much the same effect upon me.—The words are, *"Trop heureuse d'acheter au prix de ma vie le droit de t'aimer toujours sans crime et de te le dire encore une fois, avant que je meurs!"* I used to sob over this passage twenty years ago; and in this dream about it lately, I seemed to live these twenty years over again in one short moment! I do not dream ordinarily; and there are people who never could see anything in the *New Eloise.* Are we not quits!
>
> (12:24)

In this passage, Hazlitt seems to beg forgiveness from a punishing father who forbade him a life in the arts. Indeed, one might go so far as to say that his father is the absent figure symbolically removing and erasing paintings from the museum.[15] No sooner is one object of reverence removed, however, than it is replaced by another, *La Nouvelle Heloise.* The movement from painting to literature telescopes Hazlitt's choice of careers. This choice, incidentally, is conceived of as both a rebellion against the father and a fulfillment of his wishes. It is rebellious because Hazlitt's objects of veneration (paintings, literature, busts, even Napoleon and Sarah Walker herself) are profane, a rejection of the sacred text Hazlitt's Unitarian father worshiped. It is a fulfillment of the father's wishes because of the manner in which it is carried out. For Hazlitt, the objects and symbols of Catholicism which his Unitarian father repressed find their way back into the son's worship of *La Nouvelle Heloise,* or such political and artistic idols as William Wordsworth, Samuel Coleridge, Napoleon, and Sarah Walker. Hazlitt's tendency to make a fetish of art, his worship of Napoleon's bust, not only recalls his earlier career as a painter; it also forestalls sexual, political, and artistic rebellion by converting it into worship.

In an example of what I call historical chiasmus, Hazlitt's *Liber Amoris* revisits his own failure as a painter. He effectively reverses the last digits of 1820, the year he met Sarah Walker (9:120), and recalls a time, 1802, when he sat copying masterpieces in the Louvre. Eighteen years later, Hazlitt is left with only a bust of Napoleon (another reproduction!) to remind him of his former feelings for the fallen leader. Having renounced his ambitions as a philosopher and painter, he earns his living as a journalist and thinks of the commercial value of each essay he composes. He longs to abandon literary criticism and return to a more artistic vocation. *Liber Amoris* is Hazlitt's act of political nostalgia. Through writing about his infatuation with a lodging-house girl, he recalls a time when Napoleon's success made Romantic self-fashioning seem more plausible.

The importance of historical chiasmus to Hazlitt's *Liber Amoris* is never more apparent than in its opening chapter, "The Painting." H., a character loosely based on Hazlitt himself, tells S. she reminds him of a painting by Raphael, entitled "St. Cecilia, with looks commercing with the skies." S. refuses the resemblance H. tries to impose. She does not look like St. Cecilia, she declares, but manages to extract a flageolet from her middle-aged lodger as a token of his affection for her. The second, more successful exchange between H. and S. involves H.'s beloved bust. For H., the bust recalls Napoleon's career: the possibilities open to a man of talent beset by a world too inclined to estimate a man's worth by his social position. S., however, transforms the bust of Napoleon into a purely aesthetic object—perhaps even an object of commercial value. The bust is anything but the political symbol which H. sees. For S., the bronze

statue reminds her of a former lover and she requests the statue as a sentimental token, however ambiguous, of her friendship with H. H., grateful for any response from his hitherto indifferent maid, gives S. the statue. Still, she is indifferent to his advances. In the climactic scene of the novel, H. returns from a sojourn to Scotland, anxious to marry S. upon his return. When she again rejects his advances, H. smashes the bust. They are briefly reconciled and S. promises to repair the statue, which has been broken in three places. The novel ends when H. discovers S. walking with another man, presumably the man she has been in love with all along.

Both Hazlitt and the literary projection of him which appears in *Liber Amoris* are ignorant in the extreme about the political motivations (not to mention the economic and psychological ones) that have set this romance afoot. H.'s love for Napoleon has become fetishized after Napoleon's defeat: he now worships a statue rather than the emperor. So charged is his admiration for the fallen leader that the bust of Napoleon becomes a mediating device in his affiar with S. By worshiping S., H. is fulfilling the leveling ideology of the French revolution: liberty, fraternity, equality.[16] In this allegorical reading, Hazlitt and Sarah meet as members of the bourgeoisie and proletariat, respectively, occupying the upstairs and downstairs of the house, but struggling, despite the stairs and social class that separate them, to come to some kind of understanding. The bust of Napoleon presides over their social relations and sanctions intercourse between them. Now that Napoleon has surrendered and a bust of Napoleon stands for Napoleon himself, however, other synecdochic arrangements are necessary as well. H. uses S. to recall his lost youth and the fervor connected with his artistic career, while Sarah uses the memory of her former lover, whom she claims has jilted her, to extract the bust of Napoleon from H. Using each other as means rather than as ends, they have become consumers and their consumptive practice corresponds with what we would expect of a nascent capitalist economy.[17]

At crucial points in the narrative, the bust is exchanged: first as a token of love, next as a sign of loyalty, and finally as a sign of fraud. How to legislate between these competing interpretations is both text and subtext of *Liber Amoris.* Perhaps Sarah arranged to win the statue of Napoleon to begin with, Hazlitt muses. Then Hazlitt would no longer be giving Sarah something but having it wrested from him. The friendly commerce between the bourgeoisie and the proletariat that brought Napoleon into power—symbolized by Hazlitt loaning the statue to Sarah—ends, as the French Revolution ended, with mutual recriminations.

Fraud is an essential part of capitalist exchange which, like metaphor, proceeds on the assumption that one item equals or is identical to another. In each trans-action, the object exchanged is both similar to and different from the object it is meant to replace—usually, however, it is inferior. Thus the "new" bust of Napoleon is really the old bust broken in three places; the new Pygmalion turns to stone while the old one comes to life; the "new" lovers of Hazlitt's epistolary novel are never even certain of their love, while Rousseau's St. Preux and Julie avow it all too freely. The tendency of the heroes of certain Romantic texts to reproduce themselves (Byron and the repulsive personage of Childe Harold; Byron and the naive Don Juan; Hazlitt and H.; Sarah Walker and S.) and to do so in a degraded and attenuated way, speaks powerfully to the importance of the theme of the disgusted consumer as it emerges in Romanticism.[18] Byron knows that new heroes fail to measure up to old ones in *Don Juan* (the "new one" is not the "true one"), but Hazlitt clings relentlessly to his Napoleonic ideal and makes a fetish of a commodity he is unable to exchange.

Napoleon was a leader conspicuously enthralled by commodities. Byron portrays him as a child fascinated by the "gewgaws" of republicanism (the star, the string, the crest) which he has dishonorably exchanged for the "purple robe" of empire.[19] Yet Hazlitt needed someone to believe in, a need at first supplied by Wordsworth[20] and more particularly by Coleridge,[21] whose apostasy disappointed and then enraged him. Hazlitt's infatuation with Napoleon was no less intense and perhaps a great deal more so, since one passion was expunged in an essay and the other in four volumes (*The Life of Napoleon Buonaparte*). The act of writing, however, creates its own object. No sooner has Hazlitt "lost" Coleridge, Napoleon, and Sarah as objects of worship, than he has gained them on his own terms as literary commodities: **"My First Acquaintance With the Poets,"** *The Life of Napoleon Buonaparte,* and *Liber Amoris.* Yet Hazlitt substitutes these literary commodities for people only at the price of gutting his object of reverence, hoisting Coleridge, Napoleon, and Sarah on the petard of his intellect.

In *Liber Amoris,* Hazlitt is particularly successful at capitalizing on his emotional investment. Making a fetish of S. (rather than loving her for who she truly is) enables H. to turn worship into cash: first he does this by writing the second volume of *Table-Talk* in less than a month: "I regularly do ten pages a day," he writes, "which mounts up to thirty guineas' worth a week, so that you see I should grow rich at this rate, if I could keep on so; *and I could keep on so,* if I had you with me" (9:112). Finally, he turns love into a commodity by turning his personal letters to S. into *Liber Amoris* and selling the copyright for 100 guineas.[22] In his letter to her, he seems to thank her (as if for both gifts) in advance. "I owe you more than I can ever pay" (9:113). The clearest

proof we have that this fetishistic exchange is not productive, however, is H.'s confession at the height of romantic absorption, that his heart has grown "cold and dead" (9:113). Content to be her "happy slave," he informs her he will obtain a picture of her to "kiss and talk to" (9:113). The more he achieves his fetishistic desires, however, the more inanimate S. appears to him. In the second part of *Liber Amoris,* when she has been vacated of all human meaning by H., he "wake[s] with her by my side, not as my sweet bedfellow, but as the corpse of my love, without a heart in her bosom, cold, insensible, or struggling from me" (9:125). H. blames S. for fiendish propensities, for bringing about, through witchcraft, the dehumanization of S. which his own fetish has caused (9:121).

But Freud had another way of explaining fetishism, one which may allow us to tie together the political, economic, sexual, and artistic motives behind Hazlitt's worshiping practice. For Freud, fetishism is no less brutal than capitalism in its effort to impose human significance onto an object or, conversely, to transform human beings into fixed symbols. It may be helpful here to distinguish between fetishism and idolatry. A fetish is "an inanimate object supposed to possess some magical power"[23] whereas "an idol is distinguished from the fetish, the totem, and the amulet precisely because it is worshipped as a deity."[24] Hazlitt's worship of the bust of Napoleon, interestingly enough, becomes "the little image" (9:122) when Sarah shows interest in it. What was once an idol becomes a fetish by being endowed with sexual (and for Freud, tragic) significance.

For Freud, the fetish is "a substitute for the woman's (the mother's) penis that the little boy once believed in and—for reasons familiar to us—does not want to give up." Unable to deal with the horrible thought of castration which the naked female body represents to him, the young boy substitutes an object for the woman's missing member which acts as a kind of consolation. "Yes, in his mind the woman has got a penis, in spite of everything; but this penis is no longer the same as it was before. Something else has taken its place, has been appointed its substitute, as it were, and now inherits the interest which was formerly directed to its predecessor."[25] Freud's essay on fetishism allows us to make sense of the extraordinary "interest," to use Freud's word, with which the bust of Napoleon is endowed. The statue represents not only a political idol of H.'s according to this reading—one that has been castrated, in a sense, or fallen from power—but a substitute penis that enables him to pursue a relationship with S. In fact, the moment H. exchanges his bust of Napoleon is the moment he feels closest to her. *"I got up and gave her the image, and told her it was her's [sic] by every right that was sacred. She refused at first to take so valuable a curiosity, and said she would keep it for me. But I pressed it eagerly, and she took it. She immediately came and sat down, and put her arm round my neck, and kissed me, and I said 'Is it not plain we are the best friends in the world, since we are always so glad to make it up?' . . . How I loved her at that moment!"* (9:112). By giving the bust of Napoleon to S., H. symbolically restores her lost phallus and hopes for a more normal relationship with her. He will give up his fetish, hoping to replace worship with direct sexual contact.

No sooner is he out of S.'s presence in Part II of **Liber Amoris,** however, than he begins to feel she has tricked him out of the marble bust by ascribing to it a sentimental significance which it does not in fact possess. Unable to part with his fetish or to allow S. to pursue her own, H. accuses her of theft and deception. "You see by this she always hated me, and only played with my credulity till she could find some one to supply the place of her unalterable attachment to *the little image*" (9:122). The abstract language of this sentence betrays how far removed S. is from human relations, how far along the chain of fetishistic displacement he has traveled: he hopes for a person to supply the place of an attachment to an image. Her former lover, who the statue supposedly resembles (except for the nose), is now completely out of the picture. In love with a statue, both S. and H. are incapable, or perhaps uninterested, in moving beyond that worship to love of each other.

That H. thinks he is capable of loving S. for herself is precisely his pathology. He continues to pursue S. in Part III, and when she rejects his advances, he smashes the bust of Napoleon in a fit of rage. By doing so he attempts to free her from her fetish (her attachment to her previous lover) and his own (his attachment to the idea of a substitute penis). "I then dashed the little Buonaparte on the ground, and stamped upon it, as one of the instruments of her mockery" (9:145). This is the dramatic climax of the work, the moment when H. both recognizes and disavows his fetish. Not long after he has destroyed the bust, however, he meekly collects the pieces together and reveres it anew: "I gathered up the fragments of the locket of her hair, and the little bronze statue, which were strewed about the floor, kissed them, folded them up in a sheet of paper, and sent them to her, with these lines written in pencil on the outside—*'Pieces of a broken heart, to be kept in remembrance of the unhappy. Farewell.' "* (9:148). Freud's anecdotal discussion of fetishism in Chinese culture may help in explaining the significance of H.'s action. By "mutilating the female foot and then revering it like a fetish after it has been mutilated," Freud argues, "it seems as though the Chinese male wants to thank the woman for having submitted to being castrated" (21:157). Similarly, H. reveals his desire to sustain his worship of the statue even after

it has been castrated ("broken in three pieces with a missing sword") and asks S. if she will restore it. The statue which differed from Napoleon in the nose (one phallic symbol), is now missing a sword (another). The sorry state of the statue prepares us for the castration of H. that is to occur. The very evening H. thinks S. is having the statue fixed, she actually meets another lover whom she has been seeing the entire time she has been seeing H. The object meant to replace the rift between S. and H. becomes the excuse S. uses to leave the lodging house to see her other lover.

What a Freudian reading of **Liber Amoris** never resolves, however,—what it never even manages to address—is the nature of Sarah's desire, which turns out to be as perverse as H.'s. A kind of gender-reversed voyeurism takes place in the margins of **Liber Amoris** and causes considerable anxiety for H., whose greatest fear is that of being looked at in return. After all, it is S.'s gaze that begins the pathology of **Liber Amoris** and inaugurates H.'s suffering. She looks at him, turning to stare at him directly in the face after delivering his breakfast items.[26]

One reason the pock-marked Hazlitt was attracted to S. in the first place was that she always insisted that she did not like "looks." By this she meant that she did not care about the physical appearance of a man. But "looks" has at least one other meaning, that of scopophilia (love of looking) and S.'s disavowal of her fetish is overdetermined. She says she hates "looks"; she even hates C.'s "red slippers" (9:162), but her love of looking and of looks is no less intense than H.'s. At the end of **Liber Amoris,** H. shrewdly observes that "she always hated whatever she liked most" (9:162). Like H., S. negates and defers knowledge of her own fetish.

Helpful as Freud's essay is, fetishism in **Liber Amoris** would seem to have less to do with H.'s gaze than it does with a kind of visual economy connected with consumer culture. Voyeurs proliferate in the Walker household and any discussion of scopophilia must include not only H. but S., S.'s sister, and father. It would be tempting to situate H.'s and S.'s worshiping practice in the dynamics of a consumer culture, as Colin Campbell attempts to do (without reference to Hazlitt) in *The Romantic Ethic and the Spirit of Modern Consumerism.*[27]

The very derivation of the word fetish, however, takes us back to a religious interpretation. The word "fetish" was first used by Portuguese travelers in the eighteenth century who appropriated terms from their own form of worship (Catholicism) to describe specific religious practices in West Africa.[28] "Relics of saints, rosaries, and images were then abundant all over Europe and were regarded as possessing magical virtue; they were termed by the Portuguese *feiticos* (i.e. charms). Early voyagers to West Africa applied this term to the wooden figures, stones, &c. regarded as the temporary residence of gods or spirits, and to charms . . . *Feitico* is sometimes interpreted to mean artificial, made by man, but the original sense is more probably 'magically active or artful.'"[29] Fetish, then, is a word of European, Catholic derivation that was applied to African culture, not taken from it.[30] Coleridge mistakenly reverses this chronology and sees fetishism as a form of decadence that began in Africa and threatens nineteenth-century English culture. "From the fetisch of the imbruted African to the soul-debasing errors of the proud fact-hunting materialist we may trace the various ceremonials of the same idolatry, and shall find selfishness, hate and servitude as the results."[31] As this "from-to" construction would suggest, Coleridge troped fetishism as primitive and declaimed against its appearance in political and social life.[32]

Yet the term "fetishism" as used in European culture has very little to do with the type of religion practiced in Africa. "There is no good translation for the KiKongo word *nkisi* (pl. *minkisi*) because no corresponding institution exists in European culture," Wyatt MacGaffey explains. "In Kongo thought a nkisi is a personalised force from the invisible land of the dead; this force has chosen, or been induced, to submit itself to some degree of human control effected through ritual performances. The initiated expert who conducts the ritual is the *nganga* (operator or priest) . . . of the *nkisi*."[33] The Portuguese sailors who saw African religion described it in terms of their own form of worship. "Instead of functioning as a metalanguage for the magical thinking of others," Jean Baudrillard argues, the word fetishism "turns against those who use it, and surreptitiously exposes their own magical thinking."[34]

Whether we consider Moses in Exodus smashing the golden calf or Hazlitt's father inveighing against Catholic sacraments, the moral impulse that motivates these actions is the same. A worship of painting was considered by Hazlitt's father to be a form of idolatry. Intellectually loyal to his father but determined to become an artist, Hazlitt approached art and his subsequent career as a journalist with all the enthusiasm of a religious convert.[35] He avoided the guilt of rebelling against his father's wish that he become a Unitarian minister by approaching art and journalism with a religious sensibility.[36] "The idol we fall down and worship is an image familiar to our minds," he had written in "On the Knowledge of Character" (8:311). In fact it was the practice of worship, rather than the idol itself, that gained Hazlitt's interest. His admiration of Napoleon in life, and then in the form of a bust, was deluded, the result of a residual religiosity of which this most self-conscious

of writers was not fully aware. Hazlitt could no more know Napoleon than he could know the character of Sarah Walker: "Let not that veil ever be rent entirely asunder," he wrote in *Table-Talk,* "so that those images may be left bare of reverential awe, and lose their religion: for nothing can ever support the desolation of the heart afterwards!" (8:312). Hazlitt's religious feelings, once rational and Unitarian, became degraded by 1820, precisely because he could not bear the "desolation of . . . heart" (8:312) required to rid him of his faithful admiration of Napoleon. With Napoleon's (1821) and his father's death (1820) occurring within a year of each other, Hazlitt wrote essays that, as Charles Lamb observed, adopt "the style of a discontented man."[37] But Hazlitt was not merely adopting a "style"; he did not, as David Bromwich asserts, live out the drama of Othello in *Liber Amoris,* or simply ironize love, as Marilyn Butler has argued. He did not hide behind literary postures that he himself dismissed in "On Familiar Style."[38] *Liber Amoris* taught Hazlitt something about his relationship to Napoleon that he did not know, and perhaps never learned. While H. smashes his bust of Napoleon and achieves a freedom from his worshiping practice, Hazlitt remained enslaved to his idol, even after he completed *Liber Amoris.* In a four volume *Life of Napoleon,* Hazlitt shows remarkably little critical insight into his hero[39] and lapses into the stance of adoration he had chronicled in his book of love, *Liber Amoris.*[40]

Notes

[1] William Hazlitt, *Liber Amoris* in *The Complete Works of William Hazlitt,* 21 vols., ed. P. P. Howe (London, Toronto: J. M. Dent and Sons, 1930-34). Further references to this and other works by Hazlitt will appear parenthetically in the text by volume and page numbers.

[2] Ian Jack, "Hazlitt" in *English Literature: 1815-1832* (Oxford: Clarendon Press, 1963), pp. 274-5; in *Hazlitt and the Creative Imagination* (Lawrence: Univ. of Kansas Press, 1965), W. P. Albrecht notes that *Liber Amoris* and *The Life of Napoleon* "are not highly regarded in the Hazlitt canon" and omits discussion of *Liber Amoris* entirely (p. 163). Ralph M. Wardle, in *Hazlitt* (Lincoln: Univ. of Nebraska Press, 1971), concludes that "its merit as a study of human passion" is "weakened by the sentimental rhetoric with which Hazlitt overlaid the original letters" (p. 365). But many of Hazlitt's essays display the same sentiment without being faulted for that reason. Critics who have dismissed the work, or discussed only its allusiveness, have not explained its narrative integrity.

[3] In Charles Morgan's introduction to Hazlitt's *Liber Amoris and Dramatic Criticisms* (London: Peter Nevill, 1948), p. 10. The work has had its defenders, includ-

ing Mary Russell Mitford, *Letters of Mary Russell Mitford,* 2d ser., ed. Henry Chorley, 2 vols. (London: R. Bentley and Son, 1872), 1:126; Thomas De Quincey, *Collected Writings,* ed. David Masson, 14 vols. (London: A. and C. Black, 1896-97), 3:79; P. P. Howe, *The Fortnightly Review* 105 (1916): 300-10; Paul Elmer More, *Shelburne Essays,* 2d ser. (rprt. Boston and New York: Houghton Mifflin Co., 1930), p. 84; and Charles Morgan himself, who defends Hazlitt against the Victorians. For a careful consideration of critical responses to *Liber Amoris,* see Wardle, pp. 364-5.

[4] Wardle, p. 364.

[5] Herschel Baker, *William Hazlitt* (Cambridge MA: Harvard Univ. Press, 1962), p. 410.

[6] Stanley Jones, *Hazlitt: A Life from Winterslow to Frith Street* (Oxford: Clarendon Press, 1989), p. 320. Robert Ready recognizes that personal references "embarrass" literary critics, as in the digression on Sarah Walker that appears in "Of Great and Little Things." Though not applied to *Liber Amoris,* Ready's conclusions are in line with my own: "To some readers this long set piece [in "On Great and Little Things"] has seemed an embarrassment to the essay. I would suggest that it is the intention of 'On Great and Little Things' to embarrass the tidy inversions set up in the first half of the essay. Passion wells up in a speaker who has just finished observing the passion men suffer over little things . . . This is life crowding its sticky desires through the neat ironies deployed in the first part of the essay" (*Hazlitt at Table* [Rutherford NJ: Fairleigh Dickinson Univ. Press, 1981], p. 64).

[7] Jones, p. 318.

[8] David Bromwich traces allusions to *Othello* in *Liber Amoris* in *Hazlitt: The Mind of a Critic* (Oxford: Oxford Univ. Press, 1983), pp. 436-7; Robert Ready examines the theme of the "unsympathetic imagination" and urges us to read the work in "its proper literary perspective" in "The Logic of Passion: *Liber Amoris,*" *Modern Critical Views: William Hazlitt,* ed. Harold Bloom (New York: Chelsea House Publishers, 1986), p. 51; while Marilyn Butler views the work in the context of other Romantic biographies in "Satire and the Images of Self in the Romantic Period: The Long Tradition of Hazlitt's *Liber Amoris,*" in *English Satire and the Satiric Tradition,* ed. Claude Rawson and Jenny Mezciems (Oxford: Basil Blackwell, 1984), pp. 209-25. An exception to these more literary readings is John Kinnaird's, who in *William Hazlitt: Critic of Power* (New York: Columbia Univ. Press, 1978), sees *Liber Amoris* as "less the story of man hopelessly fallen in love than of a writer struggling to come to terms with an unfulfilled dream of destiny and with

the hopeless conviction of his incurable lovelessness" (p. 266). Kinnaird, quoting Peter George Patmore, notes that the work is a reflection of Hazlitt's "morbid sensitiveness" to criticism in Tory journals. Ready and Butler offer admirable thematic and historical explications, but do not, to my mind, adequately explain its central dramatic symbol, the bust of Napoleon. *Liber Amoris* is discussed in a brief footnote in Bromwich's study (n. 10, pp. 436-7), and receives no more than a paragraph of treatment in Kinnaird's study.

[9] Robert Ready has already given considerable attention to *Table-Talk* in his book-length study, *Hazlitt at Table.*

[10] Baker, p. 28; Ready, *Hazlitt at Table,* pp. 33-4.

[11] E. Tangye Lean, *The Napoleonists: A Study in Political Disaffection 1760-1960* (London: Oxford Univ. Press, 1970), p. 210. For Hazlitt's comments on his estrangement from his father, see "On the Knowledge of Character" (8:312). See also Baker, p. 29.

[12] Lean, p. 209.

[13] Emily Apter, *Feminizing the Fetish: Psychoanalysis and Narrative Obsession in Turn-of-the-Century France* (Ithaca: Cornell Univ. Press, 1991), p. 34.

[14] In his study of *Table-Talk,* Robert Ready turns Thomas De Quincey's criticism of Hazlitt's style into a compliment. De Quincey found Hazlitt's work "insulated, capricious, nonsequacious" (p. 25). Ready argues that Hazlitt's work is "a metaphoric action against systems which operate unconscious of their own 'insulated, capricious, nonsequacious' natures" (p. 26). Roy Park, in *Hazlitt and the Spirit of the Age: Abstraction and Critical Theory* (Oxford: Clarendon Press, 1971), also explains how Hazlitt and Coleridge shared an antiempiricism and were concerned to validate the authenticity of the imaginative realm (p. 78). To read Hazlitt's essays for their metaphorical logic, as Ready and Park do, seems more in keeping with Hazlitt's own literary practice.

[15] For Hazlitt's relationship with his father, see Herschel Baker, who writes that "his intellectual independence . . . had darkened his relations with his father, so that their 'unreserved communication' was ended . . . Hazlitt blasted his own father's hopes" (p. 29). Baker further describes, as "catastrophic," the circumstances surrounding Hazlitt's departure from Hackett, where he was training to be a minister (p. 28). See also Kinnaird, pp. 1-36.

[16] I am grateful to an editorial reader at *SEL* for his/her insight that the bust is equal to "liberty, fraternity, equality" by a second fetishistic move: "Hazlitt

is one of the very few since 1802 and few enough since 1798, to identify the revolutionary slogan with Napoleon."

[17] For Marx, the fetishism of commodities is false consciousness and results in "material relations between persons and social relations between things" (Karl Marx, *Capital: A Critique of Political Economy*, trans. Samuel Moore and Edward Aveling, 2 vols. [New York: International Publishers, 1967], 1:73). This seems to describe exchanges between S. and H., which are predominantly material; only the commodities they exchange have "social relations." I thank Prof. Kostis Papadantonakis, a participant in a 1992 NEH Summer Seminar, for bringing this passage to my attention.

[18] See Colin Campbell, *The Romantic Ethic and the Spirit of Modern Consumerism* (Oxford: Oxford Univ. Press, 1987), p. 31.

[19] Byron, "Ode to Napoleon Buonaparte," in *Lord Byron: The Complete Poetical Works,* ed. Jerome J. McGann, 7 vols. (Oxford: Clarendon Press, 1980-92), 3:265, stanza 18, lines 10-8.

[20] Ready, *Hazlitt at Table,* p. 45.

[21] Baker, p. 351. Kinnaird shows that Wordsworth's apostasy was justified for Hazlitt when it ceased being a Rousseauistic retreat to innocence and became instead "a state of restorative communion for the will" (p. 45).

[22] 1893 Introduction by Richard Le Gallienne," in *Liber Amoris: The Book of Love,* ed. Michael Neves (London: Hogarth Press, 1985), p. 220.

[23] *The Columbia Encyclopedia,* 3d edn., ed. William Bridgewater and Seymour Kurtz (New York: Columbia Univ. Press, 1963), p. 712.

[24] *The Columbia Encyclopedia,* p. 1003.

[25] Sigmund Freud, "Fetishism," in *The Standard Edition of the Complete Psychoanalytical Works of Sigmund Freud,* ed. James Strachey and Anna Freud, 24 vols. (London: Hogarth Press, 1953-66), 21:153. Further references will appear parenthetically in the text by volume and page numbers.

[26] S. also does this when she returns the bust of Napoleon to him ("she looked full in my eyes . . . at the door . . . [she] looked full at me" [9:156]); the quarrel between S. and H, moreover, is precipitated by the discovery of another voyeur in the house, S.'s sister, who goes running from the keyhole, crying "He thought I did not see him!" (9:106). A final moment of anxiety for H. occurs when he

worries that S.'s father has seen them embracing in her room (9:146). He questions the father and receives an affirmative reply.

[27] Campbell, pp. 34, 176. For Campbell, romantic love and a belief in the idea of luxury fueled the rise of consumerism. I find his argument for a causal connection between romanticism and consumerism to be provocative, but less helpful than fetishism in explaining *Liber Amoris.*

[28] Robert Hamill Nassau, *Fetichism [sic] in West Africa: Forty Years' Observation of Native Customs and Superstitions* (New York: Negro Univ. Press, 1901; rprt. 1969), pp. 80-1. John Vogt, in *Portuguese Rule on the Gold Coast: 1469-1682* (Athens: Univ. of Georgia Press, 1979), notes that the Portuguese trade in beads, coral, and gold began as early as the fifteenth century (pp. 69-71).

[29] Northcote Whitbridge Thomas, "Fetishism," in *The Encyclopedia Britannica,* 11th edn. (Cambridge: Cambridge Univ. Press, 1910-1). "The word was probably brought into general use by C. de Brosses, author of *Du culture des dieux fetiches* (1760), but it is frequently used by W. Bosman in his *Description of Guinea* (1705), in the sense of 'the false god, Bossum' or 'Bohsum,' properly a tutelary deity of an individual."

[30] *Encyclopedia Britannica,* 10:295. "The term fetish is commonly understood to mean the worship of or respect for material, inanimate objects, conceived as magically active from a virtue inherent in them, temporarily or permanently, which does not arise from the fact that a god or spirit is believed to reside in them or communicate virtue to them. Taken in this sense fetishism is probably a mark of decadence. There is no evidence of any such belief in Africa or elsewhere among primitive peoples. It is only after a certain grade of culture has been attained that the belief in luck appears; the fetish is essentially an object carried for luck."

[31] *The Friend,* ed Barbara E. Rooke, in *The Collected Works of Samuel Taylor Coleridge,* 14 vols. (Princeton: Princeton Univ. Press, 1969), 4:518. For Coleridge, the "unlettered African, or rude yet musing Indian" represent the "state of learned and systematic ignorance . . . mere orderliness without METHOD!" (4:513). Both figures are saved by the "friendly missionary" who explains to them the nature of written words.

[32] David Simpson, *Fetishism and Imagination: Dickens, Melville, Conrad* (Baltimore: Johns Hopkins Univ. Press, 1982), p. 13.

[33] Wyatt MacGaffey in *Art and Healing of the Bakongo, Commented by Themselves: Minkisi from the Laman Collection* (Bloomington: Indiana Univ. Press, 1991), p. 4.

[34] Jean Baudrillard, *For a Critique of the Political Economy of the Sign,* trans. Charles Levin (St. Louis: Telos Press, 1981), p. 90.

[35] Roy Park notes that for Coleridge a fusion of the poetic and religious spheres was incompatible "with his own conception of a Christian God" (p. 87). Hazlitt, by contrast, felt that the painter fulfilled the theological vocation better than the minister. "The painter does not view things in clouds or 'mist, the common gloss of theologians,' but applies the same standard of truth and disinterested spirit of inquiry, that influence his daily practice, to other subjects" (8:10).

[36] Kinnaird, p. 30. For Hazlitt's account of this relationship, see "On the Knowledge of Character" (8:312).

[37] "Lamb's Unpublished Review of Hazlitt's *Table-Talk,*" in Robert Ready, *Hazlitt at Table,* p. 97.

[38] Ready, *Hazlitt at Table,* pp. 83-90.

[39] Albrecht, p. 163. Albrecht reports that "*Liber Amoris,* and *The Life of Napoleon,* are not highly regarded in the Hazlitt canon. The individual essay is the structural unit which displays Hazlitt's imaginative resources at their best" (p. 163). While I agree with Albrecht's view of *The Life of Napoleon,* I think that its weakness has more to do with its subject matter than its length. The reasons for Hazlitt's peculiar blindness to Napoleon's limitations are powerfully exposed in the undervalued and revelatory *Liber Amoris.*

[40] This essay was written during Professor Jerome Christensen's 1992 NEH summer seminar, "Romanticism and the Triumph of Liberalism." My thanks to members of the seminar for their helpful suggestions.

Laurie Kane Lew (essay date 1997)

SOURCE: "Collection and Recollection: William Hazlitt and the Poetics of Memory," in *Studies in Romanticism,* Vol. 36, No. 3, Fall, 1997, pp. 349-89.

[*In the following essay, Lew discusses Hazlitt's essays as a series of portraits from which Lew determines his theory of memory and his understanding of artistic appreciation.*]

"For my part," Hazlitt wrote in 1827, "I set out in life with the French Revolution, and that event had considerable influence on my early feelings, as on those of others."[1] Mourning the loss, not just of his own, but of the universal possibilities for "Life" and "Liberty," which were entailed in the failure of the French Revolution, Hazlitt continued:

> Since the future was barred to my progress, I have turned for consolation to the past, gathering up the fragments of my early recollections, and putting them into a form that might live. It is thus, when we find our personal and substantial identity vanishing from us, we strive to gain a reflected and substituted one in our thoughts. . . . (17.197)

Hazlitt announces a private retreat—into the depths of memory—only to reconfigure his identity in the realm of socially symbolic action. Through the double acts of collection and recollection, which allusively recreate Hazlitt's earliest experiences of gallery-going (at the public showing of the Orleans Collection in 1798 and in the Grand Gallery of Napoleon's Louvre in 1802) and his youthful ambitions to become a painter, the essayist connects past and present and joins the public sphere of writing and viewing to his private memories of painting.

The public, which is to say the political, implications of painting had always been primary for Hazlitt. The Orleans Collection came to England as a result of circumstances created by the French Revolution, and it was the Peace of Amiens that drew Englishmen to France to see the Italian masterpieces "collected" by Napoleon and exhibited in the Louvre. Hazlitt thematized both these events in political terms—as the transformation and elevation of the individual human spirit through the medium of ideal art—and, in the decades after Waterloo, memorialized these public experiences in some of his most deeply personal and affecting essays.[2] Yet despite their political context—and in marked contrast to the public mode and orientation of the criticism of English painters and painting Hazlitt wrote for various periodicals between 1814 and 1815—these later essays on art have the texture, as well as the unresolved quality, of memories. Accounts of exhibition and gallery-going, which had provided the occasion for critical judgment and an immediacy of response, are displaced by memories of paintings, or more specifically, by the feelings associated with viewing experiences in the distant past. As the universalist values Hazlitt associated with the "revolutionary" public space of the Louvre were variously complicated by the defeat of Napoleon, the dispersal of the Louvre's masterpieces, and a reactionary political climate at home, memory became a way of substituting a "spatial" order for both the temporal dynamic of historical process and the narrative logic of autobiography. In these late essays on art, the failures of the French Revolution and the literal and figurative displacement of art works are mapped onto Hazlitt's own failed ambitions as a painter, extending, questioning, and reshaping the generic conventions of both romantic autobiography and the critical essay.

In my essay I describe this thematics and poetics of memory in Hazlitt's writing by focusing on three interrelated issues. The first is the way in which the essays themselves, as acts of imaginative collection and recollection, can be considered as a series of portraits or self-portraits, reflections on and of the self gazing both inward (as Hazlitt examines his own history as a viewer) and outward (to publicly confront the reader/viewer). The second issue I explore is how Hazlitt's memories of paintings, standing in for past viewing experiences, achieve "public" status. Hazlitt, I will argue, conceived of memory as a mode of mental reproduction, analogous to graphic reproduction and textual inscription. These were both, moreover, interactive forms of "copying" which placed the subject in a new relation to the art work: a relation which, through the circulation of texts and pictorial reproductions, offered the possibility of creating a community of similar beholders. In doing so—and this brings me to my third point—Hazlitt sought to create new modes of access to art, most significantly in his vision of the museum as public space. For nearly a decade before England established its first public museum (the doors of the National Gallery would not be opened until 1824), the textualized museum of Hazlitt's prose both created and recreated a collection of art.

1

Hazlitt's rewriting of revolutionary history in the language of memory and of the imagination is both congruent with and a significant departure from these impulses in Rousseau and Wordsworth.[3] Roy Park's discussion of the autobiographical aspects of the later essays suggests that the significance of the past for Hazlitt is that it is fully susceptible to symbol making. "Objects" from the past, recovered through language, testify to the imaginative interaction of man's spiritual or existential being and his physical being, of the confluence of the real and the ideal. Hazlitt uses these objects either as direct embodiments of feeling (pointing to them, as it were) or, in what Park understands as a more Wordsworthian mode, as the occasion for "sentiment," in which the object itself is submerged in, and obscured by, the feelings it evokes.[4] While Hazlitt attempts to recover the revolutionary ideals of freedom and equality by objectifying them as paintings, works of sculpture such as the Elgin Marbles, or museums (which he thought of as the material embodiments of human history), their inscription as memory-images only affirms their pastness, their unavailability to the present. As Mary Jacobus has recently argued with respect to romantic autobiography, writing serves not only to bring the past into the present, but interposes itself as a "barrier" between past and present: "Ordering the chaotic multiplicity of the self, writing not only defends against incoherence, but, because it is always of and from the past, it defends against presence—and against the future too. . . . "[5] Ignoring the most expressive and

innovative artistic developments of the 1820's, a decade when English landscape painting achieved more than national recognition, Hazlitt looks back to a group of canonical masters and masterpieces of Italian painting—works by Titian, Raphael, and Domenichino. These paintings are not only "of" the past: as visual objects they are also Other both to the verbal order of language and to the cultural order of contemporary Englishness. The "presence" of the past, which would seem transparently manifest in historical art, is doubly distanced—through language and through the "shortsightedness" of (Hazlitt's) memory.

From this perspective, memory becomes a subversive strategy. Despite the highly pictorial (not just imagistic) nature of Hazlitt's memories, as they configure themselves around, or are associated with, specific works of art, his memory writings rarely succeed at, or even attempt, presenting these distant objects with precision. The reader of Hazlitt's late essays is not presented with a verbal image (a word-painting) of a Raphael or a Rembrandt, any more than she is presented with a coherent or unified "portrait" of the author, but with that complex of associated ideas and feelings which defined an experience (of viewing a painting) at a moment or moments in the past. Commenting on the way paintings offered romantic critics like Hazlitt "the occasion for imagination, dream, abstraction, reverie," Elizabeth Helsinger also notes that "such imaginative activity actually takes place in the mind of the spectator only when he stops seeing."[6] For Hazlitt and contemporaries like Lamb and Coleridge, the memories which paintings evoke are not visual but affective, as the painting brings into focus a whole complex of emotions and feelings whose "truth" is unassailable—beyond the partiality of vision and the instability of words.[7]

Because memory may be experienced not only as a kind of visual image which "reproduces" the world and its objects and can be described in words, but as a kind of sensuous "knowledge" which is essentially emotional in content, it is a mode of representation which is simultaneously public and private—at once part of the external world of perception and the senses, and the inner world of thought and feeling.[8] W. J. T. Mitchell has recently argued that "the reason . . . accounts of memory inevitably appeal to models of writing, painting, photography, sculpture, printing, etc. is that memory is an intersubjective phenomenon, a practice not only of recollection *of* a past *by* a subject, but of recollection *for* another subject."[9] Inscribed in writing, Hazlitt's private memories draw upon paintings and literary associations, connecting them to a deeply internalized and thus habitual complex of feelings. Through this complex of "second nature," Hazlitt's memories both shaped and participated in a common cultural language: his memory-images at once maintain the privacy of the self while socializing that self through the critical acts of description, recollection, and quotation.

While memory-writing can be compensatory, as recollected impressions, associated with moments of emotional intensity, and can vivify and extend Hazlitt's experience of the present,[10] memory more often occasions disappointment and the blockage of vision, as present visual sensations recall the intensity of a scene in the past. When that "scene" is a painting, this dialectic of expectation and disappointment turns into a more delicate confrontation between the privacy of past memories and the (publicly accessible) languages of presence. Almost all accounts of Hazlitt's prose style have emphasized its dialogical qualities, the way a confrontation between public discourse and private reverie is played out through self-reflexive and presentational strategies in which multiple points of view, juxtaposed temporal states, and typographical shifts which signal quotations, disrupt its linear flow.[11] Hazlitt modeled his "familiar style" on the efficacy of speech, and on an idea of language as action. While he frequently drew on the idea of conversation to illustrate this point ("To write a genuine familiar or truly English style, is to write as any one would speak in a common conversation . . ."), his most characteristic essays—those in which opposing concepts collide and interpenetrate—rise to the pitch of arguments.[12] As Graham Good notes, the "characteristic texture" of the essays is an "alternation, even struggle, between intensely particularized description and abstract thought, between the painterly and the philosophical" (77).

The analogy between the essay and the portrait has been explored, with varying degrees of analytic force, by modern critics such as Adorno, who alludes merely to the essay's "affinity to the [visual] image," and Lukács, who draws a stronger parallel between the "struggle[s] for truth, for the incarnation of a life," which both portraits and essays, in their most fully realized form, enact.[13] More recently, Michel Beaujour has argued that the literary self-portrait distinguishes itself from autobiography by the absence of a continuous narrative: rather, it "attempts to create coherence through a system of cross-references, anaphoras, superimpositions, or correspondences among homologous and substitutable elements" through the "spatialization" of the text.[14] These analogies are borne out not simply by the rhetorical figures of Hazlitt's text, but by his own life-history. His early training as a painter and his later, willed, absorption into the transhistorical order of art come together as Hazlitt imagines, and tries to recreate in his writing, an "ideal" of portrait painting.

The recreative task of writing was, for Hazlitt, played out with equal intensity in the activity of painting a portrait, in giving visible form to the inwardness of human life. Although he would associate painting with the effortless pleasure of abandoning oneself to Nature ("The mind is calm and full at the same time . . ."), his efforts to achieve such a transparent mimesis are marked by repeated failure to make the surface of the canvas conform either to the world or to what "passes" in his own mind (8.10). Hazlitt looked to portraiture as (ideally or potentially) a manifestation of the interior depths and conflicts of human consciousness—of past and present, inner soul and outward resemblance—released by the creative transaction between the artist and his subject and actualized by the beholder. These are the values that shape his description of a Titian portrait in the Louvre:

> All its faculties are collected to see what it can make of you, as if you had intruded upon it with some hostile design, it takes a defensive attitude, and shews as much vigilance as dignity. It draws itself up, as if to say, 'Well, what do you think of me?' and exercises a discretionary power over you. It has 'an eye to threaten and command,' not to be lost in idle thought, or in ruminating over some abstruse, speculative proposition. It is this intense personal character which, I think, gives the superiority to Titian's portraits over all others, and stamps them with a permanent and living interest. Of other pictures you tire, if you have them constantly before you; of his, never. (12.285-86)[15]

The intensely polyphonic quality of this passage is characteristic of Hazlitt's familiar style: it begins in a self-consciously performative manner (engaging with the portrait as if it were a real person, giving it both voice and agency), modulates into a judgment, then closes, aphoristically, by renouncing the kind of closure that comes from having exhausted a subject, or having attained a fixed structure. The quotation from *Hamlet* condenses yet another set of possibilities, reminding us that for Hazlitt, the reality of dramatic character lay in a similar confrontation and exchange of identity: "It is *we* who are Hamlet" (4.232).[16]

Within a pictorial aesthetics largely oriented toward the perspective of the reader/beholder, Hazlitt imagined portraiture as a genre which was capable of eliciting an engaged, almost dramatic, responsiveness through the depiction of human character. Hazlitt's reading of facial expressiveness as a sign, or manifestation, of the mobile interiority of an individual subject would be echoed, a century later, by Georg Simmel:

> . . . the body by its movements—perhaps equally as well as the face—can certainly express psychological processes. However, only in the face do these movements become visible in features which reveal the soul clearly and ultimately. . . . In the face alone, emotion first expressed in movement is deposited as the expression of permanent character.[17]

In portraiture, the successive mental states of a subject (the history of any human face) confront one another, complicating the demand for unified pictorial form. The confrontation Hazlitt imagined between a painter and a moving subject is then doubled, as the beholder, grounded in the historicity of his own experience, confronts the seemingly permanent and unitary moment of the portrait.

For Hazlitt, moreover, that felt reciprocity between artist and pictorial subject and viewer was "naturalized" in portraiture. Portraiture exemplified that dynamic of public and private values which Hazlitt sought from painting and worked to reproduce in his writing: the genre, that is, both valorizes and introduces into public conversation the privacies and particularities of "individual nature."[18] As Richard Brilliant has recently observed, "making portraits is a response to the natural human tendency to think about oneself, of oneself in relation to others, and of others in apparent relation to themselves and to the world."[19] Portraiture is also an effort to resist closure, to deny the temporality of human life (Brilliant 14). The desires that both painting and writing address—to wrest something significant from the undifferentiated flow of experience and to put them, as Hazlitt wants to do, "in a form that might live"—lie just below the surface of his perception of portrait painting as the imaginative organization of memory.

It is memory, then, which connects portrait painting or portrait making to Hazlitt's poetics of the essay as verbal self-portrait: both are for Hazlitt equivalent acts of coming to consciousness of the self and of the other. Like memory-writing, portrait painting is the articulation of continuity through time:

> The human face is not one thing, as the vulgar suppose, nor does it remain always the same. It has infinite varieties, which the artist is obliged to notice and to reconcile, or he will make strange work. Not only the light and shade upon it do not continue for two minutes the same: the position of the head constantly varies (or if you are strict with a sitter, he grows sullen and stupid), each feature is in motion every moment, even while the artist is working at it, and in the course of a day the whole expression of the countenance undergoes a change, so that the expression which you gave to the forehead or eyes yesterday is totally incompatible with that which you have to give to the mouth to-day. You can only bring it back again to the same point or give it a consistent construction by an effort of imagination, or a strong feeling of character. (12.287-88)

Hazlitt's long sentence (beginning "Not only the light and shade") deconstructs the simultaneity of portraiture through the linear momentum of his narrative. Hazlitt can only make sense of the portrait discursively, by positing a level of meaning beyond the work's sheer physical presence.[20] In doing so, he extends the moment of painting—not, as in conventional history painting, by reading it as a narrative representation of action—but through an understanding of painting as human activity, the compression of imagination and recollection into form. Relocating the temporality of painting from depicted gesture to the residual gesture inherent in the physical handling of paint, Hazlitt is able to read into portraiture its sense as a history of making, in which the traces of movement, the passage of time, the knowledge of character are communicated through the painter's marks.[21] In contrast to Hazlitt's narrativization of portrait painting, his memory pieces—writing as self-portraiture—elide human temporality in their longing to recover an ideal past, their displacement of visual image into feeling, and their condensation of feeling into verbal image.[22]

2

I have suggested that memory, as a sensuous medium, facilitates an almost physical connection between one's sense of self, objects outside the self, and the temporal flux of human experience. Art's capacity to return us to past experiences breaks down the barriers not only between subjective and objective realms of experience, but, by way of the painter's body or embodied feeling, between the physical world and the world as representation. Hazlitt's verbal memories of being a painter similarly work to communicate an experience of being *in* the world, as his language describes not just a range of observed sensation ("the roughness of the skin . . . the clear pearly tone of a vein"), but the continuum of mental and physical activity: "every stroke tells, as the verifying of a new truth; and every new observation, the instant it is made, passes into an act and an emanation of the will" (8.13).[23] This extension of physical sensation to emotive response, the fluid exchange of mental and bodily categories of experience, is carefully deliberated throughout Hazlitt's writing, as it too serves to reproduce or to imitate or to "copy" the world.

In Hazlitt's most memorable encounters with art, the image mirrors the very texture of his experience. "I remember," he writes in one of his "conversations" with the artist James Northcote,

> . . . being once driven by a shower of rain for shelter into a picture dealer's shop in Oxford-street, where there stood on the floor a copy of Gainsborough's 'Shepherd-boy' with the thunder-storm coming on. What a truth and beauty there was! He stands with his hands clasped, looking up with a mixture of timidity and resignation, eying [sic] a magpie chattering over his head, while the wind is rustling in the branches. It was like a vision breathed on the canvas. I have been fond of Gainsborough ever since (11.291)

It is Northcote who catches Hazlitt—and the reader—short, with the question " . . . but it was only a copy you saw?" (11.292). Hazlitt, of course, executed numerous copies as an art student—a context in which copying was understood as an act of re-creating, of coming to knowledge through touch (or feeling), even if it did not demand the same interplay of physical and mnemonic gestures called for in portraiture:

> Portrait painting is . . . painting from recollection and from a conception of character, with the object before us to assist the memory and understanding. In copying, on the contrary, one part does not run away and leave you in the lurch, while you are intent upon another. You have only to attend to what is before you, and finish it carefully a bit at a time, and you are sure that the whole will come right . . . it is the changeableness or identity of the object that chiefly constitutes the difficulty of imitating it. . . . (12.288)

Hazlitt's response to the Gainsborough suggests that he regarded pictures not only as indexical signs (the tracings of the artist's marks), but as symbolic structures (or affective signs) whose meaning and emotional resonance depends on a shared—a public—context of experience. Like quotation, which is a verbal form of repetition, the copy extends or places individual feeling within a social community through the intrinsic claim of recognizability.[24] What would remain, for a middle-class English audience, largely inaccessible (the Titian portraits in the Louvre and *their* originals) is brought to public consciousness; not, of course, as a pictorial reproduction, but as memory-writing which imaginatively "reproduces" an otherwise privileged encounter, or a series of privileged encounters (between artist and subject, between viewer and painting). Although, as I go on to show, Hazlitt's memory-inscriptions always force us to recognize the differences between the original and the (verbal or visual) copy, either one can provide the public occasion and focus for private "reverie." The significance of the Gainsborough lies not, then, in its autonomous power to represent the world, but more simply in the coincidence of a familiar pictorial image with the ordinariness of Hazlitt's own experience—so that the depicted thunder-storm and the actual shower of rain are made to exemplify one another and to create an extraordinary moment of revelation and pleasure.

Hazlitt's capacity to be emotionally transported or moved by copies, like his recurrent feelings of disappointment in the presence of an original, expresses a quintessentially romantic investment in the power of "absent things." The copy, which *manifestly* points to an absent original (one which is at least potentially recoverable—as the original of a Titian portrait is not), might be understood as the material realization and extension of cultural memory to a literate public.

Yet the memories that counted for Hazlitt were increasingly private ones, which became vividly "real" (or, in Mitchell's terms, "intersubjective") for a public audience only through the collective possibilities of print culture and the reproduced image. This indifference to the cultural status of the memory-object—the picture or image which occasioned Hazlitt's feelings—is borne out by the way in which being "moved" by an image assumes both literal and metaphorical force in his writings and has important social implications for Hazlitt's understanding of the social role of visual art in his historical epoch—an issue I will return to below. Again and again, copies transport Hazlitt not to an originary viewing moment, but to an earlier self, as in this passage, where copies of pictures lead him to memories (copies of past events) of copying:

> I should be contented with these four or five pictures, the Lady by Vandyke, the Titian, the *Presentation in the Temple,* the Rubens [*The Rainbow*], and the Poussin [*Adam and Eve in Paradise*], or even with faithful copies of them, added to the two which I have of a young Neapolitan Nobelman and of the Hippolito de Medici; and which, when I look at them, recal [sic] other times and the feelings with which they were done. It is now twenty years since I made those copies, and I hope to keep them while I live. It seems to me no longer ago than yesterday. Should the next twenty years pass as swiftly, forty years will have glided by me like a dream. By this kind of speculation I can look down as from a slippery height on the beginning, and the end of life beneath my feet, and the thought makes me dizzy! (12.292)

Copies, or Hazlitt's inscribed memory-images of them, generate an experience of overwhelming intensity, seemingly equivalent to the sublime, although the "dizzy" rapture that the beholder experiences in the mountains is of course only figurative in this account—Hazlitt's vertiginous "prospect" is in fact retrospect.[25]

This second-order sublime, a sublime of circulating images in which an intense experience is secured not by the magnitude of the object but rather from its multiplication ("four or five pictures . . . added to the two which I have") is grounded in a precisely calculated ratio of pleasure which governs Hazlitt's distinction between prints and pictures:

> Good prints are no doubt better than bad pictures; or prints, generally speaking are better than pictures; for we have *more* prints of good pictures than of bad ones; yet they are for the most part but hints, loose memorandums, outlines in *little* of what the painter has done. How often, in turning over a number of choice engravings, do we tantalize ourselves by thinking 'what a head *that* must

be',—in wondering what colour a piece of drapery is, green or black,—in wishing, in vain, to know the exact tone of the sky in a particular corner of the picture! Throw open the folding-doors of a fine Collection and you see *all* you have desired at a blow—the bright originals starting up in their own proper shape, clad with flesh and blood, and teeming with the first conceptions of the painter's mind! (10.8; my emphasis)

While prints are only pictures in "little," their very abundance and their partial nature, which creates the space for reverie, compensates for (though it cannot finally rival), the sublime totality of the original. Moreover, the last sentence suggests that *prints*—as the source or origin of desires that pictures will gratify—are also, in some sense, "originals."

The unique texture of Hazlitt's art writing emanates from these competing pleasures and irreconcilable desires. The reader experiences this as a tension between permanence and flux, between memory's connective power (that which unifies the self and marks it as an origin) and its powers of dispersing and multiplying the self through reverie. Never one given to reconciliation, Hazlitt found emblematic figures for these contrary states in portraiture and in prints. For Hazlitt, the act of painting a portrait demands the immediate recall of what is fleeting while reproductions (visual imitations, memory-inscription, and verbal quotation) are second-order memory systems, which "mirror" or recall a seemingly permanent or fixed past—a past which may be preserved through the durability of the material object or the persistence of a shared cultural tradition. One dimension of Hazlitt's art of memory lies in disrupting this monumentalizing permanence, in recovering the fluxes and refluxes of original presence through fragmentation, (mis)quotation, repetition, and revision—verbal devices which never re-present the original exactly. Like the graphic copy, or the engraved reproduction, the inexactness or instability of memory-inscription bears the "signature" of its author as well as the originating "authority."[26]

Revisiting the places and objects of memory, revising his own past in such writings as **"Fonthill Abbey,"** *Notes of a Journey through France and Italy,* and **"The Pleasures of Painting,"** Hazlitt forces our awareness of the difference between copy and original, memory and presence, earlier memories and later ones, even as these texts are prompted by the desire to blur these oppositions. He does so, moreover, without compromising or questioning the authority of these past feelings—allowing, as it were, memory to rub against memory. This conflict or tension becomes most apparent, and takes on larger intersubjective significance, at those moments when Hazlitt's pictorial memory is being used to cover his political one.

This is certainly the case with the two, nearly identical descriptions of Titian's *St. Peter Martyr* from **"Fonthill Abbey"** and *Notes:* they were written three years apart, but what is fixed "forever" in Hazlitt's mind in the first account is subtly revised by the later one.[27] The first is a memory-image ("as we see it still 'in our mind's eye,' standing on the floor of the Thuilleries, with none of its brightness impaired, through the long perspective of waning years") whose particular force is ineluctably shaped by the politics of the viewing moment. Hazlitt, writing in 1822, remembers standing in Napoleon's Louvre in 1802, and reconstructs the painting as a sublime allegory of revolution, a representation of French anti-clericalism:

> There it stands, and will forever stand in our imagination, with the dark, scowling, terrific face of the murdered monk looking up to his assassin, the horror-struck features of the flying priest, and the skirts of his vest waving in the wind, the shattered branches of the autumnal trees that feel the coming gale, with that cold convent spire rising in the distance amidst the sapphire hills and golden sky . . . (18.177)

Revolution is figured here as rupture and, in the image of the golden sky, Enlightenment. The broken trees and the wind echo and extend the human drama being played out on the violent stage of revolutionary theater—a reading Hazlitt will substantially revise when the actual painting forces his awareness of the historical actualities of the viewing moment.[28]

After 1815, *Peter Martyr* was returned to the Church of SS. Giovanni e Paolo in Venice, where Hazlitt, in 1825, saw Titian's altarpiece a second time.[29] He dramatizes this encounter, allowing the reader to experience the suspense of an initial, abortive visit (when he is turned away because of poor light) and then the final revolution:

> We returned to the charge at five in the afternoon, when the light fell upon it through a high-arched Gothic window, and it came out in all its pristine glory, with its rich, embrowned, overshadowing trees, its nobly-drawn heroic figures, its blood-stained garments, its flowers and trailing plants, and that cold-convent spire rising in the distance amidst the sapphire mountains and the golden sky. I found everything in its place and as I expected. Yet I am unwilling to say that I saw it through my former impressions: this picture suffices to itself, and fills the mind without an effort; for it contains all the mighty world of landscape and history, grandeur and breadth of form with the richest depth of colouring, an expression characteristic, powerful, that cannot be mistaken, conveying the scene at the moment, a masterly freedom and unerring truth of execution, and a subject as original as it is stately and romantic. (10.271-72)

In this later account, the idea of revolution is disembodied—the murdered monk, the fleeing priest, and the assassin have all been excised—and aestheticized. What Hazlitt remembers are colors and visual details of the landscape (the phrase he repeats, "that cold convent spire rising in the distance amidst the sapphire mountains and the golden sky," refers to the painting's background), and it is these elements that dominate the later description. The figures of revolutionary history (who also signify a spiritual history within Catholicism and confirm the sense of violently disruptive event) have been lost in Hazlitt's translation to private history: a history of recollected sensations and discrete visual images and of generalized, idealized abstractions.[30]

Hazlitt's seeming elision of actual history by means of a turn to the continuity of nature and to the "natural" history of the self, repeats in a quite deliberate way the self-representations of Rousseau in the *Confessions* and *Reveries of a Solitary Walker*—a writer whose pastoralism is the consequence of a deliberate exile from the violence of history. Hazlitt looked to Rousseau both as the origin of a certain feeling for nature and for the past[31] and as the author of the French Revolution, one whose personal feelings and personal past were brought to bear upon the most urgent public matters: it was, Hazlitt wrote, Rousseau "who brought the feeling of irreconcilable enmity to rank and privileges, *above humanity,* home to the bosom of every man—identified it with all the pride of intellect, and with the deepest yearnings of the human heart" (4.89).[32] Moreover, as Michel Beaujour has noted, Rousseau's *Reveries* are situated in "a landscape accessible to virtually all readers and readily transposable . . ." (144). Taking Rousseau's autobiographical writings as a model for the ways in which feeling can become a medium for public discourse and interiority can be made manifest through "local description" (4.91), Hazlitt constructs his own version of a lost pastoral moment around rather different scenes: using paintings more often than landscape as the background for mnemonic reverie. As Hazlitt confessed earlier, there are only four or five (or perhaps six) paintings which consolidate feeling for him in this way—paintings "accessible to virtually all readers," and made doubly familiar by Hazlitt's writing and rewriting of them.

What I earlier described as a calculated tension in Hazlitt's essays between the ostensible permanence of painting and the flux of memory-writing (which disrupts, or calls into question the stability of these objects from the past) finds its clearest expression in **"On the Pleasure of Painting,"** as the essay moves from one set of representational modes to another, juxtaposing writing and painting, copies and originals, memory and visual presence, earlier memories and later ones, in a densely associative way. While

Hazlitt begins by separating painting and writing—"'There is a pleasure in painting which none but painters know.' In writing, you have to contend with the world; in painting you have only to carry on a friendly strife with Nature"—the essay itself works to complicate such simple oppositions: the reader will already "see" that Hazlitt begins with a quotation—begins, that is, by "reproducing" the pleasure of another writer on painting, possibly the painter Richard Wilson. Hazlitt's telling and retelling of his own early efforts at painting remain as partial, as fragmentary as the borrowed quotation—remain, that is, an unfinished narrative which in its fullest elaboration contains an unfinished painting (a copy of a Rembrandt), which in turn constitutes a synecdoche for his unfinished ambition: "The picture," Hazlitt writes, "was never finished, and I might have gone on with it to the present hour. I used to set it on the ground when my day's work was done, and saw revealed to me with swimming eyes the birth of new hopes, and of a new world of objects" (8.9). The new beginnings he remembered in 1820 condense more than the lost pleasures of painting, however: the essay metaphorically links Hazlitt's youthful artistic struggles, his memories of particular paintings, and his revolutionary political values. The unfinished copy of the Rembrandt has become an ekphrastic moment ("beneath the shrivelled yellow parchment look of the skin, there was here and there a streak of blood-colour tinging the face . . ."), while Hazlitt's "unfinished" politics are similarly displaced into the "wings of imagination" (19.18).

The "reflected and substituted" identity Hazlitt sought through recollection is a precarious one; by the end of the essay, when Hazlitt recollects painting his father's portrait, the self is suspended between the enduring physical objects of the past and a longing to recover what cannot be grasped—the ruins of history:

> I think but am not sure, that I finished this portrait (or another afterwards) on the same day that the news of the battle of Austerlitz came; I walked out in the afternoon, and, as I returned, saw the evening sun set over a poor man's cottage with other thoughts and feelings than I shall ever have again. Oh for the revolution of the great Platonic year, that those times might come over again! . . . The picture is left: the table, the chair, the window where I learned to construe Livy, the chapel where my father preached, remain where they were; but he himself is gone to rest, full of years, of faith, of hope, and charity! (8. 13)

As Stanley Jones has observed, the central political imagery of this passage is borrowed from one of Hazlitt's political essays which appeared in the *Morning Chronicle* on January 28, 1814, some three months after Napoleon's defeat at Leipzig:

He who has seen the evening star set over a poor man's cottage, or has connected the feeling of hope with the heart of man, and who, although he may have lost the feeling, has never ceased to reverence it—he, Sir, with submission and without a nickname, is the *true Jacobin*. (7.370)[33]

The shift of emotional register from a somewhat belligerent hopefulness for the endurance of the revolutionary Jacobin cause in the earlier passage to a rueful nostalgia and a re-invoked sense of sublime exaltation is marked by the deletion of the word "hope" and a substitution of imagery: the evening star of 1814 has become, in 1820, the evening sun— suggesting both fulfillment (of that great day) and, in retrospect, an ending. Napoleon's triumphant victory at Austerlitz in 1805 occupied a fixed point in time (a detail Hazlitt remembers but doesn't specify in 1814); the completion of his father's picture does not. What is significant for Hazlitt is the conjunction of the epochal successes of the revolution and the triumph of his own youthful hopes within the reflexive space of remembering Austerlitz, what it meant to him once and what it means to him now. What remains—the painting, the table, the window— gives force and vividness to what is gone. The symbolic equivalence of hope = Jacobin can no longer be named, but must be recalled through the evocative and rhapsodic powers of Hazlitt's own prose.

Hazlitt's memory of painting his father's portrait is a more compressed version of his memory of reading Rousseau's *New Eloise* and the *Confessions* and both are figured as among the "happiest" years of Hazlitt's life (8.13), suggestively echoing Rousseau's own reflections on his exile to St. Peter's Island: "I consider these two months the happiest time of my life, so happy that it would have contented me for my whole existence without the desire for another state arising for a single instant in my soul."[34] The expansion of two months of happiness into a lifetime, the deliberate confusion of temporal boundaries, signals the return of Rousseau to a prelapsarian state in which human time and cosmic time are one, in which even the experience of being Other to nature is abolished. "What do we enjoy in such a situation?" Rousseau asks in his fifth walk, and replies, "Nothing external to ourselves, nothing if not ourselves and our own existence. As long as this state lasts, we are sufficient unto ourselves, like God" (69).

This extension of the self through time, as individual moments of consciousness expand into a feeling of duration, is also a way of escaping time, and it is the negation of time, not simply the absence of time, that Hazlitt associated with art. When he conjoins his father's portrait with Napoleon's victory at Austerlitz, or when he observes that the Elgin Marbles "kill Time," for instance, he refers to this state of absorp-

tion and abstraction from the habitual self. Hazlitt's 1816 essay on the Elgin Marbles points as well to a related theme, the idea that the "fine arts" are a relief from what he calls "ennui." The experience of boredom, of disaffection and alienation from the familiar, became generally understood as a problem in the eighteenth century, when the sublime was proposed as an "antidote"—transforming the undefined anxiety of boredom into the stronger, but well-defined feelings of terror or awe.[35] If boredom is a state in which we are brought to an awareness of the discontinuities of everyday life, in which an habitual, "automatic," and linear relation between sensation and reflection is disrupted, then art, insofar as it approaches the status of the sublime object, prevents boredom by filling that gap: not, however, with its own powers of signification, but by symbolically evoking what Thomas Weiskel calls the "mind's relation to a transcendent order" (23). This, I take it, is how Hazlitt wishes us to understand his somewhat reductive formulation of the moral order inherent in the fine arts: "They bribe the senses into the service of the understanding: they kill Time, the great enemy of man; they employ the mind usefully—about nothing; and by preventing ennui, promote the chief ends of virtue" (18.101).[36]

Because memory, too, takes shape not from the ordinary and habitual, but from the extraordinary, it prompts a style of writing which approaches the Longinian sublime,[37] and in which the rhapsodic invocation of feeling ("Oh for the revolution of the great Platonic Year!") cannot sustain the pressure of description—so that Hazlitt's prose inevitably collapses in the presence of the object. What Hazlitt's essays "reproduce," then, is at once his own interior state, and that "storehouse" of images which serve as a kind of public hieroglyph for Hazlitt's feelings. The idea of memory as a storehouse goes back to the memory systems devised by rhetoricians in classical antiquity: Simonides and Quintilian, for instance, instruct the would-be orator to imagine a series of places (typically architectural) and then "deposit" images in them.[38] This becomes a particularly apt metaphor for Hazlitt's pictorial memories, which are similarly structured around a system of places or commonplaces. The metaphor is extended in *Sketches of the Principal Picture Galleries in England,* a handbook intended to bring to public "view" the paintings hung in the great private and public houses of England. Yet the text's gestures of public inclusion are found side by side with the disruptive privacies of Hazlitt's own feelings—brought to the surface through the deliberated act of revisiting old places and reviewing familiar images.

The linked series of tone poems which Hazlitt uses to structure *Picture Galleries* look back to earlier moments in Hazlitt's essays when reverie fragments a discourse which is itself a reflection on memory. In **"On the Past and Future,"** for example, Hazlitt interrupted his description of Rousseau's feelings for the past to evoke and apostrophize his own landscape of memory at Tudorleigh: "Ye woods that crown the clear lone brow of Norman Court, why do I revisit ye so oft . . . that in your solitudes and tangled wilds I can wander and lose myself, as I wander on and am lost in the solitude of my own heart . . ." (8.24). But while this earlier essay enacts a visit (or a revisit) through memory, *Picture Galleries* juxtaposes a personal and a historical past against the present moment. Drawing on a tradition of viewing landscape which looked back to the eighteenth century, when the meaning of nature was enlarged to accommodate the literary and historical associations of landscape,[39] Hazlitt composes his essay by composing a place:

> Who can pass through Datchet, and the neighbouring greensward paths, and not think of Falstaff, of Ann Page, and the oak of Herne the hunter? Or if he does not, still he is affected by them as if he did . . . Pope's lines on Windsor Forest also suggest themselves to the mind in the same way . . . Gray has consecrated the same spot by his Ode on a Distant Prospect of Eton College; and the finest passage in Burke's writings is his comparison of the British Monarchy to 'the proud Keep of Windsor.' The walls and massy towers of Windsor are indeed built of solid stone, weather-beaten, time-proof; but the image answering to them in the mind's eye is woven of pure thought and the airy films of imagination—Arachne's web not finer! (10.36-37)

Like one of Rousseau's walks, the pull of Hazlitt's description is to lead the reader *through* a space whose natural pathways coincide with the figurative construction of "paths" in the lines and passages of English writers. The climax of the passage—Hazlitt's destination—is Windsor castle. But as its "massy towers" dissolve back into the mind's own structures, we see more clearly how architecture serves Hazlitt only as a place to be written on—a textual space that allows him to revisit images which are at once culturally significant and personally resonant (Yates 23-24; Beaujour 142-44).

The passage also traces a conventional movement from nature to remembered associations to feelings. But the distinction between these categories of thought is progressively complicated. Nature is experienced through a series of literary associations which are as deeply internalized or habituated as "natural" feelings. In claiming that these associations affect the beholder's response even if they remain unconscious, Hazlitt assumes a "second nature"—at once memory and imagination, natural object and literary representation. Like Wordsworth's or Burke's use of the term, Hazlitt's second nature is meant to connect an imagined depth of human identity to the real of external nature. But Hazlitt departed from Wordsworth and Burke to the extent that his second nature is not an abstract concept, designating "inborn" or "habitual" feelings, but a field of linguistic or pictorial representations that gives form or shape to shared feelings.[40] Hazlitt's inscribed memory-images, as I have been describing them, participate in this second-order system.

The concept is worked out most fully in Hazlitt's 1821 essay **"On a Landscape of Nicholas Poussin,"** where second nature is used to mediate between the art of visual imitation and the imagination's spatiality. Painting, Hazlitt insisted, was dependent on the imitation of nature—an injunction which depends on an expanded sense of nature, encompassing both the real and the ideal: "To give us nature, such as we see it, is well and deserving of praise; to give us nature, such as we have never seen, but often wished to see it, is better, and deserving of higher praise" (8.169).[41] Hazlitt's notion of a truly "universal" art is one which will transcend nature without denying it. The historic painter "clothes a dream, a phantom with form and colour and the wholesome attributes of reality. *His* art is a second nature; not a different one" (8.169-70). The opening movement of the Poussin essay explores variations on this fit between the real (that external nature to which we are habituated), the ideal (as a category of artistic representation), and the "imaginary" (the beholder's realm—the power of seeing or interpreting images as ideas).[42] If Poussin's scenery, with its "unimpaired look of original nature" gives the beholder access to "reality," it is classical legend which provides a common grammar for the imagination, enabling the beholder to go beyond the visible forms on the canvas, to recover a lost, pastoral origin. And because Hazlitt's memory tends to elide or obliterate detail, one may assume that it is the very "obscurity," the "dull light" and "shadowy" atmosphere of Poussin's canvas which enables his imaginative recall.[43] Although the essay is not strictly a memory-piece (Hazlitt represents himself as a beholder before the painting, or before an actual landscape, rather than working from a recollected image), the very scene he describes belongs to the atemporal and ideal order of memory: "one feeling of vastness, of strangeness, and of primeval forms pervades the painter's canvas, and we are thrown back upon the first integrity of things. This great and learned painter might be said to see nature through the glass of time: he alone has a right to be considered as the painter of classical antiquity" (8.169). When, in *Picture Galleries,* Hazlitt goes on to describe the literary and historical associations surrounding Windsor as "classical," he emphasizes their historicity, the temporal dimension of their pastness, *and* their public accessibility. Here, Hazlitt's second nature not only mediates between the imitation of nature and a cultivated imagination, but between a shared national past (history as the real ground of human temporal existence) and the universal and permanent domain of culture.

While Hazlitt's use of the landscape in *Picture Galleries* draws on feelings common to his age, there is a significant difference between these memorials to place, and, for example, Wordsworth's post-1810 series of poems addressed to castles, churches, fortresses, and estates. In Wordsworth's case, a resistance to the political and social changes taking place in England prompted what Lawrence Goldstein describes as a "conventional recourse to the guardian fortresses of English history" (179). The stability that Wordsworth sought in monumental structures is disrupted in Hazlitt's essays by the fluxes of memory.

Deconstructing the material substantiality of these country house collections through memory (in much the same way that Windsor was transformed into Arachne's web), Hazlitt converts a simple spatial structure—that of the gallery and its fixed pathway—into the more complex spaces of reverie or memory. He searches out familiar pictures as he would old friends, or, in the case of Ludovici Caracci's *Susannah and the Elders* (one of the paintings from the Orleans Collection), a *"first love"* whose "charms have sunk deep into our minds" (10.8-9). What begins as spontaneous interruptions, or digressions from a room-by-room account of these galleries is more firmly altered a third of the way through the book. As he explains in Lord Grosvenor's gallery:

> We must go through our account of these pictures as they start up in our memory, not according to the order of their arrangement, for want of a proper set of memorandums . . . [for] to take notes before company is a thing we abhor. It has a look of pilfering something from the pictures. While we merely enjoy the sight of the objects of art before us, or sympathise with the approving gaze of the greater beauty around us, all is well . . . but take out a pocket-book, and begin to scribble notes in it, the date of the picture, the name, the room, some paltry defect, some pitiful discovery (not worth remembering), the non-essentials, the mechanic common-places of the art, and the sentiment is gone—you show that you have a further object in view, a job to execute, a feeling foreign to the place. . . . (10.50-51)

The tension between experiencing pictures and writing-as-history (the connoisseur's factual encoding of name, date, and condition) which Hazlitt sets up in this passage must be understood as a version of other, recurrent tensions inhabiting these essays: the incommensurability between "old recollections, and present objects," between desire and its realization, between a distinctively public mode of perception (the responsive gaze) and private inscription (nota-

tion in one's pocket-book) which converts culture into a material commodity.[44] What Hazlitt longs for is not the material picture, but the experience of desire: "No one," he writes, "ever felt a longing, a sickness of the heart, to see a Dutch landscape twice; but those of Claude, after an absence of years, have this effect, and produce a kind of calenture" (10.57).

But finally, the largest tension in the book is that between narrative and remembered feeling, as the text imitates a succession of moods, voices a number of beliefs, but finds its ultimate poetic in repetition. Like the bead-word, the rosary, which is Hazlitt's metaphor for Rousseau's *Confessions*, *Picture Galleries* strings together memories from Hazlitt's past, memories, which he thought of as pictures, surely alluding to this connection in his work **"Sketches."** Indeed, he had described the *Confessions* as a book that was as temporally inexhaustible as a Claude painting: "We are never tired of this work, for it everywhere presents us with pictures which we can fancy to be counterparts of our own existence" (4.90). Yet such reminders of one's (earlier) self—vividly presented as the confrontation between the presence of pictures and the past of memory—can be disorienting, and Hazlitt admits to feeling "a little bewildered . . . with old recollections and present objects" (10.30). I take this to be Hazlitt's own "confession" of how obtrusive memory could be, in the way it dislocates or displaces the work of art by evoking desire for the self at an earlier time. Hazlitt described this movement in **"Why Distant Objects Please":** "How any object, that unexpectedly brings back to us old scenes and associations, startles the mind! What a yearning it creates within us; what a longing to leap the intermediate space! How fondly we cling to and try to revive the impression of all that we were then!" (8.256). But the feelings of loss or separation that memory evokes are much more acute, years later, when he writes *Picture Galleries*. "All is still the same" Hazlitt wrote of the pictures at Burleigh House, "but their effect is not the same upon me. I am twenty years the worse for *wear and tear*" (10.62).

As I suggested earlier, it is the experience, most significantly of loss, but also of boredom—of repetition and everydayness—that prompts Hazlitt's rhetorical evocation of the sublime: a gesture which finally obscures or defeats the physical presence of paintings. Hazlitt's response plays out a quintessentially Wordsworthian sequence in which disappointment in sublime nature is redeemed through the compensatory power of the imagination.[45] Although in Hazlitt's case the intensity is remembered rather than anticipatory, it prompts an equivalent passage from the material (the work of art, the natural monument) to the ideational or imaginative:

The Rembrandts disappointed me quite. I could hardly find a trace of the impression which had been inlaid in my imagination. I might as well

'Hunt half a day for a forgotten dream'

Instead of broken wrinkles and indented flesh, I saw hard lines and stained canvas. I had seen better Rembrandts since, and had learned to see nature better. Was it a disadvantage, then, that for twenty years I had carried this fine idea in my brain, enriching it from time to time from my observations of nature or art, and raising it as they were raised; or did it much signify that it was disturbed at last? Neither. The Picture was nothing to me: it was the idea it had suggested. The one hung on the wall at Burleigh; the other was an heir-loom in my mind. . . . This is the melancholy privilege of art; it exists chiefly in idea, and is not liable to serious reverses. (10.65)

The "idea" Hazlitt longs for is not an idea *of* the painting, but a self-reflexive mental category which encompasses that sense of self or of selves realized through engagement with the art work. What the mind seeks to recover from the past is "that image of good, which is but a reflection and configuration of its own nature" (8.256).

The way in which Hazlitt understood memory and imagination as adequate, even necessary substitutes for the painting itself, is a particular kind of critical failure, one generally 'explained' in terms of the idealist structure of romantic thought.[46] But just as Hazlitt insisted on "the real" as constitutive of the structural identity of the ideal, his understanding of memory (as an analogue of the imagination) is meant to restore the fundamental "paradox" of originality. that it is unrecognizable apart from tradition.[47] Memory acknowledges the history (and the traditions) of Hazlitt's training as a painter, his experiences as a viewer, and the historicity or intertextuality of painting: the ways in which painting's original, seemingly "natural" images often deliberately invoke or borrow or "reproduce" other paintings.[48] Hazlitt's mental copies and his verbal ones, like painterly acts of borrowing, both acknowledge the necessary "human interference" between painted image and originating object (Ayrton 154-55). Hazlitt's desire to recreate an authentic relationship to the work of art through the mediation of copies both anticipates Benjamin's anxiety over the "crisis of painting" in the nineteenth century and rejects it.[49] Celebrating the breakdown of what Benjamin called the "fabric of tradition," Hazlitt's copying worked to resituate the aura, the (public) ritual function of works of art in the substituted logic of a private cult of value.[50] Forming an "imaginary museum" or a potentially public collection by publicizing (and publishing) his own memories, Hazlitt also sought to overturn the kinds of elitist cultural practices, organized around the values of privacy and property, that still guided and limited access to art collections in England.

3

The politics of Hazlitt's art criticism surfaces most explicitly in **"Fonthill Abbey."** Written in 1822 for the *London Magazine,* a monthly founded just two years earlier as an alternative to the Tory *Blackwoods,* the essay brings together Hazlitt's thoughts on the politics of English taste and on the failures of Napoleon's European campaigns, suggesting that while the political past can neither be repossessed nor rewritten, the ordering of the arts can be in some way compensatory. The essay begins:

> The old sarcasm—*Omne ignotum pro magnifico est*—cannot be justly applied here. FONTHILL ABBEY, after being enveloped in impenetrable mystery for a length of years, has been unexpectedly thrown open to the vulgar gaze, and has lost none of its reputation for magnificence—though perhaps its visionary glory, its classic renown, have vanished from the public mind for ever. (18.173)

Hazlitt begins by invoking what I have already alluded to as the "crisis" of nineteenth-century painting: what happens when works of art are severed from tradition to confront "the masses" (Benjamin 235). But by the end of the essay, Hazlitt will have inverted the conventional wisdom about "vulgar gaze" and "visionary magnificence." Interpreting the house and its collection as an allegory of "self-love," he constructs in its stead an imaginary museum, whose contents range from copies of ancient statues (the Apollo, the Venus, the Dying Gladiator, the Antinous) to coins, bas-reliefs, Egyptian hieroglyphs, Chaldee manuscripts, even "mummies from the Pyramids" (18.175). It is important, however, to note the level of *non*-specificity in Hazlitt's description (he includes "something connected with the beautiful forms of external nature, or with what is great in the mind or memorable in the history of man" as well as "a few fine old pictures"), for his idea of a proper museum is less a hierarchical ordering of masterpieces than a collective "storehouse." Underlying Hazlitt's distinction between private property and public knowledge and the conceit of his museum, there is an assumption that art, once removed from the condition of private property, must be experienced in community with other beholders.

Hazlitt's art criticism is largely an effort to create such a community, and I have been arguing that one of the ways it does so after 1815 is by collecting the privacies of recollected experience in the publicly accessible form of the essay. Hazlitt's essays do not accurately "reproduce" paintings as visually descriptive set-pieces, but work to copy them—an acknowledged mediation Michael Ayrton has described as "an act of worship that resituates the power of the image in the activity not of beholding, but of re-membering" (154). Hazlitt's resocialization of the art work and its audience to the medium of prose was a strategy shaped by, and continuous with, his vision of the museum as an ideal and *remembered* public space. Looking back to his most formative public experiences of viewing art, at the Orleans Gallery in 1798 and the Louvre—newly enriched by the spoils of Napoleon's Italian campaigns—in 1802, Hazlitt's post-1815 writings not only equate a nominally conservative canon of masterpieces (Raphael's *Transfiguration,* Correggio's *St. Jerome,* Titian's *St. Peter Martyr* and *Hippolito de Medici*) with a revolutionary movement, but repeatedly affirm these works as a universal standard of value against an emerging national taste.[51] Just as Hazlitt's 1825 description of the resituated *Peter Martyr* aestheticized the violence of revolution, converting a political assassination into a "subject as original as it is stately and romantic," the essays as a whole depoliticize Napoleon's empire, salvaging and cleansing its fallen revolutionary ideals through the shaping fiction of the museum. Hazlitt does so first by proposing an idea of the museum as public space and then, more radically, by absorbing it into the "textualized" museum of his prose.

Critics from Quatremère de Quincy to André Malraux have written of the way museums resocialize works of art—a point Benjamin made with respect to photography, which similarly destroys the art work's unique "presence in time and space."[52] Hazlitt's history of art begins in the museum age, a world deliberately emptied of certain traditions of value but replete with political associations. In this "silent" world, as Malraux puts it, Hazlitt finds a language for art. His 'history' of the Louvre joins private feeling and public images in order to resituate his own literate and national culture in relation to a universal one:

> . . . the Gallery of the Louvre was of the greatest importance not only to France, but to Europe. It was a means to civilise the world. There Art lifted up her head and was seated on her throne, and said, All eyes shall see me, and all knees shall bow to me. Honour was done to her and all hers. There was her treasure, and there the inventory of all she had. There she had gathered together all her pomp, and there was her shrine, and there her votaries came and worshipped as in a temple. The crown she wore was brighter than that of kings. Where the triumphs of human liberty had been, there were the triumphs of human genius. For there, in the Louvre, were the precious monuments of art; there 'stood the statue that enchants the world'; there was the *Apollo,* the *Laocoon,* the *Dying Gladiator,* the *Head of the Antinous, Diana* with her *Fawn,* the Muses and the Graces in a ring, and all the glories of the antique world. . . . (18.102)

In this passage from his 1816 essay, **"The Elgin Marbles,"** Hazlitt is not simply imagining the museum as a temple, but acknowledging the most material fact about museums in the nineteenth century—that they were designed to look like classical temples.[53] Writing about the status of the museum in the mid-nineteenth century, Walter Cahn comments, "The museum formalized the experience of the masterful, and as some reports suggest, elevated it to a solemn, quasi-ritualistic act. References to museums as temples of art abound" (149). If the Louvre itself was an exception (created out of an existing royal gallery), in every other way it fulfilled the intention of neo-classical museum architecture, whose grand scale and geometrical purity was designed to evoke both universality and monumentality, as well as to command respect for the educative function of a public building.[54] That respect was assured, moreover, by a collection policy narrowly bound to an idea of the masterpiece. Only the best was sent to Paris for inclusion in what was then the Musée National—or as Hazlitt observed, "Not a first-rate picture is to be met with on the continent, but it found its way to the Louvre" (13.212).

This effort to recontextualize works of art severed from their original ritualistic function is analogous to, and historically concurrent with, the emergence of nation states in Europe. Benedict Anderson argues that the idea of the nation, as it comes to supplant such traditional cultural systems as the religious community and the dynastic realm, gave expressive form to a shared experience of contingency and desire for continuity: "If nation-states are widely conceded to be 'new' and 'historical,' the nations to which they give political expression always loom out of an immemorial past, and, still more important, glide into a limitless future."[55] **"The Elgin Marbles"** constructs a similar continuum between the idea of the nation as a cultural unit, the religious community which preceded it, and the (public) cult value of art:

> A taste for the Fine Arts . . . in periods of luxury and refinement, not ill supplies the place of religious enthusiasm. It feeds our love and admiration of the grand, the good, the beautiful. What is the respect which is felt for the names of Raphael, of Michael Angelo, of Phidias, of Homer and of Milton, but a sort of hero worship, only with this difference, that in the one case we pay an indistinct homage to the powers of the mind, whereas the worshippers of Theseus and Hercules deified the powers and virtues of the body? (18.101)

The explicit identification of art with religion leads, moreover, to the deeper connectedness which Hazlitt remembered and worked to recover between art and (a utopian) political order. The real "hero" of the essay is not Phidias, then, but Napoleon, and the sudden turn that Hazlitt's argument takes—from an aesthetic of beauty to one of power—will be duplicated in all of his writings on the Louvre. The power of art to generate an imaginative community of beholders is not simply equivalent to, but dependent on, political power. The Elgin Marbles served Hazlitt not only as a standard of artistic value, as an example of the Ideal-as-real nature, but as a lesson in the power politics of art. The museum plays a foundational role in situating national culture historically and geographically, but it often does so, as Hazlitt recognized, through acts of often violent appropriation. Hazlitt never forgave the English for burning Paris and despoiling the Louvre, and **"The Elgin Marbles"** served to remind them that Napoleon's willed destruction of the old order of art had its equivalent in Lord Elgin's 1802 "seizure" of the Parthenon marbles (18.102-3).[56]

I am not, however, concerned with the fate of the marbles (which languished in the basement of the British Museum, an institution neither devoted to the fine arts nor, in Hazlitt's time, open to the public), but with the growth of public museums in the nineteenth century. And from any number of perspectives, it is Napoleon who must be credited with this development. Even apart from the Louvre, the first great public collection of art, he was responsible for the administrative centralization of Europe which made museums possible.[57] Works of art looted from private collections took on a very different status during the Napoleonic wars, when they came to symbolize the cultural heritage of nations. The Altes Museum in Berlin, begun in 1823, was largely the result of pressure exerted on Friedrich Wilhelm III to make his collection—recently returned from Paris—available to the public.[58] In England, however, the idea of a public collection of art became associated with the French Revolution and its radical excesses, and a public collection of old masters was seen by the Royal Academy as a threat to an English school of painting still struggling for self-definition.[59] While the demand for a public collection became more focused after the exhibition and sale of the Orleans collection from December of 1798 to July of 1799, so did the reaction of the Royal Academy, which felt that if it could not control the acquisition of European masters by private collectors, it could at least discourage public interest in them.[60] Hazlitt's imaginary museum, with its origins in a very real controversy, not only compensates for what England was lacking; it resituates the public for art in a linguistic representation of national space, uncontrolled by the academy.

The history of the museum as a symbol of modern national cultural identity begins with the renaming of the Louvre in 1793: Napoleon's "Muséum National" explicitly asserts the continuity between nation and the universal order of art, a concept which would be reaffirmed, however belatedly, in 1824 with the founding and naming of the National Gallery (see Holst 215-17; 252). Douglas Crimp, in his discussion of the ideologically-charged debates surrounding the establishment of the Altes Museum, points to both the significance of naming, within the larger context of defining institutional function, and the way in which names could, intentionally or unintentionally, mask this function. The term "museum," in Crimp's reading, looks back to the academy and to the materialist view of art as *praxis,* whereas the actual function of museums in nineteenth century Europe was bound to an idealist conception of art and society (Crimp 262-63).

It is of some interest, then, that Hazlitt avoids the term "museum" in referring to Napoleon's Louvre—a museum which he places in deliberate opposition to the Academy. In his 1824 ***Journal through France and Italy,*** Hazlitt refers to Napoleon's collection of art as a "monument," a word typically reserved for commemorative sculpture or architecture, public forms which evoke the foundational ceremonies of both religion and nation (10.106) (Anderson 17-18). This metaphorical transposition forces us to recognize Hazlitt's desire to recover a deeper cultural pastness than the Academy envisioned, as if he could achieve release from the disappointments and reversals of contemporary history through the permanence of art. Hazlitt's monumentalizing gesture is intended to be triply commemorative: of the genius of the artist, the genius of Napoleon as collector, and the mythic totality of the Louvre, whose dismantling began almost immediately after Waterloo. The paintings Hazlitt had devoted himself to, and had formed his taste upon, were all removed: Raphael's *Transfiguration* and the Domenichino *St. Jerome* were returned to Rome, Titian's *St. Peter Martyr* to Venice, and his *Hippolito de Medici* to Florence (8.336n.). The promise of a universal cultural order was returned to the reactionary politics of national traditions.

Hazlitt's transformation of painting into writing must also be understood as a reaction to Burke's *Reflections on the Revolution in France,* a text in which revolutionary violence was turned into theatrical spectacle—what Tom Paine famously described as "Mr. Burke's horrid paintings."[61] Hazlitt's counter-move is to sublimate the visible artifacts of history-as-painting into a medium at once sensible and intelligible—writing.[62] Hazlitt's account of his inaugural trip to the Louvre (in the 1820 essay **"On the Pleasure of Painting"**) is told as a journey, a sequence of places discretely organized by the linear logic of narrative. The Louvre comes as the climax of a series of other, lesser, viewing experiences—Longford Castle, Wilton House, Blenheim, Knowsley, and Burleigh—all of them places Hazlitt would later write about in ***Picture-Galleries:***

> The young artist makes a pilgrimage to each of these places, eyes them wistfully at a distance . . . and feels an interest in them of which the owner is scarce

conscious. . . . He furnishes out the chambers of the mind from the spoils of time. . . . He goes away richer than he came, richer than the possessor. (8.14)

This generalized scene of instruction is followed by a highly-charged, personalized moment at the Orleans collection—Hazlitt's first serious encounter with art, an event so memorable that it confirmed his early ambition to become a painter and reappeared as the content of numerous essays in the final decade of his life. Writing about it in 1820, he acknowledges both the permanence of art—its "deathless" quality—and the instability of taste:

> My first initiation into the mysteries of the art was at the Orleans Gallery; it was there I formed my taste, such as it is; so that I am irreclaimably of the old school in painting. I was staggered when I saw the works there collected, and looked at them with wondering and with longing eyes. . . . We had all heard of the names of Titian, Raphael, Guido, Domenichino, the Caracci—but to see them face to face, to be in the same room with their deathless productions, was like breaking some mighty spell—was almost an effect of necromancy! From that time I lived in a world of pictures. Battles, sieges, speeches in parliament seemed mere idle noise and fury 'signifying nothing,' compared with those mighty works and dreaded names which spoke to me in the eternal silence of thought. (8.14)[63]

Despite Hazlitt's insistence that art is "other" to the "noise" of history, his own syntactic structure—moving from a world of pictures to battles and sieges—argues for their connectedness. It is not until the reader reaches "speeches in parliament" that it is clear Hazlitt is not describing history paintings. Using language that dramatizes the potency and wonder of entering the museum world, of crossing a magical treshold which annuls the temporality of human history—"initiation," "mystery," "deathless productions," "necromancy," "dreaded names"—Hazlitt restores to art its cult-value. "Old Time," he writes, "had unlocked his treasures, and Fame stood portress at the door" (8.14).

The sense of a liminal, revelatory experience is even more explicitly thematized in the Louvre passage, where Hazlitt must overcome a series of obstacles in order to arrive at his destination:

> The first day I got there, I was kept for some time in the French Exhibition-room, and thought I should not be able to get a sight of the Old Masters. I just caught a peep at them through the door (vile hindrance!) like looking out of purgatory into paradise—from where Poussin's noble mellow-looking landscapes to where Reubens hung out his gaudy banner, and down the glimmering vista to

the rich jewels of Titian and the Italian school. At last, by much importunity, I was admitted, and lost not an instant in making use of my new privilege. (8.15)

These passages are narratives of discovery, of seeing something never seen before and being changed in the process; but the self Hazlitt discovers at the Orleans Gallery in 1798 ("From that time I lived in a world of pictures") is unmade four years later in his 1802 trip to the Louvre. Like Wordsworth's more famous revistings of scenes in *The Prelude*, Hazlitt's memories are similarly marked by "visionary dreariness" and sharp reminders of lost power: "I had made some progress in painting when I went to the Louvre to study, and I never did any thing afterwards."[64] What survived, for Hazlitt—what he would come to take possession of—was not a world of pictures, but of language:

> I never shall forget conning over the Catalogue which a friend lent me just before I set out. The pictures, the names of the painters, seemed to relish in the mouth. There was one of Titian's Mistress at her toilette. Even the colours with which the painter had adorned her hair were not more golden, more amiable to sight, than those which played round and tantalised my fancy ere I saw the picture. There were two portraits by the same hand—'A Young Nobleman with a glove'—Another, 'A companion to it'—I read the description over and over with fond expectancy, and filled up the imaginary outline with whatever I could conceive of grace and dignity, and an antique gusto—all but equal to the original. There was the Transfiguration too. With what awe I saw it in my mind's eye, and was overshadowed with the spirit of the artist! Not to have been disappointed with these works afterwards, was the highest compliment I can pay to their transcendent merits. Indeed, it was from seeing other works of the same great masters that I had formed a vague, but no disparaging idea of these. (8.15)

This passage immediately precedes the passage (which I quoted above) of being admitted to the gallery; it constitutes, moreover, Hazlitt's only attempt to describe his response to the paintings. When he is finally admitted "into the inner room," face to face with "the greatest works," Hazlitt can only point to them: "Here the Transfiguration, the St. Peter Martyr, and the St. Jerome of Domenichino stood on the floor . . ." (8.15). Falling into the language of the guide-book, in which the name itself is a sufficient mark of value, Hazlitt's lack of response also recapitulates the logic of the negative sublime, substituting the authority of the word—the name as the most condensed form of description—for the object itself.[65] The claim "Not to have been disappointed . . ." sweeps past the overcharged atmosphere of the museum, the particular history of these paintings (whose status had been confirmed since the seventeenth century), and the workings of his own imagination, to make a subtle adjustment between painting and *its* representations. It was, Hazlitt acknowledged, his experience of "seeing other works of the same great masters . . ." that shaped his expectations of these paintings (8.15). The logic of the passage, which couples visual sensations with "vague" ideas, also suggests that Hazlitt's ideas were formed by prints: what he, in the 1824 passage I quoted earlier, describes as "hints, loose memorandums, outlines in little" (10.8). Here, however, he introduces, and privileges, the graphic sign of the letter. It is *reading* the catalogue which generates "awe." Once again, the authenticating power of the original painting is subsumed by Hazlitt's critical intuition that a world of powerful descriptions generates its own dialectic of expectation and disappointment.[66]

Six years later, Hazlitt's assertion of equivalence between the catalogue and the painting is an implicit claim for the immediacy, the material presence of the word, confirmed by his own association of writing with revolutionary activity in his 1826 *The Life of Napoleon:*

> The French Revolution might be described as a remote but inevitable result of the invention of the art of printing. The gift of speech, or the communication of thought by words, is that which distinguishes man from other animals. But this faculty is limited and imperfect without the intervention of books, which render the knowledge possessed by every one in the community accessible to all. (13.38)

The relationship Hazlitt posits between the materiality of writing and the diffusion of knowledge is reproduced in the museum, whose purpose is a similarly expansive notion of "communication," which Hazlitt focuses through the medium of print. His conning of the catalogue, for instance, reminds us that the democratic intentions of the nineteenth-century museum went beyond free admission: as a recent art historian has noted, "There was a cheap catalogue and the pictures had labels" (Selig 109). In Hazlitt's account of his trip to the Louvre, it is the written text which mediates between the outer world of history and the "inner" world of the initiate into the pleasures of the Grand Gallery. The power of books to bridge these two worlds is specifically addressed in a passage (also from Hazlitt's account of the French Revolution):

> Books alone teach us to judge of truth and good in the abstract: without a knowledge of things at a distance from us, we judge like savages or animals from our senses and appetites only; but by the aid of books and of an intercourse with the world of ideas, we are purified, raised, ennobled from savages into intellectual, and rational beings. Our impressions of what is near to us

are false, of what is distant feeble; but at last gaining strength from being united in public opinion, and expressed by the public voice, are like the congregated roar of many waters . . . (13.40)

We are now in a position to understand the rhetoric of discovery and magic which shapes all of Hazlitt's accounts of visiting art galleries, the significance of which is inscribed in the very act of writing about it. For in every case, a distance is overcome by language and a new condition—of proximity, or *knowledge*—is reproduced in the text and again in Hazlitt's reader.[67]

That Hazlitt imagined the process of cultural diffusion in material terms, as an interdependent relation between writing, the materiality of art, and the materialist implications of art as language, becomes fully evident in a crucial passage which occurs near the end of his 1826 account of the origins of the Louvre in the *Life of Napoleon.* There the struggle between tyranny and liberty—Hazlitt's master terms for understanding the French Revolution—is restaged metaphorically as the liberation of art. But in order to see the transformation of art Hazlitt adduces from the historical process, I must quote at length, and begin, as Hazlitt does, with the French campaign in Italy. Upon Napoleon's entry into Parma, he inaugurated the practice of exacting "a contribution of works of art to be sent to the Museum at Paris" (13.210). Twenty pictures were chosen, including Correggio's *St. Jerome,* which the Duke attempted (unsuccessfully) to ransom back for £80,000 (13.210). The justice of this transaction is fulfilled for Hazlitt when the painting is installed in the Louvre and the audience for painting has been enlarged from the one (Duke of Parma) to the many:

> These works, instead of being taken from their respective countries, were given to the world, and to the mind and heart of man, from whence they sprung. The shades of those who wrought these miracles might here look down pleased and satisfied to see the pure homage paid to them, not out of courtesy or as a condescension of greatness, but as due to them of right as the 'salt of the earth.' Art, no longer a bondswoman, was seated on a throne, and her sons were kings. The spirit of man walked erect, and found its true level in the triumph of real over factitious claims. Whoever felt the sense of beauty or the yearning after excellence haunt his breast, was amply avenged on the injustice of fortune, and might boldly answer those who asked what there was but birth and title in the world that was not base and sordid—'Look around! These are my inheritance; this is the class to which I belong!' He who had the hope, nay, but the earnest wish to achieve any thing like the immortal works before him, rose in imagination and in the scale of true desert above principalities and powers.

All that it had entered into his mind to conceive, his thought in tangled forests, his vision of the night, was here perfected and accomplished, was acknowledged for the fair and good, honoured with the epithet of divine, spoke an intelligible language, thundered over Europe, and received the bended knee of the universe. Those masterpieces were the true handwriting on the wall, which told the great and mighty of the earth that their empire was passed away—that empire of arrogance and frivolity which assumed all superiority to itself, and scoffed at every thing that could give a title to it. (13.210)

Bearing witness to art's transformation from private property into a collective realization of human value and cultural inheritance, to its final apotheosis as the visible writing of history's poetic justice, this is Hazlitt's most fundamental vision of the necessity of art, and the strongest available evidence that his "ideal" art was bound to a politicized vision of social life.

It is also, as I suggested earlier, the culmination of Hazlitt's response to Burke—a complicated inversion of the master trope of *Reflections*. Where Burke imagines the "atrocious spectacle of the 6th of October, 1789" as a series of history paintings, Hazlitt translates these back into the real language of history, returning his own highly figurative passage (which concludes with a striking geopolitical image of the Louvre as an adoptive "home" for art) to the firm ground of historical documentation. Quoting Napoleon's public letter to Oriani, the Italian mathematician, alongside his own impassioned prose, Hazlitt affirms the romance of revolutionary history: "'The people of France have more pride in enrolling among their citizens a skilful mathematician, a painter of reputation, a distinguished man in any class of letters, than in adding to their territories a large and wealthy city'" (13.213). What is striking here about Napoleon's political imagination is the way it sustains a balance between the nation (the people of France) and a universal order (of distinct and distinguished individuals) through the concept of "citizen." The political motives of empire—projection of national power, the acquisition of territories—are once again cleansed, or aestheticized through the Enlightenment vision of a republic of letters. Hazlitt tries to effect a similarly balanced order between the paintings in the Louvre as representative of national schools and as works of individual genius which participate in the universal order of art. Remembering the effect of the Grand Gallery in his *Life of Napoleon,* Hazlitt's description moves rapidly between the political and the aesthetic, even conflating a notion of pictorial unity with one of political detente. Here the expandable term is "school":

> The effect was not broken and frittered by being divided and taken piecemeal, but the whole was collected, heaped, massed together to a gorgeous height, so that the blow stunned you, and could

never be forgotten. . . . School called unto school; one great name answered to another, swelling the chorus of universal praise. (13.212)

Like the people of France, these works of art are bound together through a concept of universality that defines itself in terms of the nation. But like Napoleon's rhetoric of conciliation, Hazlitt's poetics of the museum succeeds only at the level of desire: just as art is inevitably contaminated by history, the dream of a universal order is contaminated by the politics of empire.

If universal art for Hazlitt is synonymous with the Italian school, the means of asserting that universality and (after the 1815 despoiling of the ideal museum) maintaining it, was through language, the medium of nation. And the "true idiom" of that language was prose. Hazlitt's sensitivity to the distinction between a poetic style and the medium of prose has a precedent in the comparison between Wordsworth and Rousseau which concludes his 1816 essay, **"On the Character of Rousseau."** The essential difference between the two writers, Hazlitt claimed, is " . . . that the one wrote in prose and the other in poetry; and that prose is perhaps better adapted to express those local and personal feelings, which are inveterate habits in the mind, than poetry, which embodies its imaginary creations" (4.92). The power of poetry to transform what was habitual and ordinary into the extraordinary had its consequent dangers, which Hazlitt took precise account of in deconstructing Burke's *Reflections on the Revolution in France:*

> A crazy, obsolete government was metamorphosed into an object of fancied awe and veneration, like a mouldering Gothic ruin, which, however delightful to look at or read of, is not at all pleasant to live under. Thus the poetry and imagination of the thing were thrown into the scale of old-fashioned barbarism and musty tradition, and turned the balance. A falser mode of judging could not be found; for things strike the imagination from privation, contrast, and suffering, which are proportionately intolerable in reality. (13.51)

In his own footnote to this passage, Hazlitt adapts a distinction between the imagination and reason which he first made in **"Coriolanus"** (1815), and by politicizing the distinction between the two faculties, Hazlitt makes his own stylistic motivations clear.[68] The imagination, he writes, "aims at aggrandizing some one object, person, or thing at the expense of others. . . . Reason, on the contrary, conquers by dividing; and instead of exaggerating and excluding, aims at universality, connection, and proportion in all its determinations"(13.51n.).

But prose is an intractable medium, and while Hazlitt tries to create, and recreate in his writing, the museum as a historical fiction, he cannot sustain the mood of

1802. His own texts, moreover, belie any simple distinction between prose and poetry, between reason and imagination. Like the rhetorical necromancy which heralded Hazlitt's "initiation into the mysteries of art" and thematized the otherness of art, his writing deliberately plays across boundaries—critically constructing and then deconstructing the difference between discursive reason (which aims at universality), and a sublime, poetic rhetoric which Hazlitt understood as a *national* style, the "natural" medium of Wordsworth and Milton and Shakespeare.

Between 1820 and 1826, we can see Hazlitt's vision of the nation as a medium of universality scaled back, as the realities of Britain's nation-empire called into question the possibility of a humanitarian and cosmopolitan order. In **"On the Pleasures of Painting"** (1820), Hazlitt had maintained that the paintings were "remains," historical artifacts whose individual coherence was less significant than the totality which could still be imagined from that: "Reader 'if thou hast not seen the Louvre, thou art damned!'—for thou hast not seen the choicest remains of the works of art; or thou hast not seen all these together, with their mutually reflected glories" (8.16). But Hazlitt's allusion (to *As You Like It*) subverts this fictive order in the same way that "remains" suggests its pastness: taking on the voice of Touchstone, whose distaste for country life matched his own, Hazlitt simultaneously announces his exile (from the universal order of the Louvre) and, by the Shakespearian overlay, embraces his nationality. Here, quite explicitly, Hazlitt seems to suggest that it is poetry, not prose, that is the touchstone of Englishness, of the national and the local—in spite of what he says, or wishes. (One might add that Hazlitt's habit of quoting Shakespeare is itself a gesture of aggrandizing the personal, of succumbing to the egotistical imagination.)

Hazlitt works to reproduce, to will into being, a sense of historical continuity in his hopeful rewriting of the ideal of a universal order in the *Life of Napoleon.* But that text, too, is interrupted by the historical realities of post-revolutionary politics, by Hazlitt's implicit recognition that the complementary values of individualism and universalism are irrevocably opposed to the homogeneous forms of social and cultural life instituted by (and affirming in turn) the various forms of European nationalism. This recognition surfaces in Hazlitt's account of how remarkably misdirected Napoleon was in imagining that Correggio's *St. Jerome* would inspire the French to paint other masterpieces:

> Vain hope! Not a ray of sentiment or beauty contained in this picture dawned upon a French canvas during the twenty years it remained there, nor ever would to the end of time. A collection of works of art is a noble ornament to a city, and

attracts strangers, but works of genius do not beget other works of genius, however they may inspire a taste for them. . . . (13.210)

As he continues, it is apparent that it is the idea of nation, defined through a sense of *difference* from other nations, that imposes not simply geographical boundaries, but the limits of the pictorial imagination. Contradicting his earlier views of art history as a system of intertextual allusion and painterly borrowing, Hazlitt declares: "No age or nation can ever ape another. The Greek sculptors copied Greek forms; the Italian painters embodied the sentiments of the Roman Catholic religion. How is it possible to arrive at the same excellence without seeing the one or feeling the other?" (13.211).[69]

What underlies this different perception of art? Eight years earlier, pressing for government acquisition of the Elgin marbles, Hazlitt had argued that a "public taste" improved through exposure to the great tradition might also stimulate the production of original works of art (18.102). But in 1824 the "progress" of taste—Hazlitt's paradoxical utopia of an egalitarian and universal high culture—was still unrealized. Despite the newly opened National Gallery, national cultural life was still marked by *inequality* and exclusiveness. Many collections and galleries remained inaccessible to the public, and the arguments that were made against admitting the "rabble" only emphasized the extent of England's difference from other nations:

> The wooden shoes and mob caps in the Louvre or Vatican do no harm to the pictures on the walls: but add a new interest to them, and throw a pleasing light on human nature. If we are behind other nations in politeness and civilization, the best way to overtake them is to tread in their steps. (20.336-37)

In his 1824 return to the Louvre, it is the physical durability of the museum itself which defers Hazlitt's recognition of the fragility and transitoriness of his political construct—so that even the distinction between art and architecture, between painting and wall is obliterated:

> To my surprise, instead of finding the whole changed, I found nearly everything in its place, as I proceeded through the first compartments, which I did slowly, reserving the Italian pictures for a *bon bouche*. The colours even seemed to have been mellowed, and to have grown to the walls in the last twenty years, as if the pictures had been fixed there by the cramping-irons of Victory, instead of hanging loose and fluttering, like so much tattered canvass, at the sound of English drums, and breath of Prussian manifestoes. (10.108)

Yet Hazlitt had signalled a very different political order at the outset, when, on his way to the Grand Gallery he passed through the modern French exhibition, with its "vile farrago of Bourbon-Restoration pictures." Moreover, as he proceeds through the French, Flemish, and Dutch galleries, noting it seems, everything, his initial perception of unity, his willed, sublimely *poetic* vision of historical continuity (reified in the museum-as-monument), dissolves or surrenders to, the evidentiary pressures of the real.

Moments such as this expose the fundamentally contradictory desires that inaugurate and structure Hazlitt's memory-writing. His textualized museum—with its discursive frame of reason, manifesting itself through gestures of universality, connection, and proportion, joined to sublime, poetic figures of durability—cannot control its own collaborative energies, and Hazlitt is finally moved to recognize analogous fissures in the actual museum. Coming to the "Antwerp pictures," he finds a "gap," a "yawning chasm," and by the time he finishes the Italian gallery, the sense of "loss" is unmistakable.

> . . . we find a want of larger pictures to answer to the magnitude of the Collection, and to sustain the balance of taste between the Italian and the other schools. We have here as fine Claudes and Poussins as any in the world, but not as fine Raphaels, Correggios, Domenichinos, as there are elsewhere—as were once here. There are wanting, to make the gallery complete, six or eight capital pictures, the Transfiguration, the St. Peter Martyr, &c; and among others (not already mentioned), the Altarpiece of St. Mark, by Tintoret, and Paul Veronese's Marriage at Cana. With these it had been perfect. . . . We still see the palace of the Thuilleries from the windows, with the white flag waving over it: but we look in vain for the Brazen Horses on its gates, or him who placed them there, or the pale bands of warriors that conquered in the name of liberty and of their country! (10.113)

The universal culture of the Louvre is fragmented by Hazlitt's own experience of history, an experience marked by discontinuity (metaphorically evoked through the absent paintings, the "gaps" which signify the failure of the French Revolution). What I have been calling the willed assertion of continuity—Hazlitt's idealization, his monumentalization of art—is a response to the actual defeat of the museum as a universal cultural order. What the museum of 1824 made possible was an increasingly nationalized perception of artistic differences.

While Hazlitt's imaginary museum is only a memory—it looks back to the Louvre, rather than forward to the National Gallery—it nevertheless begins to shape both the values and the textual practices which will enable other critics (Ruskin and Roger Fry among them) to both imagine and construct very real spaces in which art and its publics can confront one another. In this sense, the museum as imagined by Hazlitt—a potential space which joined universal and national, ideal and actual, public and private, past to present—was a cultural form analogous to, or cognate with, the work of the essay form itself. Structured by "spatializations" of memory and by the unstable rhetorical crossings and collisions of reasoned prose and sublime poetry, Hazlitt's essays work to engage the reader in the task of reconciling private taste and revolutionary politics.

Notes

[1] *The Complete Works of William Hazlitt,* ed. P. P. Howe, 21 vols. (London: J. M. Dent and Sons, 1930-34) 17.196-97. All further references to Hazlitt's works are to this edition, and will be included in the text.

[2] The groundwork for examining the recursive linkage of public and private concerns has already been laid by David Bromwich's fine book on Hazlitt, which examines the influx of critical *sensations*—Hazlitt's "use of temperament as a guide to judgment"—in the political and moral essays. See *Hazlitt: The Mind of a Critic* (New York: Oxford UP, 1983).

[3] The secondary literature on memory in Wordsworth and Rousseau is considerable. See in particular, Georges Poulet, *Studies in Human Time,* trans. Elliott Coleman (Baltimore: Johns Hopkins UP, 1956) 158-84; Christopher Salvesen, *Wordsworth: The Landscape of Memory* (Lincoln: U of Nebraska P, 1965); Margery Sabin, *English Romanticism and the French Tradition* (Cambridge: Harvard UP, 1976). The problematic relationship between revolutionary politics and romantic poetry is neatly defined in Geoffrey Hartman, "Romanticism and Anti-Self-Consciousness," in *Romanticism and Consciousness: Essays in Criticism,* ed. Harold Bloom (New York: Norton, 1970) 52 n.8. See also M. H. Abrams, "Revelation, Revolution, Imagination, and Cognition," in *Natural Supernaturalism* (New York: Norton, 1971).

[4] Roy Park, *Hazlitt: the Spirit of the Age* (Oxford: Clarendon, 1971) 66-68.

[5] Mary Jacobus, "The Art of Managing Books," in *Romanticism and Language,* ed. Arden Reed (Ithaca: Cornell UP, 1984) 219.

[6] Elizabeth Helsinger, *Ruskin and the Art of the Beholder* (Cambridge: Harvard UP, 1982) 183-84.

[7] The origins of this anti-visuality are found of course, in Wordsworth. See Geoffrey Hartman's account of the romantic imagination as a power which obscures the visual reality of the senses in *Wordsworth's Poetry, 1787-1814* (Cambridge: Harvard UP, 1971) 17-18.

[8] See Mary Warnock's discussion of the romantic uses of memory in relation to the philosophical tra-

dition of Locke, Berkeley, and Hume in *Memory* (London: Faber & Faber, 1987) 89-91.

[9] W. J. T. Mitchell, "Narrative, Memory, and Slavery," in *Picture Theory* (Chicago: U of Chicago P, 1994) 193, n.17.

[10] My understanding of the operation of memory owes a great deal to Michael Fried's discussion of this as a criterion of value in Baudelaire's art criticism. See "Painting Memories: On the Containment of the Past in Baudelaire and Manet," *Critical Inquiry* 10 (1984): 510-54.

[11] See, for example, Bromwich's discussion of Hazlitt's familiar style (345-61), and Graham Good, *The Observing Self: Rediscovering the Essay* (London: Routledge, 1988) 71-89.

[12] See, for example, "On Depth and Superficiality" (12.346-60).

[13] Theodor Adorno, "The Essay as Form," in *Notes to Literature,* trans., Rolf Tiedemann, 2 vols. (New York: Columbia UP, 1991) 1: 22. Georg Lukács, "On the Nature and Form of Essay: A Letter to Leo Popper," in *Soul and Form,* trans., Anna Bostock (Cambridge: MIT Press, 1979) 11.

[14] Michel Beaujour, *Poetics of the Literary Self-Portrait,* trans., Yara Milos (New York: New York UP, 1991) 3. The value and problematics of spatial models for texts have been explored in W. J. T. Mitchell's "Spatial Form in Literature: Toward a General Theory," in *The Language of Images,* ed., W. J. T. Mitchell (Chicago: U of Chicago P, 1980) 271-99.

[15] Hazlitt identifies the portrait only as No. 1210 in the Louvre.

[16] And, of course, for Hazlitt drama was a literary medium: the "speeches and sayings" of Hamlet are as "real to us as our thoughts. Their reality is in the reader's mind" (4.232).

[17] Georg Simmel, "The Aesthetic Significance of the Face," in *Essays on Sociology, Philosophy and Aesthetics* by Georg Simmel, et al., ed., Kurt H. Wolff (New York: Harper & Row, 1965) 278-79.

[18] Hazlitt's articulation of the value of "individual nature" and his preference for the particular over the general is worked out at some length in the four essays he wrote in response to Reynolds as both the author of the *Discourses* and—on the occasion of the first "Old Master" exhibition at the British Institution—as a portrait painter. See especially his "Introduction to an Account of Sir Joshua Reynolds' Discourses" (18: 62-63) and "On Genius and Originality" (18: 64-70).

[19] Richard Brilliant, *Portraiture* (Cambridge: Harvard UP, 1991) 14. For a more historicized view of portraiture see Richard Wendorf, *The Elements of Life: Biography and Portrait-Painting in Stuart and Georgian England* (Oxford: Clarendon, 1990).

[20] See Jean Starobinski, "The Secret of the Human Face," in *The Invention of Liberty 1700-1789* (New York: Rizzoli, 1987) 134-36.

[21] Hazlitt went considerably beyond this, insisting that portraiture *was* a mode of history painting—still, in the first quarter of the nineteenth century, considered to be the most elevated genre. The political and aesthetic significance of history painting was well documented in post-Renaissance thought: the most influential expression of this is, of course, Reynolds' *Discourses.* See Rensselaer Lee, *Ut Pictura Poesis: the Humanist Theory of Painting* (New York: Norton, 1967).

[22] On the "utopian" gesture as characteristic of literary self-portraiture, see Beaujour 16-17. Hazlitt's own "pastoral" impulses, in politics as well as art, have been thoughtfully described in Stanley Jones's biography. See *Hazlitt: A Life. From Winterslow to Frith Street* (Oxford: Oxford UP, 1991) 129.

[23] See Salvesen's chapter, "Self, Memory, and Sensuous Continuity," in *Wordsworth: The Landscape of Memory.*

[24] I draw, in part, on Bromwich's rich discussion of Hazlitt, quotation, and "the politics of allusion" (275-87).

[25] See, too, the conclusion of Hazlitt's "On Depth and Superficiality," where a typically sublime experience of visual confusion ("My head has grown giddy in following the windings of the drawing in Raphael, and I have gazed on the breadth of Titian, where infinite imperceptible gradations were blended in a common mass, as into a dazzling mirror") is triggered by an experience not of great height but of *depth*—"an abyss of colour" (12.360).

[26] Michael Ayrton, "The Translated Image," in *The Rudiments of Paradise: Various Essays on Various Arts* (New York: Weybright and Talley, 1971) 155.

[27] The "Fonthill Abbey" description was originally published in the *London Magazine* in 1822; the chapter of *Notes* was originally published in the *Morning Chronicle,* September 15 & 23, 1825.

[28] On the use of natural imagery to represent revolution, see Ronald Paulson, *Representations of Revolution (1789-1820)* (New Haven: Yale UP, 1983) 1-8.

[29] Titian's altarpiece, commissioned by the scuola of Saint Peter Martyr and unveiled in 1530, was "widely

considered Titian's greatest religious work in Venice" until it was destroyed by fire in 1867. See *Titian: Prince of Painters* (Munich: Prestel, 1990) 87. It is a work of some significance for English art critics and painters as well. Reynolds found it "eminent" among Titian's landscape backgrounds, Constable devoted one of his lectures on landscape to the painting, and Ruskin took the painting as evidence (contra Reynolds) of the significance of detail. See Joshua Reynolds, *Discourses on Art,* ed. Robert Wark (New Haven: Yale UP, 1975) 199-200; *John Constable's Discourses,* ed. R. B. Beckett (Suffolk: Suffolk Records Society, 1970) 46-49; *The Complete Works of John Ruskin,* ed. E. T. Cook and Alexander Wedderburn (London: George Allen, 1903-1912) 3: 28.

30 The "spatiality" of Hazlitt's later account can be further emphasized by comparing it with the narrative of the painting offered in John Constable's 1836 "Lectures on Landscape." After describing with some precision the setting ("the scene is on the skirts of a forest"), the time of day, and the composition, Constable tells us the "story" of the painting: "Amid this scene of amenity and repose, we are startled by the rush of an assassin on two helpless travellers, monks, one of whom is struck down, and the other wounded and flying in the utmost terror. . . . " In relation to Constable's discussion, Hazlitt's first account emphasizes foreground action; his second aestheticizes the action, turning history, in effect, into landscape. See *John Constable's Discourses* 46-47. Hazlitt's new understanding of the painting—as spatialized history—participates in a more general reconception of history painting in the nineteenth-century. For Turner, who saw the painting first in 1802 and again in Venice in 1819, *St. Peter Martyr* became a focal point in claiming the autonomy of landscape as "Subject." See Jerrold Ziff, "'Backgrounds, Introduction of Architecture and Landscape': A Lecture by J. M. W. Turner," *Journal of the Warburg and Courtauld Institutes* 26 (1963): 124-37 (135).

31 " . . . it is the past that gives me most delight and most assurance of reality," Hazlitt writes in "On the Past and Future," and he names Rousseau as one who has given expression to this sense of the reality of the past (8.24). On Rousseau's language of memory, see Salvesen 187 and Poulet 158-84.

32 Scott achieved a similar influx of personal feeling and public history (most notably the recent deaths of Pitt and Nelson) in the verse epistles to *Marmion* (1808). But Scott's Tory politics shapes his nostalgic joining of England's nationalistic past to her imperialistic present and makes his acts of recovery very different from Hazlitt's. Peter Manning has briefly but suggestively discussed this aspect of Scott's poem in relation to Byron's sa-

tiric turn on the romance mode in "Childe Harold in the Marketplace," *MLQ* 52 (1991): 170-90.

33 As Jones notes, the passage, and its precise referent, was unknown (and unfathomable) at the time and became clear only after Hazlitt's reworking appeared in 1820 (135-36). I would add that the connection between historical detail and visual detail, and memory's tendency to obscure or falsify both is made explicit in another essay from 1820s, in which Hazlitt equates distance of time with distance of space. See "Why Distant Objects Please" (8.256).

34 Jean-Jacques Rousseau, *The Reveries of the Solitary Walker,* trans. Charles E. Butterworth (New York: Harper & Row, 1982) 64.

35 Thomas Weiskel, *The Romantic Sublime: Studies in the Structure and Psychology of Transcendence* (Baltimore: Johns Hopkins UP, 1986) 18; 97.

36 The insight is philosophically developed when Hazlitt tries to describe the loss that Reynolds must have felt when he had to give up painting: "It is only those who never think at all, or else who have accustomed themselves to brood invariably on abstract ideas, that never feel *ennui*" (8.12)

37 Christopher Salvesen interprets Hazlitt's "rhapsodic style" as a kind of concentration of emotion, of feeling, offered in the knowledge that it cannot be sustained: "an energetic recognition or even welcoming of transitoriness" (190). Bruce James Smith in *Politics and Remembrance* (Princeton: Princeton UP, 1985) makes just this distinction between "custom" as a mode of the habitual and "memory" as a mode of the extraordinary (17).

38 See Francis Yates's classic study, *The Art of Memory* (Chicago: U of Chicago P, 1966) 2-3; 6-8.

39 See Helsinger, *Ruskin* 42-43; Salvesen 29-31; Lawrence Goldstein, *Ruins and Empire: The Evolution of a Theme in Augustan and Romantic Literature* (Pittsburgh: U of Pittsburgh P, 1977) 178.

40 On the concept of second nature in Wordsworth and Burke, see James K. Chandler, *Wordsworth's Second Nature: A Study of the Poetry and the Politics* (Chicago: U of Chicago P, 1984) 69-89.

41 See David Bromwich's useful discussion of Hazlitt's sense of art as "another nature" (215-17).

42 Mary Warnock, *Imagination* (Berkeley: U of California P, 1976) 102.

43 See Helsinger's fine account of Hazlitt's 1821 essay "On a Landscape of Nicolas Poussin": she notes, quite

correctly, that Hazlitt's description is not "an analysis of the painting, but a description of the idea—by no means wholly visual—evoked in the mind of a responsive spectator by light itself" (176).

[44] On Rousseau's similar attempt to "efface and naturalize the art of writing" in the fifth walk, see Beaujour 144-45.

[45] Geoffrey Hartmann, *Wordsworth's Poetry: 1789-1814* (Cambridge: Harvard UP, 1987) 46-48.

[46] A problem recognized by virtually every writer on Hazlitt. See, for instance, Park, 65-68.

[47] On the "paradox" of originality, see Thomas McFarland, *Originality and Imagination* (Baltimore: Johns Hopkins UP, 1985) 1-30.

[48] See Fried 516-19. Fried's argument is that Baudelaire's use of memory reflects the extent to which paintings in post-Renaissance culture are based on the selective imitation of other paintings or literary texts—painting, that is as a "network of associations" or a "chain of memories." Fried is interested both in the way past and present are "superimposed" and in the naturalness of the process, in its proximity to Proust's *mémoire involontaire* (516). A key text in this study of memory is E. T. A. Hoffmann's description of "true memory," which Baudelaire quotes in the *Salon of 1846.* "True memory," understood as a kind of imaginative transposition of past viewing experiences, is thus a way of accommodating the claims of genius and originality on the one hand, and the traditional practice of imitation on the other: it allows a painter access to past art at the same time that it internalizes that past—the traces of earlier art works are dissolved insofar as the memories "remain below the threshold of conscious awareness" (321).

[49] Walter Benjamin, "The Work of Art in the Age of Mechanical Reproduction," in *Illuminations: Essays and Reflections,* ed. Hannah Arendt (New York: Schocken, 1969) 234.

[50] Richard Stein has developed this argument with respect to a later group of writers on art. See in particular his analysis of Pater and Ruskin's criticism in *The Ritual of Interpretation* (Cambridge: Harvard UP, 1975).

[51] Perhaps the best reading of the contradictory political and aesthetic motives in Hazlitt's art criticism is William Kinnaird's *Hazlitt: Critic of Power* (New York: Columbia UP, 1978) 129-37. On Hazlitt's contest with Burke and Napoleon, see Bromwich 300-304. For a sense of how conventional Hazlitt's canon was, see Francis Haskell, *Rediscoveries in Art: Some Aspects of Taste, Fashion, and Collecting in England and France* (Ithaca: Cornell UP, 1976) 24-44 and Walter Cahn, *Masterpieces: Chapters on the History of an Idea* (Princeton: Princeton UP, 1979) 113-14. In working

out Hazlitt's relationship to history and politics in this section I found Kevin Gilmartin's "Hazlitt and the Politics of Contradiction" particularly helpful; see "Their Nature Contradiction: Hunt, Cobbett, Hazlitt and the Literature of Independent Opposition" (diss., U of Chicago, 1991).

[52] André Malraux, *The Voices of Silence,* trans. Gilbert Stuart (Princeton: Princeton UP, 1978). On Quatremère de Quincy, see Francis Haskell and Nicholas Penny, *Taste and the Antique: The Lure of Classical Sculpture 1500-1900* (New Haven: Yale UP, 1981) 110-11. Benjamin 220.

[53] The history of the neo-classical art museum-cum-temple began in 1769 with the first building designed as a museum, Frederick II's Museum Fridericianum at Cassel. The style was quickly duplicated, notably by the Museo Pio-Clementino in the Vatican, and the British Museum. See Niels Van Holst, *Creators, Collectors, and Connoisseurs* (New York: Putnam, 1967) 229, and Elizabeth Gilmore Holt, *From the Classicists to the Impressionists: Art and Architecture in the Nineteenth Century* (New York, Doubleday, 1966) 271-73. See also Helmut Selig, "The Genesis of the Museum," *Architectural Review* CXLI, No. 840 (February 1967): 103-13.

[54] Selig 106. See also Hugh Honour, *Neo-classicism* (Harmondsworth: Penguin, 1971) 85-87.

[55] Benedict Anderson, *Imagined Communities: Reflections on the Origin and Spread of Nationalism* (London: Verso, 1983) 19.

[56] Wiliam St. Clair, *Lord Elgin and the Marbles* (New York: Oxford UP, 1983).

[57] In the occupied Netherlands, a national gallery was established at The Hague in 1804; in 1808 it was moved to Amsterdam, becoming the basis of the Rijksmuseum in 1815. Confiscated art works which were not shipped to Paris became the basis of central museums in Brussels in 1795, and in Milan, Bologna, and Venice in 1805. After 1815, many of the art works returned to Italy were not restored to their original churches but, by decree of the Pope, remained in the Vatican collection. See Holst 221-23.

[58] Douglas Crimp, "The End of Art and the Origin of the Museum," *Art Journal* 46 (Winter 1987): 261-66 (262).

[59] Peter Fullerton, "Patronage and Pedagogy: The British Institution in the Early Nineteenth Century," *Art History* (March 1982): 59-72; 60 and 70, n.5 The argument for a public collection was argued persuasively (but fruitlessly) by Reynolds in his first discourse. Neither the Royal Academy nor the English government exerted themselves, however. In 1791 the RA declined to purchase Reynolds' collection, and in 1802

it turned down the opportunity to acquire Robert Udney's collection. Robert Hunt began his weekly art column for *The Examiner* in 1808 (the year of that journal's founding), and shortly thereafter started lobbying for a public collection of art. England's failure to establish such a collection, in marked contrast to the success of Napoleonic France, confirmed, for the liberal Hunt, the repressive hegemony of the English government, and the separation of political authority from public opinion. His argument became more pointed as the military campaign against the French dragged on; by 1813 he was writing against the diversion of public funds from "peaceful science and art" to the funding of "ruinous wars." See *The Examiner,* No. 40, October 2, 1808; No. 142, September 16, 1810; No. 309, November 23, 1813.

[60] See *Discourses* 15; see also Fullerton 59 and William Whitley, *Art in England,* 2 vols. (Cambridge: Cambridge UP, 1928; 1973) 1: 29.

[61] Quoted in W. J. T. Mitchell, *Iconology: Image, Text, Ideology* (Chicago: U of Chicago P, 1986) 143.

[62] Kevin Gilmartin makes this point in his discussion of Hazlitt's political and stylistic response to Burke's *Reflections on the Revolution in France* in "Their Nature Contradiction" 192.

[63] Interpreting Hazlitt's own self-consciousness about his taste, Francis Haskell notes, "the values exemplified by the Orleans Collection were already being challenged by December 1820 when Hazlitt wrote his article" (*Rediscoveries* 26).

[64] I am indebted to Mitchell's discussion of Wordsworth in "Narrative, Memory, and Slavery" 198-99.

[65] On the rhetoric of guidebooks in the nineteenth century, see Cahn 124-28. On the negative, or "metaphorical" sublime, see Thomas Weiskel, *The Romantic Sublime: Studies in the Structure and Psychology of Transcendence* (Baltimore: Johns Hopkins UP, 1986) 28-32.

[66] For a critical account of this general problematic of representation within romantic poetics, see Paul de Man, "The Intentional Structure of the Romantic Image," in *Romanticism and Consciousness: Essays in Criticism,* ed. Harold Bloom (New York: Norton, 1970) 65-77.

[67] My sense of the significance of discovery as both theme and narrative strategy, and its link to Hazlitt's public voice as a writer, was suggested by Gilmartin's analysis of the dialectic of "penetration and disclosure" in Hazlitt's political essays; see 196-98.

[68] See David Bromwich's account of Hazlitt's submerged contest with Burke in *The Characters of*

Shakespeare's Plays, and his reading of "Coriolanus" as an allegory of politics (314-20).

[69] Hazlitt gives expression to the same thought in one of the "Common Places" contributed to the *Literary Examiner* in 1823, no. XXVIII. All truly great works of art are *national* in their character and origin (20.125).

FURTHER READING

Biography

Baker, Herschel. *William Hazlitt.* Cambridge: Harvard University Press, 1962, 530 p.
  Critical biography that places Hazlitt "in his literary, political, and philosophical milieu," and traces "the development and expression of his main ideas, relating them to the facts of his career."

Howe, P. P. *The Life of William Hazlitt.* London: Martin Secker, 1928, 484 p.
  Sympathetic biography that quotes extensively from Hazlitt's writings and letters.

Jones, Stanley. *Hazlitt: A Life from Winterslow to Frith Street.* Oxford: Clarendon Press, 1989, 397 p.
  Examines the areas of Hazlitt's life that previous biographies have left obscure, such as the details of his disputes with his family and colleagues.

Kinnaird, John. *William Hazlitt: Critic of Power.* New York: Columbia University Press, 1978, 429 p.
  Examines Hazlitt's life as a "journey of a self-exploring mind revealed only through his works," characterizing Hazlitt as a "critic of power" whose criticism is informed by his "vision of the continuity of 'power' and its motives."

MacLean, Catherine MacDonald. *Born Under Saturn.* New York: MacMillan Co., 1944, 632 p.
  Explores Hazlitt's life in relation to political struggles in France and England during the early nineteenth century.

Priestley, J. B. *William Hazlitt.* London: Longmans, Green & Co., 1960, 38 p.
  General essay on Hazlitt's life and work.

Uphaus, Robert W. *William Hazlitt.* Boston: Twayne, 1985, 119 p.
  Critical biography that discusses Hazlitt's conception of "the moral, political, and literary uses of the imagination."

Wardle, Ralph M. *Hazlitt.* Lincoln: University of Nebraska Press, 1971, 530 p.
  Biography of Hazlitt that focuses on the influence he and his writings had on his contemporaries.

Criticism

Albrecht, W. P. "Liberalism and Hazlitt's Tragic View." *College English* 23, No. 2 (November 1961): 112-18.
    Argues that, although he largely subscribed to the social and political principles of liberalism, Hazlitt rejected the "non-tragic" world view derived from the liberal doctrine of progress.

————. "Hazlitt on Wordsworth; or, The Poetry of Paradox." In *Six Studies in Nineteenth-Century English Literature and Thought,* edited by Harold Orel and George J. Worth, pp. 1-21. Lawrence: University of Kansas Publications, 1962.
    Focuses on Hazlitt's view of Wordsworth's poetry as a "poetry of paradox," which Hazlitt defined as having "its origins in the French Revolution" and being founded "on a principle of sheer humanity, on pure nature void of art."

Archer, William. Introduction to *Hazlitt on Theater,* edited by William Archer and Robert Lowe, pp. vii-xxx. New York: Hill and Wang, 1957.
    Account of Hazlitt as a playgoer and admirer of the theater.

Bloom, Harold, ed. *William Hazlitt.* New York: Chelsea House Publishers, 1986, 184 p.
    Collection of critical essays by prominent Hazlitt scholars, including David Bromwich, John Kinnaird, and John L. Mahoney.

Bromwich, David. "The Originality of Hazlitt's Essays." *The Yale Review* 72, No. 3 (Spring 1983): 366-84.
    Discusses Hazlitt as "the first writer in English to have understood his task as the sort of trial that the word 'essay' by its etymology implies."

Bullitt, John M. "Hazlitt and the Romantic Conception of the Imagination." *Philological Quarterly* XXIV, No. 4 (October 1945): 343-61.
    Describes Hazlitt's works as among the most explicit, consistent, and detailed explorations of the concept of the imagination in English romantic criticism.

Cafarelli, Annette Wheeler. "William Hazlitt: Narrative Hieroglyphics." In *Prose in the Age of Poets: Romanticism and Biographical Narrative from Johnson to De Quincey,* pp. 113-50. Philadelphia: University of Pennsylvania Press, 1990.
    Emphasizes the formal properties of Hazlitt's essay sequences as a discontinuous narrative through which he investigated and critiqued the arts of his contemporaries.

Cecil, Lord David. "Hazlitt's Occasional Essays." In *The Fine Art of Reading, and Other Literary Studies,* pp. 243-56. Indianapolis: Bobbs-Merrill Co., 1957.
    Comments on Hazlitt's characteristics as a prose writer.

Coleridge, S. T. *Biographia Literaria,* II, edited by J. Shawcross, pp. 311-14. Oxford: Clarendon Press, 1907.
    Coleridge's response to an anonymous, unfavorable review of "Christabel" believed to have been written by Hazlitt.

Foot, Michael. "Hazlitt's Revenge on the Lakers." *The Wordsworth Circle* XIV, No. 1 (Winter 1983): 61-68.
    Briefly examines Hazlitt's career in light of his writings on the Lake poets.

Jones, Stanley. "First Flight: Image and Theme in a Hazlitt Essay." *Prose Studies* 8, No. 1 (May 1985): 35-47.
    Explores Hazlitt's imagery in "My First Acquaintance with Poets."

Lahey, Gerald. Introduction to *Liber Amoris; or, The New Pygmalion,* by William Hazlitt, pp. 1-48. New York: New York University Press, 1980.
    Discusses *Liber Amoris* as a "specifically 'Romantic' narrative expressing a notable phase of the temperament or imaginative sensibility of its period."

Mahoney, John L. *The Logic of Passion: The Literary Criticism of William Hazlitt.* New York: Fordham University Press, 1981, 125 p.
    Surveys Hazlitt's aesthetic criticism in an effort to explore its underlying themes, including what Hazlitt thought important to the critic and to the artist.

McFarland, Thomas. *Romantic Cruxes: The English Essayists and the Spirit of the Age.* Oxford: Clarendon Press, 1987, 128 p.
    Views Lamb, Hazlitt, and De Quincey as decidedly Romantic authors.

Noxon, James. "Hazlitt as Moral Philosopher." *Ethics* LXXIII, No. 4 (July 1963): 279-83.
    Discusses Hazlitt's theory of morality in *An Essay on the Principles of Human Action.*

Park, Roy. *Hazlitt and the Spirit of the Age.* Oxford: Clarendon Press, 1971, 259 p.
    Examines Hazlitt's criticism on the nature of poetry and the function of the artist, focusing particularly on Hazlitt's objections to abstract thought.

Patterson, Charles I. "William Hazlitt as a Critic of Prose Fiction." *PMLA* LXVIII, No. 5 (December 1953): 1001-16.
    Discusses Hazlitt's criticism of fiction and his influence on the development of the novel.

Ready, Robert. *Hazlitt at Table.* London: Associated University Presses, 1981, 126 p.
    Analyzes the unifying elements of the essays collected in *Table Talk.*

Schneider, Elisabeth. *The Aesthetics of William Hazlitt.* 1933. Reprint. New York: Octagon, 1952, 205 p.
    Positions Hazlitt's aesthetic philosophy within the history of aesthetic thought.

Stapleton, Laurence. "William Hazlitt: The Essayist and the Moods of the Mind." In *The Elected Circle: Studies in the Art of Prose,* pp. 93-118. New Jersey: Princeton University Press, 1973.

Briefly overviews Hazlitt's principal works.

Uphaus, Robert W. "Hazlitt, the Novel, and the French Revolution." In *Studies in Eighteenth-Century Culture* 17 (1987): 217-27.

Examines Hazlitt's reading of some of the principal texts on the French Revolution.

Additional coverage of Hazlitt's life and career is contained in the following sources published by the Gale Group: *Dictionary of Literary Biography,* Vols. 110 and 158.

John Rollin Ridge

1827-1867

(Also wrote under the pseudonym of Yellow Bird.) Cherokee novelist, poet, journalist, and editor.

INTRODUCTION

Ridge is often credited as the first Native American to write a novel, *The Life and Adventures of Joaquín Murieta, the Celebrated California Bandit* (1854). He is also remembered for his various essays concerning Native Americans and for his poetry, collected in *Poems* (1868), which is generally characterized as romantic.

Biographical Information

Ridge was born in Eastern Cherokee Nation, now Rome, Georgia, and educated in a school established by his father. Both his father, John Ridge, and his grandfather, Major Ridge, were prominent Cherokee orators and political leaders who, after failing to persuade the United States government to enforce a Supreme Court decision that protected Cherokee lands from incursions by white Georgia settlers, reluctantly signed the 1835 Treaty of New Echota. This treaty provided for the voluntary relocation of their people in exchange for money and land in the West. Ridge's family relocated to present-day Missouri in 1837. Most Cherokees, however, refused to give up their lands and many blamed the elder Ridges and other treaty signers for the brutal, forced relocations of 1838-39 known as the "Trail of Tears," during which the U.S. Army drove the majority of the Cherokee Nation westward to Oklahoma under frigid winter conditions, resulting in approximately four thousand deaths due to starvation, exhaustion, and exposure. Ridge's father and grandfather were killed by members of the anti-Treaty faction in 1839, and his mother moved the family to Arkansas. During the late 1840s, Ridge began studying law and publishing his poetry and journalism in local papers. In 1849, he returned to Cherokee territory, killed one of his father's enemies during a dispute, and fled to California to escape prosecution. After pursuing various occupations, Ridge resumed his literary career and became a prominent editor and newspaper man. He served as editor for various papers, including *California American, San Francisco Herald,* and *Trinity National,* and wrote passionate political editorials. Following the Civil War, he led an unsuccessful effort to secure federal recognition of Cherokee lands as a sovereign nation. Ridge died in 1867 in Grass Valley, California.

Major Works

Ridge's most famous work, *The Life and Adventures of Joaquín Murieta,* focuses on the exploits of its eponymous hero, a renowned (and probably fictitious) Mexican bandit and his band of robbers. Often compared with the legendary outlaw Robin Hood, Murieta is portrayed as a noble figure who turns to a life of crime after suffering numerous injustices and outrages in the mining camps of California, including an undeserved whipping, the rape of his wife, the theft of his prospecting claim, and the lynching of his half-brother. There are many parallels that can be drawn between the character Murieta and Ridge himself. The main theme that Ridge is concerned with throughout the novel is one of courage and heroism in the face of oppression.

Critical Reception

Many critics note that Ridge's novel, *Joaquín Murieta,* considered significant as the first novel written by a Native American, greatly influenced later Native American fiction. Although sometimes faulted for its stereotypical portrayal of Chinese immigrants and California Indians, *Joaquín Murieta*, as noted by critic Louis Owens, "demonstrates in fascinating fashion the tension arising from conflicting identities that would emerge as the central theme in virtually every novel by a Native American author to follow." Scholars have noted that much of Ridge's literary work deals with an internal struggle that raged within him throughout his career and life. He was very conscious of his Cherokee identity, yet he wrote in favor of assimilation of his people. His works express an internal conflict between two cultures.

PRINCIPAL WORKS

The Life and Adventures of Joaquín Murieta, the Celebrated California Bandit [under pseudonym of Yellow Bird] (novel) 1854; also published as *Joaquín Murieta: Marauder of the Mines*, 1871
Poems (poetry) 1868
A Trumpet of Our Own: Yellow Bird's Essays on the North American Indians (essays) 1981

CRITICISM

Angie Debo (essay date 1931)

SOURCE: "John Rollin Ridge," in *Southwest Review,* Vol. XVII, No. 1, Autumn, 1931, pp. 59-71.

[*In the following excerpt, Debo provides an overview of Ridge's poetry, concluding that Ridge was "a Cherokee poet only in the sense that he was both a Cherokee and a poet, and that his intellectual bent was all Christian, classical, and American rather than native".*]

Most of Ridge's literary work has been lost; probably a great deal of it was of the ephemeral sort that goes to make up much of the output of the journalist. A volume of his verse [*Poems*] was published posthumously by his wife in 1868. Although somewhat disappointing after the strength and beauty of literary style revealed by his personal correspondence, still these poems throw some additional light on his strange and many-sided personality. As most of his life was spent in banishment from what was felt to be his home, his most interesting poems have to do with the loneliness of his exile. This emotion is dominant in **"The Harp of Broken Strings,"** his best known poem, and also in a poem written when, at the age of twenty-three, exiled from his people, and with a price upon his head, he was crossing the plains to California. It begins:

> A wanderer from my distant home,
>   From those who blest me with their
>   love,
> With boundless plains beneath my feet,
>   And foreign skies my head above; . . .

The following lines, evidently written two or three years later, express the same loneliness:

> Long years have passed, and I have seen
>   thee not,
>   Save in my waking and my nightly
>   dreams,
> When rose our quiet well-remembered cot
>   In that far land of pleasant woods and
>   streams.

Ridge always felt a mystical companionship with nature that was a part of his Indian heritage. This is sometimes crudely expressed, but he always felt peace and calm descending upon his stormy spirit when he was in the presence of the intimate beauty of shaded streams, the pure remoteness of the stars, or the eternal strength of the snowcapped peaks.

One of his best expressions of this contact with nature is his **"Mount Shasta,"** which begins:

> Behold the dread Mount Shasta, where it
>   stands
> Imperial midst the lesser heights, and, like
> Some mighty unimpassioned mind,
>   companion-
>   less
> And cold. The storms of Heaven may beat in
>   wrath
> Against it, but it stands in unpolluted
> Grandeur still; and from the rolling mists up-
>   heaves
> Its tower of pride e'en purer than before.
> The wintry showers and white-winged
>   tempests
>   leave
> Their frozen tributes on its brow, and it
> Doth make of them an everlasting crown.

Then there is the **"Remembrance of a Summer's Night,"** which in its fatalism reminds one somewhat of "Thanatopsis." As the poet sat beside a lake and watched the stars come out it seemed to him that the earth must burn dimly among her sister planets because of the weight of sorrow that she carried.

> Pale thoughts around her, like a host
>   Of thronging shadows, veiled her sorrow-
>   ing head—
> Remembrance of her Eden lost,
>   The guiltless blood upon her bosom shed,

Her generations that were dust,
Her millions that were yet to join the dead!

Ridge wrote also a number of love poems, somewhat hackneyed in their forms of expression, but glowing with a tropical intensity of feeling. One can find nothing of the Indian here; either because of his habit of using conventional descriptions, or because of the mixture of white blood in his family, the subject of his admiration very often has blue eyes and golden hair, and always has a "white and stainless form", "snowy arms", a "bosom of white", and so on. Even in the **"Cherokee Love Song,"** which has no Indian characteristic except the title, the maiden has a "small white hand". Perhaps in the poem of **"The Stolen White Girl,"** who rides willingly away with her Indian lover, there is the only reflection of that wild and romantic society in which John Rollin Ridge passed his life. Nearly all of Ridge's poetry shows that his teachers had done their full duty in "civilizing" him. He receives his inspiration from the "Sacred Nine"; he hears music in the woods and attributes it to the "water sprite"; and "mild-eyed Science" and "fair Liberty" seem to be his favorite characters. "The glory that was Greece" had cast over this grandson of the aborigines the same magic spell that it has cast over other alien and distant races.

His religious education also had been thorough. No matter how far he may have strayed from the precepts of his teachers in his feeling toward his enemies, there is no doubt that Christian theology formed the background of his intellectual life. Biblical allusions are as frequent in his poetry as classical figures, and even his wilder moods have a Christian setting. In his poem on "Faith" he says:

The Tributes I bring
Are not from the regions where Cherubim
  sing,
Or glory refulgent encircles the throne
Of Him, the Almighty, th' Eternal, the
  One.

But even more deeply implanted in the mind of John Rollin Ridge than his religious and classical education was his faith in industrial progress. No American pioneer dreaming of busy cities rising from the wilderness, ever idealized more hopefully than he the material processes which were to build a brighter future for mankind. The same acceptance of the white man's way of life that had caused Major Ridge to "open up a farm" and entrust his son to the disciplines of an alien people made John Rollin Ridge an ardent believer in the religion of material development. In his poem **"The Atlantic Cable"** he reviews the epic sweep of man's mastery of communication from its primitive beginnings, glorifies the ideal of progress, glows with patriotic pride in the nationality of Franklin, Morse, and

Field, and visions in the future the coming brotherhood of man and the dawn of universal peace. The following lines are characteristic:

'Twas fitting that a great, free land like this,
Should give the lightning's voice to Liberty;
Should wing the heralds of Earth's happiness,
And sing, beneath the ever-sounding sea,
The fair, the bright millenial days to be.

One may search long in these poems for any indication that Ridge considered himself heir to a culture different from that of his fellow citizens; he glorified the American flag as the "banner that our fathers loved", honored his pioneer ancestors who

Have cities reared, the arts have spread
  And placed us where we stand,

and paid the usual tributes to Washington and such "mighty men of old" as Clay, the "God-like Webster", and even the Indian-fighter, Andrew Jackson. In only one poem does he pay tribute to the Mexican and Peruvian civilizations with any indication of racial sympathy. One is forced to the reluctant conclusion that John Rollin Ridge was a Cherokee poet only in the sense that he was both a Cherokee and a poet, and that his intellectual bent was all Christian, classical, and American rather than native. Temperamentally he was all Indian, but the forms of his thought were white.

It would be hard to trace the mingled strains of his inheritance that produced the colorful charm of his character. Against the rude background of bloody Indian feuds and frontier crudeness he stands forth as a definite personality. But the gift of expression which shows in his personal letters was not used to create an epic of his race. Although he found financial competence, and recognition, and perhaps a measure of contentment in the land of his adoption, he fell short of greatness in literature—perhaps in part because he never spoke for the Indian people. He failed to realize in his poems his ambitious plans for presenting to the world the case of the oppressed Indian tribes, and became instead tritely conventional in the white man's manner.

Franklin Walker (essay date 1937)

SOURCE: "Ridge's *Life of Joaquin Murieta*: The First and Revised Editions Compared," in *California Historical Society Quarterly,* Vol. XVI, No. 3, September, 1937, pp. 256-62.

[*In the following essay, Walker analyzes and compares the 1854 first edition of Ridge's novel* Joaquín Murieta *with the more widely-read revised 1871 edition.*]

Until recently it was feared that no copy existed of John Rollin Ridge's life of Joaquin Murieta in its original version of 1854. As late as 1932, Mr. Francis P. Farquhar, in preparing what is known as the *Police Gazette* version of the Joaquin Murieta story for a reissue by the Grabhorn Press, lamented that Ridge's first edition could not be found. This first detailed account of the career of the Mexican bandit who had been killed and beheaded but a few months before its issue was a ninety-page pamphlet which had become so rare that the only testimony to its existence was an entry in Sabin's *Dictionary of Books Relating to America* (No. 51,446). Sabin located it in the New York State Library at Albany, which has since been burned. In the meantime, Ridge's version of Murieta's career had been widely read in the third, or revised edition, first issued in 1871 and most readily available to the present-day reader in the reprint put out by the *Evening Free Lance,* of Hollister, California, in 1927. The evidence indicates, in fact, that the important details of many popular accounts and historical versions of the bandit's life, including those of Hubert Howe Bancroft and Theodore H. Hittell, have been drawn largely from this revised edition of Ridge's narrative. However, until recently no one has been able to state how many of these details were found in Ridge's original version. Since seventeen years elapsed between the appearances of the original and the revised editions of the book—years during which the Joaquin legend had grown with a number of retellings—it was possible that Ridge altered his narrative fundamentally in the revision made just before his death. Thus, how could the historian hope to know how much of the Joaquin story appeared for the first time in Ridge's original narrative?

Uncertainty on this point no longer offers a problem. Recently Mr. Henry Raup Wagner of San Marino acquired what is probably a unique copy of the original edition of Ridge's **Joaquin Murieta.** He has very kindly allowed it to be examined for this paper. Its importance to the student of the most interesting of western legends cannot easily be overestimated. The evidence in newspapers and military records concerning Joaquin is both meagre and contradictory, and there is every reason to suppose that the first book account of the bandit did more to fix the outline of the legend than any actual events in social history.

A careful examination of Ridge's first edition is essential in the study of the growth of the Murieta legend. This first edition throws light, also, on the authenticity of the *Police Gazette,* or "Carmela-Clarina" account, which appears to have been the source of many Latin-American versions of the legend. When this version appeared in 1859, Ridge charged in the Grass Valley press that it was a plagiarism of his book; and it is apparently to this version that he referred when, in the author's preface to the 1871 edition, he wrote: "A spurious edition has been foisted upon unsuspecting publishers and by them circulated, to the infringement of the author's copyright and the damage of his literary credit—the spurious work, with its crude interpolations, fictitious additions, and imperfectly designed distortions of the author's phraseology, being by many persons confounded with the original performance." The similarities in content and phraseology between the *Police Gazette* version (1859) and Ridge's revised version (1871) are sufficient to establish a close relationship between the two, but until Ridge's first account could be examined, there was no way to prove that the writer of the *Police Gazette* version pirated his story from Ridge. One could as easily contend that Ridge borrowed extensively from the *Police Gazette* version in making his revision. An examination of the first edition, however, substantiates beyond question Ridge's charge of plagiarism; the *Police Gazette* version is based upon Ridge's account, altered in sequence, occasionally garbled in text, and amended in many ways. It is probable, therefore, that the publishers of Ridge's revised history of Murieta considered the *Police Gazette* version to be so patently based upon Ridge's earlier book that they looked upon it as the second edition, and therefore called the 1871 version the third. There is no record of any other second edition of Ridge's book.

The first edition of Ridge's **Murieta** was issued as a booklet with yellow paper covers. Titled "The Life and Adventures of Joaquin Murieta, the Celebrated California Bandit," by Yellow Bird, it was published by W. B. Cooke and Company in San Francisco in 1854 and was copyrighted by Charles Lindley and John R. Bridge (sic). It contains two Anthony and Baker lithographs, one representing Murieta and one Captain Harry Love. Although its ninety pages tell approximately the same story as that of the well-known third edition, many interesting minor differences appear. A collation of the two follows.

Material in the First Edition Not Included in the Third[1]

Page 2: The first edition opens with a fairly long publisher's preface followed by a short editor's preface. The publisher's preface gives a much more detailed account of John Rollin Ridge's life among the Cherokees than is found in the revised edition. It speaks heatedly of the white man's treachery to the Cherokees, tells in melodramatic fashion of the assassination of Ridge's father and grandfather by members of a rival faction among the Indians, and hints at the bereaved son's attempts to avenge his family's wrongs. Then it openly states that the half-savage author with his early taste of persecution and violence is particularly suited to tell the story of Murieta, and ends with the words:

> The following production, aside from its intrinsic merit will, no doubt, be read with increased interest,

when it is known that the author is a *Cherokee Indian,* born in the woods—reared in the midst of the wildest scenery—and familiar with all that is thrilling, fearful, and tragical, in a forest life . . . The perusal of this work will give those who are disposed to be curious, an opportunity to estimate the character of Indian talent. The aboriginal race has produced great warriors, and powerful orators, but literary men—only a few.

The editor, in his short preface, states that, although the book was written for historical purposes, it was hoped that it would also serve to defend the reputation of the Mexicans. The reader is assured that the author was not reckless but had respect for authorities: "In the main, it will be found to be strictly true."

Page 12: The sentence in the revised version reading, "Seven men were murdered within three or four days. . . ." is enclosed in quotation marks in the original, the verb is "have been" instead of "were," and the quotation is ascribed to the Marysville *Herald* of November 13, 1851.

Page 14: After the paragraph ending "filling the heaven with his solemn presence," in the original edition Ridge inserted his poem, "Mt. Shasta, Seen from a Distance." A footnote states that the poem was written by Yellow Bird in 1852. The poem, omitted from all later versions of the **Murieta,** holds the position of honor in Ridge's collected poems.

Page 27: After the sentence ending "and were excessively glad to see him," the first edition carries a statement that Joaquin verified from Three-Fingered Jack the rumor that the latter had burned a house and had committed a particularly gruesome murder.

Page 43: After the paragraph ending "each one had a tale to tell of hairbreadth escapes and daring deeds," the first edition contains a passage in which a bandit, Valenzuela, relates one of the bloody deeds of Padre Jurata at the battle of Cerro Gordo, during the Mexican War. The presence of this item bears out further Ridge's contention that the *Police Gazette* Murieta was based upon his story, for one of the principal means of expanding the 1859 version was through inclusion of anecdotes about Padre Jurata.

Page 65: After the sentence describing the burning of the robbers' huts, ending "its sound roared among the mountains for miles around," the first edition includes the sentence: "Joaquin saw and heard it with a laugh. 'If they could only throw *us* into it now,' said he, 'it would be fine.'"

Material Added in the Revised Edition

In revising his account of Murieta, though Ridge made no major alterations in his text, he added a number of episodes and expanded others. These revisions are listed below in two groups: first, the notable changes in narrative, second, the minor alterations in wording.

Notable Changes in the Narrative

The title has been changed from "The Life and Adventures of Joaquin Murieta, the Celebrated California Bandit" to "The History of Joaquin Murieta; the King of California Outlaws, Whose Band Ravaged the State in the Early Fifties."

In the revised edition the nom-de-plume, "Yellow Bird" (Ridge's Cherokee name), has been discarded and the name of the author is given as John R. Ridge.

In the revised edition the narrative has been divided into chapters, and summaries have been provided at the head of each chapter. The original had no chapter divisions.

Page 3: The two opening paragraphs have been altered slightly in wording, but the meaning remains unchanged.

Page[s] 3-4: The two paragraphs telling of Joaquin's early life in Sonora and his love for Rosita have been added in the revised edition. They open with, "The first considerable interruption in the general smooth current of his existence," and end with, "and the trip was made with expedition."

Page[s] 5-6: The account of the indignities put upon Joaquin by the Anglo-Saxon miners, ending in the ravaging of Rosita, has been expanded and dramatized with use of dialogue in the revised version. The original states simply that Joaquin was driven from his property and that his mistress was attacked; e.g., "They tied him hand and foot, and ravaged his mistress before his eyes. They left him, but the soul of the young man was from that moment darkened." (His mistress is not mentioned by name until much later in the narrative, when, on page 31, she is called Rosita, sister of Reyes Feliz.) In the revised version the section of four paragraphs starting "One pleasant evening" and ending "for a more northern portion of the mines" is the expanded account of Joaquin's persecution.

Pages 7-8: Ridge has again enlarged his story of Joaquin's persecution, here adding detail and dialogue to the episode of the hanging of the half-brother and the whipping of Joaquin. The short original version reads:

He had gone a short distance from Murphy's Diggings to see his half-brother, who had been located in that vicinity for several months, and returned to Murphy's upon a horse which his brother had lent him. The animal proved to have been stolen, and being recognized by a number of individuals in the town, an excitement was raised on the subject. Joaquin suddenly found himself surrounded by a furious mob, and charged with the crime of theft. He told them how it happened that he was riding the horse, and in what manner his half-brother had come into possession of it. They listened to no explanation, but bound him to a tree, and publicly disgraced him with the lash. They then proceeded to the house of his half-brother and hung him without judge or jury.

It is to be noted that in the original the whipping preceded the hanging; only in the revised version did Ridge conform entirely to the romantic tradition that a whipping is the last and greatest insult to be brooked by the noble savage.

Page 8: The account of the change of Joaquin's character and his dedication to revenge has been altered in wording but not in detail in the revised version.

Page 10: The paragraph on Reyes Feliz has been expanded over the original to include references to the newly-inserted material on the Sonoran activities of the young Joaquin and Rosita.

Pages 13-14: From "Coming suddenly upon a small tent" to the end of the chapter, the incident recounting the attempt of Buchanan and Bowen to capture Murieta has been greatly expanded, chiefly through the use of dialogue. The dog has been introduced in the revision. In the original, Bowen remained ignorant that the man who shot at him was actually Joaquin.

Pages 15-18: The entire episode telling of Joaquin's rescue of Old Peter's comely daughter when she was about to be ravished by one of the outlaw band has been added in the revision; possibly it was suggested by the account of Peter the Hunter in Alonzo Delano's *Chips of the Old Block*. A section of eight paragraphs starting with "In one of the descends of the banditti" and ending with the close of the chapter has been added in the revision.

Pages 30-34: All of Chapter VI, and the part of Chapter VII up to and including the paragraph on page 34 ending "the guide left them," have been added in the revision. This account of Joaquin's adventures in the Mono Lake region was probably inserted to fill a gap in the chronology and to exploit the wonders of the east slope of the Sierra. It is interesting to note that, although Ridge did not mention the trip over the Sierra in his first edition, a brief account of it appears in the *Police Gazette* version.

Pages 65-66: The account of the fight between Woodbeck and his companion and Joaquin and Three-Fingered Jack has been expanded with addition of detail and dialogue.

Pages 76-77: Several details in the account of the forming of Love's rangers have been added in revision, e.g.: the first paragraph in Chapter XV is new. In the following paragraph the material from "The officers of the law in the different counties" to "The condition of things, in short became intolerable" is new, as is the portion of the last sentence beginning with "the object being to surprise and take" and ending with "by small bodies of men." The list and comments on the rangers have been added, starting with "The following is a list of their names" and ending "At any rate Mr. Herbert was tried and acquitted."

Page 83: The affidavits as to the identity of Joaquin's head do not appear in the original. The text from "Among the numerous affidavits" to "legal authorities of the death of the noted chieftain" has been added in revision.

Minor Alterations in Wording

Page 6: The date "1850" has been inserted after the phrase "in the month of April."

Page 9: The phrase "(an acquaintance of mine, named Burns)" has been inserted after "Said an eye witness of these events."

Page 11: The phrase at the end of the fourth paragraph, reading, "including a few renegade Americans, of desperate characters and fortunes," and all of the following short paragraph, which refers to "frail ones" among the banditti, have been inserted in the revised edition.

Page 18: The note in heavy type at the beginning of Chapter IV, telling of the location of the Arroyo Cantova, was added by the editor of the 1927 reprint.

Page 20: "To secure" at the end of the second paragraph originally read "to get hold of."

Page 21: The sentence which reads, "(This circumstance was related to the writer by a man named Brown, who was intimate with Joaquin, and to whom the robber talked freely)" has been added in the revision.

Page 23: In the final paragraph, which deals with the Digger chief, Sapatarra, three phrases have been added. In the next to the last sentence on the page, "the women included" has been inserted after "naked"; in the following sentence, "dressed for the occasion with a broad-brimmed hat and a bobtailed red flannel shirt, which gave his ancient and most venerable legs a most unique appearance" has been inserted after "Sapatarra"; and "which was a mixture of Digger and Spanish" has been inserted after "long speech."

Page 41: The sentence reading "(See newspapers of that period.)" has been inserted after "'I will give $10,000. Joaquin.'"

Page 43: Joaquin's speech in the paragraph opening "He informed them" was expressed in the first person in the original. The following paragraph, about Captain Love, has been added in the revision. The account of the attempt of Gonzales' widow to murder Guerra has been slightly altered in wording.

Page 61: Apparently, when the first edition was written Moreno had not been hanged, for the sentence at the end of the chapter first read, "It is only owing to the delay of the law, that he is not already hung."

Page 64: "G—d d—n that little Sheriff" appeared as "God damn that little Sheriff" in the first edition. (The frontier had changed between 1854 and 1871!)

Page 71: Horsely was written H——— in the original.

Page 72: Added in the revision was the sentence closing the second paragraph: "This was the end of the hitherto very lucky 'Juan,'" for the seems never to have had a surname.

Page 73: Hornitas was spelled Oanetas in the original.

Page 84: John Bigler was Colonel John Bigler in the original.

Conclusions

The collation shows that Ridge in revising the 1854 edition of his account of Joaquin Murieta added no major features to the story. The changes he made were of three kinds: (1) attempts to document his evidence by giving names in full or by referring to contemporary newspapers; (2) the addition of a few minor adventures of Murieta, such as the Mono Lake and Peter the Hunter episodes; and (3), and most significant, an expansion through addition of detail, lurid phrase, and dialogue, of the incidents dealing with Joaquin's early life and persecution. These portions of the legend, emphasizing Joaquin's purity of motives, unjust persecution at the hands of the whites, and dedication to revenge, were to become the prominent parts of the legend as time went on. They are, likewise, the parts most difficult to substantiate and the themes most suited to expansion by Ridge for personal reasons. It is interesting to note that the skeleton of the Murieta legend appeared with all of its parts in the first extensive printed account of the robber's career, and that Yellow Bird's principal changes in his story, when he revised it just before his death, were added to cover the backbone with the flesh of melodramatic fiction.

Notes

[1] The page numbers refer to the 1927 reprinting of the revised or third edition, put out by the *Evening Free Lance,* of Hollister, California, with the cover title of "California's Age of Terror: Murieta and Vasquez," included with which is the story of the "Crimes and Career of Tiburcio Vasquez."

James W. Parins (essay date 1991)

SOURCE: "Romantic Poet" and "The Romance of Joaquín Murieta" in *John Rollin Ridge: His Life and Works,* University of Nebraska Press, 1991, pp. 76-94 and 95-112.

[*Below, Parins assesses Ridge's love poetry and examines the history behind* Joaquín Murieta *and Ridge's depiction of the main character.*]

Romantic Poet

By 1851 Ridge was writing seriously and attempting to have his work published in publications that circulated more widely than local newspapers. He began writing for the *Golden Era* in its first year of publication. The *Golden Era* was begun in San Francisco in 1852 by Rollin M. Daggett and J. Macdonough Foard. The literary journal's circulation and fame went far beyond that city, however. It was popular with farmers and miners all over California, and Horace Greeley called it "the most remarkable paper."[1] Its content ranged from novels, short stories, and poems to jokes, local gossip, and rumors. Besides Ridge, other writers contributing to its pages during the 1850s include Bret Harte, Mark Twain, Joaquin Miller, Charles Warren Stoddard, Orpheus Carr, and "Old Block" Delano. In the *Golden Era,* Ridge used the pen name "Yellow Bird," as he had done earlier in Arkansas. This is a literal translation of his Cherokee name, Chees-quat-a-law-ny.

Ridge published in other California periodicals as well. His poetry appeared in *Alta California,* a popular newspaper, *Hesperian,* and *Hutchings's California Magazine. Hesperian,* which featured a cover depicting three robed maidens reaching for the golden apple of literature while the dragon of ignorance lurked nearby, was founded in 1858 as a women's magazine and featured fashions as well as literature. *Hutchings's California Magazine* was founded two years earlier by J. M. Hutchings, an Englishman who wanted to spread the word about the natural splendors of the West. He published essays on various aspects of the area's wonders and printed lithographs of spectacular scenery, such as Yosemite Valley.[2]

Ridge's poetry during this period and in his last years at Honey Creek is clearly in the romantic vein that was so popular in the middle of the nineteenth century in both Britain and America. Further, much of his writing during this tempestuous time is autobiographical and intensely personal; from it we can draw some conclusions about how he saw himself and his situation in this time of "exile." Further, the poems are helpful in understanding the man's temperament.

A poem addressed to his wife was written on his trek across the plains to California. **"To Lizzie"** gives us some insight into the early years of their marriage, especially Elizabeth's influence on her husband's mercurial tendencies. The poem shows that Ridge recognized, valued, and missed her calming influence. It also expresses Ridge's image of himself as a Cain figure, a defiant exile who is cursed with dark thoughts:

> A wanderer from my distant home,
> From those who blest me with their love,
> With boundless plains beneath my feet,
> And foreign skies my head above;
> I look around me sternly here,
> And smother feelings strong and deep,
> While o'er my brow are gathering dark
> The thoughts that from my spirit leap.
>
> > (Lines 1-8)[3]

But his wife can give peace to his tortured mind, he says, and bring out his positive qualities:

> O lovely one, that pines for me!
> How well she soothed each maddened
> thought,
> And from the ruins of my soul
> A fair and beauteous fabric wrought!
>
> > (Lines 21-24)

Ridge's self-image is revealed in another poem that is perhaps a romanticized version of his and Lizzie's courtship. **"The Stolen White Girl"** tells of a "wild half-breed" (line 1) who takes a beautiful white girl captive, not by means of the usual weapons and bonds, but by his own attractiveness. The poem predicts for the couple a future full of happiness far "down in the depths of the forest" (line 9). Each of the pair is described; first the woman:

> The contrast between them is pleasing and
> rare;
> Her sweet eye of blue, and her soft silken
> hair,
> Her beautiful waist, and her bosom of white
> That heaves to the touch with a sense of
> delight;

The following stanza takes a look at the "wild half-breed":

> His form more majestic and darker his brow,
> Where the sun has imparted its liveliest
> glow—

> An eye that grows brighter with passion's true
> fire,
> As he looks on his loved one with earnest
> desire.
>
> > (Lines 17-24)

If the poem does present the self-portrait it seems to, Ridge saw himself as a romantic hero—a dashing, passionate adventurer. Other poems, however, depict a darker side.

A work dated August 16, 1847, **"The Robber's Song to His Mistress,"** depicts a tortured soul who is wracked with guilt over his deeds. The poem may reflect Ridge's ambivalent position: his often-stated desire for revenge for his father and grandfather's assassination pitted against the desire for a happy and peaceful marriage. This short poem was not published in the posthumous 1868 edition.

In **"The Harp of Broken Strings,"** several themes emerge, the chief one being isolation. Written shortly after Ridge's arrival in California, the poem depicts an exile, "a stranger in a stranger land," as he announces in the first line. He is downhearted, saying "present joy is not for me" (line 6), and the future is no less bleak: "no hope its promise brings" (line 5). The persona recognizes his own psychic instability when he says he takes a sort of perverse delight in his misery.

Part of the pain of his isolation is caused by separation from his loved one. In his imagination he sees her:

> The beauteous one before me stands
> Pure spirit in her downcast eyes,
> And like twin doves her folded hands.
>
> > (Lines 33-35)

But she is changed, he sees, by the pangs of separation. The "bloom has left her cheek forever" (line 45), and her face is "o'errun with tears" (line 48). The situation does not promise to improve, and he broods upon his "ruined fortunes" (line 53). His pain is intense.

The power of poetic imagination is invoked throughout. His imagination can conjure up his loved one and also delivers him some "delight," even though it is the perverse variety. But included too is the threat of losing this power, since his harp bears broken strings, implying the loss of youth, potential, and opportunity, strengthened by his sense of "ruined fortunes" and "shattered feelings" (line 9).

The poem is clearly driven by the circumstances of the writer's life. Written "by Sacramento's stream" (line 28), probably in 1850 or 1851, the poem depicts Ridge's near despair over his situation. By this time he had realized that the promise of instant fortune in the goldfields was empty. He found himself adrift in an alien environment, estranged from family and friends, with little money and few prospects. Most of all, he was separated from Elizabeth, his wife of only a few years, and understandably concerned for the future of their relationship. While one may regret the strong streak of self-pity and self-centeredness in the poem, the extreme nature of Ridge's personal dilemma should be taken into account; also, this expression of his feelings probably had some therapeutic value for him.

"**The Still Small Voice**" is another poem written in Ridge's romantic period, in which he assesses his situation. Here he comments on the twin forces of fate and history that he believes govern his life. The persona asserts that wherever he goes, whatever he does, he hears a voice within him saying, "Too late! too late! the doom is set, the die is cast." This line appears as a refrain at the end of each stanza, and the word "past" is repeated at the end of the second-to-last line. Whatever he does, the persona believes, has been ordained in the past. His present and future are ruled by his own history. Applied to Ridge's own life, this theory is correct. His preoccupation with revenge, his ambition to become a "successful" man, his chronic financial instability, all had their genesis in two key events in Ridge's past: the assassination of John and Major Ridge and the related killing of David Kell. In this poem, as in "**The Harp of Broken Strings**," the persona seems to relish his despondency and the hopelessness of his situation; perhaps like a Byronic hero he considers that he is being given special attention by Fate:

> A raven-thought is darkly set
> Upon my brow—where shades are met
> Of grief, of pain, of toil, and care—
> The raven-thought of stern despair!
>
> (Lines 33-36)

But Ridge wrote of another inner voice too, a more positive one, in a poem composed on March 28, 1851, and published in the Marysville *Herald*. This work also bore the title the "**Still, Small, Voice**." Here, however, the message is one of cheer, and even though the speaker of the poem insists he is "doomed" (line 36) and "ruined" (line 27), the voice supplies the only solace he receives in his troubles:

> Then let my brow grow sadder yet,
> And mountain-high still rise regret;
> Enough for me the voice that cheers
> The woes of these my darker years.
>
> (Lines 37-40)

These autobiographical poems seem to give us some idea what John Rollin Ridge thought of himself at a time he certainly regarded as a turning point in his life. His future was uncertain and, to some degree at least, his self-confidence had been shaken. But he was a proud, determined man. He saw himself as an intense person who hated and loved deeply, like most heroes of literature and myth. He admitted that his passions sometimes led to reckless behavior, but his temperament could most times be calmed through his wife's influence. Probably dating from the Kell affair, he saw his life as controlled by forces outside himself, by history and fate. His concept of the romantic adventurer proved to have a dark side, and by the time he got to California he saw himself as a Cain figure, an exile who was prevented from taking his rightful place as an important leader of his people like his father and grandfather. These poems also reveal an exaggerated sense of self-importance, and the last two works, especially, demonstrate a large capacity for self-pity.

The largest group of poems written in Ridge's early manhood are love poetry. For the most part they are conventional in language, imagery, and structure; most read like the love poetry of his own and earlier times. For example, "**A Cherokee Love Song**" and "**Song—Sweet Indian Maid**" are traditional invitational poems in which the speaker urges his love to escape with him into a bower of bliss. "**Song—Sweet Indian Maid**" was published in *Hutchings's California Magazine*[4] but did not appear in the 1868 edition. Here an Indian maiden is asked to accompany the speaker on a journey on the river to an island he knows of, "Where all alone and undisturbed, / We'll talk and love as we may please" (lines 27-28). In "**A Cherokee Love Song**," another young maiden is invited to take a canoe trip to an out-of-the-way river isle, but this time she is a white girl. Nature is no less friendly, though, and as the persona is quick to point out, smiles on the couple. With nature's approval gained, he offers other arguments:

> Oh, look to heaven, how pure it seems,
> No cloud to dim, no blot, no stain,
> And say—if we refuse to love,
> Ought we to hope or smile again?
> That island green, with roses gemmed,
> Let's seek it, love—how sweet a spot?
> Then let the hours of night speed on,
> We live to love—it matters not!
>
> (Lines 25-32)

Traditionally, love verse makes use of elaborate conceits and indulges in exaggeration; Ridge's work is no exception. An example can be found in his "**To A*******," another conventional love lyric published in the April 15, 1851, edition of the Marysville *Herald,* which noted that it had appeared previously in the *Daily Union.* The poem's speaker promises that for A's love he would forfeit "a monarch's crown" (line 5); the sun, moon, and stars (lines 9-10); half the days of his life (line 15); and other valuables. "**Lines on a Humming Bird Seen at a Lady's Window**" also contains such conceits. A hummingbird sees a lady at her window and mistakes her mouth for a flower: "That ripe, red mouth he takes / For rarer flower than ever yet was quaffed" (lines 9-10). The persona identifies with the bird as a worshiper of the young lady when he says, "But, rainbow wing'ed bird, / Thou'rt not alone from those sweet lips debarred" (lines 15-16). The bird, though, has the advantage, because it can bring a smile to the woman's lips, an accomplishment that has so far eluded the man. The bird has it over the man in another way, too—it is able to escape the "enchantress" (line 28).

The man is again held in thrall by a beautiful enchantress in "Of Her I Love." His description echoes the sonneteers of the English Renaissance as he writes of "coral-hued lips" (line 5) with the texture of roses (line 7) that enclose teeth like pearls (line 6). Her bosoms are more white than the breast of a swan (stanza 3), and her form is "angel-like" (line 14). At first glance the persona knows he has been taken prisoner by love.

Other poems continue in this vein. In **"Do I Love Thee?"** the object of his love is the most sublime vision of his imagination. By the fifth stanza, the persona has worked himself into such a froth that he proclaims he ranks "disease among his friends" because she appears to him in dreams brought on by fever (line 30). This is certainly an original conceit, if a bizarre one.

Whereas most of Ridge's love lyrics are written in a highly conventional mode featuring smitten young men yearning for the affection of young women with overblown charms, two are strikingly different. **"The Forgiven Dead"** and **"False but Beautiful"** are ballads that portray the dismal side of the male-female relationship. In **"The Forgiven Dead"** the persona tells of his former love, who left him for another man who offered her riches. The woman, "pain-haunted / That truth she forsook for gold" (lines 13-14), has pined away on her expensive bed and finally died. Now, the persona says, all his anger has disappeared, and he is able to forgive her. After her death, he says that even though she had given herself to another physically, he realizes that she really belonged to him:

> To strew her tomb with roses,
> Pure-white, as virgins' tombs should be,
> I had not thought: but Fate disposes—
> Her *soul* was virgin unto *me*.
>
> (Lines 21-24)

In **"False but Beautiful"** the speaker tells of his lamialike lover, who has great physical beauty but an evil, poisonous soul. "Dark as a demon's dream is one I love— / —in soul," he says in the opening lines, "but oh, how beautiful in form!" Even though he recognizes the danger, he finds her irresistible in a perverse way:

> To wander in that wilderness of wiles
> And blissful blandishments—it is to thrill

> With subtle poison, and to feel the will
> Grow weak in that which all the veins doth fill.
>
> (Lines 11-14)

She is a "sorceress" (line 15) with a glance that fascinates him; he is like a bird that "Hangs trembling on the serpent's doomful eye" (line 22).

Ridge's love poems for the most part use traditional language, imagery, conceits and exaggeration, and structure. Some are clearly written to his wife; the objects of some others are uncertain. But for all their conventionality, the love lyrics reinforce the conception of Ridge as a passionate, emotional man.

Much of the poetry written in this period uses poetic conventions common in the works of English and American romantic poets of the early nineteenth century, poets that Ridge read at school. Themes and structures often imitate earlier writers, especially in those pieces that may be called "nature" poems. The nature poems attempt to recreate the poet's personal experiences with the natural environment, which often have mystical or transcendental qualities. In addition, imagination is nearly always the force that makes the experience possible.

"A Night Scene" is a good example. The poem is a romantic ode reminiscent of those by John Keats. It follows the same three-part structure as "Ode to a Nightingale" and other odes and contains some rather standard romantic metaphors, found throughout the poetry of Wordsworth, Shelley, and Byron.

As the poem opens, the persona waits for that Wordsworthian "impulse from the vernal wood":

> I sit
> And muse alone—the time and the place are fit—
> And summon spirits from the blue profound,
> That answer me and through my vision flit.
>
> (Lines 7-10)

At this point his vision has not yet come, but in the next stanza it appears in the guise of a maiden, "a beauteous being" "with hair night-hued, and brow and bosom white" (lines 11-12). She seems to float in the soft light and shadows of evening, and for the moment all is still. Then he hears a heavenly sound whose "tones are filling up the air, / That brings them, with the star-light blended now, / And wavelet murmurings from below" (lines 21-23). The maiden's voice and harp are making this nightingale song, and the music lures him to her. He knows there is an abyss between them, yet still he reaches out for that momentary glimpse, that fleeting perception of immortality: "But o'er that gulf my spirit loves to lean," he says (line

30). With his "spirit bride" (line 35) he senses a connection with the divine, if only in promise; but as with the Keatsian communion with the bird, the tryst is futile and it is not long before he is called back, forlorn, to his "sole self." The poem ends on a plaintive note:

> Fair words, like ripples o'er the watery deep
> When breezes softly o'er the surface play,
> In circles one by one ye stretch away,
> Till, lost to human vision's wildest sweep
> Our souls are left to darkness and dismay.
>
> (Lines 36-40)

Ridge's poem is clearly built on the model of Keats's ode. It opens with the persona outside the vision, isolated in his own humanity, but clearly reaching beyond himself. The second part of the tripartite form is the possession, the interconnection, or the communion with the object of the poem. But this union is transitory and doomed to failure, and the subject is called back to the isolation of self, at which point he contemplates the vision, the process, and the experience.

It is important to recognize that here too Ridge's diction and imagery are typically romantic. Obvious examples are his use of the "watery deep" to convey the vast immutability of eternity and the reference in the same extended metaphor to the breezes that play over the sea, changing the configuration of its surface. The wind brings to mind the "intellectual breeze" that plays on the aeolian harp, an image pervasive in English romantic poetry. The form the vision takes is important, too: it recalls the ghostly maidens of many romantic poems, such as "La Belle Dame sans Merci," "Alastor," and "Endymion."

"The Singing Spirit" is another poem that seems close to Keats's nightingale ode. Again, at the beginning of the poem the persona is in a pastoral setting, wandering with, if not a drowsy numbness, at least a feeling of sadness and melancholy. But then he hears the healing melody, the spirit song that triggers his mystical vision. He mistakes it first for the voice of a water sprite and then for the sound of "some lonely singing bird" (line 4). His response to the song is twofold. First the music helps him chase away the spirit of sadness; the shadows then leave his "sobered, pensive brow" (line 9), and his soul is refreshed as his melancholy is magically lifted.

Then the second response comes. He stands there, the song thrilling him "Along my being's inmost strings" (line 22). He listens until the music takes on new tones that seem to warn of death. The hint of death does not terrify him, however; it is more the "easeful Death" of Keats that he has intimations of, and the persona here seems more than half in love with it:

> And yet there was no dread—I thought how meet
> 'Neath such a dirge to sink and die!
> While viewless o'er was heard that harp, how sweet
> To close the dim and fading eye!
>
> (Lines 25-28)

The song continues rich and deep for a time, and he compares its sound to "the feeling of the soul / When might thoughts our natures sweep" (lines 31-32). But the singing spirit ceases before long, like the nightingale, and the persona returns homeward, sad because he hears it no longer. The poem closes, like Keats's, with his contemplation of the experience.

In Ridge's **"Remembrance of a Summer's Night"** we see another variation on the romantic experience, a Shelleyan treatment of the coming together of the mortal and the infinite. In what seems to be an argument for an epistemology based on mystical and transcendental experience, Ridge closely follows Wordsworth and Shelley.

The poem opens with a familiar setting: the persona, with his book of ancient lore, sits in the midst of a beautiful sylvan scene and muses, oblivious to the "holy spell" (line 10) being woven around him like the approach of the "awful shadow of some unseen Power" in Shelley's "Hymn to Intellectual Beauty." With the fall of night, though, he gazes on the darkened sky, on the moon and stars, where "wing'd imagination roams" (line 25). Soon he seems to rise, to "mingle with the mighty dead" (line 40), and is transported into space, into the realm of the eternal. Here he is certain that the wisdom of the universe has been opened to him:

> Upon that mighty page unrolled
> I read, bright syllabled in blazing sphere
> What science hath but feebly told
> In all the wisdom of her garnered years.
>
> (Lines 49-52)

Knowledge and wisdom can be attained by feeding one's mind with a "wise passiveness," as Wordsworth says in "Expostulation and Reply." Ridge's epistemology also seems to embrace the idea of the visionary experience in Shelley's "Hymn to Intellectual Beauty." The voice in that poem, like Ridge's persona, seeks commerce with ghosts and "high talk with the departed dead" before the transcendent moment, that feeling of intense certainty that both poets see as central to the romantic experience. Ridge's attainment of wisdom is also reminiscent of the mystical instant in Shelley's "Alastor" when

> meaning on his vacant mind
> Flashed like strong inspiration and he saw
> The thrilling secrets of the birth of time.
>
> (Lines 126-28)

"**Mount Shasta,**" the best known of Ridge's poems, is also in the romantic vein. Specifically, it closely follows Shelley's "Mont Blanc" in theme, natural description, diction, and even meter. Both poems are written in blank verse with indiscriminate rhyme. The diction in many cases is strikingly similar. For example, Ridge's "vast Reflector in / The dome of heaven" (lines 44-45) resembles Shelley's "infinite dome / Of Heaven" (lines 141-42). Shasta as a "monarch mountain" (line 35) and "Imperial midst the lesser heights" (line 2) compares with Mont Blanc towering above "Its subject mountains" (line 62). The American poem, like the English, deals with the perception of eternity in the face of the all-consuming flux of time. The mountain peaks in both cases symbolize the ultimate reality that stands behind and occasionally intrudes into this transient and mortal world. Mount Shasta is seen as "the great material symbol of eternal / Things!" (lines 56-57) in much the same way as the Alpine pinnacle is depicted as the immutable in a changing universe.

"**To a Star Seen at Twilight,**" another of Ridge's nature poems, is important for its presentation of his public persona and for its assertions about the power and role of the artist. The poem's structure is three part. In the first section, lines 1-16, the persona describes a solitary star in the twilight sky, "companionless in light," peerless and aloof. Separate from earth, the star is part of another reality; it seems to have an eternity and immutability not found in mortal realms. After the persona describes the star, he begins to meditate on the similarity between his own spirit and the distant object. Both are isolated, distant from the rest of their kind. But there the similarity ends. The spirit of the persona, anchored by his own mortality, cannot match the pureness and nobility of the star. Although his spirit can soar, can partake of the transcendental experience, it cannot sustain the vision, cannot as yet enter the eternal world permanently as the star has done.

It is at this point that Ridge makes a statement about his own poetic vision and, by implication, the ability of all poets. He wishes all people could "in their bosoms drink / Thy loveliness and light like me" (lines 31-32). Poets are special and are able to make their mystical perceptions visible to common people. The poet's role, for Ridge, is to use his special power to translate his own experiences, transcendental and otherwise, for his readers. The poet is to recreate, as far as possible, his own special insights into the universe surrounding us all. Thus Ridge establishes himself as one of the seers, one of the priests of nature. In the third section the persona exults in the star's isolation: "Thou are the throne / Of thy own spirit, star! . . . 'Tis great to be alone!" (lines 38-39, 50).

"**To a Mocking Bird Singing in a Tree**" also treats nature in the romantic vein. The speaker hears the song and identifies the bird as a "Poet" albeit a "Sarcastic" one (line 2). He wishes he might duplicate the notes he hears, sounds that show the bird is happy and "free from pain" (line 18). This ability would enable him to rise above the trials of this world. But he would not rob the bird of its song, even for such a reward.

Here the poet raises a point about artistic inspiration. He asks if birds, like people, look to heaven for their songs. There are echoes here, too, of the belief that poets and other artists can see beyond this world, can glimpse the ideal, the eternal, whose image they then pass on to other people through the work of art. Poets, in Browning's phrase, lend out their minds.

Finally Ridge takes the idealistic stance that thought never dies and but remains in the sphere of pure Idea. If this is true, he asks, should not the bird's song, like that of Browning's Abt Vogler, remain forever in the ineffable mind of the universe? The final lines of the poem express the wish that the listener might be present when those ideal notes are sounded again.

For all his idealistic writing on nature, Ridge also portrays the darker side of his romanticism. His "**A Scene along the Rio de Las Plumas**" is an inversion of his usual nature poem. Here the persona describes a walk along the banks of the Feather River near Marysville and Yuba City, California. Now, instead of depicting the nature universe as a nurturing source of inspiration, the traveler finds the world along the river hostile and menacing. As his journey continues, the hostility grows more intense. Nonetheless, nature provides inspiration here, though the images conjured up are hardly those of "**The 'Singing Spirit,'**" "**A Night Scene,**" or "**Mount Shasta.**" He describes a slimy, oozy place where "birds of sullen flight," little resembling his mockingbird, "Pierce darkness with their screams" (lines 6-7). The traveler sees creatures rising from the bottom of the swamp and watches predatory birds. What seems at first to be a spirit hovering over the scene turns out to be not a "heavenly sprite" (line 24) but a more mundane crane, who "makes his vulgar dish / Of creeping things and fish" (lines 30-31). In contrast to the nightingales and skylarks, the immortal birds of romantic literature, Ridge's owl, which "looks like a druid priest" (line 36), is in reality much less, apt to "Not higher thought inspire / Than lowest wants require" (lines 37-38), since the bird's attention is on its next meal. A pair of flaming eyes startle the persona, and in his mind images of "Dante's damned abode" (line 48).

As the wanderer travels deeper into the swamp, nature's hostility becomes more acute. Nightshade and other poisonous plants grow in his path, and he sees tarantulas, centipedes, and scorpions lurking in the undergrowth. Finally he is forced to retreat from an attack by stinging insects.

"**Humboldt River,**" too, depicts a harsher nature than is found in the more idealistic poems. A note on the poem's title reads, "For three hundred miles its banks are one continuous burying ground. Emigrants to California died on its shore by thousands." Here Ridge describes a nature that is hostile not only to mortal humans, but to their spirits as well. As the spirits of the dead emigrants guard their remains, natural forces are at work to dissipate them:

> For the elements aye are in league,
> With a patience unknowing fatigue,
> To scatter mortality's mould,
> And sweep from the graves what they hold!
> (Lines 27-30)

At night the situation is worse, for then the plants effuse gaseous vapors formed when their roots penetrate the graves. Night travelers, the poem says, face an atmosphere thus poisoned, and they themselves take on the aspect of death. Ridge finishes by comparing the Humboldt to the Styx. "**Humboldt River**" reminds one of the dark and brooding side of William Cullen Bryant's poetry. Ridge probably read Bryant's works at Great Barrington, where the older poet had lived for a number of years. The California poem's pseudoscientific aspects evoke works like Bryant's "Thanatopsis."

Similar to "**Humboldt River**" is a companion piece, "**The Humboldt Desert,**" published in an 1866 anthology, *Poetry of the Pacific,*[5] but not included in the 1868 *Poems.* The bleak landscape depicted in this poem is forever at odds with the travelers who attempt to cross it. The trail across the desert is "parched and dreary" (line 17), lined with "the bones that bleaching lie / Where fell the wearied beast o'er driven" (lines 29-30). Ridge compares the pioneer's trek across the desert to the Christian pilgrim's journey through life. For each, he predicts, there will be rest "When camped upon the heavenly River" (line 72).

Other nature poems include "**The Rainy Season in California,**" "**A June Morning,**" and "**October Hills.**" The first of these appeared in 1858 in the California magazine *Hesperian* as well as in the 1868 *Poems.* The magazine version has a note affixed to the title: "Written in a Lonely Cabin in the 'Bald Hills,' Shasta County, at the approach of and during a storm." The poem describes the tempests of the season and predicts more pleasant weather to come. The storms remind the persona of his own bleak situation in the mining camp, but he holds out hope for better times. "**October Hills**" has a Wordsworthian flavor and celebrates nature's healing of a human psyche under stress. "**A June Morning**" is an innocuous description of a pleasant outdoor scene.

Ridge's nature poems run the gamut of nineteenth-century romanticism and suggest he was familiar with major British and American romantics such as Byron, Shelley, Keats, Poe, and Bryant. Nature generally is congenial to human beings, rejuvenating both mind and spirit. It is also a source of poetic inspiration. Much of Ridge's nature poetry shares with that of other romantic writers the quest for ideality, often expressed as a spiritual figure that can be momentarily approached but not fully obtained. The true artist, however, continues the quest even though the goal is not attainable in this world; the artist then translates the experience of the quest for his audience, individuals who do not share his powers of perception. Found in Ridge's nature poetry, too, is the evil aspect of the quest. In nature is found not only the ideal, the pure and divine, but also the base and sordid. Nature can evoke hell and death as well as heaven and the eternal.

During this phase of his career, Ridge was having some success in publishing his poetic works. For example, "**The Woods**" was written on May 16, 1853, and published in the Sacramento *Union* on May 27. "**Eyes**" was printed in the *Daily Evening Herald* at Marysville on August 12, 1853, and on November 8 his famous poem on Mount Shasta was published in the same newspaper. But writing poetry for local and regional periodicals does not often pay well, and Ridge was forced to seek additional employment. His education and legal training helped him get an appointment as deputy clerk, auditor, and recorder for Yuba County at a salary of $135 a month. This, he reported in a letter to Stand Watie, was enough to give him "a pretty decent living and some surplus money." Some of that surplus was to go toward the purchase of 160 acres of government land, on which he planned to build a house as soon as his family could join him.[6] In the meantime, he was living at Tremont House on Second Street in Marysville.[7]

His plans to purchase land and build a new house in anticipation of his family's joining him in California suggest that Ridge had given up his ideas about returning to his people. Yet he reported to Stand Watie in September 1853 that he still yearned to go home:

> If I could have contented myself to remain permanently
> in the country I could have succeeded in making a
> fortune, but I have been struggling all the time to
> make one in a hurry so that I might return to Arkansas,
> and (I will say it to *you*) to the Cherokee Nation.[8]

Later in the same letter he states, "I intend some day sooner or later to plant my foot in the Cherokee nation and stay there, too, or die." He notes that he broached the subject of a return to his family earlier, with or without his fortune, but was rebuffed:

> I am tormented so by the folks at home whenever
> I talk of going back to the Nation, and they urge me
> in their letters so much not to venture to stay even

in Arkansas with my family that I am resolved to quiet their fears by providing for my family in this country so as to place them above all want; and then I will be at liberty to follow the bent of my mind which leads me back to my own people and to my own country.

His wish to return was fueled by two related things: his desire to avenge the deaths of his father, grandfather, and uncle and, just as important, his own sense that he too was the target of oppression by the Ross faction. He believed the Kell affair was only the first of actions to be taken against him by Cherokee rivals. He says,

> I had rather die than to surrender my rights. You recollect there is one gap in Cherokee history which needs filling up. Boudinot is dead, John Ridge and Major Ridge are dead, and they are but partially avenged. I don't know how you feel now Stand, but there was a time when that brave heart of yours grew dark over the memory of our wrongs.

At this point he is careful not to call Watie's bravery or loyalty into question, knowing full well that as leader of the Ridge party, Watie holds the key to his return. He says, "But we'll not talk about it because I believe you feel right yet and I admire your prudence in keeping so quiet." He then asks his cousin to let him know "how things stand, what are the prospects of coming safely out of a trial, etc., etc." He seems genuinely interested in returning home and says he would have done so before now had it not been for his mother. "It is only on my mother's account that I have stayed away so long. It was only on her account that I did not go back in '49 or the spring of '50 and risk my trial." Other members of the family apparently had also advised him to remain in California because, he says, every time he mentions the subject of returning all he hears is

> "danger, danger, danger," as though a man had to be governed by his *fears* in place of his reason and his judgment. The Lord deliver me from the advice of women. They never think of anything but the danger—the profits and advantages all go for nothing with them, if there is any risk to run at all!

Rollin's ideas on the subject of a return to Arkansas and the Cherokee Nation can best be described as ambivalent. He did write to Watie in 1855 suggesting that he return to Arkansas to establish an Indian newspaper, and he did make plans with J. W. Washbourne and E. C. Boudinot in the 1860s to form a partnership with them in the Cherokee country. On the other hand, there were the plans for the new house and the way his poetry and editorials describe California as a golden land of opportunity, an ideal place to carry out one's dreams. He seemed to be tugged in both directions.

In the fall of 1853 Ridge fell ill. His mother reported that he was suffering from "billious fever" which resulted in "ulceration of the bowels."[9] The situation was exacerbated because no family member was there to nurse him and tend to his needs; Aeneas had returned to Arkansas in August 1853. His condition was probably the immediate reason Elizabeth decided to travel to California to join her husband at that time. She and five-year-old Alice were living at Fayetteville, patiently awaiting the right opportunity for a reunion. Rollin's sickness must have been deemed dangerous, since Elizabeth set out alone, leaving Alice in the care of her grandmother, Sarah Ridge. Late in 1854 or early 1855, Alice was reunited with her parents when she traveled to California, apparently with Aeneas and his family. Lizzie left for New York in the company of a Fayetteville merchant and his wife on December 14, 1853. Once in New York, she traveled by ship to Central America, probably Nicaragua, and went overland to the Pacific Ocean. She then sailed to San Francisco, arriving early in 1854.[10] When she met her husband, she learned of his plans for a new literary venture, his story of the notorious California bandit Joaquín Murieta.

The Romance of Joaquín Murieta

John Rollin Ridge's *The Life and Adventures of Joaquín Murieta, the Celebrated California Bandit,* was published in 1854. The book was widely read and reviewed and, eventually, frequently plagiarized. Pirated versions appeared as books, were serialized in periodicals, and were translated into foreign languages. Adaptations appeared in verse, and at least one film was made based on Ridge's story. Although many of the versions were produced in the nineteenth century, others have appeared more recently, including Pablo Neruda's 1967 drama *Fulgor y Muerta de Joaquín Murieta.*

More important than the literary imitations, however, is that prominent historians of nineteenth-century California adopted Ridge's tale as an essentially true account of the affair. Ridge himself claims the story is true and important to the early history of the state. In the opening paragraph of the work he says his purpose is "to contribute my mite to those materials out of which the early history of California shall one day be composed" and asserts that Murieta's story "is a part of the most valuable history of the State."[1]

In a way it is. Murieta's story tells of the plight of "foreigners" in the goldfields of the early 1850s, of their unfair treatment by the "Americans," of resistance to the oppression, and of retaliation to the resistance. In California at the time, "Americans" were defined as white people from eastern states and territories who had settled there, but the definition also included white immigrants from Europe. The Irish,

Germans, French, and even people from Australia's convict settlements were "Americans" in the goldfields. Others, notably Peruvian, Chilean, Mexican, and Chinese newcomers to the state, were considered "foreigners," even though many of them had arrived in California before the great influx of miners known as the gold rush. Indeed, a large number of "foreign" miners were actually native Californians who had worked on the Mexican ranchos before the discovery of gold. White miners especially resented the foreigners because they believed most of them meant to mine all the gold they could and take it back to their countries rather than contributing to the growth of California as whites did. In formulating this hypothesis, the American miners conveniently overlooked the fact that most of their number had the same idea in mind; those who traveled to California, for the most part, planned to make their fortunes quickly and return home to their families and friends. Nonetheless, the resentment against non-European miners grew from 1849 on.

The problem was exacerbated by the large number of United States Army veterans of the Mexican War who became gold miners. They harbored little love for the people they had recently been fighting and probably made little distinction between Mexicans and Spanish-speaking Chileans or Peruvians. The conquerors also saw little reason to share "American" gold with the conquered, especially when the goldfields were as crowded as Ridge found the area around Placerville in 1850. The veterans' attitudes were bolstered by the actions of General Persifer F. Smith, the military commander of California, who had formerly served in Mexico. Smith, in a letter to the American consul in Panama that was widely published in South American and Mexican newspapers, declared that it was illegal for foreigners to mine for gold on public land in California.[2] His vow to enforce the law spread fear in Latin American countries and encouraged vigilantism against Spanish-speaking miners. As early as 1849, vigilantes moved against Chileans, Peruvians, and Mexicans who were digging near Sutter's Mill.[3] Violence directed at foreigners in other gold camps was common during the period.

Opposition to foreign miners spread to the state legislature. Its members sent a memorial to Congress in 1849 claiming that "during the year, swarms of foreigners had come, worked in the mines, and extracted thousands of dollars, without contributing anything to the support of the government or people."[4] When no support was forthcoming from Washington, the legislature took action and passed a law that became known as the foreign miners tax. Passed on April 13, 1850, the law provided that all foreigners pay a tax of $20 a month to allow them to mine gold. Collectors were to receive $3 for every tax paid and were empowered to seize the property of those who refused to pay. The legislature estimated that the state treasury would receive as much as $500,000 a month from the tax, but actual revenues were much lower, largely because many collectors simply pocketed the entire $20.

June 1, 1850, was the first day the tax was to be collected, and most people expected trouble. When the collectors moved into the mining camps, however, they found that the Spanish Americans were packing up and leaving the mines. Because the foreigners constituted such a large percentage of the population of the mining towns, up to half in some cases, the impact of their leaving was felt immediately and severely by the businesses that supplied the mines with goods and services. Merchants in Stockton and Sacramento, cities that depended on the mines for business, led the fight to repeal the law. Their voices were heard, and the bill was found unconstitutional by the California Supreme Court. The legislature repealed it on March 14, 1851.[5]

Repeal of the law did not end the animosity between the "Americans" and the "foreigners," however, and the violence continued. Spanish-American miners were insulted and attacked; many were unjustly accused of crimes, given summary trials by the whites, and punished. When they were effectively forced out of the mines by white violence, many Mexicans and others turned to robbery and even murder. They raided the farms and ranches of the area, stealing livestock and other valuables. For a time, open warfare existed between the two groups.

Resentment among the Spanish Americans was fueled by several factors: many of the foreign miners were veterans who had fought on the Mexican side in the recent war; most native Californians believed that the provisions of the Treaty of Guadalupe Hidalgo had not been honored completely by the United States; the large land-grant ranchos were being broken up, leaving most of their dependents destitute and homeless; and the new American California had a distinctive racial bias, especially against Spanish Americans and Orientals. Because of these factors, it is not hard to see why Spanish-speaking Californians turned outlaw and were regarded as patriots by people of similar backgrounds.[6]

Shortly after Ridge arrived in California, the newspapers were full of reports of Mexican banditti stealing livestock, holding up businesses, and waylaying travelers. Some of the bandits organized into large bands and became well known. The leaders of some of these bands have been identified as Solomon Pico, Pio Linares, Silvestrano Chavez, Jesus Castro, and Joaquín Lugo.[7] But many of the accounts identified the leader simply as "Joaquín"; as time went on and Joaquín's stature as a superbandit grew, he was assigned several surnames, including Murieta (or Murrieta or Murietta), Valenzuela, Carrillo, Ocomorenia (spelled by Ridge as O'Comorenia), and Botellier (or Botilleras). It is not known whether all five existed or whether one or more

Joaquíns operated using aliases. Ridge's explanation is that there were only two Joaquíns, the other names being aliases. Joaquín Valenzuela was merely the lieutenant of Joaquín Murieta, who, Ridge writes, was the "Rinaldo Rinaldini of California."[8] In any case, Joaquín became the scourge of the state. Such was his prowess that he seemed able to be in two places at once, robbing a saloon in one town as he terrorized miners in another. He robbed both whites and Orientals but refrained from molesting Mexicans or other Spanish Americans. In return he was protected by members of the Spanish-speaking population, who provided him with hideouts and refused to cooperate with the authorities trying to catch him.

Joaquín's career continued for three years, 1851 through 1853. Newspaper accounts and purported interviews with the bandit provide a sketchy account of his life and the events that led him into banditry.[9] Joaquín Murieta reportedly had fought in the Mexican War as one of the Jurate guerrillas. He moved to Los Angeles in 1849, where he fell in love with Rosita Felix, whose father opposed Murieta's display of affection. The couple consequently eloped and moved to Shaw's Flat, where Joaquín engaged in mining. After a short time, a group of Americans approached him and told him Mexicans were not allowed to mine for gold in that area. When Murieta protested, he was beaten and his wife was insulted. In some versions Rosita was raped in front of her husband. He started mining in another spot but was forced off that claim as well. According to the tradition, he tried gambling for a living, setting up a monte game at Murphy's Flat. But there too he ran into trouble with Americans who tried to run him out of the camp. In a final outrage, Murieta was unjustly accused of stealing by a mob who probably seized upon the first Mexican they could find. He was summarily judged guilty, tied to a tree, and flogged. In one version of the story, Joaquín's half-brother was hanged by the American mob. After this episode Joaquín, who said he had liked Americans until he moved to California, vowed to retaliate. He organized his outlaw band, drawing on desperadoes such as the notorious Manuel García, or Three-Finger Jack, and began his campaign of revenge. It was not long before Joaquín too was well known as a bandit and killer.

As his notoriety spread, so did stories concerning his exploits. George Tinkham supplies the following anecdotes, the first of which appeared in Ridge's *Joaquín Murieta:*

> Joaquín's most daring exploit was at Stockton. Upon a house there was tacked a large poster: $5000 for the body of Joaquín Murieta DEAD OR ALIVE.

> While a number of persons were standing reading the poster a Mexican rode up. Dismounting, he wrote beneath, "I will give $10,000 myself.—

Joaquín Murietta." With a quick spring he again mounted his horse and swiftly rode away.[10]

Another reported exploit concerns one of Murieta's frequent visits to Marysville about the time Ridge lived there:

> On one occasion he visited Marysville and, entering a saloon, began playing monte. During the play the conversation turned to Joaquín Murietta and his crimes. One of the braggarts at the table exclaimed, "I would give $1,000 for a shot at Murietta." The daring bandit sprung upon the table and shouted, "You cowardly gringo, look, I am Murietta." Before the astonished players could collect their senses, Joaquín jumped from the table, ran to his horse and quickly rode from sight.

Still another story of the bandit's bravery was doubtless heard by Ridge and contributed to his curiosity about Joaquín:

> At a fandango one evening it was reported that Joaquín would be present. Quietly a party was organized to catch him. The would-be detectives entered the room and made inquiry of every one present if they had seen Murietta. One dancer replied to the deputy sheriff, "Yes, I have seen him, but I do not know where he is at present." The next day the deputy was chagrined to learn that he had been conversing with the much sought bandit.

Reports like these circulated and were eagerly picked up by newspapers, as were accounts of all the crimes attributed to Murieta and his band. Citizens of various districts where Joaquín operated, particularly around Mariposa, Tuolumne, and Calaveras counties, were terrified. Enough of them left the area in fear of the bandits that local government and business became alarmed. Petitions were sent to the governor and state legislature demanding protection. Governor John Bigler announced a $1,000 reward for the capture of Joaquín, an amount deemed entirely too small by the citizens of the Mother Lode area, which had been most seriously affected. The petitions continued, and considerable pressure was put on the politicians in Sacramento by constituents and rivals. Finally, in 1853 it was proposed that a group of twenty to twenty-five men be organized to track down and capture or kill Murieta and his band. Several ad hoc posses had set out in pursuit of the bandits over the years, but they had all been spectacularly unsuccessful, adding to Joaquín's reputation for cunning and daring. On May 17, 1853, Governor Bigler signed a bill authorizing the creation of a group to be called the California Rangers, under the leadership of Captain Harry Love. The group would remain in existence for three months, and the rangers would receive $150 each. The men were also eligible for the $1,000 reward.

The call to establish the California Rangers stated that the group's purpose was to capture the robbers under the leadership of the five Joaquíns: Muriati [sic], Carillo, Ocomorenia, Valenzuela, and Botellier.[11] William Secrest reports that the problem of identification was cleared up when Valenzuela was captured at San Luis Obispo. Before he was hanged, Valenzuela, who had been Murieta's lieutenant, testified that Murieta had used the aliases Carillo, Ocomorenia, and Botellier. Newspaper reports of the time used all five names at various times, with widely variant spellings, adding to the confusion. After Ridge's book was published the identity of the bandit chief was widely accepted, though some denied he was ever caught. Ridge's spelling of his surname was accepted as well, though occasionally an extra r or t was added. William Secrest says the correct spelling is probably Murrieta.[12]

Whatever the name of the bandit chieftain, Harry Love was in charge of bringing him—or them—to justice. Love had been nominated in a petition signed by a hundred citizens of Mariposa County. A native Texan, he had been serving as deputy sheriff of Los Angeles County. He had been a scout and messenger in the Mexican War and had fought in the Texas border wars. The newly appointed captain, aided no doubt by his reputation and his six-foot-two frame, easily recruited twenty men at Quartzburgh in Mariposa County. The group included a former army colonel and two medical doctors in addition to some young adventurers.[13] Armed with pistols, rifles, and Bowie knives, the Rangers divided into scouting parties and set out to capture or kill the bandits.

For the next two months the California Rangers traveled around Mariposa County chasing bandits, recovering stolen livestock, and keeping the peace. In July they headed north tracking a suspected band of Mexican horse thieves as far as Tulare Lake. On July 24, 1853, northwest of the present city of Coalinga, they came upon a group of Mexicans camped on Cantua Creek. William Byrnes, one of Love's lieutenants, reportedly recognized Murieta from when the two had gambled in earlier days. A fight ensued, and four bandits were killed. Among the fallen were Murieta and Three-Finger Jack. Two of the band were captured and others escaped, but the rangers had done their job.

Now they needed to authenticate their victory. They decided to decapitate Murieta and García and preserve their heads in alcohol. García's mutilated hand was included for good measure. Two of the rangers were dispatched to Millerton carrying their grisly cargo in a flour sack; their orders were to find a preservative for the heads and hand. On the way, García's head began to deteriorate rapidly in the summer sun because of bullet wounds, and so it was discarded. When they reached Millerton, they deposited their trophies in a keg of whiskey. Meanwhile, Love and the rest of the rangers took off in unsuccessful pursuit of the escaped members of the band. They joined their comrades in Millerton, where the head and hand were transferred to a large glass jar of spirits. They then brought the jar back to Sacramento after collecting affidavits at Quartzburgh and Stockton stating that the head was indeed Murieta's. They collected their reward and ninety days' pay; later the legislature rewarded them with an extra $5,000. For years afterward, the preserved head was on public display in California and elsewhere. It perished in 1906 during the San Francisco earthquake and fire.

In spite of the affidavits, many people refused to believe it was Murieta who had been killed. Some, including the editor of the San Francisco *Alta California,* stated that the whole affair had been a fraud.[14] The argument went on for a while, but the outlaw depredations had largely stopped, and the legend began to grow.

For a number of reasons, it would have been hard for John Rollin Ridge to resist setting the legend down on paper. First, he lived and traveled in the region where Joaquín and other bandits operated. According to a report, Murieta had a sister in Marysville whom he visited frequently in 1850 and 1851, when Ridge was in the area.[15] It is likely that Ridge heard the stories of Murieta's exploits and read about him in the newspapers, especially when the sensational details of the Love expedition were published. Second, Ridge had already launched his writing career, having had both poetry and prose published in the *True Delta* and in various California periodicals. Here was a ready subject, since by this time he was thoroughly familiar with the background of the disputes between the "Americans" and "foreigners"; he could provide a good sense of the setting from his travels in the area; and he knew people he could model his characters on. As for the plot, it had already been supplied by the bandits, the legislature and governor, and Harry Love's rangers. Ridge knew a good story when he saw it. Another major factor in his decision to write the story was a problem that he had grappled with before and that would haunt him in the future: a shortage of money. With much of California buzzing about Murieta's exploits as reported in often conflicting newspaper accounts, the possibility of offering the whole story to an audience hungry for it must have seemed a financial opportunity too good to pass up. Finally, Joaquín himself must have fascinated Ridge. Here was a man who had tried to live peacefully despite wrongs inflicted on his family and friends. Joaquín's only crime at first was that he did not belong to the faction in power. Driven over the brink by his enemies, he had to react violently. This action forced him into exile, where his intelligence and courage let him revenge himself on his persecutors. He was admired by his own people and feared by his enemies. In many ways Joaquín's early history was much like that of the writer who was to immortalize him; his later career had to appeal to Ridge's deep thirst for revenge. More important, in Joaquín Ridge had found a kindred soul, with the same personality and motivation. Telling his story was natural.

Ridge finished his *Life and Adventures of Joaquín Murieta* in late spring 1854. The copyright was applied for on June 3. Curiously, though the copyright listed the names of both Ridge and Charles Lindley, there is no evidence that Lindley assisted Ridge at all. No subsequent claim to authorship by Lindley has ever been found.[16] The book was published on August 3, 1854, by William B. Cooke and Company, Booksellers and Stationers, of San Francisco. It apparently was widely sold around the state. References to it appear in mining district towns such as Sonora and Weaverville,[17] and an advertisement for it ran in the San Francisco *Daily Placer Times and Transcript.*[18] *The Life and Adventures of Joaquín Murieta, the Celebrated California Bandit* was ninety pages long. It was bound with yellow paper covers and contained two lithographs, one representing Joaquín and another Harry Love. The title page identified the author as "Yellow Bird."[19]

Ridge's book was reviewed by the San Francisco *Daily California Chronicle* on August 7, 1854. The review emphasizes the controversy over Joaquín Murieta, and it, along with the author's published reply, probably helped sales considerably. The *Chronicle* identifies Ridge as "a cross breed of the Cherokees." His style is "respectable, and is an argument favorable to Indian capacity." The reviewer adds, "It might be said also that the fancy of the author is undoubtedly equal to the style of his writing." This comment is interesting because it raises the issue whether Ridge was writing fiction or history. The question was to be debated until the present.

The *Chronicle* review goes on to say that there is little to commend the book for and that the reviewer has no taste for tales of horror. The *Life and Adventures of Joaquín Murieta* is full of atrocities and gratuitous violence, the reviewer says, then adds, "It leaves Jack Sheppard to the rear, and makes the sins of Bluebeard appear mere peccadillos." But the part of the review Ridge most took offense to was the following:

> The book may serve as very amusing reading for Joaquín Murieta, should he get hold of it, for notwithstanding all which has been said and published to the contrary, we have little faith in his reported death at the hands of Love's party. The whole affair savors much of gammon, and the head which was exhibited might as well have been claimed as belonging to Lopez as Joaquín.[20]

This statement expresses an opinion shared by many Californians that the real Joaquín was never captured.

Reports said he had escaped Love's rangers and had either adopted the life of a peaceful California rancher or returned in triumph to Sonora. In any event, the reviewer's words challenged Ridge's public claim of his story's authenticity, which he deemed important to the book's sales. For this reason he felt it necessary to respond to the *Chronicle* review.

He did so in a letter published in the *Daily Placer Times and Transcript* in San Francisco. The letter, sent August 21 from Marysville, was later reprinted.[21] In it Ridge recounts the *Chronicle* reviewer's contention that Joaquín is not dead. To this he retorts, "Prove it!" He then invites the reviewer to duplicate his own research, to travel over the state as he did, consult the files of different newspapers that have published authenticated accounts of Joaquín, and converse with those who knew the bandit personally. Ridge thus reveals his own research methods. He goes on to say that the governor, the legislature, and the Chinese merchants of San Francisco were convinced enough of Joaquín's death to pay Love and his men handsome rewards. He then promises, "In the next edition of my work, I shall prove that he is dead beyond all hope of resurrection."

That Ridge was contemplating a second edition a little over three weeks after the first appeared is puzzling. It may be that the copies printed had sold much more quickly than anticipated, making a second edition necessary. Ridge reported a press run of seven thousand to Stand Watie, but this number seems high, especially since only three copies still exist. That he was thinking about a second edition seems clear, however. He gives an account of his life of Joaquín to Stand Watie in a letter sent from Marysville on October 9, 1854. As in many of his letters to his cousin, he says he needs money and is beset by circumstances beyond his control. After commenting on the whereabouts of Watie's brother Charles, Ridge reports on the fortunes of his book.

> For my own part, I am struggling along with adversity as well as I may. I expected to have made a great deal of money off of my book, my life of Joaquín Murieta (a copy of which I have sent you) and my publishers, after selling 7,000 copies and putting the money in their pockets, fled bursted up *tee totally* smashed, and left me, with a hundred others, to whistle for our money! Undaunted by this streak of back luck, I have sent the work on to the Atlantic States for a new edition, and when that is sold out I will have a few thousand dollars at my command. There is not so much danger of one of those heavy eastern houses failing as these mushroom California concerns at San Francisco.[22]

There are two problems with this account. First, there is no record or subsequent mention of negotiations to publish a second edition with an eastern firm. Second, the William Cooke Company did not go out of business as Ridge asserts. No record has ever been found of the company's bankruptcy. Further, the San Francisco city directory for 1855 lists Cooke as doing business half a block from where he had been a year before.[23] If he fled, he did not go far. Ridge was doubtless trying to put the best face on his affairs. Much of the rest of the letter involves an attempt to get Watie to finance an Indian-oriented newspaper that Ridge would edit, and projecting financial success as a writer might help in this endeavor. In any case, a second edition was not immediately forthcoming.

The San Francisco *California Police Gazette* printed in ten weekly installments "The Life of Joaquín Murieta, Brigand Chief of California" in 1859. This version, obviously pirated from Ridge's account, was published from September 3 to November 5. Three weeks after the serialization, a seventy-one-page pamphlet of the pirated version appeared, illustrated by the noted California artist Charles C. Nahl.[24] This account is based on Ridge's text, but the sequence of events is altered and its language is sometimes garbled.[25] Although some of the facts have been changed, the *Police Gazette* version obviously follows Ridge's account closely. The biggest variant is the omission of Rosita as Murieta's wife and the substitution of two mistresses, Carmela and Clarita. Ridge was quick to complain about the obvious plagiarism in the pages of the Marysville *Daily National Democrat,* which he was editing by that time.[26] His complaints got him nowhere, however, and the *Police Gazette* account became very popular. It was used in many of the versions that followed.

The edition of Yellow Bird's book that appeared in 1871 was dubbed the third, perhaps a sarcastic reference to the obviously pirated *Police Gazette* version. Although the publishers claimed that before his death Ridge had "prepared a revised edition of his story of Joaquín Murieta, to which he had added much new and heretofore unpublished material," this claim has never been authenticated. Ridge, assuming he did work on the 1871 edition, comments on the plagiarism in the Author's Preface: "A spurious edition has been foisted upon unsuspecting publishers and by them circulated, to the infringement of the author's copyright and the damage of his literary credit—the spurious work, with its crude interpolations, fictitious additions, and imperfectly designed distortions of the author's phraseology, being by many persons confounded with the original performance."[27]

The 1871 edition does include some new material, including more description of the scene in which Murieta is flogged and an account of a raid at Mono Lake. In addition, it carries the Author's Preface mentioned above, supposedly written by Ridge before his death.[28] Ridge, of course, may have worked on a revised edition as early as 1854; we know he at least contemplated such a work. Ironically, the posthumous *Joaquín Murieta* was much better received than the original.

Remi Nadeau reports that the pirated *Police Gazette* version was the basis for the many subsequent Joaquín stories. Even before Ridge's "third" edition, a New York publisher came out with an adventure yarn, "Joaquín (the Claude Duval of California); or the Marauder of the Mines," in 1865. Claude Duval was a celebrated English highwayman in the seventeenth century. Joseph E. Badger, Jr., published his Joaquín story in Beadle's Dime Library in 1881; Joaquín novels were subsequently published in France and Spain. The Spanish translation was published in Santiago, Chile, and its hero is not Mexican but Chilean. Other versions included a biography by El Professor Acigar, published in Barcelona, and one by Ireneo Paz in Mexico City. By this time the tale had become greatly embellished, according to Nadeau. Whereas the *Police Gazette* edition was 71 pages long, Paz manages to extend Joaquín's life and adventures to 281 pages. As many as a dozen other versions of the story appeared in the twentieth century, including *The Robin Hood of El Dorado,* by Walter Noble Burns. Burns, a popular writer of westerns, accepted many of the additions to the story by earlier writers.[29]

The Joaquín legend extended to genres other than fiction. Cincinnatus Hiner Miller wrote a long poem called "Californian" and published it in his *Songs of the Sierras.*[30] The poem is original in the sense that though its main character is Joaquín, it depicts a wounded Joaquín fleeing his enemies and describes his eventual death. Later Miller greatly condensed "Californian" and published it as "Joaquin Murietta." At the end of the truncated version, the poet adds this note:

> The third poem in my first London book, if I remember—you see I never kept my books about me, nor indeed any books now, and have for present use only a copy that has been many times revised and cut down—was called "California," [*sic*] but it was called "Joaquin" in the Oregon book. And it was from this that I was, in derision, called "Joaquin." I kept the name and the poem too, till both were at least respected. But my brother, who had better judgment and finer taste than I, thought it too wild and bloody; and so by degrees it has been allowed to almost entirely disappear, except this fragment, although a small book of itself, to begin with.[31]

Miller kept the name Joaquin, however, and today he is known as one of the premier nineteenth-century western writers.

The story did not escape the attention of the dramatists either. In 1858 a five-act play by Charles E. B. Howe reenacted the legend. Other dramatic presentations were to follow, including a pageant in 1927 by B. Ignacio Ortega, a romantic comedy by Charles D. McGettian produced in San Francisco in 1932, and a Chilean production in 1936 by A. Acevedo Hernandez. Pablo

Neruda's 1967 play on Murieta is overtly political; it depicts Joaquín as an early victim of Yankee imperialism. In 1936 Hollywood produced a film version of the story starring Warner Baxter. At the same time, the story was serialized in newspapers by western writer Peter B. Kyne, who claimed that his series was based on Burns's earlier novel.

But not only was Ridge's tale picked up by writers of popular literature and poets like Miller and Neruda, important nineteenth-century historians, apparently believing Ridge's claim of authenticity, adopted it as real biography. Hubert Howe Bancroft, in his *History of California,* takes his "facts" from Ridge's 1871 edition, including even the episode in which Joaquín, by writing on the reward poster, offers to increase the price on his head. Theodore H. Hittell, another major historian, adopted Ridge's story as well. For chapter 4 of his *History of California,* "Joaquín Murieta and his Banditti," he extracts his information almost exclusively from the 1871 edition, as his own footnotes readily show.[32] Ridge's story, then, passed not only into the popular imagination, but into the history books as well.

In his introduction to the University of Oklahoma Press edition of Ridge's book (1986), Joseph Henry Jackson concludes that Ridge decided California needed a folk hero and set about creating one. Jackson discounts the authenticity Ridge claims, calling the Joaquín story a "myth." He does say, though, that the basic story was there: Mexicans and other "foreigners" had been mistreated, many of them had turned to crime, one of these had been named Joaquín Murieta, and Captain Love and his men did kill someone they claimed was Joaquín and pickled his head. Jackson goes on, "What form the legend might have taken if left to itself is impossible to determine, for very soon something happened to give it shape. This was the publication of the small, paper-covered book . . . the preposterous, fantastical tale out of which Californians were gradually to construct the folk hero they unconsciously wanted."[33]

Whether Californians were seeking a hero in their heart of hearts is not clear. What is clear is that John Rollin Ridge's *Life and Adventures of Joaquín Murieta* is not pure history, but it is not pure fiction, either. It is more like today's television "docudramas" or the currently fashionable news novels, productions based loosely on history but liberally sprinkled with embellishments and added emphasis designed to titillate the audience. There is no doubt that *Joaquín* was meant to be sensational. That Ridge wanted a best-seller, the equivalent of a box office smash, is clear from his letter to Stand Watie; he expected to make money from his book—if not from the first edition, then from a subsequent one. Money was his prime motivation, and his quest for literary fame was a close second.

As for the historical part of the tale, it is clear that Ridge gathered his basic information from newspaper stories of the day. The major episodes in Ridge's book had been reported, reprinted, and rehashed, with or without the gory details, in the local press. There was no need for him to invent the story out of whole cloth. The accuracy of the press accounts is another thing, however. As Angus MacLean points out, "it seems highly improbable that any one man with a following of twenty to thirty men could possibly have committed so many atrocities, over so wide a territory, in so short a time, as the hysteria of the times attributed to 'Joaquín'; so logic would say that Joaquín Murrieta and his men were getting the blame for all these crimes even though they were not the only foxes raiding the chicken coop."[34] Since Ridge relied to a large extent on contemporary newspaper accounts, it is possible and even likely that some of his facts were not straight, no matter how conscientious he had been in his research or how dedicated he was to historical accuracy. Nonetheless, the meat for his literary stew was provided to him.

That *Joaquín's* author embellished the basic story is beyond doubt. For example, he includes in his narrative verbatim records of conversations he could never have heard. In one instance Joaquín and his men come across a party of young American hunters. Although the Americans have not threatened the bandits, Joaquín suspects they have recognized him and feels his only recourse is to kill them to prevent their reporting his presence in the area. When he tells the hunters what is in store, one of them, "a young man, originally from the wilds of Arkansas, not more than eighteen years of age, [advances] in front of his trembling comrades" and bravely addresses the bandit captain. He promises not to reveal his group's encounter with Joaquín and furthermore vows to shoot any of his companions who attempts to do so. Joaquín, taken with the man's bravery, allows the hunters to leave unharmed. Ridge's comments follow: "I have never learned that the young man, or any of his party, broke their singular compact." If the hunters never broke their silence, it is difficult to understand how Ridge came upon the story, unless he was concealed nearby, close enough to overhear the conversation, and had his pencil and notebook handy. Even if one gives credence to Ridge's claim that he interviewed people acquainted with Murieta, it is difficult to account for the verbatim reports of whole conversations. It is as if Ridge were a Joseph Conrad recording one of Marlowe's incredible feats of memory.

In another episode one of the bandit chasers, a Captain Ellas, rides into Yankee camp and sees a young Mexican, who pulls down his sombrero and lays his hand on his pistol when he sees the American. But Ellas leaves without recognizing Joaquín or, Ridge reports, even knowing the bandit has been in the area. Here again it is difficult to see how the episode was brought to Ridge's attention or, for that matter, was known to anyone outside Joaquín's band. Similar problems in the book suggest the author gave himself a free hand in writing his "history." This artistic license is appropriate to an author who was out to exploit a situation in the news of the day and to present a sensational and profitable tale to an audience eager to hear about a dashing, handsome hero and his forays into romance and danger, all heavily laced with sex and violence. Writers looking for a quick profit have not changed much over the years, nor have their audiences.

One interesting aspect of Ridge's **Joaquín** is the way the author describes his hero. Physically, Joaquín bears a strong resemblance to his biographer, according to photographs and written descriptions of Ridge:

> He was then eighteen years of age, a little over the medium height, slenderly but gracefully built, and active as a young tiger. His complexion was neither very dark or very light, but clear and brilliant, and his countenance is pronounced to have been, at that time, exceedingly handsome and attractive. His large black eyes, kindling with the enthusiasm of his earnest nature, his firm and well-formed mouth, his well-shaped head from which the long, glossy, black hair hung down over his shoulders, his silvery voice full of generous utterance, and the frank and cordial bearing which distinguished him made him beloved by all with whom he came in contact.[35]

These words could have come from the pen of Sarah Ridge in a description of her eldest son. Joaquín's situation before his troubles with the Americans is also described.

> He had built him a comfortable mining residence in which he had domiciled his heart's treasure—a beautiful Sonorian girl, who had followed the young adventurer in all his wanderings with that devotedness of passion which belongs to the dark-eyed damsels of Mexico. It was at this moment of peace and felicity that a blight came over the young man's prospects.

Joaquín and his wife are in a position analogous to that of Elizabeth and Rollin Ridge at Honey Creek before the episode with Kell. It is hard to tell whether Ridge discovered similarities between himself and Joaquín in his research for the book or created Joaquín in his own image and likeness.

In any event, **The Life and Adventures of Joaquín Murieta** made an impact on the popular imagination in several countries. In addition, largely through the efforts of Bancroft and Hittell, it had an influence on California history—the book was judged by Robert Cowan to be one of "the twenty rarest and most important works dealing with the history of California."[36] The respect Ridge yearned for was achieved,

but not till six decades after his death. The profit he expected never developed, at least for him.

Notes

Romantic Poet

[1] Foreman, "Bushyhead and Ridge," 303.

[2] Walker, *Literary Frontier.*

[3] All poetry quotations are from Ridge's *Poems* (1868) unless otherwise noted.

[4] *Hutchings's California Magazine,* April 1859.

[5] May Wentworth, ed., *Poetry of the Pacific* (San Francisco: Hubert H. Bancroft, 1866). Cited in Walker, *San Francisco's Literary Frontier,* 218.

[6] Stand Watie Miscellaneous File, Western History Collections, University of Oklahoma Library, September 23, 1853.

[7] C. P. Hale and Fred Emory, *Hale and Emory's Marysville City Directory* (Marysville, Calif.: Marysville Herald Office, 1853), 38.

[8] Stand Watie Miscellaneous File, Western History Collections, University of Oklahoma Library, September 23, 1853.

[9] Cornwall School Records, S. B. N. Ridge to Eliza Northrup, January 18, 1854.

[10] Ibid.

The Romance of Joaquín Murieta

[1] Ridge, *Joaquín Murieta,* ed. Jackson, 7.

[2] Clough, *Joaquín Murieta,* xiii-xiv.

[3] Ibid., xiv.

[4] George Henry Tinkham, *California Men and Events* (Stockton, Calif.: Record, 1915), 127.

[5] Ibid., 129.

[6] Ridge, *Joaquín Murieta,* ed. Jackson, xvi-xvii.

[7] Angus MacLean, *Legends of the California Bandidos* (Fresno, Calif.: Pioneer Press, 1977), 68.

[8] Ridge, *Joaquín Murieta,* ed. Jackson, 7.

[9] Two good sources for these reports are Tinkham's book and William B. Secrest's *Joaquín* (Fresno,

Calif.: Saga-West, 1967). Both contend that Joaquín was a Mexican. Others disagree, claiming he came from South America. See Jay Monaghan, *Chile, Peru, and the California Gold Rush of 1849* (Berkeley: University of California Press, 1973), 214.

[10] Tinkham, *Men and Events,* 132-33n.

[11] Frank F. Latta, *Joaquin Murieta and His Horse Gangs* (Santa Cruz, Calif.: Bear State Books, 1980), 328.

[12] Secrest, *Joaquín,* 32.

[13] Ibid.

[14] San Francisco *Alta California,* August 23, 1853, quoted in Ridge, *Joaquín Murieta,* ed. Jackson, xxv.

[15] *History of Nevada County, California* (N.p.: Thompson and West, 1879), 115.

[16] Hugh Sanford Cheney Baker, "The Book Trade in California, 1849-1859," *California Historical Society Quarterly* 30 (December 1951): 353.

[17] Ibid., 30 (September 1951): 251.

[18] *Daily Placer Times and Transcript,* August 25-30, p. 4, col. 3.

[19] Walker, "Ridge's Editions Compared," 257.

[20] *Daily California Chronicle,* August 7, 1954, 2-3.

[21] Yellow Bird, "Joaquín Murieta," *Daily Placer Times and Transcript,* August 25, 1854, 4.

[22] Dale and Litton, *Cherokee Cavaliers,* 83.

[23] Ridge, *Joaquín Murieta,* ed. Jackson, xxxii.

[24] Nadeau, *Real Joaquín,* 123.

[25] Ridge, *Joaquín Murieta,* ed. Jackson, xxxii.

[26] Nadeau, *Real Joaquín,* 124.

[27] Ridge, *Joaquín Murieta,* ed. Jackson, xxxii.

[28] Nadeau, *Real Joaquín,* 121.

[29] Ibid., 124.

[30] Cincinnatus Hiner Miller, *Songs of the Sierras* (Boston: Roberts Brother, 1871), 67-105.

[31] Joaquin Miller, *The Complete Poetical Works* (San Francisco: Whitaker and Ray, 1897), 40.

[32] Hubert Howe Bancroft, *History of California,* vol. 7 (San Francisco: History Company, 1890), 203; and Theodore H. Hittell, *History of California,* vol. 3 (San Francisco: N. J. Stone, 1897), 712-26.

[33] Ridge, *Joaquín Murieta,* ed. Jackson, xxvii.

[34] MacLean, *Legends,* 69.

[35] Ridge, *Joaquín Murieta,* ed. Jackson, 8-9.

[36] Robert M. Cowan, "The Twenty Rarest and Most Important Works Dealing with the History of California," *California Historical Society Quarterly* 10 (March 1931): 79-83.

Peter G. Christensen (essay date 1991-1992)

SOURCE: "Minority Interaction in John Rollin Ridge's *The Life and Adventures of Joaquin Murieta,*" in *MELUS,* University of Massachusetts, Summer, 1991-1992, pp. 61-72.

[*In the following essay, Christensen analyzes Ridge's portrayal of different ethnic groups, including Mexicans, Chinese, and Native Americans, in* Joaquín Murieta.]

The Life and Adventures of Joaquin Murieta, the Celebrated California Bandit (1854) by John Rollin Ridge (1827-1867) begins two traditions in American literature. Not only is it the first novel written in English by a person of Native American ancestry, it is also the first novel by an American in English treating the Mexican community of post-Mexican War California.[1] Surprisingly, critics of the novel have as yet failed to look closely at this cultural intersection and analyze Ridge's depiction of different ethnic groups in the novel.

Increased attention is bound to come Ridge's way soon. The new *Heath Antholology of American Literature* edited by Paul Lauter includes three selections by Ridge, two poems and an essay on Indian affairs, even though there are no excerpts from *Joaquin Murieta.* In their two-page discussion of Ridge (1: 1772-73), James W. Parins and Andrew G. Wiget note four attitudes characteristic of Ridge's thought: he urges all Indians to become "civilized" and assimilate; 2) he "celebrates[s] the expansion of United States power and human technological mastery over nature"; 3) he has an "ambivalent" stance toward the traditional concerns of his people; and 4) he believes that less acculturated Indians need to be protected during the transitional period. The ambivalence of his concerns for Native Americans can be extended to other minority groups in the United States, such as Mexicans and Chinese laborers, as we find in *Joaquin Murieta.*

This dimension of the novel is not made clear in the preface to the currently available paperback edition (written for the 1955 edition) by Joseph Henry Jackson. Unfortunately, the University of Oklahoma Press has not had this essay updated and revised, and it still serves as the principal introduction to the novel, especially for students. Jackson misread the novel as a Robin Hood story, supplying an emphasis on the redistribution of wealth that is not there. In addition, he did not have available to him either the later researches of Remi Nadeau (1974) and Frank F. Latta (1980) which establish the historical basis for the Murieta gang or the collection of Ridge's essays on Native American issues, *A Trumpet of Our Own,* edited by David Farmer and Rennard Strickland in 1981.[2]

Although Ridge was dedicated to seeing justice done for the Cherokee Nation, and he hoped that it would be admitted to the Union as a state, we should not allow this attitude to cloud our evaluation of *Joaquin Murieta.* Here Ridge is not as concerned with justice to the Mexicans as he is with courage and heroism in the face of oppression. Ridge champions the Mexicans for facing the American oppressors, for they have organized a heroic resistance, even if their retaliation methods are often characterized by murder and violence aimed at innocent people. In contrast, American Indians and Chinese immigrants in the novel do not receive this praise, since they act cowardly. This lack of empathy for these unfortunates is reflected in Ridge's philosophical poem **"Mount Shasta, Seen from a Distance,"** written in 1852 and inserted early in the novel. Although this poem is not about minority groups, it praises noble isolation rather than group spirit and gives a hierarchical view of the world. A look at Ridge's essays on the so-called Digger Indians and his other poems reveals that he has a scale of values in which some Native American tribes, such as the Cherokee, Aztecs, and Incas are seen as the superior representatives of their race.

One might initially be surprised that Ridge did not choose to write a novel chiefly about injustice to American Indians or about bloodshed among the factions of the Cherokee Nation. After all, he was the son and grandson of leaders of the Treaty Party, which agreed in 1835 to removal beyond the Mississippi. His father, John Ridge, held twenty-one slaves in 1835 (Halliburton 192), and the family lived like well-off Southern planters. The elder Ridge was murdered at his home in 1839 by the rival Cherokee faction of John Ross, but his son escaped. The younger Ridge moved to Fayetteville, Arkansas, with his mother after the assassination. In his late teens he killed a member of the Ross faction and in 1850 headed for the California gold fields. After some years as a miner, he became a full-time journalist. Although as a newspaper editor Ridge denounced secession as treason (Foreman 304), he was very much opposed to Abraham Lincoln (305).

At the end of the Civil War, he led the Southern Cherokee delegates to Washington, D.C., trying "to secure federal recognition of a Southern Cherokee Nation, separate and distinct from the Cherokees under Ross" (Wilkins 344). However, his efforts were unsuccessful (see Cherokee Nation 1866) and he died in 1867, one year after Ross.

Despite these vivid events in his life, Ridge chose not to focus his novel directly on Native Americans, and American Indian themes are at the heart of only a few of his poems.[3] Probably this decision comes from the fact that he favored assimilation, and his audience was primarily white. Furthermore, Frank F. Latta suggests that he was one-eighth Cherokee (352). Ridge's skin was fairly light and except for his dark black hair, he had Caucasian features (Walker, *Literary Frontier* 49). Although Angie Debo speculated in 1932 that Ridge's concern for the Cherokee Nation was probably more sentimental than real (67), republication of some of his journalism in *A Trumpet of Our Own* shows his concern for Native Americans, while at the same time indicating how distanced he felt from such California tribes as the Digger Indians.

It might initially seem that the theme of Mexican rights in California, as treated in *Joaquin Murieta* was a projection of some of his concerns for his own race. Indeed for Franklin Walker, Ridge's support for the Mexicans was equivalent to championing the cause of his fellow Indians. There are, however, problems with this interpretation. We should remember that his hero Joaquin is presented as being of full-blooded Spanish descent, and not as part-Indian like many Mexicans.

In his preface to *Joaquin Murieta,* Ridge defends the Mexicans and champions their heroism and courage:

> Besides, it is but doing justice to a people who have so far degenerated as to have been called by many, "A Nation of Cowards," to hold up a manifest contradiction, or at least an exception to so sweeping an opinion, in the character of a man who, bad though he was, possessed a soul as full of unconquerable courage as ever belonged to a human being. Although the Mexicans may be whipped by every other nation, in a battle of two or five to one, yet no man who speaks the truth can ever deny that there lived one Mexican whose nerves were as iron in the face of danger and death. (4)

The "justice" mentioned here pertains not to Murieta's righting of social wrongs such as the exorbitant prospecting tax of 1850 used to keep the gold fields in the hands of white Americans, but rather the defense of the honor of the Mexican people. The preface also stresses the reliability of his narrative in order to indicate that the Mexicans have not "degenerated," as many have claimed.

...ta begins life as a noble-souled man willing to ...et along with the Americans, but he turns to crime for many pressing reasons. His girlfriend is raped, and his half-brother is beaten and killed as a result of a trumped-up charge of horse stealing. Murieta's prospecting claim is stolen, and he is later whipped. (The researches of Nadeau and Latta have indicated that the real Murieta bands did not have their origin in this type of direct social injustice.) The other members of his band do not have such noble instincts, and one of them, Three-Fingered Jack, is known for his particular bloodthirstiness.[4]

Murieta and his band have no sense of camaraderie with the oppressed Chinese and American Indians. In fact, the Chinese sometimes offer comic relief in the novel. As Latta points out, the Chinese were actually often victims of attacks by the Murieta band, and the unfair Foreign Miners' Tax was not the chief cause of the raids (35). Unfortunately, the humor used by Ridge in describing the Chinese has strong tones of prejudice. The first encounter between the bandits and the Chinese begins as follows:

> . . . at this place two helpless Chinamen were encamped by the foot of a sycamore tree, and, it being near eleven o'clock in the night, were sleeping off their fatigue and the effects of their luxurious pipes of opium. Their picks and prospecting pans showed them to be miners, who were most probably supplied with a due amount of cash, as Chinamen generally are. Joaquin was for riding on, but Three-Fingered Jack could not resist the temptation of at least giving their pockets an examination. He, therefore, dismounted and walked up to the unconscious Celestials, who were snoring very soundly in their blankets and shook them. They awoke, and, seeing a horrible-looking devil standing over and glaring upon them, raised a hideous shriek, and, rising, fell upon their knees before him with the most lugubrious supplications in a by no means euphonious tongue. (47)

Ridge seems to be mocking the Chinese through such phrases as "unconscious Celestials" and "by no means euphonious tongue." Their opium use has not only rendered them incapable of fighting back, but also of perceiving clearly, since they mistake Jack for a devil. After they hand over twenty or thirty dollars, Jack cuts their throats against Murieta's wishes. The Chinese are seen as rich men rather than as a transplanted minority group which might also desire to resist white American exclusion and repression.

In the next appearance of the Chinese we have another piece of racial humor:

> . . . they met a Chinaman with a long tail, carrying a large bundle suspended at each end of a stick laid across his shoulders. . . . Looking up and seeing so

large a number of armed men before him, his eyes rolled in sudden fear, and he ducked his half-shaved head in unmistakable homage and respect to—the revolvers and bowie-knives which met his vision. No one harmed him, and he shuffled on vastly gratified and relieved. He had passed only a few minutes when he was heard howling and screaming in the most harrowing manner; and, looking back, they discovered the horrified Celestial with his tail flying in the wind, running towards them at the top of his speed, with arms wildly sawing the air. . . . (63)

The stereotypically racist image of the eye-rolling victim reminds one of the image of frightened blacks in many Hollywood movies. Fortunately, this time Joaquin is able to save the Chinese man from Jack, who says, "I love to smell the blood of a Chinaman. Besides, it's such easy work to kill them. It's a kind of luxury to cut their throats" (64). Although Ridge hardly supports killing the Chinaman, he can not be completely excused from making him a laughing-stock. In a third incident, Jack humiliates the Chinese by tying their pigtails together before he splits their skulls and severs their neck-veins (133).

The Chinese seem to be the objects of a deliberate violence because they are foreigners and because they are hard-working and supposedly likely to have thousands of dollars on them.[5] At one point, another robber, Reis, commits crimes, lurking in an abandoned tunnel. These are described by Ridge in the following terms:

> All his thefts and robberies had been done in the night. The miserable Chinamen were mostly the sufferers, and they lay along the highways like so many sheep with their throats cut by the wolves. It was a politic stroke in Reis to kill Chinamen in preference to Americans, for no one cared for so alien a class, and they were left to shift for themselves. (97)

Later we learn that in February 1853, near the end of Murieta's career, a dozen Chinese camps had been plundered. The Chinese felt that "they were singled out for destruction" (139). Seized by panic, they fled to the towns. Had Ridge made some attempt to show redistribution of wealth, perhaps it would be possible to understand this event somewhat more sympathetically.

Like the Chinese, the American Indians are also presented as cowardly. In May 1852, Murieta and his men encounter the Tejon Indians led by Sapatarra:

> The cupidity of the old chief and his right-hand men was raised to the highest pitch, and they resolved to manage the matter in hand with great skill and caution; which last, by the way, is a quality that particularly distinguishes the California Indians, amounting to so extreme a degree that it might

safely be called cowardice. Joaquin and party, having ascertained that they were no longer pursued by the Oris Timbers Ranchero, and feeling perfectly secure amongst so harmless a people as the Tejons, disencumbered themselves of their weapons to spend a few days in careless repose and genuine rural enjoyment. (37)

Through deception the cowardly Indians capture Murieta's band. This is the only way they can be victorious, since had Murieta's men made any resistance, the Indians "would have left the ground on the wings of the wind—so largely developed is the bump of caution on the head of a California Indian!" (38). For a week or two the "poor, miserable, cowardly Tejons had achieved a greater triumph over them than all the Americans put together!" (38).

At other times, Ridge uses other unflattering terms to characterize the Indians. He states that the "ignorant Indians suffered for many a deed which had been perpctrated by civilized hands" (27). Is "ignorant" a term of reproach or of sympathy? If a later passage discussing superstition is a clue here, I would say the former. Ridge writes:

> To those unacquainted with California customs, it may be necessary to explain that it is common in the mountains and mining districts to employ Digger Indians as bearers of letters, or runners upon errands, from one point to another, they being very expeditious on foot and willing to travel a considerable distance for a small piece of bread, fresh meat, or a ragged shirt. I have known them to swim rivers when the waters were high and dangerous in order to carry a letter to its destination. They are exceedingly faithful in this business, having a superstitious dread of that mysterious power which makes *a paper talk without a mouth*. (130)

Although the poverty of the Indians is made clear, their naivete makes the biggest impression on us. They are also presented as subservient to a more civilized race.

Ridge's lack of human warmth toward the Native Americans and Chinese is also reflected in **"Mount Shasta, Seen from a Distance"** (23-25). This poem, the only one included in the novel, champions isolation over community effort and emotional distance over empathy. In the first of the four stanzas, Mount Shasta is praised for its solitariness:

> Behold the dread Mount Shasta, where it
> 　　stands,
> Imperial midst the lesser hight [*sic*], and like
> Some mighty, unimpassioned mind,
> 　　companionless
> And cold. The storms of Heaven may beat in
> 　　wrath

> Against it, but it stands in unpoluted [*sic*]
> Grandeur still; and from the rolling mists
> 　　up-heaves
> Its tower of pride e'en purer than before.
> 　　　　　　　　　　　　　　　　(1-7)

In a novel in which Murieta responds emotionally to the outrages committed against him and his loved ones by forming a robber band, the mountain is nevertheless championed for its stoical detachment.

In the second stanza we suspect that perhaps Mt. Shasta is being praised for its distance from humanity:

> Aspiring to the eagle's cloudless hight [*sic*],
> No human foot hath stained its snowy side,
> Nor human breath has dimmed its icy mirror
> Which it holds unto the moon, and starts [*sic*],
> 　　and sov'reign
> Sun. We may not grow familiar with the
> 　　secrets
> Of its hoary top, whereon the Genius
> Of that mountain builds his glorious throne!
> 　　　　　　　　　　　　　　　　(14-20)[6]

In these lines, man and mountain are rigidly divided despite the earlier simile comparing the mountain to a mind. Mountains were, of course, important in Romantic poetry. We need think only of Shelley's Mount Blanc and Wordsworth's Mount Snowdon. Ridge twice refers to the Romantic sublimity of Mt. Shasta, not, however, because a divine spirit infuses it (although it is made by God), but because it defies accurate representation by artists. Mt. Shasta is so great, it towers over all the other peaks near it:

> Itself all light, save when some loftiest cloud
> Doth for a while embrace its cold forbidding
> Form—that monarch-mountain casts its mighty
> Shadows down upon the crownless peaks
> 　　below,
> That, like inferior minds to some great
> Spirit, stand in strong contrasted littleness!
> 　　　　　　　　　　　　　　　　(33-38)

Although the poem here rather pessimistically indicates the failure of the human mind to attain a spiritual level, the reference to "monarch-mountain" may also reveal a hierarchy of human relationships. We have noted that "mind" in line 3 represents the human; and Genius, or Spirit, has been anthropomorphized in the second stanza. After the close of the poem we get an example of the hierarchy when the local Indians are called "human savages" and associated with "savage beasts" (26).

After this assertion of the imaginative distance between the exalted Mount Shasta and the mundane human realm, the fourth stanza again draws the two together:

Well might it win communities so blest
To loftier feelings, and to nobler thoughts—
The great material symbol of eternal
Things!

(54-57)

Although here the mountain should win communities to lofty feeling, in the puzzling closing of the poem, we find that human feelings, such as pity, must be abandoned:

And well this Golden State shall thrive, if, like

Its own Mount Shasta, sovereign law shall lift
Itself in purer atmosphere—so high
That human feeling, human passion, at its base

Shall lie subdued; e'en pity's tears shall on
Its summit freeze; to warm it, e'en the sunlight

Of deep sympathy shall fail—
Its pure administration shall be like
The snow, immaculate upon the mountain's brow!

(68-76)

The poem is inserted after Ridge recounts the unsuccessful attempt of a sheriff named Buchanan to kill or capture Murieta. Despite the romanticization of the origins of Murieta's band, for Ridge, pity can only go so far before it gets in the way of justice.

Ridge had already written against outlaws five years before. In his essay, "The Cherokee: Their History—Present Conditions and Future Prospects," which appeared in the Clarksville (Texas) *Northern Standard* on January 20, 1849, Ridge denounced banditry by members of the Cherokee Nation:

Then there is another portion of the nation, (not inconsiderable by any means) who have framed themselves into a banditti, and attracting to themselves the lawless and corrupt in the nation and on the line, both, white and red, bid defiance to society and law. Some of the banditti have recently been killed, and although their daring wickedness was everywhere acknowledged yet so numerous were the relations and friends of these lawless men, that a high excitement on their account alone arose in the nation, and the lives of prominent individuals were threatened. (Ridge, *Trumpet* 51)

Apart from the Mt. Shasta poem, such a denunciation of banditry does not appear in *Joaquin Murieta.* Perhaps this is because of the differing political situations. Ridge goes on to plead for making the Cherokee Nation an integral part of the United States, first as a territory and then as a state. Only in this way will one faction be prevented from tyrannizing another. The strong arm of the federal government is the only

answer. Ridge believes that this policy will also ultimately come as a relief to the federal government as well. The situation for other Indian tribes was quite different than that of the Cherokee, who had probably gone farther than any other tribe in adopting white ways. The 1981 collection, *A Trumpet of Our Own,* includes three articles by Ridge on the unfortunate situation of the Digger Indians in California, one from 1851 and two from 1857. Ridge thought that the best hope for these persecuted people was to be left alone on reservations where they would not be killed by whites. In the *New Orleans True Delta* of November 1, 1851, Ridge discusses the murder of Digger Indians by the whites:

I know not how to account for such inhuman acts unless I lay it to what may be called civilized ignorance, for I have remarked that these deeds of cruelty have always been committed, in this country by ignorant men. This civilized ignorance seems to destroy the finest feelings of nature, while it denies those delicate sensibilities which belong to cultivated minds. There is just sufficient civilization in such ignorance to destroy all that is worth anything in untutored nature. (62)

The idea of "civilized ignorance" has a strange ring to it. Instead of condemning the murders of the Digger Indians as brutality, Ridge does not want to give the impression that he is entirely against Euro-American society. After all, his mother was white, as was his own wife and his paternal grandfather's wife, and he chose to live among whites in California.

In addition, Ridge does not feel any special racial kinship to the Diggers, as the following passage makes clear:

Were these Indians like the genuine North American red man in the times of the bloody frontier wars of the United States, brave, subtle, and terible in their destruction, it would be a different matter. But they are a poor, humble, degraded, and cowardly race. The instances are few, where they have shown any heroism in fight. And however much military or any other kind of men, may strive to make them appear like dangerous or even respectable antagonists with their bows and arrows against muskets and Colt's revolvers, it remains nevertheless a fact, that it is no credit for a white man to kill a Digger, or even fifty of them. It requires no heroism at all, no more than to slaughter the deer in the hills, or the coyote in the plains. It is pitiful to think of so cowardly a contest on both sides—contemptible to try to make a hero out of such battles as these! (62)

This paragraph supports the idea of hierarchies of people implicit in Ridge's novel. Unlike Joaquin's band, the Diggers are incapable of fighting heroically for their freedom and rights. The Diggers are at the bottom of the Native American ladder. In an article from Ridge's own *Sacramento Bee* of July 12, 1857, he writes that the Digger "has none of the romance which gathers around the nobler savage of the western prairies—he cannot defend himself of his rights, and a prayer for mercy is his only argument against cruelty and oppression" (62). These Indians do not have the stoicism and sense of honor that Ridge praises in an article in 1862.

Not surprisingly, Ridge prefers the *ancient* Aztecs and the Incas to the *contemporary* Diggers, stressing the political power and wealth of their civilizations. In what is perhaps his most successful poem, a piece simply entitled **"Poem,"** which was "delivered before the Agricultural, Horticultural, and Mechanics' Society of the Northern District of California, on Wednesday Evening, August 5th, 1860" (*Poems* 114), Mexico is pictured as better off under the Aztecs than under the Spanish:

> Let truth impartial say, if happier now
> Is that historic land, broad Mexico,
> Than when all greenly spread the cultured
> 　plain,
> And waved the far Cordilleras with grain,
> And rolled the deep canals, with streams that
> 　blest
> A thousand homes in Eden beauty drest,
> And all the realm from mountain slope to
> 　main,
> Was fair Montezuma's golden reign?
> 　　　　　　　　　　　(*Poems* 119)

Here Ridge expresses his scorn for those who believe that the Aztecs were barbarous because they were not white. He stresses the idea that peace had brought the people prosperity; and he ignores the bloodier side of their civilization. In addition, the Aztecs are depicted as socialists:

> As all, too, labored daily for the State,
> If sickness fell or any evil fate,
> The State provided, not as charity
> But right, for him whose former industry,
> Still looking to the common weal in this,
> Had swelled her coffers and her granaries.
> 　　　　　　　　　　　(121)

The closing of the poem looks for the day when California, spurred on by agricultural achievements, can realize the dream of El Dorado that the Spanish invaders once heard from the North American Indians.
Here we have Ridge espousing propaganda for his adopted state. Law and order, according to Ridge, are the hallmark of the good society, and it is hard to believe that the author of this poem would ever have pictured an outlaw in a sympathetic light. In addition, the theme of equalized wealth is much more prominent

in this poem than it ever becomes in *Joaquin Murieta.* The robbers, unlike the Aztecs, do not redistribute wealth to the community.

Rather than think of the novel as a Robin Hood story, a reflection of Ridge's desire for revenge against the Ross faction, or a vicarious projection onto the Mexicans of his Cherokee resentment against the federal government, we need to be aware of the ambivalent position that Ridge held as a minority writer towards other minority groups of the time, including other Native American tribes. He adopted the negative Anglo perception of Chinese laborers, separated the so-called noble savage groups from the ignoble, and defended the Mexicans as a people willing to assimilate but thwarted by greedy Easterners. When we examine *Joaquin Murieta* with these thoughts of ethnic and racial interaction in mind, Ridge's romance of banditry seems more closely connected to later novels by American Indians than it usually has been taken to be.

Notes

[1] Although Ridge authored only this one book during his lifetime, many of his poems and articles appeared in periodicals. In 1868, the year after his death, his widow published a collection of forty-four of his poems, which also included part of an autobiographical letter to a friend written in 1849. Nine of his letters, written to members of his family between 1848 and 1858, are available in *Cherokee Cavaliers* (1939). Unfortunately, only one letter from this collection comes from the period during which he wrote his novel. From this we learn that his publisher cheated him out of any profits from it (82). In 1981, *A Trumpet of Our Own*, a collection of seven essays and editorials by Ridge about American Indian affairs, was edited by David Farmer and Rennard Strickland. Short uncollected articles remain in various California newspapers of the 1860s, some of which he was editor, such as the *Sacramento Bee* and *Red Bluff Beacon*. Unpublished letters and poems can be found in the manuscript collection of the University of Oklahoma Archive.

[2] From 1926 to 1937 Ridge's life was the subject of articles in historical journals by such authors as Edward Everett Dale (1926), M. A. Ranck (1932), Angie Debo (1932), Carolyn Thomas Foreman (1936), and Franklin Walker (1937). However, after the publication of both Walker's *San Francisco's Literary Frontier* and Dale and Litton's *Cherokee Cavaliers* in 1939, interest waned until the novel's centennial. Then in 1955, the University of Oklahoma Press reprinted *Joaquin Murieta* for the Western Frontier Library. The 1955 edition was based on the original version of 1854, published in San Francisco by W. B. Cooke and Company, a copy of which turned up in 1937. In 1859 the unauthorized *Police Gazette* edition appeared. According to Franklin Walker, this edition was the source

of many Latin-American variants of the legend. Ridge (although this is disputed by Nadeau) made some revisions to his novel after 1859 for the version which is now called the "third." It was published in 1871 and it "added no major features to the story" (Walker, "Ridge's Life" 262). In 1927 the *Evening Free Lance* of Hollister, California, reissued Ridge's revised edition, and in 1932 the *Police Gazette* version was republished by Grabhorn Press. Thus the 1955 edition of the 1854 version was, in a sense, overdue. James W. Parins provides biographical material in his recent book, *John Rollin Ridge: His Life & Works.*

³ In reference to black Americans, Remi Nadeau (121) quotes an unnamed detractor of Ridge's who stated that Ridge "believed negro bondage to be a divine institution; was against the war on the part of freedom, and for anything Southern. . ."

⁴ Frank F. Latta interviewed many descendants of the families who participated in the actual Murrieta (the spelling with double "r" is the true historical one) horse gangs of California. They had their base south of the border in Sonoma, Mexico, where they took horses for sale. Latta conducted extensive research between 1920 and 1970, and shows that the leader of the band was not the Joaquin killed by Harry Love. He escaped with his girlfrend Rosa but was killed soon after.

⁵ Of the real Joaquin's twenty-four known victims, nineteen were Chinese (Nadeau 145).

⁶ The misspellings are corrected in the 1868 *Poems,* where "Mount Shasta, Seen from a Distance" is the lead poem.

Works Cited

Cherokee Nation. *Comments on the Objections of Certain Cherokee Delegates to the Propositions of the Government to Separate the Hostile Parties of the Cherokee Nation.* Washington, DC: Intelligencer Printing House, 1866.

Dale, Edward Everett, "John Rollin Ridge." *Chronicles of Oklahoma* 4 (December 1926): 312-21.

Dale, Edward Everett and Gaston Litton, eds. *Cherokee Cavaliers; Forty Years of Cherokee History As Told in the Correspondence of the Ridge-Watie-Boudinot Family.* Norman: U of Oklahoma P, 1939.

Debo, Angie. "John Rollin Ridge." *Southwest Review* 17 (1932): 59-71.

Foreman, Carolyn Thomas. "Edward W. Bushyhead and John Rollin Ridge, Cherokee Editors in California." *Chronicles of Oklahoma* 14 (September 1936): 295-311.

Halliburton, R., Jr. *Red over Black: Slavery among the Cherokee Indians.* Westport, CT: Greenwood P, 1977.

Latta, Frank. F. *Joaquin Murrieta and His Horse Gangs.* Santa Cruz: Bear State Books, 1980.

Lauter, Paul, et al. *The Heath Anthology of American Literature.* 2 vols. Lexington, MA: Heath, 1990.

Nadeau, Remi. *The Real Joaquin Murieta: Robin Hood Hero or Gold Rush Gangster?* Corona del Mar, CA: Trans-Anglo, 1974.

Parins, James W. *John Rollin Ridge: His Life & Works.* Lincoln: U of Nebraska P, 1991.

Ranck, M. A. "John Rollin Ridge in California." *Chronicles of Oklahoma* 10 (December 1932): 559-69.

Ridge, John Rollin. *The Life and Adventures of Joaquin Murieta, The Celebrated California Bandit.* Introduction by Joseph Henry Jackson. Norman: U of Oklahoma P, 1955.

———. *Poems.* San Francisco: Henry Payot & Co., 1868.

———. *A Trumpet of Our Own: Yellow Bird's Essays on the North American Indian.* Ed. David Farmer and Rennard Strickland. San Francisco: Book Club of California, 1981.

Walker, Franklin. "Ridge's Life of Murieta: The First and Revised Editions Compared." *California Historical Society Quarterly* 16 (1937): 256-62.

———. *San Francisco's Literary Frontier.* New York: Knopf, 1939.

Wilkins, Thurman. *Cherokee Tragedy: The Ridge Family and the Decimation of a People.* Rev. ed. Norman: U of Oklahoma P, 1986.

Karl Kroeber (essay date 1992)

SOURCE: "American Indian Persistence and Resurgence," in *boundary 2,* Vol. XIX, No. 3, Fall, 1992, pp. 1-25.

[*In the following excerpt, Kroeber finds Ridge's novel* Joaquín Murrieta *important as a product of Ridge's cultural identity.*]

In 1854, John Rollin Ridge, a Cherokee, became the first American Indian to publish a novel, ***The Life and Adventures of Joaquin Murietta, the Celebrated Bandit.*** This blood-and-thunder potboiler will never supersede *Madame Bovary* as an object of stylistic analysis.

Its literary interest, in fact, lies in its journalistic character. Ridge wrote the novel to take advantage of the celebrity of its protagonist, a Robin Hood figure who never existed, though a man who claimed to have killed him earned a substantial reward, proving that one should never underestimate the value of myth. For California readers, some of the interest in the "bandit Murietta" may have centered on the bounty hunter who reported shooting him—and who certainly did shoot some Mexicans. At any rate, Ridge exploits every hyperbolic resource of language to render his protagonist Byronically attractive, even providing him a consort as faithful as she is beautiful.

The chief attraction of the book appears to have been the bandit himself. Murietta was a Mexican who, like many of his countrymen, had come to California to mine gold. Some were successful, and, when California became one of the "united" states, these "foreigners" were brutally and illegally dispossessed of their property, an aspect of the "gold rush" that tends to slip out of our history books but that Ridge brings to the fore. The Californians' treatment of the Mexicans parallels the Georgians' treatment of the Cherokee, whose expulsion was in part precipitated by a discovery of gold in their territory. I hesitate, however, to praise Ridge for subversively encoding a condemnation of the Americans' treatment of Indians. For one thing, his novel includes a passage of scathing ridicule of California Indians that sounds like Twainian racism. To me, *Murietta* seems more interesting in that it illuminates a complicated sociohistorical situation in which the theme of a foreign Robin Hood could be seized on as a way to make money from American readers by a Cherokee, ambitious to succeed as a California journalist. One aspect of the confusing circumstances is highlighted by the volume of Ridge's *Poems,* the first such collection by an American Indian to be published in this country. These are, with a couple of slight exceptions, typically Victorian romanticizings in rhyme, sweet sentimentalizations that include such conventionalities as reference to a Cherokee girl's "white hand."

These verses (unlike the exuberant brutalities in *Murietta*) seem inappropriate for an author whose father, grandfather, and cousin were victims of savage murders that he long dreamed of avenging—some of that bloodcurdling biography being related in the preface to his innocuous poems. In different ways, both Ridge's poetry and his novel urge us to attend to the intricacy of how acculturative forces have worked among Native Americans, an intricacy that seems (at least to someone of my limited knowledge) to distinguish the Native American experience from that of most other "minorities" struggling with dominant white culture in the United States. Central to this peculiar play of forces, I believe, is that the Indians so consciously resisted and literally fought; though physically defeated, therefore, they were able to retain a more than merely defensive commitment to their values, even while adapting shrewdly in other ways to Anglo-white society. In materially poor and relatively small societies, any individual's existence as an embodiment of a specific culture is continuously experienced with extraordinary force. So far as the culture is a vigorous one, a firm, yet flexible, system of vital processes (as many Native American ones, in fact, were and are), new ideas, and practices can be translated and structured into traditional attitudes without extreme stress and without creating too much fear or guilt in individuals engaged in this acculturative activity. . . .

Something of this intricate interplaying may be suggested by a summary of Ridge's familial-tribal background. His grandfather, Major Ridge (the title bestowed by General Andrew Jackson for his service in fighting against the Creek), was a full-blooded Cherokee who did not speak English. He sent his son John to a school in Cornwall, Connecticut, where he was a successful student and wooer of Miss Sara Northrop. Her mother was amenable to their relationship, but his father objected to it—he had expectations of a local Cherokee for a daughter-in-law. There were even more violent objections to the match in the Connecticut community. John's will prevailed, however, and he married Sara in Connecticut and brought her back to Georgia as his wife. His son, John Rollin, was born in 1827 in the large house of his father's plantation, which included slaves and a schoolhouse with an imported white teacher.

In the 1830s, the Cherokee were forcibly and, according to Supreme Court Justice John Marshall's famous decision, illegally "removed" from their prosperous farms in Georgia. John Ridge, like his father, had vigorously resisted this usurpation and believed that President Jackson would not permit it. When this hope proved illusory, and the Cherokee became increasingly subject to harassment without any legal redress, he decided it would be best to accept the unfair judgment and relocate to Indian Territory. Although he finally persuaded his father to accept this view, a majority of his people, led by John Ross, another distinguished Cherokee, continued to resist for some time. At Honey Creek, in Indian Territory (close to present-day Southwest City, Missouri), to which the Ridges traveled, John built a new house and school, and employed the same teacher whom he had employed in Georgia. In 1839, a group of Cherokee associated with the Ross party who had been forced to emigrate to Indian Territory decided to satisfy the Cherokee blood-law, which prescribed death for anyone ceding tribal land. The plotters determined to assassinate the Ridge family, who were, besides being political rivals to John Ross, convenient scapegoats for the newcomers' difficulties in the territory, especially with older Cherokee settlers. On the night of June 22, 1839, four men dragged John Ridge from his bed and stabbed him to death, while others assassinated Major Ridge and a cousin the same day. John Rollin never forgot the scene of his father's body "with blood oozing through his winding sheet, and falling drop by drop on the floor. By his side sat my mother, with hands clasped in speechless agony. . . . And bending over him was his own afflicted mother, with her long, white hair flung loose over her shoulders and bosom, crying to the Great Spirit to sustain her in that dreadful hour."

John Rollin's mother took her surviving children out of the Cherokee Nation into Arkansas. There, John Rollin received a good education, and, in 1847, he married a white woman. Two years later, within Cherokee territory through the instigation of the Ross faction, he was deliberately provoked so that he could be murdered, but he succeeded in killing the *agent provocateur* and escaped back to Arkansas. Although he was ready to stand trial for this killing, his family persuaded him not to risk putting himself in the power of his enemies. He joined a party of gold-seekers and moved to California, where he worked as a miner, a trader, an auditor, and a county recorder. Here, he also began to make money, finally, as a writer, though he was slow to give up the idea of returning to the Cherokee Nation to avenge his father's and grandfather's murders.

In the early 1850s, John Rollin became editor of the *Grass Valley Journal* and thought he might have realized a handsome sum from the *Joaquin Murietta,* had not its publisher failed. Ridge did achieve something of a literary reputation in California, and his success as an editor enabled him to establish a good home for his family in the Sacramento Valley. At this time, he conceived the idea of setting up, with a surviving cousin in Arkansas, a periodical devoted to Indian concerns. Ridge's idea was that the journal

> would be a medium not only of defending Indian rights, and of making their oppressors tremble, but of preserving the memories of the distinguished men of the race. . . . Men, governments, will be *afraid* to trample upon the rights of defenseless Indian tribes, where there is a power to hold up their deeds to execration.

Asserting that he would bring to the paper not only the "fire of my own pen" but also that of "leading minds in the different Indian nations," Ridge hoped to do "justice to a deeply wronged and injured people by impressing upon the records of the country a true . . . account of the treatment they have received at the hands of a civilized and Christian race!" He immediately added: "If I can once see the Cherokees admitted into the Union as a State, then I am satisfied." Here is displayed a paradoxical capacity of Native Americans to make use of the encroaching culture they resist. Ridge's ideal, which his father had also cherished, of the Cherokee fully realizing their tribal destiny by

becoming part of the "united" states at whose hands they had suffered so unjustly, is difficult for most of us to understand today, since the possibility of sincere belief in the United States as representing a permanent advance toward political liberty has been so successfully eroded by the contrastive efforts of jingoistic patriots and academic intellectuals. The overwhelming attention to problems of African Americans in our society, moreover, has obscured the very different situation of Indians, who are not necessarily afflicted with that "double-consciousness" so famously formulated by W. E. B. DuBois. As Ridge/Yellowbird, with a kind of spectacular simplicity, illustrates, for some Indians at least, indigenous and European cultures could be complexly reinforcing rather than simply divisive. Our current tendency, an unconscious heritage of the Cold War, is to think of political emotions in solely oppositional terms, but it seems arguable that the strength of Ridge's loyalty to his Cherokee heritage (scarcely "blind," since his family had been victimized by his own people) could give power to an idealized Americanism, and such Americanism supports his native culture. This interplay of conflictive reinforcements, rather than a merely divided consciousness, appears throughout Ridge's life and his written work, which in several ways anticipates much subsequent Indian writing in English. For example, although *Murietta* is rather overt fiction pretending to be history, it takes on the style and attributes of genuine history as it progresses toward its conclusion. Surprisingly, but revealingly, *Murietta* became the basis of what were claimed to be genuine historical accounts by white American historians.

What happened, briefly, was that Ridge's novel was pirated six years after its publication, and that popular piracy spawned others, so that three years after Ridge's death, his novel was reissued in a "third" edition, which then was used as a documentary source by California historians. This inventing of history was possible in part because of Ridge's mixing of history, biography, and fiction, a mixing that has continued to be a notable characteristic of subsequent Indian literary productions. Under modern conditions, writing produced by a member of any marginalized group is likely to be "journalistic." But this "impure" mode that allows for an individualistic perspective on some clash of diverse social forces has been peculiarly congenial to Indians—for instance, Simon Pokagon, Will Rogers, D'Arcy McNickle, and, in our own time, Gerald Vizenor. As the second and last of these names remind us, a "journalistic" approach also facilitates humorous satire, a very powerful element in much traditional Indian discourse. Ridge's humor in *Murietta* is of a frontier style that jars our more delicate sensibilities. This humor, however, manifests a fundamental self-confidence underlying not only the work of writers I have just mentioned but also that of men such as LaFlesche and George Sword, who, in different ways . . . , used writing to come to terms with the complexity of their lives on the precarious boundary between traditional, oral Indian cultures and technologically advanced, "scientific" American culture.

The importance of Ridge's writings (which include a broader range than my concentration on his novel has suggested), then lies in their revelation of the flexibly powerful sense of cultural identity that continues to undergird even recent writing in English by Indians. That strength permits Indians to confront with surprising frankness and adroitness challenges to (and even radical transformations in) what provides them with the "native" identity. By so confronting these challenges, they strengthen their opposition to Euro-American preconceptions. It makes possible the extraordinary assimilation of diverse elements from competing social entities that enables the protagonists of modern novels by Indians, such as Leslie Marmon Silko's *Ceremony* and N. Scott Momaday's *House Made of Dawn,* to survive. Ridge's work may also help us understand the spiritual appeal of the autobiography of Black Elk. This best-seller reconstitutes "Indian" religiosity effectively enough to make *Black Elk Speaks,* in the opinion of Vine Deloria, Jr., a kind of Bible for modern young Indians. As Raymond DeMallie and others have demonstrated, however, this reconstituting involved, for Black Elk, transmuting into his tradition elements of white religion absorbed through his participation in Christian services.

What is most impressive about the survival of American Indians, their success in not vanishing, is that they resist not merely by clinging to the past but by changing, accepting, even welcoming at least part of the present. Their persistence should provoke us (though so far it has not done so) to realize to what a large degree culture *is* transformation. Like homo sapiens' "big brain," every culture provides a group of human beings with supranatural means for accommodating, in an original fashion, to "random" circumstances, what cannot be accomplished by creatures without our complex brain structures and the systems beyond biology it produces. Better recognition of culture's dynamically adaptive values, offered by an understanding of the ways in which Indians managed *not* to disappear (either through genocide or assimilation), offers us, were we willing to recognize it, an escape from the banality of such currently popular enterprises as theorizings on the "poetics of culture."

Louis Owens (essay date 1992)

SOURCE: "Origin Mists: John Rollin Ridge's Masquerade and Mourning Dove's Mixed Bloods," in *Other Destinies: Understanding the American Indian Novel,* University of Oklahoma Press, 1992, pp. 32-48.

[*In the following essay, Owens discusses* Joaquín Murieta *as a work that expresses the internal conflict Ridge experienced as an individual trapped between Native and white cultures.*]

John Rollin Ridge, the first American Indian to publish a novel, arrived in California in 1850, a mixedblood Cherokee fleeing the turmoil set loose by the injustices of the Removal Act. If the "Indian Territory" that would become Oklahoma was a displaced setting wrought out of violence and confusion, however, the gold-fevered place to which Ridge fled was no promised land for Native Americans. The same year that Ridge arrived in California—a new state with an already well established history of genocide against Indians—California's governor, Peter H. Burnett, announced what amounted to a war of extermination against California's native population. In the midst of this intense Indian-hating (exemplified by the bitter racism against "Digger" Indians in Mark Twain's *Roughing It*), in 1854 the half-Cherokee Ridge published *The Life and Adventures of Joaquin Murieta, the Celebrated California Bandit,* a wild and bloody fiction purporting to be the biography of a notorious Mexican American bandit.

In this, his only novel, Ridge transforms himself and his bitterness against the oppression and displacement of Indians, becoming a haunted shapeshifter writing between the lines. The result is a deeply encoded work filled with dialogic tension, a subversive narrative in which the surface plot rides over the subtext like a palimpsest. It is a novel that stands as fascinating testimony to the conflicts and tensions within the mixedblood author, who moves easily inside the dominant white culture but cannot forget or forgive the denigration by that culture of his indigenous self. It is also a work that marks the thinly camouflaged beginning of a long campaign by Native American writers to wrench a new genre—the novel—free from the hegemony of the dominant and (to Native Americans especially) destructive culture of European America. Ridge's *Joaquin Murieta* is a disguised act of appropriation, an aggressive and subversive masquerade.

In considering Ridge's novel, the first question that arises is why an author who experienced first-hand some of the most painful oppression of Native American people in the nineteenth century should have chosen to write about a Mexican American bandit in California, a subject that seems so distant from American Indian concerns. The most obvious answer to this question is, of course, that Ridge's choice was determined by the literary marketplace: like many authors he hoped to make money quickly from a sensational potboiler. With the Gold Rush and the completion of America's transcontinental march had come a vivid interest in the far West, the frontier. Ridge's acute judgment of his audience's "apperceptive background" would have led him to expect a profitable response to the romantic tragedy of a colorful "Californio." It is also significant, however, that in the western United States at midnineteenth century, American Indians had not yet taken their stylized place in the epic drama of extinction favored in the East. There were too many actual Indians living very visible lives in California in 1854, and their removal—primarily by disease, but often through simple slaughter—was a messy and unromantic business. As the terminus for the metanarrative that provided a context for domination of the continent, California was too close to the ugly underbelly of the millenarian enterprise to find the central victim of that enterprise very charming. Ridge, a successful journalist, would certainly have recognized the poor marketability of Indian outrage in the West, and, like Native Americans and other marginalized authors writing today, he would also have recognized the necessity for writing the kind of literature that would be acceptable and publishable. To be published, he would have to mimic the discourse of the privileged center. By writing about the fictionalized Joaquin Murieta, however, Ridge could have it both ways: he could write his romantic potboiler in the language of monocentric, Euramerican consciousness while simultaneously including a non-very-veiled protest against America's treatment of Native American people.

Ridge attempts his masquerade with a straight face. "The author," declares Ridge in his "Editor's Preface" to *Joaquin Murieta,* "in presenting this book to the public, is aware that its chief merit consists in the reliability of the ground-work upon which it stands and not in the beauty of its composition." According to Ridge, "In the main, it will be found to be strictly true." In spite of this disingenuous preface, the publisher of Ridge's novel cleverly alerts readers to the narrative doubling in *Joaquin Murieta,* attempting to ensure that the epic tragedy of the American Indian would loom portentously behind the surface text. "The following production," Ridge's publisher wrote in a "Publisher's Preface," "aside from its intrinsic merit, will, no doubt, be read with increased interest when it is known that the author is a 'Cherokee Indian,' born in the woods—reared in the midst of the wildest scenery—and familiar with all that is thrilling, fearful, and tragical in a forestlife." Less dramatically, Ridge's publisher ends his preface with the suggestion that "the perusal of this work will give those who are disposed to be curious an opportunity to estimate the character of Indian talent. The aboriginal race has produced great warriors, and powerful orators, but literary men—only a few."

Despite his publisher's appeal to the reader's gothic sensibility, Ridge, who published his work as "Yellow Bird," the name under which he had also contributed a stream of poems and sketches to northern California newspapers, had not exactly been "born in the woods." Born in 1827, the grandson of the prominent and wealthy Cherokee leader Major Ridge, John Rollin Ridge had spent his first eight years in extremely privileged surroundings, in a house which, according to a visitor, swarmed with seventeen servants. If, as [Mikhail Bakhtin suggests in *The Dialogic Imagination*], "the ideological becoming of a human being is the process of selectively assimilating the words of others," John Rollin Ridge had ample opportunity—rather rare for Native Americans at the time—to thoroughly assimilate the privileged discourse of Euramerica. In this process of "ideological becoming," the "other" discourse, writes Bakhtin, "strives . . . to determine the very basis of our behavior; it performs here as *authoritative discourse,* and an *internally persuasive discourse.*" On one hand, as his publisher observes, John Rollin Ridge writes in language assimilated from the authoritative discourse of privileged "literary" America; on the other hand, the internally persuasive discourse of the oppressed and marginalized minority continually subverts the authority of the dominant discourse. As a result, like the traditional Native American trickster, the author of *Joaquin Murieta* gives ample evidence of being divided within and against himself; he embodies cultural fragmentation. In this light, Ridge's *Joaquin Murieta* can be seen as intensely dialogic, a hybridized narrative within which the author is in dialogue with himself, within which two distinct linguistic consciousnesses, two kinds of discourse, coexist in a "dialogically agitated and tension-filled environment."

To understand the tensions underlying Ridge's prose, some history is required. John Ridge, the author's father, had been sent north to the Cornwall Indian School in Connecticut for his education, there he met and married Sarah Northrup, the daughter of the school's white principal. Returning to Georgia, where John Rollin Ridge was born in 1827, John Ridge set his wife up in the style becoming a well-to-do southerner. As is common knowledge today, the prosperity and large landholdings of the so-called Five Civilized Tribes, the Cherokee and Choctaw in particular, led to conflict with whites who wanted what the Indians possessed. In 1830, Congress bowed to this pressure by passing the Indian Removal Act ordering the removal of the tribes to "Indian Territory" in the west, most of what would become Oklahoma.

In the face of increasing hostility and violence from whites, Major Ridge declared that resistance to removal was futile, a stance that put him into conflict with Cherokee leader John Ross as well as the largest portion of the Cherokee tribe. In 1835, the Ridges, their cousin Elias Boudinot (a successful journalist), and a few other prominent Cherokees signed the New Echota Treaty agreeing to the removal as the only hope for the tribe. In signing, the Ridges and others defied a tribal law making it a capital offense for any Cherokee to enter into a treaty with the United States—a law Major Ridge himself had drawn up in 1829.

Despite the opposition of the majority faction under John Ross, the largest portion of the Cherokee population was moved into stockades and concentration camps and then force-marched to Oklahoma, with as many as four thousand deaths resulting from the move. Meanwhile, a number of families of means; such as the Ridges—the core of what came to be known as the Treaty Party—had sold their Georgia holdings and moved comfortably to the Indian Territory ahead of the mass exodus, settling on choice lands and setting themselves up in livestock, farming, and merchandising businesses in the new country.

As a result of the conflict between the Ridge and Ross followers, on June 22, 1839, twelve-year-old John Rollin Ridge found himself watching as a group belonging to the antitreaty faction rode up to the family home and stabbed his father to death in the front yard. The decree of death for signers of the New Echota Treaty had been enforced. Later that night the family learned that Major Ridge and Elias Boudinot had also been murdered. Thus, by the time he was twelve years old the future author had been witness to the federal government's theft—against the ruling of the U.S. Supreme Court and by military force—of his tribe's ancestral homeland and his people's brutal removal to what was considered a worthless region. He had seen his father murdered by a political faction born from that removal and had learned of the simultaneous murders of his grandfather and cousin.

Of the murder of John Rollin Ridge's father, Franklin Walker wrote [in *San Francisco's Literary Frontier*] in the noble-savage tones common to literature about American Indians: "The boy learned that the avenging spirit of a noble line of savages was bequeathed to him that night. The deed darkened his mind with an eternal shadow; retribution for that deed remained his chief purpose in life." Joseph Henry Jackson, in his introduction to the 1955 reprint of Ridge's novel, suggests similarly that "ideas of violence, sudden death, and—more important—long-cherished revenge, might well enough have been planted in an impressionable boy's mind by such events." Though it is tempting to see the familiar "invention" of the gothic Indian in such descriptions, Ridge apparently did nurture thoughts of revenge, writing from his New England college to a famous cousin, Stand Watie, to request "an article I wish extremely that you would get for me—a Bowie knife." Before he turned twenty, Ridge had returned from his mother's home in Fayetteville, Arkansas, to the Indian Territory and, in a dispute, had killed Judge D. Kell, one of the rival faction. Subsequently, in 1850, Ridge traced the route of what had already become an American archetype: he fled westward to California, arriving at the height of the gold rush and at the birth of a California literary scene energized by such figures as Samuel Clemens and Brett Harte.

While physical and cultural displacement has been the common experience for American Indians since the sixteenth century, for Ridge's Cherokees and the other tribes "removed" to the territory, displacement was particularly abrupt and traumatic, an experience giving rise to an acute version of what has been called a "postcolonial crisis of identity": "the concern with the development or recovery of an effective identifying relationship between self and place" [Bill Ashcroft, Gareth Griffiths, and Helen Tiffin, *The Empire Writes Back*]. When Ridge was forced to remove himself yet again from Cherokee culture, he placed himself still more fully within a tense, liminal position of suspension between dialectically opposed indigenous (Indian) and colonial (Euramerican) realities. It is this intense liminality that illuminates ***Joaquin Murieta***'s transparent text.

Ridge's Joaquin Murieta arose, apparently, out of the specters of several minor California bandits named Joaquin, bearing the various surnames of Murieta, O'Comorenia, Valenzuela, Bottelier, and Carillo, all of whom Ridge collapses into two Joaquins, these two being the brilliant bandit leader Murieta and his lieutenant Valenzuela. Ridge selected one of the Joaquins—Murieta—and from scraps of information created a legend.

Again and again, throughout his novel Ridge makes it clear that Joaquin Murieta has been driven to his bloody outlaw life because of mistreatment by Anglo-Americans. As a precipitating factor, Ridge notes the Foreign Miners' Tax Law, an 1850 statute by the California legislature which made it virtually impossible for Latin Americans to mine in the state. Having been beaten and tied up and forced to watch while his young wife was raped, at age eighteen Murieta is driven from his mining claim. "They left him," Ridge writes of the scene, "but the soul of the young man was from that moment darkened. It was the first injury he had ever received at the hands of the Americans, whom he had always respected, and it wrung him to the soul as a deeper and deadlier wrong from that very circumstance."

Despite his darkened soul, Murieta swallows his rage and, with the patience of Job, settles with his beautiful Sonoran wife on a small farm in a Sierra Nevada valley. But like the agrarian Cherokees who had obligingly made room for Europeans and tolerated generations of abuse in the Southeast, Joaquin is finally driven from his homestead by whites who want the "fertile tract of land." Twice humiliated and forced out by the more powerful whites, Murieta still pursues a peaceful life, becoming a professional monte dealer in "Murphy's Diggings" in the gold fields, where "he was considered by all the very beau ideal of a gambler and the prince of clever fellows." Almost immediately, however, he is falsely charged with complicity in horse-stealing and is flogged while his half-brother, wrongly accused of stealing the animal, is hanged "without judge or jury." "It was then," writes the author, "that the character of Joaquin changed, suddenly and irrevocably. Wanton cruelty and the tyranny of prejudice had reached their climax. . . . Then it was that he declared to a friend that he would live henceforth for revenge and that his path should be marked with blood."

In spite of the superhuman carnage the noble Joaquin and his followers spill across the state, Ridge reminds us repeatedly that the bandits' actions are no more than a response to the "tyranny of prejudice" in Mexican Americans' treatment by racist whites, a race Murieta, like many American Indians, had begun by admiring and welcoming. Ultimately, Ridge explains, the young bandit would die "not as a mere outlaw, committing petty depredations and robberies, but as a *hero* who has revenged his country's wrongs and washed out her disgrace in the blood of her enemies." And finally, when his splendid bandit dies at age twenty-two, the age at which Ridge himself had become a fugitive, Ridge declares that

> in the few years which were allowed him, he displayed qualities of mind and heart which marked him as an extraordinary man, and leaving his name impressed upon the early history of this State. He also leaves behind him the important lesson that there is nothing so dangerous in its consequences as *injustice to individuals*—whether it arise from prejudice of color or from any other source; that a wrong done to one man is a wrong to society and to the world. (emphasis is Ridge's)

The authorial voice here is that of the dime-novel romance, a discourse arising from the Eurocentric conflation of heroic quest and manifest destiny, and one that Ridge appropriates to make it "bear the burden" of his subtext. Ridge's Joaquin belongs to that gothic tradition described by Michel Foucault: "the character of the black, cursed hero devoted to making the world expiate the evil done to him." It does not require a leap of imagination to conclude that Ridge, having seen his people robbed of their land and heritage and having had his father, grandfather and cousin murdered as a result, is acting out his often-sworn desire for revenge in the form of the invented bandit. At the same time, that the increasingly successful author would choose this heavily veiled medium for protest against America's treatment of Indians is not surprising. After all, with his thick black beard and urbane dress, Ridge passed easily as a Euramerican, and, more importantly, with his education and talents he was distinguishing himself amongst his "white" peers and seeing his name appearing repeatedly in association with those of the leading literati of San Francisco. Ridge, like many mixedbloods who "pass" and who have succeeded

within the parameters of the dominant culture, must have felt the conflict deeply.

More direct treatment of Indians in the novel underscores the complexity of the mixedblood author's feelings, as when Ridge introduces the "half-breeds and others at the Cherokee House" in a settlement called Cherokee Flat. Gold fever had sent a large number of Cherokees to the mountains of California. Even the prominent leader John Ross had set himself up as a dry-goods dealer proposing to sell supplies to his fellow Cherokees headed for the gold fields. In Ridge's novel, these mixedbloods eagerly and energetically assist the whites in capturing and hanging various unlucky Mexicans with little evidence of the captives' guilt. And when Ridge comes to mention the native inhabitants of California, he easily embraces the nineteenth century's racist stereotypes that reduced the many Indian cultures in California to the status of "Diggers." After referring to California Indians as "naked savages" and "ignorant Indians," Ridge describes "old Sapatarra," chief of the Tejon Nation, "seated upon his haunches in all the grandeur of 'naked majesty,' enjoying a very luxurious repast of roasted acorns and dried angle-worms." Ridge continues: "His swarthy subjects were scattered in various directions around him, engaged for the most part in the very arduous task of doing nothing. The little, smoky-looking children were sporting, like a black species of water-fowl." These Indians, he declares, always act "with great skill and caution; which last, by the way, is a quality that particularly distinguishes California Indians, amounting to so extreme a degree that it might safely be called cowardice." Finally, Ridge sums up this particular tribe as the "poor, miserable, cowardly Tejons."

While the well-educated Ridge, grandson of a tribal leader and member of the highly cultured and militantly proud Cherokee Nation, might easily look down on the oppressed and destitute California Indians, the absence of any sense of irony in his descriptions of the Tejons or "Diggers" suggests that Ridge thought primarily and perhaps almost exclusively of his own people when he addressed the concern of racial injustice through the example of Joaquin Murieta. Ridge paradoxically both embraces the racist values of his fellow Californians and protests social and racial injustice at the same time. He is divided against himself, an internal conflict further suggested in the fact that although there can be no doubt that Ridge thought California Indians to be vastly inferior to the Cherokee and other tribes to the east, he did at times defend the "Diggers" in print against Californians' depredations.

The Life and Adventures of Joaquin Murieta is at times abominably written, mimicking the romantic horrors in prose common to much nineteenth-century fiction. Nonetheless, Ridge's book marks an important moment in the development of American Indian fiction. This first novel by an Indian author demonstrates in fascinating fashion the tension arising from conflicting identities that would emerge as the central theme in virtually every novel by a Native American author to follow. Writing to his Cherokee cousin, Stand Watie, Ridge could identify himself as Indian and swear vengeance and redemption for his Cherokee relatives. When he turned to face his more privileged audience, however, Ridge was forced to veil his Indianness, to inscribe his identity within a context of sublimation and subterfuge. Following in Ridge's wake, American Indian authors would face again and again the dilemma of audience and identity, being forced to discover ways to both mimic and appropriate the language of the center and make it express a different reality, bear a different burden. Nearly a hundred years would pass before a novel written by a Native American could address the issues of injustice and genocide more directly, and even more time would pass before a work by an author recognizably Indian would gain critical acceptance. And in the novels of later generations of Indian writers, the character of the mixedblood behind the mask—Ridge himself—would move into the novel as protagonist and central concern. Out of the explosion of blood in Ridge's psychodrama of Mexican banditry and revolution would emerge a subgenre in American literature: the American Indian novel with its unceasing investigation of cultural dialectics, competing discourses, fractured identities, and historical genocide.

John Lowe (essay date 1996)

SOURCE: "I Am Joaquin!: Space and Freedom in Yellow Bird's *The Life and Adventures of Joaquin Murieta, The Celebrated California Bandit*," in *Early Native American Writing. New Critical Essays,* edited by Helen Jaskoski, Cambridge University Press, 1996, pp. 104-21.

[*In the following essay, Lowe examines Ridge's depiction of the relationship between space and identity in* Joaquin Murieta.]

Christopher Newman, that quintessential American abroad, opens Henry James's *The American* by occupying a huge circular divan at the Louvre; he sits, spreads his arms and legs, and fills up all the space he possibly can. He is, of course, from the West (where else?), where his prodigious energy and WASP identity have given him direct access to the American dream. A French aristocrat quite rightly nominates him for the title of "Duke of California."

The word "California" has always had a certain poetic resonance for Americans, partly because of the state's tremendous size but also because of its unique and abundant beauty. It is the original dream of the New World garden magnificently enlarged and gilded.

Indeed, the term "golden republic" refers not only to the native grasses, themselves emblematic of the state's general fecundity, but also to the mother lodes of gold discovered in the mid-1800s, images that underline the tensions inherent in the state's identity. Aware of these ironies, Yellow Bird (John Rollin Ridge), in *The Life and Adventures of Joaquin Murieta, the Celebrated California Bandit,* gives us a saga of space and freedom set in the golden republic's halcyon days of the 1850s. It is, to be sure, a story with a didactic purpose that pushes a moral message, and much of it is mediocre and slack. At its best, however, it is a powerful reminder of how the metaphysics of access to the American dream have always depended on the appropriation of space for the concept of identity, and how the politics of displaced and relocated peoples can give rise to heroic and sometimes mythical folk literature. Increasingly, it has been the important task of those denied the benefits of American life—the poor, the dispossessed, blacks, Native Americans, and immigrants—to remind all Americans of who they are as a people, and of what America says it is and should be. Fighting a battle for equality, armed with an awareness of our stated national principles and the demand that they be extended to all, disadvantaged Americans keep a national dynamic alive.

John Rollin Ridge (Yellow Bird was his tribal name) was born in Georgia to one of the most powerful families in the Cherokee Nation. The Ridges saw the inevitability of the federal government's plan to relocate the Nation and urged a negotiated acceptance, thus pitting themselves against the equally powerful Ross family. The issue had really been resolved, however, when gold was discovered in north Georgia.

When the Rosses killed Yellow Bird's father and grandfather, the family fled; Yellow Bird killed a man himself in a dispute and subsequently went to California to mine gold. Failing at that, he embarked on a literary career but remained obsessed with getting revenge for his relatives' murders. Meanwhile, he vented his spleen by indirectly damning U.S. imperialism in California. He did this by writing a romantic novel based on the contemporary and compelling legend of Joaquin Murieta, seeing an affinity between that figure's wronged ethnic, familial, and sexual honor and his own. Yellow Bird's publishers obviously saw the parallel, too; the "Publishers' Preface" to the original edition prominently announced that the author was "a 'Cherokee Indian' born in the woods—reared in the midst of the wildest scenery—and familiar with all that is thrilling, fearful, and tragical in a forest life" (2). The author of this mini-biography seems intent on establishing a romantic yet forbidding association between Yellow Bird and the preexisting tradition of the noble savage. This latter figure had long been connected, in the popular imagination, with the mastery of treacherous space, that is, the forest, forever linked in the Eurocentric mind with the moral "wood of error," the labyrinth, and the abode of the devil. The physical Western American counterpart of these images could easily be found in the desert, the plains, and the mountains, and all of these function in Joaquin's narrative; indeed, the expulsion from Eden/home is a constant theme.

Joaquin Murieta, branded as Cain and made to wander, unlike Christopher Newman but like Ridge himself, has had the American dream snatched from under him; a Mexican, his homestead in California has been seized by the American government. The narrative seems intent on reversing this imposed typology, on making us see Joaquin as more of an Abel/victim figure. Still, we must be careful in building this parallel; as his biographer notes, Ridge paradoxically favored assimilation as the ultimate answer to the "Indian question," and eagerly pursued wealth and position for himself and his family (Parins 2). Ridge seems to have been caught in limbo, neither inside nor outside a secure American identity; his writing resonates with that tension, which helps account for what seems his exuberant relief in the expansive spatial metaphors of Murieta's story.

The Joaquin myth was a composite of several bandits' careers. In *Joaquin,* Ridge faithfully follows the basic facts but interweaves them with details suggested by his own life; as noted, his family was originally driven, along with most other Cherokees, from northern Georgia, where the discovery of gold led to a land rush for Indian property. Ridge arrived in California in 1850, the same year that, in the novel, Joaquin rides up from Mexico. Just as Ridge's family was driven from Georgia, Joaquin is driven from his gold field claim by both predatory Anglo marauders and an equally unjust set of laws that persecuted foreign-born miners with an outrageous tax. Unlike Ridge, however, Murieta terrorizes most of California, and he is pursued and finally killed by a crude gang of deputies under the leadership of Captain Harry Love. His head and the hand of Three-Fingered Jack, his sidekick, are preserved in alcohol and then go on display for years in the sideshows and "museums" of the state as a warning to others. Rumor has it that the body parts were lost in the great San Francisco fire and earthquake, which would seem to be an appropriate coda to a heroic and brutal tale that takes much of its power from that of nature.

We might further note the metonymy involved here. The spatial confinement of the robbers' bodily parts backfires, for as the subsequent display of Joaquin's head and Three-Fingered Jack's hand across the state indicates, the "relics" are rather considered icons, retaining tremendous power. Although the bandits are dismembered and "caught" in glass jars, the meaning of their lives radiates endlessly.

What makes Ridge's Joaquin story different from its many other variants, and adds to the residual power of the myth, is his realization of this power. In his romantic and poetic evocation of Joaquin and his enchanted progress through the edenic spaces of the golden republic, Ridge similarly "caught" Joaquin and his men in the confined space of the novel but found a means to make their magical powers work anew for the readers. This aspect of the text perhaps accounts for its popularity in California, for in addition to providing the state with a heroic myth, it sets it against what Gaston Bachelard calls images of "felicitous space," which grow out of a kind of "topophilia," a mapping of space we love, space "that may be defended against adverse forces," and also space that may thus also be "eulogized" and therefore further "poeticized" (Bachelard xxxi). Anyone familiar with the similar topophilia of almost all Native American literature will immediately see the usefulness of Bachelard here, and of the centrality of *Joaquin Murieta* to that pattern. I make broad use of his theories here in an attempt to portray the meaning of Ridge's apparently random semiotics of landscape, as well as to demonstrate their metaphysical and political implications.

The Life and Adventures of Joaquin Murieta begins, traditionally but significantly, with the narrator's words: "I sit down to write somewhat concerning the life and character of *Joaquin Murieta*" (7). The sedentary stance of the author, a trite commonplace, here becomes an effective contrast to an extraordinarily mobile hero. The narrator then refers to Joaquin as a "truly wonderful man" who was nothing more or less than the "natural production of the social and moral condition of the country in which he lived, acting upon certain peculiar circumstances favorable to such a result, and consequently, his individual history is a part of the most valuable history of the State" (7). The narrator is interested in establishing Joaquin's amazing ability to range freely and quickly through the vast spaces of California. He therefore claims that although there were supposedly at least five "sanguinary devils" named Joaquin ranging the country at the same time, there was really only one: Joaquin Murieta.

Our omniscient guide then quickly sketches in the series of outrages that transformed Joaquin into an outlaw. Here the story has much in common, in a symbolic sense, with more current explorations of imperialism and empire, such as *The Jewel in the Crown* and David Lean's film of *A Passage to India,* for all three feature a cry of rape, which signifies what has been done to a country and a people. Daphne Manners, in *Crown,* actually is gang-raped, but the crime is falsely ascribed to Harry Kumar, an Indian. In *Passage,* the hysterical Adela Quested accuses her Indian friend, Dr. Aziz, of attempting to rape her. Both novels, written by Englishmen, ironically focus on unjust charges against men who represent whole cultures that have been "raped" by the British Raj. Here, the rape of Rosita (Joaquin's mistress) by Anglo-Americans similarly and ironically comments on the "rape" of displaced Hispanics in California and, obliquely, on the "rape" of the Cherokees, whose tragic story of displacement and disintegration is surely on Ridge's mind as he maps out parallel events in California.

In *Joaquin,* after the title figure has been ousted from successful ventures in mining and farming, he is forced to witness Rosita's rape, which is soon followed by the murder of his half-brother by a crazed vigilante mob. These events have a catastrophic affect on Joaquin, which is expressed in a spatial metaphor: "His soul swelled beyond its former boundaries, and the barriers of honor, rocked into atoms by the strong passion which shook his heart like an earthquake, crumbled around him. Then it was that he declared . . . he would live henceforth for revenge and that his path should be marked with blood" (12-13). Joaquin's circle of self, thwarted in its effort to grow via the traditional American way (hard work, enterprise, and democratic comradeship), has burst through into a new and larger circle through the passion of anger. His vow to cut a "bloody path" through the state as he avenges the wrongs done to him and his family presages ever-widening circles of spatial/criminal conquest. His path echoes several principles set down in the 1840s by Ralph Waldo Emerson in his seminal essay "Circles." In one of literary Transcendentalism's prime expressions, Emerson gives space and confinement elemental circular forms, first in the human eye and then, significantly, in nature, for the "horizon" formed by the eyes is the second circle man knows, a "primary figure" that is repeated "without end" in nature (263). Here and in his other essays, Emerson maps out an imperial self that properly seeks expansion and power, a process generated from and paralleled by nature itself. The concept of the self expressed by ever-expanding concentric circles has a demonic side as well; at one point in "Circles," Emerson relates his expanding circles of self to explosive anger, the kind Ridge's readers see expressed by Joaquin: "But the heart refuses to be imprisoned; in its first and narrowest pulses it already tends outward with a vast force and to immense and innumerable expansions" (Emerson 265).

Theories of "self-reliance" and the "imperial self" fed into the ideology of manifest destiny. These ideas would find magnificent expression in other key works of the period, particularly in Hawthorne's exploration of the "magic circles" of the self in *The Scarlet Letter* (1850) and in Melville's critique of unleashed darker elements of Emersonian and capitalist ideology, *Moby-Dick* (1851), books published only a few years before *Joaquin.* Although it is beyond the scope of this essay, *The Life and Adventures of Joaquin Murieta* surely demands to be studied alongside these books and other masterworks of what we have called the "American Renaissance," as well as with the works of newer members of the canon such as

Frederick Douglass, Harriet Beecher Stowe, and Harriet Jacobs. As in many of those narratives, in *Joaquin Murieta* we follow a somewhat romantic and poetic evocation of a hero through edenic spaces, but it is a vision that coexists with a gruesome litany of murders, robberies, and tortures. Yellow Bird was able to achieve this fusion, perhaps, because he was taking folkloric materials and transforming them into narrative virtually at their moment of formation. Bakhtin has demonstrated that the novel's roots must ultimately be sought in folklore, where the object of artistic representation is degraded to the level of a contemporary reality; the fluid periods of history are ideal for furnishing such material (Bakhtin 39).

Furthermore, as is often the case with an American 'classic,' *Joaquin*'s narrative charts a key moment in American history, a time when prospectors from all over the world converged on the mother lode. The gold rush as mined by Mark Twain, Bret Harte, and others quickly became the stuff of legend and literature. What has been left out of the literature, however, is the displacement of Mexican-Americans. The victory of the United States over Mexico in 1848 coincided almost exactly with the discovery of gold in California. Two years later, the state's legislature passed a "Foreign Miners' Tax Law"; ironically, Germans, French, and, for a time, Chinese were permitted to stay, but Latino miners were forced out. The great Mexican ranches in the state, with their hundreds of dependents, contributed a vast displaced population; some of these displaced individuals became outlaws who were supported by others in the Hispanic community.

The force of history seemed to accelerate drastically during these years, and *Joaquin*'s hectic narrative keeps fictional pace. As the narrator points out, one of the most amazing things about the ensuing and terrifying assassinations of the men who had brutalized Joaquin and his family is the swiftness with which the miscreants are dispatched. Throughout the tale, the banditti act swiftly; celerity works hand in hand with mastery of space. Joaquin's apparent ability to be everywhere is partially explained in the text, as the narrator conflates another Joaquin story by having the actual Joaquin Valenzuela (one of the five Joaquins) function as Joaquin's lieutenant. This also implies that Joaquin operates as part of a long line of Mexican bandits, for Valenzuela, we are told, rode with the famous guerrilla chief Padre Jurata in Mexico and presumably schooled Joaquin in the tricks of the trade.

Physical security conceived in terms of spatial refuge, frequently set as nature's bosom, also finds expression in material goods that answer immediate temporal needs. Joaquin's only safety is said, for instance, to lie "in a persistence in the unlawful course which he had begun. It was necessary that he should have horses and that he should have money" (13-14). Soon the local newspapers are full of accounts of attacks on ranchers, coaches, and travelers:

> The scenes of murder and robbery shifted with the rapidity of lightning. At one time, the northern countries [sic] would be suffering slaughters and depredations, at another the southern, and, before one would have imagined it possible, the east and the west, and every point of the compass would be in trouble . . . the country . . . was so well adapted to a business of this kind—the houses scattered at such distances along the roads, the plains so level and open in which to ride with speed, and the mountains so rugged with their ten thousand fastnesses in which to hide. (15)

As Joaquin's mastery of space expands, that of the public at large shrinks, for "all dreaded to travel the public roads" (22), a fact that contributes powerfully to the Americans' growing anger and resentment.

Joaquin's most impressive feat comes when he is surprised by a band of men in a canyon:

> His only practicable path was a narrow digger-trail which led along the side of a huge mountain, directly over a ledge of rocks a hundred yards in length, which hung beatling [sic] over the rushing stream beneath in a direct line with the hill. . . . It was a fearful gauntlet for any man to run . . . [there was] danger of falling 100 feet . . . [he] must run in a parallel line with his enemies . . . with their revolvers drawn. He dashed along that fearful trail as if he had been mounted upon a spirit-steed, shouting as he passed, "I am Joaquin! Kill me if you can!" (87)

It is hardly surprising that this is the moment in the book that artists have most often depicted (it appears on the cover of the 1955 Oklahoma Press edition), for as Ridge remarks, "It was perfectly sublime to see such super-human daring and recklessness" (87). We may read the scene's spatial semiotics both ethnically and politically. Murieta, belonging to neither the Indian nor the Anglo-American world, nor even to the community of law-abiding but oppressed Mexicans, rides a razor-thin ridge (also the author's last name) of marginality throughout the book, boldly outlined against nature, riding on it, across it, against it, supported yet threatened by the abyss. Politically, he is alien, outlaw, racial and religious other; but all this is transcended through his "sublime" mastery of American space(s), much of it forbidden. Again and again, the narrator refers to Joaquin's lightning-like ability to range across the land as "magical." He is also careful, however, to provide a counterpoint of realistic reasons for Joaquin's success, such as the general support and encouragement the protagonist receives from the rest of the Mexican community, the unsettled condition of the country, and the isolation of the mining regions. Joaquin also, like Robin Hood, deals gently with those who support him, and many ranchers buy protection by sheltering the band for the night and keeping quiet about it later.

Yellow Bird takes care to authenticate space. He understands the value time has in setting the boundaries of place, so when Joaquin is in a specific vicinity, the narrator frequently gives the precise date, quotes local newspapers for details of the location, and specifies towns, rivers, mountains, and even gullies. One may easily chart Joaquin's course across the state by following Yellow Bird's narrative mapping. Arroyos, rocks, and other prominent features in the terrain are also added, not for scenic effect but to reify the landscape. Two men are traveling on a road, specifically the one "that leads up Feather River, near to the Honcut Creek, which puts into that stream" (21). Similarly, the complementary grid of temporal reality is laid over the natural. When Joaquin is said to be in a specific locale, Ridge includes sentences supposedly taken from newspapers in passages like this: "*The Marysville Herald* of November 15, 1851, speaking of the horrible state of affairs, has the following remarkable paragraph: 'Seven men have been murdered within three or four days in a region of country not more than twelve miles in extent'" (21). All this is necessary. Joaquin's mastery of space will not be magical unless the land itself is realistic and believable.

The most important statement of this central theme comes when Joaquin relocates to a spot near Mount Shasta in the northern part of the state. The mountain, Ridge maintains, "serves at a distance of two hundred miles to direct the course of the mountain-traveler, being to him as the polar star to the mariner" (23). Mount Shasta awesomely "rears its white shaft at all seasons of the year high above every other peak . . . in its garments of snow like some mighty archangel, filling the heaven with his solemn presence" (23). This rather trite description nevertheless parallels Yellow Bird's main themes, for like Joaquin, Mount Shasta towers above its peers, is unassailable and unavoidable, and extends into space both horizontally and vertically.

The mountain creates a peak of sorts in the narrative as well, for Yellow Bird inserts into the novel his two-and-a-half-page poem, **"Mount Shasta, Seen from a Distance."** At first the mountain is personified as a proud blasphemer, a tower of pride that defies the storms of heaven that beat against it in wrath. Mount Shasta, however, is not static: "age by age" it is "still rising higher / Into Heaven!" (23). In an abrupt turn, Yellow Bird reveals that the mountain, far from being the blasphemous rebel that it seems to be, was created by God and symbolizes the higher law of God that humans should strive to attain. "And well this Golden State shall thrive, if, like / Its own Mounta Shasta, sovereign law shall lift / Itself in purer atmosphere—so high / That human feeling, human passion, at its base shall lie subdued. . . . Its pure administration shall be like / The snow, immaculate upon that mountain's brow!" (25). In his poem, Ridge points to the discrepancy between what the law should be and what it actually is.

This long apostrophe to the mountain enables Yellow Bird to take us as readers high above the state to share this lofty monarch's view of "the fertile / Vale, and undulating plains below, the grass" (25). From this vantage point we understand the purifying effect that Mount Shasta has on the land, for from its flanks come cool breezes and vapors which "guarantee . . . health and happiness" to the farms and farmers below. Even better, and more romantically, the mountain inspires "loftier feelings . . . nobler thoughts" for the humble plowman; little children, asking who made the mountain, learn from their mothers that it is God's creation. We thus, like the spotted hawk in Walt Whitman's similarly conceived *Song of Myself* (1855), aspire to "the eagle's cloudless height" and the clear-eyed perspective on American nature and the law that should proceed from the continent's grandeur and majestic space. The poem ends, in fact, by transforming this "blasphemous" Babel-like natural phenomenon into a symbol of law, a pure white shaft that towers above humanity's activities as a moral guide. It is in the shadow of this peak that Joaquin and his men take refuge for several months, descending at intervals into the valley below to steal horses with the aid of the Indians.

How does all this work in the overall scheme of the novel? Mount Shasta suggests the doubled nature of Joaquin, who as rebel against an unjust set of laws that discriminate against Mexicans actually represents a purer law. Like Mount Shasta, his freedom in space gives him a kind of vertical presence in the society of humans as well; as with most mythical bandits, his actions, which take place during hard times for many people, offer heroic and poetic imaginative space and freedom for the oppressed and the weak, who lack Joaquin's resourcefulness and courage. The fact that the mountain's base in earthly nature is frequently obscured by clouds aligns with Joaquin's mythical stance, one much like the trickster's, between God and humanity. Moreover, the cooperation with California's Indians underlines Yellow Bird's doubled role as narrator and begins a long skein of references to the shameful treatment Native Americans have received in the Golden State, both as victims and as scapegoats. Ridge will charge, in fact, that "The ignorant Indians suffered for many a deed which had been perpetrated by civilized hands. It will be recollected by many persons who resided at Yreka and on Scott's River in the fall and winter of 1851 how many 'prospecters' [sic] were lost in the mountains and never again heard from; how many were found dead, supposed to have been killed by the Indians, and yet bearing upon their bodies the marks of knives and bullets quite as frequently as arrows" (27).

Joaquin's role as trickster and his alignment with Indians dovetail in the episode where he and his men are robbed by the Tejons. The trickster, as mediator between God and humanity, usually has his way, but if he did so always, he would be too close to the status of God; therefore he, too, must occasionally come to grief, as Coyote, Raven, and Brer Rabbit all do from time to time. Moreover, it is often true that a weaker creature tricks the trickster, and that is precisely how the Tejons function here. As masters of the region's terrain and as silent, superb hunters, the Tejons have little difficulty surprising Joaquin and his band, stripping them naked, and beating them soundly with willow rods. The episode is a version of the "trickster tricked" motif that Paul Radin has identified in trickster narratives, one also found in African-American folktales and confirmed by Ridge's statement that "The robbers were robbed" (40). Joaquin, however, laughs off the episode and refuses to take revenge on Old Chief Sapatarra and his band. He knows, as we do, that they were inspired to this mischief by a wealthy white rancher, who sought their aid in retrieving stock the bandits had stolen. Moreover, when Joaquin's band, men and women alike, are stripped naked by the Tejons, the men find new clothing but the women hide themselves in the brush "like mother Eve"; the phrase points both to the regenerative nature all around them and to the parallels between their retreats and the Garden of Eden/mythical nest.

It should not be supposed, however, that Ridge is in close consort with California Indians. His portraits of them are quite mixed, perhaps because of his own ancestry in a supposedly more civilized tribe, the Georgia Cherokees, who had their own alphabet, had adopted white modes of production, and had established thriving businesses before the forced march to the West. In a later scene, he paints the Tejon Nation in lazy poses as they eat acorns and worms, and he charges them with treachery and cowardice. When they succeed in robbing Joaquin and his band, Ridge comments, "The poor, miserable, cowardly Tejons had achieved a greater triumph over them than all the Americans put together!" (38). Nor are the Tejons the only Native people who operate against Joaquin; later, some Cherokees aid the American pursuers and kill two of Murieta's band. Presumably, Ridge had in mind those renegades who sided with the Ross faction rather than with his own family; there were no good Indians, per se, for Ridge, even in his own tribe.

Similarly, Ridge's verdict on the "Digger" Indians is mixed. Like the Mark Twain of *Roughing It,* he has contempt for their supposedly low standard of living and their employment in menial positions (the term "Digger" was a derogatory label imposed by white settlers), but he admits that in their capacity as runners bearing mail, they are "very expeditious on foot and willing to travel a considerable distance for a small piece of bread, fresh meat, or a ragged shirt. I have known them to swim rivers when the waters were high and dangerous in order to carry a letter to its destination. They are exceedingly faithful in this business, having a superstitious dread of that mysterious power which makes a *paper talk without a mouth*" (130). However, although they are admired for their mastery over time and space, their ignorance, superstition, and servile natures undercut this quality. In short, Joaquin's ability to achieve his own rough version of justice in an unjust world is a beacon of hope for all oppressed Californians—exemplified in his frequent but sometimes problematic alliance with the Indians.

Joaquin and his band cannot be continually in motion; such a plot would be as exhausting to the reader as it would be to the men and would violate the traditional pattern in the Robin Hood genre that Ridge follows. Like Robin, Joaquin has a mistress, Rosita, who travels with him, like Maid Marian; his gang is full of idiosyncratic desperados; and, most important for this discussion, Murieta's band has a multitude of natural hideouts to return to for rest and recuperation. The rugged arroyos are their Sherwood Forest. Bachelard would term these hidden strongholds "nests," and indeed, that is the way Yellow Bird describes them. The most beautiful is the Arroyo Cantoova, fenced in by impenetrable mountains. It contains rich pasturage for the many animals Joaquin and his band steal from the ranchers. Entrance is limited to a narrow pass that can be guarded and defended by only a handful of men; even better, the arroyo is at least 150 miles from any human habitation. Despite these rather forbidding facts, the "nest" is attractive. "Embosomed" by the mountains, the retreat abounds in wild game and features a luxurious grove of evergreen oaks that Joaquin and his "still blooming companion," Rosita, inhabit. The refuge is the band's bower of bliss, roofed by "rich foliage," "carpeted" with grass and flowers (28).

The various nest/sanctuaries of the novel operate as many other features of Yellow Bird's poetic landscapes do; as Bachelard would say, they give us back the situations of our dreams—, in this case, the dream of security. This idea is as old as Theocritus and the pastoral tradition, where a simplification of setting and character enables the poet/writer to reduce complex ideas to essences. Attic shepherds and shepherdesses, whether inhabiting Virgil's *Eclogues,* Shakespeare's Arden Forest, or Faulkner's bucolic Mississippi, may introduce probing aesthetic and moral arguments and propositions effortlessly and clearly against the untroubled rural backdrop, whose "bosom" shelters but also nourishes the body and the spirit. An alternative to the tradition has always been the hidden refuge of the bandit, which popular novels and operas often feature; Blackmoore's *Lorna Doone,* Scott's *Rob Roy,* Bizet's *Carmen,* and Verdi's *Il Trovatore* all feature hidden banditti mountain paradises. They are places to

go when someone cries, "Flee, all is discovered!" Readers can relate to this idea of refuge; as Bachelard notes, nests are the imaginative and supremely safe childhood spaces we yearn for in daydreams (99). In political terms (and we should not forget that Murieta represents a persecuted and exiled minority and a kind of proto-guerrilla movement), the retreats are reminiscent of those of the montagnards of Vietnam or the freedom fighters in Afghanistan.

Yellow Bird, however, makes this "nest" uniquely and unforgettably American. The thrust of nature, the interplay between Mexicans and Indians, the guns and horses and sweeping rides over the vast plains of Western narrative—all these qualities and several more, linked indelibly with American republican iconography, stimulate shocks of recognition for the American reader. It is here, in this natural "house," that Joaquin promises Rosita that one day he will soon complete his revenge, take his booty, and retire to a peaceful ranch where he will build her a "pleasant home," the ultimate sacred space for Yellow Bird's domestic readers. Just three years earlier, in *Uncle Tom's Cabin,* Harriet Beecher Stowe had created parallel domestic nests for runaway slaves in properly Victorian American homes, homes purposely delineated as identical to those of her readers.

Part of Joaquin's revenge lies in the invasion of precisely this domestic space: Many of the murders he commits take place in the homes of his victims, and he delights in secret penetration of other social spaces as well. In one of the novel's most famous scenes, Joaquin, in disguise, is playing monte in a saloon in Mokelumne Hill when his fellow players begin a discussion about the dreaded Joaquin. One of them boasts that he would "just like once in his life to come across Joaquin, and that he would kill him as quick as he would a snake," whereupon Joaquin jumps up on the table, brandishes his pistol, and shouts "I am Joaquin! if there is any shooting to do, I am in" (31). He has impishly "become the game," and as so often happens in the book, his action ruptures the narrative; it precipitates a chase, hurling the reader into yet another whirlwind across the landscape. But Joaquin's escape into vast space is underlined by his preceding ability to puncture the restricted space, the "temple" of the profane urban world, the saloon. Murieta is not content merely to penetrate this sanctum sanctorum of the patriarchs; the poker table, a doubled altar with the gods of money above and guns below, is literally trampled and profaned by Joaquin's muddy boots.

However, Joaquin is not a blasphemer of the truly sacred. He and his colleagues are befriended by the Catholic Church and take shelter for weeks at a time at places like San Gabriel Mission, thereby appropriating sacred as well as secular space and adding yet another nest for rest and recuperation. More often, however, Joaquin returns to the maternal embrace of the arroyos, moving back and forth between his multidirectional raids and his secret mountain dens, "so rugged with their ten thousand fastnesses in which to hide" (15).

Who can stop this "outrageous" bandit? Clearly, only a man such as Captain Harry Love, who is as masterful as Joaquin in transcending space and time. That is exactly how the bandit's ultimate nemesis is introduced, quite early in the book, long before he is to kill Joaquin:

> Love had served as an express rider in the Mexican war and had borne dispatches from one military post to another over the most dangerous tracts of Mexico. He had traveled alone for hundreds of miles over mountains and deserts. . . . Riding fleet horses and expert in the use of the lasso, it required a well-mounted horseman to escape [bandits] on the open plains, and many a hard race with them has the Captain had to save his neck and the valuable papers in his charge. (34)

Similarly, the real Love's men succeeded in tracking Murieta partly because, as Edwin Corle has observed, they were "expert horsemen, superb marksmen and perfectly capable of handling themselves in any terrain, be it the coastal valleys, the dry deserts or the High Sierras" (Corle 270). Furthermore, Love comes from a pioneer background, and is thus suited to the hardships and dangers of border life. Finally, in his role as deputy sheriff of Los Angeles County, he is a representative of the law that Joaquin scorns.

Still, Love has difficulty finding the charmed Murieta. Throughout the book Ridge creates the impression that Joaquin is enclosed in a magical space, making him immune to legal retribution, no matter how desperate the situation has become. This theme frequently becomes interwoven with concepts of moral space as well. One evening, Joaquin, riding alone, meets Joe Lake, a friend of his "more happy and honest days." After the men exchange greetings, the text quickly becomes sentimental. Joaquin weeps, confesses that he is not the man he once was, admits that he hates almost all Americans but still loves Joe, and thus implores Joe not to betray him. "Lake assured him there was no danger, and the two parted, for the wide gulf of dishonor yawned between them, and they could never again be united" (51). Lake, unaware of Joaquin's uncanny ability to be everywhere at once, immediately betrays his friend to Americans in Ornetas while a serape-clad Mexican listens; this bystander, Joaquin's spy, reports to the master himself, who is just outside. Charging that "you have lied to me," Murieta shoots Lake dead. An instant later, he is seen on top of a nearby hill with fifty men, once again protected by "the magical luck which pursued this man, following him like an invisible guardian fiend in every hour of his peril" (51).

The passage reaffirms our sense of Joaquin's magical mastery of space, but adds the sense of moral distance and the gulfs opened up by imperialist history.

Such passages—and there are several—are more than merely adventures. They exemplify the ballooning myth of Joaquin in the state that Ridge was chronicling. As Joseph Henry Jackson has stated, "Hardly a town along the Mother Lode is without its cavern, cellar, or tunnel, in or through which Murieta dodged the law," and the tales that relate these episodes are repeated "solemnly as truth," as great myths always are (110-11). Harry Hansen's *Guide to the Golden State* lists many "shrines" to Joaquin across the state, including a resort called Murietta [sic] Hot Springs, a museum claiming to have his red sash, and various others, typified by the town of Murphys: "The town has the usual Joaquin Murrieta [sic] legend: here the ubiquitous bad man is said to have been a three-card monte dealer in 1851 and to have begun his bloody career when his brother, unjustly . . . was hanged" (446, 447, 491-4, 524). Although the various versions of the tale over the years have taken many liberties, there is one quality they all share: mastery of space. When Edwin Corle published his study of banditry in 1949, he emphasized that Joaquin's "forays ranged throughout the gold towns in the High Sierras and up and down the Royal Highway, and nobody could be sure just where he was, what he was planning or where he would strike next" (267).

One explanation for this magical space comes from the concept of banditti solidarity. Together, the band is strong, but if their principle of *e pluribus unum* falters, disaster ensues. For instance, when Joaquin and his band need to move through the Los Angeles section of the state, Love's home territory, they separate so as not to be detected. It is here that Reyes, Joaquin's friend and Rosita's brother, is captured and hanged shortly after Love has found and murdered Gonzalez. As Joaquin's band fragments and is reduced, so are his powers; it seems important that this process begins in an area where land has been massively appropriated from Hispanics and where premodern life presents obstacles, physical, social, and psychic, to the unfettered movements of the banditti. Twenty men are lost in one fight alone, including the valued lieutenant Claudio. Soon afterward, Mountain Jim is hanged in San Diego.

The differing locales for these events indicate the sweep of Joaquin's network across the state once again but also demonstrate the menace that increasing settlement and urbanization pose to space and freedom—and not just for outlaws. Joaquin astutely sees these events as an evil omen, one dictating the need to act swiftly and conclusively.

Once back in Arroyo Cantoova, he announces a master plan of destruction that will end his days as a bandit.

Now that he commands 2,000 men spread over the state, he intends to make a clean sweep of the southern counties, killing and burning as he goes on toward the refuge of Sonora. "When I do this, I shall wind up my career. My brothers, we will then be revenged for our wrongs, and some little, too, for the wrongs of our poor, bleeding country. We will divide our substance and spend the rest of our days in peace" (75). This last campaign begins in earnest with a strategic attack by Joaquin's full forces on Calaveras County, which is described by Ridge in edenic terms. The gang's terrifying assault brings on the final conflict with Captain Love, which is made possible by Joaquin's inexplicable decision to travel apart from his band and with only three followers.

Joaquin in these last pages is not the man he was, as is suggested earlier in the scene with Lake. His decision to leave a trail of scorched earth behind him actually masks what amounts to his surrender. What causes this change? Bachelard suggests that a true poetics of space is based in simple images of felicitous space; he also stresses the concepts of interiority and exteriority that exist in the human imagination, depending on how the person in question reacts to the spaces that surround him. Joaquin, an outcast in the world of people, initially poeticizes the world of nature positively in the mode of Bachelard's topophilics; he has not been "cast into the world" since he has opened it through his actions. As a master of space, he is a master of nature, and in its subservience it is beautiful proof of his identity. In his interior daydreams, the vast landscapes of California that he effortlessly covers are corresponding symbols of his interior immensity. Like a poet cited by Bachelard, Joaquin might say, "As I stood in contemplation of the garden of the wonders of space I had the feeling that I was looking into the ultimate depths, the most secret regions of my own being; and I smiled, because it had never occurred to me that I could be so pure, so great, so fair! My heart burst into singing. . . . All these constellations are yours, they exist in you" (189). It would be easy to find similar passages in Ridge's contemporaries, like Cooper, Emerson, Whitman, and Thoreau, and in other Native American writings, but let us continue in a French vein. Baudelaire writes, "In certain almost supernatural inner states, the depth of life is entirely revealed in the spectacle, however, ordinary, that we have before our eyes, and which becomes the symbol of it," thereby permitting intimate grandeur to unfold (cited in Bachelard 195). Moreover, as Bachelard suggests, movement within vastness magnifies this feeling: "When the dreamer really experiences the word immense, he sees himself liberated from his cares and thoughts, even from his dreams. He is no longer shut up in his weight, the prisoner of his own being" (195).

Unfortunately, perceptions can change. Joaquin's feeling of transcendence eventually becomes a trap; the originally authenticating sense of identification with the powers of vast landscapes pales. Bachelard quotes the poet Jules Supervielle's reactions to similarly endless rides on the South American pampas: "Precisely because of too much riding and too much freedom, and of the unchanging horizon, in spite of our desperate gallopings, the pampa assumed the aspect of a prison for me, a prison that was bigger than the others" (221). Joaquin, however, as I have suggested, possibly understands that even the vast sweep of wild California will have to submit to the American imperialist enterprise; *his* "pampas," unlike Supervielle's, are not "unchanging." Moreover, no matter how big the space, if it offers no sanctuary except in hidden enclaves, is it not still a prison, no matter how vast? Finally, of course, the ever-constricting wild landscape, always a metaphor for the mind itself, mirrors the internal constriction of identity, and the possibilities of topographic transcendence collapse.

We can only go so far, however, in reading Murieta's sensibilities. Ridge created a composite hero to command our attention but was unable to develop his psychology. To Ridge's credit, however, our interest in and frustration with the narrative are related to more important issues than the character of Joaquin. Murieta's story, calculated for popular appeal, has more to tell us than we suspect. A parallel version, the 1936 movie *The Robin Hood of El Dorado* (which, ironically and predictably, cast the Anglo Warner Baxter in Joaquin's role), was made in an escapist mode. It was also crafted, however, to speak to mainstream American concerns during a grim economic decline, when crime, be it Bonnie and Clyde's or Joaquin Murieta's, sometimes seemed justified, romantic, and peculiarly American. The movie was based on Walter Noble Burns's history/novel of the same title (1932); as Kent Steckmesser notes, Burns was following the same formula he had used in his wildly successful and historically inaccurate *Saga of Billy the Kid* (1926). Although the topic is outside the scope of this essay, one must be struck by the way Ridge inserts into the American outlaw narrative the assertion that ethnicity constitutes an affront to society, as surely as do broken laws. Joaquin speaks not only for the poor but also for the racially and ethnically oppressed, all denied "space" at the feast of America. He becomes a necessary mythic hero, who, like Robin Hood and Rob Roy, has been generated from and supported by the folk. As Lukacs has noted, both Goethe and Scott were interested in this kind of figure as demonstrative of the possibilities for "human upsurge and heroism" that are widespread among the masses (52-3); the ruptures of history, and their consequent patterns of dislocation and relocation, thus provide revolutionary possibilities for heroic behavior.

The Joaquin legend is in many ways the chief mythic nugget from the mother lode created by the birth of the state of California. For Californians, Murieta's story has become more than folklore; we may surely call it an epic. Bakhtin felt that the epic genre echoed a world of beginnings and peak times, a shared heroic past that speaks to the present. Joaquin also seems generated and nurtured by a threatened but still untamed nature. His very exteriority and marginality ironically locate him in the magical realm of spatial and imaginative freedom, and he thus personifies the dream that was felt but rarely experienced by actual miners, whose faces were averted into the mud as they panned for gold. The Chilean Pablo Neruda, one of the more recent writers to set this tale, ends his lyric poem, *Splendor and Death of Joaquin Murieta,* with a passage redolent of both Joaquin's link to the people and Bachelard's formulations. Neruda seems to suggest that Joaquin's poetic spaces still exist, most particularly in the souls of people still yearning to be free:

> Joaquin, return to your nest: gallop the air
>   toward the south
>   on your blood-colored stallion.
> The streams of the country that bore you sing
>   out of silvery
>   mouths. Your poet sings with them.
> Your fate mingled bloodshed and gall, Joaquin
>   Murieta; but
>   its sound
> is still heard. Your people repeat both your
>   song and your
>   grief, like a tolling bell struck underground.
>   The people
>   are million.

(175)

Works Cited

Bachelard, Gaston. *The Poetics of Space,* trans. Maria Jolas. Boston: Beacon Press, 1969.

Bakhtin, Mikhail. *The Dialogic Imagination: Four Essays by Mikhail Bakhtin,* ed. Michael Holquist and Caryl Emerson. Austin: University of Texas Press, 1981.

Corle, Edwin. *The Royal Highway.* Indianapolis: Bobbs-Merrill, 1949.

Emerson, Ralph Waldo. *Selected Writings of Emerson,* ed. Donald McQuade. New York: Modern Library, 1981.

Hansen, Harry, ed. *A Guide to the Golden State.* New York: Hastings House, 1969.

Jackson, Joseph Henry. *Anybody's Gold: The Story of California's Mining Towns.* San Francisco: Chronicle Books, 1970.

Lukacs, Georg. *The Historical Novel,* trans. H. and S. Mitchell. London: Merlin, 1962.

Neruda, Pablo. *The Splendor and Death of Joaquin Murieta,* trans. Ben Belitt. New York: Farrar, Straus and Giroux, 1972.

Parins, James W. *John Rollin Ridge: His Life and Works.* Lincoln: University of Nebraska Press, 1991.

Radin, Paul. *The Trickster: A Study in American Indian Mythology.* New York: Schocken Books, 1972.

Ridge, John Rollin (Yellow Bird). *The Life and Adventures of Joaquin Murieta, The Celebrated California Bandit.* 1854. Rpt. Norman: University of Oklahoma Press, 1955.

Steckmesser, Kent. *The Western Hero in History and Myth.* Norman: University of Oklahoma Press, 1965.

FURTHER READING

Biography

Walker, Franklin. "The Fifties." In his *San Francisco's Literary Frontier,* pp. 45-54. New York: Alfred A. Knopf, Inc., 1939.

> Provides a brief overview of Ridge's life as well as a discussion of some of the major features of his novel

---

Additional coverage of Ridge's life and career is contained in the following source published by the Gale Group: *Native North American Literature.*

Une Saison en enfer

Arthur Rimbaud

The following entry presents criticism of Rimbaud's prose poem *Une Saison en enfer* (1873). For information on Rimbaud's complete career, see *NCLC,* Volumes 4 and 35.

INTRODUCTION

In both style and substance, *Une Saison en enfer* (*A Season in Hell*) is considered a revolutionary work. Unlike earlier authors of prose poems, Rimbaud shunned conventional description, straightforward narrative, and didactic purpose. *Une Saison* represents a revolt against the naturalism, precision, and objectivity of the Parnassians, who dominated French poetry in the 1860s and 1870s. Its innovative reliance on suggestion and evocation rather than concrete depiction heralds the inception of the Symbolist movement, whose adherents idolized Rimbaud. In basic form, *Une Saison* is a unique confessional work in which the poet describes a harrowing emotional and spiritual struggle. Though the poem has been subject to widely divergent interpretations, most recent commentators regard it as both a sardonic account of Rimbaud's beliefs and aspirations, and a moving exploration of universal hopes and desires.

Biographical Information

Rimbaud was born on October 20, 1854, in Charleville, a town in northeastern France not far from the Belgian border. He was eighteen years old when he wrote *Une Saison,* and his literary career—inaugurated when he was fifteen—was nearly over. He began the work in April 1873, and composed most of it in the seclusion of his mother's farmhouse in Roche, near Charleville; however, he may have written parts of it in London and Brussels, where he spent brief periods in May and July with the poet Paul Verlaine. Rimbaud and Verlaine had become lovers in 1871, but their two-year affair was marked by frequent quarrels and separations. Their relationship came to a dramatic close in Brussels on July 10, 1873, when Verlaine—outraged that Rimbaud intended to leave him once again—shot him in the wrist. After recuperating in a Brussels hospital for a week, Rimbaud returned to his mother's farm and completed *Une Saison* before the month was over. The work was published in November, and Rimbaud took a few copies to Paris, seeking critical acclaim. Disappointed at the lack of interest in his latest creation, Rimbaud left France and spent much of 1874 in England. In January 1875 he began the

nomadic career that would occupy the remainder of his life. After traveling throughout Europe, he journeyed to Africa in 1880. He spent the following years chiefly in Abyssinia (modern-day Ethiopia) where he became a commercial trader, an explorer, and an arms dealer. He died in Marseilles on November 10, 1891.

Textual History

The composition dates and early publication history of *Une Saison en enfer* have been well documented by modern scholars. In a letter to his friend Ernest Delahaye, dated May of 1873 and written from Roche, Rimbaud described his progress on a prose poem that he had provisionally titled "Livre païen" ("Pagan Book") or "Livre nègre" ("Negro Book"). After completing the work in July of 1873, Rimbaud took the manuscript to a printer in Brussels, where it was published in November. His sister Isabelle fostered the story that Rimbaud was so discouraged by the lack of critical enthusiasm for *Une Saison* that he burned the entire edition, and for decades it was generally believed that there were only a few copies in existence.

However, in 1901 a Belgian bibliophile named Losseau discovered approximately five hundred copies of the book in the attics of the Brussels printer; apparently they were left in storage because Rimbaud had been unable to pay for them. Losseau shocked the literary world when, in 1915, he revealed his discovery.

Form and Content

Une Saison en enfer is framed as a literary, emotional, and spiritual autobiography. In the course of the work, Rimbaud adopted a series of narrative personas, contended with concrete and abstract protagonists, and addressed a variety of audiences. The prevailing rhetorical style follows a pattern of statement—endorsement of a proposed solution, a philosophical premise, or a moral value—followed by an antithetical or counterstatement; this, in turn, is succeeded by a rejection or dismissal of both positions. Verb tenses frequently switch from past to present, and the poetic language alternates between formal and colloquial discourse.

Commentators generally view *Une Saison* as comprising nine sections, although some regard the fourth and fifth sections—"Délires I" and "Délires II"—as a single entity. The first section, untitled, is usually referred to as the prologue or preface; here the speaker reminisces about his former life and his rebellions against authority, and sets the stage for the poem's ambiguous treatment of good and evil. In the second part, "Mauvais Sang" ("Bad Blood"), the poet explores his pre-Christian, Gallic origins and emphasizes his alienation from modern civilization. "Nuit de l'enfer" ("Night of Hell") is a tortured account of hallucinations, spiritual combat, and damnation, in which the narrator parodies his attempts to become a semi-divine being and change the world. "Délires I" ("Deliriums I") subtitled "Vierge folle—l'Époux infernal" ("Foolish Virgin—The Infernal Bridegroom")—is generally agreed to be an ironic presentation of the failed relationship between Verlaine and Rimbaud, although several critics have asserted that the two personas also represent the feminine and masculine aspects of the author's temperament. "Délires II"—subtitled "Alchimie du verbe" ("Alchemy of the Word")—evokes Rimbaud's failed literary experiment to find, through the role of *voyant* or seer, a new mode of poetic expression; it includes seven of the poems he wrote the previous year, in slightly altered form. "L'Impossible" ("The Impossible") is highly intense, abstract, and metaphysical; here the author bitterly denounces nineteenth-century Western civilization, mourns the loss of purity, and acknowledges that his dreams of escape are futile. "L'Éclair" ("The Flash [of Lightning or Insight]") is alternately hopeful and mocking, remorseful and defiant, as it considers alternatives to traditional modes of religion, art, and cultural institutions. In "Matin" ("Morning"), the narrator reflects on his past even as he looks to the future; he appears to accept, with resignation, the necessity of adapting to life's realities. In the final section, "Adieu" ("Farewell"), the speaker advances the possibility of finding a new way of achieving truth and then expressing it in innovative language; the narrator mocks this effort, too, and points out that the search will be a lonely venture.

Major Themes

Perhaps because it is a richly complex work, there is no critical consensus regarding the principal motifs in *Une Saison en enfer*. Some critics emphasize the theme of evil, others focus on the topic of alienation, and still others stress the significance of sin and redemption in the poem. Many scholars have called attention to the narrator's struggle to reconcile the ideals of Christianity with the hypocrisy and corruption of Western civilization. The poem presents a myriad of dualities or conflicting themes, most of which have their origin in the Christian opposition of body and spirit. The attempt to resolve these dualities—to achieve salvation through some yet unknown means—is diffused throughout the work. The motif of damnation occurs repeatedly and is variously met with hope, despair, mockery, and resignation. The poem's title itself suggests the theme of time and the different stages of life, including innocence as well as corruption. Although the issue of literary aspirations is dealt with most extensively in "Délires II," it appears frequently throughout the poem, as the narrator alternately speaks with pride of his earlier verses and denigrates these lyrics as failures. Whether "Adieu" presents the poet as vowing never to write again, resigned to his role as an ordinary man, or still hopeful that he can find a way to express the ineffable and achieve personal salvation, is unclear. Alluding to the essential ambiguities of *Une Saison en enfer*, C. W. Hackett has asserted that, like most of Rimbaud's work, it is "both 'closed' and 'open,' final and provisional, an end and a beginning."

Critical Reception

The earliest critical appraisals of *Une Saison en enfer* almost invariably disparaged the poem as the confession of a debauched scoundrel. In the 1890s, however, commentators began to perceive in it a deep spirituality. Late nineteenth- and early twentieth-century critics generally believed the myth that Rimbaud personally destroyed every copy of the poem, and they were unaware of the likelihood that he continued working on his other major prose poem, the *Illuminations*, after completing this work. Thus they viewed *Une Saison* as Rimbaud's final, emphatic farewell to literature. Throughout the first half of the twentieth century, commentators frequently adopted a biographical approach to the poem, tracing—or hypothesizing—connections between the text and Rimbaud's life. This approach yielded a variety of judgments, as various critics concluded that *Une Saison* reveals its author as a mystic and a blasphemer, an atheist and a devout Catholic, a bourgeois and a communist. To some degree, explications of the poem's biographical resonances are still being proposed; in the 1960s, for example, Enid Starkie asserted that the work demonstrates the nexus between Rimbaud's poetic doctrines and his religious beliefs, and that he was chiefly concerned with the issues of sin, his personal belief in God, and his compromised principles. Similarly interested in the link between art and religion in *Une Saison,* W. M. Frohock proposed that while the poem displays Rimbaud's rejection of both Catholicism and the poetry he wrote before 1873, it also reveals his determination to continue searching for a new path to wisdom and a new way of expressing the realities of human existence. The 1970s marked the beginning of a movement away from the critical preoccupation with the link between Rimbaud's life and his poetry. In 1979, C. Chadwick adopted a more formal approach to *Une Saison,* comparing it with Rimbaud's other work and focusing on such issues as structure, tone, and vocabulary. Soon thereafter C. A. Hackett continued this trend, emphasizing Rimbaud's artistry and the unique dramatic technique he devised for *Une Saison.* In 1987 Jonathan Monroe evaluated the poem's formal and thematic structure, particularly its fragmented narrative and its disjointed presentation of time and space. And in the early 1990s, James Lawler analyzed the self-dramatizing nature of *Une Saison,* calling attention to its pervasive emotional ambiguities. Common strains running through recent criticism have included a focus on Rimbaud's dramatic technique and on his juxtaposition of pagan and Christian thought, together with forceful assertions about the universal ramifications of this acutely personal narrative.

CRITICISM

Enid Starkie (essay date 1961)

SOURCE: *"Une Saison en enfer,"* in *Arthur Rimbaud,* New Directions, 1961, pp. 287-313.

[*In the following excerpt from her book-length treatment of Rimbaud's life and works, Starkie identifies three principal themes in* Une Saison en enfer: *sin, belief in God, and conformity to the realities of human existence. She asserts that* Une Saison *reveals Rimbaud's inability either to resolve the conflict between good and evil, trade personal freedom for the love of God, or compromise his idealistic principles.*]

With *Le Bateau Ivre, Mémoire* and certain poems from *Illuminations, Une Saison en Enfer* ranks as Rimbaud's greatest work. It contains some very lovely passages of writing which are prose poems in themselves, and could be printed as such, taken from their context.

In August 1873, after many weeks of anguish, he finished the work. We do not know how much there was still left to write when he returned wounded from Belgium at the end of July, nor how much he had written in London, nor yet how much he re-wrote of what he had already written, after his tragic experience. From the comparison of the rough draft—of which we have only two chapters—with the final version, we suspect that any changes he made must have been stylistic with a view to simplifying his vision and taking from it what was not necessary, rather than to altering the initial inspiration.

We know definitely—of this there can be no doubt—that *Une Saison en Enfer* was the book on which he had been at work since April, the 'Livre Païen ou Livre Nègre,' which he had mentioned in his letter to Delahaye in May, and of which three chapters were already written when he went to England with Verlaine. He might subsequently have scrapped these three chapters, but this supposition is unlikely since he would then scarcely have dated the finished work 'April-August 1873'. It can therefore safely be assumed that *Une Saison en Enfer* was begun in April and that even as early as that he intended to make a complete break with his past, with everything that he had hitherto prized and on which he had built his hopes. This point needs emphasizing since it is tempting to believe that it was the Brussels drama that drove him into relating his season in Hell and to say farewell to literature. It is naturally very probable that the events in Belgium gave a new poignancy and a fresh anguish to the struggle. Yet one of the more tragic chapters, **"Nuit de l'Enfer,"** was written in London in July.

Une Saison en Enfer is composed of nine chapters of varying lengths, each, with the exception of the first, **"Mauvais Sang,"** relating some single aspect of the struggle. There is no justification for printing—as Paterne Berrichon has done in the 1912 edition for *Le Mercure de France*—the prose poem describing Christ's first miracle, as an introduction, on no better grounds than that it was written on the reverse side of the rough draft of a chapter of the work. Rimbaud himself published *Une Saison en Enfer* and had he wished the poem to serve as a prologue he would have included it. Delahaye tells us in any case that this was a poem in the series he was projecting under the title *Photographies du Temps Passé.*[1]

For alchemists the descent into Hell was symbolical for the descent into oneself. This is a terrifying experience and there is the psychological danger of the complete dissolution of the human personality, disintegration. Rimbaud's *Saison en Enfer* was the record of such a descent into himself and with him there was the danger of this disintegration of his personality, but he rose in the end victorious. According to the alchemists the Hermetic Philosopher makes this descent as a 'redeemer'. Rimbaud hoped that he might be such a redeemer.

Une Saison en Enfer is difficult to interpret as a whole for Rimbaud has described, simultaneously, the past, the present and the future and he has omitted all the connecting links. The *leit motiven* of the various problems which are besetting him surge each in turn and subside, only to burst out again with renewed force, at a later part of the work; or else they mingle together so as to form an intricate and bewildering fugue. The nature of the problems is mainly spiritual for it was spiritual aspiration which had driven him to adopt his particular form of art and so his failure was a spiritual rather than artistic failure. Thus the problem on which so many critics concentrate—the question of whether or not he intended to continue being a poet—pales into insignificance beside the greater spiritual problem. What was chiefly occupying him was his attitude to God and his previous doctrine of art had been closely linked with his religious conceptions. When he discovered that all his aspirations and hopes had been based on falsehood, he cast aside the art and the philosophy which had deceived him, but there was nothing to prevent his still being a poet, if a poet of a different kind.

The three important *leit motiven* in *Une Saison en Enfer* are the problem of sin, the problem of God—his personal need to believe in God—and finally the problem of life, the acceptance of life. These thread their way backwards and forwards through the texture of the work, and only, at the very end, are brought to full conclusion.

Rimbaud had previously imagined that with his art he had soared into the beyond, but he discovered now that it was not Heaven into which he had penetrated, but Hell; it had verily been a season in Hell. It was his pride and arrogance which had brought him to such a pass and had led him into the deepest state of sin. This brought him face to face with the problem of evil. What was sin and did it really exist? At the time of the first *Illuminations* he had thought that the tree of Good and Evil could finally be cut down.

But this had been an illusion like all his other illusions, for the tree had sent out sucker shoots that had grown big enough to destroy him. 'Le vice qui a poussé ses racines à mon côté, dès l'âge de raison,—qui monte au ciel, me bat, me renverse, me traîne.'[2]

One of his main reasons for beginning to write *Une Saison en Enfer* was to solve, once and for all, the problem of this conflict between Good and Evil. He

had meant by his first title, 'Livre Païen ou Livre Nègre,' to indicate that his intention was to return to the days before the advent of Christianity, before there had existed the tragic dilemma of right and wrong. Pagans and Negroes can still live in blissful ignorance knowing nothing of the problem of good and evil; the tree of knowledge, with its heavy sickly shade, does not yet darken their lives. Rimbaud refused to accept the ideals of Christianity and intended to return to the real kingdom of the children of Ham.[3] 'Prêtres, professeurs, maîtres, vous vous trompez en me livrant à la justice. Je n'ai jamais été de ce peuple-ci; je n'ai jamais été chrétien; je ne comprends pas les lois; je n'ai pas le sens moral, je suis une brute, vous vous trompez.

'Oui, j'ai les yeux fermés à votre lumière. Je suis une bête, un nègre. Mais je puis être sauvé.'[4]

This was in the early days of composition. But, as he worked at the book and pondered on the problem, he discovered—to his great anguish—that he was, after all, like all the others, that he could not escape his hereditary taint, that he could not wipe out the traces of his baptism, that no one of the west could ever eradicate the imprint left by two thousand years of Christianity. His whole nature, his mind and soul, had been formed and moulded by the civilization from which he had thought he could escape. With the food he ate, the water he drank, the very air he breathed, he absorbed into his being the tainted ideals of Christianity. Long before he had been conceived it had been decreed that he should be born a westerner and there was no way of escaping this fatality however passionate might be his longing. The characteristic sign of westerners, of Christians, is their consciousness of sin. Baudelaire's poetry had been the expression of the conflict between *Spleen* and *Idéal*. Rimbaud's work now becomes the expression of a similar conflict—between God and Satan, between good and evil. The two voices rise one after the other, sometimes in unison, sometimes mingling in a strange duet. With Baudelaire we have no doubt on which side he would wish to weight the scales; but with Rimbaud we do not know which voice is stronger, nor which is divine, that of God or Satan, and even he himself is uncertain.

The second *leit motif* is that of Rimbaud's longing for God, for a belief in God. His need of God was one of the fundamental needs of his nature and when he found that he could no longer accept the God of his Catholic teaching he could not rest until he had found a God which would satisfy his spiritual aspirations. He had staked everything on expressing God and the infinite, on becoming like unto God himself. When this conviction failed he was left bewildered and lost. His problem was now whether he could return to the humble Christian position in front of God. From the beginning to the end of *Une Saison en Enfer* we find expressed his burning longing for a religion in which to lose himself, but his longing is damped down by his inability to accept the loss of personality and liberty, by his desire to keep *'la liberté dans le salut'*. He was incapable of the simple trusting faith of Verlaine; he would not be God's humble servant, nor the patient little donkey of the Lord. And seeing in himself the longing and the desire for faith he cried, 'Je reconnais là ma sale éducation d'enfance.'[5]

In spite of what Catholic critics allege, Rimbaud came out of his season in Hell determined to leave God's love behind him and to keep his personal freedom at all costs. That was part of the victory on which, at the end, he prided himself; he had not yielded in spite of his longing to give in; God fought him with all His powers of persuasion, with all the weight of His arm, but he had stood firm till the end and kept himself intact. Nevertheless his later career was to prove that his victory had left him mutilated and that by stifling the voice of God in himself he condemned himself to live out his life spiritually maimed and crippled.

The third big problem is that of the acceptance or endurance of life as we have to live it in the world. The manner in which Rimbaud approached this problem and tried to solve it reveals his fundamental inability to accept life as it is and to live like all those ordinary human beings whom he so deeply despised. ***Une Saison en Enfer*** is, for the greater part, an acute expression of the idealism of youth hurt by the ugliness which it encounters and which it cannot explain, since it has not yet learnt—the bitterest of all the lessons which we have to learn—to make concessions with our ideals and principles, and to accept the second best. Rimbaud never learned to make concessions and since he was not able to possess what he believed was *la vraie vie* he would have nothing. In the days of his pride and his belief in his powers he refused life as it was given to him; he intended to create his own life, on his own conditions. He would destroy everything that existed naturally in himself; he would build everything again and transform life. And so he spurned and refused all the things which made life sweet for ordinary simple human beings—work, love and hope. 'Quant au bonheur établi, domestique ou non. . . . Non je ne peux pas!'[6] he exclaimed. Slowly, and by degrees he destroyed all the things in him which had made him a human being, and in this struggle he became willingly, with masochistic delight, a new kind of martyr. But this martyrdom eventually led him only to the dead end of the acceptance of the inevitable, to the grudging acceptance of reality, of perpetual slavery. He belonged to the slave race and so it did not behove him to curse life. 'Esclaves, ne maudissons pas la vie!'[7]

Rimbaud's *bateau ivre,* instead of bearing him into the centre of the ocean of infinity, or as Baudelaire's boat to the shores at least of that endless sea, had merely described a complete circle, bringing him back to the reality from which he had fled, from which he had imagined he had escaped, to revolting reality. That was the final port into which his boat sailed after all the storms and the return was not easy. Whatever he might say or think, reality was what Rimbaud was never able—and never would be able—to accept. 'L'automne déjà, notre barque élevée dans les brumes immobiles tourne vers le port de la misère, la cité énorme au ciel taché de feu et de boue.'[8] . . .

Notes

[1] *Rimbaud* [1923], pp. 45-6.

[2] *Mauvais Sang (Une Saison en Enfer)* (*Oeuvres Complètes* [ed. Jules Mouquet and Roll and de Renéville, Bibliothèque de la Pléiade, 1946], p. 208).

[3] Ham's descendants were thought to be the negro race.

[4] *Mauvais Sang (Une Saison en Enfer)* (*Oeuvres Complètes,* p. 208).

[5] *L'Eclair (Une Saison en Enfer)* (*Oeuvres Complètes,* p. 227).

[6] *Mauvais Sang (Une Saison en Enfer)* (*Oeuvres Complètes,* p. 211).

[7] *Matin (Une Saison en Enfer)* (*Oeuvres Complètes,* p. 228).

[8] Ibid. . . .

W. M. Frohock (essay date 1963)

SOURCE: "From the Far Side of Despair," in *Rimbaud's Poetic Practice: Image and Theme in the Major Poems,* Harvard University Press, 1963, pp. 201-22.

[*In the following essay, Frohock disputes the view—held by many earlier critics—that in* Une Saison en enfer *Rimbaud irrevocably rejected both the world around him and his literary aspirations. Frohock maintains that although Rimbaud condemned both the Christian tradition and his personal experiment with voyancy, he accepted the challenge of dealing with reality and searching for a new form of poetic expression.*]

Nothing could be more natural than that our time should have made Rimbaud one of its special heroes. We have been aware of ourselves as living in—perhaps living through—an age of anxiety, and identified him as typically anxious. The heroes of our fiction have been alienated figures, and we know that Rimbaud's alienation was deep. We have honored, above all, those who have

shown themselves capable of pronouncing a total refusal of the world in which we have no choice but to
live, and written down Rimbaud as one of the most
exemplary of such *révoltés*. Discussions of his work as
a "poetry of revolt" have abounded, especially since
the brave days of Existentialism and the publication by
Albert Camus of *The Rebel,* and the importance of
Une Saison en enfer has been emphasized, at times
out of proportion.

Revolt, once defined by Camus as the utterance of a
universal No—example: Ivan Karamazov's rejection of
a world made good by one child's suffering—is distin-
guishable from mere rebellion by its absoluteness, philosophical seriousness, and cosmic scope. The most co-
gent metaphysical statement is perhaps contained in
André Malraux's demonstration, in *The Voices of Silence,* that the function of art has always been to express man's refusal of "the human condition." How
Rimbaud—especially the Rimbaud "with the wind in
his heels" of the various biographies—could have come
to be seen as the ancestor of all who held such views
is easy to understand. Had he not written a book which
was a complete rejection of the world as he had known
it? And had he not, having written it, followed word
with deed, simply walking out and slamming the door
definitively behind him? If he had not actually expressed
the theory of revolt, he had, according to this view,
furnished a classic example of the practice.

It can at least be said in favor of such a notion that,
even if closer inspection reveals that Rimbaud fell rather
short of being the model he has been said to be, his
example made it considerably easier for the latter-day
stereotype of the *révolté* to come into existence. But
before more than this can be granted, certain critical
distinctions are in order: we are not free to forget,
though some have managed to do so, that Rimbaud
himself speaks, in *Une Saison en enfer,* of never having understood "la révolte." That he was violently repelled at times by the world around him no one who
can read would conceivably deny. He has looked on
life and not found it invariably good. With so many
poets of his time, from Hugo to Tennyson, he can
imagine a rationally organized political future in which
ordinary human beings would be allowed to realize
their innate potentialities and a society in which love
would replace greed and cupidity. Of this what he sees
about him falls heart-breakingly short—as it falls short
also of the world of the innocent child, who now is
doomed to be contaminated and degraded by the mere
process of growing up. Anyone could imagine something better, such as his imaginary "Orient," exempt
from the devastation of commerce, industry, colonial-
ism, and what his time thinks of as science. The effort
of creating a more habitable world would not be great,
even if the difficulty had been increased by the consciousness of accumulated guilts which apparently strike
him as the principal heritage of a Christian society.

But this is only one of the several "visages" of Rimbaud
which appear in *Une Saison en enfer.* This is also the
youth who is at the end of his liaison with Verlaine,
who begins his account of his personal hell just before,
and finishes it just after, the shooting in Brussels. In
addition, this is the poet who has staked so much on
poetry and fallen far short of the goal; the failure
half-foreseen in the **"Lettre du voyant"** has become a
part of the reality in which he must manage to live. He
has, finally, had the experience of the brink of insanity, to which he has been led perilously close by the
practice of his method. The mixed nature of his spiritual and physical predicament, with the disaffections
which turn inward as well as outward, radically complicates the question of Rimbaud's revolt.

2

Human life, as Sartre's Oreste was not the first to observe, begins on the far side of despair. Rimbaud's
account of his spiritual experience follows him not only
down through the Slough of Despond but up again on
the far side and onto the firm ground beyond. This
"collection of a few pages from the notebook of the
Damned" does reveal a progress, however incoherent
and tortured the account may be: it takes its reader
from the utter despair of the earlier sections through
to a mood of acceptance (however unwilling) and of
reconciliation (at least partial). The impression that
Rimbaud's intention, together with his feelings, un-
derwent some modification while his book was in the
writing is, almost certainly, well grounded: there may
well have been a moment, after his break with Verlaine,
when he could see no exit from his predicament, and
another, subsequent one when some hope was once
again possible. We may not, after all, neglect that he
finally called his book a *Season,* after toying with such
titles as *Livre païen* and *Livre nègre;* the characteristic
of seasons is that they have a beginning and an end.

It is incontestable that places in *Une Saison en enfer*
are expressions of complete revolt. But a review of the
entire book leaves the feeling that the mood of revolt
is not everywhere present and that it does not prevail
in the end.

A majority opinion among Rimbaud specialists holds
that the opening section is an introduction written after
the shooting scrape in Belgium, and contains a preliminary statement of the major themes. The time had
been, the text says, when everything was good, when
all hearts were open and every wine flowed free, a
time of a fine party—"un festin"—when, in short, he
had been happy. But subsequently he had lost the "key"
to the "festin" and had, so to speak, shot his albatross,
by taking Beauty upon his knees and insulting her.
Now, having realized his mistake *in extremis*—on the
point of "the last quack," a possible allusion to what
might have happened if Verlaine had been a better

hand with firearms—he would like to find the "key" again. The key is charity, he says. But thinking that he can recover it is a delusion; Satan is there to tell him that he must remain a "hyena" to the end. So at the end of the passage he offers Satan his notes on the experience.

It is just as likely that the second section, **"Mauvais sang,"** was written before the final visit to Verlaine which culminated in the shooting, or at least that it was conceived if not actually written before these events, since it alone contains the material which would justify his having written a friend about the titles he later discarded. Here Rimbaud is attributing his faults to his belonging to an "inferior race"—seeing himself at first as a descendant of the old, conquered Gauls and subsequently as a Negro in some distant country about to be colonized by Europeans. In either of these avatars he belongs to those who do not choose Christianity but have it forced upon them and become its prisoners. Momentarily his imagination plays with the idea of being born a true and complete pagan, ignorant of and thus unplagued by the ideas of good and evil and the "torments of the soul which is almost dead to the Good." But this vision dissolves like the previous ones and the section ends with an image of himself marching like a soldier into combat.

"Nuit de l'Enfer" is devoted to the reality of the hell where he now finds himself. Directly now, not through metaphors, he describes his plight. He is indeed a victim of Christianity in that, without being able to divest himself of his sins, he is still aware of them as sins and as condemning him to eternal punishment. If he seems relatively untroubled by the loss of heaven he is remarkably conscious of the pains of hell. This section is more intelligible to those who accept the hypothesis that after Verlaine shot him, Rimbaud, under the shock of having come close to death and at the same time seeing all his projects collapse entirely, went through a religious crisis which very nearly resulted in a return to the Catholic practices of his childhood.

In the following section, **"Délires,"** he turns violently to self-accusation. The first of its two subdivisions, the celebrated **"Epoux infernal,"** the account of his life with Verlaine, uses the noteworthy literary strategy of giving the point of view to the other member of the couple. Verlaine is characterized by his voice, which is full of self-pity, nagging, and female weakness. He comes off poorly, a pitiable if not despicable picture. The technique lets Rimbaud appear as he imagines he must have looked to Verlaine, extraordinarily cruel and revoltingly sadistic, as well as perversely vicious. Rimbaud's judgment of himself is no less severe for being indirect. And the second subsection, **"L'Alchimie du verbe,"** goes on, with the poet speaking in his own person, to condemn him as thoroughly as poet as he has been condemned just before

as moral individual. There is a fair possibility that the second subsection was written before the first and before the rupture with Verlaine; it seems hardly possible, on the other hand, that the first can have been written before the two poets separated for good and all. Thus, if this assumption is correct, Rimbaud would first have contemplated reasons for the unsatisfactoriness of his poetry, and then have looked for the reasons in his own moral inadequacy.

But the "Orient" section, which follows next, turns attention from the defective poet to the defective world, setting up a contrast between an "Orient" which he imagines and an "Occident" which is the world he lives in and tolerates so little. This section has given encouragement to exegetes who, like Rolland de Renéville, interpret Rimbaud's poetry as' implying close familiarity with Eastern philosophy. But what Orient is Rimbaud talking about? The whole subject remains vague. Actually, in the full thematic development of the *Saison,* what is important is less an East that never was than a West which the poet knows well and detests thoroughly. The East has negative virtues only: the absence of the "false elect," of a bourgeois society, of a Christianity which is also bourgeois, of western commerce and industry, art, and philosophy. We have returned, in other words, to the theme first stated in **"Mauvais sang,"** and to a material which permits us to talk about a revolt against life. But here again, self-accusation complicates the picture: if only, he says, he had had the eyes to see the truth of all this while there was still time. And once again, for all his savagery, there is audible the faintest note of self-pity.

The themes now having been stated, and developed as far as they will ever be, Rimbaud returns to the violent, almost frenetic tone of **"Mauvais sang,"** and in **"L'Eclair"** protests against the empty notion of salvation through work. He can admit that all human effort may not be vanity, and he recalls his moments of socialist idealism when the dignity of labor appealed to him, but he rejects the possibility of redemption by such effort as too slow. He puts the thought away along with his attempts to attain the Unknown, and also dismisses the solution of religion as a hangover from childhood. He simply does not want to die; he wants to go on and live his "twenty years," meaning the two decades he allows himself as a future. And if eternity is thus lost—a sarcastic final exclamation—so much for that!

Thus he comes to the point, in **"Matin,"** of measuring his final degradation. The promise of youth, by whatever crime or error of his, has not been kept. Let anyone who will tell the story; he has, himself, passed beyond the limit of communication. "I no longer know how to speak." And yet, he continues, the story of his suffering is now finished. He has been through the real hell, the one, he insists, of which the Son of Man burst the gates. There is open before him a kind of vision of Bethlehem, with the star always before his eyes and the Magi of heart, soul, and spirit, together with the promise of a "new work, new wisdom, the confusion of tyrants, and the end of superstition." The section ends by picking up the theme of the "pagan" and "Negro" sections: "Slaves, let us not curse life." The tone is quieter now than it has been previously, and he mentions his lassitude.

In the final section, **"Adieu,"** it is "already autumn," but why, he asks, regret a waning earthly sun when one is in search of a divine light? Yet autumn calls up a picture of intense suffering, and distress, followed by the thought that if this is bad, comfort is hardly better. He passes into a tone of resignation, and the words he uses are famous. "J'ai créé toutes les fêtes, tous les triomphes, tous les drames: J'ai essayé d'inventer de nouvelles fleurs, de nouveaux astres, de nouvelles chairs, de nouvelles langues. J'ai cru acquérir des pouvoirs surnaturels. Eh bien! je dois enterrer mon imagination et mes souvenirs!" And on this note of acceptance of his lot, with all this implies in respect to the themes which run through his book, his season ends. He had thought himself seer or angel, and created his own feasts and triumphs and dramas, a new nature, a new heaven, new bodies, and new languages; he has returned to earth, to the new duty he must find, with a harsh reality to embrace.

3

In order to make sense of these texts in their totality, one must be alert to their falling at times into a dramatic form: it should be recognized that Rimbaud is speaking here in more than one voice. If what he says means anything at all, he has been on the threshold of madness. There can be very little doubt of what kind of insanity he had contemplated so closely. **"L'Alchimie du verbe"** makes it abundantly clear that his visionary experiments had not been far from breaking his contact with the world in which men live and to which their dreams ordinarily refer. There can come a moment when the subject merely turns his face to the wall, refuses to know people around him, becomes unable to take food and finally succumbs to inanition. How close to the edge the author of the *Illuminations* actually came, in that moment when he was "waiting to become a dangerous madman," nobody can say, but he leaves no doubt that it was close enough to give him a severe fright. Thus it is no surprise to detect at times in the *Saison en enfer* one voice which is savage, sarcastic, ironic, and occasionally brutal, which keeps speaking up in the name of harsh reality—the reality which must at all costs be embraced, and which replies to the other voice, that of the poet-*voyant.*

Critics who from the internal evidence of the *Illuminations* and *Une Saison en enfer* tend to the persuasion that it is possible to divide Rimbaud's life as poet into sharply defined periods, are also fond of the idea that he went through a moment of violent hallucination and delusion during the spring of 1872, at the moment of the last inchoate poems in verse. It is true that his illustrations of his "madness," which he quotes in **"L'Alchimie du verbe,"** are from these writings, but nothing proves that the time of the writing was his only one of precarious mental balance. Isabelle Rimbaud may not be the most dependable of witnesses, the best interpreter of her brother's poems or the significance of various events in his life, but there is little reason to think that what she says of his behavior during the writing of these pages in the attic of the farmhouse at Roche—the shouts and groans from above stairs, the unpredictable conduct and erratic moods—is an invention. The story is true because she would have no object in telling a false one: the struggle to keep a grip on reality was grim. Her story is confirmed by the texts themselves—which Isabelle long failed to realize that the world would ever read.

An example can be the evocation of childhood in **"Nuit de l'Enfer,"** where his imaginations of hell are particularly vivid. "La peau de ma tête se dessèche. Pitié! Seigneur, j'ai peur. J'ai soif, si soif. Ah! l'enfance, l'herbe, la pluie, le lac sur les pierres, *le clair de lune quand le clocher sonnait douze . . .* le diable est au clocher, à cette heure. Marie! Sainte-Vierge!" (The italics are in the text.) This voice belongs to the hallucinated poet. To it the voice of the man in contact with reality answers abruptly and with impatience: "Horreur de ma bêtise."

One could be tempted to identify the two voices with the two parts of the divided personality of the **"Lettre du voyant"**—the "JE" who is "autre" and the "je" who is not. The first of the two speeches follows the then-and-now pattern familiar from some of the *Illuminations:* opposed to the frightening dryness of the infernal present are childhood and the sweetness of nature, and the moonlit sounds of the midnight belfry which have now been replaced by Satan. Thus, the second voice can be read as rejecting the "stupidity" of the poems—as well as that of the poet.

Another example occurs in the introductory passage. The poet has explained how he has lost the key to the great feast and sunk into various sorts of depravity; now, at the point of death, he would like to recover the key which is Charity.

> Or, tout dernièrement m'étant trouvé sur le point de faire le dernier *couac!* j'ai songé à rechercher la clef de l'ancien festin, où je reprendrais peut-être appétit.

> La Charité est cette clef.

So far, this is the voice of the *voyant,* desperately seeking salvation. But now the other voice interrupts: "Cette inspiration prouve que j'ai rêvé." Here again, and as always, the second voice is the voice of reality and sanity.

This technique is standard with Romantic ironists from Stendhal to Henri de Montherlant. "Aedificabo et destruam," writes Montherlant, "I shall construct, but to destroy." The procedure has nothing new for confirmed readers of Rimbaud. "And what about my job?" asks the voice of Nina at the end of **"Les Réparties,"** and the down-to-earth question brings to an abrupt close that most detailed phantasy about love in a benevolent nature. At the end of **"Roman,"** it will be remembered, the poet returns from flights of erotic reverie to the realization that he must look like something of a puppy. And though the words of **"Le Cœur supplicié"** speak of complete disgust with life, the lilting rhythm reminds us that the poet is conscious of being a bit too intensely eloquent for his years and stature. The same effect is produced in the poem that begins, "Qu'est-ce pour nous, mon cœur," when the poet emerges from a dream of global holocaust into an awareness that after all nothing has happened.

In *Une Saison en enfer,* each of the persistent themes—Christian religion, childhood, hostile external world, romantic travel, and so forth—occasions a renewal of the same treatment.

4

The religious crisis Rimbaud is supposed to have passed through in the hospital in Brussels is psychologically possible. Although his wound itself was minor, the experience of being shot was not. Rimbaud could have died without opportunity to confess his sins, do penance, and amend his life. To one brought up a Catholic, the thought is sobering. But the experience can only have sent him more precipitately along a way already chosen: he had begun *Une Saison* before this episode and is in a mood to examine his conscience.

Once he had committed himself to the ancient metaphor which equates suffering with the Nether Pit, he had almost no choice but to continue in the language of the Judaeo-Christian tradition. Suffering being hell, and hell being in turn punishment, the question, old as Job, arises inevitably: What have I done to merit this? The tone necessarily becomes one of self-recrimination and confession. Nothing could be less surprising than that readers like Claudel, Daniel-Rops, and Jacques Rivière, already predisposed to see every conflict stated in Christian terms, should have discovered in Rimbaud a kind of crypto-Catholic. To agree with them, however, requires resolute inattention to the contexts of the passages that they cite most often in defense of their view.

If there is any validity to the claim, put forth above, that the *Saison* frequently falls into the form of a dialogue

between two voices which are both the poet's, then it must be significant that the voice that is aware of the claims of reality intervenes most often when the other voice has embarked on the subject of salvation through religion. In the introduction, Charity appears to be represented as the key to the lost "feast," but it is not entirely true that at that point the poet represents himself as having lost two of the three theological virtues: while he has been through a period of despair, *part* of him lives in hope of finding his key again; and it is now that the other voice denies the hope, telling him that he will always remain the "hyena." We may conclude from this that the religious urge is only one velleity among others. And each time the Christian solution is mentioned in the pages that follow, this conclusion is reconfirmed; the voice of reason and reality reminds him that he is losing the indispensable contact.

Throughout Rimbaud's confession such phrases occur as the famous: "I await God with *gourmandise,*" an expression more easily understood by those familiar with the language of Catholic mysticism and the doctrine of transubstantiation. (Saint Teresa of Avila is known to have preferred the largest possible hosts at communion.) "God is my strength," he declares in another place, "And I praise God." No more is required to send those who are predisposed to do so off on an orgy of rereading the *Illuminations,* to make such discoveries as that the "Génie," otherwise identifiable with the *voyant* side of the poet's personality, is really Jesus Christ. But even those of such readers who are willing to admit that Rimbaud reveals himself to them as a Christian only upon fleeting occasion are bound to encounter very serious obstacles.

Rimbaud's cry about waiting for God with *gourmandise* is followed in the next sentence by the statement that he belongs "to an inferior race throughout eternity," and the ellipsis between the two declarations can hardly be filled by anything but a statement of causal relationship, either "because" or "consequently." The often quoted: "De profundis, domine," in **"Mauvais sang,"** is followed immediately by words less often cited: "Am I stupid!" The words following his remark in **"L'Eclair"** about the odor of incense coming so strong to his bed in the hospital are to the effect that he recognizes "in this the filthy education of my childhood."

In texts written, most likely, both before and after the shooting, he associates Christianity with the idea of an inferior race. His feeling that he descends directly from the old Gauls, with all their bad habits and their vices, including laziness, seems less incongruous when one remembers that he was a contemporary of determinists like Taine. As one of the conquered people, he sees himself in a series of atavistic incarnations: pilgrim, leprous beggar, foot soldier, all playing subordinate roles, never members of the "councils." And historically, he reminds himself, the Gauls did not exactly seek Christianity, but had it forced upon them by their conquerors. At the same time, God is the refuge of the inferior.

When he sees himself not as a son of old Gaul but as a Negro in a country about to be invaded by Europeans, the connecting theme is inferiority. The whites come ashore, the cannon fire: one must submit, dress oneself in clothes, go to work. Not even those most persuaded of Rimbaud's Catholicism will argue that such a page constitutes a cry of Christian triumph. To accept Christianity, in this purview, implies an irrevocable admission not only of defeat but of one's having been defeated from the start. His playing with the idea that if one is genuinely exempt from all the inhibitions of a Christian civilization one is better off constitutes another flight from reality. The reader who submits scrupulously to the meaning of the total work recognizes that occasional velleities of submission and acceptance are counterbalanced by velleities of rejection.

The general theme persists in **"Nuit de l'enfer,"** and in an even more desperate tone. He is trapped in his Christian tradition, the "slave of his baptism." He has had the vision of peace and bliss which would go with reconciliation to his faith: "Millions of charming creatures, a suave spiritual concert, strength and peace, noble ambitions, and so forth." But here the paragraph ends. The new one, which consists only of a repetition of "noble ambitions," but this time written with an exclamation point, can only be read as ironical: the voice of sanity has intervened again to collapse the vision; one who has been trained a Christian must live with what he has learned in his catechism; only the true, born pagan is safe from hell; the poet's parents have wrought his misfortune as well as their own.

And at the end of the book, in **"Matin,"** in spite of the references to the star, the desert, and the Magi, the "Noël on earth" he speaks of is surely not the Christian one. New work and new wisdom, flight of tyrants and demons, and an end to superstition, go well of course with the idea of peace to men of good will—but these are men whose ideal of good will is, most likely, the far off, divine event of nineteenth-century idealistic socialism. The acceptance which the last pages of Rimbaud's book may be said to breathe is not an acceptance of Christianity. He is talking, rather, about a world which would be of a quality such that he would not feel himself preternaturally alienated from it.

What makes Rimbaud seem, at moments, so close to Christianity is, more than anything, his capacity for self-accusation. But in the last accounting, even this leaves one a bit suspicious. The very violence of the language he uses to call himself a fool, a knave, and

a scoundrel has a touch of masochism about it. There is too good a chance that this self-laceration brings satisfactions and reliefs of its own. To be a fool and a failure is not, of itself, a sin. The frustration which comes from knowing that one has failed and been foolish can be as real as any other. Rimbaud, as we know, had the habit of lashing out when he was frustrated and does so now, when the source of the trouble is inside himself. Religion need not enter the discussion at this point. He may still be, quite simply, the young poet who tolerated nothing that came between him and felicity.

5

The world Rimbaud seems to have wanted would have had to be entirely different from the one he was in. He knows that in this present one the inferior race has inherited the earth. The last century has seen, he says, the victory of the People, of reason, of the nation, of knowledge. But knowledge—science to his contemporaries—seems to be nothing more than medicine, which is the codifying of old wives' remedies, and philosophy, which is the rearrangement of the sentiments of popular songs. For progress he has only scorn. "We are headed for the conquest of matter by mind," he declares, and the irony emerges as it develops that in his visions the priests and professors are always opposed to him. The leaders of the modern world—merchants, magistrates, generals, and emperors—are "faux nègres," he says, inspired by fever and cancer. It would be best to quit this continent and go off to "the true kingdom of the children of Cham" and, like them, be a cannibal. He gives to the devil the martyrs, the art, the inventions, and the ardor of those he calls the "pillagers"—his fellow Europeans. These aggressively commercial proprietors own everything, including Christianity.

To the characteristic delusions of the West, that nothing is vain, that knowledge is progress, and that work is good, he remains closed: no subterfuge can hide the fact that the trouble with the workaday world is work, the progress of the snail toward something which will never take place. The glimpses of the great modern city, probably London, are again—as in the *Illuminations*—reminiscent of Blake.

Rimbaud is no more specific on the world he detests than on any other of the half-dozen subjects which preoccupy him in *Une Saison.* Whether or not it is true that he now has no gift for description, as he says on the opening page, he clearly has no desire to describe. As always, his focus is not on objects but on his feeling about them. He wants no part of this world he finds about him; it makes him ill and all his instinct is to reject it. Yet he also has to face his situation: this world is a part of the reality which he must bring himself, at the end, to embrace. For the sake of his sanity and perhaps of his life he must accept it, though we may remember that to embrace is not always, and necessarily, a sign of love.

The opening pages of this book, plus the happy tone of some of the *Illuminations* in which the visions are reminiscences of childhood, has led some readers to believe that the *Saison* should be read as a rejection of the *adult* world and an expression of the wish to return, or regress, to childhood. In favor of this view, there is ample evidence in the *Illuminations* that as Rimbaud got older some early moment in life looked increasingly attractive to him. But on the other hand, the more one examines his biography, the harder it is to find any moment in his own life which would fit the description.

The children in his poems are not particularly happy either. Those in **"Les Etrennes des orphelins"** are in a pitiable plight; the group in **"Les Effarés"** are poor and cold. Those in the more autobiographical poems, **"Les Poètes de sept ans,"** and **"Les Premières Communions,"** are abjectly wretched. The only happy figure in Rimbaud's poems, actually, is the young poet who has momentarily contrived an evasion either through a real life fugue or through one of the imagination. And the author of *Une Saison en enfer* is by no means persuaded that the author of **"Ma bohème"** was on the road to happiness. "Ah, the life of my childhood, the open road in every weather, naturally sober, caring less than the best of beggars, proud of having neither country or friends, what stupidity it was!"

On the whole, it seems more likely that childhood appeared to him less as a specific refuge than as a time when, innocence and purity not having been contaminated by a specific vice, he had not departed on a course of scattering his talent to the winds. In a sense, *Une Saison en enfer* repeats the burden of the **"Chanson de la plus haute tour"**:

> Oisive jeunesse
> A tout asservie,
> Par délicatesse
> J'ai perdu ma vie.

Rimbaud seems considerably more willing than some of his admirers have been since to face the fact of his vice. In the fugitive piece called **"Les Déserts de l'amour,"** he is entirely explicit: "Not having loved women—though full of blood—his soul and heart, his strength, were brought up in strange errors." The author of the **"Délires"** chapter and of the *Illumination* called **"Vagabonds,"** hard as he may be on poor Verlaine, does not spare himself.

But his vice is not his only reason for looking on his own character with disgust. He speaks of others: his proneness for anger and his delight in immorally soft living, his laziness and his lying. Here, as usual, he veils his terms and it is hard to know what he means in every case. It is not surprising if his experiments in voyancy put his nerves in a state such that he was subject to flare-ups of very bad temper; on the other hand, he and Verlaine were always so short of money that it is hard to imagine what experience he had of sybaritic living. Lying, since the French "mensonge" includes the lie which is lived as well as the lie which is told, may refer to the whole quality of his life during these years.

We do know what he meant by laziness. Rimbaud had never had any patience with work. Back in 1871 his mother had left him both frightened and indignant with her threats to make him get a job. He was always instinctively orthodox on this point: work was the primeval curse laid upon the race. His momentary exaltation over human labor was probably an expression of his sympathy for the laboring class during the months when he was intent on joining the Commune, rather than a personal commitment to toil. He says that he has all the laziness of the old Gauls, and part of his horror at discovering himself to be a member of the inferior race he connects with the state of being a slave: slaves are condemned to work.

We may wonder whether, in addition, he meant that he had not done faithfully the work of the poet. It is true that, unless there is poetry written in the interval of which we know nothing, he had done relatively little since mid-1872. As compared with Verlaine, at least, he had not much to show. But the conclusion is ours alone, and one which he does not endorse, that the practice of voyancy gradually incapacitated him for poetry.

In any case, along with all the other reasons for his self-revulsion there is the paramount one that, from his angle, the great experiment of voyancy had not succeeded. No document connected with modern French poetry is more often cited than **"L'Alchimie du verbe."** It has been taken as a faithful report of what he had been trying to do ever since the letter to Demeny. This is reasonable so long as the report is recognized as retrospective, and as an explanation of what he had meant in the letter itself. He is certainly saying that, looking back upon it, his enterprise was a great mistake. The attempt to induce hallucinations resulted in nothing more than induced hallucinations. The "sacred disorder of his mind" had given the world nothing that was not paltry. The project of tapping the irrational sources of poetry turned out to have been an immense, nearly fatal, self-deception.

But he exaggerates, somewhat, the case against his own work. Looking back over the poems in verse of 1872, one simply does not find the trace of all the trivialities which he says fascinated him during his period of disorder. Nor does one find them in the prose *Illuminations,* whenever it may be that these were written. Where, for example, is the evidence of his pleasure in church Latin, except possibly in the *Saison* itself? There is disagreement as to how much of his poetry he includes in his condemnation. The traditional view, that he had in mind everything he had ever written, has given way to one which has at least the merit of not going miles beyond what **"L'Alchimie du verbe"** actually says: it holds that he was saying farewell only to the *kind* of poetry which was to have been the glory of the "voyant." But this opens new questions.

Either we have to believe that this impulsive young man, having had his great inspiration no later than May 15, 1871, waited almost a year to explore the possibilities of hallucination, or else that he condemned virtually all his poetry written before the *Saison.* A year in the accelerated life of Rimbaud is the equivalent of a cycle in that of almost any other poet. Moreover, the *Saison* itself confirms what one gathers elsewhere about his impatience when moved by an impulse. And we have seen that some of the poems written within short months after the **"Lettre du voyant"** are more easily interpreted if one presupposes the practice of the program it sets forth. Moreover, we know that by June 10, 1871, he was urging Demeny to burn all the early poems which subsequently went not into the fire but into the "Collection Demeny." The request suggests strongly that the poet was persuaded of the superior value of poems of a new sort; and poems like **"Le Cœur supplicié"** and **"Voyelles,"** whatever the present estimate of their value, already reveal an irrationality which has yet to be proved *not* to be the result of applying the famous method. The thesis advanced in an earlier chapter, that the **"Bateau Ivre"** is a report on systematically contrived hallucinations, is not widely supported by respected experts in the subject, but the evidence stands by itself. No one contests that in Roche, in 1872, Rimbaud brought on himself a crisis which frightened him considerably—even though the evidence is nothing more than a line left in one of his drafts—but this makes it no easier to concede that his renunciation in **"L'Alchimie du verbe"** applies only to a very small part of his total output.

The poems which he sprinkles through this chapter are, obviously, the work of 1872, and mostly of the first half of that year. But he also condemns **"Voyelles"** as a characteristic product of his enterprise, and this poem is surely earlier. That he now scorns the poems of 1872 is very likely, since either he does not go to the bother of copying them into his new work in correct form or else quotes them defectively on purpose. But this does not have to mean that only these poems were included in his condemnation.

It should be remembered that Rimbaud was in the habit of abandoning his poetry. The injunction to Demeny was a formal act, covering the poems up to that time. The sudden cessation, about a year later, of the flow of poems in syntactically solid verse would seem to be a second, this time informal, renunciation. *Une Saison en enfer* now appears as the third in a series, almost indicative of a habit. The fact that he does not specifically include in his renunciation the prose *Illuminations* may be taken to confirm Bouillane de Lacoste's view that these last had not been written, or may, on the other hand, simply show that in 1873 Rimbaud did not recognize that the texts formed a unified collection. Everything testifies that Rimbaud had no objections to publishing his work; it seems likely that in 1875, when he wanted to recover the manuscripts from Verlaine, his intention of sending them to be printed was very real. The possibility that Rimbaud did not repudiate the prose *Illuminations* simply because he was not aware that there was anything there to repudiate is not entirely to be dismissed.

Everything considered, however, we may as well assume that Rimbaud's declaration regards only the poetry he has written up to 1873—whatever may be included in this list. It does not constitute a promise never to write poetry again, and cannot be considered a general farewell to the activity of writing. Rimbaud is simply giving up writing a kind of poetry which he has now outgrown, just as he had done once before in his life and quite possibly twice. Few poets have not had moments of discouragement when they felt that their work to date amounted to less than nothing, and yet not hoped, perhaps without daring to say so, that in future they might yet realize their promise.

The scandal of *Une Saison,* if scandal there is, lies in Rimbaud's having been so willing to abandon poems which must be counted, by any standard, among the finest in French poetry. Here at last the Romantic has been divorced from the oratorical and the grand manner (which had hampered Baudelaire and sometimes Gérard de Nerval) and is not inferior to the best English and German Romanticism. It is a pity that Rimbaud did not know it.

But he is now very completely trapped in a machine of his own making. Poetry—at least his poetry—now takes its place as a means of eluding "harsh reality." Among other ways of doing so are those pictured in the vision of the *Saison,* in which he sees himself hardened by travel and adventure. These are often brought forward by interpreters who neglect to add, because they do not notice, that these things are introduced into the book only so that Rimbaud can reject them.

One of these is the celebrated "prophecy" of his own future: "I have put in my time. I am leaving Europe. The sea air will burn my lungs; far climates will bronze me . . . I shall return with iron muscles, skin darkened, fury in my eye: by my features people will take me for one of the strong race. I shall have gold, and be lazy and brutal. Women care for these strange invalids who are back from the hot countries. I shall have a hand in politics. Saved!" Biographers like Berrichon and Madame Maléra have been tremendously impressed by this passage and, by such devices as harmlessly increasing the total of Rimbaud's savings in Abyssinia, have made it sound like an uncanny prevision of what actually happened to him. But it is the voice of the *voyant* which has taken over the dialogue here. There is a break in the text in a moment, and then the voice speaks which values reality: "One does not leave." This vision is herewith rejected just as he had rejected Christianity, and just as he had rejected the method when it did not lead to happiness. There is no escape.

The more one ponders this enigmatic text, the more one has trouble believing that escapes were what Rimbaud felt he needed, and the harder it becomes, accordingly, to read *Une Saison en enfer* as the preface to a departure for Abyssinia. So far as the testimony of the book goes, he has come to see that he is engaged, as he had thought long ago he might be, in an unsuccessful enterprise. Now he admits the truth and, at the end of the book, is ready to go on living.

This does not sound like the work of a poet in revolt so much as it sounds, as does everything else he wrote, like the work of a very great poet.

C. Chadwick (essay date 1979)

SOURCE: *"Une Saison en enfer,"* in *Rimbaud,* Athlone Press, 1979, pp. 112-35.

[*In the following essay, Chadwick argues that Rimbaud demonstrated a much firmer sense of artistic control in the two parts of "Délires" than he did in other sections of the poem. The critic further contends that in "Délires I and II," the principal themes of spiritual alienation, the search for a new verse form, and the impulse to reshape Western society are more fully articulated than in the preceding or following sections.*]

Publication and Composition

With the exception of a few of his early poems, *Une Saison en enfer* is the only one of Rimbaud's works to have been published immediately after its composition. But even so, its publication, in the autumn of 1873, was accompanied by a number of complications, not the least of which is that it is not strictly correct to say that *Une Saison en enfer* was *published;* in actual fact five hundred copies were *printed* but they were not then offered for sale to the public. Rimbaud received his half-dozen author's copies, but all the others were left in the hands of the printers, presumably because Rimbaud was unable or unwilling to pay for them. It goes without saying that the publication of work such as *Une Saison en enfer* must have been undertaken at the author's expense and Rimbaud was no doubt required, as is the usual practice, to pay part of the cost in advance and the rest on completion. It is this latter part of the agreement that he presumably failed to observe and in consequence the printers concerned, M. J. Poot & Co., 37 rue aux Choux, Brussels, took no further steps to distribute the copies to the general public. Rimbaud sent his half-dozen complimentary copies to various friends, including Verlaine and Delahaye, none of whom appear to have urged him or helped him to bring his volume to the notice of the press or the public, with the result that, as Verlaine put it ten years later in *Les Poètes maudits* in 1883: '*Une Saison en enfer* sombra corps et biens dans un oubli monstrueux'.

It was not until 1901, quite by chance, that the remainder of the five hundred copies was discovered in the storeroom of Poot & Co., but in the meantime, the picturesque legend had been launched, by Isabelle Rimbaud and her husband Paterne Berrichon, that Rimbaud had burned all the copies of *Une Saison en enfer* in 1873 in a superb gesture of renunciation, a mere half-dozen having been saved from the flames. It was not until after 1914, when the discoverer of the five hundred copies made his discovery generally known that this legend began to disappear from biographies of Rimbaud.[1]

Not only do complications thus surround the initial printing and ultimate publication of *Une Saison en enfer,* but further complications surround the circumstances of its composition. At the end of the last chapter Rimbaud adds the dates: 'Avril-août, 1873' and it is generally agreed that these dates refer, as is customary with indications of this kind, to the period of composition. N. Osmond's suggestion that these dates 'correspond to the duration of Rimbaud's season in hell, not to the actual composition of the work', is difficult to accept, not only because this is not the usual significance of a dating of this sort, but also because the period April-August 1873 does not form a single, distinctive phase in Rimbaud's life. On the contrary, it is divided into two very different parts—the six weeks from 11 April to 24 May when he was with his family at Roche,[2] and the eight weeks from 24 May to the end of July when he had rejoined Verlaine and was with him in London and Brussels during the final unhappy stage of their relationship. The duration of Rimbaud's season in hell could therefore be regarded either as these last few disastrous weeks with Verlaine from late May to late July, or as the much longer period covering the whole of the time they spent together from late 1871 to mid 1873, but there seems to be no good reason for drawing a line somewhere between the two.

On the other hand it may be thought that the five months from April to August 1873 form too long a time for the composition of a work which is a mere twenty-five pages long and gives the impression of having been written under intense emotional pressure. The solution to this problem may be that when Rimbaud parted from Verlaine after crossing the Channel with him on 4 April and arrived home at Roche on 11 April he regarded his attempt during the previous months to create a new morality and a new poetry as having failed.[3] The postscript of his letter of 18 May to Delahaye makes it clear that he had no wish to meet Verlaine again, even though the latter was a mere thirty miles away staying with relatives at Jehonville in south-east Belgium, and that he had every intention of staying in Roche or Charleville for some considerable time: 'Je rouvre ma lettre. Verlaine doit t'avoir proposé un rendez-vol au dimanche 18, à Boulion. Moi je ne puis y aller. Si tu y vas il te chargera probablement de quelques fraguemants en prose de moi ou de lui, à me retourner. La mère Rimb. Retournera à Charlestown dans le courant de juin. C'est sûr, et je tâcherai de rester dans cette jolie ville quelque temps'.[4] Moreover, it is generally agreed that he is referring to what was ultimately to become *Une Saison en enfer* when he writes, in the same letter: 'Je travaille pourtant assez régulièrement, je fais de petites histoires en prose, titre général: Livre païen, ou Livre nègre . . . ' It is true that, as N. Osmond points out,[5] the term 'petites histoires' does not apply particularly well to *Une Saison en enfer* in its final form, but at this early stage Rimbaud may have intended his 'Livre païen ou Livre nègre' to have a different structure more suited to such a description. More important than the question of form is the undoubted fact that the opposition between Christianity and paganism and between white civilization and black primitivism, implicit in the earlier titles, remains one of the principal themes of *Une Saison en enfer.*

But although it therefore seems probable that Rimbaud felt, during the last two weeks in April and the first three weeks of May 1873, that his brave attempt to create a new world had ended in failure and although it seems certain that he had already begun to adopt the ideas that were to dominate *Une Saison en enfer,* he suddenly changed his mind and not only went to meet Verlaine at Bouillon on 24 May but promptly set off for London with him to resume their interrupted relationship which finally came to an end with the shooting incident and Verlaine's arrest in Brussels on 10 July. When Rimbaud once more returned to Roche towards the end of July the disillusionment and disappointment he had felt in April must have been all the stronger now that yet another effort to forge a lasting relationship with Verlaine had ended so disastrously. It could well be therefore that, under the impact of this second traumatic separation from Verlaine, he returned to the 'Livre païen ou Livre Nègre' that he had begun three months before

and completed it in a different form and under the new title of *Une Saison en enfer.*

Before turning to a discussion of the sense of *Une Saison en enfer,* mention must be made of three short passages that Rimbaud also wrote about this time. These are the texts generally known as the 'proses évangéliques' based on the fourth and fifth chapters of *The Gospel according to St John.* Since they are written on one side only of two sheets of paper having on the other side rough drafts of two parts of *Une Saison en enfer* it seems certain that they must have been written before these rough drafts which would otherwise have flowed over on to the blank reverse sides, as is in fact the case with the rough draft of a third part of *Une Saison en enfer.* There is, of course, no means of knowing just how long before the rough drafts the 'proses évangéliques' were written, but it seems reasonable to suggest that it cannot have been long before. It is even possible that these three short texts may be the 'petites histoires en prose' to which Rimbaud refers in his letter of 18 May as forming part of his 'Livre païen ou Livre nègre' especially since, at the end of the letter, he states that he has already written three of them. They undoubtedly fit the description of 'petites histoires' since they describe three incidents in the life of Christ, namely his revelation of his identity to the woman of Samaria, the miracle by which he cured the son of a nobleman from Capernaum and the miracle by which he cured a cripple at the pool of Bethsaïda. Whether or not they could also be seen as forming part of a 'Livre païen' depends on how these curious and enigmatic passages are interpreted, for although they are based on the Bible they have a strange twist to them which suggests to many critics that Rimbaud is denying that Christ possessed any miraculous gifts. Other critics, however, do not see them as anti-Christian but simply as somewhat elliptic renderings of the original Bible stories. Whatever view one takes of them their fundamental significance no doubt lies in the fact that they are concerned with the question of the power of the Christian faith. Their ambiguity may therefore be a reflection of the anxiety that Rimbaud felt on this issue in April and May 1873 and that can also be perceived in *Une Saison en enfer.*

Changed Attitudes

Although *Une Saison en enfer* is divided into seven chapters preceded by a brief preface it can also be divided into three distinct parts dealing with quite different and virtually unrelated themes. The long first chapter, **'Mauvais Sang'**, the short second chapter **'Nuit de l'enfer'**, the equally short fourth chapter, **'L'Impossible,'** and the even shorter fifth, sixth and seventh chapters, **'L'Eclair', 'Matin'** and **'Adieu',** are all concerned with moral and religious issues. The third chapter, however, **'Délires'**, forms a parenthesis interrupting, for no apparent reason, the tumultuous flow of Rimbaud's thoughts and feelings on these issues so as to deal with two quite different matters in the two fairly lengthy sections into which it is sub-divided.

'Drôle de ménage'

The first of these sections, which bears the sub-heading **'Vierge folle—l'époux infernal'**, is generally agreed to be, as has already been suggested on a number of occasions in the course of the preceding pages, a disenchanted account of the relationship between Rimbaud and Verlaine.[6] It is written in the form of a monologue by the latter, introduced by a single opening line spoken by the former:[7] 'Ecoutons la confession d'un compagnon d'enfer', and brought to a close by a final caustic comment by Rimbaud: 'Drôle de ménage!' All the rest of the text in between these opening and closing lines is in inverted commas and is therefore the confession of the 'compagnon d'enfer', within which there are further sets of inverted commas as the 'vierge folle' quotes the ideas and opinions of 'l'époux infernal'.

By means of these somewhat complex methods **'Délires I'** paints a vivid portrait of Rimbaud, emphasizing certain aspects of his character that have already been noted elsewhere in his work. His sense of living in an alien world, apparent in such texts as **'Soleil et chair'** and **'Après le déluge'**, is repeated even more forcefully in **'Délires I'**:

> . . . Je suis de race lointaine: mes pères étaient Scandinaves: ils se perçaient les côtes, buvaient leur sang . . .

This claim, which is also made in other chapters of *Une Saison en enfer,* is clearly symbolical of Rimbaud's conviction that he does not by nature belong to modern, Christian civilization and it is the consequent sense of frustration and anger that drives him into a masochistic rage:

> . . . Je me ferai des entailles partout le corps, je me tatouerai, je veux devenir hideux comme un Mongol: tu verras, je hurlerai dans les rues. Je veux devenir bien fou de rage . . .

But his anger can be directed against others as well as himself and, like the prince in 'Conte', he derives a sadistic pleasure from terrifying others, as the 'vierge folle' sadly complains:

> Je l'écoute faisant de l'infamie une gloire, de la cruauté un charme . . . Les nuits, souvent, ivre, il se poste dans des rues ou dans des maisons, pour m'épouvanter mortellement.

In sharp contrast to this side of Rimbaud's character the extraordinary tenderness towards less fortunate members of society that is revealed in such early poems as **'Les Effarés'** and **'Le Dormeur du val'** is again emphasized by the words of the 'vierge folle':

> . . . Dans les bouges où nous nous enivrions, il pleurait en considérant ceux qui nous entouraient, bétail de la misère. Il relevait les ivrognes dans les rues noires. Il avait la pitié d'une mère méchante pour les petits enfants . . .

This feeling of pity for the downtrodden leads him to protest, as he had done in **'Les Pauvres à l'"eglise'**, about the treatment sometimes meted out to women in nineteenth-century society:

> . . . Je vois des femmes, avec les signes du bonheur, dont, moi, j'aurais pu faire de bonnes camarades, dévorées tout d'abord par des brutes sensibles comme des bûchers . . .

But despite this sympathy for women on the social level, his attitude towards them on the emotional level remains the same as in **'Les Sœurs de charité'**, **'Conte'** and **'Génie'** since he categorically states:

> . . . Je n'aime pas les femmes. L'amour est à réinventer, on le sait.

This scarcely veiled reference to Rimbaud's homosexuality is followed by much more specific references when the 'vierge folle' talks of the 'baisers' and the 'étreintes amies' of the 'époux infernal' and describes a moment of understanding between them that is reminscent of **'Veillées I'**:

> . . . Nous nous accordions. Bien émus nous travaillions ensemble. Mais, après une pénétrante caresse, il disait: 'Comme ça te paraîtra drôle, quand je n'y serai plus, ce par quoi tu as passé. Quand tu n'auras plus mes bras sous ton cou, ni mon cœur pour t'y reposer, ni cette bouche sur tes yeux. Parce qu'il faudra que je m'en aille très loin un jour. Puis il faut que j'en aide d'autres: c'est mon devoir . . . '

But the suggestion of a separation in these lines and of a duty to be accomplished indicates that Rimbaud's homosexuality was not solely a personal matter and that, as is implied in **'Chanson de la plus haute tour'**, **'L'Eternité'** and in so many of the *Illuminations* his ambition was to change society in order to accommodate 'le nouvel amour'. This ambition is specifically referred to by the 'vierge folle' who wonders whether 'l'époux infernal' possesses 'des secrets pour changer la vie' and recognizes that this is the only alternative to moving to another country with different laws and customs:

> . . . lui me rendra forte, nous voyagerons, nous chasserons dans les déserts, nous dormirons sur les

pavés des villes inconnues, sans soins, sans peines.
Ou je me réveillerai, et les lois et les mœurs auront
changé,—grâce à son pouvoir magique,—le monde,
en restant le même, me laissera à mes désirs, joies,
nonchalances.

Implicit in this desire for change on Rimbaud's part
there is the same sense of dissatisfaction with the relationship with Verlaine that is so often apparent in the
Illuminations and it is not therefore surprising that the
'vierge folle' should also refer to another of the principle themes of the *Illuminations* and of much of
Rimbaud's earlier poetry, namely his escape into the
world of the imagination:

Je voyais tout le décor dont, en esprit, il s'entourait;
vêtements, draps, meubles . . . A côté de son cher
corps endormi, que d'heures des nuits j'ai veillé,
cherchant pourquoi il voulait tant s'évader de la
réalité.

Not only does '**Délires I**' thus paint a vivid portrait of
Rimbaud, it also paints a no less vivid portrait of
Verlaine, constantly stressing his extraordinary weakness of character which made him quite unable to overcome his Christian scruples about his relationship with
Rimbaud and yet, at the same time, made him equally
unable to break free from the latter's extraordinary
power over him:

'O divin époux, mon Seigneur, ne refusez pas la
confession de la plus triste de vos servantes. Je suis
perdue. Je suis perdue. Je suis soûle. Je suis impure.
Quelle vie!

'Pardon, divin Seigneur, pardon! Ah! pardon! Que
de larmes! Et que de larmes encore plus tard,
j'espère!

Plus tard, je connaîtrai le divin Epoux! Je suis
née soumise à Lui.—L'autre peut me battre
maintenant! . . .

Je suis esclave de l'Epoux infernal, celui qui a perdu
les vierges folles. C'est bien ce démon-là . . . J'ai
oublié tout mon devoir humain pour le suivre. Quelle
vie! La vraie vie est absente. Nous ne sommes pas
au monde. Je vais où il va, il le faut. Et souvent il
s'emporte contre moi, *moi, la pauvre âme.*[8] Le
Démon!—C'est un Démon, vous savez, *ce n'est pas
un homme.*

The opposition here, in the opening lines of '**Délires
I**', between the 'divin époux' and the 'époux infernal' echoes the last two stanzas of Verlaine's 'Birds
in the Night', written some six months before in
September-October 1872 and included in *Romances
sans paroles,* where he vacillates between his anxiety
as a Christian and his enthusiasm as a convert to the

ideas advanced by Rimbaud, whom he sees as a new
Jesus with himself as the first of his disciples:[9]

Par instants je meurs la mort du pécheur
Qui se sait damné s'il n'est confessé,
Et, perdant l'espoir de nul confesseur,
Se tord dans l'Enfer qu'il a devancé.

O mais! par instants, j'ai l'extase rouge
Du premier chrétien, sous la dent rapace,
Qui rit à Jésus témoin, sans que bouge
Un poil de sa chair, un nerf de sa face.

The other, related aspect of Verlaine's character that
emerges from '**Délires I**' is his lack of any real understanding of Rimbaud and the realization of this fact by
both of them:

. . . Hélas! je dépendais bien de lui. Mais que
voulait-il avec mon existence terne et lâche? Il ne
me rendait pas meilleure, s'il ne me faisait pas
mourir! Tristement dépitée je lui dis quelquefois:
'Je te comprends.' Il haussait les épaules . . .

. . . Je lui faisais promettre qu'il ne me lâcherait
pas. Il l'a faite vingt fois, cette promesse d'amant.
C'était aussi frivole que moi lui disant: 'Je te
comprends' . . . S'il m'expliquait ses tristesses,
les comprendrais-je plus que ses railleries? Il
m'attaque, il passe des heures à me faire honte de
tout ce qui m'a pu toucher au monde, et s'indigne
si je pleure . . .

Matters had obviously deteriorated to breaking point at
the time to which these words refer and it is not surprising that, looking back over the months they had
managed to live together, despite the prodigious differences between them in terms of intellectual ability and
strength of character, Rimbaud should have described
their relationship as a 'drôle de ménage'.

'Alchimie du verbe'

The Second section of '**Délires**', sub-titled '**Alchimie
du verbe**', is another disenchanted account of an episode now belonging to the past, but this 'histoire d'une
de mes folies', as Rimbaud describes it in the opening line, is very different from the first section of
'**Délires**' in that it is concerned not with his moral
and emotional difficulties during the preceding months
but with his literary activities. A number of the poems
of 1872 are quoted—or rather misquoted, for reasons which
will be explored later—as examples of what he now regards as his foolish excursion into verbal alchemy, namely
'**Larme**', '**Bonne Pensée du matin**', '**Chanson de la
plus haute tour**', '**Faim**', '**Le loup criait**', '**L'Eternité**'
and '**O saisons, ô châteaux**'. In between these poems
Rimbaud gives a brief and broken account of the poetic
theory they are intended to illustrate, but he does so in

his usual elliptic and enigmatic fashion so that it is not always clear what he is referring to. He writes, for example:

> . . . J'écrivais des silences, des nuits, je notais l'inexprimable. Je fixais des vertiges.

He then quotes **'Larme'** and **'Bonne Pensée du matin'**, although nothing in either poem particularly fits this description. In the *Illuminations,* however, there are several passages to which these words could readily be applied. **'Enfance V'**, for example, contains a very similar phrase: 'Je suis maître du silence', and more-over, as indicated above, it paints an impressive picture of the darkness and silence surrounding Rimbaud's basement room. **'Veillées'** and **'Nocturne vulgaire'** also seem to bear some relation to Rimbaud's claim to have written about night effects, at least as far as their titles are concerned, and several of the short passages in **'Phrases'** could well be said to 'noter l'inexprimable'. As for Rimbaud's final claim: 'Je fixais des vertiges', one has only to think of such passages as **'Mystique'** or **'Being Beauteous'** to appreciate how accurately these words describe their extraordinarily dynamic qualities.

Elsewhere in **'Délires II'** Rimbaud writes:

> Je rêvais croisades, voyages de découvertes dont on n'a pas de relations, républiques sans histoires, guerres de religion étouffées, révolutions de mœurs, déplacements de races et de continents: je croyais à tous les enchantements.

It is true that these 'croisades' might be those of the warriors of **'Michel et Christine'**, mounted on their 'pâles coursiers', and that the 'voyages de découvertes' might be an allusion to the fantastic wanderings of **'Le Bateau ivre'.** But it is equally true that 'la levée des nouveaux hommes et leur en-marche' in **'A une Raison'** could also be one of these crusades, and that the voyages of discovery could refer to **'Mouvement'** whose 'voyageurs' set off 'dans l'héroïsme de la découverte'. Similarly the 'républiques sans histoires' may refer to Rimbaud's dream of destroying the 'républiques de ce monde' in **'Qu'est-ce pour nous'** and the 'guerres de religion étouffées' may refer to the 'religieuse après-midi d'orage' that sweeps over Europe in **'Michel et Christine'**. But again it is equally true that these phrases also call to mind such passages as **'Démocratie'**, **'Guerre'** and **'Soir historique'** in the *Illuminations.* As for the 'révolutions de mœurs' of which Rimbaud dreamed, these call to mind very strongly indeed the 'révolutions de l'amour' in **'Conte'**, just as the 'déplacements de races' echo the 'migrations plus énormes que les anciennes invasions' of **'Génie'**, and the 'déplacement de continents', the cosmic destruction visualized towards the end of **'Soir historique'.**

A little later in **'Délires II'** Rimbaud returns to this idea that he had lived in a dream world with the words: 'Je m'habituai à l'hallucination simple', a statement which may well be a less vivid and less immediate version of the last of the short passages in 'Phrases':

> Je baisse les feux du lustre, je me jette sur le lit, et, tourné du côté de l'ombre, je vous vois, mes filles! mes reines!

He then goes on to give examples of these hallucinations to which he became accustomed. 'Je voyais très franchement une mosquée à la place d'une usine' is the first of these examples, but since it does not actually exist anywhere in Rimbaud's work it is clearly meant as a specimen of the kind of imaginative transformation to which he subjected the world around him. It is true that, as has been shown throughout the preceding pages, this is a constant feature of Rimbaud's work, but it is also true that some of the recreative passages in the *Illuminations* spring particularly to mind in this connection, especially **'Villes I'** where the substitution of a palm tree for a lamp-post and of a 'boulevard de Bagdad' for a London street offer close parallels to the substitution of a mosque for a factory. Similarly Rimbaud's claim to have seen 'les monstres, les mystères' could refer to the exotic sea creatures encountered by **'Le Bateau ivre'** in its mysterious voyages, but it could equally well refer to the fantasy figures in **'Antique'** and **'Being Beauteous'** and to such mysterious scenes as the one depicted in **'Parade'** which ends with Rimbaud's statement that he alone holds the key to the mystery: 'J'ai seul la clef de cette parade sauvage'.

In the case of these examples it does therefore seem that Rimbaud may be referring to his imaginative powers both in his earlier poetry and in the *Illuminations.* But in the case of another example of the kind of hallucinations to which he became accustomed: '[Je voyais] un salon au fond d'un lac', there seems to be so clear an echo of a phrase in **'Soir historique'**: 'On joue aux cartes au fond de l'étang', that it is difficult to deny that he must have been thinking solely and specifically of this particular passage.

Yet although Rimbaud thus seems to be including the *Illuminations* along with his earlier poetry as part of the foolish excursion into verbal alchemy which he now deplores, he does not quote a single passage from the *Illuminations* alongside the seven poems of 1872 that are so extensively quoted. This is obviously a strong argument against the suggestion that **'Délires II'** refers in part to the *Illuminations* and consequently against the belief that the latter were written before *Une Saison en enfer.* It should be noted, however, that Rimbaud is clearly quoting his poems from memory and thus makes a considerable number of mistakes. The second and third stanzas of **'Larme'**, for example, are imperfectly recollected and the final quatrain has disappeared altogether save for a single line very different from the original. Only two of the original six stanzas of **'Chanson de la plus haute tour'** are quoted and the refrain contains an unwarranted subjunctive resulting from the fact that Rimbaud has remembered the rhyme but not the way he arrived at it:

> Qu'il vienne, qu'il vienne
> Le temps dont on s'éprenne.

Two of the stanzas of **'L'Eternité'** are switched round, the regular five syllable rhythm of the earlier version is interrupted on three occasions by four syllable lines being substituted instead, and a number of the lines are poorly remembered. The sixth couplet of **'O saisons, ô châteaux'** has been completely forgotten and the eighth couplet, crossed out on the original manuscript, has been quoted, or misquoted, in its stead. If Rimbaud could not therefore remember accurately the poems he had written twelve months before, despite the aids to memory that rhyme and rhythm undoubtedly constitute, it is perhaps not so surprising that none of the prose passages of the **Illuminations** should be quoted in **'Délires II'** and that he should have preferred to define the methods he had used rather than to quote the results.

But although no actual passage from the **Illuminations** is to be found in **'Délires II'**, a short passage in prose is nevertheless quoted that reads very much like the beginning of one of Rimbaud's prose poems:

> 'Genéral, s'il reste un vieux canon sur tes remparts en ruines, bombarde nous avec des blocs de terre sèche. Aux glaces des magasins splendides! dans les salons! Fais manger sa poussière à la ville. Oxyde les gargouilles. Emplis les boudoirs de poudre de rubis brûlante . . .'

Such exclamatory commands are typical of several passages of the **Illuminations**—'Gracieux fils de Pan . . . promène-toi la nuit' (**'Antique'**); 'Ecume, roule sur le pont et par-dessus les bois' (**'Après le déluge'**) 'Aux pays poivrés et détrempés!' (**'Démocratie'**); 'Arrière ces superstitions!' (**'Génie'**); 'Change nos lots, crible les fléaux' (**'A une raison'**). As for the vocabulary, it is a curious fact that most of the words in this prose passage can be found in the **Illuminations**—'général', 'vieux', 'remparts' and 'terre' all occur within the space of a few lines in **'Enfance II'** which goes on to describe a dilapidated castle, even though the words 'en ruines' are not actually used; 'canon' occurs in **'Being Beauteous'**; 'glaces' in **'Après le déluge'**, **'Nocturne vulgaire'**, **'Métropolitain'** and **'Dévotion'**; 'salon' in **'Enfance V'** and **'Scènes'**; 'gargouille' in **'Nocturne vulgaire'**; 'poudre' in **'Phrases'** and 'rubis' in **'Fleurs'**.

Most significant of all, the passage has that surreal quality that characterizes so many of the **Illuminations,** with the logic of the opening words disintegrating as the sentences follow one another. It does therefore seem possible that in this quotation Rimbaud may be making up a specimen passage typical of the **Illuminations** to illustrate the kind of prose writing in which he had engaged after the free verse poems of 1872.

All such participation in experimental writing appears now, however, to be dismissed in peremptory fashion in the final line of **'Délires II'** in favour of a passive recognition of the virtues of more formal qualities:

> Cela s'est passé, je sais aujourd'hui saluer la beauté.

A somewhat longer phrase towards the end of the rough draft of **'Délires II'** seems to confirm this interpretation:

> Je hais maintenant les élans mystiques et les bizarreries de style. Maintenant je puis dire que l'art est une sottise.

But although the phrase 'les élans mystiques et les bizarreries de style' seems to be an excellent definition not only of such poems as **'L'Eternité'**, **'Larme'** and **'O Saisons, ô châteaux'** but also of such prose passages as **'Mystique'**, **'Matinée d'ivresse'**, **'Barbare'** and **'Génie'**, and although the phrase 'l'art est une sottise' appears to mean that Rimbaud has decided to give up writing altogether, such an interpretation assumes that Rimbaud had already written the **Illuminations** before 1873 and that after that date he gave up all forms of literary activity. Those who believe that some of the **Illuminations** were written after **Une Saison en enfer** are therefore obliged to interpret the final lines of **'Délires II'** and of the rough draft in a very different sense and to argue, as does Suzanne Bernard,[10] that Rimbaud is not bidding farewell to all literary activity and that, moreover, it is solely the poetry of 1872 that is to be equated with the 'art' which he now dismisses and with 'les élans mystiques et les bizarreries de style' which he now rejects. But if this is the case, it is difficult to see how Rimbaud could then have proceeded to write the **Illuminations** which, as has been shown above, are a natural extension of the 'vers nouveaux' of 1872. One would have expected him, on the contrary, to revert to the kind of poetry, conventional in both form and content, that he had written in 1870 and 1871, such as **'Le Dormeur du val'** and **'Les Sœurs de charité'**. It is interesting, in this connection, to note that Verlaine, whose poetry in 1872 and early 1873 kept pace with that of Rimbaud and became much more free than it had been hitherto, reverted to a more formal kind of style once the episode with Rimbaud was over.[11]

The pursuit of happiness

Rimbaud's dismissal, in the two sections of **'Délires'**, of his life with Verlaine and of his poetic experiments of 1872-3 is parallelled, in the rest of *Une Saison en enfer,* by his dismissal of other aspects of his revolt against society.

After a short preface, almost certainly written after the Brussels incident, introducing 'ces quelques hideux feuillets de mon carnet de damné', he begins by describing and justifying his one-time attitude in the long first chapter, **'Mauvais sang'**, which is in the present tense, either because Rimbaud wanted to make his account more vivid, or because this chapter was written early enough for him still not to have entirely rejected his ideas, that is to say in late April or early May 1873, before the final break with Verlaine. The particular theme to which he constantly returns is that he does not belong to modern civilization but that he is a kind of throw-back to a pre-Christian era. From the very first line he stresses the fact that he is descended fro m the Gauls and possesses both their physical and their mental characteristics:

> J'ai de mes ancêtres gaulois l'œil bleu et blanc, la cervelle étroite et la maladresse dans la lutte . . .

> D'eux, j'ai: l'idolâtrie et l'amour du sacrilège;— oh! tous les vices, colère, luxure,—magnifique, la luxure;—surtout mensonge et paresse.

At the beginning of the second of the eight sections into which **'Mauvais sang'** is divided, he denies that he has any links with France after the period of the Gauls and insists that he has always belonged to a different race:

> Si j'avais des antécédents à un point quelconque de l'histoire de France!

> Mais non, rien.

> Il m'est bien évident que j'ai toujours été race inférieure . . .

This expression about belonging to a 'race inférieure' is repeated on two further occasions in the second section and the similar idea of having in one's veins the 'mauvais sang' of the title is repeated when Rimbaud states, in the third section, that, despite the advent of Christianity, 'le sang païen revient'. He feels a certain regret that he is therefore excluded from the Christian community, but he is also determined that his 'race inférieure' will one day be transformed into a 'race forte' and that he himself will no longer be an outcast:

> Ma journée est faite; je quitte l'Europe. L'air marin brûlera mes poumons; les climats perdus me tanneront . . .

> Je reviendrai avec des membres de fer, la peau sombre, l'œil furieux: sur mon masque, on me jugera d'une race forte . . .

These optimistic lines are followed, in the fourth section, by a sudden realization that such a transformation is not easy and that for the present he is a prisoner in an alien society, bearing the mark of a vice which remains unspecified but which most commentators agree must refer to his homosexuality:

> On ne part pas. Reprenons le chemin d'ici, chargé de mon vice, le vice qui a poussé ses racines de souffrance à mon côté dès l'âge de raison—qui monte au ciel, me bat, me renverse, me traîne . . .

This interpretation seems to be confirmed by Rimbaud's frank statement in the fifth section that 'l'orgie et la camaraderie des femmes m'étaient interdites' which leads into a renewed insistence on his paganism:

> . . . Je n'ai jamais été de ce peuple-ci; je n'ai jamais été thrétien; je suis de la race qui chantait dans le supplice; je ne comprends pas les lois; je n'ai pas le sens moral, je suis une brute . . .

But instead of associating himself with a people outside Christianity in terms of time, he now sees himself as belonging to a race outside Christianity in terms of space:

> Oui, j'ai les yeux fermés à votré lumière. Je suis une bête, un nègre . . .

If he is a 'negro' however, so too, under their veneer of Christianity, are the members of western civilization:

> . . . Marchand, tu es nègre; magistrat, tu es nègre; général, tu es nègre . . .

He again feels the longing to leave Europe for the 'vrai royaume des enfants de Cham', tempted by the primitive quality of life there: 'Faim, soif, cris, danse, danse, danse, danse!'.

But just as his previous departure was suddenly halted, so too this dream of a new life is abruptly destroyed at the beginning of the sixth section by the invading forces of white civilization:

> Les blancs débarquent. Le canon! Il faut se soumettre au baptême, s'habiller, travailler.

Rimbaud appears to yield to the pressures to which he is thus subjected and the sixth section ends with a temporary return to the Christian faith:

La raison m'est née. Le monde est bon. Je bénirai
la vie. J'aimerai mes frères. Ce ne sont plus des
promesses d'enfance. Ni l'espoir d'échapper à la
vieillesse et à la mort. Dieu fait ma force, et je loue
Dieu.

This feeling of salvation and of having put behind
him his recent past is continued at the beginning of
the seventh section:

> L'ennui n'est plus mon amour. Les rages, les
> débauches, la folie, dont je sais tous les élans et les
> désastres,—tout mon fardeau est déposé. Apprécions
> sans vertige l'étendue de mon innocence.

He no longer takes any comfort from being at odds
with the world:

> Je ne serais plus capable de demander le réconfort
> d'une bastonnade.

Nor is his Christianity of a purely sentimental nature:

> . . . Je ne me crois pas embarqué pour une noce
> avec Jésus-Christ pour beau-père.

On the other hand, however, he has no wish to remain
a prisoner of his rediscovered faith: 'Je veux la liberté
dans le salut'. This phrase marks a new direction in
Rimbaud's thoughts as the attractions of a quietly Christian way of life begin to fade:

> Quant au bonheur établi, domestique ou non . . .
> non, je ne peux pas. Je suis trop dissipé, trop
> faible.

The section then ends with Rimbaud spurning the innocence that he has just begun to appreciate and returning to his mood of cynical contempt for life:

> . . . Mon innocence me ferait pleurer. La vie est la
> farce à mener par tous.

His hope of salvation and his prospect of returning
to the Christian community has thus been quickly
dispelled and the eighth and final section of **'Mauvais
sang'** conjures up, in a few vivid and staccato phrases,
the image of punishment as an alternative means by
which he can be brought back to what he sarcastically calls, in an echo of the 'gaulois' theme of the
beginning of the chapter, 'la vie française, le sentier
de l'honneur'.

The second chapter, **'Nuit de l'enfer'**, resembles
'Mauvais sang' in that it too deals with the theme of
Christianity and paganism, but Rimbaud's attitude has
now changed and instead of emphasizing that he does
not belong to the Christian community, he stresses, on
the contrary, the fact that he cannot escape from it:

> . . . Je suis esclave de mon baptême. Parents, vous
> avez fait mon malheur et vous avec fait le vôtre.
> Pauvre innocent! L'enfer ne peut attaquer les païens.

Consequently the dream of abolishing the distinction
between good and evil to which he had referred in
'Matinée d'ivresse' and to which Verlaine was to refer in 'Crimen amoris' is now over:

> J'avais entrevu la conversion au bien et au bonheur,
> le salut. Puis-je décrire le vision, l'air de l'enfer ne
> souffre pas les hymnes! C'était des millions de
> créatures charmantes, un suave concert spirituel, la
> force et la paix, les nobles ambitions, que sais-je?
> Les nobles ambitions!

The 'poison' of the **'lettre du voyant'** and **'Matinée
d'ivresse'** which was ultimately to have had beneficial
results, is now seen to have had no such effect. On the
contrary, the torture through which Rimbaud was to
have passed to reach his state of bliss has now been
revealed as endless:

> J'ai avalé une fameuse gorgée de poison.—Trois
> fois béni soit le conseil qui m'est arrivé!—Les
> entrailles me brûlent. La violence du venin tord mes
> membres, me rend difforme, me terrasse. Je meurs
> de soif, j'étouffe, je ne puis crier. C'est l'enfer,
> l'éternelle peine!

He recognizes that his inordinate ambition to reform
the world sprang from a pride and vanity which he
now mocks:

> . . . Je suis maître en fantasmagories.

> Ecoutez!

> J'ai tous les talents . . .

He parodies his former vision of himself as a new
Christ:

> Fiez-vous donc à moi, la foi soulage, guide, guérit.
> Tous, venez,—même les petits enfants,—que je vous
> console, qu'on répande pour vous son cœur,—le
> cœur merveilleux!—Pauvres hommes, travailleurs!
> Je ne demande pas de prières; avec votre confiance
> seulement je serai heureux.

He now acknowledges that his dream of a 'conversion
au bien et au bonheur' was a 'fausse conversion' to
use the abandoned title of the first draft of this chapter
and that he has, on the contrary, been plunged into the
'nuit de l'enfer' of the final title.

Like the second chapter, the fourth chapter, **'L'Impossible'**,
as the title implies, is concerned with the reasons why
Rimbaud found it impossible to achieve his goal and

once again he emphasizes the fact that he does not by nature belong to western civilization:

> . . . Je vois que mes malaises viennent de ne m'être pas figuré assez tôt que nous sommes à l'Occident . . . J'envoyais au diable les palmes des martyrs, les rayons de l'art, l'orgueil des inventeurs, l'ardeur des pillards; je retournais à l'Orient et à la sagesse première et éternelle.

But his refusal to conform to conventional opinion in matters of religion, aesthetics, scientific discoveries and commercial exploitation meant that the kind of life he led was dismissed as 'un rêve de paresse grossière'.

There is, however, one way out of the difficulty faced by someone who feels alienated from the world around him: 'Vous êtes en Occident mais libre d'habiter dans votre Orient'. That is to say that the era of primitive innocence to which Rimbaud wants to return, the garden of Eden he is looking for, in short the kind of God that he is seeking, can be found through a life of the mind, irrespective of material surroundings. It is this realization which leads him to declare, at the end of the chapter: 'Par l'esprit on va à Dieu', and to describe as a 'déchirante infortune' the fact that this realization has come so late.

In one of those sudden changes of direction that characterize *Une Saison en enfer,* the fifth chapter, **'L'Eclair'**, abruptly proposes an alternative route towards the new world that Rimbaud wants:

> Le travail humain! c'est l'explosion qui éclaire mon abîme de temps en temps.

But he rejects this solution as quickly as the related alternative of progress through science: 'Je connais le travail et la science est trop lente'. This leads into a moment of extreme pessimism:

> Ma vie est usée. Allons! feignons, fainéantons, ô pitié! Et nous existerons en nous amusant, en rêvant amours monstres et univers fantastiques.

In what is almost certainly an allusion to the brief period he spent in hospital in Brussels after the shooting incident of July 1873, he moves towards accepting the idea of death as a means of escape:

> Sur mon lit d'hôpital, l'odeur de l'encens m'est revenue si puissante; gardien des aromates sacrés, confesseur, martyr . . .

But his fundamentally rebellious nature brusquely erupts again:

> Je reconnais là ma sale éducation d'enfance. Puis quoi!
> . . . Aller mes vingt ans, si les autres vont vingt ans . . .

> Non! non! à présent je me révolte contre la mort!

He seems therefore determined to continue his life as an outcast in society, even if this means that the new era that he longs for will never be reached:

> Alors,—oh!—chère pauvre âme, l'éternité serait-elle pas perdue pour nous!

With this question at the end of the fifth chapter Rimbaud plumbs the depths of despair in *Une Saison en enfer.* In the sixth chapter, **'Matin',** he recognizes that he has no more to say about his situation and his past experiences:

> Pourtant, aujourd'hui, je crois avoir fini la relation de mon enfer. C'était bien l'enfer; l'ancien, celui dont le fils de l'homme ouvrit les portes.

This sentence clearly links up with the reference in **'Nuit de l'enfer'** to pagans being free from the idea of hell and with the general theme of the previous chapters that Rimbaud is an outcast from the Christian community. But the previous chapters have also shown his stubborn refusal to surrender and once again he looks forward to the advent of the new era he is seeking:

> . . . Quand irons-nous, par-delà les grèves et les monts, saluer la naissance du travail nouveau, la sagesse nouvelle, la fuite des tyrans et des démons, la fin de la superstition, adorer—les premiers! Noël sur la terre!

> Le chant des cieux, la marche des peuples! Esclaves, ne maudissons pas la vie.

In the final chapter, appropriately entitled **'Adieu'**, this mixture of optimism and pessimism continues as Rimbaud reflects that, although autumn, with all its symbolic significance, was drawing near as he was completing *Une Saison en enfer,*[12] he has no need to regret the darkening days since he is seeking a spiritual rather than a physical source of light:

> L'automne déjà!—Mais pourquoi regretter un éternel soleil, si nous sommes engagés à la découverte de la clarté divine,—loin des gens qui meurent sur les saisons.

But the thought of autumn and more particularly, no doubt, of the previous autumn of 1872 when he and Verlaine had set sail from Ostend for Dover on 7 September on the way to London, leads to a paragraph full of darkness and bitterness as he recalls that unhappy period:

> L'automne. Notre barque élevée dans les brumes immobiles tourne vers le port de la misère, la cité énorme au ciel taché de feu et de boue. Ah!

les haillons pourris, le pain trempé de pluie, l'ivresse, les mille amours qui m'ont crucifié!

These sombre reflections on the past are, however, counterbalanced by a radiant picture of the promised land and by a series of comments on his past achievements which seem to define with a remarkable accuracy certain passages of the *Illuminations:*

—Quelquefois je vois au ciel des plages sans fin couvertes de blanches nations en joie. Un grand vaisseau d'or, au-dessus de moi, agite ses pavillons multicolores sous les brises du matin. J'ai créé toutes les fêtes, tous les triomphes, tous les drames. J'ai essayé d'inventer de nouvelles fleurs, de nouveaux astres, de nouvelles chairs, de nouvelles langues. J'ai cru acquérir des pouvoirs surnaturels . . . [13]

But again the plunge into pessimism occurs as he realizes that all this creative activity, not only in the realm of literature but also in the realm of ideas, is now ended:

. . . Eh bien! je dois enterrer mon imagination et mes souvenirs. Une belle gloire de conteur et d'artiste emportée!

Moi! moi qui me suis dit mage ou ange, dispensé de toute morale, je suis rendu au sol, avec un devoir à chercher, et la réalité rugueuse à étreindre. Paysan!

Furthermore, not only have all his high hopes been dashed, but he now feels, after the break with Verlaine, entirely alone with no one to help him out of his difficulties:

Mais pas une main amie! et où puiser le secours?

Yet despite this feeling of failure and solitude, he paradoxically claims, in the final paragraphs of *Une Saison en enfer,* that he has won a kind of victory in the sense that he has now recovered from his anger, regret and grief at what has occurred and can put all this past history behind him:

Car je puis dire que la victoire m'est acquise: les grincements de dents, les sifflements de feu, les soupirs empestés se modèrent. Tous les souvenirs immondes s'effacent. Mes derniers regrets détalent . . .

This leads into another radiant picture of the promised land that he feels convinced will one day be reached:

. . . Recevons tous les influx de vigueur et de tendresse réelle. Et à l'aurore, armés d'une ardente patience, nous entrerons aux splendides villes.

As for the means by which it is to be attained, Rimbaud's conclusion, in the last paragraph of *Une*

Saison en enfer, is that he no longer believes in the concept of 'l'amour universel'. His solitude no longer appears to him as a cause for complaint:

Que parlais-je de main amie! Un bel avantage, c'est que je puis rire des vieilles amours mensongères, et frapper de honte ces couples menteurs . . .

There can be little doubt that these lines refer to the relationship with Verlaine, despite the fact that Rimbaud then adds the somewhat surprising phrase: 'J'ai vu l'enfer des femmes là-bas'. Suzanne Bernard suggests that this may be a reference to the 'vierge folle', but it may also be an admission by Rimbaud that he does not regard heterosexuality as an alternative to homosexuality but simply as another aspect of 'l'amour universel' which must therefore be rejected so that he can pursue his own solitary path towards true happiness:

. . . et il me sera loisible de *posséder la vérité dans une âme et un corps.*

Old and New Techniques

If *Une Saison en enfer* is an account of the new attitudes Rimbaud adopted in the summer of 1873 towards the three-fold ambition he had once had of forging a lasting relationship with Verlaine, of writing a new kind of poetry and of reforming the moral basis on which western society is founded, it is only to be expected that this rejection of his earlier ideas should be expressed in ways very different from those which he had previously used and which are condemned with such scorn in **'Alchimie du verbe'**. One immediately obvious difference is that *Une Saison en enfer* is very much a prose work and although, on occasions, there are passages that have a poetic quality, such as the lines at the end of **'Matin'** looking forward to the advent of a new era, or the sombre opening paragraphs of **'Adieu'**, recalling the despondent weeks in London, or the later paragraph of **'Adieu'** painting a radiant picture of the promised land, on the whole Rimbaud seems to make little or no attempt to achieve the poetic effects that have been analysed in the *Illuminations.* On the contrary, he not infrequently lapses into language of a clumsy banality, as when he writes, in **'Mauvais sang'**:

. . . C'est très-certain, c'est oracle, ce que je dis. Je comprends, et ne sachant m'expliquer sans paroles païennes, je voudrais me taire;

or as when he writes in **'L'Impossible'**:

Mes deux sous de raison sont finis!—L'esprit est autorité. Il veut que je sois en Occident. Il faudrait le faire taire pour conclure comme je voulais.

Not only does *Une Saison en enfer* thus use language for the purpose of 'reportage' as Mallarmé put it, rather than for the purpose of poetry, but it also, in consequence, abandons, for the most part, the idea advanced in the **'lettre du voyant'** that the poet is a passive instrument played upon by outside forces. The first section of **'Délires'** in particular is far removed from such free-flowing passages as **'Barbare'** and **'Ville'** and such inconsequential poems as **'Chant de guerre parisien'** and **'Entends comme brame'**. The technique of ostensibly quoting the 'vierge folle' who, in turn, ostensibly quotes the 'époux infernal' is clearly a complex one that cannot have sprung from any 'désordre de l'esprit' but must, on the contrary, have resulted from a conscious control as rigorous as in such conventional poems of 1870 and 1871 as **'Le Forgeron'** and **'Les Premières Communions'**. The second section of **'Délires'** too is coherently organized and pursues a clear line of argument as Rimbaud amplifies his opening statement that he is going to recount 'l'histoire d'une de mes folies', even if the poems he quotes do not always illustrate his points particularly well.

The remaining chapters of *Une Saison en enfer,* as has just been shown, also pursue a theme to which Rimbaud constantly returns, developing successive stages in his argument so as to arrive at his conclusion. But in matters of detail these chapters are much less carefully ordered than the two sections of **'Délires'** and they frequently give the impression that Rimbaud is allowing his thoughts to stray from the essential point, distracted by associated ideas and images. In the opening lines of **'Mauvais sang'** for example, his contention that he is descended from the Gauls leads him to drift into details about them that are irrelevant to his argument:

> J'ai de mes ancêtres gaulois l'œil bleu blanc, la cervelle étroite, et la maladresse dans la lutte. Je trouve mon habillement aussi barbare que le leur. Mais je ne beurre pas ma chevelure.

> Les Gaulois étaient des écorcheurs de bêtes, les brûleurs d'herbes les plus ineptes de leur temps . .

Towards the end of the same chapter Rimbaud's lack of conscious control over what Suzanne Bernard calls 'ce texte chaotique' takes a different form as he vividly but far from coherently conveys his sense of being forced, like an unwilling conscript, to fight for a cause he does not support:

> Assez! voici la punition. *En marche!*

> Ah! les poumons brûlent, les tempes grondent! la nuit roule dans mes yeux, par ce soleil! le cœur . . . les membres . . .

> Où va-t-on? au combat? Je suis faible! les autres avancent. Les outils, les armes . . . le temps!

> Feu! feu sur moi! Là ou je me rends.—Lâches!—Je me tue! Je me jette aux pieds des chevaux!

> Ah! . . .

> —Je m'y habituerai.

> Ce serait la vie francaise, le sentier de l'honneur!

This kind of style, strongly reminiscent of such texts as **'L'Orgie parisienne'** and **'Démocratie'**, is to be found in other chapters of *Une Saison en enfer* where Rimbaud allows his thoughts and feelings to pour out, as in the following paragraph from **'Nuit de l'enfer'**:

> Tais-toi, mais tais-toi! . . . C'est la honte, le reproche, ici: Satan qui dit que le feu est ignoble, que ma colère est affreusement sotte.—Assez! . . . Des erreurs qu'on me souffle, magies, parfums faux, musiques puériles.—Et dire que je tiens la vérité, que je vois la justice: j'ai un jugement sain et arrêté, jé suis prêt pour la perfection . . . Orgueil.—La peau de ma tête se dessèche. Pitié! Seigneur, j'ai peur. J'ai soif, si soif! Ah! l'enfance, l'herbe, la pluie, le lac sur les pierres, *le clair de lune quand le clocher sonnait douze* . . . le diable est au clocher, à cette heure. Marie! Sainte-Vierge! . . . —Horreur de ma bêtise.

In **'L'Impossible'** too, despite the fact that the general theme of the chapter is fairly clear, there are many passages where Rimbaud's ideas appear to have run away with him so that the reader is left far behind, as in the following paragraph:

> Hier encore je soupirais: 'Ciel! sommes-nous assez de damnés ici-bas! Moi j'ai tant de temps déjà dans leur troupe. Je les connais tous. Nous nous reconnaissons toujours; nous nous dégoûtons. La charité nous est inconnue. Mais nous sommes polis, nos relations avec le monde sont très-convenables'. Est-ce étonnant? Le monde! les marchands, les naïfs!—Nous ne sommes pas déshonorés.—Mais les élus, comment nous recevraient-ils? Or il y a des gens hargneux et joyeux, de faux élus, puisqu'il nous faut de l'audace ou de l'humilité pour les aborder. Ce sont les seuls élus. Ce ne sont pas des bénisseurs!

If the two sections of **'Délires'** are as carefully composed as the conventional poems of 1870 and 1871, the remaining chapters of *Une Saison en enfer* may therefore be compared to **'Le Bateau ivre'** and other poems of late 1871 in that, although they have a fairly clear overall pattern, within this framework there is evidence of a decided 'désordre de l'esprit'. The Rimbaud of the **'lettre du voyant'** thus still persists in *Une Saison en enfer,* standing aside on occasions and allowing his thoughts and feelings to unfold; but the earlier Rimbaud of the period before the **'lettre du voyant'** has begun to re-assert his authority, ordering every detail of the two sections of **'Délires'** and consciously shaping the outline of the other chapters so that their logical train of thought, however much it may be interrupted, is never entirely lost.[14]

Notes

[1] A more detailed account of the events surrounding the publication of *Une Saison en enfer* can conveniently be found in the 1954 edition of the *Oeuvres complètes*. The *Oeuvres complètes [O.C.] 1972* edition [edited by Antoine Adams, Gallimard, Bibliothèque de la Pléiade] gives a much briefer account.

[2] Vitalie Rimbaud notes in her diary her brother's arrival at Roche on Good Friday 11 April 1873 (see *O.C. 1972* p. 819); it should be noted that on p. 817 this section of Vitalie's diary is wrongly headed 'août 1874' when it should read 'avril-septembre 1873'.

[3] It is interesting to note that Verlaine too seems to have regarded April 1873 as marking a distinct break in his life and work. Hence the fact that *Romances sans paroles* has no poems in it dating from after April and that *Sagesse* has several poems in it written between April and July. So that although, with the benefit of hindsight, July 1873 now appears to mark the end of the Verlaine-Rimbaud relationship, it seems clear that they themselves thought that this particular chapter in their lives was finished in April and that they did not, at that time, expect to come together again for a final few weeks from 24 May to 20 July. For further details on this point see C. Chadwick, *Verlaine* (Athlone French Poets), The Athlone Press, University of London, 1973, pp. 51-3.

[4] The incorrect spellings are, of course, deliberate and form part of the adolescent style that Rimbaud adopted in his letters at this time.

[5] See N. Osmond, ed. [*Illuminations* (Athlone French Poets), The Athlone Press, University of London, 1976, Introduction, p. 7.

[6] In 1968 M. Ruff in his *Rimbaud* [Hatier], pp. 173-5, revived a suggestion made by R. Clauzel in 1931 that the 'vierge folle' and 'l'époux infernal' were not Verlaine and Rimbaud but were two aspects of the latter's character. Antoine Adam, in *O.C. 1972*, p. 962, gives the suggestion his approval, but few, if any, other critics regard it as tenable.

[7] M. Ruff puzzles over why the words 'l'époux infernal' are in smaller lettering than the words 'vierge folle' and are placed below rather than beside the latter. The reason may be to indicate that they do not form part of the sub-title of the passage but are used, as in a play, to designate the person who speaks the first line and, indirectly, the whole passage.

[8] 'Pourquoi souligner *"moi, la pauvre âme' "* , asks M. Ruff, op. cit., p. 174. The most likely explanation is that these words are quoted from an earlier poem by Rimbaud, 'Chanson de la plus haute tour', in which, with reference to Verlaine, he had talked of the 'mille veuvages de la si pauvre âme', the notion of 'veuvage' also being repeated in 'Délires I'.

[9] For further discussion of this point see C. Chadwick, *Verlaine*, p. 42 and *Etudes sur Rimbaud* [Nizet, 1960], p. 50.

[10] See Suzanne Bernard, ed. [Rimbaud, *Oeuvres* Garnier, 1960], p. 473, note 29.

[11] See C. Chadwick, *Verlaine,* pp. 68-9.

[12] It is interesting to note that, at about the same time, Verlaine gave a similar significance to autumn in the final line of his sonnet 'L'espoir luit . . . ' (see Paul Verlaine, *Sagesse,* edited by C. Chadwick (Athlone French Poets), The Athlone Press, University of London, 1973, pp. 91-3).

[13] These 'nouvelles fleurs' seem to echo the 'fleurs de rêve' of Enfance I and the 'fleurs magiques' of 'Enfance II', as well as the exotic flowers of the passage 'Fleurs'. The 'nouveaux astres' may well refer to the 'lunes et comètes' and the 'boules de saphir, de métal' that Rimbaud imagines in the centre of the earth in 'Enfance V'. The 'nouvelles chairs' seem to be an apt description of the fantasy creatures of 'Antique' and 'Being Beauteous'.

[14] C. A. Hackett reaches a similar conclusion in *Une Saison en enfer: frénésie et structure:* 'Ainsi, *Une Saison en enfer,* malgré la frénésie présente dans les conflits qui s'y trouvent retracés, nous apparaît comme une construction très concertée et même un peu trop linéaire. Au lieu de créer et de suggérer comme dans les *Illuminations,* Rimbaud raconte, affirme, explique. Cette œuvre est bien, comme il l'a écrit lui-même, la "relation" de son enfer' (*La Revue des Lettres Modernes,* Nos. 370-3, 1973, pp. 7-15).

C. A. Hackett (essay date 1981)

SOURCE: "Une Saison en enfer," in *Rimbaud: A Critical Introduction,* Cambridge University Press, 1981, pp. 85-119.

[*In the essay below, Hackett emphasizes the technical artistry and universal implications of* Une Saison en enfer. *Discussing each section in turn, the critic examines Rimbaud's language and imagery; his rhetorical method of statement and counterstatement; his use of certain structural devices to achieve coherence; and his ambiguous treatment of the motifs of time, salvation, the search for truth, and the essential duality of body and spirit.*]

Poésies, Derniers vers or ***Vers nouveaux et chansons,*** and ***Illuminations*** are collections or groups of poems which have been arranged in a certain order, and given those titles, by various editors. ***Une Saison en enfer,*** on the other hand, is a work which, from its inception to its publication, was under Rimbaud's control. It was he who decided the order of the nine sections, gave them their titles, dated the work, found a publisher in Brussels, corrected the proofs and saw it through the press. As well as being his only sustained and completed work—his only *œuvre*—*Une Saison en enfer* is the work which Rimbaud himself considered, perhaps for personal reasons, of supreme importance. Some of the sections were written before, and some after the quarrel in Brussels in which Verlaine shot and wounded him, an event which may have suggested the title, ***Une Saison en enfer,*** in place of the ones originally thought of—'Livre païen' and 'Livre nègre'.

More is known about ***Une Saison en enfer*** than about ***Poésies*** or the ***Illuminations.*** We have drafts of three sections, and an invaluable letter to Ernest Delahaye, written in May 1873, which shows Rimbaud at the family farm at Roche, in the act of composing the work which was later to become ***Une Saison en enfer.*** The poet's attitude to his work in progress is revealing. He has already thought about a title, and about the length and the structure of the book: nine 'petites histoires en prose', three of which he has finished and half-a-dozen he still has to 'faire' or 'inventer'. The use of these verbs, in particular the second, and his reference to the stories as 'histoires atroces' and 'atrocités', suggest the attitude of a writer who is conscious of his craft and of the effect he hopes to produce. The letter also reveals frenzied activity, total absorption and a sense of crisis. When Rimbaud declares, 'Mon sort dépend de ce livre', one feels that he is thinking not only of literary glory but of some kind of human fate or 'salvation'.

Une Saison en enfer can be read as a self-contained narration, with a beginning, a middle and an end, as a work of art complete in itself; but it does not fit neatly into any definite genre. It defies classification, and even today critics are divided, not only about its meaning and the exact nature of its 'hell', but also about its importance and value as a literary text. Like the ***Illuminations,*** it has been interpreted in widely divergent and even more extreme ways, ranging from a spiritual conversion and a 'return to God', to a rejection of poetry and a 'return to reality'; so that for generations of readers, it has been a Bible or, more often, an anti-Bible. Verlaine, in his enthusiastic uncritical way, probably came nearest to defining its particular nature and style when he wrote, in his article, 'Arthur Rimbaud "1884"', that it was an 'espèce de prodigieuse autobiographie', written in a 'prose de diamant'. Even if the work is not an autobiography in the customary sense and does not tell accurately and in detail the story of Rimbaud's life, it is a comprehensive survey of his beliefs and ambitions. A narrative element is felt in the recurrence of explicit statements, and is heightened by the almost total absence of certain images, notably those of the stage and theatre, which are pervasive in the ***Illuminations.*** There, they had been used to create a multiplicity of viewpoints and perspectives, suggesting the mind's limitless possibilities. Here, our attention is confined to the actor himself and to emotions and ideas which—at one time projected into imaginary figures and dramas—are now locked in conflict within his own mind. Whereas in the ***Illuminations*** Rimbaud's spirit was always 'en avant', reaching into the future, in ***Une Saison en enfer*** the first movement is a turning to the past and a regret for a 'festin'.[1]

The whole of ***Une Saison en enfer*** is, of course, rooted in the past, in what Rimbaud calls his 'sale éducation d'enfance' and his Catholic upbringing. One of his most profound statements, 'Je suis esclave de mon baptême' in the ***'Nuit de l'enfer',*** is immediately followed by a statement attributing all the blame to his parents: 'Parents, vous avez fait mon malheur et vous avez fait le vôtre. Pauvre innocent!' The same psychological mechanism which we noted in the early poems and in the ***Lettre du voyant*** is at work in ***Une Saison en enfer.*** Rimbaud is fascinated by what revolts him; and he is both attracted and repelled by the doctrines of Catholicism. Religious images and expressions constantly recur, but these, like the Latin of the Liturgy to which at times he has recourse (for example, *De profundis Domine* in ***'Mauvais sang',*** *ad matutinum* and *Christus venit* in ***'Délires II. Alchimie du verbe',*** *Pater* and *Ave Maria* in ***'Matin'***), are ridiculed and dismissed. He still needs what he claims to reject, and his 'slavery' is necessary so that he can affirm his passionate desire for freedom, whether through the dream of a mythical past—a lost paradise or the golden age of youth—or through an aspiration to an idealised and impossible future.

Une Saison en enfer can perhaps be best seen as a dramatised confession, or the parody of a confession, in which Rimbaud is both guilty and innocent, a 'damné' and a 'pauvre innocent'. Yet, in this confession, there is nothing normal, calm or passive; it is an upheaval, a volcanic eruption. Themes that had been suppressed or transcended in the ***Illuminations*** invade the poet's mind with unparalleled force, and he is suddenly confronted with all the antitheses, antinomies and dualisms which are inherent in the condition of Western man. *Une Saison en enfer* is in fact much more than a confession. It is a spiritual battle in which the protagonists are God and Satan, Good and Evil, Sin and Innocence, Past and Future, the Occident and the Orient, Body and Mind, and at least thirty other antithetical couples. The title, as brilliant a *trouvaille* as Baudelaire's *Les Fleurs du mal,* indicates the nature of the work, the brevity and intensity of the poet's suffering. As the 'ivresse' of the *voyant* had lasted only for a 'matinée', so the anguish is only for a 'saison'; and in the title, 'Saison', the less dramatic of the two words, is the more important. The idea of a 'season' as a part of the year, or a symbolic season of ecstasy, loss or despair, and more generally as a period of time—real time and the poet's emotional time—is present from the first to the last section and, with its store of lyrical associations, is a unifying theme.

Une Saison en enfer has a logical plan and a coherent structure. Even the titles of the sections—'**Mauvais sang**', '**Nuit de l'enfer**', '**Délires I**', '**Délires II**', '**L'Impossible**', '**L'Éclair**', '**Matin**', and '**Adieu**'—show a concern for an artistic effect, and they delineate the general development and the external structure. This and the inner structure are most clearly seen in the prologue, 'Jadis, si je me souviens bien'; in the long central movement consisting of the two 'délires' ('**Vierge folle—L'Époux infernal**' and '**Alchimie du verbe**'); and in the conclusion '**Adieu**', which is both a summing up and a dénouement. In each of these sections, an allusion to a season—spring in the prologue, summer in the '**Délires**', autumn and winter in '**Adieu**'—marks a significant phase in Rimbaud's 'hell'. *Une Saison en enfer* has often been seen as an uncontrolled upsurge of ideas and feelings; but one is as conscious of Rimbaud's art as of the tumultuous nature of his emotions. The pervasive repetition, for example, of words, motifs and rhythms, which denotes a frenzied obsession with certain ideas and states of mind, is also used as a structural device.

This balance and sense of structure are felt in the opening section where, as Ernest Delahaye noted, albeit somewhat fancifully, sentences and paragraphs follow each other 'with the elegance of a minuet'.[2] This is untitled, and is usually called the prelude or prologue. It sets the ironic tone and introduces some of the main themes: childhood, time, duality, suffering, death. Above all, it indicates, in the first two sentences, where the stress will fall throughout the work: first on life, in particular Rimbaud's own life ('ma vie était un festin où s'ouvraient tous les cœurs, où tous les vins coulaient'), and then on literature, especially his own poetry and poetic beliefs ('Un soir, j'ai assis la Beauté sur mes genoux.—Et je l'ai trouvée amère.—Et je l'ai injuriée'). Always, literature is

secondary and is seen in terms of life. The reference to Beauty is reminiscent of the passage in the second section of Vigny's 'La Maison du berger', where he attacks those who have defiled the Muse of poetry ('un vieillard, t'enivrant de son baiser jaloux, / Releva le premier ta robe de prêtresse, / Et, parmi les garçons, t'assit sur ses genoux'). The image may be similar, but the sense is different; and Rimbaud rejects what Vigny had always defended, namely, a moral and didactic view of poetry, 'perle de la Pensée'.

This introductory section prepares the stage for the beginning of a battle or drama, in which Rimbaud directs his attack against moral virtues and normal human emotions. Brutal sado-masochistic sentences express feelings that surge from one extreme to another; and a savage thrust at the external world and its values is immediately followed by self-laceration and a desire for punishment:

> Je me suis armé contre la justice.
>
> Je me suis enfui. Ô sorcières, ô misère, ô haine, c'est à vous que mon trésor a été confié!
>
> Je parvins à faire s'évanouir dans mon esprit toute l'espérance humaine. Sur toute joie pour l'étrangler j'ai fait le bond sourd de la bête féroce.
>
> J'ai appelé les bourreaux pour, en périssant, mordre la crosse de leurs fusils. J'ai appelé les fléaux, pour m'étouffer avec le sable, le sang. Le malheur a été mon dieu. Je me suis allongé dans la boue. Je me suis séché à l'air du crime.

These violent, yet controlled, fluctuations are characteristic of the whole work, as are the two roles which Rimbaud adopts. He is both the 'bête féroce' ('hyène', Satan calls him) and at the same time, as is evident from his bantering address to the Devil, the detached cynical observer. But he is also the poet, a different one from the *voyant* who, in the *Illuminations,* had proudly proclaimed that he had discovered 'quelque chose comme la clef de l'amour'. Now, referring to the incident in Brussels when he imagined himself on the point of death ('tout dernièrement m'étant trouvé sur le point de faire le dernier *couae!*'), he is preoccupied with finding again 'la clef du festin ancien'. Charity, which might be the key, is at once rejected because of its Christian associations, and satirised as an 'inspiration'. Statement followed by counter-statement, affirmation by denial, acceptance by rejection, may be the sign of a profound spiritual conflict, but it is also a conscious literary device which enables Rimbaud to examine, criticise and attack opposed attitudes, and to reveal absurdities in established values. In the same way Time, the most inexorable of the antagonists, is used as a structural device to give the work coherence and unity. 'Jadis' opens the section; and 'le printemps' divides it into equal parts, the first dealing with a remote, imagined past, and the second with a recent past and also with the present, when Rimbaud has become aware of good and evil and the many other dualities in life.

The prologue recalls 'Au Lecteur', Baudelaire's preface to *Les Fleurs du mal;* but Rimbaud adopts a different, perverse convention, addressing not the reader but himself and Satan—to whom he appropriately offers his work in ironic homage:

> Mais, cher Satan, . . . vous qui aimez dans l'écrivain l'absence des facultés descriptives ou instructives, je vous détache ces quelques hideux feuillets de mon carnet de damné.

He flatters Satan by attributing to him literary tastes, and the flattery is the more subtle because these are precisely the tastes to which Rimbaud's own best work bears witness: absence of description and of didacticism. The absence of these two features characterises the *Illuminations,* for example in **'Jeunesse'** the 'voix instructives' are exiled, and in **'Vies'** the poet asks, 'Qu'a-t-on fait du brahmane qui m'expliqua les Proverbes?' Yet in *Une Saison en enfer* there *is* description, not it is true of the external world, but of the poet's own mind, and inevitably the meaning of the work becomes 'instructive' not only for Rimbaud but also for the reader.

In the prologue, as elsewhere, Rimbaud's attitude to Satan is equivocal. He allies himself with the arch-rebel the better to express his defiance of Christ; but as his damnation is only for a season, he can, at the same time, taunt and provoke him, and finally show him to be a myth, or, to borrow Renan's expression, an 'excellent fiction'. Later, he uses Christ in the same ambiguous way. In **'Nuit de l'enfer'**, for example, he identifies himself with Him, assuming His role, and paraphrasing His words, but only in order to undermine the belief in His divinity: 'Fiez-vous donc à moi . . . Tous, venez,—même les petits enfants . . . Je ne demande pas de prières; avec votre confiance seulement, je serai heureux.' Again, in **'Délires I. Vierge folle—L'Époux infernal'**, based on the parable of the ten foolish virgins, the perverse identification of the 'Époux infernal' with the heavenly bridegroom is used to parody and destroy the belief in the divinity of Christ. This identification, first with Satan then with Christ, the extremes of evil and good, followed by mockery and rejection, reflects Rimbaud's search for a solution acceptable on his own terms. But he is equally equivocal towards himself, and as he constantly eludes any rational examination of his dilemma—'Je suis caché et je ne le suis pas', he says in **'Nuit de l'enfer'**—it is difficult to be certain that his solution is not another 'attitude' or evasion. That uncertainty, which

has made possible so many varied interpretations of *Une Saison en enfer,* does not however in any way diminish our appreciation of the extraordinary skill and beauty of Rimbaud's ambiguous art.

The sweeping, dogmatic statements of an essentially personal kind used in the prologue (only one sentence is impersonal: 'La charité est cette clef') are one of the most obvious features of *Une Saison en enfer.* In the next section, **'Mauvais sang'**, however, one becomes conscious of a more subtle feature—the occasional use of an impersonal statement at an important point in the text: for instance, 'La main à plume vaut la main à charrue', 'Le monde marche! Pourquoi ne tournerait-il pas?', 'L'amour divin seul octroie les clefs de la science', 'La vie est la farce à mener par tous.' This strategic placing of impersonal, epigrammatic statements among predominantly personal utterances is a means Rimbaud adopts to give an ordered pattern to the expression of a disordered mind. Moreover, as well as telling about himself, it enables him to comment on the human condition and so give universality to his work.

Delahaye's word 'menuet' may not be the most appropriate term to describe the prologue; but **'Mauvais sang'**, consisting of numerous interwoven variations on a single theme, could be likened to a fugue. The 'mauvais sang' is 'le sang païen', the blood which is the sign of Rimbaud's innocence because, through no fault of his, he is a heathen; and the sign of his guilt, because he is not a Christian. As the blood circulates and returns—'le sang païen revient!', he exclaims—it brings images of other blood, and of salvation through sacrifice. Rimbaud begins by making his ancestors, the barbaric Gauls, responsible for his faults, vices and sins; and for his being 'race inférieure'. They were destroyers, and their stupid descendants had infected the earth with materialism, reason, nineteenth-century positivism, so-called progress and science, ironically described as 'la nouvelle noblesse'. As the poet recalls the history of France, he sees himself in many roles, but always as an alien and an outcast—serf, leper, mercenary, convict, savage, negro. In his imagination, he has been everywhere, seen and known everything; but he is rootless, 'toujours seul, sans famille'. In a desperate longing for a true spiritual nobility, he turns momentarily to Christianity and thinks of the Holy Ghost, Christ, the Gospel, and God. 'J'attends Dieu avec gourmandise', he declares, and while waiting, he finds consolation in thinking of conventional success, with values acceptable to society: virility, money, women, politics. 'Sauvé!' he mockingly exclaims, and then, without transition, he returns to his present state—'maudit'—and to a desire, viewed sardonically, for oblivion in a drunken sleep. In the next passage, realising that no escape is possible and that the conflict cannot be disposed of by sleep, he appears to accept the burden of his sin and his human condition, 'Allons! La marche, le fardeau, le désert, l'ennui et la colère . . . La vie dure . . . '—a statement to which his life was later to give reality. But simplification by action is no more efficacious than forgetfulness through sleep. The repressed torment breaks through in a series of questions which reveal the extent of Rimbaud's solitude and the disordered state of his mind:

> À qui me louer? Quelle bête faut-il adorer? Quelle sainte image attaque-t-on? Quels cœurs briserai-je? Quel mensonge dois-je tenir?—Dans quel sang marcher?

Torn between extremes, 'le ciel' and 'ici-bas', he thinks again of charity and the Christian virtues. This solution is rejected as soon as it is entertained, and he exclaims: *'De profundis Domine,* suis-je bête!' Invariably, anything associated with religion is followed by savage dismissal; a longing for God being the surest proof of weakness and degradation.

In the fifth part of **'Mauvais sang'**, Rimbaud plays out in dramatic form several complementary themes: guilt and innocence, damnation and salvation, passivity and aggression, masochism and sadism, etc. He recalls the time when, as a child, he had felt so alienated from society that he had identified himself with the convict, like him an outcast and a rebel, seeing towns and 'civilised' life through his eyes and with his mentality. On winter nights his suffering left him with a death-like appearance which by morning made him almost unrecognisable to those he met: 'Au matin j'avais le regard si perdu et la contenance si morte, que ceux que j'ai rencontrés *ne m'ont peut-être pas vu.'* Then, as though extreme privation had quickened the senses and produced enrichment, the outcast with 'le regard si perdu' suddenly sees with the eyes of the *voyant,* and the narrative is interrupted by a passage leading through a series of images to an apocalyptic vision:

> Dans les villes la boue m'apparaissait soudainement rouge et noire, comme une glace quand la lampe circule dans la chambre voisine, comme un trésor dans la forêt! Bonne chance, criais-je, et je voyais une mer de flammes et de fumée au ciel; et, à gauche, à droite, toutes les richesses flambant comme un milliard de tonnerres.

This extract is similar to the evocation in the fifth section of 'Enfance' of the 'ville monstrueuse', the town where the mud is 'rouge ou noire'; but it has a closer resemblance to another of the **Illuminations,** **'Mystique'**, where there is a similar 'situating' of the scene ('A gauche le terreau de l'arête . . . Derrière l'arête de droite . . . '), and a similar fiery vision ('Des prés de flammes bondissent jusqu'au sommet

du mamelon . . . '). But the scene in **'Mauvais sang'** is the demonic counterpart of **'Mystique'**, with fire no longer just part of a unified verbal pattern, but dominant and destructive of 'toutes les richesses'. Moments of imagery and vision such as this are relatively rare in *Une Saison en enfer* which is, as Rimbaud himself says in **'Matin'**, a 'relation', a narration. In a draft version of **'Nuit de l'enfer'** he is more explicit: 'Puis-je décrire la vision, on n'est pas poète en enfer'; and in the final text: 'Puis-je décrire la vision, l'air de l'enfer ne souffre pas les hymnes!' Even images of fire, which one might expect to be numerous in the scenario and story of this period in hell, are infrequent; and their appearance at this point is not only unexpected but significant. The effect of surprise and suddenness, conveyed by both verb—'apparaissait'—and adverb—'soudainement'—is followed by a rapid expansion of space from a 'chambre' to a 'forêt' to a 'mer de flammes et de fumée au ciel', from the confined and familiar to the vast and strange—a *fluid* conflagration. In 'mer de flammes', water and fire unite to evoke a Dante-like inferno, as, later, at the end of **'Nuit de l'enfer'**, the same two elements are fused in a minute, but equally original image, 'une goutte de feu'. These are two examples of how one, or more, of the four elements—earth, water, air, fire—can nourish and re-energise the poetic imagination, as Gaston Bachelard has shown.[3] They have a special significance in *Une Saison en enfer,* where water and fire symbolise not only baptism and hell, but also transformation and regeneration.

Again Rimbaud returns to the solitude of his childhood:

> Pas même un compagnon. Je me voyais devant une foule exaspérée, en face du peloton d'exécution, pleurant du malheur qu'ils n'aient pu comprendre, et pardonnant!—Comme Jeanne d'Arc!—«Prêtres, professeurs, maîtres, vous vous trompez en me livrant à la justice. Je n'ai jamais été de ce peuple-ci; je n'ai jamais été chrétien; je suis de la race qui chantait dans le supplice; je ne comprends pas les lois; je n'ai pas le sens moral, je suis une brute: vous vous trompez . . . »

> Oui, j'ai les yeux fermés à votre lumière. Je suis une bête, un nègre. Mais je puis être sauvé. Vous êtes de faux nègres, vous maniaques, féroces, avares. Marchand, tu es nègre; magistrat, tu es nègre; général, tu es nègre; empereur, vieille démangeaison, tu es nègre . . .

Like Joan of Arc, also a rebel, he is condemned to death for his visions. In protesting his innocence, he attacks those who have judged and sentenced him—priests, teachers, merchants, magistrates, generals—all, like his 'Homme juste', hypocrites and pillars of a Christian society. And he asserts that they are mistaken in their condemnation because he does not belong to their race, has never been a Christian, and so cannot be judged by standards and laws he does not accept. This obsession with innocence, suffering and martyrdom is a complex and ambiguous theme, and the negro who embodies it represents both primitive man in his purity, the noble savage, and the unclean, guilty child. Rimbaud feels, however, that he himself is the true primitive and so may yet be saved. His judges and executioners, on the other hand, are 'faux nègres' who, by the 'light' of their reason, have misunderstood him. They are the adults who have betrayed the visionary light of childhood which he, at least in his poetry, has preserved intact. Despite the over-emphasis, and the melodramatic nature of the scene, this is one of the moments in *Une Saison en enfer* where Rimbaud's vehement attack is convincing, and where the 'je' takes on more than personal significance and becomes representative of the individual in his struggle against an uncomprehending and corrupt society. The revolt is followed by disgust, and he thinks of leaving Europe, but finds instead a more profound escape in a return to a physical elemental state, and an ecstasy of forgetfulness through gesture and action: 'Faim, soif, cris, danse, danse, danse, danse!'

In the next passage, he presents in two images a simplified version of the main theme of salvation and damnation. The first image is of the white race landing from their ship to 'save' him by forcing him at the point of the gun to be baptised. The other is of a 'navire sauveur', the ship of salvation, symbol of divine love, which, dispensing with military formalities, rescues him, but leaves the others, his friends, to drown. The ironic presentation (reminiscent of the shipwreck incident in the fifth chapter of Voltaire's *Candide*), the contrasts and similarities between these two orders and two kinds of love, human and divine, make one realise that if Rimbaud were to accept salvation it would be on his own terms. Nevertheless, he decides that, for the time being, he will love his fellow men and praise God. But again, no sooner has he accepted this salvation than he rejects it and demands the impossible, 'la liberté' dans le salut'. Nothing must constrain his spirit, yet innocent or guilty, he is obliged to accept, with the rest of us, the inescapable burden of life itself; and in an aphoristic statement he expresses his philosophy of the Absurd: 'La vie est la farce à mener par tous.' The farce is then illustrated in the conclusion by a satirical picture of Rimbaud seeking salvation in the despised French way of life— as a soldier facing death in battle.

'Nuit de l'enfer' which, as we know from the draft, had originally been called 'Fausse Conversion' (perhaps too obvious a key to the meaning) begins with the statement 'J'ai avalé une fameuse gorgée de poison.' In tone and style, this beginning is typical. By this kind of short sentence, with a normal word order of subject, verb, object, Rimbaud achieves some of his most forceful and sardonic effects. The physical and mental results of this 'poison' seem to bring the full realisation that he is enduring hell fire and eternal damnation. The poison which is ironically welcomed and blessed at the beginning, is, at the end, equated with a kiss, 'ce baiser mille fois maudit'; and whereas the 'mauvais sang' was the blood of the heathen, the kiss is the poison of Christianity, the 'Baiser putride de Jésus' of 'Les Premières communions'. Rimbaud is, as he himself puts it, the slave of his baptism. In **'Mauvais sang',** he referred to the 'chant raisonnable' of the angels and declared, 'la raison m'est née'; but now he has moved into an irrational realm of darkness and hallucinations, an ostensibly deeper experience, which he views with detachment and irony. The hell which is portrayed is mocked in a parody of Cartesian logic, 'Je me crois en enfer, donc j'y suis.' This melodramatic section, beginning and ending with poison, fire and damnation, is like a mosaic or synthesis of parodies—of the mystic's Dark Night of the Soul, Dante's *Inferno* and a Catholic version of Hell. 'La théologie est sérieuse, l'enfer est certainement *en bas*—et le ciel en haut', says Rimbaud, and to show how 'serious' he is, he affirms, 'Je brûle comme il faut.' Throughout this long soliloquy, more than anywhere else in *Une Saison en enfer,* he is the actor conscious of the effect he wishes to create through tone of voice, asides, studied gestures, and 'toutes les grimaces imaginables'. By the same means, he peoples the stage of his solitude with spectres from his past, and the principal figures of the Christian drama, the Devil, God, Christ, the Virgin Mary.

He makes repeated appeals to his audience to look— 'Voyez comme le feu se relève!'; to agree—'Un homme qui veut se mutiler est bien damnè, n'est-ce pas?'; to keep away—'Qu'on n'approche pas'; to listen—'Écoutez!'; to reply—'Veut-on des chants nègres, des danses de houris?'; and to have faith in him (and here he identifies himself with Christ)— 'Fiez-vous donc à moi . . . tous, venez, même les petits enfants . . . '. The final appeal is to God, 'Mon Dieu, pitié, cachez-moi, je me tiens trop mal.' Here, Rimbaud plays on two meanings of 'se tenir'—his behaviour as a human being, and his bearing as an actor, which have both been bad because his attitude has been equivocal and, as he says in the next sentence, because he has neither concealed nor revealed himself. Like the ideal actor of Diderot's *Paradoxe sur le comédien,* he has tried to hide his real feelings, but some of the roles he has attempted to portray have not yet been written and cannot therefore be learned and imitated. Moreover, he has suddenly been confronted with a new element in the drama, 'l'Orgueil', his own besetting sin and, according to Saint Gregory the Great, the general commanding the devil's army of deadly sins.

'**Mauvais sang**' showed the individual opposed to society as a whole. '**Nuit de l'enfer**' shows him in conflict with its moral values and religious beliefs. Special emphasis is given to Pride because this is one of the causes of his present hell, and the source of his human and literary ambitions. 'Nobles ambitions', he exclaims ironically, and later says, 'Je vais dévoiler tous les mystères: mystères religieux ou naturels, mort, naissance, avenir, passé, cosmogonie, néant. Je suis maître en fantasmagories . . . J'ai tous les talents . . . '. The naturalness and the poignancy of cries which spring from the memory of childhood, such as, 'Ah! l'enfance, l'herbe, la pluie, le lac sur les pierres . . . ', emphasise not only the artificiality of his posturing but also what lies beneath it, namely, the desperate need to find a way out of his dilemma. The lucid, if cynical, realisation of his over-weening pride leads directly to a detailed appraisal in the next two sections, '**Délires I**' and '**Délires II**'; and points the way to a resolution, or at least an 'attitude', that is finally reached in '**Adieu**', the concluding section.

'**Délires**' is the centre and climax of *Une Saison en enfer;* and, in structural terms, it forms the keystone of the work. It consists of two parts, '**Vierge folle— L'Époux infernal**' and '**Alchimie du verbe**'; and if the experience described in them can be qualified as 'delirious', it is a delirium controlled and mastered by art. Despite the title, this is the most objective and the most rigorously constructed of all the sections. To change the metaphor, '**Délires**' resembles a diptych with one panel depicting the Infernal Bridegroom (Rimbaud), his life and human ambitions, and his relationship with the Foolish Virgin (Verlaine); and the other portraying his literary ideals, illustrated by examples taken from his own poetry. Both are pictures of failure; but they are presented in so many varying lights and analysed with such penetrating detail that they are among Rimbaud's most brilliant achievements. The rigour and the beauty of the composition are evident not only in each separate 'délire' but also in their reciprocal relationships, the literary failure contrasting with, and at the same time illustrating, the human failure.

After a long monologue addressed to an imaginary companion, the Devil, Rimbaud introduces into his hell a 'real' companion; a device which gives the work a human quality, and greater narrative and dramatic potentiality. The first of the 'délires', based on the parable of the Foolish Virgins, is a confession—and the parody of a confession—within the general confessional framework of *Une Saison en enfer.* While seeing Verlaine with the utmost clarity, Rimbaud sees himself looking at Verlaine, who in turn is looking at him; and at the same time he sees Verlaine looking at both of them in their homosexual relationship. As the creator and script-writer of this drama, Rimbaud could say, as Monsieur Teste

does in Valéry's *La Soirée avec Monsieur Teste,* 'Je suis étant, et me voyant; me voyant me voir, et ainsi de suite . . . '. As far as one can judge from available sources, in particular Verlaine's letters to Rimbaud and the numerous poems in which he alludes to himself, Rimbaud has caught every trait of his character: the sentimentality, the pleading, the weeping, the self-pity, the religiosity, the childishness, the passivity, the dependence, the helplessness of mind and body, the fear and the bewilderment, the incomprehension, even the tone of his insinuating voice. In a sentence, Rimbaud has summed up Verlaine's desertion of wife and child, and the tragedy of his life: 'J'ai oublié tout mon devoir humain pour le suivre.' But the portrait, as well as being cruel and sadistic, is incomplete and one-sided. There is no hint of the other Verlaine, the poet, only the Verlaine whom Claudel, in his poem 'Verlaine', was to describe as 'faible', 'lamentable' and an 'espèce de soudard immonde'.

In '**Vierge folle—L'Époux infernal**', Verlaine is seen as the Foolish Virgin enslaved by Catholicism, torn between a love of God, the 'divin Époux', and a desire for Rimbaud, the 'Époux infernal'. Weak and helpless, he is tossed to and fro, as in the 'bon délire' of his own poem, 'Le Bon Disciple'. At various points in Verlaine's confession, which typically is often a maudlin 'confidence', Rimbaud puts into the mouth of his companion words and phrases similar to those he has previously used about himself. This simple verbal artifice is an unusually effective means of emphasising the extent of Verlaine's submissiveness, which is evident throughout the section. In addition, by making slight but significant changes, such as the omission of a forceful adjective, adverb, or image, Rimbaud 'dilutes' Verlaine's language, so that the Foolish Virgin's suffering is expressed in a series of enfeebled, prosaic statements, which reveal fundamental differences in the intensity, quality, and even in the 'temperature' of the reactions of the two partners. The Foolish Virgin's exclamation, 'Ah! je souffre, je crie. Je souffre vraiment', expresses the suffering of a weak and submissive character; whereas, in '**Nuit de l'enfer**', Rimbaud reenacts his anguish in virile, masculine language which is itself a liberating force: 'Les entrailles me brûlent. La violence du venin tord mes membres, me rend difforme, me terrasse.'

A particularly interesting passage (put in quotation marks to indicate that the words are those of the Infernal Bridegroom as reported by the Foolish Virgin) refers back to what Rimbaud had said in '**Jadis**' and at the beginning of '**Mauvais sang**' about his barbarous ancestors. Retransmitted through the mind of the Foolish Virgin, everything is confused, facts are inaccurate, and actions either exaggerated or trivialised; for example, the Gauls who buttered their hair become Scandinavians who drank their own blood. Rimbaud, who had declared, 'J'ai appelé les fléaux, pour m'étouffer avec le sable, le sang', is made to utter the absurdity, ' "je me tatouerai . . . je ramperais [a characteristic Verlaine verb of action] et me tordrais sur le tapis" '; and his image 'Je n'aurais jamais ma main' becomes the flat statement ' "Jamais je ne travaillerai." ' This passage illustrates one of the main functions of the Foolish Virgin persona: purgation through ridicule and a fearless, lucid vision. While satirising the Foolish Virgin's muddled mind and the masochistic need to see the Infernal Bridegroom as a terrifying figure, the device also enables the Infernal Bridegroom to see again and criticise, in a different perspective, his own ideas and actions. Similarly, the Foolish Virgin is made to report in 'her' own words some of the Infernal Bridegroom's ideas about social questions, such as the dependent position of woman in society and man's attitude towards her:

> 'Tu vois cet élégant jeune homme, entrant dans la belle et calme maison: il s'appelle Duval, Dufour, Armand, Maurice, que sais-je? Une femme s'est dévouée à aimer ce méchant idiot: elle est morte, c'est certes une sainte au ciel, à présent.'

That passage, apparently casual and offhand, sums up with merciless clarity social attitudes and a whole ethos. It is also an ironic comment on Rimbaud's own attitude, on the apathy and cynicism which, because of the relationship with Verlaine, had overtaken him since the time of the *Lettre du voyant.* Then, he had prophesied that woman's endless servitude would be broken so that she too could become a person in her own right, even a poet, and discover the new and the unknown.

Despite pious utterance about God, and tears of penitence, the Foolish Virgin is concerned only with this world, its opinions and values, and, above all, with self and carnal satisfactions. 'Her' horizon is so limited that, while being totally dependent on the Infernal Bridegroom, 'she' is unable to understand him; the bewildered questions about his wish to escape from reality and to change life reveal chasms of incomprehension. 'J'ignore son idéal', 'she' concludes. 'She' believes that, without any effort, a new life, virile and adventurous, will be given 'her' as a present to a child; or that one day, on awaking from sleep, she will find, thanks to the Infernal Bridegroom's magic power, that laws and customs have changed and that she will be free to satisfy every whim and desire. Even when the Infernal Bridegroom demonstrates some of his ideas, his actions are as misconstrued as his thoughts; yet, in spite of apparent weaknesses and limitations, the Foolish Virgin, with shrewd feminine intuition, sees through him and judges him: 'Il feignait d'être éclairé sur tout, commerce, art, médecine.' She knows that his omnipotence was only a pretence, and that he was still searching for what he

claimed to possess already, namely, secrets for changing life: 'Il a peut-être des secrets pour *changer la vie?* Non, il ne fait qu'en chercher, me répliquais-je.' This insight is all the more ironic because the image of the Foolish Virgin was obviously inspired by Rimbaud's disgust at Verlaine's inability to understand anything about his ideas, aims, and ideals, an inability paralleled by Rimbaud's own failure to understand, until too late, Verlaine. He sees in him not only the example of an abject, irredeemable human being, but also his own image as a failed prophet and *voyant.* If he could not change Verlaine, how could he change life? This first 'délire', although ostensibly objective, expresses Rimbaud's personal involvement, and reflects in dramatic form the conflicts of his divided nature. If on one level, the Foolish Virgin is Verlaine, on another, 'she' is Rimbaud's projection of the passive 'feminine' half of his own personality. In many ways **'Délires I'** is a masterpiece of indirect self-confession because, in making the Foolish Virgin confess, the Infernal Bridegroom also confesses.

Rimbaud's presentation of himself as the highly ambiguous figure of the Infernal Bridegroom raises many questions. Is the Infernal Bridegroom a portrait of himself seen through Verlaine's eyes? Or does it serve a double purpose and give also a self-portrait, concealed beneath the mask of the supposedly fictional character? Or is the Infernal Bridegroom a more complex and equivocal figure, a mixture of Rimbaud's own ideas about himself and those of Verlaine about him, to which are added elements of a fantasy figure, half-demon, half-angel, which Rimbaud has created in response to his own and Verlaine's eccentric desires and satisfactions?

Having considered how Rimbaud makes Verlaine, as the Foolish Virgin, see him in his fictional guise of the Infernal Bridegroom, it is revealing to look at some of Verlaine's poems in which it can be seen how Verlaine in turn, and in other contexts, sees Rimbaud. The agreement between the two portraits is remarkable. Every detail in **'Délires I'** has its parallel in a Verlaine text: Rimbaud's strange beauty ('très beau d'une beauté paysanne et rusée'); his adolescence and his rage ('cet enfant de colère'); his strength and virility ('un Hercule'); his posturings and grimaces ('viles simagrées'); his arrogance and his gestures ('de satyre'); and, above all, the two poles of his nature ('Ange et Démon'). The 'nuits de noce' of 'Le Poète et la Muse', and the 'roman de vivre à deux hommes', so joyfully recounted in 'Laeti et errabundi', are the ironic counterpart of the concubinage in hell. For Verlaine, Rimbaud is his 'grand péché radieux'.[4]

In **'Délires I',** the Foolish Virgin and the Infernal Bridegroom express in concrete and dramatic form a struggle which has previously been carried on between Rimbaud and abstract antagonists. These two fictional figures, at once insignificant and tremendous, stand out against a vast context, and they throw lights of evil and of good backwards and forwards over the whole work. The Foolish Virgin expresses 'her' feelings about the relationship in an image of a place which emphasises the sense of isolation and loneliness, 'J'étais dans son âme comme dans un palais qu'on a vidé pour ne pas voir une personne si peu noble que vous.' The Infernal Bridegroom expresses his isolation and indifference with a shrug of the shoulders; and finally, with an ironic exclamation, a masterpiece of understatement, the relationship is dismissed as a 'Drôle de ménage!'. In rejecting it, he reveals, in a grotesque and perverted way, the pathos and tragedy of a human situation, with the dreams and fantasies of each of the partners, the frustrated aspirations, the impossibility of communication, the misunderstandings and conflicts, and the ultimate loneliness of the individual as each uses the other in a search for some kind of salvation.

In **'Délires II'** (**'Alchimie du verbe'**), Rimbaud considers what he feels to be equally 'drôle': his poetic ambitions, his verbal alchemy, and the influence this revolutionary poetic activity had had on his life. As if relieved at having finished with alibis, personae, and the 'folie' of the Foolish Virgin, he turns to himself, 'À moi. L'histoire d'une de mes folies'. From the literary point of view, this is the most interesting of all the sections. Although more personal than the previous 'délire', it is just as dramatic, for Rimbaud has replaced the Foolish Virgin by a fresh protagonist: his own poetry. At intervals, he introduces, with minor changes, seven of the verse poems composed in May and June 1872: **'Larme'** (**'Loin des oiseaux . . .'**), **'Chanson de la plus haute tour'**, **'Fêtes de la faim'** (**'Faim'**), **'Le loup criait sous les feuilles'**, **'L'Éternité'** (**'Elle est retrouvée'**), **'Ô Saison, ô châteaux!'**. This use of specimens from his own work is reminiscent of a similar technique in the *Lettre du voyant*, where they illustrated the birth of a new *art poétique*. Here, however, they represent the literary failure of his ideal to find a language, just as in the previous section the Foolish Virgin embodied the human failure to change life. It is possible that Rimbaud chose these particular poems rather than, for example, **'Le Dormeur du val'**, **'Ophélie'**, or **'Le Buffet'**, because they represent a crucial and transitional phase in his evolution between the early verse poems in stanza form and the prose poems of the *Illuminations*, when he was experimenting with what Verlaine termed verses that were 'délicieusement faux exprès'.

Rimbaud's attitude to these naive lyrics and 'romances' is ambiguous and the attention they receive suggests that, although half-ironically, he is exhibiting with a certain pride what he also condemns. Visually and rhythmically, the poems form a contrast within the text. The effect is a kind of *trompe l'oeil* for, although functioning as a background to the prose commentary, they stand out in relief from it; and by their apparent calm and freshness they both counterbalance and heighten the anguish of the poet's self-criticism. All seven are related to the sources of Rimbaud's poetry, and they mark stages or 'seasons' in his development from poet to *voyant*. Although they are used to illustrate the past, all, except the first, evoke a present moment—an eternal present—whether of ecstatic joy ('Elle est retrouvée! Quoi? L'éternité') or of suffering ('le supplice est sûr'). There is, in fact, a subtle interplay between the time when the poems were written (a recent past, but treated as remote), the tenses used in them (mainly the present), and the tenses in the prose text which, though obviously more recent, are almost entirely in the past. In the prose commentary, Rimbaud examines in a measured and logical way the claims he had made in the *Lettre du voyant*, and his achievements since that time. He is now as ironical and contemptuous towards himself and his poetic work as he had been, only two years before, towards his predecessors and contemporaries. He sees his earlier claims as arrogant, and his attempts at visionary poetry a failure. As he is now dealing with concrete particularities (at least when talking about his own poems) rather than metaphysical problems, his 'confession' has the touch and feel of sincerity. More self-critical than elsewhere in *Une Saison en enfer*, he realises, but without any accompanying suggestion of penitence, that he has been guilty, not only of self-deception, but also of bluff and falsity. He recalls that, at the beginning of his career, he had revolted against the generally accepted values of modern art and had found all sources of inspiration within himself; or in things outmoded, commonplace, strange, childlike, that had been neglected or not even noticed by the famous and the philistines:

> Depuis longtemps je me vantais de posséder tous les paysages possibles, et trouvais dérisoires les célébrités de la peinture et de la poésie moderne.
>
> J'aimais les peintures idiotes, dessus de portes, décors, toiles de saltimbanques, enseignes, enluminures populaires; la littérature démodée, latin d'église, livres érotiques sans orthographe, romans de nos aïeules; contes de fées, petits livres de l'enfance, opéras vieux, refrains niais, rhythmes naïfs.

This rediscovery of the childlike and the primitive was regarded by André Breton as one of Rimbaud's most challenging and exalting statements, and in it the Surrealists found some of their main themes.

Then, in a short passage which echoes themes in **'Les Poètes de sept ans'** and **'Le Bateau ivre'**, Rimbaud tells of ranging through time and space in dreams of evasion and revolt, of visions of social and geographical upheavals, of his belief in all enchantments. Coming to his actual achievements, he makes a reference to the sonnet **'Voyelles'**, and to his experiments with vowels, consonants, rhythms: 'J'inventai la couleur des voyelles!—*A* noir, *E* blanc, *I* rouge, *O* bleu, *U* vert.—Je réglai la forme et le mouvement de chaque consonne, et, avec des rhythmes instinctifs, je me flattai d'inventer un verbe poétique accessible, un jour ou l'autre, à tous les sens.' The statement makes it clear that **'Voyelles'** had been part of his aim to find a rational and sensuous language which would be more fully and more directly 'accessible' to everyone than any previous means of communication— a communication of meanings and also a communication to all the senses ('sens' here has a double meaning). Rimbaud realises too that the sonnet **'Voyelles'** was a part, perhaps the very basis, of his most exciting and humanitarian vision. He now considers all that a mystification; but, as the self-defensive mockery shows, he is only too aware that in deriding vowels, consonants and rhythms he is attacking the poet's raw material, the elements of language itself. Three rapid sentences reflect the speed of his passage from experiments and study to capturing in words silence, night, delirium, and the inexpressible. These are followed by quoting in full, and not quite accurately, possibly because from memory, two of the 1872 verse poems, **'Larme'** and **'Bonne pensée du matin'** (here not titled). These make an effective contrast, the first being a lyric about the poet himself, and the second, more general and social, about workers. Taken together, the poems illustrate several of the sources and themes that Rimbaud has enumerated and, because of their rhymes and stanza form, they may also be intended to serve as examples of his statement: 'La vieillerie poétique avait une bonne part dans mon alchimie du verbe.' He continues:

> Je m'habituai à l'hallucination simple: je voyais très franchement une mosquée à la place d'une usine, une école de tambours faite par des anges, des calèches sur les routes du ciel, un salon au fond d'un lac; les monstres, les mystères; un titre de vaudeville dressait des épouvantes devant moi.

> Puis j'expliquai mes sophismes magiques avec l'hallucination des mots!

> Je finis par trouver sacré le désordre de mon esprit.

In those statements, all in a past tense, Rimbaud reviews briefly in a logical order, three phases or aspects of his poetry and *art poétique:* first 'la vieillerie poétique', that is, the poems written before the *Illuminations;* next the poetry of his *voyance*—the seeing of visions, 'L'hallucination simple'; and lastly their expression in words, 'L'hallucination des mots'.

'Vieillerie'—'out-of-date', 'old fashioned'—is pejorative, and suggests contempt for the type of lyrical poetry in rhymed stanza form, such as the 1872 verse poems (of which he has just given two examples), as well as for the earlier more conventional pieces of 1870. In thinking of these early periods, he may also be experiencing some of the affection and nostalgia with which, in **'Le Buffet'** (1870), he viewed the jumble of interesting old objects, the 'fouillis de vieilles vieilleries'.

The examples he gives of 'l'hallucination simple' illustrate the nature of his first and simplest visions, passively received or deliberately induced, in which one object replaced another, or was suddenly transformed, or appeared in an unexpected place or context. In the first example, where a mosque takes the place of a factory, the link between word and object has been severed and the purely representational function of the word destroyed; yet, by the very fact of their being mentioned, they 'exist' together and suggest some of the extremes in *Une Saison en enfer* and in Rimbaud's life: religion and materialism, East and West, two irreconcilable civilisations or worlds. In 'Une école de tambours faite par des anges', drummers are replaced by angels; but the 'school' remains as a link between them, as does the idea of music. The vision is therefore more stable and less arresting than the previous one. These angel musicians, although playing unusual instruments, remind us of those we already know from paintings and carvings, and so cause little more than amused surprise. They have none of the liberating impact of the drum image in one of the *Illuminations:* 'Un coup de ton doigt sur le tambour décharge tous les sons et commence la nouvelle harmonie' ('À une raison'). Yet this transformation of the ordinary, and in particular the placing of the heavenly in an everyday human context, is characteristic of Rimbaud's visionary techniques. The next two examples, 'des calèches sur les routes du ciel' and 'un salon au fond d'un lac', may be allusions to the *Illuminations,* the first to **'Nocturne vulgaire'** (but the relationship is tenuous), the second to **'Soir historique'** ('on joue aux cartes au fond de l'étan•). But, more important, these are the kinds of visions that characterise the anti-natural, upsidedown world of the *Illuminations,* where a cathedral comes down, and a lake rises up. Critics have suggested that the 'vaudeville' mentioned in the last example may be Scribe's comedy, *Michel et Christine,* a title which Rimbaud had used for one of his 1872 verse poems. The example has, however, a more general significance in showing how a banal or incongruous source, perhaps in this case a poster, could act upon the poet's overwrought mind. One thinks of Apollinaire who later found a lyrical beauty (without any accompanying terror) in 'les prospectus les catalogues les affiches qui chantent tout haut' ('Zone').

Rimbaud quickly realised, however, that to translate hallucinatory visions by hallucinatory words was to be caught in the magic web of a new convention, and to turn in a vicious circle. The poetic method he had formulated in the **Lettre du voyant** as a 'raisonné *dérèglement* de *tous les sens*' had resulted in a disordering of the mind, which, as if in ironic consolation, he describes as 'sacré'. In this state, he had envied the 'félicité' of insects and animals. The contrast between his mental torment and their mindless bliss is conveyed by the word 'félicité', which has a deeper meaning than 'bonheur', and normally describes an inner, spiritual happiness. The irony is intensified by the examples: caterpillars, to represent the innocence of the unbaptised in limbo; and moles, to represent unawakened virginity, 'le sommeil de la virginité'— an ironic echo of his own very different sleep, 'un sommeil dans un nid de flammes', in **'Nuit de l'enfer'**. In this embittered state, he had said farewell to the world in 'romances', or ballad-like poems. 'Chanson de la plus haute tour', the poem he quotes next, is a typical example. The theme of impatient longing for an ecstatic happiness links it to the two previous poems; and its thrice-repeated couplet, 'Qu'il vienne, qu'il vienne, / Le temps dont on s'éprenne', is an illustration of the 'refrains niais' and 'rhythmes naïfs' to which reference is made at the beginning of this 'délire'.

As if commenting on the poem, Rimbaud in a prose passage gives examples of his unconventional poetic tastes for the arid, the parched, the faded and the tepid. He then relates how he had, in the stinking alleys of cities, offered himself, like a sacrificial victim, to the sun, imploring the god of fire (apostrophised as 'Général') to attack and destroy the world:

> Bombarde-nous avec des blocs de terre sèche. Aux glaces des magasins splendides! dans les salons! Fais manger sa poussière à la ville. Oxyde les gargouilles. Emplis les boudoirs de poudre de rubis brûlante . . .

Then, in a swift and brilliant transition from the great to the small—from the sun bombarding the earth and its towns to a sunbeam 'dissolving' a gnat in a urinal—he underlines his bitterness by expressing, this time in original anti-aesthetic terms, the envy he felt for the curiously ecstatic, if ephemeral happiness of the lesser animals:

> Oh! le moucheron enivré à la pissotière de l'auberge, amoureux de la bourrache, et que dissout un rayon!

The 'moucheron', appropriately enamoured of the diuretic borage, recalls the 'sales mouches' mentioned in the **'Chanson'** and leads to further animal imagery in the second of the next two poems, **'Faim'** and **'Le loup criait sous les feuilles'**. The first develops the theme of aridity and hardness and evokes in rhythmically stressed simple words, like those of a *comptine* (a child's counting-out rhyme), the poet's virile hunger:

"Faim"

Si j'ai du goût, ce n'est guère
Que pour la terre et les pierres.
Je déjeune toujours d'air,
De roc, de charbons, de fer.

Mes faims, tournez. Paissez, faims,
    Le pré des sons.
Attirez le gai venin
    Des liserons.

Mangez les cailloux qu'on brise,
Les vieilles pierres d'églises;
Les galets des vieux déluges,
Pains semés dans les vallées grises.

This frustrated hunger has resulted in an example of what Rimbaud had earlier called 'd'espèces de romances'. It differs, however, from the usual *romance* in being vital and entirely unsentimental. The poet's hunger has impelled him to reject the clichés and stale symbols of generations of writers who had been 'inspired' by nature, and to rediscover her in the harshest as well as in the most ethereal of her features. The concluding stanza, with its thrice-repeated affirmation that stone is the poet's bread, also implies his rejection of traditional religious symbols, such as Christ 'the bread of life'.

'Le loup criait sous les feuilles' continues, once more through animal images (wolf, fowl, spider), the theme of hunger and frustration. In the last stanza, the mocking jingle of rhymes and assonances ('Le b*ou*illon c*ou*rt sur la r*ou*ille') surprisingly mingles 'broth' and 'rust' with the idea of death; and the biblical allusions to the altars of Solomon and the brook of Cedron (which Christ crossed on his way to betrayal and crucifixion) again suggest Rimbaud in the role of sacrificial victim:

> Que je dorme! que je bouille
> Aux autels de Salomon.
> Le bouillon court sur la rouille
> Et se mêle au Cédron.

The prose passage which makes a transition to the next poem, **'L'Éternité'**, stresses, on the other hand, purity, gold and life: 'Je vécus étincelle d'or de la lumière *nature*'; and the poem itself, in lyrical yet semi-ironic tones, implies that this fleeting union of the individual with nature could be made universal and eternal. But it also emphasises patience, tenacity, mental anguish, and all that must be endured before we can say:

> Elle est retrouvée!
> —Quoi?—l'éternité.

> C'est la mer mêlée
> 　Au soleil.

In the last part of '**Délires II**', Rimbaud refers to himself as an 'opéra fabuleux', a striking expression which could apply to the world of the *Illuminations,* where he had illustrated the human comedy; but, in the context, it refers to his 'folie' and to his particular kind of imagination, the opposite of empathic. Instead of enabling him to project feelings on to people and external phenomena, his imagination had absorbed everything into his inner life, transforming it and driving him to the confines of the world and to the verge of madness. This was the final and anguished consequence of the statement he had made at the beginning of the section about possessing all possible landscapes within his own mind. Everything was then *in* his mind; and its state resembled the 'tempête sous un crâne' described by Hugo in *Les Misérables,* with its 'chaos des chimères', its 'fournaise des rêves' and its 'pandemonium des sophismes'—an analogy that could be pressed more closely, for Rimbaud may well have considered his *Saison en enfer* to be what Hugo terms 'le poème de la conscience humaine'. At all events, this particular 'délire' is both a storm inside Rimbaud's skull and a coherent poem; and, paradoxically, the climax is expressed in intellectually controlled rhythms, sound patterns and arabesques of magnificent prose:

> Ma santé fut menacée. La terreur venait. Je tombais dans des sommeils de plusieurs jours, et, levé, je continuais les rêves les plus tristes. J'étais mûr pour le trépas, et par une route de dangers ma faiblesse me menait aux confins du monde et de la Cimmérie, patrie de l'ombre et des tourbillons.

> Je dus voyager, distraire les enchantements assemblés sur mon cerveau. Sur la mer, que j'aimais comme si elle eût dû me laver d'une souillure, je voyais se lever la croix consolatrice. J'avais été damné par l'arc-en-ciel. Le Bonheur était ma fatalité, mon remords, mon ver: ma vie serait toujours trop immense pour être dévouée à la force et à la beauté.

Claudel has written an enthusiastic commentary on the beauty of the sounds, the rhythms and the melodic line in this 'miracle' of French prose, selecting for special praise the sentence about the 'confins du monde', and the sentence ('si grand et si pathétique') about the cross—which ends with the perfect alexandrine: 'je voyais se lever la croix consolatrice'.[5] The appearance of the cross over the sea, the sea which in '**Le Bateau ivre**' had produced so many visions, is both surprising and ironic. Like the rainbow, it is a religious symbol, reminding Rimbaud of his enslavement to his baptism and the beliefs of the Catholic Church, and therefore powerless to help him. It is the symbol of his damnation; but the damnation, which before was expressed in

terms of Catholic iconography, of the Devil and hell fire, is now of a less melodramatic but more insidious kind. It is the inescapable happiness into which every human being is fated to descend. Happiness is, in fact, the main subject of the prose passage (the word 'bonheur' occurs three times) and also of the poem, where it is the theme. This is not, however, the ecstatic happiness of '**L'Éternité**', but the drab happiness of ordinary mortals, 'une fatalité de bonheur!':

> Ô saisons, ô châteaux!
> Quelle âme est sans défauts?
> J'ai fait la magique étude
> Du bonheur, qu'aucun n'élude.

The poem links Rimbaud's season in hell to the world of our seasons, where the 'châteaux' (prestigious refuges for alchemists, mystics, mortals—and for the soul) are as transient as time itself. The question 'Quelle âme est sans défauts?' is rhetorical. No soul is flawless; and this universal statement is, in its lyrical simplicity, the most poignant of Rimbaud's confessions. The final sentences, 'Cela s'est passé. Je sais aujourd'hui saluer la beauté', are typical of what one might call Rimbaud's method of resolution through calculated, or perhaps unconscious, ambiguities. Beauty may be here a eulogistic or a derogatory word (the reference to beauty in the prologue suggests the latter); and 'saluer' can be used to greet and welcome, or to say farewell and dismiss (the draft indicates the second). In fact, the beauty in question is, like the happiness Rimbaud has discussed, a bourgeois value and pursuit; and his conclusion is both contemptuous and definitive.

After the two long and detailed accounts of his 'délires', Rimbaud takes, in '**L'impossible**', a broader and a more searching view of himself and of nineteenth-century civilisation. His conflict, although no less intense, now takes place on an abstract, metaphysical plane. The title refers to the impossibility of recapturing various forms of a lost purity: a human purity—the innocence of childhood; a spiritual purity—a pre-Christian state before man's mind had been poisoned by ideas of good and evil; and a philosophic purity—the primitive wisdom of the East. It also suggests the impossibility of finding in the future, either by reason or by faith, any other kind of purity. In a particularly lucid moment, Rimbaud has realised that his deliriums and all his mental aberrations have their source in a corrupt civilisation, which he equates with Christianity. Reason has shown him that everything in his life—childhood, education, religion, behaviour, thoughts, and even dreams, including in particular his dream of evasion and of purity—has been conditioned, and vitiated, by the values of Christian civilisation. His contempt is expressed in an epigrammatic statement, in which the birth of the prototype bourgeois is made to coincide with the birth of Christ: 'M.

Prudhomme est né avec le Christ.'⁶ But the poet's reason, referred to ironically as 'deux sous de raison', while revealing his own place—and dilemma—in bourgeois society, does not offer a solution; and a characteristic double movement of acceptance followed by rejection of a solution through religion ends the section:

> Ô pureté! pureté!
> C'est cette minute d'éveil qui m'a donné la
>   vision de la
>   pureté!
> —Par l'esprit on va à Dieu!
> Déchirante infortune!

'Déchirante', which describes the 'infortune', also sums up the state of the poet's mind, *torn* between the extremes of a continuing conflict.

'L'Éclair', a section as brief and as explosive as the title, begins with the exclamation, 'Le travail humain!' The idea of work, Rimbaud states, had illuminated from time to time the depths of his hell; and one remembers other occasions such as his cynical references in **'Mauvais sang'** to work, science and progress in our 'siècle à mains'. Once more, however, he considers the slogan of the modern world which, with an ironic reversal of the words of the Preacher in the Bible 'All is vanity' (Eccles. 1:2), he formulates as: 'Rien n'est vanité; à la science, et en avant!' But this solution is too simple; and, like others he has examined, it has only been proposed in order to be ridiculed and dismissed. Moreover, his impatient, lucid mind sees through these palliatives and distractions (*divertissements,* as Pascal called them) to the inescapable end which they hide from others, namely death. He will therefore continue to protest against the human condition by playing a succession of roles—mountebank, beggar, artist, bandit, and even priest; and at the hour of death, at the risk of losing all hope of eternal salvation, he will launch a desperate attack:

> Non! Non! à présent je me révolte contre la mort! Le travail paraît trop léger à mon orgueil: ma trahison au monde serait un supplice trop court. Au dernier moment, j'attaquerais à droite, à gauche . . .
>
> Alors,—oh! chère pauvre âme, l'éternité serait-elle pas perdue pour nous!

No solution has been found and the conclusion seems a sombre denial of the title. Yet in **'L'Éclair'** the forces of childhood and religion, which were pulling Rimbaud back and binding him to the past, have become less potent; and the last sentence where, in 'chère pauvre âme', we hear the cautious voice of the 'Vierge folle', could be read as a defiant challenge rather than as an exclamation of regret.

'**Matin**' is a pause in the drama and 'aujourd'hui', in the middle of the section, is the pivotal point from which Rimbaud looks back and then forward, as he prepares for the final struggle in '**Adieu**':

"Matin"

N'eus-je pas *une fois* une jeunesse aimable, héroïque, fabuleuse, à écrire sur des feuilles d'or,—trop de chance! Par quel crime, par quelle erreur, ai-je mérité ma faiblesse actuelle? Vous qui prétendez que des bêtes poussent des sanglots de chagrin, que des malades désespèrent, que des morts rêvent mal, tâchez de raconter ma chute et mon sommeil. Moi, je ne puis pas plus m'expliquer que le mendiant avec ses continuels *Pater* et *Ave Maria. Je ne sais plus parler!*

Pourtant, aujourd'hui, je crois avoir fini la relation de mon enfer. C'était bien l'enfer; l'ancien, celui dont le fils de l'homme ouvrit les portes.

Du même désert, à la même nuit, toujours mes yeux las se réveillent à l'étoile d'argent, toujours, sans que s'émeuvent les Rois de la vie, les trois mages, le coeur, l'âme, l'esprit. Quand irons-nous, par delà les grèves et les monts, saluer la naissance du travail nouveau, la sagesse nouvelle, la fuite des tyrans et des démons, la fin de la superstition, adorer—les premiers!—Noël sur la terre!

Le chant des cieux, la marche des peuples! Esclaves, ne maudissons pas la vie.

After '**L'Éclair**' and the flashes that have by turns lit up then darkened the hell of the poet's mind, '**Matin**' brings light from the outside world, and a sustaining vision. It is the most moving of the nine sections because in it the rhetoric is never gratuitous, but is used to temper and control Rimbaud's agitated emotions, and to give to uniquely personal themes a universal significance. '**Matin**' is an unusually poised and harmonious prose poem, and while it appears to be self contained in its structured symmetry, it is at the same time expansive and resonant with meanings. Closely linked to all that has preceded, it reechoes the prologue, the beginning of the drama, 'Jadis, si je me souviens bien . . . ' and points to the last act and dénouement in '**Adieu**'. It is also related thematically to some of the early poems (one thinks of '**Les Effarés**'), to several of the 1872 verse poems (for example, '**Bonne pensée du matin**', '**Fêtes de la patience**'), and to some of the *Illuminations* (in particular, '**Jeunesse**' and '**Génie**').

The title has several meanings. As well as 'the first hours of the day', and 'morning', it has the figurative sense of 'the morning of life', and 'jeunesse'—to which Rimbaud refers in the opening sentence. More important perhaps, and permeating the text, is the idea of a morning prayer, the first prayer of the day in the divine service of Matins—but here transposed into non-religious, anti-Catholic terms. The poem is divided into two equal parts, at once opposed and complementary. The first, static and reflective, looks back to the beginning of time, to a lost paradise; the second looks forward to the new beginning to which the whole of *Une Saison en enfer* is leading.

Rimbaud begins not with any sign of penitence or gratitude, nor with a request for help; but, characteristically, with a protestation uttered in a tone of aggrieved indignation. His protest is ingeniously presented as a rhetorical question, where the italicised *'une fois'* suggests the possibility of two opposed meanings: *once* and *never*. The elegant first-person inverted form of the question, 'N'eus-je pas *une fois* une jeunesse aimable, héroïque, fabuleuse, . . . ', implies, however, a mock-heroic attitude, and a negation, which is made explicit by the sardonic 'trop de chance!'. The sentence is an interesting example of Rimbaud's use of linguistic contrast between the formal and the colloquial to give vitality to his narration and a sharper point to his meaning. Similarly, in the second sentence, the preciosity of the inversion 'ai-je' is again used in a mocking way, and with a negating force, to disclaim all personal responsibility or guilt for his present weakness. He then turns to his audience, and ironically challenges us, with our 'wisdom', to relate *his* 'chute'— his fall from grace, and his 'sommeil'—the many moments of weariness, physical and mental, to which he has succumbed during his season in hell; and he states that he himself is no more capable of giving an explanation than the beggar mouthing everlasting Paternosters and Ave Marias. But this is a pretence, a rhetorical device, for he knows that the end is in sight, and that there is now little need for further speech or narration: 'Pourtant, aujourd'hui, je crois avoir fini la relation de mon enfer. C'était bien l'enfer; l'ancien, celui dont le fils de l'homme ouvrit les portes.' The affirmation suggests relief; but it also implies that his *Saison en enfer,* although as 'real' as the biblical hell, is an 'invention', a work of art which will end when his account of it—his 'relation'—ends. The statement also reflects the belief underlying this poem, and indeed the entire work, that damnation is not eternal, hell is only for a 'season'. It is a personal affair, 'mon enfer', as he says here; a state of mind, 'Je me crois en enfer, donc j'y suis', as he said in **'Nuit de l'enfer'.** This belief (or arrogant assumption) of the non-believer is the mainspring of *Une Saison en enfer.*

In the opening of the second part of the poem, the twice repeated 'même' and the twice repeated 'toujours' emphasise the monotony of a vigil which has so far produced mainly frustration and lassitude. But the rhythm has changed and, despite the biblical allusions, the accent is on this earth and this life, on the human

as opposed to the divine. The Son of God has become the 'fils de l'homme', and the three wise men are three 'Rois de la vie'—heart, soul and mind. The star shines not for the birth of the Christ child, but for the birth of a new kind of work and a new wisdom, for the end of tyrannies and superstition. Even if the question 'Quand irons-nous . . . ' is left unanswered, the movement is towards the future and a new Noël, or 'day of birth', in the original sense of the word, when the song of the heavens will be identified with the progress of humanity. Inspired and sustained by this vision, Rimbaud is able to accept, in common with others, his condition as one of life's 'slaves'—slaves of the work to which our 'chute' (original sin) has condemned us. He ends, as he began, with an equivocal figure of rhetoric, 'Esclaves, ne maudissons pas la vie', a litotes in which 'ne maudissons pas' could be read as 'bénissons'; but the command, although expressing hope, is tinged with reproof and resignation.

In the last section, **'Adieu',** the opening words 'L'automne déjà!' convey Rimbaud's startled awakening to the present and to reality; and the theme of the seasons, and more generally of time, announced in the first section and heard repeatedly throughout the work, becomes fully orchestrated. As he had previously played at being others but never himself, so, living in a mythical past, an impossible future, and an imaginary present, he had played with all the fictional devices of time. Now, in a succession of allusions to the seasons, light, the sun, morning, night, the eve, dawn and 'l'heure nouvelle', he expresses the reality of time's irreversible flow. He can, at last, accept 'real' time because, although it reveals his failure as a *voyant,* it offers hope of a tangible victory, in the life of this world. The autumn may be, as for the Romantic poets, the season of melancholy and nostalgia; but it is also the moment for action and a definitive turning towards the future. Moreover, the idea of autumn brings fresh inspiration, and introduces two singularly appropriate images which dominate the section and are intimately related to many of the main themes—the quest, the town, and *voyance.*

The first image, associated with mists, a city-port, poverty and degradation, is that of a boat, symbol of the journeys through life:

> Notre barque élevée dans les brumes immobiles tourne vers le port de la misère, la cité énorme au ciel taché de feu et de boue.

The second, preceded by an apocalyptic vision reminiscent of **'Matin',** is of a golden boat, symbol of the journeys he has made in his imagination since **'Le Bateau ivre'**:

> Quelquefois je vois au ciel des plages sans fin couvertes de blanches nations en joie. Un grand

vaisseau d'or, au-dessus de moi, agite ses pavillons
multicolores sous les brises du matin.

These particular images echo and sum up the two
'délires', the 'barque' corresponding to human 'madness'; the 'vaisseau d'or' to literary 'madness', the
'alchimie du verbe', appropriately demonstrated here,
as the ship of life is metamorphosed into the ship of
beauty. In addition, they reach further back to the very
beginning of *Une Saison en enfer,* where Rimbaud
had indicated that the stress throughout his work would
fall first on life ('ma vie') and then on literature ('la
Beauté').

The second image, the golden ship with its many-coloured
flags fluttering in the morning breeze, is linked, by
references to 'matin' and 'or', to the previous poem,
'Matin'; and its 'pavillons' recall those in the *Illuminations.* Indeed, this unusually potent image represents all that Rimbaud had created or attempted to
create; as well as the godlike powers he thought he
had acquired, and which he now renounces:

> J'ai créé toutes les fêtes, tous les triomphes, tous
> les drames. J'ai essayé d'inventer de nouvelles fleurs,
> de nouveaux astres, de nouvelles chairs, de nouvelles
> langues. J'ai cru acquérir des pouvoirs surnaturels.
> Eh bien! je dois enterrer mon imagination et mes
> souvenirs! Une belle gloire d'artiste et de conteur
> emportée!

> Moi! moi qui me suis dit mage ou ange, dispensé
> de toute morale, je suis rendu au sol, avec un devoir
> à chercher, et la réalité rugueuse à étreindre! Paysan!

The poet who had imagined that he was a seer, an
angel, a Promethean stealer of fire and omnipotent, is
now forced to realise that he is no more than a 'Paysan!'

Paradoxically, Rimbaud signals this renunciation of
his poetic ambitions with a remarkable series of images: on his face, 'le sang séché fume'; behind him
stands the 'horrible arbrisseau' of good and evil; above
him, 'un grand vaisseau d'or' and 'des plages sans
fin couvertes de blanches nations en joie'; and in front
and all around him, 'la réalité rugueuse'. This return
to earth from the peaks of ambition is harsh and brutal; and the identification with the peasant, who embodies what Rimbaud most despised—manual work,
'la main à charrue' and our 'siècle à mains'—is exceptionally ironical. But 'paysan' can still mean, as it
once did, someone who belongs to a 'pays', who has
a country, a background and a human context. Instead of provoking a rhetorical outburst of indignation, as one might have expected, this ironic revelation becomes the occasion for a display of controlled
artistry, and Rimbaud uses the image of the 'paysan',
the last of a series of related images—the convict, the
serf, the mercenary, the outcast, the damned, the negro,

the infernal bridegroom—to obtain effects of repetition, alliteration and, above all, contrast. For this
ignoble creature is also a heroic figure who grapples
with reality and moves onward with a firm unwavering tread. Hence, if the realisation that he is a peasant
is a defeat, it is also the signal for another departure.
This 'départ' becomes an adieu to the emotions and
sensations he had written about in the *Illuminations.*
Henceforth he will rely on the common virtues of
duty, patience, and tenacity. Disillusioned by the cities and towns of his imagination, he prepares to enter
(and the verb can be taken in its literal sense) other
towns 'splendides villes', which, stripped of the illusions of literature, shine with the light of their own
reality:

> Cependant c'est la veille. Recevons tous les influx
> de vigueur et de tendresse réelle. Et à l'aurore,
> armés d'une ardente patience, nous entrerons aux
> splendides villes.

> Que parlais-je de main amie! Un bel avantage, c'est
> que je puis rire des vieilles amours mensongères,
> et frapper de honte ces couples menteurs,—j'ai vu
> l'enfer des femmes là-bas;—et il me sera loisible
> de *posséder la vérité dans une âme et un corps.*

In the *Illuminations* Rimbaud had explored the limits of
the known and the imaginary and, as he declared in
'Enfance', he had frequently been near to the abyss: 'Ce
ne peut être que la fin du monde en avançant.' Now,
however, he has no need of help or of a 'main amie'.
Unaided he will find the truth, not through poetry, but in
himself. The ultimate identification does indeed seem to
be with himself, with the fundamental duality of body
and spirit, which is the source of all the dualities and
conflicting themes in *Une Saison en enfer.* In stressing
this concluding statement, he is also stressing the unity
underlying the extraordinary diversity of his personality
and his work. But what is meant by 'posséder la vérité'?
What is this truth, and how can it be possessed? Is
Rimbaud thinking of yet another quest, or does he intend
to remain intact and keep, 'avare comme la mer', what he
already possesses? In the previous sections he has touched
upon, highlighted and dramatised countless emotions, conflicts, clashes of opposites and dualities; but nothing has
been developed or fully explored. The final declaration is
as abstract and general as his other statements—and it is
projected into the future. Everything has been said, but
everything still remains to be done. Since **'Les Déserts
de l'amour',** a short earlier prose work, Rimbaud has,
however, transformed his solitude, with its vulnerability
as well as its potential strength, into the semblance of a
hard-won victory, *Une Saison en enfer,* like most of his
work, is both 'closed' and 'open', final and provisional,
an end and a beginning.

Une Saison en enfer has ended, as it began, with
the emphasis on the 'je' and the 'moi'—on Rimbaud

himself. The plural form of the pronoun, however, is also used in alternation with the 'je'; and although the 'nous' is often only a rhetorical artifice to express a personal attitude of irony, disdain, false modesty, imperiousness or feigned politeness, it refers at times to us, to mankind. Indeed, Rimbaud shows by the tone he adopts, by the nature of some of his visions, and by lapidary statements and wide-ranging generalisations, that he is himself aware that his work has universal significance. In the last section, as if fully conscious of this, and of the importance and majesty of his **'Adieu',** he begins, for the first time, with 'nous': 'Nous sommes engagés à la découverte de la clarté divine . . . ' And he does not speak for himself alone when he affirms: 'Recevons tous les influx de vigueur et de tendresse réelle. Et à l'aurore, armés d'une ardente patience, nous entrerons aux splendides villes.' His words voice the age-long hope that man will one day enter into his full human heritage. The stress finally falls on the one fundamental duality, that of mind and body—as old as man himself; and on a quest that is eternal—the quest for truth.

Reference was made at the beginning of this chapter to the letter of May 1873 in which Rimbaud, feverishly composing the work that was to become **Une Saison en enfer,** declared: 'Mon sort dépend de ce livre.' At the time, he may have been thinking that the book, when finished, would enable him to escape finally from 'la *mother*' (as he calls her in the same letter), and from Roche, the 'triste trou' where she had confined him. But, as the work progressed, he must have realised that his 'fate', and that of his book, were destined to be more than personal or local. Everything in the interrelated aspects of its content and structure, especially the movement between the 'I' and 'others', between the particular and the general, suggests that he is speaking not only as an individual but also as a representative, or at least a member, of modern society. We are never allowed to forget the social context within which he writes, and that his conflicts spring from its divisions. In his journey of self-discovery, Rimbaud has touched on, and laid bare, most of the conflicts, ambivalent emotions, and dualisms that exist in Western man. Now, at a distance of more than a century, we can see that, if at one level **Une Saison en enfer** expresses the crisis in the life of an adolescent struggling for self-fulfilment in the year 1873, at another level it represents a crisis in our own materialistic civilisation.

Notes

¹ René Char's aphorism about his own dynamic spirit could be applied to the Rimbaud of *Illuminations:* 'Être du bond. N'être pas du festin, son épilogue' *(Feuillets d'Hypnos).*

² E. Delahaye, *Les Illuminations et Une Saison en enfer* (Paris, 1927), p. 199.

³ G. Bachelard, *L'Eau et les rêves* (Paris, 1942), 132-3.

⁴ This quotation and the quotations in parentheses are from 'Poèmes de Verlaine inspirés par Rimbaud', in J. Mouquet, *Rimbaud raconté par Paul Verlaine* (Paris, 1934), pp. 211-41.

⁵ Paul Claudel, *Œuvres en prose* (Pléiade edition, Paris, 1965), pp. 37-8.

⁶ Monsieur Prudhomme is a character created by Henri Monnier. He represents the complacent, pompous bourgeois of the regin of Louis-Philippe. He first appeared briefly in *Scènes populaires, dessinées à· la plume* (1830); and his philistine opinions and grandiloquent utterances are fully recorded in *Mémoires de Monsieur Joseph Prudhomme* (1857).

James Lawler (essay date 1992)

SOURCE: "Conclusion," in *Rimbaud's Theatre of the Self,* Harvard University Press, 1992, pp. 201-19.

[*In the following essay, Lawler examines the self-reflexive nature of* Une Saison en enfer, *suggesting that like all Rimbaud's work, its essential purpose is dramatic rather than descriptive or didactic. The critic also points out the influence of Baudelaire's* Les Fleurs du mal *on Rimbaud's depiction of a soul in anguish—though he argues that unlike* Les Fleurs, Une Saison *ultimately expresses belief in the possibility of deliverance.*]

"Bah! faisons toutes les grimaces imaginables" 'So what! let us make all conceivable grimaces'.¹ Rimbaud projected himself in a series of roles that allowed him to act out a multiple relationship with the world. Self-reflexive images, warring affections, refashioned myths: his poetry is complex representation.

The element of play was no doubt central to such a venture as it had been for the schoolboy who shone by his Latin hexameters and who· later pastiched the Romantics and Parnassians. What could give more pleasure than to write these variations in which he was visible and invisible like a magician: "Ecoutez . . . J'ai tous les talents!—Il n'y a personne ici et il y a quelqu'un . . . Je suis caché et je ne le suis pas" 'Listen! . . . I have all talents! There is no one here and there is someone . . . I am hidden and not hidden'.² He could take each part while keeping a distance from any single one. Nevertheless we know that his poetry was not only play, for it resulted in one of the truly tragic expressions of literature that confronts futility, anguish, madness, death. The work shows a coherent ambition by which he rebelled against fatal constraints; and the tensions were all the more violent as he grew more impatient of repression.

The theatrical enterprise found mature focus in 1871. *The Drunken Boat* tropes past, present, future, its voice being that of a visionary plenitude which is forced to discover narrower limits. No single unilinear reading—for instance, a recently proposed Marxist scheme[3]—can do justice to a poem whose five parts image forth the antagonisms of strength and weakness: "Je ne puis plus, baigné de vos langueurs, ô lames . . ."

This is the lucid pattern that Rimbaud amplifies in the several voices of his later poems. The Inventor of **"Voyelles"** writes the language of anger and penitence, brilliance and shadow, silence and noise; the Memorialist of **"Mémoire"** poignantly moves between twin flowers; the Ingénu of **"Michel et Christine"**, solemn yet tender, concludes his poem on the uncertain postulate of naive hope. Carrying these dramatizations still further into the formal freedoms of the prose poem, the *Illuminations* develops with every text a manner, a style, a highly individual dramatic action. Rimbaud commanded his various modes ("J'ai essayé d'inventer de nouvelles fleurs, de nouveaux astres, de nouvelles chairs, de nouveaux langages" 'I tried to invent new flowers, new stars, new flesh, new languages')[4] by which he could each time realize himself provisionally. Thus the poet pronounces the admirable monologue of Self-aware Creator, Critic and Ironist; the Floodmaker intones the litany of rupture and possible recovery; the Storyteller presents the despot who finds and loses what he seeks; the Dreamer is torn between contradictory dreams; the Agonist chooses to go to the depths of suffering; the Lover lives at one and the same time by music and death, gravity and wit. A theatre is animated by the protean self as it struggles with final dualities.

Yet what of *Une Saison en enfer,* about which Rimbaud said: "Ma vie dépend de ce livre" 'My life hangs on this book'?[5] The manuscripts and other indices show that it does not postdate the *Illuminations,* as was originally thought on the combined authority of Rimbaud's sister and Paul Claudel. The two works were no doubt written in some part simultaneously. But, such being the case, how are we to reconcile their apparent contradictions? The interpretation that saw *Une Saison en enfer* as Rimbaud's account of his farewell to poetry and his salute to a life of action had been at least intellectually satisfying.

I would wish to propose that the very simultaneity of the texts underlines their theatrical character. Each answers each: whereas the *Illuminations* is fragmented, *Une Saison en enfer* is unitary; and whereas the former tends to the universal, the latter explores the intimate.

The descent into hell answers the *Illuminations,* which answers it. Rimbaud enacts yet again, in a new way, the *absolute* and the *conditional* of his thought.

The presence of various models has been canvased, including the Gnostic Gospels, the *Æneid,* the *Divine Comedy* and Nerval's *Aurélia,* each of which is a commanding treatment of the scheme of *katabasis.* It seems to me, however, that the essential intertext is *Les Fleurs du mal,* no longer considered with respect to individual poems of the collection such as "Le Voyage" or "Correspondances" or "Spleen" but considered rather as an undivided whole. Rimbaud responds to Baudelaire's large compass by his own long multifaceted confession placed under the sign of Satan, a crafted book which shows from one end to the other—to recall Baudelaire's own words—"the agitation of the Spirit in the throes of Evil" ('l'agitation de l'Esprit dans le Mal'). The soul struggles inside a Christian worldview of sin and salvation from which it is unable to break free, and which takes it to the depths of despair before allowing a final glimpsed resolution. All is ordered according to a total rhythm—six parts and a liminary poem in *Les Fleurs du mal,* eight parts and a preface in *Une Saison en enfer*—that has its full resonance solely when read in sequence from start to finish. How, indeed, could Rimbaud, having faced immediate death by Verlaine's revolver in July 1873, not have turned to the poet who had shown poetry, from one end of *Les Fleurs du mal* to another, to be here and now a matter of life and death? Could he, too, not write a confession that would both indict and engage himself? No less than *Les Fleurs du mal, Une Saison en enfer* is the poem of the crisis of an individual soul, which also expresses a society ("Maîtres et ouvriers, tous paysans, ignobles" 'Masters and workers, all peasants, ignoble') and a culture ("Pas une famille d'Europe que je ne connaisse" 'Not one European family that I do not know") that have been subjected to spiritual, emotional and economic alienation ("Quel siècle à mains!—Je n'aurai jamais ma main" 'What a century of hands!—I shall never have my hand').

The constant lucidity of Rimbaud's art of dramatic composition has been evident from our analyses. Yet *Une Saison en enfer* brings this mastery to new fruition. The anguish is acute which translates the progression from a historically determined ill chance (**"Mauvais Sang"**) to present passion (**"Nuit de l'enfer"**), from the companion's suffering (**"Délires I"**) to the poet's overweening ambition and self-destructiveness (**"Délires II"**), from exotic dream (**"L'Impossible"**) to illusory labor (**"L'Eclair"**), from nostalgia (**"Matin"**) to autumnal hope (**"Adieu"**). The binary pattern, through an unswerving rhythm, spells out the vision in its grand design. At the same time, the prose weaves a furious dialectic with every sentence.

The preface begins on inverted commas that are never closed. They designate an actor who speaks his role in two separate tones and with respect to two separate moments in time—"jadis" in the first seven paragraphs, "tout dernièrement" in the second four. Turning with nostalgia to the almost forgotten past, he evokes a graduated self-violence: present and imperfect tenses are replaced by perfect and historical; beauty, justice, hope, joy are denied; suffering and madness are part of a scenario in which the self bites the executioners' rifles and grovels in the mud. The imagination and diction are passionately theatrical.

> Jadis, si je me souviens bien, ma vie était un festin où s'ouvraient tous les cœurs, où tous les vins coulaient.
>
> Un soir, j'ai assis la Beauté sur mes genoux.—Et je l'ai trouvée amère.—Et je l'ai injuriée.
>
> Je me suis armé contre la justice.
> Je me suis enfui. O sorcières, ô misère, ô haine, c'est à vous que mon trésor a été confié!
>
> Je parvins à faire s'évanouir dans mon esprit toute l'espérance humaine. Sur toute joie pour l'étrangler j'ai fait le bond sourd de la bête féroce.
>
> J'ai appelé les bourreaux pour, en périssant, mordre la crosse de leurs fusils. J'ai appelé les fléaux, pour m'étouffer avec le sable, le sang. Le malheur a été mon dieu. Je me suis allongé dans la boue. Je me suis séché à l'air du crime. Et j'ai joué de bons tours à la folie.
>
> Et le printemps m'a apporté l'affreux rire de l'idiot.[6]

> *Once, if my memory serves me, my life was a banquet at which all hearts opened, all wines flowed.*
>
> *One evening, I sat Beauty on my knees.—And I found her bitter.—And I reviled her.*
>
> *I took arms against justice.*
>
> *I fled. O witches, O poverty, O hatred, it was to you that my treasure was entrusted!*
>
> *I managed to make all human hope vanish from my mind. Upon every joy, to strangle it, I made the noiseless leap of the wild beast.*
>
> *I summoned the executioners so as to bite their gun-butts as I lay dying. I summoned scourges so as to suffocate with sand, with blood. Misery was my god. I stretched out in the mud. I dried myself in the air of crime. And I played fine tricks on madness.*
>
> *And spring brought me the idiot's frightful laughter.*

Qualis artifex pereo: the self articulates its Baudelairean anguish. Alliteration continues from start to finish; a

set of antagonisms gauges the emotions (sweetness/ bitterness, treasure/poverty, joy/ferocity, laughter/terror); syntactic parellelisms and phonetic insistence tell of fatal decline. The second part, however, moves in a wholly different way and, instead of developing narrative intensity, *reacts* to what has been said. All is now treated with black humor ("le dernier *couac!*"), cool aplomb ("j'ai rêvé"), ironic gratitude ("de si aimables pavots"), assumed affection ("cher Satan"), false baroque ("une prunelle moins irritée"). The now anti-Baudelairean speaker follows a dramatic—that is, nondescriptive and noninstructive—mode to please this demon who, on one legendary occasion, became a talking serpent. He will give back to Satan, without any self-indulgence, what is properly Satan's.

> Or, tout dernièrement m'étant trouvé sur le point de faire le dernier *couac!* j'ai songé à rechercher la clef du festin ancien, où je reprendrais peut-être appétit.
>
> La charité est cette clef.—Cette inspiration prouve que j'ai eêvé!
>
> "Tu resteras hyène, etc. . . . ", se récrie le démon qui me couronna de si aimables pavots. "Gagne la mort avec tous tes appétits, et ton égoïsme et tous les péchés capitaux."
>
> Ah! j'en ai trop pris:—Mais, cher Satan, je vous en conjure, une prunelle moins irritée! et en attendant les quelques petites lâchetés en retard, vous qui aimez dans l'écrivain l'absence des facultés descriptives ou instructives, je vous détache ces quelques hideux feuillets de mon carnet de damné.

> *Now, just lately, finding myself about to make a last croak! I thought of looking for the key to the old banquet, where I might perhaps recover my appetite.*
>
> *Charity is that key.—That inspiration proves I have been dreaming!*
>
> *"You will remain a hyena, etc. . . . ", protests the demon who wreathed me with such pleasant poppies. "Earn your death with all your appetites, and your selfishness and all the deadly sins."*
>
> *Ah! I have suffered too much:—But, my dear Satan, I beg you, a gentler eye! and in the expectation of a few more small cowardly acts that are late to bloom, I tear out for you—you who love a writer's lack of descriptive or instructive talents—these few horrible pages from my notebook of a damned soul.*

The lines bring a reversal of attitudes like those crucial reversals that so suddenly break into **"Le Bateau ivre"** and the other great Rimbaud works we have read: the poem turns back on itself in an act of self-reflection. Anguish loses its sting for a speaker who can announce his new resolution while predicting some further irresoluteness on his part, and who can play the devil by voicing a threat ("Tu resteras hyène . . .") or a temptation ("Gagne la mort . . ."). The preface thus ironically—such tragic irony is the nexus of *Une Saison en enfer*—places damnation under the sign of salvation: it puts the divided sensibility and intellect *on stage* according to a foreshadowed plot.

The first of the eight parts, **"Mauvais Sang"**, has eight sections of widely varying lengths ranging from five paragraphs to ten. It begins with a mock-heroic genealogy, passes to a poignant dream of happiness, the awareness of inescapable solitude, an imagined primitive nature, a future conversion, an evocation of fresh innocence yet the farce of such innocence, finally a vision of martyrdom. Nothing is more agitated than this self caught between its hope and fear, whose only constancy is self-contradiction. Yet if the opening is matter-of-fact ("J'ai de mes ancêtres gaulois l'œil bleu blanc" 'From my Gaulish ancestors I have my blue-white eyes'), the other sections trace a mounting passion like that of a monologuist who exhausts every note of his register, from poignancy to hallucination: "Si j'avais des antécédents à un point quelconque de l'histoire de France! . . .", "Le sang revient! . . .", "On ne part pas . . .", "Encore tout enfant, j'admirais le forçat intraitable sur qui se referme toujours le bagne . . .", "Les blancs débarquent. Le canon! . . .", "L'ennui n'est plus mon amour . . .", "Assez! Voici la punition . . ."

After this rapid succession of conflicting passages, **"Nuit de l'enfer"** is a single long piece that enunciates hellfire. Across twenty carefully ordered paragraphs, the soul acts out its dual consciousness of being damned yet potentially saved. For, by a dramatic irony parallel to that of the preface, damnation and salvation are felt together like simultaneous torture and blessing. Whereas **"Mauvais Sang"** proceeded by fragments arranged in a temporal sequence, these lines move in an undivided moment: "J'ai avalé une fameuse gorgée de poison.—Trois fois béni le conseil qui m'est arrivé" 'I swallowed a famous mouthful of poison.—Thrice blessed be the good counsel that came to me'. The self gives us a drama in which error implies truth as hell implies heaven: "Des erreurs qu'on me souffle, magies, parfums faux, musiques puériles.—Et dire que je tiens la vérité, que je vois la justice . . ." 'Errors that are whispered to me, magic, false perfumes, childish music.—And to think that I possess the truth, that I perceive justice . . .'; again: "Marie! Sainte-Vierge!—Horreur de ma bêtise" 'Mary! Holy Virgin!—The horror of my stupidity'. Language works against itself as goodness is juxtaposed to selfishness, ecstasy to nightmare, miraculous powers (the self will be a charitable Christ: "Tous, venez,—même les petits enfants, que je

vous console . . ." 'All of you, come—even the little children, let me comfort you . . . ') to dejection, pride to dissolution. Poetic force derives from these contradictory exclamatives, but also from the immobile nature of a soliloquy burning with the flame of paradox, which introduces in the first lines a delirious vision—"Voyez comme le feu se relève" 'See how the fire rises up again'—and closes on the symmetrical counterpart of this vision—"C'est le feu qui se relève avec son damné" 'It is fire that rises up again with its damned soul'.

The third and fourth sections, **"Délires I"** and **"Délires II"**, break into the sequence with a radical modification of the speaking voice. In the former the role is that of a man/woman, both companion ("un compagnon d'enfer") and foolish virgin ("vierge folle")—a male playing a female part, who construes all self-references in the feminine ("la plus triste de vos servantes . . perdue . . . soûle . . . impure . . . veuve . . . jalouse . . . soumise . . . folle . . ."). The new voicing distances the immediate crisis, so that what is tragic in **"Mauvais Sang"** and **"Nuit de l'enfer"** is here treated with a measure of light relief; but this lightness is relative, for it serves finally to reveal still more desperately the failure of the demonic project when seen from an external vantage point.

Thus past anguish is transmuted into a mixture of comedy and pathos. The pseudowoman who has put her destiny in the hands of the Spouse uses an unintentionally farcical language that figures Verlaine in his religious nostalgia yet carnal weakness ("Je suis née soumise à Lui!—L'autre peut me battre maintenant!" 'I was born subject to Him!—The other one can beat me now!'), his self-abasement yet pleasure in self-abasement ("Que de larmes! Et que de larmes encore plus tard, j'espère!" 'How many tears! And how many more tears later, I hope!'), his sexuality yet censorship of sexual identity ("O mes amies! . . . non, pas mes amies . . ." 'O my girlfriends! . . . no, not my girlfriends . . . '), his sadness yet indulgence in melancholy ("Enfin, faisons cette confidence, quitte à la répéter vingt fois—aussi morne, aussi insignifiante!" 'So let us make this confession, while being ready to repeat it twenty times over—just as melancholy, just as insignificant!'), his true naiveté yet self-conscious cult of naiveté ("moi, *moi, la pauvre âme*" 'I, *I, the poor soul*'). For the foolish virgin, God exists and there is no quarrel, but He can be postponed for more pressing needs. That such a profile corresponds to the "Pauvre Lélian" of Verlaine's verse and prose is clear: no less than the nervous rhythms and sinuous phrasing, a precise vocabulary signals the author of *Poèmes saturniens* and *Romances sans paroles:* "triste", "tristement", "tristesses", "le Paradis de la tristesse", "chagrin", "douceur", "sagesse" . . .

Yet the goal is surely not to write a portrait of Verlaine as such but to judge the madness of an enterprise that involves both the Infernal Spouse and his companion. He who sought to save himself and others, to go beyond reality, *to change life,* is shown with his shortcomings. The woman declares both her own torment and the less than noble contradictions of the Spouse, whose words are mimed in yet another voice of misogyny, cruelty, terror, charity, sadness, indignation, mockery, gentleness. The Mad Virgin sees the sham, and forgives; trembles, and follows; imagines, and despairs; admires, and deems herself unworthy; twice says "Je te comprends", and does not understand; and although she calls him devilish, she expects that he may ascend one day divinely into heaven in some messianic assumption. We are held by a suffering that is unfolded in its hopelessness, all the more so since we recognize before we are told—as we shall be told in **"Délires II"**—the self-destructiveness that underlies the Spouse's ambition to save the world. By dramatic irony, we see more than the woman herself sees, since she does not comprehend the gulf. The last words, of the section ("Drôle de ménage!" 'Funny couple!') put the crisis with terrible understatement.

"Délires II" points up ludically from the start the changed voice ("A moi" 'Now it's my turn'): a freshly poised self, direct, calmly analytical, describes the ways it has sought to achieve verbal alchemy. In a controlled temporal order ("Depuis longtemps je me vantais . . . J'aimais . . . Je rêvais . . . je croyais . . . J'inventai . . ."), the imperfect tense of habit becomes the past definite of event, just as pride gives way to invention—"J'inventai la couleur des voyelles!" 'I invented the color of vowels!'—and dreams of invention—"je me flattai d'inventer un verbe poétique accessible, un jour ou l'autre, à tous les sens" 'I flattered myself that I was inventing a poetic language that would one day or other be accessible to all the senses'. Moving forward like an intellectual autobiography, the narrative places the writing of **"Voyelles"** in the line of a lucid undertaking. "Ce fut d'abord une étude" 'It was first of all an investigation'. Nevertheless, at this point, the monologue is interrupted by the first of seven poems that appear in forms different in each case from those of other manuscripts. Rimbaud gives us edited texts as if he had taken pains to fit them to his argument. For if the commentary follows a plot ("histoire"), the poems may be said to constitute a dramatic progression. In this *itinerarium mentis* or spiritual *chantefable*[7] the first two pieces are vertigos ("Je fixais des vertiges") after the fashion of Poe's Maëlstrom or House of Usher or Tell-tale Heart, although for Rimbaud the whirlpool's center is the soul.

> Loin des oiseaux, des troupeaux, des
>   villageoises,
> Que buvais-je, à genoux dans cette bruyère
> Entourée de tendres bois de noisetiers,
> Dans un brouillard d'après-midi tiède et vert?

Far from birds, herds, village-maids, / what was I drinking on my knees in that heath / surrounded by tender woods of hazel-trees, / in a warm green afternoon fog?

We read, written in the rare hendecasyllabic meter, a poem that tells of unfathomed and unfathomable thirst in the midst of an abundant nature—heather, hazel trees, warm green vapor. The interrogatives, the meter, the negatives and implied negatives unsettle expectations, trope uncertainty ("Je faisais une louche enseigne d'auberge" 'I was an ambiguous inn sign'). Equivocalness reaches a climax, which is totally swept aside in a broad vision of storm and sky.

> —Un orage vint chasser le ciel. Au soir
> L'eau des bois se perdait sur les sables
>   vierges,
> Le vent de Dieu jetait des glaçons aux mares;
> Pleurant, je voyais de l'or—et ne pus boire.—

—A storm came to cleanse the sky. In the evening / water from the woods spilt down on virgin sands, / God's wind cast icy blocks at the ponds; Weeping, / I saw gold—and could not drink.—

Warmth gives way to bitter cold, afternoon to evening, as if God were chastizing nature. The thirst for the absolute ends in frustrated desire.

The second poem answers this vertigo by a vertigo of a different kind: not solitude but love, not afternoon but morning, not sadness but happiness. A festive world blesses the lovers and, at the same time, as if from an overflowing heart, blesses the workers who recover their spirits (playfully, "eau-de-vie") by the intercession of the star of love, and who rejoice in the prospect of a future sea-change.

> A quatre heures du matin, l'été,
> Le sommeil d'amour dure encore.
> Sous les bocages s'évapore
>   L'odeur du soir fêté.
>
> Là-bas, dans leur vaste chantier
> Au soleil des Hespérides,
> Déjà s'agitent—en bras de chemise—
>   Les Charpentiers.
>
> Dans leurs Déserts de mousse, tranquilles,
> Ils préparent les lambris précieux
>   Où la ville
>   Peindra de faux cieux.
>
> O, pour ces Ouvriers charmants
> Sujets d'un roi de Babylone,
> Vénus! quitte un instant les Amants
>   Dont l'âme est en couronne.

O Reine des Bergers,
Porte aux travailleurs l'eau-de-vie,
Que leurs forces soient en paix
En attendant le bain dans la mer à midi.

At four o'clock in the morning, in summer, / love's
sleep still lasts. / Beneath the groves evaporates /
the smell of the festive evening.

Down there, in their vast workshop / in the sunlight
of the Hesperides, / already in their shirtsleeves—
the Carpenters / are active.

In their mossy Deserts, calmly, / they ready the
costly panels / on which the city / will paint false
skies.

O, for these magical Workers / subjects of a
Babylonian King, / Venus! leave for a moment
the Lovers / whose souls are wreathed.

O Queen of Shepherds, / bring to the workmen the
water-of-life, / may their strength be at peace / while
they wait to bathe in the sea at Midday.

The self and legendary nature are held in a dream,
sustained by rhythms that do not count their numbers.

Prose intervenes to record the continuing alchemy
of and by the word, which is this experiment in
self-transformation. But verse soon returns, this time
to capture the insouciance of caterpillars and moles.
"Chanson de la plus haute tour" expresses, again in
song form, a vagueness as undirected as nature, a simplicity as effortless as prayer, for thirst has become
revolt against all conscious application.

Qu'il vienne, qu'il vienne,
Le temps dont on s'éprenne.

J'ai tant fait patience
Qu'à jamais j'oublie.
Craintes et souffrances
Aux cieux sont parties.
Et la soif malsaine
Obscurcit mes veines.
Qu'il vienne, qu'il vienne,
Le temps dont on s'éprenne.

Let it come, let it come, / the time you will cherish.

I have been so patient / that forever I forget. /
Fears and sufferings / have gone to the sky. / And
unhealthy thirst / darkens my veins.

Let it come, let it come, / the time you will cherish.

Two earlier versions read: "Ah! que le temps vienne /
Où les cœurs s'éprennent" 'Ah! let the time come /

when hearts fall in love', which is no less melodious
than the final version but more concrete. "Temps" will
replace "cœur", and the hypothetical subjunctive will
replace the possible indicative; for it is precisely such
weightlessness that is at this point the goal of ***Une***
Saison en enfer.

The search for unreason is brought to a high point as
the poet turns to images of devastation: the world must
be "bombarded", "pulverized", "oxidized", "dissolved".
Two poems treat the theme of bitter consumption in
complementary fashion, the first projecting a violence
that seeks to reduce reality to nothingness and adopting as it goes the phonetic and semantic insistence of
nonsensical children's rounds:

Mangez les cailloux qu'on brise,
Les vieilles pierres d'églises;
Les galets des vieux déluges,
Pains semés dans les vallées grises.

Eat the broken pebbles, / the old church stones; /
the shingles from old floods, / loaves strewn in the
gray valleys.

the second recalling Gautier in its Parnassian emphasis, yet signifying the wish, no longer to consume, but
to be consumed.

Que je dorme! que je bouille
Aux autels de Salomon.
Le bouillon court sur la rouille,
Et se mêle au Cédron.

Let me sleep! let me boil / on the altars of Solomon.
/ The broth flows on the rust / and mingles with the
Kedron.

The references call up a large space and time that
merges with legend, like the self that merges with sleep,
broth with river. The twin orgies—active and passive—
carry no joy, however, so that we must wait until the
following poem, one of Rimbaud's most extraordinary,
in which sea and sun, day and night, concrete and
abstract combine in an ecstatic sequence. Hope no
longer exists, since eternity is achieved here and now.

Elle est retrouvée!
Quoi? l'éternité.
C'est la mer mêlée
Au soleil.

Mon âme éternelle,
Observe ton vœu
Malgré la nuit seule
Et le jour en feu.

Donc tu te dégages
Des humains suffrages,

Des communs élans!
Tu voles selon . . .

—Jamais l'espérance.
  Pas d'*orietur*.
Science et patience,
Le supplice est sûr.

Plus de lendemain,
Braises de satin,
  Votre ardeur
  Est le devoir.

Elle est retrouvée!
—Quoi?—l'Eternité.
C'est la mer mêlée
  Au soleil.

It is found again! / What? eternity. / It is the sea mingling / with the sun.

My eternal soul, / follow your wish / despite lonely night / and fiery day.

So you free yourself / from human wills, / from common passions! / You fly at your whim . . .

—Never a hope. / No desire. / Science and patience, / the punishment is sure.

No tomorrow, / satin embers, / your present ardor / is your duty.

It is found again! / What? Eternity. / It is the sea mingling / with the sun.

The meter is pentasyllabic, although broken by three trisyllables and a tetrasyllable in a rapid movement that Claudel might well describe by his favorite Zen term "Ah! awareness" or *ahité:* the self escapes from time to eternity in the way sea fuses with sun, Christian expectancy ("espérance" *"orietur"*) with immediate experience. The fire metaphor ("soleil", "feu", "braises") becomes internalized as the poet's only responsibility and goal ("Votre ardeur / Est le devoir"), which rejects laborious science and long-suffering patience. It is the mystical song of eternity possessed.

Yet happiness—"le Bonheur"—is taken up in the last poem in quite different terms. Again the meter is light, with ten seven-syllable lines arranged in rhyming couplets; but a rhythmic counterpoint is introduced by four hexasyllables which catch the tenderly nostalgic note of an unexplained lovesong—"O saisons, ô châteaux"—like a fragment from Gérard de Nerval's "Chansons et Légendes du Valois".[8] Answer is made to the previous poem by the sudden apprehension of loss. If the first, second and third pieces of the sequence treat the motif of thirst as frustration, then fulfillment, then bitter

rejection of the world, and the fourth and fifth treat hunger as cruel consumption of external nature and the inner self, the last two present the contrasting images of flight as eternity, then—here—as mortality of the heart.

O saisons, ô châteaux!
Quelle âme est sans défauts?

J'ai fait la magique étude
Du bonheur, que nul n'élude.

Salut à lui, chaque fois
Que chante son coq gaulois.

Ah! je n'aurai plus d'envie:
Il s'est chargé de ma vie.

Ce charme a pris âme et corps
Et dispersé les efforts.

  O saisons, ô châteaux!

L'heure de sa fuite, hélas!
Sera l'heure du trépas.

  O saisons, ô châteaux!

O seasons, O castles! / What soul is without stain? / I have pursued the magical study / of happiness, that no man avoids. / Hail to it, each time / the Gallic cock crows. / Ah! no longer shall I want: it has assumed my life. / This charm has become body and soul / and dispersed all toil. / O seasons, O castles! / The hour of its flight, alas! / will be the hour of death. / O seasons, O castles!

The fragile matter of song recalls the whole sequence of **"Délires II"**—study, pleasure, dissolution, death. At the same time, enlarging the drama to universal dimensions ("qu'aucun n'élude"), it announces the failure of all future endings. The conclusion is, however, immediately ironized by the poet who speaks with hindsight: "Cela s'est passé. Je sais aujourd'hui saluer la beauté" 'That is over and done with. Today I can greet beauty'. From the present he deflates the past with confidence, for he believes that he has emerged from the burden of remorse as he had foretold in the preface. The drama he has played in life and literature would seem to be over. Yet this we are unable wholly to accept since there has been no resolution of any clear kind, so that if all may be right, all may still be terribly wrong. In the four remaining sections of *Une Saison en enfer* anguish will not cease, the soul being in constant jeopardy. The performance has not come to a close.

With **"L'Impossible"** the poem becomes a monologue of the abstract mind emblematic of Western culture.

The confident declaration at the end of **"Délires II"** opens the way for reason which, finding the failure of reason, nevertheless affirms as it goes: "J'ai eu raison . . . J'ai eu raison . . . Je m'explique . . ." The self will return not to past wanderings that proved all too deceptive ("Quelle sottise c'était . . ."), or to more recent experiences of the venal or puerile ways of society ("Le monde! les marchands, les naïfs!"), but to Oriental wisdom. The Orient here provides Rimbaud with an imaginative pole of knowledge beyond knowledge: "sagesse"—the word occurs four times—would appear to offer an escape from Christian guilt and Western stagnation ("Les marais occidentaux!"). The poverty of religion, nationalism, middle-class conventions is associated with Christianity, since M. Prudhomme—the epitome of the nineteenth-century French bourgeois—"est né avec le Christ" 'was born at the same time as Christ'. Will not Oriental wisdom, on the contrary, allow the self to quit the spiritual mists in which it has lived too long? The Church has an answer: the imagined Orient does not belong to the East, for the Orient is nothing but the Eden of the Bible and, therefore, the common property of all. Western philosophy also: Oriental philosophy can be discovered in the West by way of the imagination and need not be sought *in situ*. The mind recognizes its own facile exoticism and decides for one brief moment that it can accomplish itself here and now: "Par l'esprit on va à Dieu" 'By our minds we go to God'. The words appear to come as an epiphany, but the question-begging nature of the argument is only too apparent inasmuch as *esprit* slips from signifying intelligence to spirit. The "impossible" of the title is, then, this blockage of reason caught in the net of its own aporias—"Déchirante infortune!" 'Grievous misfortune!'

So, after the madness of **"Délires II"**, the self has grappled with reason and with reason's shortcomings. But now, after reason, work: the sixth part entitled **"L'Eclair"** weighs the virtues of labor. Rimbaud takes for a moment the voice of society which, as it denies the *vanitas vanitatum* of the biblical Preacher, espouses the cult of progress. "Le travail humain! c'est l'explosion qui éclaire mon abîme de temps en temps" 'Human labor! that is the explosion which illuminates my abyss from time to time'; again: "Rien n'est vanité; à la science, et en avant!" 'Nothing is vanity; to knowledge, forward march!' But humor subverts such a project, for the self declares that it will respect work in an absolute way—by not doing it ("en le mettant de côté"). It can playfully assume any number of gratuitous roles ("saltimbanque, mendiant, artiste, bandit,—prêtre!" 'acrobat, beggar, artist, bandit,—priest!') which would define poetry as detached theatre. Nevertheless, with a brusque shift, the serious nature of such a theatrical enterprise is realized in terms all the more touching in that they announce, twenty years before the event, Rimbaud's last days at the Hôpital de la Conception:

"Sur mon lit d'hôpital, l'odeur de l'encens m'est revenue si puissante; gardien des aromates sacrés, confesseur, martyr . . ." 'On my hospital bed the smell of incense came back to me so powerfully; keeper of the holy aromatics, confessor, martyr . . . ' The religious terms carry the notions of sin and salvation that the self thought to have avoided ("Je reconnais là ma sale éducation d'enfance" 'I recognize my rotten childhood upbringing'). Anguish must be defused; a conventional life can be lived: "Aller mes vingt ans, si les autres vont vingt ans . . ." 'Let us be twenty if others are twenty . . . ' Yet neither work nor the refusal to work suffices, since either choice merely postpones the realization of the meaninglessness of life, which is death. The speaker addresses his own soul—"chère pauvre âme"—with the knowledge that, whatever his choice, eternity is lost. From initial enthusiasm he is led by the self-critical intellect to despair.

"Matin", although the shortest of the sections, is crucial in opening the doors of the sensibility to past and future. The title posits an imaginary fulfillment which the four paragraphs trope in two even surges of past and present, present and future. The sum of desire is expressed in a plaintive confession that calls to witness the unseen audience of all humanity.

> N'eus-je pas *une fois* une jeunesse aimable, héroïque, fabuleuse, à écrire sur des feuilles d'or,—trop de chance! Par quel crime, par quelle erreur, ai-je mérité ma faiblesse actuelle? Vous qui prétendez que des bêtes poussent des sanglots de chagrin, que des malades désespèrent, que des morts rêvent mal, tâchez de raconter ma chute et mon sommeil. Moi, je ne puis pas plus m'expliquer que le mendiant avec ses continuels *Pater* et *Ave Maria. Je ne sais plus parler!*

> Pourtant, aujourd'hui, je crois avoir fini la relation de mon enfer. C'était bien l'enfer; l'ancien, celui dont le fils de l'homme ouvrit les portes.

> *Did I not have at one time a pleasant childhood, heroic, fabulous, to be inscribed on gold leaves,— too lucky! By what crime, by what error did I merit my present weakness? You who claim that animals sob with grief, that invalids despair, that dead men have bad dreams, try to tell of my fall and my sleep. I cannot explain myself any more than the beggar with his ceaselles* Our Father's *and* Hail Mary's. *I can no longer speak!*

> *And yet today I think I have finished the account of my hell. It was indeed hell, the old hell, whose gates were opened by the son of man.*

A fall has taken place like the mythical fall of man, the word "chance" already containing the paradox of luck and loss (Latin: *cadens*) in the midst of youth. Those who feel compassion for, and an instinctive identification with, animals as well as the sick and dead can perhaps explain the speaker to himself, since he himself has become brutish: he has reached the end of reasoned discourse, like a man who can only mumble his prayers as circular as madness.

Yet, at a time when there seems to be nowhere to turn, the speaker recognizes that his tale has been told. A new morning of freedom like that of youth before the fall can be imagined: if the anguish associated with Christianity is synonymous with the infernal round of sin and salvation, cannot the cycle be broken once and for all by the birth of another Messiah?

> Du même désert, à la même nuit, toujours mes yeux las se réveillent à l'étoile d'argent, toujours, sans que s'émeuvent les rois de la vie, les trois mages, le cœur, l'âme, l'esprit. Quand irons-nous, par delà les grèves et les monts, saluer la naissance du travail nouveau, la sagesse nouvelle, la fuite des tyrans et des démons, la fin de la superstition, adorer—les premiers!—Noël sur la terre!

> Le chant des cieux, la marche des peuples! Esclaves, ne maudissons pas la vie.

> *From the same desert to the same night, my eyes forever waken to the silver star, and forever the three magi, the kings of life—heart, soul, mind,—are not stirred. When shall we go, beyond shores and mountains, to salute the birth of the new work, the new wisdom, the flight of tyrants and demons, the end of superstition, and worship—for the first time!—Christmas on earth!*

> *The song of heaven, the progress of peoples! Slaves, let us not curse life.*

The biblical echoes are clear, yet this is less parody than pastiche. The images answer those of the previous sections in an organic way: "la naissance du travail nouveau" answers **"L'Eclair"**, which turned on the notion of work; "la sagesse nouvelle" answers **"L'Impossible"**, which vainly sought wisdom; "la fuite des tyrans et des démons" answers **"Nuit de l'enfer"**, in which God and Satan exercized their powers of domination; while "la fin de la superstition" refers back to **"Mauvais Sang"**, its idolatries, Sabbaths, sacrileges, conversion. The inverse order sums up past conflicts while proposing the cult of another Christ untouched by Christianity. The tone is one of confidence: the protagonist has immersed himself in a chiliastic vision as compelling as it is unreasoned. He can look to future vigor like that of the "Million d'oiseaux d'or" of **"Le Bateau ivre"**; he can imagine heaven and earth moving to the harmony of song ("chant"), to the rhythms of collective progress ("marche"). The future appears as fair as the imagined past at the beginning of

"Matin". The last words, however, rediscover the tension of present with future in which the negative command—"Esclaves, ne maudissons pas la vie"—includes statement and virtual counterstatement; for with what strength, and how durably, can the enslaved self wage its impossible conflict?

The poet changes stance and mode one last time to elaborate the tenuous image of liberation. On the one hand, autumn has come ("L'automne déjà . . .", "L'automne . . ."), and approaching winter is to be feared; on the other, night no doubt heralds a new morning. The two parts of the section comprising six, then eight paragraphs (they recall the binary structure of the preface) move in antithetical ways—first, from confidence to helplessness ("où puiser le secours?" 'where can help be found?'), then from loss to putative gain ("il me sera loisible de *posséder la vérité dans une âme et un corps*" 'I shall be able to *possess truth in a soul and a body*'). Contrasting with the hortatory character of the last line of **"Matin"**, **"Adieu"** finds a lyrical pattern and tone. The title sums up an emotional ambiguity which is both farewell to suffering and salute ("Adieu", "A Dieu") to the unknown god—"clarté divine"—that is *beyond*. (Not without relevance perhaps, Littré tells us that provincial French in Rimbaud's time still used "Adieu" both as goodbye and hello; thus, "Adieu, comment vous portez-vous?")

The combat of the entire poem is focused in this passion. Yet the time has come for the supernatural to be rejected ("je suis rendu au sol" 'I am returned to the earth'), for the Infernal Spouse to be exorcized ("je puis rire des vieilles amours mensongères" 'I can laugh at the old deceptive loves'), for the self's own peasant origins that were castigated in **"Mauvais Sang"** to be affirmed anew ("la réalité rugueuse à étreindre! Paysan!" 'rough-skinned reality to be embraced! Peasant!'). The "horrible bush" of Christianity must be left behind. Nevertheless the last lines do not reject in any rational way the aporia of sin and salvation but rather musicalize it in a finale that pits truth against lie, strength against weakness, tenderness against fear, warmth against cold. Not forgetful of unanswerable arguments, the actor who is the self as post-Baudelairean Confessor precariously affirms the *possibility* of escape by way of his resurgent moral strength and lucid courage.[9]

Paul Valéry was severe in his judgment of *Une Saison en enfer,* which he considered to be the product of an easily imitable rhetoric: "Ce ne sont qu'expressions directes, jaculations, intensité" 'There are only direct statements, jaculations, intensity'.[10] He preferred the *Illuminations.* Paul Claudel, on the other hand, put *Une Saison en enfer* above the *Illuminations* for its theme ("ce document incomparable")[11] no less than its style: "Il est certain que Rimbaud a beaucoup travaillé les *Illuminations,* mais beaucoup moins sur le papier que sur son âme. Comme style je les trouve inférieures à la *Saison,* qui, elle, est tout entière pénétrée par l'âme. Là plus aucune trace d'effort de bizarreries (comme l'indique le passage des brouillons), à ce moment dépassées et condamnées' 'It is certain that Rimbaud reworked the *Illuminations* a great deal, but much less in his manuscripts than in his soul. Stylistically I find them inferior to the *Saison,* which is wholly permeated by the soul. No longer does one find in it any trace of effort, of bizarreness (as indicated by the passage in the drafts), which is henceforth abandoned and condemned'.[12] Must we side with Claudel or Valéry? Or shall we say that their differences are comparable to those of René Char with Yves Bonnefoy by reason of basic incompatibilities? Surely both are right to underline the relative lack of complexity of *Une Saison en enfer* with respect to the *Illuminations,* Valéry pointing to the mode, Claudel to the sense. Nevertheless the uniqueness of *Une Saison en enfer* results not merely from its directness of language and emotion, nor from its valorization of a role that embraces the Christian tradition, but also from the admirable intellectual and emotional passion of a performance that brings into question the stylistic obliqueness of the *Illuminations* as it does the formalism of *Les Fleurs du mal.* (We recall that Rimbaud had written in his letter of May 1871: "la forme si vantée en lui est mesquine" 'his [Baudelaire's] much-praised form is puny').[13]

Does this, then, set *Une Saison en enfer* apart from the rest of the work? We are struck by a movement we take to be characteristic: Rimbaud on every occasion beginning with **"Le Bateau ivre"** writes *his last poem.* We think back to the pieces studied here and to others that might well have been chosen. The loss/gain scheme is at the heart of the poetry, not as a simplistic axis of resolution, but—this is Rimbaud's integrity—as drama. Although *Une Saison en enfer* mediates the antagonisms of intellect and sensibility within a religious scheme, it differs in kind and compass rather than in tension.

For each of his compositions, whether in verse or prose, Rimbaud lends an individual voice and setting to the dilemma. The good that is revolt, departure, creation, the evil that is conventionality, stasis, custom, are found at one extreme in the non-Christian frame of **"Le Bateau ivre"**, the **"Derniers Vers"** and the *Illuminations,* at the other in the properly Christian frame of *Une Saison en enfer.* Language grasps irreducible contradictions that are taken to the limits of Rimbaud's imaginative and ironic powers. When we look at isolated lines we have no difficulty in identifying a number of profiles like those of "everybody's favorite hippy", or the "mystique à l'état sauvage", or the "Communard", or any other of the univocal models that have been suggested. But he goes beyond them by a self-awareness that recreates the theatre. If the subject on occasion may appear to be less than grave, we recognize as we read further the tragic urgency of this poet who forever broaches the issue of spiritual and social renewal and assumes his role as sacrificer and sacrificed. (I think of Nietzsche's words on Rousseau that point to "the magnanimity with which, as a man of knowledge, he dauntlessly, often with embarrassment, often with sublime mockery and smiling, offers himself and his life as sacrifice".)[14] Rimbaud could abandon literature at the age of twenty, feeling no doubt that he had expressed in the many ways of which he was capable—"toutes les énergies chorales et orchestrales et leurs applications instantanées" 'all choral and orchestral energies and their instantaneous applications'[15]—his dedication to poetry as vision and act.

Notes

[1] "Nuit de l'enfer", *Une Saison en enfer,* p. 222. Verlaine puts the same thought in musical terms when he writes: "La Muse . . . de M. Arthur Rimbaud prend tous les tons, pince toutes les cordes de la harpe, gratte toutes celles de la guitare et caresse le rebec d'un archet agile s'il en fut" 'Mr. Arthur Rimbaud's Muse . . . catches all the tones, plucks all the harp strings, scrapes all the guitar strings, and fondles the fiddle with as agile a bow as ever there was' ("Arthur Rimbaud", *Œuvres en prose complètes,* p. 645).

[2] Ibid., p. 221.

[3] Thus, Kristin Ross (*The Emergence of Social Space: Rimbaud and the Paris Commune,* Minneapolis: University of Minnesota Press, 1988) evokes "this new 'emancipated' subjectivity that takes as its point of departure the radical atomization or isolation of the worker, and proceeds by *heightening* or exaggerating that atomization rather than masking it in a myth of workers' community . . ." (p. 119).

[4] "Adieu", *Une Saison en enfer, Œuvres,* p. 240.

[5] Letter to Ernest Delahaye, May 1873, *Œuvres,* p. 355. A facsimile of the first page, with a Rimbaud self-portrait, is to be found in the *Album Rimbaud,* ed. Henri Matarasso and Pierre Petitfils, Paris: Gallimard, "Pléiade", 1967, p. 159. Steve Murphy published a facsimile of the complete letter in *Parade sauvage: revue d'études rimbaldiennes,* no. 1, 1984.

[6] The text is that of the Bernard-Guyaux *Œuvres,* pp. 211-241. For the most detailed critical edition, see Pierre Brunel, *Une Saison en enfer,* Paris: Corti, 1987.

[7] I refer to the medieval genre which alternates prose and song.

[8] See Paul Bénichou, *Nerval et la chanson folklorique,* Paris: Corti, 1970. Mallarmé, Laforgue, Claudel and

Apollinaire were, among Rimbaud's contemporaries and immediate successors, especially sensitive to the poetic charge of folksongs. Thus the ultrarefined Mallarmé said that he wanted to plunge verse back into the spring waters of folksong so that it would be "mystérieux et natif" (Stéphane Mallarmé, *Correspondance,* vol. 3, p. 316); while Guillaume Apollinaire, at the other end of the poetic spectrum, spoke similarly of folksong as "la source la plus limpide où puisse s'étancher la soif lyrique" 'the clearest source in which lyrical thirst may be quenched' (*Vers et prose,* June 1908).

[9] Nothing seems to me further from solipsism, or a pathological narcissism, than the poetry of Rimbaud. I cannot therefore agree with Harold Bloom's remarks concerning the conclusion of *Une Saison en enfer:* "Possessing the truth in a single mind and a single body—one's own—is a narcissistic revelation akin to that of Walt Whitman at the close of *Song of Myself*" (*Arthur Rimbaud,* p. 5).

[10] *Cahiers,* Paris: Centre National de la Recherche Scientifique, 29 vols., 1957-1961, vol. 29, p. 871.

[11] "Verlaine poète de la nature et poète chrétien", *Œuvres en prose,* p. 494.

[12] F. Petralia: "Lettere inedite di Paul Claudel a Paterne Berrichon", *Rivista di letterature moderne e comparate,* vol. 8, nos. 3-4, p. 236. Claudel's letter is dated 13 August 1913. His reference to the "brouillon" concerns the section originally entitled "Fausse Conversion", which includes much that was later to be elaborated in "Délires II". Rimbaud writes: "Je hais maintenant les élans mystiques et les bizarreries de style" 'I now hate mystical enthusiasms and bizarreness of style' (*Œuvres,* p. 340).

[13] *Œuvres,* p. 351.

[14] Friedrich Nietzsche, *Morgenröthe,* in *Werke,* Leipzig: Kröner, 20 vols., 1900-1926, vol. 4, p. 310. Verlaine admirably points to the fatal necessity that distinguishes Rimbaud's life and poetry: "la vie, à lui qu'on a voulu travestir en loup-garou, est toute en avant dans la lumière et la force, belle de logique et d'unité comme son œuvre" 'the life of one who has been presented in the guise of a werewolf is wholly turned toward light and strength, beautiful in its logic and unity like his work' ("Arthur Rimbaud '1884'", *Œuvres en prose complètes,* p. 801).

[15] "Solde", *Œuvres,* p. 293.

FURTHER READING

Bloom, Harold, ed. *Arthur Rimbaud.* New York: Chelsea House, 1988, 240 p.

A collection of late twentieth-century essays on Rimbaud and his writings, reprinted from various books and periodicals.

Bonnefoy, Yves. "*A Season in Hell.*" In *Rimbaud,* trans. Paul Schmidt, pp. 82-105. New York: Harper & Row, 1973.

Interprets *Une Saison en enfer* as a tortured account of Rimbaud's moral and spiritual alienation. Bonnefoy declares that as it swings between nihilism and "aspirations toward the sacred," the poem depicts its author's struggle to resolve the contradictions of human existence.

Cohn, Robert Greer. "*Une Saison en enfer.*" In *The Poetry of Rimbaud,* pp. 401-38. Princeton: Princeton University Press, 1973.

Objects to extravagant praise of Rimbaud and *Une Saison en enfer.* Although Cohn describes some sections of the poem as masterful, he contends that it lacks structural coherence and is obsessively self-absorbed. Also includes detailed commentary on important passages in each of the poem's nine sections. Cohn's explication of these lines is contained in pp. 413-38 of the chapter.

Fowlie, Wallace. "*Une Saison en enfer.*" In *Rimbaud,* pp. 87-96. Chicago: University of Chicago Press, 1965.

Discusses the poem as a confessional narrative in which the author alternately sees himself as a scapegoat, a criminal, and a sinner. In Fowlie's judgment, the poet ultimately concedes that he is not a visionary with supernatural powers but merely an ordinary man.

Houston, John Porter. "The Symbolic Structure of Rimbaud's Hell." *Modern Language Quarterly* XXI, No. 1 (March 1960): 69-72.

Focuses on the symbolic language and formal design of *Une Saison en enfer.* Houston declares that while the poem embodies the conventional myth of fall and redemption, it presents a unique vision of the state of grace.

———. "*Une Saison en enfer* and the Dialectics of Damnation." In *The Design of Rimbaud's Poetry,* pp. 137-200. New Haven: Yale University Press, 1963.

Analyzes the theological framework of *Une Saison en enfer,* arguing that Rimbaud rejected Christian dualism and replaced it with a new ideology—one in which the traditional antitheses of spirit and body, good and evil, are synthesized and presented as equally valid ideals.

Peschel, Enid Rhodes. "Rimbaud's Life and Work." In *A Season in Hell—The Illuminations,* by Arthur Rimbaud, trans. Enid Rhodes Peschel, pp. 3-33. New York: Oxford University Press, 1973.

In addition to reviewing the known facts of Rimbaud's life, his "*lettre du voyant,*" and his literary influence, Peschel also discusses *A Season in Hell* in terms of the poet's emotional and spiritual development.

St. Aubyn, F. C. "Songs of a Private Hell" and "More Songs of a Private Hell." In *Arthur Rimbaud,* pp. 73-94 and 95-111. Boston: Twayne, 1975.

Provides a detailed gloss on the text of *Une Saison en enfer.* St. Aubyn maintains that the poem's chief concern is loss of innocence, yet he also notes other significant themes, including Christianity, social justice, and immortality.

Wing, Nathaniel. "The Autobiography of Rhetoric: On Reading Rimbaud's *Une Saison en enfer.*" *French Forum* 9, No. 1 (January 1984): 42-58.

Evaluates *Une Saison en enfer* as a deeply subversive examination of the relation between literature and reality. In Wing's judgment, Rimbaud demonstrated that the search for a "new modernity" is fruitless, for the poet/narrator cannot elude the strictures and authority of Western thought and discourse.

Additional coverage of Rimbaud's life and career is contained in the following sources published by the Gale Group: *Nineteenth-Century Literature Criticism,* Vols. 4 and 35; *Poetry Criticism,* Vol. 3; *DISCovering Authors;* and *World Literature Criticism, 1500 to the Present.*

Constance Fenimore Woolson

1840-1894

American novelist and short story writer.

INTRODUCTION

Defining herself in opposition to typical American female sentimental writers, Constance Fenimore Woolson became one of the most well-known and respected women authors of nineteenth-century America. Woolson is frequently described as a "local colorist" due to her vivid evocations of such settings as the Great Lakes, Florida, Tennessee, and Italy. In contrast to most regional writers, she does not write about her "native" homes—New Hampshire and Cleveland; Peter Caccavari thus modulates this identification by describing her as a "traveling regionalist." Woolson is also noted for her subtle characterizations that emerge out of the interaction with these physical locales. Widely popular during her lifetime, Woolson remains popular among scholars today for her talented use of locale and character and for her struggle to reconcile the role of female author with nineteenth-century conceptions of woman's place in society.

Biographical Information

Born in Claremont, New Hampshire, on March 5, 1840, Woolson survived all five of her sisters, a biographical detail which pivotally shaped Woolson's experience. After the death of one of her sisters in New Hampshire her family moved to Ohio. Woolson received her education in Cleveland and later in New York City, far exceeding that of many women of her day. Woolson began traveling with her mother and sister after her father's death in 1869. It was during this period that Woolson produced her first short stories, set in Michigan and the American South. In 1875, her first collection of short stories, *Castle Nowhere: Lake-Country Sketches* was published, after appearing piecemeal in journals such as *Atlantic Monthly* and *Harper's*. Her mother's death in 1879 spurred Woolson to travel abroad with her sister. Publicity for her first novel, *Anne* (1882), emphasized her kinship with James Fenimore Cooper, a maternal great-uncle. She spent time in England, Switzerland, and Italy, the last forming the backdrop to some of her later short stories. Introduced to Henry James in 1880, Woolson sustained a supportive literary correspondence with him until her death in Venice in 1894. It is not clear whether she died during a bout with fever or if her death was a suicide.

Major Works

Woolson is commonly described as a "local color" author, yet her settings vary from the contemporary streets of Rome to the wilderness camps of the Lake Huron region. Her attention to locale is not merely descriptive, however; character development often emerges primarily in interaction with the physical features of the environment. Many of her narratives, particularly her short stories set in Italy, focus on characters who are not native to the environs. The principal figures are often foreigners who have assimilated into Italian society. Woolson's depictions of exile in conjunction with her description of locale function as metaphors which reveal the emotions and motivations of her characters. In many stories, the plot is driven by the "troubled personal relations," as Alexander Cowie has suggested, between genders. Woolson inherits the figure of the self-sacrificing woman bound by romantic entanglements from the sentimental tradition. Although most of her main characters are women, her novel *Horace Chase* (1894) is, in Arthur Hobson Quinn's words, "a study of the [eponymous] self-made man." Woolson's novels and short stories do not lend themselves to political or social criticism although many deal with potentially controversial issues like Reconstruction ("Old Gardiston" and *Anne*)—and Anglo-American interactions with Native Americans in the Great Lakes Region ("The Lady of Little Fishing"). Instead, most of Woolson's works involve struggles of virtue and personal relationships. In her portrayals of these struggles, which appear throughout her stories, there is often a decision to be made between independence, which signifies a certain isolation, and belonging, which often stifles individuality.

Critical Reception

The popular and critical success of Woolson's short stories and novels provided her with financial stability and allowed her to cultivate friendships with Henry James, the poet Paul Hamilton Hayne, and other contemporary literary figures. Yet, in this century, Woolson's work has attracted less attention from critics until recent feminist interest in Woolson's work and life, and in her attempts to negotiate the sometimes conflicting demands of nineteenth-century womanhood and artistic imagination. Of many favorable reviews in her time, Henry James' reflections on her later works, particularly *East Angels* (1886) and *For the Major* (1883) remain among the most frequently cited. James writes, "what is most substantial to me in the book [*East Angels*] is the writer's general conception of her task, her general attitude of watching life, waiting upon it, and trying to catch it in the fact." For James, Woolson only partially succeeds in leaving behind the sentimentalism and conventionalism that marks most writing by American women in the nineteenth century. The naturalism of her characters and her precise study of human relationships are often praised by critics, in addition to her ability to evoke a particular setting and allow that setting to figure crucially in the narrative. Quinn attests, "what distinguishes Miss Woolson's stories from the usual magazine fiction is the way she can fix a character with one brief sentence." Readers generally agree that her shorter work tends to be more cohesive and well-paced because her skill lies more with characterization than with elaborate plotting.

Contrary to James' conclusion that Woolson is conservative in her concept of gender roles, recent feminists such as Victoria Brehm have argued that her stories self-consciously depict the dilemmas of the woman author: "[Woolson] did write one story over and over, and it was about the cost and gains to women who refused to go along with the obligatory domestic femininity of their time." Although her popular success has faded with that of the sentimental writers she strove to surpass, Woolson's indirect depictions of her own struggles and complex use of setting lend a naturalism to her work that has earned her critical praise.

PRINCIPAL WORKS

The Old Stone House [as Anne March] (juvenilia) 1872
Castle Nowhere: Lake-Country Sketches (short stories) 1875
Rodman the Keeper: Southern Sketches (short stories) 1880
Anne (novel) 1882
For the Major: A Novelette (novel) 1883
East Angels (novel) 1886
Jupiter Lights: A Novel (novel) 1889
Horace Chase (novel) 1894
The Front Yard and Other Italian Stories (short stories) 1895
Dorothy and Other Italian Stories (short stories) 1896

CRITICISM

Henry James (essay date 1887)

SOURCE: "Miss Constance Fenimore Woolson," *Harper's Weekly* Vol. XXXI, No. 1573, February 12, 1887, pp. 114-15.

[*In the essay that follows, James evaluates Woolson's writing as possessed by "a spirit singularly and essentially conservative," opposed to the entrance of women into public life.*]

Flooded as we have been in these latter days with copious discussion as to the admission of women to various offices, colleges, functions, and privileges, singularly little attention has been paid, by themselves at least, to the fact that in one highly important department of human affairs their cause is already gained—gained in such a way as to deprive them largely of their ground, formerly so substantial, for complaining of the intolerance of man. In America, in England, today, it is no longer a question of their admission into the world of literature: they are there in force; they have been admitted with all the honors, on a perfectly equal footing. In America, at least, one feels tempted at moments to exclaim that they are in themselves the world of literature. In Germany and in France, in this line of production, their presence is less to be perceived. To speak only of the latter country, France has brought forth in the persons of Madame De Sévigne, Madame De Stael, and Madame Sand three female writers of the first rank; without counting a hundred ladies to whom we owe charming memoirs and volumes of reminiscence; but in the table of contents of the *Revue des Deux Mondes,* that epitome of the literary movement (as regards everything, at least, but the famous doctrine, in fiction, of "naturalism"), it is rare to encounter the name of a female contributor. The covers of American and English periodicals tell a different story; in these monthly sections of the ladder of fame the ladies stand as thick as on the staircase at a crowded evening party.

There are, of course, two points of view from which this free possession of the public ear may be considered—as regards its effect upon the life of women; and as regards its effect upon literature. I hasten to add that I do not propose to consider either, and I touch on the general fact simply because the writer whose name I have placed at the head of these remarks happens to be a striking illustration of it. The work of Miss Constance Fenimore Woolson is an excellent example of the way the door stands open between the personal life of American women and the immeasurable world of print, and what makes it so is the particular quality that this work happens to possess. It breathes a spirit singularly and essentially conservative—the sort of spirit which, but for a special indication pointing the other way, would in advance seem most to oppose itself to the introduction into the feminine lot of new and complicating elements. Miss Woolson evidently thinks that lot sufficiently complicated, with the sensibilities which even in primitive ages women were acknowledged to possess; fenced in by the old disabilities and prejudices, they seem to her to have been, by the very nature of their being, only too much exposed, and it would never occur to her to lend her voice to the plea for further exposure—for a revolution which should place her sex in the thick of the struggle for power. She sees it in preference surrounded certainly by plenty of doors and windows (she has not, I take it, a love of bolts and Oriental shutters), but distinctly on the private side of that somewhat evasive and exceedingly shifting line which divides, human affairs into the profane and the sacred. Such is the turn of mind of the author of *Rodman the Keeper* and *East Angels,* and if it has not prevented her from writing books, from competing for the literary laurel, this is a proof of the strength of the current which to-day carries both sexes alike to that mode of expression.

It would not be hidden from a reader of *Anne* and *East Angels* that the author is a native of New England, who may have been transplanted to a part of the country open in some degree to the imputation of being "out West," who may then have lived for a considerable time in the South, and who may meanwhile constantly have retained as a part of her essence certain mysterious and not unvalued affinities

with the State of New York. Such, in fact, so far as my knowledge goes, has been the succession of events in Miss Woolson's history. She was born, like her father, Dr. Charles Jarvis Woolson, before her, at Claremont, New Hampshire, and taken as a child to live at Cleveland. She was educated partly in that city and partly at a French school in New York—an establishment which she has sketchily commemorated (if, indeed, the term "sketchy" may ever be applied to her earnest, lingering manner) in certain chapters of *Anne.* Such at least is my inference; the charming figure of Madame Moreau, in that novel, may be assumed to be a reminiscence of the late celebrated Madame Chegaray. On the death of her father, in 1869, she entered with her mother upon an unbroken residence of several years in the Southern States, principally in Florida, where, as is manifest in every page of *East Angels,* she conceived a high appreciation of orange gardens and white beaches, pine-barrens and rivers smothered in jungles, and a peculiar affection for that city of the past, so rapidly becoming a city of the future, St. Augustine. Her early summers she was accustomed to spend, in the Cleveland phrase, "up the lakes," and particularly amid the beautiful scenery of Mackinaw, in the straits between Michigan and Huron. Mackinaw is obviously the rather tormentingly nameless island represented in the early chapters of *Anne,* represented with a vividness which causes the reader of that story to rage not a little at the perversity which leads the author to desert the brilliant frozen straits and the little snow-bound United States military post for scenes less remunerative—the only case that I can remember, by-the-way, in which she has abandoned an opportunity without having conscientiously pressed it out. Miss Woolson must have known Mackinaw by winter as well as by summer, and none of her novels contains an episode better executed than those interrupted pages of *Anne* which give the sense of the snowglare beating into small, hot, bare interiors, the dog trains jogging over the white expanse, and the black forests staring for long months at the channel of ice. When it is added that Miss Woolson is by her mother a grandniece of Fenimore Cooper, and that she cherishes a devotion for the charming little town on Lake Otsego which bears, for good reasons, the name of the great romancer, her stories will have been accounted for so far as the distribution of her years, superficially speaking, may account for them.

That is, there is only one element unaccounted for— the inevitable European element, which, oddly enough, is nowadays almost the sign and hallmark of American experience. Miss Woolson has, I believe, of late years lived much in Europe, and yet there is nothing about Europe in her writings. She has not pressed it into service; she appears to have an unassuming suspicion that she can get on without it. Her characters sometimes sail for foreign countries (in general they move about a great deal, and take many journeys), but she does not even accompany them to the plank of the Steamer to the office where they take their berths; it is the most if she will renew acquaintance with them when they come back. Has she a story about Europe in reserve (I remember two or three very short ones, which, apparently, she has been shy of republishing), or does she propose to maintain her distinguished Independence? It will be interesting to see, and meanwhile we may note this Independence as an unusual phenomenon, taken in connection with her personal familiarity with Rome, Florence, Venice, and other irrepressible cities. The habit of introducing these cities usually exhibits itself in connection with a want of familiarity with them.

Miss Woolson's first productions were two collections of short tales, published in 1876 and 1880, and entitled respectively **Castle Nowhere** and **Rodman the Keeper.** I may not profess and acquaintance with the former of these volumes, but the latter is full of interesting, artistic work. Miss Woolson has done nothing better than the best pages in this succession of careful, strenuous studies of certain aspects of life, after the war, in Florida, Georgia, and the Carolinas. As the fruit of a remarkable minuteness of observation and tenderness of feeling on the part of one who evidently did not glance and pass, but lingered and analyzed, they have a high value, especially when regarded in the light of the *voicelessness* of the conquered and reconstructed South. Miss Woolson strikes the reader as having a compassionate sense of this pathetic dumbness—having perceived that no social revolution of equal magnitude had ever reflected itself so little in literature, remained so unrecorded, so unpainted and unsung. She has attempted to give an impression of this circumstance, among others, and a sympathy altogether feminine has guided her pen. She loves the whole region, and no daughter of the land could have handled its peculiarities more indulgently or communicated to us more of the sense of close observation and intimate knowledge. Nevertheless, it must be confessed that the picture, on the whole, is a picture of dreariness—of impressions that may have been gathered in the course of lonely afternoon walks at the end of hot days, when the sunset was wan, on the edge of rice-fields, dismal swamps, and other brackish inlets. The author is to be congratulated in so far as such expeditions may have been the source of her singularly exact familiarity with the "natural objects" of the region, including the negro of reality. She knows every plant and flower, every vague odor and sound, the song and flight of every bird, every tint of the sky and murmur of the forest, and she has noted scientifically the dialect of the freedmen. It is not too much to say that the negroes in **Rodman the Keeper** and in **East Angels** are a careful philological study, and that if Miss Woolson preceded Uncle Remus

by a considerable interval, she may have the credit of the initiative—of having been the first to take their words straight from their lips.

No doubt that if in **East Angels,** as well as in the volume of tales, the sadness of Miss Woolson's South is more striking than its high spirits, this is owing somewhat to the author's taste in the way of subject and situation, and especially to her predilection for cases of heroic sacrifice—sacrifice sometimes unsuspected, and always unappreciated. She is fond of irretrievable personal failures, of people who have had to give up even the memory of happiness, who love and suffer in silence, and minister in secret to the happiness of those who look over their heads. She is interested in general in secret histories, in the "inner life" of the weak, the superfluous, the disappointed, the bereaved, the unmarried. She believes in personal renunciation, in its frequency as well as its beauty. It plays a prominent part in each of her novels, especially in the last two, and the interest of **East Angels** at least is largely owing to her success in having made an extreme case of the virtue in question credible to the reader. Is it because this element is weaker in **Anne,** which was published in 1882, that **Anne** strikes me as the least happily composed of the author's works? The early chapters are charming and full of promise, but the story wanders away from them, and the pledge is not taken up. The reader has built great hopes upon Tita, but Tita vanishes into the vague, after putting him out of countenance by an infant marriage—an accident in regard to which, on the whole, throughout her stories, Miss Woolson shows perhaps an excessive indulgence. She likes the unmarried, as I have mentioned, but she likes marriages even better, and also sometimes hurries them forward in advance of the reader's forecast. The only complaint it would occur to me to make of **East Angels** is that Garda Thorne, whom we cannot think of as anything but a little girl, discounts the projects we have formed for her by marrying twice; and somehow the case is not bettered by the fact that nothing is more natural than that she *should* marry twice, unless it be that she should marry three times. We have perceived her, after all, from the first, to be peculiarly adapted to a succession of pretty widowhoods.

For the Major has an idea, a little fantastic perhaps, but eminently definite. This idea is the secret effort of an elderly woman to appear really as young to her husband as (owing to peculiar circumstances) he believed her to be when he married her. Nature helps her (she happens to preserve, late in life, the look of comparative youth), and art helps nature, and her husband's illusions, fostered by failing health and a weakened brain, help them both, so that she is able to keep on the mask till his death, when she pulls it off with a passionate cry of relief—ventures at last, gives herself the luxury, to be old. The sacrifice in this case has been the sacrifice of the maternal instinct, she having had a son, now a man grown, by a former marriage, who reappears after unsuccessful wanderings in far lands, and whom she may not permit herself openly to recognize. The sacrificial attitude is indeed repeated on the part of her step-daughter, who, being at last taken into Madam Carroll's confidence, suffers the young man—a shabby, compromising, inglorious acquaintance—to pass for her lover, thereby discrediting herself almost fatally (till the situation is straightened out) with the Rev. Frederick Owen, who has really been marked out by Providence for the character, and who cannot explain on any comfortable hypothesis her relations with the mysterious Bohemian. Miss Woolson's women in general are capable of these refinements of devotion and exaltations of conscience, and she has a singular talent for making our sympathies go with them. The conception of Madam Carroll is highly ingenious and original, and the small stippled portrait has a real fascination. It is the first time that a woman has been represented as painting her face, dyeing her hair, and "dressing young" out of tenderness for another; the effort usually has its source in tenderness for herself. But Miss Woolson has done nothing of a neater execution than this fanciful figure of the little ringleted, white-frocked, falsely juvenile lady, who has the toilet-table of an actress and the conscience of a Puritan.

The author likes a glamour, and by minute touches and gentle, conciliatory arts she usually succeeds in producing a valid one. If I had more space I should like to count over these cumulative strokes, in which a delicate manipulation of the real is mingled with an occasionally frank appeal to the romantic muse. But I can only mention two of the most obvious: one the frequency of her reference to the Episcopal Church, as an institution giving a tone to American life (the sort of tone which it is usually assumed that we must seek in civilizations more permeated with ecclesiasticism); the other her fondness for family histories—for the idea of perpetuation of race, especially in the backward direction. I hasten to add that there is nothing of the crudity of sectarianism in the former of these manifestations, or of the dreariness of the purely genealogical passion in the latter; but none the less is it clear that Miss Woolson likes little country churches that are dedicated to saints not vulgarized by too much notoriety, that are dressed with greenery (and would be with holly if there were any) at Christmas and Easter; that have "rectors," well connected, who are properly garmented, and organists, slightly deformed if possible, and addicted to playing Gregorian chants in the twilight, who are adequately artistic; likes also generations that have a pleasant consciousness of a few warm generations behind them, screening them in from too bleak a past, from vulgar draughts in the rear. I know not whether for the most part we are either so Episcopal or so long-descended as in Miss

Woolson's pages we strike ourselves as being, but it is certain that as we read we protest but little against the soft impeachment. She represents us at least as we would like to be, and she does so with such discretion and taste that we have no fear of incurring ridicule by assent. She has a high sense of the picturesque, and cannot get on without a social atmosphere. Once, I think, she has looked for these things in the wrong place—at the country boarding-house denominated Caryl's—in *Anne,* where there must have been flies and grease in the dining-room, and the ladies must have been overdressed; but as a general thing her quest is remarkably happy. She stays at home, and yet gives us a sense of being "abroad"; she has a remarkable faculty, of making the New World seem old. She succeeds in representing Far, Edgerly, the mountain village in *For the Major,* as bathed in the precious medium I speak of. Where is it meant to be, and where was the place that gave her the pattern of it? We gather vaguely, though there are no negroes, that it is in the South; but this, after all, is a tolerably indefinite part of the United States. It is somewhere in the midst of forests, and yet it has as many idiosyncrasies as Mrs. Gaskell's *Cranford,* with added possibilities of the pathetic and the tragic. What new town is so composite? what composite town is so new? Miss Woolson anticipates these questions; that is, she prevents us from asking them; we swallow Far Edgerly whole, or say at most, with a sigh, that if it couldn't have been like that, it certainly ought to have been.

It is, however,, in *East Angels* that she has been most successful in this feat of evoking a local tone, and this is a part of the general superiority of that very interesting work, which to my mind represents a long stride of her talent, and has more than the value of all else she has done. In *East Angels* the attempt to create an atmosphere has had, to a considerable degree, the benefit of the actual quality of things in the warm, rank peninsula which she has studied so exhaustively and loves so well. Miss Woolson found an atmosphere in Florida, but it is not too much to say that she has left it still more agreeably dense—converted it into a fine golden haze. Wonderful is the tact with which she has pressed it into the service of her story, draped the bare spots of the scene with it, and hung it there half as a curtain and half as a background. *East Angels* is a performance which does Miss Woolson the highest honor, and if her talent is capable, in another novel, of making an advance equal to that represented by this work in relation to its predecessors, she will have made a substantial contribution to our new literature of fiction. Long, comprehensive, copious, still more elaborate than her other elaborations, *East Angels* presents the interest of a large and well-founded scheme. The result is not flawless at every point, but the undertaking is of a fine, high kind, and for the most part the effect produced is thoroughly worthy of it. The author has, in other words, proposed to give us the complete natural history, as it were, of a group of persons collected, in a complicated relationship, in a little winter city on a Southern shore, and she has expended on her subject stores of just observation and an infinite deal of the true historical spirit. How much of this spirit and of artistic feeling there is in the book only an attentive perusal will reveal. The central situation is a very interesting one, and is triumphantly treated, but I confess that what is most substantial to me in the book is the writer's general conception of her task, her general attitude of watching life, waiting upon it, and trying to catch it in the fact. I know not what theories she may hold in relation to all this business, to what camp or league she may belong; my impression, indeed, would be that she is perfectly free—that she considers that though camps and leagues may be useful organizations for looking for the truth, it is not in their own bosom that it is usually to be found. However this may be, it is striking that, artistically, she has had a fruitful instinct in seeing the novel as a picture of the actual, of the characteristic—a study of human types and passions, of the evolution of personal relations.

In *East Angels* the sacrifice, as all Miss Woolson's readers know, is the great sacrifice of Margaret Harold, who immolates herself—there is no other word—deliberately, completely, and repeatedly, to a husband whose behavior may as distinctly be held to have absolved her. The problem was a very interesting one, and worthy to challenge a superior talent—that of making real and natural a transcendent, exceptional act representing a case in which the sense of duty is raised to exaltation. What makes Margaret Harold's behavior exceptional and transcendent is that, in order to render the barrier between herself and the man who loves her, and whom she loves, absolutely insurmountable, she does her best to bring about his marriage, and endeavors to put another woman into the frame of mind to respond to him in the event (possible, as she is a woman whom he once appeared to love) of his attempting to console himself for a bitter failure. The care, the ingenuity, the precautions, the author has exhibited to make us accept Mrs. Harold in her integrity are perceptible on every page, and they leave us finally no alternative but to accept her. She remains exalted, but she remains at the same time thoroughly sound; for it is not a simple question of cleverness of detail, but a question of the larger sort of imagination, and Margaret Harold would have halted considerably if her creator had not taken the supreme precaution of all, and conceived her from the germ as capable of a certain heroism—of clinging at the cost of a grave personal loss to an idea which she believes to be a high one, and taking such a fancy to it that she endeavors to paint it, by a refinement of magnanimity, with still richer hues. She is a picture,

not of a woman indulging in a great spasmodic flight or moral *tour de force,* but of a nature bent upon looking at life from a high point of view, an attitude in which there is nothing abnormal, and which the author illustrates, as it were, by a test case. She has drawn Margaret with so close and firm and living a line that she seems to put us in the quandary, if we repudiate her, of denying that a woman *may* look at life from a high point of view. She seems to say to us: "Are there distinguished natures, or are there not? Very well, if there are, that's what they can do—they can try and provide for the happiness of others (when they adore them) even to their own injury." And we feel that we wish to be the first to agree that there *are* distinguished natures.

Garda Thorne is the next best thing in the book to Margaret, and she is indeed equally good in this, that she is conceived with an equal clearness. But Margaret produces her impression upon us by moving before us and doing certain things, whereas Garda is more explained, or rather she explains herself more, tells us more about herself. She says somewhere, or some one says of her, that she doesn't narrate, but in fact she does narrate a good deal, for the purpose of making the reader understand her. This the reader does, very constantly, and Garda is a brilliant success. I must not, however, touch upon the different parts of *East Angels,* because in a work of so much patience and conscience a single example carries us too far. I will only add that in three places in especial the author has been so well inspired as to give a definite pledge of high accomplishment in the future. One of these salient passages is the description of the closing days of Mrs. Thorne, the little starved yet ardent daughter of the Puritans, who has been condemned to spend her life in the land of the relaxed, and who, before she dies, pours out her accumulations of bitterness—relieves herself in a passionate confession of everything she has suffered and missed, of how she has hated the very skies and fragrances of Florida, even when, as a consistent Christian, thankful for every mercy, she has pretended most to appreciate them. Mrs. Thorne is the pathetic, tragic form of the type of which Mrs. Stowe's Miss Ophelia was the comic. In almost all of Miss Woolson's stories the New England woman is represented as regretting the wholesome austerities of the region of her birth. She reverts to them, in solemn hours, even when, like Mrs. Thorne, she may appear for a time to have been converted to mild winters. Remarkably fine is the account of the expedition undertaken by Margaret Harold and Evert Winthrop to look for Lanse in the forest, when they believe him, or his wife thinks there may be reason to believe him, to have been lost and overtaken by a storm. The picture of their paddling the boat by torchlight into the reaches of the river, more or less smothered in the pestilent jungle, with the personal drama, in the unnatural place, reaching an acute stage between them—this whole episode is in a high degree vivid, strange, and powerful. Lastly, Miss Woolson has risen altogether to the occasion in the scene in which Margaret "has it out," as it were, with Evert Winthrop, parts from him, and leaving him baffled and unsurpassably sore, gives him the measure of her determination to accept the necessity of her fate. These three episodes are not alike, yet they have, in the high finish of Miss Woolson's treatment of them, a family resemblance. Moreover, they all have the stamp which I spoke of at first—the stamp of the author's conservative feeling, the implication that for her the life of a woman is essentially an affair of private relations.

Arthur Hobson Quinn (essay date 1936)

SOURCE: "Place and Race in American Fiction," in *American Fiction: An Historical and Critical Survey,* D. Appleton-Century Company, 1936, pp. 332-42.

[*In the following excerpt, Quinn discusses Woolson's ability to blend vibrant descriptions of physical settings with the actions of realistic characters.*]

Usually a novelist's impulse to deal with the life of a locality was confined to one section, but Constance Fenimore Woolson dealt not only with the North-west and the South but also with the European scene. She was born in Claremont, New Hampshire, in 1840, her mother, Hannah Cooper Pomeroy Woolson, being the niece of James Fenimore Cooper. She was educated in Cleveland, Ohio, and as a girl spent her summers at Mackinac Island in the straits between Lake Huron and Lake Michigan. In 1858 she graduated from Madame Chegary's school in New York City, which was to appear in her novel *Anne,* and began her contributions to periodicals with a sketch, **"The Happy Valley,"** in *Harper's* for July, 1870. This description of a German community on the Tuscarawas River in Ohio, which she used later in a short story, **"Wilhemina,"** was her first article to be written and shows how like Howells she began with an interest in the scene, out of which characters later developed. In the same month her sketch, **"The Fairy Island,"** a description of Mackinac Island, appeared in *Putnam's.* With this Lake region she was thoroughly familiar, and when she turned to it as material for fiction, after a few preliminary stories of a somewhat conventional character, it is interesting to see how the quality of her work improved. Even in a comparatively poor story, **"One Versus Two,"** the writing becomes alive when the characters reach the Lake country.[2] From 1872 to 1878 she made the Lake country the background for twenty-three stories.[3]

Miss Woolson had the rare gift of self-criticism, and her selection for her first volume of stories, *Castle*

Nowhere; Lake Country Sketches (1875), includes the most significant of her early work, although **"A Flower of the Snow,"**[4] might easily have been included. How far she had come in three years may be seen by comparing this book with her first published volume, *The Old Stone House* (1873), a rather pietistic story for children. How strong Bret Harte's influence was upon her is seen in the story **"Misery Landing,"** in which the hero, who has fled from a love he does not wish to pursue, tells in his diary his admiration for Harte, "who shows us the good in the heart of the outcast," and who makes the shrewd observation that "everywhere it is the cultivated people only who are taken with Bret." **"The Lady of Little Fishing"** shows even more clearly Harte's influence. The narrator, Mitchell, tells of the saintly woman who suddenly appeared among the rough hunters and trappers, thirty years before, and preached to them, so that they worshipped her. The relapse of the rough men when they discover their idol is simply a woman, is not badly done, and the fact that the narrator is the one she loved is concealed to make a dramatic ending. It is the "moral contrast" again. Some of the stories deal with Mackinac Island, some with the shores of Lake Superior, some with Ohio. Nearly always, however, the scenery is the background; the central character is an outsider who proves sometimes a disturbing influence or, as in **"The Old Agency,"** in which she describes from real life the courtly French priest who forms such a contrast to his parishioners, he is a mystery and a benediction. Miss Woolson, like Bret Harte, remains an observer rather than a partaker of the life. But her descriptions of the marshes in **"St. Clair Flats"** or of the fog in **"Castle Nowhere"** are masterly.

On account of her mother's health, Miss Woolson was constantly traveling, and between 1873 and 1879 she spent her time largely in Florida and the Carolinas. The result came, as before, in the form of travel sketches, short stories, and novels. Between 1875 and 1879 she published fourteen short stories with a Southern background. The best of these are included in *Rodman the Keeper* (1880). She used first the Florida scene. **"Miss Elisabetha,"** laid before the Civil War, is a tragic story of the efficient Northern woman who manages the life of her ward, "Doro," keeps him from his proper career and sees him sink into contented laziness. **"The South Devil"** is one of her finest achievements. The way she establishes the mystical relation between the great swamp and Carl, the young musician who hears the harmonies the swamp sings only to him, and who cannot keep away from it though it may mean death to him, reveals her great power of understanding the relations of place and human character. It is not only vivid descriptions of the "rank luxuriance of the heart of the swamp, a riot of intoxicating, steaming, swarming, fragrant, beautiful tropical life, without man to make* or mar it. All the world was once so, before man was made." The swamp is active, living. When Mark goes into it to save his brother, "the matted water vines caught at his boat like hundreds of hands; the great lily leaves slowly sank and let the light boat glide over them." In **"Sister St. Luke,"** a story of the boundless courage of a timid Spanish nun who saves two shipwrecked men from the tornado, Miss Woolson not only showed her knowledge of the seacoast of Florida, but also revealed the breadth of her understanding of races not her own. So in **"Felipa,"** the passionate devotion of a little Minorcan girl to a man and a woman, themselves lovers, whom she adores in different ways, is rendered powerfully and objectively.

Next Miss Woolson turned to the mountain regions of Tennessee and western North Carolina. But in her first story of this region, "Crowder's Cove,"[5] the mountaineer, John Crowder, appears only as a "neutral" in the Civil War, and the main characters are a New England woman and a Southern girl of very different origin from the mountain people. Even in **"Up in the Blue Ridge,"** which appeared in *Appleton's* for August, 1878, three months after Miss Murfree's first story had been published in the *Atlantic,* the mountaineers are described but are only the background. The conflict is between the Northern characters like Stephen Wainwright and John Royce, and the Southerner Richard Eliot, who, though he is associated with a gang of moonshiners, is distinctly one of the planter class. The story is really a study of the reactions of Wainwright, who risks his life to save Eliot, because of his interest in Honor Dooris, Eliot's cousin.

Much more significant than her stories of the mountaineers are Miss Woolson's sympathetic revelations of the conditions in Reconstruction days in the South. **"Old Gardiston,"** laid in no very definite spot in the rice lands of the Carolinas, is a touching picture of a girl's proud resistance to her growing love for a Northern officer, made real by the description of brave economies a man could not have imagined. **"In the Cotton Country,"** on the other hand, is a story of a woman's hopeless suffering from the effects of war, without any expectation of the future, a woman whose husband had been called away at the altar and whom she had never seen again. This picture of apathy, of courage only to endure, is as realistic as it well can be. It is to her credit also that while Negro rule was still being imposed upon the South with Federal bayonets, a Northern woman told through her fictional characters the truth. She made it even more evident in 1878 in **"King David,"** a story of a New England teacher who goes South to educate the Negroes and fails hopelessly because of their shiftlessness and drunkenness. It is another Northerner, a liquor-seller and political organizer, who helps to defeat him, but King David's failure is inherent because he tries to treat the Negroes as his equals. The very title shows her skill in her implication of the magnitude of the

problem. These, together with **"Rodman the Keeper,"** a study in the isolation of a Northern officer who becomes the warden of a Union cemetery in a Southern community, are the best of the post-war stories.

Miss Woolson began her first novel, *Anne* (1882), on the island of Mackinac, which she knew so well, and the scenes of Anne's girlhood as she grows up, a strong, tender, brave nature, meeting the responsibilities of her young step-sister Tita and the boys, when her father's death leaves them to her, have been the favorite portions of the book. There are remarkable character portraits in Miss Lois, a New England Puritan who had come out to convert the Indians, and the two clergymen, Père Michaux and Dr. Gaston, who watch over Anne. It seems a pity that after establishing so well these characters and the atmosphere of an army post in the 'fifties, Miss Woolson should have taken Anne away to New York City, to the school she herself had attended, but after all she builds up by deft touches the girl's reaction to the social organization which meets her with the cruelty which is the lot of "the islander." Her life under the patronage of her wealthy aunt gives Miss Woolson ample opportunity for keen social satire, and there has hardly ever been written a better picture of an American girl of character and natural breeding thrown into unconscious rivalry with women of the world, first suffering defeat and finally accomplishing victory. Anne's relations with Helen Lorrington and their rivalry for the love of Heathcote are developed with that insight into the capacity of women for friendship, love, and hate in which the realist again shone. There is, of course, too much in the novel, especially at the end, where Helen's murderer is brought to confession by means hardly credible; but the novel created marked critical approval even in its serial form in *Harper's Magazine.*[6]

In *For the Major* (1883) Miss Woolson showed none of the faults but all the virtues of *Anne.* It is much shorter, and the tone is kept with a restrained power that is almost beyond praise. The people are Southerners with high standards of conduct, living in **"Far Edgerley,"** a hill town on the eastern flank of **"Chillawassee Mountain"** in North Carolina. They are not mountaineers, however, but a little group of survivals from the past of the South. Major Scarborough Carroll; his second wife, Madam Marion Carroll; Sara, his daughter by his first wife; and **"Scar,"** his little son by his second, live on the Farms. He has been a distinguished man, but he is beginning to fail. The skill with which Marion Carroll guards the Major from the townspeople, so that his mental faltering shall not be apparent, even more the way she keeps Sara from tiring her father by insistence on his preserving the high ideals which Sara has had from her childhood about him, is unusual. Gradually through the conversations of different characters we learn, just as we do in real life, how Major Carroll has married

Marion, a widow much younger than himself, how her first husband had fled, after a shooting affray, taking their boy away with him, and how she had heard of the pursuit and the drowning of both of them. Beginning with gratitude, her love for the Major has grown into a devotion that makes her an epic figure. How she conceals her real age, not from vanity but because of the Major's delight in her youth, how her blonde beauty lends itself to her brave artifices, above all how her unwavering watchfulness fights for the security and peace which her earlier life makes precious to her, is told with an art that no one of that day could surpass. Then into that security comes the disturbing element. Her eldest son, who is not dead, finds her and, under an assumed name, comes to Far Edgerley. She cannot acknowledge him, and here Sara plays her part, acting as go-between and almost killing her own chance of happiness with the young rector, Frederick Owen, so that her father will not suffer. There is a remarkable scene in which Marion Carroll waits until the Major is asleep to go to the death-bed of her son, which for quiet heroism is hard to surpass. Then when the Major's mind finally fails and he becomes like a child, Mrs. Carroll at once relaxes her vigilance of years, becomes overnight her real age, and tells her story to Owen. The passage in which she reveals to Owen her well-guarded secret, is an example of the art of fiction in which a great novelist pays a tribute to the imaginative power of her reader:

> " . . . And now I must come to my second reason for telling you. You remember I said that there were two. This is something which even Sara does not know—I would not give her any of that burden; she could not help me, and she had enough to bear. She could not help me; but now you can. It is something I want you to do for me. It could not be done before, it could not be done until the Major became as he is at present. No one now living knows; still, as you are to be one of us, I should like to have you do it for me."

And then she told him.

Miss Woolson scorns to spoil her effect by explanations. But when Owen marries the Major to Marion, the reader suddenly realizes that this is the last gesture of a great soul, who, having learned from her son that her first husband was alive at the time of her marriage to Major Carroll, does what she can to make herself in truth the wife of the man she has loved so dearly. All her life she has lived for others; this at least she can do for herself.

If *For the Major* reminds one of an etching in which one central figure stands out in exquisite proportions against a background whose very limitations present that figure to perfection, *East Angels* (1886) is a glowing canvas, rich with color, where the characters gain each in his own way in vividness from their contrast or association with the rich languor of the Florida landscape. The principal actors are from the North. Miss Woolson proceeds to build up slowly a strong moral contrast between two groups of characters, those who insist upon doing right even at the cost of happiness and those who demand their own happiness and sweep ruthlessly aside anyone in their way. Margaret Harold, married at seventeen to a charming, selfish husband who leaves her for a French-woman shortly after their union, is one of those women who builds her life on self-sacrifice. Not only does she crush down the love she begins to feel for Evert Winthrop, but she does the harder thing—she bears quietly the implicit blame of the separation. Miss Woolson shows how the others, led by Mrs. Rutherford, a professional invalid who succeeds in making the attentions she demands from Margaret seem like a favor to her, all expect Margaret to "do her duty." Even Evert Winthrop is deceived at first, but when Lance Harold returns to Margaret, leaves her again and once more comes back, an invalid, Margaret has to combat not only her own desire but also Winthrop's determined passion. To draw a character whose achievement lies in renunciation is not easy, for her very inarticulate acceptance of the path she has chosen forbids the expression of her deep feeling. Winthrop's final restraint and respect for her determination are not so credible, but, as he is drawn, they were at least possible.

Mrs. Thorne, the owner of East Angels, is another illustration of self-sacrifice. A New England school teacher who had married a Southern planter of English descent, she is described delightfully by her neighbor, Mrs. Carew:

> " . . . However, I ought to say that poor little Mistress Thorne has certainly done her very best to acquire our Southern ways; she has actually tried to make herself over, root, stem, and branch, from her original New England sharpness to our own softer temperament, though I always feel sure, at the same moment, that, in the core of the rock, the old sap burns still—like the soul under the ribs of death, you know; not that I mean that exactly (though she *is* thin), but simply that the leopard cannot change his spots, nor the zebra his stripes, nor," added the good lady—altering her tone to solemnity as she perceived that her language was becoming Biblical—"the wild *cony* her *young.* . . . "

Mrs. Thorne's desperate sense of duty, which makes her try to become a Southern woman, while she prays secretly during the Civil War for "her own people," leads to a remarkable scene on her death-bed when she confides to Margaret how she has loathed the life she has had to live. Opposed to these stern self-schooled people are not only Lance Harold and Mrs. Rutherford, who are drawn with malicious insight, but, more important, Garda Thorne, Mrs. Thorne's daughter. With a good deal of Spanish blood, her beauty, her utter selfishness and her rapidly changing emotional reactions make her very much alive. Miss Woolson does not draw any conclusions or preach any lesson; nor does she reward her good characters, like George Eliot, with the satisfaction of self-respect. They are unhappy, but they cannot do otherwise. Marriage, to Margaret Harold, is for better or worse, and divorce is out of the question.

There are some remarkable scenes, as usual, in *East Angels.* The landscape plays its part in the nightlong search of Winthrop and Margaret for Lance in the great swamp with its deadly poisonous sweetness. And how well Miss Woolson conveys her knowledge of woman's nature in the conversation between Margaret and Winthrop concerning Garda:

> "We seem to have much the same idea of her," said Winthrop. "I shouldn't have thought it possible," he added.
>
> "That we should agree in anything?" said Margaret, with a faint smile.
>
> "No, not that; but a woman so seldom has the same idea of another woman that a man has. And—if you will allow me to say it—I think the man's idea often the more correct one, for a woman will betray (confide, if you like the term better) more of her inner nature, her real self, to a man, when she knows him well and likes him, than she ever will to any woman, no matter how well she may know and like her."
>
> Margaret concurred in this.
>
> "So you agree with me there too? Another surprise! What I have said is true enough, but women generally dispute it."
>
> "What you have said is true, after a fashion," Margaret answered. "But the inner feelings you speak of, the real self, which a woman confides to the man she likes rather than to a woman, these are generally her ideal feelings, her ideal self; what she thinks she feels, or hopes to feel, rather than the actual feeling; what she wishes to be, rather than what she is. She may or may not attain her ideal; but in the mean time she is judged, by those of her own sex at least, according to her present qualities, what she has already attained; what she is practically, and every day."

In *Jupiter Lights* (1889), Miss Woolson combined the coast of Georgia and the Lake country, but as usual the characters dominate the scene. In Eve Bruce, a Northern woman who comes to Romney Island in the sounds south of Savannah, Miss Woolson depicted a strong-willed nature, impatient of the weaker but none the

less tenacious Southern woman, her brother's widow. Her horror when she finds Cicely has remarried, her rescue of Cicely and her little nephew from the crazed dipsomaniac husband, her flight with them to Port aux Pins on Lake Superior, and her own ultimate love story make up a novel with more action than is usual with Miss Woolson, some of it, especially the final scenes in Italy, being too melodramatic. It is, however, a fine study of the havoc made by any woman who tries to manage another's life.

So far Miss Woolson had made a woman the central character of her novels, but in her last, *Horace Chase* (1894), she presented a study of the self-made man, thirty-seven years old, who marries a girl of nineteen, Ruth Franklin. The Franklins are from New York but live either in Asheville, North Carolina, or at St. Augustine because they have been left property there by an aunt who belonged to a North Carolina family. The situation is one of frequent occurrence in which a family without much energy depend upon a strong nature and at the same time secretly look down upon him as beneath their social stratum. Horace Chase dominates the novel, and his reception of Ruth's confession of her infatuation for a younger man, and her journey to her lover only to find he has forgotten her, is quite in keeping with a largeness of view which success has given Chase. But while there is good character analysis, especially of the women, who care more for the son and brother than they do for each other, *Horace Chase* does not leave the same sense of artistic completeness as do the earlier novels.

Miss Woolson's later short stories were concerned largely with European scenes. After her mother's death in 1879, she went to England and the Continent, staying most frequently in Italy. Her first short story written abroad, **"Miss Grief,"**[7] is of special interest because the central character is a woman who dies of privation rather than change her powerful but crude drama to suit the critical judgment of a popular author. Curiously enough, it was not included in either of the two collections published after her death, *The Front Yard and Other Italian Stories* (1895) and *Dorothy and Other Italian Stories* (1896), for it is one of the best. The similarity of this theme to some of those used later by Henry James is also noteworthy, since it was in 1880, under his guidance, that she grew to know Florence, her favorite among Italian cities. In these later stories, the American characters are the most important; sometimes indeed they are the only ones. The European scene remains the background, but it is an integral part of the narrative. Sometimes, as in **"The Street of the Hyacinth,"**[8] it is the belief that she can paint which brings an American girl to Rome, but it is her poise and courage under disappointment that lend distinction to the narrative. In **"The Front Yard"**[9] not only the scene but also the Italian characters form a contrast to the

American. This is a fine study of a New England woman, Prudence Wilkins, who has married an Italian and who takes care of his family after his death, including a terrible old woman, the grandmother of his first wife. Living in Assisi, Prudence is oblivious to its meaning. To her life is not beauty but duty. The one thing she longs for is a "front yard" such as she had had in New Hampshire, but each time she saves up enough to start one, she makes a new sacrifice for her adopted family. Courage and fixity of purpose make the Americans in the later stories memorable. The way Mrs. Azubah Ash, an elderly woman, rises to command the situation after her son has killed his rival in **"Neptune's Shore,"**[10] the clear grit of the fourteen-year-old lad in **"A Transplanted Boy,"**[11] who plays a man's part, without heroics; both are revelations of a power that showed no sign of weakening.

When the social scene is important, her Americans are never the vague uncertain figures of Henry James. Even the expatriated Americans like Mrs. Churchill in **"A Pink Villa"** are real. But what distinguishes Miss Woolson's stories from the usual magazine fiction is the way she can fix a character with one brief sentence. "No vulgar affluence oppressed Isabella. She had six hundred dollars a year of her own and each dollar was well bred." Her art is a fine art; one returns to her fiction for the sheer joy in well-controlled creation. She knew her own limitations as well as those of her characters. For the daring female of literature she had no respect, and she puts the case for her own manner brilliantly in one of her short stories, **"At the Chateau of Corinne."** In her delicate and distinguished art, she and Miss Jewett represented at its height that ability to guide with a firm hand the steeds of imagination and introspection which carried the so-called feminine impulse in American fiction very far toward perfection. Henry James in his *Partial Portraits* chose to place her with George Eliot, Trollope, and Turgenev, and his judgment was sounder than that which has apparently forgotten her. But at the time of her death (she fell or threw herself from her window in Venice in 1894), she was recognized as one of the most consummate artists in that great epoch of the novel.

Notes

. . . .[2] *Lippincott's,* August, 1872.

[3] See Kern, John D., *Constance Fenimore Woolson* (1934), for a complete analysis of these stories.

[4] *Galaxy,* January, 1874.

[5] *Appleton's Journal,* March 18, 1876.

[6] See J. Henry Harper, *The House of Harper,* 484-487.

[7] *Lippincott's Magazine,* May, 1880.

[8] *Century Magazine,* May-June, 1882.

[9] *Harper's Magazine,* December, 1888.

[10] *Harper's Magazine,* October, 1888.

[11] *Harper's Magazine,* February, 1894.

Alexander Cowie (essay date 1948)

SOURCE: "Local-Color, Frontier and Regional Fiction," in *The Rise of the American Novel,* American Book Company, 1948, pp. 568-78.

[*In the following essay, Cowie studies Woolson's five novels and argues that their principal qualities are simplicity of plot, realism of character and dialogue, and precision of description.*]

An author able to elicit the high praise of so austere a critic as Henry James may be assumed to have mastered important elements in the technique of writing.[84] Praise from such a quarter would indeed for some people be presumptive evidence that the writer was more skilled than readable. Yet Constance Fenimore Woolson was not only an able craftsman but also in the 1880's and 1890's a popular writer, especially with that relatively superior audience comprised in part of readers of magazines such as *Harper's,* in which many of her stories first appeared. Her popularity of course has long since waned, and she is now in the familiar category of the superior minor writer who is periodically "rediscovered" by a sensitive critic or a zealous historian. No number of such discoveries, of course, can make her over into a major novelist. At best her art was extremely sensitive and delicate. True, she undoubtedly won many readers by the sensational, even melodramatic, materials which she sometimes ineptly introduced into her work. Yet vigorous action was not her forte: it is vain to look in her work for any suggestion of the broad powers of her illustrious kinsman (her mother was a niece of James Fenimore Cooper). The structure of a long narrative she never mastered. It is her distinction, rather, that she skilfully employed some aspects of that type of impressionistic technique which was one of the principal interests of the more serious post-Victorian novelists. She also added to the domain of the local-color writers who were prominent in the seventies and eighties.

Miss Woolson was born in New Hampshire, educated in Ohio, "finished" at a school in New York City, lived for several years in the South (Florida and the Carolinas), and traveled extensively in Europe.[85] She practiced writing at an early age, producing rapidly a considerable number of tales and sketches, the more successful of which are set in the Great Lakes country, where she spent her childhood. Her first volume of short stories, **Castle Nowhere; Lake Country Sketches** (1875), reprinted a number of pieces that had won favorable comment upon their first appearance in *Harper's, Lippincott's, The Galaxy,* and elsewhere. Her first novel, **Anne,** was published in 1882, and her last, **Horace Chase,** in 1894, the year of her death.

Anne is a long book, presumably autobiographical in the first part and certainly set in a region which the author well knew. Its action, surprisingly enough, is often sentimental, morbid, and melodramatic. The heroine is Anne Douglas, at sixteen a very large girl regarded as a conscientious but somewhat colorless person. Unlike her immediate predecessors in popular fiction, she is not superficially alluring: "This unwritten face, with its direct gaze, so far neutralized the effect of the Diana-like form that the girl missed beauty on both sides."[86] The devoted daughter of a cultivated and amiable but eccentric old gentleman no longer gainfully employed, she does her best to stabilize his shaky personality and to bring up the four somewhat difficult children of his second marriage. Comforts are few and life is slow for Anne Douglas on the remote island (Mackinac) which is her home. Romance crosses her path in the person of a village lad named Rast, who asks her hand in marriage. But Rast must go off to college and, her father dying suddenly, Anne feels that she must accept the offer of a relative in New York who wishes to give her a year of tony schooling to the end that she may later become a teacher. New York itself proves to be a school of experience of more consequence to the story than the fussy little establishment of Mme Moreau, and Anne is involved with two men, one of them a millionaire who wishes to marry her. The other (Heathcote), to whom Anne is more drawn, is prevented from offering marriage by reason of a commitment to one of Anne's friends, Helen Lorrington. Anne, like a good domestic heroine, runs away. But Heathcote later comes back into her life: he has married Helen but loves Anne! Though now freed from her somewhat tepid engagement to Rast—whose heart has been successfully stormed by one of Anne's stepsisters, the bewitching, ruthless little quarter-breed Tita—Anne resists the entreaties of Heathcote. Ultimately the story broadens into melodrama: Helen is found murdered and it devolves upon Anne to do enough amateur detective work to prove that Heathcote did not perpetrate the deed: the real murderer was left-handed! And Anne gets Heathcote—or vice versa. The story is much too diffuse. It is best in the first part-in the charming description of Anne's circumscribed life on the island. Her queer old father is a more satisfactory character than Heathcote. The portrait of the housekeeper, Lois Hinsdale, is fine: a New England spinster whose severity in the kitchen is balanced by her High Church religious preference. Un-

consciously in love with Douglas, she has bitterly resented his (second) marriage to a giddy female of French and Indian blood and of Catholic faith; but she does not weary of caring for his children, and she helps to bind together a story that often threatens to break completely into fragments.

Yet some of the fragments are precious. The opening of the story provides an excellent illustration of Miss Woolson's meticulous impressionistic method. Eschewing the traditional (Victorian) type of beginning—in which the author plainly states what he regards as essential facts for the reader: where the scene is, what sorts of persons are in it, what the time is, what the activity of the moment is, etc.—Miss Woolson, like James, begins at once to communicate an experience *in the present*. She does not wish to tell or relate an action but to present it; not to "introduce" a story but to begin it. Necessary facts will be found as experience is unfolded. Characters are not summarized but will grow out of detailed impressions.[87] The quality of the whole book will be felt from the very beginning: indeed Miss Woolson at her best concretely illustrates James's opinion that

> A novel is a living thing, all one and continuous, like any other organism, and in proportion as it lives will it be found, I think, that in each of the parts there is something of each of the other parts.[88]

Thus Miss Woolson does not begin with a statement of the "inorganic" facts (1) that it was Christmas Eve on Mackinac Island; (2) that a father was conversing affectionately with his daughter while she was decorating a provincial church; (3) that they have different opinions about a valued housekeeper named Lois, etc. etc. Instead, she opens a dialogue which begins to reveal the characters not only of the speakers but of the third person as well. It will be seen that the quality of these paragraphs is precisely that of all other valid parts of the book:

> "Does it look well, father?"
>
> "What, child?"
>
> "Does this look well?"
>
> William Douglas stopped playing for a moment, and turned his head toward the speaker, who, standing on a ladder, bent herself to one side, in order that he might see the wreath of evergreen, studded with cones, which she had hung on the wall over one of the small arched windows.
>
> "It is too compact, Anne, too heavy. There should be sprays falling from it here and there, like a real vine. The greenery, dear, should be either growing naturally upward or twining; large branches standing

in the corners like trees, or climbing vines. Stars, stiff circles, and set shapes should be avoided. That wreath looks as though it had been planed by a carpenter."

"Miss Lois made it."

"Ah," said William Douglas, something which made you think of a smile, although no smile was there, passing over his face, "it looks like her work; it will last a long time. And there will be no need to remove it for Ash-Wednesday, Anne; there is nothing joyous about it."

"I did not notice that it was ugly," said the girl, trying in her bent posture to look at the wreath, and bringing one eye and a portion of anxious forehead to bear upon it.

"That is because Miss Lois made it," replied William Douglas, returning to his music.[89]

It would be hard to find in fiction of the time an example of more skilful indirect characterization than is here presented. True, the reader must wait for the gradual absorption of these details into the whole body of the work to understand their full relationship to structure. True, also, Miss Woolson falls away, as *Anne* proceeds, from the high technical standard here exemplified, but the same method reappears, more evenly sustained, in her next long narrative, *For the Major* (1883).

For the Major (called by the author a "novelette") is more successful as a whole than *Anne* perhaps because its action is simpler and, except for a few exciting episodes, more suited to her special talent for finely discriminating effects. The situation fundamentally involves two venial deceptions that undoubtedly appealed to Henry James. The first is revealed shortly after Sara Carroll returns from Connecticut to Far Edgerley, a small secluded community presumably set in the mountains of North Carolina. She at first feels queerly frustrated in her attempt to resume the filial relationship with her father which had always been such a joy to her. Jealously she blames Madam Carroll, Major Carroll's second wife. When, however, the latter finally explains that the Major's mind is beginning to fail, Sara promptly co-operates with her in devising every protection for him. This involves coping with an unforeseen crisis that calls for a second deception. The appearance in Far Edgerley of a poverty-stricken, impudently vagabondish musician called Louis Dupont arouses the resentment of Far Edgerley, but Sara's step-mother astonishingly takes him up. Even more incredible to Mr. Owen, the Episcopal clergyman in love with Sara, is the fact that Sara has several clandestine meetings with the gay but sinister Bohemian. As if to end all gossip, Sara stuns the community by announcing her engagement to Dupont.

Actually she has no intention of marrying him: he is the son of her step-mother! She has been conspiring with her step-mother to take care of him without revealing to the Major (or to the gossipy village) the true facts concerning Madam Carroll's first marriage. Her husband had been a rotter who had finally killed a man in a duel and fled from the law, taking their boy with him. Both were reported drowned. Left with a ten-year-old girl to support, the mother passed herself off as twenty-three (though she was thirty-five) when the Major courted her, her excuse being that she couldn't bear to destroy the pleasure the Major took in her "youth" and that she needed protection for her daughter who, however, soon died. The stratagem thus begun has to be carried out through the ensuing years by means of dye, rouge, and kindred arts. When the son turned up, the critical condition of the Major forbade an explanation. The son presently dies, but on his deathbed reports that the father had also escaped death by drowning, and was living at the time of his mother's marriage to the Major. This intelligence necessitates a formal marriage with the Major. But the Major happily wakes up one morning with his mind almost completely gone, and it is easy to arrange a ceremony in which he takes part pleasantly with no knowledge of what it signifies. Madam Carroll has had to take Mr. Owen the clergyman into her confidence, of course, but that is now an easy matter, for he will soon himself belong to the family—as the husband of Sara.

Obviously *For the Major* contains plot material which would forbid the author's throwing stones at the artificial structures of the domestic novelists. Yet in this book as in others, it is not finally the exciting plot materials that the author is concerned with, but the motives of the characters.[90] The difference between Miss Woolson and the domestic sisterhood lies in her comparatively condensed treatment of crude plot material and her artful elaboration of ethical problems created in the minds first of Madam Carroll and then of Sara. The impressionistic characterizations of the step-mother pleased Henry James:

> The conception of Madam Carroll is highly ingenious and original, and the small stippled portrait has a real fascination . . . Miss Woolson has done nothing of a neater execution than this fanciful figure of the little ringleted, white-frocked, falsely juvenile lady, who has the toilet-table of an actress and the conscience of a Puritan.[91]

Sara Carroll is almost equally well characterized, though allowed less space. Despite temperamental differences between her and the Major's wife, she willingly shares in the bizarre fiction on which the Major's tenuous happiness rests. Even when her rôle calls for action that seriously damages her in the eyes of her lover, she does not flinch. The key to her character as to that of so many characters in the novels of Henry James is high-minded renunciation.

But quite as fascinating to watch as the raveling of the fantastic fabrication of Madam Carroll is the revelation of the nature of the community in which the story takes place. Far Edgerley, as James has implied, may be a bit too steeped in Anglicanism and provided with more suggested past than a town in the New World can actually be possessed of:

> . . . Miss Woolson likes little country churches that are dedicated to saints not vulgarised by too much notoriety, that are dressed with greenery (and would be with holly if there were any), at Christmas and Easter; that have "rectors," well connected, who are properly garmented, and organists, slightly deformed if possible, and addicted to playing Gregorian chants in the twilight, who are adequately artistic; likes also generations that have a pleasant consciousness of a few warm generations behind them, screening them in from too bleak a past, from vulgar draughts in the rear.[92]

Far Edgerley is brought to life perfectly with brush-strokes that are as faultless as they are gentle. Cranford is not more authentic. Much can be done by patience in a quiet community where the church is the centre of social life and where manners are so conservative that "There were persons in the congregation who considered whist-playing a test of the best churchmanship."[93] Genteel though these mountain folk be, they are so avid of personalia that the rector's every move coins local comment. Without effort Miss Woolson adjusts her tempo to miniature incident which, as in the following example, she often reports with genuine humor:

> Far Edgerley was deprived of its rector. Mr. Owen had gone to the coast to attend the Diocesan Convention. But as he had started more than a week before the time of its opening, and had remained a week after its sessions were ended, Mrs. General Hibbard was of the opinion that he was attending to other things as well. She had, indeed, heard a rumor before he came that there was *some one* (some one in whom he felt an interest) elsewhere. Now it is well known that there is nothing more depressing for a parish than a rector with an interest, large or small, "elsewhere." St. John in the Wilderness was therefore much relieved when its rector returned, with no signs of having left any portion of himself or his interest behind him. And Mrs. General Hibbard lost ground.[94]

The subsequent novels of Miss Woolson do not vary greatly in quality from her first two. Her principal theme continued to be magnanimity expressed in one form or another. In *East Angels* (1886) the main character is a dauntless, an almost incredible, illustra-

tion of self-sacrifice. Margaret, the wife of Lansing Harold, has every reason in the conduct of her husband to break with him and marry the affluent and cultivated Evert Winthrop. Instead she willingly shoulders the blame for her unharmonious marriage, resists the agreeable approaches of Winthrop, and when her husband finally returns as an invalid, devotes herself to nursing him. Isabel Archer in James's *The Portrait of a Lady* (1881) is not more heroic, though she is perhaps more real. But the unhappy marriage of the Harolds is only part of the excellent social study of St. Augustine which comprises *East Angels.* The novel also reports the affairs of a giddy group of pleasure-seekers of whom the most conspicuous, Garda Thorne, is a vivacious beauty who manages to get married twice. Her wanton conduct and obvious glamour make her a foil for the resolute Margaret. The book is comprehensive in its dramatis personae, being provided also with (principal) characters from the North, as well as full-blooded Spaniards, and the quarter-Spanish Garda. The characters, though individually well done, have a certain detached or "shipwrecked air"[95] but the Floridan mise-en-scène is firmly established in all its opulence and fascination. Yet by a very fine contrast which is perhaps referable to Miss Woolson's own origin in New England, the author draws one of her most successful characters in the exiled New Englander, Mrs. Thorne, who wholeheartedly hates the entire (Florida) section. Before her death she pours out all her long repressed love of her native region in a finely conceived speech which serves to emphasize the disparities that existed in "American" character in the 1870's. Mrs. Thorne, said James, is the "tragic form of the type of which Mrs. Stowe's Miss Ophelia was the comic."[95a] Against these and other characters Margaret Harold is seen, the utmost symbol of renunciation in personal relationships. *East Angels* is perhaps the fullest, the roundest, the most significant of Miss Woolson's novels.

With what fine integrity Miss Woolson observed her own principles as a writer was amusingly illustrated in a letter written in response to one from a young person who, like a majority of popular readers, would have preferred a happy ending in *East Angels*—a consummation that could easily have been arranged if the author had been willing to decree the death of Lansing Harold. Miss Woolson replies:

> My dear Miss Ethel.
>
> Your letter made me laugh,—it was so frank! It would indeed have been more agreeable for everyone, if Lansing Harold could have been (as you express it) "taken." But, in real life, such fortunate takings-off seldom occur, & it is real life I was endeavoring to picture. It is seldom indeed that I ask anyone to write to me, as I find it almost impossible to answer the letters I receive. But you are so honest that I propose that, after my next novel, you send

a few lines more; what do you say? About "the happy ending" you ask for, we will see![96]

As it happens Miss Woolson's next novel, *Jupiter Lights* (1889), is equipped with a "happy ending" but only after a great quantity of trouble has been seen. The novel is interesting as a local color story "with scenes from each of the three regions with which Miss Woolson is associated: the South, the lake country, and Italy." Miss Woolson is particularly successful in her delineation of the South during Reconstruction.[97] Yet the chief power of *Jupiter Lights* derives from the concentrated study of troubled personal relations, being in this case a study of a woman who interfered disastrously in the affairs of another. A whole train of difficulty is set in motion when Eve Bruce undertakes to meddle in the affairs of Cicely Morrison, formerly the widow of Eve's dead brother, now the wife of a dipsomaniac in a small rundown town on an island off the coast of Georgia during the period of Reconstruction. Results include a shooting, a flight to the Lake Superior region, the death of the degraded husband, a love affair for Eve, her retirement to a convent in Italy, and—the happy ending—her lover's arrival at the convent, where he "batters his way to her and takes her in his arms."[98] Hemingway could have handled this strong plot in its externals much more plausibly than Miss Woolson: he might even have strengthened it by tossing in a few more shootings, stronger drinks, and more general violence. But he would have been puzzled by the ethical problems of Eve who is so troubled about a point of honor (her part in the episode that resulted in Morrison's death) that, like James's high-minded Strether, she wants to have gained nothing for herself "out of the whole affair."[99] "Can have and will not"—that would be Hemingwayese for the attitude of many of the characters in Woolson. And it is precisely in the mental struggles of persons involved in such cases of casuistry that Miss Woolson, like James, succeeds most notably. In *Jupiter Lights,* however, the problem is largely lost in the frequently improbable action, and the book remains her least valuable novel. Miss Woolson can render setting and she can characterize quiet, well-bred people, but high tensions are likely to induce erratic fluctuations in the delicate instruments of her art.

Horace Chase (1894) marks a return to the narrower scope of action in which Miss Woolson moved with greatest freedom and sureness. Fundamentally it suffers from being too studied, too conscientious. It is unique among her novels in having for its centre of interest a man instead of a woman—in this case a successful businessman of considerable intelligence but of no great refinement. In type he is not far removed from James's Christopher Newman. His language is robust and colloquial. He is frankly interested in making money for the satisfaction of his ego: "For a big pile is something more than a pile; it's

a proof that a man's got brains."[100] The time comes when he must prove whether he has fineness of character as well as practical intelligence. His wife becomes infatuated with another man to the point of following him to the house of a friend—only to learn (what except for her blindness she should have known before) that he is interested not in her but in another girl, whom he is about to marry. No simple return to her own hearth is possible, for her husband untimely arrives at the house. A way out of making the embarrassing disclosure of her folly is devised by her sister, but doggedly the wife prefers to face the music, expecting to be sent away by an outraged husband. Instead, Horace Chase magnanimously but quietly indicates that he wishes her to stay: "Have I been so faultless myself that I have any right to judge *you?*"[101] This is a typical situation with Woolson: a character proves his fineness by making a difficult decision when, so far as external pressure is concerned, he is a perfectly free agent. In this case the gesture is one of forbearance rather than of renunciation. To make the scene a mess of sentimentality based upon incredible self-sacrifice would have been easy, but the author prefers to handle the situations with the quiet restraint befitting a realist. The story, she revealed in a letter to the publishers, was based on an instance "from actual life."[102] Her aim in the settings (Asheville, North Carolina, and St. Augustine) is to be utterly faithful to fact. The whole is a good miniature, possessed of much, perhaps too much, well-wrought detail. Yet that subtle process of artistic enlargement by which a work passes out of the specific into the universal is lacking in this book, as well as in most of Miss Woolson's work.

In Miss Woolson's novels the narrative situation is the thing. She carried no banners, religious, political, or sociological. Digressions seldom occur and such social criticism as she indulges in takes a subordinate place on her page. Yet her writing is informed with a realistic spirit that is gradually felt to be characteristic of her nature. Her childhood nickname "And why?" suggests in exaggerated form her critical proclivities. Thus she sees the beauty of the country but she realizes how a rural life limits the opportunities of the individual and intensifies the provincialism of the group, especially on the frontier. When in a minor matter Mlle Pitre fails to conform to village expectations, there is doubt about her integrity:

> Simple comment swelled into suspicion; the penny-saving old maid was now considered a dark and mysterious person at Lancaster. Opinions varied as to whether she had committed a crime in her youth, or intended to commit one in her age. At any rate, she was not like other people—in the country a heinous crime.[103]

The border Indians of the Great Lakes region were not only part of her story in *Anne* but also a sociological problem. Without sentiment or romance Miss Woolson candidly reports the difficulty experienced by white folk who attempted to civilize them:

> Years before, missionaries had been sent from New England to work among the Indians of this neighborhood, who had obtained their ideas of Christianity, up to that time, solely from the Roman Catholic priests, who had succeeded each other in an unbroken line from that adventurous Jesuit, the first explorer of these inland seas, Father Marquette. The Presbyterians came, established their mission, built a meeting-house, a school-house, and a house for their pastor, the buildings being as solid as their belief. Money was collected for this enterprise from all over New England, that old-time, devout, self-sacrificing community whose sternness and faith were equal; tall spare men came westward to teach the Indians, earnest women with bright steadfast eyes and lath-like forms were their aiders, wives, and companions . . . The missionaries worked faithfully; but, as the Indians soon moved further westward, the results of their efforts can not be statistically estimated now, or the accounts balanced.
>
> "The only good Indian is a dead Indian," is a remark that crystallizes the floating opinion of the border. But a border population has not a missionary spirit. New England, having long ago chased out, shot down, and exterminated all her own Indians, had become peaceful and pious, and did not agree with these Western carriers of shot-guns. Still, when there were no more Indians to come to this island school, it was of necessity closed, no matter which side was right.[104]

Occasionally she pauses to correct false notions implanted in the popular mind by more sensational writers. When, for example, Anne takes her place in a fashionable school in New York, her fine character does not make her either hated or sanctified. An intermediate reaction on the part of Anne's mates seems more natural to Miss Woolson:

> It was soon understood that "the islander" could sing as well as study. Tolerance was therefore accorded to her. But not much more. It is only in "books for the young" that poorly clad girls are found leading whole schools by the mere power of intellectual or moral supremacy. The emotional type of boarding-school, also, is seldom seen in cities; its home is amid the dead lethargy of a winter-bound country village.[105]

Similarly, the common conception of a nurse's romantic rôle during the Civil War is revised when a novice reaches the front:

> But during that day, not only did the promised nurse from the Rivertown Aid Society arrive, but with her

a volunteer assistant, a young girl, her face flushed with exaltation and excitement over the opportunity afforded her to help and comfort "our poor dear wounded heroes." The wounded heroes were not poetical in appearance; they were simply a row of ordinary sick men, bandaged in various ways, often irritable, sometimes profane; their grammar was defective, and they cared more for tobacco than for texts, or even poetical quotations.[106]

A fine restraint, then, distinguishes the realistic Miss Woolson from those scores of novelists who have erred on the opposite side of prolonged naturalistic descriptions of the horrors of war. Yet she does not lean over backward in this respect; and her sense of balance is shown by the fact that the same novice who found "her romance rudely dispelled" rose adequately to her situation; and since "there was good stuff in her, she would do useful work yet, although shorn of many illusions."[107] This is typical of the author in her better works: she prefers decent proportion to cheap intensity.

On the positive side (for Miss Woolson was not one to spend much time or effort upon correcting others) there was her original and vivid treatment of comparatively new regions; her pioneer studies of the difference between "the Anglo-Saxon and the Latin temperaments" in the South;[108] her faithful recording of Negro speech,[109] and her use of natural if unusually sensitive girls as heroines in place of the pasteboard saints of the popular novelists.[110] It was finally these heroines who inspired most of what was distinguished in the work of Constance Fenimore Woolson. She described their persons with a critical eye, understood the crises of their "private relations" with fine intuition, recorded their self-immolations with a quiet intensity that often lends exaltation to her page. Dynamic action jeopardized her art; larger structural units never quite found their equilibrium. But in the nooks and recesses of human experience she was wholly masterful. In *Anne* there is a church "whose steeple threw a slow-moving shadow across its garden, like a great sundial, all day." In some such sequestered place, where action is natural but unhurried, where light and shadow fulfill each other, belongs the special art of Miss Woolson.

Notes

[84] See James's *Partial Portraits,* London, 1888, Chapter VI.

[85] For a study of her life and writings see John Dwight Kern, *Constance Fenimore Woolson: Literary Pioneer,* Philadelphia, 1934. For such autobiography as is available in the abridged letters of Miss Woolson, see Clare Benedict (ed.), *Constance Fenimore Woolson,* London [1930]. This latter work is the second part of a three-volume study entitled *Five Generations (1785-1923).* For a brief biographi-

cal and critical study, see Lyon N. Richardson, "Constance Fenimore Woolson, 'Novelist Laureate' of America," *South Atlantic Quarterly* (January, 1940), XXXIX, 18-36.

[86] *Anne, A Novel,* New York, 1882, pp. 2, 3.

[87] Cf. an observation in one of her notebooks: "Character . . . should . . . grow and develop on the scene; in the book. Not to be introduced completely formed in the beginning." Clare Benedict (ed.), *Constance Fenimore Woolson,* p. 99. Few novelists of the nineteenth century (except Hawthorne and James) have left such copious laboratory or workshop notes—comment on technique, ideas for stories, etc.—as Miss Woolson . . . At many points her notes distinctly show her kinship with Hawthorne and James. Hawthorne might have been interested by this (*ibid.,* p. 137): "To imagine in an old Italian palace or villa a bell which rang at the top of a very high ceiling, now and then. No one can find any cord or handle to it!" A turn of thought that James might have found interesting (*ibid.,* p. 138): "An American who has lived so long abroad that he is almost de-nationalized, and *conscious of it fully;* which makes him an original figure."

[88] "The Art of Fiction," *Partial Portraits,* p. 392.

[89] *Anne,* pp. 1, 2.

[90] Cf. a comment in her notebook: "I care only for motives; why a man or woman does or has done so and so. Ditto a nation. It is the mental state—the mental problem that interests me." *Constance Fenimore Woolson,* pp. 118-19.

[91] *Partial Portraits,* p. 183. As it happens, James achieves this neat antithesis at some slight expense of truth. It was the daughter who was really the Puritan, as Madam makes it clear when she says in discussing her stratagem with Sara: "Under the same circumstances you would never have done it, nor under twenty times the same circumstances. But I am not you; I am not anybody but myself. That lofty kind of vision which sees only the one path, and that the highest, is not mine; I always see . . . the cross-cuts." *For the Major,* New York, 1883, p. 160.

[92] *Partial Portraits,* p. 184.

[93] *For the Major,* p. 179.

[94] *Ibid.,* p. 131.

[95] James, *op. cit.,* p. 187.

[95a] *Ibid.,* p. 191.

[96] Kern, *op. cit.,* p. 88.

[97] Indeed among Northern writers it was Miss Woolson who had the "surest grip upon a mood of plantation life, the bewildering numbness of that civilization after the full import of the change was realized." Gaines, *The Southern Plantation,* pp. 68-69. The poignant suffering of the South (spiritual and material) after the War is brought out in an almost perfect short story, "Old Gardiston" (published first in *Harper's Magazine* in 1876; collected in *Rodman the Keeper,* 1880).

[98] Kern, *op. cit.,* p. 91.

[99] Cf. below, p. 723.

[100] *Horace Chase, A Novel,* New York, 1894, pp. 269-70.

[101] *Ibid.,* p. 419.

[102] Kern, *op. cit.,* p. 94.

[103] *Anne,* pp. 185-86.

[104] *Ibid.,* pp. 53-54.

[105] *Ibid.,* p. 156.

[106] *Ibid.,* p. 368.

[107] *Ibid.*

[108] Cf. Kern, *op. cit.,* p. 176.

[109] In this, observed James, Miss Woolson antedated J. C. Harris. *Partial Portraits,* pp. 180-81.

[110] Cf. Miss Vanhorn's comment on another character in *Anne,* a character who reminds her of the "creole" type of beauty: "It is a novelty . . . which has made its appearance lately; a reaction after the narrow-chested type which has so long in America held undisputed sway. We absolutely take a quadroon to get away from the consumptive, blue-eyed saint, of whom we are all desperately tired." *Anne,* p. 196. The Creole was at about the same time making her fascinating appearance, it may be noted, in the works of G. W. Cable. . . .

Rayburn S. Moore (essay date 1963)

SOURCE: "The 'Immeasurable World of Print': The Short Fiction," in *Constance Fenimore Woolson,* Twayne Publishers, 1963, pp. 41-50.

[*In the essay that follows, Moore discusses Woolson's first collection of short stories and examines its increasingly sophisticated character development.*]

Constance Woolson's first contributions to the great national magazines were descriptive articles in the guise of fiction. She wrote of the Zoar Community in the Tuscarawas Valley of Ohio, of Mackinac in the far north of the Lake country, and of Lake Otsego near the ancestral home of the Coopers. Gradually she began to concentrate more on her characters and less on description, though she never lost her concern for setting and background even after she had lived for years in Europe. Her first sketches and stories dealt, with few exceptions, with the country she knew best—the Great Lakes area, Ohio, and New York. Later, after she had lived for some time in the South, she began to treat Southern characters and scenes in her fiction. Finally, when she had spent many years in Europe, she began to use European (especially Italian) characters and setting in her tales, though her favorite approach at this point in her career was to place Americans in Old World backgrounds. Thus she took advantage of her experience and of her knowledge of place to produce more than enough fiction to comprise four volumes of short stories: *Castle Nowhere* (1875); *Rodman the Keeper* (1880); *The Front Yard* (1895); and *Dorothy* (1896).

I. Castle Nowhere

Though she had won a prize for a volume she had written for children in 1872, Miss Woolson considered *Castle Nowhere: Lake-Country Sketches* her first book.[1] In it she brought together nine stories, all of which (with the exception of the title piece which was appearing for the first time) had been published first in the pages of the *Atlantic Monthly, Scribner's Monthly, Harper's New Monthly,* the *Galaxy,* and *Appletons' Journal*. These pieces, selected from a number of sketches dealing with lake-country settings and characters, represent, on the whole, her best work in this vein, though there are several other stories that might have been included in this volume.[2]

James R. Osgood, the Boston publisher, apparently suggested to Miss Woolson in 1874 that he would be interested in bringing out a collection of her best sketches. After an agreement was reached, the volume was scheduled for publication in 1875. On January 20 of that year she wrote Stedman about her forthcoming book: "I do not know whether you will approve of my volume, or rather, of any volume at all from me at present. But it seemed to me best to make a beginning, and it is a modest one, the best of my stories led by one which gives the name to the collection. Please keep this secret at present, as I have told no one. . . . The whole collection belongs to the lake-country."

The book appeared a month or two later and was, on the whole, favorably received by the critics. A reviewer in *Appletons' Journal*, April 3, 1875, thought, for example, that the "promise" of this early work presaged a "very bright" literary future and that Miss Woolson had made "a contribution of something fresh and vigorous beyond the common" (439). Howells' criticism in the June *Atlantic* found much to praise in many of the stories—especially those which had first appeared in the *Atlantic's* own pages—and in the author's concern for "truth to human nature," though the champion of realism was "harassed . . . by a disagreeable fantasticality" in **"Castle Nowhere."**

That sketch, by the way, had been written especially for this collection and had therefore not appeared first in a magazine. If one needed to advance other reasons for the story's failure to come out in one of the great monthlies, they are ready at hand. It is, for example, very long (it runs to ninety-one pages in book form), and the central character espouses principles repugnant to the family reading circles so important to magazine circulation in the late nineteenth century. Furthermore, the story centers around a love that supersedes moral principles, but this is no ordinary love story, for the love described is that of a foster father for the child he has reared.

In order to get away from the trappings of civilization, Jarvis Waring goes into the wilderness "bordering the head of Lake Michigan." There he chances to meet an old man named Amos Fog, who steals certain of Waring's possessions. In his search for the thief, Waring discovers a beautiful girl named Silver living in a log fortress called Castle Nowhere. (At this point readers of Cooper are likely to recall the "castle" in *The Deerslayer*.) Waring locates his stolen treasures and remains to find that Silver considers Fog her father and to be told Fog's story: he is an escaped murderer performing expiation through his loving concern for the girl—"a life for a life." Fog will do anything for Silver. He lures lake steamers to their doom in order to provide for her needs, telling himself that the crews lost are nothing to Silver's "delicate life." Yet he refuses to let her know the Bible, for "religion is fancy."

Before Waring becomes completely enthralled by Silver's naïveté, he leaves the castle, but is later rescued by Fog from the ice and cold. Finally surrendering to his feelings for the girl, Waring agrees to marry her, but he insists that they return to civilization after the ceremony. After leaving, however, Silver persuades him to return to Castle Nowhere, where they find Fog dying. They watch over the old man in his last hours, and he tells them he is "content," though his last words—"Is it expiated, O God?"—receive "no answer . . . on earth." With the death of Fog, the lovers leave the castle to fall in ruin and to become "indeed Nowhere."

Fog's lack of regard for conventional religion and his adoption of any means to a good end (i.e., the comfort and protection of Silver) did not endear him as a character to Miss Woolson's readers, a number of whom wrote to her questioning this aspect of his make-up. In an undated letter presumably written in 1875, Miss Woolson took up this matter with her friend Mrs. Washburn:

> At least twenty awful letters have I received because I made 'Old Fog' say he did not believe in eternal punishment. Is it possible that I am to be held personally responsible for the theology and morality of all my characters? I want you to think of me not as your old friend, when you read my writings, but as a 'writer,' like anyone else. For instance, take 'Adam Bede.' . . . Would you like to have a friend of yours the author of such a story? Dealing with such subjects? And yet it was a great book. . . . The truth is, Belle, whatever one does must be done with one's might and I would rather be strong than beautiful, or even good, provided the 'good' must be dull. All this applies more to what I hope to do in the future, of course, than to the slight sketches I have already brought out [Benedict, II, 20].

Even the critics were concerned. Howells' review in the *Atlantic* put it this way:

> A subtle confusion of all the conceptions of right and wrong is wrought by this old reprobate's devotion to the child, and his inability to feel that any means to her pleasure and comfort can be bad; but we doubt whether this is an intended effect, and if it is, we think it not worth the writer's or reader's pains. Castle Nowhere is the least satisfactory of the stories . . . [XXXV, 736].[3]

This aspect of Fog's character is hardly likely to disturb the modern reader. It is Fog's eagerness to sacrifice himself for the girl that may now arouse the wonder of readers, though it should be added that Fog's actions have been provided for in the motivation and analysis of his character. In this sense, Fog takes his place in a long line of Woolson characters who devote themselves to some unselfish goal. Fog is not altogether credible as a character, but neither is he completely "fantastical." The sketch's chief failure lies not so much in his confusion of right and wrong as it does in the failure of Waring and Silver to come off as believable human beings and in the introduction, as Kern has pointed out, of an "improbable series of events" into the narrative. Waring's conventional cynicism and Silver's wraithlike quality make the old outcast's elements of humanity appear all the more realistic by contrast. In the end, the sketch, though it is something less than an unqualified artistic success, is saved from total failure by the portrait of Fog and the vivid realization of the lake-country setting.

The next two pieces, **"Peter the Parson"** and **"Jeannette,"** both appeared first in *Scribner's Monthly.*[4]

"Peter the Parson" capitalizes, as the title implies, on the author's interest in Episcopal clergymen and is a study in dramatic contrast. The Reverend Herman W. Peters, a high-church Anglican priest, has come to a raw little settlement on Lake Superior as a missionary of his church; but he finds himself ridiculed by the Harte-like miners who inhabit the place and whose interest in religion can only be aroused by Brother Saul, a miner himself who enjoys "a-holding forth" among his comrades. The contrast between the two men themselves and the two widely divergent approaches to the faith they represent, to say nothing of the implied contrast between frontier and civilization, makes for a story rich in suggestion and overtone. Seldom in her tales did Miss Woolson elaborate anything more carefully fashioned than the poignant but never sentimental contrast she drew between the brawling, lusty settlement and the little, ascetic Anglican priest who, though he failed to convert the miners to his faith, lived up to it and died for it himself.[5]

Contrast is also vital in **"Jeannette,"** in which a French half-breed girl is the central character. Her beauty and coquetry attract the attention of Rodney Prescott, the scion of an old New England family and an officer in the army at Mackinac Island, Miss Woolson's favorite summer resort and a natural background for much of her early fiction.[6] The contrast between Jeannette's ignorance and natural grace and Prescott's culture and acquired polish is skillfully developed in this sketch, and her scornful rejection of his suit in favor of one of her own kind is brought off nicely.

"The Old Agency," although it was published in the *Galaxy,* appeared in December, 1874, the same month as **"Jeannette,"** and is a sort of companion piece to that tale. The setting and background of **"The Old Agency"** is Mackinac Island, and the narrator in both stories is Mrs. Sarah Corlyne, the aunt of an army officer at Fort Mackinac. In this work, however, the point of view is that of Father Piret, a beloved Roman Catholic priest whose aristocratic bearing and mysterious past have cast a romantic aura about a personality that is mythic in nature and substance. Piret's tale is about Jacques, an old and penniless soldier of the French Empire who has sought a place of refuge where he may dream of the glories of the past and prepare to die. The use of the double point of view in this instance provides less contrast than one might imagine, since Mrs. Corlyne is entirely sympathetic to Father Piret's qualities and to the loyalties of Jacques. If this point of contrast is not realized, the effort of the gentle old priest to infuse Christian precepts and attitudes into the grenadier's pagan worship of Napoleon affords Miss Woolson an opportunity subtly to contrast the two men as aliens and brothers and to show their different religions as expressive of two approaches to faith that are universal and timeless and that transcend the immediacy of the nineteenth century and Mackinac Island.

"Misery Landing," published in *Harper's* in May, 1874, is the only sketch in this collection to appear first in the monthly organ of the publishing firm with which Miss Woolson later made such pleasant arrangements concerning the publication of her work. Though its setting is an island near the western end of Lake Superior, its central character, John Jay, is from the metropolitan centers of sophistication and, in many ways, resembles Jarvis Waring in his cynical attitude. The contrast is strong between civilization and frontier, but the story does not quite come off because Jay fails to come alive, though his efforts to help others suggest some quality of humanity. The piece is chiefly interesting because of Jay's remarks regarding Bret Harte. In an entry in his diary, for example, he discusses Harte's "deep-hearted prose." "After all," he writes, "as long as I can read his pages, I can not be so bad as I seem, since, to my idea, there is more of goodness and generosity and courage in his words than in many a sermon. He shows us the good in the heart of the outcast." Later, he observes:

> I read aloud last evening. George [an ignorant boy of the region whom Jay has befriended] did not seem much interested in Bret Harte, but was captivated with the pageantry of 'Ivanhoe.' Strange that it should be so, but everywhere it is the cultivated people only who are taken with Bret. But they must be imaginative as well as cultivated; routine people, whether in life or in literature, dislike any thing unconventional or new [219].

Remembering her letter to Mrs. Washburn and not taking these views expressed by Jay as being too literally hers, one might yet suspect from reading this and other passages indicating similar opinions that Miss Woolson herself accepted the general tenor of these remarks.

The only sketch in this volume to have appeared originally in *Appletons' Journal* (October 4, 1873), **"St. Clair Flats"** contains some of Miss Woolson's most interesting early work, a view shared by her and expressed in a letter to Samuel Mather written in 1875: "I have all along cherished a special regard for '**St. Clair Flats**,' and have felt troubled because no one else seemed to care for the poor thing; now here comes along a young man, for whose literary taste I have a sincere respect, and this delightful young man picks out my poor neglected sketch for special commendation!" (Benedict, II, 22-23).

In this piece, two men, one of whom narrates the story, visit the flats of the St. Clair River, near Detroit, to fish and hunt; and they find a place to stay with Waiting Samuel, an eloquent but uneducated religious fa-

natic whose religion is compounded of "a strange mixture of Jacob Boehmen, chiliastic dreams, Christianity, sun-worship, and modern spiritualism," and his wife Roxana, a native of Maine. Roxana tells her story to the visitors, and the reader becomes aware that Miss Woolson has deftly sketched a memorable character. Because of her great love for her husband, Roxana has given up her own name, her family, and her native heath. She is lonely and sometimes memories of the past overwhelm her, but she is steadfast in her faith in Samuel's "great gifts" (one cannot help thinking here of Deerslayer "Christian's gifts" and "white gifts") and in her love for him; and she does not seriously consider returning to the land of lost content. Thus, the author turns to contrast again in showing the differences between these two wedded for life, the one poetic and prophetic and the other prosaic and pathetic; yet these two accept their lot and neither complains of incompatibility.

The treatment of the background also adds distinction to this sketch. Miss Woolson is at her best in describing the natural features of the St. Clair Flats.

> The word "marsh" does not bring up a beautiful picture to the mind, and yet the reality was as beautiful as anything I have ever seen—an enchanted land, whose memory haunts me as an idea unwritten, a melody unsung, a picture unpainted, haunts the artist, and will not away. On each side and in front, as far as the eye could reach, stretched the low green land which was yet no land, intersected by hundreds of channels, narrow and broad, whose waters were green as their shores. In and out, now running into each other for a moment, now setting off each for himself again, these many channels flowed along with a rippling current; zigzag as they were, they never seemed to loiter, but, as if knowing just where they were going and what they had to do, they found time to take their own pleasant roundabout way, visiting the secluded households of their friends the flags, who, poor souls, must always stay at home. These currents were as clear as crystal, and green as the water-grasses that fringed their miniature shores. The bristling reeds, like companies of free-lances, rode boldly out here and there into the deeps, trying to conquer more territory for the grasses, but the currents were hard to conquer; they dismounted the free-lances, and flowed over their submerged heads; they beat them down with assaulting ripples; they broke their backs so effectually that the bravest had no spirit left, but trailed along, limp and bedraggled. And, if by chance the lances succeeded in stretching their forces across from one little shore to another, then the unconquered currents forced their way between the closely serried ranks of the enemy, and flowed on as gayly as ever, leaving the grasses sitting hopeless on the bank; for they needed solid ground for their delicate feet, these graceful ladies in green [306-7].[7]

"St. Clair Flats" is, on the whole, an interesting sketch which gives promise of better work to come.

The remaining sketches in the collections were all published first in the *Atlantic*.[8] Howells thought these three the "best in this book." Two of these—"**Solomon**" and "**Wilhelmina**"—are set in the Zoar Community in Ohio and are not strictly lake-country work. In his review of *Castle Nowhere,* Howells describes "**Solomon**" as

> a triumph of its kind—a novel kind, as simple as it is fresh. The Zoar Community, with its manners and customs, and that quaint mingling of earthy good-feeling and mild, coarse kindliness with forms of austere religious and social discipline, which seems to characterize all the peculiar German sectarians, has had the fortune to find an artist in the first who introduces us to its life. Solomon's character is studied with a delicate and courageous sympathy, which spares us nothing of his grotesqueness, and yet keenly touches us with his pathetic history. An even greater success of literary art is his poor, complaining wife, the faded parody of the idol of his young love, still beautiful in his eyes, and the inspiration of all his blind, unguided efforts in painting. His death, after the first instruction has revealed his powers to himself, is affectingly portrayed, without a touch of sentimentalistic insistence. It is a very complete and beautiful story [737].

In "**Wilhelmina**," Miss Woolson apparently described too accurately some of her originals at Zoar, for the publication of the piece disturbed people at the Community, as she acknowledged in a letter to Samuel Mather in 1875. "Some one sent me a New Philadelphia paper containing a savage article on '**Wilhelmina**,' based upon the idea that my characters were all from life, and consequently 'the leathery woman' was the good Mrs. Beiter, the gardener's wife, etc., etc. Of course the article in the country paper was of no consequence, but I was distressed to think that perhaps the Beiters, always good friends of mine, thought so, too. I therefore wrote to Mr. Beiter telling him it was but a fancy sketch" (Benedict, II, 22).

Howells thought "**Wilhelmina**" "not quite so good" as "**Solomon.**" The reason is not far to seek. Wilhelmina herself somehow fails to come alive, and her emotional attachment to her lover Gustav never seems quite real. The use of a detached observer-character to narrate the story also influences adversely the credibility and effectiveness of Wilhelmina as a character. In this instance, as Claude M. Simpson has pointed out in another connection, the "personality" of the narrator becomes a "formidable barrier between reader and scene." Despite these handicaps, Miss Woolson does manage, as Kern has maintained, to stimulate some sympathy in the reader for the plight of the "pathetic girl at the apathy of her erstwhile lover."

"**The Lady of Little Fishing**," the last story in the collection—though it had appeared concurrently with

"**Peter the Parson**"—is in many ways also the best. The Lady is a beautiful Scottish missionary who appears suddenly one night among the rough trappers and hunters of Little Fishing, a camp on an island in Lake Superior, and whose beneficent influence on their lives reminds one of the "Luck's" impact on the miners of Harte's Roaring Camp. Almost as rapidly as her influence has waxed does it wane, when the men discover that she has fallen in love with one of their number (ironically, the only man there who is not in love with her); and thus, in Miss Woolson's sketch, "the problem of their unnaturally restrained behavior," as Simpson puts it, is resolved "by the strictly human device of disenchantment, where Harte resorted to chance calamity."[9]

Pattee, in his *Development of the American Short Story,* compares Miss Woolson's story with Harte's and then generalizes briefly on her artistry in the short story:

> '**The Lady of Little Fishing**,' . . . greatly surpassed in short-story art Harte's 'Luck of Roaring Camp.' The motif of Harte's piece centers about the abnormality of a group of men isolated completely from all feminine and domestic influences and the grotesque extremes to which such a group may go when such an element appears suddenly among them. . . . Miss Woolson does all that Harte does, and then she adds a touch that makes her work a model short story, as Harte's is not. All the men but one are in love with the Lady, and she is forced to choose one from among them. She chooses Mitchell, who refuses her absolutely, and then explains himself to the amazed group whom she had rejected: '*I* never gave in to her influence; *I* was never under her thumb. *I* was the only man in Little Fishing who cared nothing for her.' 'And that is the secret of *her* liking,' murmured the Doctor. 'O woman! woman! the same the world over!'

> This is the real motif of the story; not the mere grotesqueness of an abnormal situation presented merely for entertainment and wonder. The story is not finished when the reader has read it: it becomes with him a haunting suspicion, a peep into the heart of life [255].

Pattee concludes that Miss Woolson "must be rated with James and Aldrich as a strong influence toward more careful short-story workmanship at a moment when such influence peculiarly was needed" (255). There is little one may add to this critical and historical appraisal today. In this story Miss Woolson's insight has touched upon the universal, and she has bettered the work of one of her masters.

As a whole, *Castle Nowhere* (1875) is a good first book. In comparison with Sarah Orne Jewett's *Deephaven* (1877) and Mary N. Murfree's *In the Tennessee Mountains* (1884), to choose only two titles of similar quality from among the first books of Miss Woolson's feminine contemporaries, **Castle Nowhere** holds its own pretty well. In treatment and development of character and in the realization of background and locale, these early sketches give promise of the work to come. They are pioneer work, a fact one should not forget in assessing their value. "The ground is new," Howells wrote in the *Atlantic* in 1875, "and Miss Woolson gathers from it a harvest out of which the grain had not been threshed long ago." That the granaries were later to be filled to overflowing from the work of many harvesters should not obscure the fact that Miss Woolson made a distinct contribution in this book and others to follow both in local-color fiction and in analysis of character. . . .

Notes

[1] Benedict, II (1932), 553. Miss Woolson's juvenile, called *The Old Stone House,* was written under the pseudonym of Anne March. D. Lothrop & Company published it in Boston, 1872.

[2] See, for example, "Margaret Morris," *Appletons' Journal,* VII (April 13, 1872), 394-99; "Ballast Island," *Appletons',* IX (June 28, 1873), 833-39; and "A Flower of the Snow," *The Galaxy,* XVII (January, 1874), 76-85. The first of these concerns a proud young lady from New England who feels contempt for her fellow passengers on a lake steamer. She comes to her senses only after a storm sinks the vessel and she discovers that those whom she had despised have more courage in the face of danger than she has. The account of the sinking of the *Chippewa* is the best part of this piece.

"Ballast Island" contains within its conventional love-story framework one of the most memorable sketches of character in Miss Woolson's early work: Miss Jonah, a North Georgia woman who leaves her home for an island in Lake Erie so that her fiancé may marry her sister. In the treatment of Miss Jonah's character and dialect, this work looks forward to the Southern sketches to come; in the development of the theme of self-sacrifice, it also anticipates the novels.

Like "Ballast Island," "A Flower of the Snow" is a love story; and, like so many of the lake-country sketches, it has a Mackinac setting. Flower Moran, a plain little teacher from New England, falls in love with Lieutenant Maxwell Ruger, a "stalwart young Saxon" at Fort Holmes, who at first takes the romance rather lightly. When, however, Flower, feeling that he does not truly love her, leaves the village with the mail pack, Max follows her in the knowledge that he loves her enough to brave a blinding snowstorm. He catches up with her after both have been almost frozen by the storm, and they are married by Père Ronan, a hermit priest who reminds one of both Père

Piret and Père Michaux in other lake-country fiction and whose portrait in this piece may well be a preparatory study for the later characterizations of Piret and Michaux.

[3] In a letter of June 15, 1875, to Hayne, Miss Woolson remarks on Howell's review of the book in general and his criticism of "Castle Nowhere" in particular:

> But the criticism, as a whole, was very high praise, I thought; of course I am smarting a little about the 'Castle,' which, to tell the truth, *was* something of an ideal, instead of a *real* tale—like the others. But then I had been abused so for writing such deadly 'real' stories, that I did branch out, in that one, into the realm of the imagination. Still, Mr. Howells is mistaken in thinking that situation fantastic; the islands, the fogs, the false lights, the wreckers, the Mormons are all exactly from real life, true descriptions.

[4] VIII (September, 1874), 600-10 and IX (December, 1874), 232-43. "Peter the Parson" has recently been reprinted in *American Local-Color Stories* (1941).

E. C. Stedman apparently persuaded Richard Watson Gilder, one of the editors of *Scribner's,* to publish both stories. Miss Woolson refers to them in a letter to Stedman of April 13, 1874: "I shall be ever so glad if you can stir up Mr. Gilder to publish 'Jeannette.' Not that it is a good story; but it is weary waiting for a first appearance." A few lines later, she points out that the editors "don't like" "Peter the Parson" and concludes: " . . . in my opinion it is the most powerful thing I have ever written." This letter and another of October 10, 1876, are in the Yale University Library.

[5] Miss Woolson was criticized for allowing the minister to be killed in the story. Her reaction was expressed in a letter of April 25 [1875?] to Samuel Mather: "Under the abuse which has been showered upon me for my 'brutal' killing of 'Peter the Parson,' I have steadily maintained to myself that both in an artistic and truthful-to-life point of view, my ending of the story was better than the conversion of the miners, the plenty to eat, and the happy marriage proposed by my critics." Part of this letter has been printed in Benedict, II, 23.

[6] Despite her modest reference to "Jeannette" in her letter to Stedman, Miss Woolson liked the story, as she wrote James R. Osgood, because it was "such an accurate picture of Mackinac" (Kern, p. 25).

[7] "St. Clair Flats" has been reprinted in Benedict, II (1932), 431-57.

[8] "Solomon," XXXII (October, 1873), 413-24; "Wilhelmina," XXXV (January, 1875), 44-55; and

"The Lady of Little Fishing," XXXV (September, 1874), 293-305. The first of these has been reprinted in *American Local-Color Stories* (1941), pp. 188-206; the last, in *The Local Colorists: American Short Stories, 1857-1900* (1960), pp. 130-51.

[9] *The Local Colorists,* p. 130. For other views of "Solomon" and "Wilhelmina," see p. 129 and Kern, pp. 33-34.

Robert L. White (essay date 1967)

SOURCE: "Cultural Ambivalence in Constance Fenimore Woolson's Italian Tales," in *Tennessee Studies in Literature,* edited by Richard Beale Davis and Kenneth L. Knickerbocker, Vol. XII, University of Tennessee Press, 1967, pp. 121-29.

[*In the following essay, White considers Woolson's letters and short stories as expressions of American ambivalence toward "the foreign" in general and Italy in particular.*]

Until recently, Constance Fenimore Woolson, grand-niece of Fenimore Cooper and a respected authoress in her own right during the 1870's and '80's, was a figure but dimly remembered by most students of American literature, a figure occupying one of the shadowier niches in the gallery of "local color writers." In the past couple of years, however, her name has been broadcast by two separate scholars. Professor Rayburn Moore has published a book-length study of Miss Woolson which asserts she was a writer of modest but genuine talent who produced, along with a variety of readable short fiction, several novels of merit and substance. And Professor Leon Edel, in his continuing biography of Henry James, has made us aware of the long and pathetic intimacy which existed between the two writers, and of the extent to which James' fiction reverberates with his slow realization of Miss Woolson's would-be love for him.[1]

My concern with Miss Woolson is neither biographical nor strictly literary—although I suppose I should remark my agreement with Mr. Edel's assessment of her as a dispiritingly banal writer. Instead, I should like to discuss the ways in which a distinctive portion of her work lights up one of the most intriguing facets of America's involved relationship with Europe—how a number of her tales are symptomatic of the ambivalent responses of nineteenth-century Americans to Italy: the European land which, simultaneously, United States citizens found the most attractive and most repulsive.[2] (Although Miss Woolson's literary merit is questionable, it is certain that she was a writer whose tales about Italy were popular with magazine editors and, presumably, magazine readers. It seems proper, then, to assume that the attitudes toward Italy to be dis-

cerned in her work are symptomatic of the middle-class culture in which she found her audience. Simply because her tales are so mediocre and lacking in individual lustre, they can all the more properly be viewed as an index to the culture which produced and ingested them.[3])

One of a host of nineteenth-century American sojourners abroad, Miss Woolson sailed for Europe in 1879 and remained there until her death in Venice fifteen years later. She was never an expatriate, in the twentieth-century sense of the term, but she seems to have enjoyed keenly her succession of *outre-mer* years. She passed most of those years in Italy, and it was Italy, among all the lands of Europe, which most engaged her affections. Once, after a visit to England, she wrote relatives that she was "very fond of the misty, green island" but that she was happy to be returning to Italy; Italy was, she said, "the country I love best of all European ones. It comes next in my heart after Florida."[4]

Miss Woolson's letters home and her published travel sketches constantly descant upon the charms of Italy; several of her short stories, however, reveal an anxious revulsion from Italy. They suggest that the witchery of Italy is not altogether wholesome and that perhaps Americans would be better off if they were not so fascinated by the grace and beauty of Italian life and landscape. These tales, all very unimpressive as fiction, are nevertheless intriguing as documents which reveal the deep-seated distrust with which Americans have always been inclined to regard Europe—and the o'erweening pride with which they flesh out their own inadequacies. Many Americans, of course, have been scornfully leery of Europe; in Miss Woolson's case, what is interesting is not so much the revulsion from Italy discernible in her fiction as the fact that the dark undercurrent of the stories runs counter to her elsewhere expressed affection for Italy. Her letters and travel sketches voice a willed and conscious love; the stories embody doubts, suppressed but nonetheless real, of the worthiness of that love.[5]

Not long after her arrival in the Old World, Miss Woolson announced, in a letter from Florence, that attitude toward Italy she was to maintain outwardly the rest of her life. "Florence is," she wrote, "all that I have dreamed and more. . . . Here I have attained that old-world feeling I used to dream about, a sort of enthusiasm made up of history, mythology, old churches, pictures, statues, vineyards, the Italian sky, dark-eyed peasants, opera music, Raphael and old Michael, 'Childe Harold,' the 'Marble Faun,' 'Romola,' and ever so many more ingredients—the whole having, I think, taken me pretty well off my feet." Miss Woolson's continuing infatuation with Italy found outlets all up and down the peninsula. After one of her first walks in Rome, she wrote: "I come home so excited with it all that I fairly glow! For it *is* so interesting, so wonderful, so beautiful. You see I have 'gone over' body and soul to *Rome!*" In Venice, some years afterward, she exclaimed: "Venice is enchanting. Last night, in the full moon, the canal was dotted with gondolas, and music filled the air. It was beautiful as a dream." And in 1887, after she had taken up residence atop the heights of Bellosguardo, she told one of her friends back in America: "Everywhere . . . I see the most enchanting landscape spread out before me; mountains, hills, river, city, villages, old castles, towns, campaniles, olive groves, almond trees and all the thousand divine 'bits' that make up Italian scenery."[6]

Miss Woolson's persistent love affair with Italy is evident in most of her letters home, but perhaps it is most strikingly revealed in one addressed to an old teacher. She musingly recalls how she had been fascinated by the name of one of her classmates, *"Italia Beatrice,"* and then goes on to remark: "Since then, I have lived much in Italy itself. But it still remains fully as beautiful and romantic as it seemed in imagination, then."[7]

Given the fervor of Miss Woolson's professed enchantment with life in Italy, one might expect her Italian tales to be imbued with a like affection for the land and its people. The short stories do depict a land which is "beautiful and romantic"—but they also project an Italy with imaginative contours strikingly similar to those which coil about the Italy of Hawthorne's *The Marble Faun*. The Italy of both authors is compellingly beautiful, but beneath the mask of beauty lurk violence and evil. Miss Woolson's stories, like Hawthorne's novel, do not deny the charm of Italy; several of the stories, however, suggest that the charm is unwholesome and that, on the moral plane at least, the plain simplicity of America is superior to the beguiling loveliness of Italy.

Altogether, Miss Woolson published, in such major periodicals as *The Century, The Atlantic Monthly,* and *Harper's Magazine,* eleven long tales with Italian settings. Not all display ambivalent attitudes toward Italy; several are merely saccharine love tales set against Florentine and Roman backdrops. Generally, these neutral tales date from the first years of her stay abroad. It was only when her absence from America grew apace, and while she was seemingly growing more fixed in her love for Italy, that her stories begin increasingly to suggest that she was not really convinced of the propriety of her affections. Generally, in these later fictions the note of doubt is expressed in one of two fashions. Several stories intimate that Italians, seemingly the embodiments of charm and grace, are depraved and animalistically vicious beneath the veneer of their picturesque attractiveness. In other stories, the hero or heroine brought forward for our admiration is a person representative of strictly American virtues, one who is unswayed by the spell of Italy and steadfast in his or her upright Americanism.

This second motif is sounded for the first time in a story titled **"In Venice."** The tale is filled with visits to San Marco, gondola rides, and excursions through the lagoons; but it is centrally concerned with the seeming struggle of a quiet and aging American wife to safeguard her husband's love against the blandishments of a younger and more beautiful woman. The struggle is "seeming" in that the wife knows there is no danger her husband will prove unfaithful; the young girl, however, pathetically thinks it is her destiny to rescue the man, a would-be artist, from what she takes to be the mediocrity and dullness of his wife. Given the straight-laced tone of Miss Woolson's "love" tales with an American setting, it is perhaps noteworthy that something about the atmosphere of Venice prompted her to essay a tale which hints at illicit sex; even more significant, however, is her handling of the differing responses of her two female protagonists, both Americans, to the charms of Italy. Claudia, the young girl, is particularly enamoured of Venice and wishes she could have been a citizen of the Republic during the fifteenth century. The wife, Mrs. Lenox, harbors no such fond desires. She is happy to admit that she and her husband are "very completely of this poor nineteenth century." When Claudia compares the prow of a gondola to "the shining blade of St. Theodore," Mrs. Lenox suggests that "it looks a good deal like the hammer of a sewing-machine." Mrs. Lenox is respectful of the beauty of Venice, but she confesses that she "would give it all for the fresh odor of the fields at home, and the old scent of lilacs."[8]

Claudia is scornful of Mrs. Lenox's response to Venice. She feels that the wife, who spends most of her time caring for a sickly nephew, ought to devote more attention to her husband. During a visit to San Marco, she luxuriates in the warm and magical darkness of the interior and unabashedly observes: "I do believe that if some of our thin, anxious-faced American women could only be induced to come and sit here quietly several hours a day they would soon grow serene and physically opulent, like . . . the women of Veronese." Claudia, convinced of her own Veronesque sumptuousness, feels that Mrs. Lenox's thinness could be modified by a proper diet of Italian art and romance; but the story proceeds toward a dramatization of Mrs. Lenox's heroic New England virtues and toward Claudia's realization that her own enthusiasm for Italy has led her astray. At the end of the tale, after Mrs. Lenox has had singlehandedly to watch the death and burial of her little nephew because Claudia has dispatched the husband on a futile quest after some rumored Titian drawings, Claudia admits the wife's superiority, and the Lenoxes decide to return to America. The stay in Venice has not been harmful to them, but they have no desire to cut themselves off from America. The husband says: "We may return some time . . . but at present I think we want a home."[9] The clear implication is that, for Americans, a *palazzo* in Venice cannot be a home.

Two other stories similarly suggest that Italy is a land of dangerous passions and similarly employ figures of Americans impervious to the spell of Italy to suggest the basic wholesomeness of American values. In "Neptune's Shore," a lurid tale of jealousy, attempted murder, and suicide, Miss Woolson devotes much time to describing the splendors of the Mediterranean landscape, but her chief concern is a sympathetic portrait of the mother of the violent man who, within that landscape, tries to murder a rival in love and then destroys himself. Though older, Azubel Ash is much like the Mrs. Lenox of **"In Venice."** She is totally oblivious to the heralded charms of Italian scenery and classic architecture. At her hotel in Salerno, she spends most of her time gazing upon the kitchen garden. Indifferent to the view of the sea from the front terrace, she apologetically observes, "I don't know as I care about the sea; it's all water—nothing to look at," and explains that she sits by the back garden because she likes "ter see the things grow." At the end of the story, after a night spent by the side of her dead son, she has moved from a position of obliviousness to the Italian landscape to a lonely domination of that landscape. Her stature is rivalled only by the ancient Greek temples which have long brooded over the countryside—and Miss Woolson consciously couples the grandeur of the temples with the dignity of the American woman who has turned her back on them: "The sun, rising, shed his fresh golden light on the tall lonely figure with its dark hair uncovered. . . . Looking the other way, one could see in the south the beautiful temples of Paestum, that have gazed over that plain for more than two thousand years."[10]

The other story, **"A Pink Villa,"** differs from the general run of Miss Woolson's Italian tales in that it employs a masculine figure to exemplify the peculiar virtues of Americans. David Rod, a young planter from Florida, enters the pink villa on the Sorrentine cliffs to disrupt the plans of an ambitious American mother to marry her daughter to a foppish European nobleman. When Eva, the daughter, meets Rod she immediately falls in love with him—even though his clothes are unfashionable, his hands are brown and hardened, and his mission in Italy is not the pursuit of culture but the recruitment of laborers for his Everglades plantation. The mother struggles against her daughter's love for the young American, but the forthright Rod imbues Eva with his own firmness. The story ends happily with the departure of the wedded lovers for Florida—with Eva's ultimate decision to abandon a life of ease in Italy for a life of striving in America.

Although the young planter is depicted as a man of discrimination and foresight, some of Miss Woolson's other tales might lead readers to think him ill-advised in coming to Italy to seek laborers for his Florida acres. The Italians of these stories are handsome, colorfully picturesque, and seemingly gracious and amenable; beneath their smiling exteriors, however, they are selfish, dishonest, treacherous, animally sensual, and brutally violent. The duplicitous nature of Italian character is explicitly outlined in three of Miss Woolson's tales. In two, **"A Christmas Party"** and **"A Waitress,"** Americans who have naïvely been taken in by the winning ways of Italian servants suddenly discover that the domestics in whom they have put their trust are capable of horrifyingly passionate criminality.

Modesta, the Tuscan servant in **"A Waitress,"** is a good cook, loyal to her employer, kind to animals and old men, and fervent in her religious devotions; the American tourist who thinks her such a gem learns, however, that she is capable of sensual abandon and insane jealousy. One fiesta night, she attempts to stiletto a Swedish maidservant who is dancing with her betrothed, and the American tourist looks on as the countenance of the good Italian servant is animally transformed: "It was like nothing human; her head was thrust out, the eyes were narrowed and glittering, the nostrils flattened, and the lips drawn up and back from the set, fierce teeth; . . . she was like a wild beast who had made one spring and is about to make another."[11] In **"A Christmas Party,"** the seemingly perfect Italian servant is not so much transformed as literally undisguised. Carmela is a pert and handsome maid whose only concern seems to be the care and feeding of her American employers. Her real concern, however, is the safety of her son, a thief and murderer, and she coolly deceives the Americans while helping her son escape the police. When her complicity is finally detected, Carmela's façade crumples before the eyes of the police and her employers. She is not young and handsome, but old and withered— and it seems not amiss to infer that Miss Woolson is troubledly suggesting, in the image of the unmasked Carmela, that beneath the shell of Italian loveliness fester decrepitude and ugliness: "What was left was an old, old woman, small and withered, her feeble chest rising and falling in convulsions under her coarse chemise, and the rest of her little person scantily covered with a patched, poverty-stricken underskirt."[12]

"The Front Yard," title story of the first collection of Miss Woolson's Italian tales, doubly calls into question the putative fascination of Italy by coupling sketches of deceitfully charming Italians with an idealized portrait of a simple American heroine unmoved by the supposed wonders of Italian scenery and culture. The heroine of the tale, Prudence Wilkins

Guadagni, has received her surname from a handsome Italian waiter who beguiled her into marriage and then soon after left her a widow—with a stepfamily of seven children by a previous wife, a wastrel nephew, a sonnet-writing uncle, and a querulous grandmother to take care of.

In an exaggerated fashion, the characteristics of the American heroines of **"In Venice"** and **"Neptune's Shore"**—a disregard for the attractions of Italy and a homesick longing for the domestic niceties of New England—provide the basis for the narrative action of **"The Front Yard."** In Prudence's eyes, Italy is primarily a land of "indecent Antiquity," a land where everything is "old and dirty." In picturesque Assisi, where she lives with her new family, she finds these qualities heightened to "a degree that the most profligate imagination of Ledham (New Hampshire) would never have been able to conceive." Her most intense disgust, however, is reserved for a fragment of Antiquity strewn at her very door—a ramshackle stable and pigsty surrounded by heaps of refuse and manure. Her great ambition is to earn enough money to have the eyesore removed and a proper New England front yard laid out. In her dreams she envisions "a nice straight path going down to the front gate, set in a new paling fence; along the sides currant bushes; and in the open spaces to the right and left a big flowerin' shrub—snowballs, or Missouri currant; near the house a clump of matrimony, perhaps; and in the flower beds on each side of the path bachelor's-buttons, chiny-asters, lady's slippers, and pinks; the edges bordered with box."[13]

Prudence's hopes, however, are repeatedly frustrated by the machinations of the Italians whom she toils to support. Working from dawn to dusk to accumulate enough money to fulfill her vision, she sees her savings again and again depleted by the importunities and treacheries of her in-laws. The grandmother repeatedly demands costly foodstuffs, one son plunders a carefully watched fig crop, another extorts money from her to go off to Florence, the uncle must be rescued from debt, one of the daughters, a shiftless and vain creature, wheedles money from Prudence for a trousseau and then refuses to invite her to the wedding feast. Finally, after several years of constant toil, just when she is on the verge of realizing her goal, another son, a handsome creature upon whom Prudence has lavished a mother's love, steals all the money and flings it away in a bout of dissipation.

Eventually, Prudence Guadagni does get her front yard landscaped after a New England pattern, but only after she has been taken under the care of an American tourist who finds her tottering about Assisi and only after long years of unceasing labor have brought her to her death bed. When she finally does look upon her renovated front yard, she approvingly sighs, "It's mighty purty." The American lady who has wrought the miracle for Prudence also observes that the view has been much improved since the removal of the pigsty, but her view is that of the "great landscape all about," the landscape which she opines is "the very loveliest view in the whole world." Prudence, however, in spite of her companion's efforts to point out the beauties of the vistas unfolding on every side, will not lift her eyes beyond her new front yard. She will not be taken in by the reputed excellences of the larger view, and the judgment she passes on the Italian countryside may very well echo sentiments deep-rooted within the breast of the maiden American lady who had created her—and who, outwardly at least, was never uncertain of her love for Italy: "The truth is," Prudence says, "I don't care much for these Eyetalian views; it seems to me a poor sort of country, and always did."[14]

Notes

[1] Rayburn S. Moore, *Constance Fenimore Woolson* (New York, 1963); Leon Edel, *Henry James*, vols. 2 and 3 (London, 1963).

[2] As yet, there is no adequate account of American fascination with Italy during the nineteenth century. Van Wyck Brook's impressionistic *The Dream of Arcadia* (New York, 1958) and Paul R. Baker's pedestrian *The Fortunate Pilgrims* (Cambridge, 1964) are surpassed in many respects by earlier works by two Italian scholars: Giuseppe Prezzolini's *Come gli Americani scoprirono l'Italia* (Milano, 1933) and Angelina La Piana's *La cultura americana e l'Italia* (Torino, 1938). For a discerning account of the reactions of American novelists to Italy during the early and middle years of the nineteenth century, see Nathalia Wright, *American Novelists in Italy; The Discoverers; Allston to James* (Philadelphia, 1965).

[3] For a discussion of the ways in which literary documents may be utilized as indices of cultural assumptions see the stimulating essay by Bernard Bowron, Leo Marx, and Arnold Rose, "Literature and Covert Culture," in *Studies in American Culture,* edited by Joseph Kwiat and Mary Turpie (Minneapolis, 1960), 84-95.

[4] Clare Benedict, *Constance Fenimore Woolson* (London, 1930), pp. 292-93. Miss Benedict's memorial volume is mostly a compilation of letters and journal entries. It has obviously been selectively edited, but it seems unlikely that the relevant material about Miss Woolson's responses to Italy has been grossly tampered with.

[5] In a previous article, "Washington Allston: Banditti in Arcadia," *American Quarterly,* XIII (1961), 387-401,

I have attempted to demonstrate how a similar pattern of ambivalence is to be discerned in the paintings and fiction of one of the first American travellers to Italy. Although he does not develop the point, Umberto Mariani suggests that Henry James also was torn between his expressed love for Italy and his tendency, in his fiction, always to image Italy as a "ruffled nymph": "The Italian Experience of Henry James," *Nineteenth-Century Fiction,* XIX (1964), 237-54.

[6] Benedict, pp. 184-85, 242, 273, 298.

[7] *Ibid.,* p. 45.

[8] Constance Fenimore Woolson, *The Front Yard and Other Italian Stories* (New York, 1895), pp. 242, 244, 255. Miss Woolson's Italian tales were brought together in two books published shortly after her death in 1894.

[9] *Ibid.,* pp. 252, 266.

[10] *Ibid.,* pp. 64, 89-90.

[11] Constance Fenimore Woolson, *Dorothy and Other Italian Stories* (New York, 1896), p. 229.

[12] *The Front Yard,* p. 231.

[13] *Ibid.,* pp. 3, 16.

[14] *Ibid.,* pp. 47-48.

Rayburn S. Moore (essay date 1967)

SOURCE: "Editor's Introduction," in *For the Major and Selected Short Stories,* College & University Press, 1967, pp. 7-22.

[*In the essay that follows, Moore provides a general introduction to Woolson's short stories.*]

I

In her own day Constance Fenimore Woolson (1840-1894) was popular with both public and critics. Many American and British readers read her work when it first appeared in *Harper's New Monthly* and other literary magazines, and incomplete figures from her publishers Harper and Brothers on the sale of eight of her twelve volumes show that more than one hundred thousand copies of these books were sold. *Anne,* her first novel, accounted for almost sixty thousand copies of this total.

The critics were also enthusiastic about Miss Woolson's fiction. A writer in the *New York Tribune* asserted that the author of *Anne* stood "without question at the head of American woman novelists"; a reviewer in the *Century* remarked that "a fragment, and not an inferior fragment, of the mantle of George Eliot" had come to rest on Constance Woolson's "capable shoulders"; and a critic in the *Boston Globe* conjectured that she might "easily become the novelist laureate." Nor were her fellow artists slow to offer their praise. Edmund Clarence Stedman, William Dean Howells, and Henry James expressed their approval in various ways—Stedman in personal letters and in several editorial capacities; Howells in the critical columns and editorial departments of the *Atlantic* and *Harper's;* and James in a warm friendship during the last fourteen years of her life and in perceptive criticism of her work.

Despite this friendly reception by her contemporaries, Miss Woolson has not been widely read in the twentieth century. Readers of fiction have allowed her books to languish on library shelves, one suspects, because they smack too much of Victorian taste and morals. Scholars and critics, however, have from time to time expressed interest; and over the past forty years Fred L. Pattee, John D. Kern, Arthur H. Quinn, Lyon N. Richardson, Jay B. Hubbell, Van Wyck Brooks, Alexander Cowie, and Edward Wagenknecht have all discussed Miss Woolson's fiction favorably. But her novels and stories have, with the exception of two or three anthology pieces, remained out of print for years prior to this present collection.[1] . . .

II

Constance Woolson began taking a serious interest in writing in the late 1860's, and her articles and stories appeared in prominent magazines in 1870 and thereafter. These pieces were at first a clumsy combination of fact and fiction, the result of an explorative creative effort to deal with imaginary characters and situations (sometimes thinly disguised treatments of her own experience) in authentic backgrounds and settings. She learned gradually to handle these elements more gracefully and to motivate and analyze her characters on the basis of commonsense experience and a knowledge of psychology. By 1875 when **Castle Nowhere: Lake-Country Sketches** (her first volume of fiction for adults) was published, she had written a number of respectable short stories and sketches. These pieces are set either in the Great Lakes country or in a German Pietist settlement in eastern Ohio; and they reveal a knowledge and appreciation of locale, manners, customs, and people that led many to consider her primarily a local colorist and to compare her work with that of Bret Harte. Few were inclined to disagree with this view when D. Appleton brought out in 1880 her next collection, **Rodman the Keeper: Southern Sketches.** But many were amazed that she, a staunch Unionist and descendant of New

England forebears, could treat so dispassionately and sympathetically the land of the recent "rebellion" and its people.

By 1880, when *Rodman* appeared, Miss Woolson had sailed to Europe and had turned to the novel. She continued to write short fiction, but no collections appeared until after her death, though she had agreed to select enough stories for a volume or two for Harper before she died. These books—*The Front Yard and Other Italian Stories* (1895) and *Dorothy and Other Italian Stories* (1895)—contain (with one or two exceptions) the best tales she wrote during her European period and deal mainly with American characters in European settings. They reflect her interest in the contrast between the cultures of the Old World and the New, and especially in the effect the Old World has on Americans who have lived there for some time. In this way Constance Woolson contributed to another important literary current of her day—the fiction of international incident, a theme that had also fascinated James and Howells.

After her arrival in Europe near the end of 1879, Miss Woolson concentrated chiefly on the novel, a literary development coinciding with the beginning of the serialization of *Anne* in *Harper's* in December, 1880. She had thought about writing a novel as early as 1874 and several years later had expressed her interest in such a project to her friends Edmund Clarence Stedman and Paul Hamilton Hayne. *Anne* was finished by the spring of 1878; but since James R. Osgood, the Boston publisher for whom it was intended, failed to bring it out and since Harper, the New York firm which accepted the manuscript, wanted to begin to serialize the work in the first issue of the English edition of its monthly magazine, the novel did not appear until two and one-half years later.

Anne was well received by all, and Miss Woolson thereafter devoted her creative energies to long fiction, working slowly but steadily and publishing the fruits of her labor first in *Harper's* and then in book form. In this manner she produced *For the Major* (1883); *East Angels* (1886); *Jupiter Lights* (1889); and *Horace Chase* (1894). During this period she did not entirely neglect short fiction, but she found it difficult to write many sketches while working on a novel. In fact, she published only thirteen stories after *Rodman* appeared in 1880.

Her fiction of the 1880's is distinguished chiefly by an interest in local color, in analysis of character, and in relationships between Europe and America. Local color and character analysis manifest themselves principally in the long fiction, and international relationships are most clearly developed in the short stories. In the materials of the present collection, *For the Major* and later pieces such as **"The Street of the Hyacinth"** and **"The Front Yard"** amply illustrate these qualities.

During a sojourn of more than fourteen years abroad, Miss Woolson lived in Florence and Venice, in London and Oxford, and spent some time in Switzerland, Germany, and France. She read widely among the nineteenth-century European writers of fiction and admired especially the work of George Eliot and Ivan Turgenev. She became the intimate friend of Henry James, a fellow artist whose principles and craftsmanship appealed to her and whose influence on her later work, along with that of Eliot and Turgenev, was extensive. Her literary tastes and standards were cosmopolitan; but, unlike James, she was no expatriate in either a literary or a political sense. She loved her Uncle Fenimore's novels and Bret Harte's early stories, and throughout her long stay in Europe she constantly wrote to friends and relatives at home of her love for her country and of her ambition to return to it for a leisurely retirement in Florida.

In January, 1894, after a debilitating bout with influenza the previous summer and after completing the galley proofs of *Horace Chase,* Constance Woolson contracted the flu for the second and last time. On January 24 (slightly more than a month before her fifty-fourth birthday) in a state of delirium she either fell or threw herself from her bedroom window while her nurse was momentarily out of the room. She died before daybreak without having regained consciousness.[2]

III

As a book of local-color sketches *Castle Nowhere* (1875) compares favorably with the first collections of such work in the 1870's by Miss Woolson's contemporaries: Bret Harte, Sarah Orne Jewett, and George W. Cable. The better stories in *Castle Nowhere*—**"Peter the Parson," "Solomon," "St. Clair Flats,"** and **"The Lady of Little Fishing"**—offer an effective treatment of Lake-country setting, plausible interpretations of human nature in various situations, and a growing mastery of technique and material. **"The Lady of Little Fishing"** represents the author at her best during this early period.

Published first in the *Atlantic* for September, 1874, and praised by both Howells and Stedman, this tale of the influence of a beautiful woman on the miners and trappers of a camp on an island in Lake Superior reflects Miss Woolson's interest in the work of Harte. The Lady is a Scottish missionary who appears suddenly one night in Little Fishing, and her beneficent reign over the men of the settlement cannot help reminding one of the "Luck's" impact on the roughs of Roaring Camp. The Lady's power declines, however, when the men discover that she has fallen in love with one of their number (ironically, the only man who fails to be bewitched by her spell). But, as both Fred L. Pattee and Claude R. Simpson have pointed out, Constance Woolson went beyond the work of her master. In her sketch the problem of the "unnaturally restrained behavior of the men," as Simpson explains in *The Local Colorists* (1960), is resolved "by the strictly human device of disenchantment, where Harte resorted to chance calamity." Pattee had earlier remarked in his *Development of the American Short Story* (1923) on the keenness of Miss Woolson's insight into human nature in the tale, and he concluded that it "greatly surpassed in short-story art" Harte's "Luck of Roaring Camp."

These comments are valid despite the Lady's failure to become anything more than a shadowy figure and the absence of a necessary robustness in both the narrator and the rough men of this wilderness. The author's purpose, however, lies in another direction: she is concerned with setting, situation, and universal human emotions, and she handles these with assurance and skill. The situation is carefully developed, and the resolution is achieved by a reasonable treatment of the foibles and perversities of human nature. Indeed, in **"The Lady of Little Fishing"** Miss Woolson has wrought the particular into the universal and produced a work worthy of Harte himself.

In the fall of 1873 Constance Woolson made the first of a number of long seasonal visits to the South, where she spent much of the next six years. In the spring of 1875 she began publishing short fiction with Southern scenes and characters in *Appletons' Journal, Harper's,* the *Atlantic,* and other Northern literary magazines. She thus became, along with John W. De Forest, one of the first Northern writers of any significance to deal with such material on a large scale. Ten of these pieces were brought together in **Rodman the Keeper: Southern Sketches** (1880), her best collection in this vein and one which Henry James found "full of interesting artistic work." *Rodman,* like *Castle Nowhere,* clearly exhibits Miss Woolson's interest in local color, analysis of character, and the impingement of one culture upon another; but it also reveals a maturity of insight and a sureness of technique that mark it as an advance over the first volume. Three sketches—**"Old Gardiston," "Rodman the Keeper,"** and **"King David"**—represent these qualities in the present edition.

"Old Gardiston" first appeared in *Harper's* in April, 1876, before Federal troops were removed from South Carolina and before the flag of reconciliation had been very far advanced in either section. Yet, as Kern and others have suggested, the point of view developed in the sketch is basically sympathetic to the region, which was hardly the case with many of Constance Woolson's Northern contemporaries who were writing about the South during the seventies. Old Gardiston is a home in the rice country not far from Charleston, but it also symbolizes a family whose vitality has reached a low ebb at the time the story begins. The only surviving members—Gardis Duke, a beautiful but proud young belle, and her cousin, Copeland Gardiston, a gentle old dreamer whose primary interest in life is genealogy—seek to maintain some dignity in the midst of the poverty-stricken times of the Yankee occupation. The action revolves around the efforts of Gardis to live according to family custom and tradition despite war's impoverishment and the presence of Federal troops. When, however, Cousin Copeland dies and the old house is destroyed by fire, Gardis accepts the inevitable in the form of a proposal from Captain Newell, the commander of the occupation forces in the locality and a faithful admirer. Thus the work ends on a note of national harmony, but one of larger scope than that found in the mere bonds of matrimony; indeed, this reconciliation results in the union of the pride and courage of the South with the generosity and forbearance of the North.

One of Miss Woolson's contemporaries, Thomas Sergeant Perry, did not like **"Old Gardiston."** In a review of *Rodman* published in the *Atlantic* in July, 1880, Perry condemned the story chiefly on the grounds of the characterization of Gardis Duke, a "little chit" whose "cantrips . . . read like what one finds oftener in poor novels than in real life." But later critics have found much to praise in this work. Kern remarks on the "understanding and deep sympathy" of the author for the "stricken people" of the area; and Cowie, who touches on the same point, concludes that **"Old Gardiston"** is "an almost perfect short story." If the heroine's pride has become stereotyped and the reconciliation theme shopworn, one must grant that Miss Woolson was a pioneer in the treatment of these matters in fiction, that she achieved a nice balance between objectivity and sentiment, and that she managed her characters (Northern and Southern) and her material with a comprehension and tolerance worthy of attention today.

"Rodman the Keeper," which appeared about a year later, also deals with reconstruction in the South in a more objective manner than that in "Old Gardiston." It is a tale which depends on character and situation for its effect and, one might add, on the author's knowledge and understanding of both. The central character, a former Federal officer turned keeper of a national cemetery in Georgia after the war, exhibits the aspects of courage and devotion Miss Woolson admired in people in difficult situations, yet he seems altogether plausible without being in the least sentimental. The crux comes when Rodman, though ignored by the community, puts himself in a new relation to it by nursing a wounded ex-Confederate soldier who has returned to his ruined plantation to die. The materials are again available for a symbolic reunion of the states through an understanding established by the two former soldiers. Contrary to the acquiescence eventually achieved in **"Old Gardiston,"** Miss Woolson has no intention of dealing with the theme in this way in **"Rodman the Keeper."** Rodman and De Rosset never fall on each other's necks and never mention the matter of reconciliation. The former, indeed, may give vent to a modicum of sentiment at the end when he seeks to acquire the piazza greenery from the old De Rosset place, but even this whim is treated ironically when the Maine man who now owns the place offers to sell the vines to him.

The sketch was well received by contemporary critics, and its merits led one publisher (presumably Harper) to offer to take "every line" Constance Woolson wrote and to allow her "to set" her "own price" for her work. Twentieth-century scholars have also thought well of it. Pattee, Richardson, and Hubbell have commented on it favorably; and Quinn has characterized it, along with **"Old Gardiston"** and **"King David,"** as the best of the author's "post-war stories." More recently, Edel, in the second volume of his biography of James, has cited the piece as "one of her most celebrated sketches," though he has also mentioned its "limitations."

"King David" repeats with some variation the theme of **"Old Gardiston"** and **"Rodman the Keeper,"** the contrast between Northern and Southern political views of reconstruction in the old Confederacy and the well-meaning efforts of Northern idealists to do something constructive in a land which is quite strange to them and amongst a people whom they do not understand. David King, a "narrow-chested" young man from New Hampshire, feels "called" upon to go south after the war and to teach the "blacks." He settles in a plantation community, establishes a school for the freedmen, and proceeds to try to inculcate both the three R's and morals in his pupils; but he discovers after months of patient labor that his lessons have little effect on his child-like charges of Jubilee Town, that a "glib-tongued" compatriot from the North ("knighted with the initials C. B.") has more influence over them with his demagoguery and liquor, and that a retired planter of the neighborhood (who thinks the blacks an "inferior race by nature") nevertheless understands and appreciates the Negroes and their needs better than either Yankee visitor. Giving up and returning home in the hope that a colored "minister-teacher" will be sent in his place, King David (the Negroes themselves had given him the name) accepts defeat. His mission to the Israelites elicits a final ironic comment from a New England gossip: "'Didn't find the blacks what he expected, I guess.'" King fails, as the narrative makes quite clear, because he understands neither the region nor the Negro and because he "shrinks from personal contact" with the black man (though he is a staunch believer in equality) and goes about his work from a sense of "duty, not liking."

Again, as in **"Rodman,"** the artist has shown her strong interest in contrast; in each case Miss Woolson examines a character out of his proper element, an idealistic Yankee in the devastated South. Rodman, of course, is made of sterner stuff than King, and he comes closer to success, though he is dealing not with Negroes but with white Southerners; still, he manages to reach only an uneasy armistice with Bettina Ward, De Rosset's cousin and a hearty hater of anything representing the Federal government or the Union cause.

Interestingly enough, though T. S. Perry liked neither **"Old Gardiston"** nor **"Rodman the Keeper,"** he thought that "King David" was "very good" and that it contained no "exaggeration" and no "inclination toward the use of melodramatic devices, such as are only too apt to make their appearance in the other stories." Kern, Quinn, and Hubbell have also found the sketch to their liking. Certainly, it reveals a knowledge and an understanding rarely manifested in the work of other Northern writers of the day and an objectivity seldom achieved by Southerners in their fictional treatments of the particular problem.

The other stories in the present collection all have European settings. The earliest of these was " 'Miss Grief'," a tale never reprinted by Miss Woolson though it later appeared in the fourth volume of a Scribner's series entitled *Stories by American Authors* (1884). Published first by *Lippincott's Magazine* in May, 1880, only six months after her arrival in Europe, " 'Miss Grief' " is the author's first effort to deal with Americans abroad (the scene is Rome), and it is interesting to note that the piece appeared shortly before Constance Woolson had either been to Rome or met Henry James, though both these "deficiencies" were speedily remedied. James, for example, came to visit her in Florence at about the same time that the May issue of *Lippincott's* was appearing in America. He was, as she wrote home, "perfectly charming" to her and a "delightful companion" during a month of trips to museums and churches, of walks in the Cascine and on Bellosguardo, and of discussions about art and literature.[3]

Miss Woolson had, of course, long known his work and admired it—a fact which perhaps explains certain aspects of " 'Miss Grief.' " The narrative itself concerns an American woman who goes to Rome to seek literary advice from an expatriated American author who has found financial success in Europe. Aaronna Crief (Moncrief, one learns later) is no longer young, but she has written a drama of great power, something immediately recognized by the expatriate who has only reluctantly undertaken to read the manuscript. The sketch develops as the mentor (who also narrates the proceedings) fails either to improve the play or to get it published. As interesting as the work itself is the resemblance between the narrator and Henry James. Both are men who have inherited money and know the "way of society"; both model their work a "little on Balzac"; both are interested in analysis and motivation in their fiction; and both use the term "the figure in the carpet" in similar ways.

Moreover, " 'Miss Grief' " bears some interesting marks of similarity to **"The Street of the Hyacinth"** (also set in Rome and brought out after Miss Woolson had not only visited the Holy City several times but had on at least one occasion in the spring of 1881 enjoyed the sights there in the company of James himself). In both stories the chief male character is an American expatriate writer and critic whom an inexperienced and naïve American female seeks out for counsel about work or culture. Both women feel they can get what they need from their advisers, but there are some differences. First, Ettie Macks in **"The Street of the Hyacinth"** has no artistic talent and Miss Grief has; and, second, Ettie finds her fulfillment in a marriage with her mentor, whereas Miss Grief fulfills herself in her work. Both men remind one of Henry James. They possess Jamesian qualities of aesthetic sophistication and perhaps something akin to his literary position in the early 1880's, and each, indeed, may have been in part modeled on James himself. Also, as both Kern and Richardson have suggested, there is something of the method of James in the telling of these two tales.

Contemporary critics had little to say about either story, but later students of Miss Woolson's fiction have commented on both. Kern, for example, notes that the "central problem" of " 'Miss Grief' " anticipates by eight years James's "Lesson of the Master" and remarks that "the sketch is wholly a study of character and of artistic method in the manner later made famous by James." Richardson describes **"The Street of the Hyacinth"** and two other late stories as "especially noteworthy." Despite the Jamesian characters and method, however, these pieces are Miss Woolson's own, particularly the later one in which the careful development of character and the treatment of the background reveal the hand of a mature artist at work. Both sketches place characters (chiefly American) in an appropriate Old World setting and allow them to grow within the context of a dramatic contrast between the new and the old, between innocence and experience, between shallowness and depth.

"The Front Yard" also deals with American characters in a European background, but it concerns itself with a social and economic level of life seldom examined by James or Howells. Prudence Wilkin, a plain New England woman of humble class, finds herself stranded in Italy upon the death of her wealthy cousin whom she served as "companion and attendant." She marries an Italian waiter who offers her the only romance she has ever known and who dies after a year, leaving her to care for his large and demanding family. Accepting with stoicism the duty imposed on her, she struggles for years rearing the numerous progeny of her dead husband and dreaming of replacing the "noisome" cowshed in the front yard with a gate and fence, a "straight path," "currant bushes," and "box-bordered flower beds." The glories of Italy which figure so prominently in fiction by James and Howells (and also in " 'Miss Grief' " and **"The Street of the Hyacinth"**) fail to stir in Prudence the conventional response of the Jamesian "passionate pilgrim." Rather, she is a Pilgrim of another sort: a New Hampshire Prudence whose "idea of Antiquity" is anything that is "old and dirty." This is the way she views Assisi, her present home, and its "picturesque" environs. She never notices the "serene vast Umbrian plain," she never enters the church of St. Francis, and she is of course unaware of Giotto, whose frescoes adorn the walls of that edifice. Yet she has her own notions of beauty, and her dream of establishing a colorful New England front yard on her hill in Italy suggests a different esthetic from that of the cultural antiquity and artistry of the Old World.

Another idea dear to Miss Woolson's heart is developed in **"The Front Yard"**: the theme of "high-minded renunciation" (also typical of Jamesian women), as Cowie characterizes it. Prudence Wilkin spends the best years of her life rearing her dead husband's children and caring for several elderly members of his first wife's family, but she considers this a responsibility incurred by her marriage vows and acts on this obligation until she breaks down after working fourteen hours a day for sixteen years trying to support these largely worthless people. Prudence's notions of honor and duty may appear quixotic to some, but they are basic to her character and so consistently maintained that even the reader who is unwilling to suspend his disbelief is bound to admit that such a nature is possible or, if not, run the risk, as James says in regard to another of Miss Woolson's characters, "of denying that a woman *may* look at life from a high point of view."

At least one contemporary reviewer thought well of this story. Writing in the *Critic* for December 28, 1895, he pointed out that **"The Front Yard"** was a "brilliant piece of genre-painting executed by an artist who understood her subject to the heart." He was also pleased that its "originality of invention" reflected not "the least straining after effect," and he concluded that its method was "entirely adequate" to its "idea." Many years later Kern cited the piece as one of the best of Miss Woolson's "Italian tales" and described Prudence Wilkin as one of her "finest creations," a view with which Quinn and Richardson have concurred. **"The Front Yard"** deserves a high place in the canon of the author's short fiction on the basis of a memorable characterization of the protagonist, the effective use of contrast on the levels of both character and culture, and a discriminating treatment of a dominant theme in the whole corpus of her work.

Though **"A Transplanted Boy"** appeared in *Harper's* several months before Miss Woolson's last published story, it is said by some to have been the last tale she wrote. . . . A bit long for a short story—its almost eighteen thousand words make it longer by about one thousand than **"The Street of the Hyacinth"** and, therefore, the longest work in the present collection save *For the Major*—its length approximates the *nouvelle* rather than the novelette and its scope gives the author ample opportunity to examine her chief character in terms of the influences on him and to show his native self-reliance in response to a situation that steadily grows worse for him. Maso's predicament, of course, is that he has been "transplanted"; and when he is left to his own devices in Pisa, he discovers that Americans think him Italian and that Italians think him American and that, consequently, neither assistance nor sanctuary is likely. He nevertheless "plays a man's part, without heroics," as Quinn puts it; and the author's restrained treatment of his sturdy courage and perseverance in the face of his plight, despite the sentiment inherent in several aspects of the situation, gives distinction to this poignant tale.

Miss Woolson's readers have liked this story and so have some of the critics. After reading over the letters she received in response to the distribution of her *Five Generations* (the piece is reprinted in the second volume), Clare Benedict reported in her foreword to *Appreciations* (1941) that **"A Transplanted Boy,"** along with **"Old Gardiston"** and **"Rodman the Keeper,"** were "favourites" with her aunt's public. The critics have been generous in their praise. Writing in the *New York Times Saturday Review* under the pseudonym of Leigh North, Mrs. Elizabeth Steward Phelps commended the author for a "divine gift of sympathy" which enabled her "to put herself in the place of someone else, to look at life through his lens, for the time being." In 1929 Miss May Harris remarked on Miss Woolson's "magical Italian stories" in the *Saturday Review of Literature* and cited **"A Transplanted Boy"** as one of five "perfect or finished examples of what a short story should be." Several years later Kern characterized as "notable" the author's "interpretation of the effect of long-continued foreign association upon an American boy," and Quinn observed that the tale was a revelation of a "power that showed no sign of weakening." The sketch of Maso is a memorable one, and the artist's

careful use of point of view suggests indeed that her command of technique was as sure as ever.

For the Major, Miss Woolson's only novelette, appeared as a serial in *Harper's* and then was brought out in book form in 1883. Contrary to the episodic quality of *Anne* (1882) and the panoramic sweep involved in its three basic changes of scene, *For the Major* offers a unity and concentration in structure and setting, though the theme of self-sacrifice runs through both stories. The idea in the shorter work, as James describes it, is that of the "secret effort of an elderly woman to appear really as young to her husband as (owing to peculiar circumstance) he believed her to be when he married her." Complications force Madam Carroll to solicit help from her stepdaughter Sara and to practice a few deceptions, all for the best of reasons. Sara herself is put in an awkward position before her lover, the Reverend Frederick Owen. Such material, to be sure, may not seem very promising to the modern reader, but Miss Woolson is concerned more specifically with matters of character, background, and idea.

Madam Carroll's actions are carefully analyzed and well motivated, and her portrait is a well-rounded one. Henry James found its conception "highly ingenious and original" and concluded that the author had "done nothing of a neater execution." The treatment of Sara Carroll is hardly less successful, although she is definitely secondary to her stepmother in Miss Woolson's scheme. Major Carroll is an early sketch of a Southern aristocrat in decay but one without moral or sociological overtones. The contrast indeed between the Major's noble and chivalrous earlier life and his present serene senility assures the reader that his wife's sacrifice has a worthy object.

Even the minor characters, as is frequently the case in Miss Woolson's longer fiction, are among her best achievements. Senator Ashley, Mrs. Greer, and other parishioners of St. John in the Wilderness make the North Carolina mountain village of Far Edgerley come to abundant life. These village folk also provide the author with frequent opportunities for an unpretentious display of quiet humor in the conversation of Senator Ashley, a garrulous elderly gentleman of the old school whose favorite topic is the Crimean War; in the gossip of Mrs. Greer who considers "whist-playing a test of the best churchmanship" and whose talent for talk is subtly exploited by Madam Carroll when she wishes certain news spread throughout the town; and in the antics of the members of the choir at St. John's, whose musical and other qualities are universal enough to shock even readers of today into amused recognition.

Despite her own remark that the novelette was a "little genre picture of village life, with strong local color,"

Miss Woolson is not merely concerned with local color *per se* (Kern, as a matter of fact, has asserted that the "element" of local color is "more faint" in this work than in any of her novels). Far Edgerley is also characterized by its people in a manner reminiscent of Jane Austen. The reader's view of the community takes on dimensions as he observes the people's conservative temper, as he becomes aware of their hospitality and concern for others, even strangers, and as he comes to know their customs and manners and attitudes. As Cowie points out, the "revelation of the nature" of Far Edgerley is as "fascinating to watch as the raveling of the fantastic fabrication of Madam Carroll."

In matters of style and technique, **For the Major** is assuredly the author's most impressive performance in short fiction, and to some, it is the best work she ever did. The omniscient point of view is concentrated on Madam Carroll and her affairs, but since the narrative is developed from the outside, the totality of village and characters can be easily surveyed and assessed. This portrayal is accomplished with a minimum of commentary, and the story line is seldom obstructed by excessive analysis, digression, or asides by the author. The central situation is handled with restraint and economy, and the concluding scenes are treated in a rather unconventional manner for romantic fiction of the 1880's, for Miss Woolson refuses to spell out Madam Carroll's appeal to Owen to make her an "honest" woman. This aspect of the work alone, as clearly as anything else, suggests the writer's quality as an artist.

The critical reaction to **For the Major** was immediate. Reviewers in *Harper's* for July, 1883, and in the *Century* the following December were enthusiastic; and though critics in the *Atlantic* for July and in *Lippincott's* for August were not so warm in their praise, the former admitted that the novelette was "very ingenious" and "skillfully managed" and the latter thought it "rare, delicate, and exquisitely told." Miss Woolson herself considered it the best piece of work she had done. More recent opinions have also been favorable, although Wagenknecht has expressed a few reservations. Hubbell cites it as "probably the best of her novels," and Kern characterizes it as a "distinguished little book" and as "one of the finest American novels of the time." Quinn is reminded of an "etching" in which "one central figure stands out in exquisite proportion against a background whose very limitations present that figure to perfection." Cowie comments on the author's "special talent for finely discriminating effects," her "artful elaboration of ethical problems," and her ability to bring Far Edgerley to "life perfectly with brush-strokes that are as faultless as they are gentle." In this work Miss Woolson has successfully created a community which, though based on solid reality, has a fictional validity of its own and is inhabited by characters whose motives and actions play an integral part in establishing the credibility of this world of the imagination. **For the Major** is, in its own quiet way, a little masterpiece.

Notes

[1] See Pattee's appraisal in *The Development of the American Short Story* (1923) and in "Constance Fenimore Woolson and the South," *South Atlantic Quarterly,* XXXVIII (April, 1939), 130-41; Kern's in *Constance Fenimore Woolson: Literary Pioneer* (1934); Quinn's in *American Fiction* (1936); Richardson's in "Constance Fenimore Woolson, 'Novelist Laureate' of America," *South Atlantic Quarterly,* XXXIX (January, 1940), 18-36; Hubbell's in "Some New Letters of Constance Fenimore Woolson," *New England Quarterly,* XIV (December, 1941), 715-35, and in *The South in American Literature, 1607-1900* (1954); Brooks's in *The Times of Melville and Whitman* (1947); Cowie's in *The Rise of the American Novel* (1948); and Wagenknecht's in *Cavalcade of the American Novel* (1952). More recently, Leon Edel has considered, albeit generally unfavorably, some of Miss Woolson's fiction in the second and third volumes of his biography of Henry James: *The Conquest of London: 1870-1881* (1962) and *The Middle Years: 1882-1895* (1962). These discussions—together with Clare Benedict's *Five Generations* (3 vols., 1929-1932), the second volume of which deals entirely with Constance Woolson, and Rayburn S. Moore's *Constance Fenimore Woolson* (1963) and "The Full Light of a Higher Criticism: Edel's Biography and Other Recent Studies of Henry James," *South Atlantic Quarterly,* LXIII (Winter, 1964), 105-14—comprise the chief twentieth-century considerations of Miss Woolson's work. James's "Miss Constance Fenimore Woolson" (*Harper's Weekly,* XXXI [February 12, 1887], 114-15; reprinted with a few changes in *Partial Portraits,* 1888) is the most authoritative treatment of the nineteenth century and remains today the best essay on his friend's fiction, though for obvious reasons it contains no discussion of her work after *East Angels* (1886).

[2] For varying opinions regarding Miss Woolson's death, see Kern, pp. 159-62; Edel, *The Middle Years,* pp. 356 *passim;* and Moore, *Constance Fenimore Woolson,* pp. 8, 36-39.

[3] For the fullest account of this friendship, see the second and third volumes of Edel's biography of James; for disagreement with some of Edel's interpretations (especially in regard to his inferences concerning Miss Woolson's part in the relationship), see Moore, "The Full Light of a Higher Criticism"; and for earlier treatments of this matter, see the second and third volumes of Clare Benedict's *Five Generations* and Kern's study.

Sharon L. Dean (essay date 1986)

SOURCE: "Constance Woolson's Southern Sketches," *Southern Studies,* Vol. XXV, No. 3, Fall 1986, pp. 274-83.

[*In the following essay, Dean praises Woolson's sensitivity to the complex position of women in the South which is evident through her fictional accounts of Southern society during Reconstruction.*]

Constance Woolson was not a Southerner. Born in Claremont, New Hampshire, on March 5, 1840, she moved that winter to Cleveland where she lived, aside from schooling in New York and summer visits to Mackinac Island, Michigan, until her first of many extended visits South in 1873. From 1873 to 1879, she spent much of her time in Florida, Virginia, the Carolinas, Tennessee, and Georgia, and from 1879 until her death in 1894, she lived in Europe, particularly in Italy. Typically writing about the places where she lived and visited, Woolson published her stories in regional collections: *Castle Nowhere: Lake Country Sketches* (1875), *Rodman the Keeper: Southern Sketches* (1888), *The Front Yard and Other Italian Stories* (1895), and *Dorothy and Other Italian Stories* (1896). Though her novels move from place to place, several are set primarily in the South: *For the Major,* (1883), *East Angels* (1886), *Jupiter Lights* (1889), and *Horace Chase* (1894). As a result of her interest in the South, Woolson has been numbered as a Southern, as well as a Lakes Country, local colorist, as one of the more successful Northerners to write about the South during Reconstruction, and as a writer with the ability to understand, without sentimentalism, the social conditions of the South.[1] In *Partial Portraits* Henry James, early on an admirer of Woolson, said of *Rodman the Keeper:*

> Miss Woolson has done nothing better than the best pages in this succession of careful, strenuous studies of certain aspects of life, after the war, in Florida, Georgia and the Carolinas. As the fruit of a remarkable minuteness of observation and tenderness of feeling on the part of one who evidently did not glance and pass, but lingered and analysed, they have a high value, especially when regarded in the light of the *voicelessness* of the conquered and reconstructed South. Miss Woolson strikes the reader as having a compassionate sense of this pathethic dumbness—having perceived that no social revolution of equal magnitude had ever reflected itself so little in literature, remained so unrecorded and unsung. She has attempted to give an impression of this circumstance, among others, and a sympathy altogether feminine has guided her pen. She loves the whole region, and no daughter of the land could have handled its peculiarities more indulgently, or communicated to us more of the sense of close observation and intimate knowledge.[2]

James's assessment is astute, for what emerges in nearly every story of *Rodman the Keeper* is the voice of one who loves and understands the South and can assess the position of women within the South. Though James notes a "dreariness" in her sketches, as if she gathered her impressions "on the edge of rice-fields, dismal swamps, and other brackish inlets,"[3] Woolson also treats the South with humorous indulgence instead of maudlin pity at its condition during Reconstruction. Perhaps because she was not a Southerner, she can keep a distance which enables her to reveal a living and complex region. Woolson exposes the kinds of extremism, both Northern and Southern, that led to the Civil War and that blocked Reconstruction, and she examines both the extremism and sensitivity of Southern religious attitudes. Beyond these perspectives on the South, Woolson finds in the region a metaphor for art and an ideal medium to reflect her concern about women's tendency to perpetuate their limited role in society.

As a Northerner come South in 1873, Woolson is quick to see the havoc the war has played on the Southern way of life, the inefficiency and unwillingness to accommodate of both Northerners and Southerners during Reconstruction. She never looks with a blaming eye on either side; rather she portrays people's inability to change, more than their overt resistance. She captures the typical rigid Northerner in her portrait of Stephen Wainwright and his handwriting in **"Up in the Blue Ridge."** Stephen's "letters carried themselves crookedly, and never twice alike; but owing to their extreme smallness, and the careful way in which they stood on the line, rigidly particular as to their feet, although their spines were misshapen, they looked not unlike a regiment of little humpbacked men, marching with extreme precision, and daring you to say that they were crooked" (276).[4] The Southern woman in that story represents Woolson's typical portrait of a rigid Southerner as she works diligently on a composition called "Reflections on the Book of Job," complete with references to "authorities" and "dictionaries" (290). Whether male or female, both Northerners and Southerners represent extreme forms of behavior. As strangers to the South, Northerners like Woolson must necessarily play the part of foreigners; in turn, as soon as they come in contact with a Northerner, Southerners themselves adopt a role of conquered but still proud enemy.

The advantage of Woolson's outsidedness—and her own role-playing as an outsider—is that she can exaggerate the foibles of both North and South to make the point that their enmity represents any kind of destructive and self-destructive extremism. In fact, this may be the real issue of a curious story called **"Felipa"** where the young girl named Felipa loves an engaged Northern couple, loves the male and the female equally. This is, says Woolson's narrator, "a case of color-blindness, as it were—supposing [the] two were colors" (216). Not only does the love reflect color-blindness, with all its implications for abolition, but it also represents the kind of love/hate relationship involved in the Civil War. Felipa tries to kill one of the lovers, themselves engaged in a love/hate relationship, when she feels they do not collectively return her love. She had for them "two loves, and the strongest thrust the knife" (220); that is, the one that most desired union between North and South would rather kill than separate.

This ambivalent love/hate between North and South is captured strongly in the story **"King David."** The hate is muted here because David King is a well-meaning Northerner who simply cannot understand and, therefore, really love the South. For all his Northern philanthropic notions, King's prejudice runs rampant, and Woolson leaves no doubt that she wishes us to see through his false altruism in coming South to educate the Negro. Aloud, he calls his scholars "colored" or "the Children of Ham" because he doesn't want to call them what they are, "black—black as the ace of spades" (254). He considers the blacks "ignorant, childish, irresponsible" (256), thinks in terms of their "animal features" (263), and lives and eats always a little distant from them. Woolson's perception here is far in advance of someone like Harriet Beecher Stowe who could call the Northerners to arms with the kind of philanthropy David himself displays. Nor is she simplistic, simply poking snide remarks at Northern do-gooders. It is, after all, David King that she has voice a warning to the South, represented by the Southern planter to whom he is speaking: "But if you, sir, and the class to which you belong would exert yourselves, I am inclined to think much might be done. The breach will only grow broader every year; act now, while you still have influence left" (266). Of course, they do not act; the Northern carpetbaggers have their day, the Southerners nod their I-told-you-so's, and only David King is duly humbled because he knows the "lesson of failure" (274). In her study of Woolson, Anne Rowe notices that the North has dropped its self righteousness and is ready to hear this kind of softened attitude toward Northern culpability.[5] Perhaps for this reason Woolson can treat the very real problems of Reconstruction with humor and understanding.

In part, David King cannot respond to the Southern world because he cannot accept its climate and the casual attitudes that climate seems to darken the work ethic with. This same inability to respond is displayed by the keeper of a cemetery dedicated to Union soldiers in **"Rodman the Keeper."** Here, Woolson plays up the natural environment and the way it mirrors, and perhaps even engenders, the extremism of North and South and the extremism within the South, par-

ticularly on the part of Southern women who have lost so much in the war. Returning to the South after the war, Rodman has no intention of exploiting it or even aiding it, though he is not indifferent to its charms: his "New England eyes" have seen "the magnificence and carelessness of the South, her splendour and negligence, her wealth and thriftlessness" (11). His mission, to bring his Northern sense of order to the cemetery, is, of course, not embraced by the Southerners who vent their bitterness on him "not in words, but in averted looks, in sudden silences when he approached, in withdrawals and avoidance, until he lived and moved in a vacuum" (11-12), finally withdrawing totally to the solitude of his cemetery, content to keep it and its records with the "infinite pains and labor" (13) of his Northern meticulousness. Woolson captures Rodman's alienation from the whole Southern landscape in an episode where a young Negro brings his supplies from town, "whistling and shuffling along, gay as a lark" (15-16), offending Rodman merely because he is "stirring up the heat" (16). What Woolson implies in the story is that until Northerners accept this Southern way of life instead of trying to impose on it the energy of their Northern work-ethic, they will remain outsiders to the South.

Much of **"Rodman the Keeper"** centers as well on the loss of ancestral homes and the whole way of life this loss represents. Rodman comes across a wreck of a house, inhabited by a wreck of a Confederate soldier, whom he slowly nurses to a peaceful death, over the objections of the soldier's never-relenting female cousin. This experience prompts him to accept the South so that his final act in the story is to buy a vine from the soldier's home to plant as symbol of the indolent but graceful South to soften his Northern cemetery. This house, however, represents Woolson's perspective on the man-made things of place that create so poignant a picture of the Southern past and its loss, a perspective that Rowe has also identified as typical of Woolson's Northern contemporaries.[6] The house, its doors barred and windows blinded, its "clapboards gray and mossy," its piazza floor "fallen in here and there from decay" (17) is a monument to Southern loss just as the cemetery, significantly to Rodman a "more cheerful place" (17), is a monument to the less devastating losses of the North. To clinch the loss, Woolson has the dilapidated house bought, in the end, by an "energetic Maine" (41) man who, always ready to make a profit, sells Rodman the vine.

Woolson uses the symbol of fallen house to its greatest advantage in the story **"Old Gardiston,"** a story Henry James may have had in mind when he wrote *The Spoils of Poynton*. Old Gardiston is a "Manor house down in the rice-lands six miles from a Southern seaport" (105), a house dating back to Colonial days. The church that was once part of the house is gone, the road to it overgrown, and the ancestral members of the family are all buried in the church-yard. The house still has its latticed windows and Chinese ornamental vases and "spindle-legged side-board, covered with dark-colored plates and platters ornamented with dark-blue dragons going out to walk, and crocodiles circling around fantastically roofed temples as though they were waiting for the wor-shippers to come out in order to make a meal of them" (106). These cannot mask the house's decay, its "sunken and defaced" marble floor, its dampness, its hearth fireless because wood is too expensive. Woolson fills her story with marvelous details of the faded South, none better than the portrait of the mis-tress of the house who one day is forced to entertain Union soldiers and serves them using the four forks that are left of the family silver. For the occasion, she wears an old-fashioned gown and mildewed, blue kid slippers that she has "bravely" (121) mended. As her name suggests, the mistress of the house, Gardis Duke, is guardian of the noble Southern past, joined in her endeavors by her cousin whose life's work has been to keep a genealogy. But it is the house that is in some sense the main character of the story, certainly the major symbol. The denouement of "Old Gardiston" involves the burning of the house, complete with the footnoted and red-inked genealogy. In the process of invoking this loss, Woolson is gentle, understanding, and very funny. Her meaning is clear, and it is the meaning only someone who remains distant from the Southern pain could voice. This past, she implies, cannot be guarded but it can be loved, and in loving it, it should not be transformed, as was the house in **"Rodman the Keeper"** by social climbing Northern-ers. Better to burn than to sell. Further, only when there is a true union between North and South, when the old South symbolized by the cousin and the gene-alogy is dead, can a new South be formed. That South is symbolized here in, for Woolson, a rare happy ending where Gardis accepts the offer of marriage to a Union officer.

Woolson's sense of the South's permanent beauty is directed at the landscape rather than at the houses that suggest a past that must be let go. Through the landscape, the artistic soul can respond to the South. In the story **"Miss Elisabetha,"** for instance, Woolson paints a typical shabby gentility and the humor of a cultivated artistic response to the silvery loveliness of lagoon and ocean. Miss Elisabetha's nephew, Theodore, is a student who has been under her tutelage for six-teen years. When he nearly sucumbs to the snares of a famous singer who wants to correct his "bad" method (95) of singing and make him her protégé, Woolson lets us see that this is no more true than the heart-felt response Elisabetha has tried to instill in Theodore toward the land. Woolson is not measuring profound responses to the South, but true ones, and perhaps this genuineness is what caused her to number this story as one of her "favorites."[7] Miss Elisabetha has

her crisis, and her martyrdom. She watches Theodore marry a Minorcan girl and their children wreck havoc in the house, especially on the piano, but neither she nor Woolson judge against his adoption of Minorcan care-lessness, for his life is filled with love, if not with art. As for Miss Elisabetha, though she is ever the North-erner, an "old, old woman, but working still" (104), she has been enriched by pain and her response to the South, however shallow artistically, remains genuine.

A more profound artistic response to the South emerges as the dominant note in **"The South Devil"** where Woolson best defines the quality of Florida that so attracts her. Here a Florida swamp serves as metaphor for the Southern natural beauty that in-trigues the receptive Northern mind. As always, Woolson deals with Northerners come South, but here she defines more clearly what separates the true responders to the South, like Miss Elisabetha and the soldier in **"Old Gardiston,"** from the false or incom-plete, like David King and Rodman. In this story, Mark Deal is the workaholic Northerner who has brought his stepbrother Carl Brenner to recuperate on an old Spanish plantation. While Carl lies under a majestic, symmetrical live-oak tree listening to the call of the swamp and even sneaking away to its unhealthy depths, Mark energetically cleans up its overgrown orange grove. Woolson uses Mark and Carl to pinpoint responses to the South. Carl can respond to the artistic mystery of the swamp because he can accept the South as it is. However, Woolson recog-nizes that Carl's response is not necessarily "better" than Mark's. It is he who gambles away Mark's money and who instigates Mark's marriage to a Northern woman who will be the final cold insurance that Mark will never learn a more genuine artistic appreciation. Woolson is also clear that the Southern swamp repre-sents a stifling, sinister quality, a spur to the exploit-ative, nonproductive side of Carl's character, a qual-ity that also became dominant in Theodore in **"Miss Elisabetha."** This danger, Woolson implies, must be courted. The artist must be open to beauty. It may paralyze him but without it he can never get his art right. Woolson develops this concept in analogous experiences of Mark and Carl. Mark, before coming South, had nearly died on an ice-island in the Arctic where he had spent a whole day and night drifting among dead bodies. Carl had a similar experience alone, with-out the dead bodies, in the Florida swamp. Mark's ex-perience does not enrich him. Only for a fleeting mo-ment, before he accepts his Northern wife, does he feel the power of the swamp, the aloneness and mystery and threat that is the lot of the artist. Carl, on the other hand, takes his experience and finally produces from it. He not only hears music in the swamp, but he gets the music right, though it is too late for him to write it down. And so on his last journey, when dead, he rides through the swamp with his eyes open to a South that Woolson knows can touch the soul.

Woolson uses the South to point not only to the dichotomy between Northern and Southern attitudes and artistic and nonartistic responses, but also to serve as the perfect ground to laugh at religious extremism and hypocrisy. Again, as she laughs, she also understands and sees that sincerity is valid even when it lacks brilliance. Where David King is the young Israelite with courage and good intentions come to deliver a people from the Philistines, Sister St. Luke, in the story of that name, is the epitome of religious patience. In this case, the industrious Northerner is a woman who marries a Spaniard, but rather than be married in a Catholic church she is married by a justice of the peace because she considers "the padre of the little parish and one or two attendant priests as so much dust to be trampled energetically under her shoes, Protestant and number six and half double-soled [pun intended?] mediums" (43). Again the South serves as the perfect place for Woolson's humor toward extremism. Here there are dilettantish city men enjoying country living for a time and unable to take seriously Sister St. Luke's religious sincerity. Small wonder, for this little nun parrots a faith she blindly obeys. She keeps for "her most precious treasures—a bead of rosary that had belonged to some saint who lived somewhere some time" (62), a prayer in the handwriting of an early-dead nun, and a list of her own faults. Yet for all this poking fun at Sister St. Luke, Woolson sees a kind of mystical power in her simplicity when a tornado calls her to walk across water she fears in order to save her friends. She is dull, certainly, but there is a power that can move her. Rayburn Moore captures the essence of her religious nature and Woolson's portrait of it: "She is gentle and sentimental, yet her character is not developed sentimentally; and she represents the best qualities of any religious order; that is, she is kind and thinks of others before herself, she is brave and courageous in the face of dangers that frighten her, and she possesses a simple and abiding faith in her order and church. . . . "[8] After the rescue episode, when Sister St. Luke returns to her convent, she returns not just to dull-wittedness and shelter but also to peace and beauty, to what Woolson might have defined as the calm, not ignorant, Southern nature that has nurtured her religion.

The story "Sister St. Luke" is thrown nicely into relief by "Up in the Blue Ridge" where Woolson pokes wonderful fun at religious fanaticism. The treatise writer Honor Dooris prays hourly for a person who turns out to be a renegade cousin; her supporter Brother Bethue, one of nine ministers on a stagecoach that the story opens with, is a man so engulfed by religion that he gets drunk on five drinks of spring water. Woolson extends the extremism to matters nonreligious as well and has a melodramatic heyday with the story's bootlegger and federal agent plot. Like the stories "Rodman the Keeper" and "Old Gardiston," beneath its humor, "Up in the Blue

Ridge" emphasizes the crushing power of extremism on a woman's world. Gardis Duke may find her way to a union with a Northern moderate and point the way for a new Southern woman, not bound to the loyalties of a lost cause, but the self-imprisoned woman in "Rodman the Keeper" is a more typical portrait for Woolson. In fact, it is Rodman who best voices the real issue in his frustrated response to the dying soldier who has been listening to his female cousin's Southern viewpoint: "Bringing you here. . .

here; that is my offense, is it? There they lie, fourteen thousand brave men and true. Could they come back to earth they would be the first to pity and aid you, now that you are down. So would it be with you if the case were reversed; for a soldier is generous to a soldier. It was not your own spoke then; it was the small venom of a woman, that here, as everywhere through the South, is playing its rancorous part" (27). Unlike Gardis, that woman never forgives, and when she takes her last leave of Rodman she still cannot bring herself to sign the register book that would indicate that she has been willing to visit at least the cemetery on whose premises her old cousin has been cared for in death.

Through this kind of extremism, Woolson portrays the trap that Southern women build for themselves in their preference for living in a lost past rather than building a future for themselves as vital women. Perhaps this sense of a preference for the honor of suffering is what is at the heart of Woolson's maudlin language in the worst story of the collection, "In the Cotton Country." Here Woolson beautifically describes a young/old woman and her massive sadness, the fruit of losses in the war. When Woolson has the woman tell her own version of the cruelty of war, which takes up the majority of this story, the language is untypical of any of the other pieces. It has no humor and is unconvincingly sentimental, enough different from the rest of the collection that one must wonder if Woolson was not, as Moore points out, drawing on a true story and showing sympathy for Southern pain,[9] but was purposely showing the futility of living in the past.

Far more successful than the sympathy of "In the Cotton Country" is the humor that pervades "Up in the Blue Ridge" and Honor's betrayal of her sense of honor by turning in her bootlegging cousin rather than allowing him to murder the man she loves. Later, she marries that man, a Southerner to whom she becomes subservient. After her marriage, she never realizes her potential for beauty, at least in the eyes of the manipulative Northern lady who is left with Honor's rejected Northern choice, Stephen Wainwright. Woolson ends the story by commenting that this woman could give Stephen love where Honor could give him only gratitude, and by asking "What would you have?" (339). One would like, as Woolson surely must, to say neither, for the choice offered here is between the manipulative North or the fanatical South, not the kind of union into a more wholesome future seen in **"Old Gardiston."**

The kind of imprisonment of women typical in the South is perhaps best represented in the story **"Bro"** which concerns a love triangle between Marion Manning, whose mother is worried because she is not married, a faithful but silent admirer Bro, and Lawrence Vickery, the returned grandson of an established family. The story is conventional enough: Marion loves Vickery; Bro uses money from an invention to buy land anonymously from Vickery for ten thousand dollars so Vickery will stay in town and marry Marion; Vickery complies and, years later, learns of Bro's purchase when Bro wills the land to Marion. Bro, an inventor, knows that with the loss of Marion his inspiration for inventing is gone, and he dismantles his workroom. Through the Marion-Bro relationship, Woolson provides insight into Marion's position as a member of an old, impoverished Southen family and into the reason why this position has shaped her attitudes so that she never will rise out of it. She is Bro's inspiration, but she is also his mathematician, the one person who can figure the math so that Bro can get an invention patented. Lawrence Vickery is duly impressed with Marion's ability, and Woolson delights in exposing the kind of mentality that spurs his comment, "What will you do next? . . . Build a stone-wall—or vote? Imagine a girl taking light recreation in equations, and letting her mind run hilariously among groves of triangles on a rainy day!" (240). The response is doubly amusing when we learn that Marion's mathematical ability is not so good after all, for *this* invention of Bro's is not accepted for patent. The pleasure of arithmetic learned from a teacher at the Episcopal seminary in town is really no more than a Southern lady's idle hobby and Marion shows her feminine weakness when, well-timed, she swoons at the false news that Vickery is dead. What, Woolson seems to be saying, can one expect from a woman who "had never said 'don't' or 'can't' in [her life]" (235)? The freedom to accept such language is all that the liberated Vickery delivers.

All of Woolson's fiction deals in some way with the position of women in nineteenth-century society. It is not didactic; it does not call women to join in any kind of reform movement any more than the stories in **Rodman the Keeper** pretend to offer a plan for Reconstruction. This quiet, amazed view of the well-intentioned but mundane behavior of individuals gives Woolson's writing the subtlety and power that Henry James was so quick to recognize. The South serves her especially well because in it she can capture a whole spectrum of human perspectives: the pride and humility of a defeated culture; the indolence of a land whose beauty can also trigger the energy of art; the

ambiguity of sincerity and fanaticism in a religious milieu; the self-inflicted role of women as subservient creatures, and the endurance that women can display in the face of great suffering. Woolson shows all this and, in the tradition that James after her perfected, she never judges. Nor could she judge the South her fiction celebrates.

Notes

[1] Fullest early discussions are John Dwight Kern, *Constance Fenimore Woolson: Literary Pioneer* (Philadelphia, 1934), Jay B. Hubbell, "Northern Writers: Constance Fenimore Woolson," in *The South in American Literature 1607-1900* Durham, 1954), 733-37, and Claude M. Simpson, ed., *The Local Colorists: American Short Stories 1857-1900* (New York, 1960), 129-51. At this time, the most valuable book-length source is Rayburn S. Moore's Twayne Series, *Constance F. Woolson* (New Haven, 1963). Sybil Weir has studied some of Woolson's Southern women in "Southern Womanhood in the Novels of Constance Fenimore Woolson," *Mississippi Quarterly,* 29 (1976), 559-68, and Anne Rowe has written on Woolson as one of a number of Northern writers in the South (*The Enchanted Country: Northern Writers in the South, 1865-1910*, Baton Rouge, 1978).

[2] Henry James, *Partial Portraits* (New York, 1888), 179-80.

[3] James, p. 180.

[4] Page references are to Constance F. Woolson, *Rodman the Keeper: Southern Sketches* in *The American Short Story Series,* v. 87 (New York, 1880; 1969).

[5] Rowe, pp. 57-58.

[6] Rowe, pp. 62-65.

[7] Moore, p. 54.

[8] Moore, p. 53.

[9] Moore, p. 57.

Joan Myers Weimer (essay date 1986)

SOURCE: "Women Artists as Exiles in the Fiction of Constance Fenimore Woolson," *Legacy: A Journal of Nineteenth-Century American Women Writers,* Vol. 3, No. 2, Fall 1986, pp. 3-15.

[*In the essay that follows, Weimer studies Woolson's reflections on the extent to which "women artists . . . are ultimately exiled from their own art."*]

American women starting to write just after the Civil War found themselves standing on uneven new ground. Not because it was an act of daring for women to present themselves as professional writers: women novelists of the previous generation had broken that ground, and some, like Susan Warner and Maria Cummins, had written best sellers. These "literary domestics," however, had atoned for their presumption in departing from women's sphere; they made domesticity their subject matter, and justified their work by its moral uplift (Kelley 335, 329).

But among this new generation of women, many writers, like Mary E. Wilkins Freeman, Sarah Orne Jewett, Kate Chopin, and Constance Fenimore Woolson, made no excuses for themselves. They rejected the commitment to moral uplift along with the domestic ideology of the literary domestics. Irony, not sentimentality, characterized the realistic fiction they rooted in the regions they knew best. Labelling them as "regionalists" and "local colorists" has trivialized their work and obscured its universality and artistry. For they were the first American women writers of fiction who saw themselves not just as professionals but as artists, and who saw themselves competing with male writers not just for readers but for laurels.

One of these writers has left a remarkable record of a woman artist's struggle to place herself in relation to the literary domestics, to the male and female giants of literature, to her material, her society, and her sexuality. Constance Fenimore Woolson (1840-1894) published five novels and four volumes of short stories, as well as numerous reviews, sketches and poems, in her short life. Her work deserves to be better known for its complexity, ambiguity, irony, and wit; for its close observation of people and their environments; for its keen analysis of unacknowledged motives; and for the range of voices and tones its style accommodates.[1]

Woolson is of particular interest in women's literary history because she was acutely conscious of her situation as a woman writer. She could hardly be anything else, as the great-niece of James Fenimore Cooper, whose name she bore, and as the "extremely intimate" friend of Henry James (Edel 160), who wrote an admiring essay about her work which he included with his 1888 *Partial Portraits* of Turgenev and George Eliot. These connections forced her to compare herself with major male writers, and raised urgent questions about women and art which she dramatized in a group of short stories.

If a woman wants passionately to be an artist, but lacks talent, what kind of life can she make for herself in the shadow of great art and criticism by men? Or in the shadow of a woman genius of another age? If a woman writer has enormous power, would her work be perceived as being so flawed by the anomaly of genius in woman that it would fail to find an audience? Would her genius be so deforming that it would deprive her of men's love as well as success? If she is drawn to women but loses them to male rivals, would not her loveless state limit her as an artist? If she allows herself to love a man, won't she become an ordinary woman whose words have no weight with men?

In working out these chilling questions, Woolson's fiction presents only once a character who is successful both as woman and as artist. She is a figure of fantasy who materializes on a Florida beach sitting on a tiger skin, wearing purple velvet, and singing operatic arias (**"Miss Elizabetha,"** *Rodman the Keeper*). When Woolson presents women artists realistically, rather than fantastically, she envisions them as she does most of her women characters—as exiles. And she furthers her exploration of alienation by presenting their proper subject matter as other exiles.

Some of Woolson's female characters begin as voluntary exiles, leaving their homes in order to become painters or preachers, only to find themselves involuntarily exiled from love and self-respect. Some are exiles from their own painful feelings of inadequacy; some from self-knowledge; some from relationships whose loss leads to such devastation that solitude is preferable. The women artists, whether mediocre or brilliant, are ultimately exiled from their own art.

Woolson felt herself an exile for much of her life, her wanderings associated with bereavements. When three of her five older sisters died of scarlet fever in Woolson's first month of life, her parents left their home in New Hampshire with its unbearable memories and moved to Cleveland.[2] When Woolson was 12, her oldest sister contracted tuberculosis from her husband of a few months and died. The next year, her remaining older sister died in childbirth. She learned to be cautious of all attachments, and wary of marriage; by her early twenties she declared herself a spinster. When her father died in her twenty-ninth year, Woolson gave up an independent life in New York to begin a decade of wandering with her mother in the South. Although she found excellent material for fiction in the post-Reconstruction South, she complained to the poet Paul Hamilton Hayne that "a trunk is all the home I have had," and that "I am so eager to go north that I can scarcely wait; an 'exile longing for home.' I like the South; no Yankee-born northerner ever liked it better; but, the years away from home! I have no real home, however" (Hubbell 720, 731).

That nomadic period ended with her mother's death, which destroyed even the fragile home they had built out of their trunks. Abruptly on her own at 39, Woolson was devastated. To bring her out of her depression, her one surviving sister took her to Europe—a removal which turned out to be a permanent exile. While there, she wrote to her fellow expatriate Henry James, who became her first close friend in Europe, that his writings "are my true country, my real home. And nothing else ever fully is—try as I may to think so" (Edel 93).

At the same time that Woolson was describing herself as a rather pathetic, homeless creature, she was developing her phenomenal powers of observation of people and places and learning to transform this raw material into fiction which brought her recognition and an independent income. Her women characters reflect Woolson's sense of exile but not her success. A remarkable distance exists between Woolson's authorial voice—assured, ironic, in control—and the debilitated lives she assigns to women artists, or to women whose intense interest in human feeling, behavior and motivation identifies them with the writer. These characters' situations seem to reflect her deepest feelings about women and art, convictions which persist from her earliest stories despite the improvement in her own circumstances.

Woolson set many of her early stories in the American equivalents of desert islands: Fort Mackinac on Lake Michigan; a closed community of Zoarites in Ohio; a mining camp on an island in Lake Superior; a solitary house in a salt marsh on Lake Huron; an abandoned cotton plantation after Sherman's march. These isolated settings justify the intensity of the relationships among the castaways who meet there, and function as metaphors for women's various forms of exile. Several stories that are not explicitly about women artists probe the limits of subject matter available to women writers. They present the woman writer as an outsider among outsiders, driven by her own isolation to prey on, even cannibalize, the lives and passions of other women.[3]

The narrator of **"Jeannette"** (1874) is the widowed aunt of a young lieutenant at Fort Mackinac, where she fills some lonely hours trying to teach a beautiful half-breed woman to read, and encouraging a cold young surgeon to fall in love with her protégée. She seems to expect the doctor to seduce and abandon the girl, so that she can enjoy vicariously the thrill of romantic heart-break. Instead, the surgeon becomes obsessed with the girl and decides to lower himself to marry this "ignorant half-breed" (**Castle Nowhere** 171). The girl escapes his condescension and the woman's manipulation by refusing to marry the doctor. But if the narrator has missed the opportunity to enjoy the girl's broken heart, she still has the pleasure of feeding on the doctor's pain and passion, wondering "how long the feeling lived,—the feeling that swept me along in its train down to the beach-cottage that wild night" (175). She admits no responsibility for the doctor's

suffering, nor any inclination to imagine Jeannette's pain had her plot turned out more predictably. She believes she has fallen "into the habit of studying persons very closely" (154), but Woolson's irony shows clearly that she has failed to include herself in her scrutiny.

Despite this distance from her narrator, Woolson seems also to share her fascination with a woman who is everything she and the narrator are not—beautiful, gay, proud, vital, daring—and who therefore attracts and experiences violent romantic passions. Woolson's interest in such women recurs in other stories. It is a complex mixture of envy and attraction, which never evolves into romantic friendship or into the love between kindred spirits which many nineteenth-century women freely enjoyed (Faderman 161, 205). No doubt the deaths of her five sisters made Woolson fearful of devastating loss following intimacy with women. Through women narrators who distance themselves from both men and women, she explores the fictive possibilities and psychological risks in the position of the solitary outsider, the literal or emotional exile.

The narrator of a weak but revealing early tale, **"Wilhemena"** (1874), is like the narrator of **"Jeannette"** in her unsettling mixture of manipulation and vicarious romantic involvement, although, unlike the lonely widow, she is a "romantic wife" whose "heart went out to all lovers" (**Castle Nowhere** 273). She tells herself that her interest in Wilhemena is to help her leave her closed Zoarite community to marry her beloved Gustav, who will have none of the community's restrictions now that the Civil War has shown him more of the world. When she runs to tell Wilhemena the news of Gustav's arrival, however, it is in order to experience both the girl's passions and those of her lover: "Her emotion resembled the intensest fire of fever, and yet it seemed natural . . . her slender form throbbed, and pulses were beating under my hands wherever I touched her" (285).

Like the narrator of **"Jeannette,"** this woman is strongly attracted to the woman whose life she manipulates. When Gustav predictably leaves without her, and the girl cries out after him, the woman "drew her head down on my shoulder to stifle the sound; it was better the soldier should not hear it, and its anguish thrilled my own heart also (300). In reserving for herself the cry meant for Wilhemena's lover, the narrator plays his role. Because she admits to none of her real motives, she is driven to practice a rather chilling form of possession of both lovers, trying like the narrator of **"Jeannette"** to expropriate the passions—even the painful ones—that are absent from her own life.

In a fine early tale, **"In the Cotton Country"** (1876), the passion preyed upon is not love, but the despair of a woman who has lost everything and everyone in the Civil War. The predatory narrator is a Northern woman whose own life is so empty that she spends much of it as a "solitary pedestrian," and whose own sense of homelessness is so great that she follows a flock of crows, thinking, "The crows at home—that would be something worth seeing" (***Rodman the Keeper*** 179). They lead her not to their home but to a "solemn, lonely old house" whose wretched isolation fascinates her: "Now if there had been two, I should not have gone on. . . . Two houses are sociable and commonplace; but one all alone on a desolate waste like that inspired me with—let us call it interest, and I went forward" (181).

What else might one call it? Certainly a compulsive fascination with solitude perhaps greater than her own, as well as a need to feel someone else's pain. This narrator excuses her own prying into the Southern woman's tragic story by telling herself she is a "Sister of Charity . . . bearing balm and wine and oil for those who suffer" (184). But in fact, she is testing her own tendency toward solitude, wondering how great a deprivation could be endured.

Ann Douglas Wood finds in this "superb story" the narrator's "almost uncontrollable need to . . . get at some stifled part of herself, mysteriously locked in the other woman's past and capable not only of pain but of creativity" (30). Wood is certainly right about the narrator's deprivation and need: she is so fascinated with the other woman's "dry, still eyes of immovable, helpless grief" that she admits, "I used to wait impatiently for the hour when I could enter into the presence of her great silence," even though the other woman's eyes ask, "'By what right are you here?'" (***Rodman the Keeper*** 182). But while Woolson can find powerful material in the Southern woman's tragedy, her narrator finds only confirmation of her unstated beliefs that human connection cannot last but can only betray, and that the best protection against such loss is accepting homelessness and habitual solitude. She allows herself only the tenuous, temporary connection that a woman exiled from herself can make with other such exiles.

These narrators, along with their vicarious experience of women's passions, obviously reveal an author in search of material. But they also reveal a guilty awareness that such "material" is the experience of other human beings who cannot be intimately observed without damaging their lives and the observer's own integrity. This was the dilemma Hawthorne had dramatized in tales like "Ethan Brand," "The Birthmark," "Rappaccini's Daughter," and in *The Scarlet Letter*. Since Woolson said that Hawthorne was "always" one of her "gods" (Moore 23), she must have studied eagerly and apprehensively his uneasy "burrowing" into the secret caverns of human nature (Hawthorne 590).[4] She would have recognized her own anxiety in his. But she would have seen too that as a single woman artist she ran risks that Hawthorne did not. He felt rescued from the worst of his isolation, if not from his guilt, by love and marriage. For Woolson, however, love of women threatened devastating disappointment, while love of men, if it didn't kill women outright, could be a trap for the woman who wanted to be an artist.

This dilemma is dramatized in **"The Lady of Little Fishing"** (1874), one of Woolson's most admired and most misread tales. Here, the central character is a Scottish woman missionary whose power over language links her with the woman artist; her words have such immense authority that they transform the behavior of a group of brutal hunters camped on an island in Lake Superior. The men, awed by her pale, nun-like beauty, call her "Our Lady" (***Castle Nowhere*** 359) and treat her like the Madonna. But the moment they discover that she has fallen in love with one of them, her influence is destroyed.

Critics who admire the story tend to take as its theme one character's observation that women perversely care only for the men who care nothing for them: "'O woman! woman! the same the world over!'" (383). But the story is ultimately not about love or women's choices of love objects, but about the perception that a woman's words have weight just so long as she is seen as an angel, a madonna, a sexless, wholly spiritual being. Then she is safe among wolfish men, who will even cook for her, nurse her when she's ill, build a meeting-house for her to conduct services, and build themselves new houses to hold their new, clean, orderly selves. For this mother, sibly, or angel, men become good children, docile, domestic, and sexless. They are spellbound by "that spotless woman standing alone in the glare of the fire" (361), whose severe words hold back not "one grain of denunciation, one iota of future punishment" (360).

This powerful figure is barely recognizable after she falls in love. Once the men see that she is "common flesh and blood" (379), she is "our Lady no longer; only a woman like any other,—weak and fickle" (392). The Madonna has become Eve, and powerless. The change is not only in the men's perception of her, but in herself, most dramatically in her language. Her "steady voice" becomes "softer, the words at times faltering" (374). When she throws herself at the feet of the man who does not love her, her rhetorical degradation is as great as her personal fall: "Oh, take me with you! Let me be your servant—your slave—anything—anything, so that I am not parted from you, my lord and master, my only, only love" (384). Love is a terrible affliction of which people die—in this case, I think, of shame.

Love leads the Lady not only to the loss of her dignity and verbal power, but to a devastating revelation. She learns that she was deluded in thinking of herself as God's instrument in the wilderness of America and of men's hearts. Since the men reform only out of their idolatrous adoration of her, their reform ends when she falls from her niche. The story thus comments on the contemporary ideology of womanhood and on the strategy of the literary domestics who excused their unladylike entry into man's public sphere by claiming to be God's instruments called to save souls (Kelley 295). Woolson suggests not only that God's instruments may be deluded, but that they can retain their power only by sacrificing their capacity for passionate love.

The story also subverts the nineteenth-century belief that a woman's selfless love of one man gives her power over him, and through him, in the world. Instead, love robs a woman of her integrity and power. The story even undercuts the ideology of "the angel of the house." Despite her silvery paleness, her devotion to religion, her strenuous efforts to redeem fallen men, this angel is confined to no home, but takes the whole American wilderness as her sphere. Her role is not to sacrifice herself for men, but to save them by her preaching. They in fact sacrifice for her, giving up their liquor, fights, and dirt, giving her their food and labor. They do give her worshipful love and a home in the wilderness. But Woolson's point is that women's words have power only as long as they are indifferent to these traditional sources of women's power. The lovelessness and homelessness that torment the narrators of **"In the Cotton Country,"** **"Jeannette,"** and **"Wilhemena"** here have at least the potential for artistic success.

Another early story, however, which deals explicitly with a woman artist, finds lovelessness as disabling as love. Catherine, the narrator of **"Felipa"** (1876), has never known the success and power of the Lady of Little Fishing. She describes herself as "an artist, poor and painstaking" (***Rodman the Keeper*** 199) who lives a "poor gray life" (218). Her obvious foil is her beautiful friend Christine, whose arrogant power over her lover Edward makes Catherine say to herself, "Fate, in the next world make me one of those long, lithe, light-haired women, will you? I want to see how it feels" (216). But Catherine has a true alter-ego in Felipa, the Minorcan child they meet in Florida. She shares the sexual amiguity implied by Felipa's name and made explicit by the child's passionate attachment to *both* Christine and Edward—an attachment which amuses and puzzles the adults, but which in fact expresses Catherine's own unacknowledged feelings.

Perhaps because of this repression of her passions, Catherine lacks Felipa's Orpheus-like power over na-

ture. The child dances in circles of pine cones and knows the trees listen when she talks to them. Felipa's artistic powers are still developing, but she worships them in the form of a goddess she has made of saw palmetto pieces and crowned with flowers, and to whom she offers food and other treasures. Catherine does not acknowledge Felipa's artistic gifts, but tries systematically to socialize the child into a properly repressed female like herself who is "gentle," "quiet and good" (209), giving her a "respectable, orderly doll" (217) to replace the palmetto goddess. For such efforts, Catherine wins exactly nothing—"I was forgotten as usual" (210)—and turns to her painting to escape her pain and anger at being rejected by both children and adults. She sanitizes these emotions as "cynicism" which she calls "a small brass field-piece that eventually bursts and kills the artilleryman. I knew this, having blown up myself more than once; so I went back to my painting and forgot the world" (211). We might also identify these explosives as sexual longings, directed toward women as well as men, which Catherine uses art to evade rather than to express, understand, or transform.

When Christine finally accepts Edward's proposal, Catherine tells herself that she is "glad that the old simple-hearted love was not entirely gone from our tired metallic world" (218). But Felipa recognizes and deals directly with the self-hatred and rage they both feel. She eats the "poison things" (219) in Catherine's paint box, grasping what the woman artist does not— that art can poison when it is used to repress rather than to express honest feeling. Seriously ill, Felipa responds to Edward's attempts to comfort her by stabbing his arm with Catherine's little dagger.

Catherine tells the child's grandfather that since Felipa loved Edward and Christine "both alike," her love "is nothing; she does not know." The old man agrees that Felipa doesn't know the meaning of her attachments, "but *I* know. It was two loves, and the stronger thrust the knife" (220). The stronger love was the one for Christine; the attack was on the man who chose her instead of Felipa, and who also took away the woman she loved. Catherine truly "does not know" what she feels.[5] Using art to deny unfulfillable longings, Catherine finds her attempts to capture on canvas Felipa's complex character or the subtleties of the salt-marsh are "hopeless efforts" (296). Denial of her complicated feelings dooms her as woman and as artist.

Two years after writing **"Felipa,"** Woolson drew attention to the power of women's love for each other in a review she wrote for *The Atlantic* of *Esther Pennefather*. She called the novel a ridiculous book but one with an original subject: "The singular power one woman sometimes has over another. . . . I myself have seen tears of joy, the uttermost faith, and deepest devotion, in mature, well-educated and cultivated women, for some other woman whom they adored" (503). Although Woolson says that as soon as an agreeable man appears, "the whole cloud structure topples over, its battlements dissolve" (503), she does not quite present women's love for each other as "a rehearsal in girlhood of the great drama of woman's life," as Longfellow did in his 1849 novel *Kavanaugh* (Faderman 170). Instead, Woolson describes such women lovers as thinking after marriage "of that old adoration which was so intense and so pure, so self-sacrificing and so far away" (503). But her imagery of cloud castles indicates what her stories dramatize, that women who love women lose them to men.

The troubled relationship between love and art became even more urgent for Woolson when she moved to Europe in 1879 and developed an intense friendship with Henry James.[6] Three stories she wrote in the next three years place an American woman artist in Europe, and in the shadow of a successful male writer or critic who resembles James. Although her Continental scenes offer women more options than the American desert islands of her earlier fiction, none of these women find success in art or love. This, despite the warmth of James's friendship and her own success as a writer. Her first novel *Anne* came out during her first year abroad, and was one of Harper's best-sellers. But Woolson apparently mistrusted her success. When she imagined a woman writer of real genius, she called her **"Miss Grief"** and made her work incomprehensible to the reading public. Her other women artists attract the love of masterful men who insist they give up art. Their decisions to marry these men are presented as a "great downfall" (*Dorothy* 193).

Ettie Macks, the heroine of **"The Street of the Hyacinth"** (1882) has a complexly developed consciousness that shows James's influence on Woolson's work.[7] At the same time, this heroine has important resemblances to the shadowy, mythic Lady of Woolson's earlier tale. Like the Lady, out of place among the savage hunters of Lake Superior, Ettie Macks is an exile in Rome. She has rented the family farm in her tiny Western town of Tuscolee Falls so she can come with her mother to live on the dirty, narrow street of the Hyacinth in the shadow of the Pantheon, to study male masterpieces as part of her education as an artist. In this dedication to her goal, and in her impersonal indifference to the men around her except as they can help her to reach it, Ettie is again like the Lady. Like her too, Ettie has seriously overestimated her own powers. She is finally persuaded by a series of male mentors that she has not a shred of talent.

Although Ettie resembles the Lady in loving a man who doesn't love her, she retains more of her self-

respect and dignity than the woman missionary did. When the James-like Raymond Noel, an aloof and successful art critic, proposes marriage not because he loves her but because he is eager to receive her ardent love, Ettie refuses him. Admitting she loves him, she tells Noel she's ashamed to love a man she can't respect or admire, and will learn to overcome her feeling for him. Ettie's honesty and pride shock Noel into realizing he does indeed love this remarkable woman. She agrees to marry him only when she is persuaded she cannot be an artist, and is worn down by his persistence and her mother's, by her strenuous labors to support herself and her mother by teaching, and by her own reluctant love of Noel. Rayburn Moore concludes that Ettie has found "fulfillment in a marriage to her mentor" (67). But Noel's ironic remark that in marrying him Ettie has suffered "a great downfall" from her "superhuman" heights of integrity (193) is closer to the truth. The imagery of hyacinths makes Woolson's intention clear.

Ettie's "downfall" is linked with the demolition of the Street of the Hyacinth, which "experienced a great downfall, also" (193), pulled down so it would no longer "disfigure" the Pantheon, "the magificent old Pagan temple" (191) it adjoined. In "Pagan" mythology, Hyacinthus suffered a downfall worse than Ettie's at the hands of his loving mentor, Apollo, who accidentally killed him while teaching him to throw the discus. The street where Ettie came to live is named for the doomed Hyacinthus because Ettie's mentor has slain his beloved's faith in herself as artist and woman. Such female self-assertion would evidently "disfigure" the monumental principles of male culture which Noel upholds both as art critic and as suitor. When Ettie marries him, her integrity, which had survived her admission that she had no talent as an artist, suffers a genuine "downfall."

Woolson imagined another male mentor persuading a woman to give up her artistic ambitions, not because her writing is bad—Woolson never reveals its quality—but because he believes that genius in women is a disfigurement or a delusion. In **"At The Chateau of Corinne"** (1880), Katherine Winthrop has to choose between her literary ambitions, symbolized by Madame de Staël, whose home on Lake Lehman provides the setting and title of the story, and marriage to John Ford, who cannot abide Madame de Staël or any other literary woman. Ford offers marriage on condition that Katherine cultivate the "simple and retiring womanly graces" and "write no more" (*Dorothy* 263, 285). Katherine's acquiescence, like Ettie's, is a "downfall."

Ford loathes Madame de Staël. His stated objections are personal: she wore a turban, forced her guests to discuss the subject she was writing about, made egotistical demands for sympathy. But his serious, unspoken objections are to de Staël and her heroine Corinne as models of female greatness. Woolson's admiration of them was shared by contemporaries as different as Elizabeth Cady Stanton and Harriet Beecher Stowe (Parker 13, 37). Margaret Fuller, another "martyr to her own uniqueness" (Welter 78), was known as "the American Corinne." But a real cultural ambivalence about these female geniuses emerges in the warning in a popular magazine that while women with minds "equal to any human undertaking" exist, "happily these giants of their kind are rare" (*Young Lady's Companion* qtd. in Welter 76). Such women have unsexed themselves. By going beyond male-defined limitations, they have become monsters, not women at all.

Ford would emphatically have agreed. He responds to Katherine's defense of Madame de Staël as "a woman of genius" by exclaiming, "'A woman of genius! And what is the very term but a stigma? No woman is so proclaimed by the great brazen tongue of the Public unless she has thrown away her birthright of womanly seclusion for the miserable mess of pottage called "fame."' "'The seclusion of a convent? or a prison?'" asks Katherine (263). This exchange is a fair example of her witty defense of women and Ford's bombastic severity. Yet she masochistically chooses Ford to tell her "the truth, your real opinion" (265) of the volume of poetry she has written and published anonymously. Ford responds with a remarkable outburst of misogyny which seeks to disguise itself as a generous masculine desire to save women from themselves:

> We do not expect great poems from women any more than we expect great pictures; we do not expect strong logic any more than we expect brawny muscle. A woman's poetry is subjective. But what cannot be forgiven—at least in my opinion—is . . . a certain sort of daring. This is its essential, unpardonable sin . . . because it comes . . . from the lips of a woman. For a woman should not dare in that way. Thinking to soar, she invariably descends. . . . And to see her leave [her sphere], and come in all her white purity, which must inevitably be soiled, to the garish arena where men are contending, where the dust is rising, and the air is tainted and heavy—this is indeed a painful sight. Every honest man feels like going to her, poor mistaken sibyl that she is, closing her lips with gentle hand, and leading her away to some far spot among the quiet fields, where she can learn her error, and begin her life anew. (268)

Remarkable words from a man who devotes himself to exposing other people's posturing, and prides himself on male logic.

Ford's misogyny is so overwhelming that it suggests a tangle of motives. Perhaps he wants to punish Katherine for making him a "victim" of her charms while she is engaged to someone else. Perhaps he wants to offend her so as to put distance between himself and a woman whose independence frightens him. Perhaps he wants to set the terms under which he would feel safe enough to marry her. In any case, the violence of his opinions and the space Woolson gives to them indicate that she believed opinions like his were a real obstacle to women writers. The overblown rhetoric she assigns him is a clear sign of her disapproval of this stereotypical masculinity, just as the Lady's romantic effusions signalled the demise of her integrity

When she loses her fiancé and her fortune and decides she must marry Ford, Katherine agrees without much of a struggle to his conditions that she "write no more" (285). Her greater conflict is over losing the independence which wealth had given her, and which Ford saw as an equally serious obstacle to their marriage. He prefers her impoverished, so that she will "in a measure be dependent upon your husband, and that is very sweet to a self-willed man like myself. Perhaps in time I can even make it sweet to you" (281).

Katherine is not so sure. She tells him, "You are narrow, prejudiced; you do not believe in progress of any kind. You would keep women down with an iron hand" (284). It seems she is right. After their marriage Ford keeps in his study a complete set of Madame de Staël's works as a kind of trophy of what he took from his wife: her independence of mind, her literary aspirations.

The structure of the story indicates Woolson's regret that modern women lack the genius and the independence of Madame de Staël. The story is built on four visits to Coppet, each of which marks a decline in de Staël's prestige and Katherine's independence. In the first, Katherine's fiancé praises Madame de Staël's genius. In the second, Ford savages Katherine's poem. In the third, Katherine has been jilted. And in the fourth, which takes place on a comfortless, wet, cold day, Katherine has lost her fortune, her fiancé, and her hopes for herself as a writer, and accepts Ford's proposal. Katherine's story, worked out in the shadow of a great woman's place of exile, has the same outcome as Ettie's, in the shadow of the Pantheon and the galleries of great male painters. Neither male nor female models of greatness seem of much help to women who would be artists, but who are persuaded that they have no talent and that their only recourse is marriage to men unable to accept independence or talent in women.

By taking Ford's misogynistic, manipulative opinions as Woolson's own, her literary biographer Rayburn Moore mistakenly concludes that she shared his "entire disbelief in the possibility of true fiery genius in women" (157, n. 35).[8] Evidence that Woolson believed in and was inspired by women of genius is found both inside and outside the story. She made her own pilgrimage to Coppet "to stand there just for its association with [Madame de Staël]" (Benedict 226), and placed Charlotte Brontë and George Eliot among her literary luminaries. And in her journal, Woolson objected to the critic Edmund C. Stedman for his condescension to Elizabeth Barrett Browning: "Mr. Stedman does not really believe in woman's genius. His disbelief peeps through every line of the criticism below, whose essence is—'She did wonderfully well for a woman'" (Benedict 93). Since Stedman was her own first literary mentor, she must herself have felt the sting of his condescension. **"At the Chateau of Corinne"** should be read as a critique of men who belittle women writers.

Woolson wrote one tale about a woman writer of genius. Although **"Miss Grief"** (1880) is generally considered Woolson's best story, Harper and Brothers did not include it in the two anthologies of her stories they issued shortly after her death, which included every other story she had published since the last collection of her short fiction in 1880. Since the story depicts a woman genius whose tragic failure is the fault of her society and not of herself, perhaps the publishers felt that like Miss Grief's own work, Woolson's account would not be acceptable to the public.

"Miss Grief" is narrated by a male writer who is everything the woman writer is not: "Young, well and strong, passably good-looking, with some money that one has inherited and more that one has earned," the narrator admits that he takes a "deep, although of course carefully concealed, satisfaction in my own little fame" (574), and in his popularity in the superficial American and English society in Rome. The woman who seeks his help in getting her work published is not young, though younger at 43 than she looks. (Woolson was then 40.) Miss Aaronna Crief, whose name the narrator misreads as "Grief," is not good-looking or well dressed, because she is poor and suffering from hunger and cold. For these reasons, the narrator repeatedly refuses to see her, smugly telling himself that "Grief has not so far visited me here . . . and she shall not now" (574). He assumes she wants to sell him something, and when he learns she is a writer, exclaims, "An authoress! This is worse than old lace" (576).

When the narrator is finally shamed into reading her play, he recognizes that it is "inspired," full of earnestness, passion and "power" which "thrill" him as evidence that she has the "divine spark of genius" (578). But he finds her work deeply flawed "by some fault or lack which seemed wilful perversity, like the work of an evil sprite. It was like a case of jeweller's wares set before you, with each ring unfinished, each bracelet too large or too small for its purpose, each breastpin without its fastening, each necklace purposely broken" (581). This view of the work's fatal flaws is supported by male publishers to whom the narrator sends it. It is never clear whether this judgment is a fair one or whether the woman genius is writing in a way that the men cannot comprehend.

When the narrator overcomes Miss Grief's proud refusal to let him change so much as a "comma," and tries to correct these faults, he finds the flaws inseparable from the genius. It is like "taking out one especial figure in a carpet: that is impossible unless you unravel the whole" (583). As Leon Edel has observed, Henry James took Woolson's metaphor of the "figure in a carpet" for the title of his own tale about the elusive nature of genius. But James's male genius, Hugh Vereker, had fame and disciples. Miss Grief has neither, because in a woman genius is perceived as deforming. An imagination that is "unrestrained, large, vast, like the skies or the wind" (583) makes her too eccentric to communicate with the public she needs.

While the narrator sends out her work to publishers, Miss Grief lies dying. He discovers this through an accidental meeting with her aunt, for he has forgotten all about her. Recognizing her deathbed not only as a scene of desperate poverty but as a sacred shrine, he brings wine, flowers, and candles, and tells himself that lying to her about the fate of her drama is one of his "few good deeds" (584). Believing it is to be published, she says, "I have never known what it was . . . to be fully happy until now . . . Yes, I am happy," (584) she tells herself in amazement.

But it is the narrator's turn for grief, although he tells himself that the reason he has kept her rejected drama in a locked case, and reads it over "once in a while," is that it is a "memento of my own good fortune, for which I should continually give thanks. The want of one grain made all her work void, and that one grain was given to me. She, with the greater power, failed—I with the less, succeeded" (585). Thus he admits the truth of Miss Grief's dying words: "You had success—but I had the greater power" (585).

If successful mediocrity is better than unsuccessful greatness, then he is indeed fortunate. He has married a trivial, narrow-minded society woman, and written trivial, popular books. But secretly, he has made the greater writer "my . . . Miss Grief" (585), has taken into himself the grief of recognizing like Henry James's failed "master" what it means to have everything but "the great thing . . . the sense of having done the best" (James 135).

Woolson herself made no compromises with "the best" she could do. She put her work ahead of everything else, working long days and revising tirelessly. Her considerable success as a writer, however, did not prevent grief from being her regular companion. She struggled all her life with bouts of acute depression which she thought she inherited from her father. She wrote in her journal, "When she woke in the morning not haunted by care or trouble or grief or pain, it was a new sensation, it was a relief. Still it made her feel strange—*old, strangely* indifferent. 'I wonder if I am going to die soon?' she thought" (Benedict 147). Haunted by grief and probably guilt at having survived five of her sisters, securing less of Henry James's time and attention than she wanted, lonely and vulnerable to depressions during a second bout of influenza, she may have committed suicide. Delirious with fever, she either fell or leapt from her balcony in Venice in January of 1894.

But it would be a mistake to see her death as a mark of professional despair. Although her stories show that both genius and mediocrity, love and lovelessness, disabled women artists, she herself managed not to be disabled but to remain productive and successful by making art out of those dilemmas. And it would be equally wrong to dismiss her analysis of the excruciating dilemmas of women artists as merely a symptom of her own depressions. Several of her women contemporaries depicted those struggles as equally harrowing.

Both Rebecca Harding Davis and Elizabeth Stuart Phelps portray talented women artists who find they cannot combine art with love and the responsibilities of marriage. While Davis affirms the struggle of an impoverished male artist, Hugh Wolfe in *Life in the Iron Mills* (1861), to express his tragic vision, in "The Wife's Story" (1864) she rejects a woman's attempts to fulfill her artistic potential, even though—or perhaps because—she has a chance to succeed. The story concludes instead that "a woman has no better work in life than . . . to make herself a visible Providence to her husband and child" (19). While the story supports the prevailing domestic ideology that women who stray outside the domestic sphere bring misery to themselves and others, it also testifies eloquently to the agony of having to choose between art and love.[9]

Elizabeth Stuart Phelps's *The Story of Avis* (1877) differs from "The Wife's Tale" in affirming its talented heroine's right to pursue a life of art, but concurs that women cannot combine art with family life. If they want to be artists, they should not marry. At the same time, Phelps insists that the often painful experiences of marriage and motherhood enlarge the sympathies that are the basis of great art—even while they consume a woman's time and energy and prevent her from producing that art. Evidently, this bind ensures that we cannot have the best work of which women are capable.

Unmarried women devoted to art appear in Mary E. Wilkins Freeman's stories, but these women are distinguished by their devotion to art rather than by their talent. The women in "A Village Singer" and "A Poetess" (1891) find their reason for living in their passion for singing and writing. When their work is rejected, the process is not enough to sustain them, and despite their rugged independence, they die.

Although these authors are better known than Woolson, none of their fictions about women artists is more powerful or complex than hers. While she displays strong anxiety that solitary observers may become predators of the lives of others, lacking the self-knowledge that is an indispensible ingredient of great art, she also shows how women who would be artists are coerced by the male-established and male-maintained canon, and punished for the distance between their own vision and male-defined taste. Woolson's fiction shows that withdrawal into voluntary exile from such painful contradictions can become an involuntary separation from oneself, while insisting at the same time that the more pernicious isolation is from one's art, an exile in which all society conspires.

Nevertheless, Woolson believed that women were capable of distinctive greatness in art. She wrote a remarkable sonnet **"To George Eliot"** (1876) which insists that a woman genius combines the "colossal" power of a Michelangelo with the "finely traced" beauty created by "woman-hands":

> O wondrous woman! shaping with thy pen
> As Michael Angelo did shape from stone,
> Colossal forms of clear-cut outline, when
> We dwell upon thy pages, not alone
> The beauty of thy rose we see, as finely traced
> As roses drawn by other woman-hands
> Who spend their lives in shaping them, but
>   faced
> We find ourselves with giant's work, that
>   stands
> Above us as a mountain lifts its brow,
> Grand, unapproachable, yet clear in view
> To lowliest eyes that upward look. O, how
> Hast thou shed radiance as thy finger drew
> Its shapes! A myriad women light have seen,
> And courage taken, because *thou* hast been![10]

This mixture of power and tenderness is what she hoped her own legacy would be. A month before her death, she thought again of the "giant's work" that a woman could do, and wrote, "I should like to turn into a peak when I die, to be a beautiful purple mountain, which would please the tired, sad eyes of thousands of human beings for ages" (Benedict xvi). Woolson's mountain is metaphorically further from Shelley's Mont Blanc, which embodies the male poet's verbal and sexual power, than her grave is from his in the beautiful Protestant Cemetery in Rome, where she rests a few feet lower than he on the bank that slopes down from the ancient wall. Woolson's purple mountain is instead like her conception of George Eliot's genius, both maternal and phallic. It suggests that at the end of her life she saw the tensions surrounding love and gender identity dramatized in her early fiction as possible sources of distinctive female artistry. Her courage and skill in exploring these and other conflicts faced by the first generation of American women artists should recommend her to modern readers who seek to understand the conditions under which nineteenth-century women wrote.

Notes

[1] I am editing a volume of Woolson's short fiction for the American Women Writers series published by Rutgers University Press. It is scheduled to appear in 1988.

[2] All biographical information is from Rayburn S. Moore, Clare Benedict, and Jay B. Hubbell's published work, as well as Doris Faber's unpublished biography.

[3] Ann Douglas Wood finds a pattern among the women local colorists of "spying or even preying upon their subject matter" (29).

[4] Woolson's "Castle Nowhere" is an elaborate reworking of Hawthorne's "Rappaccini's Daughter." Like Hawthorne, she also gives her preachers characteristics of artists; see "The Lady of Little Fishing" and "Peter the Parson," both in *Rodman the Keeper.*

[5] A similar unacknowledged attraction exists between the women in Woolson's "A Florentine Experiment" (1880), *Dorothy and Other Italian Stories.*

[6] Leon Edel gives extensive but negatively biased consideration to Woolson's relationship with Henry James in Volume III of his biography of James.

[7] Two articles consider the influence of James and Woolson on each other's work: Rayburn S. Moore, "The Strange Irregular Rhythm of Life: James's Late Tales and Constance Woolson." *South Atlantic Bulletin* 41 (1976): 86-93; and Sharon Dean, "Constance Fenimore Woolson and Henry James: The Literary Relationship." *Massachusetts Studies in English* 71.3 (1980): 1-9.

[8] Moore finds "little room to question the views expressed here concerning the literary amateur and the limitations of certain types of female writers" (74). He ignores the fact that Ford here rejects *all* types of female writers.

[9] Although Davis's heroine is happiest when her husband calls her "Hetty," a name which signifies her contentment with domestic affection, her real name, Hester, points to Hawthorne's Hester Prynne, another woman with an artistic talent and temperament, blighted and warped by the harsh Puritanical attitudes that condemned her sexuality and forced her to use her artistic needlework as her only link to the society that rejected her. Davis saves her Hetty from the agonies—and the stature—of a Hester Prynne.

[10] Woolson was clearly aware that this view of woman's genius was not going to suit traditional sensibilities. She published it not in *Harper's, Appelton's, Lippincott's,* or the *Atlantic,* her usual outlets, but in *The New Century for Woman.*

Works Cited

Benedict, Clare, ed. *Constance Fenimore Woolson.* London: Ellis, 1929. Vol. II of *Five Generations (1785-1923).*

Davis, Rebecca Harding. "The Wife's Story." *Atlantic Monthly* (July 1864): 1-19.

Edel, Leon. *Henry James.* Vol. III. New York: J. P. Lippincott, 1962, 1964.

Faderman, Lillian. *Surpassing the Love of Men: Romantic Friendship and Love between Women from the Renaissance to the Present.* New York: Morrow, 1981.

Freeman, Mary E. Wilkins. *A New England Nun and Other Stories.* New York: Harper and Bros., 1891.

Hawthorne, Nathaniel. Preface. *The Snow Image and Other Twice-Told Tales. Nathaniel Hawthorne: Selected Tales and Sketches.* Ed. Hyatt Waggoner. New York: Holt, Rinehart, and Winston, 1970.

Hubbell, Jay B. "Some New Letters of Constance Fenimore Woolson." *New England Quarterly* XIV (December 1941): 715-35.

James, Henry. "The Lesson of the Master." 1888. *Henry James: Stories of Writers and Artists.* Ed. F. O. Matthiessen. New York: New Directions, n.d.

Kelley, Mary. *Private Woman, Public Stage: Literary Domesticity in Nineteenth-Century America.* New York: Oxford Univ. Press, 1984.

Moore, Rayburn S. *Constance Fenimore Woolson.* New York: Twayne, 1963.

Parker, Gail, ed. *The Oven Birds: American Women on Womanhood 1820-1920.* New York: Doubleday, 1972.

Phelps, Elizabeth Stuart. *The Story of Avis.* 1877. New Brunswick: Rutgers Univ. Press, 1985.

Welter, Barbara. "Anti-Intellectualism and the American Woman 1800-1860." *Dimity Convictions: The American Woman in the Nineteenth Century.* Athens: Ohio Univ. Press, 1976.

Wood, Ann Douglas. "The Literature of Impoverishment: the Women Local Colorists in America 1865-1914." *Women's Studies* I (1972): 3-45.

Woolson, Constance Fenimore. *Castle Nowhere: Lake-Country Sketches.* Boston: J. R. Osgood & Co., 1875.

CCC. *Dorothy and Other Italian Stories.* New York: Harper and Bros., 1896, 1899.

Rev. of *Esther Pennefather,* by Constance Fenimore Woolson. *The Atlantic* (October 1878): 503.

CCC. *The Front Yard and Other Italian Stories.* New York: Harper and Bros., 1895.

CCC. "Miss Grief." *Lippincott's Magazine* (May 1880): 574-585.

CCC. *Rodman the Keeper: Southern Sketches.* New York: D. Appleton and Co., 1880; New York: Harper and Bros., 1886, 1899.

CCC. "To George Eliot." *The New Century for Woman.* 2 (May 20, 1876): 1.

Sharon L. Dean (essay date 1989)

SOURCE: "Homeward Bound: The Novels of Constance Fenimore Woolson," *Legacy: A Journal of Nineteenth-Century American Women Writers,* Vol. 6, No. 2, Fall 1989, pp. 17-28.

[*In the following essay, Dean explores the idea of independence which is developed in Woolson's later novels.*]

When Henry James wrote his generally favorable review of Constance Woolson in the February 12, 1887, edition of *Harper's Weekly,* he criticized her for limiting women's choices by too often having them choose marriage: Miss Woolson, he says, "likes the unmarried . . . but she likes marriages even better" (182). For him, Woolson was not revolutionary in her portraits of women: rather than adding further complications to women's lives, she was content to explore the complications that already existed for women "fenced in by the old disabilities and prejudices" (179). Critics like Mary Kelley and Nina Baym

who have studied a broad range of nineteenth-century works have helped us define these "disabilities and prejudices" which allowed women to write but limited them to domestic fiction that endorsed women's roles in holding together homes, whether those homes involved marriage or some other kind of extended family. Woolson herself struggled with these attitudes toward women writers and was especially pointed in her criticism of women's limited sphere for writing in her late story "In Sloane Street" (1892) where a character actually says that "Women can't write. And they ought not to try. . . . Children's stories—yes; they can write for children and for young girls, extremely well. And they can write little sketches and episodes if they will confine themselves rigidly to the things they thoroughly know, such as love stories, and so forth" (474).

James seems to have thought that Woolson and other women writers avoided notions of power in favor of notions of love or of domesticity. What he failed to see is that Woolson's ability to criticize the limitations placed on women allowed her to subvert the fences that surrounded women writers. The issue of home and homelessness constitutes a primary and powerful imaginative focus in Woolson's work. Joan Weimer has located in Woolson's short fiction a larger dimension than one that involves purely domestic or relational matters, a pattern of female artists who choose "homelessness and habitual solitude" (6) over human relationships, male or female, which often threaten betrayal. One of the aspects of "homelessness" that Weimer emphasizes is the lack of family ties, particularly ties of marriage.[1] However, while in the short fiction the female artists often choose a lonely independence and in the novels many interesting minor characters do the same, the major female characters in the novels almost always choose a home equated with marriage. Woolson is not here abandoning the broader sphere of the female artist that she developed in her short fiction; rather she is using the longer novel form to reconcile independence with the "'longing for home'"[2] that she spoke about in her letters to her relatives, with whom she kept a close correspondence.

Because she was also quite aware that "nine-tenths of the great mass of readers care only for the love story" (Benedict 103) and because she had to please these readers to maintain her financial independence, she needed to reconcile her sense of the rewards of independence despite loneliness with the tastes of the audience of her day. As she wrestles in each of her novels with the expectations of her audience and her own conflicting needs for home and independence, Woolson breaks out the "old disabilities and prejudices" by stepping back to observe the implications of the choice for a home that is equated with marriage. Because she continued to long for a home outside of marriage, she also asks, particularly in her last novel, how a woman can possess a home that is not equated with marriage.

Like so much of the fiction written by males canonized in American literature, each of Woolson's longer pieces of fiction juxtaposes naive or shallow girl-women with women more aware of the ambiguities of life. The girl figures always choose marriage and through them, Woolson reveals her ability to understand why women did not often exercise other kinds of choices. Woolson's niece Clare Benedict describes her aunt's capacity for understanding all types of women as an "intense sympathy with and understanding of all . . . moral and intellectual aspirations, that [enabled her] to draw out of people the best that was in them, while giving them in return the most inspiring and comforting comprehension" (xiv). Such a capacity for comprehension is even more apparent in Woolson's portraits of complex women. While the girl-women in the novels are interesting but similar, each of the complex heroines provides a different focus on the issues involved when a woman desires or is expected by her society to desire a home. An examination of Woolson's character pairings shows her observing closely how women compromise as they seek homes and shows her struggling with issues involving kinship, sexuality, violence, and loneliness.

In her first novel, *Anne* (1882), Woolson explores a society where women exist for marriage or can find financial security only within marriage. Because the possibility of home is equated with marriage, Woolson reveals how ruthless women can be in their pursuit of a husband, but because she observes so well what leads to this ruthlessness she refuses to denounce it. The novel's shallow, though hardly naive, girl figure, Helen Lorrington, articulates the feelings that plague all of women's relationships: Helen befriends the title character Anne because "Anne admired her, and was at the same time neither envious nor jealous, and from her youth she [Helen] had been troubled by the sure development of these two feelings, sooner or later, in all her girl companions" (161). Several plot complications suggest how often women's jealousy or fear leads them to betray one another if they equate home with marriage. Anne's aunt subverts Anne's engagement because her fiancé is the son of the man her aunt once loved and had hoped to make a home with, and Anne's half-sister Angelique elopes with Anne's fiancé. An even worse betrayal comes from Helen, who tells Ward Heathcote, the man both she and Anne have fallen in love with, that the Angelique whose marriage notice has appeared in the newspaper is really Anne and thereby wins Heathcote for her own husband. Woolson might have ended this novel with Helen Lorrington's marriage to the man Anne loves, thus being consistent with her versions of exiles from home in the short fiction. Instead, she reunites Anne and Helen. Believing Heathcote dead, they become honest with each other and share the bond of suffering. Through their bond, Woolson suggests that although women often betray each other in their search for the security of home, that betrayal can also unite them in a closer relationship than they might otherwise have had.

Woolson completes the plot of *Anne* as if it were a nineteenth-century Agatha Christie mystery. Learning that Heathcote is alive, Helen goes to him, only to be murdered under circumstances that lead to Heathcote being accused of the murder. This is more than a convenient way to provide *Anne* with a happy ending by having the heroine marry the man she loves. While Woolson can satisfy her audience by concluding her novel with this marriage, she can also satisfy herself by examining one of the compensations for remaining unmarried; that is, the compensation of being independent. The task of proving Heathcote's innocence falls to Anne and a spinster friend, Miss Lois, whom she has known since girlhood. These two maiden ladies act out the kind of adventure Twain gives to Huck Finn three years later. They disguise their identity, track strangers through the town where the murder occurred, and row alone on a river in pursuit of a suspicious fisherman. They have to call in a priest to confront the murderer, but they have had the adventure of completing the detective work, an adventure they have pursued with intelligence and courage.

Adventure is the reward Woolson gives these two unmarried women, but the freedom for adventure carries the price of loneliness. Miss Lois has had a permanent but precarious home as a spinster, but in her own words the unmarried life has been one of "loneliness" and "misunderstoodness" that has contributed to her "general sense of a useless ocean within [her], its breaking waves dashed high on a stern and rock-bound coast" (135). Anne has felt even more keenly this metaphor of thwarted life, for she has been both unmarried and homeless. Still, the two join in a common cause they would have been denied had they been married: "No man being there to weigh [their plan] with a cooler masculine judgment, it seemed to them a richly promising one" (492). Through this adventure, Woolson emphasizes that the home marriage may provide can be an imprisoning one and that the loneliness of spinsterhood may be compensated for by its accompanying freedom. Imprisoned at first by her engagement, Anne gains the freedom of temporary spinsterhood and is able to free Heathcote from the prison of his marriage that has been represented metaphorically in his literal imprisonment. Woolson has spent so much time on Anne's and Miss Lois's detective work in order to provide options that allow women to break out of imprisoning roles.

Once Anne proves Heathcote's innocence, they join together in a marriage that is liberating rather than imprisoning. Although this marriage may not be a wise choice and one of Anne's former suitors, the stable Gregory Dexter, might have proved a better husband, Anne's choice of Heathcote is similar to her half-sister Angelique's elopement, a choice made despite what society defines as sensible. A significant difference in the choice, however, is that society would certainly define Anne's choice as morally acceptable. It is important that the marriage takes place on the little Michigan island that was Anne's girlhood home and that would have been a limiting home had she married her girlhood fiancé. Because Anne has been independent and intelligent, hers is not the limiting fate that fulfills women like Helen and Angelique; rather, it is one that combines freedom and responsibility at the same time that it satisfies a reader's desire for romantic adventure within or outside of marriage.

Although Woolson is radical in *Anne* in refusing to criticize Helen for betraying friendship and Angelique for betraying kinship, her overall conception of the novel endorses the heroine who follows the conventionally moral path no matter the cost to herself and rewards this heroine by providing her a mature, satisfactory, even romantic, home within marriage. In *For the Major* (1883), she continues to explore the kinds of choices women make to establish marital homes, but now with a heroine whose behavior might be considered less socially acceptable.[3] Again, Woolson juxtaposes the girl figure with a woman whose life circumstances are more complex. Sara Carroll is one of Woolson's least complex girl figures, and her virtue is rewarded by marriage to the man she loves. She is of minor interest in the novella, far more conventional than Angelique or Helen, but providing her with a home via marriage enables Woolson to validate Sara's simplicity because it is accompanied by honesty. In her conventional morality, Sara is more like Anne than Helen or Angelique, but this morality is never really tempted. Sara's stepmother, Madame Carroll, might be compared to Helen and Angelique in the sense that she must compromise standards of behavior in order to gain a husband. However, because Woolson has focused on Madame Carroll, we see her not just following self-gratification but weighing the consequences of her actions within both a social and familial context. Unlike Helen and Angelique, Madame Carroll is honest with herself even though she is not truthful with those around her.

For the Major explores an interesting angle toward marriage and home because Madame Carroll articulates so explicitly the reasons why many women act the way they do. Through her, Woolson finds a voice that helps us to understand her own unwillingness to belittle any of the decisions her female characters make regarding marriage. In order to persuade Major Carroll to marry her and to provide her sickly daughter with a home, Madame Carroll pretends to be younger than she is. She also leads Major Carroll to believe she has had only one child who dies shortly after her marriage to the Major. In reality, she also has a son who finds her at Far Edgerley, Major Carroll's home. When the son dies and the Major's ill-health deteriorates into senility, Madame Carroll reveals the truth to Sara. In a final plot twist, we learn that Madame Carroll has either never married the Major or, more likely, married him not knowing her first husband was still alive. Woolson downplays the bigamy, revealing it only when Madame Carroll (re)-marries the senile Major at a bedside ceremony.

Madame Carroll's actions have hardly been what we want to admire: living a lie based on feminine appearance to satisfy a man. Yet the portrait is sympathetic because Woolson has shown us that although loving has required Madame Carroll to be false, it has not required hypocrisy. Explaining her position to Sara, Madame Carroll displays the kind of integrity Woolson wanted us to see in her:

> [The Major] saw in me a little blue-eyed, golden-haired girl-mother, unacquainted with the dark side of life, trusting, sweet. It was this very youth and child-like look which had attracted him, man of the world as he was himself, and no longer young. I feared to shatter his dream. In addition, that part did not seem to me of any especial consequence; I knew that I should be able to live up to his ideal, to maintain it not only fully, but longer, probably, than as though I had been in reality the person he supposed me to be. (341)

By having Madame Carroll become only superficially a child-wife, permanently youthful and beautiful but also fully aware of the implications of her pretense, Woolson has focused on her observations about the things that matter to the Major's kind of world. Is it really so awful, Woolson seems to be suggesting, to choose honest pretense and service as a more viable way of living than loneliness and poverty? Madame Carroll is not, at the core, false or child-like, for she knows that she is not a person who possesses a "lofty kind of vision which sees only the one path, and that the highest." Instead, she sees "all the shorter paths, lower down, that lead to the same place—the crosscuts." "The great things, the wide view," says Madame Carroll, "are beyond me." She is not fitted for "struggle" but can "work and plan and accomplish . . . only when sheltered—sheltered in a home, no matter how plain, protected from actual contact with the crowd" where there is always "brutality" (342-43). Although some of Woolson's more limited characters may take a superficial kind of high road, Madame Carroll outdistances them because she understands how much societal expectations have shaped her own decisions in securing a home.

In *East Angels* (1886), Woolson returns to a view of a girl-woman who defies society's mores to pursue the man she loves. Garda Thorne's defiance makes her, like Angelique and Helen in Woolson's first novel, more interesting than the simply virtuous Sara Carroll. Through both Garda and Margaret Harold, the more complex heroine of *East Angels,* Woolson hints at the sexual dimension implied in a marital home and at how that home may fulfill or stifle a woman's sexuality. One of the reasons Garda pursues marriage is that she is pursuing her sexuality, a trait most of Woolson's contemporaries denied their fictional girl figures. In fact, Nina Baym's research on reviews of post-Civil War novels finds hostility among reviewers to any treatment of sexuality (*Novels* 181-90). Woolson may be subverting nineteenth-century literary models and expectations by suggesting that sexuality fulfills these limited women precisely because they do not need wider avenues for fulfillment. Furthermore, Woolson suggests that beautiful women have greater choices in finding their ideal marriage/sex partners. The beginning of *East Angels* contains a passage that articulates this view:

> For in their hearts women always know that of all the gifts bestowed upon their sex that of beauty has so immeasurably the greatest power that nothing else can for one moment be compared with it, that all other gifts of whatsoever nature and extent, sink into insignificance and powerlessness beside it. (19)[4]

The question *East Angels* poses at first is what will become of the beautiful, sheltered, natural, naive, restless Garda Thorne. Encouraged by her mother to become interested in a rich Northerner, 35-year-old Evert Winthrop, Garda complies. But enter Lucian Spencer who engages in a brief flirtation with Garda. Spenser soon leaves Florida, the setting for the novel, and is enticed into marriage by a woman who has told him she is dying, but gets well after their marriage. This relationship is not central to the novel; however, it again reflects Woolson's sense of the tricks women use to achieve marriage. When Garda can no longer pretend to love Winthrop, she breaks her engagement, taking what would seem a noble stance: "Everybody in the world seems to tell lies but me. . . . And everybody else seems to prefer it" (392). But nobility requires deeper feelings than Woolson develops in Garda. Because she does not have these deeper feelings, Woolson can reward her truthfulness simply by having Spenser's wife die and Garda marry him. In an unexpected plot twist, Spenser himself dies, but Garda finds a suitable second marriage to a handsome former admirer. Given the dashing manners and physical handsomeness of both Garda's husbands, Woolson seems to be implying that being an honest and virtuous girl-wife is compatible with sexuality. If one must marry to find a home, the sexual dimension to marriage can be fulfilling rather than endured for the sake of that home.

Unlike Garda, Margaret Harold does not find a fulfilling sexuality within her marital home but, instead, discovers how sexuality threatens to destroy a home. Margaret's husband Lanse has had a long-standing affair in Europe. He eventually returns to America and Margaret but remains oblivious to Margaret's needs. He cannot understand that his presence may be painful to her, for he is willing to allow her to lead the life she is used to while he leads the life he wants. Thus, he believes, they can have a model marriage. Yet Lanse immediately contradicts this notion by insisting that Margaret conform to his notions of how she should dress, turning her into an ornament much as Henry James's Gilbert Osmond tried to turn Isabel Archer into an object for his collection. After all, Lanse has married Margaret for "her profile" (438) rather than for love. He dresses her according to his wishes and is pleased that she is such a "beautiful object" (440). While Madame Carroll in *For the Major* finds this kind of role a satisfying one, Margaret finds it stifling, especially because she has fallen in love with Evert Winthrop during Lanse's absence. A scene between Margaret and Winthrop exudes the kind of passion Margaret is capable of feeling and that Garda's more fulfilling marriages seem to contain. They are lost in a lush swamp that serves as a metaphor for sexuality. Woolson uses no heavy-handed symbolism—just an atmosphere of heat, fertility, danger, fear, passion. Eventually Margaret and Winthrop acknowledge their mutual passion, but this is never consummated because Margaret chooses to keep her home with Lanse who has left her a second time only to return as an invalid, his illness suggesting that the marriage will remain non-sexual.

Woolson uses Margaret's decision not to divorce Lanse, despite her unhappiness within the marriage, to illustrate how complex women's tendency to self-sacrifice can be. In an otherwise favorable review of *East Angels,* William Dean Howells criticizes Woolson's portrayal of Margaret as a sacrificial woman: "Neither Margaret nor Winthrop her lover appeals to our sympathy, perhaps because we cannot believe in them; they form for us the one false note of the book" (Petry 88). Woolson objects in a letter to John Hay that she "could not expect Mr. Howells to like 'Margaret,' for he does not believe in 'Margarets,'—he has never perceived they exist" (Petry 87). Nor, it seems, does Rayburn Moore believe they exist. He admits his own impatience with Margaret even as he recognizes the problem of dismissing her and thus denying the "generous impulses of feminine nature" (97). Aside from the sexism underlying such a statement, to accept Howells's or Moore's view is to dismiss Woolson's subtle portrayal of self-sacrifice, especially when the stakes of finding a satisfactory home are so high for women. Although Henry James believes Woolson spends too much time in *East Angels* on feminine matters of love, he also sees that if we "repudiate"

Margaret, we deny "that a woman may look at life from a high point of view," deny "that there are distinguished natures" (190).

By recognizing that there is a temptation to repudiate Margaret's choice to remain in her marital home, James suggests that Woolson is ambivalent about the value of women's sacrificial nature. A narrative passage from *East Angels* about Margaret's sacrifice and her friend Dr. Kirby's response to it illustrates one side of the issue:

> There are women who are capable of sacrificing themselves, with the noblest unselfishness in great causes, who yet, as regards the small matters of every-day life, are rather uncomfortable to live with; so much so, indeed, that those who are under the same roof with them are driven to reflect now and then upon the merits of the ancient hermitages and caves to which in former ages such characters were accustomed to retire. . . .

> The Doctor had had these saints as his patients more than once, he knew them perfectly. But here was a woman who had sacrificed her whole life to duty, who felt constantly the dreary ache of deprivation; but who yet did not think in the least, apparently, that these things freed her from the kindly efforts, the patience, the small sweet friendly attempts which made *home* comfortable. (565-66, emphasis mine)

Although Woolson seems here to be stressing the value of sacrifice for the sake of home, she also knows the doctor's view is only one part of the issue. Garda takes an opposite view, believing that sacrifice is silly, that "two whole lives [have been] wasted—and all for the sake of an idea" (579). Winthrop takes yet another angle: "Women are better than men; in some things they are stronger. But that's because they are sustained . . . by their terrible love of self-sacrifice; I absolutely believe there are women who *like* to be tortured" (588).

Had Woolson simply admired sacrifice and seen it played out in martyrdom, she might have chosen to end her novel with either reward or doom. Instead, the ambiguous last lines of *East Angels* show Margaret still married to Lanse, never again meeting Winthrop, engaged in this cutting dialogue:

> "Do you know that you've grown old, Madge, before your time?"

> "Yes, I know it."

> "Well—you're a good woman," said Lanse. (591)

Margaret has sacrificed and lost love, has been tempted into the "terrible love of self-sacrifice" that is the mark of the "good" martyr. But something stronger than martyrdom also works in Margaret much as it works in James's Isabel Archer whose apparent choice to return to her marriage Woolson echoes. Like Isabel, Margaret had married naively believing in fidelity only to discover opposing values in her husband and, again like Isabel, when she chooses with full knowledge to remain married, she upholds the value she believes reflected in the marriage vow, no matter her husband's cynicism about such vows. She wishes she could be like Garda who "puts the rest of us (women, I mean) to shame—the rest of us with our complicated motives, and involved consciences" (244). But Margaret knows society too well to be like Garda and can analyze what lies beneath society's codes. She understands that part of the necessity to remain married comes from the stigma that would have been attached to her divorcing a man who, in her words, has not been physically abusive, who has not been an alcoholic, and who has not exerted a negative influence on any children (531).[5]

An interesting commentary on society's attitudes occurs in *East Angels* when Winthrop overhears an older woman speaking to a younger one on a train: "We [women] do not exhibit our charms—which should be sacred to the privacy of the boudoir [i.e., the home]—in the glare of lecturerooms; *we* prefer to be, and to *remain,* the low-voiced retiring mothers of a race of giant sons whom the Muse of History will immortalize in the character of soldier, statesman, and divine" (536). Given this attitude, Margaret must struggle to find a place for herself in a society that allows her neither divorce nor a public sphere. While Woolson clearly does not endorse this attitude, she may be suggesting that change can come only from a younger generation of women. Through Margaret's "complicated motives, and involved conscience" and Garda's naiveté, she may also be suggesting that as the younger generation carves a public sphere for women it consider the implications of this on the private sphere. To widen society's acceptance of divorce for reasons of incompatibility would be to undermine the value of home in maintaining the private sphere even as a more public sphere is opened for women.

In *East Angels,* Woolson shows the price Margaret pays for upholding the sanctity of marriage her readers expected her to uphold. But she does not do this by making Margaret only a "good" woman who submits to her husband with no gain for herself, and thus she subverts the most negative implications of her society's mores. Although Margaret's continued marriage to Lanse and, along with this, her relationship to his hostile aunt are clearly painful, she also has gained something for herself. Three months before Lanse's return to the marriage, Margaret decides not to return to the isolated New England home of the deceased grandmother who raised her and has instead purchased East Angels in her own name. Knowing that a sense of place may help her replace her lack of a satisfying home, she tells Winthrop, "I shall do very well here if I have the place to think about . . . I shall have the land cultivated; perhaps I shall start a new orange grove" (524). At the same time, she also accuses Winthrop of wanting "no woman to lead a really independent life" (524). Lanse's return undercuts Margaret's independence, but, given the fact that he is now an invalid, she can still maintain control over her property. In fact, Woolson mentions a new orange grove just before Margaret tells Winthrop that she will remain married to Lanse (538). As much as Margaret sacrifices, her choice has had its compensations. We know that she has learned to live with the pain of Winthrop's loss because she counsels Garda that she, too, will learn to live with the loss of her first husband. She is even willing to have Winthrop marry Garda, and Winthrop reads this as a reflection of how much "you women think . . . of a home" (587). By the end of *East Angels,* Margaret has gained a richer home than she had in the past because both Lanse and his aunt have learned to treat her more kindly and because Garda, whom she cares about, is also likely to return to Florida and add the rootedness of place to the home she has in her new marriage. Most important, Margaret has gained the integrity of the self-knowledge that if she is old before her time, she has become so for reasons that go beyond her personal happiness.

If addressing, however subtly, the sexual dimension to marriage was risky for Woolson, equating home with violence, as she does in *Jupiter Lights* (1889) was even more daring. This novel's girl figure, Cicely Bruce Morrison, is faced with a choice not between sexuality and home or sexuality or home, but between sexuality/violence/home and loneliness. The book is Woolson's most problematic, for it seems to endorse stereotypical attitudes about women as martyrs. And yet its subject matter—wife and child abuse—is her most provocative, and beneath its surface we see her struggling against the conventional attitudes her characters too often display. The widowed Cicely has remarried, and her second husband, Ferdinand Morrison, when drunk, abuses both Cicely and Jack, the child of her first marriage. Although everyone who knows him loves and defends Ferdie, he misuses other people's money, misuses alcohol, misuses women, misuses children, misuses himself. The qualities Cicely and the others love in Ferdie—his vitality, his handsome devil-may-care passion—are the very qualities that lead him to violence. Woolson seems to accept the misconception that to break the violence may well be to break the man, but despite this misrepresentation of male violence, she shows a clear understanding of the effects of abusiveness on women. Ferdie's half-brother, for example, says that "Drunkards are death to the women—to the wives and mothers and sisters; but some of 'em are more lovable than lots of the moral skinflints that go nagging about, saving a penny, and grinding everybody but themselves. The trouble with Ferdie was that he was born without any conscience, just as some people have no ear for music; it was a case of heredity . . ." (339).[6] Heredity or not, lovable or not, Woolson sees the danger of adopting Cicely's attitude of pretending that violence within the home does not exist by never speaking of the violence.

Centering on the issues of home as kindred and home as violence, Woolson deepens the question of how women pursue homes in her portrait of Cicely's more complex counterpart, Eve Bruce, her sister-in-law by her first marriage. Eve comes to meet Cicely for the first time after her brother's death, already disliking her for having married her brother and causing her, she believes, to lose the only family and connection to the feeling of home she has had. In fact, Eve's motive is to take her nephew Jack from his mother and build a home for herself with the child. Instead, she shoots Ferdie and rescues Cicely and Jack from one of Ferdie's rampages. Soon Eve herself falls in love with Ferdie's half-brother, Paul Tennant, a device Woolson uses to put Eve into a situation similar to Cicely's. Early on, Eve thinks of Cicely's wish that she drop her cold demeanor and learn the power of love: "To wish her [Eve] a love like her [Cicely's] own, this seemed almost a curse, a malediction; . . . to love any man so submissively was weakness, but to love as Cicely loved, that was degradation" (90). Eve's anger here at Cicely is a revolt "against the injustice of all the ages, past, present, and to come, towards women" (90). But Eve's love for Paul is just as powerful as Cicely's for Ferdie. Although he does not have Ferdie's outward abusiveness, he does have faults that Eve knows about, condemns, and loves him in spite of. He trifles with other women and he trifles with her. Once he admits he loves her, he treats her like a child and like a person who will, of course, bend to his will.

Only by having Eve love Paul can Woolson provide a way for her to understand how Cicely can continue to desire a home with Ferdie. But because she is not naive, Eve refuses to be bound to Paul in contrast to Cicely's bondage in love. She fears she will become a woman whose love will destroy her integrity and make her yet another victim of love, another woman who will accept a marital home, whatever the cost to her personal safety and integrity. "Once your wife," she says to Paul, "I know that I should stay on, even if it were only to fold your clothes,—to touch them; to pick up the burnt match-ends you had dropped, and your newspapers; to arrange the chairs as you like to have them. I should be weak, weak—I should follow you about" (324).

Woolson makes Eve's decision to leave Paul, because she believes she has killed his half-brother, strong enough that we have no question about its seriousness. Eve cannot marry Paul until Woolson provides a *deus ex machina* revealing that Eve did not murder Ferdie. The question we must ask is why provide this. On a simple level, the answer may be that Woolson knew her readers would expect it. But as concerned as she was with the question of home, it is consistent that Woolson find a way to provide Eve a home that will not be one of bondage. She cannot give her Jack, for she needs Jack to provide Cicely with a home and for Eve to make her own home with them would be to enter into a different kind of bondage with a woman who hates her. Nor does Woolson want Eve to marry Paul's friend, a man who loves her but whom she does not love in return. The only home Eve can have consistent with her character is with Paul, but on her terms, not his.

Woolson reunites Paul and Eve at the end of *Jupiter Lights* in a scene that allows her to speak out against violence, suggesting that women like Cicely who have been tempted to tolerate violence for the sake of love and home have traded too much. Paul knocks down a priest at a charitable institution to get to Eve to tell her the truth about the real cause of Ferdie's death. The woman in charge of the institution stops Paul just as he is about to force open the door that is blocking him from Eve: "Your violence has been unnecessary—the violence of a boor!" (347). Paul "laugh[s] in her face," opens the door, and takes "Eve in his arms" (347). Like the woman who blocks the door, we want to say, yes, his violence is, like Ferdie's, "the violence of a boor." But we also must surmise that despite, or maybe even because of, this display of violence, Paul wins Eve in a way that Woolson's readers might find satisfyingly dramatic. Woolson does not naively dismiss Paul's violence but, instead, shows the extent to which women commit themselves to relationships and the extent to which readers romanticize this kind of violence as evidence of love. But because Woolson has linked violence to Ferdie in a more instructive way, she forces us to remember that to be bound to home can constitute the kind of bondage that love has been for Cicely. Because she has earlier made Eve strong enough to resist the bondage of love, we also hope that she will marry Paul in a union that will allow him to see that violence should not be equated with loving passion.

In her portrait of the girl-woman in *Horace Chase* (1894), Woolson does not expand on issues she has previously addressed, but she does again link sexuality with naiveté. Ruth Franklin is spoiled, indulged, entirely natural; she is unconcerned about the implications of sexuality and acts however she wants without thinking about social forms. Like an indulged child, she has her way in marrying Horace Chase, who is much her senior, not in any search for home, but because she finds him fun to be with. Woolson

does not deepen Ruth's character even when she has her discover her sexual attraction to Horace's partner, Walter Willoughby, a man who flirts with her but ultimately marries the woman he really loves. Ruth's awakening to her sexuality, late and outside her "happy" marriage, anticipates by five years Kate Chopin's theme in *The Awakening*. But Ruth, because she remains a child character, never gains Edna Pontellier's awareness of the implications of sexuality outside of marriage. Horace, the father-figure, is really the right man for this non-speculative woman whose limited view of happiness is so different from Chopin's and from Woolson's own. Still, Woolson refuses to condescend: given her upbringing and personality, Ruth is suited only for play love. If Ruth is not cut out for a higher view of life or for enduring and growing through suffering, she at least has the integrity of her feelings and whims. Honest and fresh, she can attain the kind of happiness denied the person who possesses the deeper intelligence Woolson may have felt cursed by herself.

Woolson's own character is apparent in all her complex heroines, but the personal connection seems the strongest in her portrait of Ruth's sister, Dolly Franklin. She is the only major character in the novels who remains unmarried and through her Woolson looks again at how the idea of home includes the importance of kindred and the importance of place. She had touched on both these issues before—in *Jupiter Lights,* for example, through Eve's longing for her dead brother in the guise of his child and in *East Angels* in Margaret's purchase of a house—but never without involving as well the idea of a marital home. Dolly stands out even more oddly as an unmarried woman because this novel contains a number of other women who associate home with marriage. Dolly's sister-in-law, Genevieve, gains the kind of home she wants in marriage, but she forces her husband, Jared Franklin, into a life style he is unsuited for and thinks so little of his well-being that she is indirectly responsible for his death. And yet, in her limited way, Genevieve loves Jared and even as Woolson blames her, she sees both her and Jared as victims of society's expectations. Society has taught them to value men according to how successfully they provide for a family, whether or not this material dimension provides a satisfying marital relationship, a sense of kinship, or even a permanent place to live. Jared's mother has valued the male within the home so much that she dotes on her son as the only male left in the family and even dies when he dies, as if to say that without a male there can be no home. It is not without significance that the name of her home is L'Hommedieu, for home equates with the men she thinks necessary to support it.

Dolly stands in contrast not only to the other female members of her family but also to three female aquaintances who represent some of Woolson's best comic portraits of women. Woolson often seems to use the comic portrait to control her bitterness over society's lessons that women should define themselves in terms of men. Mrs. Kip has learned society's lesson well: she has been married twice and is about to marry a third time because marriage is what she thrives on. Similarly, the spinster Miss Billy, significantly given a male's name because she has never caught a male, spends her life pining for a man. Balancing these portraits of marriage-hungry women is the most comic portrait in all of Woolson's novels, that of feminist Maud Murial who defies patriarchy by modelling male behavior. She is a sculptor who tries to learn to smoke cigars and sculpts only the ugly because that is what she sees around her. In the portraits of Mrs. Kip, Miss Billy, and Maud Murial, Woolson has shown what she saw in too many of her contemporaries: women made silly because no one has shown them how not to be silly; women whose choice is to dote on men or become men because they have not yet found a better way. These are the kinds of women she complained of in a letter to her niece by marriage Flora [Mrs. Samuel] Mather as lacking "broad, reasonable, solid views," but they are also women she sympathizes with because, as she continues to Flora, their failure is not from inferior minds but from lack of appropriate education (Benedict 49).

As the only unmarried woman in her novels not treated comically, Dolly Franklin may be Woolson's answer for how to reconcile home and independence, a reconciliation closest to the one Woolson sought for herself. She represents the same kind of strong woman that Woolson provides in her other novels in the portraits of Anne, Madame Carroll, Margaret Harold, and Eve Bruce. However, Dolly hasn't the sexual passion of any of these women. Speculation about Henry James to the contrary, at this point in her life Woolson seems less interested in seeing what passion calls forth in a woman than what steadfast intelligence calls forth. Dolly's intelligence is especially nurtured because her arthritis-like condition, perhaps a metaphor for Woolson's tendency to depression and her habit of loneliness, has limited her options even more than society has limited them. Woolson surely intended Dolly's name to be ironic, for she is no pale, doll-like invalid, but with her acute and lively observations sounds much like Alice James. Even though Horace Chase dismisses her as a meddling spinster, she has superior insight about others and sees why Ruth and many like her need to marry men who will indulge them. At the end of the novel, Dolly reveals not just intelligence but also physical and moral strength when during a storm she saves Ruth, who has tried to run to Walter Willoughby. Dolly returns her to Horace, cautioning her not to tell him the truth because she underestimates his integrity and believes

he, like most of society, will reject Ruth. Instead, Horace forgives Ruth and continues to love and value her as his wife. Because Ruth and Horace will now leave L'Hommedieu for Europe, Dolly has saved Ruth's marital home at the price of her own last ties to kindred.

Early in *Horace Chase,* Dolly articulates her understanding of how women tend to find homes and, therefore, of why Ruth's marital home is so important. In her comments, she locates the theme that permeates all of Woolson's novels: "Have you ever noticed . . . that the women who sacrifice their lives so nobly to help humanity seldom sacrifice one small thing, and that is a happy home? Either they do not possess such an article, or else they have spoiled it by quarrelling with every individual member of their families" (19). Through all her novels, Woolson presents a consistent vision of women who are homeward bound in the sense that they fight to find or to keep a home. When they sacrifice at all, as in the cases of Anne for Helen's marriage and Eve Bruce for her own integrity, they do so before they have found a home or, as with Madame Carroll's sacrifice of conventional honesty and Margaret Harold's sacrifice of love, they do so for a home. A passage from a letter Woolson wrote to John Hay in 1883 captures the importance of this theme: "I should say I was a trifle homesick—only how can one be homesick who has'nt a 'home[']? Be thankful that you have one; & keep kindly thoughts for the less fortunate" (Petry 48).

Read in the light of Dolly's need to reconcile home and independence, the last paragraph of *Horace Chase* seems more that just melodrama: "Horace Chase put Dolly aside—put her aside forever. He lifted his wife in his arms, and silently bent his head over hers as it lay on his breast" (419). The image of a cast-aside woman is a fitting one in a society where women have been so bound to the need for home that many feared that to remain unmarried was to bind them to homelessness and loneliness. Marriage represented to most of Woolson's contemporaries less the danger of limitedness and compromise than the promise of legitimized sexuality, social status, or security. But Woolson's portrait of Dolly Franklin, the woman who by the death of her parents and her brother and the marriage of her younger sister becomes the owner of L'Hommedieu, represents a different way to find a home, one that Woolson had touched on most explicitly in *East Angels.* In that novel, not only does Margaret Harold become rooted to East Angels, but Garda Thorne returns to it, and, before her death, Garda's widowed mother found satisfaction in performing household maintenance normally associated with men. That Dolly is cast aside by Horace, that she has no husband and now will lose her tie to kindred, just as

Woolson had lost so many of her own ties to kindred, does not mean that she must be homeless. Woolson did not live to write a novel where she examined closely the struggles a woman like Dolly Franklin might confront as she becomes bound to a home defined as the rootedness of place. But she clearly looked forward to this kind of home for herself, hoping to buy her own little cottage in Florida. Had illness, and possibly suicide brought on by her sense of homelessness, not cut short her life, she may have found herself bound to a home that did not limit her as it limited so many of her characters.

Notes

[1] Weimer believes this is an understandable theme for Woolson, given the deaths of five sisters and both parents by the time she was 39. One of Woolson's infant sisters also died and, when Woolson was in her early 40s, her brother Charley died, probably a suicide.

[2] The phrase comes from a letter Woolson wrote to Hamilton Hayne in 1876 in which she calls herself an "'exile longing for home'" (Hubbell 731).

[3] I follow Moore's precedent here in considering *For the Major* with the novels because of its full development. Its treatment of home is also of a piece with that in the longer novels.

[4] The implications of physical beauty seem to have plagued Woolson who, according to Clare Benedict, had a "curiously low opinion of her own personal appearance" (xv).

[5] See Woolson's notebook entry for a story about society's rejection of a divorced woman (Benedict 134). Nina Baym also notes the negative responses to divorce given by book reviewers in the nineteenth century (*Novels* 184).

[6] Woolson believed in the hereditary nature of certain psychological traits and thought her own bouts of depression to be hereditary (Moore 36). In an 1876 letter to Hamilton Hayne, she links "'Depression,' that evil spirit that haunts all creative minds" with the need for "the close appreciative warm belief & praise of . . . family" (Hubbell 728-29).

Works Cited

Baym, Nina. *Novels, Readers, and Reviewers: Responses to Fiction in Antebellum America*. Ithaca: Cornell UP, 1984.

CCC. *Woman's Fiction: A Guide to Novels by and about Women in America, 1820-1870*. Ithaca: Cornell UP, 1978.

Benedict, Clare. *Constance Fenimore Woolson*. London: Ellis, 1929. Vol. 2 of *Five Generations (1785-1923)*. 1929-30.

Edel, Leon. *The Middle Years (1882-1895)*. New York: Lippincott, 1962. Vol. 3 of *Henry James*. 1962-64.

Hubbell, Jay B. "Some New Letters of Constance Fenimore Woolson." *New England Quarterly* 14 (1941): 715-35.

James, Henry. *Partial Portraits*. 1887. Ann Arbor: U of Michigan P, 1970.

Kelley, Mary. *Private Woman, Public Stage: Literary Domesticity in Nineteenth-Century America*. New York: Oxford UP, 1984.

Kern, John Dwight. *Constance Fenimore Woolson: Literary Pioneer*. Philadelphia: U of Pennsylvania P, 1934.

Moore, Rayburn S. *Constance F. Woolson*. New York: Twayne, 1963.

Petry, Alice Hall. "'Always Your Attached Friend': The Unpublished Letters of Constance Fenimore Woolson to John and Clara Hay." *Books at Brown* 29-30 (1982-83): 11-107.

Weimer, Joan Myers. "Women Artists as Exiles in the Fiction of Constance Fenimore Woolson." *Legacy* 3.1 (1986): 3-15.

Woolson, Constance Fenimore. *Anne*. 1882. Intro. Elizabeth Hardwick. New York: Arno, 1977.

CCC. *East Angels*. New York: Harper, 1886.

CCC. *For the Major*. 1883. Rpt. in *For the Major and Selected Short Stories*. Ed. Rayburn S. Moore. New Haven: College and University P, 1967.

CCC. *Horace Chase*. 1894. Upper Saddle River: Literature House, 1970.

CCC. "In Sloane Street." *Harper's Bazar* 11 June 1892: 473-78.

CCC. *Jupiter Lights*. 1889. New York: AMS, 1971.

Cheryl B. Torsney (essay date 1989)

SOURCE: "*Anne*: Woolson's Portrait of a Lady," in *Constance Fenimore Woolson: The Grief of Artistry*, University of Georgia Press, 1989, pp. 34-49.

[*In the essay that follows, Torsney compares Woolson's first novel* Anne *with Henry James's* Portrait of a Lady,

*and contends that Woolson "adapted her literary in-
heritance from the domestics of earlier in the century
to suit her original purposes."*]

Woolson's transitional position—on the one hand a
member of the "scribbling" sorority, on the other an
exile who isolated herself from society in order to
devote herself to art—is best demonstrated, perhaps,
by example. Woolson's earliest stories are reminiscent of the earlier fashions in women's writing discussed so thoroughly by Mary Kelly and Nina Baym,
among others.[1] For example, the early piece **"Duets"**
(1874) features two friends, Olive and Helena, who
get what the other wants in a husband.[2] And although
"Weighed in the Balance" (1872) takes up women's
suffrage as a topic during a lake voyage—one gentleman believes that only when men recognize their
"soul-companions . . . will woman reach her apotheosis" and "human intellect, embodied in the clear crys-
tals of woman's mind, rise to its true place," while
another maintains "that love is her power, and we
love her, not for her mind, but rather for her heart"—
a quiet girl, in the manner of a domestic romance,
saves the day when a sudden storm threatens the
outing.[3] In **"The Lady of Little Fishing"** (1874), the
opening story of Woolson's first collection of short
fiction, *Castle Nowhere: Lake Country Sketches,* a
beautiful spiritlike woman civilizes a rough logging
camp, and in **"Old Gardiston"** (1876) a vanquished
Confederate belle finds herself in love with a Yankee
officer, happily capitulating to him in the end.[4]

To demonstrate further Woolson's debt to the women
fiction writers who preceded her and to highlight her
own internalization of women's culture, it is instructive to consider her first long work and most popular
piece of fiction, *Anne.*[5] By reading the novel in terms
of another novel of the period, Henry James's *The
Portrait of a Lady,* we will see even more clearly
how Woolson used the earlier women's fiction tradition in order to find a voice and how she later adapted
it to make statements about the possibility for women's
artistry in her world, about the powerless position of
female artists in a patriarchal culture.[6]

My purpose here, however, is not to create more anxiety by arguing influence. I see neither Woolson nor
James as derivative: both are part of the same textual
fabric. Rather, I think it more valuable to examine
how, as a result of their shared cultural milieu, they
focus on similar themes yet produce gender-inflected
results. Whether or not, like Alfred Habegger, we see
James as an effeminate "sissy," he is still a man
writing from his own gender perspective.[7] Likewise,
Woolson is a woman writing from hers.

Both Henry James's and Constance Fenimore Woolson's
first important novels were published serially, his in the
Atlantic (from November 1880 to December 1881) and

hers in *Harper's New Monthly Magazine* (from December 1880 to May 1882). Both are novels of love
and marriage, a theme as old as the genre itself. Both
The Portrait of a Lady and *Anne* present female protagonists akin to the prototypical women's heroine
whose characteristics, "intelligence, will, resourcefulness, and courage," have been outlined by Nina Baym.[8]
Isabel Archer and Anne Douglas are provincial or-
phans who are adopted by eccentric aunts after the
deaths of parents with whom the aunts had argued.
Both young women make a successful entry into society after being taken in by their relations, and both
marry men of questionable virtue. In each character's
case another man, Ralph Touchett and Gregory Dexter, respectively, at some point provides for the
heroine's material well-being. Although the novels
share structural similarities and a relation to the
Ur-plot of trial and triumph as elucidated by Baym,
they are based on different gender assumptions, traditions, and development.

Carren Kaston has defended James against the charges
of some hostile feminist criticism by noting that "James
wrote regularly with a profound sensitivity to what it
was and very often still is like to be a woman."[9]
Although, as Alfred Habegger asserts, James was
"in sympathy with the best feminine values," he was
nonetheless male, still on the outside.[10] Still, his effort
to understand is genuine, his understanding as certain as possible. From his own hegemonic position,
he presents a woman of imagination who, because
of the constraints of the male world in which she
lives, cannot realize the triumph of that imagination.
As Kaston puts it, "Such independence to which
Isabel at first aspires is unattainable not only because of the existence of others, who constitute society and exert pressure on her, but because of conditions within Isabel herself."[11] It is Isabel's tragedy that
she cannot really act independently. She can only be
managed. As James writes, "Madame Merle had married her" (430). Even grammatically Isabel is an object,
not a subject. She is passive, not active, as a male culture expected a woman in her place to be.

Keys to Isabel's failure lie in her own habits of mind,
habits born of reading two classes of literature: romances by and about women and texts from the transcendentalist tradition. These two sources of Isabel's
ideas suggest what Kaston calls her "conflicting attitudes toward power: her desire for self-origination on
the one hand and, on the other, her attraction to dependency."[12] Isabel (as well as James, of course) is not at
fault; rather, as Kaston puts it, "given the powerlessness women frequently feel, the challenge of self-origination could not easily be met by any woman, even
one as generously conceived as Isabel is by James."[13]

From the beginning Isabel understands her world in
textual terms. On her arrival at Gardencourt, she is

thrilled to meet Lord Warburton: "Oh, I hoped there would be a lord; it's just like a novel!" she gushes (27). Indeed, in the following flashback to Lydia Touchett's visit to Albany to fetch her niece, Isabel is ensconced in the library, where she reads indiscriminately, "guided in the selection chiefly by the frontispiece" (33). Her reading includes "the London *Spectator*" and "the latest publications" (41-42), both of which would have treated women's issues. Other evidence demonstrates, however, that Isabel has been reading romantic women's novels as well. These unnamed novels help to set up her expectations only to have reality decimate the tenderly held images.

Mr. Touchett, sensing Isabel's impending disaster, raises the issue of the discrepancy between fantasy and reality in women's fiction, but Isabel either does not hear or does not heed the warning. Their discussion begins with Isabel's wondering whether English character confirms what she has read in books. Her uncle replies that he is unfamiliar with what appears in novels, that he believes only what he has learned from firsthand experience. But Isabel continues to push the question of novelistic representations of reality by asking how she will be treated in society. "I don't believe they're [the English] very nice to girls; they're not nice to them in novels" (58). Daniel Touchett's response might have served to warn Isabel, but finding herself in a situation usually reserved for novels, her ears are deaf to her uncle's warnings.

> "I don't know about the novels," said Mr. Touchett. "I believe the novels have a great deal of ability, but I don't suppose they're very accurate. We once had a lady who wrote novels staying here; she was a friend of Ralph's and he asked her down. She was very positive, quite up to everything; but she was not the sort of person you could depend on for evidence. Too free a fancy—I suppose that was it. She afterwards published a work of fiction in which she was understood to have given a representation . . . of my unworthy self. . . . Well, it was not at all accurate; she couldn't have listened very attentively. . . . I don't talk like the old gentleman in that lady's novel. . . . I just mention that fact to show you that they're not always accurate." (58-59)

Isabel might have taken to heart James's ironic joke about people who think that novels faithfully record experience, but she does not. Throughout the early sections of the novel, she reads real-life situations according to women's writing conventions: she sees Warburton "as a hero of romance" rather than as a troubled man caught in a changing political order and his home "as a castle in a legend"; she has read that the English "are at bottom the most romantic of races"; she identifies herself as a young woman being made love to by a nobleman in a "deeply romantic"

situation (66, 75, 77, 96). When Henrietta Stackpole tries to penetrate Isabel's novelistically clouded vision by asking her "Don't you know where you're drifting?" Isabel replies: "No, I haven't the least idea, and I find it very pleasant not to know. A swift carriage, of a dark night, rattling with four horses over roads that one can't see—that's my idea of happiness." Henrietta responds that her language sounds like that of "the heroine of an immoral novel" (146).

That Isabel uses such language should come as no surprise since she understands her world in part through the filter of the romance tradition of women's novels. As William Veeder observes, Isabel talks a conventional line, using the extravagant language of women's fiction. Like women's heroines, she relies "upon the pretty set-speeches conventional with pretty heroines."[14] Her own naive reading deceives her and tricks her into marriage with a man whose name, Gilbert, suggests the heroes of romances written by both Sir Walter Scott and Susan Dudley Warner.[15] At the end, still following the literary convention of her romance novels, Isabel is left with only one way out, self-sacrifice. Ironically, it has been another convention of women's fiction, the sickly, feminized Ralph Touchett, himself a writer (and reader) of the genre, who prepared Isabel for her downfall when he convinced his father to provide for the requirements of his cousin's imagination, thus authoring the pre-text of her disaster.

But the romance tradition is not the only literary tradition that fails Isabel. When Mrs. Touchett first meets Isabel in the family library in Albany, the girl has been "trudging over the sandy plains of a history of German Thought" (34). She takes to heart the superiority of the male virtues of logic, reason, and mind over the female ones of emotion, sensitivity, and heart. Had she been conscious enough to note that her reading was indicting her own character, she might have become a resisting reader, recognizing that the texts she was reading made her own gender into the enemy.[16] Isabel's transcendentalist reading tricks her into believing in the possibilities for her own independence, possibilities reserved, according to the American tradition of idealism, for men. Emerson, one of Isabel's heroes, for instance, as Joyce Warren notes, was "unable to see women as individuals like himself." "It is clear that his philosophy [of self-reliance and insistence on high goals] was not intended to apply to women."[17] In the beginning of the novel Isabel is the embodiment of the Emersonian idealist: she believes in the world "as a place of brightness, of free expansion, of irresistible action" (54); she believes in "the continuity between the movements of her own soul and the agitations of the world" (41). But Isabel is a woman, as James well knows—as Kaston remarks, "Isabel Archer is more than incidentally female."[18] Her reading of a male intellectual philosophy does not serve her. As she laments: "She had desired a large acquaintance with human life, and in spite of her having flattered herself that she cultivated it with some success this elementary privilege had been denied her" (431). The "privilege" is denied her because of her sex and her goodness, and both the reader and James mourn her lost opportunity.

Thus, Isabel's naïveté fails her on two levels. First, she thinks the world of the romance novel real, allowing it to dictate experience to her, revealing her dependency; second, she thinks male transcendentalism and idealism written for her, thus revealing her paradoxical desire to write her own text of self. James does not condemn the romance vision itself; however, he thinks that the tradition of German-Concord transcendentalism was responsible for Isabel's naive perception of reality and for her failure to allow her imagination free rein. But finally, Isabel, as a woman in a man's world, a woman written by a man (sympathetic though he be), can only respond as she does: as a mostly passive participant whose glorious imagination will never experience free rein though it may triumph over some of the obstacles it confronts.

Nearly three-quarters of a very long letter from Woolson to James, dated 12 February 1882, is taken up with her criticism of *Portrait.* By far the most telling of Woolson's responses to the novel is the whole of her last paragraph:

> How did you ever dare write a portrait of a lady? Fancy any woman's attempting a portrait of a gentleman! Would'nt there be a storm of ridicule! . . . For my own part, in my small writings, I never dare put down what men are thinking, but confine myself simply to what they do and say. For, long experience has taught me that whatever I suppose them to be thinking at any especial time, that is sure to be exactly what they are *not* thinking. What they *are* thinking, however, nobody but a ghost could know.[19]

Woolson, of course, is making a mild joke, and, in fact, she does attempt several portraits of gentlemen, both in her last novel, **Horace Chase,** and in **"'Miss Grief,'"** a narrative told from a male first-person perspective. Yet, just as James's *Portrait,* though about a woman, presents a heroine from a male tradition where women, even admirable, imaginative ones, are in a sense forcedly passive, Woolson's narratives featuring male characters evolve from the women's writing tradition we see described, for example, by Nina Baym in *Woman's Fiction* and by Mary Kelley in *Private Woman, Public Stage.*[20] In this tradition the female character is active, not passive; the protagonist is the writer's alter ego rather than a female character for whom the male author has a large degree of sympathy. In a letter dated 30 August 1882, Woolson compares her work to James's:

> All the money that I have received, and shall receive, from my long novel, does not equal probably the half of the sum you received for your first, or shortest. It is quite right that it should be so. And, even if a story of mine should have a large "popular" sale (which I do not expect), that could not alter the fact that the utmost best of my work cannot touch the hem of your first or poorest. My work is coarse beside yours. Of entirely another grade. The two should not be mentioned on the same day. Do pray believe how acutely I know this. If I feel anything in the world with earnestness it is the beauty of your writings, and any little thing I may say about my own comes from entirely another stratum; and is said because I live so alone, as regards to my writing, that sometimes when writing to you, or speaking to you—out it comes before I know it. You see,—I like so few people! Though I pass for a constantly smiling, ever-pleased person! My smile is the basest hypocrisy.[21]

That her writing cannot compare to James's is undeniable: hers is the writing of a woman, as the passage abundantly demonstrates. It is cautious, modest, self-effacing, yet the turn at the end, the suggestion of wearing a mask, even in comparing her work with his, is reminiscent of a familiar strategy used in American women's writing since the time of Woolson's sister New Englander Anne Bradstreet. Like her letter to James, Woolson's writing employs women's writing traditions, such as the writer's identification with her heroine and the widespread use of feminine archetypal patterns and images; and like the domestic writings from the earlier part of the century, Woolson's works empower women in many ways rather than lament their powerlessness in the outer world while compensating them with an imaginative inner life.[22]

Anne, the novel about which Woolson wrote to James, is the first of her strong women narratives. It was printed in several editions during her life, again after her death, and just recently with a new introduction.[23] Although past critics have praised *Anne* primarily for its local-color descriptions of Mackinac Island, Michigan, many agree that because the novel is replete with issues of self-identity, it deserves renewed attention. The issue of identity is the same one James treats in *Portrait,* yet since male and female definitions of identity and power differ, the thread is spun out with differing tension by male and female writers.

One of the ways that male and female texts differ is in the identification of the writer with the protagonist. Isabel is not James, nor was she meant to be, and Woolson teases James about his attempt to paint the portrait of a woman. Anne, however, is in many ways Woolson herself, substantiating Judith Kegan Gardiner's hypothesis that a woman writer "uses her text, particularly one centering on a female hero, as part of a continuing process involving her own self-definition and her empathic identification with her character. Thus, the text and its female hero begin as narcissistic extensions of the author."[24]

Anne Douglas and Constance Fenimore Woolson share interests and background, not the least of which is the name *Anne,* which Woolson adopted as a pseudonym for her first publication, **The Old Stone House** (1872). Both Anne and Woolson were New Hampshire natives and as children spent periods on the upper peninsula of Michigan, where a memorial to Woolson with the name *Anne* at the head of the tablet was erected in 1916. Both young women, though accomplished in the liberal and fine arts, protest that they are ugly. Woolson's portraits and her descriptions of Anne, however, belie such evaluation. Perhaps as a reaction against her sense that she falls short of the American ideal of beauty, Woolson develops a love of letter writing, the art of communicating without being seen. Anne shares that love. Just as Woolson tells James that she writes to him for her own amusement, Anne, in writing to her fiancé, Rast Pronando, finds that through the use of language she may assert a control over her life. (It is, on the other hand, the workings of language in literature that represent Isabel's inability to control her life.)

Both Woolson and her textual daughter also assert power and identity in physical activity and exertion. Throughout her life Woolson rowed to release energy as well as to pass a pleasant Saturday afternoon. Near the end of **Anne,** the heroine uses rowing as a release and as a means of coming to terms with her identity. In addition to rowing, Woolson loved any sort of physical activity, especially walking, and her letters are filled with references to hour-long morning jaunts and afternoon treks of six to eight miles. The place of physical exercise in Anne's and Woolson's lives is reflected in Ellen Moers's reading of walking as a recurring pattern in women's writing, signaling feminist independence and drive.[25]

Woolson's use of archetypal patterns and images in women's writing further identifies her (and **Anne**) with the women's writing tradition, gaining for Woolson depth and power. Among the archetypes Woolson's novel uses in some fashion are those of the green world epiphany (the coming to self in nature) and the green world lover (the coming to passion in nature), both elements of the archetypal feminine *Bildungsroman* as discussed by Annis Pratt. As Pratt explains, in nature, the stage for growth, activity, and confirmation of self-identity, women find "solace, companionship, and independence."[26] An important distinction is to be made here: for the transcendentalists (and for Isabel) nature is intellectualized, as evidenced by the analytic presentation of the subject in Emerson's famous "Nature" essay. Nature is a representative force rather than a fundamentally real part of our lives. In women's writing, however, nature is a personified friend. In the female *Bildungsroman* the girl takes possession of herself in taking possession of nature. Anne loves the trees so much she talks to them. Like her heroine, Woolson feels most independent and powerful—most herself— out in nature.[27]

The green world is the most important setting in Woolson's novel. In a culminating scene, Anne recognizes her friend's killer and is thus empowered to exonerate her lover through knowledge gained while rowing on a lake. In another of her green world epiphanies "among the arbor vitae, where there was an opening, like a green window overlooking the harbor," Anne agrees to marry young Rast Pronando, after his near drowning (132). But Rast is not Anne's green world lover. That figure, associated with the mythic dying god, appears in the person of Ward Heathcote, whose surname is Woolson's adaptation of another famous woman's green world lover. She retailors a rather wild, uncivilized Heathcliff into a more civilized, well-bred Heathcote. A Union captain in the Civil War, he is wounded in West Virginia, and, nearly dead, is restored to life by Anne.

In the archetype, the restorer is a goddess: Aphrodite, Ishtar, or Isis. Anne, in fact, is endowed with similar mythic resonance tying her to the power of the archetypes. From the second page of the narrative, Anne is described as "a young Diana," an allusion that reverberates throughout the novel. Both James and Woolson play on the allusion with their respective heroines; however, James's use is disguised in Isabel's last name, whereas Woolson's use is overt, appealing directly to the women's literary tradition of using goddess archetypes. James uses it from a male perspective to suggest Isabel Archer's female virtue, an abstract idea; Woolson uses it to suggest Anne's physical "vigor" and "elasticity," a concrete description. Their use of the references to Diana echoes their differing versions of transcendental nature: for James and Isabel it is intellectual; for Woolson and Anne it is sensate.

Anne, posed braiding her hair, is also called Ariadne, a figure as familiar as Diana in the women's literary tradition. Indeed, she is both: in her guise as Diana, she is the huntress who dwells alone in the woods and mountains; as Ariadne, she is abandoned by Rast Pronando. But Anne (Woolson) is also Ariadne, a weaver, a domestic maker of fictions, who grows in that capacity over the course of the novel. Early in her recognition that she enjoys writing, we are told that "she never put down any of her own thoughts, opinions, or feelings: Her letters were curious examples of purely impersonal objective writing." Woolson continues:

Egotism, the under-current of most long letters as of most long conversations also, the telling of how this or that was due to us, affected us, was regarded by us, was prophesied, was commended, was objected to, was feared, was thoroughly understood, was held in restraint, was despised or scorned by us, and all our opinions on the subject, which, however important in itself, we present always surrounded by a large indefinite aureolaCthis of our own personalityCthis was entirely wanting in Anne Douglas's letters and conversation. (98)

Throughout the course of *Anne* the heroine's narrative talents grow until, at the climax of the novel, Anne demonstrates her new mastery of narrative form by weaving on the witness stand the fabric of truth, designed to acquit her lover. When the jury cannot arrive at a verdict, Anne rereads the text of the murder herself, discovering the killer. Finally, in the last pages of the novel, the passive voice of her early reflection on writing is rewritten in the active, identifying herself as the star of the show: "I, Anne, take thee, Ward, to be my wedded husband, to have and to hold, from this day forward" (539). Unlike Isabel, Anne can assert her identity in the real world, as suggested by her new command of language. To the end, Isabel, given her circumstances, cannot vigorously and independently pursue her dream. She remains, in the last words she utters in the novel, an object, as she implores Caspar Goodwood, "As you love me, as you pity me, leave me alone!" (489).

Writing her own text of self and arriving at her own identity have not been easy for Anne. At every turn in the novel someone is attempting to appropriate her by stripping her of her linguistic being. Rast calls her Diana; Mrs. Vanhorn calls her Phyllis; Helen calls her Crystal (a particularly suggestive nickname since it implies a reflective relationship between Anne and Helen, one with a singularly complex inner composition and transparency); Miss Lois calls her Ruth Young. Her egotistical assertion at the end, "I, Anne," both defines her powerful new statement of identity and marks an assertion of Woolson's fictional power. Tied into archetypal patterns, that power strengthens the weave.

Before we leave *Anne* and the way it works with the women's literary tradition, we need to consider the function of Anne's half sister Tita. Much intrigued by the French-American half-breed with more than a trace of Indian blood, Henry James thought highly of Tita as a literary creation, as he writes in his *Partial Portraits* sketch of Woolson. That Tita "vanishes into the vague" after the reader has "built great hopes" on her is problematic, however.[28] What James does not understand is that Tita is a nineteenth-century women's literary archetype: the madwoman in the attic, or, in the case of *Anne,* the wild child on the island. She cannot be

permitted any more narrative space than she has or she would take over. After fulfilling her purpose, she can be dispensed with.

Tita is the madwoman from the other side of the mirror Woolson holds up to herself in her projection of Anne. In *The Madwoman in the Attic* Sandra M. Gilbert and Susan Gubar describe the dynamics of such a mirroring:

> Even the most apparently conservative and decorous women writers obsessively create fiercely independent characters who seek to destroy all the patriarchal structures which both their authors and their authors' submissive heroines seem to accept as inevitable. Of course, by projecting their rebellious impulses not into their heroines but into mad or monstrous women . . . female authors dramatize their own self-division, their desire both to accept the strictures of patriarchal society and to reject them. What this means, however, is that the madwoman in literature by women is not merely, as she might be in male literature, an antagonist or foil to the heroine. Rather, she is usually in some sense the *author's* double, an image of her own anxiety and rage.[29]

Tita is truly Anne's mad double. Born of the same father (the same patriarchal structure) but of different mothers, Tita and Anne are both intimately related and decidedly divergent. Whereas Anne was born an Episcopalian in civilized New Hampshire, Tita is the Catholic daughter of his second wife, a French woman with Indian blood, whom he married in the uncivilized territory of the Western Reserve. Her religion, region, and language make Tita a dark unknown, a marginal Gothic figure from the very beginning.

Her personality reinforces her "otherness" vis-à-vis her older sister. While we first see Anne actively hanging Christmas wreaths at the church, Tita is "basking in the glow" of the fireplace, looking up listlessly (9). Anne's eyes are "wide open, and frank" (2), and the "adjective generally applied to her was 'big'" (3). Her heavy hair is demurely braided and pinned up in the fashion Woolson herself adopted. Tita, on the other hand, is "small—a strange little creature, with braids of black hair hanging down behind almost to her ankles, half-closed black eyes, little hands and feet, a low soft voice, and the grace of a young panther" (9). Anne has the blush of a peach, but Tita's complexion is pallid. Anne maternally cares for her half brothers; Tita threatens violence: "If you come any nearer," she tells one, " . . . I shall lay open the side of your head" (9-10). Tita rules the boys like a king, exhorting them with foul language and avenging herself against them for invading the privacy of her fur-carpeted lair near the fire:

> When they had been unbearably troublesome she stole into their room at night in her little white

nightgown, with all her long thick black hair loose, combed all over her face, and hanging down round her nearly to her feet. . . . she left a lamp in the hall outside, so that they could dimly see her, and then she stood and swayed toward them slowly, backward and forward, without a sound, all the time coming nearer and nearer, until they shrieked aloud in terror, and Anne, hurrying to the rescue, found only three frightened little fellows cowering together in their broad bed, and the hairy ghost gone. (10)

Elsewhere, too, Tita is depicted as a ghost. On the same Christmas Eve that Anne hangs the wreath, Tita steals into the sitting room to examine the contents of her stocking. When she does not find the hair ribbons she wants, she writes a letter to Santa asking for them and puts it in her father's way. Her mission complete, she goes back to her own room "like a small white ghost" (23). Anne, innocent of Tita's machinations, provides the ribbons for her sister's pleasure after consulting with her father. Tita's ghostly image is a correlative for the "uneasy sense of trouble" that surfaces "like a veiled, formless shape" (20) whenever William Douglas thinks of Tita. "The sins of the fathers," he reflects.

Compared to both a cat and an embalmed monkey of the Nile, Tita at thirteen years old, neither child nor woman, is a preternatural, mythic, dangerous, mysterious force. She dresses entirely inappropriately for a Christmas dance in "a fantastic short skirt of black cloth barred with scarlet, and a little scarlet bodice" (33). When Tita is said to look like a circus rider in such a thin costume—the colors of blood and passion, we note—Anne confesses that she knew nothing of her sister's plan to dress in such an outfit.

But Anne should know, if not consciously, then unconsciously; for if Anne is her father's favorite and Rast Pronando's sweetheart, Tita is her rival. The small, ghostly half-breed sister is the locus for the virginal Diana's displaced feelings not only of violence, manipulation, and jealousy, but also of selfhood and passion. Père Michaux, Tita's confessor, is the first to identify Tita's "strong selfism" in her understanding of religious ideas: "Whatever was said to her in the way of correction she turned and adjusted to suit herself; her mental ingenuity was extraordinary" (74). Obedient Anne just "listened to the child with wonder" (74) as her sister revolts against the patriarchy of the Catholic Church.

But it is Rast, Anne's fiancé, who evokes the passion primary in Tita's nature and hidden in Anne's in a particularly telling scene, which occurs as Rast prepares to leave the island for college. As he bids farewell to Anne, she appears calm rather than sad, a reaction that annoys him. Tita, on the other hand, drops out of a tree into his arms. After giving her a kiss and stroking her hair, Rast is forced to pry her arms from him. Although Woolson is probably conscious only of how the scene prepares the way for Rast and Tita's marriage at the end, her language illuminates Tita's role as Anne's (and Woolson's) mad double crazed by passion:

> Tita, left alone, looked at her arms, reddened by the force with which she had resisted his efforts to unclasp them. They had been pressed so closely against the rough woollen cloth of his coat that the brown flesh showed the mark of the diagonal pattern.
>
> "It is a hurt," she said, passionately—"it is a hurt." Her eyes flashed, and she shook her small fist at the retreating figure. (120)

As Anne grows into selfhood, recognizing and acting on her own passions for Heathcote, Tita marries the colorless Rast, companion of her sister's youth, and then disappears from the scene. We learn of the marriage through a traditional women's writing strategy of concentric narratives.[30] Chapter 22 of *Anne* reproduces four different letters notifying the heroine of the events leading up to the marriage, which ironically frees her to act on her own passion.

Tita, whose real name is *Angélique* (like her mother's), is Anne's dark angel as well as nemesis. Diminutive Tita, full of strength of identity, is indeed, as William Douglas had noted, a product of some patriarchal sin. We read that sin as the father's denial of personhood for his daughters. Because of that sin, exemplified by his refusal to allow Anne to learn Greek, Tita rises to assert her own identity violently and passionately.

Despite their other differences, constituted in part by their differing gender viewpoints, Woolson and James are each concerned with the silencing of female figures. Tita, whose passionate nature presents a distinct threat to domesticity as constituted by the patriarchy, is silenced, and though Anne becomes an active asserter of selfhood at the end of the novel, in marrying she will be subjugating her own identity to her husband's.

Woolson's power, in *Anne* as well as in other fictions, derives from traditions of women's writing as well as from her own unique talent. The tradition is the most important element differentiating her from Henry James, a man who generally chose (the notable exception being George Eliot, a curious case given her choice of pseudonym) male writers as his models. We realize that Emerson spoke to him, not to women, like Woolson, when he wrote: "The Poet is representative. He stands among partial men for the complete man." One of Isabel Archer's mistakes is in thinking that Emerson wrote to her. Women, as Ellen Moers suggests by her recasting of Emerson in her headnote to Chapter I of *Literary Women,* are themselves forced to rewrite Emerson because they belong to a variant tradition.[31] Constance Fenimore Woolson found her representative poets in that tradition, in the works of Elizabeth Barrett Browning, George Sand, George Eliot, and the Brontës. Her individual talent is remarkable, too, not simply for her vivid local-color descriptions of Michigan, Ohio, North Carolina, Florida, and Europe (those landscapes which form the boundaries of her career) but also for her energetic struggle with issues of identity, language, and art.

Anne clearly exemplifies how Woolson adapted her literary inheritance from the domestics of earlier in the century to suit her original purposes. And indeed, her later novels take up that same women's tradition to tell stories of strong girls who triumph over obstacles to make their ways in the world. In her short fiction, however, Woolson treats issues other than marrying well. In fact, in several of her best fictions, marriage becomes the lesser of two evils, the other being destitution. Her artist-heroines are forced, in choosing it—and survival—to sacrifice self and art.

Notes

[1] Mary Kelley, *Private Woman, Public Stage* (New York: Oxford University Press, 1984) and Nina Baym, *Woman's Fiction: Novels by and About Women in America* (Ithaca: Cornell University Press, 1978).

[2] Constance Fenimore Woolson, "Duets," *Harper's New Monthly Magazine* 49 (September 1874): 579-585.

[3] Constance Fenimore Woolson, "Weighed in the Balance," *Appleton's Journal* 7 (1 June 1872): 590.

[4] Constance Fenimore Woolson, *Castle Nowhere: Lake Country Sketches* (Boston: J. R. Osgood and Company, 1875).

[5] Constance Fenimore Woolson, *Anne* (New York: Harper and Brothers, 1882). Page numbers are cited parenthetically within the text.

[6] Henry James, *The Portrait of a Lady*, ed. Robert D. Bamberg (New York: W. W. Norton, 1975). I have chosen to use the Norton Critical Edition since it offers a list of textual variants from the first edition of 1881 in addition to the text of the later New York edition. Because the 1908 edition differs from the original, written while Woolson was at work on *Anne*, the reader should consult the 1881 first edition variants, as I have done. Page numbers are cited parenthetically within the text.

[7] Alfred Habegger refers to Henry James and William Dean Howells as sissies in chapter 7 of *Gender, Fantasy, and Realism in American Literature* (New York: Columbia University Press, 1982), pp. 56-65.

[8] Baym, *Woman's Fiction*, p. 22.

[9] Carren Kaston, *Imagination and Desire in the Novels of Henry James* (New Brunswick, N.J.: Rutgers University Press, 1984), p. 40.

[10] Habegger, *Gender, Fantasy*, p. 56.

[11] Kaston, *Imagination and Desire*, p. 41.

[12] Ibid., p. 41.

[13] Ibid., p. 41.

[14] William Veeder, *Henry James—The Lessons of the Master: Popular Fiction and Personal Style in the Nineteenth Century* (Chicago: University of Chicago Press, 1975), p. 71.

[15] Veeder, *Henry James*, p. 120.

[16] For the idea of the resisting reader, I am indebted to Judith Fetterley, *The Resisting Reader: A Feminist Approach to American Fiction* (Bloomington: Indiana University Press, 1978).

[17] Joyce Warren, *The American Narcissus: Individualism and Women in Nineteenth-Century Fiction* (New Brunswick, N.J.: Rutgers University Press, 1984), pp. 43, 49.

[18] Kaston, *Imagination and Desire*, p. 40.

[19] Henry James, *Henry James Letters*, vol. 3 (1883-1895), ed. Leon Edel (Cambridge, Mass.: Belknap Press, 1980), p. 535.

[20] See Baym, *Woman's Fiction*, and Kelley, *Private Woman*.

[21] *Henry James Letters*, 3:544-545.

[22] For extensive discussions of how women's writing empowers its female readers, see for example, Baym, *Woman's Fiction*, and Kelley, *Private Woman*.

[23] *Anne* was published by Harper and Brothers in 1882, 1903, and 1910, and by Sampson and Low (London) in 1883. The Arno Press has reprinted the Harper's text with a new introduction by Elizabeth Hardwick.

[24] Judith Kegan Gardiner, "On Female Identity and Writing by Women," in *Writing and Sexual Difference*, ed. Elizabeth Abel (Chicago: University of Chicago Press, 1982), p. 187.

[25] Ellen Moers, *Literary Women: The Great Writers* (1976: rpt., New York: Oxford University Press, 1985), p. 130.

[26] Annis Pratt, *Archetypal Patterns in Women's Fiction* (Bloomington: Indiana University Press, 1981), p. 21.

[27] I located a list of wildflowers Woolson had seen, written in the back cover of a wildflower text in the holdings of the Olin Library at Rollins College, Winter Park, Florida, where I also found two unpublished Woolson poems, "Ferns" and "Fern Fragments," tucked in the back of a book.

[28] James, "Miss Woolson," *Literary Criticism: Essays on Literature, American, English Writers* (New York: Library of America, 1984), p. 642.

[29] Sandra M. Gilbert and Susan Gubar, *The Madwoman in the Attic: The Woman Writer and the Nineteenth-Century Literary Imagination* (New Haven: Yale University Press, 1979), pp. 77-78.

[30] Ibid., p. 249.

[31] Moers, *Literary Women,* p. 1.

Victoria Brehm (essay date 1990)

SOURCE: "Island Fortresses: The Landscape of the Imagination in the Great Lakes Fiction of Constance Fenimore Woolson," *American Literary Realism: 1870-1910,* Vol. 22, No. 3, Spring 1990, pp. 51-66.

[*In the following essay, Brehm contests the idea that Woolson is either "a failed realist or a failed sentimentalist" and argues that Woolson's writing reflects her own conflicts and renunciations as a female author.*]

Henry James noted only two "defects" in Constance Fenimore Woolson's 1889 novel ***Jupiter Lights:*** "One is that the group on which she has bent her lens strikes us as too detached, too isolated, too much a desert island. . . . The other fault is that the famous 'tender sentiment' usurps among them a place even greater perhaps than that which it holds in real life. . . . "[1] Although James rightly spotted two unresolved problems in Woolson's work, he did not understand that there was a connection between them, nor could he have perceived how they were an attempt to resolve a personal conflict. ***Jupiter Lights*** was only the most recent manifestation of a theme Woolson had repeated obsessively in more than twenty Great Lakes stories, where she tried to solve the problem of being a single, self-supporting woman as well as a serious artist in the two decades after the Civil War. Her solution, perhaps unconscious, was to encode her painful struggle in stories with conventional romantic patterns, using idiosyncratic motifs of character and landscape to undercut the promised marriage her readers expected.

Unfortunately, Woolson left little record of this early struggle except her stories. Her career spanned several decades—she was the first woman to write maritime fiction about the Great Lakes, the first writer to chronicle the Reconstruction South, and one of the first to describe American expatriate life in Europe—before she died suddenly at age 54, perhaps a suicide, in Venice in 1894. Because she did not live to write an autobiography and always requested that her correspondents destroy her letters, we seldom know how close she was to the themes in her work. The biography compiled by her niece is a potpourri of fragments of Woolson's work and undated excerpts from surviving letters, thus compounding the difficulties of scholarly investigation of this reticent, retiring woman.[2] Nevertheless, there is enough evidence to suggest that she contended all her life with the dilemma of wanting to be part of her nineteenth-century world and yet needing to remain aloof from it. If she fulfilled the expectations of her society to marry and have children, her freedom, both personal and professional, would be severely restricted. To ignore those social expectations was to condemn herself to loneliness, to become, as she wrote late in her life, a "very quiet person whose circle constantly narrows around her."[3] Yet she had early revealed a reluctance toward the conventional feminine role; in her twenties she wrote to a friend who had recently married, "Although I am willing to settle down after thirty years are told, I do not care to be forced into quiescence yet awhile."[4] As her many travel articles attest, she never stayed anywhere long, even in places she loved. She gave up her prized apartment in the Villa Brichieri in Florence, where she had settled after seventeen years of wandering Europe and the Middle East, to take lodgings in England because

> I have come here to do a long job of literary work. I could do almost nothing in Florence; there were such endless numbers of people to receive & to go and see. . . . I hated to give up the beautiful Bellosguardo View; it tore me to pieces to do it. But after a struggle to write & attend to social duties at the same time through three long years, I at last recognized that it was impossible. At least impossible for *me.*[5]

At this time (1890), Woolson was artistically and financially successful, yet the societal world still seemed threatening. And when she first began to write, she could not have had the bulwark of success. Her struggle shows in her first stories, where she approached her problem by creating characters who did what she was trying to do, who served as the examples she lacked in life. She projected her conflict into her characters and onto the landscape of her imagination, creating singular, isolated individuals who find an island refuge. In her fiction she found the freedom to envision another life, one that anticipated what her own would become.

Her personal conflict of longing for complete independence, but fearing its price, was compounded by her public relations. She despised the predictable, romantic fiction that appealed to what she witheringly referred to as "the public," once relating how she had flung a popular novel across the room.[6] Elsewhere she wrote, "I have such a horror of 'pretty,' 'sweet' writing that I should almost prefer a style that was ugly and bitter, provided it was also *strong*."[7] But many of her early stories are constructed with a conventional romantic plot that ends in marriage, and her first novel, *Anne* (1882), was a best-selling model in the genre, reminiscent of the domestic novels already popular for three decades. This paradox can be explained only partly by the demands of the marketplace. When she did risk "going back to nature and exact reality"[8] in stories like **"Castle Nowhere"** (1875) and **"Peter the Parson"** (1874) her readers complained:

> At least twenty awful letters have I received because I made Old Fog (**"Castle Nowhere"**) say he did not believe in eternal punishment. Is it possible that I am to be held personally responsible for the morality of my characters? I want you to think of me not as your old friend, when you read my writings, but as a "writer," like anyone else. . . . The truth is . . . whatever one does must be done with one's might and I would rather be strong than beautiful, or even good, provided the "good" must be dull.

> And, under the abuse which has been showered upon me for my "brutal killing of Peter the Parson," I have steadily maintained to myself that both in an artistic and truthful-to-life point of view, my ending of the story was better than the conversion of the miners, "the plenty to eat and the happy marriage" proposed by my critics.[9]

The second comment suggests that Woolson's first readers disliked not only her refusal to write saccharin stories, but her use of isolato figures as a contrast to the romance, characters who chose not to conform and often felt no need to justify themselves. Set down amidst the trappings of romance, their examples flash like buoys marking the hidden rocks in a placid channel, warning readers that below the surface prettiness of wedding plans lies another, more disturbing, reality.

Despite her questioning of fictional conventions, Woolson has been shunned by many recent feminist critics in favor of other nineteenth-century women writers whose work falls into the patterns of "women's fiction" currently in fashion. If they judge her at all, it is as a "serious" writer whose use of a love plot undercuts her intentions.[10] Thus to them she is either a failed realist or a failed sentimentalist, and her ability to use both conventions equally well is considered a fault rather than a vir-

tue. Other critics have categorized her as a local colorist,[11] or as straddling "the border between local color and realism."[12] These conclusions are based on the inference that since she wrote about the Great Lakes and then the South and then Europe and described each setting with fidelity of detail, realistic evocation of place was her major talent. But the many differences in her work and her life that distinguish her from women local colorists should by now have made such categorization fallacious.[13] Some critics have noted that she always wrote about characters who sacrifice what they love so that others can be happy.[14] Few have considered how her use of this familiar renunciation theme differs from the ordinary, and none how inseparable it is from her use of landscape. She did write one story over and over, and it was about the cost and gains to women who refused to go along with the obligatory domestic femininity of their time. Few American women had written it before.

I

The landscapes of the Great Lakes stories are remote, as those who class Woolson with the local colorists commonly point out, settings more common to that mode than to the "inner spaces" of the domestic fiction of the 1840s and 1850s. But remoteness of place or the use of curious characters does not necessarily make a local color story. Woolson uses dialects sparingly; she shows little or no nostalgia for a vanished way of life. Unlike the work of Rose Terry Cooke, Mary Wilkins Freeman, Sarah Orne Jewett, or Mary Murfree, Woolson's stories are as likely to be narrated by men as by women and to have both male and female protagonists. Moreover, Woolson's stories of women seldom depict them retreating to their native villages, a common theme in feminine local color writing; rather, especially in the early stories, they trace the fates of those who do not follow husbands into the wilderness but go alone, a different pattern from what Annette Kolodny describes[15] or from what Margaret Fuller had noticed when she was traveling in Great Lakes country in 1843.[16]

Raised in Cleveland, Woolson never wrote about her native city because, she said, "there was no 'background' there but the lights from the blast-furnaces at Newburgh on a dark night."[17] Woolson's territory, her imaginative landscape, is the Michigan wilderness, what might more properly be called the Old Northwest Territory. To her it seemed not a sparsely settled frontier but often a true wilderness, a place "where man himself is a visitor and does not remain."[18] What Woolson does not admit is that this wilderness had not existed since she was a child, and hardly then. Even before the Civil War Michigan was being lumbered, mined, settled, and rapidly transformed into a tourist mecca. Caroline Kirkland's *A New Home—Who'll Follow?*[19] had described the Michigan frontier a year before Woolson was born in 1840. When Woolson began to write, Kirkland's frontier was comfortably settled and Michigan had been a state for over thirty years. A recent historian half-humorously describes the Great Lakes shortly after Woolson's birth this way:

> In 1845 . . . approximately 200,000 passengers crossed the upper Lakes bound for Chicago, Milwaukee, and other western ports. Tourist excursions by steamboat to Green Bay and other points of interest in the near North had become fashionable: wealthy New Yorkers engaged in Great Circle tours—up the Mississippi by steamboat, a short rail or stage transfer to the Lakes at Chicago, down the Lakes by luxury liner to Buffalo, and thence by train or Erie Canal packet boat to the Hudson and home. It had been just twenty-five years since the Cass expedition had found most of the Lakes a howling wilderness. Now they were seeing women in evening gowns and men in tails on promenade decks lined with plush cushions. Henry Schoolcraft, now the Indian Agent at Mackinac, quit his post and went home in disgust to write his memoirs. Civilization, he thought, had taken over far too completely.[20]

Woolson wrote several travel pieces about the Lakes, one a humorous debunking of just such luxury excursions. Yet with few exceptions, the majority of her fictional settings are not only wild, but beyond history. Her descriptions of nature may be beautiful, evocative of a rapidly disappearing paradise that Champlain had called *la Mer douce,* the sweet sea. But her land is a land of imagination, not experience. From her childhood memories of the Lakes, she created a landscape to serve as the stage for her actions, a wilderness that is frequently an island where social expectations need not be honored, where those who have fled society make their refuges.

"Ballast Island" (1873), an early piece, begins, like many of these stories, with a storm on the Lakes and a lover's quarrel. Elizabeth, fleeing from her betrothed, Frederick, is caught in a storm on Lake Erie and her boat is blown ashore on Ballast Island. Frederick pursues her and they are both taken care of by Miss Jonah, the solitary middle-aged woman who has kept the light there for many years. The lovers' quarrel resolved and the wedding date set, Miss Jonah's tale is then revealed at the center of the story. After a long engagement she had discovered that her betrothed loved her younger sister, so Miss Jonah faked her own drowning and stole away, leaving her farm to the lovers, and wandered until she came to the island. Determined not to be found and brought back into the family circle where she would either marry a man she knew did not love her or be forced to watch him marry someone else, she changed her name, taking that of a mountain near her home, "Yonah." But the people of Lake Erie mispronounced it and she became "Miss Jonah," a mistake she never corrected. Although

Elizabeth and Frederick plead with her to come with them to the city, she refuses: "Here I'm going to stay. I like it. It's lonely, but I'm best alone. . . . I have a fancy I shall not live long, and I want to be buried here on Ballast. There mustn't be any stone or even a mound, for I want to be clean forgotten; and this is what I ask you two to do for me."[21]

Superficially, this story appears to resemble the Shell Heap Island episodes in Sarah Orne Jewett's *The Country of the Pointed Firs,* but there are significant differences. "Poor Joanna" is rejected by her lover, whereas Miss Jonah sacrifices herself for his happiness. Joanna isolates herself on an island, but Shell Heap is within sight and sound of her former home and people frequently sail their boats near or stop and leave packages for her. She remains emotionally, if not physically, within her former society. But Woolson's Miss Jonah changes her name and flees north. When she dies only three people bury her, not the whole town. More important, while Jewett constantly refers to Joanna as "poor Joanna," Woolson does not pity Miss Jonah any more than Miss Jonah pities herself. She is described as strong and competent as a man, capable of handling any emergency, but also still feminine, a good cook and a lover of flowers. She chides Elizabeth's dainty femininity with "What's the good of your hands?" and her one culinary accomplishment, cream pies, with "Cream pies! . . . Will *they* save the nation?"

At first glance **"Ballast Island"** may seem only a love story with a spinster figure for contrast, a common type before the Civil War. But Miss Jonah is much more than simply a Wise Aunt. Woolson is careful to make her life an alternative to marriage, an example of how a woman can thrive without love. In earlier women's fiction, the so-called "handbooks of feminine revolt"[22] and stories of the "philosophy of the fortunate fall,"[23] the heroine often renounced love, only to have it restored to her when the plot threads were neatly tied. But Woolson is concerned with what happens to women who renounce and then discover there is no restoration. The woman local colorists explored this theme repeatedly, but their women wither away in dark, decaying houses or, like Poor Joanna, immolate themselves in sight of the community.[24] Miss Jonah does neither. Like so many of Woolson's heroines who sacrifice themselves for another's happiness, she leaves without good-byes and begins life over in another place, becoming stronger for her struggle.

She does not, however, necessarily become happier in a conventional sense. True to her Biblical namesake, Miss Jonah has sacrificed her own joy for a greater good, but her renunciation was not without pain and she still weeps when she considers all that she lost. At the same time, her hard-won strength and wisdom overshadow Elizabeth's naive romantic posturings with an example of how fragile romantic happiness truly is, how quickly a young woman can be forced to create another life for herself. Yet Miss Jonah has not become bitter, nor does she begrudge the young lovers their happiness. As they leave, she "climbed upon a rock and stood gazing after the sloop, her tall form outlined against the gloomy sky," becoming like the mountain whose name she had chosen, rather than the grim prophet whose name society had given her.

The metaphor of Miss Jonah as mountain is interesting because it prefigures the last entry in Woolson's journal before she died in 1894:

> Upon seeing the sharp peaks of the Dolomites and the great snow masses of the Alps from the point of the Lido on Christmas Eve, 1893, the thought came to me that they are riding along through immeasurable space, they are the outer edge of our star, they cut the air as they fly. They are the rim of the world. I should like to turn into a peak when I die: to be a beautiful purple mountain, which would please the tired, sad eyes of thousands of human beings for the ages.[25]

Woolson wrote that passage twenty years after **"Ballast Island,"** but the metaphors in question had not changed. By 1893 she too had become isolated, and while that isolation often made her weary, as it did Miss Jonah, she had made for herself an artist's life, distinct from conventional married lives.[26]

In *The Experience of Landscape,* Jay Appleton suggests that like most animals we prefer landscapes where we feel secure. Landscapes which offer protection—high hills, the edges of forests, or islands—which allow us to detect strangers long before they arrive, are more attractive than other landforms. He suggests that this atavistic instinct for "prospect and refuge" explains many configurations in landscape paintings we find pleasing, and that this instinct operates even more powerfully in the symbolic language of literature. The act of reading forces the reader to produce a landscape from the cues of the writer's imagination and thus to participate in the experience of place more intimately than he may when presented with the accomplished facts of pictorial representations.[27] If Appleton is right, it seems reasonable to believe that a writer who creates fictional landscapes also completes such an inferential process. And so Woolson's late journal entry seems a residual form of such operations she had conducted when writing her fiction, where an isolato on an island, often an island with a high escarpment, appears in almost every Great Lakes story after **"Ballast Island."** Through her landscapes she gains symbolic power and control outdoors and far away, rather than in what Henry Nash Smith has called "the middle landscape" of small towns and gentle spaces.[28] Woolson's response is more like that of her grand-uncle James

Fenimore Cooper, what Richard Slotkin has described as "the characteristic American gesture in the face of adversity . . . immersion in the native element, the wilderness, as the solution to all problems, the balm to all wounds of the soul, the restorative for failing fortunes."[29] For a woman writer who felt the conventional feminine role as a restriction on her freedom—"I do not care to be forced into quiescence"—the usual female, domestic, fictional setting with its garden was an anathema.

Edith Cobb claims that resort to a landscape known earlier is common among persons of genius, where it takes the form of an imaginative return to a "middle age of childhood, approximately from five or six to eleven to twelve . . . when the natural world is experienced in some highly evocative way, producing in the child a sense of some profound continuity with natural processes . . . when what a child wanted to do most of all was to make a world in which to find a place to discover a self." The recreation of this landscape in later life is an attempt to renew at its source the impulse and power to create.[30] For Woolson, this meant a return to the Great Lakes islands she had visited as a child, particularly the Wine Islands of Lake Erie (of which Ballast Island is one) and Mackinac Island at the Straights. During the next five years before she wrote her first novel, *Anne* (partly set on Mackinac Island), Woolson would write nine more stories set on Great Lakes islands, moving the settings generally north and west farther into the wilderness until she reached the Apostle Islands in western Lake Superior. With **"Ballast Island"** the group is:

"Ballast Island"	1873 Wine Islands	Lake Erie
"St. Clair Flats"	1873 Lake St. Clair	Lake Huron
"A Flower of the Snow"	1874 Mackinac	Lake Huron
"Jeannette"	1874 Mackinac	Lake Huron
"The Old Agency"	1874 Mackinac	Lake Huron
"Misery Landing"	1874 Apostles	Lake Superior
"The Lady of Little Fishing"	1874 Apostles	Lake Superior
"Mission Endeavor"	1874 Apostles	Lake Superior
"Castle Nowhere"	1876 Hog Island?	Lake Michigan
"Raspberry Island"	1877 Bois Blanche?	Lake Huron

Many of these islands rise like cliffs from the water, particularly Mackinac, which was a military garrison chosen for the impregnability of its ramparts when Indians had attacked Fort Michilimackinac on the mainland across the Straits, and the Apostles in Lake Superior. The protagonist of **"Misery Landing"** (1874), John Jay, builds an eyrie on one of the Apostles, "fortified by a high stockade across the land side; the other three sides were cliffs rising from the deep water,"[31] a setting more convenient for eagles than for a man.

Those islands not described as cliff-like are fortresses hidden in labyrinths. Waiting Samuel, a crazed religious prophet, and his long-suffering wife Roxanna of **"St. Clair Flats"** (1873) live in the great marsh on Lake St. Clair, surrounded by channels so confusing that only by trailing string behind can outsiders find their way back to the island house.[32] Old Fog of **"Castle Nowhere"** (1875) has so cleverly camouflaged his inland house with floating sedge that one can approach it only by knowing just which piece of sedge to move.[33] All these island isolatos have been unhappy, sometimes persecuted wanderers in the world, until they find their islands where they are free and safe. Even the members of the garrison at Mackinac, secure in a military society, mourn when they must leave for other posts; in **"Jeannette"** (1874) a mixed-race island girl gives up a chance to marry the garrison doctor who will educate her and take her traveling with him to stay at Mackinac and marry a local boy who is as wild and free as she.[34]

In contrast, those characters in stories not set on islands but in wilderness clearings, isolated by the lake on one side and impenetrable timber on the other, are quite different. The setting of Pine City in **"Hepzibah's Story,"** an early, unpublished manuscript, is typical:

> [It was] a small settlement gathered around the sawmills; back on the ridge there was a row of white houses, a long dock ran out into the lake, and on all sides stood the woods, the great trees so close together that I could not see between them, stretching down to the water's edge and closing around the clearing like a well.[35]

Significantly, the characters in these "clearing" stories do not fare so well as Miss Jonah or Old Fog. Hepzibah returns to New England when she finds her betrothed loves another, the only one of Woolson's heroines to retreat. Peter, the ascetic Episcopal priest of **"Peter the Parson"** (1874), is mocked by the rough miners of his congregation, even as he gives his life to save a thief who once maimed him. Peter's sacrifice is neither appreciated nor avenged, and the young girl who loved him promptly marries his replacement. Unlike Miss Jonah, he reaps no

satisfaction from his sacrifice: "I have failed in my work, I have failed in myself, I am of all men the most miserable!"[36]

Even Woolson's infrequent pastoral landscape of small towns and settled fields is not a good place, particularly for women. Her two stories of the Zoar Community of Ohio, **"Solomon"** (1873) and **"Wilhelmina"** (1875), are set in the archetypal middle landscape, yet both describe the lives of doomed and suffering characters. Solomon, a talented but untutored artist, paints the same picture repeatedly, trying to create what he sees only in his imagination. Once given a lesson, he realizes his vision on canvas, only to die the next day in a mining accident. His wife, who understood neither his genius nor his desire, pities only herself.[37] Wilhelmina waits steadfastly for her lover to return from the Civil War so they may marry, but when he marches home, he abandons her. Forced to marry a man she doesn't love, she dies soon after.[38] For Woolson, society, and often love or marriage, equalled loss of power and loss of self. There is no "prospect" or "refuge" where one who falls outside the social norm can feel confident; the forest or the fields suffocate, "closing around [like] a well."[39]

II

Like Miss Jonah, however, none of Woolson's island isolatos, man or woman, is happy in a conventional sense. At best they are aware that their lives, cut off from society, can make truce with loneliness only by strength and resignation. Even though their social isolation is not always pleasant, however, it does give them independence, and this is the key to Woolson's obsession with her theme. To define herself as an artist took courage in a time when most women defined themselves as daughters, wives, and mothers, particularly when, as in Woolson's case, there was no nurturing group of other writers around her. James and Howells, who faced the same difficulty in becoming serious artists during a period awash in conventional fiction, lived in urban centers. Woolson had no such support. That she missed it is evident from letters even late in her life: "I am terribly alone in my literary work. There seems to be no one for me to turn to. It is true that there are only two or three to whom I wd. turn!"[40]

And so Woolson respectfully projects her strong, singular, independent men and women, particularly women, who are proud, willing to settle for less than their due and yet able to take the consequences. Whereas John Jay gives up his Misery Landing to return to the city and marry a woman he loves but whom he knows wants only his money, Woolson's women seldom capitulate, even if it means permanent isolation or death. When Miriam, the heroine of **"Mission Endeavor"** (1876), abandons a man she has saved from execution by agreeing to marry him, she leaves him to a lesser woman in an explanatory letter. Like many other Woolson heroines, Miriam has sailed off into a lake without saying good-bye, but she gives a parting shot:

> I hate hypocrisy. Therefore I wish to say that it was not religious enthusiasm or self-sacrifice that made me try to save you when Ruth failed. (For she did fail; you can never alter that.) I *was* religious—once. I had deep religious enthusiasms—once. I was capable of making just such a sacrifice for a doomed criminal—once. But that was long ago—before I loved you!

> Yes, Richard Herndon, I loved you, I love you now. But through all the complications and temptations of my fate I am coming out right; I am leaving you forever.

> Go back to Ruth if you like; I do not care, nor shall I know. For I can not marry you if I would, being a wife, at least in name already; and I would not if I could, being very proud. For you did not love me first, Richard; therefore you shall not love me last.[41]

Richard's reaction to this unexpected feminine independence is that he has had a "happy escape; she would have been very inconvenient." To which Woolson as narrator adds her last line, like an ironic smile, "And so she would I fear."

It is intriguing to compare **"Mission Endeavor"** with an earlier tale considered among Woolson's best, **"The Lady of Little Fishing"** (1874). This story, which she patterned after Bret Harte's "The Luck of Roaring Camp," was far more appealing to nineteenth-century readers than **"Mission Endeavor,"** for obvious reasons. Yet Woolson seems to have felt compelled to reconsider the Bret Harte materials in the later story, to restructure the sentimental plot in a less romantic manner more aligned with her own philosophy. Nowhere else in her work does she create two stories with characters and situations so similar but with such different endings. The Lady of Little Fishing, a missionary to a camp of trappers, falls in love with the only man who does not love her. When he rejects her, she weakens and dies, murmuring that although she had "held herself above her kind," God had shown her that she was "the weakest of them all."[42] In both stories the group of men who rule are initially afraid of the woman missionary because of her strength and saintly demeanor. But both the Lady and Miriam "fall," experiencing unrequited love and showing that they are human after all. The significant difference in **"Mission Endeavor"** is that Miriam does not die from loss of love; she sails off into the lake, presumably to become an isolato, and leaves her erstwhile lover to walk along the beach for twelve hours to reach a settlement. Woolson's message is again that love is capricious and that the best way for a woman to cope, particularly if her love is unreturned, is to gather strength and make another life. To refuse to do that, to continue expecting that somehow fate will restore happiness, is death.

As Ann Douglas has pointed out, in the post-Civil War years many women faced just such a possibility, for there were relatively few available men. She suggests that local colorists recognized a statistical probability in cataloguing lonely women left at home with no alternatives except death or a mouldering, witch-like insanity.[43] But Woolson creates an alternative: sane women, secure in what they know they must do to survive, realistic about their chances for happiness. In so doing she also shows that by freeing herself from the constraints of self-destructive love, a woman can avail herself of men's personal freedom to travel, to explore, to become competent at taking care of herself. Woolson's strong women may be uppity and unpredictable, like Miriam; they may have their moments of deep regret, like Miss Jonah; but they endure in a hostile world. Margaret Morris survives after a shipwreck on Lake Michigan through sheer anger at a fellow survivor's condescension: "The pride and high temper of Margaret Morris, lashed into vigor by the sharp questions of the stranger, saved the life of her exhausted body, and the two were still talking when the cold dawn rose slowly into sight, revealing the gray surface of the stormy lake and the blue line of distant shore."[44] Contrary to convention, moreover, Margaret does not marry her raftmate, but soon boards another steamer and continues to Chicago. Flower Moran, of **"A Flower of the Snow"** (1874), is another strong woman willing to be alone. Believing the man she loves does not love her, she sets off into a blizzard. Her guide gives up, the dog train is close to exhaustion, but Flower trudges on. "I am not a coward," she replies to a seductive voice in her head, which urges her to lie down in the snow and sleep into certain death. "'What have *you* to live for?' pursued the voice. 'To conquer myself. . . . Do I not know that I am unloved and unlovable? Am I not trying to do right? Have I not left all that is dear to me in life to follow my wretched, lonely way through the world?'" After continuing to walk, despite the pain of cold and exhaustion, Flower suddenly remembers a Bible verse, "As if written in letters of fire in the air. . . . He that overcometh shall inherit all things."[45] Much has been written about the covert feminism of the women's literature of the 1840s and 1850s, but recent critics have suggested that after the Civil War, when feminism moved out of books and into the streets, literature became regressive.[46] Woolson's stories prove this is not completely accurate. Moreover, Woolson's feminism is of a different character than that of the Sentimentalists, who were intent on giving women power within the home.

III

But Woolson's pattern of story—a character who begins in a love, loses the love, creates another self in nature in response to loss, but then is alone—can become an imaginative dead-end. Woolson's "Natalie Bumppos" have only a single story, and its repetitions can pall. As Kolodny writes of Leatherstocking, the price for returning to the womb of the wilderness is "adult sexuality and much of what we know of civilized norms. Natty can never experience adult human relations within the social community."[47] Woolson's growing recognition of the limitations in her early theme becomes apparent in one of her last Great Lakes isolato portraits, the title story to her collection of Lake Country sketches, *Castle Nowhere*.[48] Old Fog has left civilization for the fog-shrouded northern reaches of Lake Michigan, where for many years he secretly wrecks ships to obtain food and clothing for his beloved foundling child, Silver. When a wealthy stranger from the city happens on Fog's "castle," Silver is grown, but she is still a joyful child who knows nothing of death or evil because of Fog's protection. As Silver comes to know and love the stranger, her naiveté vanishes. "Frightened, shy, bewildered, she fled away from all her dearest joys, and stayed by herself in the flower-room with the bar across the door, only emerging timidly at meal-times and stealing into the long room like a little wraith; a rosy wraith now, for at last she had learned to blush." When they marry and prepare to leave the island, Fog dies, and on her wedding day Silver learns her first lesson of death. Although her husband dutifully teaches her the Christian doctrine of the resurrection, the reader is left wondering if marriage and religion, however laudatory, compensate for Silver's losses. She has learned of evil, and in Woolson's island paradise, evil comes from civilization to take away childlike joy and replace it with a controlling husband who suggests to Fog that, "Of course it is a great thing for you to have the child off your hands and placed in a home so high above your expectations."

At the same time, Woolson clearly portrays the danger Fog courted by remaining isolated in his castle, for if no stranger had ever come for Silver, when Fog died of old age she would have starved to death. In this paradox of strength and naiveté inevitably forced to face death or return to society, Woolson admits that to remain an isolato on an island is to refuse to acknowledge reality. Painful as that reality may be, the person, or the artist, who shuns it will forever remain a child, trapped in a dream of landscape that will one day destroy by psychic starvation.

By the time Woolson came to write *Anne* she had been living in the South for nearly ten years and setting fiction there for five. Thus it was logical that she should try to use both island and Southern settings as she did later in *Jupiter Lights*. The combination is not satisfactory, however, as nearly every critic notes.[49] The first section of *Anne*, set on Mackinac, is universally praised, but once the heroine leaves the Strait, the novel becomes episodic, unfocused, and traditionally sentimental. The large middle section of *Jupiter Lights*, set on Lake Superior, lies incongruously between the southern beginning and close. In both books Woolson seems caught in transition between two different metaphors of landscape, a North of escape and retreat, and a South of closeness and familial tradition.

The North remains, in both novels, a place of safety and power. Anne, like Silver before her, is forced by circumstances from her island paradise at Mackinac, and the rest of the novel traces her attempt to make her way in the world alone. When finally she succeeds, she returns to the island to be married, high within the ramparts of the fort that crowns the escarpment overlooking the water. The whole cast of *Jupiter Lights* flees north to escape danger; most of the resolution of the plot takes place near the Lake, and the return to the South at the end is only a return to a stable family situation. But in neither novel does Woolson achieve the dramatic power of Great Lakes landscape and character as she had in her stories. There is no isolato on an island at the center, no conflict between remaining within a social world and rejecting it. These novels are apprentice-pieces for Woolson's later work as a novelist of manners and they reveal her growing recognition that the metaphorical structure she had imposed on her childhood country was no longer sufficient for her imagination. The magic that had come from a seamless blending of character and place was gone; she had grown beyond it.

Rather than boredom with her local color materials, as most critics have suggested, this is the major reason why Woolson stopped writing about the Great Lakes country. In the post-Reconstruction South she could explore the isolato's position within an established society; like Henry James, she would create a complex investigation of the outsider in a social setting. In her Southern stories, and her later European stories as well, this outsider is often a northerner or a Yankee set down in a foreign culture. Although she still wrote of isolated houses by the water, they were filled with family life. She still described mountains, but they provided comfort and shelter for the towns set down among them; they had no escarpments to keep away the world. Throughout her life, she created characters who sacrifice themselves for another's happiness, but in her later stories, they do not run away after having done so; they remain in their society, tied by bonds of kinship and affection.

Woolson had created her singular Great Lakes island wilderness as a projection of and solution for her dilemma as woman and artist, using landscape to help her escape the mores and tropes of sentimental fiction while she drew inspiration from her childhood memories of place. Once she had explored the implications of the isolato on an island, she could leave her island fortresses behind; she had internalized their strength. Like Miss Jonah, Woolson had become a mountain and she could reside in the world on her own terms: a woman who had chosen to become an artist and succeeded in publishing frequently and well. She was then ready to learn to create characters who could defy convention without denying social relationships. When she wrote the closing line of "Castle Nowhere," she anticipated her farewell to the Great Lakes landscape she would soon abandon: "The fogs still steal across the lake, and wave their gray draperies up into the northern curve; but the sedge-gate is gone, and the castle is indeed nowhere."

Notes

[1] Henry James, "Miss Woolson," in *Partial Portraits* (London: Macmillan & Co., 1988), pp. 177-192.

[2] Claire Benedict, *Constance Fenimore Woolson* (London: Ellis, 1929-1930). The most recent, and by far the best, critical biography of Woolson is *Constance Fenimore Woolson: the Grief of Artistry* by Cheryl B. Torsney (Athens: Univ. of Georgia Press, 1989).

[3] Alice Hall Petry, "Always, Your Attached Friend': The Unpublished Letters of Constance Fenimore Woolson to John and Clara Hay," *Books at Brown,* 29-30 (1982-1983), 74.

[4] Benedict, p. 19.

[5] Petry, p. 104. Woolson's italics.

[6] Rayburn S. Moore, *Constance Fenimore Woolson* (New York: Twayne, 1963), p. 130.

[7] Benedict, pp. 21-22. Woolson's italics.

[8] Benedict, p. 21.

[9] Benedict, p. 23.

[10] Elizabeth Hardwick, "Introduction," *Anne* (New York: Arno Press, 1977), pp. i-ii.

[11] There are three significant studies of Woolson as a local colorist: Fred Lewis Pattee, *The Development of the American Short Story* (New York: Harper & Brothers, 1923); John Kern, *Constance Fenimore Woolson: Literary Pioneer,* dissertation, Univ. of Pennsylvania, 1934; Ann Douglas [Wood], "The Literature of Impoverishment: The Women Local Colorists in America 1865-1914," *Women's Studies,* 1 (1972), 2-40.

[12] Alfred Habegger, *Gender, Fantasy and Realism in American Literature* (New York: Columbia Univ. Press, 1982), p. 105.

[13] Ann Douglas (see note 10) groups Woolson with the local colorists, often women, who retreated to remote parts of the country, often failed to make a financial success of their writing, and lacked any sustained productivity, none of which applies to Woolson. Douglas also notes the "conspicuous absence of male romantic leads" in the local colorists' settings of backward towns and villages, again a point that fits Woolson's work haphazardly.

[14] Moore, p. 127.

[15] Annette Kolodny, *The Land Before Her* (Chapel Hill: Univ. of North Carolina Press, 1984), Chapters 6 and 7.

[16] S. M. Fuller [Margaret Fuller], *Summer on the Lakes, in 1843* (New York: Charles S. Francis and Co., 1844).

[17] Petry, p. 51.

[18] Roderick Nash, *Wilderness and the American Mind* (New Haven: Yale Univ. Press, 1967), p. 5.

[19] [Caroline Kirkland], *A New Home—Who'll Follow? Or, Glimpses of Western Life. By Mrs. Mary Clavers. An Actual Settler* (1839; rpt. New York: Garrett Press, 1969).

[20] William Ashworth, *The Late Great Lakes: An Environmental History* (New York: Knopf, 1986), p. 97.

[21] *Appleton's Journal,* 9 (28 June 1873), 833-839.

[22] Helen Waite Papishvily, *All the Happy Endings* (New York: Harper and Brothers, 1952), Chapter 1.

[23] Nina Baym, *Women's Fiction* (New York: Cornell Univ. Press, 1978), p. 20.

[24] Douglas, pp. 18-19.

[25] Benedict, p. 411.

[26] Woolson's history of depression and her probable suicide suggest that, as she grew older, her personal metaphors of strength became less efficacious. Other American writers have relied on paradigms of character they created while young, only to find themselves without materials for fiction as they aged. Woolson won her struggle for independence, but undoubtedly discovered that strength seldom suffices past youth.

[27] Jay Appleton, *The Experience of Landscape* (London: Wiley & Sons, 1975), Chapters 4 and 7.

[28] Henry Nash Smith, *Virgin Land: The American West as Symbol and Myth* (Cambridge, Massachusetts: Harvard Univ. Press, 1950), Chapters 11 and 12.

[29] Richard Slotkin, *Regeneration Through Violence: The Mythology of the American Frontier 1600-1860* (Middletown, Connecticut: Wesleyan Univ. Press, 1973), p. 267.

[30] Edith Cobb, "The Ecology of Imagination in Childhood," *Daedalus* 88 (1959), 537-548. For another discussion of this concept see Judith Fryer, *Felicitous Space: The Imaginative Structures of Edith Wharton and Willa Cather* (Chapel Hill and London: Univ. of North Carolina Press, 1986), Chapter 1.

[31] *Harper's New Monthly Magazine,* 48 (May 1874), 864-870.

[32] *Appleton's Journal,* 10 (4 October 1873), 419-426.

[33] *Castle Nowhere* (Boston: J. R. Osgood & Company, 1875), pp. 7-98.

[34] *Scribner's Monthly,* 9 (December 1874), 232-243.

[35] Robert Gingras, "Hepzibah's Story': An Unpublished Work by Constance Fenimore Woolson," *Resources for American Literary Study,* 10 (1980), 33-46.

[36] *Scribner's Monthly,* 8 (September 1874), 293-305.

[37] *Atlantic Monthly,* 32 (October 1873), 413-424.

[38] *Castle Nowhere,* pp. 270-303.

[39] Gingras, p. 35.

[40] Petry, p. 65.

[41] *Harper's New Monthly Magazine,* 53 (November 1876), 886-893.

[42] *Atlantic Monthly,* 34 (September 1874), 293-305.

[43] Douglas, pp. 28-30.

[44] *Appleton's Journal,* 7 (13 April 1872), 394-399.

[45] *Galaxy,* 17 (January 1874), 76-85.

[46] For example, see Douglas, p. 13.

[47] Annette Kolodny, *The Lay of the Land* (Chapel Hill: Univ. of North Carolina Press, 1975), p. 114.

[48] *Castle Nowhere,* p. 98.

[49] For example, see the Henry James review cited above.

Peter Caccavari (essay date 1998)

SOURCE: "Exile, Depatriation and Constance Fenimore Woolson's Traveling Regionalism," in *Women, America, and Movement: Narratives of Relocation,* edited by Susan L. Roberson, University of Missouri Press, 1998, pp. 19-37.

[*In the following essay, Caccavari examines Woolson's attempt at being a "writer in exile" and her simultaneous yearning for homecoming.*]

In a letter she wrote as a young girl to a friend who was about to be married and then live in Europe, Constance Fenimore Woolson touched on issues that would preoccupy her writing life throughout her adulthood: exile, travel, place, freedom, art, patriarchy, and depatriation:

> To Miss Flora Payne, afterwards, Mrs. William C. Whitney.
>
> "Seems to me if *I* had a friend in exile across the ocean"—In *exile!* I wish I could be in "exile" too, if I could visit the most beautiful and famous places the world can show! You are the most fortunate young lady I know, and ought to be the *happiest.* I envy you to that extent that the tenth commandment makes me shudder, for although I am willing to settle down after thirty years are told, I do not care to be forced into quiescence yet awhile.[1]

For the young Woolson, exile appears not to be a lonely state but one that offers freedom through mobility. For her, exile represents a desire for place—not a single, fixed, familiar place but many, sequential, unfamiliar places. She wants not to "settle down" for thirty years, and yet the enviable state she is describing is made possible by her friend's marriage, her settling down. It is clearly not her friend's marriage that is the object of longing for Woolson; it is the apparent freedom and reconfiguration of attachment to place(s) that the marriage allows. Indeed, Woolson's letter demonstrates an early attempt at envisioning a depatriation of both place and subjectivity. She thinks that through expatriation she will gain a fresh look at the world, giving her a different perspective on her own land when she returns to it in quiescence. The young Woolson also thinks that even in marriage exile will escape the boundaries of patriarchy. Yet Woolson would come to see that such an exile could be possible without marriage, that the gendered obligations of husband and family actually prevent such exile from coming to fruition, and that even when achieved, exile involves conditions that are anything but enviable.

Even today Woolson as a writer is in exile, little known despite success in her own day. A self-enforced exile from home and nation both within the United States and abroad, she sought as well to distance herself from cultural and gendered constraints upon her writing and life. Known, when she is thought of at all, as a regionalist, Woolson wrote about a variety of places where she had lived or visited, including the Great Lakes (**Castle Nowhere,** 1875), the South (**Rodman the Keeper: Southern Sketches,** 1880), and Italy (**The Front Yard and Other Italian Stories,** 1895, and **Dorothy and Other Italian Stories,** 1896). However, while regionalism is usually predicated on belonging to one particular place in some self-contained and highly demarcated construction of "authenticity," Woolson achieved something quite different: she created a permeable regionalism that brings into question the very ideas of regional and national, national and international, local and global, inside and outside, private and public, participant and observer. Rather than writing a regionalism about *becoming-in-place,* she developed a kind of regionalism based on *becoming-through-placings.* Like Frantz Fanon, who wrote, "In the world through which I travel, I am endlessly creating myself,"[2] Woolson used travel to both create herself over and over again and to depict characters made anew by place, placement, and replacement. The self-creations reflected in Woolson's "traveling regionalism" are, however, conflicted with the tension between the potential for unprecedented freedom (political, social, economic, and geographic) for women in the late nineteenth century and the constraints of domestic ideology that, while in the process of being critiqued and dismantled, still held powerful sway over women.

Indeed, it is the cultural conflation of woman and home that makes Woolson's brand of regionalism so radical and so conservative, so expansive and so located. As Jane Marcus points out, "A woman exile is, in addition, an uncanny figure, in Freud's formulation, for her very body means home and hearth, the womb/home of humankind. If she is homeless, lost, wandering, where are we, her daughters and sons?"[3] Woolson was a contradiction of woman's role in domestic ideology because of her professional status as writer, her "homelessness" in travel, and her unmarried and childless state. She attempted to exchange her womb/home identity as woman for a mind/movement identity that sought to re-create woman through intellectual depatriation, forsaking fatherlands and exploring borderlands. Even so, Woolson could not eradicate the pull of domestic ideology and fashion herself as a subject of unrestrained freedom. Her life and her fiction became contested domains where home and world, rootedness and transience, vied for dominance. Although Woolson wanted to deconstruct the binary oppositions of home/exile, wife/writer, and womb/mind, she was ultimately unable to get beyond these oppositions, and so found herself and her art between them.

A logical extension of the relationship between woman and home is the relationship between exile and nation. Looking at the Modernist women who would be the successors of Woolson and her generation, Shari Benstock recognizes that women often experience an internal exile:

> For women, the definition of patriarchy already assumes the reality of expatriate *in patria;* for women, this expatriation is internalized, experienced as an exclusion imposed from the outside and lived from the inside in such a way that the separation of outside from inside, patriarchal dicta from female decorum, cannot be easily distinguished.

Woolson did not have to wait until she traveled to Europe to experience exile; this was the stuff of her everyday life in the United States. As Benstock goes on to say of woman, as did Marcus about the womb and home, "Her very body is the 'native land' on which patriarchy stakes its claims."[4]

Similarly, Cheryl Torsney locates Woolson in a state of betweenness historically and psychologically. Torsney conjectures that part of the explanation for Woolson's literary neglect since her death is that "she comes of age as a writer just after the heyday of domestic fiction . . . and dies in 1894 just before the maturation of the New Woman. Thus, her professional career is interposed between two periods when women wrote from positions of secure identity and power." It was this period "between the weakening of the bonds of womanhood and the freedom of the New Woman" when "local color writing comes to the fore." Like the period, Woolson herself was caught between bonds and freedom, in the complicated interplay of bonds both constrictive and expansive, of freedoms both liberating and debilitating. As Torsney observes, Woolson's characters "often take on Woolson's own fragmented identity, rehearsing both her transitional generational position and her individual history of family disaster and exile. Woolson's artist-heroines can neither entirely align themselves with the Cult of True Womanhood nor fully reject their upbringing . . . and become New Women."[5] It is thus between bonds and freedom, between home and exile, that Woolson and her characters create a traveling regionalism that is neither here nor there, yet also both here and there. Woolson portrays regions as places where cultures and ideologies meet and blend in ways that make identity—both regional and individual—ambivalent and unsettled. Part of this blending and ambivalence comes from a confusion of outside and inside, of internal exile; but part also comes from Woolson's taking stock of her situation, of assuming agency, and reconstructing a place, or rather, a series of places, from which she can speak in exile. She would find a way to transform expatriation through depatriation. And yet, even this achievement would be incomplete, caught between two worlds as she was.

Woolson's traveling regionalism initially developed out of the transition from her stories set in the Great Lakes region to those set in the South during Reconstruction and the migration of Northerners to the South following the Civil War. Often known collectively by Southerners as "carpetbaggers" (a term deriving from the belief that a person can be identified by place), these transplants began an unprecedented mobility to settled parts of the United States, breaking down regional coherence and creating a decentered sense of place. Woolson's writing of this period, itself a kind of literary carpetbagging, reflected this mobility and confluence.

In her story, **"Old Gardiston,"** in *Rodman the Keeper,* the narrator refers to "double-faced, conscienceless whites" who "were sometimes emigrant Northerners, sometimes renegade Southerners, but always rascals" (116). The narrator intends "double-faced" to mean duplicity with its usual pejorative implications, but it is also an apt description for the Janus-like literary carpetbagging that Woolson engages in, embodying multiple identities, resulting in a variety of complications and contradictions. In a letter to Paul Hamilton Hayne, she speaks of her Southern stories: "I have tried to 'put myself in their place', and at least to be fair." Whereas the typical regionalist is supposedly already "there," Woolson must "put" herself in that place. And yet, she does not thereby become *of* that place in a nativist sense. Instead, she engages in a cultural alibi that positions her both here and elsewhere, constructing multiple levels of place and identity that replace the carpetbagger's image of deceit with ambiguity and decenteredness.[6]

Reconstruction taught Woolson much about a changing sense of place. Judith Kinsolving, a Southern woman who is the focus of Woolson's story, **"In the Cotton Country,"** has lost everything in the Civil War and tells the story's northern-born narrator: "I do not know anything certainly any more, for my world has been torn asunder, and I am uprooted and lost. No, you can not help me, no one can help me. I can not adjust myself to the new order of things; I can not fit myself in new soil; the fibers are broken."[7] While much regional fiction exhibited a rooted sense of place and mourned, like Kinsolving, its disintegration in a modern mobile culture, Woolson took the rootlessness to be a part of her contemporary condition. She saw it as an opportunity for self-reconstruction.

Many of the stories in *Rodman the Keeper,* like **"Old Gardiston"** and **"In the Cotton Country,"** deal with dislocation caused by war and internal (that is, domestic) exile caused by a civil war. The images of disloca-

tion and dividedness (and reconciliation) exemplify Woolson's sense of regionalism and gender as she attempts to create new spaces and new selves by crossing distances and chasms, trying to bring exiles to a new home. Kinsolving experiences a profound sense of loss—of home, region, nation, and identity—as someone who has been depatriated from the United States through secession, depatriated from the Confederate States of America through surrender, and repatriated to the United States. In her concluding dialogue Kinsolving says, "I will abide in my own country" (148), and we are left wondering which country she is talking about, thinking perhaps that ultimately she is referring to the new country of her reconstructed self.

Writing about her Southern fiction, Fred Lewis Pattee called Woolson "an unlocalized soul," who, unlike other American regionalists, was "bounded each by a single horizon," but, "like Henry James, was rooted nowhere." As a refinement of Pattee's idea, I would suggest that Woolson is a *polylocalized* soul—someone who is in some sense "native" to a number of places, not by birth or even duration of habitation, but by observation and imagination. In part, she sought the reconstruction of place through and in writing. She wrote Henry James in 1883: "Well—that is my feeling with regard to your writings; they are my true country, my real home. And nothing else ever is fully—try as I may to think so."[8]

It was not only James's writings, however, in which Woolson found a home; her own provided one too. The title of her story, **"Castle Nowhere,"** is a telling image of both her own rootlessness and her dwelling in/on her fiction. In that story, a man who has committed murder goes off with his older sister to a remote part of the head of Lake Michigan. With them they have brought a foundling child whom the man raises as his own. In that place the man comes to be known as Fog, his sister as Shadow, and the girl as Silver. To feed and clothe them, he periodically sets a beacon for ships lost in storms to follow into reefs so that the vessels are destroyed, the crews killed, and their supplies washed up on shore for the family's use. After a time Shadow dies. Into this wilderness wanders an explorer, Jarvis Waring, who uncovers Fog's past, and eventually marries Silver. Fog dies, and Waring and Silver leave Castle Nowhere, which goes to ruins and falls into the lake.

Joan Myers Weimer identifies this story as a justification of regionalism and its particularization of locale and culture:

Woolson also entertained and rejected the possibility of being "nowhere" rather than one particular "somewhere"—a possibility that challenges the basis of regionalist writing. "Nowhere" is outside geography, history, religion, society, and culture. There, sinful father and innocent daughter can live happily together until "somebody"—a potential suitor for the daughter—invades, bringing with him a variety of cultural "somewheres" that eventually destroy "nowhere."

Woolson's project in **"Castle Nowhere"** is similar to that in **"In the Cotton Country"**; both affirm the portrayal of locale within the regionalist tradition while at the same time engaging in a reconstruction of place in a modern sense. **"Castle Nowhere"** opens narratively in the present remarking about the past: "Not many years ago the shore bordering the head of Lake Michigan . . . was a wilderness unexplored. It is a wilderness still. . . . "[9] Although it may be a wilderness still, it is not as remote as it once was, and we are to understand that it is part of a vanishing frontier. Not only does the castle become "nowhere," but the wilderness itself is becoming "nowhere" as well. Indeed, regionalism is not beyond the reach of the outside, which inevitably breaks into its pristine landscape.

Moreover, the gender issues that Woolson's story raises demonstrate the hold of patriarchy even in remote places. Silver is handed off from Fog to Waring and is portrayed as utterly malleable in the hands of both men. Starting life as a homeless foundling, then taken to a place that is no place, she will finally be taken away by Waring, it is presumed, to what is supposed to be her rightful place, as the angel of a house somewhere rather than a castle nowhere. Silver is supposed to be an exile who is in some ways being returned home by Waring, and yet, we cannot help but see her as returning to the same exile, simply in a different location. She is repatriated in terms of returning to "civilization," but she has never been away from patriarchs. This would be the last time Woolson did not interrogate the cultural assumptions and contradictions implicit in marriage plots and domesticity. In her later fiction marriage would appear, to take an image from **"Castle Nowhere,"** as the deceptive beacon, as "a false light" (44) where women's vessels are dashed on the reefs and men collect for their own benefit the remains that drift ashore.

The home that does arise, however, out of **"Castle Nowhere"** is the home that writing provides Woolson. Her admiration for James's work was a writer's admiration, her appreciation for James's fiction a validation of her own seriousness as a writer. Yet her questioning of identity and relation to place made her question, as well, James's understanding of these issues. In a letter to James, she tells him: "But if you had never left the banks of the Maumee, you would still have been, dumbly, an 'alienated American' (I suppose you have no idea where the Maumee is!)." Moreover, as a literary carpetbagger, Woolson found

her regional doubleness as a Northerner in the South already compounded into a plurality by her identity with New England and the Great Lakes. By the time Woolson went to live in Europe, especially Italy, she had developed a plurality of identities rooted in region and gender in her writing. Weimer observes of this aspect of Woolson's life and writing: "Her psychological doubleness—anguished and amused, home-rooted and restless—was underlined by her complicated dual national identities—a Northerner in the South, an American in Europe. She transforms these facts of her life into the insights of her fiction."[10] I agree with Weimer but would push the "complicated" nature of Woolson's national identities further, saying that her identity, even as a Northerner, is at least dual—born in New Hampshire and having lived in Ohio—and that from that point on there is compounding of identities rather than merely dualities. Indeed, Woolson's polylocalism and ambivalence emerge out of a sense of multiple identity rather than an organic unity lost or idealized, making her traveling regionalism permeable and fluid.

In "The 'Mechanics' of Fluids" Luce Irigaray observes that metonymy is "closely allied to fluids" and helps to characterize women's sexuality. This characterization, according to Irigaray, applies to women's discourse as well. "Woman never speaks the same way. What she emits is flowing, fluctuating. *Blurring*." Boundaries are not fixed but permeable: "Fluid—like that other, inside/outside of philosophical discourse—is, by nature, unstable." Similarly, Woolson destabilizes regions and cultures, blurring sectional and community boundaries, undermining insider/outsider distinctions, creating a metonymic regionalism that emphasizes connection and intersection. Irigaray's framework relates to Benstock's ideas about exile and expatriation. Women's sexuality and discourse may blur boundaries between inside and outside, but so does the internalization of patriarchal assumptions about women and home. The multiplicity of women's identities that Irigaray has spent much time examining—"this sex which is not one"—is, for Benstock, the basis for understanding Modernism, women, and exile: "The standard definitions of the terms *expatriate* and *exile* suggest the cultural assumptions of coextensive self-identity, of coherent subjectivity, of the singular 'I' that Modernism so ruthlessly questions."[11] Just as Benstock rewrites the definitions of *expatriate* and *exile* to reflect women Modernists' experience, Woolson did her own rewriting of *expatriate* and *exile* earlier, in part by rewriting the singular *I* and the regionalism that accompanied it into a serial *I* and a regionalism that reflected the cycles of dislocation and relocation that increasingly were becoming the norm of life in the United States.

James Clifford's concept of "traveling cultures" can shed some light on Woolson's traveling regionalism.

He writes that "I'm trying to sketch a comparative cultural studies approach to specific histories, tactics, everyday practices of dwelling *and* traveling: traveling-in-dwelling, dwelling-in-traveling." Woolson's work and life exemplify Clifford's notion of "dwelling-in-traveling." Like the fluidity that Irigaray says destabilizes the inside/outside of philosophical discourse, or like the disintegration of inside/outside boundaries of internal and internalized exile under patriarchy that Benstock observes, Clifford seeks to blur the participant/observer distinctions of ethnography. "In the history of twentieth-century anthropology, 'informants' first appear as natives; they emerge as travelers. In fact, . . . they are specific mixtures of the two roles."[12] The relation of Woolson's fiction to ethnography would make a valuable study all its own. While Woolson is not self-consciously acting as an ethnographer, her work addresses such ethnographic issues as the constructions of native, informant, and authenticity.

The regionalist is typically seen as the "native," the one born to a place and culture and fluent in the local knowledge. But writing about a region also makes the native an informant and threatens the authenticity of the report. The regionalist as chronicler of a region becomes, then, something of a hybrid, both a native and an informant, one whose reliability is and is not in question. Woolson alludes to the complexity of regionalist writing in her story **"In Venice"** from ***The Front Yard and Other Italian Stories***. An American, Claudia Marcy, observes that "these Venetians of to-day . . . do not appreciate in the least their wonderful water-city— scarcely know what it is." According to Miss Marcy, an outsider can best observe what is actually there, what to the insider is invisible. Another American, Elizabeth Lenox, replies: "They don't study 'Venice' because they are Venice—isn't that it?" (241). For Mrs. Lenox, the Venetians' immediacy and immersion in place makes them the more authentic precisely because they do not observe. Woolson negotiates between both these stances, and, like Clifford, dwells on the specific mixtures of the two roles, making the informant one who lives between and among different cultures.

Not only does the role of informant reveal aspects of Woolson's regionalism, it also shows the part that gender plays in that regionalism. While the subject position of the native is the privileged position of the regionalist, the woman traveler is an uncanny figure who has abandoned her "sphere," who has transgressed by crossing the threshold of home into a world that is supposedly not her own. Traditionally men have been allowed to move freely between the public and the private without the permeability of these spheres threatening their identities. But when a woman engages in physical and cultural mobility, she becomes an informant, someone who ceases to be the pristine native, the angel in the house, without, however, quite becoming a traveler, a "man" of the world. Either way, if she stays at home or goes out into the world, she is an exile, banished culturally if not geographically. And just as homelessness makes a woman an uncanny figure, so narrative, the work of the mind and not of the womb, exiles her from traditional female identifications. Thus, woman is like the Venetian who is most Venetian in silence. Woolson, however, wanted to legitimize women's use of narrative without quite relinquishing home and the feminine. As informant, she sought to create a na(rra)tive that moves frequently (if not freely) across boundaries and borders, even if she could not fully free herself from the ideology she critiqued.

Woolson addresses the issue of the exiled woman writer in **"At the Château of Corinne"** from ***Dorothy and Other Italian Stories***. In this story, Katharine Winthrop, an American widow living on Lake Leman (Lake Geneva) in Switzerland, visits Coppet, the house in which lived the exiled Madame de Staël, who wrote *Corinne, or Italy* (1807). Visiting Coppet with her is another American, John Ford, who has some very definite ideas about women and narrative. When Katharine calls Madame de Staël "a woman of genius," John replies:

> "A woman of genius! And what is the very term but a stigma! No woman is so proclaimed by the great brazen tongue of the Public unless she has thrown away her birthright of womanly seclusion for the miserable mess of pottage called 'fame'."

> "The seclusion of a convent? or a prison?"

> "Neither. Of a home." (263)

Katharine is a poet and so has much at stake in this discussion under Madame de Staël's roof. She says to John, "You dislike literary women very much," to which he responds, "I pity them" (264). When Katharine asks John to comment on her book of poetry, he notes that "the distinguishing feature of the volume" is "a certain sort of daring. This is its essential, unpardonable sin." Such a woman who dares in this way is a "poor mistaken sibyl"—literally an uncanny figure (268). The act of narration itself, for John, makes a woman an exile from her proper sphere of domesticity. She becomes a witchlike figure, with all the ostracism and power that such a figure embodies, someone both repugnant and fearsome. The sibyl is a sage, but as a woman she must be seen as lonely and deformed. John's patriarchal gaze can only frame women in dualities: home or exile, womb or mind.[13]

The talk about home in the exile's house resonates on a number of levels. John tells Katharine and the others of their party that "Madame de Staël detested the country; to the last, Coppet remained to her a dreary exile" (262). It was a house but not a home; Madame de Staël was a woman but not feminine. In John's view, narrative itself, which unfeminized Madame de Staël, threatens to do the same to Katharine. As informants, Madame de Staël and Katharine dwell in two worlds, and between two worlds, the private and public worlds. In John's eyes, narrative in the hands of women exchanges a home for a prison-house of language. For Katharine, however, home is a prison, a place with impermeable borders, where a person is one thing and not any other. The château of Coppet makes a stark contrast to another castle, the Castle Nowhere, showing how far Woolson had come in delineating the complexities and contradiction of home and exile, captivity and freedom.

At the turning point in the story when Katharine and John are once again at Coppet, this time professing a love for each other that hinges on Katharine's economic dependence—she has lost her fortune—and her renunciation of narrative. Speaking again of her book of poetry, Katharine asks John: "But you do not forgive the book?" He responds: "I will forget it instead. You will write no more" (285). Katharine concedes, and the story ends with their return to John's home in the United States as man and wife.

The images in the final few paragraphs are dense: "In the library of Mr. John Ford, near New York, there hangs in the place of honor a water-color sketch of an old yellow château. Beneath it, ranged by themselves, are all the works of that eloquent authoress and noble woman, Madame de Staël" (287). The château of exile is contrasted to the American home. The public character of Madame de Staël is contrasted to the private setting of the library. It is clear that although the narrator calls Madame de Staël a "noble woman," we are to understand that as a technical term, referring to her aristocratic origins. From John's perspective, Katharine is the truly noble woman for she has renounced narrative and public life. As Cheryl Torsney points out, it is in this house "that both Katharine, metaphorically, and Mme de Staël, literally, are brought into line."[14] The narratives of Madame de Staël have been contained, her works "ranged by themselves," as Katharine has been contained in this home-turned-prison. In fact, Katharine loses all power of narration, for in this scene she is not heard from at all; she is silenced, and the library, with its knowledge and narrative, is identified with John, who is the legitimate guardian of narrative. The "home" is to be Katharine's, although the "house" is John's; Katharine resumes her traditional place and role, and will be only an observer of Madame de Staël's narrative achievements (if she ever opens those books again), not a participant in narrative herself. Katharine's repatriation has re-placed an exile of words with a homecoming of silence.

Even though her heroine returns to a traditional and confining home, one of Woolson's goals was to recon-struct home and narrative as compatible for the woman writer. In the letter to Henry James where Woolson says that his writings are "my true country, my real home," she explicitly conflates home and narrative. However, this narrative home is James's writing, not her own. Again, the man is the guardian of narrative: the "home" is Woolson's, but the narrative "house" is James's. Although Katharine is not Woolson, Katharine is a warning of the allure that home has for women, including Woolson, and its potential to silence them. Despite Katharine's repatriation—both physical and patriarchal—and Woolson's gendered displacement in this letter to James, in her own works Woolson asserts the right of claiming narrative for women, making her own words both her home and house.

In another letter to James, this one written in 1882 in Dresden, Woolson noted that she had been thirteen years "without a home," and talked about being an American abroad:

> But I suppose there never was a woman so ill fitted to do without a home as I am. . . . Like a poor old bird shut up in a cage, who tries to make a nest out of two wisps of straw. Or the beaver I saw in the Zoological Gardens here, who had constructed a most pathetic little dam out of a few poor fragments of old boughs. I stood and looked at that beaver a long time. He is an American—as I am?[15]

This passage invokes several of Woolson's frequent themes—homes, boundaries, and the nature of being American. We can see Woolson's anxiety of exile, fearing the loss of national identity and home. She wonders whether she is any longer an American and considers her homes abroad akin to the beaver's "most pathetic little dam." She seems to feel much like John's portrayal of Madame de Staël at Coppet, viewing her own expatriation as "a dreary exile." Rather than the home being a prison, as Katharine initially feared, this letter imagines exile to be a prison, a cage. Her greatest freedom seemed at times to be her greatest confinement, indicating her own ambivalence about her position as a woman exile. She feels an anxiety of depatriation, not in a gendered sense, but in a nationalistic one, wondering aloud if she is still an American.

Indeed, when she wrote James, "But I suppose there never was a woman so ill fitted to do without a home as I am," she indicated that women are especially in need of homes. She had written to him earlier that year about the death of a parent: "A daughter feels it more than a son, of course, because her life is so limited, bounded by home-love. . . . "[16] The Victorian image of the home-bound woman is evident here. Yet Woolson is able to both imagine and resist that image by expanding the private sphere of the home in both her writing and her life by moving home from place to place, thus lessening its confinement and pushing back its boundaries. It is no coincidence that the death of her father opened the way to her move from Cleveland to Florida and that the death of her mother allowed her the chance to live in Europe. The death of her parents, while making her emotional reactions painful because of "home-love," made her less bound, less limited by home. Moreover, Woolson did not exchange her parent's home for a husband's home, remaining single all her life. By dwelling-in-traveling, Woolson was able to create greater freedom for herself than she would have had in a more conventional Victorian life as a woman. In the childhood letter Woolson wrote to her friend Flora, who was about to be married, she did not see Flora's marriage as an impediment to the exile Woolson so longed for; as an adult who at last came to experience that exile, she realized that marriage and home were not compatible with the freedom that exile represented for her. No doubt she feared becoming like Katharine, a woman writer silenced by home-love. Yet she regretted not having a home. While the price Katharine paid for a home was too high for Woolson, its appeal never seemed to fade. In her life, she felt the elegiac loss of place depicted in regional fiction, even as she was forging a more modern sense of transition and mobility.

Woolson used images of boundaries to explore her ambivalence about home. As the narrator of **"In the Cotton Country"** comes upon Judith Kinsolving's house, the former comments that there is no fence around the house: "Take away the fence from a house, and you take away its respectability; it becomes at once an outlaw" (136). In **"The Front Yard,"** Prudence Wilkin, a New Hampshire woman transplanted to Assisi, Italy, when she marries an Italian, Antonio Guadagni, is quickly widowed and spends the next sixteen years taking care of his large and largely ungrateful family. Despite her poverty and exhaustion, what she wants most in the world is a proper front yard. She scrimps and saves so that she can remove the pig shed in front of her house and replace it with

> a nice straight path going down to the front gate, set in a new paling fence; along the sides currant bushes; and in the open spaces to the right and left a big flowerin' shrub—snowballs, or Missouri currant; near the house a clump of matrimony, perhaps; and in the flower beds on each side of the path bachelor's-buttons, Chiny-asters, lady's slippers, and pinks; the edges bordered with box. (16)

In the two stories, fences define both a sense of home as a place within and a sense of the alien without. In keeping with the traditional and gendered separation of the private and public spheres, these fences seek to maintain a purity of place. In **"In the Cotton Country,"** this endeavor is unsuccessful; the fence has been

destroyed, the South defeated, and the Northerners have come. In **"The Front Yard,"** Prudence finally gets her front yard, which, thanks to three American women, is successful in creating a pure place for her. Not only does she physically re-create a corner of New England in her Italian home, but she maintains her cultural identity as well. She considers the Italian language to be "simply lunatic English, English spoiled" (8). Of her stepson, whom she calls "Jo Vanny" rather than Giovanni, she says: "'He's sort of American, anyhow.' It was the highest praise she could give" (18). Despite her sixteen years in Italy, Prudence is resolutely American, a cultural purity maintained, like her Missouri currants within the yard fence. In this way, Prudence is also like the beaver in the Dresden zoo, fenced in, building a "home" in that boundary that is reminiscent of its indigenous place, but surrounded by foreign environs.

And yet, Prudence is not meant to be a paragon of cultural virtue. Her distaste for everything Italian and refusal to assimilate in any manner, paralleled by the Italians' dislike of her American qualities and habits, shows two cultures in a stand-off. Home is both sanctuary and prison, both a remembrance of things past and, like the beaver's in the Dresden zoo, "a most pathetic little dam" constructed from "a few poor fragments of old boughs." Whereas Torsney argues that Prudence's sacrifice "is not that of self to a generalized and all-consuming love of family,"[17] attempting to show that Prudence is not a traditional domestic woman-as-martyr, it strikes me that her sacrifice is indeed that of self-renunciation, but, as with Prudence's xenophobia, it is not a trait Woolson wants emulated. Woolson is criticizing Prudence's attempt at repatriation in exile, with its fierce, immobile regionalism and its acceptance of patriarchal values (indicated by her caring for her husband's family and the "matrimony" flowers she plants in her front yard).

In **"A Pink Villa,"** also from *The Front Yard and Other Italian Stories,* young Eva Churchill, who was born in the United States but has lived in Italy for fifteen of her nearly eighteen years, falls in love with David Rod, an American from Florida. Although she has lived most of her life in Italy, she has been protected by her mother "like a hot-house flower" (124). The pink villa, Italian in design but housing Americans and keeping American culture intact abroad, is the hothouse. As with Prudence's front yard or the beaver at the Dresden zoo, we have another image of a boundary keeping its inhabitants from contact with the outside and creating an artificial atmosphere for them within.

With Eva's marriage to David, it seems that Woolson will break down boundaries, will free her heroine from the house that keeps her from the outside world and from herself. Indeed, David, derided for being a "backwoodsman" (117) without refinement and called "Signor Ra" (125) after the Egyptian god of the sun, seems to be the catalyst for Eva's journey to the naturalness of the Florida wilderness. Eva, the hothouse flower, is being recalled to the unmediated sun. Thus, her going with David, while still within the context of marriage and its restraints, offers the hope of greater freedom with a broader horizon. And yet, any notion of "nativeness" or even "nature" is immediately called into question. Eva may be returning to her "native" country, but Florida is by no means her native land. David may be the outdoors type, but he is cultivating the land, not letting it remain in any kind of natural state. Eva and David will make a home, not find one. Eva appears to be following in the footsteps of Katharine; hers would seem to be an act of repatriation, a returning to the United States after having been married. But here the home becomes as big as the wilderness, appearing to be physically without boundaries, while still maintaining the cultural boundaries that home has come to represent.

"A Transplanted Boy" from *Dorothy and Other Italian Stories*

"A Transplanted Boy" from *Dorothy and Other Italian Stories* is perhaps Woolson's most explicit and most complex examination of home, exile, and depatriation. In that story, an American mother, Violet Roscoe, and her son, Maso, live in Pisa. Her actual name is Violet Coe (Mrs. Thomas Ross Coe) but people changed it in conversation to "Roscoe," and Maso's name has been Italianized from Thomas. On their own, with little money since her husband's death six months after Maso's birth, Violet and Maso live in Pisa and "had often followed a nomadic life for a while when funds were low . . ." (87). A devoted mother, Violet is also fiercely independent, and rather than return to New Hampshire where her husband's family lives and from which her meager finances come, she prefers to do as she pleases. She forsakes the New England sense of duty that Prudence Guadagni feels and lives her life on her own terms. Her exile is not dreary: "I have a better time abroad than I do at home . . ." (74). Their lives have been one of dwelling-in-traveling, making a home not so much in a place as among themselves in a private but distinctly undomestic sphere (both in terms of household and nationality). Like Eva Churchill, Violet makes a home rather than finds one. Unlike Eva, and much like Woolson herself, she does so on her own.

But Violet becomes ill, and for her health she must go north, leaving Maso with a tutor. When the tutor abruptly leaves, Maso does not send his mother the tutor's letter about his departure. Rather than disrupt his mother's recuperation, Maso tries to live on his own until he becomes increasingly destitute and ill. At last, Violet returns and finds Maso. The story ends with their return to New Hampshire, home of her brother-in-law, Reuben Coe:

A month later Mr. Reuben J. Coe, of Coesville, New Hampshire, said to his brother David: "That foolish wife of Tom's is coming home at last. In spite of every effort on my part, she has made ducks and drakes of almost all her money."

"Is that why she is coming back?"
"No; thinks it will be better for the boy. But I'm afraid it's too late for that." (121)

Reuben Coe finds Violet to be a "foolish wife" who has denied both her nation and her womanly responsibilities, but it seems that he is uneasy that the boy has lived abroad in an untraditional domestic arrangement. Concern for Maso's health may inform Coe's comment, but it seems that Coe and Woolson are also concerned with issues of identity.

Indeed, when the destitute boy turned to the U.S. consul in Leghorn for help, Woolson brings these issues of identity to the fore. The consul, a Michigan man named Maclean, does not immediately recognize Maso as an American: "And of what nation are you?" he asks (102). Moreover, because Maso has had no formal education, he does not even recognize that the day of his encounter with the consul, the Fourth of July, is a celebration of American independence and national identity. Learning of Maso's nomadic history, the consul says: "I see— one of the expatriated class" (105). Perhaps this is why it may be "too late" for Maso, not that he was so desperately ill but that he has become too thoroughly Italianized. It is just this ambiguity on which the meaning of the story hinges. Entitled **"A Transplanted Boy,"** it very obviously suggests that Maso is an American "transplanted" in Italy. That is certainly Reuben Coe's understanding. However, the title could also suggest that Maso is transplanted when he returns to the United States. He is a hybrid, a new creation, who is as American as he is Italian. Woolson's line about the beaver in the Dresden zoo—"He is an American—as I am?"—is as applicable to Maso as to herself, for while he continually thinks of himself as an American, much of his situation points to his being polylocalized in a way that defies neat categorization.

In an article disparaging Woolson, Robert White raises two important issues relevant to Woolson's Italian stories. First, White asserts that Woolson "was never an expatriate, in the twentieth-century sense of the term, but she seems to have enjoyed keenly her succession of *outre-mer* years." White does not go on to explain why Woolson is not an expatriate in the Modernist sense, but Benstock clarifies this point. According to Benstock, "Female Modernists were expatriated (if this term is even applicable) differently than their male counterparts," and she places this difference at the site of gender. She goes on to assert that even "[t]he definitions of *exile* and *expatriate* were different for men and women. . . . "[18] White is correct that Woolson was not an expatriate in the *male* twentieth-century sense of the term; she was much closer to the *female* one. As the traveling in her life increased, the obligations to home decreased, and her depiction of these locales reflected a new relationship between dweller and place. It is precisely the "succession" that White notes that made Woolson's expatriation an extension of her regional writing set in the United States, the kind of metonymy and fluidity that Irigaray saw as characteristic of women's ways of knowing and narrating.

In her expatriation, Woolson explored the idea of repatriation as a gendered event. In **"At the Château of Corinne,"** Katharine is returned to the United States as John's wife. No longer an expatriate, she is also no longer a writer, and Katharine returns to her homeland replacing exile with home, narrative with silence. Eva of **"A Pink Villa"** likewise returns to the United States as a wife, and although their home seems to be an expression of a belonging that is constructed by the two of them rather than received from society and imposed on the woman, we are left with doubt as to whether Eva will find as much freedom as her physically boundless home would seem to promise. Finding her fullest self-expression in exile and a succession of homes, Violet of **"A Transplanted Boy"** remakes the idea of home into a family without a husband, a home without permanence. Unlike Woolson, Violet expresses no regrets for having chosen an unconventional lifestyle, even if her return for Maso's sake may arise from such a regret. Violet's forced return to the United States and a brother-in-law (the law of the husband) makes her defeat as devastating as Katharine's, with the significant exception that Violet is aware of her confinement, of being homeward bound.

Woolson was concerned with the idea of self-consciousness as an aspect of the expatriate experience. In her notebooks Woolson had written an idea for a story: "An American who has lived so long abroad that he is almost de-nationalized, and *conscious of it fully;* which makes him an original figure."[19] In a sense this expatriate would become a depatriate, decentering national identity and bringing to its logical conclusion in the form of dwelling-in-traveling abroad the traveling regionalism begun in the United States. Woolson compounds this depatriation, moreover, with gender as she attempts in her writings and in her life to free herself of the patriarchal country of letters and culture. Despite her declaration to James that she found her "true country, [her] real home" in his writings, she was aware of the dangers of women finding their homes in men's houses and fictions, of the dangers of

patriation and repatriation, and so she tried to become a depatriate, with mixed results and feelings.

The second point in White's article which has important implications for the study of Woolson's Italian stories derives from his title, "Cultural Ambivalence in Constance Fenimore Woolson's Italian Tales." White argues that, despite her stated love for Italy as a country, Woolson actually had conflicted attitudes about the people and culture. White erroneously reads Woolson's characters as espousing Woolson's own views. Moreover, White misplaces the location of this cultural ambivalence, characterizing it as xenophobia. Rather, Woolson's cultural ambivalence lies in her position as a woman within American culture in the last half of the nineteenth century, caught between the Cult of the True Woman and the New Woman. Her portrayals of home and exile, marriage and independence, reflect this ambivalence. In addition, she delineated in her fiction the ambivalence of culture itself, how it is not unitary or fragmented but, like Irigaray's representation of women's psychology and discourse, plural. Even representing certain historical/social periods as being defined by ideas called the "Cult of the True Woman" and the "New Woman" is a falsely homogenizing schematic that Woolson would have recognized as erasing the multiplicity of voices that formed those periods; for her, regionalism embodied pluralities that defied easy categorization.

While dwelling-in-traveling proved beneficial for Woolson's writing, it was a strain on her life. She wrote, "I should like to turn into a peak when I die, to be a beautiful purple mountain, which would please the tired, sad eyes of thousands of human beings for ages." Her image of death is one of place, not movement. James recognized this desire for home, for placement, and when she died he wrote to John Hay in 1894: "The only image I can evoke that interposes at all is that of the blest Roman cemetery that she positively *desired*—I mean in her extreme love of it—and of her intensely consenting and more than reconciled rest under the Roman sky. *Requiescat.*"[20] The quiescence that Woolson so wished to put off as a girl writing to her friend Flora had come at last. Whether it was forced or embraced may never be known, and the ambiguity of her end is a fitting emblem of the conflicting forces of home and exile that characterized her life.

Notes

[1] Clare Benedict, ed., *Constance Fenimore Woolson* (London: Ellis, [1932]), 16-17.

[2] Constance Fenimore Woolson, *Dorothy and Other Italian Stories* (New York: Harper and Brothers, 1896); *The Front Yard and Other Italian Stories* (New York: Harper and Brothers, 1895); *Rodman the Keeper: Southern Sketches* (1880; reprint, New

York: Garrett Press, 1969). Subsequent citations will appear parenthetically in the text. Frantz Fanon, *Black Skin, White Masks,* trans. Charles Lam Markmann (New York: Grove Press, 1967), 229.

[3] Jane Marcus, "Alibis and Legends: The Ethics of Elsewhereness, Gender, and Estrangement," in *Women's Writing in Exile,* ed. Mary Lynn Broe and Angela Ingram (Chapel Hill: University of North Carolina Press, 1989), 272-73.

[4] Shari Benstock, "Expatriate Modernism: Writing on the Cultural Rim," in *Women's Writing in Exile,* ed. Mary Lynn Broe and Angela Ingram (Chapel Hill: University of North Carolina Press, 1989), 20, 26.

[5] Cheryl B. Torsney, *Constance Fenimore Woolson: The Grief of Artistry* (Athens: University of Georgia Press, 1989), 7, 8, 33.

[6] Jay B. Hubbell, "Some New Letters of Constance Fenimore Woolson," *New England Quarterly* 14 (1941): 731; Jane Marcus discusses alibi in the context of exile in a very different way than I do here, but it is worth noting that she wants to keep the deceitful and criminal connotations of alibi in literary criticism as a reminder of when scholars usurp the voice of others disingenuously and act in bad faith, both outside and inside feminist scholarship.

[7] Constance Fenimore Woolson, "In the Cotton Country," in *Women Artists, Women Exiles: "Miss Grief" and Other Stories,* ed. Joan Myers Weimer (New Brunswick: Rutgers University Press, 1988), 147. Subsequent citations will appear parenthetically in the text.

[8] Fred Lewis Pattee, "Constance Fenimore Woolson and the South," *South Atlantic Quarterly* 38 (1939): 131; Leon Edel, ed., *Henry James: Letters,* vol. 3, 1883-1895 (Cambridge: Harvard University Press, Belknap Press, 1980), 551.

[9] Joan Myers Weimer, ed., *Women Artists, Women Exiles: "Miss Grief" and Other Stories* (New Brunswick: Rutgers University Press, 1988), xxviii; Constance Fenimore Woolson, "Castle Nowhere," in *Women Artists,* ed. Weimer, 25. Subsequent citations will appear parenthetically in the text.

[10] Edel, *James,* 527; Weimer, *Women Artists,* xxiii.

[11] Luce Irigaray, *This Sex Which Is Not One,* trans. Catherine Porter (Ithaca: Cornell University Press, 1985), 110, 112; Benstock, "Expatriate Modernism," 23.

[12] James Clifford, "Traveling Cultures," in *Cultural Studies,* ed. Lawrence Grossberg, Cary Nelson, and Paula A. Treichler (New York: Routledge, 1992), 108, 97.

[13] Elizabeth Barrett Browning's *Aurora Leigh* (1857) has a scene between Romney and Aurora in book 2 that is very similar to the scene between John and Katharine in terms of women's relationship to art in general, and the woman artist as witch in particular. For a discussion of "At the Château of Corinne" and *Aurora Leigh,* see Torsney, *Constance Fenimore Woolson,* 97, 104, 106-7. For a discussion of *Aurora Leigh,* especially the scene between Romney and Aurora, in the context of Italy, *Corinne,* and gender, see Sandra M. Gilbert, "From *Patria* to *Matria:* Elizabeth Barrett Browning's Risorgimento," *PMLA* 99 (1984): 196-98, 201-2.

[14] Torsney, *Constance Fenimore Woolson,* 95.

[15] Edel, *James,* 539, 540.

[16] Ibid., 536.

[17] Torsney, *Constance Fenimore Woolson,* 149.

[18] Robert L. White, "Cultural Ambivalence in Constance Fenimore Woolson's Italian Tales," reprint in *Critical Essays on Constance Fenimore Woolson,* ed. Cheryl Torsney (New York: G. K. Hall, 1992), 133; Benstock, "Expatriate Modernism," 23.

[19] Benedict, *Woolson,* 138. Emphasis is in the original text.

[20] Ibid., xvi; Edel, *James,* 460.

FURTHER READING

Biography

Alden, Henry Mills. "Constance Fenimore Woolson." *Harper's Weekly* XXXVIII, No. 1937 (February 3, 1894): 113-14.
> An obituary that traces the late stages of Woolson's literary career.

Criticism

Dean, Sharon. "Constance Fenimore Woolson and Henry James: The Literary Relationship." *Massachusetts Studies in English* VII, No. 3 (1998): 1-9.
> Details the mutual influence of Woolson and Henry James.

Gingras, Robert. "'Hepzibah's Story': An Unpublished Work by Constance Fenimore Woolson." *Resources for American Literary Study* X, No. 1 (Spring 1980): 33-46.

Introduces an early short story by Woolson which is set in the Great Lakes region.

Hubbell, Jay B., ed. "Some New Letters of Constance Fenimore Woolson." *The New England Quarterly* XIV, No. 4 (December 1941): 715-35.
Woolson's correspondence with Southern poet Paul Hamilton Hayne between 1875 and 1880.

Kern, John Dwight. *Constance Fenimore Woolson: Literary Pioneer,* Ph.D. dissertation, University of Birmingham, 1934, 198 p.
Examines Woolson's use of Great Lakes settings in two novels and numerous short stories.

Kitterman, Mary P. Edwards. "Henry James and the Artist-Heroine in the Tales of Constance Fenimore Woolson." In *Nineteenth-Century Woman Writers of the English-Speaking World,* edited by Rhoda B. Nathan, pp. 45-59. New York: Greenwood Press, 1986.

Studies Woolson's relationship with Henry James and its impact on her literary and emotional life.

Rowe, Anne. "Constance Woolson and Southern Local Color." In *The Enchanted Country: Northern Writers in the South: 1865-1910,* pp. 54-73. Baton Rouge: Louisiana State University Press, 1978.
Describes Woolson's sensitive depiction of the South during Reconstruction.

Torsney, Cheryl B. Introduction to "Miss Grief." *Legacy* 4, No. 1 (Spring 1987): 11-25.
Argues that this short story can be read as a study in class conflict as well as one in literary influence.

Weir, Sybil B. "Southern Womanhood in the Novels of Constance Fenimore Woolson." *The Mississippi Quarterly* XXIX, No. 4 (Fall 1976): 559-68.
Contests the notion that Woolson was uncritically sympathetic toward Southern culture.

Nineteenth-Century Literature Criticism

Cumulative Indexes
Volumes 1-82

How to Use This Index

Alberti, Rafael 1902-   **CLC 7**
   See also CA 85-88; CANR 81; DLB 108; HW
   2
Albert the Great 1200(?)-1280   **CMLC 16**
   See also DLB 115
Alcala-Galiano, Juan Valera y
   See Valera y Alcala-Galiano, Juan
Alcott, Amos Bronson 1799-1888   **NCLC 1**
   See also DLB 1
Alcott, Louisa May 1832-1888   **NCLC 6, 58;**
   **DA; DAB; DAC; DAM MST, NOV; SSC
   27; WLC**
   See also AAYA 20; CDALB 1865-1917; CLR
   1, 38; DA3; DLB 1, 42, 79; DLBD 14; JRDA;
   MAICYA; SATA 100; YABC 1
Aldanov, M. A.
   See Aldanov, Mark (Alexandrovich)
Aldanov, Mark (Alexandrovich) 1886(?)-1957
   TCLC 23
   See also CA 118; 181
Aldington, Richard 1892-1962   **CLC 49**
   See also CA 85-88; CANR 45; DLB 20, 36, 100,
   149
Aldiss, Brian W(ilson) 1925-   **CLC 5, 14, 40;**
   DAM NOV; SSC 36
   See also CA 5-8R; CAAS 2; CANR 5, 28, 64;
   DLB 14; MTCW 1, 2; SATA 34
Alegria, Claribel 1924-**CLC 75; DAM MULT;**
   HLCS 1; PC 26
   See also CA 131; CAAS 15; CANR 66; DLB
   145; HW 1; MTCW 1
Alegria, Fernando 1918-   **CLC 57**
   See also CA 9-12R; CANR 5, 32, 72; HW 1, 2
Aleichem, Sholom   **TCLC 1, 35; SSC 33**
   See also Rabinovitch, Sholem
Aleixandre, Vicente 1898-1984
   See also CANR 81; HLCS 1; HW 2
Alepoudelis, Odysseus
   See Elytis, Odysseus
Aleshkovsky, Joseph 1929-
   See Aleshkovsky, Yuz
   See also CA 121; 128
Aleshkovsky, Yuz   **CLC 44**
   See also Aleshkovsky, Joseph
Alexander, Lloyd (Chudley) 1924-   **CLC 35**
   See also AAYA 1, 27; CA 1-4R; CANR 1, 24,
   38, 55; CLR 1, 5, 48; DLB 52; JRDA;
   MAICYA; MTCW 1; SAAS 19; SATA 3, 49,
   81
Alexander, Meena 1951-   **CLC 121**
   See also CA 115; CANR 38, 70
Alexander, Samuel 1859-1938   **TCLC 77**
Alexie, Sherman (Joseph, Jr.) 1966- **CLC 96;**
   DAM MULT
   See also AAYA 28; CA 138; CANR 65; DA3;
   DLB 175, 206; MTCW 1; NNAL
Alfau, Felipe 1902-   **CLC 66**
   See also CA 137
Alger, Horatio, Jr. 1832-1899   **NCLC 8**
   See also DLB 42; SATA 16
Algren, Nelson 1909-1981**CLC 4, 10, 33; SSC
   33**
   See also CA 13-16R; 103; CANR 20, 61;
   CDALB 1941-1968; DLB 9; DLBY 81, 82;
   MTCW 1, 2
Ali, Ahmed 1910-   **CLC 69**
   See also CA 25-28R; CANR 15, 34
Alighieri, Dante
   See Dante
Allan, John B.
   See Westlake, Donald E(dwin)
Allan, Sidney
   See Hartmann, Sadakichi

Allan, Sydney
   See Hartmann, Sadakichi
Allen, Edward 1948-   **CLC 59**
Allen, Fred 1894-1956   **TCLC 87**
Allen, Paula Gunn 1939-   **CLC 84; DAM
   MULT**
   See also CA 112; 143; CANR 63; DA3; DLB
   175; MTCW 1; NNAL
Allen, Roland
   See Ayckbourn, Alan
Allen, Sarah A.
   See Hopkins, Pauline Elizabeth
Allen, Sidney H.
   See Hartmann, Sadakichi
Allen, Woody 1935- **CLC 16, 52; DAM POP**
   See also AAYA 10; CA 33-36R; CANR 27, 38,
   63; DLB 44; MTCW 1
Allende, Isabel 1942- **CLC 39, 57, 97; DAM
   MULT, NOV; HLC 1; WLCS**
   See also AAYA 18; CA 125; 130; CANR 51,
   74; DA3; DLB 145; HW 1, 2; INT 130;
   MTCW 1, 2
Alleyn, Ellen
   See Rossetti, Christina (Georgina)
Allingham, Margery (Louise) 1904-1966**CLC
   19**
   See also CA 5-8R; 25-28R; CANR 4, 58; DLB
   77; MTCW 1, 2
Allingham, William 1824-1889   **NCLC 25**
   See also DLB 35
Allison, Dorothy E. 1949-   **CLC 78**
   See also CA 140; CANR 66; DA3; MTCW 1
Allston, Washington 1779-1843   **NCLC 2**
   See also DLB 1
Almedingen, E. M.   **CLC 12**
   See also Almedingen, Martha Edith von
   See also SATA 3
Almedingen, Martha Edith von 1898-1971
   See Almedingen, E. M.
   See also CA 1-4R; CANR 1
Almodovar, Pedro 1949(?)-**CLC 114; HLCS 1**
   See also CA 133; CANR 72; HW 2
Almqvist, Carl Jonas Love 1793-1866**NCLC 42**
Alonso, Damaso 1898-1990   **CLC 14**
   See also CA 110; 131; 130; CANR 72; DLB
   108; HW 1, 2
Alov
   See Gogol, Nikolai (Vasilyevich)
Alta 1942-   **CLC 19**
   See also CA 57-60
Alter, Robert B(ernard) 1935-   **CLC 34**
   See also CA 49-52; CANR 1, 47
Alther, Lisa 1944-   **CLC 7, 41**
   See also CA 65-68; CAAS 30; CANR 12, 30,
   51; MTCW 1
Althusser, L.
   See Althusser, Louis
Althusser, Louis 1918-1990   **CLC 106**
   See also CA 131; 132
Altman, Robert 1925-   **CLC 16, 116**
   See also CA 73-76; CANR 43
Alurista 1949-
   See Urista, Alberto H.
   See also DLB 82; HLCS 1
Alvarez, A(lfred) 1929-   **CLC 5, 13**
   See also CA 1-4R; CANR 3, 33, 63; DLB 14,
   40
Alvarez, Alejandro Rodriguez 1903-1965
   See Casona, Alejandro
   See also CA 131; 93-96; HW 1
Alvarez, Julia 1950-   **CLC 93; HLCS 1**
   See also AAYA 25; CA 147; CANR 69; DA3;
   MTCW 1

Alvaro, Corrado 1896-1956   **TCLC 60**
   See also CA 163
Amado, Jorge 1912- CLC 13, 40, 106; DAM
   MULT, NOV; HLC 1
   See also CA 77-80; CANR 35, 74; DLB 113;
   HW 2; MTCW 1, 2
Ambler, Eric 1909-1998   **CLC 4, 6, 9**
   See also CA 9-12R; 171; CANR 7, 38, 74; DLB
   77; MTCW 1, 2
Amichai, Yehuda 1924-   **CLC 9, 22, 57, 116**
   See also CA 85-88; CANR 46, 60; MTCW 1
Amichai, Yehudah
   See Amichai, Yehuda
Amiel, Henri Frederic 1821-1881   **NCLC 4**
Amis, Kingsley (William) 1922-1995**CLC 1, 2,
   3, 5, 8, 13, 40, 44; DA; DAB; DAC; DAM
   MST, NOV**
   See also AITN 2; CA 9-12R; 150; CANR 8, 28,
   54; CDBLB 1945-1960; DA3; DLB 15, 27,
   100, 139; DLBY 96; INT CANR-8; MTCW
   1, 2
Amis, Martin (Louis) 1949-**CLC 4, 9, 38, 62,
   101**
   See also BEST 90:3; CA 65-68; CANR 8, 27,
   54, 73; DA3; DLB 14, 194; INT CANR-27;
   MTCW 1
Ammons, A(rchie) R(andolph) 1926-**CLC 2, 3,
   5, 8, 9, 25, 57, 108; DAM POET; PC 16**
   See also AITN 1; CA 9-12R; CANR 6, 36, 51,
   73; DLB 5, 165; MTCW 1, 2
Amo, Tauraatua i
   See Adams, Henry (Brooks)
Amory, Thomas 1691(?)-1788   **LC 48**
Anand, Mulk Raj 1905-   **CLC 23, 93; DAM
   NOV**
   See also CA 65-68; CANR 32, 64; MTCW 1, 2
Anatol
   See Schnitzler, Arthur
Anaximander c. 610B.C.-c. 546B.C.**CMLC 22**
Anaya, Rudolfo A(lfonso) 1937-   **CLC 23;
   DAM MULT, NOV; HLC 1**
   See also AAYA 20; CA 45-48; CAAS 4; CANR
   1, 32, 51; DLB 82, 206; HW 1; MTCW 1, 2
Andersen, Hans Christian 1805-1875**NCLC 7,
   79; DA; DAB; DAC; DAM MST, POP;
   SSC 6; WLC**
   See also CLR 6; DA3; MAICYA; SATA 100;
   YABC 1
Anderson, C. Farley
   See Mencken, H(enry) L(ouis); Nathan, George
   Jean
Anderson, Jessica (Margaret) Queale 1916-
   CLC 37
   See also CA 9-12R; CANR 4, 62
Anderson, Jon (Victor) 1940-   **CLC 9; DAM
   POET**
   See also CA 25-28R; CANR 20
Anderson, Lindsay (Gordon) 1923-1994**CLC
   20**
   See also CA 125; 128; 146; CANR 77
Anderson, Maxwell 1888-1959**TCLC 2; DAM
   DRAM**
   See also CA 105; 152; DLB 7; MTCW 2
Anderson, Poul (William) 1926-   **CLC 15**
   See also AAYA 5; CA 1-4R; 181; CAAE 181;
   CAAS 2; CANR 2, 15, 34, 64; CLR 58; DLB
   8; INT CANR-15; MTCW 1, 2; SATA 90;
   SATA-Brief 39; SATA-Essay 106
Anderson, Robert (Woodruff) 1917-**CLC 23;
   DAM DRAM**
   See also AITN 1; CA 21-24R; CANR 32; DLB 7
Anderson, Sherwood 1876-1941 **TCLC 1, 10,
   24; DA; DAB; DAC; DAM MST, NOV;**

SSC 1; WLC
 See also AAYA 30; CA 104; 121; CANR 61;
   CDALB 1917-1929; DA3; DLB 4, 9, 86;
   DLBD 1; MTCW 1, 2
Andier, Pierre
 See Desnos, Robert
Andouard
 See Giraudoux, (Hippolyte) Jean
Andrade, Carlos Drummond de   **CLC 18**
 See also Drummond de Andrade, Carlos
Andrade, Mario de 1893-1945   **TCLC 43**
Andreae, Johann V(alentin) 1586-1654 **LC 32**
 See also DLB 164
Andreas-Salome, Lou 1861-1937   **TCLC 56**
 See also CA 178; DLB 66
Andress, Lesley
 See Sanders, Lawrence
Andrewes, Lancelot 1555-1626   **LC 5**
 See also DLB 151, 172
Andrews, Cicily Fairfield
 See West, Rebecca
Andrews, Elton V.
 See Pohl, Frederik
Andreyev, Leonid (Nikolaevich) 1871-1919
   TCLC 3
 See also CA 104
Andric, Ivo 1892-1975   **CLC 8; SSC 36**
 See also CA 81-84; 57-60; CANR 43, 60; DLB
   147; MTCW 1
Androvar
 See Prado (Calvo), Pedro
Angelique, Pierre
 See Bataille, Georges
Angell, Roger 1920-   **CLC 26**
 See also CA 57-60; CANR 13, 44, 70; DLB 171,
   185
Angelou, Maya 1928-**CLC 12, 35, 64, 77; BLC
   1; DA; DAB; DAC; DAM MST, MULT,
   POET, POP; WLCS**
 See also AAYA 7, 20; BW 2, 3; CA 65-68;
   CANR 19, 42, 65; CDALBS; CLR 53; DA3;
   DLB 38; MTCW 1, 2; SATA 49
Anna Comnena 1083-1153   **CMLC 25**
Annensky, Innokenty (Fyodorovich) 1856-1909
   TCLC 14
 See also CA 110; 155
Annunzio, Gabriele d'
 See D'Annunzio, Gabriele
Anodos
 See Coleridge, Mary E(lizabeth)
Anon, Charles Robert
 See Pessoa, Fernando (Antonio Nogueira)
Anouilh, Jean (Marie Lucien Pierre) 1910-1987
   CLC 1, 3, 8, 13, 40, 50; DAM DRAM; DC 8
 See also CA 17-20R; 123; CANR 32; MTCW
   1, 2
Anthony, Florence
 See Ai
Anthony, John
 See Ciardi, John (Anthony)
Anthony, Peter
 See Shaffer, Anthony (Joshua); Shaffer, Peter
   (Levin)
Anthony, Piers 1934-   **CLC 35; DAM POP**
 See also AAYA 11; CA 21-24R; CANR 28, 56,
   73; DLB 8; MTCW 1, 2; SAAS 22; SATA 84
Anthony, Susan B(rownell) 1916-1991**TCLC 84**
 See also CA 89-92; 134
Antoine, Marc
 See Proust, (Valentin-Louis-George-Eugene-)
   Marcel
Antoninus, Brother
 See Everson, William (Oliver)

Antonioni, Michelangelo 1912-   **CLC 20**
 See also CA 73-76; CANR 45, 77
Antschel, Paul 1920-1970
 See Celan, Paul
 See also CA 85-88; CANR 33, 61; MTCW 1
Anwar, Chairil 1922-1949   **TCLC 22**
 See also CA 121
Anzaldua, Gloria 1942-
 See also CA 175; DLB 122; HLCS 1
Apess, William 1798-1839(?)**NCLC 73; DAM
   MULT**
 See also DLB 175; NNAL
Apollinaire, Guillaume 1880-1918**TCLC 3, 8,
   51; DAM POET; PC 7**
 See also Kostrowitzki, Wilhelm Apollinaris de
 See also CA 152; MTCW 1
Appelfeld, Aharon 1932-   **CLC 23, 47**
 See also CA 112; 133; CANR 86
Apple, Max (Isaac) 1941-   **CLC 9, 33**
 See also CA 81-84; CANR 19, 54; DLB 130
Appleman, Philip (Dean) 1926-   **CLC 51**
 See also CA 13-16R; CAAS 18; CANR 6, 29,
   56
Appleton, Lawrence
 See Lovecraft, H(oward) P(hillips)
Apteryx
 See Eliot, T(homas) S(tearns)
Apuleius, (Lucius Madaurensis) 125(?)-175(?)
   CMLC 1
 See also DLB 211
Aquin, Hubert 1929-1977   **CLC 15**
 See also CA 105; DLB 53
Aquinas, Thomas 1224(?)-1274   **CMLC 33**
 See also DLB 115
Aragon, Louis 1897-1982   **CLC 3, 22; DAM
   NOV, POET**
 See also CA 69-72; 108; CANR 28, 71; DLB
   72; MTCW 1, 2
Arany, Janos 1817-1882   **NCLC 34**
Aranyos, Kakay
 See Mikszath, Kalman
Arbuthnot, John 1667-1735   **LC 1**
 See also DLB 101
Archer, Herbert Winslow
 See Mencken, H(enry) L(ouis)
Archer, Jeffrey (Howard) 1940-   **CLC 28;
   DAM POP**
 See also AAYA 16; BEST 89:3; CA 77-80;
   CANR 22, 52; DA3; INT CANR-22
Archer, Jules 1915-   **CLC 12**
 See also CA 9-12R; CANR 6, 69; SAAS 5;
   SATA 4, 85
Archer, Lee
 See Ellison, Harlan (Jay)
Arden, John 1930-**CLC 6, 13, 15; DAM DRAM**
 See also CA 13-16R; CAAS 4; CANR 31, 65,
   67; DLB 13; MTCW 1
Arenas, Reinaldo 1943-1990 **CLC 41; DAM
   MULT; HLC 1**
 See also CA 124; 128; 133; CANR 73; DLB
   145; HW 1; MTCW 1
Arendt, Hannah 1906-1975   **CLC 66, 98**
 See also CA 17-20R; 61-64; CANR 26, 60;
   MTCW 1, 2
Aretino, Pietro 1492-1556   **LC 12**
Arghezi, Tudor 1880-1967   **CLC 80**
 See also Theodorescu, Ion N.
 See also CA 167
Arguedas, Jose Maria 1911-1969**CLC 10, 18;
   HLCS 1**
 See also CA 89-92; CANR 73; DLB 113; HW 1
Argueta, Manlio 1936-   **CLC 31**
 See also CA 131; CANR 73; DLB 145; HW 1

Arias, Ron(ald Francis) 1941-
 See also CA 131; CANR 81; DAM MULT; DLB
   82; HLC 1; HW 1, 2; MTCW 2
Ariosto, Ludovico 1474-1533   **LC 6**
Aristides
 See Epstein, Joseph
Aristophanes 450B.C.-385B.C.**CMLC 4; DA;
   DAB; DAC; DAM DRAM, MST; DC 2;
   WLCS**
 See also DA3; DLB 176
Aristotle 384B.C.-322B.C.   **CMLC 31; DA;
   DAB; DAC; DAM MST; WLCS**
 See also DA3; DLB 176
Arlt, Roberto (Godofredo Christophersen)
   1900-1942**TCLC 29; DAM MULT; HLC 1**
 See also CA 123; 131; CANR 67; HW 1, 2
Armah, Ayi Kwei 1939-   **CLC 5, 33; BLC 1;
   DAM MULT, POET**
 See also BW 1; CA 61-64; CANR 21, 64; DLB
   117; MTCW 1
Armatrading, Joan 1950-   **CLC 17**
 See also CA 114
Arnette, Robert
 See Silverberg, Robert
**Arnim, Achim von (Ludwig Joachim von
   Arnim)** 1781-1831   **NCLC 5; SSC 29**
 See also DLB 90
Arnim, Bettina von 1785-1859   **NCLC 38**
 See also DLB 90
Arnold, Matthew 1822-1888**NCLC 6, 29; DA;
   DAB; DAC; DAM MST, POET; PC 5;
   WLC**
 See also CDBLB 1832-1890; DLB 32, 57
Arnold, Thomas 1795-1842   **NCLC 18**
 See also DLB 55
Arnow, Harriette (Louisa) Simpson 1908-1986
   CLC 2, 7, 18
 See also CA 9-12R; 118; CANR 14; DLB 6;
   MTCW 1, 2; SATA 42; SATA-Obit 47
Arouet, Francois-Marie
 See Voltaire
Arp, Hans
 See Arp, Jean
Arp, Jean 1887-1966   **CLC 5**
 See also CA 81-84; 25-28R; CANR 42, 77
Arrabal
 See Arrabal, Fernando
Arrabal, Fernando 1932-   **CLC 2, 9, 18, 58**
 See also CA 9-12R; CANR 15
Arreola, Juan Jose 1918-
 See also CA 113; 131; CANR 81; DAM MULT;
   DLB 113; HLC 1; HW 1, 2
Arrick, Fran   **CLC 30**
 See also Gaberman, Judie Angell
Artaud, Antonin (Marie Joseph) 1896-1948
   TCLC 3, 36; DAM DRAM
 See also CA 104; 149; DA3; MTCW 1
Arthur, Ruth M(abel) 1905-1979   **CLC 12**
 See also CA 9-12R; 85-88; CANR 4; SATA 7,
   26
Artsybashev, Mikhail (Petrovich) 1878-1927
   TCLC 31
 See also CA 170
Arundel, Honor (Morfydd) 1919-1973**CLC 17**
 See also CA 21-22; 41-44R; CAP 2; CLR 35;
   SATA 4; SATA-Obit 24
Arzner, Dorothy 1897-1979   **CLC 98**
Asch, Sholem 1880-1957   **TCLC 3**
 See also CA 105
Ash, Shalom
 See Asch, Sholem
Ashbery, John (Lawrence) 1927-**CLC 2, 3, 4,
   6, 9, 13, 15, 25, 41, 77, 125; DAM POET;**

DA3; DLB 14, 207; MTCW 1, 2; SATA 93

Balmont, Konstantin (Dmitriyevich) 1867-1943
TCLC 11
See also CA 109; 155

Baltausis, Vincas
See Mikszath, Kalman

Balzac, Honore de 1799-1850**NCLC 5, 35, 53;**
DA; DAB; DAC; DAM MST, NOV; SSC
5; WLC
See also DA3; DLB 119

Bambara, Toni Cade 1939-1995 **CLC 19, 88;**
BLC 1; DA; DAC; DAM MST, MULT;
SSC 35; WLCS
See also AAYA 5; BW 2, 3; CA 29-32R; 150;
CANR 24, 49, 81; CDALBS; DA3; DLB 38;
MTCW 1, 2

Bamdad, A.
See Shamlu, Ahmad

Banat, D. R.
See Bradbury, Ray (Douglas)

Bancroft, Laura
See Baum, L(yman) Frank

Banim, John 1798-1842 **NCLC 13**
See also DLB 116, 158, 159

Banim, Michael 1796-1874 **NCLC 13**
See also DLB 158, 159

Banjo, The
See Paterson, A(ndrew) B(arton)

Banks, Iain
See Banks, Iain M(enzies)

Banks, Iain M(enzies) 1954- **CLC 34**
See also CA 123; 128; CANR 61; DLB 194;
INT 128

Banks, Lynne Reid **CLC 23**
See also Reid Banks, Lynne
See also AAYA 6

Banks, Russell 1940- **CLC 37, 72**
See also CA 65-68; CAAS 15; CANR 19, 52,
73; DLB 130

Banville, John 1945- **CLC 46, 118**
See also CA 117; 128; DLB 14; INT 128

Banville, Theodore (Faullain) de 1832-1891
NCLC 9

Baraka, Amiri 1934 **CLC 1, 2, 3, 5, 10, 14, 33,**
115; BLC 1; DA; DAC; DAM MST, MULT,
POET, POP; DC 6; PC 4; WLCS
See also Jones, LeRoi
See also BW 2, 3; CA 21-24R; CABS 3; CANR
27, 38, 61; CDALB 1941-1968; DA3; DLB
5, 7, 16, 38; DLBD 8; MTCW 1, 2

Barbauld, Anna Laetitia 1743-1825**NCLC 50**
See also DLB 107, 109, 142, 158

Barbellion, W. N. P. **TCLC 24**
See also Cummings, Bruce F(rederick)

Barbera, Jack (Vincent) 1945- **CLC 44**
See also CA 110; CANR 45

Barbey d'Aurevilly, Jules Amedee 1808-1889
NCLC 1; SSC 17
See also DLB 119

Barbour, John c. 1316-1395 **CMLC 33**
See also DLB 146

Barbusse, Henri 1873-1935 **TCLC 5**
See also CA 105; 154; DLB 65

Barclay, Bill
See Moorcock, Michael (John)

Barclay, William Ewert
See Moorcock, Michael (John)

Barea, Arturo 1897-1957 **TCLC 14**
See also CA 111

Barfoot, Joan 1946- **CLC 18**
See also CA 105

Barham, Richard Harris 1788-1845**NCLC 77**
See also DLB 159

Baring, Maurice 1874-1945 **TCLC 8**
See also CA 105; 168; DLB 34

Baring-Gould, Sabine 1834-1924 **TCLC 88**
See also DLB 156, 190

Barker, Clive 1952- **CLC 52; DAM POP**
See also AAYA 10; BEST 90:3; CA 121; 129;
CANR 71; DA3; INT 129; MTCW 1, 2

Barker, George Granville 1913-1991 **CLC 8,**
48; DAM POET
See also CA 9-12R; 135; CANR 7, 38; DLB
20; MTCW 1

Barker, Harley Granville
See Granville-Barker, Harley
See also DLB 10

Barker, Howard 1946- **CLC 37**
See also CA 102; DLB 13

Barker, Jane 1652-1732 **LC 42**

Barker, Pat(ricia) 1943- **CLC 32, 94**
See also CA 117; 122; CANR 50; INT 122

Barlach, Ernst (Heinrich) 1870-1938**TCLC 84**
See also CA 178; DLB 56, 118

Barlow, Joel 1754-1812 **NCLC 23**
See also DLB 37

Barnard, Mary (Ethel) 1909- **CLC 48**
See also CA 21-22; CAP 2

Barnes, Djuna 1892-1982 **CLC 3, 4, 8, 11, 29;**
SSC 3
See also CA 9-12R; 107; CANR 16, 55; DLB
4, 9, 45; MTCW 1, 2

Barnes, Julian (Patrick) 1946- **CLC 42; DAB**
See also CA 102; CANR 19, 54; DLB 194;
DLBY 93; MTCW 1

Barnes, Peter 1931- **CLC 5, 56**
See also CA 65-68; CAAS 12; CANR 33, 34,
64; DLB 13; MTCW 1

Barnes, William 1801-1886 **NCLC 75**
See also DLB 32

Baroja (y Nessi), Pio 1872-1956**TCLC 8; HLC**
1
See also CA 104

Baron, David
See Pinter, Harold

Baron Corvo
See Rolfe, Frederick (William Serafino Austin
Lewis Mary)

Barondess, Sue K(aufman) 1926-1977 **CLC 8**
See also Kaufman, Sue
See also CA 1-4R; 69-72; CANR 1

Baron de Teive
See Pessoa, Fernando (Antonio Nogueira)

Baroness Von S.
See Zangwill, Israel

Barres, (Auguste-) Maurice 1862-1923**TCLC**
47
See also CA 164; DLB 123

Barreto, Afonso Henrique de Lima
See Lima Barreto, Afonso Henrique de

Barrett, (Roger) Syd 1946- **CLC 35**

Barrett, William (Christopher) 1913-1992
CLC 27
See also CA 13-16R; 139; CANR 11, 67; INT
CANR-11

Barrie, J(ames) M(atthew) 1860-1937 **TCLC**
2; DAB; DAM DRAM
See also CA 104; 136; CANR 77; CDBLB 1890-
1914; CLR 16; DA3; DLB 10, 141, 156;
MAICYA; MTCW 1; SATA 100; YABC 1

Barrington, Michael
See Moorcock, Michael (John)

Barrol, Grady
See Bograd, Larry

Barry, Mike
See Malzberg, Barry N(athaniel)

Barry, Philip 1896-1949 **TCLC 11**
See also CA 109; DLB 7

Bart, Andre Schwarz
See Schwarz-Bart, Andre

Barth, John (Simmons) 1930-**CLC 1, 2, 3, 5, 7,**
9, 10, 14, 27, 51, 89; DAM NOV; SSC 10
See also AITN 1, 2; CA 1-4R; CABS 1; CANR
5, 23, 49, 64; DLB 2; MTCW 1

Barthelme, Donald 1931-1989**CLC 1, 2, 3, 5, 6,**
8, 13, 23, 46, 59, 115; DAM NOV; SSC 2
See also CA 21-24R; 129; CANR 20, 58; DA3;
DLB 2; DLBY 80, 89; MTCW 1, 2; SATA 7;
SATA-Obit 62

Barthelme, Frederick 1943- **CLC 36, 117**
See also CA 114; 122; CANR 77; DLBY 85;
INT 122

Barthes, Roland (Gerard) 1915-1980**CLC 24,**
83
See also CA 130; 97-100; CANR 66; MTCW
1, 2

Barzun, Jacques (Martin) 1907- **CLC 51**
See also CA 61-64; CANR 22

Bashevis, Isaac
See Singer, Isaac Bashevis

Bashkirtseff, Marie 1859-1884 **NCLC 27**

Basho
See Matsuo Basho

Basil of Caesaria c. 330-379 **CMLC 35**

Bass, Kingsley B., Jr.
See Bullins, Ed

Bass, Rick 1958- **CLC 79**
See also CA 126; CANR 53; DLB 212

Bassani, Giorgio 1916- **CLC 9**
See also CA 65-68; CANR 33; DLB 128, 177;
MTCW 1

Bastos, Augusto (Antonio) Roa
See Roa Bastos, Augusto (Antonio)

Bataille, Georges 1897-1962 **CLC 29**
See also CA 101; 89-92

Bates, H(erbert) E(rnest) 1905-1974**CLC 46;**
DAB; DAM POP; SSC 10
See also CA 93-96; 45-48; CANR 34; DA3;
DLB 162, 191; MTCW 1, 2

Bauchart
See Camus, Albert

Baudelaire, Charles 1821-1867 **NCLC 6, 29,**
55; DA; DAB; DAC; DAM MST, POET;
PC 1; SSC 18; WLC
See also DA3

Baudrillard, Jean 1929- **CLC 60**

Baum, L(yman) Frank 1856-1919 **TCLC 7**
See also CA 108; 133; CLR 15; DLB 22; JRDA;
MAICYA; MTCW 1, 2; SATA 18, 100

Baum, Louis F.
See Baum, L(yman) Frank

Baumbach, Jonathan 1933- **CLC 6, 23**
See also CA 13-16R; CAAS 5; CANR 12, 66;
DLBY 80; INT CANR-12; MTCW 1

Bausch, Richard (Carl) 1945- **CLC 51**
See also CA 101; CAAS 14; CANR 43, 61; DLB
130

Baxter, Charles (Morley) 1947- **CLC 45, 78;**
DAM POP
See also CA 57-60; CANR 40, 64; DLB 130;
MTCW 2

Baxter, George Owen
See Faust, Frederick (Schiller)

Baxter, James K(eir) 1926-1972 **CLC 14**
See also CA 77-80

Baxter, John
See Hunt, E(verette) Howard, (Jr.)

Bayer, Sylvia
See Glassco, John

Baynton, Barbara 1857-1929   **TCLC 57**
Beagle, Peter S(oyer) 1939-   **CLC 7, 104**
   See also CA 9-12R; CANR 4, 51, 73; DA3;
   DLBY 80; INT CANR-4; MTCW 1; SATA
   60
Bean, Normal
   See Burroughs, Edgar Rice
Beard, Charles A(ustin) 1874-1948 TCLC 15
   See also CA 115; DLB 17; SATA 18
Beardsley, Aubrey 1872-1898   **NCLC 6**
Beattie, Ann 1947-CLC 8, 13, 18, 40, 63; DAM
   NOV, POP; SSC 11
   See also BEST 90:2; CA 81-84; CANR 53, 73;
   DA3; DLBY 82; MTCW 1, 2
Beattie, James 1735-1803   **NCLC 25**
   See also DLB 109
Beauchamp, Kathleen Mansfield 1888-1923
   See Mansfield, Katherine
   See also CA 104; 134; DA; DAC; DAM MST;
   DA3; MTCW 2
Beaumarchais, Pierre-Augustin Caron de 1732-
   1799   **DC 4**
   See also DAM DRAM
Beaumont, Francis 1584(?)-1616LC 33; DC 6
   See also CDBLB Before 1660; DLB 58, 121
**Beauvoir, Simone (Lucie Ernestine Marie
   Bertrand) de** 1908-1986CLC 1, 2, 4, 8, 14,
   **31, 44, 50, 71, 124; DA; DAB; DAC; DAM
   MST, NOV; SSC 35; WLC**
   See also CA 9-12R; 118; CANR 28, 61; DA3;
   DLB 72; DLBY 86; MTCW 1, 2
Becker, Carl (Lotus) 1873-1945   **TCLC 63**
   See also CA 157; DLB 17
Becker, Jurek 1937-1997   **CLC 7, 19**
   See also CA 85-88; 157; CANR 60; DLB 75
Becker, Walter 1950-   **CLC 26**
Beckett, Samuel (Barclay) 1906-1989 CLC 1,
   2, 3, 4, 6, 9, 10, 11, 14, 18, 29, 57, 59, 83;
   **DA; DAB; DAC; DAM DRAM, MST,
   NOV; SSC 16; WLC**
   See also CA 5-8R; 130; CANR 33, 61; CDBLB
   1945-1960; DA3; DLB 13, 15; DLBY 90;
   MTCW 1, 2
Beckford, William 1760-1844   **NCLC 16**
   See also DLB 39
Beckman, Gunnel 1910-   **CLC 26**
   See also CA 33-36R; CANR 15; CLR 25;
   MAICYA; SAAS 9; SATA 6
Becque, Henri 1837-1899   **NCLC 3**
   See also DLB 192
Becquer, Gustavo Adolfo 1836-1870
   See also DAM MULT; HLCS 1
Beddoes, Thomas Lovell 1803-1849 NCLC 3
   See also DLB 96
Bede c. 673-735   **CMLC 20**
   See also DLB 146
Bedford, Donald F.
   See Fearing, Kenneth (Flexner)
Beecher, Catharine Esther 1800-1878 N C L C
   30
   See also DLB 1
Beecher, John 1904-1980   **CLC 6**
   See also AITN 1; CA 5-8R; 105; CANR 8
Beer, Johann 1655-1700   **LC 5**
   See also DLB 168
Beer, Patricia 1924-   **CLC 58**
   See also CA 61-64; CANR 13, 46; DLB 40
Beerbohm, Max
   See Beerbohm, (Henry) Max(imilian)
Beerbohm, (Henry) Max(imilian) 1872-1956
   TCLC 1, 24
   See also CA 104; 154; CANR 79; DLB 34, 100
Beer-Hofmann, Richard 1866-1945TCLC 60

   See also CA 160; DLB 81
Begiebing, Robert J(ohn) 1946-   **CLC 70**
   See also CA 122; CANR 40
Behan, Brendan 1923-1964 CLC 1, 8, 11, 15,
   79; DAM DRAM
   See also CA 73-76; CANR 33; CDBLB 1945-
   1960; DLB 13; MTCW 1, 2
Behn, Aphra 1640(?)-1689 LC 1, 30, 42; DA;
   **DAB; DAC; DAM DRAM, MST, NOV,
   POET; DC 4; PC 13; WLC**
   See also DA3; DLB 39, 80, 131
Behrman, S(amuel) N(athaniel) 1893-1973
   CLC 40
   See also CA 13-16; 45-48; CAP 1; DLB 7, 44
Belasco, David 1853-1931   **TCLC 3**
   See also CA 104; 168; DLB 7
Belcheva, Elisaveta 1893-   **CLC 10**
   See Bagryana, Elisaveta
Beldone, Phil "Cheech"
   See Ellison, Harlan (Jay)
Beleno
   See Azuela, Mariano
Belinski, Vissarion Grigoryevich 1811-1848
   NCLC 5
   See also DLB 198
Belitt, Ben 1911-   **CLC 22**
   See also CA 13-16R; CAAS 4; CANR 7, 77;
   DLB 5
Bell, Gertrude (Margaret Lowthian) 1868-1926
   TCLC 67
   See also CA 167; DLB 174
Bell, J. Freeman
   See Zangwill, Israel
Bell, James Madison 1826-1902   **TCLC 43;
   BLC 1; DAM MULT**
   See also BW 1; CA 122; 124; DLB 50
Bell, Madison Smartt 1957-   **CLC 41, 102**
   See also CA 111; CANR 28, 54, 73; MTCW 1
Bell, Marvin (Hartley) 1937-CLC 8, 31; DAM
   POET
   See also CA 21-24R; CAAS 14; CANR 59; DLB
   5; MTCW 1
Bell, W. L. D.
   See Mencken, H(enry) L(ouis)
Bellamy, Atwood C.
   See Mencken, H(enry) L(ouis)
Bellamy, Edward 1850-1898   **NCLC 4**
   See also DLB 12
Belli, Gioconda 1949-
   See also CA 152; HLCS 1
Bellin, Edward J.
   See Kuttner, Henry
**Belloc, (Joseph) Hilaire (Pierre Sebastien Rene
   Swanton)** 1870-1953 TCLC 7, 18; DAM
   POET; PC 24
   See also CA 106; 152; DLB 19, 100, 141, 174;
   MTCW 1; YABC 1
Belloc, Joseph Peter Rene Hilaire
   See Belloc, (Joseph) Hilaire (Pierre Sebastien
   Rene Swanton)
Belloc, Joseph Pierre Hilaire
   See Belloc, (Joseph) Hilaire (Pierre Sebastien
   Rene Swanton)
Belloc, M. A.
   See Lowndes, Marie Adelaide (Belloc)
Bellow, Saul 1915-CLC 1, 2, 3, 6, 8, 10, 13, 15,
   **25, 33, 34, 63, 79; DA; DAB; DAC; DAM
   MST, NOV, POP; SSC 14; WLC**
   See also AITN 2; BEST 89:3; CA 5-8R; CABS
   1; CANR 29, 53; CDALB 1941-1968; DA3;
   DLB 2, 28; DLBD 3; DLBY 82; MTCW 1, 2
Belser, Reimond Karel Maria de 1929-
   See Ruyslinck, Ward

   See also CA 152
Bely, Andrey   **TCLC 7; PC 11**
   See also Bugayev, Boris Nikolayevich
   See also MTCW 1
Belyi, Andrei
   See Bugayev, Boris Nikolayevich
Benary, Margot
   See Benary-Isbert, Margot
Benary-Isbert, Margot 1889-1979   **CLC 12**
   See also CA 5-8R; 89-92; CANR 4, 72; CLR
   12; MAICYA; SATA 2; SATA-Obit 21
Benavente (y Martinez), Jacinto 1866-1954
   TCLC 3; DAM DRAM, MULT; HLCS 1
   See also CA 106; 131; CANR 81; HW 1, 2;
   MTCW 1, 2
Benchley, Peter (Bradford) 1940- CLC 4, 8;
   DAM NOV, POP
   See also AAYA 14; AITN 2; CA 17-20R; CANR
   12, 35, 66; MTCW 1, 2; SATA 3, 89
Benchley, Robert (Charles) 1889-1945 T C L C
   1, 55
   See also CA 105; 153; DLB 11
Benda, Julien 1867-1956   **TCLC 60**
   See also CA 120; 154
Benedict, Ruth (Fulton) 1887-1948 TCLC 60
   See also CA 158
Benedict, Saint c. 480-c. 547   **CMLC 29**
Benedikt, Michael 1935-   **CLC 4, 14**
   See also CA 13-16R; CANR 7; DLB 5
Benet, Juan 1927-   **CLC 28**
   See also CA 143
Benet, Stephen Vincent 1898-1943 TCLC 7;
   DAM POET; SSC 10
   See also CA 104; 152; DA3; DLB 4, 48, 102;
   DLBY 97; MTCW 1; YABC 1
Benet, William Rose 1886-1950   **TCLC 28;
   DAM POET**
   See also CA 118; 152; DLB 45
Benford, Gregory (Albert) 1941-   **CLC 52**
   See also CA 69-72; 175; CAAE 175; CAAS 27;
   CANR 12, 24, 49; DLBY 82
Bengtsson, Frans (Gunnar) 1894-1954 T C L C
   48
   See also CA 170
Benjamin, David
   See Slavitt, David R(ytman)
Benjamin, Lois
   See Gould, Lois
Benjamin, Walter 1892-1940   **TCLC 39**
   See also CA 164
Benn, Gottfried 1886-1956   **TCLC 3**
   See also CA 106; 153; DLB 56
Bennett, Alan 1934- CLC 45, 77; DAB; DAM
   MST
   See also CA 103; CANR 35, 55; MTCW 1, 2
Bennett, (Enoch) Arnold 1867-1931 TCLC 5,
   20
   See also CA 106; 155; CDBLB 1890-1914;
   DLB 10, 34, 98, 135; MTCW 2
Bennett, Elizabeth
   See Mitchell, Margaret (Munnerlyn)
Bennett, George Harold 1930-
   See Bennett, Hal
   See also BW 1; CA 97-100
Bennett, Hal   **CLC 5**
   See also Bennett, George Harold
   See also DLB 33
Bennett, Jay 1912-   **CLC 35**
   See also AAYA 10; CA 69-72; CANR 11, 42,
   79; JRDA; SAAS 4; SATA 41, 87; SATA-
   Brief 27
Bennett, Louise (Simone) 1919-CLC 28; BLC
   1; DAM MULT

See also BW 2, 3; CA 151; DLB 117

Benson, E(dward) F(rederic) 1867-1940
TCLC 27
See also CA 114; 157; DLB 135, 153

Benson, Jackson J. 1930-　　　　　　　**CLC 34**
See also CA 25-28R; DLB 111

Benson, Sally 1900-1972　　　　　　　**CLC 17**
See also CA 19-20; 37-40R; CAP 1; SATA 1,
35; SATA-Obit 27

Benson, Stella 1892-1933　　　　　　　**TCLC 17**
See also CA 117; 155; DLB 36, 162

Bentham, Jeremy 1748-1832　　　　　　**NCLC 38**
See also DLB 107, 158

Bentley, E(dmund) C(lerihew) 1875-1956
TCLC 12
See also CA 108; DLB 70

Bentley, Eric (Russell) 1916-　　　　　**CLC 24**
See also CA 5-8R; CANR 6, 67; INT CANR-6

Beranger, Pierre Jean de 1780-1857**NCLC 34**

Berdyaev, Nicolas
See Berdyaev, Nikolai (Aleksandrovich)

Berdyaev, Nikolai (Aleksandrovich) 1874-1948
TCLC 67
See also CA 120; 157

Berdyayev, Nikolai (Aleksandrovich)
See Berdyaev, Nikolai (Aleksandrovich)

Berendt, John (Lawrence) 1939-　　　　**CLC 86**
See also CA 146; CANR 75; DA3; MTCW 1

Beresford, J(ohn) D(avys) 1873-1947　**TCLC 81**
See also CA 112; 155; DLB 162, 178, 197

Bergelson, David 1884-1952　　　　　　**TCLC 81**

Berger, Colonel
See Malraux, (Georges-)Andre

Berger, John (Peter) 1926-　　　　　　**CLC 2, 19**
See also CA 81-84; CANR 51, 78; DLB 14, 207

Berger, Melvin H. 1927-　　　　　　　**CLC 12**
See also CA 5-8R; CANR 4; CLR 32; SAAS 2;
SATA 5, 88

Berger, Thomas (Louis) 1924-**CLC 3, 5, 8, 11,
18, 38; DAM NOV**
See also CA 1-4R; CANR 5, 28, 51; DLB 2;
DLBY 80; INT CANR-28; MTCW 1, 2

Bergman, (Ernst) Ingmar 1918-　　**CLC 16, 72**
See also CA 81-84, CANR 33, 70; MTCW 2

Bergson, Henri(-Louis) 1859-1941　**TCLC 32**
See also CA 164

Bergstein, Eleanor 1938-　　　　　　　**CLC 4**
See also CA 53-56; CANR 5

Berkoff, Steven 1937-　　　　　　　　**CLC 56**
See also CA 104; CANR 72

Bermant, Chaim (Icyk) 1929-　　　　　**CLC 40**
See also CA 57-60; CANR 6, 31, 57

Bern, Victoria
See Fisher, M(ary) F(rances) K(ennedy)

Bernanos, (Paul Louis) Georges 1888-1948
TCLC 3
See also CA 104; 130; DLB 72

Bernard, April 1956-　　　　　　　　**CLC 59**
See also CA 131

Berne, Victoria
See Fisher, M(ary) F(rances) K(ennedy)

Bernhard, Thomas 1931-1989　**CLC 3, 32, 61**
See also CA 85-88; 127; CANR 32, 57; DLB
85, 124; MTCW 1

Bernhardt, Sarah (Henriette Rosine) 1844-1923
TCLC 75
See also CA 157

Berriault, Gina 1926-　　**CLC 54, 109; SSC 30**
See also CA 116; 129; CANR 66; DLB 130

Berrigan, Daniel 1921-　　　　　　　　**CLC 4**
See also CA 33-36R; CAAS 1; CANR 11, 43,
78; DLB 5

Berrigan, Edmund Joseph Michael, Jr.　1934-
1983
See Berrigan, Ted
See also CA 61-64; 110; CANR 14

Berrigan, Ted　　　　　　　　　　　　**CLC 37**
See also Berrigan, Edmund Joseph Michael, Jr.
See also DLB 5, 169

Berry, Charles Edward Anderson　1931-
See Berry, Chuck
See also CA 115

Berry, Chuck　　　　　　　　　　　　**CLC 17**
See also Berry, Charles Edward Anderson

Berry, Jonas
See Ashbery, John (Lawrence)

Berry, Wendell (Erdman)　1934-　**CLC 4, 6, 8,
27, 46; DAM POET; PC 28**
See also AITN 1; CA 73-76; CANR 50, 73; DLB
5, 6; MTCW 1

Berryman, John　1914-1972**CLC 1, 2, 3, 4, 6, 8,
10, 13, 25, 62; DAM POET**
See also CA 13-16; 33-36R; CABS 2; CANR
35; CAP 1; CDALB 1941-1968; DLB 48;
MTCW 1, 2

Bertolucci, Bernardo　1940-　　　　　**CLC 16**
See also CA 106

Berton, Pierre (Francis Demarigny)　1920-
CLC 104
See also CA 1-4R; CANR 2, 56; DLB 68; SATA
99

Bertrand, Aloysius　1807-1841　　　　**NCLC 31**

Bertran de Born　c. 1140-1215　　　　**CMLC 5**

Besant, Annie (Wood)　1847-1933　　　**TCLC 9**
See also CA 105

Bessie, Alvah　1904-1985　　　　　　　**CLC 23**
See also CA 5-8R; 116; CANR 2, 80; DLB 26

Bethlen, T. D.
See Silverberg, Robert

Beti, Mongo　　　　**CLC 27; BLC 1; DAM MULT**
See also Biyidi, Alexandre
See also CANR 79

Betjeman, John　1906-1984　**CLC 2, 6, 10, 34,
43; DAB; DAM MST, POET**
See also CA 9-12R, 112, CANR 33, 56, CDBLB
1945-1960; DA3; DLB 20; DLBY 84;
MTCW 1, 2

Bettelheim, Bruno　1903-1990　　　　　**CLC 79**
See also CA 81-84; 131; CANR 23, 61; DA3;
MTCW 1, 2

Betti, Ugo　1892-1953　　　　　　　　**TCLC 5**
See also CA 104; 155

Betts, Doris (Waugh)　1932-　　**CLC 3, 6, 28**
See also CA 13-16R; CANR 9, 66, 77; DLBY
82; INT CANR-9

Bevan, Alistair
See Roberts, Keith (John Kingston)

Bey, Pilaff
See Douglas, (George) Norman

Bialik, Chaim Nachman　1873-1934　**TCLC 25**
See also CA 170

Bickerstaff, Isaac
See Swift, Jonathan

Bidart, Frank　1939-　　　　　　　　**CLC 33**
See also CA 140

Bienek, Horst　1930-　　　　　　　　**CLC 7, 11**
See also CA 73-76; DLB 75

Bierce, Ambrose (Gwinett)　1842-1914(?)
**TCLC 1, 7, 44; DA; DAC; DAM MST; SSC
9; WLC**
See also CA 104; 139; CANR 78; CDALB
1865-1917; DA3; DLB 11, 12, 23, 71, 74,
186

Biggers, Earl Derr　1884-1933　　　　**TCLC 65**
See also CA 108; 153

Billings, Josh
See Shaw, Henry Wheeler

Billington, (Lady) Rachel (Mary)　1942-　**C L C
43**
See also AITN 2; CA 33-36R; CANR 44

Binyon, T(imothy) J(ohn)　1936-　　　**CLC 34**
See also CA 111; CANR 28

Bioy Casares, Adolfo　1914-1999**CLC 4, 8, 13,
88; DAM MULT; HLC 1; SSC 17**
See also CA 29-32R; 177; CANR 19, 43, 66;
DLB 113; HW 1, 2; MTCW 1, 2

Bird, Cordwainer
See Ellison, Harlan (Jay)

Bird, Robert Montgomery　1806-1854**NCLC 1**
See also DLB 202

Birkerts, Sven　1951-　　　　　　　　**CLC 116**
See also CA 128; 133; 176; CAAE 176; CAAS
29; INT 133

Birney, (Alfred) Earle　1904-1995**CLC 1, 4, 6,
11; DAC; DAM MST, POET**
See also CA 1-4R; CANR 5, 20; DLB 88;
MTCW 1

Biruni, al　973-1048(?)　　　　　　　**CMLC 28**

Bishop, Elizabeth　1911-1979　**CLC 1, 4, 9, 13,
15, 32; DA; DAC; DAM MST, POET; PC
3**
See also CA 5-8R; 89-92; CABS 2; CANR 26,
61; CDALB 1968-1988; DA3; DLB 5, 169;
MTCW 1, 2; SATA-Obit 24

Bishop, John　1935-　　　　　　　　　**CLC 10**
See also CA 105

Bissett, Bill　1939-　　　　　　**CLC 18; PC 14**
See also CA 69-72; CAAS 19; CANR 15; DLB
53; MTCW 1

Bissoondath, Neil (Devindra)　1955-**CLC 120;
DAC**
See also CA 136

Bitov, Andrei (Georgievich)　1937-　　**CLC 57**
See also CA 142

Biyidi, Alexandre　1932-
See Beti, Mongo
See also BW 1, 3; CA 114; 124; CANR 81;
DA3; MTCW 1, 2

Bjarme, Brynjolf
See Ibsen, Henrik (Johan)

Bjoernson, Bjoernstjerne (Martinius)　1832-
1910　　　　　　　　　　　　　　**TCLC 7, 37**
See also CA 104

Black, Robert
See Holdstock, Robert P.

Blackburn, Paul　1926-1971　　　　**CLC 9, 43**
See also CA 81-84; 33-36R; CANR 34; DLB
16; DLBY 81

Black Elk　1863-1950　**TCLC 33; DAM MULT**
See also CA 144; MTCW 1; NNAL

Black Hobart
See Sanders, (James) Ed(ward)

Blacklin, Malcolm
See Chambers, Aidan

Blackmore, R(ichard) D(oddridge)　1825-1900
TCLC 27
See also CA 120; DLB 18

Blackmur, R(ichard) P(almer)　1904-1965
CLC 2, 24
See also CA 11-12; 25-28R; CANR 71; CAP 1;
DLB 63

Black Tarantula
See Acker, Kathy

Blackwood, Algernon (Henry)　1869-1951
TCLC 5
See also CA 105; 150; DLB 153, 156, 178

Blackwood, Caroline　1931-1996**CLC 6, 9, 100**
See also CA 85-88; 151; CANR 32, 61, 65; DLB

14, 207; MTCW 1

Blade, Alexander
See Hamilton, Edmond; Silverberg, Robert

Blaga, Lucian 1895-1961 **CLC 75**
See also CA 157

Blair, Eric (Arthur) 1903-1950
See Orwell, George
See also CA 104; 132; DA; DAB; DAC; DAM MST, NOV; DA3; MTCW 1, 2; SATA 29

Blair, Hugh 1718-1800 **NCLC 75**

Blais, Marie-Claire 1939-**CLC 2, 4, 6, 13, 22; DAC; DAM MST**
See also CA 21-24R; CAAS 4; CANR 38, 75; DLB 53; MTCW 1, 2

Blaise, Clark 1940- **CLC 29**
See also AITN 2; CA 53-56; CAAS 3; CANR 5, 66; DLB 53

Blake, Fairley
See De Voto, Bernard (Augustine)

Blake, Nicholas
See Day Lewis, C(ecil)
See also DLB 77

Blake, William 1757-1827 **NCLC 13, 37, 57; DA; DAB; DAC; DAM MST, POET; PC 12; WLC**
See also CDBLB 1789-1832; CLR 52; DA3; DLB 93, 163; MAICYA; SATA 30

Blasco Ibanez, Vicente 1867-1928 **TCLC 12; DAM NOV**
See also CA 110; 131; CANR 81; DA3; HW 1, 2; MTCW 1

Blatty, William Peter 1928-**CLC 2; DAM POP**
See also CA 5-8R; CANR 9

Bleeck, Oliver
See Thomas, Ross (Elmore)

Blessing, Lee 1949- **CLC 54**

Blish, James (Benjamin) 1921-1975 **CLC 14**
See also CA 1-4R; 57-60; CANR 3; DLB 8; MTCW 1; SATA 66

Bliss, Reginald
See Wells, H(erbert) G(eorge)

Blixen, Karen (Christentze Dinesen) 1885-1962
See Dinesen, Isak
See also CA 25-28; CANR 22, 50; CAP 2; DA3; MTCW 1, 2; SATA 44

Bloch, Robert (Albert) 1917-1994 **CLC 33**
See also AAYA 29; CA 5-8R, 179; 146; CAAE 179; CAAS 20; CANR 5, 78; DA3; DLB 44; INT CANR-5; MTCW 1; SATA 12; SATA-Obit 82

Blok, Alexander (Alexandrovich) 1880-1921 **TCLC 5; PC 21**
See also CA 104

Blom, Jan
See Breytenbach, Breyten

Bloom, Harold 1930- **CLC 24, 103**
See also CA 13-16R; CANR 39, 75; DLB 67; MTCW 1

Bloomfield, Aurelius
See Bourne, Randolph S(illiman)

Blount, Roy (Alton), Jr. 1941- **CLC 38**
See also CA 53-56; CANR 10, 28, 61; INT CANR-28; MTCW 1, 2

Bloy, Leon 1846-1917 **TCLC 22**
See also CA 121; DLB 123

Blume, Judy (Sussman) 1938- **CLC 12, 30; DAM NOV, POP**
See also AAYA 3, 26; CA 29-32R; CANR 13, 37, 66; CLR 2, 15; DA3; DLB 52; JRDA; MAICYA; MTCW 1, 2; SATA 2, 31, 79

Blunden, Edmund (Charles) 1896-1974 **CLC 2, 56**
See also CA 17-18; 45-48; CANR 54; CAP 2;

DLB 20, 100, 155; MTCW 1

Bly, Robert (Elwood) 1926-**CLC 1, 2, 5, 10, 15, 38; DAM POET**
See also CA 5-8R; CANR 41, 73; DA3; DLB 5; MTCW 1, 2

Boas, Franz 1858-1942 **TCLC 56**
See also CA 115; 181

Bobette
See Simenon, Georges (Jacques Christian)

Boccaccio, Giovanni 1313-1375 **CMLC 13; SSC 10**

Bochco, Steven 1943- **CLC 35**
See also AAYA 11; CA 124; 138

Bodel, Jean 1167(?)-1210 **CMLC 28**

Bodenheim, Maxwell 1892-1954 **TCLC 44**
See also CA 110; DLB 9, 45

Bodker, Cecil 1927- **CLC 21**
See also CA 73-76; CANR 13, 44; CLR 23; MAICYA; SATA 14

Boell, Heinrich (Theodor) 1917-1985 **CLC 2, 3, 6, 9, 11, 15, 27, 32, 72; DA; DAB; DAC; DAM MST, NOV; SSC 23; WLC**
See also CA 21-24R; 116; CANR 24; DA3; DLB 69; DLBY 85; MTCW 1, 2

Boerne, Alfred
See Doeblin, Alfred

Boethius 480(?)-524(?) **CMLC 15**
See also DLB 115

Boff, Leonardo (Genezio Darci) 1938-
See also CA 150; DAM MULT; HLC 1; HW 2

Bogan, Louise 1897-1970 **CLC 4, 39, 46, 93; DAM POET; PC 12**
See also CA 73-76; 25-28R; CANR 33, 82; DLB 45, 169; MTCW 1, 2

Bogarde, Dirk 1921-1999 **CLC 19**
See also Van Den Bogarde, Derek Jules Gaspard Ulric Niven
See also CA 179; DLB 14

Bogosian, Eric 1953- **CLC 45**
See also CA 138

Bograd, Larry 1953- **CLC 35**
See also CA 93-96; CANR 57; SAAS 21; SATA 33, 89

Boiardo, Matteo Maria 1441-1494 **LC 6**

Boileau-Despreaux, Nicolas 1636-1711 **LC 3**

Bojer, Johan 1872-1959 **TCLC 64**

Boland, Eavan (Aisling) 1944- **CLC 40, 67, 113; DAM POET**
See also CA 143; CANR 61; DLB 40; MTCW 2

Boll, Heinrich
See Boell, Heinrich (Theodor)

Bolt, Lee
See Faust, Frederick (Schiller)

Bolt, Robert (Oxton) 1924-1995**CLC 14; DAM DRAM**
See also CA 17-20R; 147; CANR 35, 67; DLB 13; MTCW 1

Bombal, Maria Luisa 1910-1980 **SSC 37; HLCS 1**
See also CA 127; CANR 72; HW 1

Bombet, Louis-Alexandre-Cesar
See Stendhal

Bomkauf
See Kaufman, Bob (Garnell)

Bonaventura **NCLC 35**
See also DLB 90

Bond, Edward 1934- **CLC 4, 6, 13, 23; DAM DRAM**
See also CA 25-28R; CANR 38, 67; DLB 13; MTCW 1

Bonham, Frank 1914-1989 **CLC 12**
See also AAYA 1; CA 9-12R; CANR 4, 36;

JRDA; MAICYA; SAAS 3; SATA 1, 49; SATA-Obit 62

Bonnefoy, Yves 1923- **CLC 9, 15, 58; DAM MST, POET**
See also CA 85-88; CANR 33, 75; MTCW 1, 2

Bontemps, Arna(ud Wendell) 1902-1973**CLC 1, 18; BLC 1; DAM MULT, NOV, POET**
See also BW 1; CA 1-4R; 41-44R; CANR 4, 35; CLR 6; DA3; DLB 48, 51; JRDA; MAICYA; MTCW 1, 2; SATA 2, 44; SATA-Obit 24

Booth, Martin 1944- **CLC 13**
See also CA 93-96; CAAS 2

Booth, Philip 1925- **CLC 23**
See also CA 5-8R; CANR 5; DLBY 82

Booth, Wayne C(layson) 1921- **CLC 24**
See also CA 1-4R; CAAS 5; CANR 3, 43; DLB 67

Borchert, Wolfgang 1921-1947 **TCLC 5**
See also CA 104; DLB 69, 124

Borel, Petrus 1809-1859 **NCLC 41**

Borges, Jorge Luis 1899-1986**CLC 1, 2, 3, 4, 6, 8, 9, 10, 13, 19, 44, 48, 83; DA; DAB; DAC; DAM MST, MULT; HLC 1; PC 22; SSC 4; WLC**
See also AAYA 26; CA 21-24R; CANR 19, 33, 75; DA3; DLB 113; DLBY 86; HW 1, 2; MTCW 1, 2

Borowski, Tadeusz 1922-1951 **TCLC 9**
See also CA 106; 154

Borrow, George (Henry) 1803-1881 **NCLC 9**
See also DLB 21, 55, 166

Bosch (Gavino), Juan 1909-
See also CA 151; DAM MST, MULT; DLB 145; HLCS 1; HW 1, 2

Bosman, Herman Charles 1905-1951 **TCLC 49**
See also Malan, Herman
See also CA 160

Bosschere, Jean de 1878(?)-1953 **TCLC 19**
See also CA 115

Boswell, James 1740-1795**LC 4, 50; DA; DAB; DAC; DAM MST; WLC**
See also CDBLB 1660-1789; DLB 104, 142

Bottoms, David 1949- **CLC 53**
See also CA 105; CANR 22; DLB 120; DLBY 83

Boucicault, Dion 1820-1890 **NCLC 41**

Boucolon, Maryse 1937(?)-
See Conde, Maryse
See also BW 3; CA 110; CANR 30, 53, 76

Bourget, Paul (Charles Joseph) 1852-1935 **TCLC 12**
See also CA 107; DLB 123

Bourjaily, Vance (Nye) 1922- **CLC 8, 62**
See also CA 1-4R; CAAS 1; CANR 2, 72; DLB 2, 143

Bourne, Randolph S(illiman) 1886-1918 **TCLC 16**
See also CA 117; 155; DLB 63

Bova, Ben(jamin William) 1932- **CLC 45**
See also AAYA 16; CA 5-8R; CAAS 18; CANR 11, 56; CLR 3; DLBY 81; INT CANR-11; MAICYA; MTCW 1; SATA 6, 68

Bowen, Elizabeth (Dorothea Cole) 1899-1973 **CLC 1, 3, 6, 11, 15, 22, 118; DAM NOV; SSC 3, 28**
See also CA 17-18; 41-44R; CANR 35; CAP 2; CDBLB 1945-1960; DA3; DLB 15, 162; MTCW 1, 2

Bowering, George 1935- **CLC 15, 47**
See also CA 21-24R; CAAS 16; CANR 10; DLB 53

Bowering, Marilyn R(uthe) 1949- **CLC 32**
See also CA 101; CANR 49
Bowers, Edgar 1924- **CLC 9**
See also CA 5-8R; CANR 24; DLB 5
Bowie, David **CLC 17**
See also Jones, David Robert
Bowles, Jane (Sydney) 1917-1973 **CLC 3, 68**
See also CA 19-20; 41-44R; CAP 2
Bowles, Paul (Frederick) 1910- **CLC 1, 2, 19, 53; SSC 3**
See also CA 1-4R; CAAS 1; CANR 1, 19, 50, 75; DA3; DLB 5, 6; MTCW 1, 2
Box, Edgar
See Vidal, Gore
Boyd, Nancy
See Millay, Edna St. Vincent
Boyd, William 1952- **CLC 28, 53, 70**
See also CA 114; 120; CANR 51, 71
Boyle, Kay 1902-1992 **CLC 1, 5, 19, 58, 121; SSC 5**
See also CA 13-16R; 140; CAAS 1; CANR 29, 61; DLB 4, 9, 48, 86; DLBY 93; MTCW 1, 2
Boyle, Mark
See Kienzle, William X(avier)
Boyle, Patrick 1905-1982 **CLC 19**
See also CA 127
Boyle, T. C. 1948-
See Boyle, T(homas) Coraghessan
Boyle, T(homas) Coraghessan 1948- **CLC 36, 55, 90; DAM POP; SSC 16**
See also BEST 90:4; CA 120; CANR 44, 76; DA3; DLBY 86; MTCW 2
Boz
See Dickens, Charles (John Huffam)
Brackenridge, Hugh Henry 1748-1816 **NCLC 7**
See also DLB 11, 37
Bradbury, Edward P.
See Moorcock, Michael (John)
See also MTCW 2
Bradbury, Malcolm (Stanley) 1932- **CLC 32, 61; DAM NOV**
See also CA 1-4R; CANR 1, 33; DA3; DLB 14, 207; MTCW 1, 2
Bradbury, Ray (Douglas) 1920- **CLC 1, 3, 10, 15, 42, 98; DA; DAB; DAC; DAM MST, NOV, POP; SSC 29; WLC**
See also AAYA 15; AITN 1, 2; CA 1-4R; CANR 2, 30, 75; CDALB 1968-1988; DA3; DLB 2, 8; MTCW 1, 2; SATA 11, 64
Bradford, Gamaliel 1863-1932 **TCLC 36**
See also CA 160; DLB 17
Bradley, David (Henry), Jr. 1950- **CLC 23, 118; BLC 1; DAM MULT**
See also BW 1, 3; CA 104; CANR 26, 81; DLB 33
Bradley, John Ed(mund, Jr.) 1958- **CLC 55**
See also CA 139
Bradley, Marion Zimmer 1930- **CLC 30; DAM POP**
See also AAYA 9; CA 57-60; CAAS 10; CANR 7, 31, 51, 75; DA3; DLB 8; MTCW 1, 2; SATA 90
Bradstreet, Anne 1612(?)-1672 **LC 4, 30; DA; DAC; DAM MST, POET; PC 10**
See also CDALB 1640-1865; DA3; DLB 24
Brady, Joan 1939- **CLC 86**
See also CA 141
Bragg, Melvyn 1939- **CLC 10**
See also BEST 89:3; CA 57-60; CANR 10, 48; DLB 14
Brahe, Tycho 1546-1601 **LC 45**
Braine, John (Gerard) 1922-1986 **CLC 1, 3, 41**

See also CA 1-4R; 120; CANR 1, 33; CDBLB 1945-1960; DLB 15; DLBY 86; MTCW 1
Bramah, Ernest 1868-1942 **TCLC 72**
See also CA 156; DLB 70
Brammer, William 1930(?)-1978 **CLC 31**
See also CA 77-80
Brancati, Vitaliano 1907-1954 **TCLC 12**
See also CA 109
Brancato, Robin F(idler) 1936- **CLC 35**
See also AAYA 9; CA 69-72; CANR 11, 45; CLR 32; JRDA; SAAS 9; SATA 97
Brand, Max
See Faust, Frederick (Schiller)
Brand, Millen 1906-1980 **CLC 7**
See also CA 21-24R; 97-100; CANR 72
Branden, Barbara **CLC 44**
See also CA 148
Brandes, Georg (Morris Cohen) 1842-1927 **TCLC 10**
See also CA 105
Brandys, Kazimierz 1916- **CLC 62**
Branley, Franklyn M(ansfield) 1915- **CLC 21**
See also CA 33-36R; CANR 14, 39; CLR 13; MAICYA; SAAS 16; SATA 4, 68
Brathwaite, Edward (Kamau) 1930- **CLC 11; BLCS; DAM POET**
See also BW 2, 3; CA 25-28R; CANR 11, 26, 47; DLB 125
Brautigan, Richard (Gary) 1935-1984 **CLC 1, 3, 5, 9, 12, 34, 42; DAM NOV**
See also CA 53-56; 113; CANR 34; DA3; DLB 2, 5, 206; DLBY 80, 84; MTCW 1; SATA 56
Brave Bird, Mary 1953-
See Crow Dog, Mary (Ellen)
See also NNAL
Braverman, Kate 1950- **CLC 67**
See also CA 89-92
Brecht, (Eugen) Bertolt (Friedrich) 1898-1956 **TCLC 1, 6, 13, 35; DA; DAB; DAC; DAM DRAM, MST; DC 3; WLC**
See also CA 104; 133; CANR 62; DA3; DLB 56, 124; MTCW 1, 2
Brecht, Eugen Berthold Friedrich
See Brecht, (Eugen) Bertolt (Friedrich)
Bremer, Fredrika 1801-1865 **NCLC 11**
Brennan, Christopher John 1870-1932 **TCLC 17**
See also CA 117
Brennan, Maeve 1917-1993 **CLC 5**
See also CA 81-84; CANR 72
Brent, Linda
See Jacobs, Harriet A(nn)
Brentano, Clemens (Maria) 1778-1842 **NCLC 1**
See also DLB 90
Brent of Bin Bin
See Franklin, (Stella Maria Sarah) Miles (Lampe)
Brenton, Howard 1942- **CLC 31**
See also CA 69-72; CANR 33, 67; DLB 13; MTCW 1
Breslin, James 1930-1996
See Breslin, Jimmy
See also CA 73-76; CANR 31, 75; DAM NOV; MTCW 1, 2
Breslin, Jimmy **CLC 4, 43**
See also Breslin, James
See also AITN 1; DLB 185; MTCW 2
Bresson, Robert 1901- **CLC 16**
See also CA 110; CANR 49
Breton, Andre 1896-1966 **CLC 2, 9, 15, 54; PC 15**
See also CA 19-20; 25-28R; CANR 40, 60; CAP

2; DLB 65; MTCW 1, 2
Breytenbach, Breyten 1939(?)- **CLC 23, 37, 126; DAM POET**
See also CA 113; 129; CANR 61
Bridgers, Sue Ellen 1942- **CLC 26**
See also AAYA 8; CA 65-68; CANR 11, 36; CLR 18; DLB 52; JRDA; MAICYA; SAAS 1; SATA 22, 90; SATA-Essay 109
Bridges, Robert (Seymour) 1844-1930 **TCLC 1; DAM POET; PC 28**
See also CA 104; 152; CDBLB 1890-1914; DLB 19, 98
Bridie, James **TCLC 3**
See also Mavor, Osborne Henry
See also DLB 10
Brin, David 1950- **CLC 34**
See also AAYA 21; CA 102; CANR 24, 70; INT CANR-24; SATA 65
Brink, Andre (Philippus) 1935- **CLC 18, 36, 106**
See also CA 104; CANR 39, 62; INT 103; MTCW 1, 2
Brinsmead, H(esba) F(ay) 1922- **CLC 21**
See also CA 21-24R; CANR 10; CLR 47; MAICYA; SAAS 5; SATA 18, 78
Brittain, Vera (Mary) 1893(?)-1970 **CLC 23**
See also CA 13-16; 25-28R; CANR 58; CAP 1; DLB 191; MTCW 1, 2
Broch, Hermann 1886-1951 **TCLC 20**
See also CA 117; DLB 85, 124
Brock, Rose
See Hansen, Joseph
Brodkey, Harold (Roy) 1930-1996 **CLC 56**
See also CA 111; 151; CANR 71; DLB 130
Brodskii, Iosif
See Brodsky, Joseph
Brodsky, Iosif Alexandrovich 1940-1996
See Brodsky, Joseph
See also AITN 1; CA 41-44R; 151; CANR 37; DAM POET; DA3; MTCW 1, 2
Brodsky, Joseph 1940-1996 **CLC 4, 6, 13, 36, 100; PC 9**
See also Brodskii, Iosif; Brodsky, Iosif Alexandrovich
See also MTCW 1
Brodsky, Michael (Mark) 1948- **CLC 19**
See also CA 102; CANR 18, 41, 58
Bromell, Henry 1947- **CLC 5**
See also CA 53-56; CANR 9
Bromfield, Louis (Brucker) 1896-1956 **TCLC 11**
See also CA 107; 155; DLB 4, 9, 86
Broner, E(sther) M(asserman) 1930- **CLC 19**
See also CA 17-20R; CANR 8, 25, 72; DLB 28
Bronk, William (M.) 1918-1999 **CLC 10**
See also CA 89-92; 177; CANR 23; DLB 165
Bronstein, Lev Davidovich
See Trotsky, Leon
Bronte, Anne 1820-1849 **NCLC 71**
See also DA3; DLB 21, 199
Bronte, Charlotte 1816-1855 **NCLC 3, 8, 33, 58; DA; DAB; DAC; DAM MST, NOV; WLC**
See also AAYA 17; CDBLB 1832-1890; DA3; DLB 21, 159, 199
Bronte, Emily (Jane) 1818-1848 **NCLC 16, 35; DA; DAB; DAC; DAM MST, NOV, POET; PC 8; WLC**
See also AAYA 17; CDBLB 1832-1890; DA3; DLB 21, 32, 199
Brooke, Frances 1724-1789 **LC 6, 48**
See also DLB 39, 99
Brooke, Henry 1703(?)-1783 **LC 1**
See also DLB 39

Cayer, D. M.
See Duffy, Maureen
Cayrol, Jean 1911-　　　　　CLC 11
See also CA 89-92; DLB 83
Cela, Camilo Jose 1916- CLC **4, 13, 59, 122;**
DAM MULT; HLC 1
See also BEST 90:2; CA 21-24R; CAAS 10;
CANR 21, 32, 76; DLBY 89; HW 1; MTCW
1, 2
Celan, Paul　　　CLC **10, 19, 53, 82; PC 10**
See also Antschel, Paul
See also DLB 69
Celine, Louis-Ferdinand CLC **1, 3, 4, 7, 9, 15,**
47, 124
See also Destouches, Louis-Ferdinand
See also DLB 72
Cellini, Benvenuto 1500-1571　　　LC 7
Cendrars, Blaise 1887-1961　　CLC **18, 106**
See also Sauser-Hall, Frederic
Cernuda (y Bidon), Luis 1902-1963 CLC **54;**
DAM POET
See also CA 131; 89-92; DLB 134; HW 1
Cervantes, Lorna Dee 1954-
See also CA 131; CANR 80; DLB 82; HLCS 1;
HW 1
Cervantes (Saavedra), Miguel de 1547-1616
LC **6, 23; DA; DAB; DAC; DAM MST,**
NOV; SSC 12; WLC
Cesaire, Aime (Fernand) 1913- CLC **19, 32,**
112; BLC 1; DAM MULT, POET; PC 25
See also BW 2, 3; CA 65-68; CANR 24, 43,
81; DA3; MTCW 1, 2
Chabon, Michael 1963-　　　CLC 55
See also CA 139; CANR 57
Chabrol, Claude 1930-　　　CLC 16
See also CA 110
Challans, Mary 1905-1983
See Renault, Mary
See also CA 81-84; 111; CANR 74; DA3;
MTCW 2; SATA 23; SATA-Obit 36
Challis, George
See Faust, Frederick (Schiller)
Chambers, Aidan 1934-　　　CLC 35
See also AAYA 27; CA 25-28R; CANR 12, 31,
58; JRDA; MAICYA; SAAS 12; SATA 1,
69, 108
Chambers, James 1948-
See Cliff, Jimmy
See also CA 124
Chambers, Jessie
See Lawrence, D(avid) H(erbert Richards)
Chambers, Robert W(illiam) 1865-1933
TCLC 41
See also CA 165; DLB 202; SATA 107
Chamisso, Adelbert von 1781-1838 NCLC 82
See also DLB 90
Chandler, Raymond (Thornton) 1888-1959
TCLC **1, 7; SSC 23**
See also AAYA 25; CA 104; 129; CANR 60;
CDALB 1929-1941; DA3; DLBD 6; MTCW
1, 2
Chang, Eileen 1920-1995　　　SSC 28
See also CA 166
Chang, Jung 1952-　　　CLC 71
See also CA 142
Chang Ai-Ling
See Chang, Eileen
Channing, William Ellery 1780-1842 NCLC 17
See also DLB 1, 59
Chao, Patricia 1955-　　　CLC 119
See also CA 163
Chaplin, Charles Spencer 1889-1977 CLC 16
See also Chaplin, Charlie

Chaplin, Charlie
See Chaplin, Charles Spencer
See also DLB 44
Chapman, George 1559(?)-1634 LC **22; DAM**
DRAM
See also DLB 62, 121
Chapman, Graham 1941-1989　　CLC 21
See also Monty Python
See also CA 116; 129; CANR 35
Chapman, John Jay 1862-1933　　TCLC 7
See also CA 104
Chapman, Lee
See Bradley, Marion Zimmer
Chapman, Walker
See Silverberg, Robert
Chappell, Fred (Davis) 1936-　　CLC **40, 78**
See also CA 5-8R; CAAS 4; CANR 8, 33, 67;
DLB 6, 105
Char, Rene(-Emile) 1907-1988 CLC **9, 11, 14,**
55; DAM POET
See also CA 13-16R; 124; CANR 32; MTCW
1, 2
Charby, Jay
See Ellison, Harlan (Jay)
Chardin, Pierre Teilhard de
See Teilhard de Chardin, (Marie Joseph) Pierre
Charles I 1600-1649　　　LC 13
Charriere, Isabelle de 1740-1805　NCLC 66
Charyn, Jerome 1937-　　　CLC **5, 8, 18**
See also CA 5-8R; CAAS 1; CANR 7, 61;
DLBY 83; MTCW 1
Chase, Mary (Coyle) 1907-1981　　DC 1
See also CA 77-80; 105; SATA 17; SATA-Obit 29
Chase, Mary Ellen 1887-1973　　CLC 2
See also CA 13-16; 41-44R; CAP 1; SATA 10
Chase, Nicholas
See Hyde, Anthony
Chateaubriand, Francois Rene de 1768-1848
NCLC 3
See also DLB 119
Chatterje, Sarat Chandra 1876-1936(?)
See Chatterji, Saratchandra
See also CA 109
Chatterji, Bankim Chandra 1838-1894
NCLC 19
Chatterji, Saratchandra　　　TCLC 13
See also Chatterje, Sarat Chandra
Chatterton, Thomas 1752-1770　LC **3, 54;**
DAM POET
See also DLB 109
Chatwin, (Charles) Bruce 1940-1989 CLC **28,**
57, 59; DAM POP
See also AAYA 4; BEST 90:1; CA 85-88; 127;
DLB 194, 204
Chaucer, Daniel
See Ford, Ford Madox
Chaucer, Geoffrey 1340(?)-1400 LC **17; DA;**
DAB; DAC; DAM MST, POET; PC 19;
WLCS
See also CDBLB Before 1660; DA3; DLB 146
Chavez, Denise (Elia) 1948-
See also CA 131; CANR 56, 81; DAM MULT;
DLB 122; HLC 1; HW 1, 2; MTCW 2
Chaviaras, Strates 1935-
See Haviaras, Stratis
See also CA 105
Chayefsky, Paddy　　　CLC 23
See also Chayefsky, Sidney
See also DLB 7, 44; DLBY 81
Chayefsky, Sidney 1923-1981
See Chayefsky, Paddy
See also CA 9-12R; 104; CANR 18; DAM DRAM

Chedid, Andree 1920-　　　CLC 47
See also CA 145
Cheever, John 1912-1982 CLC **3, 7, 8, 11, 15,**
25, 64; DA; DAB; DAC; DAM MST, NOV,
POP; SSC 1; WLC
See also CA 5-8R; 106; CABS 1; CANR 5, 27,
76; CDALB 1941-1968; DA3; DLB 2, 102;
DLBY 80, 82; INT CANR-5; MTCW 1, 2
Cheever, Susan 1943-　　　CLC **18, 48**
See also CA 103; CANR 27, 51; DLBY 82; INT
CANR-27
Chekhonte, Antosha
See Chekhov, Anton (Pavlovich)
Chekhov, Anton (Pavlovich) 1860-1904 TCLC
3, 10, 31, 55, 96; DA; DAB; DAC; DAM
DRAM, MST; DC 9; SSC 2, 28; WLC
See also CA 104; 124; DA3; SATA 90
Chernyshevsky, Nikolay Gavrilovich 1828-1889
NCLC 1
Cherry, Carolyn Janice 1942-
See Cherryh, C. J.
See also CA 65-68; CANR 10
Cherryh, C. J.　　　CLC 35
See also Cherry, Carolyn Janice
See also AAYA 24; DLBY 80; SATA 93
Chesnutt, Charles W(addell) 1858-1932
TCLC **5, 39; BLC 1; DAM MULT; SSC 7**
See also BW 1, 3; CA 106; 125; CANR 76; DLB
12, 50, 78; MTCW 1, 2
Chester, Alfred 1929(?)-1971　　CLC 49
See also CA 33-36R; DLB 130
Chesterton, G(ilbert) K(eith) 1874-1936
TCLC **1, 6, 64; DAM NOV, POET; PC 28;**
SSC 1
See also CA 104; 132; CANR 73; CDBLB
1914-1945; DLB 10, 19, 34, 70, 98, 149,
178; MTCW 1, 2; SATA 27
Chiang, Pin-chin 1904-1986
See Ding Ling
See also CA 118
Ch'ien Chung-shu 1910-　　　CLC 22
See also CA 130; CANR 73; MTCW 1, 2
Child, L. Maria
See Child, Lydia Maria
Child, Lydia Maria 1802-1880　NCLC **6, 73**
See also DLB 1, 74; SATA 67
Child, Mrs.
See Child, Lydia Maria
Child, Philip 1898-1978　　　CLC **19, 68**
See also CA 13-14; CAP 1; SATA 47
Childers, (Robert) Erskine 1870-1922
TCLC 65
See also CA 113; 153; DLB 70
Childress, Alice 1920-1994 CLC **12, 15, 86, 96;**
BLC 1; DAM DRAM, MULT, NOV; DC 4
See also AAYA 8; BW 2, 3; CA 45-48; 146;
CANR 3, 27, 50, 74; CLR 14; DA3; DLB 7,
38; JRDA; MAICYA; MTCW 1, 2; SATA 7,
48, 81
Chin, Frank (Chew, Jr.) 1940-　　DC 7
See also CA 33-36R; CANR 71; DAM MULT;
DLB 206
Chislett, (Margaret) Anne 1943-　CLC 34
See also CA 151
Chitty, Thomas Willes 1926-　　CLC 11
See also Hinde, Thomas
See also CA 5-8R
Chivers, Thomas Holley 1809-1858 NCLC 49
See also DLB 3
Choi, Susan　　　CLC 119
Chomette, Rene Lucien 1898-1981
See Clair, Rene
See also CA 103

Chopin, Kate TCLC 5, 14; DA; DAB; SSC 8; WLCS
See also Chopin, Katherine
See also CDALB 1865-1917; DLB 12, 78
Chopin, Katherine 1851-1904
See Chopin, Kate
See also CA 104; 122; DAC; DAM MST, NOV; DA3
Chretien de Troyes c. 12th cent. - **CMLC 10**
See also DLB 208
Christie
See Ichikawa, Kon
Christie, Agatha (Mary Clarissa) 1890-1976
CLC 1, 6, 8, 12, 39, 48, 110; DAB; DAC; DAM NOV
See also AAYA 9; AITN 1, 2; CA 17-20R; 61-64; CANR 10,37; CDBLB 1914-1945; DA3; DLB 13, 77; MTCW 1, 2; SATA 36
Christie, (Ann) Philippa
See Pearce, Philippa
See also CA 5-8R; CANR 4
Christine de Pizan 1365(?)-1431(?)   **LC 9**
See also DLB 208
Chubb, Elmer
See Masters, Edgar Lee
Chulkov, Mikhail Dmitrievich 1743-1792**LC 2**
See also DLB 150
Churchill, Caryl 1938-   **CLC 31, 55; DC 5**
See also CA 102; CANR 22, 46; DLB 13; MTCW 1
Churchill, Charles 1731-1764   **LC 3**
See also DLB 109
Chute, Carolyn 1947-   **CLC 39**
See also CA 123
Ciardi, John (Anthony) 1916-1986 **CLC 10, 40, 44; DAM POET**
See also CA 5-8R; 118; CAAS 2; CANR 5, 33; CLR 19; DLB 5; DLBY 86; INT CANR-5; MAICYA; MTCW 1, 2; SAAS 26; SATA 1, 65; SATA-Obit 46
Cicero, Marcus Tullius 106B.C.-43B.C.
CMLC 3
See also DLB 211
Cimino, Michael 1943-   **CLC 16**
See also CA 105
Cioran, E(mil) M. 1911-1995   **CLC 64**
See also CA 25-28R; 149
Cisneros, Sandra 1954- **CLC 69, 118; DAM MULT; HLC 1; SSC 32**
See also AAYA 9; CA 131; CANR 64; DA3; DLB 122, 152; HW 1, 2; MTCW 2
Cixous, Helene 1937-   **CLC 92**
See also CA 126; CANR 55; DLB 83; MTCW 1, 2
Clair, Rene   **CLC 20**
See also Chomette, Rene Lucien
Clampitt, Amy 1920-1994   **CLC 32; PC 19**
See also CA 110; 146; CANR 29, 79; DLB 105
Clancy, Thomas L., Jr. 1947-
See Clancy, Tom
See also CA 125; 131; CANR 62; DA3; INT 131; MTCW 1, 2
Clancy, Tom **CLC 45, 112; DAM NOV, POP**
See also Clancy, Thomas L., Jr.
See also AAYA 9; BEST 89:1, 90:1; MTCW 2
Clare, John 1793-1864 NCLC 9; DAB; DAM POET; PC 23
See also DLB 55, 96
Clarin
See Alas (y Urena), Leopoldo (Enrique Garcia)
Clark, Al C.
See Goines, Donald
Clark, (Robert) Brian 1932-   **CLC 29**

See also CA 41-44R; CANR 67
Clark, Curt
See Westlake, Donald E(dwin)
Clark, Eleanor 1913-1996   **CLC 5, 19**
See also CA 9-12R; 151; CANR 41; DLB 6
Clark, J. P.
See Clark, John Pepper
See also DLB 117
Clark, John Pepper 1935- **CLC 38; BLC 1; DAM DRAM, MULT; DC 5**
See also Clark, J. P.
See also BW 1; CA 65-68; CANR 16, 72; MTCW 1
Clark, M. R.
See Clark, Mavis Thorpe
Clark, Mavis Thorpe 1909-   **CLC 12**
See also CA 57-60; CANR 8, 37; CLR 30; MAICYA; SAAS 5; SATA 8, 74
Clark, Walter Van Tilburg 1909-1971**CLC 28**
See also CA 9-12R; 33-36R; CANR 63; DLB 9, 206; SATA 8
Clark Bekederemo, J(ohnson) P(epper)
See Clark, John Pepper
Clarke, Arthur C(harles) 1917-**CLC 1, 4, 13, 18, 35; DAM POP; SSC 3**
See also AAYA 4; CA 1-4R; CANR 2, 28, 55, 74; DA3; JRDA; MAICYA; MTCW 1, 2; SATA 13, 70
Clarke, Austin 1896-1974   **CLC 6, 9; DAM POET**
See also CA 29-32; 49-52; CAP 2; DLB 10, 20
Clarke, Austin C(hesterfield) 1934-**CLC 8, 53; BLC 1; DAC; DAM MULT**
See also BW 1; CA 25-28R; CAAS 16; CANR 14, 32, 68; DLB 53, 125
Clarke, Gillian 1937-   **CLC 61**
See also CA 106; DLB 40
Clarke, Marcus (Andrew Hislop) 1846-1881
NCLC 19
Clarke, Shirley 1925-   **CLC 16**
Clash, The
See Headon, (Nicky) Topper; Jones, Mick; Simonon, Paul; Strummer, Joe
Claudel, Paul (Louis Charles Marie) 1868-1955
TCLC 2, 10
See also CA 104; 165; DLB 192
Claudius, Matthias 1740-1815   **NCLC 75**
See also DLB 97
Clavell, James (duMaresq) 1925-1994**CLC 6, 25, 87; DAM NOV, POP**
See also CA 25-28R; 146; CANR 26, 48; DA3; MTCW 1, 2
Cleaver, (Leroy) Eldridge 1935-1998**CLC 30, 119; BLC 1; DAM MULT**
See also BW 1, 3; CA 21-24R; 167; CANR 16, 75; DA3; MTCW 2
Cleese, John (Marwood) 1939-   **CLC 21**
See also Monty Python
See also CA 112; 116; CANR 35; MTCW 1
Cleishbotham, Jebediah
See Scott, Walter
Cleland, John 1710-1789   **LC 2, 48**
See also DLB 39
Clemens, Samuel Langhorne 1835-1910
See Twain, Mark
See also CA 104; 135; CDALB 1865-1917; DA; DAB; DAC; DAM MST, NOV; DA3; DLB 11, 12, 23, 64, 74, 186, 189; JRDA; MAICYA; SATA 100; YABC 2
Cleophil
See Congreve, William
Clerihew, E.
See Bentley, E(dmund) C(lerihew)

Clerk, N. W.
See Lewis, C(live) S(taples)
Cliff, Jimmy   **CLC 21**
See also Chambers, James
Cliff, Michelle 1946-   **CLC 120; BLCS**
See also BW 2; CA 116; CANR 39, 72; DLB 157
Clifton, (Thelma) Lucille 1936- CLC 19, 66; **BLC 1; DAM MULT, POET; PC 17**
See also BW 2, 3; CA 49-52; CANR 2, 24, 42, 76; CLR 5; DA3; DLB 5, 41; MAICYA; MTCW 1, 2; SATA 20, 69
Clinton, Dirk
See Silverberg, Robert
Clough, Arthur Hugh 1819-1861   **NCLC 27**
See also DLB 32
Clutha, Janet Paterson Frame 1924-
See Frame, Janet
See also CA 1-4R; CANR 2, 36, 76; MTCW 1, 2
Clyne, Terence
See Blatty, William Peter
Cobalt, Martin
See Mayne, William (James Carter)
Cobb, Irvin S(hrewsbury) 1876-1944 **TCLC 77**
See also CA 175; DLB 11, 25, 86
Cobbett, William 1763-1835   **NCLC 49**
See also DLB 43, 107, 158
Coburn, D(onald) L(ee) 1938-   **CLC 10**
See also CA 89-92
Cocteau, Jean (Maurice Eugene Clement) 1889-1963**CLC 1, 8, 15, 16, 43; DA; DAB; DAC; DAM DRAM, MST, NOV; WLC**
See also CA 25-28; CANR 40; CAP 2; DA3; DLB 65; MTCW 1, 2
Codrescu, Andrei 1946- **CLC 46, 121; DAM POET**
See also CA 33-36R; CAAS 19; CANR 13, 34, 53, 76; DA3; MTCW 2
Coe, Max
See Bourne, Randolph S(illiman)
Coe, Tucker
See Westlake, Donald E(dwin)
Coen, Ethan 1958-   **CLC 108**
See also CA 126; CANR 85
Coen, Joel 1955-   **CLC 108**
See also CA 126
The Coen Brothers
See Coen, Ethan; Coen, Joel
Coetzee, J(ohn) M(ichael) 1940- CLC 23, 33, **66, 117; DAM NOV**
See also CA 77-80; CANR 41, 54, 74; DA3; MTCW 1, 2
Coffey, Brian
See Koontz, Dean R(ay)
Coffin, Robert P(eter) Tristram 1892-1955
TCLC 95
See also CA 123; 169; DLB 45
Cohan, George M(ichael) 1878-1942**TCLC 60**
See also CA 157
Cohen, Arthur A(llen) 1928-1986 **CLC 7, 31**
See also CA 1-4R; 120; CANR 1, 17, 42; DLB 28
Cohen, Leonard (Norman) 1934- CLC 3, 38; **DAC; DAM MST**
See also CA 21-24R; CANR 14, 69; DLB 53; MTCW 1
Cohen, Matt 1942-   **CLC 19; DAC**
See also CA 61-64; CAAS 18; CANR 40; DLB 53
Cohen-Solal, Annie 19(?)-   **CLC 50**
Colegate, Isabel 1931-   **CLC 36**

See also CA 17-20R; CANR 8, 22, 74; DLB 14; INT CANR-22; MTCW 1

Coleman, Emmett
See Reed, Ishmael

Coleridge, M. E.
See Coleridge, Mary E(lizabeth)

Coleridge, Mary E(lizabeth) 1861-1907 **TCLC 73**
See also CA 116; 166; DLB 19, 98

Coleridge, Samuel Taylor 1772-1834 **NCLC 9, 54; DA; DAB; DAC; DAM MST, POET; PC 11; WLC**
See also CDBLB 1789-1832; DA3; DLB 93, 107

Coleridge, Sara 1802-1852 **NCLC 31**
See also DLB 199

Coles, Don 1928- **CLC 46**
See also CA 115; CANR 38

Coles, Robert (Martin) 1929- **CLC 108**
See also CA 45-48; CANR 3, 32, 66, 70; INT CANR-32; SATA 23

Colette, (Sidonie-Gabrielle) 1873-1954 **TCLC 1, 5, 16; DAM NOV; SSC 10**
See also CA 104; 131; DA3; DLB 65; MTCW 1, 2

Collett, (Jacobine) Camilla (Wergeland) 1813-1895 **NCLC 22**

Collier, Christopher 1930- **CLC 30**
See also AAYA 13; CA 33-36R; CANR 13, 33; JRDA; MAICYA; SATA 16, 70

Collier, James L(incoln) 1928- **CLC 30; DAM POP**
See also AAYA 13; CA 9-12R; CANR 4, 33, 60; CLR 3; JRDA; MAICYA; SAAS 21; SATA 8, 70

Collier, Jeremy 1650-1726 **LC 6**

Collier, John 1901-1980 **SSC 19**
See also CA 65-68; 97-100; CANR 10; DLB 77

Collingwood, R(obin) G(eorge) 1889(?)-1943 **TCLC 67**
See also CA 117; 155

Collins, Hunt
See Hunter, Evan

Collins, Linda 1931- **CLC 44**
See also CA 125

Collins, (William) Wilkie 1824-1889 **NCLC 1, 18**
See also CDBLB 1832-1890; DLB 18, 70, 159

Collins, William 1721-1759 **LC 4, 40; DAM POET**
See also DLB 109

Collodi, Carlo 1826-1890 **NCLC 54**
See also Lorenzini, Carlo
See also CLR 5

Colman, George 1732-1794
See Glassco, John

Colt, Winchester Remington
See Hubbard, L(afayette) Ron(ald)

Colter, Cyrus 1910- **CLC 58**
See also BW 1; CA 65-68; CANR 10, 66; DLB 33

Colton, James
See Hansen, Joseph

Colum, Padraic 1881-1972 **CLC 28**
See also CA 73-76; 33-36R; CANR 35; CLR 36; MAICYA; MTCW 1; SATA 15

Colvin, James
See Moorcock, Michael (John)

Colwin, Laurie (E.) 1944-1992 **CLC 5, 13, 23, 84**
See also CA 89-92; 139; CANR 20, 46; DLBY 80; MTCW 1

Comfort, Alex(ander) 1920- **CLC 7; DAM POP**
See also CA 1-4R; CANR 1, 45; MTCW 1

Comfort, Montgomery
See Campbell, (John) Ramsey

Compton-Burnett, I(vy) 1884(?)-1969 **CLC 1, 3, 10, 15, 34; DAM NOV**
See also CA 1-4R; 25-28R; CANR 4; DLB 36; MTCW 1

Comstock, Anthony 1844-1915 **TCLC 13**
See also CA 110; 169

Comte, Auguste 1798-1857 **NCLC 54**

Conan Doyle, Arthur
See Doyle, Arthur Conan

Conde (Abellan), Carmen 1901-
See also CA 177; DLB 108; HLCS 1; HW 2

Conde, Maryse 1937- **CLC 52, 92; BLCS; DAM MULT**
See also Boucolon, Maryse
See also BW 2; MTCW 1

Condillac, Etienne Bonnot de 1714-1780 **LC 26**

Condon, Richard (Thomas) 1915-1996 **CLC 4, 6, 8, 10, 45, 100; DAM NOV**
See also BEST 90:3; CA 1-4R; 151; CAAS 1; CANR 2, 23; INT CANR-23; MTCW 1, 2

Confucius 551B.C.-479B.C. **CMLC 19; DA; DAB; DAC; DAM MST; WLCS**
See also DA3

Congreve, William 1670-1729 **LC 5, 21; DA; DAB; DAC; DAM DRAM, MST, POET; DC 2; WLC**
See also CDBLB 1660-1789; DLB 39, 84

Connell, Evan S(helby), Jr. 1924- **CLC 4, 6, 45; DAM NOV**
See also AAYA 7; CA 1-4R; CAAS 2; CANR 2, 39, 76; DLB 2; DLBY 81; MTCW 1, 2

Connelly, Marc(us Cook) 1890-1980 **CLC 7**
See also CA 85-88; 102; CANR 30; DLB 7; DLBY 80; SATA-Obit 25

Connor, Ralph **TCLC 31**
See also Gordon, Charles William
See also DLB 92

Conrad, Joseph 1857-1924 **TCLC 1, 6, 13, 25, 43, 57; DA; DAB; DAC; DAM MST, NOV; SSC 9; WLC**
See also AAYA 26; CA 104; 131; CANR 60; CDBLB 1890-1914; DA3; DLB 10, 34, 98, 156; MTCW 1, 2; SATA 27

Conrad, Robert Arnold
See Hart, Moss

Conroy, Pat
See Conroy, (Donald) Pat(rick)
See also MTCW 2

Conroy, (Donald) Pat(rick) 1945- **CLC 30, 74; DAM NOV, POP**
See also Conroy, Pat
See also AAYA 8; AITN 1; CA 85-88; CANR 24, 53; DA3; DLB 6; MTCW 1

Constant (de Rebecque), (Henri) Benjamin 1767-1830 **NCLC 6**
See also DLB 119

Conybeare, Charles Augustus
See Eliot, T(homas) S(tearns)

Cook, Michael 1933- **CLC 58**
See also CA 93-96; CANR 68; DLB 53

Cook, Robin 1940- **CLC 14; DAM POP**
See also AAYA 32; BEST 90:2; CA 108; 111; CANR 41; DA3; INT 111

Cook, Roy
See Silverberg, Robert

Cooke, Elizabeth 1948- **CLC 55**
See also CA 129

Cooke, John Esten 1830-1886 **NCLC 5**
See also DLB 3

Cooke, John Estes

See Baum, L(yman) Frank

Cooke, M. E.
See Creasey, John

Cooke, Margaret
See Creasey, John

Cook-Lynn, Elizabeth 1930- **CLC 93; DAM MULT**
See also CA 133; DLB 175; NNAL

Cooney, Ray **CLC 62**

Cooper, Douglas 1960- **CLC 86**

Cooper, Henry St. John
See Creasey, John

Cooper, J(oan) California (?)- **CLC 56; DAM MULT**
See also AAYA 12; BW 1; CA 125; CANR 55; DLB 212

Cooper, James Fenimore 1789-1851 **NCLC 1, 27, 54**
See also AAYA 22; CDALB 1640-1865; DA3; DLB 3; SATA 19

Coover, Robert (Lowell) 1932- **CLC 3, 7, 15, 32, 46, 87; DAM NOV; SSC 15**
See also CA 45-48; CANR 3, 37, 58; DLB 2; DLBY 81; MTCW 1, 2

Copeland, Stewart (Armstrong) 1952- **CLC 26**

Copernicus, Nicolaus 1473-1543 **LC 45**

Coppard, A(lfred) E(dgar) 1878-1957 **TCLC 5; SSC 21**
See also CA 114; 167; DLB 162; YABC 1

Coppee, Francois 1842-1908 **TCLC 25**
See also CA 170

Coppola, Francis Ford 1939- **CLC 16, 126**
See also CA 77-80; CANR 40, 78; DLB 44

Corbiere, Tristan 1845-1875 **NCLC 43**

Corcoran, Barbara 1911- **CLC 17**
See also AAYA 14; CA 21-24R; CAAS 2; CANR 11, 28, 48; CLR 50; DLB 52; JRDA; SAAS 20; SATA 3, 77

Cordelier, Maurice
See Giraudoux, (Hippolyte) Jean

Corelli, Marie 1855-1924 **TCLC 51**
See also Mackay, Mary
See also DLB 34, 156

Corman, Cid 1924- **CLC 9**
See also Corman, Sidney
See also CAAS 2; DLB 5, 193

Corman, Sidney 1924-
See Corman, Cid
See also CA 85-88; CANR 44; DAM POET

Cormier, Robert (Edmund) 1925- **CLC 12, 30; DA; DAB; DAC; DAM MST, NOV**
See also AAYA 3, 19; CA 1-4R; CANR 5, 23, 76; CDALB 1968-1988; CLR 12, 55; DLB 52; INT CANR-23; JRDA; MAICYA; MTCW 1, 2; SATA 10, 45, 83

Corn, Alfred (DeWitt III) 1943- **CLC 33**
See also CA 179; CAAE 179; CAAS 25; CANR 44; DLB 120; DLBY 80

Corneille, Pierre 1606-1684 **LC 28; DAB; DAM MST**

Cornwell, David (John Moore) 1931- **CLC 9, 15; DAM POP**
See also le Carre, John
See also CA 5-8R; CANR 13, 33, 59; DA3; MTCW 1, 2

Corso, (Nunzio) Gregory 1930- **CLC 1, 11**
See also CA 5-8R; CANR 41, 76; DA3; DLB 5, 16; MTCW 1, 2

Cortazar, Julio 1914-1984 **CLC 2, 3, 5, 10, 13, 15, 33, 34, 92; DAM MULT, NOV; HLC 1; SSC 7**
See also CA 21-24R; CANR 12, 32, 81; DA3; DLB 113; HW 1, 2; MTCW 1, 2

Corties, Hernan 1484-1547   LC 31
Corvinus, Jakob
    See Raabe, Wilhelm (Karl)
Corwin, Cecil
    See Kornbluth, C(yril) M.
Cosic, Dobrica 1921-   CLC 14
    See also CA 122; 138; DLB 181
Costain, Thomas B(ertram) 1885-1965CLC 30
    See also CA 5-8R; 25-28R; DLB 9
Costantini, Humberto 1924(?)-1987 CLC 49
    See also CA 131, 122; HW 1
Costello, Elvis 1955-   CLC 21
Costenoble, Philostene
    See Ghelderode, Michel de
Cotes, Cecil V.
    See Duncan, Sara Jeannette
Cotter, Joseph Seamon Sr. 1861-1949 TCLC
    28; BLC 1; DAM MULT
    See also BW 1; CA 124; DLB 50
Couch, Arthur Thomas Quiller
    See Quiller-Couch, SirArthur (Thomas)
Coulton, James
    See Hansen, Joseph
Couperus, Louis (Marie Anne) 1863-1923
    TCLC 15
    See also CA 115
Coupland, Douglas 1961-   CLC 85; DAC;
    DAM POP
    See also CA 142; CANR 57
Court, Wesli
    See Turco, Lewis (Putnam)
Courtenay, Bryce 1933-   CLC 59
    See also CA 138
Courtney, Robert
    See Ellison, Harlan (Jay)
Cousteau, Jacques-Yves 1910-1997 CLC 30
    See also CA 65-68; 159; CANR 15, 67; MTCW
    1; SATA 38, 98
Coventry, Francis 1725-1754   LC 46
Cowan, Peter (Walkinshaw) 1914-   SSC 28
    See also CA 21-24R; CANR 9, 25, 50, 83
Coward, Noel (Peirce) 1899-1973CLC 1, 9, 29,
    51; DAM DRAM
    See also AITN 1; CA 17-18; 41-44R; CANR
    35; CAP 2; CDBLB 1914-1945; DA3; DLB
    10; MTCW 1, 2 ·
Cowley, Abraham 1618-1667   LC 43
    See also DLB 131, 151
Cowley, Malcolm 1898-1989   CLC 39
    See also CA 5-8R; 128; CANR 3, 55; DLB 4,
    48; DLBY 81, 89; MTCW 1, 2
Cowper, William 1731-1800 NCLC 8; DAM
    POET
    See also DA3; DLB 104, 109
Cox, William Trevor 1928-   CLC 9, 14, 71;
    DAM NOV
    See also Trevor, William
    See also CA 9-12R; CANR 4, 37, 55, 76; DLB
    14; INT CANR-37; MTCW 1, 2
Coyne, P. J.
    See Masters, Hilary
Cozzens, James Gould 1903-1978 CLC 1, 4,
    11, 92
    See also CA 9-12R; 81-84; CANR 19; CDALB
    1941-1968; DLB 9; DLBD 2; DLBY 84, 97;
    MTCW 1, 2
Crabbe, George 1754-1832   NCLC 26
    See also DLB 93
Craddock, Charles Egbert
    See Murfree, Mary Noailles
Craig, A. A.
    See Anderson, Poul (William)
Craik, Dinah Maria (Mulock) 1826-1887

NCLC 38
    See also DLB 35, 163; MAICYA; SATA 34
Cram, Ralph Adams 1863-1942   TCLC 45
    See also CA 160
Crane, (Harold) Hart 1899-1932 TCLC 2, 5,
    80; DA; DAB; DAC; DAM MST, POET;
    PC 3; WLC
    See also CA 104; 127; CDALB 1917-1929;
    DA3; DLB 4, 48; MTCW 1, 2
Crane, R(onald) S(almon) 1886-1967CLC 27
    See also CA 85-88; DLB 63
Crane, Stephen (Townley) 1871-1900 T C L C
    11, 17, 32; DA; DAB; DAC; DAM MST,
    NOV, POET; SSC 7; WLC
    See also AAYA 21; CA 109; 140; CANR 84;
    CDALB 1865-1917; DA3; DLB 12, 54, 78;
    YABC 2
Cranshaw, Stanley
    See Fisher, Dorothy (Frances) Canfield
Crase, Douglas 1944-   CLC 58
    See also CA 106
Crashaw, Richard 1612(?)-1649   LC 24
    See also DLB 126
Craven, Margaret 1901-1980 CLC 17; DAC
    See also CA 103
Crawford, F(rancis) Marion 1854-1909
    TCLC 10
    See also CA 107; 168; DLB 71
Crawford, Isabella Valancy 1850-1887
    NCLC 12
    See also DLB 92
Crayon, Geoffrey
    See Irving, Washington
Creasey, John 1908-1973   .CLC 11
    See also CA 5-8R; 41-44R; CANR 8, 59; DLB
    77; MTCW 1
Crebillon, Claude Prosper Jolyot de (fils) 1707-
    1777   LC 1, 28
Credo
    See Creasey, John
Credo, Alvaro J. de
    See Prado (Calvo), Pedro
Creeiey, Robert (White) 1926-CLC 1, 2, 4, 8,
    11, 15, 36, 78; DAM POET
    See also CA 1-4R; CAAS 10; CANR 23, 43; DA3;
    DLB 5, 16, 169; DLBD 17; MTCW 1, 2
Crews, Harry (Eugene) 1935- CLC 6, 23, 49
    See also AITN 1; CA 25-28R; CANR 20, 57;
    DA3; DLB 6, 143, 185; MTCW 1, 2
Crichton, (John) Michael 1942-CLC 2, 6, 54,
    90; DAM NOV, POP
    See also AAYA 10; AITN 2; CA 25-28R; CANR
    13, 40, 54, 76; DA3; DLBY 81; INT CANR-
    13; JRDA; MTCW 1, 2; SATA 9, 88
Crispin, Edmund   CLC 22
    See also Montgomery, (Robert) Bruce
    See also DLB 87
Cristofer, Michael 1945(?)-   CLC 28; DAM
    DRAM
    See also CA 110; 152; DLB 7
Croce, Benedetto 1866-1952   TCLC 37
    See also CA 120; 155
Crockett, David 1786-1836   NCLC 8
    See also DLB 3, 11
Crockett, Davy
    See Crockett, David
Crofts, Freeman Wills 1879-1957   TCLC 55
    See also CA 115; DLB 77
Croker, John Wilson 1780-1857   NCLC 10
    See also DLB 110
Crommelynck, Fernand 1885-1970   CLC 75
    See also CA 89-92
Cromwell, Oliver 1599-1658   LC 43

Cronin, A(rchibald) J(oseph) 1896-1981
    CLC 32
    See also CA 1-4R; 102; CANR 5; DLB 191;
    SATA 47; SATA-Obit 25
Cross, Amanda
    See Heilbrun, Carolyn G(old)
Crothers, Rachel 1878(?)-1958   TCLC 19
    See also CA 113; DLB 7
Croves, Hal
    See Traven, B.
Crow Dog, Mary (Ellen) (?)-   CLC 93
    See also Brave Bird, Mary
    See also CA 154
Crowfield, Christopher
    See Stowe, Harriet (Elizabeth) Beecher
Crowley, Aleister   TCLC 7
    See also Crowley, Edward Alexander
Crowley, Edward Alexander 1875-1947
    See Crowley, Aleister
    See also CA 104
Crowley, John 1942-   CLC 57
    See also CA 61-64; CANR 43; DLBY 82;
    SATA 65
Crud
    See Crumb, R(obert)
Crumarums
    See Crumb, R(obert)
Crumb, R(obert) 1943-   CLC 17
    See also CA 106
Crumbum
    See Crumb, R(obert)
Crumski
    See Crumb, R(obert)
Crum the Bum
    See Crumb, R(obert)
Crunk
    See Crumb, R(obert)
Crustt
    See Crumb, R(obert)
Cruz, Victor Hernandez 1949-
    See also BW 2; CA 65-68; CAAS 17; CANR
    14, 32, 74; DAM MULT, POET; DLB 41;
    HLC 1; HW 1, 2; MTCW 1
Cryer, Gretchen (Kiger) 1935-   CLC 21
    See also CA 114; 123
Csath, Geza 1887-1919   TCLC 13
    See also CA 111
Cudlip, David R(ockwell) 1933-   CLC 34
    See also CA 177
Cullen, Countee 1903-1946TCLC 4, 37; BLC
    1; DA; DAC; DAM MST, MULT, POET;
    PC 20; WLCS
    See also BW 1; CA 108; 124; CDALB 1917-
    1929; DA3; DLB 4, 48, 51; MTCW 1, 2;
    SATA 18
Cum, R.
    See Crumb, R(obert)
Cummings, Bruce F(rederick) 1889-1919
    See Barbellion, W. N. P.
    See also CA 123
Cummings, E(dward) E(stlin) 1894-1962CLC
    1, 3, 8, 12, 15, 68; DA; DAB; DAC; DAM
    MST, POET; PC 5; WLC
    See also CA 73-76; CANR 31; CDALB 1929-
    1941; DA3; DLB 4, 48; MTCW 1, 2
Cunha, Euclides (Rodrigues Pimenta) da 1866-
    1909   TCLC 24
    See also CA 123
Cunningham, E. V.
    See Fast, Howard (Melvin)
Cunningham, J(ames) V(incent) 1911-1985
    CLC 3, 31
    See also CA 1-4R; 115; CANR 1, 72; DLB 5

Cunningham, Julia (Woolfolk) 1916- **CLC 12**
See also CA 9-12R; CANR 4, 19, 36; JRDA; MAICYA; SAAS 2; SATA 1, 26

Cunningham, Michael 1952-   **CLC 34**
See also CA 136

Cunninghame Graham, R(obert) B(ontine) 1852-1936   **TCLC 19**
See also Graham, R(obert) B(ontine) Cunninghame
See also CA 119; DLB 98

Currie, Ellen 19(?)-   **CLC 44**

Curtin, Philip
See Lowndes, Marie Adelaide (Belloc)

Curtis, Price
See Ellison, Harlan (Jay)

Cutrate, Joe
See Spiegelman, Art

Cynewulf c. 770-c. 840   **CMLC 23**

Czaczkes, Shmuel Yosef
See Agnon, S(hmuel) Y(osef Halevi)

Dabrowska, Maria (Szumska) 1889-1965
CLC 15
See also CA 106

Dabydeen, David 1955-   **CLC 34**
See also BW 1; CA 125; CANR 56

Dacey, Philip 1939-   **CLC 51**
See also CA 37-40R; CAAS 17; CANR 14, 32, 64; DLB 105

Dagerman, Stig (Halvard) 1923-1954
TCLC 17
See also CA 117; 155

Dahl, Roald 1916-1990 **CLC 1, 6, 18, 79; DAB; DAC; DAM MST, NOV, POP**
See also AAYA 15; CA 1-4R; 133; CANR 6, 32, 37, 62; CLR 1, 7, 41; DA3; DLB 139; JRDA; MAICYA; MTCW 1, 2; SATA 1, 26, 73; SATA-Obit 65

Dahlberg, Edward 1900-1977 **CLC 1, 7, 14**
See also CA 9-12R; 69-72; CANR 31, 62; DLB 48; MTCW 1

Daitch, Susan 1954-   **CLC 103**
See also CA 161

Dale, Colin   **TCLC 18**
See also Lawrence, T(homas) E(dward)

Dale, George E.
See Asimov, Isaac

Dalton, Roque 1935-1975
See also HLCS 1; HW 2

Daly, Elizabeth 1878-1967   **CLC 52**
See also CA 23-24; 25-28R; CANR 60; CAP 2

Daly, Maureen 1921-   **CLC 17**
See also AAYA 5; CANR 37, 83; JRDA; MAICYA; SAAS 1; SATA 2

Damas, Leon-Gontran 1912-1978 **CLC 84**
See also BW 1; CA 125; 73-76

Dana, Richard Henry Sr. 1787-1879 **NCLC 53**

Daniel, Samuel 1562(?)-1619   **LC 24**
See also DLB 62

Daniels, Brett
See Adler, Renata

Dannay, Frederic 1905-1982 **CLC 11; DAM POP**
See also Queen, Ellery
See also CA 1-4R; 107; CANR 1, 39; DLB 137; MTCW 1

D'Annunzio, Gabriele 1863-1938 **TCLC 6, 40**
See also CA 104; 155

Danois, N. le
See Gourmont, Remy (-Marie-Charles) de

Dante 1265-1321   **CMLC 3, 18; DA; DAB; DAC; DAM MST, POET; PC 21; WLCS**
See also DA3

d'Antibes, Germain

See Simenon, Georges (Jacques Christian)

Danticat, Edwidge 1969-   **CLC 94**
See also AAYA 29; CA 152; CANR 73; MTCW 1

Danvers, Dennis 1947-   **CLC 70**

Danziger, Paula 1944-   **CLC 21**
See also AAYA 4; CA 112; 115; CANR 37; CLR 20; JRDA; MAICYA; SATA 36, 63, 102; SATA-Brief 30

Da Ponte, Lorenzo 1749-1838   **NCLC 50**

Dario, Ruben 1867-1916   **TCLC 4; DAM MULT; HLC 1; PC 15**
See also CA 131; CANR 81; HW 1, 2; MTCW 1, 2

Darley, George 1795-1846   **NCLC 2**
See also DLB 96

Darrow, Clarence (Seward) 1857-1938
TCLC 81
See also CA 164

Darwin, Charles 1809-1882   **NCLC 57**
See also DLB 57, 166

Daryush, Elizabeth 1887-1977   **CLC 6, 19**
See also CA 49-52; CANR 3, 81; DLB 20

Dasgupta, Surendranath 1887-1952 **TCLC 81**
See also CA 157

Dashwood, Edmee Elizabeth Monica de la Pasture 1890-1943
See Delafield, E. M.
See also CA 119; 154

Daudet, (Louis Marie) Alphonse 1840-1897
NCLC 1
See also DLB 123

Daumal, Rene 1908-1944   **TCLC 14**
See also CA 114

Davenant, William 1606-1668   **LC 13**
See also DLB 58, 126

Davenport, Guy (Mattison, Jr.) 1927- **CLC 6, 14, 38; SSC 16**
See also CA 33-36R; CANR 23, 73; DLB 130

Davidson, Avram (James) 1923-1993
See Queen, Ellery
See also CA 101; 171; CANR 26; DLB 8

Davidson, Donald (Grady) 1893-1968 **CLC 2, 13, 19**
See also CA 5-8R; 25-28R; CANR 4, 84; DLB 45

Davidson, Hugh
See Hamilton, Edmond

Davidson, John 1857-1909   **TCLC 24**
See also CA 118; DLB 19

Davidson, Sara 1943-   **CLC 9**
See also CA 81-84; CANR 44, 68; DLB 185

Davie, Donald (Alfred) 1922-1995 **CLC 5, 8, 10, 31**
See also CA 1-4R; 149; CAAS 3; CANR 1, 44; DLB 27; MTCW 1

Davies, Ray(mond Douglas) 1944-   **CLC 21**
See also CA 116; 146

Davies, Rhys 1901-1978   **CLC 23**
See also CA 9-12R; 81-84; CANR 4; DLB 139, 191

Davies, (William) Robertson 1913-1995 **C L C 2, 7, 13, 25, 42, 75, 91; DA; DAB; DAC; DAM MST, NOV, POP; WLC**
See also BEST 89:2; CA 33-36R; 150; CANR 17, 42; DA3; DLB 68; INT CANR-17; MTCW 1, 2

Davies, Walter C.
See Kornbluth, C(yril) M.

Davies, William Henry 1871-1940 **TCLC 5**
See also CA 104; 179; DLB 19, 174

Davis, Angela (Yvonne) 1944-   **CLC 77; DAM MULT**

See also BW 2, 3; CA 57-60; CANR 10, 81; DA3

Davis, B. Lynch
See Bioy Casares, Adolfo; Borges, Jorge Luis

Davis, B. Lynch
See Bioy Casares, Adolfo

Davis, H(arold) L(enoir) 1894-1960 **CLC 49**
See also CA 178; 89-92; DLB 9, 206

Davis, Rebecca (Blaine) Harding 1831-1910
TCLC 6
See also CA 104; 179; DLB 74

Davis, Richard Harding 1864-1916 **TCLC 24**
See also CA 114; 179; DLB 12, 23, 78, 79, 189; DLBD 13

Davison, Frank Dalby 1893-1970   **CLC 15**
See also CA 116

Davison, Lawrence H.
See Lawrence, D(avid) H(erbert Richards)

Davison, Peter (Hubert) 1928-   **CLC 28**
See also CA 9-12R; CAAS 4; CANR 3, 43, 84; DLB 5

Davys, Mary 1674-1732   **LC 1, 46**
See also DLB 39

Dawson, Fielding 1930-   **CLC 6**
See also CA 85-88; DLB 130

Dawson, Peter
See Faust, Frederick (Schiller)

Day, Clarence (Shepard, Jr.) 1874-1935
TCLC 25
See also CA 108; DLB 11

Day, Thomas 1748-1789   **LC 1**
See also DLB 39; YABC 1

Day Lewis, C(ecil) 1904-1972 **CLC 1, 6, 10; DAM POET; PC 11**
See also Blake, Nicholas
See also CA 13-16; 33-36R; CANR 34; CAP 1; DLB 15, 20; MTCW 1, 2

Dazai Osamu 1909-1948   **TCLC 11**
See also Tsushima, Shuji
See also CA 164; DLB 182

de Andrade, Carlos Drummond 1892-1945
See Drummond de Andrade, Carlos

Deane, Norman
See Creasey, John

Deane, Seamus (Francis) 1940-   **CLC 122**
See also CA 118; CANR 42

de Beauvoir, Simone (Lucie Ernestine Marie Bertrand)
See Beauvoir, Simone (Lucie Ernestine Marie Bertrand) de

de Beer, P.
See Bosman, Herman Charles

de Brissac, Malcolm
See Dickinson, Peter (Malcolm)

de Chardin, Pierre Teilhard
See Teilhard de Chardin, (Marie Joseph) Pierre

Dee, John 1527-1608   **LC 20**

Deer, Sandra 1940-   **CLC 45**

De Ferrari, Gabriella 1941-   **CLC 65**
See also CA 146

Defoe, Daniel 1660(?)-1731   **LC 1, 42; DA; DAB; DAC; DAM MST, NOV; WLC**
See also AAYA 27; CDBLB 1660-1789; CLR 61; DA3; DLB 39, 95, 101; JRDA; MAICYA; SATA 22

de Gourmont, Remy(-Marie-Charles)
See Gourmont, Remy (-Marie-Charles) de

de Hartog, Jan 1914-   **CLC 19**
See also CA 1-4R; CANR 1

de Hostos, E. M.
See Hostos (y Bonilla), Eugenio Maria de

de Hostos, Eugenio M.
See Hostos (y Bonilla), Eugenio Maria de

Deighton, Len   **CLC 4, 7, 22, 46**

Drabble, Margaret 1939-CLC 2, 3, 5, 8, 10, 22, 53; DAB; DAC; DAM MST, NOV, POP
See also CA 13-16R; CANR 18, 35, 63; CDBLB 1960 to Present; DA3; DLB 14, 155; MTCW 1, 2; SATA 48
Drapier, M. B.
See Swift, Jonathan
Drayham, James
See Mencken, H(enry) L(ouis)
Drayton, Michael 1563-1631   LC 8; DAM POET
See also DLB 121
Dreadstone, Carl
See Campbell, (John) Ramsey
Dreiser, Theodore (Herman Albert) 1871-1945
TCLC 10, 18, 35, 83; DA; DAC; DAM MST, NOV; SSC 30; WLC
See also CA 106; 132; CDALB 1865-1917; DA3; DLB 9, 12, 102, 137; DLBD 1; MTCW 1, 2
Drexler, Rosalyn 1926-   CLC 2, 6
See also CA 81-84; CANR 68
Dreyer, Carl Theodor 1889-1968   CLC 16
See also CA 116
Drieu la Rochelle, Pierre(-Eugene) 1893-1945
TCLC 21
See also CA 117; DLB 72
Drinkwater, John 1882-1937   TCLC 57
See also CA 109; 149; DLB 10, 19, 149
Drop Shot
See Cable, George Washington
Droste-Hulshoff, Annette Freiin von 1797-1848
NCLC 3
See also DLB 133
Drummond, Walter
See Silverberg, Robert
Drummond, William Henry 1854-1907
TCLC 25
See also CA 160; DLB 92
Drummond de Andrade, Carlos 1902-1987
CLC 18
See also Andrade, Carlos Drummond de
See also CA 132; 123
Drury, Allen (Stuart) 1918-1998   CLC 37
See also CA 57-60; 170; CANR 18, 52; INT CANR-18
Dryden, John 1631-1700LC 3, 21; DA; DAB; DAC; DAM DRAM, MST, POET; DC 3; PC 25; WLC
See also CDBLB 1660-1789; DLB 80, 101, 131
Duberman, Martin (Bauml) 1930-   CLC 8
See also CA 1-4R; CANR 2, 63
Dubie, Norman (Evans) 1945-   CLC 36
See also CA 69-72; CANR 12; DLB 120
Du Bois, W(illiam) E(dward) B(urghardt) 1868-1963   CLC 1, 2, 13, 64, 96; BLC 1; DA; DAC; DAM MST, MULT, NOV; WLC
See also BW 1, 3; CA 85-88; CANR 34, 82; CDALB 1865-1917; DA3; DLB 47, 50, 91; MTCW 1, 2; SATA 42
Dubus, Andre 1936-1999   CLC 13, 36, 97; SSC 15
See also CA 21-24R; 177; CANR 17; DLB 130; INT CANR-17
Duca Minimo
See D'Annunzio, Gabriele
Ducharme, Rejean 1941-   CLC 74
See also CA 165; DLB 60
Duclos, Charles Pinot 1704-1772   LC 1
Dudek, Louis 1918-   CLC 11, 19
See also CA 45-48; CAAS 14; CANR 1; DLB 88
Duerrenmatt, Friedrich 1921-1990 CLC 1, 4, 8, 11, 15, 43, 102; DAM DRAM

See also CA 17-20R; CANR 33; DLB 69, 124; MTCW 1, 2
Duffy, Bruce 1953(?)-   CLC 50
See also CA 172
Duffy, Maureen 1933-   CLC 37
See also CA 25-28R; CANR 33, 68; DLB 14; MTCW 1
Dugan, Alan 1923-   CLC 2, 6
See also CA 81-84; DLB 5
du Gard, Roger Martin
See Martin du Gard, Roger
Duhamel, Georges 1884-1966   CLC 8
See also CA 81-84; 25-28R; CANR 35; DLB 65; MTCW 1
Dujardin, Edouard (Emile Louis) 1861-1949
TCLC 13
See also CA 109; DLB 123
Dulles, John Foster 1888-1959   TCLC 72
See also CA 115; 149
Dumas, Alexandre (pere)
See Dumas, Alexandre (Davy de la Pailleterie)
Dumas, Alexandre (Davy de la Pailleterie) 1802-1870NCLC 11, 71; DA; DAB; DAC; DAM MST, NOV; WLC
See also DA3; DLB 119, 192; SATA 18
Dumas, Alexandre (fils) 1824-1895NCLC 71; DC 1
See also AAYA 22; DLB 192
Dumas, Claudine
See Malzberg, Barry N(athaniel)
Dumas, Henry L. 1934-1968   CLC 6, 62
See also BW 1; CA 85-88; DLB 41
du Maurier, Daphne 1907-1989CLC 6, 11, 59; DAB; DAC; DAM MST, POP; SSC 18
See also CA 5-8R; 128; CANR 6, 55; DA3; DLB 191; MTCW 1, 2; SATA 27; SATA-Obit 60
Dunbar, Paul Laurence 1872-1906 TCLC 2, 12; BLC 1; DA; DAC; DAM MST, MULT, POET; PC 5; SSC 8; WLC
See also BW 1, 3; CA 104; 124; CANR 79; CDALB 1865-1917; DA3; DLB 50, 54, 78; SATA 34
Dunbar, William 1460(?)-1530(?)   LC 20
See also DLB 132, 146
Duncan, Dora Angela
See Duncan, Isadora
Duncan, Isadora 1877(?)-1927   TCLC 68
See also CA 118; 149
Duncan, Lois 1934-   CLC 26
See also AAYA 4; CA 1-4R; CANR 2, 23, 36; CLR 29; JRDA; MAICYA; SAAS 2; SATA 1, 36, 75
Duncan, Robert (Edward) 1919-1988 CLC 1, 2, 4, 7, 15, 41, 55; DAM POET; PC 2
See also CA 9-12R; 124; CANR 28, 62; DLB 5, 16, 193; MTCW 1, 2
Duncan, Sara Jeannette 1861-1922 TCLC 60
See also CA 157; DLB 92
Dunlap, William 1766-1839   NCLC 2
See also DLB 30, 37, 59
Dunn, Douglas (Eaglesham) 1942- CLC 6, 40
See also CA 45-48; CANR 2, 33; DLB 40; MTCW 1
Dunn, Katherine (Karen) 1945-   CLC 71
See also CA 33-36R; CANR 72; MTCW 1
Dunn, Stephen 1939-   CLC 36
See also CA 33-36R; CANR 12, 48, 53; DLB 105
Dunne, Finley Peter 1867-1936   TCLC 28
See also CA 108; 178; DLB 11, 23
Dunne, John Gregory 1932-   CLC 28
See also CA 25-28R; CANR 14, 50; DLBY 80
Dunsany, Edward John Moreton Drax Plunkett 1878-1957

See Dunsany, Lord
See also CA 104; 148; DLB 10; MTCW 1
Dunsany, Lord   TCLC 2, 59
See also Dunsany, Edward John Moreton Drax Plunkett
See also DLB 77, 153, 156
du Perry, Jean
See Simenon, Georges (Jacques Christian)
Durang, Christopher (Ferdinand) 1949-C L C 27, 38
See also CA 105; CANR 50, 76; MTCW 1
Duras, Marguerite 1914-1996CLC 3, 6, 11, 20, 34, 40, 68, 100
See also CA 25-28R; 151; CANR 50; DLB 83; MTCW 1, 2
Durban, (Rosa) Pam 1947-   CLC 39
See also CA 123
Durcan, Paul 1944-CLC 43, 70; DAM POET
See also CA 134
Durkheim, Emile 1858-1917   TCLC 55
Durrell, Lawrence (George) 1912-1990 C L C 1, 4, 6, 8, 13, 27, 41; DAM NOV
See also CA 9-12R; 132; CANR 40, 77; CDBLB 1945-1960; DLB 15, 27, 204; DLBY 90; MTCW 1, 2
Durrenmatt, Friedrich
See Duerrenmatt, Friedrich
Dutt, Toru 1856-1877   NCLC 29
Dwight, Timothy 1752-1817   NCLC 13
See also DLB 37
Dworkin, Andrea 1946-   CLC 43
See also CA 77-80; CAAS 21; CANR 16, 39, 76; INT CANR-16; MTCW 1, 2
Dwyer, Deanna
See Koontz, Dean R(ay)
Dwyer, K. R.
See Koontz, Dean R(ay)
Dwyer, Thomas A. 1923-   CLC 114
See also CA 115
Dye, Richard
See De Voto, Bernard (Augustine)
Dylan, Bob 1941-   CLC 3, 4, 6, 12, 77
See also CA 41-44R; DLB 16
E. V. L.
See Lucas, E(dward) V(errall)
Eagleton, Terence (Francis) 1943-
See Eagleton, Terry
See also CA 57-60; CANR 7, 23, 68; MTCW 1, 2
Eagleton, Terry   CLC 63
See also Eagleton, Terence (Francis)
See also MTCW 1
Early, Jack
See Scoppettone, Sandra
East, Michael
See West, Morris L(anglo)
Eastaway, Edward
See Thomas, (Philip) Edward
Eastlake, William (Derry) 1917-1997 CLC 8
See also CA 5-8R; 158; CAAS 1; CANR 5, 63; DLB 6, 206; INT CANR-5
Eastman, Charles A(lexander) 1858-1939
TCLC 55; DAM MULT
See also CA 179; DLB 175; NNAL; YABC 1
Eberhart, Richard (Ghormley) 1904- CLC 3, 11, 19, 56; DAM POET
See also CA 1-4R; CANR 2; CDALB 1941-1968; DLB 48; MTCW 1
Eberstadt, Fernanda 1960-   CLC 39
See also CA 136; CANR 69
Echegaray (y Eizaguirre), Jose (Maria Waldo) 1832-1916   TCLC 4; HLCS 1
See also CA 104; CANR 32; HW 1; MTCW 1

Echeverria, (Jose) Esteban (Antonino) 1805-1851   **NCLC 18**

Echo
See Proust, (Valentin-Louis-George-Eugene-) Marcel

Eckert, Allan W. 1931-   **CLC 17**
See also AAYA 18; CA 13-16R; CANR 14, 45; INT CANR-14; SAAS 21; SATA 29, 91; SATA-Brief 27

Eckhart, Meister 1260(?)-1328(?)   **CMLC 9**
See also DLB 115

Eckmar, F. R.
See de Hartog, Jan

Eco, Umberto 1932-**CLC 28, 60; DAM NOV, POP**
See also BEST 90:1; CA 77-80; CANR 12, 33, 55; DA3; DLB 196; MTCW 1, 2

Eddison, E(ric) R(ucker) 1882-1945**TCLC 15**
See also CA 109; 156

Eddy, Mary (Ann Morse) Baker 1821-1910 **TCLC 71**
See also CA 113; 174

Edel, (Joseph) Leon 1907-1997   **CLC 29, 34**
See also CA 1-4R; 161; CANR 1, 22; DLB 103; INT CANR-22

Eden, Emily 1797-1869   **NCLC 10**

Edgar, David 1948-   **CLC 42; DAM DRAM**
See also CA 57-60; CANR 12, 61; DLB 13; MTCW 1

Edgerton, Clyde (Carlyle) 1944-   **CLC 39**
See also AAYA 17; CA 118; 134; CANR 64; INT 134

Edgeworth, Maria 1768-1849   **NCLC 1, 51**
See also DLB 116, 159, 163; SATA 21

Edison, Thomas 1847-1931   **TCLC 96**

Edmonds, Paul
See Kuttner, Henry

Edmonds, Walter D(umaux) 1903-1998 **CLC 35**
See also CA 5-8R; CANR 2; DLB 9; MAICYA; SAAS 4; SATA 1, 27; SATA-Obit 99

Edmondson, Wallace
See Ellison, Harlan (Jay)

Edson, Russell   **CLC 13**
See also CA 33-36R

Edwards, Bronwen Elizabeth
See Rose, Wendy

Edwards, G(erald) B(asil) 1899-1976**CLC 25**
See also CA 110

Edwards, Gus 1939-   **CLC 43**
See also CA 108; INT 108

Edwards, Jonathan 1703-1758**LC 7, 54; DA; DAC; DAM MST**
See also DLB 24

Efron, Marina Ivanovna Tsvetaeva
See Tsvetaeva (Efron), Marina (Ivanovna)

Ehle, John (Marsden, Jr.) 1925-   **CLC 27**
See also CA 9-12R

Ehrenbourg, Ilya (Grigoryevich)
See Ehrenburg, Ilya (Grigoryevich)

Ehrenburg, Ilya (Grigoryevich) 1891-1967 **CLC 18, 34, 62**
See also CA 102; 25-28R

Ehrenburg, Ilyo (Grigoryevich)
See Ehrenburg, Ilya (Grigoryevich)

Ehrenreich, Barbara 1941-   **CLC 110**
See also BEST 90:4; CA 73-76; CANR 16, 37, 62; MTCW 1, 2

Eich, Guenter 1907-1972   **CLC 15**
See also CA 111; 93-96; DLB 69, 124

Eichendorff, Joseph Freiherr von 1788-1857 **NCLC 8**
See also DLB 90

Eigner, Larry   **CLC 9**
See also Eigner, Laurence (Joel)
See also CAAS 23; DLB 5

Eigner, Laurence (Joel) 1927-1996
See Eigner, Larry
See also CA 9-12R; 151; CANR 6, 84; DLB 193

Einstein, Albert 1879-1955   **TCLC 65**
See also CA 121; 133; MTCW 1, 2

Eiseley, Loren Corey 1907-1977   **CLC 7**
See also AAYA 5; CA 1-4R; 73-76; CANR 6; DLBD 17

Eisenstadt, Jill 1963-   **CLC 50**
See also CA 140

Eisenstein, Sergei (Mikhailovich) 1898-1948 **TCLC 57**
See also CA 114; 149

Eisner, Simon
See Kornbluth, C(yril) M.

Ekeloef, (Bengt) Gunnar 1907-1968 **CLC 27; DAM POET; PC 23**
See also CA 123; 25-28R

Ekelof, (Bengt) Gunnar
See Ekeloef, (Bengt) Gunnar

Ekelund, Vilhelm 1880-1949   **TCLC 75**

Ekwensi, C. O. D.
See Ekwensi, Cyprian (Odiatu Duaka)

Ekwensi, Cyprian (Odiatu Duaka) 1921-**CLC 4; BLC 1; DAM MULT**
See also BW 2, 3; CA 29-32R; CANR 18, 42, 74; DLB 117; MTCW 1, 2; SATA 66

Elaine   **TCLC 18**
See also Leverson, Ada

El Crummo
See Crumb, R(obert)

Elder, Lonne III 1931-1996   **DC 8**
See also BLC 1; BW 1, 3; CA 81-84; 152; CANR 25; DAM MULT; DLB 7, 38, 44

Elia
See Lamb, Charles

Eliade, Mircea 1907-1986   **CLC 19**
See also CA 65-68; 119; CANR 30, 62; MTCW 1

Eliot, A. D.
See Jewett, (Theodora) Sarah Orne

Eliot, Alice
See Jewett, (Theodora) Sarah Orne

Eliot, Dan
See Silverberg, Robert

Eliot, George 1819-1880 **NCLC 4, 13, 23, 41, 49; DA; DAB; DAC; DAM MST, NOV; PC 20; WLC**
See also CDBLB 1832-1890; DA3; DLB 21, 35, 55

Eliot, John 1604-1690   **LC 5**
See also DLB 24

Eliot, T(homas) S(tearns) 1888-1965**CLC 1, 2, 3, 6, 9, 10, 13, 15, 24, 34, 41, 55, 57, 113; DA; DAB; DAC; DAM DRAM, MST, POET; PC 5; WLC**
See also AAYA 28; CA 5-8R; 25-28R; CANR 41; CDALB 1929-1941; DA3; DLB 7, 10, 45, 63; DLBY 88; MTCW 1, 2

Elizabeth 1866-1941   **TCLC 41**

Elkin, Stanley L(awrence) 1930-1995 **CLC 4, 6, 9, 14, 27, 51, 91; DAM NOV, POP; SSC 12**
See also CA 9-12R; 148; CANR 8, 46; DLB 2, 28; DLBY 80; INT CANR-8; MTCW 1, 2

Elledge, Scott   **CLC 34**

Elliot, Don
See Silverberg, Robert

Elliott, Don
See Silverberg, Robert

Elliott, George P(aul) 1918-1980   **CLC 2**
See also CA 1-4R; 97-100; CANR 2

Elliott, Janice 1931-   **CLC 47**
See also CA 13-16R; CANR 8, 29, 84; DLB 14

Elliott, Sumner Locke 1917-1991   **CLC 38**
See also CA 5-8R; 134; CANR 2, 21

Elliott, William
See Bradbury, Ray (Douglas)

Ellis, A. E.   **CLC 7**

Ellis, Alice Thomas   **CLC 40**
See also Haycraft, Anna
See also DLB 194; MTCW 1

Ellis, Bret Easton 1964-**CLC 39, 71, 117; DAM POP**
See also AAYA 2; CA 118; 123; CANR 51, 74; DA3; INT 123; MTCW 1

Ellis, (Henry) Havelock 1859-1939 **TCLC 14**
See also CA 109; 169; DLB 190

Ellis, Landon
See Ellison, Harlan (Jay)

Ellis, Trey 1962-   **CLC 55**
See also CA 146

Ellison, Harlan (Jay) 1934-   **CLC 1, 13, 42; DAM POP; SSC 14**
See also AAYA 29; CA 5-8R; CANR 5, 46; DLB 8; INT CANR-5; MTCW 1, 2

Ellison, Ralph (Waldo) 1914-1994 **CLC 1, 3, 11, 54, 86, 114; BLC 1; DA; DAB; DAC; DAM MST, MULT, NOV; SSC 26; WLC**
See also AAYA 19; BW 1, 3; CA 9-12R; 145; CANR 24, 53; CDALB 1941-1968; DA3; DLB 2, 76; DLBY 94; MTCW 1, 2

Ellmann, Lucy (Elizabeth) 1956-   **CLC 61**
See also CA 128

Ellmann, Richard (David) 1918-1987**CLC 50**
See also BEST 89:2; CA 1-4R; 122; CANR 2, 28, 61; DLB 103; DLBY 87; MTCW 1, 2

Elman, Richard (Martin) 1934-1997 **CLC 19**
See also CA 17-20R; 163; CAAS 3; CANR 47

Elron
See Hubbard, L(afayette) Ron(ald)

Eluard, Paul   **TCLC 7, 41**
See also Grindel, Eugene

Elyot, Sir Thomas 1490(?)-1546   **LC 11**

Elytis, Odysseus 1911-1996 **CLC 15, 49, 100; DAM POET; PC 21**
See also CA 102; 151; MTCW 1, 2

Emecheta, (Florence Onye) Buchi 1944-**CLC 14, 48; BLC 2; DAM MULT**
See also BW 2, 3; CA 81-84; CANR 27, 81; DA3; DLB 117; MTCW 1, 2; SATA 66

Emerson, Mary Moody 1774-1863 **NCLC 66**

Emerson, Ralph Waldo 1803-1882 **NCLC 1, 38; DA; DAB; DAC; DAM MST, POET; PC 18; WLC**
See also CDALB 1640-1865; DA3; DLB 1, 59, 73

Eminescu, Mihail 1850-1889   **NCLC 33**

Empson, William 1906-1984   **CLC 3, 8, 19, 33, 34**
See also CA 17-20R; 112; CANR 31, 61; DLB 20; MTCW 1, 2

Enchi, Fumiko (Ueda) 1905-1986   **CLC 31**
See also CA 129; 121; DLB 182

Ende, Michael (Andreas Helmuth) 1929-1995 **CLC 31**
See also CA 118; 124; 149; CANR 36; CLR 14; DLB 75; MAICYA; SATA 61; SATA-Brief 42; SATA-Obit 86

Endo, Shusaku 1923-1996 **CLC 7, 14, 19, 54, 99; DAM NOV**
See also CA 29-32R; 153; CANR 21, 54; DA3; DLB 182; MTCW 1, 2

Fecamps, Elise
  See Creasey, John
Federman, Raymond 1928-   **CLC 6, 47**
  See also CA 17-20R; CAAS 8; CANR 10, 43,
  83; DLBY 80
Federspiel, J(uerg) F. 1931-   **CLC 42**
  See also CA 146
Feiffer, Jules (Ralph) 1929-   **CLC 2, 8, 64;**
    DAM DRAM
  See also AAYA 3; CA 17-20R; CANR 30, 59;
  DLB 7, 44; INT CANR-30; MTCW 1; SATA
  8, 61, 111
Feige, Hermann Albert Otto Maximilian
  See Traven, B.
Feinberg, David B. 1956-1994   **CLC 59**
  See also CA 135; 147
Feinstein, Elaine 1930-   **CLC 36**
  See also CA 69-72; CAAS 1; CANR 31, 68;
  DLB 14, 40; MTCW 1
Feldman, Irving (Mordecai) 1928-   **CLC 7**
  See also CA 1-4R; CANR 1; DLB 169
Felix-Tchicaya, Gerald
  See Tchicaya, Gerald Felix
Fellini, Federico 1920-1993   **CLC 16, 85**
  See also CA 65-68; 143; CANR 33
Felsen, Henry Gregor 1916-1995   **CLC 17**
  See also CA 1-4R; 180; CANR 1; SAAS 2;
  SATA 1
Fenno, Jack
  See Calisher, Hortense
Fenollosa, Ernest (Francisco) 1853-1908
    TCLC 91
Fenton, James Martin 1949-   **CLC 32**
  See also CA 102; DLB 40
Ferber, Edna 1887-1968   **CLC 18, 93**
  See also AITN 1; CA 5-8R; 25-28R; CANR 68;
  DLB 9, 28, 86; MTCW 1, 2; SATA 7
Ferguson, Helen
  See Kavan, Anna
Ferguson, Samuel 1810-1886   **NCLC 33**
  See also DLB 32
Fergusson, Robert 1750-1774   **LC 29**
  See also DLB 109
Ferling, Lawrence
  See Ferlinghetti, Lawrence (Monsanto)
Ferlinghetti, Lawrence (Monsanto) 1919(?)-
    CLC 2, 6, 10, 27, 111; DAM POET; PC 1
  See also CA 5-8R; CANR 3, 41, 73; CDALB
  1941-1968; DA3; DLB 5, 16; MTCW 1, 2
Fernandez, Vicente Garcia Huidobro
  See Huidobro Fernandez, Vicente Garcia
Ferre, Rosario 1942-   **SSC 36; HLCS 1**
  See also CA 131; CANR 55, 81; DLB 145; HW
  1, 2; MTCW 1
Ferrer, Gabriel (Francisco Victor) Miro
  See Miro (Ferrer), Gabriel (Francisco Victor)
Ferrier, Susan (Edmonstone) 1782-1854
    NCLC 8
  See also DLB 116
Ferrigno, Robert 1948(?)-   **CLC 65**
  See also CA 140
Ferron, Jacques 1921-1985   **CLC 94; DAC**
  See also CA 117; 129; DLB 60
Feuchtwanger, Lion 1884-1958   **TCLC 3**
  See also CA 104; DLB 66
Feuillet, Octave 1821-1890   **NCLC 45**
  See also DLB 192
Feydeau, Georges (Leon Jules Marie) 1862-
  1921   **TCLC 22; DAM DRAM**
  See also CA 113; 152; CANR 84; DLB 192
Fichte, Johann Gottlieb 1762-1814 **NCLC 62**
  See also DLB 90
Ficino, Marsilio 1433-1499   **LC 12**

Fiedeler, Hans
  See Doeblin, Alfred
Fiedler, Leslie A(aron) 1917-   **CLC 4, 13, 24**
  See also CA 9-12R; CANR 7, 63; DLB 28, 67;
  MTCW 1, 2
Field, Andrew 1938-   **CLC 44**
  See also CA 97-100; CANR 25
Field, Eugene 1850-1895   **NCLC 3**
  See also DLB 23, 42, 140; DLBD 13; MAICYA;
  SATA 16
Field, Gans T.
  See Wellman, Manly Wade
Field, Michael 1915-1971   **TCLC 43**
  See also CA 29-32R
Field, Peter
  See Hobson, Laura Z(ametkin)
Fielding, Henry 1707-1754   **LC 1, 46; DA;**
    DAB; DAC; DAM DRAM, MST, NOV;
    WLC
  See also CDBLB 1660-1789; DA3; DLB 39,
  84, 101
Fielding, Sarah 1710-1768   **LC 1, 44**
  See also DLB 39
Fields, W. C. 1880-1946   **TCLC 80**
  See also DLB 44
Fierstein, Harvey (Forbes) 1954-   **CLC 33;**
    DAM DRAM, POP
  See also CA 123; 129; DA3
Figes, Eva 1932-   **CLC 31**
  See also CA 53-56; CANR 4, 44, 83; DLB 14
Finch, Anne 1661-1720   **LC 3; PC 21**
  See also DLB 95
Finch, Robert (Duer Claydon) 1900- **CLC 18**
  See also CA 57-60; CANR 9, 24, 49; DLB 88
Findley, Timothy 1930- **CLC 27, 102; DAC;**
    DAM MST
  See also CA 25-28R; CANR 12, 42, 69; DLB 53
Fink, William
  See Mencken, H(enry) L(ouis)
Firbank, Louis 1942-
  See Reed, Lou
  See also CA 117
Firbank, (Arthur Annesley) Ronald 1886-1926
    TCLC 1
  See also CA 104, 177; DLB 36
Fisher, Dorothy (Frances) Canfield 1879-1958
    TCLC 87
  See also CA 114; 136; CANR 80; DLB 9, 102;
  MAICYA; YABC 1
Fisher, M(ary) F(rances) K(ennedy) 1908-1992
    CLC 76, 87
  See also CA 77-80; 138; CANR 44; MTCW 1
Fisher, Roy 1930-   **CLC 25**
  See also CA 81-84; CAAS 10; CANR 16;
  DLB 40
Fisher, Rudolph 1897-1934 **TCLC 11; BLC 2;**
    DAM MULT; SSC 25
  See also BW 1, 3; CA 107; 124; CANR 80; DLB
  51, 102
Fisher, Vardis (Alvero) 1895-1968   **CLC 7**
  See also CA 5-8R; 25-28R; CANR 68; DLB
  9, 206
Fiske, Tarleton
  See Bloch, Robert (Albert)
Fitch, Clarke
  See Sinclair, Upton (Beall)
Fitch, John IV
  See Cormier, Robert (Edmund)
Fitzgerald, Captain Hugh
  See Baum, L(yman) Frank
FitzGerald, Edward 1809-1883   **NCLC 9**
  See also DLB 32
Fitzgerald, F(rancis) Scott (Key) 1896-1940

TCLC 1, 6, 14, 28, 55; DA; DAB; DAC;
    DAM MST, NOV; SSC 6, 31; WLC
  See also AAYA 24; AITN 1; CA 110; 123;
  CDALB 1917-1929; DA3; DLB 4, 9, 86;
  DLBD 1, 15, 16; DLBY 81, 96; MTCW
  1, 2
Fitzgerald, Penelope 1916-   **CLC 19, 51, 61**
  See also CA 85-88; CAAS 10; CANR 56, 86;
  DLB 14, 194; MTCW 2
Fitzgerald, Robert (Stuart) 1910-1985 **CLC 39**
  See also CA 1-4R; 114; CANR 1; DLBY 80
FitzGerald, Robert D(avid) 1902-1987 **CLC 19**
  See also CA 17-20R
Fitzgerald, Zelda (Sayre) 1900-1948 **TCLC 52**
  See also CA 117; 126; DLBY 84
Flanagan, Thomas (James Bonner) 1923-
    CLC 25, 52
  See also CA 108; CANR 55; DLBY 80; INT
  108; MTCW 1
Flaubert, Gustave 1821-1880 **NCLC 2, 10, 19,**
    62, 66; DA; DAB; DAC; DAM MST, NOV;
    SSC 11; WLC
  See also DA3; DLB 119
Flecker, Herman Elroy
  See Flecker, (Herman) James Elroy
Flecker, (Herman) James Elroy 1884-1915
    TCLC 43
  See also CA 109; 150; DLB 10, 19
Fleming, Ian (Lancaster) 1908-1964   **CLC 3,**
    30; DAM POP
  See also AAYA 26; CA 5-8R; CANR 59;
  CDBLB 1945-1960; DA3; DLB 87, 201;
  MTCW 1, 2; SATA 9
Fleming, Thomas (James) 1927-   **CLC 37**
  See also CA 5-8R; CANR 10; INT CANR-10;
  SATA 8
Fletcher, John 1579-1625   **LC 33; DC 6**
  See also CDBLB Before 1660, DLB 58
Fletcher, John Gould 1886-1950   **TCLC 35**
  See also CA 107; 167; DLB 4, 45
Fleur, Paul
  See Pohl, Frederik
Flooglebuckle, Al
  See Spiegelman, Art
Flying Officer X
  See Bates, H(erbert) E(rnest)
Fo, Dario 1926- **CLC 32, 109; DAM DRAM;**
    DC 10
  See also CA 116; 128; CANR 68; DA3; DLBY
  97; MTCW 1, 2
Fogarty, Jonathan Titulescu Esq.
  See Farrell, James T(homas)
Follett, Ken(neth Martin) 1949-   **CLC 18;**
    DAM NOV, POP
  See also AAYA 6; BEST 89:4; CA 81-84; CANR
  13, 33, 54; DA3; DLB 87; DLBY 81; INT
  CANR-33; MTCW 1
Fontane, Theodor 1819-1898   **NCLC 26**
  See also DLB 129
Foote, Horton 1916- **CLC 51, 91; DAM DRAM**
  See also CA 73-76; CANR 34, 51; DA3; DLB
  26; INT CANR-34
Foote, Shelby 1916- **CLC 75; DAM NOV, POP**
  See also CA 5-8R; CANR 3, 45, 74; DA3; DLB
  2, 17; MTCW 2
Forbes, Esther 1891-1967   **CLC 12**
  See also AAYA 17; CA 13-14; 25-28R; CAP 1;
  CLR 27; DLB 22; JRDA; MAICYA; SATA
  2, 100
Forche, Carolyn (Louise) 1950- **CLC 25, 83,**
    86; DAM POET; PC 10
  See also CA 109; 117; CANR 50, 74; DA3; DLB
  5, 193; INT 117; MTCW 1

Gay, John 1685-1732 **LC 49; DAM DRAM**
    See also DLB 84, 95
Gay, Oliver
    See Gogarty, Oliver St. John
Gaye, Marvin (Penze) 1939-1984 **CLC 26**
    See also CA 112
Gebler, Carlo (Ernest) 1954- **CLC 39**
    See also CA 119; 133
Gee, Maggie (Mary) 1948- **CLC 57**
    See also CA 130; DLB 207
Gee, Maurice (Gough) 1931- **CLC 29**
    See also CA 97-100; CANR 67; CLR 56; SATA
    46, 101
Gelbart, Larry (Simon) 1923- **CLC 21, 61**
    See also CA 73-76; CANR 45
Gelber, Jack 1932- **CLC 1, 6, 14, 79**
    See also CA 1-4R; CANR 2; DLB 7
Gellhorn, Martha (Ellis) 1908-1998**CLC 14, 60**
    See also CA 77-80; 164; CANR 44; DLBY
    82, 98
Genet, Jean 1910-1986**CLC 1, 2, 5, 10, 14, 44,**
    46; DAM DRAM
    See also CA 13-16R; CANR 18; DA3; DLB 72;
    DLBY 86; MTCW 1, 2
Gent, Peter 1942- **CLC 29**
    See also AITN 1; CA 89-92; DLBY 82
Gentile, Giovanni 1875-1944 **TCLC 96**
    See also CA 119
Gentlewoman in New England, A
    See Bradstreet, Anne
Gentlewoman in Those Parts, A
    See Bradstreet, Anne
George, Jean Craighead 1919- **CLC 35**
    See also AAYA 8; CA 5-8R; CANR 25; CLR 1;
    DLB 52; JRDA; MAICYA; SATA 2, 68
George, Stefan (Anton) 1868-1933**TCLC 2, 14**
    See also CA 104
Georges, Georges Martin
    See Simenon, Georges (Jacques Christian)
Gerhardi, William Alexander
    See Gerhardie, William Alexander
Gerhardie, William Alexander 1895-1977
    CLC 5
    See also CA 25-28R; 73-76; CANR 18; DLB 36
Gerstler, Amy 1956- **CLC 70**
    See also CA 146
Gertler, T. **CLC 34**
    See also CA 116; 121; INT 121
Ghalib **NCLC 39, 78**
    See also Ghalib, Hsadullah Khan
Ghalib, Hsadullah Khan 1797-1869
    See Ghalib
    See also DAM POET
Ghelderode, Michel de 1898-1962 **CLC 6, 11;**
    DAM DRAM
    See also CA 85-88; CANR 40, 77
Ghiselin, Brewster 1903- **CLC 23**
    See also CA 13-16R; CAAS 10; CANR 13
Ghose, Aurabinda 1872-1950 **TCLC 63**
    See also CA 163
Ghose, Zulfikar 1935- **CLC 42**
    See also CA 65-68; CANR 67
Ghosh, Amitav 1956- **CLC 44**
    See also CA 147; CANR 80
Giacosa, Giuseppe 1847-1906 **TCLC 7**
    See also CA 104
Gibb, Lee
    See Waterhouse, Keith (Spencer)
Gibbon, Lewis Grassic **TCLC 4**
    See also Mitchell, James Leslie
Gibbons, Kaye 1960- **CLC 50, 88; DAM POP**
    See also CA 151; CANR 75; DA3; MTCW 1
Gibran, Kahlil 1883-1931 **TCLC 1, 9; DAM**

POET, POP; PC 9
    See also CA 104; 150; DA3; MTCW 2
Gibran, Khalil
    See Gibran, Kahlil
Gibson, William 1914- **CLC 23; DA; DAB;**
    DAC; DAM DRAM, MST
    See also CA 9-12R; CANR 9, 42, 75; DLB 7;
    MTCW 1; SATA 66
Gibson, William (Ford) 1948- **CLC 39, 63;**
    DAM POP
    See also AAYA 12; CA 126; 133; CANR 52;
    DA3; MTCW 1
Gide, Andre (Paul Guillaume) 1869-1951
    TCLC 5, 12, 36; DA; DAB; DAC; DAM
    MST, NOV; SSC 13; WLC
    See also CA 104; 124; DA3; DLB 65; MTCW
    1, 2
Gifford, Barry (Colby) 1946- **CLC 34**
    See also CA 65-68; CANR 9, 30, 40
Gilbert, Frank
    See De Voto, Bernard (Augustine)
Gilbert, W(illiam) S(chwenck) 1836-1911
    TCLC 3; DAM DRAM, POET
    See also CA 104; 173; SATA 36
Gilbreth, Frank B., Jr. 1911- **CLC 17**
    See also CA 9-12R; SATA 2
Gilchrist, Ellen 1935-**CLC 34, 48; DAM POP;**
    SSC 14
    See also CA 113; 116; CANR 41, 61; DLB 130;
    MTCW 1, 2
Giles, Molly 1942- **CLC 39**
    See also CA 126
Gill, Eric 1882-1940 **TCLC 85**
Gill, Patrick
    See Creasey, John
Gilliam, Terry (Vance) 1940- **CLC 21**
    See also Monty Python
    See also AAYA 19; CA 108; 113; CANR 35;
    INT 113
Gillian, Jerry
    See Gilliam, Terry (Vance)
Gilliatt, Penelope (Ann Douglass) 1932-1993
    CLC 2, 10, 13, 53
    See also AITN 2; CA 13-16R; 141; CANR 49;
    DLB 14
Gilman, Charlotte (Anna) Perkins (Stetson)
    1860-1935 **TCLC 9, 37; SSC 13**
    See also CA 106; 150; MTCW 1
Gilmour, David 1949- **CLC 35**
    See also CA 138; 147
Gilpin, William 1724-1804 **NCLC 30**
Gilray, J. D.
    See Mencken, H(enry) L(ouis)
Gilroy, Frank D(aniel) 1925- **CLC 2**
    See also CA 81-84; CANR 32, 64, 86; DLB 7
Gilstrap, John 1957(?)- **CLC 99**
    See also CA 160
Ginsberg, Allen 1926-1997**CLC 1, 2, 3, 4, 6, 13,**
    36, 69, 109; DA; DAB; DAC; DAM MST,
    POET; PC 4; WLC
    See also AITN 1; CA 1-4R; 157; CANR 2, 41,
    63; CDALB 1941-1968; DA3; DLB 5, 16,
    169; MTCW 1, 2
Ginzburg, Natalia 1916-1991**CLC 5, 11, 54, 70**
    See also CA 85-88; 135; CANR 33; DLB 177;
    MTCW 1, 2
Giono, Jean 1895-1970 **CLC 4, 11**
    See also CA 45-48; 29-32R; CANR 2, 35; DLB
    72; MTCW 1
Giovanni, Nikki 1943- **CLC 2, 4, 19, 64, 117;**
    BLC 2; DA; DAB; DAC; DAM MST,
    MULT, POET; PC 19; WLCS
    See also AAYA 22; AITN 1; BW 2, 3; CA 29-

32R; CAAS 6; CANR 18, 41, 60; CDALBS;
CLR 6; DA3; DLB 5, 41; INT CANR-18;
MAICYA; MTCW 1, 2; SATA 24, 107
Giovene, Andrea 1904- **CLC 7**
    See also CA 85-88
Gippius, Zinaida (Nikolayevna) 1869-1945
    See Hippius, Zinaida
    See also CA 106
Giraudoux, (Hippolyte) Jean 1882-1944
    TCLC 2, 7; DAM DRAM
    See also CA 104; DLB 65
Gironella, Jose Maria 1917- **CLC 11**
    See also CA 101
Gissing, George (Robert) 1857-1903**TCLC 3,**
    24, 47; SSC 37
    See also CA 105; 167; DLB 18, 135, 184
Giurlani, Aldo
    See Palazzeschi, Aldo
Gladkov, Fyodor (Vasilyevich) 1883-1958
    TCLC 27
    See also CA 170
Glanville, Brian (Lester) 1931- **CLC 6**
    See also CA 5-8R; CAAS 9; CANR 3, 70; DLB
    15, 139; SATA 42
Glasgow, Ellen (Anderson Gholson) 1873-1945
    TCLC 2, 7; SSC 34
    See also CA 104; 164; DLB 9, 12; MTCW 2
Glaspell, Susan 1882(?)-1948**TCLC 55; DC 10**
    See also CA 110; 154; DLB 7, 9, 78; YABC 2
Glassco, John 1909-1981 **CLC 9**
    See also CA 13-16R; 102; CANR 15; DLB 68
Glasscock, Amnesia
    See Steinbeck, John (Ernst)
Glasser, Ronald J. 1940(?)- **CLC 37**
Glassman, Joyce
    See Johnson, Joyce
Glendinning, Victoria 1937- **CLC 50**
    See also CA 120; 127; CANR 59; DLB 155
Glissant, Edouard 1928- **CLC 10, 68; DAM**
    MULT
    See also CA 153
Gloag, Julian 1930- **CLC 40**
    See also AITN 1; CA 65-68; CANR 10, 70
Glowacki, Aleksander
    See Prus, Boleslaw
Gluck, Louise (Elisabeth) 1943-**CLC 7, 22, 44,**
    81; DAM POET; PC 16
    See also CA 33-36R; CANR 40, 69; DA3; DLB
    5; MTCW 2
Glyn, Elinor 1864-1943 **TCLC 72**
    See also DLB 153
Gobineau, Joseph Arthur (Comte) de 1816-
    1882 **NCLC 17**
    See also DLB 123
Godard, Jean-Luc 1930- **CLC 20**
    See also CA 93-96
Godden, (Margaret) Rumer 1907-1998**CLC 53**
    See also AAYA 6; CA 5-8R; 172; CANR 4, 27,
    36, 55, 80; CLR 20; DLB 161; MAICYA;
    SAAS 12; SATA 3, 36; SATA-Obit 109
Godoy Alcayaga, Lucila 1889-1957
    See Mistral, Gabriela
    See also BW 2; CA 104; 131; CANR 81; DAM
    MULT; HW 1, 2; MTCW 1, 2
Godwin, Gail (Kathleen) 1937-**CLC 5, 8, 22,**
    31, 69, 125; DAM POP
    See also CA 29-32R; CANR 15, 43, 69; DA3;
    DLB 6; INT CANR-15; MTCW 1, 2
Godwin, William 1756-1836 **NCLC 14**
    See also CDBLB 1789-1832; DLB 39, 104, 142,
    158, 163
Goebbels, Josef
    See Goebbels, (Paul) Joseph

Goebbels, (Paul) Joseph 1897-1945 **TCLC 68**
See also CA 115; 148
Goebbels, Joseph Paul
See Goebbels, (Paul) Joseph
Goethe, Johann Wolfgang von 1749-1832
**NCLC 4, 22, 34; DA; DAB; DAC; DAM
DRAM, MST, POET; PC 5; WLC**
See also DA3; DLB 94
Gogarty, Oliver St. John 1878-1957 **TCLC 15**
See also CA 109; 150; DLB 15, 19
Gogol, Nikolai (Vasilyevich) 1809-1852 **NCLC
5, 15, 31; DA; DAB; DAC; DAM DRAM,
MST; DC 1; SSC 4, 29; WLC**
See also DLB 198
Goines, Donald 1937(?)-1974 **CLC 80; BLC 2;
DAM MULT, POP**
See also AITN 1; BW 1, 3; CA 124; 114; CANR
82; DA3; DLB 33
Gold, Herbert 1924- **CLC 4, 7, 14, 42**
See also CA 9-12R; CANR 17, 45; DLB 2;
DLBY 81
Goldbarth, Albert 1948- **CLC 5, 38**
See also CA 53-56; CANR 6, 40; DLB 120
Goldberg, Anatol 1910-1982 **CLC 34**
See also CA 131; 117
Goldemberg, Isaac 1945- **CLC 52**
See also CA 69-72; CAAS 12; CANR 11, 32;
HW 1
Golding, William (Gerald) 1911-1993 **CLC 1,
2, 3, 8, 10, 17, 27, 58, 81; DA; DAB; DAC;
DAM MST, NOV; WLC**
See also AAYA 5; CA 5-8R; 141; CANR 13,
33, 54; CDBLB 1945-1960; DA3; DLB 15,
100; MTCW 1, 2
Goldman, Emma 1869-1940 **TCLC 13**
See also CA 110; 150
Goldman, Francisco 1954- **CLC 76**
See also CA 162
Goldman, William (W.) 1931- **CLC 1, 48**
See also CA 9-12R; CANR 29, 69; DLB 44
Goldmann, Lucien 1913-1970 **CLC 24**
See also CA 25-28; CAP 2
Goldoni, Carlo 1707-1793 **LC 4; DAM DRAM**
Goldsberry, Steven 1949- **CLC 34**
See also CA 131
Goldsmith, Oliver 1728-1774 **LC 2, 48; DA;
DAB; DAC; DAM DRAM, MST, NOV,
POET; DC 8; WLC**
See also CDBLB 1660-1789; DLB 39, 89, 104,
109, 142; SATA 26
Goldsmith, Peter
See Priestley, J(ohn) B(oynton)
Gombrowicz, Witold 1904-1969 **CLC 4, 7, 11,
49; DAM DRAM**
See also CA 19-20; 25-28R; CAP 2
Gomez de la Serna, Ramon 1888-1963 **CLC 9**
See also CA 153; 116; CANR 79; HW 1, 2
Goncharov, Ivan Alexandrovich 1812-1891
NCLC 1, 63
Goncourt, Edmond (Louis Antoine Huot) de
1822-1896 **NCLC 7**
See also DLB 123
Goncourt, Jules (Alfred Huot) de 1830-1870
NCLC 7
See also DLB 123
Gontier, Fernande 19(?)- **CLC 50**
Gonzalez Martinez, Enrique 1871-1952
TCLC 72
See also CA 166; CANR 81; HW 1, 2
Goodman, Paul 1911-1972 **CLC 1, 2, 4, 7**
See also CA 19-20; 37-40R; CANR 34; CAP 2;
DLB 130; MTCW 1
Gordimer, Nadine 1923- **CLC 3, 5, 7, 10, 18, 33,**

51, 70; **DA; DAB; DAC; DAM MST, NOV;
SSC 17; WLCS**
See also CA 5-8R; CANR 3, 28, 56; DA3; INT
CANR-28; MTCW 1, 2
Gordon, Adam Lindsay 1833-1870 **NCLC 21**
Gordon, Caroline 1895-1981 **CLC 6, 13, 29, 83;
SSC 15**
See also CA 11-12; 103; CANR 36; CAP 1;
DLB 4, 9, 102; DLBD 17; DLBY 81; MTCW
1, 2
Gordon, Charles William 1860-1937
See Connor, Ralph
See also CA 109
Gordon, Mary (Catherine) 1949- **CLC 13, 22**
See also CA 102; CANR 44; DLB 6; DLBY
81; INT 102; MTCW 1
Gordon, N. J.
See Bosman, Herman Charles
Gordon, Sol 1923- **CLC 26**
See also CA 53-56; CANR 4; SATA 11
Gordone, Charles 1925-1995 **CLC 1, 4; DAM
DRAM; DC 8**
See also BW 1, 3; CA 93-96, 180; 150;
CAAE 180; CANR 55; DLB 7; INT 93-
96; MTCW 1
Gore, Catherine 1800-1861 **NCLC 65**
See also DLB 116
Gorenko, Anna Andreevna
See Akhmatova, Anna
Gorky, Maxim 1868-1936 **TCLC 8; DAB; SSC
28; WLC**
See also Peshkov, Alexei Maximovich
See also MTCW 2
Goryan, Sirak
See Saroyan, William
Gosse, Edmund (William) 1849-1928 **TCLC 28**
See also CA 117; DLB 57, 144, 184
Gotlieb, Phyllis Fay (Bloom) 1926- **CLC 18**
See also CA 13-16R; CANR 7; DLB 88
Gottesman, S. D.
See Kornbluth, C(yril) M.; Pohl, Frederik
Gottfried von Strassburg fl. c. 1210-
CMLC 10
See also DLB 138
Gould, Lois **CLC 4, 10**
See also CA 77-80; CANR 29; MTCW 1
Gourmont, Remy (-Marie-Charles) de 1858-
1915 **TCLC 17**
See also CA 109; 150; MTCW 2
Govier, Katherine 1948- **CLC 51**
See also CA 101; CANR 18, 40
Goyen, (Charles) William 1915-1983 **CLC 5, 8,
14, 40**
See also AITN 2; CA 5-8R; 110; CANR 6, 71;
DLB 2; DLBY 83; INT CANR-6
Goytisolo, Juan 1931- **CLC 5, 10, 23; DAM
MULT; HLC 1**
See also CA 85-88; CANR 32, 61; HW 1, 2;
MTCW 1, 2
Gozzano, Guido 1883-1916 **PC 10**
See also CA 154; DLB 114
Gozzi, (Conte) Carlo 1720-1806 **NCLC 23**
Grabbe, Christian Dietrich 1801-1836
NCLC 2
See also DLB 133
Grace, Patricia Frances 1937- **CLC 56**
See also CA 176
Gracian y Morales, Baltasar 1601-1658 **LC 15**
Gracq, Julien **CLC 11, 48**
See also Poirier, Louis
See also DLB 83
Grade, Chaim 1910-1982 **CLC 10**
See also CA 93-96; 107

Graduate of Oxford, A
See Ruskin, John
Grafton, Garth
See Duncan, Sara Jeannette
Graham, John
See Phillips, David Graham
Graham, Jorie 1951- **CLC 48, 118**
See also CA 111; CANR 63; DLB 120
Graham, R(obert) B(ontine) Cunninghame
See Cunninghame Graham, R(obert) B(ontine)
See also DLB 98, 135, 174
Graham, Robert
See Haldeman, Joe (William)
Graham, Tom
See Lewis, (Harry) Sinclair
Graham, W(illiam) S(ydney) 1918-1986
CLC 29
See also CA 73-76; 118; DLB 20
Graham, Winston (Mawdsley) 1910- **CLC 23**
See also CA 49-52; CANR 2, 22, 45, 66;
DLB 77
Grahame, Kenneth 1859-1932 **TCLC 64; DAB**
See also CA 108; 136; CANR 80; CLR 5; DA3;
DLB 34, 141, 178; MAICYA; MTCW 2;
SATA 100; YABC 1
Granovsky, Timofei Nikolaevich 1813-1855
NCLC 75
See also DLB 198
Grant, Skeeter
See Spiegelman, Art
Granville-Barker, Harley 1877-1946 **TCLC 2;
DAM DRAM**
See also Barker, Harley Granville
See also CA 104
Grass, Guenter (Wilhelm) 1927- **CLC 1, 2, 4, 6,
11, 15, 22, 32, 49, 88; DA; DAB; DAC;
DAM MST, NOV; WLC**
See also CA 13-16R; CANR 20, 75, DA3; DLB
75, 124; MTCW 1, 2
Gratton, Thomas
See Hulme, T(homas) E(rnest)
Grau, Shirley Ann 1929- **CLC 4, 9; SSC 15**
See also CA 89-92; CANR 22, 69; DLB 2; INT
CANR-22; MTCW 1
Gravel, Fern
See Hall, James Norman
Graver, Elizabeth 1964- **CLC 70**
See also CA 135; CANR 71
Graves, Richard Perceval 1945- **CLC 44**
See also CA 65-68; CANR 9, 26, 51
Graves, Robert (von Ranke) 1895-1985 **C L C
1, 2, 6, 11, 39, 44, 45; DAB; DAC; DAM
MST, POET; PC 6**
See also CA 5-8R; 117; CANR 5, 36; CDBLB
1914-1945; DA3; DLB 20, 100, 191; DLBD
18; DLBY 85; MTCW 1, 2; SATA 45
Graves, Valerie
See Bradley, Marion Zimmer
Gray, Alasdair (James) 1934- **CLC 41**
See also CA 126; CANR 47, 69; DLB 194; INT
126; MTCW 1, 2
Gray, Amlin 1946- **CLC 29**
See also CA 138
Gray, Francine du Plessix 1930- **CLC 22;
DAM NOV**
See also BEST 90:3; CA 61-64; CAAS 2;
CANR 11, 33, 75, 81; INT CANR-11;
MTCW 1, 2
Gray, John (Henry) 1866-1934 **TCLC 19**
See also CA 119; 162
Gray, Simon (James Holliday) 1936- **CLC 9,
14, 36**
See also AITN 1; CA 21-24R; CAAS 3; CANR

32, 69; DLB 13; MTCW 1

Gray, Spalding 1941-**CLC 49, 112; DAM POP; DC 7**
See also CA 128; CANR 74; MTCW 2

Gray, Thomas 1716-1771**LC 4, 40; DA; DAB; DAC; DAM MST; PC 2; WLC**
See also CDBLB 1660-1789; DA3; DLB 109

Grayson, David
See Baker, Ray Stannard

Grayson, Richard (A.) 1951- **CLC 38**
See also CA 85-88; CANR 14, 31, 57

Greeley, Andrew M(oran) 1928- **CLC 28; DAM POP**
See also CA 5-8R; CAAS 7; CANR 7, 43, 69; DA3; MTCW 1, 2

Green, Anna Katharine 1846-1935 **TCLC 63**
See also CA 112; 159; DLB 202

Green, Brian
See Card, Orson Scott

Green, Hannah
See Greenberg, Joanne (Goldenberg)

Green, Hannah 1927(?)-1996 **CLC 3**
See also CA 73-76; CANR 59

Green, Henry 1905-1973 **CLC 2, 13, 97**
See also Yorke, Henry Vincent
See also CA 175; DLB 15

Green, Julian (Hartridge) 1900-1998
See Green, Julien
See also CA 21-24R; 169; CANR 33; DLB 4, 72; MTCW 1

Green, Julien **CLC 3, 11, 77**
See also Green, Julian (Hartridge)
See also MTCW 2

Green, Paul (Eliot) 1894-1981**CLC 25; DAM DRAM**
See also AITN 1; CA 5-8R; 103; CANR 3; DLB 7, 9; DLBY 81

Greenberg, Ivan 1908-1973
See Rahv, Philip
See also CA 85-88

Greenberg, Joanne (Goldenberg) 1932- **C L C 7, 30**
See also AAYA 12; CA 5-8R; CANR 14, 32, 69; SATA 25

Greenberg, Richard 1959(?)- **CLC 57**
See also CA 138

Greene, Bette 1934- **CLC 30**
See also AAYA 7; CA 53-56; CANR 4; CLR 2; JRDA; MAICYA; SAAS 16; SATA 8, 102

Greene, Gael **CLC 8**
See also CA 13-16R; CANR 10

Greene, Graham (Henry) 1904-1991**CLC 1, 3, 6, 9, 14, 18, 27, 37, 70, 72, 125; DA; DAB; DAC; DAM MST, NOV; SSC 29; WLC**
See also AITN 2; CA 13-16R; 133; CANR 35, 61; CDBLB 1945-1960; DA3; DLB 13, 15, 77, 100, 162, 201, 204; DLBY 91; MTCW 1, 2; SATA 20

Greene, Robert 1558-1592 **LC 41**
See also DLB 62, 167

Greer, Richard
See Silverberg, Robert

Gregor, Arthur 1923- **CLC 9**
See also CA 25-28R; CAAS 10; CANR 11; SATA 36

Gregor, Lee
See Pohl, Frederik

Gregory, Isabella Augusta (Persse) 1852-1932 **TCLC 1**
See also CA 104; DLB 10

Gregory, J. Dennis
See Williams, John A(lfred)

Grendon, Stephen

See Derleth, August (William)

Grenville, Kate 1950- **CLC 61**
See also CA 118; CANR 53

Grenville, Pelham
See Wodehouse, P(elham) G(renville)

Greve, Felix Paul (Berthold Friedrich) 1879-1948
See Grove, Frederick Philip
See also CA 104; 141; 175; CANR 79; DAC; DAM MST

Grey, Zane 1872-1939 **TCLC 6; DAM POP**
See also CA 104; 132; DA3; DLB 212; MTCW 1, 2

Grieg, (Johan) Nordahl (Brun) 1902-1943 **TCLC 10**
See also CA 107

Grieve, C(hristopher) M(urray) 1892-1978 **CLC 11, 19; DAM POET**
See also MacDiarmid, Hugh; Pteleon
See also CA 5-8R; 85-88; CANR 33; MTCW 1

Griffin, Gerald 1803-1840 **NCLC 7**
See also DLB 159

Griffin, John Howard 1920-1980 **CLC 68**
See also AITN 1; CA 1-4R; 101; CANR 2

Griffin, Peter 1942- **CLC 39**
See also CA 136

Griffith, D(avid Lewelyn) W(ark) 1875(?)-1948 **TCLC 68**
See also CA 119; 150; CANR 80

Griffith, Lawrence
See Griffith, D(avid Lewelyn) W(ark)

Griffiths, Trevor 1935- **CLC 13, 52**
See also CA 97-100; CANR 45; DLB 13

Griggs, Sutton Elbert 1872-1930(?)**TCLC 77**
See also CA 123; DLB 50

Grigson, Geoffrey (Edward Harvey) 1905-1985 **CLC 7, 39**
See also CA 25-28R; 118; CANR 20, 33; DLB 27; MTCW 1, 2

Grillparzer, Franz 1791-1872**NCLC 1; SSC 37**
See also DLB 133

Grimble, Reverend Charles James
See Eliot, T(homas) S(tearns)

Grimke, Charlotte L(ottie) Forten 1837(?)-1914
See Forten, Charlotte L.
See also BW 1; CA 117; 124; DAM MULT, POET

Grimm, Jacob Ludwig Karl 1785-1863**NCLC 3, 77; SSC 36**
See also DLB 90; MAICYA; SATA 22

Grimm, Wilhelm Karl 1786-1859**NCLC 3, 77; SSC 36**
See also DLB 90; MAICYA; SATA 22

Grimmelshausen, Johann Jakob Christoffel von 1621-1676 **LC 6**
See also DLB 168

Grindel, Eugene 1895-1952
See Eluard, Paul
See also CA 104

Grisham, John 1955- **CLC 84; DAM POP**
See also AAYA 14; CA 138; CANR 47, 69; DA3; MTCW 2

Grossman, David 1954- **CLC 67**
See also CA 138

Grossman, Vasily (Semenovich) 1905-1964 **CLC 41**
See also CA 124; 130; MTCW 1

Grove, Frederick Philip **TCLC 4**
See also Greve, Felix Paul (Berthold Friedrich)
See also DLB 92

Grubb
See Crumb, R(obert)

Grumbach, Doris (Isaac) 1918-**CLC 13, 22, 64**

See also CA 5-8R; CAAS 2; CANR 9, 42, 70; INT CANR-9; MTCW 2

Grundtvig, Nicolai Frederik Severin 1783-1872 **NCLC 1**

Grunge
See Crumb, R(obert)

Grunwald, Lisa 1959- **CLC 44**
See also CA 120

Guare, John 1938- **CLC 8, 14, 29, 67; DAM DRAM**
See also CA 73-76; CANR 21, 69; DLB 7, MTCW 1, 2

Gudjonsson, Halldor Kiljan 1902-1998
See Laxness, Halldor
See also CA 103; 164

Guenter, Erich
See Eich, Guenter

Guest, Barbara 1920- **CLC 34**
See also CA 25-28R; CANR 11, 44, 84; DLB 5, 193

Guest, Edgar A(lbert) 1881-1959 **TCLC 95**
See also CA 112; 168

Guest, Judith (Ann) 1936- **CLC 8, 30; DAM NOV, POP**
See also AAYA 7; CA 77-80; CANR 15, 75; DA3; INT CANR-15; MTCW 1, 2

Guevara, Che **CLC 87; HLC 1**
See also Guevara (Serna), Ernesto

Guevara (Serna), Ernesto 1928-1967**CLC 87; DAM MULT; HLC 1**
See also Guevara, Che
See also CA 127; 111; CANR 56; HW 1

Guicciardini, Francesco 1483-1540 **LC 49**

Guild, Nicholas M. 1944- **CLC 33**
See also CA 93-96

Guillemin, Jacques
See Sartre, Jean-Paul

Guillen, Jorge 1893-1984 **CLC 11; DAM MULT, POET; HLCS 1**
See also CA 89-92; 112; DLB 108; HW 1

Guillen, Nicolas (Cristobal) 1902-1989 **C L C 48, 79; BLC 2; DAM MST, MULT, POET; HLC 1; PC 23**
See also BW 2; CA 116; 125; 129; CANR 84; HW 1

Guillevic, (Eugene) 1907- **CLC 33**
See also CA 93-96

Guillois
See Desnos, Robert

Guillois, Valentin
See Desnos, Robert

Guimaraes Rosa, Joao 1908-1967
See also CA 175; HLCS 2

Guiney, Louise Imogen 1861-1920 **TCLC 41**
See also CA 160; DLB 54

Guiraldes, Ricardo (Guillermo) 1886-1927 **TCLC 39**
See also CA 131; HW 1; MTCW 1

Gumilev, Nikolai (Stepanovich) 1886-1921 **TCLC 60**
See also CA 165

Gunesekera, Romesh 1954- **CLC 91**
See also CA 159

Gunn, Bill **CLC 5**
See also Gunn, William Harrison
See also DLB 38

Gunn, Thom(son William) 1929-**CLC 3, 6, 18, 32, 81; DAM POET; PC 26**
See also CA 17-20R; CANR 9, 33; CDBLB 1960 to Present; DLB 27; INT CANR-33; MTCW 1

Gunn, William Harrison 1934(?)-1989
See Gunn, Bill

See also AITN 1; BW 1, 3; CA 13-16R; 128;
CANR 12, 25, 76

Gunnars, Kristjana 1948-   **CLC 69**
See also CA 113; DLB 60

Gurdjieff, G(eorgei) I(vanovich) 1877(?)-1949
TCLC 71
See also CA 157

Gurganus, Allan 1947- **CLC 70; DAM POP**
See also BEST 90:1; CA 135

Gurney, A(lbert) R(amsdell), Jr. 1930- **C L C
32, 50, 54; DAM DRAM**
See also CA 77-80; CANR 32, 64

Gurney, Ivor (Bertie) 1890-1937   **TCLC 33**
See also CA 167

Gurney, Peter
See Gurney, A(lbert) R(amsdell), Jr.

Guro, Elena 1877-1913   **TCLC 56**

Gustafson, James M(oody) 1925- **CLC 100**
See also CA 25-28R; CANR 37

Gustafson, Ralph (Barker) 1909-   **CLC 36**
See also CA 21-24R; CANR 8, 45, 84; DLB 88

Gut, Gom
See Simenon, Georges (Jacques Christian)

Guterson, David 1956-   **CLC 91**
See also CA 132; CANR 73; MTCW 2

Guthrie, A(lfred) B(ertram), Jr. 1901-1991
CLC 23
See also CA 57-60; 134; CANR 24; DLB 212;
SATA 62; SATA-Obit 67

Guthrie, Isobel
See Grieve, C(hristopher) M(urray)

Guthrie, Woodrow Wilson 1912-1967
See Guthrie, Woody
See also CA 113; 93-96

Guthrie, Woody   **CLC 35**
See also Guthrie, Woodrow Wilson

Gutierrez Najera, Manuel 1859-1895
See also HLCS 2

Guy, Rosa (Cuthbert) 1928-   **CLC 26**
See also AAYA 4; BW 2; CA 17-20R; CANR
14, 34, 83; CLR 13; DLB 33; JRDA;
MAICYA; SATA 14, 62

Gwendolyn
See Bennett, (Enoch) Arnold

H. D.   **CLC 3, 8, 14, 31, 34, 73; PC 5**
See also Doolittle, Hilda

H. de V.
See Buchan, John

Haavikko, Paavo Juhani 1931-   **CLC 18, 34**
See also CA 106

Habbema, Koos
See Heijermans, Herman

Habermas, Juergen 1929-   **CLC 104**
See also CA 109; CANR 85

Habermas, Jurgen
See Habermas, Juergen

Hacker, Marilyn 1942- **CLC 5, 9, 23, 72, 91;
DAM POET**
See also CA 77-80; CANR 68; DLB 120

Haeckel, Ernst Heinrich (Philipp August) 1834-
1919   **TCLC 83**
See also CA 157

Hafiz c. 1326-1389   **CMLC 34**

Hafiz c. 1326-1389(?)   **CMLC 34**

Haggard, H(enry) Rider 1856-1925 **TCLC 11**
See also CA 108; 148; DLB 70, 156, 174, 178;
MTCW 2; SATA 16

Hagiosy, L.
See Larbaud, Valery (Nicolas)

Hagiwara Sakutaro 1886-1942 **TCLC 60;
PC 18**

Haig, Fenil
See Ford, Ford Madox

Haig-Brown, Roderick (Langmere) 1908-1976
CLC 21
See also CA 5-8R; 69-72; CANR 4, 38, 83; CLR
31; DLB 88; MAICYA; SATA 12

Hailey, Arthur 1920-**CLC 5; DAM NOV, POP**
See also AITN 2; BEST 90:3; CA 1-4R; CANR
2, 36, 75; DLB 88; DLBY 82; MTCW 1, 2

Hailey, Elizabeth Forsythe 1938-   **CLC 40**
See also CA 93-96; CAAS 1; CANR 15, 48;
INT CANR-15

Haines, John (Meade) 1924-   **CLC 58**
See also CA 17-20R; CANR 13, 34; DLB 212

Hakluyt, Richard 1552-1616   **LC 31**

Haldeman, Joe (William) 1943-   **CLC 61**
See Graham, Robert
See also CA 53-56, 179; CAAE 179; CAAS 25;
CANR 6, 70, 72; DLB 8; INT CANR-6

Hale, Sarah Josepha (Buell) 1788-1879
NCLC 75
See also DLB 1, 42, 73

Haley, Alex(ander Murray Palmer) 1921-1992
**CLC 8, 12, 76; BLC 2; DA; DAB; DAC;
DAM MST, MULT, POP**
See also AAYA 26; BW 2, 3; CA 77-80; 136;
CANR 61; CDALBS; DA3; DLB 38; MTCW
1, 2

Haliburton, Thomas Chandler 1796-1865
NCLC 15
See also DLB 11, 99

Hall, Donald (Andrew, Jr.) 1928- **CLC 1, 13,
37, 59; DAM POET**
See also CA 5-8R; CAAS 7; CANR 2, 44, 64;
DLB 5; MTCW 1; SATA 23, 97

Hall, Frederic Sauser
See Sauser-Hall, Frederic

Hall, James
See Kuttner, Henry

Hall, James Norman 1887-1951   **TCLC 23**
See also CA 123; 173; SATA 21

Hall, Radclyffe
See Hall, (Marguerite) Radclyffe
See also MTCW 2

Hall, (Marguerite) Radclyffe 1886-1943
TCLC 12
See also CA 110; 150; CANR 83; DLB 191

Hall, Rodney 1935-   **CLC 51**
See also CA 109; CANR 69

Halleck, Fitz-Greene 1790-1867   **NCLC 47**
See also DLB 3

Halliday, Michael
See Creasey, John

Halpern, Daniel 1945-   **CLC 14**
See also CA 33-36R

Hamburger, Michael (Peter Leopold) 1924-
CLC 5, 14
See also CA 5-8R; CAAS 4; CANR 2, 47;
DLB 27

Hamill, Pete 1935-   **CLC 10**
See also CA 25-28R; CANR 18, 71

Hamilton, Alexander 1755(?)-1804 **NCLC 49**
See also DLB 37

Hamilton, Clive
See Lewis, C(live) S(taples)

Hamilton, Edmond 1904-1977   **CLC 1**
See also CA 1-4R; CANR 3, 84; DLB 8

Hamilton, Eugene (Jacob) Lee
See Lee-Hamilton, Eugene (Jacob)

Hamilton, Franklin
See Silverberg, Robert

Hamilton, Gail
See Corcoran, Barbara

Hamilton, Mollie
See Kaye, M(ary) M(argaret)

Hamilton, (Anthony Walter) Patrick 1904-1962
CLC 51
See also CA 176; 113; DLB 191

Hamilton, Virginia 1936-   **CLC 26; DAM
MULT**
See also AAYA 2, 21; BW 2, 3; CA 25-28R;
CANR 20, 37, 73; CLR 1, 11, 40; DLB 33,
52; INT CANR-20; JRDA; MAICYA;
MTCW 1, 2; SATA 4, 56, 79

Hammett, (Samuel) Dashiell 1894-1961 **C L C
3, 5, 10, 19, 47; SSC 17**
See also AITN 1; CA 81-84; CANR 42; CDALB
1929-1941; DA3; DLBD 6; DLBY 96;
MTCW 1, 2

Hammon, Jupiter 1711(?)-1800(?)   **NCLC 5;
BLC 2; DAM MULT, POET; PC 16**
See also DLB 31, 50

Hammond, Keith
See Kuttner, Henry

Hamner, Earl (Henry), Jr. 1923-   **CLC 12**
See also AITN 2; CA 73-76; DLB 6

Hampton, Christopher (James) 1946- **CLC 4**
See also CA 25-28R; DLB 13; MTCW 1

Hamsun, Knut   **TCLC 2, 14, 49**
See also Pedersen, Knut

Handke, Peter 1942-**CLC 5, 8, 10, 15, 38; DAM
DRAM, NOV**
See also CA 77-80; CANR 33, 75; DLB 85, 124;
MTCW 1, 2

Handy, W(illiam) C(hristopher) 1873-1958
TCLC 97
See also BW 3; CA 121; 167

Hanley, James 1901-1985   **CLC 3, 5, 8, 13**
See also CA 73-76; 117; CANR 36; DLB 191;
MTCW 1

Hannah, Barry 1942-   **CLC 23, 38, 90**
See also CA 108; 110; CANR 43, 68; DLB 6;
INT 110; MTCW 1

Hannon, Ezra
See Hunter, Evan

Hansberry, Lorraine (Vivian) 1930-1965**CLC
17, 62; BLC 2; DA; DAB; DAC; DAM
DRAM, MST, MULT; DC 2**
See also AAYA 25; BW 1, 3; CA 109; 25-28R;
CABS 3; CANR 58; CDALB 1941-1968;
DA3; DLB 7, 38; MTCW 1, 2

Hansen, Joseph 1923-   **CLC 38**
See also CA 29-32R; CAAS 17; CANR 16, 44,
66; INT CANR-16

Hansen, Martin A(lfred) 1909-1955**TCLC 32**
See also CA 167

Hanson, Kenneth O(stlin) 1922-   **CLC 13**
See also CA 53-56; CANR 7

Hardwick, Elizabeth (Bruce) 1916- **CLC 13;
DAM NOV**
See also CA 5-8R; CANR 3, 32, 70; DA3; DLB
6; MTCW 1, 2

Hardy, Thomas 1840-1928**TCLC 4, 10, 18, 32,
48, 53, 72; DA; DAB; DAC; DAM MST,
NOV, POET; PC 8; SSC 2; WLC**
See also CA 104; 123; CDBLB 1890-1914;
DA3; DLB 18, 19, 135; MTCW 1, 2

Hare, David 1947-   **CLC 29, 58**
See also CA 97-100; CANR 39; DLB 13;
MTCW 1

Harewood, John
See Van Druten, John (William)

Harford, Henry
See Hudson, W(illiam) H(enry)

Hargrave, Leonie
See Disch, Thomas M(ichael)

Harjo, Joy 1951-**CLC 83; DAM MULT; PC 27**
See also CA 114; CANR 35, 67; DLB 120, 175;

MTCW 2; NNAL

Harlan, Louis R(udolph) 1922- **CLC 34**
See also CA 21-24R; CANR 25, 55, 80

Harling, Robert 1951(?)- **CLC 53**
See also CA 147

Harmon, William (Ruth) 1938- **CLC 38**
See also CA 33-36R; CANR 14, 32, 35; SATA 65

Harper, F. E. W.
See Harper, Frances Ellen Watkins

Harper, Frances E. W.
See Harper, Frances Ellen Watkins

Harper, Frances E. Watkins
See Harper, Frances Ellen Watkins

Harper, Frances Ellen
See Harper, Frances Ellen Watkins

Harper, Frances Ellen Watkins 1825-1911 **TCLC 14; BLC 2; DAM MULT, POET; PC 21**
See also BW 1, 3; CA 111; 125; CANR 79; DLB 50

Harper, Michael S(teven) 1938- **CLC 7, 22**
See also BW 1; CA 33-36R; CANR 24; DLB 41

Harper, Mrs. F. E. W.
See Harper, Frances Ellen Watkins

Harris, Christie (Lucy) Irwin 1907- **CLC 12**
See also CA 5-8R; CANR 6, 83; CLR 47; DLB 88; JRDA; MAICYA; SAAS 10; SATA 6, 74

Harris, Frank 1856-1931 **TCLC 24**
See also CA 109; 150; CANR 80; DLB 156, 197

Harris, George Washington 1814-1869 **NCLC 23**
See also DLB 3, 11

Harris, Joel Chandler 1848-1908 **TCLC 2; SSC 19**
See also CA 104; 137; CANR 80; CLR 49; DLB 11, 23, 42, 78, 91; MAICYA; SATA 100; YABC 1

Harris, John (Wyndham Parkes Lucas) Beynon 1903-1969
See Wyndham, John
See also CA 102; 89-92; CANR 84

Harris, MacDonald **CLC 9**
See also Heiney, Donald (William)

Harris, Mark 1922- **CLC 19**
See also CA 5-8R; CAAS 3; CANR 2, 55, 83; DLB 2; DLBY 80

Harris, (Theodore) Wilson 1921- **CLC 25**
See also BW 2, 3; CA 65-68; CAAS 16; CANR 11, 27, 69; DLB 117; MTCW 1

Harrison, Elizabeth Cavanna 1909-
See Cavanna, Betty
See also CA 9-12R; CANR 6, 27, 85

Harrison, Harry (Max) 1925- **CLC 42**
See also CA 1-4R; CANR 5, 21, 84; DLB 8; SATA 4

Harrison, James (Thomas) 1937- **CLC 6, 14, 33, 66; SSC 19**
See also CA 13-16R; CANR 8, 51, 79; DLBY 82; INT CANR-8

Harrison, Jim
See Harrison, James (Thomas)

Harrison, Kathryn 1961- **CLC 70**
See also CA 144; CANR 68

Harrison, Tony 1937- **CLC 43**
See also CA 65-68; CANR 44; DLB 40; MTCW 1

Harriss, Will(ard Irvin) 1922- **CLC 34**
See also CA 111

Harson, Sley
See Ellison, Harlan (Jay)

Hart, Ellis

See Ellison, Harlan (Jay)

Hart, Josephine 1942(?)- **CLC 70; DAM POP**
See also CA 138; CANR 70

Hart, Moss 1904-1961 **CLC 66; DAM DRAM**
See also CA 109; 89-92; CANR 84; DLB 7

Harte, (Francis) Bret(t) 1836(?)-1902 **TCLC 1, 25; DA; DAC; DAM MST; SSC 8; WLC**
See also CA 104; 140; CANR 80; CDALB 1865-1917; DA3; DLB 12, 64, 74, 79, 186; SATA 26

Hartley, L(eslie) P(oles) 1895-1972 **CLC 2, 22**
See also CA 45-48; 37-40R; CANR 33; DLB 15, 139; MTCW 1, 2

Hartman, Geoffrey H. 1929- **CLC 27**
See also CA 117; 125; CANR 79; DLB 67

Hartmann, Eduard von 1842-1906 **TCLC 97**

Hartmann, Sadakichi 1867-1944 **TCLC 73**
See also CA 157; DLB 54

Hartmann von Aue c. 1160-c. 1205 **CMLC 15**
See also DLB 138

Hartmann von Aue 1170-1210 **CMLC 15**

Haruf, Kent 1943- **CLC 34**
See also CA 149

Harwood, Ronald 1934- **CLC 32; DAM DRAM, MST**
See also CA 1-4R; CANR 4, 55; DLB 13

Hasegawa Tatsunosuke
See Futabatei, Shimei

Hasek, Jaroslav (Matej Frantisek) 1883-1923 **TCLC 4**
See also CA 104; 129; MTCW 1, 2

Hass, Robert 1941- **CLC 18, 39, 99; PC 16**
See also CA 111; CANR 30, 50, 71; DLB 105, 206; SATA 94

Hastings, Hudson
See Kuttner, Henry

Hastings, Selina **CLC 44**

Hathorne, John 1641-1717 **LC 38**

Hatteras, Amelia
See Mencken, H(enry) L(ouis)

Hatteras, Owen **TCLC 18**
See also Mencken, H(enry) L(ouis); Nathan, George Jean

Hauptmann, Gerhart (Johann Robert) 1862-1946 **TCLC 4; DAM DRAM; SSC 37**
See also CA 104; 153; DLB 66, 118

Havel, Vaclav 1936- **CLC 25, 58, 65; DAM DRAM; DC 6**
See also CA 104; CANR 36, 63; DA3; MTCW 1, 2

Haviaras, Stratis **CLC 33**
See also Chaviaras, Strates

Hawes, Stephen 1475(?)-1523(?) **LC 17**
See also DLB 132

Hawkes, John (Clendennin Burne, Jr.) 1925-1998 **CLC 1, 2, 3, 4, 7, 9, 14, 15, 27, 49**
See also CA 1-4R; 167; CANR 2, 47, 64; DLB 2, 7; DLBY 80, 98; MTCW 1, 2

Hawking, S. W.
See Hawking, Stephen W(illiam)

Hawking, Stephen W(illiam) 1942- **CLC 63, 105**
See also AAYA 13; BEST 89:1; CA 126; 129; CANR 48; DA3; MTCW 2

Hawkins, Anthony Hope
See Hope, Anthony

Hawthorne, Julian 1846-1934 **TCLC 25**
See also CA 165

Hawthorne, Nathaniel 1804-1864 **NCLC 39; DA; DAB; DAC; DAM MST, NOV; SSC 3, 29; WLC**
See also AAYA 18; CDALB 1640-1865; DA3; DLB 1, 74; YABC 2

Haxton, Josephine Ayres 1921-
See Douglas, Ellen
See also CA 115; CANR 41, 83

Hayaseca y Eizaguirre, Jorge
See Echegaray (y Eizaguirre), Jose (Maria Waldo)

Hayashi, Fumiko 1904-1951 **TCLC 27**
See also CA 161; DLB 180

Haycraft, Anna 1932-
See Ellis, Alice Thomas
See also CA 122; CANR 85; MTCW 2

Hayden, Robert E(arl) 1913-1980 **CLC 5, 9, 14, 37; BLC 2; DA; DAC; DAM MST, MULT, POET; PC 6**
See also BW 1, 3; CA 69-72; 97-100; CABS 2; CANR 24, 75, 82; CDALB 1941-1968; DLB 5, 76; MTCW 1, 2; SATA 19; SATA-Obit 26

Hayford, J(oseph) E(phraim) Casely
See Casely-Hayford, J(oseph) E(phraim)

Hayman, Ronald 1932- **CLC 44**
See also CA 25-28R; CANR 18, 50; DLB 155

Haywood, Eliza (Fowler) 1693(?)-1756 **LC 1, 44**
See also DLB 39

Hazlitt, William 1778-1830 **NCLC 29, 82**
See also DLB 110, 158

Hazzard, Shirley 1931- **CLC 18**
See also CA 9-12R; CANR 4, 70; DLBY 82; MTCW 1

Head, Bessie 1937-1986 **CLC 25, 67; BLC 2; DAM MULT**
See also BW 2, 3; CA 29-32R; 119; CANR 25, 82; DA3; DLB 117; MTCW 1, 2

Headon, (Nicky) Topper 1956(?)- **CLC 30**

Heaney, Seamus (Justin) 1939- **CLC 5, 7, 14, 25, 37, 74, 91; DAB; DAM POET; PC 18; WLCS**
See also CA 85-88; CANR 25, 48, 75; CDBLB 1960 to Present; DA3; DLB 40; DLBY 95; MTCW 1, 2

Hearn, (Patricio) Lafcadio (Tessima Carlos) 1850-1904 **TCLC 9**
See also CA 105; 166; DLB 12, 78, 189

Hearne, Vicki 1946- **CLC 56**
See also CA 139

Hearon, Shelby 1931- **CLC 63**
See also AITN 2; CA 25-28R; CANR 18, 48

Heat-Moon, William Least **CLC 29**
See also Trogdon, William (Lewis)
See also AAYA 9

Hebbel, Friedrich 1813-1863 **NCLC 43; DAM DRAM**
See also DLB 129

Hebert, Anne 1916- **CLC 4, 13, 29; DAC; DAM MST, POET**
See also CA 85-88; CANR 69; DA3; DLB 68; MTCW 1, 2

Hecht, Anthony (Evan) 1923- **CLC 8, 13, 19; DAM POET**
See also CA 9-12R; CANR 6; DLB 5, 169

Hecht, Ben 1894-1964 **CLC 8**
See also CA 85-88; DLB 7, 9, 25, 26, 28, 86

Hedayat, Sadeq 1903-1951 **TCLC 21**
See also CA 120

Hegel, Georg Wilhelm Friedrich 1770-1831 **NCLC 46**
See also DLB 90

Heidegger, Martin 1889-1976 **CLC 24**
See also CA 81-84; 65-68; CANR 34; MTCW 1, 2

Heidenstam, (Carl Gustaf) Verner von 1859-1940 **TCLC 5**
See also CA 104

Heifner, Jack 1946-　　　　　　**CLC 11**
　See also CA 105; CANR 47
Heijermans, Herman 1864-1924　**TCLC 24**
　See also CA 123
Heilbrun, Carolyn G(old) 1926-　　**CLC 25**
　See also CA 45-48; CANR 1, 28, 58
Heine, Heinrich 1797-1856**NCLC 4, 54; PC 25**
　See also DLB 90
Heinemann, Larry (Curtiss) 1944-　**CLC 50**
　See also CA 110; CAAS 21; CANR 31, 81;
　DLBD 9; INT CANR-31
Heiney, Donald (William) 1921-1993
　See Harris, MacDonald
　See also CA 1-4R; 142; CANR 3, 58
Heinlein, Robert A(nson) 1907-1988**CLC 1, 3,
　8, 14, 26, 55; DAM POP**
　See also AAYA 17; CA 1-4R; 125; CANR 1,
　20, 53; DA3; DLB 8; JRDA; MAICYA;
　MTCW 1, 2; SATA 9, 69; SATA-Obit 56
Helforth, John
　See Doolittle, Hilda
Hellenhofferu, Vojtech Kapristian z
　See Hasek, Jaroslav (Matej Frantisek)
Heller, Joseph 1923-**CLC 1, 3, 5, 8, 11, 36, 63;
　DA; DAB; DAC; DAM MST, NOV, POP;
　WLC**
　See also AAYA 24; AITN 1; CA 5-8R; CABS
　1; CANR 8, 42, 66; DA3; DLB 2, 28; DLBY
　80; INT CANR-8; MTCW 1, 2
Hellman, Lillian (Florence) 1906-1984**CLC 2,
　4, 8, 14, 18, 34, 44, 52; DAM DRAM; DC 1**
　See also AITN 1, 2; CA 13-16R; 112; CANR
　33; DA3; DLB 7; DLBY 84; MTCW 1, 2
Helprin, Mark 1947-**CLC 7, 10, 22, 32; DAM
　NOV, POP**
　See also CA 81-84; CANR 47, 64; CDALBS;
　DA3; DLBY 85; MTCW 1, 2
Helvetius, Claude-Adrien 1715-1771　**LC 26**
Helyar, Jane Penelope Josephine 1933-
　See Poole, Josephine
　See also CA 21-24R; CANR 10, 26; SATA 82
Hemans, Felicia 1793-1835　　　　**NCLC 71**
　See also DLB 96
Hemingway, Ernest (Miller) 1899-1961　**C L C
　1, 3, 6, 8, 10, 13, 19, 30, 34, 39, 41, 44, 50,
　61, 80; DA; DAB; DAC; DAM MST, NOV;
　SSC 1, 25, 36; WLC**
　See also AAYA 19; CA 77-80; CANR 34;
　CDALB 1917-1929; DA3; DLB 4, 9, 102,
　210; DLBD 1, 15, 16; DLBY 81, 87, 96, 98;
　MTCW 1, 2
Hempel, Amy 1951-　　　　　　**CLC 39**
　See also CA 118; 137; CANR 70; DA3;
　MTCW 2
Henderson, F. C.
　See Mencken, H(enry) L(ouis)
Henderson, Sylvia
　See Ashton-Warner, Sylvia (Constance)
Henderson, Zenna (Chlarson) 1917-1983
　SSC 29
　See also CA 1-4R; 133; CANR 1, 84; DLB 8;
　SATA 5
Henkin, Joshua　　　　　　　　**CLC 119**
　See also CA 161
Henley, Beth　　　　　　**CLC 23; DC 6**
　See also Henley, Elizabeth Becker
　See also CABS 3; DLBY 86
Henley, Elizabeth Becker 1952-
　See Henley, Beth
　See also CA 107; CANR 32, 73; DAM DRAM,
　MST; DA3; MTCW 1, 2
Henley, William Ernest 1849-1903　**TCLC 8**
　See also CA 105; DLB 19

Hennissart, Martha
　See Lathen, Emma
　See also CA 85-88; CANR 64
Henry, O.　　　　**TCLC 1, 19; SSC 5; WLC**
　See also Porter, William Sydney
Henry, Patrick 1736-1799　　　　**LC 25**
Henryson, Robert 1430(?)-1506(?)　**LC 20**
　See also DLB 146
Henry VIII 1491-1547　　　　　**LC 10**
　See also DLB 132
Henschke, Alfred
　See Klabund
Hentoff, Nat(han Irving) 1925-　　**CLC 26**
　See also AAYA 4; CA 1-4R; CAAS 6; CANR
　5, 25, 77; CLR 1, 52; INT CANR-25; JRDA;
　MAICYA; SATA 42, 69; SATA-Brief 27
Heppenstall, (John) Rayner 1911-1981
　CLC 10
　See also CA 1-4R; 103; CANR 29
Heraclitus c. 540B.C.-c. 450B.C.　**CMLC 22**
　See also DLB 176
Herbert, Frank (Patrick) 1920-1986**CLC 12,
　23, 35, 44, 85; DAM POP**
　See also AAYA 21; CA 53-56; 118; CANR 5,
　43; CDALBS, DLB 8, INT CANR-5; MTCW
　1, 2; SATA 9, 37; SATA-Obit 47
Herbert, George 1593-1633　　**LC 24; DAB;
　DAM POET; PC 4**
　See also CDBLB Before 1660; DLB 126
Herbert, Zbigniew 1924-1998　　**CLC 9, 43;
　DAM POET**
　See also CA 89-92; 169; CANR 36, 74;
　MTCW 1
Herbst, Josephine (Frey) 1897-1969　**CLC 34**
　See also CA 5-8R; 25-28R; DLB 9
Heredia, Jose Maria 1803-1839
　See also HLCS 2
Hergesheimer, Joseph 1880-1954　**TCLC 11**
　See also CA 109; DLB 102, 9
Herlihy, James Leo 1927-1993　　　**CLC 6**
　See also CA 1-4R; 143; CANR 2
Hermogenes fl. c. 175-　　　　　**CMLC 6**
Hernandez, Jose 1834-1886　　　**NCLC 17**
Herodotus c. 484B.C.-429B.C.　**CMLC 17**
　See also DLB 176
Herrick, Robert 1591-1674**LC 13; DA; DAB;
　DAC; DAM MST, POP; PC 9**
　See also DLB 126
Herring, Guilles
　See Somerville, Edith
Herriot, James 1916-1995**CLC 12; DAM POP**
　See also Wight, James Alfred
　See also AAYA 1; CA 148; CANR 40; MTCW
　2; SATA 86
Herrmann, Dorothy 1941-　　　　**CLC 44**
　See also CA 107
Herrmann, Taffy
　See Herrmann, Dorothy
Hersey, John (Richard) 1914-1993**CLC 1, 2, 7,
　9, 40, 81, 97; DAM POP**
　See also AAYA 29; CA 17-20R; 140; CANR
　33; CDALBS; DLB 6, 185; MTCW 1, 2;
　SATA 25; SATA-Obit 76
Herzen, Aleksandr Ivanovich 1812-1870
　NCLC 10, 61
Herzl, Theodor 1860-1904　　　　**TCLC 36**
　See also CA 168
Herzog, Werner 1942-　　　　　**CLC 16**
　See also CA 89-92
Hesiod c. 8th cent. B.C.-　　　　**CMLC 5**
　See also DLB 176
Hesse, Hermann 1877-1962**CLC 1, 2, 3, 6, 11,
　17, 25, 69; DA; DAB; DAC; DAM MST,**

NOV; SSC 9; WLC
　See also CA 17-18; CAP 2; DA3; DLB 66;
　MTCW 1, 2; SATA 50
Hewes, Cady
　See De Voto, Bernard (Augustine)
Heyen, William 1940-　　　　**CLC 13, 18**
　See also CA 33-36R; CAAS 9; DLB 5
Heyerdahl, Thor 1914-　　　　　**CLC 26**
　See also CA 5-8R; CANR 5, 22, 66, 73; MTCW
　1, 2; SATA 2, 52
Heym, Georg (Theodor Franz Arthur) 1887-
　1912　　　　　　　　　　**TCLC 9**
　See also CA 106; 181
Heym, Stefan 1913-　　　　　　**CLC 41**
　See also CA 9-12R; CANR 4; DLB 69
Heyse, Paul (Johann Ludwig von) 1830-1914
　TCLC 8
　See also CA 104; DLB 129
Heyward, (Edwin) DuBose 1885-1940
　TCLC 59
　See also CA 108; 157; DLB 7, 9, 45; SATA 21
Hibbert, Eleanor Alice Burford 1906-1993
　CLC 7; DAM POP
　See also BEST 90:4; CA 17-20R; 140; CANR
　9, 28, 59; MTCW 2; SATA 2; SATA-Obit 74
Hichens, Robert (Smythe) 1864-1950**TCLC 64**
　See also CA 162; DLB 153
Higgins, George V(incent) 1939-　**CLC 4, 7,
　10, 18**
　See also CA 77-80; CAAS 5; CANR 17, 51;
　DLB 2; DLBY 81, 98; INT CANR-17;
　MTCW 1
Higginson, Thomas Wentworth 1823-1911
　TCLC 36
　See also CA 162; DLB 1, 64
Highet, Helen
　See MacInnes, Helen (Clark)
Highsmith, (Mary) Patricia 1921-1995**CLC 2,
　4, 14, 42, 102; DAM NOV, POP**
　See also CA 1-4R; 147; CANR 1, 20, 48, 62;
　DA3; MTCW 1, 2
Highwater, Jamake (Mamake) 1942(?)-**CLC
　12**
　See also AAYA 7; CA 65-68; CAAS 7; CANR
　10, 34, 84; CLR 17; DLB 52; DLBY 85;
　JRDA; MAICYA; SATA 32, 69; SATA-Brief
　30
Highway, Tomson 1951-**CLC 92; DAC; DAM
　MULT**
　See also CA 151; CANR 75; MTCW 2; NNAL
Higuchi, Ichiyo 1872-1896　　　　**NCLC 49**
Hijuelos, Oscar 1951-　**CLC 65; DAM MULT,
　POP; HLC 1**
　See also AAYA 25; BEST 90:1; CA 123; CANR
　50, 75; DA3; DLB 145; HW 1, 2; MTCW 2
Hikmet, Nazim 1902(?)-1963　　　**CLC 40**
　See also CA 141; 93-96
Hildegard von Bingen 1098-1179　**CMLC 20**
　See also DLB 148
Hildesheimer, Wolfgang 1916-1991　**CLC 49**
　See also CA 101; 135; DLB 69, 124
Hill, Geoffrey (William) 1932-　**CLC 5, 8, 18,
　45; DAM POET**
　See also CA 81-84; CANR 21; CDBLB 1960
　to Present; DLB 40; MTCW 1
Hill, George Roy 1921-　　　　　**CLC 26**
　See also CA 110; 122
Hill, John
　See Koontz, Dean R(ay)
Hill, Susan (Elizabeth) 1942-　　**CLC 4, 113;
　DAB; DAM MST, NOV**
　See also CA 33-36R; CANR 29, 69; DLB 14,
　139; MTCW 1

Hillerman, Tony 1925- **CLC 62; DAM POP**
See also AAYA 6; BEST 89:1; CA 29-32R;
CANR 21, 42, 65; DA3; DLB 206; SATA 6
Hillesum, Etty 1914-1943 **TCLC 49**
See also CA 137
Hilliard, Noel (Harvey) 1929- **CLC 15**
See also CA 9-12R; CANR 7, 69
Hillis, Rick 1956- **CLC 66**
See also CA 134
Hilton, James 1900-1954 **TCLC 21**
See also CA 108; 169; DLB 34, 77; SATA 34
Himes, Chester (Bomar) 1909-1984**CLC 2, 4,
7, 18, 58, 108; BLC 2; DAM MULT**
See also BW 2; CA 25-28R; 114; CANR 22;
DLB 2, 76, 143; MTCW 1, 2
Hinde, Thomas **CLC 6, 11**
See also Chitty, Thomas Willes
Hine, (William) Daryl 1936- **CLC 15**
See also CA 1-4R; CAAS 15; CANR 1, 20; DLB
60
Hinkson, Katharine Tynan
See Tynan, Katharine
Hinojosa(-Smith), Rolando (R.) 1929-
See Hinojosa-Smith, Rolando
See also CA 131; CAAS 16; CANR 62; DAM
MULT; DLB 82; HLC 1; HW 1, 2; MTCW 2
Hinojosa-Smith, Rolando 1929-
See Hinojosa(-Smith), Rolando (R.)
See also CAAS 16; HLC 1; MTCW 2
Hinton, S(usan) E(loise) 1950- **CLC 30, 111;
DA; DAB; DAC; DAM MST, NOV**
See also AAYA 2; CA 81-84; CANR 32, 62;
CDALBS; CLR 3, 23; DA3; JRDA;
MAICYA; MTCW 1, 2; SATA 19, 58
Hippius, Zinaida **TCLC 9**
See also Gippius, Zinaida (Nikolayevna)
Hiraoka, Kimitake 1925-1970
See Mishima, Yukio
See also CA 97-100; 29-32R; DAM DRAM;
DA3; MTCW 1, 2
Hirsch, E(ric) D(onald), Jr. 1928- **CLC 79**
See also CA 25-28R; CANR 27, 51; DLB 67;
INT CANR-27; MTCW 1
Hirsch, Edward 1950- **CLC 31, 50**
See also CA 104; CANR 20, 42; DLB 120
Hitchcock, Alfred (Joseph) 1899-1980**CLC 16**
See also AAYA 22; CA 159; 97-100; SATA 27;
SATA-Obit 24
Hitler, Adolf 1889-1945 **TCLC 53**
See also CA 117; 147
Hoagland, Edward 1932- **CLC 28**
See also CA 1-4R; CANR 2, 31, 57; DLB 6;
SATA 51
Hoban, Russell (Conwell) 1925- **CLC 7, 25;
DAM NOV**
See also CA 5-8R; CANR 23, 37, 66; CLR 3;
DLB 52; MAICYA; MTCW 1, 2; SATA 1,
40, 78
Hobbes, Thomas 1588-1679 **LC 36**
See also DLB 151
Hobbs, Perry
See Blackmur, R(ichard) P(almer)
Hobson, Laura Z(ametkin) 1900-1986**CLC 7,
25**
See also CA 17-20R; 118; CANR 55; DLB 28;
SATA 52
Hochhuth, Rolf 1931- **CLC 4, 11, 18; DAM
DRAM**
See also CA 5-8R; CANR 33, 75; DLB 124;
MTCW 1, 2
Hochman, Sandra 1936- **CLC 3, 8**
See also CA 5-8R; DLB 5
Hochwaelder, Fritz 1911-1986 **CLC 36;**

DAM DRAM
See also CA 29-32R; 120; CANR 42; MTCW 1
Hochwalder, Fritz
See Hochwaelder, Fritz
Hocking, Mary (Eunice) 1921- **CLC 13**
See also CA 101; CANR 18, 40
Hodgins, Jack 1938- **CLC 23**
See also CA 93-96; DLB 60
Hodgson, William Hope 1877(?)-1918 **TCLC
13**
See also CA 111; 164; DLB 70, 153, 156, 178;
MTCW 2
Hoeg, Peter 1957- **CLC 95**
See also CA 151; CANR 75; DA3; MTCW 2
Hoffman, Alice 1952- **CLC 51; DAM NOV**
See also CA 77-80; CANR 34, 66; MTCW 1, 2
Hoffman, Daniel (Gerard) 1923-**CLC 6, 13, 23**
See also CA 1-4R; CANR 4; DLB 5
Hoffman, Stanley 1944- **CLC 5**
See also CA 77-80
Hoffman, William M(oses) 1939- **CLC 40**
See also CA 57-60; CANR 11, 71
Hoffmann, E(rnst) T(heodor) A(madeus) 1776-
1822 **NCLC 2; SSC 13**
See also DLB 90; SATA 27
Hofmann, Gert 1931- **CLC 54**
See also CA 128
Hofmannsthal, Hugo von 1874-1929**TCLC 11;
DAM DRAM; DC 4**
See also CA 106; 153; DLB 81, 118
Hogan, Linda 1947- **CLC 73; DAM MULT**
See also CA 120; CANR 45, 73; DLB 175;
NNAL
Hogarth, Charles
See Creasey, John
Hogarth, Emmett
See Polonsky, Abraham (Lincoln)
Hogg, James 1770-1835 **NCLC 4**
See also DLB 93, 116, 159
Holbach, Paul Henri Thiry Baron 1723-1789
LC 14
Holberg, Ludvig 1684-1754 **LC 6**
Holden, Ursula 1921- **CLC 18**
See also CA 101; CAAS 8; CANR 22
Holderlin, (Johann Christian) Friedrich 1770-
1843 **NCLC 16; PC 4**
Holdstock, Robert
See Holdstock, Robert P.
Holdstock, Robert P. 1948- **CLC 39**
See also CA 131; CANR 81
Holland, Isabelle 1920- **CLC 21**
See also AAYA 11; CA 21-24R; 181; CAAE
181; CANR 10, 25, 47; CLR 57; JRDA;
MAICYA; SATA 8, 70; SATA-Essay 103
Holland, Marcus
See Caldwell, (Janet Miriam) Taylor (Holland)
Hollander, John 1929- **CLC 2, 5, 8, 14**
See also CA 1-4R; CANR 1, 52; DLB 5; SATA
13
Hollander, Paul
See Silverberg, Robert
Holleran, Andrew 1943(?)- **CLC 38**
See also CA 144
Hollinghurst, Alan 1954- **CLC 55, 91**
See also CA 114; DLB 207
Hollis, Jim
See Summers, Hollis (Spurgeon, Jr.)
Holly, Buddy 1936-1959 **TCLC 65**
Holmes, Gordon
See Shiel, M(atthew) P(hipps)
Holmes, John
See Souster, (Holmes) Raymond
Holmes, John Clellon 1926-1988 **CLC 56**

See also CA 9-12R; 125; CANR 4; DLB 16
Holmes, Oliver Wendell, Jr. 1841-1935**TCLC
77**
See also CA 114
Holmes, Oliver Wendell 1809-1894**NCLC 14,
81**
See also CDALB 1640-1865; DLB 1, 189;
SATA 34
Holmes, Raymond
See Souster, (Holmes) Raymond
Holt, Victoria
See Hibbert, Eleanor Alice Burford
Holub, Miroslav 1923-1998 **CLC 4**
See also CA 21-24R; 169; CANR 10
Homer c. 8th cent. B.C.- **CMLC 1, 16; DA;
DAB; DAC; DAM MST, POET; PC 23;
WLCS**
See also DA3; DLB 176
Hongo, Garrett Kaoru 1951- **PC 23**
See also CA 133; CAAS 22; DLB 120
Honig, Edwin 1919- **CLC 33**
See also CA 5-8R; CAAS 8; CANR 4, 45; DLB
5
Hood, Hugh (John Blagdon) 1928-**CLC 15, 28**
See also CA 49-52; CAAS 17; CANR 1, 33;
DLB 53
Hood, Thomas 1799-1845 **NCLC 16**
See also DLB 96
Hooker, (Peter) Jeremy 1941- **CLC 43**
See also CA 77-80; CANR 22; DLB 40
hooks, bell **CLC 94; BLCS**
See also Watkins, Gloria
See also MTCW 2
Hope, A(lec) D(erwent) 1907- **CLC 3, 51**
See also CA 21-24R; CANR 33, 74; MTCW 1,
2
Hope, Anthony 1863-1933 **TCLC 83**
See also CA 157; DLB 153, 156
Hope, Brian
See Creasey, John
Hope, Christopher (David Tully) 1944- **CLC
52**
See also CA 106; CANR 47; SATA 62
Hopkins, Gerard Manley 1844-1889 **NCLC
17; DA; DAB; DAC; DAM MST, POET;
PC 15; WLC**
See also CDBLB 1890-1914; DA3; DLB 35,
57
Hopkins, John (Richard) 1931-1998 **CLC 4**
See also CA 85-88; 169
Hopkins, Pauline Elizabeth 1859-1930**TCLC
28; BLC 2; DAM MULT**
See also BW 2, 3; CA 141; CANR 82; DLB 50
Hopkinson, Francis 1737-1791 **LC 25**
See also DLB 31
Hopley-Woolrich, Cornell George 1903-1968
See Woolrich, Cornell
See also CA 13-14; CANR 58; CAP 1; MTCW
2
Horatio
See Proust, (Valentin-Louis-George-Eugene-)
Marcel
Horgan, Paul (George Vincent O'Shaughnessy)
1903-1995 **CLC 9, 53; DAM NOV**
See also CA 13-16R; 147; CANR 9, 35; DLB
212; DLBY 85; INT CANR-9; MTCW 1, 2;
SATA 13; SATA-Obit 84
Horn, Peter
See Kuttner, Henry
Hornem, Horace Esq.
See Byron, George Gordon (Noel)
**Horney, Karen (Clementine Theodore
Danielsen)** 1885-1952 **TCLC 71**

See also CA 114; 165

Hornung, E(rnest) W(illiam) 1866-1921
TCLC 59
See also CA 108; 160; DLB 70

Horovitz, Israel (Arthur) 1939-**CLC 56; DAM DRAM**
See also CA 33-36R; CANR 46, 59; DLB 7

Horvath, Odon von
See Horvath, Oedoen von
See also DLB 85, 124

Horvath, Oedoen von 1901-1938   **TCLC 45**
See also Horvath, Odon von
See also CA 118

Horwitz, Julius 1920-1986   **CLC 14**
See also CA 9-12R; 119; CANR 12

Hospital, Janette Turner 1942-   **CLC 42**
See also CA 108; CANR 48

Hostos, E. M. de
See Hostos (y Bonilla), Eugenio Maria de

Hostos, Eugenio M. de
See Hostos (y Bonilla), Eugenio Maria de

Hostos, Eugenio Maria
See Hostos (y Bonilla), Eugenio Maria de

Hostos (y Bonilla), Eugenio Maria de 1839-1903
TCLC 24
See also CA 123; 131; HW 1

Houdini
See Lovecraft, H(oward) P(hillips)

Hougan, Carolyn 1943-   **CLC 34**
See also CA 139

Household, Geoffrey (Edward West) 1900-1988
CLC 11
See also CA 77-80; 126; CANR 58; DLB 87;
SATA 14; SATA-Obit 59

Housman, A(lfred) E(dward) 1859-1936
TCLC 1, 10; DA; DAB; DAC; DAM MST,
POET; PC 2; WLCS
See also CA 104; 125; DA3; DLB 19; MTCW
1, 2

Housman, Laurence 1865-1959   **TCLC 7**
See also CA 106; 155; DLB 10; SATA 25

Howard, Elizabeth Jane 1923-   **CLC 7, 29**
See also CA 5-8R; CANR 8, 62

Howard, Maureen 1930-   **CLC 5, 14, 46**
See also CA 53-56; CANR 31, 75; DLBY 83;
INT CANR-31; MTCW 1, 2

Howard, Richard 1929-   **CLC 7, 10, 47**
See also AITN 1; CA 85-88; CANR 25, 80; DLB
5; INT CANR-25

Howard, Robert E(rvin) 1906-1936   **TCLC 8**
See also CA 105; 157

Howard, Warren F.
See Pohl, Frederik

Howe, Fanny (Quincy) 1940-   **CLC 47**
See also CA 117; CAAS 27; CANR 70; SATA-
Brief 52

Howe, Irving 1920-1993   **CLC 85**
See also CA 9-12R; 141; CANR 21, 50; DLB
67; MTCW 1, 2

Howe, Julia Ward 1819-1910   **TCLC 21**
See also CA 117; DLB 1, 189

Howe, Susan 1937-   **CLC 72**
See also CA 160; DLB 120

Howe, Tina 1937-   **CLC 48**
See also CA 109

Howell, James 1594(?)-1666   **LC 13**
See also DLB 151

Howells, W. D.
See Howells, William Dean

Howells, William D.
See Howells, William Dean

Howells, William Dean 1837-1920   **TCLC 7,**
17, 41; SSC 36

See also CA 104; 134; CDALB 1865-1917;
DLB 12, 64, 74, 79, 189; MTCW 2

Howes, Barbara 1914-1996   **CLC 15**
See also CA 9-12R; 151; CAAS 3; CANR 53;
SATA 5

Hrabal, Bohumil 1914-1997   **CLC 13, 67**
See also CA 106; 156; CAAS 12; CANR 57

Hroswitha of Gandersheim c. 935-c. 1002
CMLC 29
See also DLB 148

Hsun, Lu
See Lu Hsun

Hubbard, L(afayette) Ron(ald) 1911-1986
CLC 43; DAM POP
See also CA 77-80; 118; CANR 52; DA3;
MTCW 2

Huch, Ricarda (Octavia) 1864-1947**TCLC 13**
See also CA 111; DLB 66

Huddle, David 1942-   **CLC 49**
See also CA 57-60; CAAS 20; DLB 130

Hudson, Jeffrey
See Crichton, (John) Michael

Hudson, W(illiam) H(enry) 1841-1922 **TCLC**
29
See also CA 115; DLB 98, 153, 174; SATA 35

Hueffer, Ford Madox
See Ford, Ford Madox

Hughart, Barry 1934-   **CLC 39**
See also CA 137

Hughes, Colin
See Creasey, John

Hughes, David (John) 1930-   **CLC 48**
See also CA 116; 129; DLB 14

Hughes, Edward James
See Hughes, Ted
See also DAM MST, POET; DA3

Hughes, (James) Langston 1902-1967**CLC 1,**
5, 10, 15, 35, 44, 108; BLC 2; DA; DAB;
DAC; DAM DRAM, MST, MULT, POET;
DC 3; PC 1; SSC 6; WLC
See also AAYA 12; BW 1, 3; CA 1-4R; 25-28R;
CANR 1, 34, 82; CDALB 1929-1941; CLR
17; DA3; DLB 4, 7, 48, 51, 86; JRDA;
MAICYA; MTCW 1, 2; SATA 4, 33

Hughes, Richard (Arthur Warren) 1900-1976
CLC 1, 11; DAM NOV
See also CA 5-8R; 65-68; CANR 4; DLB 15,
161; MTCW 1; SATA 8; SATA-Obit 25

Hughes, Ted 1930-1998   **CLC 2, 4, 9, 14, 37,**
119; DAB; DAC; PC 7
See also Hughes, Edward James
See also CA 1-4R; 171; CANR 1, 33, 66; CLR
3; DLB 40, 161; MAICYA; MTCW 1, 2,
SATA 49; SATA-Brief 27; SATA-Obit 107

Hugo, Richard F(ranklin) 1923-1982 **CLC 6,**
18, 32; DAM POET
See also CA 49-52; 108; CANR 3; DLB 5, 206

Hugo, Victor (Marie) 1802-1885**NCLC 3, 10,**
21; DA; DAB; DAC; DAM DRAM, MST,
NOV, POET; PC 17; WLC
See also AAYA 28; DA3; DLB 119, 192; SATA
47

Huidobro, Vicente
See Huidobro Fernandez, Vicente Garcia

Huidobro Fernandez, Vicente Garcia 1893-
1948   **TCLC 31**
See also CA 131; HW 1

Hulme, Keri 1947-   **CLC 39**
See also CA 125; CANR 69; INT 125

Hulme, T(homas) E(rnest) 1883-1917   **TCLC**
21
See also CA 117; DLB 19

Hume, David 1711-1776   **LC 7**

See also DLB 104

Humphrey, William 1924-1997   **CLC 45**
See also CA 77-80; 160; CANR 68; DLB 212

Humphreys, Emyr Owen 1919-   **CLC 47**
See also CA 5-8R; CANR 3, 24; DLB 15

Humphreys, Josephine 1945-   **CLC 34, 57**
See also CA 121; 127; INT 127

Huneker, James Gibbons 1857-1921**TCLC 65**
See also DLB 71

Hungerford, Pixie
See Brinsmead, H(esba) F(ay)

Hunt, E(verette) Howard, (Jr.) 1918- **CLC 3**
See also AITN 1; CA 45-48; CANR 2, 47

Hunt, Francesca
See Holland, Isabelle

Hunt, Kyle
See Creasey, John

Hunt, (James Henry) Leigh 1784-1859**NCLC**
1, 70; DAM POET
See also DLB 96, 110, 144

Hunt, Marsha **CLC 70**
See also BW 2, 3; CA 143; CANR 79

Hunt, Violet 1866(?)-1942   **TCLC 53**
See also DLB 162, 197

Hunter, E. Waldo
See Sturgeon, Theodore (Hamilton)

Hunter, Evan 1926- **CLC 11, 31; DAM POP**
See also CA 5-8R; CANR 5, 38, 62; DLBY 82;
INT CANR-5; MTCW 1; SATA 25

Hunter, Kristin (Eggleston) 1931-   **CLC 35**
See also AITN 1; BW 1; CA 13-16R; CANR
13; CLR 3; DLB 33; INT CANR-13;
MAICYA; SAAS 10; SATA 12

Hunter, Mary
See Austin, Mary (Hunter)

Hunter, Mollie 1922-   **CLC 21**
See McIlwraith, Maureen Mollie Hunter
See also AAYA 13; CANR 37, 78; CLR 25; DLB
161; JRDA; MAICYA; SAAS 7; SATA 54,
106

Hunter, Robert (?)-1734   **LC 7**

Hurston, Zora Neale 1903-1960**CLC 7, 30, 61;**
BLC 2; DA; DAC; DAM MST, MULT,
NOV; SSC 4; WLCS
See also AAYA 15; BW 1, 3; CA 85-88; CANR
61; CDALBS; DA3; DLB 51, 86; MTCW 1,
2

Huston, John (Marcellus) 1906-1987**CLC 20**
See also CA 73-76; 123; CANR 34; DLB 26

Hustvedt, Siri 1955-   **CLC 76**
See also CA 137

Hutten, Ulrich von 1488-1523   **LC 16**
See also DLB 179

Huxley, Aldous (Leonard) 1894-1963 **CLC 1,**
3, 4, 5, 8, 11, 18, 35, 79; DA; DAB; DAC;
DAM MST, NOV; WLC
See also AAYA 11; CA 85-88; CANR 44;
CDBLB 1914-1945; DA3; DLB 36, 100,
162, 195; MTCW 1, 2; SATA 63

Huxley, T(homas) H(enry) 1825-1895 **NCLC**
67
See also DLB 57

Huysmans, Joris-Karl 1848-1907**TCLC 7, 69**
See also CA 104; 165; DLB 123

Hwang, David Henry 1957-   **CLC 55; DAM**
DRAM; DC 4
See also CA 127; 132; CANR 76; DA3; DLB
212; INT 132; MTCW 2

Hyde, Anthony 1946-   **CLC 42**
See also CA 136

Hyde, Margaret O(ldroyd) 1917-   **CLC 21**
See also CA 1-4R; CANR 1, 36; CLR 23; JRDA;
MAICYA; SAAS 8; SATA 1, 42, 76

Hynes, James 1956(?)- CLC 65
See also CA 164
Hypatia c. 370-415 CMLC 35
Ian, Janis 1951- CLC 21
See also CA 105
Ibanez, Vicente Blasco
See Blasco Ibanez, Vicente
Ibarbourou, Juana de 1895-1979
See also HLCS 2; HW 1
Ibarguengoitia, Jorge 1928-1983 CLC 37
See also CA 124; 113; HW 1
Ibsen, Henrik (Johan) 1828-1906 TCLC 2, 8,
16, 37, 52; DA; DAB; DAC; DAM DRAM,
MST; DC 2; WLC
See also CA 104; 141; DA3
Ibuse, Masuji 1898-1993 CLC 22
See also CA 127; 141; DLB 180
Ichikawa, Kon 1915- CLC 20
See also CA 121
Idle, Eric 1943- CLC 21
See also Monty Python
See also CA 116; CANR 35
Ignatow, David 1914-1997 CLC 4, 7, 14, 40
See also CA 9-12R; 162; CAAS 3; CANR 31,
57; DLB 5
Ignotus
See Strachey, (Giles) Lytton
Ihimaera, Witi 1944- CLC 46
See also CA 77-80
Ilf, Ilya TCLC 21
See also Fainzilberg, Ilya Arnoldovich
Illyes, Gyula 1902-1983 PC 16
See also CA 114; 109
Immermann, Karl (Lebrecht) 1796-1840
NCLC 4, 49
See also DLB 133
Ince, Thomas H. 1882-1924 TCLC 89
Inchbald, Elizabeth 1753-1821 NCLC 62
See also DLB 39, 89
Inclan, Ramon (Maria) del Valle
See Valle-Inclan, Ramon (Maria) del
Infante, G(uillermo) Cabrera
See Cabrera Infante, G(uillermo)
Ingalls, Rachel (Holmes) 1940- CLC 42
See also CA 123; 127
Ingamells, Reginald Charles
See Ingamells, Rex
Ingamells, Rex 1913-1955 TCLC 35
See also CA 167
Inge, William (Motter) 1913-1973 CLC 1, 8,
19; DAM DRAM
See also CA 9-12R; CDALB 1941-1968; DA3;
DLB 7; MTCW 1, 2
Ingelow, Jean 1820-1897 NCLC 39
See also DLB 35, 163; SATA 33
Ingram, Willis J.
See Harris, Mark
Innaurato, Albert (F.) 1948(?)- CLC 21, 60
See also CA 115; 122; CANR 78; INT 122
Innes, Michael
See Stewart, J(ohn) I(nnes) M(ackintosh)
Innis, Harold Adams 1894-1952 TCLC 77
See also CA 181; DLB 88
Ionesco, Eugene 1909-1994 CLC 1, 4, 6, 9, 11,
15, 41, 86; DA; DAB; DAC; DAM DRAM,
MST; WLC
See also CA 9-12R; 144; CANR 55; DA3;
MTCW 1, 2; SATA 7; SATA-Obit 79
Iqbal, Muhammad 1873-1938 TCLC 28
Ireland, Patrick
See O'Doherty, Brian
Iron, Ralph
See Schreiner, Olive (Emilie Albertina)

Irving, John (Winslow) 1942-CLC 13, 23, 38,
112; DAM NOV, POP
See also AAYA 8; BEST 89:3; CA 25-28R;
CANR 28, 73; DA3; DLB 6; DLBY 82;
MTCW 1, 2
Irving, Washington 1783-1859 NCLC 2, 19;
DA; DAB; DAC; DAM MST; SSC 2, 37;
WLC
See also CDALB 1640-1865; DA3; DLB 3, 11,
30, 59, 73, 74, 186; YABC 2
Irwin, P. K.
See Page, P(atricia) K(athleen)
Isaacs, Jorge Ricardo 1837-1895 NCLC 70
Isaacs, Susan 1943- CLC 32; DAM POP
See also BEST 89:1; CA 89-92; CANR 20, 41,
65; DA3; INT CANR-20; MTCW 1, 2
Isherwood, Christopher (William Bradshaw)
1904-1986 CLC 1, 9, 11, 14, 44; DAM
DRAM, NOV
See also CA 13-16R; 117; CANR 35; DA3;
DLB 15, 195; DLBY 86; MTCW 1, 2
Ishiguro, Kazuo 1954- CLC 27, 56, 59, 110;
DAM NOV
See also BEST 90:2; CA 120; CANR 49; DA3;
DLB 194; MTCW 1, 2
Ishikawa, Hakuhin
See Ishikawa, Takuboku
Ishikawa, Takuboku 1886(?)-1912 TCLC 15;
DAM POET; PC 10
See also CA 113; 153
Iskander, Fazil 1929- CLC 47
See also CA 102
Isler, Alan (David) 1934- CLC 91
See also CA 156
Ivan IV 1530-1584 LC 17
Ivanov, Vyacheslav Ivanovich 1866-1949
TCLC 33
See also CA 122
Ivask, Ivar Vidrik 1927-1992 CLC 14
See also CA 37-40R; 139; CANR 24
Ives, Morgan
See Bradley, Marion Zimmer
Izumi Shikibu c. 973-c. 1034 CMLC 33
J. R. S.
See Gogarty, Oliver St. John
Jabran, Kahlil
See Gibran, Kahlil
Jabran, Khalil
See Gibran, Kahlil
Jackson, Daniel
See Wingrove, David (John)
Jackson, Jesse 1908-1983 CLC 12
See also BW 1; CA 25-28R; 109; CANR 27; CLR
28; MAICYA; SATA 2, 29; SATA-Obit 48
Jackson, Laura (Riding) 1901-1991
See Riding, Laura
See also CA 65-68; 135; CANR 28; DLB 48
Jackson, Sam
See Trumbo, Dalton
Jackson, Sara
See Wingrove, David (John)
Jackson, Shirley 1919-1965 CLC 11, 60, 87;
DA; DAC; DAM MST; SSC 9; WLC
See also AAYA 9; CA 1-4R; 25-28R; CANR 4,
52; CDALB 1941-1968; DA3; DLB 6;
MTCW 2; SATA 2
Jacob, (Cyprien-)Max 1876-1944 TCLC 6
See also CA 104
Jacobs, Harriet A(nn) 1813(?)-1897 NCLC 67
Jacobs, Jim 1942- CLC 12
See also CA 97-100; INT 97-100
Jacobs, W(illiam) W(ymark) 1863-1943
TCLC 22

See also CA 121; 167; DLB 135
Jacobsen, Jens Peter 1847-1885 NCLC 34
Jacobsen, Josephine 1908- CLC 48, 102
See also CA 33-36R; CAAS 18; CANR 23, 48
Jacobson, Dan 1929- CLC 4, 14
See also CA 1-4R; CANR 2, 25, 66; DLB 14,
207; MTCW 1
Jacqueline
See Carpentier (y Valmont), Alejo
Jagger, Mick 1944- CLC 17
Jahiz, al- c. 780-c. 869 CMLC 25
Jakes, John (William) 1932- CLC 29; DAM
NOV, POP
See also AAYA 32; BEST 89:4; CA 57-60;
CANR 10, 43, 66; DA3; DLBY 83; INT
CANR-10; MTCW 1, 2; SATA 62
James, Andrew
See Kirkup, James
James, C(yril) L(ionel) R(obert) 1901-1989
CLC 33; BLCS
See also BW 2; CA 117; 125; 128; CANR 62;
DLB 125; MTCW 1
James, Daniel (Lewis) 1911-1988
See Santiago, Danny
See also CA 174; 125
James, Dynely
See Mayne, William (James Carter)
James, Henry Sr. 1811-1882 NCLC 53
James, Henry 1843-1916 TCLC 2, 11, 24, 40,
47, 64; DA; DAB; DAC; DAM MST, NOV;
SSC 8, 32; WLC
See also CA 104; 132; CDALB 1865-1917;
DA3; DLB 12, 71, 74, 189; DLBD 13;
MTCW 1, 2
James, M. R.
See James, Montague (Rhodes)
See also DLB 156
James, Montague (Rhodes) 1862-1936 TCLC
6; SSC 16
See also CA 104; DLB 201
James, P. D. 1920- CLC 18, 46, 122
See also White, Phyllis Dorothy James
See also BEST 90:2; CDBLB 1960 to Present;
DLB 87; DLBD 17
James, Philip
See Moorcock, Michael (John)
James, William 1842-1910 TCLC 15, 32
See also CA 109
James I 1394-1437 LC 20
Jameson, Anna 1794-1860 NCLC 43
See also DLB 99, 166
Jami, Nur al-Din 'Abd al-Rahman 1414-1492
LC 9
Jammes, Francis 1868-1938 TCLC 75
Jandl, Ernst 1925- CLC 34
Janowitz, Tama 1957- CLC 43; DAM POP
See also CA 106; CANR 52
Japrisot, Sebastien 1931- CLC 90
Jarrell, Randall 1914-1965 CLC 1, 2, 6, 9, 13,
49; DAM POET
See also CA 5-8R; 25-28R; CABS 2; CANR 6,
34; CDALB 1941-1968; CLR 6; DLB 48, 52;
MAICYA; MTCW 1, 2; SATA 7
Jarry, Alfred 1873-1907 TCLC 2, 14; DAM
DRAM; SSC 20
See also CA 104; 153; DA3; DLB 192
Jaynes, Roderick
See Coen, Ethan
Jeake, Samuel, Jr.
See Aiken, Conrad (Potter)
Jean Paul 1763-1825 NCLC 7
Jefferies, (John) Richard 1848-1887 NCLC 47
See also DLB 98, 141; SATA 16

Jeffers, (John) Robinson 1887-1962 **CLC 2, 3, 11, 15, 54; DA; DAC; DAM MST, POET; PC 17; WLC**
See also CA 85-88; CANR 35; CDALB 1917-1929; DLB 45, 212; MTCW 1, 2

Jefferson, Janet
See Mencken, H(enry) L(ouis)

Jefferson, Thomas 1743-1826 **NCLC 11**
See also CDALB 1640-1865; DA3; DLB 31

Jeffrey, Francis 1773-1850 **NCLC 33**
See also DLB 107

Jelakowitch, Ivan
See Heijermans, Herman

Jellicoe, (Patricia) Ann 1927- **CLC 27**
See also CA 85-88; DLB 13

Jen, Gish **CLC 70**
See also Jen, Lillian

Jen, Lillian 1956(?)-
See Jen, Gish
See also CA 135

Jenkins, (John) Robin 1912- **CLC 52**
See also CA 1-4R; CANR 1; DLB 14

Jennings, Elizabeth (Joan) 1926- **CLC 5, 14**
See also CA 61-64; CAAS 5; CANR 8, 39, 66; DLB 27; MTCW 1; SATA 66

Jennings, Waylon 1937- **CLC 21**

Jensen, Johannes V. 1873-1950 **TCLC 41**
See also CA 170

Jensen, Laura (Linnea) 1948- **CLC 37**
See also CA 103

Jerome, Jerome K(lapka) 1859-1927 **TCLC 23**
See also CA 119; 177; DLB 10, 34, 135

Jerrold, Douglas William 1803-1857 **NCLC 2**
See also DLB 158, 159

Jewett, (Theodora) Sarah Orne 1849-1909 **TCLC 1, 22; SSC 6**
See also CA 108; 127; CANR 71; DLB 12, 74; SATA 15

Jewsbury, Geraldine (Endsor) 1812-1880 **NCLC 22**
See also DLB 21

Jhabvala, Ruth Prawer 1927- **CLC 4, 8, 29, 94; DAB; DAM NOV**
See also CA 1-4R; CANR 2, 29, 51, 74; DLB 139, 194; INT CANR-29; MTCW 1, 2

Jibran, Kahlil
See Gibran, Kahlil

Jibran, Khalil
See Gibran, Kahlil

Jiles, Paulette 1943- **CLC 13, 58**
See also CA 101; CANR 70

Jimenez (Mantecon), Juan Ramon 1881-1958 **TCLC 4; DAM MULT, POET; HLC 1; PC 7**
See also CA 104; 131; CANR 74; DLB 134; HW 1; MTCW 1, 2

Jimenez, Ramon
See Jimenez (Mantecon), Juan Ramon

Jimenez Mantecon, Juan
See Jimenez (Mantecon), Juan Ramon

Jin, Ha 1956- **CLC 109**
See also CA 152

Joel, Billy **CLC 26**
See also Joel, William Martin

Joel, William Martin 1949-
See Joel, Billy
See also CA 108

John, Saint 7th cent. - **CMLC 27**

John of the Cross, St. 1542-1591 **LC 18**

Johnson, B(ryan) S(tanley William) 1933-1973 **CLC 6, 9**
See also CA 9-12R; 53-56; CANR 9; DLB 14, 40

Johnson, Benj. F. of Boo

See Riley, James Whitcomb

Johnson, Benjamin F. of Boo
See Riley, James Whitcomb

Johnson, Charles (Richard) 1948- **CLC 7, 51, 65; BLC 2; DAM MULT**
See also BW 2, 3; CA 116; CAAS 18; CANR 42, 66, 82; DLB 33; MTCW 2

Johnson, Denis 1949- **CLC 52**
See also CA 117; 121; CANR 71; DLB 120

Johnson, Diane 1934- **CLC 5, 13, 48**
See also CA 41-44R; CANR 17, 40, 62; DLBY 80; INT CANR-17; MTCW 1

Johnson, Eyvind (Olof Verner) 1900-1976 **CLC 14**
See also CA 73-76; 69-72; CANR 34

Johnson, J. R.
See James, C(yril) L(ionel) R(obert)

Johnson, James Weldon 1871-1938 **TCLC 3, 19; BLC 2; DAM MULT, POET; PC 24**
See also BW 1, 3; CA 104; 125; CANR 82; CDALB 1917-1929; CLR 32; DA3; DLB 51; MTCW 1, 2; SATA 31

Johnson, Joyce 1935- **CLC 58**
See also CA 125; 129

Johnson, Judith (Emlyn) 1936- **CLC 7, 15**
See also Sherwin, Judith Johnson
See also CA 25-28R, 153; CANR 34

Johnson, Lionel (Pigot) 1867-1902 **TCLC 19**
See also CA 117; DLB 19

Johnson, Marguerite (Annie)
See Angelou, Maya

Johnson, Mel
See Malzberg, Barry N(athaniel)

Johnson, Pamela Hansford 1912-1981 **CLC 1, 7, 27**
See also CA 1-4R; 104; CANR 2, 28; DLB 15; MTCW 1, 2

Johnson, Robert 1911(?)-1938 **TCLC 69**
See also BW 3; CA 174

Johnson, Samuel 1709-1784 **LC 15, 52; DA; DAB; DAC; DAM MST; WLC**
See also CDBLB 1660-1789; DLB 39, 95, 104, 142

Johnson, Uwe 1934-1984 **CLC 5, 10, 15, 40**
See also CA 1-4R; 112; CANR 1, 39; DLB 75; MTCW 1

Johnston, George (Benson) 1913- **CLC 51**
See also CA 1-4R; CANR 5, 20; DLB 88

Johnston, Jennifer 1930- **CLC 7**
See also CA 85-88; DLB 14

Jolley, (Monica) Elizabeth 1923- **CLC 46; SSC 19**
See also CA 127; CAAS 13; CANR 59

Jones, Arthur Llewellyn 1863-1947
See Machen, Arthur
See also CA 104; 179

Jones, D(ouglas) G(ordon) 1929- **CLC 10**
See also CA 29-32R; CANR 13; DLB 53

Jones, David (Michael) 1895-1974 **CLC 2, 4, 7, 13, 42**
See also CA 9-12R; 53-56; CANR 28; CDBLB 1945-1960; DLB 20, 100; MTCW 1

Jones, David Robert 1947-
See Bowie, David
See also CA 103

Jones, Diana Wynne 1934- **CLC 26**
See also AAYA 12; CA 49-52; CANR 4, 26, 56, CLR 23; DLB 161; JRDA; MAICYA; SAAS 7; SATA 9, 70, 108

Jones, Edward P. 1950- **CLC 76**
See also BW 2, 3; CA 142; CANR 79

Jones, Gayl 1949- **CLC 6, 9; BLC 2; DAM MULT**

See also BW 2, 3; CA 77-80; CANR 27, 66; DA3; DLB 33; MTCW 1, 2

Jones, James 1921-1977 **CLC 1, 3, 10, 39**
See also AITN 1, 2; CA 1-4R; 69-72; CANR 6; DLB 2, 143; DLBD 17; DLBY 98; MTCW 1

Jones, John J.
See Lovecraft, H(oward) P(hillips)

Jones, LeRoi **CLC 1, 2, 3, 5, 10, 14**
See also Baraka, Amiri
See also MTCW 2

Jones, Louis B. 1953- **CLC 65**
See also CA 141; CANR 73

Jones, Madison (Percy, Jr.) 1925- **CLC 4**
See also CA 13-16R; CAAS 11; CANR 7, 54, 83; DLB 152

Jones, Mervyn 1922- **CLC 10, 52**
See also CA 45-48; CAAS 5; CANR 1; MTCW 1

Jones, Mick 1956(?)- **CLC 30**

Jones, Nettie (Pearl) 1941- **CLC 34**
See also BW 2; CA 137; CAAS 20

Jones, Preston 1936-1979 **CLC 10**
See also CA 73-76; 89-92; DLB 7

Jones, Robert F(rancis) 1934- **CLC 7**
See also CA 49-52; CANR 2, 61

Jones, Rod 1953- **CLC 50**
See also CA 128

Jones, Terence Graham Parry 1942- **CLC 21**
See also Jones, Terry; Monty Python
See also CA 112; 116; CANR 35; INT 116

Jones, Terry
See Jones, Terence Graham Parry
See also SATA 67; SATA-Brief 51

Jones, Thom 1945(?)- **CLC 81**
See also CA 157

Jong, Erica 1942- **CLC 4, 6, 8, 18, 83; DAM NOV, POP**
See also AITN 1; BEST 90:2; CA 73-76; CANR 26, 52, 75; DA3; DLB 2, 5, 28, 152; INT CANR-26; MTCW 1, 2

Jonson, Ben(jamin) 1572(?)-1637 **LC 6, 33; DA; DAB; DAC; DAM DRAM, MST, POET; DC 4; PC 17; WLC**
See also CDBLB Before 1660; DLB 62, 121

Jordan, June 1936- **CLC 5, 11, 23, 114; BLCS; DAM MULT, POET**
See also AAYA 2; BW 2, 3; CA 33-36R; CANR 25, 70; CLR 10; DLB 38; MAICYA; MTCW 1; SATA 4

Jordan, Neil (Patrick) 1950- **CLC 110**
See also CA 124; 130; CANR 54; INT 130

Jordan, Pat(rick M.) 1941- **CLC 37**
See also CA 33-36R

Jorgensen, Ivar
See Ellison, Harlan (Jay)

Jorgenson, Ivar
See Silverberg, Robert

Josephus, Flavius c. 37-100 **CMLC 13**

Josipovici, Gabriel 1940- **CLC 6, 43**
See also CA 37-40R; CAAS 8; CANR 47, 84; DLB 14

Joubert, Joseph 1754-1824 **NCLC 9**

Jouve, Pierre Jean 1887-1976 **CLC 47**
See also CA 65-68

Jovine, Francesco 1902-1950 **TCLC 79**

Joyce, James (Augustine Aloysius) 1882-1941 **TCLC 3, 8, 16, 35, 52; DA; DAB; DAC; DAM MST, NOV, POET; PC 22; SSC 3, 26; WLC**
See also CA 104; 126; CDBLB 1914-1945; DA3; DLB 10, 19, 36, 162; MTCW 1, 2

Jozsef, Attila 1905-1937 **TCLC 22**
See also CA 116

Kennedy, Joseph Charles 1929-
See Kennedy, X. J.
See also CA 1-4R; CANR 4, 30, 40; SATA 14, 86

Kennedy, William 1928-   **CLC 6, 28, 34, 53; DAM NOV**
See also AAYA 1; CA 85-88; CANR 14, 31, 76; DA3; DLB 143; DLBY 85; INT CANR-31; MTCW 1, 2; SATA 57

Kennedy, X. J.   **CLC 8, 42**
See Kennedy, Joseph Charles
See also CAAS 9; CLR 27; DLB 5; SAAS 22

Kenny, Maurice (Francis) 1929-   **CLC 87; DAM MULT**
See also CA 144; CAAS 22; DLB 175; NNAL

Kent, Kelvin
See Kuttner, Henry

Kenton, Maxwell
See Southern, Terry

Kenyon, Robert O.
See Kuttner, Henry

Kepler, Johannes 1571-1630   **LC 45**

Kerouac, Jack   **CLC 1, 2, 3, 5, 14, 29, 61**
See also Kerouac, Jean-Louis Lebris de
See also AAYA 25; CDALB 1941-1968; DLB 2, 16; DLBD 3; DLBY 95; MTCW 2

Kerouac, Jean-Louis Lebris de 1922-1969
See Kerouac, Jack
See also AITN 1; CA 5-8R; 25-28R; CANR 26, 54; DA; DAB; DAC; DAM MST, NOV, POET, POP; DA3; MTCW 1, 2; WLC

Kerr, Jean 1923-   **CLC 22**
See also CA 5-8R; CANR 7; INT CANR-7

Kerr, M. E.   **CLC 12, 35**
See also Meaker, Marijane (Agnes)
See also AAYA 2, 23; CLR 29; SAAS 1

Kerr, Robert   **CLC 55**

Kerrigan, (Thomas) Anthony 1918-   **CLC 4, 6**
See also CA 49-52; CAAS 11; CANR 4

Kerry, Lois
See Duncan, Lois

Kesey, Ken (Elton) 1935-   **CLC 1, 3, 6, 11, 46, 64; DA; DAB; DAC; DAM MST, NOV, POP; WLC**
See also AAYA 25; CA 1-4R; CANR 22, 38, 66; CDALB 1968-1988; DA3; DLB 2, 16, 206; MTCW 1, 2; SATA 66

Kesselring, Joseph (Otto) 1902-1967**CLC 45; DAM DRAM, MST**
See also CA 150

Kessler, Jascha (Frederick) 1929-   **CLC 4**
See also CA 17-20R; CANR 8, 48

Kettelkamp, Larry (Dale) 1933-   **CLC 12**
See also CA 29-32R; CANR 16; SAAS 3; SATA 2

Key, Ellen 1849-1926   **TCLC 65**

Keyber, Conny
See Fielding, Henry

Keyes, Daniel 1927-**CLC 80; DA; DAC; DAM MST, NOV**
See also AAYA 23; CA 17-20R; CANR 10, 26, 54, 74; DA3; MTCW 2; SATA 37

Keynes, John Maynard 1883-1946 **TCLC 64**
See also CA 114; 162, 163; DLBD 10; MTCW 2

Khanshendel, Chiron
See Rose, Wendy

Khayyam, Omar 1048-1131 **CMLC 11; DAM POET; PC 8**
See also DA3

Kherdian, David 1931-   **CLC 6, 9**
See also CA 21-24R; CAAS 2; CANR 39, 78; CLR 24; JRDA; MAICYA; SATA 16, 74

Khlebnikov, Velimir   **TCLC 20**
See also Khlebnikov, Viktor Vladimirovich

Khlebnikov, Viktor Vladimirovich 1885-1922
See Khlebnikov, Velimir
See also CA 117

Khodasevich, Vladislav (Felitsianovich) 1886-1939   **TCLC 15**
See also CA 115

Kielland, Alexander Lange 1849-1906 **TCLC 5**
See also CA 104

Kiely, Benedict 1919-   **CLC 23, 43**
See also CA 1-4R; CANR 2, 84; DLB 15

Kienzle, William X(avier) 1928-   **CLC 25; DAM POP**
See also CA 93-96; CAAS 1; CANR 9, 31, 59; DA3; INT CANR-31; MTCW 1, 2

Kierkegaard, Soren 1813-1855 **NCLC 34, 78**

Kieslowski, Krzysztof 1941-1996   **CLC 120**
See also CA 147; 151

Killens, John Oliver 1916-1987   **CLC 10**
See also BW 2; CA 77-80; 123; CAAS 2; CANR 26; DLB 33

Killigrew, Anne 1660-1685   **LC 4**
See also DLB 131

Kim
See Simenon, Georges (Jacques Christian)

Kincaid, Jamaica 1949- **CLC 43, 68; BLC 2; DAM MULT, NOV**
See also AAYA 13; BW 2, 3; CA 125; CANR 47, 59; CDALBS; DA3; DLB 157; MTCW 2

King, Francis (Henry) 1923-**CLC 8, 53; DAM NOV**
See also CA 1-4R; CANR 1, 33; DLB 15, 139; MTCW 1

King, Kennedy
See Brown, George Douglas

King, Martin Luther, Jr. 1929-1968 **CLC 83; BLC 2; DA; DAB; DAC; DAM MST, MULT; WLCS**
See also BW 2, 3; CA 25-28; CANR 27, 44; CAP 2; DA3; MTCW 1, 2; SATA 14

King, Stephen (Edwin) 1947-**CLC 12, 26, 37, 61, 113; DAM NOV, POP; SSC 17**
See also AAYA 1, 17; BEST 90:1; CA 61-64; CANR 1, 30, 52, 76; DA3; DLB 143; DLBY 80; JRDA; MTCW 1, 2; SATA 9, 55

King, Steve
See King, Stephen (Edwin)

King, Thomas 1943-   **CLC 89; DAC; DAM MULT**
See also CA 144; DLB 175; NNAL; SATA 96

Kingman, Lee   **CLC 17**
See Natti, (Mary) Lee
See also SAAS 3; SATA 1, 67

Kingsley, Charles 1819-1875   **NCLC 35**
See also DLB 21, 32, 163, 190; YABC 2

Kingsley, Sidney 1906-1995   **CLC 44**
See also CA 85-88; 147; DLB 7

Kingsolver, Barbara 1955-**CLC 55, 81; DAM POP**
See also AAYA 15; CA 129; 134; CANR 60; CDALBS; DA3; DLB 206; INT 134; MTCW 2

Kingston, Maxine (Ting Ting) Hong 1940-
CLC 12, 19, 58, 121; DAM MULT, NOV; WLCS
See also AAYA 8; CA 69-72; CANR 13, 38, 74; CDALBS; DA3; DLB 173, 212; DLBY 80; INT CANR-13; MTCW 1, 2; SATA 53

Kinnell, Galway 1927- **CLC 1, 2, 3, 5, 13, 29; PC 26**

See also CA 9-12R; CANR 10, 34, 66; DLB 5; DLBY 87; INT CANR-34; MTCW 1, 2

Kinsella, Thomas 1928-   **CLC 4, 19**
See also CA 17-20R; CANR 15; DLB 27; MTCW 1, 2

Kinsella, W(illiam) P(atrick) 1935- **CLC 27, 43; DAC; DAM NOV, POP**
See also AAYA 7; CA 97-100; CAAS 7; CANR 21, 35, 66, 75; INT CANR-21; MTCW 1, 2

Kinsey, Alfred C(harles) 1894-1956**TCLC 91**
See also CA 115; 170; MTCW 2

Kipling, (Joseph) Rudyard 1865-1936 **TCLC 8, 17; DA; DAB; DAC; DAM MST, POET; PC 3; SSC 5; WLC**
See also AAYA 32; CA 105; 120; CANR 33; CDBLB 1890-1914; CLR 39; DA3; DLB 19, 34, 141, 156; MAICYA; MTCW 1, 2; SATA 100; YABC 2

Kirkup, James 1918-   **CLC 1**
See also CA 1-4R; CAAS 4; CANR 2; DLB 27; SATA 12

Kirkwood, James 1930(?)-1989   **CLC 9**
See also AITN 2; CA 1-4R; 128; CANR 6, 40

Kirshner, Sidney
See Kingsley, Sidney

Kis, Danilo 1935-1989   **CLC 57**
See also CA 109; 118; 129; CANR 61; DLB 181; MTCW 1

Kivi, Aleksis 1834-1872   **NCLC 30**

Kizer, Carolyn (Ashley) 1925-**CLC 15, 39, 80; DAM POET**
See also CA 65-68; CAAS 5; CANR 24, 70; DLB 5, 169; MTCW 2

Klabund 1890-1928   **TCLC 44**
See also CA 162; DLB 66

Klappert, Peter 1942-   **CLC 57**
See also CA 33-36R; DLB 5

Klein, A(braham) M(oses) 1909-1972**CLC 19; DAB; DAC; DAM MST**
See also CA 101; 37-40R; DLB 68

Klein, Norma 1938-1989   **CLC 30**
See also AAYA 2; CA 41-44R; 128; CANR 15, 37; CLR 2, 19; INT CANR-15; JRDA; MAICYA; SAAS 1; SATA 7, 57

Klein, T(heodore) E(ibon) D(onald) 1947-
CLC 34
See also CA 119; CANR 44, 75

Kleist, Heinrich von 1777-1811 **NCLC 2, 37; DAM DRAM; SSC 22**
See also DLB 90

Klima, Ivan 1931-   **CLC 56; DAM NOV**
See also CA 25-28R; CANR 17, 50

Klimentov, Andrei Platonovich 1899-1951
See Platonov, Andrei
See also CA 108

Klinger, Friedrich Maximilian von 1752-1831
NCLC 1
See also DLB 94

Klingsor the Magician
See Hartmann, Sadakichi

Klopstock, Friedrich Gottlieb 1724-1803
NCLC 11
See also DLB 97

Knapp, Caroline 1959-   **CLC 99**
See also CA 154

Knebel, Fletcher 1911-1993   **CLC 14**
See also AITN 1; CA 1-4R; 140; CAAS 3; CANR 1, 36; SATA 36; SATA-Obit 75

Knickerbocker, Diedrich
See Irving, Washington

Knight, Etheridge 1931-1991**CLC 40; BLC 2; DAM POET; PC 14**
See also BW 1, 3; CA 21-24R; 133; CANR 23,

DLB 41; MTCW 2

Knight, Sarah Kemble 1666-1727   **LC 7**
See also DLB 24, 200

Knister, Raymond 1899-1932   **TCLC 56**
See also DLB 68

Knowles, John 1926-   **CLC 1, 4, 10, 26; DA;
DAC; DAM MST, NOV**
See also AAYA 10; CA 17-20R; CANR 40, 74,
76; CDALB 1968-1988; DLB 6; MTCW 1,
2; SATA 8, 89

Knox, Calvin M.
See Silverberg, Robert

Knox, John c. 1505-1572   **LC 37**
See also DLB 132

Knye, Cassandra
See Disch, Thomas M(ichael)

Koch, C(hristopher) J(ohn) 1932-   **CLC 42**
See also CA 127; CANR 84

Koch, Christopher
See Koch, C(hristopher) J(ohn)

Koch, Kenneth 1925-   **CLC 5, 8, 44; DAM
POET**
See also CA 1-4R; CANR 6, 36, 57; DLB 5;
INT CANR-36; MTCW 2; SATA 65

Kochanowski, Jan 1530-1584   **LC 10**

Kock, Charles Paul de 1794-1871   **NCLC 16**

Koda Shigeyuki 1867-1947
See Rohan, Koda
See also CA 121

Koestler, Arthur 1905-1983 **CLC 1, 3, 6, 8, 15,
33**
See also CA 1-4R; 109; CANR 1, 33; CDBLB
1945-1960; DLBY 83; MTCW 1, 2

Kogawa, Joy Nozomi 1935-   **CLC 78; DAC;
DAM MST, MULT**
See also CA 101; CANR 19, 62; MTCW 2;
SATA 99

Kohout, Pavel 1928-   **CLC 13**
See also CA 45-48; CANR 3

Koizumi, Yakumo
See Hearn, (Patricio) Lafcadio (Tessima Carlos)

Kolmar, Gertrud 1894-1943   **TCLC 40**
See also CA 167

Komunyakaa, Yusef 1947-**CLC 86, 94; BLCS**
See also CA 147; CANR 83; DLB 120

Konrad, George
See Konrad, Gyoergy

Konrad, Gyoergy 1933-   **CLC 4, 10, 73**
See also CA 85-88

Konwicki, Tadeusz 1926- **CLC 8, 28, 54, 117**
See also CA 101; CAAS 9; CANR 39, 59;
MTCW 1

Koontz, Dean R(ay) 1945-   **CLC 78; DAM
NOV, POP**
See also AAYA 9, 31; BEST 89:3, 90:2; CA 108;
CANR 19, 36, 52; DA3; MTCW 1; SATA 92

Kopernik, Mikolaj
See Copernicus, Nicolaus

Kopit, Arthur (Lee) 1937-**CLC 1, 18, 33; DAM
DRAM**
See also AITN 1; CA 81-84; CABS 3; DLB 7;
MTCW 1

Kops, Bernard 1926-   **CLC 4**
See also CA 5-8R; CANR 84; DLB 13

Kornbluth, C(yril) M. 1923-1958   **TCLC 8**
See also CA 105; 160; DLB 8

Korolenko, V. G.
See Korolenko, Vladimir Galaktionovich

Korolenko, Vladimir
See Korolenko, Vladimir Galaktionovich

Korolenko, Vladimir G.
See Korolenko, Vladimir Galaktionovich

Korolenko, Vladimir Galaktionovich 1853-

1921   **TCLC 22**
See also CA 121

Korzybski, Alfred (Habdank Skarbek) 1879-
1950   **TCLC 61**
See also CA 123; 160

Kosinski, Jerzy (Nikodem) 1933-1991**CLC 1,
2, 3, 6, 10, 15, 53, 70; DAM NOV**
See also CA 17-20R; 134; CANR 9, 46; DA3;
DLB 2; DLBY 82; MTCW 1, 2

Kostelanetz, Richard (Cory) 1940-   **CLC 28**
See also CA 13-16R; CAAS 8; CANR 38, 77

Kostrowitzki, Wilhelm Apollinaris de 1880-
1918
See Apollinaire, Guillaume
See also CA 104

Kotlowitz, Robert 1924-   **CLC 4**
See also CA 33-36R; CANR 36

Kotzebue, August (Friedrich Ferdinand) von
1761-1819   **NCLC 25**
See also DLB 94

Kotzwinkle, William 1938-   **CLC 5, 14, 35**
See also CA 45-48; CANR 3, 44, 84; CLR 6;
DLB 173; MAICYA; SATA 24, 70

Kowna, Stancy
See Szymborska, Wislawa

Kozol, Jonathan 1936-   **CLC 17**
See also CA 61-64; CANR 16, 45

Kozoll, Michael 1940(?)-   **CLC 35**

Kramer, Kathryn 19(?)-   **CLC 34**

Kramer, Larry 1935-**CLC 42; DAM POP; DC
8**
See also CA 124; 126; CANR 60

Krasicki, Ignacy 1735-1801   **NCLC 8**

Krasinski, Zygmunt 1812-1859   **NCLC 4**

Kraus, Karl 1874-1936   **TCLC 5**
See also CA 104; DLB 118

Kreve (Mickevicius), Vincas 1882-1954**TCLC
27**
See also CA 170

Kristeva, Julia 1941-   **CLC 77**
See also CA 154

Kristofferson, Kris 1936-   **CLC 26**
See also CA 104

Krizanc, John 1956-   **CLC 57**

Krleza, Miroslav 1893-1981   **CLC 8, 114**
See also CA 97-100; 105; CANR 50; DLB 147

Kroetsch, Robert 1927- **CLC 5, 23, 57; DAC;
DAM POET**
See also CA 17-20R; CANR 8, 38; DLB 53;
MTCW 1

Kroetz, Franz
See Kroetz, Franz Xaver

Kroetz, Franz Xaver 1946-   **CLC 41**
See also CA 130

Kroker, Arthur (W.) 1945-   **CLC 77**
See also CA 161

Kropotkin, Peter (Alekseievich) 1842-1921
   TCLC 36
See also CA 119

Krotkov, Yuri 1917-   **CLC 19**
See also CA 102

Krumb
See Crumb, R(obert)

Krumgold, Joseph (Quincy) 1908-1980 **C L C
12**
See also CA 9-12R; 101; CANR 7; MAICYA;
SATA 1, 48; SATA-Obit 23

Krumwitz
See Crumb, R(obert)

Krutch, Joseph Wood 1893-1970   **CLC 24**
See also CA 1-4R; 25-28R; CANR 4; DLB 63,
206

Krutzch, Gus

See Eliot, T(homas) S(tearns)

Krylov, Ivan Andreevich 1768(?)-1844**N C L C
1**
See also DLB 150

Kubin, Alfred (Leopold Isidor) 1877-1959
   TCLC 23
See also CA 112; 149; DLB 81

Kubrick, Stanley 1928-1999   **CLC 16**
See also AAYA 30; CA 81-84; 177; CANR 33;
DLB 26

Kumin, Maxine (Winokur) 1925- **CLC 5, 13,
28; DAM POET; PC 15**
See also AITN 2; CA 1-4R; CAAS 8; CANR 1,
21, 69; DA3; DLB 5; MTCW 1, 2; SATA 12

Kundera, Milan 1929- **CLC 4, 9, 19, 32, 68,
115; DAM NOV; SSC 24**
See also AAYA 2; CA 85-88; CANR 19, 52,
74; DA3; MTCW 1, 2

Kunene, Mazisi (Raymond) 1930-   **CLC 85**
See also BW 1, 3; CA 125; CANR 81; DLB
117

Kunitz, Stanley (Jasspon) 1905-**CLC 6, 11, 14;
PC 19**
See also CA 41-44R; CANR 26, 57; DA3; DLB
48; INT CANR-26; MTCW 1, 2

Kunze, Reiner 1933-   **CLC 10**
See also CA 93-96; DLB 75

Kuprin, Aleksandr Ivanovich 1870-1938
   TCLC 5
See also CA 104; 182

Kureishi, Hanif 1954(?)-   **CLC 64**
See also CA 139; DLB 194

Kurosawa, Akira 1910-1998 **CLC 16, 119;
DAM MULT**
See also AAYA 11; CA 101; 170; CANR 46

Kushner, Tony 1957(?)-**CLC 81; DAM DRAM;
DC 10**
See also CA 144; CANR 74; DA3; MTCW 2

Kuttner, Henry 1915-1958   **TCLC 10**
See Vance, Jack
See also CA 107; 157; DLB 8

Kuzma, Greg 1944-   **CLC 7**
See also CA 33-36R; CANR 70

Kuzmin, Mikhail 1872(?)-1936   **TCLC 40**
See also CA 170

Kyd, Thomas 1558-1594**LC 22; DAM DRAM;
DC 3**
See also DLB 62

Kyprianos, Iossif
See Samarakis, Antonis

La Bruyere, Jean de 1645-1696   **LC 17**

Lacan, Jacques (Marie Emile) 1901-1981
   CLC 75
See also CA 121; 104

Laclos, Pierre Ambroise Francois Choderlos de
1741-1803   **NCLC 4**

La Colere, Francois
See Aragon, Louis

Lacolere, Francois
See Aragon, Louis

La Deshabilleuse
See Simenon, Georges (Jacques Christian)

Lady Gregory
See Gregory, Isabella Augusta (Persse)

Lady of Quality, A
See Bagnold, Enid

**La Fayette, Marie (Madelaine Pioche de la
Vergne Comtes** 1634-1693   **LC 2**

Lafayette, Rene
See Hubbard, L(afayette) Ron(ald)

La Fontaine, Jean de 1621-1695   **LC 50**
See also MAICYA; SATA 18

Laforgue, Jules 1860-1887**NCLC 5, 53; PC 14;**

SSC 20

Lagerkvist, Paer (Fabian) 1891-1974 **CLC 7, 10, 13, 54; DAM DRAM, NOV**
See also Lagerkvist, Par
See also CA 85-88; 49-52; DA3; MTCW 1, 2

Lagerkvist, Par **SSC 12**
See also Lagerkvist, Paer (Fabian)
See also MTCW 2

Lagerloef, Selma (Ottiliana Lovisa) 1858-1940 **TCLC 4, 36**
See also Lagerlof, Selma (Ottiliana Lovisa)
See also CA 108; MTCW 2; SATA 15

Lagerlof, Selma (Ottiliana Lovisa)
See Lagerloef, Selma (Ottiliana Lovisa)
See also CLR 7; SATA 15

La Guma, (Justin) Alex(ander) 1925-1985 **CLC 19; BLCS; DAM NOV**
See also BW 1, 3; CA 49-52; 118; CANR 25, 81; DLB 117; MTCW 1, 2

Laidlaw, A. K.
See Grieve, C(hristopher) M(urray)

Lainez, Manuel Mujica
See Mujica Lainez, Manuel
See also HW 1

Laing, R(onald) D(avid) 1927-1989 **CLC 95**
See also CA 107; 129; CANR 34; MTCW 1

Lamartine, Alphonse (Marie Louis Prat) de 1790-1869 **NCLC 11; DAM POET; PC 16**

Lamb, Charles 1775-1834 **NCLC 10; DA; DAB; DAC; DAM MST; WLC**
See also CDBLB 1789-1832; DLB 93, 107, 163; SATA 17

Lamb, Lady Caroline 1785-1828 **NCLC 38**
See also DLB 116

Lamming, George (William) 1927- **CLC 2, 4, 66; BLC 2; DAM MULT**
See also BW 2, 3; CA 85-88; CANR 26, 76; DLB 125; MTCW 1, 2

L'Amour, Louis (Dearborn) 1908-1988 **C L C 25, 55; DAM NOV, POP**
See also AAYA 16; AITN 2; BEST 89:2; CA 1-4R; 125; CANR 3, 25, 40; DA3; DLB 206; DLBY 80; MTCW 1, 2

Lampedusa, Giuseppe (Tomasi) di 1896-1957 **TCLC 13**
See also Tomasi di Lampedusa, Giuseppe
See also CA 164; DLB 177; MTCW 2

Lampman, Archibald 1861-1899 **NCLC 25**
See also DLB 92

Lancaster, Bruce 1896-1963 **CLC 36**
See also CA 9-10; CANR 70; CAP 1; SATA 9

Lanchester, John **CLC 99**

Landau, Mark Alexandrovich
See Aldanov, Mark (Alexandrovich)

Landau-Aldanov, Mark Alexandrovich
See Aldanov, Mark (Alexandrovich)

Landis, Jerry
See Simon, Paul (Frederick)

Landis, John 1950- **CLC 26**
See also CA 112; 122

Landolfi, Tommaso 1908-1979 **CLC 11, 49**
See also CA 127; 117; DLB 177

Landon, Letitia Elizabeth 1802-1838 **N C L C 15**
See also DLB 96

Landor, Walter Savage 1775-1864 **NCLC 14**
See also DLB 93, 107

Landwirth, Heinz 1927-
See Lind, Jakov
See also CA 9-12R; CANR 7

Lane, Patrick 1939- **CLC 25; DAM POET**
See also CA 97-100; CANR 54; DLB 53; INT 97-100

Lang, Andrew 1844-1912 **TCLC 16**
See also CA 114; 137; CANR 85; DLB 98, 141, 184; MAICYA; SATA 16

Lang, Fritz 1890-1976 **CLC 20, 103**
See also CA 77-80; 69-72; CANR 30

Lange, John
See Crichton, (John) Michael

Langer, Elinor 1939- **CLC 34**
See also CA 121

Langland, William 1330(?)-1400(?) **LC 19; DA; DAB; DAC; DAM MST, POET**
See also DLB 146

Langstaff, Launcelot
See Irving, Washington

Lanier, Sidney 1842-1881 **NCLC 6; DAM POET**
See also DLB 64; DLBD 13; MAICYA; SATA 18

Lanyer, Aemilia 1569-1645 **LC 10, 30**
See also DLB 121

Lao-Tzu
See Lao Tzu

Lao Tzu fl. 6th cent. B.C.- **CMLC 7**

Lapine, James (Elliot) 1949- **CLC 39**
See also CA 123; 130; CANR 54; INT 130

Larbaud, Valery (Nicolas) 1881-1957 **TCLC 9**
See also CA 106; 152

Lardner, Ring
See Lardner, Ring(gold) W(ilmer)

Lardner, Ring W., Jr.
See Lardner, Ring(gold) W(ilmer)

Lardner, Ring(gold) W(ilmer) 1885-1933 **TCLC 2, 14; SSC 32**
See also CA 104; 131; CDALB 1917-1929; DLB 11, 25, 86; DLBD 16; MTCW 1, 2

Laredo, Betty
See Codrescu, Andrei

Larkin, Maia
See Wojciechowska, Maia (Teresa)

Larkin, Philip (Arthur) 1922-1985 **CLC 3, 5, 8, 9, 13, 18, 33, 39, 64; DAB; DAM MST, POET; PC 21**
See also CA 5-8R; 117; CANR 24, 62, CDBLB 1960 to Present; DA3; DLB 27; MTCW 1, 2

Larra (y Sanchez de Castro), Mariano Jose de 1809-1837 **NCLC 17**

Larsen, Eric 1941- **CLC 55**
See also CA 132

Larsen, Nella 1891-1964 **CLC 37; BLC 2; DAM MULT**
See also BW 1; CA 125; CANR 83; DLB 51

Larson, Charles R(aymond) 1938- **CLC 31**
See also CA 53-56; CANR 4

Larson, Jonathan 1961-1996 **CLC 99**
See also AAYA 28; CA 156

Las Casas, Bartolome de 1474-1566 **LC 31**

Lasch, Christopher 1932-1994 **CLC 102**
See also CA 73-76; 144; CANR 25; MTCW 1, 2

Lasker-Schueler, Else 1869-1945 **TCLC 57**
See also DLB 66, 124

Laski, Harold 1893-1950 **TCLC 79**

Latham, Jean Lee 1902-1995 **CLC 12**
See also AITN 1; CA 5-8R; CANR 7, 84; CLR 50; MAICYA; SATA 2, 68

Latham, Mavis
See Clark, Mavis Thorpe

Lathen, Emma **CLC 2**
See also Hennissart, Martha; Latsis, Mary J(ane)

Lathrop, Francis
See Leiber, Fritz (Reuter, Jr.)

Latsis, Mary J(ane) 1927(?)-1997
See Lathen, Emma

See also CA 85-88; 162

Lattimore, Richmond (Alexander) 1906-1984 **CLC 3**
See also CA 1-4R; 112; CANR 1

Laughlin, James 1914-1997 **CLC 49**
See also CA 21-24R; 162; CAAS 22; CANR 9, 47; DLB 48; DLBY 96, 97

Laurence, (Jean) Margaret (Wemyss) 1926-1987 **CLC 3, 6, 13, 50, 62; DAC; DAM MST; SSC 7**
See also CA 5-8R; 121; CANR 33; DLB 53; MTCW 1, 2; SATA-Obit 50

Laurent, Antoine 1952- **CLC 50**

Lauscher, Hermann
See Hesse, Hermann

Lautreamont, Comte de 1846-1870 **NCLC 12; SSC 14**

Laverty, Donald
See Blish, James (Benjamin)

Lavin, Mary 1912-1996 **CLC 4, 18, 99; SSC 4**
See also CA 9-12R; 151; CANR 33; DLB 15; MTCW 1

Lavond, Paul Dennis
See Kornbluth, C(yril) M.; Pohl, Frederik

Lawler, Raymond Evenor 1922- **CLC 58**
See also CA 103

Lawrence, D(avid) H(erbert Richards) 1885-1930 **TCLC 2, 9, 16, 33, 48, 61, 93; DA; DAB; DAC; DAM MST, NOV, POET; SSC 4, 19; WLC**
See also CA 104; 121; CDBLB 1914-1945; DA3; DLB 10, 19, 36, 98, 162, 195; MTCW 1, 2

Lawrence, T(homas) E(dward) 1888-1935 **TCLC 18**
See also Dale, Colin
See also CA 115; 167; DLB 195

Lawrence of Arabia
See Lawrence, T(homas) E(dward)

Lawson, Henry (Archibald Hertzberg) 1867-1922 **TCLC 27; SSC 18**
See also CA 120; 181

Lawton, Dennis
See Faust, Frederick (Schiller)

Laxness, Halldor **CLC 25**
See also Gudjonsson, Halldor Kiljan

Layamon fl. c. 1200- **CMLC 10**
See also DLB 146

Laye, Camara 1928-1980 **CLC 4, 38; BLC 2; DAM MULT**
See also BW 1; CA 85-88; 97-100; CANR 25; MTCW 1, 2

Layton, Irving (Peter) 1912- **CLC 2, 15; DAC; DAM MST, POET**
See also CA 1-4R; CANR 2, 33, 43, 66; DLB 88; MTCW 1, 2

Lazarus, Emma 1849-1887 **NCLC 8**

Lazarus, Felix
See Cable, George Washington

Lazarus, Henry
See Slavitt, David R(ytman)

Lea, Joan
See Neufeld, John (Arthur)

Leacock, Stephen (Butler) 1869-1944 **TCLC 2; DAC; DAM MST**
See also CA 104; 141; CANR 80; DLB 92; MTCW 2

Lear, Edward 1812-1888 **NCLC 3**
See also CLR 1; DLB 32, 163, 166; MAICYA; SATA 18, 100

Lear, Norman (Milton) 1922- **CLC 12**
See also CA 73-76

Leautaud, Paul 1872-1956 **TCLC 83**

MTCW 1, 2; SATA 66

Levin, Meyer 1905-1981   **CLC 7; DAM POP**
See also AITN 1; CA 9-12R; 104; CANR 15; DLB 9, 28; DLBY 81; SATA 21; SATA-Obit 27

Levine, Norman 1924-   **CLC 54**
See also CA 73-76; CAAS 23; CANR 14, 70; DLB 88

Levine, Philip 1928-   **CLC 2, 4, 5, 9, 14, 33, 118; DAM POET; PC 22**
See also CA 9-12R; CANR 9, 37, 52; DLB 5

Levinson, Deirdre 1931-   **CLC 49**
See also CA 73-76; CANR 70

Levi-Strauss, Claude 1908-   **CLC 38**
See also CA 1-4R; CANR 6, 32, 57; MTCW 1, 2

Levitin, Sonia (Wolff) 1934-   **CLC 17**
See also AAYA 13; CA 29-32R; CANR 14, 32, 79; CLR 53; JRDA; MAICYA; SAAS 2; SATA 4, 68

Levon, O. U.
See Kesey, Ken (Elton)

Levy, Amy 1861-1889   **NCLC 59**
See also DLB 156

Lewes, George Henry 1817-1878   **NCLC 25**
See also DLB 55, 144

Lewis, Alun 1915-1944   **TCLC 3**
See also CA 104; DLB 20, 162

Lewis, C. Day
See Day Lewis, C(ecil)

Lewis, C(live) S(taples) 1898-1963   **CLC 1, 3, 6, 14, 27, 124; DA; DAB; DAC; DAM MST, NOV, POP; WLC**
See also AAYA 3; CA 81-84; CANR 33, 71; CDBLB 1945-1960; CLR 3, 27; DA3; DLB 15, 100, 160; JRDA; MAICYA; MTCW 1, 2; SATA 13, 100

Lewis, Janet 1899-1998   **CLC 41**
See also Winters, Janet Lewis
See also CA 9-12R; 172; CANR 29, 63; CAP 1; DLBY 87

Lewis, Matthew Gregory 1775-1818   **NCLC 11, 62**
See also DLB 39, 158, 178

Lewis, (Harry) Sinclair 1885-1951   **TCLC 4, 13, 23, 39; DA; DAB; DAC; DAM MST, NOV; WLC**
See also CA 104; 133; CDALB 1917-1929; DA3; DLB 9, 102; DLBD 1; MTCW 1, 2

Lewis, (Percy) Wyndham 1882(?)-1957   **TCLC 2, 9; SSC 34**
See also CA 104; 157; DLB 15; MTCW 2

Lewisohn, Ludwig 1883-1955   **TCLC 19**
See also CA 107; DLB 4, 9, 28, 102

Lewton, Val 1904-1951   **TCLC 76**

Leyner, Mark 1956-   **CLC 92**
See also CA 110; CANR 28, 53; DA3; MTCW 2

Lezama Lima, Jose 1910-1976   **CLC 4, 10, 101; DAM MULT; HLCS 2**
See also CA 77-80; CANR 71; DLB 113; HW 1, 2

L'Heureux, John (Clarke) 1934-   **CLC 52**
See also CA 13-16R; CANR 23, 45

Liddell, C. H.
See Kuttner, Henry

Lie, Jonas (Lauritz Idemil) 1833-1908(?)   **TCLC 5**
See also CA 115

Lieber, Joel 1937-1971   **CLC 6**
See also CA 73-76; 29-32R

Lieber, Stanley Martin
See Lee, Stan

Lieberman, Laurence (James) 1935-   **CLC 4, 36**
See also CA 17-20R; CANR 8, 36

Lieh Tzu fl. 7th cent. B.C.-5th cent. B.C.   **CMLC 27**

Lieksman, Anders
See Haavikko, Paavo Juhani

Li Fei-kan 1904-
See Pa Chin
See also CA 105

Lifton, Robert Jay 1926-   **CLC 67**
See also CA 17-20R; CANR 27, 78; INT CANR-27; SATA 66

Lightfoot, Gordon 1938-   **CLC 26**
See also CA 109

Lightman, Alan P(aige) 1948-   **CLC 81**
See also CA 141; CANR 63

Ligotti, Thomas (Robert) 1953-   **CLC 44; SSC 16**
See also CA 123; CANR 49

Li Ho 791-817   **PC 13**

Liliencron, (Friedrich Adolf Axel) Detlev von 1844-1909   **TCLC 18**
See also CA 117

Lilly, William 1602-1681   **LC 27**

Lima, Jose Lezama
See Lezama Lima, Jose

Lima Barreto, Afonso Henrique de 1881-1922   **TCLC 23**
See also CA 117; 181

Limonov, Edward 1944-   **CLC 67**
See also CA 137

Lin, Frank
See Atherton, Gertrude (Franklin Horn)

Lincoln, Abraham 1809-1865   **NCLC 18**

Lind, Jakov   **CLC 1, 2, 4, 27, 82**
See also Landwirth, Heinz
See also CAAS 4

Lindbergh, Anne (Spencer) Morrow 1906-   **CLC 82; DAM NOV**
See also CA 17-20R; CANR 16, 73; MTCW 1, 2; SATA 33

Lindsay, David 1878-1945   **TCLC 15**
See also CA 113

Lindsay, (Nicholas) Vachel 1879-1931   **TCLC 17; DA; DAC; DAM MST, POET; PC 23; WLC**
See also CA 114; 135; CANR 79; CDALB 1865-1917; DA3; DLB 54; SATA 40

Linke-Poot
See Doeblin, Alfred

Linney, Romulus 1930-   **CLC 51**
See also CA 1-4R; CANR 40, 44, 79

Linton, Eliza Lynn 1822-1898   **NCLC 41**
See also DLB 18

Li Po 701-763   **CMLC 2**

Lipsius, Justus 1547-1606   **LC 16**

Lipsyte, Robert (Michael) 1938-   **CLC 21; DA; DAC; DAM MST, NOV**
See also AAYA 7; CA 17-20R; CANR 8, 57; CLR 23; JRDA; MAICYA; SATA 5, 68

Lish, Gordon (Jay) 1934-   **CLC 45; SSC 18**
See also CA 113; 117; CANR 79; DLB 130; INT 117

Lispector, Clarice 1925(?)-1977   **CLC 43; HLCS 2; SSC 34**
See also CA 139; 116; CANR 71; DLB 113; HW 2

Littell, Robert 1935(?)-   **CLC 42**
See also CA 109; 112; CANR 64

Little, Malcolm 1925-1965
See Malcolm X
See also BW 1, 3; CA 125; 111; CANR 82; DA;

DAB; DAC; DAM MST, MULT; DA3; MTCW 1, 2

Littlewit, Humphrey Gent.
See Lovecraft, H(oward) P(hillips)

Litwos
See Sienkiewicz, Henryk (Adam Alexander Pius)

Liu, E 1857-1909   **TCLC 15**
See also CA 115

Lively, Penelope (Margaret) 1933-   **CLC 32, 50; DAM NOV**
See also CA 41-44R; CANR 29, 67, 79; CLR 7; DLB 14, 161, 207; JRDA; MAICYA; MTCW 1, 2; SATA 7, 60, 101

Livesay, Dorothy (Kathleen) 1909-   **CLC 4, 15, 79; DAC; DAM MST, POET**
See also AITN 2; CA 25-28R; CAAS 8; CANR 36, 67; DLB 68; MTCW 1

Livy c. 59B.C.-c. 17   **CMLC 11**
See also DLB 211

Lizardi, Jose Joaquin Fernandez de 1776-1827   **NCLC 30**

Llewellyn, Richard
See Llewellyn Lloyd, Richard Dafydd Vivian
See also DLB 15

Llewellyn Lloyd, Richard Dafydd Vivian 1906-1983   **CLC 7, 80**
See also Llewellyn, Richard
See also CA 53-56; 111; CANR 7, 71; SATA 11; SATA-Obit 37

Llosa, (Jorge) Mario (Pedro) Vargas
See Vargas Llosa, (Jorge) Mario (Pedro)

Lloyd, Manda
See Mander, (Mary) Jane

Lloyd Webber, Andrew 1948-
See Webber, Andrew Lloyd
See also AAYA 1; CA 116; 149; DAM DRAM; SATA 56

Llull, Ramon c. 1235-c. 1316   **CMLC 12**

Lobb, Ebenezer
See Upward, Allen

Locke, Alain (Le Roy) 1886-1954   **TCLC 43; BLCS**
See also BW 1, 3; CA 106; 124; CANR 79; DLB 51

Locke, John 1632-1704   **LC 7, 35**
See also DLB 101

Locke-Elliott, Sumner
See Elliott, Sumner Locke

Lockhart, John Gibson 1794-1854   **NCLC 6**
See also DLB 110, 116, 144

Lodge, David (John) 1935-   **CLC 36; DAM POP**
See also BEST 90:1; CA 17-20R; CANR 19, 53; DLB 14, 194; INT CANR-19; MTCW 1, 2

Lodge, Thomas 1558-1625   **LC 41**
See also DLB 172

Loennbohm, Armas Eino Leopold 1878-1926
See Leino, Eino
See also CA 123

Loewinsohn, Ron(ald William) 1937-   **CLC 52**
See also CA 25-28R; CANR 71

Logan, Jake
See Smith, Martin Cruz

Logan, John (Burton) 1923-1987   **CLC 5**
See also CA 77-80; 124; CANR 45; DLB 5

Lo Kuan-chung 1330(?)-1400(?)   **LC 12**

Lombard, Nap
See Johnson, Pamela Hansford

London, Jack   **TCLC 9, 15, 39; SSC 4; WLC**
See also London, John Griffith
See also AAYA 13; AITN 2; CDALB 1865-1917; DLB 8, 12, 78, 212; SATA 18

London, John Griffith 1876-1916

See also DLBD 6

MacDougal, John
  See Blish, James (Benjamin)

MacEwen, Gwendolyn (Margaret) 1941-1987
  CLC 13, 55
  See also CA 9-12R; 124; CANR 7, 22; DLB
  53; SATA 50; SATA-Obit 55

Macha, Karel Hynek 1810-1846   **NCLC 46**

Machado (y Ruiz), Antonio 1875-1939 **T C L C
3**
  See also CA 104; 174; DLB 108; HW 2

Machado de Assis, Joaquim Maria 1839-1908
  TCLC 10; BLC 2; HLCS 2; SSC 24
  See also CA 107; 153

Machen, Arthur   **TCLC 4; SSC 20**
  See also Jones, Arthur Llewellyn
  See also CA 179; DLB 36, 156, 178

Machiavelli, Niccolo 1469-1527 **LC 8, 36; DA;
  DAB; DAC; DAM MST; WLCS**

MacInnes, Colin 1914-1976   **CLC 4, 23**
  See also CA 69-72; 65-68; CANR 21; DLB 14;
  MTCW 1, 2

MacInnes, Helen (Clark) 1907-1985 **CLC 27;
  39; DAM POP**
  See also CA 1-4R; 117; CANR 1, 28, 58, DLB
  87; MTCW 1, 2; SATA 22; SATA-Obit 44

Mackenzie, Compton (Edward Montague)
  1883-1972   **CLC 18**
  See also CA 21-22; 37-40R; CAP 2; DLB 34,
  100

Mackenzie, Henry 1745-1831   **NCLC 41**
  See also DLB 39

Mackintosh, Elizabeth 1896(?)-1952
  See Tey, Josephine
  See also CA 110

MacLaren, James
  See Grieve, C(hristopher) M(urray)

Mac Laverty, Bernard 1942-   **CLC 31**
  See also CA 116; 118; CANR 43; INT 118

MacLean, Alistair (Stuart) 1922(?)-1987 **C L C
  3, 13, 50, 63; DAM POP**
  See also CA 57-60; 121; CANR 28, 61; MTCW
  1; SATA 23; SATA-Obit 50

Maclean, Norman (Fitzroy) 1902-1990 **C L C
  78; DAM POP; SSC 13**
  See also CA 102; 132; CANR 49; DLB 206

MacLeish, Archibald 1892-1982 **CLC 3, 8, 14,
  68; DAM POET**
  See also CA 9-12R; 106; CANR 33, 63;
  CDALBS; DLB 4, 7, 45; DLBY 82; MTCW
  1, 2

MacLennan, (John) Hugh 1907-1990 **CLC 2,
  14, 92; DAC; DAM MST**
  See also CA 5-8R; 142; CANR 33; DLB 68;
  MTCW 1, 2

MacLeod, Alistair 1936- **CLC 56; DAC; DAM
  MST**
  See also CA 123; DLB 60; MTCW 2

Macleod, Fiona
  See Sharp, William

MacNeice, (Frederick) Louis 1907-1963 **C L C
  1, 4, 10, 53; DAB; DAM POET**
  See also CA 85-88; CANR 61; DLB 10, 20;
  MTCW 1, 2

MacNeill, Dand
  See Fraser, George MacDonald

Macpherson, James 1736-1796   **LC 29**
  See also Ossian
  See also DLB 109

Macpherson, (Jean) Jay 1931-   **CLC 14**
  See also CA 5-8R; DLB 53

MacShane, Frank 1927-   **CLC 39**
  See also CA 9-12R; CANR 3, 33; DLB 111

Macumber, Mari
  See Sandoz, Mari(e Susette)

Madach, Imre 1823-1864   **NCLC 19**

Madden, (Jerry) David 1933-   **CLC 5, 15**
  See also CA 1-4R; CAAS 3; CANR 4, 45;
  DLB 6; MTCW 1

Maddern, Al(an)
  See Ellison, Harlan (Jay)

Madhubuti, Haki R. 1942- **CLC 6, 73; BLC 2;
  DAM MULT, POET; PC 5**
  See also Lee, Don L.
  See also BW 2, 3; CA 73-76; CANR 24, 51,
  73; DLB 5, 41; DLBD 8; MTCW 2

Maepenn, Hugh
  See Kuttner, Henry

Maepenn, K. H.
  See Kuttner, Henry

Maeterlinck, Maurice 1862-1949   **TCLC 3;
  DAM DRAM**
  See also CA 104; 136; CANR 80; DLB 192;
  SATA 66

Maginn, William 1794-1842   **NCLC 8**
  See also DLB 110, 159

Mahapatra, Jayanta 1928-   **CLC 33; DAM
  MULT**
  See also CA 73-76; CAAS 9; CANR 15, 33, 66

Mahfouz, Naguib (Abdel Aziz Al-Sabilgi)
  1911(?)-
  See Mahfuz, Najib
  See also BEST 89:2; CA 128; CANR 55; DAM
  NOV; DA3; MTCW 1, 2

Mahfuz, Najib   **CLC 52, 55**
  See also Mahfouz, Naguib (Abdel Aziz Al-
  Sabilgi)
  See also DLBY 88

Mahon, Derek 1941-   **CLC 27**
  See also CA 113; 128; DLB 40

Mailer, Norman 1923- **CLC 1, 2, 3, 4, 5, 8, 11,
  14, 28, 39, 74, 111; DA; DAB; DAC; DAM
  MST, NOV, POP**
  See also AAYA 31; AITN 2; CA 9-12R; CABS
  1; CANR 28, 74, 77; CDALB 1968-1988;
  DA3; DLB 2, 16, 28, 185; DLBD 3; DLBY
  80, 83; MTCW 1, 2

Maillet, Antonine 1929- **CLC 54, 118; DAC**
  See also CA 115; 120; CANR 46, 74, 77; DLB
  60; INT 120; MTCW 2

Mais, Roger 1905-1955   **TCLC 8**
  See also BW 1, 3; CA 105; 124; CANR 82; DLB
  125; MTCW 1

Maistre, Joseph de 1753-1821   **NCLC 37**

Maitland, Frederic 1850-1906   **TCLC 65**

Maitland, Sara (Louise) 1950-   **CLC 49**
  See also CA 69-72; CANR 13, 59

Major, Clarence 1936- **CLC 3, 19, 48; BLC 2;
  DAM MULT**
  See also BW 2, 3; CA 21-24R; CAAS 6; CANR
  13, 25, 53, 82; DLB 33

Major, Kevin (Gerald) 1949- **CLC 26; DAC**
  See also AAYA 16; CA 97-100; CANR 21, 38;
  CLR 11; DLB 60; INT CANR-21; JRDA;
  MAICYA; SATA 32, 82

Maki, James
  See Ozu, Yasujiro

Malabaila, Damiano
  See Levi, Primo

Malamud, Bernard 1914-1986 **CLC 1, 2, 3, 5,
  8, 9, 11, 18, 27, 44, 78, 85; DA; DAB; DAC;
  DAM MST, NOV, POP; SSC 15; WLC**
  See also AAYA 16; CA 5-8R; 118; CABS 1;
  CANR 28, 62; CDALB 1941-1968; DA3;
  DLB 2, 28, 152; DLBY 80, 86; MTCW 1, 2

Malan, Herman
  See Bosman, Herman Charles; Bosman, Herman
  Charles

Malaparte, Curzio 1898-1957   **TCLC 52**

Malcolm, Dan
  See Silverberg, Robert

Malcolm X   **CLC 82, 117; BLC 2; WLCS**
  See also Little, Malcolm

Malherbe, Francois de 1555-1628   **LC 5**

Mallarme, Stephane 1842-1898 **NCLC 4, 41;
  DAM POET; PC 4**

Mallet-Joris, Francoise 1930-   **CLC 11**
  See also CA 65-68; CANR 17; DLB 83

Malley, Ern
  See McAuley, James Phillip

Mallowan, Agatha Christie
  See Christie, Agatha (Mary Clarissa)

Maloff, Saul 1922-   **CLC 5**
  See also CA 33-36R

Malone, Louis
  See MacNeice, (Frederick) Louis

Malone, Michael (Christopher) 1942- **CLC 43**
  See also CA 77-80; CANR 14, 32, 57

Malory, (Sir) Thomas 1410(?)-1471(?) **LC 11;
  DA; DAB; DAC; DAM MST; WLCS**
  See also CDBLB Before 1660; DLB 146; SATA
  59; SATA-Brief 33

Malouf, (George Joseph) David 1934- **CLC 28,
  86**
  See also CA 124; CANR 50, 76; MTCW 2

Malraux, (Georges-)Andre 1901-1976 **CLC 1,
  4, 9, 13, 15, 57; DAM NOV**
  See also CA 21-22; 69-72; CANR 34, 58; CAP
  2; DA3; DLB 72; MTCW 1, 2

Malzberg, Barry N(athaniel) 1939-   **CLC 7**
  See also CA 61-64; CAAS 4; CANR 16; DLB 8

Mamet, David (Alan) 1947- **CLC 9, 15, 34, 46,
  91; DAM DRAM; DC 4**
  See also AAYA 3; CA 81-84; CABS 3; CANR
  15, 41, 67, 72; DA3; DLB 7; MTCW 1, 2

Mamoulian, Rouben (Zachary) 1897-1987
  CLC 16
  See also CA 25-28R; 124; CANR 85

Mandelstam, Osip (Emilievich) 1891(?)-1938(?)
  TCLC 2, 6; PC 14
  See also CA 104; 150; MTCW 2

Mander, (Mary) Jane 1877-1949   **TCLC 31**
  See also CA 162

Mandeville, John fl. 1350-   **CMLC 19**
  See also DLB 146

Mandiargues, Andre Pieyre de   **CLC 41**
  See also Pieyre de Mandiargues, Andre
  See also DLB 83

Mandrake, Ethel Belle
  See Thurman, Wallace (Henry)

Mangan, James Clarence 1803-1849 **NCLC 27**

Maniere, J.-E.
  See Giraudoux, (Hippolyte) Jean

Mankiewicz, Herman (Jacob) 1897-1953
  TCLC 85
  See also CA 120; 169; DLB 26

Manley, (Mary) Delariviere 1672(?)-1724 **L C
  1, 42**
  See also DLB 39, 80

Mann, Abel
  See Creasey, John

Mann, Emily 1952-   **DC 7**
  See also CA 130; CANR 55

Mann, (Luiz) Heinrich 1871-1950   **TCLC 9**
  See also CA 106; 164; 181; DLB 66, 118

Mann, (Paul) Thomas 1875-1955 **TCLC 2, 8,
  14, 21, 35, 44, 60; DA; DAB; DAC; DAM
  MST, NOV; SSC 5; WLC**
  See also CA 104; 128; DA3; DLB 66; MTCW

See also CA 97-100; CANR 19, 41; DLB 27

Matsuo Basho 1644-1694 **PC 3**
See also DAM POET

Mattheson, Rodney
See Creasey, John

Matthews, Brander 1852-1929 **TCLC 95**
See also DLB 71, 78; DLBD 13

Matthews, Greg 1949- **CLC 45**
See also CA 135

Matthews, William (Procter, III) 1942-1997
CLC 40
See also CA 29-32R; 162; CAAS 18; CANR 12, 57; DLB 5

Matthias, John (Edward) 1941- **CLC 9**
See also CA 33-36R; CANR 56

Matthiessen, Peter 1927-GLC 5, 7, 11, 32, 64;
DAM NOV
See also AAYA 6; BEST 90:4; CA 9-12R; CANR 21, 50, 73; DA3; DLB 6, 173; MTCW 1, 2; SATA 27

Maturin, Charles Robert 1780(?)-1824NCLC 6
See also DLB 178

Matute (Ausejo), Ana Maria 1925- **CLC 11**
See also CA 89-92; MTCW 1

Maugham, W. S.
See Maugham, W(illiam) Somerset

Maugham, W(illiam) Somerset 1874-1965
CLC 1, 11, 15, 67, 93; DA; DAB; DAC; DAM DRAM, MST, NOV; SSC 8; WLC
See also CA 5-8R; 25-28R; CANR 40; CDBLB 1914-1945; DA3; DLB 10, 36, 77, 100, 162, 195; MTCW 1, 2; SATA 54

Maugham, William Somerset
See Maugham, W(illiam) Somerset

Maupassant, (Henri Rene Albert) Guy de 1850-1893NCLC 1, 42; DA; DAB; DAC; DAM MST; SSC 1; WLC
See also DA3; DLB 123

Maupin, Armistead 1944-CLC 95; DAM POP
See also CA 125; 130; CANR 58; DA3; INT 130; MTCW 2

Maurhut, Richard
See Traven, B

Mauriac, Claude 1914-1996 **CLC 9**
See also CA 89-92; 152; DLB 83

Mauriac, Francois (Charles) 1885-1970 C L C 4, 9, 56; SSC 24
See also CA 25-28; CAP 2; DLB 65; MTCW 1, 2

Mavor, Osborne Henry 1888-1951
See Bridie, James
See also CA 104

Maxwell, William (Keepers, Jr.) 1908-CLC 19
See also CA 93-96; CANR 54; DLBY 80; INT 93-96

May, Elaine 1932- **CLC 16**
See also CA 124; 142; DLB 44

Mayakovski, Vladimir (Vladimirovich) 1893-1930 **TCLC 4, 18**
See also CA 104; 158; MTCW 2

Mayhew, Henry 1812-1887 **NCLC 31**
See also DLB 18, 55, 190

Mayle, Peter 1939(?)- **CLC 89**
See also CA 139; CANR 64

Maynard, Joyce 1953- **CLC 23**
See also CA 111; 129; CANR 64

Mayne, William (James Carter) 1928-CLC 12
See also AAYA 20; CA 9-12R; CANR 37, 80; CLR 25; JRDA; MAICYA; SAAS 11; SATA 6, 68

Mayo, Jim
See L'Amour, Louis (Dearborn)

Maysles, Albert 1926- **CLC 16**
See also CA 29-32R

Maysles, David 1932- **CLC 16**

Mazer, Norma Fox 1931- **CLC 26**
See also AAYA 5; CA 69-72; CANR 12, 32, 66; CLR 23; JRDA; MAICYA; SAAS 1; SATA 24, 67, 105

Mazzini, Guiseppe 1805-1872 **NCLC 34**

McAlmon, Robert (Menzies) 1895-1956TCLC 97
See also CA 107; 168; DLB 4, 45; DLBD 15

McAuley, James Phillip 1917-1976 **CLC 45**
See also CA 97-100

McBain, Ed
See Hunter, Evan

McBrien, William Augustine 1930- **CLC 44**
See also CA 107

McCaffrey, Anne (Inez) 1926-CLC 17; DAM NOV, POP
See also AAYA 6; AITN 2; BEST 89:2; CA 25-28R; CANR 15, 35, 55; CLR 49; DA3; DLB 8; JRDA; MAICYA; MTCW 1, 2; SAAS 11; SATA 8, 70

McCall, Nathan 1955(?)- **CLC 86**
See also BW 3; CA 146

McCann, Arthur
See Campbell, John W(ood, Jr.)

McCann, Edson
See Pohl, Frederik

McCarthy, Charles, Jr. 1933-
See McCarthy, Cormac
See also CANR 42, 69; DAM POP; DA3; MTCW 2

McCarthy, Cormac 1933- CLC 4, 57, 59, 101
See also McCarthy, Charles, Jr.
See also DLB 6, 143; MTCW 2

McCarthy, Mary (Therese) 1912-1989CLC 1, 3, 5, 14, 24, 39, 59; SSC 24
See also CA 5-8R; 129; CANR 16, 50, 64; DA3; DLB 2; DLBY 81; INT CANR-16; MTCW 1, 2

McCartney, (James) Paul 1942- **CLC 12, 35**
See also CA 146

McCauley, Stephen (D.) 1955- **CLC 50**
See also CA 141

McClure, Michael (Thomas) 1932-CLC 6, 10
See also CA 21-24R; CANR 17, 46, 77; DLB 16

McCorkle, Jill (Collins) 1958- **CLC 51**
See also CA 121; DLBY 87

McCourt, Frank 1930- **CLC 109**
See also CA 157

McCourt, James 1941- **CLC 5**
See also CA 57-60

McCourt, Malachy 1932- **CLC 119**

McCoy, Horace (Stanley) 1897-1955TCLC 28
See also CA 108; 155; DLB 9

McCrae, John 1872-1918 **TCLC 12**
See also CA 109; DLB 92

McCreigh, James
See Pohl, Frederik

McCullers, (Lula) Carson (Smith) 1917-1967
CLC 1, 4, 10, 12, 48, 100; DA; DAB; DAC; DAM MST, NOV; SSC 9, 24; WLC
See also AAYA 21; CA 5-8R; 25-28R; CABS 1, 3; CANR 18; CDALB 1941-1968; DA3; DLB 2, 7, 173; MTCW 1, 2; SATA 27

McCulloch, John Tyler
See Burroughs, Edgar Rice

McCullough, Colleen 1938(?)- **CLC 27, 107; DAM NOV, POP**
See also CA 81-84; CANR 17, 46, 67; DA3; MTCW 1, 2

McDermott, Alice 1953- **CLC 90**
See also CA 109; CANR 40

McElroy, Joseph 1930- **CLC 5, 47**
See also CA 17-20R

McEwan, Ian (Russell) 1948- CLC 13, 66; **DAM NOV**
See also BEST 90:4; CA 61-64; CANR 14, 41, 69; DLB 14, 194; MTCW 1, 2

McFadden, David 1940- **CLC 48**
See also CA 104; DLB 60; INT 104

McFarland, Dennis 1950- **CLC 65**
See also CA 165

McGahern, John 1934-CLC 5, 9, 48; SSC 17
See also CA 17-20R; CANR 29, 68; DLB 14; MTCW 1

McGinley, Patrick (Anthony) 1937- **CLC 41**
See also CA 120; 127; CANR 56; INT 127

McGinley, Phyllis 1905-1978 **CLC 14**
See also CA 9-12R; 77-80; CANR 19; DLB 11, 48; SATA 2, 44; SATA-Obit 24

McGinniss, Joe 1942- **CLC 32**
See also AITN 2; BEST 89:2; CA 25-28R; CANR 26, 70; DLB 185; INT CANR-26

McGivern, Maureen Daly
See Daly, Maureen

McGrath, Patrick 1950- **CLC 55**
See also CA 136; CANR 65

McGrath, Thomas (Matthew) 1916-1990CLC 28, 59; **DAM POET**
See also CA 9-12R; 132; CANR 6, 33; MTCW 1; SATA 41; SATA-Obit 66

McGuane, Thomas (Francis III) 1939-CLC 3, 7, 18, 45
See also AITN 2; CA 49-52; CANR 5, 24, 49; DLB 2, 212; DLBY 80; INT CANR-24; MTCW 1

McGuckian, Medbh 1950- **CLC 48; DAM POET; PC 27**
See also CA 143; DLB 40

McHale, Tom 1942(?)-1982 **CLC 3, 5**
See also AITN 1; CA 77-80; 106

McIlvanney, William 1936- **CLC 42**
See also CA 25-28R; CANR 61; DLB 14, 207

McIlwraith, Maureen Mollie Hunter
See Hunter, Mollie
See also SATA 2

McInerney, Jay 1955-CLC 34, 112; **DAM POP**
See also AAYA 18; CA 116; 123; CANR 45, 68; DA3; INT 123; MTCW 2

McIntyre, Vonda N(eel) 1948- **CLC 18**
See also CA 81-84; CANR 17, 34, 69; MTCW 1

McKay, ClaudeTCLC 7, 41; **BLC 3; DAB; PC 2**
See also McKay, Festus Claudius
See also DLB 4, 45, 51, 117

McKay, Festus Claudius 1889-1948
See McKay, Claude
See also BW 1, 3; CA 104; 124; CANR 73; DA; DAC; DAM MST, MULT, NOV, POET; MTCW 1, 2; WLC

McKuen, Rod 1933- **CLC 1, 3**
See also AITN 1; CA 41-44R; CANR 40

McLoughlin, R. B.
See Mencken, H(enry) L(ouis)

McLuhan, (Herbert) Marshall 1911-1980
CLC 37, 83
See also CA 9-12R; 102; CANR 12, 34, 61; DLB 88; INT CANR-12; MTCW 1, 2

McMillan, Terry (L.) 1951- CLC 50, 61, 112; **BLCS; DAM MULT, NOV, POP**
See also AAYA 21; BW 2, 3; CA 140; CANR 60; DA3; MTCW 2

McMurtry, Larry (Jeff) 1936-**CLC 2, 3, 7, 11, 27, 44; DAM NOV, POP**
See also AAYA 15; AITN 2; BEST 89:2; CA 5-8R; CANR 19, 43, 64; CDALB 1968-1988; DA3; DLB 2, 143; DLBY 80, 87; MTCW 1, 2

McNally, T. M. 1961- **CLC 82**

McNally, Terrence 1939- **CLC 4, 7, 41, 91; DAM DRAM**
See also CA 45-48; CANR 2, 56; DA3; DLB 7; MTCW 2

McNamer, Deirdre 1950- **CLC 70**

McNeal, Tom **CLC 119**

McNeile, Herman Cyril 1888-1937
See Sapper
See also DLB 77

McNickle, (William) D'Arcy 1904-1977 **CLC 89; DAM MULT**
See also CA 9-12R; 85-88; CANR 5, 45; DLB 175, 212; NNAL; SATA-Obit 22

McPhee, John (Angus) 1931- **CLC 36**
See also BEST 90:1; CA 65-68; CANR 20, 46, 64, 69; DLB 185; MTCW 1, 2

McPherson, James Alan 1943- **CLC 19, 77; BLCS**
See also BW 1, 3; CA 25-28R; CAAS 17; CANR 24, 74; DLB 38; MTCW 1, 2

McPherson, William (Alexander) 1933- **CLC 34**
See also CA 69-72; CANR 28; INT CANR-28

Mead, George Herbert 1873-1958 **TCLC 89**

Mead, Margaret 1901-1978 **CLC 37**
See also AITN 1; CA 1-4R; 81-84; CANR 4; DA3; MTCW 1, 2; SATA-Obit 20

Meaker, Marijane (Agnes) 1927-
See Kerr, M. E.
See also CA 107; CANR 37, 63; INT 107; JRDA; MAICYA; MTCW 1; SATA 20, 61, 99; SATA-Essay 111

Medoff, Mark (Howard) 1940- **CLC 6, 23; DAM DRAM**
See also AITN 1; CA 53-56; CANR 5; DLB 7; INT CANR-5

Medvedev, P. N.
See Bakhtin, Mikhail Mikhailovich

Meged, Aharon
See Megged, Aharon

Meged, Aron
See Megged, Aharon

Megged, Aharon 1920- **CLC 9**
See also CA 49-52; CAAS 13; CANR 1

Mehta, Ved (Parkash) 1934- **CLC 37**
See also CA 1-4R; CANR 2, 23, 69; MTCW 1

Melanter
See Blackmore, R(ichard) D(oddridge)

Melies, Georges 1861-1938 **TCLC 81**

Melikow, Loris
See Hofmannsthal, Hugo von

Melmoth, Sebastian
See Wilde, Oscar

Meltzer, Milton 1915- **CLC 26**
See also AAYA 8; CA 13-16R; CANR 38; CLR 13; DLB 61; JRDA; MAICYA; SAAS 1; SATA 1, 50, 80

Melville, Herman 1819-1891 **NCLC 3, 12, 29, 45, 49; DA; DAB; DAC; DAM MST, NOV; SSC 1, 17; WLC**
See also AAYA 25; CDALB 1640-1865; DA3; DLB 3, 74; SATA 59

Menander c. 342B.C.-c. 292B.C. **CMLC 9; DAM DRAM; DC 3**
See also DLB 176

Menchu, Rigoberta 1959-
See also HLCS 2

Menchu, Rigoberta 1959-
See also CA 175; HLCS 2

Mencken, H(enry) L(ouis) 1880-1956 **TCLC 13**
See also CA 105; 125; CDALB 1917-1929; DLB 11, 29, 63, 137; MTCW 1, 2

Mendelsohn, Jane 1965(?)- **CLC 99**
See also CA 154

Mercer, David 1928-1980 **CLC 5; DAM DRAM**
See also CA 9-12R; 102; CANR 23; DLB 13; MTCW 1

Merchant, Paul
See Ellison, Harlan (Jay)

Meredith, George 1828-1909 **TCLC 17, 43; DAM POET**
See also CA 117; 153; CANR 80; CDBLB 1832-1890; DLB 18, 35, 57, 159

Meredith, William (Morris) 1919-**CLC 4, 13, 22, 55; DAM POET; PC 28**
See also CA 9-12R; CAAS 14; CANR 6, 40; DLB 5

Merezhkovsky, Dmitry Sergeyevich 1865-1941 **TCLC 29**
See also CA 169

Merimee, Prosper 1803-1870**NCLC 6, 65; SSC 7**
See also DLB 119, 192

Merkin, Daphne 1954- **CLC 44**
See also CA 123

Merlin, Arthur
See Blish, James (Benjamin)

Merrill, James (Ingram) 1926-1995**CLC 2, 3, 6, 8, 13, 18, 34, 91; DAM POET; PC 28**
See also CA 13-16R; 147; CANR 10, 49, 63; DA3; DLB 5, 165; DLBY 85; INT CANR-10; MTCW 1, 2

Merriman, Alex
See Silverberg, Robert

Merriman, Brian 1747-1805 **NCLC 70**

Merritt, E. B.
See Waddington, Miriam

Merton, Thomas 1915-1968 **CLC 1, 3, 11, 34, 83; PC 10**
See also CA 5-8R; 25-28R; CANR 22, 53; DA3; DLB 48; DLBY 81; MTCW 1, 2

Merwin, W(illiam) S(tanley) 1927- **CLC 1, 2, 3, 5, 8, 13, 18, 45, 88; DAM POET**
See also CA 13-16R; CANR 15, 51; DA3; DLB 5, 169; INT CANR-15; MTCW 1, 2

Metcalf, John 1938- **CLC 37**
See also CA 113; DLB 60

Metcalf, Suzanne
See Baum, L(yman) Frank

Mew, Charlotte (Mary) 1870-1928 **TCLC 8**
See also CA 105; DLB 19, 135

Mewshaw, Michael 1943- **CLC 9**
See also CA 53-56; CANR 7, 47; DLBY 80

Meyer, Conrad Ferdinand 1825-1905 **NCLC 81**
See also DLB 129

Meyer, June
See Jordan, June

Meyer, Lynn
See Slavitt, David R(ytman)

Meyer-Meyrink, Gustav 1868-1932
See Meyrink, Gustav
See also CA 117

Meyers, Jeffrey 1939- **CLC 39**
See also CA 73-76, 181; CAAE 181; CANR 54; DLB 111

Meynell, Alice (Christina Gertrude Thompson) 1847-1922 **TCLC 6**
See also CA 104; 177; DLB 19, 98

Meyrink, Gustav **TCLC 21**
See also Meyer-Meyrink, Gustav
See also DLB 81

Michaels, Leonard 1933- **CLC 6, 25; SSC 16**
See also CA 61-64; CANR 21, 62; DLB 130; MTCW 1

Michaux, Henri 1899-1984 **CLC 8, 19**
See also CA 85-88; 114

Micheaux, Oscar (Devereaux) 1884-1951 **TCLC 76**
See also BW 3; CA 174; DLB 50

Michelangelo 1475-1564 **LC 12**

Michelet, Jules 1798-1874 **NCLC 31**

Michels, Robert 1876-1936 **TCLC 88**

Michener, James A(lbert) 1907(?)-1997 **CLC 1, 5, 11, 29, 60, 109; DAM NOV, POP**
See also AAYA 27; AITN 1; BEST 90:1; CA 5-8R; 161; CANR 21, 45, 68; DA3; DLB 6; MTCW 1, 2

Mickiewicz, Adam 1798-1855 **NCLC 3**

Middleton, Christopher 1926- **CLC 13**
See also CA 13-16R; CANR 29, 54; DLB 40

Middleton, Richard (Barham) 1882-1911 **TCLC 56**
See also DLB 156

Middleton, Stanley 1919- **CLC 7, 38**
See also CA 25-28R; CAAS 23; CANR 21, 46, 81; DLB 14

Middleton, Thomas 1580-1627 **LC 33; DAM DRAM, MST; DC 5**
See also DLB 58

Migueis, Jose Rodrigues 1901- **CLC 10**

Mikszath, Kalman 1847-1910 **TCLC 31**
See also CA 170

Miles, Jack **CLC 100**

Miles, Josephine (Louise) 1911-1985**CLC 1, 2, 14, 34, 39; DAM POET**
See also CA 1-4R; 116; CANR 2, 55; DLB 48

Militant
See Sandburg, Carl (August)

Mill, John Stuart 1806-1873 **NCLC 11, 58**
See also CDBLB 1832-1890; DLB 55, 190

Millar, Kenneth 1915-1983 **CLC 14; DAM POP**
See also Macdonald, Ross
See also CA 9-12R; 110; CANR 16, 63; DA3; DLB 2; DLBD 6; DLBY 83; MTCW 1, 2

Millay, E. Vincent
See Millay, Edna St. Vincent

Millay, Edna St. Vincent 1892-1950 **TCLC 4, 49; DA; DAB; DAC; DAM MST, POET; PC 6; WLCS**
See also CA 104; 130; CDALB 1917-1929; DA3; DLB 45; MTCW 1, 2

Miller, Arthur 1915-**CLC 1, 2, 6, 10, 15, 26, 47, 78; DA; DAB; DAC; DAM DRAM, MST; DC 1; WLC**
See also AAYA 15; AITN 1; CA 1-4R; CABS 3; CANR 2, 30, 54, 76; CDALB 1941-1968; DA3; DLB 7; MTCW 1, 2

Miller, Henry (Valentine) 1891-1980**CLC 1, 2, 4, 9, 14, 43, 84; DA; DAB; DAC; DAM MST, NOV; WLC**
See also CA 9-12R; 97-100; CANR 33, 64; CDALB 1929-1941; DA3; DLB 4, 9; DLBY 80; MTCW 1, 2

Miller, Jason 1939(?)- **CLC 2**
See also AITN 1; CA 73-76; DLB 7

Miller, Sue 1943- **CLC 44; DAM POP**
See also BEST 90:3; CA 139; CANR 59; DA3; DLB 143

Miller, Walter M(ichael), Jr.) 1923-**CLC 4, 30**
See also CA 85-88; DLB 8

Millett, Kate 1934-   **CLC 67**
See also AITN 1; CA 73-76; CANR 32, 53, 76;
DA3; MTCW 1, 2

Millhauser, Steven (Lewis) 1943-**CLC 21, 54,
109**
See also CA 110; 111; CANR 63; DA3; DLB 2;
INT 111; MTCW 2

Millin, Sarah Gertrude 1889-1968   **CLC 49**
See also CA 102; 93-96   .

Milne, A(lan) A(lexander) 1882-1956**TCLC 6,
88; DAB; DAC; DAM MST**
See also CA 104; 133; CLR 1, 26; DA3; DLB
10, 77, 100, 160; MAICYA; MTCW 1, 2;
SATA 100; YABC 1

Milner, Ron(ald) 1938-**CLC 56; BLC 3; DAM
MULT**
See also AITN 1; BW 1; CA 73-76; CANR 24,
81; DLB 38; MTCW 1

Milnes, Richard Monckton 1809-1885 **NCLC
61**
See also DLB 32, 184

Milosz, Czeslaw 1911- **CLC 5, 11, 22, 31, 56,
82; DAM MST, POET; PC 8; WLCS**
See also CA 81-84; CANR 23, 51; DA3, MTCW
1, 2

Milton, John 1608-1674 **LC 9, 43; DA; DAB;
DAC; DAM MST, POET; PC 19; WLC**
See also CDBLB 1660-1789; DA3; DLB 131,
151

Min, Anchee 1957-   **CLC 86**
See also CA 146

Minehaha, Cornelius
See Wedekind, (Benjamin) Frank(lin)

Miner, Valerie 1947-   **CLC 40**
See also CA 97-100; CANR 59

Minimo, Duca
See D'Annunzio, Gabriele

Minot, Susan 1956-   **CLC 44**
See also CA 134

Minus, Ed 1938-   **CLC 39**

Miranda, Javier
See Bioy Casares, Adolfo

Mirbeau, Octave 1848-1917   **TCLC 55**
See also DLB 123, 192

Miro (Ferrer), Gabriel (Francisco Victor) 1879-
1930   **TCLC 5**
See also CA 104

Mishima, Yukio 1925-1970**CLC 2, 4, 6, 9, 27;
DC 1; SSC 4**
See also Hiraoka, Kimitake
See also DLB 182; MTCW 2

Mistral, Frederic 1830-1914   **TCLC 51**
See also CA 122

Mistral, Gabriela   **TCLC 2; HLC 2**
See also Godoy Alcayaga, Lucila
See also MTCW 2

Mistry, Rohinton 1952-   **CLC 71; DAC**
See also CA 141; CANR 86

Mitchell, Clyde
See Ellison, Harlan (Jay); Silverberg, Robert

Mitchell, James Leslie 1901-1935
See Gibbon, Lewis Grassic
See also CA 104; DLB 15

Mitchell, Joni 1943-   **CLC 12**
See also CA 112

Mitchell, Joseph (Quincy) 1908-1996**CLC 98**
See also CA 77-80; 152; CANR 69; DLB 185;
DLBY 96

Mitchell, Margaret (Munnerlyn) 1900-1949
TCLC 11; DAM NOV, POP
See also AAYA 23; CA 109; 125; CANR 55;
CDALBS; DA3; DLB 9; MTCW 1, 2

Mitchell, Peggy

See Mitchell, Margaret (Munnerlyn)

Mitchell, S(ilas) Weir 1829-1914   **TCLC 36**
See also CA 165; DLB 202

Mitchell, W(illiam) O(rmond) 1914-1998**CLC
25; DAC; DAM MST**
See also CA 77-80; 165; CANR 15, 43; DLB
88

Mitchell, William 1879-1936   **TCLC 81**

Mitford, Mary Russell 1787-1855   **NCLC 4**
See also DLB 110, 116

Mitford, Nancy 1904-1973   **CLC 44**
See also CA 9-12R; DLB 191

Miyamoto, (Chujo) Yuriko 1899-1951 **T C L C
37**
See also CA 170, 174; DLB 180

Miyazawa, Kenji 1896-1933   **TCLC 76**
See also CA 157

Mizoguchi, Kenji 1898-1956   **TCLC 72**
See also CA 167

Mo, Timothy (Peter) 1950(?)-   **CLC 46**
See also CA 117; DLB 194; MTCW 1

Modarressi, Taghi (M.) 1931-   **CLC 44**
See also CA 121; 134; INT 134

Modiano, Patrick (Jean) 1945-   **CLC 18**
See also CA 85-88; CANR 17, 40; DLB 83

Moerck, Paal
See Roelvaag, O(le) E(dvart)

Mofolo, Thomas (Mokopu) 1875(?)-1948
TCLC 22; BLC 3; DAM MULT
See also CA 121; 153; CANR 83; MTCW 2

Mohr, Nicholasa 1938-**CLC 12; DAM MULT;
HLC 2**
See also AAYA 8; CA 49-52; CANR 1, 32, 64;
CLR 22; DLB 145; HW 1, 2; JRDA; SAAS
8; SATA 8, 97

Mojtabai, A(nn) G(race) 1938- **CLC 5, 9, 15,
29**
See also CA 85-88

Moliere 1622-1673**LC 10, 28; DA; DAB; DAC;
DAM DRAM, MST; WLC**
See also DA3

Molin, Charles
See Mayne, William (James Carter)

Molnar, Ferenc 1878-1952   **TCLC 20; DAM
DRAM**
See also CA 109; 153; CANR 83

Momaday, N(avarre) Scott 1934- **CLC 2, 19,
85, 95; DA; DAB; DAC; DAM MST,
MULT, NOV, POP; PC 25; WLCS**
See also AAYA 11; CA 25-28R; CANR 14, 34,
68; CDALBS; DA3; DLB 143, 175; INT
CANR-14; MTCW 1, 2; NNAL; SATA 48;
SATA-Brief 30

Monette, Paul 1945-1995   **CLC 82**
See also CA 139; 147

Monroe, Harriet 1860-1936   **TCLC 12**
See also CA 109; DLB 54, 91

Monroe, Lyle
See Heinlein, Robert A(nson)

Montagu, Elizabeth 1720-1800   **NCLC 7**

Montagu, Mary (Pierrepont) Wortley 1689-
1762   **LC 9; PC 16**
See also DLB 95, 101

Montagu, W. H.
See Coleridge, Samuel Taylor

Montague, John (Patrick) 1929- **CLC 13, 46**
See also CA 9-12R; CANR 9, 69; DLB 40;
MTCW 1

Montaigne, Michel (Eyquem) de 1533-1592
LC 8; DA; DAB; DAC; DAM MST; WLC

Montale, Eugenio 1896-1981**CLC 7, 9, 18; PC
13**
See also CA 17-20R; 104; CANR 30; DLB 114;

MTCW 1

Montesquieu, Charles-Louis de Secondat 1689-
1755   **LC 7**

Montgomery, (Robert) Bruce 1921(?)-1978
See Crispin, Edmund ──
See also CA 179; 104

Montgomery, L(ucy) M(aud) 1874-1942
TCLC 51; DAC; DAM MST
See also AAYA 12; CA 108; 137; CLR 8; DA3;
DLB 92; DLBD 14; JRDA; MAICYA;
MTCW 2; SATA 100; YABC 1

Montgomery, Marion H., Jr. 1925-   **CLC 7**
See also AITN 1; CA 1-4R; CANR 3, 48; DLB
6

Montgomery, Max
See Davenport, Guy (Mattison, Jr.)

Montherlant, Henry (Milon) de 1896-1972
CLC 8, 19; DAM DRAM
See also CA 85-88; 37-40R; DLB 72; MTCW
1

Monty Python
See Chapman, Graham; Cleese, John
(Marwood); Gilliam, Terry (Vance); Idle,
Eric; Jones, Terence Graham Parry; Palin,
Michael (Edward)
See also AAYA 7

Moodie, Susanna (Strickland) 1803-1885
NCLC 14
See also DLB 99

Mooney, Edward 1951-
See Mooney, Ted
See also CA 130

Mooney, Ted   **CLC 25**
See also Mooney, Edward

Moorcock, Michael (John) 1939-**CLC 5, 27, 58**
See also Bradbury, Edward P.
See also AAYA 26; CA 45-48; CAAS 5; CANR
2, 17, 38, 64; DLB 14; MTCW 1, 2; SATA
93

Moore, Brian 1921-1999**CLC 1, 3, 5, 7, 8, 19,
32, 90; DAB; DAC; DAM MST**
See also CA 1-4R; 174; CANR 1, 25, 42, 63;
MTCW 1, 2

Moore, Edward
See Muir, Edwin

Moore, G. E. 1873-1958   **TCLC 89**

Moore, George Augustus 1852-1933**TCLC 7;
SSC 19**
See also CA 104; 177; DLB 10, 18, 57, 135

Moore, Lorrie   **CLC 39, 45, 68**
See also Moore, Marie Lorena

Moore, Marianne (Craig) 1887-1972**CLC 1, 2,
4, 8, 10, 13, 19, 47; DA; DAB; DAC; DAM
MST, POET; PC 4; WLCS**
See also CA 1-4R; 33-36R; CANR 3, 61;
CDALB 1929-1941; DA3; DLB 45; DLBD
7; MTCW 1, 2; SATA 20

Moore, Marie Lorena 1957-
See Moore, Lorrie
See also CA 116; CANR 39, 83

Moore, Thomas 1779-1852   **NCLC 6**
See also DLB 96, 144

Mora, Pat(ricia) 1942-
See also CA 129; CANR 57, 81; CLR 58; DAM
MULT; DLB 209; HLC 2; HW 1, 2; SATA
92

Moraga, Cherrie 1952-**CLC 126; DAM MULT**
See also CA 131; CANR 66; DLB 82; HW 1, 2

Morand, Paul 1888-1976   **CLC 41; SSC 22**
See also CA 69-72; DLB 65

Morante, Elsa 1918-1985   **CLC 8, 47**
See also CA 85-88; 117; CANR 35; DLB 177;
MTCW 1, 2

Moravia, Alberto 1907-1990 **CLC 2, 7, 11, 27, 46; SSC 26**
See also Pincherle, Alberto
See also DLB 177; MTCW 2

More, Hannah 1745-1833 **NCLC 27**
See also DLB 107, 109, 116, 158

More, Henry 1614-1687 **LC 9**
See also DLB 126

More, Sir Thomas 1478-1535 **LC 10, 32**

Moreas, Jean **TCLC 18**
See also Papadiamantopoulos, Johannes

Morgan, Berry 1919- **CLC 6**
See also CA 49-52; DLB 6

Morgan, Claire
See Highsmith, (Mary) Patricia

Morgan, Edwin (George) 1920- **CLC 31**
See also CA 5-8R; CANR 3, 43; DLB 27

Morgan, (George) Frederick 1922- **CLC 23**
See also CA 17-20R; CANR 21

Morgan, Harriet
See Mencken, H(enry) L(ouis)

Morgan, Jane
See Cooper, James Fenimore

Morgan, Janet 1945- **CLC 39**
See also CA 65-68

Morgan, Lady 1776(?)-1859 **NCLC 29**
See also DLB 116, 158

Morgan, Robin (Evonne) 1941- **CLC 2**
See also CA 69-72; CANR 29, 68; MTCW 1; SATA 80

Morgan, Scott
See Kuttner, Henry

Morgan, Seth 1949(?)-1990 **CLC 65**
See also CA 132

Morgenstern, Christian 1871-1914 **TCLC 8**
See also CA 105

Morgenstern, S.
See Goldman, William (W.)

Moricz, Zsigmond 1879-1942 **TCLC 33**
See also CA 165

Morike, Eduard (Friedrich) 1804-1875 **NCLC 10**
See also DLB 133

Moritz, Karl Philipp 1756-1793 **LC 2**
See also DLB 94

Morland, Peter Henry
See Faust, Frederick (Schiller)

Morley, Christopher (Darlington) 1890-1957 **TCLC 87**
See also CA 112; DLB 9

Morren, Theophil
See Hofmannsthal, Hugo von

Morris, Bill 1952- **CLC 76**

Morris, Julian
See West, Morris L(anglo)

Morris, Steveland Judkins 1950(?)-
See Wonder, Stevie
See also CA 111

Morris, William 1834-1896 **NCLC 4**
See also CDBLB 1832-1890; DLB 18, 35, 57, 156, 178, 184

Morris, Wright 1910-1998 **CLC 1, 3, 7, 18, 37**
See also CA 9-12R; 167; CANR 21, 81; DLB 2, 206; DLBY 81; MTCW 1, 2

Morrison, Arthur 1863-1945 **TCLC 72**
See also CA 120; 157; DLB 70, 135, 197

Morrison, Chloe Anthony Wofford
See Morrison, Toni

Morrison, James Douglas 1943-1971
See Morrison, Jim
See also CA 73-76; CANR 40

Morrison, Jim **CLC 17**
See also Morrison, James Douglas

Morrison, Toni 1931- **CLC 4, 10, 22, 55, 81, 87; BLC 3; DA; DAB; DAC; DAM MST, MULT, NOV, POP**
See also AAYA 1, 22; BW 2, 3; CA 29-32R; CANR 27, 42, 67; CDALB 1968-1988; DA3; DLB 6, 33, 143; DLBY 81; MTCW 1, 2; SATA 57

Morrison, Van 1945- **CLC 21**
See also CA 116; 168

Morrissy, Mary 1958- **CLC 99**

Mortimer, John (Clifford) 1923- **CLC 28, 43; DAM DRAM, POP**
See also CA 13-16R; CANR 21, 69; CDBLB 1960 to Present; DA3; DLB 13; INT CANR-21; MTCW 1, 2

Mortimer, Penelope (Ruth) 1918- **CLC 5**
See also CA 57-60; CANR 45

Morton, Anthony
See Creasey, John

Mosca, Gaetano 1858-1941 **TCLC 75**

Mosher, Howard Frank 1943- **CLC 62**
See also CA 139; CANR 65

Mosley, Nicholas 1923- **CLC 43, 70**
See also CA 69-72; CANR 41, 60; DLB 14, 207

Mosley, Walter 1952- **CLC 97; BLCS; DAM MULT, POP**
See also AAYA 17; BW 2; CA 142; CANR 57; DA3; MTCW 2

Moss, Howard 1922-1987 **CLC 7, 14, 45, 50; DAM POET**
See also CA 1-4R; 123; CANR 1, 44; DLB 5

Mossgiel, Rab
See Burns, Robert

Motion, Andrew (Peter) 1952- **CLC 47**
See also CA 146; DLB 40

Motley, Willard (Francis) 1909-1965 **CLC 18**
See also BW 1; CA 117; 106; DLB 76, 143

Motoori, Norinaga 1730-1801 **NCLC 45**

Mott, Michael (Charles Alston) 1930- **CLC 15, 34**
See also CA 5-8R; CAAS 7; CANR 7, 29

Mountain Wolf Woman 1884-1960 **CLC 92**
See also CA 144; NNAL

Moure, Erin 1955- **CLC 88**
See also CA 113; DLB 60

Mowat, Farley (McGill) 1921- **CLC 26; DAC; DAM MST**
See also AAYA 1; CA 1-4R; CANR 4, 24, 42, 68; CLR 20; DLB 68; INT CANR-24; JRDA; MAICYA; MTCW 1, 2; SATA 3, 55

Mowatt, Anna Cora 1819-1870 **NCLC 74**

Moyers, Bill 1934- **CLC 74**
See also AITN 2; CA 61-64; CANR 31, 52

Mphahlele, Es'kia
See Mphahlele, Ezekiel
See also DLB 125

Mphahlele, Ezekiel 1919- **CLC 25; BLC 3; DAM MULT**
See also Mphahlele, Es'kia
See also BW 2, 3; CA 81-84; CANR 26, 76; DA3; MTCW 2

Mqhayi, S(amuel) E(dward) K(rune Loliwe) 1875-1945 **TCLC 25; BLC 3; DAM MULT**
See also CA 153

Mrozek, Slawomir 1930- **CLC 3, 13**
See also CA 13-16R; CAAS 10; CANR 29; MTCW 1

Mrs. Belloc-Lowndes
See Lowndes, Marie Adelaide (Belloc)

Mtwa, Percy (?)- **CLC 47**

Mueller, Lisel 1924- **CLC 13, 51**
See also CA 93-96; DLB 105

Muir, Edwin 1887-1959 **TCLC 2, 87**

See also CA 104; DLB 20, 100, 191

Muir, John 1838-1914 **TCLC 28**
See also CA 165; DLB 186

Mujica Lainez, Manuel 1910-1984 **CLC 31**
See also Lainez, Manuel Mujica
See also CA 81-84; 112; CANR 32; HW 1

Mukherjee, Bharati 1940- **CLC 53, 115; DAM NOV**
See also BEST 89:2; CA 107; CANR 45, 72; DLB 60; MTCW 1, 2

Muldoon, Paul 1951- **CLC 32, 72; DAM POET**
See also CA 113; 129; CANR 52; DLB 40; INT 129

Mulisch, Harry 1927- **CLC 42**
See also CA 9-12R; CANR 6, 26, 56

Mull, Martin 1943- **CLC 17**
See also CA 105

Muller, Wilhelm **NCLC 73**

Mulock, Dinah Maria
See Craik, Dinah Maria (Mulock)

Munford, Robert 1737(?)-1783 **LC 5**
See also DLB 31

Mungo, Raymond 1946- **CLC 72**
See also CA 49-52; CANR 2

Munro, Alice 1931- **CLC 6, 10, 19, 50, 95; DAC; DAM MST, NOV; SSC 3; WLCS**
See also AITN 2; CA 33-36R; CANR 33, 53, 75; DA3; DLB 53; MTCW 1, 2; SATA 29

Munro, H(ector) H(ugh) 1870-1916
See Saki
See also CA 104; 130; CDBLB 1890-1914; DA; DAB; DAC; DAM MST, NOV; DA3; DLB 34, 162; MTCW 1, 2; WLC

Murdoch, (Jean) Iris 1919-1999 **CLC 1, 2, 3, 4, 6, 8, 11, 15, 22, 31, 51; DAB; DAC; DAM MST, NOV**
See also CA 13-16R; 179; CANR 8, 43, 68; CDBLB 1960 to Present; DA3; DLB 14, 194; INT CANR-8; MTCW 1, 2

Murfree, Mary Noailles 1850-1922 **SSC 22**
See also CA 122; 176; DLB 12, 74

Murnau, Friedrich Wilhelm
See Plumpe, Friedrich Wilhelm

Murphy, Richard 1927- **CLC 41**
See also CA 29-32R; DLB 40

Murphy, Sylvia 1937- **CLC 34**
See also CA 121

Murphy, Thomas (Bernard) 1935- **CLC 51**
See also CA 101

Murray, Albert L. 1916- **CLC 73**
See also BW 2; CA 49-52; CANR 26, 52, 78; DLB 38

Murray, Judith Sargent 1751-1820 **NCLC 63**
See also DLB 37, 200

Murray, Les(lie) A(llan) 1938- **CLC 40; DAM POET**
See also CA 21-24R; CANR 11, 27, 56

Murry, J. Middleton
See Murry, John Middleton

Murry, John Middleton 1889-1957 **TCLC 16**
See also CA 118; DLB 149

Musgrave, Susan 1951- **CLC 13, 54**
See also CA 69-72; CANR 45, 84

Musil, Robert (Edler von) 1880-1942 **TCLC 12, 68; SSC 18**
See also CA 109; CANR 55, 84; DLB 81, 124; MTCW 2

Muske, Carol 1945- **CLC 90**
See also Muske-Dukes, Carol (Anne)

Muske-Dukes, Carol (Anne) 1945-
See Muske, Carol
See also CA 65-68; CANR 32, 70

Musset, (Louis Charles) Alfred de 1810-1857

O Nuallain, Brian 1911-1966
  See O'Brien, Flann
  See also CA 21-22; 25-28R; CAP 2
Ophuls, Max 1902-1957   **TCLC 79**
  See also CA 113
Opie, Amelia 1769-1853   **NCLC 65**
  See also DLB 116, 159
Oppen, George 1908-1984   **CLC 7, 13, 34**
  See also CA 13-16R; 113; CANR 8, 82; DLB
  5, 165
Oppenheim, E(dward) Phillips 1866-1946
   TCLC 45
  See also CA 111; DLB 70
Opuls, Max
  See Ophuls, Max
Origen c. 185-c. 254   **CMLC 19**
Orlovitz, Gil 1918-1973   **CLC 22**
  See also CA 77-80; 45-48; DLB 2, 5
Orris
  See Ingelow, Jean
Ortega y Gasset, Jose 1883-1955   **TCLC 9;**
  DAM MULT; HLC 2
  See also CA 106; 130; HW 1, 2; MTCW 1, 2
Ortese, Anna Maria 1914-   **CLC 89**
  See also DLB 177
Ortiz, Simon J(oseph) 1941- **CLC 45; DAM**
  MULT, POET; PC 17
  See also CA 134; CANR 69; DLB 120, 175;
  NNAL
Orton, Joe   **CLC 4, 13, 43; DC 3**
  See also Orton, John Kingsley
  See also CDBLB 1960 to Present; DLB 13;
  MTCW 2
Orton, John Kingsley 1933-1967
  See Orton, Joe
  See also CA 85-88; CANR 35, 66; DAM
  DRAM; MTCW 1, 2
Orwell, George **TCLC 2, 6, 15, 31, 51; DAB;**
  WLC
  See also Blair, Eric (Arthur)
  See also CDBLB 1945-1960; DLB 15, 98, 195
Osborne, David
  See Silverberg, Robert
Osborne, George
  See Silverberg, Robert
Osborne, John (James) 1929-1994**CLC 1, 2, 5,**
  11, 45; DA; DAB; DAC; DAM DRAM,
  MST; WLC
  See also CA 13-16R; 147; CANR 21, 56;
  CDBLB 1945-1960; DLB 13; MTCW 1, 2
Osborne, Lawrence 1958-   **CLC 50**
Osbourne, Lloyd 1868-1947   **TCLC 93**
Oshima, Nagisa 1932-   **CLC 20**
  See also CA 116; 121; CANR 78
Oskison, John Milton 1874-1947   **TCLC 35;**
  DAM MULT
  See also CA 144; CANR 84; DLB 175; NNAL
Ossian c. 3rd cent. -   **CMLC 28**
  See also Macpherson, James
Ostrovsky, Alexander 1823-1886**NCLC 30, 57**
Otero, Blas de 1916-1979   **CLC 11**
  See also CA 89-92; DLB 134
Otto, Rudolf 1869-1937   **TCLC 85**
Otto, Whitney 1955-   **CLC 70**
  See also CA 140
Ouida   **TCLC 43**
  See also De La Ramee, (Marie) Louise
  See also DLB 18, 156
Ousmane, Sembene 1923-   **CLC 66; BLC 3**
  See also BW 1, 3; CA 117; 125; CANR 81;
  MTCW 1
Ovid 43B.C.-17 **CMLC 7; DAM POET; PC 2**
  See also DA3; DLB 211

Owen, Hugh
  See Faust, Frederick (Schiller)
Owen, Wilfred (Edward Salter) 1893-1918
  TCLC 5, 27; DA; DAB; DAC; DAM MST,
  POET; PC 19; WLC
  See also CA 104; 141; CDBLB 1914-1945;
  DLB 20; MTCW 2
Owens, Rochelle 1936-   **CLC 8**
  See also CA 17-20R; CAAS 2; CANR 39
Oz, Amos 1939-**CLC 5, 8, 11, 27, 33, 54; DAM**
  NOV
  See also CA 53-56; CANR 27, 47, 65; MTCW
  1, 2
Ozick, Cynthia 1928- **CLC 3, 7, 28, 62; DAM**
  NOV, POP; SSC 15
  See also BEST 90:1; CA 17-20R; CANR 23,
  58; DA3; DLB 28, 152; DLBY 82; INT
  CANR-23; MTCW 1, 2
Ozu, Yasujiro 1903-1963   **CLC 16**
  See also CA 112
Pacheco, C.
  See Pessoa, Fernando (Antonio Nogueira)
Pacheco, Jose Emilio 1939-
  See also CA 111; 131; CANR 65; DAM MULT;
  HLC 2; HW 1, 2
Pa Chin   **CLC 18**
  See also Li Fei-kan
Pack, Robert 1929-   **CLC 13**
  See also CA 1-4R; CANR 3, 44, 82; DLB 5
Padgett, Lewis
  See Kuttner, Henry
Padilla (Lorenzo), Heberto 1932-   **CLC 38**
  See also AITN 1; CA 123; 131; HW 1
Page, Jimmy 1944-   **CLC 12**
Page, Louise 1955-   **CLC 40**
  See also CA 140; CANR 76
Page, P(atricia) K(athleen) 1916- **CLC 7, 18;**
  DAC; DAM MST; PC 12
  See also CA 53-56; CANR 4, 22, 65; DLB 68;
  MTCW 1
Page, Thomas Nelson 1853-1922   **SSC 23**
  See also CA 118; 177; DLB 12, 78; DLBD 13
Pagels, Elaine Hiesey 1943-   **CLC 104**
  See also CA 45-48; CANR 2, 24, 51
Paget, Violet 1856-1935
  See Lee, Vernon
  See also CA 104; 166
Paget-Lowe, Henry
  See Lovecraft, H(oward) P(hillips)
Paglia, Camille (Anna) 1947-   **CLC 68**
  See also CA 140; CANR 72; MTCW 2
Paige, Richard
  See Koontz, Dean R(ay)
Paine, Thomas 1737-1809   **NCLC 62**
  See also CDALB 1640-1865; DLB 31, 43, 73,
  158
Pakenham, Antonia
  See Fraser, (Lady) Antonia (Pakenham)
Palamas, Kostes 1859-1943   **TCLC 5**
  See also CA 105
Palazzeschi, Aldo 1885-1974   **CLC 11**
  See also CA 89-92; 53-56; DLB 114
Pales Matos, Luis 1898-1959
  See also HLCS 2; HW 1
Paley, Grace 1922- **CLC 4, 6, 37; DAM POP;**
  SSC 8
  See also CA 25-28R; CANR 13, 46, 74; DA3;
  DLB 28; INT CANR-13; MTCW 1, 2
Palin, Michael (Edward) 1943-   **CLC 21**
  See also Monty Python
  See also CA 107; CANR 35; SATA 67
Palliser, Charles 1947-   **CLC 65**
  See also CA 136; CANR 76

Palma, Ricardo 1833-1919   **TCLC 29**
  See also CA 168
Pancake, Breece Dexter 1952-1979
  See Pancake, Breece D'J
  See also CA 123; 109
Pancake, Breece D'J   **CLC 29**
  See also Pancake, Breece Dexter
  See also DLB 130
Panko, Rudy
  See Gogol, Nikolai (Vasilyevich)
Papadiamantis, Alexandros 1851-1911**TCLC**
  29
  See also CA 168
Papadiamantopoulos, Johannes 1856-1910
  See Moreas, Jean
  See also CA 117
Papini, Giovanni 1881-1956   **TCLC 22**
  See also CA 121; 180
Paracelsus 1493-1541   **LC 14**
  See also DLB 179
Parasol, Peter
  See Stevens, Wallace
Pardo Bazan, Emilia 1851-1921   **SSC 30**
Pareto, Vilfredo 1848-1923   **TCLC 69**
  See also CA 175
Parfenie, Maria
  See Codrescu, Andrei
Parini, Jay (Lee) 1948-   **CLC 54**
  See also CA 97-100; CAAS 16; CANR 32
Park, Jordan
  See Kornbluth, C(yril) M.; Pohl, Frederik
Park, Robert E(zra) 1864-1944   **TCLC 73**
  See also CA 122; 165
Parker, Bert
  See Ellison, Harlan (Jay)
Parker, Dorothy (Rothschild) 1893-1967**CLC**
  15, 68; DAM POET; PC 28; SSC 2
  See also CA 19-20; 25-28R; CAP 2; DA3; DLB
  11, 45, 86; MTCW 1, 2
Parker, Robert B(rown) 1932-**CLC 27; DAM**
  NOV, POP
  See also AAYA 28; BEST 89:4; CA 49-52;
  CANR 1, 26, 52; INT CANR-26; MTCW 1
Parkin, Frank 1940-   **CLC 43**
  See also CA 147
Parkman, Francis Jr., Jr. 1823-1893**NCLC 12**
  See also DLB 1, 30, 186
Parks, Gordon (Alexander Buchanan) 1912-
  CLC 1, 16; BLC 3; DAM MULT
  See also AITN 2; BW 2, 3; CA 41-44R; CANR
  26, 66; DA3; DLB 33; MTCW 2; SATA 8,
  108
Parmenides c. 515B.C.-c. 450B.C. **CMLC 22**
  See also DLB 176
Parnell, Thomas 1679-1718   **LC 3**
  See also DLB 94
Parra, Nicanor 1914-   **CLC 2, 102; DAM**
  MULT; HLC 2
  See also CA 85-88; CANR 32; HW 1; MTCW
  1
Parra Sanojo, Ana Teresa de la 1890-1936
  See also HLCS 2
Parrish, Mary Frances
  See Fisher, M(ary) F(rances) K(ennedy)
Parson
  See Coleridge, Samuel Taylor
Parson Lot
  See Kingsley, Charles
Partridge, Anthony
  See Oppenheim, E(dward) Phillips
Pascal, Blaise 1623-1662   **LC 35**
Pascoli, Giovanni 1855-1912   **TCLC 45**
  See also CA 170

Pasolini, Pier Paolo 1922-1975   **CLC 20, 37, 106; PC 17**
See also CA 93-96; 61-64; CANR 63; DLB 128, 177; MTCW 1

Pasquini
See Silone, Ignazio

Pastan, Linda (Olenik) 1932-   **CLC 27; DAM POET**
See also CA 61-64; CANR 18, 40, 61; DLB 5

Pasternak, Boris (Leonidovich) 1890-1960   **CLC 7, 10, 18, 63; DA; DAB; DAC; DAM MST, NOV, POET; PC 6; SSC 31; WLC**
See also CA 127; 116; DA3; MTCW 1, 2

Patchen, Kenneth 1911-1972   **CLC 1, 2, 18; DAM POET**
See also CA 1-4R; 33-36R; CANR 3, 35; DLB 16, 48; MTCW 1

Pater, Walter (Horatio) 1839-1894   **NCLC 7**
See also CDBLB 1832-1890; DLB 57, 156

Paterson, A(ndrew) B(arton) 1864-1941   **TCLC 32**
See also CA 155; SATA 97

Paterson, Katherine (Womeldorf) 1932-**C L C 12, 30**
See also AAYA 1, 31; CA 21-24R; CANR 28, 59; CLR 7, 50; DLB 52; JRDA; MAICYA; MTCW 1; SATA 13, 53, 92

Patmore, Coventry Kersey Dighton 1823-1896   **NCLC 9**
See also DLB 35, 98

Paton, Alan (Stewart) 1903-1988   **CLC 4, 10, 25, 55, 106; DA; DAB; DAC; DAM MST, NOV; WLC**
See also AAYA 26; CA 13-16; 125; CANR 22; CAP 1; DA3; DLBD 17; MTCW 1, 2; SATA 11; SATA-Obit 56

Paton Walsh, Gillian 1937-
See Walsh, Jill Paton
See also CANR 38, 83; JRDA; MAICYA; SAAS 3; SATA 4, 72, 109

Patton, George S. 1885-1945   **TCLC 79**

Paulding, James Kirke 1778-1860   **NCLC 2**
See also DLB 3, 59, 74

Paulin, Thomas Neilson 1949-
See Paulin, Tom
See also CA 123; 128

Paulin, Tom   **CLC 37**
See also Paulin, Thomas Neilson
See also DLB 40

Pausanias c. 1st cent. -   **CMLC 36**

Paustovsky, Konstantin (Georgievich) 1892-1968   **CLC 40**
See also CA 93-96; 25-28R

Pavese, Cesare 1908-1950   **TCLC 3; PC 13; SSC 19**
See also CA 104; 169; DLB 128, 177

Pavic, Milorad 1929-   **CLC 60**
See also CA 136; DLB 181

Pavlov, Ivan Petrovich 1849-1936   **TCLC 91**
See also CA 118; 180

Payne, Alan
See Jakes, John (William)

Paz, Gil
See Lugones, Leopoldo

Paz, Octavio 1914-1998**CLC 3, 4, 6, 10, 19, 51, 65, 119; DA; DAB; DAC; DAM MST, MULT, POET; HLC 2; PC 1; WLC**
See also CA 73-76; 165; CANR 32, 65; DA3; DLBY 90, 98; HW 1, 2; MTCW 1, 2

p'Bitek, Okot 1931-1982   **CLC 96; BLC 3; DAM MULT**
See also BW 2, 3; CA 124; 107; CANR 82; DLB 125; MTCW 1, 2

Peacock, Molly 1947-   · **CLC 60**
See also CA 103; CAAS 21; CANR 52, 84; DLB 120

Peacock, Thomas Love 1785-1866   **NCLC 22**
See also DLB 96, 116

Peake, Mervyn 1911-1968   **CLC 7, 54**
See also CA 5-8R; 25-28R; CANR 3; DLB 15, 160; MTCW 1; SATA 23

Pearce, Philippa   **CLC 21**
·See also Christie, (Ann) Philippa
See also CLR 9; DLB 161; MAICYA; SATA 1, 67

Pearl, Eric
See Elman, Richard (Martin)

Pearson, T(homas) R(eid) 1956-   **CLC 39**
See also CA 120; 130; INT 130

Peck, Dale 1967-   **CLC 81**
See also CA 146; CANR 72

Peck, John 1941-   **CLC 3**
See also CA 49-52; CANR 3

Peck, Richard (Wayne) 1934-   **CLC 21**
See also AAYA 1, 24; CA 85-88; CANR 19, 38; CLR 15; INT CANR-19; JRDA; MAICYA; SAAS 2; SATA 18, 55, 97; SATA-Essay 110

Peck, Robert Newton 1928-   **CLC 17; DA; DAC; DAM MST**
See also AAYA 3; CA 81-84, 182; CAAE 182; CANR 31, 63; CLR 45; JRDA; MAICYA; SAAS 1; SATA 21, 62, 111; SATA-Essay 108

Peckinpah, (David) Sam(uel) 1925-1984 **C L C 20**
See also CA 109; 114; CANR 82 ·

Pedersen, Knut 1859-1952
See Hamsun, Knut
See also CA 104; 119; CANR 63; MTCW 1, 2

Peeslake, Gaffer
See Durrell, Lawrence (George)

Peguy, Charles Pierre 1873-1914   **TCLC 10**
See also CA 107

Peirce, Charles Sanders 1839-1914 **TCLC 81**

Pellicer, Carlos 1900(?)-1977
See also CA 153; 69-72; HLCS 2; HW 1

Pena, Ramon del Valle y
See Valle-Inclan, Ramon (Maria) del

Pendennis, Arthur Esquir
See Thackeray, William Makepeace

Penn, William 1644-1718   **LC 25**
See also DLB 24

PEPECE
See Prado (Calvo), Pedro

Pepys, Samuel 1633-1703   **LC 11; DA; DAB; DAC; DAM MST; WLC**
See also CDBLB 1660-1789; DA3; DLB 101

Percy, Walker 1916-1990**CLC 2, 3, 6, 8, 14, 18, 47, 65; DAM NOV, POP**
See also CA 1-4R; 131; CANR 1, 23, 64; DA3; DLB 2; DLBY 80, 90; MTCW 1, 2

Percy, William Alexander 1885-1942**TCLC 84**
See also CA 163; MTCW 2

Perec, Georges 1936-1982   **CLC 56, 116**
See also CA 141; DLB 83

Pereda (y Sanchez de Porrua), Jose Maria de 1833-1906   **TCLC 16**
See also CA 117

Pereda y Porrua, Jose Maria de
See Pereda (y Sanchez de Porrua), Jose Maria de

Peregoy, George Weems
See Mencken, H(enry) L(ouis)

Perelman, S(idney) J(oseph) 1904-1979 **C L C 3, 5, 9, 15, 23, 44, 49; DAM DRAM; SSC 32**

See also AITN 1, 2; CA 73-76; 89-92; CANR 18; DLB 11, 44; MTCW 1, 2

Peret, Benjamin 1899-1959   **TCLC 20**
See also CA 117

Peretz, Isaac Loeb 1851(?)-1915   **TCLC 16; SSC 26**
See also CA 109

Peretz, Yitzhok Leibush
See Peretz, Isaac Loeb

Perez Galdos, Benito 1843-1920   **TCLC 27; HLCS 2**
See also CA 125; 153; HW 1

Peri Rossi, Cristina 1941-
See also CA 131; CANR 59, 81; DLB 145; HLCS 2; HW 1, 2

Perrault, Charles 1628-1703   **LC 3, 52**
See also MAICYA; SATA 25

Perry, Anne 1938-   **CLC 126**
See also CA 101; CANR 22, 50, 84

Perry, Brighton
See Sherwood, Robert E(mmet)

Perse, St.-John
See Leger, (Marie-Rene Auguste) Alexis Saint-Leger

Perutz, Leo(pold) 1882-1957   **TCLC 60**
See also CA 147; DLB 81

Peseenz, Tulio F.
See Lopez y Fuentes, Gregorio

Pesetsky, Bette 1932-   **CLC 28**
See also CA 133; DLB 130

Peshkov, Alexei Maximovich 1868-1936
See Gorky, Maxim
See also CA 105; 141; CANR 83; DA; DAC; DAM DRAM, MST, NOV; MTCW 2

Pessoa, Fernando (Antonio Nogueira) 1888-1935**TCLC 27; DAM MULT; HLC 2; PC 20**
See also CA 125

Peterkin, Julia Mood 1880-1961   **CLC 31**
See also CA 102; DLB 9

Peters, Joan K(aren) 1945-   **CLC 39**
See also CA 158

Peters, Robert L(ouis) 1924-   **CLC 7**
See also CA 13-16R; CAAS 8; DLB 105

Petofi, Sandor 1823-1849   **NCLC 21**

Petrakis, Harry Mark 1923-   **CLC 3**
See also CA 9-12R; CANR 4, 30, 85

Petrarch 1304-1374 **CMLC 20; DAM POET; PC 8**
See also DA3

Petronius c. 20-66   **CMLC 34**
See also DLB 211

Petrov, Evgeny   **TCLC 21**
See·also Kataev, Evgeny Petrovich

Petry, Ann (Lane) 1908-1997   **CLC 1, 7, 18**
See also BW 1, 3; CA 5-8R; 157; CAAS 6; CANR 4, 46; CLR 12; DLB 76; JRDA; MAICYA; MTCW 1; SATA 5; SATA-Obit 94

Petursson, Halligrimur 1614-1674   **LC 8**

Peychinovich
See Vazov, Ivan (Minchov)

Phaedrus c. 18B.C.-c. 50   **CMLC 25**
See also DLB 211

Philips, Katherine 1632-1664   **LC 30**
See also DLB 131

Philipson, Morris H. 1926-   **CLC 53**
See also CA 1-4R; CANR 4

Phillips, Caryl 1958-   **CLC 96; BLCS; DAM MULT**
See also BW 2; CA 141; CANR 63; DA3; DLB 157; MTCW 2

Phillips, David Graham 1867-1911 **TCLC 44**
See also CA 108; 176; DLB 9, 12

Phillips, Jack
See Sandburg, Carl (August)
Phillips, Jayne Anne 1952-CLC 15, 33; SSC 16
See also CA 101; CANR 24, 50; DLBY 80; INT
CANR-24; MTCW 1, 2
Phillips, Richard
See Dick, Philip K(indred)
Phillips, Robert (Schaeffer) 1938-　　**CLC 28**
See also CA 17-20R; CAAS 13; CANR 8; DLB
105
Phillips, Ward
See Lovecraft, H(oward) P(hillips)
Piccolo, Lucio 1901-1969　　　**CLC 13**
See also CA 97-100; DLB 114
Pickthall, Marjorie L(owry) C(hristie) 1883-
1922　　　　**TCLC 21**
See also CA 107; DLB 92
Pico della Mirandola, Giovanni 1463-1494LC
15
Piercy, Marge 1936- CLC 3, 6, 14, 18, 27, 62
See also CA 21-24R; CAAS 1; CANR 13, 43,
66; DLB 120; MTCW 1, 2
Piers, Robert
See Anthony, Piers
Pieyre de Mandiargues, Andre 1909-1991
See Mandiargues, Andre Pieyre de
See also CA 103; 136; CANR 22, 82
Pilnyak, Boris　　　　　**TCLC 23**
See also Vogau, Boris Andreyevich
Pincherle, Alberto 1907-1990　**CLC 11, 18;**
DAM NOV
See also Moravia, Alberto
See also CA 25-28R; 132; CANR 33, 63;
MTCW 1
Pinckney, Darryl 1953-　　　**CLC 76**
See also BW 2, 3; CA 143; CANR 79
Pindar 518B.C.-446B.C.　**CMLC 12; PC 19**
See also DLB 176
Pineda, Cecile 1942-　　　**CLC 39**
See also CA 118
Pinero, Arthur Wing 1855-1934　**TCLC 32;**
DAM DRAM
See also CA 110; 153; DLB 10
Pinero, Miguel (Antonio Gomez) 1946-1988
CLC 4, 55
See also CA 61-64; 125; CANR 29; HW 1
Pinget, Robert 1919-1997　　**CLC 7, 13, 37**
See also CA 85-88; 160; DLB 83
Pink Floyd
See Barrett, (Roger) Syd; Gilmour, David; Ma-
son, Nick; Waters, Roger; Wright, Rick
Pinkney, Edward 1802-1828　　**NCLC 31**
Pinkwater, Daniel Manus 1941-　　**CLC 35**
See also Pinkwater, Manus
See also AAYA 1; CA 29-32R; CANR 12, 38;
CLR 4; JRDA; MAICYA; SAAS 3; SATA 46,
76
Pinkwater, Manus
See Pinkwater, Daniel Manus
See also SATA 8
Pinsky, Robert 1940- CLC 9, 19, 38, 94, 121;
DAM POET; PC 27
See also CA 29-32R; CAAS 4; CANR 58; DA3;
DLBY 82, 98; MTCW 2
Pinta, Harold
See Pinter, Harold
Pinter, Harold 1930-CLC 1, 3, 6, 9, 11, 15, 27,
58, 73; DA; DAB; DAC; DAM DRAM,
MST; WLC
See also CA 5-8R; CANR 33, 65; CDBLB 1960
to Present; DA3; DLB 13; MTCW 1, 2
Piozzi, Hester Lynch (Thrale) 1741-1821
NCLC 57

See also DLB 104, 142
Pirandello, Luigi 1867-1936TCLC 4, 29; DA;
DAB; DAC; DAM DRAM, MST; DC 5;
SSC 22; WLC
See also CA 104; 153; DA3; MTCW 2
Pirsig, Robert M(aynard) 1928-CLC 4, 6, 73;
DAM POP
See also CA 53-56; CANR 42, 74; DA3; MTCW
1, 2; SATA 39
Pisarev, Dmitry Ivanovich 1840-1868 N C L C
25
Pix, Mary (Griffith) 1666-1709　　　**LC 8**
See also DLB 80
Pixerecourt, (Rene Charles) Guilbert de 1773-
1844　　　　　　**NCLC 39**
See also DLB 192
Plaatje, Sol(omon) T(shekisho) 1876-1932
TCLC 73; BLCS
See also BW 2, 3; CA 141; CANR 79
Plaidy, Jean
See Hibbert, Eleanor Alice Burford
Planche, James Robinson 1796-1880NCLC 42
Plant, Robert 1948-　　　　**CLC 12**
Plante, David (Robert) 1940- CLC 7, 23, 38;
DAM NOV
See also CA 37-40R; CANR 12, 36, 58, 82;
DLBY 83; INT CANR-12; MTCW 1
Plath, Sylvia 1932-1963 CLC 1, 2, 3, 5, 9, 11,
14, 17, 50, 51, 62, 111; DA; DAB; DAC;
DAM MST, POET; PC 1; WLC
See also AAYA 13; CA 19-20; CANR 34; CAP
2; CDALB 1941-1968; DA3; DLB 5, 6, 152;
MTCW 1, 2; SATA 96
Plato 428(?)B.C.-348(?)B.C.　　**CMLC 8; DA;**
DAB; DAC; DAM MST; WLCS
See also DA3; DLB 176
Platonov, Andrei　　　　　**TCLC 14**
See also Klimentov, Andrei Platonovich
Platt, Kin 1911-　　　　　**CLC 26**
See also AAYA 11; CA 17-20R; CANR 11;
JRDA; SAAS 17; SATA 21, 86
Plautus c. 251B.C.-184B.C.　**CMLC 24; DC 6**
See also DLB 211
Plick et Plock
See Simenon, Georges (Jacques Christian)
Plimpton, George (Ames) 1927-　　**CLC 36**
See also AITN 1; CA 21-24R; CANR 32, 70;
DLB 185; MTCW 1, 2; SATA 10
Pliny the Elder c. 23-79　　　**CMLC 23**
See also DLB 211
Plomer, William Charles Franklin 1903-1973
CLC 4, 8
See also CA 21-22; CANR 34; CAP 2; DLB
20, 162, 191; MTCW 1; SATA 24
Plowman, Piers
See Kavanagh, Patrick (Joseph)
Plum, J.
See Wodehouse, P(elham) G(renville)
Plumly, Stanley (Ross) 1939-　　　**CLC 33**
See also CA 108; 110; DLB 5, 193; INT 110
Plumpe, Friedrich Wilhelm 1888-1931T C L C
53
See also CA 112
Po Chu-i 772-846　　　　　**CMLC 24**
Poe, Edgar Allan 1809-1849 NCLC 1, 16, 55,
78; DA; DAB; DAC; DAM MST, POET;
PC 1; SSC 34; WLC
See also AAYA 14; CDALB 1640-1865; DA3;
DLB 3, 59, 73, 74; SATA 23
Poet of Titchfield Street, The
See Pound, Ezra (Weston Loomis)
Pohl, Frederik 1919-　　　**CLC 18; SSC 25**
See also AAYA 24; CA 61-64; CAAS 1; CANR

11, 37, 81; DLB 8; INT CANR-11; MTCW
1, 2; SATA 24
Poirier, Louis 1910-
See Gracq, Julien
See also CA 122; 126
Poitier, Sidney 1927-　　　　**CLC 26**
See also BW 1; CA 117
Polanski, Roman 1933-　　　**CLC 16**
See also CA 77-80
Poliakoff, Stephen 1952-　　　**CLC 38**
See also CA 106; DLB 13
Police, The
See Copeland, Stewart (Armstrong); Summers,
Andrew James; Sumner, Gordon Matthew
Polidori, John William 1795-1821 NCLC 51
See also DLB 116
Pollitt, Katha 1949-　　　**CLC 28, 122**
See also CA 120; 122; CANR 66; MTCW 1, 2
Pollock, (Mary) Sharon 1936-CLC 50; DAC;
DAM DRAM, MST
See also CA 141; DLB 60
Polo, Marco 1254-1324　　　**CMLC 15**
Polonsky, Abraham (Lincoln) 1910- CLC 92
See also CA 104; DLB 26; INT 104
Polybius c. 200B.C.-c. 118B.C.　　**CMLC 17**
See also DLB 176
Pomerance, Bernard 1940-　　**CLC 13; DAM**
DRAM
See also CA 101; CANR 49
Ponge, Francis (Jean Gaston Alfred) 1899-1988
CLC 6, 18; DAM POET
See also CA 85-88; 126; CANR 40, 86
Poniatowska, Elena 1933-
See also CA 101; CANR 32, 66; DAM MULT;
DLB 113; HLC 2; HW 1, 2
Pontoppidan, Henrik 1857-1943　**TCLC 29**
See also CA 170
Poole, Josephine　　　　　**CLC 17**
See also Helyar, Jane Penelope Josephine
See also SAAS 2; SATA 5
Popa, Vasko 1922-1991　　　　**CLC 19**
See also CA 112; 148; DLB 181
Pope, Alexander 1688-1744 LC 3; DA; DAB;
DAC; DAM MST, POET; PC 26; WLC
See also CDBLB 1660-1789; DA3; DLB 95,
101
Porter, Connie (Rose) 1959(?)-　　**CLC 70**
See also BW 2, 3; CA 142; SATA 81
Porter, Gene(va Grace) Stratton 1863(?)-1924
TCLC 21
See also CA 112
Porter, Katherine Anne 1890-1980CLC 1, 3, 7,
10, 13, 15, 27, 101; DA; DAB; DAC; DAM
MST, NOV; SSC 4, 31
See also AITN 2; CA 1-4R; 101; CANR 1, 65;
CDALBS; DA3; DLB 4, 9, 102; DLBD 12;
DLBY 80; MTCW 1, 2; SATA 39; SATA-
Obit 23
Porter, Peter (Neville Frederick) 1929-CLC 5,
13, 33
See also CA 85-88; DLB 40
Porter, William Sydney 1862-1910
See Henry, O.
See also CA 104; 131; CDALB 1865-1917; DA;
DAB; DAC; DAM MST; DA3; DLB 12, 78,
79; MTCW 1, 2; YABC 2
Portillo (y Pacheco), Jose Lopez
See Lopez Portillo (y Pacheco), Jose
Portillo Trambley, Estela 1927-1998
See also CANR 32; DAM MULT; DLB 209;
HLC 2; HW 1
Post, Melville Davisson 1869-1930 TCLC 39
See also CA 110

Potok, Chaim 1929- **CLC 2, 7, 14, 26, 112;**
DAM NOV
See also AAYA 15; AITN 1, 2; CA 17-20R;
CANR 19, 35, 64; DA3; DLB 28, 152; INT
CANR-19; MTCW 1, 2; SATA 33, 106
Potter, Dennis (Christopher George) 1935-1994
CLC 58, 86
See also CA 107; 145; CANR 33, 61; MTCW 1
Pound, Ezra (Weston Loomis) 1885-1972**CLC**
1, 2, 3, 4, 5, 7, 10, 13, 18, 34, 48, 50, 112;
DA; DAB; DAC; DAM MST, POET; PC
4; WLC
See also CA 5-8R; 37-40R; CANR 40; CDALB
1917-1929; DA3; DLB 4, 45, 63; DLBD 15;
MTCW 1, 2
Povod, Reinaldo 1959-1994 **CLC 44**
See also CA 136; 146; CANR 83
Powell, Adam Clayton, Jr. 1908-1972**CLC 89;**
BLC 3; DAM MULT
See also BW 1, 3; CA 102; 33-36R; CANR 86
Powell, Anthony (Dymoke) 1905-**CLC 1, 3, 7,**
9, 10, 31
See also CA 1-4R; CANR 1, 32, 62; CDBLB
1945-1960; DLB 15; MTCW 1, 2
Powell, Dawn 1897-1965 **CLC 66**
See also CA 5-8R; DLBY 97
Powell, Padgett 1952- **CLC 34**
See also CA 126; CANR 63
Power, Susan 1961- **CLC 91**
Powers, J(ames) F(arl) 1917-1999**CLC 1, 4, 8,**
57; SSC 4
See also CA 1-4R; 181; CANR 2, 61; DLB 130;
MTCW 1
Powers, John J(ames) 1945-
See Powers, John R.
See also CA 69-72
Powers, John R. **CLC 66**
See also Powers, John J(ames)
Powers, Richard (S.) 1957- **CLC 93**
See also CA 148; CANR 80
Pownall, David 1938- **CLC 10**
See also CA 89-92, 180; CAAS 18; CANR 49;
DLB 14
Powys, John Cowper 1872-1963**CLC 7, 9, 15,**
46, 125
See also CA 85-88; DLB 15; MTCW 1, 2
Powys, T(heodore) F(rancis) 1875-1953
TCLC 9
See also CA 106; DLB 36, 162
Prado (Calvo), Pedro 1886-1952 **TCLC 75**
See also CA 131; HW 1
Prager, Emily 1952- **CLC 56**
Pratt, E(dwin) J(ohn) 1883(?)-1964 **CLC 19;**
DAC; DAM POET
See also CA 141; 93-96; CANR 77; DLB 92
Premchand **TCLC 21**
See also Srivastava, Dhanpat Rai
Preussler, Otfried 1923- **CLC 17**
See also CA 77-80; SATA 24
Prevert, Jacques (Henri Marie) 1900-1977
CLC 15
See also CA 77-80; 69-72; CANR 29, 61;
MTCW 1; SATA-Obit 30
Prevost, Abbe (Antoine Francois) 1697-1763
LC 1
Price, (Edward) Reynolds 1933-**CLC 3, 6, 13,**
43, 50, 63; DAM NOV; SSC 22
See also CA 1-4R; CANR 1, 37, 57; DLB 2;
INT CANR-37
Price, Richard 1949- **CLC 6, 12**
See also CA 49-52; CANR 3; DLBY 81
Prichard, Katharine Susannah 1883-1969
CLC 46

See also CA 11-12; CANR 33; CAP 1; MTCW
1; SATA 66
Priestley, J(ohn) B(oynton) 1894-1984**CLC 2,**
5, 9, 34; DAM DRAM, NOV
See also CA 9-12R; 113; CANR 33; CDBLB
1914-1945; DA3; DLB 10, 34, 77, 100, 139;
DLBY 84; MTCW 1, 2
Prince 1958(?)- **CLC 35**
Prince, F(rank) T(empleton) 1912- **CLC 22**
See also CA 101; CANR 43, 79; DLB 20
Prince Kropotkin
See Kropotkin, Peter (Alekseevich)
Prior, Matthew 1664-1721 **LC 4**
See also DLB 95
Prishvin, Mikhail 1873-1954 **TCLC 75**
Pritchard, William H(arrison) 1932- **CLC 34**
See also CA 65-68; CANR 23; DLB 111
Pritchett, V(ictor) S(awdon) 1900-1997 **C L C**
5, 13, 15, 41; DAM NOV; SSC 14
See also CA 61-64; 157; CANR 31, 63; DA3;
DLB 15, 139; MTCW 1, 2
Private 19022
See Manning, Frederic
Probst, Mark 1925- **CLC 59**
See also CA 130
Prokosch, Frederic 1908-1989 **CLC 4, 48**
See also CA 73-76; 128; CANR 82; DLB 48;
MTCW 2
Propertius, Sextus c. 50B.C.-c. 16B.C.**CMLC**
32
See also DLB 211
Prophet, The
See Dreiser, Theodore (Herman Albert)
Prose, Francine 1947- **CLC 45**
See also CA 109; 112; CANR 46; SATA 101
Proudhon
See Cunha, Euclides (Rodrigues Pimenta) da
Proulx, Annie
See Proulx, E(dna) Annie
Proulx, E(dna) Annie 1935- **CLC 81; DAM**
POP
See also CA 145; CANR 65; DA3; MTCW 2
Proust, (Valentin-Louis-George-Eugene-)
Marcel 1871-1922 **TCLC 7, 13, 33; DA;**
DAB; DAC; DAM MST, NOV; WLC
See also CA 104; 120; DA3; DLB 65; MTCW
1, 2
Prowler, Harley
See Masters, Edgar Lee
Prus, Boleslaw 1845-1912 **TCLC 48**
Pryor, Richard (Franklin Lenox Thomas) 1940-
CLC 26
See also CA 122; 152
Przybyszewski, Stanislaw 1868-1927**TCLC 36**
See also CA 160; DLB 66
Pteleon
See Grieve, C(hristopher) M(urray)
See also DAM POET
Puckett, Lute
See Masters, Edgar Lee
Puig, Manuel 1932-1990**CLC 3, 5, 10, 28, 65;**
DAM MULT; HLC 2
See also CA 45-48; CANR 2, 32, 63; DA3; DLB
113; HW 1, 2; MTCW 1, 2
Pulitzer, Joseph 1847-1911 **TCLC 76**
See also CA 114; DLB 23
Purdy, A(lfred) W(ellington) 1918- **CLC 3, 6,**
14, 50; DAC; DAM MST, POET
See also CA 81-84; CAAS 17; CANR 42, 66;
DLB 88
Purdy, James (Amos) 1923- **CLC 2, 4, 10, 28,**
52
See also CA 33-36R; CAAS 1; CANR 19, 51;

DLB 2; INT CANR-19; MTCW 1
Pure, Simon
See Swinnerton, Frank Arthur
Pushkin, Alexander (Sergeyevich) 1799-1837
NCLC 3, 27; DA; DAB; DAC; DAM
DRAM, MST, POET; PC 10; SSC 27;
WLC
See also DA3; DLB 205; SATA 61
P'u Sung-ling 1640-1715 **LC 49; SSC 31**
Putnam, Arthur Lee
See Alger, Horatio Jr., Jr.
Puzo, Mario 1920-1999 **CLC 1, 2, 6, 36, 107;**
DAM NOV, POP
See also CA 65-68; CANR 4, 42, 65; DA3; DLB
6; MTCW 1, 2
Pygge, Edward
See Barnes, Julian (Patrick)
Pyle, Ernest Taylor 1900-1945
See Pyle, Ernie
See also CA 115; 160
Pyle, Ernie 1900-1945 **TCLC 75**
See also Pyle, Ernest Taylor
See also DLB 29; MTCW 2
Pyle, Howard 1853-1911 **TCLC 81**
See also CA 109; 137; CLR 22; DLB 42, 188;
DLBD 13; MAICYA; SATA 16, 100
Pym, Barbara (Mary Crampton) 1913-1980
CLC 13, 19, 37, 111
See also CA 13-14; 97-100; CANR 13, 34; CAP
1; DLB 14, 207; DLBY 87; MTCW 1, 2
Pynchon, Thomas (Ruggles, Jr.) 1937-**CLC 2,**
3, 6, 9, 11, 18, 33, 62, 72; DA; DAB; DAC;
DAM MST, NOV, POP; SSC 14; WLC
See also BEST 90:2; CA 17-20R; CANR 22,
46, 73; DA3; DLB 2, 173; MTCW 1, 2
Pythagoras c. 570B.C.-c. 500B.C. **CMLC 22**
See also DLB 176
Q
See Quiller-Couch, SirArthur (Thomas)
Qian Zhongshu
See Ch'ien Chung-shu
Qroll
See Dagerman, Stig (Halvard)
Quarrington, Paul (Lewis) 1953- **CLC 65**
See also CA 129; CANR 62
Quasimodo, Salvatore 1901-1968 **CLC 10**
See also CA 13-16; 25-28R; CAP 1; DLB 114;
MTCW 1
Quay, Stephen 1947- **CLC 95**
Quay, Timothy 1947- **CLC 95**
Queen, Ellery **CLC 3, 11**
See also Dannay, Frederic; Davidson, Avram
(James); Lee, Manfred B(ennington);
Marlowe, Stephen; Sturgeon, Theodore
(Hamilton); Vance, John Holbrook
Queen, Ellery, Jr.
See Dannay, Frederic; Lee, Manfred
B(ennington)
Queneau, Raymond 1903-1976 **CLC 2, 5, 10,**
42
See also CA 77-80; 69-72; CANR 32; DLB 72;
MTCW 1, 2
Quevedo, Francisco de 1580-1645 **LC 23**
Quiller-Couch, SirArthur (Thomas) 1863-1944
TCLC 53
See also CA 118; 166; DLB 135, 153, 190
Quin, Ann (Marie) 1936-1973 **CLC 6**
See also CA 9-12R; 45-48; DLB 14
Quinn, Martin
See Smith, Martin Cruz
Quinn, Peter 1947- **CLC 91**
Quinn, Simon
See Smith, Martin Cruz

Quintana, Leroy V. 1944-
See also CA 131; CANR 65; DAM MULT; DLB 82; HLC 2; HW 1, 2

Quiroga, Horacio (Sylvestre) 1878-1937
TCLC 20; DAM MULT; HLC 2
See also CA 117; 131; HW 1; MTCW 1

Quoirez, Francoise 1935- **CLC 9**
See also Sagan, Francoise
See also CA 49-52; CANR 6, 39, 73; MTCW 1, 2

Raabe, Wilhelm (Karl) 1831-1910 **TCLC 45**
See also CA 167; DLB 129

Rabe, David (William) 1940- **CLC 4, 8, 33; DAM DRAM**
See also CA 85-88; CABS 3; CANR 59; DLB 7

Rabelais, Francois 1483-1553 **LC 5; DA; DAB; DAC; DAM MST; WLC**

Rabinovitch, Sholem 1859-1916
See Aleichem, Sholom
See also CA 104

Rabinyan, Dorit 1972- **CLC 119**
See also CA 170

Rachilde 1860-1953 **TCLC 67**
See also DLB 123, 192

Racine, Jean 1639-1699 **LC 28; DAB; DAM MST**
See also DA3

Radcliffe, Ann (Ward) 1764-1823 **NCLC 6, 55**
See also DLB 39, 178

Radiguet, Raymond 1903-1923 **TCLC 29**
See also CA 162; DLB 65

Radnoti, Miklos 1909-1944 **TCLC 16**
See also CA 118

Rado, James 1939- **CLC 17**
See also CA 105

Radvanyi, Netty 1900-1983
See Seghers, Anna
See also CA 85-88, 110, CANR 82

Rae, Ben
See Griffiths, Trevor

Raeburn, John (Hay) 1941- **CLC 34**
See also CA 57-60

Ragni, Gerome 1942-1991 **CLC 17**
See also CA 105; 134

Rahv, Philip 1908-1973 **CLC 24**
See Greenberg, Ivan
See also DLB 137

Raimund, Ferdinand Jakob 1790-1836 **NCLC 69**
See also DLB 90

Raine, Craig 1944- **CLC 32, 103**
See also CA 108; CANR 29, 51; DLB 40

Raine, Kathleen (Jessie) 1908- **CLC 7, 45**
See also CA 85-88; CANR 46; DLB 20; MTCW 1

Rainis, Janis 1865-1929 **TCLC 29**
See also CA 170

Rakosi, Carl 1903- **CLC 47**
See also Rawley, Callman
See also CAAS 5; DLB 193

Raleigh, Richard
See Lovecraft, H(oward) P(hillips)

Raleigh, Sir Walter 1554(?)-1618 **LC 31, 39**
See also CDBLB Before 1660; DLB 172

Rallentando, H. P.
See Sayers, Dorothy L(eigh)

Ramal, Walter
See de la Mare, Walter (John)

Ramana Maharshi 1879-1950 **TCLC 84**

Ramoacn y Cajal, Santiago 1852-1934 **TCLC 93**

Ramon, Juan
See Jimenez (Mantecon), Juan Ramon

Ramos, Graciliano 1892-1953 **TCLC 32**
See also CA 167; HW 2

Rampersad, Arnold 1941- **CLC 44**
See also BW 2, 3; CA 127; 133; CANR 81; DLB 111; INT 133

Rampling, Anne
See Rice, Anne

Ramsay, Allan 1684(?)-1758 **LC 29**
See also DLB 95

Ramuz, Charles-Ferdinand 1878-1947 **TCLC 33**
See also CA 165

Rand, Ayn 1905-1982 **CLC 3, 30, 44, 79; DA; DAC; DAM MST, NOV, POP; WLC**
See also AAYA 10; CA 13-16R; 105; CANR 27, 73; CDALBS; DA3; MTCW 1, 2

Randall, Dudley (Felker) 1914- **CLC 1; BLC 3; DAM MULT**
See also BW 1, 3; CA 25-28R; CANR 23, 82; DLB 41

Randall, Robert
See Silverberg, Robert

Ranger, Ken
See Creasey, John

Ransom, John Crowe 1888-1974 **CLC 2, 4, 5, 11, 24; DAM POET**
See also CA 5-8R; 49-52; CANR 6, 34; CDALBS; DA3; DLB 45, 63; MTCW 1, 2

Rao, Raja 1909- **CLC 25, 56; DAM NOV**
See also CA 73-76; CANR 51; MTCW 1, 2

Raphael, Frederic (Michael) 1931- **CLC 2, 14**
See also CA 1-4R; CANR 1, 86; DLB 14

Ratcliffe, James P.
See Mencken, H(enry) L(ouis)

Rathbone, Julian 1935- **CLC 41**
See also CA 101; CANR 34, 73

Rattigan, Terence (Mervyn) 1911-1977 **CLC 7; DAM DRAM**
See also CA 85-88; 73-76; CDBLB 1945-1960; DLB 13; MTCW 1, 2

Ratushinskaya, Irina 1954- **CLC 54**
See also CA 129; CANR 68

Raven, Simon (Arthur Noel) 1927- **CLC 14**
See also CA 81-84; CANR 86

Ravenna, Michael
See Welty, Eudora

Rawley, Callman 1903-
See Rakosi, Carl
See also CA 21-24R; CANR 12, 32

Rawlings, Marjorie Kinnan 1896-1953 **TCLC 4**
See also AAYA 20; CA 104; 137; CANR 74; DLB 9, 22, 102; DLBD 17; JRDA; MAICYA; MTCW 2; SATA 100; YABC 1

Ray, Satyajit 1921-1992 **CLC 16, 76; DAM MULT**
See also CA 114; 137

Read, Herbert Edward 1893-1968 **CLC 4**
See also CA 85-88; 25-28R; DLB 20, 149

Read, Piers Paul 1941- **CLC 4, 10, 25**
See also CA 21-24R; CANR 38, 86; DLB 14; SATA 21

Reade, Charles 1814-1884 **NCLC 2, 74**
See also DLB 21

Reade, Hamish
See Gray, Simon (James Holliday)

Reading, Peter 1946- **CLC 47**
See also CA 103; CANR 46; DLB 40

Reaney, James 1926- **CLC 13; DAC; DAM MST**
See also CA 41-44R; CAAS 15; CANR 42; DLB 68; SATA 43

Rebreanu, Liviu 1885-1944 **TCLC 28**

See also CA 165

Rechy, John (Francisco) 1934- **CLC 1, 7, 14, 18, 107; DAM MULT; HLC 2**
See also CA 5-8R; CAAS 4; CANR 6, 32, 64; DLB 122; DLBY 82; HW 1, 2; INT CANR-6

Redcam, Tom 1870-1933 **TCLC 25**

Reddin, Keith **CLC 67**

Redgrove, Peter (William) 1932- **CLC 6, 41**
See also CA 1-4R; CANR 3, 39, 77; DLB 40

Redmon, Anne **CLC 22**
See also Nightingale, Anne Redmon
See also DLBY 86

Reed, Eliot
See Ambler, Eric

Reed, Ishmael 1938- **CLC 2, 3, 5, 6, 13, 32, 60; BLC 3; DAM MULT**
See also BW 2, 3; CA 21-24R; CANR 25, 48, 74; DA3; DLB 2, 5, 33, 169; DLBD 8; MTCW 1, 2

Reed, John (Silas) 1887-1920 **TCLC 9**
See also CA 106

Reed, Lou **CLC 21**
See also Firbank, Louis

Reeve, Clara 1729-1807 **NCLC 19**
See also DLB 39

Reich, Wilhelm 1897-1957 **TCLC 57**

Reid, Christopher (John) 1949- **CLC 33**
See also CA 140; DLB 40

Reid, Desmond
See Moorcock, Michael (John)

Reid Banks, Lynne 1929-
See Banks, Lynne Reid
See also CA 1-4R; CANR 6, 22, 38; CLR 24; JRDA; MAICYA; SATA 22, 75, 111

Reilly, William K.
See Creasey, John

Reiner, Max
See Caldwell, (Janet Miriam) Taylor (Holland)

Reis, Ricardo
See Pessoa, Fernando (Antonio Nogueira)

Remarque, Erich Maria 1898-1970 **CLC 21; DA; DAB; DAC; DAM MST, NOV**
See also AAYA 27; CA 77-80; 29-32R; DA3; DLB 56; MTCW 1, 2

Remington, Frederic 1861-1909 **TCLC 89**
See also CA 108; 169; DLB 12, 186, 188; SATA 41

Remizov, A.
See Remizov, Aleksei (Mikhailovich)

Remizov, A. M.
See Remizov, Aleksei (Mikhailovich)

Remizov, Aleksei (Mikhailovich) 1877-1957 **TCLC 27**
See also CA 125; 133

Renan, Joseph Ernest 1823-1892 **NCLC 26**

Renard, Jules 1864-1910 **TCLC 17**
See also CA 117

Renault, Mary **CLC 3, 11, 17**
See also Challans, Mary
See also DLBY 83; MTCW 2

Rendell, Ruth (Barbara) 1930- **CLC 28, 48; DAM POP**
See also Vine, Barbara
See also CA 109; CANR 32, 52, 74; DLB 87; INT CANR-32; MTCW 1, 2

Renoir, Jean 1894-1979 **CLC 20**
See also CA 129; 85-88

Resnais, Alain 1922- **CLC 16**

Reverdy, Pierre 1889-1960 **CLC 53**
See also CA 97-100; 89-92

Rexroth, Kenneth 1905-1982 **CLC 1, 2, 6, 11, 22, 49, 112; DAM POET; PC 20**

Sapphire, Brenda 1950- **CLC 99**
Sappho fl. 6th cent. B.C.- **CMLC 3; DAM POET; PC 5**
See also DA3; DLB 176
Saramago, Jose 1922- **CLC 119; HLCS 1**
See also CA 153
Sarduy, Severo 1937-1993 **CLC 6, 97; HLCS 1**
See also CA 89-92; 142; CANR 58, 81; DLB 113; HW 1, 2
Sargeson, Frank 1903-1982 **CLC 31**
See also CA 25-28R; 106; CANR 38, 79
Sarmiento, Domingo Faustino 1811-1888
See also HLCS 2
Sarmiento, Felix Ruben Garcia
See Dario, Ruben
Saro-Wiwa, Ken(ule Beeson) 1941-1995 **CLC 114**
See also BW 2; CA 142; 150; CANR 60; DLB 157
Saroyan, William 1908-1981 **CLC 1, 8, 10, 29, 34, 56; DA; DAB; DAC; DAM DRAM, MST, NOV; SSC 21; WLC**
See also CA 5-8R; 103; CANR 30; CDALBS; DA3; DLB 7, 9, 86; DLBY 81; MTCW 1, 2; SATA 23; SATA-Obit 24
Sarraute, Nathalie 1900- **CLC 1, 2, 4, 8, 10, 31, 80**
See also CA 9-12R; CANR 23, 66; DLB 83; MTCW 1, 2
Sarton, (Eleanor) May 1912-1995 **CLC 4, 14, 49, 91; DAM POET**
See also CA 1-4R; 149; CANR 1, 34, 55; DLB 48; DLBY 81; INT CANR-34; MTCW 1, 2; SATA 36; SATA-Obit 86
Sartre, Jean-Paul 1905-1980 **CLC 1, 4, 7, 9, 13, 18, 24, 44, 50, 52; DA; DAB; DAC; DAM DRAM, MST, NOV; DC 3; SSC 32; WLC**
See also CA 9-12R; 97-100; CANR 21; DA3; DLB 72; MTCW 1, 2
Sassoon, Siegfried (Lorraine) 1886-1967 **CLC 36; DAB; DAM MST, NOV, POET; PC 12**
See also CA 104; 25-28R; CANR 36; DLB 20, 191; DLBD 18; MTCW 1, 2
Satterfield, Charles
See Pohl, Frederik
Saul, John (W. III) 1942- **CLC 46; DAM NOV, POP**
See also AAYA 10; BEST 90:4; CA 81-84; CANR 16, 40, 81; SATA 98
Saunders, Caleb
See Heinlein, Robert A(nson)
Saura (Atares), Carlos 1932- **CLC 20**
See also CA 114; 131; CANR 79; HW 1
Sauser-Hall, Frederic 1887-1961 **CLC 18**
See also Cendrars, Blaise
See also CA 102; 93-96; CANR 36, 62; MTCW 1
Saussure, Ferdinand de 1857-1913 **TCLC 49**
Savage, Catharine
See Brosman, Catharine Savage
Savage, Thomas 1915- **CLC 40**
See also CA 126; 132; CAAS 15; INT 132
Savan, Glenn 19(?)- **CLC 50**
Sayers, Dorothy L(eigh) 1893-1957 **TCLC 2, 15; DAM POP**
See also CA 104; 119; CANR 60; CDBLB 1914-1945; DLB 10, 36, 77, 100; MTCW 1, 2
Sayers, Valerie 1952- **CLC 50, 122**
See also CA 134; CANR 61
Sayles, John (Thomas) 1950- **CLC 7, 10, 14**
See also CA 57-60; CANR 41, 84; DLB 44
Scammell, Michael 1935- **CLC 34**
See also CA 156

Scannell, Vernon 1922- **CLC 49**
See also CA 5-8R; CANR 8, 24, 57; DLB 27; SATA 59
Scarlett, Susan
See Streatfeild, (Mary) Noel
Scarron
See Mikszath, Kalman
Schaeffer, Susan Fromberg 1941- **CLC 6, 11, 22**
See also CA 49-52; CANR 18, 65; DLB 28; MTCW 1, 2; SATA 22
Schary, Jill
See Robinson, Jill
Schell, Jonathan 1943- **CLC 35**
See also CA 73-76; CANR 12
Schelling, Friedrich Wilhelm Joseph von 1775-1854 **NCLC 30**
See also DLB 90
Schendel, Arthur van 1874-1946 **TCLC 56**
Scherer, Jean-Marie Maurice 1920-
See Rohmer, Eric
See also CA 110
Schevill, James (Erwin) 1920- **CLC 7**
See also CA 5-8R; CAAS 12
Schiller, Friedrich 1759-1805 **NCLC 39, 69; DAM DRAM**
See also DLB 94
Schisgal, Murray (Joseph) 1926- **CLC 6**
See also CA 21-24R; CANR 48, 86
Schlee, Ann 1934- **CLC 35**
See also CA 101; CANR 29; SATA 44; SATA-Brief 36
Schlegel, August Wilhelm von 1767-1845 **NCLC 15**
See also DLB 94
Schlegel, Friedrich 1772-1829 **NCLC 45**
See also DLB 90
Schlegel, Johann Elias (von) 1719(?)-1749 **LC 5**
Schlesinger, Arthur M(eier), Jr. 1917- **CLC 84**
See also AITN 1; CA 1-4R; CANR 1, 28, 58; DLB 17; INT CANR-28; MTCW 1, 2; SATA 61
Schmidt, Arno (Otto) 1914-1979 **CLC 56**
See also CA 128; 109; DLB 69
Schmitz, Aron Hector 1861-1928
See Svevo, Italo
See also CA 104; 122; MTCW 1
Schnackenberg, Gjertrud 1953- **CLC 40**
See also CA 116; DLB 120
Schneider, Leonard Alfred 1925-1966
See Bruce, Lenny
See also CA 89-92
Schnitzler, Arthur 1862-1931 **TCLC 4; SSC 15**
See also CA 104; DLB 81, 118
Schoenberg, Arnold 1874-1951 **TCLC 75**
See also CA 109
Schonberg, Arnold
See Schoenberg, Arnold
Schopenhauer, Arthur 1788-1860 **NCLC 51**
See also DLB 90
Schor, Sandra (M.) 1932(?)-1990 **CLC 65**
See also CA 132
Schorer, Mark 1908-1977 **CLC 9**
See also CA 5-8R; 73-76; CANR 7; DLB 103
Schrader, Paul (Joseph) 1946- **CLC 26**
See also CA 37-40R; CANR 41; DLB 44
Schreiner, Olive (Emilie Albertina) 1855-1920 **TCLC 9**
See also CA 105; 154; DLB 18, 156, 190
Schulberg, Budd (Wilson) 1914- **CLC 7, 48**
See also CA 25-28R; CANR 19; DLB 6, 26, 28; DLBY 81

Schulz, Bruno 1892-1942 **TCLC 5, 51; SSC 13**
See also CA 115; 123; CANR 86; MTCW 2
Schulz, Charles M(onroe) 1922- **CLC 12**
See also CA 9-12R; CANR 6; INT CANR-6; SATA 10
Schumacher, E(rnst) F(riedrich) 1911-1977 **CLC 80**
See also CA 81-84; 73-76; CANR 34, 85
Schuyler, James Marcus 1923-1991 **CLC 5, 23; DAM POET**
See also CA 101; 134; DLB 5, 169; INT 101
Schwartz, Delmore (David) 1913-1966 **CLC 2, 4, 10, 45, 87; PC 8**
See also CA 17-18; 25-28R; CANR 35; CAP 2; DLB 28, 48; MTCW 1, 2
Schwartz, Ernst
See Ozu, Yasujiro
Schwartz, John Burnham 1965- **CLC 59**
See also CA 132
Schwartz, Lynne Sharon 1939- **CLC 31**
See also CA 103; CANR 44; MTCW 2
Schwartz, Muriel A.
See Eliot, T(homas) S(tearns)
Schwarz-Bart, Andre 1928- **CLC 2, 4**
See also CA 89-92
Schwarz-Bart, Simone 1938- **CLC 7; BLCS**
See also BW 2; CA 97-100
Schwitters, Kurt (Hermann Edward Karl Julius) 1887-1948 **TCLC 95**
See also CA 158
Schwob, Marcel (Mayer Andre) 1867-1905 **TCLC 20**
See also CA 117; 168; DLB 123
Sciascia, Leonardo 1921-1989 **CLC 8, 9, 41**
See also CA 85-88; 130; CANR 35; DLB 177; MTCW 1
Scoppettone, Sandra 1936- **CLC 26**
See also AAYA 11; CA 5-8R; CANR 41, 73; SATA 9, 92
Scorsese, Martin 1942- **CLC 20, 89**
See also CA 110; 114; CANR 46, 85
Scotland, Jay
See Jakes, John (William)
Scott, Duncan Campbell 1862-1947 **TCLC 6; DAC**
See also CA 104; 153; DLB 92
Scott, Evelyn 1893-1963 **CLC 43**
See also CA 104; 112; CANR 64; DLB 9, 48
Scott, F(rancis) R(eginald) 1899-1985 **CLC 22**
See also CA 101; 114; DLB 88; INT 101
Scott, Frank
See Scott, F(rancis) R(eginald)
Scott, Joanna 1960- **CLC 50**
See also CA 126; CANR 53
Scott, Paul (Mark) 1920-1978 **CLC 9, 60**
See also CA 81-84; 77-80; CANR 33; DLB 14, 207; MTCW 1
Scott, Sarah 1723-1795 **LC 44**
See also DLB 39
Scott, Walter 1771-1832 **NCLC 15, 69; DA; DAB; DAC; DAM MST, NOV, POET; PC 13; SSC 32; WLC**
See also AAYA 22; CDBLB 1789-1832; DLB 93, 107, 116, 144, 159; YABC 2
Scribe, (Augustin) Eugene 1791-1861 **NCLC 16; DAM DRAM; DC 5**
See also DLB 192
Scrum, R.
See Crumb, R(obert)
Scudery, Madeleine de 1607-1701 **LC 2**
Scum
See Crumb, R(obert)
Scumbag, Little Bobby

See Crumb, R(obert)

Seabrook, John
  See Hubbard, L(afayette) Ron(ald)

Sealy, I. Allan 1951-   **CLC 55**

Search, Alexander
  See Pessoa, Fernando (Antonio Nogueira)

Sebastian, Lee
  See Silverberg, Robert

Sebastian Owl
  See Thompson, Hunter S(tockton)

Sebestyen, Ouida 1924-   **CLC 30**
  See also AAYA 8; CA 107; CANR 40; CLR 17;
  JRDA; MAICYA; SAAS 10; SATA 39

Secundus, H. Scriblerus
  See Fielding, Henry

Sedges, John
  See Buck, Pearl S(ydenstricker)

Sedgwick, Catharine Maria 1789-1867 **NCLC
  19**
  See also DLB 1, 74

Seelye, John (Douglas) 1931-   **CLC 7**
  See also CA 97-100; CANR 70; INT 97-100

Seferiades, Giorgos Stylianou 1900-1971
  See Seferis, George
  See also CA 5-8R; 33-36R; CANR 5, 36;
  MTCW 1

Seferis, George   **CLC 5, 11**
  See also Seferiades, Giorgos Stylianou

Segal, Erich (Wolf) 1937-   **CLC 3, 10; DAM
  POP**
  See also BEST 89:1; CA 25-28R; CANR 20,
  36, 65; DLBY 86; INT CANR-20; MTCW 1

Seger, Bob 1945-   **CLC 35**

Seghers, Anna   **CLC 7**
  See also Radvanyi, Netty
  See also DLB 69

Seidel, Frederick (Lewis) 1936-   **CLC 18**
  See also CA 13-16R; CANR 8; DLBY 84

Seifert, Jaroslav 1901-1986   **CLC 34, 44, 93**
  See also CA 127; MTCW 1, 2

Sei Shonagon c. 966-1017(?)   **CMLC 6**

Séjour, Victor 1817-1874   **DC 10**
  See also DLB 50

Sejour Marcou et Ferrand, Juan Victor
  See Séjour, Victor

Selby, Hubert, Jr. 1928- **CLC 1, 2, 4, 8; SSC 20**
  See also CA 13-16R; CANR 33, 85; DLB 2

Selzer, Richard 1928-   **CLC 74**
  See also CA 65-68; CANR 14

Sembene, Ousmane
  See Ousmane, Sembene

Senancour, Etienne Pivert de 1770-1846
  NCLC 16
  See also DLB 119

Sender, Ramon (Jose) 1902-1982 **CLC 8; DAM
  MULT; HLC 2**
  See also CA 5-8R; 105; CANR 8; HW 1;
  MTCW 1

Seneca, Lucius Annaeus c. 1-c. 65 **CMLC 6;
  DAM DRAM; DC 5**
  See also DLB 211

Senghor, Leopold Sedar 1906- **CLC 54; BLC
  3; DAM MULT, POET; PC 25**
  See also BW 2; CA 116; 125; CANR 47, 74;
  MTCW 1, 2

Senna, Danzy 1970-   **CLC 119**
  See also CA 169

Serling, (Edward) Rod(man) 1924-1975 **CLC
  30**
  See also AAYA 14; AITN 1; CA 162; 57-60;
  DLB 26

Serna, Ramon Gomez de la
  See Gomez de la Serna, Ramon

Serpieres
  See Guillevic, (Eugene)

Service, Robert
  See Service, Robert W(illiam)
  See also DAB; DLB 92

Service, Robert W(illiam) 1874(?)-1958 **TCLC
  15; DA; DAC; DAM MST, POET; WLC**
  See also Service, Robert
  See also CA 115; 140; CANR 84; SATA 20

Seth, Vikram 1952- **CLC 43, 90; DAM MULT**
  See also CA 121; 127; CANR 50, 74; DA3; DLB
  120; INT 127; MTCW 2

Seton, Cynthia Propper 1926-1982   **CLC 27**
  See also CA 5-8R; 108; CANR 7

Seton, Ernest (Evan) Thompson 1860-1946
  TCLC 31
  See also CA 109; CLR 59; DLB 92; DLBD 13;
  JRDA; SATA 18

Seton-Thompson, Ernest
  See Seton, Ernest (Evan) Thompson

Settle, Mary Lee 1918-   **CLC 19, 61**
  See also CA 89-92; CAAS 1; CANR 44; DLB
  6; INT 89-92

Seuphor, Michel
  See Arp, Jean

**Sevigne, Marie (de Rabutin-Chantal) Marquise
  de** 1626-1696   **LC 11**

Sewall, Samuel 1652-1730   **LC 38**
  See also DLB 24

Sexton, Anne (Harvey) 1928-1974 **CLC 2, 4, 6,
  8, 10, 15, 53; DA; DAB; DAC; DAM MST,
  POET; PC 2; WLC**
  See also CA 1-4R; 53-56; CABS 2; CANR 3,
  36; CDALB 1941-1968; DA3; DLB 5, 169;
  MTCW 1, 2; SATA 10

Shaara, Jeff 1952-   **CLC 119**
  See also CA 163

Shaara, Michael (Joseph, Jr.) 1929-1988 **CLC
  15; DAM POP**
  See also AITN 1; CA 102; 125; CANR 52, 85;
  DLBY 83

Shackleton, C. C.
  See Aldiss, Brian W(ilson)

Shacochis, Bob   **CLC 39**
  See also Shacochis, Robert G.

Shacochis, Robert G. 1951-
  See Shacochis, Bob
  See also CA 119; 124; INT 124

Shaffer, Anthony (Joshua) 1926-   **CLC 19;
  DAM DRAM**
  See also CA 110; 116; DLB 13

Shaffer, Peter (Levin) 1926- **CLC 5, 14, 18, 37,
  60; DAB; DAM DRAM, MST; DC 7**
  See also CA 25-28R; CANR 25, 47, 74; CDBLB
  1960 to Present; DA3; DLB 13; MTCW 1, 2

Shakey, Bernard
  See Young, Neil

Shalamov, Varlam (Tikhonovich) 1907(?)-1982
  CLC 18
  See also CA 129; 105

Shamlu, Ahmad 1925-   **CLC 10**

Shammas, Anton 1951-   **CLC 55**

Shange, Ntozake 1948- **CLC 8, 25, 38, 74, 126;
  BLC 3; DAM DRAM, MULT; DC 3**
  See also AAYA 9; BW 2; CA 85-88; CABS 3;
  CANR 27, 48, 74; DA3; DLB 38; MTCW 1,
  2

Shanley, John Patrick 1950-   **CLC 75**
  See also CA 128; 133; CANR 83

Shapcott, Thomas W(illiam) 1935-   **CLC 38**
  See also CA 69-72; CANR 49, 83

Shapiro, Jane   **CLC 76**

Shapiro, Karl (Jay) 1913- **CLC 4, 8, 15, 53;
  PC 25**
  See also CA 1-4R; CAAS 6; CANR 1, 36, 66;
  DLB 48; MTCW 1, 2

Sharp, William 1855-1905   **TCLC 39**
  See also CA 160; DLB 156

Sharpe, Thomas Ridley 1928-
  See Sharpe, Tom
  See also CA 114; 122; CANR 85; INT 122

Sharpe, Tom   **CLC 36**
  See also Sharpe, Thomas Ridley
  See also DLB 14

Shaw, Bernard   **TCLC 45**
  See also Shaw, George Bernard
  See also BW 1; MTCW 2

Shaw, G. Bernard
  See Shaw, George Bernard

Shaw, George Bernard 1856-1950 **TCLC 3, 9,
  21; DA; DAB; DAC; DAM DRAM, MST;
  WLC**
  See also Shaw, Bernard
  See also CA 104; 128; CDBLB 1914-1945;
  DA3; DLB 10, 57, 190; MTCW 1, 2

Shaw, Henry Wheeler 1818-1885   **NCLC 15**
  See also DLB 11

Shaw, Irwin 1913-1984 **CLC 7, 23, 34; DAM
  DRAM, POP**
  See also AITN 1; CA 13-16R; 112; CANR 21;
  CDALB 1941-1968; DLB 6, 102; DLBY 84;
  MTCW 1, 21

Shaw, Robert 1927-1978   **CLC 5**
  See also AITN 1; CA 1-4R; 81-84; CANR 4;
  DLB 13, 14

Shaw, T. E.
  See Lawrence, T(homas) E(dward)

Shawn, Wallace 1943-   **CLC 41**
  See also CA 112

Shea, Lisa 1953-   **CLC 86**
  See also CA 147

Sheed, Wilfrid (John Joseph) 1930- **CLC 2, 4,
  10, 53**
  See also CA 65-68; CANR 30, 66; DLB 6;
  MTCW 1, 2

Sheldon, Alice Hastings Bradley 1915(?)-1987
  See Tiptree, James, Jr.
  See also CA 108; 122; CANR 34; INT 108;
  MTCW 1

Sheldon, John
  See Bloch, Robert (Albert)

Shelley, Mary Wollstonecraft (Godwin) 1797-
  1851 **NCLC 14, 59; DA; DAB; DAC; DAM
  MST, NOV; WLC**
  See also AAYA 20; CDBLB 1789-1832; DA3;
  DLB 110, 116, 159, 178; SATA 29

Shelley, Percy Bysshe 1792-1822   **NCLC 18;
  DA; DAB; DAC; DAM MST, POET; PC
  14; WLC**
  See also CDBLB 1789-1832; DA3; DLB 96,
  110, 158

Shepard, Jim 1956-   **CLC 36**
  See also CA 137; CANR 59; SATA 90

Shepard, Lucius 1947-   **CLC 34**
  See also CA 128; 141; CANR 81

Shepard, Sam 1943- **CLC 4, 6, 17, 34, 41, 44;
  DAM DRAM; DC 5**
  See also AAYA 1; CA 69-72; CABS 3; CANR
  22; DA3; DLB 7, 212; MTCW 1, 2

Shepherd, Michael
  See Ludlum, Robert

Sherburne, Zoa (Lillian Morin) 1912-1995
  CLC 30
  See also AAYA 13; CA 1-4R; 176; CANR 3,
  37; MAICYA; SAAS 18; SATA 3

Sheridan, Frances 1724-1766   **LC 7**

See also DLB 39, 84

Sheridan, Richard Brinsley 1751-1816 **N C L C 5; DA; DAB; DAC; DAM DRAM, MST; DC 1; WLC**
See also CDBLB 1660-1789; DLB 89

Sherman, Jonathan Marc   **CLC 55**

Sherman, Martin 1941(?)-   **CLC 19**
See also CA 116; 123; CANR 86

Sherwin, Judith Johnson 1936-
See Johnson, Judith (Emlyn)
See also CANR 85

Sherwood, Frances 1940-   **CLC 81**
See also CA 146

Sherwood, Robert E(mmet) 1896-1955 **T C L C 3; DAM DRAM**
See also CA 104; 153; CANR 86; DLB 7, 26

Shestov, Lev 1866-1938   **TCLC 56**

Shevchenko, Taras 1814-1861   **NCLC 54**

Shiel, M(atthew) P(hipps) 1865-1947 **TCLC 8**
See also Holmes, Gordon
See also CA 106; 160; DLB 153; MTCW 2

Shields, Carol 1935-   **CLC 91, 113; DAC**
See also CA 81-84; CANR 51, 74; DA3; MTCW 2

Shields, David 1956-   **CLC 97**
See also CA 124; CANR 48

Shiga, Naoya 1883-1971   **CLC 33; SSC 23**
See also CA 101; 33-36R; DLB 180

Shikibu, Murasaki c. 978-c. 1014   **CMLC 1**

Shilts, Randy 1951-1994   **CLC 85**
See also AAYA 19; CA 115; 127; 144; CANR 45; DA3; INT 127; MTCW 2

Shimazaki, Haruki 1872-1943
See Shimazaki Toson
See also CA 105; 134; CANR 84

Shimazaki Toson 1872-1943   **TCLC 5**
See also Shimazaki, Haruki
See also DLB 180

Sholokhov, Mikhail (Aleksandrovich) 1905-1984   **CLC 7, 15**
See also CA 101; 112; MTCW 1, 2; SATA-Obit 36

Shone, Patric
See Hanley, James

Shreve, Susan Richards 1939-   **CLC 23**
See also CA 49-52; CAAS 5; CANR 5, 38, 69; MAICYA; SATA 46, 95; SATA-Brief 41

Shue, Larry 1946-1985 **CLC 52; DAM DRAM**
See also CA 145; 117

Shu-Jen, Chou 1881-1936
See Lu Hsun
See also CA 104

Shulman, Alix Kates 1932-   **CLC 2, 10**
See also CA 29-32R; CANR 43; SATA 7

Shuster, Joe 1914-   **CLC 21**

Shute, Nevil   **CLC 30**
See also Norway, Nevil Shute
See also MTCW 2

Shuttle, Penelope (Diane) 1947-   **CLC 7**
See also CA 93-96; CANR 39, 84; DLB 14, 40

Sidney, Mary 1561-1621   **LC 19, 39**

Sidney, Sir Philip 1554-1586 **LC 19, 39; DA; DAB; DAC; DAM MST, POET**
See also CDBLB Before 1660; DA3; DLB 167

Siegel, Jerome 1914-1996   **CLC 21**
See also CA 116; 169; 151

Siegel, Jerry
See Siegel, Jerome

Sienkiewicz, Henryk (Adam Alexander Pius) 1846-1916   **TCLC 3**
See also CA 104; 134; CANR 84

Sierra, Gregorio Martinez
See Martinez Sierra, Gregorio

Sierra, Maria (de la O'LeJarraga) Martinez
See Martinez Sierra, Maria (de la O'LeJarraga)

Sigal, Clancy 1926-   **CLC 7**
See also CA 1-4R; CANR 85

Sigourney, Lydia Howard (Huntley) 1791-1865   **NCLC 21**
See also DLB 1, 42, 73

Siguenza y Gongora, Carlos de 1645-1700 **L C 8; HLCS 2**

Sigurjonsson, Johann 1880-1919   **TCLC 27**
See also CA 170

Sikelianos, Angelos 1884-1951   **TCLC 39**

Silkin, Jon 1930-   **CLC 2, 6, 43**
See also CA 5-8R; CAAS 5; DLB 27

Silko, Leslie (Marmon) 1948-**CLC 23, 74, 114; DA; DAC; DAM MST, MULT, POP; SSC 37; WLCS**
See also AAYA 14; CA 115; 122; CANR 45, 65; DA3; DLB 143, 175; MTCW 2; NNAL

Sillanpaa, Frans Eemil 1888-1964   **CLC 19**
See also CA 129; 93-96; MTCW 1

Sillitoe, Alan 1928-   **CLC 1, 3, 6, 10, 19, 57**
See also AITN 1; CA 9-12R; CAAS 2; CANR 8, 26, 55; CDBLB 1960 to Present; DLB 14, 139; MTCW 1, 2; SATA 61

Silone, Ignazio 1900-1978   **CLC 4**
See also CA 25-28; 81-84; CANR 34; CAP 2; MTCW 1

Silver, Joan Micklin 1935-   **CLC 20**
See also CA 114; 121; INT 121

Silver, Nicholas
See Faust, Frederick (Schiller)

Silverberg, Robert 1935- **CLC 7; DAM POP**
See also AAYA 24; CA 1-4R; CAAS 3; CANR 1, 20, 36, 85; CLR 59; DLB 8; INT CANR-20; MAICYA; MTCW 1, 2; SATA 13, 91; SATA-Essay 104

Silverstein, Alvin 1933-   **CLC 17**
See also CA 49-52; CANR 2; CLR 25; JRDA; MAICYA; SATA 8, 69

Silverstein, Virginia B(arbara Opshelor) 1937- **CLC 17**
See also CA 49-52; CANR 2; CLR 25; JRDA; MAICYA; SATA 8, 69

Sim, Georges
See Simenon, Georges (Jacques Christian)

Simak, Clifford D(onald) 1904-1988 **CLC 1, 55**
See also CA 1-4R; 125; CANR 1, 35; DLB 8; MTCW 1; SATA-Obit 56

Simenon, Georges (Jacques Christian) 1903-1989   **CLC 1, 2, 3, 8, 18, 47; DAM POP**
See also CA 85-88; 129; CANR 35; DA3; DLB 72; DLBY 89; MTCW 1, 2

Simic, Charles 1938-   **CLC 6, 9, 22, 49, 68; DAM POET**
See also CA 29-32R; CAAS 4; CANR 12, 33, 52, 61; DA3; DLB 105; MTCW 2

Simmel, Georg 1858-1918   **TCLC 64**
See also CA 157

Simmons, Charles (Paul) 1924-   **CLC 57**
See also CA 89-92; INT 89-92

Simmons, Dan 1948- **CLC 44; DAM POP**
See also AAYA 16; CA 138; CANR 53, 81

Simmons, James (Stewart Alexander) 1933- **CLC 43**
See also CA 105; CAAS 21; DLB 40

Simms, William Gilmore 1806-1870 **NCLC 3**
See also DLB 3, 30, 59, 73

Simon, Carly 1945-   **CLC 26**
See also CA 105

Simon, Claude 1913-1984   **CLC 4, 9, 15, 39; DAM NOV**
See also CA 89-92; CANR 33; DLB 83;

MTCW 1

Simon, (Marvin) Neil 1927-**CLC 6, 11, 31, 39, 70; DAM DRAM**
See also AAYA 32; AITN 1; CA 21-24R; CANR 26, 54; DA3; DLB 7; MTCW 1, 2

Simon, Paul (Frederick) 1941(?)-   **CLC 17**
See also CA 116; 153

Simonon, Paul 1956(?)-   **CLC 30**

Simpson, Harriette
See Arnow, Harriette (Louisa) Simpson

Simpson, Louis (Aston Marantz) 1923-**CLC 4, 7, 9, 32; DAM POET**
See also CA 1-4R; CAAS 4; CANR 1, 61; DLB 5; MTCW 1, 2

Simpson, Mona (Elizabeth) 1957-   **CLC 44**
See also CA 122; 135; CANR 68

Simpson, N(orman) F(rederick) 1919-**CLC 29**
See also CA 13-16R; DLB 13

Sinclair, Andrew (Annandale) 1935-   **CLC 2, 14**
See also CA 9-12R; CAAS 5; CANR 14, 38; DLB 14; MTCW 1

Sinclair, Emil
See Hesse, Hermann

Sinclair, Iain 1943-   **CLC 76**
See also CA 132; CANR 81

Sinclair, Iain MacGregor
See Sinclair, Iain

Sinclair, Irene
See Griffith, D(avid Lewelyn) W(ark)

Sinclair, Mary Amelia St. Clair 1865(?)-1946
See Sinclair, May
See also CA 104

Sinclair, May 1863-1946   **TCLC 3, 11**
See also Sinclair, Mary Amelia St. Clair
See also CA 166; DLB 36, 135

Sinclair, Roy
See Griffith, D(avid Lewelyn) W(ark)

Sinclair, Upton (Beall) 1878-1968 **CLC 1, 11, 15, 63; DA; DAB; DAC; DAM MST, NOV; WLC**
See also CA 5-8R; 25-28R; CANR 7; CDALB 1929-1941; DA3; DLB 9; INT CANR-7; MTCW 1, 2; SATA 9

Singer, Isaac
See Singer, Isaac Bashevis

Singer, Isaac Bashevis 1904-1991 **CLC 1, 3, 6, 9, 11, 15, 23, 38, 69, 111; DA; DAB; DAC; DAM MST, NOV; SSC 3; WLC**
See also AAYA 32; AITN 1, 2; CA 1-4R; 134; CANR 1, 39; CDALB 1941-1968; CLR 1; DA3; DLB 6, 28, 52; DLBY 91; JRDA; MAICYA; MTCW 1, 2; SATA 3, 27; SATA-Obit 68

Singer, Israel Joshua 1893-1944   **TCLC 33**
See also CA 169

Singh, Khushwant 1915-   **CLC 11**
See also CA 9-12R; CAAS 9; CANR 6, 84

Singleton, Ann
See Benedict, Ruth (Fulton)

Sinjohn, John
See Galsworthy, John

Sinyavsky, Andrei (Donatevich) 1925-1997 **CLC 8**
See also CA 85-88; 159

Sirin, V.
See Nabokov, Vladimir (Vladimirovich)

Sissman, L(ouis) E(dward) 1928-1976 **CLC 9, 18**
See also CA 21-24R; 65-68; CANR 13; DLB 5

Sisson, C(harles) H(ubert) 1914-   **CLC 8**
See also CA 1-4R; CAAS 3; CANR 3, 48, 84; DLB 27

Sitwell, Dame Edith 1887-1964 **CLC 2, 9, 67; DAM POET; PC 3**
See also CA 9-12R; CANR 35; CDBLB 1945-1960; DLB 20; MTCW 1, 2

Siwaarmill, H. P.
See Sharp, William

Sjoewall, Maj 1935- **CLC 7**
See also CA 65-68; CANR 73

Sjowall, Maj
See Sjoewall, Maj

Skelton, John 1463-1529 **PC 25**

Skelton, Robin 1925-1997 **CLC 13**
See also AITN 2; CA 5-8R; 160; CAAS 5; CANR 28; DLB 27, 53

Skolimowski, Jerzy 1938- **CLC 20**
See also CA 128

Skram, Amalie (Bertha) 1847-1905 **TCLC 25**
See also CA 165

Skvorecky, Josef (Vaclav) 1924- **CLC 15, 39, 69; DAC; DAM NOV**
See also CA 61-64; CAAS 1; CANR 10, 34, 63; DA3; MTCW 1, 2

Slade, Bernard **CLC 11, 46**
See also Newbound, Bernard Slade
See also CAAS 9; DLB 53

Slaughter, Carolyn 1946- **CLC 56**
See also CA 85-88; CANR 85

Slaughter, Frank G(ill) 1908- **CLC 29**
See also AITN 2; CA 5-8R; CANR 5, 85; INT CANR-5

Slavitt, David R(ytman) 1935- **CLC 5, 14**
See also CA 21-24R; CAAS 3; CANR 41, 83; DLB 5, 6

Slesinger, Tess 1905-1945 **TCLC 10**
See also CA 107; DLB 102

Slessor, Kenneth 1901-1971 **CLC 14**
See also CA 102; 89-92

Slowacki, Juliusz 1809-1849 **NCLC 15**

Smart, Christopher 1722-1771 **LC 3; DAM POET; PC 13**
See also DLB 109

Smart, Elizabeth 1913-1986 **CLC 54**
See also CA 81-84; 118; DLB 88

Smiley, Jane (Graves) 1949- **CLC 53, 76; DAM POP**
See also CA 104; CANR 30, 50, 74; DA3; INT CANR-30

Smith, A(rthur) J(ames) M(arshall) 1902-1980 **CLC 15; DAC**
See also CA 1-4R; 102; CANR 4; DLB 88

Smith, Adam 1723-1790 **LC 36**
See also DLB 104

Smith, Alexander 1829-1867 **NCLC 59**
See also DLB 32, 55

Smith, Anna Deavere 1950- **CLC 86**
See also CA 133

Smith, Betty (Wehner) 1896-1972 **CLC 19**
See also CA 5-8R; 33-36R; DLBY 82; SATA 6

Smith, Charlotte (Turner) 1749-1806 **NCLC 23**
See also DLB 39, 109

Smith, Clark Ashton 1893-1961 **CLC 43**
See also CA 143; CANR 81; MTCW 2

Smith, Dave **CLC 22, 42**
See also Smith, David (Jeddie)
See also CAAS 7; DLB 5

Smith, David (Jeddie) 1942-
See Smith, Dave
See also CA 49-52; CANR 1, 59; DAM POET

Smith, Florence Margaret 1902-1971
See Smith, Stevie
See also CA 17-18; 29-32R; CANR 35; CAP 2; DAM POET; MTCW 1, 2

Smith, Iain Crichton 1928-1998 **CLC 64**
See also CA 21-24R; 171; DLB 40, 139

Smith, John 1580(?)-1631 **LC 9**
See also DLB 24, 30

Smith, Johnston
See Crane, Stephen (Townley)

Smith, Joseph, Jr. 1805-1844 **NCLC 53**

Smith, Lee 1944- **CLC 25, 73**
See also CA 114; 119; CANR 46; DLB 143; DLBY 83; INT 119

Smith, Martin
See Smith, Martin Cruz

Smith, Martin Cruz 1942- **CLC 25; DAM MULT, POP**
See also BEST 89:4; CA 85-88; CANR 6, 23, 43, 65; INT CANR-23; MTCW 2; NNAL

Smith, Mary-Ann Tirone 1944- **CLC 39**
See also CA 118; 136

Smith, Patti 1946- **CLC 12**
See also CA 93-96; CANR 63

Smith, Pauline (Urmson) 1882-1959 **TCLC 25**

Smith, Rosamond
See Oates, Joyce Carol

Smith, Sheila Kaye
See Kaye-Smith, Sheila

Smith, Stevie **CLC 3, 8, 25, 44; PC 12**
See also Smith, Florence Margaret
See also DLB 20; MTCW 2

Smith, Wilbur (Addison) 1933- **CLC 33**
See also CA 13-16R; CANR 7, 46, 66; MTCW 1, 2

Smith, William Jay 1918- **CLC 6**
See also CA 5-8R; CANR 44; DLB 5; MAICYA; SAAS 22; SATA 2, 68

Smith, Woodrow Wilson
See Kuttner, Henry

Smolenskin, Peretz 1842-1885 **NCLC 30**

Smollett, Tobias (George) 1721-1771 **LC 2, 46**
See also CDBLB 1660-1789; DLB 39, 104

Snodgrass, W(illiam) D(e Witt) 1926- **CLC 2, 6, 10, 18, 68; DAM POET**
See also CA 1-4R; CANR 6, 36, 65, 85; DLB 5; MTCW 1, 2

Snow, C(harles) P(ercy) 1905-1980 **CLC 1, 4, 6, 9, 13, 19; DAM NOV**
See also CA 5-8R; 101; CANR 28; CDBLB 1945-1960; DLB 15, 77; DLBD 17; MTCW 1, 2

Snow, Frances Compton
See Adams, Henry (Brooks)

Snyder, Gary (Sherman) 1930- **CLC 1, 2, 5, 9, 32, 120; DAM POET; PC 21**
See also CA 17-20R; CANR 30, 60; DA3; DLB 5, 16, 165, 212; MTCW 2

Snyder, Zilpha Keatley 1927- **CLC 17**
See also AAYA 15; CA 9-12R; CANR 38; CLR 31; JRDA; MAICYA; SAAS 2; SATA 1, 28, 75, 110

Soares, Bernardo
See Pessoa, Fernando (Antonio Nogueira)

Sobh, A.
See Shamlu, Ahmad

Sobol, Joshua **CLC 60**

Socrates 469B.C.-399B.C. **CMLC 27**

Soderberg, Hjalmar 1869-1941 **TCLC 39**

Sodergran, Edith (Irene)
See Soedergran, Edith (Irene)

Soedergran, Edith (Irene) 1892-1923 **TCLC 31**

Softly, Edward
See Lovecraft, H(oward) P(hillips)

Sokolov, Raymond 1941- **CLC 7**
See also CA 85-88

Solo, Jay
See Ellison, Harlan (Jay)

Sologub, Fyodor **TCLC 9**
See also Teternikov, Fyodor Kuzmich

Solomons, Ikey Esquir
See Thackeray, William Makepeace

Solomos, Dionysios 1798-1857 **NCLC 15**

Solwoska, Mara
See French, Marilyn

Solzhenitsyn, Aleksandr I(sayevich) 1918- **CLC 1, 2, 4, 7, 9, 10, 18, 26, 34, 78; DA; DAB; DAC; DAM MST, NOV; SSC 32; WLC**
See also AITN 1; CA 69-72; CANR 40, 65; DA3; MTCW 1, 2

Somers, Jane
See Lessing, Doris (May)

Somerville, Edith 1858-1949 **TCLC 51**
See also DLB 135

Somerville & Ross
See Martin, Violet Florence; Somerville, Edith

Sommer, Scott 1951- **CLC 25**
See also CA 106

Sondheim, Stephen (Joshua) 1930- **CLC 30, 39; DAM DRAM**
See also AAYA 11; CA 103; CANR 47, 68

Song, Cathy 1955- **PC 21**
See also CA 154; DLB 169

Sontag, Susan 1933- **CLC 1, 2, 10, 13, 31, 105; DAM POP**
See also CA 17-20R; CANR 25, 51, 74; DA3; DLB 2, 67; MTCW 1, 2

Sophocles 496(?)B.C.-406(?)B.C. **CMLC 2; DA; DAB; DAC; DAM DRAM, MST; DC 1; WLCS**
See also DA3; DLB 176

Sordello 1189-1269 **CMLC 15**

Sorel, Georges 1847-1922 **TCLC 91**
See also CA 118

Sorel, Julia
See Drexler, Rosalyn

Sorrentino, Gilbert 1929- **CLC 3, 7, 14, 22, 40**
See also CA 77-80; CANR 14, 33; DLB 5, 173; DLBY 80; INT CANR-14

Soto, Gary 1952- **CLC 32, 80; DAM MULT; HLC 2; PC 28**
See also AAYA 10; CA 119; 125; CANR 50, 74; CLR 38; DLB 82; HW 1, 2; INT 125; JRDA; MTCW 2; SATA 80

Soupault, Philippe 1897-1990 **CLC 68**
See also CA 116; 147; 131

Souster, (Holmes) Raymond 1921- **CLC 5, 14; DAC; DAM POET**
See also CA 13-16R; CAAS 14; CANR 13, 29, 53; DA3; DLB 88; SATA 63

Southern, Terry 1924(?)-1995 **CLC 7**
See also CA 1-4R; 150; CANR 1, 55; DLB 2

Southey, Robert 1774-1843 **NCLC 8**
See also DLB 93, 107, 142; SATA 54

Southworth, Emma Dorothy Eliza Nevitte 1819-1899 **NCLC 26**

Souza, Ernest
See Scott, Evelyn

Soyinka, Wole 1934- **CLC 3, 5, 14, 36, 44; BLC 3; DA; DAB; DAC; DAM DRAM, MST, MULT; DC 2; WLC**
See also BW 2, 3; CA 13-16R; CANR 27, 39, 82; DA3; DLB 125; MTCW 1, 2

Spackman, W(illiam) M(ode) 1905-1990 **CLC 46**
See also CA 81-84; 132

Spacks, Barry (Bernard) 1931- **CLC 14**
See also CA 154; CANR 33; DLB 105

See Campbell, Maria
Stifter, Adalbert 1805-1868 NCLC 41; SSC 28
See also DLB 133
Still, James 1906-   CLC 49
See also CA 65-68; CAAS 17; CANR 10, 26;
DLB 9; SATA 29
Sting 1951-
See Sumner, Gordon Matthew
See also CA 167
Stirling, Arthur
See Sinclair, Upton (Beall)
Stitt, Milan 1941-   CLC 29
See also CA 69-72
Stockton, Francis Richard 1834-1902
See Stockton, Frank R.
See also CA 108; 137; MAICYA; SATA 44
Stockton, Frank R.   TCLC 47
See also Stockton, Francis Richard
See also DLB 42, 74; DLBD 13; SATA-Brief
32
Stoddard, Charles
See Kuttner, Henry
Stoker, Abraham 1847-1912
See Stoker, Bram
See also CA 105; 150; DA; DAC; DAM MST,
NOV; DA3; SATA 29
Stoker, Bram 1847-1912 TCLC 8; DAB; WLC
See also Stoker, Abraham
See also AAYA 23; CDBLB 1890-1914; DLB
36, 70, 178
Stolz, Mary (Slattery) 1920-   CLC 12
See also AAYA 8; AITN 1; CA 5-8R; CANR
13, 41; JRDA; MAICYA; SAAS 3; SATA 10,
71
Stone, Irving 1903-1989   CLC 7; DAM POP
See also AITN 1; CA 1-4R; 129; CAAS 3;
CANR 1, 23; DA3; INT CANR-23; MTCW
1, 2; SATA 3; SATA-Obit 64
Stone, Oliver (William) 1946-   CLC 73
See also AAYA 15; CA 110; CANR 55
Stone, Robert (Anthony) 1937- CLC 5, 23, 42
See also CA 85-88; CANR 23, 66; DLB 152;
INT CANR-23; MTCW 1
Stone, Zachary
See Follett, Ken(neth Martin)
Stoppard, Tom 1937- CLC 1, 3, 4, 5, 8, 15, 29,
34, 63, 91; DA; DAB; DAC; DAM DRAM,
MST; DC 6; WLC
See also CA 81-84; CANR 39, 67; CDBLB
1960 to Present; DA3; DLB 13; DLBY 85;
MTCW 1, 2
Storey, David (Malcolm) 1933- CLC 2, 4, 5, 8;
DAM DRAM
See also CA 81-84; CANR 36; DLB 13, 14, 207;
MTCW 1
Storm, Hyemeyohsts 1935-   CLC 3; DAM
MULT
See also CA 81-84; CANR 45; NNAL
Storm, Theodor 1817-1888   SSC 27
Storm, (Hans) Theodor (Woldsen) 1817-1888
NCLC 1; SSC 27
See also DLB 129
Storni, Alfonsina 1892-1938   TCLC 5; DAM
MULT; HLC 2
See also CA 104; 131; HW 1
Stoughton, William 1631-1701   LC 38
See also DLB 24
Stout, Rex (Todhunter) 1886-1975   CLC 3
See also AITN 2; CA 61-64; CANR 71
Stow, (Julian) Randolph 1935- CLC 23, 48
See also CA 13-16R; CANR 33; MTCW 1
Stowe, Harriet (Elizabeth) Beecher 1811-1896
NCLC 3, 50; DA; DAB; DAC; DAM MST,

NOV; WLC
See also CDALB 1865-1917; DA3; DLB 1, 12,
42, 74, 189; JRDA; MAICYA; YABC 1
Strachey, (Giles) Lytton 1880-1932 TCLC 12
See also CA 110; 178; DLB 149; DLBD 10;
MTCW 2
Strand, Mark 1934- CLC 6, 18, 41, 71; DAM
POET
See also CA 21-24R; CANR 40, 65; DLB 5;
SATA 41
Straub, Peter (Francis) 1943-   CLC 28, 107;
DAM POP
See also BEST 89:1; CA 85-88; CANR 28, 65;
DLBY 84; MTCW 1, 2
Strauss, Botho 1944-   CLC 22
See also CA 157; DLB 124
Streatfeild, (Mary) Noel 1895(?)-1986 CLC 21
See also CA 81-84; 120; CANR 31; CLR 17;
DLB 160; MAICYA; SATA 20; SATA-Obit
48
Stribling, T(homas) S(igismund) 1881-1965
CLC 23
See also CA 107; DLB 9
Strindberg, (Johan) August 1849-1912 TCLC
1, 8, 21, 47; DA; DAB; DAC; DAM DRAM,
MST; WLC
See also CA 104; 135; DA3; MTCW 2
Stringer, Arthur 1874-1950   TCLC 37
See also CA 161; DLB 92
Stringer, David
See Roberts, Keith (John Kingston)
Stroheim, Erich von 1885-1957   TCLC 71
Strugatskii, Arkadii (Natanovich) 1925-1991
CLC 27
See also CA 106; 135
Strugatskii, Boris (Natanovich) 1933- CLC 27
See also CA 106
Strummer, Joe 1953(?)-   CLC 30
Strunk, William, Jr. 1869-1946   TCLC 92
See also CA 118; 164
Stryk, Lucien 1924-   PC 27
See also CA 13-16R; CANR 10, 28, 55
Stuart, Don A.
See Campbell, John W(ood, Jr.)
Stuart, Ian
See MacLean, Alistair (Stuart)
Stuart, Jesse (Hilton) 1906-1984 CLC 1, 8, 11,
14, 34; SSC 31
See also CA 5-8R; 112; CANR 31; DLB 9, 48,
102; DLBY 84; SATA 2; SATA-Obit 36
Sturgeon, Theodore (Hamilton) 1918-1985
CLC 22, 39
See also Queen, Ellery
See also CA 81-84; 116; CANR 32; DLB 8;
DLBY 85; MTCW 1, 2
Sturges, Preston 1898-1959   TCLC 48
See also CA 114; 149; DLB 26
Styron, William 1925- CLC 1, 3, 5, 11, 15, 60;
DAM NOV, POP; SSC 25
See also BEST 90:4; CA 5-8R; CANR 6, 33,
74; CDALB 1968-1988; DA3; DLB 2, 143;
DLBY 80; INT CANR-6; MTCW 1, 2
Su, Chien 1884-1918
See Su Man-shu
See also CA 123
Suarez Lynch, B.
See Bioy Casares, Adolfo; Borges, Jorge Luis
Suassuna, Ariano Vilar 1927-
See also CA 178; HLCS 1; HW 2
Suckow, Ruth 1892-1960   SSC 18
See also CA 113; DLB 9, 102
Sudermann, Hermann 1857-1928   TCLC 15
See also CA 107; DLB 118

Sue, Eugene 1804-1857   NCLC 1
See also DLB 119
Sueskind, Patrick 1949-   CLC 44
See also Suskind, Patrick
Sukenick, Ronald 1932-   CLC 3, 4, 6, 48
See also CA 25-28R; CAAS 8; CANR 32; DLB
173; DLBY 81
Suknaski, Andrew 1942-   CLC 19
See also CA 101; DLB 53
Sullivan, Vernon
See Vian, Boris
Sully Prudhomme 1839-1907   TCLC 31
Su Man-shu   TCLC 24
See also Su, Chien
Summerforest, Ivy B.
See Kirkup, James
Summers, Andrew James 1942-   CLC 26
Summers, Andy
See Summers, Andrew James
Summers, Hollis (Spurgeon, Jr.) 1916- CLC 10
See also CA 5-8R; CANR 3; DLB 6
**Summers, (Alphonsus Joseph-Mary Augustus)
Montague** 1880-1948   TCLC 16
See also CA 118; 163
Sumner, Gordon Matthew   CLC 26
See also Sting
Surtees, Robert Smith 1803-1864   NCLC 14
See also DLB 21
Susann, Jacqueline 1921-1974   CLC 3
See also AITN 1; CA 65-68; 53-56; MTCW 1,
2
Su Shih 1036-1101   CMLC 15
Suskind, Patrick
See Sueskind, Patrick
See also CA 145
Sutcliff, Rosemary 1920-1992 CLC 26; DAB;
DAC; DAM MST, POP
See also AAYA 10; CA 5-8R; 139; CANR 37;
CLR 1, 37; JRDA; MAICYA; SATA 6, 44,
78; SATA-Obit 73
Sutro, Alfred 1863-1933   TCLC 6
See also CA 105; DLB 10
Sutton, Henry
See Slavitt, David R(ytman)
Svevo, Italo 1861-1928   TCLC 2, 35; SSC 25
See also Schmitz, Aron Hector
Swados, Elizabeth (A.) 1951-   CLC 12
See also CA 97-100; CANR 49; INT 97-100
Swados, Harvey 1920-1972   CLC 5
See also CA 5-8R; 37-40R; CANR 6; DLB 2
Swan, Gladys 1934-   CLC 69
See also CA 101; CANR 17, 39
Swarthout, Glendon (Fred) 1918-1992 CLC 35
See also CA 1-4R; 139; CANR 1, 47; SATA 26
Sweet, Sarah C.
See Jewett, (Theodora) Sarah Orne
Swenson, May 1919-1989 CLC 4, 14, 61, 106;
DA; DAB; DAC; DAM MST, POET; PC
14
See also CA 5-8R; 130; CANR 36, 61; DLB 5;
MTCW 1, 2; SATA 15
Swift, Augustus
See Lovecraft, H(oward) P(hillips)
Swift, Graham (Colin) 1949-   CLC 41, 88
See also CA 117; 122; CANR 46, 71; DLB 194;
MTCW 2
Swift, Jonathan 1667-1745   LC 1, 42; DA;
DAB; DAC; DAM MST, NOV, POET; PC
9; WLC
See also CDBLB 1660-1789; CLR 53; DA3;
DLB 39, 95, 101; SATA 19
Swinburne, Algernon Charles 1837-1909
TCLC 8, 36; DA; DAB; DAC; DAM MST,

Thomas, D(onald) M(ichael) 1935- **CLC 13, 22, 31**
See also CA 61-64; CAAS 11; CANR 17, 45, 75; CDBLB 1960 to Present; DA3; DLB 40, 207; INT CANR-17; MTCW 1, 2

Thomas, Dylan (Marlais) 1914-1953TCLC 1, **8, 45; DA; DAB; DAC; DAM DRAM, MST, POET; PC 2; SSC 3; WLC**
See also CA 104; 120; CANR 65; CDBLB 1945-1960; DA3; DLB 13, 20, 139; MTCW 1, 2; SATA 60

Thomas, (Philip) Edward 1878-1917 **TCLC 10; DAM POET**
See also CA 106; 153; DLB 98

Thomas, Joyce Carol 1938- **CLC 35**
See also AAYA 12; BW 2, 3; CA 113; 116; CANR 48; CLR 19; DLB 33; INT 116; JRDA; MAICYA; MTCW 1, 2; SAAS 7; SATA 40, 78

Thomas, Lewis 1913-1993 **CLC 35**
See also CA 85-88; 143; CANR 38, 60; MTCW 1, 2

Thomas, M. Carey 1857-1935 **TCLC 89**
Thomas, Paul
See Mann, (Paul) Thomas

Thomas, Piri 1928- **CLC 17; HLCS 2**
See also CA 73-76; HW 1

Thomas, R(onald) S(tuart) 1913- **CLC 6, 13, 48; DAB; DAM POET**
See also CA 89-92; CAAS 4; CANR 30; CDBLB 1960 to Present; DLB 27; MTCW 1

Thomas, Ross (Elmore) 1926-1995 **CLC 39**
See also CA 33-36R; 150; CANR 22, 63

Thompson, Francis Clegg
See Mencken, H(enry) L(ouis)

Thompson, Francis Joseph 1859-1907TCLC 4
See also CA 104; CDBLB 1890-1914; DLB 19

Thompson, Hunter S(tockton) 1939- **CLC 9, 17, 40, 104; DAM POP**
See also BEST 89:1; CA 17-20R; CANR 23, 46, 74, 77; DA3; DLB 185; MTCW 1, 2

Thompson, James Myers
See Thompson, Jim (Myers)

Thompson, Jim (Myers) 1906-1977(?)CLC 69
See also CA 140

Thompson, Judith **CLC 39**

Thomson, James 1700-1748 **LC 16, 29, 40; DAM POET**
See also DLB 95

Thomson, James 1834-1882 NCLC 18; **DAM POET**
See also DLB 35

Thoreau, Henry David 1817-1862NCLC 7, 21, **61; DA; DAB; DAC; DAM MST; WLC**
See also CDALB 1640-1865; DA3; DLB 1

Thornton, Hall
See Silverberg, Robert

Thucydides c. 455B.C.-399B.C. **CMLC 17**
See also DLB 176

Thurber, James (Grover) 1894-1961 **CLC 5, 11, 25, 125; DA; DAB; DAC; DAM DRAM, MST, NOV; SSC 1**
See also CA 73-76; CANR 17, 39; CDALB 1929-1941; DA3; DLB 4, 11, 22, 102; MAICYA; MTCW 1, 2; SATA 13

Thurman, Wallace (Henry) 1902-1934TCLC **6; BLC 3; DAM MULT**
See also BW 1, 3; CA 104; 124; CANR 81; DLB 51

Tibullus, Albius c. 54B.C.-c. 19B.C.CMLC 36
See also DLB 211

Ticheburn, Cheviot
See Ainsworth, William Harrison

Tieck, (Johann) Ludwig 1773-1853 **NCLC 5, 46; SSC 31**
See also DLB 90

Tiger, Derry
See Ellison, Harlan (Jay)

Tilghman, Christopher 1948(?)- **CLC 65**
See also CA 159

Tillinghast, Richard (Williford) 1940-CLC 29
See also CA 29-32R; CAAS 23; CANR 26, 51

Timrod, Henry 1828-1867 **NCLC 25**
See also DLB 3

Tindall, Gillian (Elizabeth) 1938- **CLC 7**
See also CA 21-24R; CANR 11, 65

Tiptree, James, Jr. **CLC 48, 50**
See also Sheldon, Alice Hastings Bradley
See also DLB 8

Titmarsh, Michael Angelo
See Thackeray, William Makepeace

Tocqueville, Alexis (Charles Henri Maurice Clerel, Comte) de 1805-1859NCLC 7, 63

Tolkien, J(ohn) R(onald) R(euel) 1892-1973 **CLC 1, 2, 3, 8, 12, 38; DA; DAB; DAC; DAM MST, NOV, POP; WLC**
See also AAYA 10; AITN 1; CA 17-18; 45-48; CANR 36; CAP 2; CDBLB 1914-1945; CLR 56; DA3; DLB 15, 160; JRDA; MAICYA; MTCW 1, 2; SATA 2, 32, 100; SATA-Obit 24

Toller, Ernst 1893-1939 **TCLC 10**
See also CA 107; DLB 124

Tolson, M. B.
See Tolson, Melvin B(eaunorus)

Tolson, Melvin B(eaunorus) 1898(?)-1966 **CLC 36, 105; BLC 3; DAM MULT, POET**
See also BW 1, 3; CA 124; 89-92; CANR 80; DLB 48, 76

Tolstoi, Aleksei Nikolaevich
See Tolstoy, Alexey Nikolaevich

Tolstoy, Alexey Nikolaevich 1882-1945TCLC **18**
See also CA 107; 158

Tolstoy, Count Leo
See Tolstoy, Leo (Nikolaevich)

Tolstoy, Leo (Nikolaevich) 1828-1910TCLC 4, **11, 17, 28, 44, 79; DA; DAB; DAC; DAM MST, NOV; SSC 9, 30; WLC**
See also CA 104; 123; DA3; SATA 26

Tomasi di Lampedusa, Giuseppe 1896-1957
See Lampedusa, Giuseppe (Tomasi) di
See also CA 111

Tomlin, Lily **CLC 17**
See also Tomlin, Mary Jean

Tomlin, Mary Jean 1939(?)-
See Tomlin, Lily
See also CA 117

Tomlinson, (Alfred) Charles 1927-CLC 2, 4, 6, **13, 45; DAM POET; PC 17**
See also CA 5-8R; CANR 33; DLB 40

Tomlinson, H(enry) M(ajor) 1873-1958TCLC **71**
See also CA 118; 161; DLB 36, 100, 195

Tonson, Jacob
See Bennett, (Enoch) Arnold

Toole, John Kennedy 1937-1969 **CLC 19, 64**
See also CA 104; DLBY 81; MTCW 2

Toomer, Jean 1894-1967CLC 1, 4, 13, 22; BLC **3; DAM MULT; PC 7; SSC 1; WLCS**
See also BW 1; CA 85-88; CDALB 1917-1929; DA3; DLB 45, 51; MTCW 1, 2

Torley, Luke
See Blish, James (Benjamin)

Tornimparte, Alessandra
See Ginzburg, Natalia

Torre, Raoul della
See Mencken, H(enry) L(ouis)

Torrence, Ridgely 1874-1950 **TCLC 97**
See also DLB 54

Torrey, E(dwin) Fuller 1937- **CLC 34**
See also CA 119; CANR 71

Torsvan, Ben Traven
See Traven, B.

Torsvan, Benno Traven
See Traven, B.

Torsvan, Berick Traven
See Traven, B.

Torsvan, Berwick Traven
See Traven, B.

Torsvan, Bruno Traven
See Traven, B.

Torsvan, Traven
See Traven, B.

Tournier, Michel (Edouard) 1924-CLC 6, 23, **36, 95**
See also CA 49-52; CANR 3, 36, 74; DLB 83; MTCW 1, 2; SATA 23

Tournimparte, Alessandra
See Ginzburg, Natalia

Towers, Ivar
See Kornbluth, C(yril) M.

Towne, Robert (Burton) 1936(?)- **CLC 87**
See also CA 108; DLB 44

Townsend, Sue **CLC 61**
See also Townsend, Susan Elaine
See also AAYA 28; SATA 55, 93; SATA-Brief 48

Townsend, Susan Elaine 1946-
See Townsend, Sue
See also CA 119; 127; CANR 65; DAB; DAC; DAM MST

Townshend, Peter (Dennis Blandford) 1945- **CLC 17, 42**
See also CA 107

Tozzi, Federigo 1883-1920 **TCLC 31**
See also CA 160

Traill, Catharine Parr 1802-1899 **NCLC 31**
See also DLB 99

Trakl, Georg 1887-1914 **TCLC 5; PC 20**
See also CA 104; 165; MTCW 2

Transtroemer, Tomas (Goesta) 1931-CLC 52, **65; DAM POET**
See also CA 117; 129; CAAS 17

Transtromer, Tomas Gosta
See Transtroemer, Tomas (Goesta)

Traven, B. (?)-1969 **CLC 8, 11**
See also CA 19-20; 25-28R; CAP 2; DLB 9, 56; MTCW 1

Treitel, Jonathan 1959- **CLC 70**

Tremain, Rose 1943- **CLC 42**
See also CA 97-100; CANR 44; DLB 14

Tremblay, Michel 1942- **CLC 29, 102; DAC; DAM MST**
See also CA 116; 128; DLB 60; MTCW 1, 2

Trevanian **CLC 29**
See also Whitaker, Rod(ney)

Trevor, Glen
See Hilton, James

Trevor, William 1928-CLC 7, 9, 14, 25, 71, 116; **SSC 21**
See also Cox, William Trevor
See also DLB 14, 139; MTCW 2

Trifonov, Yuri (Valentinovich) 1925-1981 **CLC 45**
See also CA 126; 103; MTCW 1

Trilling, Lionel 1905-1975 **CLC 9, 11, 24**
See also CA 9-12R; 61-64; CANR 10; DLB 28, 63; INT CANR-10; MTCW 1, 2

Trimball, W. H.
See Mencken, H(enry) L(ouis)
Tristan
See Gomez de la Serna, Ramon
Tristram
See Housman, A(lfred) E(dward)
Trogdon, William (Lewis) 1939-
See Heat-Moon, William Least
See also CA 115; 119; CANR 47; INT 119
Trollope, Anthony 1815-1882 **NCLC 6, 33; DA; DAB; DAC; DAM MST, NOV; SSC 28; WLC**
See also CDBLB 1832-1890; DA3; DLB 21, 57, 159; SATA 22
Trollope, Frances 1779-1863 **NCLC 30**
See also DLB 21, 166
Trotsky, Leon 1879-1940 **TCLC 22**
See also CA 118; 167
Trotter (Cockburn), Catharine 1679-1749 **LC 8**
See also DLB 84
Trotter, Wilfred 1872-1939 **TCLC 99**
Trout, Kilgore
See Farmer, Philip Jose
Trow, George W. S. 1943- **CLC 52**
See also CA 126
Troyat, Henri 1911- **CLC 23**
See also CA 45-48; CANR 2, 33, 67; MTCW 1
Trudeau, G(arretson) B(eekman) 1948-
See Trudeau, Garry B.
See also CA 81-84; CANR 31; SATA 35
Trudeau, Garry B. **CLC 12**
See also Trudeau, G(arretson) B(eekman)
See also AAYA 10; AITN 2
Truffaut, Francois 1932-1984 **CLC 20, 101**
See also CA 81-84; 113; CANR 34
Trumbo, Dalton 1905-1976 **CLC 19**
See also CA 21-24R; 69-72; CANR 10; DLB 26
Trumbull, John 1750-1831 **NCLC 30**
See also DLB 31
Trundlett, Helen B.
See Eliot, T(homas) S(tearns)
Tryon, Thomas 1926-1991 **CLC 3, 11; DAM POP**
See also AITN 1; CA 29-32R; 135; CANR 32, 77; DA3; MTCW 1
Tryon, Tom
See Tryon, Thomas
Ts'ao Hsueh-ch'in 1715(?)-1763 **LC 1**
Tsushima, Shuji 1909-1948
See Dazai Osamu
See also CA 107
Tsvetaeva (Efron), Marina (Ivanovna) 1892-1941 **TCLC 7, 35; PC 14**
See also CA 104; 128; CANR 73; MTCW 1, 2
Tuck, Lily 1938- **CLC 70**
See also CA 139
Tu Fu 712-770 **PC 9**
See also DAM MULT
Tunis, John R(oberts) 1889-1975 **CLC 12**
See also CA 61-64; CANR 62; DLB 22, 171; JRDA; MAICYA; SATA 37; SATA-Brief 30
Tuohy, Frank **CLC 37**
See also Tuohy, John Francis
See also DLB 14, 139
Tuohy, John Francis 1925-1999
See Tuohy, Frank
See also CA 5-8R; 178; CANR 3, 47
Turco, Lewis (Putnam) 1934- **CLC 11, 63**
See also CA 13-16R; CAAS 22; CANR 24, 51; DLBY 84
Turgenev, Ivan 1818-1883 **NCLC 21; DA;**

DAB; DAC; DAM MST, NOV; DC 7; SSC 7; WLC
Turgot, Anne-Robert-Jacques 1727-1781 **LC 26**
Turner, Frederick 1943- **CLC 48**
See also CA 73-76; CAAS 10; CANR 12, 30, 56; DLB 40
Tutu, Desmond M(pilo) 1931- **CLC 80; BLC 3; DAM MULT**
See also BW 1, 3; CA 125; CANR 67, 81
Tutuola, Amos 1920-1997 **CLC 5, 14, 29; BLC 3; DAM MULT**
See also BW 2, 3; CA 9-12R; 159; CANR 27, 66; DA3; DLB 125; MTCW 1, 2
Twain, Mark **TCLC 6, 12, 19, 36, 48, 59; SSC 34; WLC**
See also Clemens, Samuel Langhorne
See also AAYA 20; CLR 58, 60; DLB 11, 12, 23, 64, 74
Tyler, Anne 1941- **CLC 7, 11, 18, 28, 44, 59, 103; DAM NOV, POP**
See also AAYA 18; BEST 89:1; CA 9-12R; CANR 11, 33, 53; CDALBS; DLB 6, 143; DLBY 82; MTCW 1, 2; SATA 7, 90
Tyler, Royall 1757-1826 **NCLC 3**
See also DLB 37
Tynan, Katharine 1861-1931 **TCLC 3**
See also CA 104; 167; DLB 153
Tyutchev, Fyodor 1803-1873 **NCLC 34**
Tzara, Tristan 1896-1963 **CLC 47; DAM POET; PC 27**
See also CA 153; 89-92; MTCW 2
Uhry, Alfred 1936- **CLC 55; DAM DRAM, POP**
See also CA 127; 133; DA3; INT 133
Ulf, Haerved
See Strindberg, (Johan) August
Ulf, Harved
See Strindberg, (Johan) August
Ulibarri, Sabine R(eyes) 1919- **CLC 83; DAM MULT; HLCS 2**
See also CA 131; CANR 81; DLB 82; HW 1, 2
Unamuno (y Jugo), Miguel de 1864-1936 **TCLC 2, 9; DAM MULT, NOV; HLC 2; SSC 11**
See also CA 104; 131; CANR 81; DLB 108; HW 1, 2; MTCW 1, 2
Undercliffe, Errol
See Campbell, (John) Ramsey
Underwood, Miles
See Glassco, John
Undset, Sigrid 1882-1949 **TCLC 3; DA; DAB; DAC; DAM MST, NOV; WLC**
See also CA 104; 129; DA3; MTCW 1, 2
Ungaretti, Giuseppe 1888-1970 **CLC 7, 11, 15**
See also CA 19-20; 25-28R; CAP 2; DLB 114
Unger, Douglas 1952- **CLC 34**
See also CA 130
Unsworth, Barry (Forster) 1930- **CLC 76**
See also CA 25-28R; CANR 30, 54; DLB 194
Updike, John (Hoyer) 1932- **CLC 1, 2, 3, 5, 7, 9, 13, 15, 23, 34, 43, 70; DA; DAB; DAC; DAM MST, NOV, POET, POP; SSC 13, 27; WLC**
See also CA 1-4R; CABS 1; CANR 4, 33, 51; CDALB 1968-1988; DA3; DLB 2, 5, 143; DLBD 3; DLBY 80, 82, 97; MTCW 1, 2
Upshaw, Margaret Mitchell
See Mitchell, Margaret (Munnerlyn)
Upton, Mark
See Sanders, Lawrence
Upward, Allen 1863-1926 **TCLC 85**
See also CA 117; DLB 36

Urdang, Constance (Henriette) 1922- **CLC 47**
See also CA 21-24R; CANR 9, 24
Uriel, Henry
See Faust, Frederick (Schiller)
Uris, Leon (Marcus) 1924- **CLC 7, 32; DAM NOV, POP**
See also AITN 1, 2; BEST 89:2; CA 1-4R; CANR 1, 40, 65; DA3; MTCW 1, 2; SATA 49
Urista, Alberto H. 1947-
See Alurista
See also CA 45-48, 182; CANR 2, 32; HLCS 1; HW 1
Urmuz
See Codrescu, Andrei
Urquhart, Guy
See McAlmon, Robert (Menzies)
Urquhart, Jane 1949- **CLC 90; DAC**
See also CA 113; CANR 32, 68
Usigli, Rodolfo 1905-1979
See also CA 131; HLCS 1; HW 1
Ustinov, Peter (Alexander) 1921- **CLC 1**
See also AITN 1; CA 13-16R; CANR 25, 51; DLB 13; MTCW 2
U Tam'si, Gerald Felix Tchicaya
See Tchicaya, Gerald Felix
U Tam'si, Tchicaya
See Tchicaya, Gerald Felix
Vachss, Andrew (Henry) 1942- **CLC 106**
See also CA 118; CANR 44
Vachss, Andrew H.
See Vachss, Andrew (Henry)
Vaculik, Ludvik 1926- **CLC 7**
See also CA 53-56; CANR 72
Vaihinger, Hans 1852-1933 **TCLC 71**
See also CA 116; 166
Valdez, Luis (Miguel) 1940- **CLC 84; DAM MULT; DC 10; HLC 2**
See also CA 101; CANR 32, 81; DLB 122; HW 1
Valenzuela, Luisa 1938- **CLC 31, 104; DAM MULT; HLCS 2; SSC 14**
See also CA 101; CANR 32, 65; DLB 113; HW 1, 2
Valera y Alcala-Galiano, Juan 1824-1905 **TCLC 10**
See also CA 106
Valery, (Ambroise) Paul (Toussaint Jules) 1871-1945 **TCLC 4, 15; DAM POET; PC 9**
See also CA 104; 122; DA3; MTCW 1, 2
Valle-Inclan, Ramon (Maria) del 1866-1936 **TCLC 5; DAM MULT; HLC 2**
See also CA 106; 153; CANR 80; DLB 134; HW 2
Vallejo, Antonio Buero
See Buero Vallejo, Antonio
Vallejo, Cesar (Abraham) 1892-1938 **TCLC 3, 56; DAM MULT; HLC 2**
See also CA 105; 153; HW 1
Valles, Jules 1832-1885 **NCLC 71**
See also DLB 123
Vallette, Marguerite Eymery
See Rachilde
Valle Y Pena, Ramon del
See Valle-Inclan, Ramon (Maria) del
Van Ash, Cay 1918- **CLC 34**
Vanbrugh, Sir John 1664-1726 **LC 21; DAM DRAM**
See also DLB 80
Van Campen, Karl
See Campbell, John W(ood, Jr.)
Vance, Gerald
See Silverberg, Robert

Vosce, Trudie
See Ozick, Cynthia
Voznesensky, Andrei (Andreievich) 1933-
    CLC 1, 15, 57; DAM POET
    See also CA 89-92; CANR 37; MTCW 1
Waddington, Miriam 1917-   **CLC 28**
    See also CA 21-24R; CANR 12, 30; DLB 68
Wagman, Fredrica 1937-   **CLC 7**
    See also CA 97-100; INT 97-100
Wagner, Linda W.
    See Wagner-Martin, Linda (C.)
Wagner, Linda Welshimer
    See Wagner-Martin, Linda (C.)
Wagner, Richard 1813-1883   **NCLC 9**
    See also DLB 129
Wagner-Martin, Linda (C.) 1936-   **CLC 50**
    See also CA 159
Wagoner, David (Russell) 1926- **CLC 3, 5, 15**
    See also CA 1-4R; CAAS 3; CANR 2, 71; DLB
    5; SATA 14
Wah, Fred(erick James) 1939-   **CLC 44**
    See also CA 107; 141; DLB 60
Wahloo, Per 1926-1975   **CLC 7**
    See also CA 61-64; CANR 73
Wahloo, Peter
    See Wahloo, Per
Wain, John (Barrington) 1925-1994 **CLC 2,
    11, 15, 46**
    See also CA 5-8R; 145; CAAS 4; CANR 23,
    54; CDBLB 1960 to Present; DLB 15, 27,
    139, 155; MTCW 1, 2
Wajda, Andrzej 1926-   **CLC 16**
    See also CA 102
Wakefield, Dan 1932-   **CLC 7**
    See also CA 21-24R; CAAS 7
Wakoski, Diane 1937- **CLC 2, 4, 7, 9, 11, 40;
    DAM POET; PC 15**
    See also CA 13-16R; CAAS 1; CANR 9, 60;
    DLB 5; INT CANR-9; MTCW 2
Wakoski-Sherbell, Diane
    See Wakoski, Diane
Walcott, Derek (Alton) 1930-**CLC 2, 4, 9, 14,
    25, 42, 67, 76; BLC 3; DAB; DAC; DAM
    MST, MULT, POET; DC 7**
    See also BW 2; CA 89-92; CANR 26, 47, 75,
    80; DA3; DLB 117; DLBY 81; MTCW 1, 2
Waldman, Anne (Lesley) 1945-   **CLC 7**
    See also CA 37-40R; CAAS 17; CANR 34, 69;
    DLB 16
Waldo, E. Hunter
    See Sturgeon, Theodore (Hamilton)
Waldo, Edward Hamilton
    See Sturgeon, Theodore (Hamilton)
Walker, Alice (Malsenior) 1944- **CLC 5, 6, 9,
    19, 27, 46, 58, 103; BLC 3; DA; DAB;
    DAC; DAM MST, MULT, NOV, POET,
    POP; SSC 5; WLCS**
    See also AAYA 3; BEST 89:4; BW 2, 3; CA
    37-40R; CANR 9, 27, 49, 66, 82; CDALB
    1968-1988; DA3; DLB 6, 33, 143; INT
    CANR-27; MTCW 1, 2; SATA 31
Walker, David Harry 1911-1992   **CLC 14**
    See also CA 1-4R; 137; CANR 1; SATA 8;
    SATA-Obit 71
Walker, Edward Joseph 1934-
    See Walker, Ted
    See also CA 21-24R; CANR 12, 28, 53
Walker, George F. 1947- **CLC 44, 61; DAB;
    DAC; DAM MST**
    See also CA 103; CANR 21, 43, 59; DLB 60
Walker, Joseph A. 1935-   **CLC 19; DAM
    DRAM, MST**
    See also BW 1, 3; CA 89-92; CANR 26; DLB

38
Walker, Margaret (Abigail) 1915-1998**CLC 1,
    6; BLC; DAM MULT; PC 20**
    See also BW 2, 3; CA 73-76; 172; CANR 26,
    54, 76; DLB 76, 152; MTCW 1, 2
Walker, Ted   **CLC 13**
    See also Walker, Edward Joseph
    See also DLB 40
Wallace, David Foster 1962-   **CLC 50, 114**
    See also CA 132; CANR 59; DA3; MTCW 2
Wallace, Dexter
    See Masters, Edgar Lee
Wallace, (Richard Horatio) Edgar 1875-1932
    TCLC 57
    See also CA 115; DLB 70
Wallace, Irving 1916-1990 **CLC 7, 13; DAM
    NOV, POP**
    See also AITN 1; CA 1-4R; 132; CAAS 1;
    CANR 1, 27; INT CANR-27; MTCW 1, 2
Wallant, Edward Lewis 1926-1962**CLC 5, 10**
    See also CA 1-4R; CANR 22; DLB 2, 28, 143;
    MTCW 1, 2
Wallas, Graham 1858-1932   **TCLC 91**
Walley, Byron
    See Card, Orson Scott
Walpole, Horace 1717-1797   **LC 49**
    See also DLB 39, 104
Walpole, Hugh (Seymour) 1884-1941**TCLC 5**
    See also CA 104; 165; DLB 34; MTCW 2
Walser, Martin 1927-   **CLC 27**
    See also CA 57-60; CANR 8, 46; DLB 75, 124
Walser, Robert 1878-1956 **TCLC 18; SSC 20**
    See also CA 118; 165; DLB 66
Walsh, Jill Paton   **CLC 35**
    See also Paton Walsh, Gillian
    See also AAYA 11; CLR 2; DLB 161; SAAS 3
Walter, Villiam Christian
    See Andersen, Hans Christian
Wambaugh, Joseph (Aloysius, Jr.) 1937-**CLC
    3, 18; DAM NOV, POP**
    See also AITN 1; BEST 89:3; CA 33-36R;
    CANR 42, 65; DA3; DLB 6; DLBY 83;
    MTCW 1, 2
Wang Wei 699(?)-761(?)   **PC 18**
Ward, Arthur Henry Sarsfield 1883-1959
    See Rohmer, Sax
    See also CA 108; 173
Ward, Douglas Turner 1930-   **CLC 19**
    See also BW 1; CA 81-84; CANR 27; DLB 7,
    38
Ward, E. D.
    See Lucas, E(dward) V(errall)
Ward, Mary Augusta
    See Ward, Mrs. Humphry
Ward, Mrs. Humphry 1851-1920   **TCLC 55**
    See also DLB 18
Ward, Peter
    See Faust, Frederick (Schiller)
Warhol, Andy 1928(?)-1987   **CLC 20**
    See also AAYA 12; BEST 89:4; CA 89-92; 121;
    CANR 34
Warner, Francis (Robert le Plastrier) 1937-
    CLC 14
    See also CA 53-56; CANR 11
Warner, Marina 1946-   **CLC 59**
    See also CA 65-68; CANR 21, 55; DLB 194
Warner, Rex (Ernest) 1905-1986   **CLC 45**
    See also CA 89-92; 119; DLB 15
Warner, Susan (Bogert) 1819-1885 **NCLC 31**
    See also DLB 3, 42
Warner, Sylvia (Constance) Ashton
    See Ashton-Warner, Sylvia (Constance)
Warner, Sylvia Townsend 1893-1978 **CLC 7,**

19; SSC 23
    See also CA 61-64; 77-80; CANR 16, 60; DLB
    34, 139; MTCW 1, 2
Warren, Mercy Otis 1728-1814   **NCLC 13**
    See also DLB 31, 200
Warren, Robert Penn 1905-1989**CLC 1, 4, 6,
    8, 10, 13, 18, 39, 53, 59; DA; DAB; DAC;
    DAM MST, NOV, POET; SSC 4; WLC**
    See also AITN 1; CA 13-16R; 129; CANR 10,
    47; CDALB 1968-1988; DA3; DLB 2, 48,
    152; DLBY 80, 89; INT CANR-10; MTCW
    1, 2; SATA 46; SATA-Obit 63
Warshofsky, Isaac
    See Singer, Isaac Bashevis
Warton, Thomas 1728-1790   **LC 15; DAM
    POET**
    See also DLB 104, 109
Waruk, Kona
    See Harris, (Theodore) Wilson
Warung, Price 1855-1911   **TCLC 45**
Warwick, Jarvis
    See Garner, Hugh
Washington, Alex
    See Harris, Mark
Washington, Booker T(aliaferro) 1856-1915
    TCLC 10; BLC 3; DAM MULT
    See also BW 1; CA 114; 125; DA3; SATA 28
Washington, George 1732-1799   **LC 25**
    See also DLB 31
Wassermann, (Karl) Jakob 1873-1934 **TCLC
    6**
    See also CA 104; 163; DLB 66
Wasserstein, Wendy 1950- **CLC 32, 59, 90;
    DAM DRAM; DC 4**
    See also CA 121; 129; CABS 3; CANR 53, 75;
    DA3; INT 129; MTCW 2; SATA 94
Waterhouse, Keith (Spencer) 1929- **CLC 47**
    See also CA 5-8R; CANR 38, 67; DLB 13, 15;
    MTCW 1, 2
Waters, Frank (Joseph) 1902-1995   **CLC 88**
    See also CA 5-8R; 149; CAAS 13; CANR 3,
    18, 63; DLB 212; DLBY 86
Waters, Roger 1944-   **CLC 35**
Watkins, Frances Ellen
    See Harper, Frances Ellen Watkins
Watkins, Gerrold
    See Malzberg, Barry N(athaniel)
Watkins, Gloria 1955(?)-
    See hooks, bell
    See also BW 2; CA 143; MTCW 2
Watkins, Paul 1964-   **CLC 55**
    See also CA 132; CANR 62
Watkins, Vernon Phillips 1906-1967 **CLC 43**
    See also CA 9-10; 25-28R; CAP 1; DLB 20
Watson, Irving S.
    See Mencken, H(enry) L(ouis)
Watson, John H.
    See Farmer, Philip Jose
Watson, Richard F.
    See Silverberg, Robert
Waugh, Auberon (Alexander) 1939- **CLC 7**
    See also CA 45-48; CANR 6, 22; DLB 14, 194
Waugh, Evelyn (Arthur St. John) 1903-1966
    **CLC 1, 3, 8, 13, 19, 27, 44, 107; DA; DAB;
    DAC; DAM MST, NOV, POP; WLC**
    See also CA 85-88; 25-28R; CANR 22; CDBLB
    1914-1945; DA3; DLB 15, 162, 195; MTCW
    1, 2
Waugh, Harriet 1944-   **CLC 6**
    See also CA 85-88; CANR 22
Ways, C. R.
    See Blount, Roy (Alton), Jr.
Waystaff, Simon

Author Index

Whitehead, Alfred North 1861-1947**TCLC 97**
See also CA 117; 165; DLB 100

Whitehead, E(dward) A(nthony) 1933-**CLC 5**
See also CA 65-68; CANR 58

Whitemore, Hugh (John) 1936-   **CLC 37**
See also CA 132; CANR 77; INT 132

Whitman, Sarah Helen (Power) 1803-1878
NCLC 19
See also DLB 1

Whitman, Walt(er) 1819-1892**NCLC 4, 31, 81;**
DA; DAB; DAC; DAM MST, POET; PC
3; WLC
See also CDALB 1640-1865; DA3; DLB 3, 64;
SATA 20

Whitney, Phyllis A(yame) 1903-   **CLC 42;**
DAM POP
See also AITN 2; BEST 90:3; CA 1-4R; CANR
3, 25, 38, 60; CLR 59; DA3; JRDA;
MAICYA; MTCW 2; SATA 1, 30

Whittemore, (Edward) Reed (Jr.) 1919-**CLC 4**
See also CA 9-12R; CAAS 8; CANR 4; DLB 5

Whittier, John Greenleaf 1807-1892**NCLC 8,**
59
See also DLB 1

Whittlebot, Hernia
See Coward, Noel (Peirce)

Wicker, Thomas Grey 1926-
See Wicker, Tom
See also CA 65-68; CANR 21, 46

Wicker, Tom   **CLC 7**
See also Wicker, Thomas Grey

Wideman, John Edgar 1941-**CLC 5, 34, 36, 67,**
122; BLC 3; DAM MULT
See also BW 2, 3; CA 85-88; CANR 14, 42,
67; DLB 33, 143; MTCW 2

Wiebe, Rudy (Henry) 1934-   **CLC 6, 11, 14;**
DAC; DAM MST
See also CA 37-40R; CANR 42, 67; DLB 60

Wieland, Christoph Martin 1733-1813**NCLC**
17
See also DLB 97

Wiene, Robert 1881-1938   **TCLC 56**
Wieners, John 1934-   **CLC 7**
See also CA 13-16R; DLB 16

Wiesel, Elie(zer) 1928- **CLC 3, 5, 11, 37; DA;**
DAB; DAC; DAM MST, NOV; WLCS
See also AAYA 7; AITN 1; CA 5-8R; CAAS 4;
CANR 8, 40, 65; CDALBS; DA3; DLB 83;
DLBY 87; INT CANR-8; MTCW 1, 2; SATA
56

Wiggins, Marianne 1947-   **CLC 57**
See also BEST 89:3; CA 130; CANR 60

Wight, James Alfred 1916-1995
See Herriot, James
See also CA 77-80; SATA 55; SATA-Brief 44

Wilbur, Richard (Purdy) 1921-**CLC 3, 6, 9, 14,**
53, 110; DA; DAB; DAC; DAM MST,
POET
See also CA 1-4R; CABS 2; CANR 2, 29, 76;
CDALBS; DLB 5, 169; INT CANR-29;
MTCW 1, 2; SATA 9, 108

Wild, Peter 1940-   **CLC 14**
See also CA 37-40R; DLB 5

Wilde, Oscar 1854(?)-1900**TCLC 1, 8, 23, 41;**
DA; DAB; DAC; DAM DRAM, MST,
NOV; SSC 11; WLC
See also CA 104; 119; CDBLB 1890-1914;
DA3; DLB 10, 19, 34, 57, 141, 156, 190;
SATA 24

Wilder, Billy   **CLC 20**
See also Wilder, Samuel
See also DLB 26

Wilder, Samuel 1906-

See Wilder, Billy
See also CA 89-92

Wilder, Thornton (Niven) 1897-1975**CLC 1, 5,**
6, 10, 15, 35, 82; DA; DAB; DAC; DAM
DRAM, MST, NOV; DC 1; WLC
See also AAYA 29; AITN 2; CA 13-16R; 61-
64; CANR 40; CDALBS; DA3; DLB 4, 7, 9;
DLBY 97; MTCW 1, 2

Wilding, Michael 1942-   **CLC 73**
See also CA 104; CANR 24, 49

Wiley, Richard 1944-   **CLC 44**
See also CA 121; 129; CANR 71

Wilhelm, Kate   **CLC 7**
See also Wilhelm, Katie Gertrude
See also AAYA 20; CAAS 5; DLB 8; INT
CANR-17

Wilhelm, Katie Gertrude 1928-
See Wilhelm, Kate
See also CA 37-40R; CANR 17, 36, 60; MTCW
1

Wilkins, Mary
See Freeman, Mary E(leanor) Wilkins

Willard, Nancy 1936-   **CLC 7, 37**
See also CA 89-92; CANR 10, 39, 68; CLR 5;
DLB 5, 52; MAICYA; MTCW 1; SATA 37,
71; SATA-Brief 30

William of Ockham 1285-1347   **CMLC 32**
Williams, Ben Ames 1889-1953   **TCLC 89**
See also DLB 102

Williams, C(harles) K(enneth) 1936-**CLC 33,**
56; DAM POET
See also CA 37-40R; CAAS 26; CANR 57; DLB
5

Williams, Charles
See Collier, James L(incoln)

Williams, Charles (Walter Stansby) 1886-1945
TCLC 1, 11
See also CA 104; 163; DLB 100, 153

Williams, (George) Emlyn 1905-1987**CLC 15;**
DAM DRAM
See also CA 104; 123; CANR 36; DLB 10, 77;
MTCW 1

Williams, Hank 1923-1953   **TCLC 81**
Williams, Hugo 1942-   **CLC 42**
See also CA 17-20R; CANR 45; DLB 40

Williams, J. Walker
See Wodehouse, P(elham) G(renville)

Williams, John A(lfred) 1925-**CLC 5, 13; BLC**
3; DAM MULT
See also BW 2, 3; CA 53-56; CAAS 3; CANR
6, 26, 51; DLB 2, 33; INT CANR-6

Williams, Jonathan (Chamberlain) 1929-
CLC 13
See also CA 9-12R; CAAS 12; CANR 8; DLB
5

Williams, Joy 1944-   **CLC 31**
See also CA 41-44R; CANR 22, 48

Williams, Norman 1952-   **CLC 39**
See also CA 118

Williams, Sherley Anne 1944-**CLC 89; BLC 3;**
DAM MULT, POET
See also BW 2, 3; CA 73-76; CANR 25, 82;
DLB 41; INT CANR-25; SATA 78

Williams, Shirley
See Williams, Sherley Anne

Williams, Tennessee 1911-1983**CLC 1, 2, 5, 7,**
8, 11, 15, 19, 30, 39, 45, 71, 111; DA; DAB;
DAC; DAM DRAM, MST; DC 4; WLC
See also AAYA 31; AITN 1, 2; CA 5-8R; 108;
CABS 3; CANR 31; CDALB 1941-1968;
DA3; DLB 7; DLBD 4; DLBY 83; MTCW
1, 2

Williams, Thomas (Alonzo) 1926-1990**CLC 14**

See also CA 1-4R; 132; CANR 2

Williams, William C.
See Williams, William Carlos

Williams, William Carlos 1883-1963**CLC 1, 2,**
5, 9, 13, 22, 42, 67; DA; DAB; DAC; DAM
MST, POET; PC 7; SSC 31
See also CA 89-92; CANR 34; CDALB 1917-
1929; DA3; DLB 4, 16, 54, 86; MTCW 1, 2

Williamson, David (Keith) 1942-   **CLC 56**
See also CA 103; CANR 41

Williamson, Ellen Douglas 1905-1984
See Douglas, Ellen
See also CA 17-20R; 114; CANR 39

Williamson, Jack   **CLC 29**
See also Williamson, John Stewart
See also CAAS 8; DLB 8

Williamson, John Stewart 1908-
See Williamson, Jack
See also CA 17-20R; CANR 23, 70

Willie, Frederick
See Lovecraft, H(oward) P(hillips)

Willingham, Calder (Baynard, Jr.) 1922-1995
CLC 5, 51
See also CA 5-8R; 147; CANR 3; DLB 2, 44;
MTCW 1

Willis, Charles
See Clarke, Arthur C(harles)

Willis, Fingal O'Flahertie
See Wilde, Oscar

Willy
See Colette, (Sidonie-Gabrielle)

Willy, Colette
See Colette, (Sidonie-Gabrielle)

Wilson, A(ndrew) N(orman) 1950-   **CLC 33**
See also CA 112; 122; DLB 14, 155, 194;
MTCW 2

Wilson, Angus (Frank Johnstone) 1913-1991
CLC 2, 3, 5, 25, 34; SSC 21
See also CA 5-8R; 134; CANR 21; DLB 15,
139, 155; MTCW 1, 2

Wilson, August 1945-   **CLC 39, 50, 63, 118;**
BLC 3; DA; DAB; DAC; DAM DRAM,
MST, MULT; DC 2; WLCS
See also AAYA 16; BW 2, 3; CA 115; 122;
CANR 42, 54, 76; DA3; MTCW 1, 2

Wilson, Brian 1942-   **CLC 12**
Wilson, Colin 1931-   **CLC 3, 14**
See also CA 1-4R; CAAS 5; CANR 1, 22, 33,
77; DLB 14, 194; MTCW 1

Wilson, Dirk
See Pohl, Frederik

Wilson, Edmund 1895-1972**CLC 1, 2, 3, 8, 24**
See also CA 1-4R; 37-40R; CANR 1, 46; DLB
63; MTCW 1, 2

Wilson, Ethel Davis (Bryant) 1888(?)-1980
CLC 13; DAC; DAM POET
See also CA 102; DLB 68; MTCW 1

Wilson, John 1785-1854   **NCLC 5**
Wilson, John (Anthony) Burgess 1917-1993
See Burgess, Anthony
See also CA 1-4R; 143; CANR 2, 46; DAC;
DAM NOV; DA3; MTCW 1, 2

Wilson, Lanford 1937- **CLC 7, 14, 36; DAM**
DRAM
See also CA 17-20R; CABS 3; CANR 45; DLB
7

Wilson, Robert M. 1944-   **CLC 7, 9**
See also CA 49-52; CANR 2, 41; MTCW 1

Wilson, Robert McLiam 1964-   **CLC 59**
See also CA 132

Wilson, Sloan 1920-   **CLC 32**
See also CA 1-4R; CANR 1, 44

Wilson, Snoo 1948-   **CLC 33**

Literary Criticism Series
Cumulative Topic Index

This index lists all topic entries in Gale's *Classical and Medieval Literature Criticism, Contemporary Literary Criticism, Literature Criticism from 1400 to 1800, Nineteenth-Century Literature Criticism,* and *Twentieth-Century Literary Criticism.*

Topic Index

Topic Index

Topic Index

NCLC Cumulative Nationality Index

Hebbel, Friedrich 43
Hegel, Georg Wilhelm Friedrich 46
Heine, Heinrich **4, 54**
Hoffmann, E(rnst) T(heodor) A(madeus) 2
Holderlin, (Johann Christian) Friedrich 16
Immermann, Karl (Lebrecht) **4, 49**
Jean Paul 7
Kant, Immanuel **27, 67**
Kleist, Heinrich von **2, 37**
Klinger, Friedrich Maximilian von 1
Klopstock, Friedrich Gottlieb **11**
Kotzebue, August (Friedrich Ferdinand) von **25**
Ludwig, Otto 4
Marx, Karl (Heinrich) **17**
Meyer, Conrad Ferdinand 81
Morike, Eduard (Friedrich) 10
Novalis 13
Schelling, Friedrich Wilhelm Joseph von 30
Schiller, Friedrich **39, 69**
Schlegel, August Wilhelm von 15
Schlegel, Friedrich 45
Schopenhauer, Arthur 51
Storm, (Hans) Theodor (Woldsen) 1
Tieck, (Johann) Ludwig **5, 46**
Wagner, Richard 9
Wieland, Christoph Martin 17

GREEK
Solomos, Dionysios 15

HUNGARIAN
Arany, Janos **34**
Madach, Imre **19**
Petofi, Sandor **21**

INDIAN
Chatterji, Bankim Chandra 19
Dutt, Toru 29
Ghalib **39, 78**

IRISH
Allingham, William 25
Banim, John 13
Banim, Michael 13
Boucicault, Dion 41
Carleton, William 3
Croker, John Wilson 10
Darley, George 2
Edgeworth, Maria **1, 51**
Ferguson, Samuel 33
Griffin, Gerald 7
Jameson, Anna 43
Le Fanu, Joseph Sheridan **9, 58**
Lever, Charles (James) 23
Maginn, William 8
Mangan, James Clarence 27

Maturin, Charles Robert 6
Merriman, Brian 70
Moore, Thomas 6
Morgan, Lady 29
O'Brien, Fitz-James 21

ITALIAN
Collodi, Carlo 54
Foscolo, Ugo 8
Gozzi, (Conte) Carlo 23
Leopardi, (Conte) Giacomo 22
Manzoni, Alessandro 29
Mazzini, Guiseppe 34
Nievo, Ippolito 22

JAPANESE
Higuchi, Ichiyo **49**
Motoori, Norinaga **45**

LITHUANIAN
Mapu, Abraham (ben Jekutiel) 18

MEXICAN
Lizardi, Jose Joaquin Fernandez de 30

NORWEGIAN
Collett, (Jacobine) Camilla (Wergeland) **22**
Wergeland, Henrik Arnold 5

POLISH
Fredro, Aleksander 8
Krasicki, Ignacy 8
Krasinski, Zygmunt 4
Mickiewicz, Adam 3
Norwid, Cyprian Kamil **17**
Slowacki, Juliusz 15

ROMANIAN
Eminescu, Mihail 33

RUSSIAN
Aksakov, Sergei Timofeyvich 2
Bakunin, Mikhail (Alexandrovich) **25, 58**
Dashkirtseff, Marie 27
Belinski, Vissarion Grigoryevich 5
Chernyshevsky, Nikolay Gavrilovich 1
Dobrolyubov, Nikolai Alexandrovich 5
Dostoevsky, Fedor Mikhailovich **2, 7, 21,
33, 43**
Gogol, Nikolai (Vasilyevich) **5, 15, 31**
Goncharov, Ivan Alexandrovich **1, 63**
Granovsky, Timofei Nikolaevich 75
Herzen, Aleksandr Ivanovich **10, 61**
Karamzin, Nikolai Mikhailovich 3
Krylov, Ivan Andreevich 1
Lermontov, Mikhail Yuryevich 5

Leskov, Nikolai (Semyonovich) 25
Nekrasov, Nikolai Alekseevich 11
Ostrovsky, Alexander **30, 57**
Pisarev, Dmitry Ivanovich 25
Pushkin, Alexander (Sergeyevich) **3, 27**
Saltykov, Mikhail Evgrafovich 16
Smolenskin, Peretz 30
Turgenev, Ivan 21
Tyutchev, Fyodor **34**
Zhukovsky, Vasily (Andreevich) **35**

SCOTTISH
Baillie, Joanna 2
Beattie, James 25
Blair, Hugh 75
Campbell, Thomas 19
Carlyle, Thomas **22, 70**
Ferrier, Susan (Edmonstone) 8
Galt, John 1
Hogg, James 4
Jeffrey, Francis 33
Lockhart, John Gibson 6
Mackenzie, Henry 41
Oliphant, Margaret (Oliphant Wilson) **11,
61**
Scott, Walter **15, 69**
Stevenson, Robert Louis (Balfour) **5, 14, 63**
Thomson, James, 18
Wilson, John 5
Wright, Frances 74

SPANISH
Alarcon, Pedro Antonio de 1
Caballero, Fernan 10
Castro, Rosalia de **3, 78**
Espronceda, Jose de 39
Larra (y Sanchez de Castro), Mariano Jose de
17
Tamayo y Baus, Manuel 1
Zorrilla y Moral, Jose 6

SWEDISH
Almqvist, Carl Jonas Love 42
Bremer, Fredrika 11
Stagnelius, Eric Johan 61
Tegner, Esaias 2

SWISS
Amiel, Henri Frederic 4
Burckhardt, Jacob (Christoph) 49
Keller, Gottfried 2
Meyer, Conrad Ferdinand 81
Wyss, Johann David Von 10

UKRAINIAN
Shevchenko, Taras 54

Nationality Index

NCLC-82 Title Index

Title Index

ISBN 0-7876-3258-9

90000